1993

Michelangelo's Drawings

MICHELANGELO'S DRAWINGS

The Science of Attribution

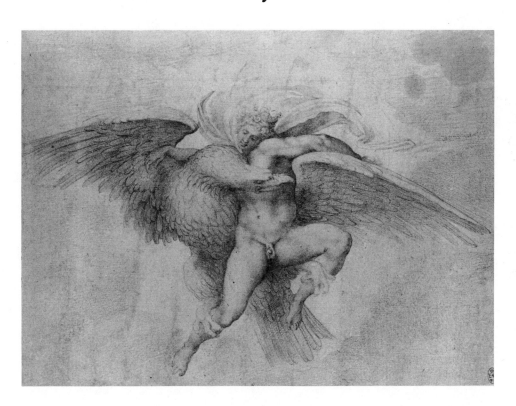

ALEXANDER PERRIG

TRANSLATED BY MICHAEL JOYCE

Yale University Press   New Haven and London

Published with the assistance of
the F. B. Adams, Jr., Publication
Fund.

Designed by Richard Hendel.
Set in Aldus type by
G&S Typesetters, Inc.,
Austin, Texas.

Printed in the United States of
America by Halliday Lithograph,
West Hanover, Massachusetts.

Library of Congress Cataloging-
in-Publicaton Data

Perrig, Alexander.
    Michelangelo's drawings :
the science of attribution /
Alexander Perrig ; translated
by Michael Joyce.
        p.   cm.
    Translated from German.
    Includes bibliographical
references and index.
    ISBN 0-300-03948-4 (alk.
paper)
    1. Michelangelo
Buonarroti, 1475–1564—
Authorship.   I. Title.
NC257.B8P48   1991
741'.092—dc20   90-44417
                    CIP

The paper in this book meets the
guidelines for permanence and
durability of the Committee on
Production Guidelines for Book
Longevity of the Council on
Library Resources.

10 9 8 7 6 5 4 3 2 1

Title page illustration:
Michelangelo, *The Rape of
Ganymede*. Windsor Castle,
Royal Library. Copyright 1990
by Her Majesty Queen
Elizabeth II.

Contents

List of Illustrations   vii

Introduction   1

PART I: THE SCIENCE OF DRAWING ANALYSIS

1. Drawing and How It Is Produced   15

PART II: THE DRAWINGS AND DRAWING TECHNIQUE OF MICHELANGELO

2. Authenticated Drawings and Criteria for Authentication   37

3. Michelangelo's Way of Drawing   57

4. What Finally Can Be Attributed to Michelangelo?   67

PART III: SOME VICTIMS OF THE MICHELANGELO CULT

5. Tommaso de' Cavalieri (ca. 1509/10–1587)   75

6. Ascanio Condivi (1524–1574)   86

7. Marcello Venusti (1512/15–1579) and the Crucifixion Drawings   94

8. Daniele Ricciarelli da Volterra (1509–1566) and the

      Expulsion of the Moneychangers   102

Excursus   111

Notes   119

Bibliography   153

Index   163

Illustrations

following page 168

MICHELANGELO

1. Florence, Archivio Buonarroti, II/III, Fol. 3v: practice sketches, writing exercises; pen and ink; 27.5 × 21.5 cm. Photo: Pineider, Florence.

2. Paris, Louvre, no. 685v: preface of a current account ledger, kneeling girl, eagle head, vessel; pen and ink, in part over black chalk (contour of the girl); 32.5 × 26.1 cm; cut (recto: fig. 4). Photo: Giraudon, Paris.

3. London, British Museum, no. 1895-9-15-498r: draped male figure; pen and ink; 32.8 × 21.2 cm; cut. Photo: Courtesy of the Trustees of the British Museum.

4. Paris, Louvre, no. 685r: St. Anne, male nude, head in profile, manuscript texts; pen and ink, in part over black chalk (hatching of St. Anne); 32.5 × 26.1 cm; cut (verso: fig. 2). Photo: Giraudon, Paris.

5. Paris, Louvre, no. 714r: arm study, David sketch, manuscript texts; pen and ink; 26.5 × 18.8 cm; cut. Photo: Service de Documentation photographique, Paris.

6. Oxford, Ashmolean Museum, Parker no. 297: studies for the Libyan sibyl's companion and for the sibyl's right hand (red chalk); six slaves, entablature piece (pen and ink); 28.8 × 19.4 cm; cut. Photo: Ashmolean Museum.

7. Florence, Uffizi, no. 2318F: studies for the Libyan sibyl (copy); red chalk; 28.7 × 21.5 cm; cut. Photo: Soprintendenza no. 71171.

8. New York, Metropolitan Museum, no. 24.197.2r: studies for the Libyan sibyl (copy); red chalk; 28.8 × 21.3 cm; cut. The Metropolitan Museum of Art, Purchase, 1984, Joseph Pulitzer Bequest.

9. Boston, Isabella Stewart Gardner Museum, B400: studies for the crucified Haman (copy); red chalk; 36.3 × 19 cm; cut. Photo: Isabella Stewart Gardner Museum.

10. London, British Museum, no. 1895-9-15-497r: studies for the crucified Haman (copy); red chalk; 40.5 × 20.6 cm; cut. Photo: Courtesy of the Trustees of the British Museum.

11. Windsor Castle, Royal Library, no. 0435r: studies for the crucified Haman (copy); red chalk; 39 × 22.2 cm; cut. Copyright 1989 Her Majesty Queen Elizabeth II.

12. London, British Museum, no. 1859-6-25-543r: sketch of a double tomb for Lorenzo the Magnificent and his brother Giuliano de' Medici, annotation; pen and ink; 21 × 16 cm; cut. Photo: Courtesy of the Trustees of the British Museum.

13. Florence, Casa Buonarroti, no. 2F: bust of Cleopatra (copy); black chalk; 23.2 × 18.2 cm; cut. Photo: Soprintendenza no. 4721.

14. London, British Museum, no. 1895-9-15-501r: *Christ Descending to Hell* (copy); black chalk; 40.5 × 26.5 cm; cut. Photo: Courtesy of the Trustees of the British Museum.

15. Frankfurt, Städelsches Kunstinstitut, no. 3976: *Christ Descending to Hell* (copy); black chalk; 37.3 × 22.1 cm; cut. Photo: by U. Edelmann, courtesy of Städelsches Kunstinstitut.

16. Windsor Castle, Royal Library, no. 12768: *Risen Christ* (copy); black chalk; 37.3 × 22.1 cm; cut. Copyright 1989 Her Majesty Queen Elizabeth II.

17. Cambridge, Massachusetts, Fogg Art Museum, no. 1955.750: *The Rape of Ganymede*; black chalk; 36.1 × 27.5 cm; cut. Photo: Courtesy of The Fogg Art Museum, Harvard University.

18. Windsor Castle, Royal Library, no. 13036: *The Rape of Ganymede* (copy); black chalk; 19.2 × 26 cm; cut. Copyright 1989 Her Majesty Queen Elizabeth II.

19. Windsor Castle, Royal Library, no. 12771r: *The Punishment of Tityos*; black chalk; 19 × 33 cm; cut (verso: fig. 61). Copyright 1989 Her Majesty Queen Elizabeth II.

20. Windsor Castle, Royal Library, no. 0472r: *The Punishment of Tityos* (copy, signed on the verso by Clovio); black chalk; 20.3 × 29 cm; cut. Copyright 1989 Her Majesty Queen Elizabeth II.

21. Windsor Castle, Royal Library, no. 12778r: *The Archers* (copy, signed on the verso by Clovio); red chalk; 21.9 × 32.3 cm; cut. Copyright 1989 Her Majesty Queen Elizabeth II.

22. Windsor Castle, Royal Library, no. 0442r: *The Archers* (copy, signed on the verso by Bernardino Cesari); red chalk; 25.7 × 37.2 cm. Copyright 1989 Her Majesty Queen Elizabeth II.

23. London, British Museum, no. 1895-9-15-517: *The Fall of Phaeton*, annotation; black chalk; 31.3 × 21.7 cm; cut. Photo: Courtesy of the Trustees of the British Museum.

24. Windsor Castle, Royal Library, no. 12766r: *The Fall of Phaeton*; black chalk; 41.3 × 23.4 cm; cut (verso: fig. 50). Copyright 1989 Her Majesty Queen Elizabeth II.

25. Windsor Castle, Royal Library, no. 12777: *The Children's Bacchanal* (copy); red chalk over black chalk; 27.4 × 38.8 cm; cut. Copyright 1989 Her Majesty Queen Elizabeth II.

26. Berlin-Dahlem, Kupferstichkabinett, KdZ no. 17358: *The Children's Bacchanal* (copy); red chalk; 28.8 × 40.1 cm; cut. Photo: Staatliche Museen Preussischer Kulturbesitz, Kupferstichkabinett, Berlin.

27. London, British Museum, no. 1860-6-16-133: *Resurrection of Christ* (copy); black chalk; 32.7 × 28.9 cm; cut. Photo: Courtesy of the Trustees of the British Museum.

28. Frankfurt, Städelsches Kunstinstitut, no. 3975: *Resurrection of Christ* (copy); black chalk; 32 × 24.4 cm; cut. Photo: Städelsches Kunstinstitut.

29. Oxford, Ashmolean Museum, Parker no. 318r: Plague of Serpents and Worship of the Brazen Serpent (copy); red chalk over black chalk; 24.5 × 33.5 cm; cut. Photo: Ashmolean Museum.

30. Florence, Casa Buonarroti, no. 65F-r: *Last Judgment*; black chalk; 41.4 × 30 cm; cut (verso: fig. 59). Photo: G.F.S.G., Florence.

31. Windsor Castle, Royal Library, no. 12776r: partial sketch for the *Last Judgment* with subsidiary sketches, male torso; black chalk; 27.7 × 41.9 cm; cut (verso: fig. 71). Copyright 1989 Her Majesty Queen Elizabeth II.

32. London, British Museum, no. 1895-9-15-518r: partial sketch for the *Last Judgment* with subsidiary sketches, figure studies; black chalk; 38.2 × 24.7 cm; cut. Photo: Courtesy of the Trustees of the British Museum.

33. London, British Museum, no. 1895-9-15-504: Christ on the cross between two hovering angels (copy); 37.2 × 27.2 cm; cut. Photo: Courtesy of the Trustees of the British Museum.

34. Naples, Museo Nazionale, no. 398: cartoon fragment for the fresco of the *Crucifixion of Peter* in the Pauline Chapel; black chalk; 263 × 156 cm; perforated. Photo: Albertini.

35. Oxford, Ashmolean Museum, Parker no. 339: five sketches for an Entombment or a Pietà; black chalk; 10.8 × 28.2 cm; cut. Photo: Ashmolean Museum.

36. Oxford, Ashmolean Museum, Parker no. 340: sketches for the apostles of a Gethsemane scene; black chalk; 10.8 × 32.7 cm; cut. Photo: Ashmolean Museum.

37. Oxford, Ashmolean Museum, Parker no. 345: *Annunciation*, manuscript text; black chalk; 22 × 20 cm; cut. Photo: Ashmolean Museum.

38. London, British Museum, no. 1859-6-25-562: standing woman with child; black chalk; 26.7 × 11.8 cm; cut. Photo: Courtesy of the Trustees of the British Museum.

39. Florence, Archivio Buonarroti, XIII, Fol. 111: sonnet with marginal sketch; pen and ink; 28.3 × 20 cm. Photo: Pineider, Florence.

40. London, British Museum, no. 1859-6-25-544r: block sketches for a river god; pen and ink; 13.8 × 21 cm; cut. Photo: Courtesy of the Trustees of the British Museum.

41. Florence, Archivio Buonarroti, XIII, Fol. 169v: left hand pointing to the right, verse fragments; pen and ink; 29 × 17.3 cm. Photo: Pineider, Florence.

42. Rome, Vatican Library, Cod. Vat. 3211, Fol. 74r: right hand holding a book, verse fragments; pen and ink; 21.2 × 14.4 cm; cut. Photo: Gabinetto Fotografico Nazionale, Rome.

43. Florence, Archivio Buonarroti, X, Fol. 578v: notes on purchases with accompanying sketches; pen and ink; 21.3 × 14.5 cm; cut. Photo: Pineider, Florence.

44. Rome, Conservatory Palace: *Hercules of the Forum Boarium* (2d half of 2d century); bronze; larger than life. Photo: Alinari.

SEBASTIANO DEL PIOMBO

45. Windsor Castle, Royal Library, no. 4815: hovering God the Father; black chalk; 30 × 27.3 cm; cut. Copyright 1989 Her Majesty Queen Elizabeth II.

46. Bayonne, Musée Bonnat, no. 682: three sketches for the risen Lazarus; red chalk; 20 × 33 cm; cut. Photo: Aubert, Bayonne.

47. London, British Museum, no. 1860-7-14-1: the risen Lazarus with two helpers; red chalk; 25 × 14.5 cm; cut. Photo: Courtesy of the Trustees of the British Museum.

48. Florence, Casa Buonarroti, no. 66F: male nude; black chalk; 32.5 × 19 cm; cut. Photo: Alinari.

49. Florence, Casa Buonarroti, no. 61F-v: male nude; black chalk; 38 × 25.2 cm; cut. Photo: G.F.S.G., Florence.

ANTONIO MINI

50. Windsor Castle, Royal Library, no. 12766v: half-length portrait of a girl with mirror, left ear; red chalk; 41.3 × 23.4 cm; cut (recto: fig. 24). Copyright 1989 Her Majesty Queen Elizabeth II.

51. London, British Museum, no. 1859-6-25-561: girl with distaff; black chalk; 28.5 × 18.2 cm; cut. Photo: Courtesy of the Trustees of the British Museum.

52. Paris, Louvre, no. 684r: faun's head; ink over red chalk; 27.5 × 21 cm; cut. Photo: Roger-Viollet.

53. Munich, Staatliche Graphische Sammlung, no. 2191r: two arm studies, red chalk; St. Peter after Masaccio's *Tribute Money*, ink over red chalk; 31.7 × 19.7 cm; cut. Photo: Staatliche Graphische Sammlung.

54. Oxford, Ashmolean Museum, Parker no. 324: draped old woman with cane, accompanied by a boy; ink over black chalk; 32.9 × 19.2 cm; cut. Photo: Ashmolean Museum.

55. London, British Museum, no. 1859-5-14-818r: four sketches of a Madonna with child, ink or red chalk (square net in black chalk); manuscript text, pen and ink; 40 × 26.9 cm; cut. Photo: Courtesy of the Trustees of the British Museum.

56. Oxford, Ashmolean Museum, Parker no. 325: seated female draped figure ("Sibyl"); pen and ink; 26.3 × 20 cm; cut. Photo: Ashmolean Museum.

57. London, formerly Collection Woolf Posner: seated Madonna with Christ Child and St. John; tempera on wood; 94 × 75 cm. Reproduced courtesy of the owner.

TOMMASO DE' CAVALIERI

58. Florence, Uffizi, no. 611E: *The Rape of Ganymede*; red chalk; 31 × 22.5 cm; cut. Photo: G.F.S.G., Florence.

59. Florence, Casa Buonarroti, no. 65F-v: *Risen Christ*; black chalk; 41.4 × 30 cm; cut (recto: fig. 30). Photo: Alinari.

60. Florence, Archivio Buonarroti, VI, Fol. 24v: *Risen Christ*; black chalk; manuscript text, pen and ink; 21 × 13.8 cm; cut. Photo: Pineider, Florence.

61. Windsor Castle, Royal Library, no. 12771v: two sketches of a Risen Christ; black chalk; 33 × 19 cm; cut (recto: fig. 19). Copyright 1989 Her Majesty Queen Elizabeth II.

62. Oxford, Ashmolean Museum, Parker no. 311v: *Risen Christ*; black chalk; 27.3 × 15.7 cm; cut. Photo: Ashmolean Museum.

63. Florence, Uffizi, no. 1450S: *Risen Christ*; black chalk; cut. Photo: G.F.S.G., Florence.

64. Windsor Castle, Royal Library, no. 12764r: head of a youth with cap; black chalk; 21.2 × 14.2 cm; cut. Copyright 1989 Her Majesty Queen Elizabeth II.

65. Oxford, Ashmolean Museum, Parker no. 315: bust of a youth in fantastic dress; red chalk; 20.5 × 16.5 cm; cut. Photo: Ashmolean Museum.

66. Venice, Academy, no. 177: *Fall of Phaeton*; black chalk; 39.4 × 25.5 cm; cut. Photo: Umberto Rossi, Venice.

67. Bayonne, Musée Bonnat, no. 1217: partial sketch of a Last Judgment; black chalk; 34.4 × 29 cm. Photo: Aubert, Bayonne.

68. Florence, Uffizi, no. 170S: partial sketch of a Last Judgment; black chalk; 19 × 28.7 cm; cut. Photo: G.F.S.G., Florence.

69. Florence, Casa Buonarroti, no. 69F-v: arm and knee studies, male torso, nude seen from the rear, and head; black chalk; 39.8 × 28.2 cm; cut. Photo: G.F.S.G., Florence.

70. Bayonne, Musée Bonnat, no. 681: partial sketch of a Last Judgment; black chalk; 17.9 × 23.8 cm. Photo: Aubert, Bayonne.

71. Windsor Castle, Royal Library, no. 12776v: four limb studies, two male nudes; black chalk; 27.7 × 41.9 cm; cut (recto: fig. 31). Copyright 1989 Her Majesty Queen Elizabeth II.

BENVENUTO CELLINI

72. Paris, Louvre, no. 689v: two seated female nudes, one with a suckling child; ink over metal point; 25 × 17 (sheet excerpt) or 37.5 × 19.5 cm (whole sheet). Photo: Giraudon, Paris.

73. Vienna, Albertina, Sc.R.152v: seated Madonna with suckling child; pen and ink; 39 × 19.5 cm; cut. Photo: Alpenland, Vienna.

74. London, British Museum, no. 1895-9-15-496r: sketch of battling horsemen, two statue sketches; pen and ink; 18.6 × 18.3 cm; cut. Photo: Courtesy of the Trustees of the British Museum.

75. Paris, Louvre, R.F. 70-1068v: male nude, arm study, bearded male head, manuscript texts; pen and ink; 34 × 16.8 cm; cut (recto: fig. 79). Photo: Giraudon, Paris.

76. London, British Museum, no. 1859-6-25-564v: fragmentary group of three male nudes (black chalk), leg study, verse fragment (pen and ink), two standing

boys (ink over metal point); 31.5 × 27.8 cm; cut. Photo: Courtesy of the Trustees of the British Museum.

77. Oxford, Ashmolean Museum, Parker no. 291 v: male nude seen from the rear, half-length figure of a youth, four heads, manuscript texts; pen and ink; 25.7 × 17.5 cm; cut. Photo: Ashmolean Museum.

78. Florence, Casa Buonarroti, no. 73F-r: male nude seen from the rear; ink over black chalk; 40.8 × 28.4 cm; cut. Photo: G.F.S.G., Florence.

79. Paris, Louvre, R.F. 70-1068r: striding nude youth; pen and ink; 34 × 16.8 cm; cut (verso: fig. 75). Photo: Giraudon, Paris.

80. London, British Museum, no. 1887-5-2-117r: youth hurrying to the left (pen and ink), leg study (black chalk), manuscript texts (pen and ink or black chalk); 37.5 × 23 cm; cut. Photo: Courtesy of the Trustees of the British Museum.

GIULIO CLOVIO

81. Windsor Castle, Royal Library, no. 12767r: *Resurrection of Christ*; black chalk; 24 × 34.8 cm; cut (verso: fig. 82). Copyright 1989 Her Majesty Queen Elizabeth II.

82. Windsor Castle, Royal Library, no. 12767v: study of a right arm with shoulder, two shoulder studies (black chalk), "D. Giulio Clovio" (pen and ink); 24 × 34.8 cm; cut (recto: fig. 81). Copyright 1989 Her Majesty Queen Elizabeth II.

83. Florence, Casa Buonarroti, no. 32F: seated male nude; red chalk; 13.5 × 19.5 cm; cut. Photo: G.F.S.G., Florence.

84. Cambridge, Massachusetts, Fogg Art Museum, no. 1943.125: *Resurrection of Christ*; oil on wood; 60 × 40 cm. Photo: Courtesy of The Fogg Art Museum, Harvard University.

85. New York Public Library, Towneley Lectionary, Fol. 16v: *Resurrection of Christ*; miniature. Photo: DiRicci 91, Rare Books and Manuscripts Division, The New York Public Library Astor, Lenox and Tilden Foundations.

86. Giulio Romano. Berlin-Dahlem, Kupferstichkabinett, KdZ no. 26368: *Resurrection of Christ*; pen and ink and brush; washed; 27.9 × 40.7 cm; cut. Photo: Staatliche Museen, Berlin.

87. London, British Museum, no. 1895-9-15-654: *Lamentation of Christ*; signed by Giulio Clovio; black chalk; 25 × 12 cm; cut. Photo: Courtesy of the Trustees of the British Museum.

88. London, British Museum, no. 1859-5-14-820: left leg and left foot; red chalk; 21.4 × 16.1 cm; cut. Photo: Courtesy of the Trustees of the British Museum.

89. Oxford, Ashmolean Museum, Parker no. 309r: reclining male nude, manuscript texts; black chalk; 25.8 × 33.2 cm. Photo: Ashmolean Museum.

90. Florence, Casa Buonarroti, no. 44F: lower half of a reclining nude; pen and ink; 14.5 × 19.3 cm; cut. Photo: G.F.S.G., Florence.

ASCANIO CONDIVI

91. Cambridge, Fitzwilliam Museum, no. 3056r: draped male figure, two arm sketches; black chalk; 26.5 × 16.2 cm; cut. Photo: Fitzwilliam Museum.

92. Oxford, Ashmolean Museum, Parker no. 335: striding male nude; black chalk; 18.1 × 8.7 cm; cut. Photo: Ashmolean Museum.

93. Oxford, Ashmolean Museum, Parker no. 334v: striding draped figure, column niche, ground plan; black chalk; 20 × 12 cm; cut. Photo: Ashmolean Museum.

94. Oxford, Ashmolean Museum, Parker no. 337r: male head; black chalk; 23.8 × 20.1 cm; cut. Photo: Ashmolean Museum.

95. London, British Museum, no. 1895-9-15-518+: "*Epiphany*"; black chalk; 232.7 × 165.6 cm; cut. Photo: Courtesy of the Trustees of the British Museum.

96. London, British Museum, no. 1895-9-15-518+: "*Epiphany*" (detail). Photo: Courtesy of the Trustees of the British Museum.

97. London, British Museum, no. 1895-9-15-518+: "*Epiphany*" (detail). Photo: Courtesy of the Trustees of the British Museum.

98. Florence, Casa Buonarroti: "*Epiphany*"; tempera on wood; 240 × 187 cm. Photo: G.F.S.G., Florence.

99. Oxford, Ashmolean Museum, no. 278: ambiguous scene; bistre over a green plaster ground on wood; 66 × 53 cm. Photo: Ashmolean Museum.

MARCELLO VENUSTI

100. London, British Museum, no. 1895-9-15-516r: *Annunciation*; black chalk; 28.3 × 19.6 cm; cut. Photo: Courtesy of the Trustees of the British Museum.

101. New York, Pierpont Morgan Library, no. IV, 7: *Annunciation*; black chalk; 38.2 × 29.6 cm; cut. Photo: Pierpont Morgan Library.

102. Florence, Uffizi, no. 229F: *Annunciation*; black chalk; 40.5 × 54.7 cm; cut. Photo: G.F.S.G., Florence.

103. Florence, Uffizi, no. 230F: *Christ in Gethsemane*; black chalk; 36 × 60 cm; cut. Photo: G.F.S.G., Florence.

104. Paris, Louvre, no. 720v: male nude looking upward; black chalk; 23 × 11 cm; cut (recto: fig. 112). Photo: Cliché des Musées Nationaux.

105. Oxford, Ashmolean Museum, Parker no. 343r: Christ on the cross between two secondary figures; black chalk, treated in some places with white lead (oxidized); 27.8 × 23.4 cm; cut. Photo: Ashmolean Museum.

106. Windsor Castle, Royal Library, no. 12775: Christ on the cross between Mary and John; black chalk, treated in some places with white lead (oxidized); 38.2 × 21 cm; cut. Copyright 1989 Her Majesty Queen Elizabeth II.

107. Windsor Castle, Royal Library, no. 12761r: Christ on the cross between Mary and John; black chalk; 40.5 × 21.8 cm; cut. Copyright 1989 Her Majesty Queen Elizabeth II.

108. Paris, Louvre, no. 842r: Christ on the cross; black chalk; 25.5 × 13.5 cm; cut. Photo: Cliché des Musées Nationaux.

109. London, British Museum, no. 1895-9-15-510: Christ on the cross between Mary and John; black chalk treated in some places with white lead (oxidized); 41.2 × 27.9 cm. Photo: Courtesy of the Trustees of the British Museum.

110. Paris, Louvre, no. 700: Christ on the cross between Mary and John; black chalk, treated in some places with white lead (oxidized) and ink; 43.3 × 29 cm; cut. Photo: Cliché des Musées Nationaux.

111. London, British Museum, no. 1895-9-15-509: Christ on the cross between Mary and John; black chalk, treated in some places with white lead (oxidized); 41.3 × 28.6 cm; cut. Photo: Courtesy of the Trustees of the British Museum.

112. Paris, Louvre, no. 720r: Mary looking up (at the crucified Christ); black chalk; 23 × 11 cm; cut (verso: fig. 104). Photo: Cliché des Musées Nationaux.

113. Paris, Louvre, no. 698: John (under the cross); black chalk; 25 × 8.2 cm; cut. Photo: Cliché des Musées Nationaux.

114. Paris, Louvre, no. 843: crucified Christ with crown of thorns (copy); black chalk; 29 × 23 cm; cut. Photo: Cliche des Musées Nationaux.

115. Philipp Soye. Christ on the cross between Mary and John and two angels; copper engraving, dated 1568. Photo: Bibliothèque Nationale, Paris.

116. Frankfurt, Städelsches Kunstinstitut, no. 3978: Christ on the cross (copy); black chalk; cut. Photo: Städelsches Kunstinstitut.

117. Rome, Galleria Doria-Pamphili, no. 340: Christ on the cross between Mary and John and two angels; oil on wood; 51 × 33 cm. Photo: Georg Kamp.

118. Forlì Pinacoteca: *Resurrection of Christ*; oil on wood; 72 × 44 cm; cut. Photo: Pinacoteca.

DANIELE DA VOLTERRA

119. London, British Museum, no. 1946-7-13-114: draped male figure with book (apostle), left leg; black chalk; 37.2 × 22.8 cm; cut. Photo: Courtesy of the Trustees of the British Museum.

120. London, British Museum, no. 1956-10-13-13: upward-glancing man being undressed by a naked boy (Aeneas and Ascanius); black chalk; 14 × 10.1 cm; cut (copy). Photo: Courtesy of the Trustees of the British Museum.

121. Haarlem, Teylers Museum, A32-v: upward-glancing man being undressed by a naked boy in front of a bed occupied by a figure (Aeneas, Ascanius, and Dido), architectural profiles and frameworks; black chalk; 18 × 13.6 cm; cut (recto: fig. 126). Photo: Teylers Museum.

122. Vienna, Albertina, no. 497: upward-glancing man being undressed by a naked boy (Aeneas and Ascanius); black chalk; 52.1 × 34.6 cm; cut. Photo: Alpenland, Vienna.

123. Oxford, Ashmolean Museum, Parker no. 328r: seven sketches for a battle group, four sketches for an *Expulsion of the Moneychangers*; black chalk; 21 × 24.5 cm; cut. Photo: Ashmolean Museum.

124. London, British Museum, no. 1895-9-15-513: standing male nude; black chalk; 17 × 5.5 cm; cut. Photo: Courtesy of the Trustees of the British Museum.

125. Haarlem, Teylers Museum, A29v: seven figural sketches, niche frames; black chalk; 39.9 × 23.5 cm; cut. Photo: Teylers Museum.

126. Haarlem, Teylers Museum, A32r: two sketches of a standing man with open book (apostle), architectural sketches; black chalk; 18 × 13.6 cm; cut (verso: fig. 121). Photo: Teylers Museum.

127. London, British Museum, no. 1860-6-16-2/3v: sketches for an *Expulsion of the Moneychangers*; black chalk; 17.8 × 30.2 cm; cut (recto: fig. 130). Photo: Courtesy of the Trustees of the British Museum.

128. London, British Museum, no. 1860-6-16-2/2v: sketches for an *Expulsion of the Moneychangers*; black chalk; 14.8 × 27.6 cm; cut (recto: fig. 129). Photo: Courtesy of the Trustees of the British Museum.

129. London, British Museum, no. 1860-6-16-2/2r: two sketches for an *Expulsion of the Moneychangers*; black chalk; 14.8 × 27.6 cm; cut (verso: fig. 128). Photo: Courtesy of the Trustees of the British Museum.

130. London, British Museum, no. 1860-6-16-2/3r: *Expulsion of the Moneychangers*; black chalk; 17.8 × 37.2 cm; cut (verso: fig. 127). Photo: Courtesy of the Trustees of the British Museum.

131. Giulio Clovio. *Expulsion of the Moneychangers*; London, National Gallery, no. 1194; oil on wood; 60 × 38 cm. Photo: National Gallery, London.

FORGERY

132. Vienna, Albertina, Sc.R.155r: "studies" for the ignudo to the right above the Persica of the Sistine ceiling; red chalk over metal point, highlighted in white; 27 × 19 cm; cut. Photo: Alpenland, Vienna.

Introduction

Michelangelo spent the last third of his long life (1534–64) in Rome, on the Macel de' Corvi, near Trajan's Forum, where he owned a house, complete with workshop and stables. He lived there, along with several servants, until his death at approximately 4:45 P.M. on 18 February 1564.[1] As soon as presiding doctors and friends had confirmed his death, measures were taken to safeguard his works. The following morning a commission from the Roman governor arrived to conduct the official inventory. In the process it became apparent that except for ten cartoons of various sizes no drawings had been left behind. Interrogation of his servants revealed that the artist had burned almost everything in two lots shortly before his death.[2] The news spread like wildfire, evoking disappointment, astonishment, indeed indignation. "It did not appear to us to be an action worthy of him, to have surrendered them [the drawings] to the fire," wrote the duke of Florence, Cosimo I de' Medici, in his answer of 5 March to the report of his ambassador in Rome.[3]

It is understandable that Cosimo was angry. During the artist's life the duke had been unable to get anything out of him, neither his return to Florence, nor his willingness to deliver the plans needed to complete the Medici Chapel and the Laurentian Library, not to mention a single contribution for the ducal collection of drawings. As a result, he had placed his last hope in Michelangelo's estate. And yet he appears to have been aware of the fruitless nature of this hope, as his measures for secret surveillance of the artist prove.[4] For decades Michelangelo had been known for his contempt for those products (drawings, cartoons, wax and clay models) that served merely as preparatory stages for works of art. The letter of a confidant, Lionardo del Sellaio (or Compagno), indicates that he had arranged for the burning of all the *cartoni* left in his house in Rome when he moved to Florence in the spring of 1518.[5] Neither then nor later could he restrain himself from such destructive activities. At least twice—in 1538 and 1546—Pietro Aretino had tried, from Venice, to wrest from the famous man something that he otherwise was "wont [to give] so freely to the fire."[6] In the end Aretino was forced to content himself with a chalk drawing of Saint Catherine, presumably from Michelangelo's youth, which had been given to him by his friend and countryman Giorgio Vasari in 1535 and which he afterward treated "like a relic" (lost).[7] Vasari himself, the sixteenth century's most knowledgeable and passionate collector of drawings, seems to have fared similarly. Although he was the artist's frequent companion and enjoyed Michelangelo's affection and trust,[8] he apparently never succeeded in convincing his idol that preliminary sketches, studies, and cartoons were also worthy of a long life. To be sure, he owned a handful of the master's sketches, but none of them had been obtained from Michelangelo himself. The most splendid, in Vasari's eyes, was a present from Michelangelo's boyhood friend Francesco Granacci. It was a pen-and-ink drawing by a student of Ghirlandaio corrected by the young Michelangelo (lost).[9] The other sketches were discovered by Vasari after Michelangelo's death, in the long-abandoned Florentine workshop.[10] It is unlikely that all of them are by the master, if for no other reason than that only one of them—a sketch showing an intended suspension device for the transport of the marble *David* (1504, now lost)—appeared to the biographer to be worth mentioning by name.[11]

Despite his failure, Vasari was clever enough—in contrast to Duke Cosimo—not to view Michelangelo's behavior through the eyes of a collector or potential heir. He viewed it realistically—as the natural result of that artistic compulsion for perfection which led the master, throughout his life, to regard as perfect only those works from which every trace of labor had been expunged. Michelangelo had, Vasari wrote in 1568, always shrunk from letting an outsider see "the pains suffered by him and the manner and means by which he made visible his genius. For he wanted nothing other than to appear perfect" ("le fatiche durate da lui et i modi di tentare l'ingegno suo, per non apparire se non perfetto").[12] No one was supposed to learn how the work, which in its perfection appeared to be created as if by itself, had been created in reality.

Fortuitously preserved documents, such as a vexed letter from Rome on 4 October 1511, in which Michelangelo strictly forbids his father (for the second time) from letting anyone touch his drawings left for safekeeping in Florence, are not the only evidence that Vasari's view corresponded to the facts.[13] The few cases in which the artist gave away sketches, studies, or cartoons instead of destroying them are also revealing. As far as can be determined, he did this exclusively within the circle of his closest friends and always after considerable deliberation. Studies and sketches for his *own* works were given only to friends who were themselves artistically active—never to those whose relation to art was merely passive. The latter received, if anything, only perfect drawings, that is, specific highly finished drawings or cartoons that represent a stage immediately preliminary to a painted work.

The first among the privileged was Sebastiano del Piombo (ca. 1485–1547), the good-natured and somewhat lazy painter from Venice who had settled in Rome in 1511.[14] More gifted in portraiture than in history painting, he felt himself dependent on the imagination and anatomical knowledge of his great friend and accordingly often received Michelangelo's help—in the form of drawings that were especially tailored to his commissions for paintings, or occasionally in the form of studies for Michelangelo's own completed works.[15] His successor as recipient of drawings was Michelangelo's assistant and pupil Antonio Mini. When Mini left the master's workshop in November 1531 to try his luck in France after nearly nine years' service, he probably owned more Michelangelo drawings than all the other friends who ever received gifts combined.[16] To be sure, not much of this collection survives (among others, figs. 2, 4–6). Part was lost through theft even before Mini's early death.[17] The first to take custody of what was left behind was Giovanni Francesco Rustici (1474–1554), the Florentine sculptor, admirer of Michelangelo, and resident of Paris.[18] He owned an impressive number of cartoons, five of which—the cartoon for the *Leda* and four cartoons for the *ignudi* and prophets of the Sistine Chapel ceiling—were entrusted to his colleague Benvenuto Cellini between 1540 and 1544; Cellini, after returning to his native city of Florence, in turn sold them to Bernardo Vecchietti and Girolamo degli Albizzi (all lost).[19] Rustici returned the remaining cartoons to their creator on 31 August 1544.[20] Michelangelo seems thereupon to have burned them, except for the cartoon for the *Drunkenness of Noah*. In any case, none is thereafter mentioned in the sources; nor does it appear that any survived. Michelangelo gave the only cartoon not burned to his and Vasari's friend Bindo Altoviti (1491–1556), the banker, patron, and member of the anti-Medici faction living in exile in Rome (lost).[21] This gift was unique in its kind. Neither before nor after does the master appear to have given a non-artist a "used" cartoon. The cartoon for the *Venus and Amor*, which his friend the banker Bartolommeo Bettini received, had been prepared at Bettini's request and may well have been, from Michelangelo's point of view, just as much a commissioned work, complete in itself, as the *Noli me tangere* cartoon, which he had recently (1531) created for the Marchese del Vasto (both lost).[22] The former passed into the possession of that same Farnese librarian, Fulvio Orsini (1529–1600), whose collection contained the only *extant* Michelangelo cartoon—the Neapolitan fragment for the fresco of the *Crucifixion of Peter* in the Pauline Chapel, which was begun circa 1547 (fig. 34).[23]

After Antonio Mini's departure, Tommaso de' Cavalieri, an educated Roman nobleman renowned for his beauty, entered the artist's circle. He became Michelangelo's most beloved friend. Personally instructed in drawing by Michelangelo, in the course of his "apprenticeship" (1533) he received, in addition to a portrait drawn of himself (lost), at least seven highly finished drawings executed with the utmost care (including figs. 17, 19, and 24), together with some preliminary sketches for these same compositions (fig. 23).[24] Although it was small, contemporaries praised the collection as unique, and a large number of copies (including figs. 13, 16, 18, 20–22, 25) carried its fame far beyond the borders of Italy. The collection was subsequently enlarged by sketches for the *Last Judgment* (figs. 30–32),[25] by the Michelangelo sheets acquired by Cavalieri following the death of Sebastiano del Piombo,[26] and by the cartoon for a planned painting of *Christ's Farewell to His Mother* (lost).[27] Alessandro Farnese considered the drawings so valuable that he paid Cavalieri's heirs the then unprecedented sum of five hundred gold ducats for the complete collection—the price of at least two life-size marble sculptures.[28]

Compared with Cavalieri and Mini, Michelangelo's other artistically active friends came away virtually empty-handed. The sculptor and architect Jacopo del Duca (ca. 1520–after 1601) and the unknown Sicilian painter who ground the pigments for Michelangelo during the painting of the *Last Judgment* appear to have been the only friends between 1534 and 1564 who received a few remnants from the mass of sketches and studies otherwise destined for burning. Jacopo del Duca received "certain small drawings" for two paintings of the *Annunciation* and a painting of *Christ at the Mount of Olives* (figs. 36–37),[29] and the Sicilian painter "sketches and various drawings" for the fresco of the *Fall of the Rebel Angels* planned originally for the altar wall of the Sistine Chapel (lost).[30] All others—Alfonso Lombardi, Giuliano Bugiardini, Daniele da Volterra, and Marcello Venusti, indeed even the master's devoted pupil and biographer Ascanio Condivi—apparently had to content themselves with the few ad hoc sketches that Michelangelo occasionally drew to assist them.[31]

Even so, they were lucky. Many of Michelangelo's admirers passed their lives without even seeing one of their idol's drawings. To some, such frustration appears to have been so unbearable that they were driven to crime. In July 1529, according to a *ricordo* probably written by Mini, "Michelangelo's workshop in the Via Mozza [was] broken open with chisels, and about fifty sheets with figures were taken from it, including those with the Medici tombs and many drawings of great value" (presumably including figs. 2–4, 12).[32] The thieves were nevertheless so careless that they could be identified by the traces left behind. They were two otherwise up-

right young Michelangelo fans, the future sculptors Bartolommeo Ammannati and Nanni di Baccio Bigio. They had to return the stolen items.[33]

After Michelangelo's burial, when nothing more was to be expected much less stolen from the workshops in Rome and Florence, increasing demand for examples of the master's draftsmanship could be satisfied only with drawings allegedly by Michelangelo. One of the first to be taken in by these was Cosimo de' Medici. He plainly regarded as authentic—and thus "as jewels"—the two small cartoons (figs. 102–03) that Lionardo Buonarroti, who lived in Florence and knew little of his dead uncle's artistic practices, had brought with him from Rome (where he had hurried because of the inheritance) in May 1564. Cosimo's shrewd adviser Vasari, who as a close friend of Lionardo had arranged for the gift, could not bring himself to enlighten the duke. He only cryptically expressed his knowledge that the real author was Marcello Venusti by employing an unusual vagueness and circumlocution in the relevant report in the *Lives*.[34]

So much for the fate of Michelangelo's drawings according to the testimony of the written sources. The testimony, although laconic, leaves scarcely anything to be desired in clarity. It is therefore all the more astonishing how little importance present-day literature attaches to it. Delacre's bulky opus, *Le Dessin de Michel-Ange* (1938), the catalogue of the large anniversary exhibition at the British Museum in 1975 (Bib. 77), and Tolnay's four-volume *Corpus dei disegni di Michelangelo* (1975–80) refrain from any mention of Michelangelo's burning his drawings. In his *Drawings of Michelangelo* (1971, 19–20), Hartt at least mentions the later of the two documented burnings in a small aside indicating it took place "according to Vasari," but apparently only in order to sow doubt as to its actually having occurred.[35] And he maintains that there could have been no burning besides this one because Michelangelo was a person with a "jealous concern for the welfare of his drawings during his youth and maturity"—exactly the opposite of what Michelangelo appeared to be to Lionardo del Sellaio, Pietro Aretino, and Giorgio Vasari. Hartt does not tell us how he knows this, but the numbers of his catalogue are revealing. The catalogue contains 548 entries, which corresponds to about 410 sheets (one number equals one side of a sheet). If the drawings not included in the catalogue itself but described by Hartt as authentic in a table of concordance are added to the total, we arrive at a grand total of approximately 465 sheets, the majority of which are described as "undoubtedly" by Michelangelo.

The number of drawings Hartt attributes to Michelangelo exceeds the total number of extant drawings by nearly every other Italian Renaissance master. Nevertheless, to Tolnay this tally appeared too small. In his *Corpus*, he expanded it to approximately 630 sheets. The justification is found in the catalogue for the anniversary exhibition held in Florence in 1975 (bib. 318, n.p.). In this catalogue we learn that there had indeed been—as Vasari claimed—burnings of drawings "arranged" by Michelangelo. But these burnings had involved "disegni lascivi," not the sketches, studies, and cartoons regularly associated with the master's commissions. The artist was ashamed of these "disegni lascivi" and not, as Vasari maintained, of the normal preparatory drawings that bore witness to his labor.[36] Up to the time of this sensational revelation nothing was known about "disegni lascivi" by Michelangelo. Certainly the *Leda* was and is known—from engravings, paintings, and drawn copies. But this was not what Tolnay had in mind, for he was, like all Michelangelo scholars, well aware that Michelangelo gave both the painting and the corresponding cartoon to Antonio Mini—without any discernible fear of corrupting a minor.[37] Tolnay apparently had something spicier in mind: something "along the lines of erotic Renaissance graphics" à la Giulio Romano—something traded *under* the counter. Unfortunately he was unable to say what these drawings looked like. We learn only that they "contrasted with the religiosity of his last years" and, moreover, were burned immediately. Nevertheless, our curiosity is given one consolation: the letter written by Lionardo del Sellaio.[38] Seen in the light of Tolnay's assertions, it indicates that Michelangelo's pornographic works were the size of cartoons and must have been available in large quantities as early as 1518.

tory drawings. Taken together, however, they point to a mass of sketches and studies of unique dimensions. In any case, they could well exceed all other products of the master's draftsmanship several times over.

Let us assume that this overwhelming volume of sketches and studies was actually preserved by Michelangelo—as Tolnay speculated—so as to give them as presents on occasion. Of course no one would expect all of them to have survived into our time. But in such a case one could well expect that their quantitative preponderance over the architectural sketches, anatomical studies, presentation sheets, and quisquilia sketches would be reflected in the extant drawings. But such is not the case. In fact, Tolnay's *Corpus* (bib. 319) provides precisely the opposite ratio. Of the 633 catalogue numbers, at most 140 are related to Michelangelo's huge production of sculpture and painting, according to Tolnay's commentaries. Over 75 percent consist of sketches for architecture, furniture, and marble blocks (about 190 catalogue numbers), anatomical studies (14 numbers), studies and sketches without recognizable reference to Michelangelo's works (about 180 numbers), presentation sheets (about 40 numbers), sketches for works by other artists (about 40 numbers), and quisquilia sketches. The user of Tolnay's *Corpus* is confronted with a dilemma: Either the bulk of sketches, studies, and cartoons related to his works was destroyed by Michelangelo himself—leaving one to wonder why Tolnay used so much cleverness to dispute the claim. Or these drawings were destroyed by their owners—leaving us with the riddle of why they directed their destructive rage primarily at the drawings related to sculpture and painting, and why Michelangelo was given the blame. It is left to the reader to solve this dilemma for himself. In any case, there is one thing at which he can rejoice: sheets by the master still exist. The only question is, how many?

Let us pause for a moment at the sculptures and paintings of the artist. This oeuvre contains, when the few lost pieces are included, approximately twenty-four marble sculptures, most of them larger than life-size and some consisting of several figures; four marble reliefs; two bronze statues; and one wooden crucifix; four gigantic frescoes with many hundreds of figures; four large tempera paintings; and the cartoons for at least three other paintings that were not executed (including one for the fresco of the "Bathing Soldiers").[39] Each of these works required a more or less extensive set of prepara-

Tolnay was not always of the opinion that there were 630 sheets by the master. In 1960 he reckoned the number at around 250.[40] Fifty years before, Frey (bib. 101) had proposed a similarly modest number (244, although some are *different* sheets), while his contemporary Thode (bib. 294) had at the same time (1913) catalogued twice as many, namely 494 sheets. Thode's total was impressive for the time, but under Berenson's critical eye (bib. 37) it shrank back to 288 sheets—a shocking reversal when one considers that several dozen new sheets, unknown to Thode and Frey, had surfaced in the intervening years (including figs. 42, 121, 125–26).[41] That same year, Delacre reversed the contractionist tendency by presenting a body of sheets, the number of which is not precisely determinable but whose total certainly exceeds Thode's record. This was based on enumerating sheets that filled the "schoolwork" portfolios in the collections. Initially, most scholars reacted with skepticism.[42] In 1959 Dussler (bib. 80) shortened the tally to about 350 sheets and declared an equally large number to be "apocryphal." Keller (bib. 156) went even further in 1975 and declared only "around three hundred" sheets to be authentic. First Hartt (bib. 130) and then Tolnay (bib. 319) dropped all earlier reservations and presented—each with his own method and with his own totals—their expanded views on the authentic Michelangelo corpus.

Every non-expert has much the same feeling when he consults one of the many available catalogues and reads, for example, that "this undoubtedly genuine drawing" was possibly created if not for the Sistine Chapel ceiling then for the tomb of Julius II or for an unknown relief. He feels something akin to satisfaction—satisfaction that the author in question could readily prove the authenticity of this masterpiece if he wanted to; and that the only reason he did not was because others had long since provided the conclusive evidence. The amateur does not know who the others are. But he feels that they must and do exist, and is grateful for this feeling for reasons of comfort alone. As a rule, he remains grateful, too—unless he is overcome by the desire to get to the root of the matter.

Let us assume we have by chance taken a glance at the verso of the famous Windsor sheet number 12767, where the signature "D. Giulio Clouio" stands (fig. 82), and are now eager to know why the drawing of the *Resurrection* on the front (fig. 81) is considered a product of Michelangelo. We consult the most recent relevant publication, the second volume of Tolnay's sumptuous *Corpus* (bib. 319). Under number 255 we find an extensive commentary, divided into the sections "Description" and "Dating and Attribution." We skim the first section and plunge into the second. We learn the following: (1) The composition fits "perfectly into a lunette"; (2) "This fact" proves that the drawing—as Popp (bib. 241) had already assumed—is a sketch by Michelangelo for the lunette above the Medici tombs in the New Sacristy of San Lorenzo; (3) The sketches on the back are likewise

"originals"; (4) The signature serves to "indicate the name of the owner."

By chance, we know that the sources report nothing about a plan to paint the lunettes of the Medici Chapel. We therefore find it difficult to accept Tolnay's assertion that the drawing's "perfect" conformity to a lunette format is proof that it was drawn for such a project. We find it even more difficult to imagine how Clovio's signature can vouch for Michelangelo's authorship. To be sure, this most famous of all sixteenth-century miniaturists and Michelangelo-imitators was also the owner of about a dozen Michelangelo sketches, as is documented in an inventory of his possessions made on 31 December 1577, conducted while he was still alive.[43] But these sketches contained everything imaginable: a candleholder, a window, a door, a sarcophagus, two prophets, a Madonna, various arms and legs, everything but a *Resurrection of Christ*. Not that Clovio didn't own any sheets with such a subject. On the contrary: he owned six of them. But he had, according to his inventory, drawn them himself. We are, in short, no wiser. By consulting Tolnay's *Corpus*, we can only derive the challenge to research further. And Tolnay is helpful to the extent that he appended to his own commentary a list of what he considered the most important earlier commentaries.

Tolnay's bibliographical appendix lists eleven titles. The most recent is the catalogue of the London anniversary exhibition in 1975. But there is no commentary under number 46 of this catalogue, merely a cross-reference to number 42. There the Windsor drawing is not explicitly mentioned in a discussion of "fourteen studies for a Risen Christ for a composition of the *Resurrection*." These studies are—the catalogue reports—listed in full in Wilde (bib. 344). We duly consult Wilde's list and ascertain, to our amazement, that it in no way contains only "studies" and still less for only *one* composition of the *Resurrection*. Curious to know what intrinsically holds the fourteen drawings (including figs. 14, 16, 27, 59–63, 81), we garner the information, written between the lines by Wilde, that it is the hand of Michelangelo. Sighing, we return to number 42 of the 1975 catalogue. "It seems clear," we read there, "that the project in connexion with which they [the fourteen "studies"] were made was one to which Michelangelo devoted particular trouble." The question is *what* project it was. Hirst offers the "most convincing solution" to this question in his essay "The Chigi Chapel in Santa Maria della Pace" (bib. 133). Hirst's essay does not appear in Tolnay's bibliographic list. His "solution" is significantly different from Tolnay's: Michelangelo did not draw these "studies" for himself and for a painting in the lunette of the Medici Chapel, but for an altar painting by his friend Sebastiano del Piombo (a labor of love that was nevertheless futile, since the painting was never executed).[44] After this information we have two contradictory answers, but none to the question that interests *us*. Still curious, we reach for the second-most-recent title in Tolnay's list, Hartt's *Michelangelo Drawings*. Under number 256 we learn that "this wonderful drawing has never been placed in question," and that "contrary to some statements, it fits perfectly into a semicircle"; number 124 has this to say about the verso (fig. 82): "Hitherto unrecognized, these strong studies can be connected only with the aged Boaz, Michelangelo's fierce caricature of Julius II." We are not advised about the signature "D. Giulio Clouio."

We turn to the third authority, Luciano Berti (bib. 40, 454), where we learn that the Windsor drawing is a study "for a Resurrection dated circa 1532–33."

Thereafter we turn to Tolnay's essay "Morte e Resurrezione in Michelangelo" (bib. 307–08), which states that Michelangelo "modeled the naked bodies with a masterful chiaroscuro," and that he "succeeded . . . in giving an impression of the softness of the skin." Especially noteworthy is the "expressive value" of Christ's gesture. For it breaks "with a centuries-old tradition, according to which Christ's gesture in such a scene was merely the adaptation of a conventional posture." The guards react "not only to the unexpected event; they also evoke earthly sensuality in contrast to the spiritual striving of Christ." Does the proof of authenticity ultimately lie in the statement that the chiaroscuro is masterful and Christ's gesticulation revolutionary and "spiritual?"

The fifth authority, Brugnoli's volume on Michelangelo's drawings (bib. 50), seems to harden this suspicion. Numbers 36–38 confirm what we already know: that there is nothing to substantiate the lunette theory. But then she gets to the point: "The eternal dualism between spirit and matter" is "paradigmatically evident" in the Windsor drawing. Christ is a "picture of pure spiritual beauty, free of every earthly chain," while the guards are "hopelessly [entangled] in the corruptible matter of their bodies. . . . The black chalk, masterfully applied in the shading of light and dark," is a medium intimately meshed with Michelangelo's imagination" and achieves "effects of simultaneously external plastic evidence and the softest light-dark shading."

A bit confused by so much angelic music devoted to a human product composed of strokes, we knock on the door of the sixth authority, Dussler's *Kritischer Katalog* (bib. 80). We enter, yet become even more confused. There we find the Windsor drawing—number 239—classified among the "authentic" products by Michelangelo's "own hand," and simultaneously learn that it actually bears no resemblance whatsoever to other authentic sheets. It exhibits "effects . . . that exceed his [Michelangelo's] strictly plastic composition. . . . The soft, dim modeling and material characteristics" in particular are "surprising" for Michelangelo.

With growing discouragement, we pore through the remaining authorities. In Wilde (bib. 343a, no. 427), we learn again that "there exist . . . further representations of the Resurrection," and that "there are various grounds, both external and internal, for connecting all these sheets [including figs. 14, 16, 27, 59–63, 81] with the years 1532–33." In Tolnay (bib. 219, no. 109) we are informed that "the movement and emotion in the center of the composition . . . are the most intense, and both become less intense towards the periphery." In Gamba (bib. 106, xxxii) we receive the information that Christ "rises up like an athlete shaking off his chains, to the irritation of his suddenly awoken guards," and that he appears "like a giant struggling with the elements." After consulting Tolnay's earliest commentary (bib. 296, 438–40) and upon reaching Popp's *Medici-Kapelle* (bib. 241), the eleventh and last authority and the wellspring of all theories concerning the owner-signature on the verso and the lunette destination for the composition on the recto, we are ready to give up. We have heard everything conceivable from Tolnay and from every other important expert he lists—everything but this: how a sheet signed by Giulio Clovio, bearing a drawing of the *Resurrection* outside the scope of Michelangelo's "strictly plastic composition," is supposed to be an authentic Michelangelo sheet.

Amateurs that we are, we are reluctant to do any expert an injustice. We patiently await the desired proof of authenticity and therefore again make our way through the authorities—those authorities not listed in Tolnay's bibliographic appendix. This time we proceed chronologically and begin with Berenson (bib. 34). Under catalogue number 1612 we learn that the Windsor drawing is "indeed a marvel of dramatic force" and could by all means have been made for Cavalieri, were it not that "internal evidence alone" gives one cause "to believe it of slightly earlier date." Then we turn to Frey (bib. 101, 19), who assures us that the drawing is the "result of a spontaneous impulse." From Frey the trail leads to Thode, Panofsky, and Brinckmann. Brinckmann (no. 47) thinks the drawing is "perhaps even more pictorially suggestive" than the Madonna studies X and Y, while Panofsky (bib. 202, 29) speaks laconically of a "high point" in the development of the "twenties and early 'thirties." Next come Popham, Delacre,

Degenhart, Kleiner, Kirschenbaum, Goldscheider, Einem, Schmidt, and Keller. Each contributes a morsel to our knowledge. Keller (bib. 101), in conclusion, ties the details together: "Yes, occasionally in such 'master drawings' Michelangelo far exceeded the bounds that characterize the majority of his graphic creations. The sheet with the *Resurrection of Christ* in Windsor is complete in itself. Material charm is wrung from the soft matt chalk like a dim trail of light—the outstretched arms of the Risen Christ direct one to the fall of divine light. Perhaps the unusual character of the sheet, and also its perfect execution, can be explained thus: the drawing was intended to be shown to the client, who was meant to be moved to select such a magnificently closed semicircular composition for execution in one of the lunettes of the Medici tombs."

After this summary in the twenty-sixth authority, we finally know this for sure: the Windsor sheet with the signature "D. Giulio Clouio" is an "undoubtedly genuine" Michelangelo (Popp, bib. 246, 65) because—as Hartt so aptly remarked—its authenticity has never been doubted. The proof of authenticity is based on the fact that in the course of seventy-five years of balloting only yes-votes were cast.

Because of the illustrious scholarly reputations of the participants, we take this balloting seriously. But since it has produced no insights regarding the attribution, we begin to conduct some research for ourselves. We glance at the small *Resurrection* painting in the Fogg Museum in Cambridge (fig. 84). We see that ten of its fourteen small figures are based on the Windsor drawing, but that the other four are based on another *Resurrection* composition authenticated as Michelangelo's (figs. 27–28). We consult the literature and are informed that the painting is by Venusti and is a combination of two *Resurrection* compositions by Michelangelo.[45] That's odd, we think. How is it that Venusti is associated with this combination when one of the two drawings belonged not to him, but to Clovio? We search a little, and behold, it turns out that Clovio was also acquainted with the other drawing (figs. 27–28), since he selected two figures from it for his *Resurrection* miniature in the Towneley Lectionary (fig. 85). The main figure even appears with the same preposterous shroud flowing over the thick-walled sarcophagus. Could it be that the painting in the Fogg Museum is *not* by Venusti? We duly compare it with Venusti's authenticated paintings, including his small *Resurrection* picture in Forlì (fig. 118). As different as night and day. We compare it with Clovio's *Resurrection* miniature (fig. 85). We see not only almost the same number of soldiers, similarly clothed, in a similar jumble of dozing and agitated postures, not only a similar setting and a similar lavish array of colors; we also see the same types of faces—compact oval faces with full cheeks, widely spaced cow-eyes, and heavily dimpled mouths. Is attributing the painting to Venusti a feint meant to deflect our attention from Clovio?

Honi soit qui mal y pense, we think, and search Michelangelo's works for compositions bearing more resemblance to the composition of the Windsor drawing than Michelangelo's *Resurrection* sketch (figs. 27–28). The search proves fruitless, so we look to other artists. We finally come across something, in the work of Giulio Romano (1492–1546). Romano's *Resurrection* drawing in Berlin (fig. 86) exhibits the same spatial conception as the Windsor composition, the same limited depth. Furthermore, it shows a Christ figure that climbs out of the large sarcophagus in nearly the same way—turned with a similarly prominent corner jutting out toward the viewer. We have found no mention whatsoever of this drawing in the literature on the Windsor drawing. No wonder: Giulio Romano was Clovio's teacher. In his honor Clovio changed his baptized name Giorgio for Giulio.[46]

"Il faudrait que notre lecteur put se faire une religion avec notre seul livre," Delacre says in the preface to his thick volume (bib. 66, xxii). The sentence could just as easily come from any other publications. For ultimately every author expects from his public the same faith that he possesses himself. Of course the reader is permitted to ask questions. But they should, if possible, be questions the author can answer—for example: whether the Windsor drawing might not just as well fit into a semicircular framework as into a vertical or horizontal one. To ask for proof of authenticity in cases where authenticity has never been doubted is a sign of irreverence.

There have of course always been scholars who embraced their public and also attempted to explore its skepticism. One of the most prominent was Luitpold Dussler. He was not satisfied with shrugging his shoulders at the ebbs and flows in the inventories of genuine sheets. He felt that this ebb-and-flow phenomenon was caused by methodological faults. Scholars for the most part seem to have forgotten that, in order to become acquainted with Michelangelo's way of drawing, one must first gather together those drawings whose authenticity is warranted by any external evidence—no matter what that evidence is. Instead of undertaking this most urgent and obvious of tasks, scholars continued to stare as though hypnotized into the monumental stew in which the genuine and the dubious bubble together, and selected from it whatever seemed especially appetizing—sometimes more, sometimes less, according to one's taste. Dussler saw that this method, which merely dished out smaller stews (the selections presented in various catalogues) from the contents of the large stew (the sum of what is gathered in museums and private collections under the rubric "Michelangelo"), was incapable of solving problems of attribution—unless a scholar succeeded in the impossible task of demonstrating that *his* taste was the correct one. Dussler (bib. 80) tried to rectify what had so far been lacking. He sorted the piles of so-called Michelangelo drawings into three categories: "The genuine drawings by his own hand," "the attributed drawings," and "the apocryphal sheets." And so, for the first time, a scientific organizing principle found its way into the practice of cataloguing.[47]

But it was just as quickly dropped. Dussler's successors apparently found nothing to like in a method of presentation that put the public in the position—even if only theoretically—of testing the validity of their attributions against what was known to be genuine. As a body they returned to the stew principle, as though there had never been an attempt to make things transparent. Hartt, Tolnay, and Hirst withhold all information about which sheets are really—that is, independent of their subjective and differing tastes—"undoubtedly" by Michelangelo. The reader is left with the impression that practically all of them are. Unfortunately Dussler himself was partly responsible for this return to the status quo ante—because of the inconsistency with which he put his methodological theory into practice. Dussler knew that "in the strict sense of the word . . . extremely few drawings [can be] classified as 'genuine.'"[48] But he did not list the few by number and name. He did not even list the criteria for their verification. As though his tripartite organizing principle was merely the judgment of the eye, he filled the first and most important chapter of his *Kritischer Katalog*—containing the supposedly genuine drawings—with drawings (nos. 1–243) of which at least half cannot be categorized as "genuine" in either the strict or loose sense of the word. His only comment on the subject: "who would like to argue here, when the impression provided by the style is absolutely compelling?"!

If such were the case, no one would like to argue. But unfortunately there is no drawing style that would say for itself:

"I am typical for XY"—only its interpreter can express such a view.[49] But how can the statement of an interpreter of style be "compelling" when it exists only in the form of an assertion? We heard it claimed twenty-six times (by Dussler, among others) that the *Resurrection* drawing in Windsor (fig. 81) is "undoubtedly" a genuine product of Michelangelo. Are we now convinced? Perhaps we *were* once—when we heard the claim for the first time, when it still had its magic. Unfortunately a claim retains its magical force only as long as proof can be assumed to lie behind it.

Admittedly, there is no field of scholarly inquiry in which everything is provable. But this fact can never serve as an excuse for abandoning proper methodology. For the scholarly value of a hypothesis is measured solely by the solidity of its premises and the type and scope of the phenomenon it is meant to explain. The value of a hypothesis does not depend on who believes in it. A field of scholarship that erects its most basic hypotheses on shifting methodological sands is open to suspicion of acting opportunistically.

To select out what is genuine means putting everything else into question, that is, *almost everything*. It is readily understandable why no one likes to do that. One either owns *genuine* Michelangelo drawings or none at all. No value is placed on those whose authenticity is a passing possibility. They would become negligible quantities if measured by the yardstick of those declared genuine "in the strict sense of the word"—and of what use are they? Is this rigorous measure really practicable when everyone swears there's a much gentler one: the "compelling statement of the style," which guarantees that not only famed pieces like the *Resurrection* drawing in Windsor (fig. 81), but also stylistic detritus (including figs. 82–83, 88–90) remain in the Michelangelo corpus. It affords long-term protection against defoliation to the tree that shot so mysteriously out of the scorched earth.

No one disagrees that the number of leaves on this Michelangelo tree varies. Sometimes there is a stormy autumn, sometimes an especially bountiful spring. But is this worth squabbling over? Is it not insignificant to know how many Michelangelo sheets actually exist, when all the world claims there are "hundreds?" The medieval world hardly worried over the fact that all the relics of John the Baptist venerated in the Western world combined were more likely to produce a mammoth than a preacher in the desert. The miraculous pieces of fur and bones were needed—so they existed. Only the malicious or the insane would have robbed such possessions of their holiness by doubting their authenticity. Should the present-day needs be any less worthy of respect?

Of course not. But a drawing is not a bone displayed for veneration. It embodies a piece of the imaginative world of its creator. It makes visible the intimate mental spheres otherwise closed to all biographers. It can offer insight into modalities of artistic thought and processes of composition, into methods of construction and differentiation, into ways of assimilating reality, and into the secrets of the birth of an idea. It is more personal, more multilayered, more revealing than any work of art that is complete in itself. For that reason it is entitled to recognition and respect as an expression of the personality of its creator. Every misattribution tends to distort historical reality as a whole by imputing to an artist someone else's thoughts, the ways of imagining and expression that are the property of another. It saddles the creativity of the assumed creator with contradictions that did not exist, and at the same time makes the art of the actual creator appear more one-sided and insignificant than it actually was. Instead of illuminating at least one of the two personalities examined, it obscures both. In the end, when misattributions follow their natural course, proliferate to produce volumes, and the unintended defamation becomes a system, both the plucked and the foreign-feathered individual cease being intelligible. Both become inaccessible to research—the former for lack of concrete objects, the latter because it appears undefinable in the tangle of contradictions.

It is not hard to discover how far the confusion in Michelangelo research has already progressed. We need only ask the authors of our catalogues what constitutes the common, Michelangelo-like characteristics of their many entries, what sort of development these entries suggest, or what they say about methods of Michelangelo's conception, experimentation, and composition. We notice immediately that every such question reveals an Achilles' heel. The literature provides no coherent, conclusive answer.[50] The sum of scholars' efforts over many years is in large part merely a modification of the initial capital: a new catalogue with new numbers. As a rule the user can only hope that the individual pieces of the puzzle, correctly assembled, will produce something that looks like Michelangelo.

Let us assume we would like to learn which are the con-

stant characteristics of Michelangelo's draftsmanship, and how they were modified in certain periods of the artist's life. In one of the most recent catalogues we select two drawings that are attributed to different periods but otherwise suited for the best possible comparison. Our choices are the famous St. Peter in Munich copied from Masaccio (fig. 53) and the hunchbacked old woman in Oxford (fig. 54)—both hatched pen-and-ink drawings of the same format with similar draperies and poses. The first was—we are assured—created about 1490, the second at least a quarter-century later.[51]

The two drawings therefore stand nearly ten times as long apart as the *Zacharias* and the *Jonah* at either ends of the Sistine Chapel ceiling. But amazingly, there is nothing to indicate it. In both cases we see the same lack of proportion between effort and effect, the same expansive hatching. In both cases the same higgledy-piggledy confusion of long and short, bold and thin, "wet" and "dry" strokes, of large and tiny, brittle and soft, widely and narrowly meshed hatching groups; a confusing alternation of extremely thin and boldly reinforced contour parcels composed of single and multi-track strokes, defining sometimes summarily, sometimes punctiliously, a multiplicity of patches and seams and small smudged areas. In both cases a drapery whose flat mass is crisscrossed by numerous knife-edge folds and split by absurdly deep indentations, and a body that atrophies to a spatially nonexistent model under this dismembered mass. Even the structureless fraying of the figure toward the lower edge of the sheet is present in both examples, producing a similar obscuring of the figure's stance and position in space.

How is this stylistic conformity to be explained? Did Michelangelo develop only as a sculptor, painter, architect, and poet? Did he, as a draftsman, spend thirty years treading the same ground? Before we begin to pity him as the victim of partial early senility, we would like to know how he drew in the intervening years. Our glance falls on the two pen-and-ink drawings occupying the recto of Louvre sheet 714 (fig. 5), a study for the marble *David* and a sketch for the bronze *David* created circa 1501–02. We don't trust our eyes. The *David* sketch is smaller than the midget that accompanies the old woman on the Oxford sheet (fig. 54), but what a difference in economy and precision, in the proportioning, plasticity, and solidity of the figure, in the purposefulness and energy of the contours and hatching. What a difference also between the malleable, finely differentiated hatching texture of the arm study and the coarse, flat lattices that flatten the naked body parts of the hunchbacked old hag and her companion. Out of simple fear of being tricked by an optical illusion, we consult another sheet, the Oxford sheet with the red-chalk studies for the companion of the Libyan sibyl and the right hand of the sibyl herself, as well as the pen-and-ink drawings of slaves for the Julius tomb (fig. 6). Scholars date the sheet circa 1510–13,[52] therefore chronologically closer to the old woman in Oxford. But behold, the differences are even more striking. The studies for the Libyan sibyl and the slave studies are completely congruent with the arm study and the *David* sketch (fig. 5). Indeed, they are even more economically and more precisely articulated, are even more dynamic in their appearance. There is nothing reminiscent of the copy after Masaccio (fig. 53), nothing suggestive of the old woman in Oxford (fig. 54). We are confronted with a biological monster: a Michelangelo who circa 1501 had far outgrown the level of the Masaccio copy and who circa 1515–25 unexpectedly reverted to the level of 1490. We ask for an explanation. Hartt, Tolnay, Hirst (bib. 139a), and the London exhibition catalogue of 1975[53] offer no comment. Only Wilde found a helpful explanation. "It reverts," he wrote in 1953 in reference to a drawing of a prophet stylistically similar to the old woman in Oxford, "to a linear system long abandoned."[54]

Thus a deliberate return to the pen-and-ink excesses characteristic of the drawing style of his youth, to a neophyte style. This is not really an explanation, but it remains a possibility. If need be we could even resign ourselves to it, if this reversion—motivated by who knows what—were a unique event in Michelangelo's career. But it apparently was not. Insofar as scholarly attribution seems to indicate, the steps backward must have been habitual; Michelangelo must have hopped here and there like a frightened mouse. What the old woman in Oxford (fig. 54) and its related drawings (fig. 52–53, 55–56) show us is only one among many renaissances of his beginner's style—if we can judge from the catalogues—experienced in his mature years.[55] One of the last he suffered circa 1550, on the occasion of preparing the cartoon (fig. 95) for Condivi's *Epiphany* (fig. 98), now in the British Museum. The good spirits of economy, concentration, and self-assurance, which only a few years before had guided Michelangelo's hand in drawing the cartoon for the *Crucifixion of Peter* (fig. 34), seem to have deserted him once again. This ensemble of curiously boneless and jointless musclemen (figs. 95–97)—whose meaning has caused so much consternation—was drawn in repeated attempts, with hesitant, painstaking patching, and with an infinite number of spindly, broken strokes.

Condivi might have stood before this cartoon with the feeling that he saw in it a piece of himself. It seems no master was ever as comprehensively empathetic as Michelangelo.

When doing work for a pupil, he not only drew like a pupil himself, but he was capable of even more. He even denied what Bernhard Degenhart claims cannot be denied, that is, his own drawing dialect.

Degenhart discovered in the 1930s that every artist who received his basic training as a draftsman in a local workshop in his native region was marked accordingly for the rest of his life.[56] An artist who had learned to draw in Florence thereafter drew in the "Florentine" style, that is, with clear, sharply defined contours and tectonically constructed, "solid" hatchings. His drawings were different, independent of where and when they were made, from those of every Sienese, Roman, or Venetian. They possess their own dialect, discernible in certain functional characteristics of their components.

Degenhart considered it impossible for the characteristics he discovered to be altered by the conscious mind (these characteristics are used today to classify anonymous Italian drawings according to "local" schools). But he seemingly underestimated the chameleon-like genius of our master. To judge from what is attributed to him, Michelangelo was, without trouble, also able to draw in a non-Florentine style, in the styles of the Marches, Siena, Venice, or Milan—depending on whom he drew for. He was never in Milan and spent only a short time in Venice. But whenever he helped Venusti (fig. 100), his friend from Como, he lapsed into Venusti's own "milanese" drawing dialect and created products that are "especially rich in constant change, indeed surprises in the arrangement of strokes" and characterized by "their charm of a certain mystery," by "surprising changes of direction of the strokes, color character and low statics," as well as "an uninhibited fall of the stroke groups and a swaying steepness of the lines."[57] Similarly, he lapsed into the Venetian dialect as soon as he allegedly took pen to hand to assist the Venetian Sebastiano del Piombo (figs. 46–47). His shadings suddenly became long and broad marks that merged with the contours and, in their contrast to the unshaded parts, caused the bodies to appear as if they were radiated by an atmospheric light. Apparently Michelangelo suffered the same fate as the stigmatic Resl von Konnersreuth, who now and again took to spouting in foreign tongues even though she had only learned to speak Bavarian.

Let us suppose that a scholar unexpectedly succeeded in proving that the *Lazarus* or *Annunciation* sketches in London (figs. 46–47, 100) or the copy after Masaccio and the old woman in Oxford (figs. 53–54) were products of Michelangelo's hand. Suspicion would suddenly evaporate that the dialect and revival miracles in Michelangelo's career as a draftsman were of natural origin, that is, simply the result of arbitrary attributions. A sensational result, certainly. But one thing would not change: we would still have the most difficult task ahead of us—that of explaining the miracle of survival and disappearance. According to current attributions an enormous mass of sheets must simply have appeared one day, although Michelangelo, according to the sources, convinced his contemporaries that he had burned them. And at the same time the sheets of Cellini, Clovio, Daniele da Volterra, Mini, Sebastiano, or Venusti must have evaporated by the hundreds into thin air—those of Michelangelo's pupils Cavalieri and Condivi even vanished completely—without any documentable injury ever having been done to them.

As long as the many small miracles cannot be explained, we would do better not to believe in the big one. For it could well be that the big miracle occurred merely as a result of the many small ones, in other words: the allegedly lost sheets are among the extant ones. This possibility exists. Let us test it.

Testing has some requirements. It is of little use to name criteria for authentication and then select out what is authenticated for A or B when we do not know what to do with what has been selected out and with what is left over. What we need first and foremost is a method of evaluation. It must provide us with the means to separate the whole corpus into individual "hands" independent of what has been authenticated for whom, by showing us how to identify an individual style in the first place. And at the same time, it must be transparent. It must not lead to mere assertions about concepts like "quality," "technique," "ductus," or "lineament." For assessments of quality do not have much relevant to say about the subject itself. The style of a Michelangelo drawing can hardly be distilled with the tautological statement that the strokes are "on target," "dynamic," or simply "magnificent." The method we need should not grade the specifics of the drawing. It should explain them.

This method is developed in the first part of this book.[58] It attempts to make things sufficiently clear that the reader can draw his own conclusions and will not feel at a disadvantage when the second and third parts discuss specific examples from the "Michelangelo" corpus rather than the whole. This approach was unavoidable. The planned scope of the book allowed for one of two approaches: the writing of a new Michelangelo catalogue *or* an introduction to the science of drawing analysis using examples from "Michelangelo's" corpus. The decision was *necessarily* in favor of the second course. For the layman has a right to know, for once, *how* an attribution is made and the usefulness of making one.

I

The Science of Drawing Analysis

1

Drawing and How
It Is Produced

Drawing as the Product of Movement

Many people use the word *paint* when they mean *draw* and take no notice when Albrecht Dürer calls a pen-and-ink sketch like the *Twins of Ertingen* a "painting."[1] They are right insofar as drawing and painting are in principle similar processes. Both can be described as manual movements that are transferred to a mark-producing or color-releasing medium (brush, pen, chalk, and so forth), by means of which color material is deposited on a surface (wood, linen, paper, and so forth). The error begins in confounding the properties of the products of these movements. Drawing does not produce a continuum of color, but instead a stroke system, a purposefully organized system of movement traces that do not completely lose their linear integrity even when they are extremely concentrated. Painting, on the other hand, produces a color system whose purpose is precisely the elimination of the integrity of the individual strokes. The difference might appear insignificant to iconographers or lovers of pastels. But for art historians it is fundamental.[2] For it means nothing less than that the "style" of a drawing and that of a painting are manifested on different levels, and that different investigative methods are required to grasp those styles.

The style of a drawing is manifested in the stroke system. Like the color system, its purpose is to depict a certain thing—a figure, a "story," or a landscape. But the essence of the stroke system is not identical with that of the thing depicted. The characteristics of the stroke system refer to the movement traces themselves, to contour and hatching structures. Movement reflexes are never wholly subject to conscious control (no draftsman thinks of the quality of strokes and intervals between strokes when drawing a figure!). Therefore—in contrast to the styles of objects, figures, and composition—they cannot be imitated. The characteristics of the stroke system are the most important basis for determining authorship, and practically the only relevant one for answering the question of authenticity (original or copy?). But they cannot be systematically studied until we have a knowledge of the relationships between manual movement and its traces on a surface.

PRESSURE AND COURSE

In both writing and drawing two different directional components are at work: a course component parallel to the drawing surface and a pressure component acting vertical to the drawing surface. Their interaction is the precondition for the creation of the stroke; the way they interact is the origin of all shapes of single strokes and stroke assemblages. The course component without the pressure component produces no visible stroke, the pressure component without the course component only a point. During the act of drawing the two components interact neither uniformly nor continuously. Movement phases during which the medium in fact touches the drawing surface ("marking phases") alternate with phases during which it glides over the surface without touching it ("unmarked phases"). The clearest expression of this alternation is in hatchings, where the connections between two parallels are often partially (fig. 5, *David*) or completely (fig. 55) missing, as well as in those contours, which are interspersed with large or small gaps (figs. 4, 6, and elsewhere). The pressure component itself acts with varying intensity, producing sometimes weak, sometimes bold strokes. Its behavior can change even within one and the same stroke and thereby result in the creation of a special stroke type. This is distinguished from the "normal" or threadlike stroke drawn with uniform pressure because it increases and/or decreases in volume and girth/breadth. We therefore designate it as a modulated stroke. Modulated strokes and thread strokes are seldom equally represented in a drawing. As a rule, one or the other dominates. Drawings with a preponderance of modulated strokes are most frequent in authenticated Michelangelo drawings (for example, figs. 4–6); those in which thread strokes predominate are found exclusively in the corpus of attributed drawings (for example, figs. 51, 61, 72, 83, 88, 90, 92, 94, 104). The stroke system of the former are more elastic, those of the latter more brittle.

DIRECTION AND SHAPE

In contrast to handwriting, movement during drawing does not have to conform to a definite direction (for example, from left to right) and to a set of basic shapes (letters or characters). The course of movement is defined only by the draftsman's intention—which is not to say that the directions and shapes of strokes within a drawing are absolutely equivalent. They *are* equivalent to the extent that they produce aesthetic effects, but not as products of movements subject to the laws of joint mechanics. The variation of strokes produced by wrist movements is limited in both shape and direction. These strokes resemble flat sections of circles whose radii are at an oblique angle to the axis of the draftsman's forearm. On a sheet of paper this means either that they normally incline steeply and are bent to the left (fig. 6: hatching of the boy; fig. 46: hatching of the sarcophagus; fig. 51) or that they decline steeply and are bent to the right, depending on

whether the draftsman is right- or left-handed. Any deviation from this norm (for example, a straight line or a stroke that is bent toward the wrist) presupposes that additional mechanisms—the finger, elbow, and shoulder joints—are involved and that additional control energies are required.

A comparison between the contours of the pair of Madonnas in figure 72 and the contour of the David in figure 5 demonstrates how useful distinguishing between different types of movement can be. Most of the components of the Madonna contours are bent in the same way, while most of those of the David contour vary. According to current opinion this difference in shape is attributable to a change in speed: the Madonna contours were sketched—so it is argued—more quickly and more "vigorously" than the David contour.[3] But this explanation overlooks the reality of draftsmanship. Increasing speed is reflected primarily by an increase of discontinuity phenomena (gaps in the contours, crossed strokes, shifts in axes, and so forth) and not by changing straight or irregularly bent strokes into uniform segmental arches. No one would argue that the sketches in figure 6 (slaves) or figure 40 were drawn more slowly than the two Madonnas, although the number of uniformly bent strokes in the former is smaller and those of straight and irregularly bent strokes is larger. The difference must accordingly lie, first and foremost, in the different *types* of movement. Whereas the draftsman of the David (and the sketches in figures 6 and 40) continuously activated all his arm joints (and in particular his finger joints), the Madonna draftsman in executing the contour parts that are bent to the left exploited, insofar as possible, the freedom of movement allowed by his wrist joints.[4] These halfway mechanically drawn contour parts became the quality of patterns that are recognizable even in those parts of the contour that are essentially based on combined movements of the finger and arm joints (strokes that are horizontal or bent to the right). In the following we will call strokes based primarily on wrist movements and functioning as patterns formulaic strokes. They appear conspicuously frequently in the unauthenticated drawings of the "Michelangelo" corpus (for example, figs. 46–49, 60–62, 73–76, 79–80, 82–83, 92–94, 96–97, 100, 104, 124), but in the authenticated corpus we find them only sporadically (for example, figs. 30, 36: small figure standing up; fig. 39).

RHYTHM

As a function of time, drawing is a movement whose speed periodically increases and decreases. This change in speed is linked to the way in which ideas are converted into controlled manual movements. This conversion is not continuous but occurs in segments, because the draftsman can control the movement of his medium only over relatively short stretches. As a result, these movements become even less subject to conscious control the more he feels forced to give expression to his idea and the more impulsively he draws. His movements need (like speech) a periodic "pause" during which the next stroke (sentence) is planned and new energy is gathered. This pausing can assume various forms, each depending on the individual draftsman's habits, on his "fluency," and on the purposes of drawing. Each type of pause corresponds to a special rhythm.

The simplest type of pause is the standstill, whereby the medium stops briefly between two marked phases. In this case each movement phase begins and ends at zero speed and proceeds cautiously. The corresponding rhythm is ponderous and halting; it resembles a closely packed series of arches and can therefore be called an "arcade rhythm." Because the pressure component is not interrupted it results in long, ornamental, continuous strokes that reveal a tapeworm structure consisting of small parts when examined under a magnifying glass (for example, the shroud contours in fig. 16, or the vulture feathers in fig. 20). A subcategory of this rhythm, a "pseudo-arcade rhythm," is produced when the pausing is accomplished by a short reverse stroke along the axis of the existing main stroke. The linear continuum then has small stretches of more intensive shading at certain intervals—along those stretches where the medium passed over three times (for example, the forehead contour of the head study or the buttocks contour in fig. 8, or the body contours in fig. 16). In most such cases there is also a "sawtooth" profile—an indication that either the reverse strokes or the new stroke phases departed slightly from the axes of the preexisting strokes.

Arcade and pseudo-arcade rhythms are not habitual types of rhythms. They are principally found in the contours of beginners and copyists and reflect the extremely inhibited movements characteristic of those who draw from models and need to pause from stroke to stroke in order to get a closer look at the part of the object they are reproducing. This does not mean that under normal circumstances pauses always and everywhere occur in the course of smoothly proceeding movement. Every draftsman interrupts the flow of movement from time to time; the draftsman using pen and ink *must* interrupt his movement at regular intervals in order to refill his pen. Evidence of a fully stopped movement—lumpy thickenings (called "stroke heads" in the following) or sharp breaks at the beginnings or ends of ink, chalk, lead, or silverpoint strokes—can therefore be found even in quickly drawn sketches (figs. 39, 74, or 83, 88, 92, 124). Such stopping traces

say less about a draftsman's habit of movement the more sporadically they occur. Under normal circumstances the movement between two controlled phases tends to be interrupted by a "neutral phase," during which the pressure component is intermittent, at least over some stretches. This neutral phase can be extremely slow and short or extremely fast and extensive, but it nevertheless always seems to have a certain fixed relationship to the speed and course of the controlled phases. In the contours in figure 72 it took the form of a tiny, largely unmarked connecting loop, which was produced almost organically from the formulaic curve model of the controlled phases. The corresponding rhythm is either sedately or animatedly gliding—depending on the speed (its acceleration is reflected in the fact that the segmented strokes lose their threadlike character and slightly increase and decrease in volume toward the middle—see figure 74). This could be called an "arch-loop rhythm." In hatching it is found in the straight or slightly bent individual hatching strokes that are cleanly separated from each other (figs. 55, 72, 83).

Whereas a conspicuously large number of alleged Michelangelo drawings (including figs. 73, 75–80) are characterized by arch-loop rhythms, the drawings authenticated as originals by Michelangelo exhibit a different rhythm. Their contour strokes possess—regardless of how fast (fig. 40) or how slowly (fig. 4: male nude) they were drawn—a more finely articulated, more "individual" volume and course than the contour strokes in figures 74 or 72. Furthermore, they are only sporadically close enough together to make a simple, small connecting loop possible. The frequency of contour gaps, of hook- and tail-shaped stroke ends, of crossed strokes and shifts in axes, on the other hand, proves that controlled phases alternated with longer and more complex unmarked phases even at relatively slow speeds (fig. 6: slave sketches) than was the case in figure 72 or 74. At the same time, the transition from one phase to the other was more fluid. Sometimes the pressure component was suspended "too late" (after the controlled phase was already exhausted), sometimes it was reintroduced "too early" (even before the planning phase was completed). The rhythm is accordingly more intricate than the "arch-loop rhythm"; it affects both the pressure and course components of movement. It is vital, pulsating, and resembles a river whose course is alternately tamed and wild.

The Contour

At its simplest, a contour is a stroke that defines shape. It is what makes a "thing" selected out from the abstract surface identifiable as such. Although by its nature it tends toward linear continuity, in reality it is a composite of single strokes. As such it can be viewed in two ways. Seen from that of its components, it is either a modulated-stroke or thread-stroke contour; viewed from the aspect of type of composition, it is either a closed contour or a contour with gaps, either a single- or multiple-line contour, either a simple or a strengthened contour.

MODULATED-STROKE AND THREAD-STROKE CONTOURS

Since modulated strokes as well as thread strokes can dominate in a contour, we must ask whether a different aesthetic orientation lies behind the dominance of one or the other type. Scholars have always indirectly answered no to this question by not distinguishing between strokes drawn with constant pressure and those drawn with variable pressure. But the drawings themselves provide a different answer. The fact that the ink contours in figure 4 and the chalk contours in figure 38 largely consist of modulated strokes, whereas most of the ink contours in figure 72 and the chalk contours in figure 100 consist of thread strokes, ultimately has grave consequences. The different types of contour strokes can define the area of the sheet and that of the object in opposite ways. Whereas the contours in figures 4 and 38 transform the surface into a quasi-space in which the outlined object appears as a three-dimensional object, those in figures 72 and 100 leave the surface intact. The outlined object acts more like a silhouette than an object displacing space. Thread-stroke and modulated-stroke contours thus exhibit different boundary functions. Thread-stroke contours function only as boundaries between surfaces, modulated-stroke contours simultaneously as borders between surfaces and bodies. But this fact presupposes a different subjective attitude toward the object to be outlined. It is hard to imagine, behind the contours in figures 72 and 100, a conception of the human body that was determined primarily by haptic characteristics; it is equally hard to imagine that the contours in figures 4 and 38 were determined only by optical characteristics.

Both pairs of examples are contradictory in a further regard. Whereas the contour components in figures 72 and 100 differ from each other only slightly in thickness, those in figures 4 and 38 have a broad range of thicknesses—ranging from a delicate, almost bodiless hairstroke to a thickly swollen "monocellular" stroke. In the first case there is no point in asking about the purpose of the stroke volume. The question is relevant only in those cases where it actually

changes, whether from stroke to stroke or within the strokes themselves.

Even a fleeting glance at the male nude in figure 4 shows that the strongest modulated strokes are not distributed arbitrarily; most of them are on the left side of the body. This one-sided distribution, however, acts like a concentration of shadings compressed onto the stroke width. The outlined object is set off against the surface as if it were a plastically shaded body. The thickenings on the right side of the body, on the shoulder, upper arm, hip, and legs, contribute their own part to this effect. They all model not only the body as a whole but also its parts, its limbs and muscles. Each individual increase in stroke volume seems to register a concrete imaginative impulse, a sudden vision of a curved or indented corporeal detail.

It is obvious that the pressure components in this case were used deliberately to achieve the desired effect—how deliberately is shown by a comparison with the two Madonnas in figure 72. There the contours of the right and left halves of the body, as well as of the outer and inner contours of the extremities, are equivalent. The comparatively weak increases in stroke thickness are distributed almost randomly over the stroke system. To be sure, they do produce rounding effects here and there, but for the most part they appear to be unintentional. In any case, precisely those contour sections that were meant to delimit shaded parts (to judge from what was hatched) exhibit some strokes that are thinner than strokes that border on "lighted" areas, while some of the most strikingly voluminous strokes (for example, on the left shoulder of the left Madonna) owe their thickness to the happenstance of a freshly filled pen. The author of these Madonna sketches neglected the possibilities of plastic expression inherent in the variation of stroke volume—even though he had drawn preliminary contours for the sketches in metal point before he used his pen.

CLOSED CONTOURS AND CONTOURS WITH GAPS

The male nude in figure 4 and the pair of river gods in figure 40 are among the pen-and-ink drawings that are authenticated as originals by Michelangelo. Nevertheless, their contours appear to have nothing in common. The contour of the male nude is fully articulated and closed, whereas that of the two river gods is summary and extremely discontinuous. How is this to be explained?

The answer must begin with a correction of the optical impression. The contour of the male nude is less closed, that of the two river gods less full of gaps, than they seem at first glance. The former has a large number of inconspicuous gaps, whereas the latter has some very conspicuous gaps, but over large stretches none at all. Nevertheless—and this is the point—neither the closed contour parts nor those with gaps are produced in the same way in the two examples. In the case of the male nude the contours with gaps are produced because the ends of the relevant strokes almost converge, while the closed contour parts are produced because the ends completely converge. In the case of the two river gods, on the other hand, the contour parts with gaps are produced by stroke ends that show no tendency to converge, while the closed contour parts are formed by stroke ends that cross. This difference in what produces continuity or discontinuity in the two cases reflects nothing more than differing degrees of efficiency in movement control. The contour of the male nude suggests a movement whose pressure component usually started and stopped with such precise timing that only tiny solder points or inconspicuous gaps resulted. On the other hand, the contours of the river gods suggest a movement whose marked phases resulted in gaping empty areas or aesthetically inappropriate cross-seams—depending on whether they passed into the neutral phases too early or too late. But in both cases the shape and length of the individual movement phases are in the same proportion to each other: short, highly articulated strokes and simple neutral phases in the case of the male nude; long, less articulated strokes and tortuous neutral phases in the case of the river gods. This fact is important, for it proves that differing speed is the sole reason for the significant differences between the two drawings.

Things take another turn when the comparison is extended to the sketch of the battle of horsemen in London (fig. 74), which has been questionably attributed to Michelangelo.[5] To be sure, this sketch has the same alternation of tightly closed and widely gaping contour parts, the same predominance of weakly articulated, curved long strokes as in the pair of river gods. And, to be sure, it was outlined with the same quickness. But this similarity ends with the shape of the contour components. Instead of a balance between crooked and straight shapes there is a predominance of formulaic curves that—as the contour of the left horseman shows—are extracts of simple spiral movements. The sketch has a different relationship to the male nude than the river gods. It resembles the river gods in that it was drawn at a faster speed, but it is the product of a different type of rhythm. The horsemen sketch bears the same relationship to the two Madonnas in the Louvre (fig. 72) as the river gods bear to the male nude.

The correctness of this equation is also reflected in the details. The horsemen sketches and the Madonnas have almost no "axial shifts," whereas in the river gods and the male nude they abound (left river god: at the inner and outer contours of the legs; male nude: at the outer contour of the left arm and leg). These phenomena of discontinuity are attributable to a lightning-quick, conscious reaction to a looming error in proportion. They presuppose an especial sharpness of conception—something that cannot be inferred from the formulaic nature of the strokes in the horsemen and Madonna sketches. Their appearance seems to be bound to a functional rhythm and has nothing to do with speed. The speed with which the river gods (or the slaves in figure 6) were sketched resulted in an enlargement of this special shape of gap, not its elimination. In the case of the male nude the pen effortlessly ran back a bit without pressure when it reached the end of the stroke needing correction, in order to begin the correcting stroke at a little distance; in the case of the river god (or the slaves) it could make its way from the end of one stroke to the beginning of the next only by detours. In neither the first nor the second case did the movement take the shape of a spiral.

SINGLE AND MULTIPLE-LINE CONTOURS

In contrast to handwriting, drawing is largely an exploratory process whereby the draftsman probes the most appropriate expression of an idea. It therefore tends to be accompanied by a conscious or unconscious self-criticism that examines what has been transcribed onto the paper for inner appropriateness and—depending on the results of the examination—leads to revisions. A revision need not necessarily be carried out on a new sheet and in the form of a new sketch. It can just as easily be performed ad hoc and be restricted to an individual stroke, a small assemblage of strokes, or the contour as a whole.

The axial shifts in the stroke sequence just discussed are the most elementary types of revision. Nevertheless, they occur only in connection with certain rhythms and when the draftsman has already developed a certain level of self-assurance. Far more common is a type of doubling: one and the same thing—a single stroke, a sequence of strokes, a whole contour—is drawn two or more times in more or less changed shape and position. It occurs in "states" or layers. The newer or subsequent state or layer is called "pentimento"; it is a correction of older states.

In the normal course of events, and in particular in the case of chalk, silver-point, or lead-point drawings, corrections occur on a massive scale, and the course of the original layer is no longer recognizable in detail. Even such an apparently simple stroke system as that in figure 83 turns out, under closer observation, to be a multilayered formation whose individual layers lie not only next to each other, but also, at some points, on top of each other (for example, in the left arm). In this case the contour becomes a three-dimensional composite. It is composed not only of its length, but also of its width and depth—the product of whole generations of corrections.

According to certain manuals the number of revisions has a fixed relationship to certain phases of the exploratory process: large numbers of pentimenti are—they say—typical for preliminary sketches, whereas the opposite holds for more mature sketches.[6] This postulate flies in the face of reality. The Madonna in figure 73 has *more* corrections than its predecessors in figure 72; the sketch for the *Last Judgment* in figure 32, which is largely ready for execution, has *more* than the corresponding preliminary sketch in figure 30 and at the same time less than the sketch for the "Expulsion of the Moneychangers" in figure 130, which has fewer figures and less action. Figure 130 was preceded by at least six similar compositional sketches, while its main figure was additionally explored by at least twelve single-figure sketches (including figs. 123, 127–29), most of which have fewer pentimenti than the final product! The connoisseur's naive rule of thumb—the more pentimenti, the earlier the drawing—can be turned on its head without hesitation. But even then it does little to clarify matters, for the question is not how many pentimenti a drawing has, but how they relate to each other structurally and topographically.

Each revision implies that the draftsman distanced himself from the previous state or layer. The topographic relationship between the first and the subsequent states therefore reveals the range of development of the subjective idea during the course of outlining an object. Minimal deviations imply that the idea was relatively stable, if not rigid. They are therefore most frequently found where the drawing is based on something already available—a basic sketch or a mature preliminary sketch, a drawing to be copied or a model, that is, in advanced sketches (figs. 4, 23), in studies (figs. 1, 6, 9–11, 52, 78–79, 119, 122), highly finished drawings (figs. 19, 58, 63–64, 87), cartoons (fig. 34), or copies (figs. 3, 53, 89). In the early stages of sketching, minimal deviations occur at best where corrections are restricted to individual strokes or smaller complexes of strokes (fig. 6: slaves; fig. 74). On the other hand, deviations on the scale represented in figures 46 (figure in the center), 48–49, 100, or 106–107 (Christ) point to a correspondingly large range and accordingly to an unstable, fluctuating idea. If they occur in highly finished

drawings—as is occasionally the case in Michelangelo's works (figs. 16, 24)—they indicate that these drawings are still components of the sketching process and identical with its last phase.

In Michelangelo's *Fall of Phaeton* (fig. 24) the beginning and end of the conceptual development carried out during the execution are obvious. No one could fail to distinguish between the first and the final state. This obviousness might appear to be a matter of course considering that the final state is identical to the absolutely definitive one. But any excerpt from the cartoon for Condivi's painting of the *Epiphany* (figs. 95–97) refutes this assumption. There the beginning and end of the development process cannot be separated, because first and subsequent layers look to the eye to be largely interchangeable—in contrast to their equivalents in Michelangelo's cartoon fragment for the *Crucifixion of Peter* (fig. 34), where they are distinguished by sharp differences in strength. The only thing that can be detected from the structural relationship between the individual layers in the *Epiphany* cartoon is that the draftsman's idea remained diffuse wherever precision was required—a curious phenomenon when one considers the advanced stage a cartoon represents in the exploratory process.

A comparison between the two *Annunciation* sketches in figures 37 and 100 is as revealing for the earliest stage of the sketching process as the comparison between the *Epiphany* and *Crucifixion of Peter* cartoons is for the most advanced stage. Both "Annunciation" sketches exhibit a considerable range in the development of an idea. The angle of the sketch in figure 37 (authenticated as a work by Michelangelo) was originally drawn standing, while the Madonna was placed lower and in a pose that differs totally from her final one.[7] These preliminary states, however, were literally drowned out by corrections drawn with heavy pressure. The exploratory process ended with a clear result. In the case of the (unauthenticated) sketch in figure 100 there are a number of results; that is, the process ended ambiguously. Mary's face, which is glancing down to the left, competes with one looking up to the right; the left arm grasping at the shoulder contrasts with an arm lifted in amazement situated above it. Because of the position of the angel one automatically perceives the layer with the upturned face and the raised hand as the first one. The highly finished drawing (fig. 101) nevertheless proves that it was the last one in the eyes of the draftsman.

Bearing these examples in mind, even such an unbalanced and mottled distribution of pentimenti as that in figures 48 and 49 can easily be explained. Here too the individual states differ greatly from each other without being differentiated in their strength. Moreover, there is a total lack of inner coherence between the areas with few pentimenti and those overloaded with them, thus excluding the possibility that the draftsman had any independent notion of how to draw the human body. The individual states of the arms and legs, along with their related corrections, attempt to explore several, in part heterogeneous motifs of movement without taking into account a logical overall pose. They resemble pieces of a child's construction kit. The motif of the outstretched arm with an opened hand or that of the non-supporting leg bent at a right angle are tested like protheses, sometimes attached to the right side of the body, sometimes to the left. Within the changing overall conception of the body, both motifs remain invariable, indicating that they are quoted from a preexisting figure. Both sketches are attempts at compilation. Their starting point was apparently Michelangelo's highly finished drawing of *Christ in Limbo* (figs. 14–15). The head, torso, and arm position was copied from it, first in the same perspective, then in a mirror image.[8]

SIMPLE AND STRENGTHENED CONTOURS

In addition to the shape, the intensity of a contour or a contour section can be the object of a revision. The correction then follows the course of the primary version and functions as its strengthening. Contour strengthenings are important for us because in many cases they have the same characteristics as the original sequence of strokes, which is often no longer recognizable. The contours of the river god and heliads in figure 23 are reminiscent in their nuanced thicknesses and volumes of the contours of the slave sketches in figure 6 or of the male nude in figure 4; like them, they function as modeling factors. Nevertheless, the linear "concentrations of shadows" in figure 23 are largely attributable to a revision that fixed and clarified the original layers. They are more consciously and more clearly intended as aesthetic effects than those in figures 4 and 6. On the other hand, the contour strengthenings in figures 81 or 83 appear haphazard and purposeless. Along many stretches—for example, in the case of the rising Christ from the left shoulder to the beginning of the left thigh—they produce a viscous, straplike continuum that has a more or less exact equivalent on the other side of the body. These strengthenings have no plastically shaping force; they merely serve to clarify the linear course of the contour.

An unbalanced linear function of this type can—depending on how the object is hatched—lead to aesthetic contradictions. In the pen-and-ink drawings in figures 78 and 79

(torso) the uniformly strengthened contour looks like a narrow coastal strip forming a belt around a hilly island. It diametrically opposes the effect of the hatching and makes the body look as if its back side were flat—in contrast to the contour of Michelangelo's "Philosopher" (fig. 3), which is only partially strengthened.[9] The same applies to the contours of the Windsor specimen of Michelangelo's Haman studies (fig. 11). Compared to the elastic contour of the Libyan sibyl's companion in figure 6, they look like rigid wire ornaments framing a bas-relief. They also differ noticeably from the contours in the examples in London and Boston (figs. 9, 10), which, if they did not have a revealing sawtooth profile here and there in their strengthened parts, could be mistaken for the original contours.

Hatching

Except for the purposes of practicing, a draftsman does not hatch on a tabula rasa. Hatching is introduced onto a quasi-spatial field that consists of the "surface of an object" enclosed by a contour and of the area that surrounds the contour.[10] The hatching is called "internal" or "external" hatching depending on which of these two zones is treated. Hatching "in itself" does not exist in the field of figural draftsmanship.

A transformation of the colored substance of the ground occurs wherever hatching is present. This transformation is also extended to the area between and around the hatching. White paper no longer appears as white paper but as the surface of an object shaded in some way or other. But this effect, unlike that of watercolors, is produced by lines and not by surfaces of color. These lines follow a definite principle of parallelism. Instead of continuously coloring the ground, they enclose it in cages. The shading effect is therefore simultaneously a structural effect.

The relationship between these two effects is subject to certain laws. It is determined on the one hand by the occasional purposes of drawing and on the other by the draftsman's individual aesthetic conceptions. Whereas a structural effect usually predominates in hatched sketches (fig. 23: heliads; fig. 121), in more mature drawings (figs. 24, 122) the hatching tends to both expansion and compression, resulting in a diminution of the structural in favor of the shading effect. However, independently of this "law," within every drawing these two very general effects are further individualized so as to produce tectonic or atectonic, painterly or sculptural, material or atmospheric effects that define the individual hatching style. An individual's hatching style can be defined by a number of aspects, the most important of which are density, strength, direction, basic shape, composition, and distribution.

DENSITY

Hatching density is a function of the distance between axes and the width of the hatching strokes. It can only be described; it cannot be measured. At best, the absolute number of hatching strokes is only an indirect indicator of hatching density. If the stroke width varies, the same number of strokes per unit of surface can lead to different effects of compression, while an unequal number of strokes can lead to similar ones. Moreover, the distances between hatching strokes tend to change inconspicuously while a drawing is being hatched. Distances between strokes often determine the character of the stroke system more through the way they vary than because of abstract averages.

There appears to be no difference in density between the hatching of Michelangelo's David in figure 5 and that of the youth in figure 75. In each the hatching appears to be equally loose. The overall impression is hardly affected by the fact that the distances between hatching strokes in relation to the stroke widths are on the average somewhat closer in the case of David than in the case of the youth. What makes a greater impression is that, in the David, they seem more uniform. Most variations occur within the individual assemblages and are therefore better suited to increasing rather than diminishing the impression of regularity. In contrast, the variations in distance in the youth in figure 75 account for the varying densities from assemblage to assemblage. The assemblage of ringlets on the lower left leg is noticeably denser than the parallel assemblages on the thigh, on the right leg, and on the abdomen. And the distances between strokes within these parallel assemblages are sometimes almost twice as great as those on the lower jaw or on the right arm. The conspicuously large number of small assemblages (neck, chest, hip, knee, feet, and so forth) also have varying densities. A comparison between the arm studies of the David and the youth produces the same result. In the first case (fig. 5) the hatching as a whole resembles an elastic tissue in varying states of tension. In the second (fig. 75) it seems to vary between dense and loose without any tension.

Such differences can be found even in the smallest details of a drawing. In the case of the sketches in figures 41 and 88 or the apparently identical hand studies in figures 6 and 8, the hatching is restricted to a few assemblages consisting of short strokes. Whereas these assemblages in figures 41 and 6 ex-

hibit the same taut density as in the David (fig. 5), those in figure 88 appear unbalanced and scattered—precisely because of the unrelated juxtaposition of zigzag and ladderlike strokes. In figure 8 most of these strokes are so tightly packed that the structural effect only sporadically wins out over the shading effect (thumb).

Most of these examples have one layer of hatching, and condensing is accomplished almost exclusively by reducing the distance between strokes. But hatching can also be condensed—as in the case of the arm studies in figures 5 and 75—by drawing one or more layers in a different direction over the existing layer of hatching. The hatching then becomes multilayered ("cross-hatching"). A net or grid effect replaces the simple "picket" effect. How such a hatching has to be judged depends in large part on the medium with which it was executed: pen and ink, or a dry medium. Pen-and-ink hatchings cannot be placed all that closely together because otherwise they fuse and form blotches without structure (figs. 3, 52–54, 56). They *must* be condensed with cross-strokes when the purpose is to achieve higher degrees of shading. In the case of dry media, cross-strokes are theoretically dispensable. Nevertheless, if they do occur, their presence can indicate a special aesthetic intention—but just as easily a lack of routine and economy. Chalk hatchings with two and more layers can be found in figures 50 (face), 81, 87, 91, 95, 100–03, 105–13, 119, and 122. They deserve attention especially because they extend over wide areas of the figure, and sometimes even over the whole surface of the sheet (figs. 81, 87). In this regard they cannot be compared with the hatchings of the sketches in figures 23, 30–32, 38, or 46–47, or with those of the red-chalk studies in figure 6, or even with the finished-drawing hatchings of the *Tityos* (fig. 19) or the *Fall of Phaeton* (fig. 24). Even when compared with each other they differ markedly. The hatching in figure 119 makes a more systematic impression than those in figures 50, 81, 87, 91, 95, or 100. The parallelism of their assemblage components is as strict and consistent as in the terrain hatching in figure 19, the layering process is firmly governed by a clear tectonic "structuralism." It is thus curious that this process ultimately resulted in a condensation that dissolved the individual strokes in a dim continuum! But this continuum is a story in itself. Its plastic and material articulation exceeds even that achieved in figure 24. The robe, which bulges in deep, heavy folds, looks like glittering silk, the foot has the soft tautness of skin, the beard the unkempt waves of exuberantly growing hair. In figures 81 and 87, on the other hand, the body, robe, sarcophagus, and landscape are of one and same spotty substance, sometimes gelatinous, sometimes scratchy and brittle. In this case the hatching was a kind of careless dotting that aimed more at achieving abstract differences in color than at materially and plastically qualifying what was shaded. This had little to do with "painterly" intentions—as figures 44 and 47 show, single-layer chalk hatchings can produce more effective chiaroscuro contrasts. More likely it indicates a certain indifference to the expressive possibilities of chalk.

In Daniele's apostle's robe and Aeneas study (figs. 119, 122), as well as in the bodies of Michelangelo's *Tityos* and *Fall of Phaeton* (figs. 19, 24), the linear substance of the individual hatching strokes occasionally dissolves in a collection of microscopically fine points—because the hatchings are wiped.[11] And not accidentally. Wiping is a more economical condensation process for achieving certain smoothness effects than is pushing hatching to the point where strokes converge—as well as being the easiest technique one can imagine. Nevertheless, wiping alone could never achieve such fineness of effect unless the wiped hatching itself were as finely articulated as the unwiped terrain hatching of the *Tityos* (fig. 19). The Christ figure in figure 81 provides a contrasting example. Its surface is roughened, in some places even scratched. Once in place, the thicket of zigzag and spiral assemblages, haphazardly drawn over and through each other, could not be smoothed out.

STRENGTH

Michelangelo's male nude in figure 4 demonstrates what pressure-sensitive outlining can achieve. Michelangelo's David (fig. 5) is just as exemplary in showing what pressure-sensitive hatching can accomplish. The hatching of the David is as full of nuances as the contour, sometimes exhibiting delicate assemblages (neck), sometimes forcefully swelling ones (lower left arm). These nuances appear to have been determined by a haptic principle, for they go hand in hand with a discernible concentration of heavily drawn assemblages on the left, "shaded" side of the body. The hatching of the David makes explicit what the contour of the male nude expresses implicitly.

The hatching of the youth in figure 75 relates to the David hatching in the same way as the contours of the Madonnas in figure 72 relate to the contour of the male nude. The scale of thicknesses is comparatively small and without relation to the corporeality of the figure. Lightly and heavily drawn hatchings are distributed as if by chance over the stroke system. The plastic effect they produce bears no relationship to the space-defining potential of the motif of movement. It corre-

sponds to the schematic bas-relief effect of the hatching in the adjacent arm study.[12]

One might think that hatching with soft chalk would generally produce a finer gradation of thicknesses than hatching with a pen. But that is a deception. Compared with Michelangelo's ink hatchings in figures 5 or 41, the chalk assemblages in figures 45–47, 51, 83, or 93–97 make a monotonous impression. This monotony is even more striking because it is coupled with a much greater compression than is the case in figures 6 or 38; it presupposes ideas about the function of hatching that are incompatible with figures 6 and 38. Nevertheless, even in those two figures the range between minimum and maximum values is small compared with the range in figures 89 or 132. The reason for this difference is that in figures 6 and 38 the range reflects a genuine, original regulation of pressure, whereas the harsh contrast between light and dark that dapples the figure in figures 89 and 132 is largely attributable to a subsequent *strengthening* of the hatching, that is, to repeated layering maneuvers. These layering maneuvers are mainly identifiable in that the lattice or grid effect of the hatching is dissolved into amorphous smudges in many places. They were necessary on such a scale only because the hatching process was carried out without an appropriate gradation of pressure. As the still untouched-up parallel assemblages of the first layer demonstrate, the layering process proceeded as monotonously as in figures 83 or 101.

Massive strengthenings of the hatching also characterize the *Resurrection* in Windsor (fig. 81), where they extend even to nonfigural areas—a phenomenon that cannot be found even in highly finished drawings, let alone in Michelangelo's sketches (in figures 19 and 24 the strengthenings of the external hatchings are restricted to tiny cast-shadow zones). To judge from the low pressure and uniform flatness of all the unretouched primary layers, this strengthening mania was caused by a lack of a clear conception of space and volume. The draftsman was forced to use successive attempts at shading in order to give plastic qualification to what was depicted. This is remarkable because such a technique is usually employed by beginners and copyists,[13] whereas the Windsor drawing does not have characteristics specific to a beginner or the general qualities of a copy. The solution to the riddle is supplied by the signature on the verso (fig. 82). As a miniaturist and copyist of drawings, Clovio was accustomed to proceeding in little paces and thus unable to ease up even when he drew on his own. The technique of his highly finished drawing of the Lamentation in London (fig. 87) differs only minimally from that of his Tityos copy (fig. 20).

DIRECTION

That such dissimilar drawings as figures 6 (study of a boy), 30, 38, 46–47, 51, or 67 are hatched at such a similar angle of inclination is not accidental but attributable to the draftsman's righthandedness. The ascending slanting position of the hatching strokes corresponds to a direction of movement that is more or less vertical to the axis of the forearm and spontaneously generated by the movement of the wrist joint. This direction is the normal or basic hatching movement, and it usually remains predominant even when the overall hatching is determined by *changes* in direction (figs. 45, 54, 64–65, 72–74, 81).

The upper pen-and-ink sketch in figure 55, the red-chalk sketches in figure 47, and Michelangelo's red-chalk study for the Libyan sibyl's companion in figure 6 demonstrate what hatchings with consistent direction can and cannot achieve. The hatching strokes in these figures are for the most part too short to make their unintentional crookedness noticeable. All in all they give an impression of straightness. Accordingly, the individual assemblages as such have only a minimal capability to define space. As long as the distances between and the strengths of the individual hatching strokes remain constant, they appear as flat lattices parallel to the picture plane. Due to their shading effect they can give plastic qualification to the figure, but only at the cost of an adequate impression of materiality, because areas with and without lattices bump into each other like crystal facets. In figure 55 the lattices take absolutely no account of corporeal reality. Instead they combine whole limb complexes as uniformly structured surfaces of an abstract figural block. In figure 47, because of their crowdedness, they produce large shadow areas that, so to speak, overlay the body. Only in figure 6 are the distances between and the thickness of the hatching strokes so finely tuned that everything hard-edged gives way to taut, organic roundings. The three examples demonstrate that hatchings with consistent directions can also efficiently perform heterogeneous functions (tectonization, modeling, or chiaroscuro of the figure)—provided that the individual assemblages, which are parallel to the picture plane, do not conflict with the intention of the contour. This type of conflict arises when the contour defines the figure as a block or prism formation, as in the cases of the sarcophagus in figure 46 or Phaeton's chariot in figure 66. In these two cases the hatching would have to run parallel to the contours of the edge in order to harmonize with the perspectival circumstances; in other words, it would have to have the same kind of changes in direction as in the hatching of the chariot in Michelangelo's *Fall of Phaeton* (figs. 23–24). This is accomplished only partially in

figure 66, and not at all in figure 46. As a result, what is outlined and what is hatched seem to be independent of each other. Although this lack of harmony remains inconspicuous in figure 66, in figure 46 it results in aesthetic nonsense. The hatching negates and flattens the volume suggested by the contour of the sarcophagus, producing an unbalanced cast-shadow effect and thereby unmasking the draftsman's "painterly" intent.

External hatching demonstrates the fundamental significance of the hatching direction for spatial expression. It serves to qualify either the location or the background, depending on its topographical relationship to what is outlined. It is used as location hatching in figures 3 and 38. In figure 3 it is characterized by a large horizontal assemblage which is crossed by aesthetically subordinate, slanting hatching strokes, in figure 38 by a single, slightly inclining slanted assemblage. The difference in direction might appear to be unimportant, but it expresses a difference in content. In figure 3 the surface on which the figure stands appears flat as a board and thereby suggests an independent piece of ground. In figure 38, on the other hand, the quality of the ground is undefined. The hatching assemblage creates a fusion of "shadow" and "place" from the standing of the figure itself. In the case of David in figure 5 the location hatching consists of small assemblages on either side of Goliath's head. Whereas the left assemblage slightly descends, the right one inclines slightly. The ground accordingly seems to form a gentle, almost undetectable trough. It simultaneously acts as a symbol for "terrain" and anchors the figure.

Figures 33 and 107 demonstrate the importance of directional relationships in the case of background hatchings. In figure 33 the area on both sides of the crucified figure is uniformly hatched with horizontal assemblages. This hatched area suggests a fluid wall constructed from delicate, transparent layers that surrounds the crucifix and hill of Golgotha at an undefined depth. The two angels rise out of it like fabulous creatures from a rippled sea. In figure 107, on the other hand, the effect is contradictory because the directions of the hatching strokes to the left and right of the crucified figure are contrary. The slightly wobbling vertical hatching strokes to the left form a veil-like, wafting area that seems to hang in the same plane as the crucified figure, whereas the inclining slanted hatching strokes to the right seem to be situated a great distance away.

As the unusual density and thinness of the internal hatching strokes, even in the first stages (Mary and John) indicate, the author of this Crucifixion drawing was primarily interested in "coloring" effects. Unconcerned with the expressive possibilities of hatchings with consistent directions, from the start he let himself be guided by whatever limitations were placed on his freedom of movement. He hatched vertically, horizontally, or at a slant, depending on which direction allowed him to move uninhibitedly. In figure 111 all three directions are represented simultaneously. The aesthetic fragmentation of the background is complete.

The ground hatching of the David sketch (fig. 5) already demonstrated that changes of direction can express artistic intentions and need not be involuntary. The hatching of the body makes this obvious. Although drawn with the right hand, descending hatching strokes clearly predominate within a multiplicity of directions. But these downward strokes are contrasted with inclining ones in such a way that an alternation of light and heavy or active and passive limbs are produced, as is appropriate for the motif of movement. Because of the descending slanted strokes the forearms and weight-supporting leg seem more passive and heavier than the active leg, which is hatched with a large, upward spiral assemblage. The inert body seems about to engage in animated action.

What the loose hatching of the David drawing demonstrates for sketches, the highly concentrated hatching of the "Philosopher" (fig. 3) demonstrates for advanced drawings. The directional contrasts in figure 3 transform the drapery landscape into a stage for a subtle dialectic between standing and hanging, light and heavy, inwardly and outwardly striving shapes. The multilayered rhythm of large and small surfaces, smooth plateaus and fissured depressions, buttress-like vertical paths and mobile basins seems to be charged with dynamic forces. Nothing of the kind is to be seen in the hatchings of St. Anne (fig. 4), the Masaccio copy in Munich (fig. 53), or the lower Madonna in figure 55: their changes in direction seem accidental and without function, and they tend more to rigidify than to vitalize the figure. In the case of the Madonna in figure 55 this is especially curious, because the multiplicity of directions within its assemblages ostentatiously contrasts with the uniform direction of the hatching of the upper Madonna, thereby suggesting the procedure was intentional. Actually what we have here is a perfect example of a pupil's behavior. The hatching abounds with contradictions. The two assemblages in the Madonna's face, with their steeply descending slanted strokes, take no account of the fact that the face is foreshortened. Instead of rounding the face they flatten it. The slightly declining slanted assemblage on the neck is executed correctly, but fails to act as a modeling factor because it is contradicted by the adjacent inclining slanted assemblage which flattens the lower part of the neck and the left shoulder. The flat lattices at the right arm and

left calf of the Christ Child and the two vertical assemblages at the right thigh, which stare at each other like combs, are also ineffective as modeling factors. The rising slantedness of the hatching strokes below the Madonna's right arm is extended without reason into the piece of drapery laid across the Madonna's lap, and conflicts with the drapery's perspectival foreshortening. All in all the changes in direction fail to register plastic or dynamic conceptions. The result is a hopeless frittering away of the spatial structure. Michelangelo had every reason to write his famous admonition next to the drawing: "Draw, Antonio, draw, Antonio, draw and lose no time!"[14]

SHAPE

The spatial effect evoked by hatching depends not only on direction and density, but also on whether the assemblages consist of straight or curved elements. If the pressure and distance are varied, straight hatching strokes can produce spherical effects; if not they produce flat surface effects. The reverse is also true: by their nature curved hatching strokes lead only to spherical effects, although these effects remain inconspicuous in certain hatching arrangements.

In the case of the lower Madonna in figure 55 the inconsistency of the hatching can already be seen in its elementary form. Curved hatching strokes that make a rounding visible are suddenly crossed through by rigid flat lattices or become straight lines without reason. Both shapes act against each other's aesthetic forces. Only the segmented-arch assemblage at the left forearm of the Madonna is consistent along the whole length of the limb, although even it is disturbed on the right side by the juxtaposition of an unmotivated straight, vertical hatching assemblage. As a factor in achieving a rounding effect it remains isolated in the stroke system. Most of the hatching strokes tend to straightness—in contrast to those in Michelangelo's David and hand sketches (figs. 5, 41).

This tendency to straightness necessarily led to the formation of numerous sharp angles between the hatchings and contours and thereby to an additional rigidification of the stroke system. In this respect the drawing is related to the arm study in figure 75, which seems so much more brittle than the arm study in figure 5 (whose motif is so similar) because the hatching strokes on the left side puncture the contour like a battery of thorns, whereas in figure 5 their equivalents are buffered on the contour side by hook-shaped relics of kinetic neutral phases or by narrow "buffer zones" without hatching. This thorn effect does not occur in the adjacent youth (with the exception of the left shin) because the individual strokes are highly curved. The hatching seems more flexible. Apparently it was the custom of this draftsman (Cellini) to reduce the modeling function of the individual hatching strokes as the hatching density increased and to delegate this function to the hatching assemblages. In fact, in figure 77 the curved hatching strokes of the nude seen from the rear, which were just as characteristic of the first hatching layer as they are for the head in profile bent forward (see also the left shoulder-blade area), were successively absorbed by straight hatching strokes. In figure 80 this absorption process, which leads to rigidification of the hatching, can be followed exactly. The assemblages at the neck, shoulders, clavicle, and lower legs indicate that the youth was originally hatched in the same way as the figures in figures 72, 75, and 76 (youths). Subsequently, however, its spherical curved strokes were covered over and buried by the second and third layers consisting of straight strokes. They unintentionally reveal what they were for the draftsman in reality: mere transitional phases on the way to the "real" hatching, provisional initial states that became functionless in the course of fine hatching. And thus the opposite of what they are in Michelangelo's David and hand sketches (figs. 5, 41), where the rounded hatchings have the quality of something final. Their striking volume alone makes them seem indestructible. They could have been covered over only at the cost of the intended overall effect. But this final character is also indicated by their survival in the studies. The hatching of the arm study (fig. 5) is essentially determined by curved hatching strokes and indicates that the hatching process was guided by haptic impulses.

COMPOSITION

As a rule, the hatching of a drawing consists not of individual hatching strokes but of hatching assemblages. It is a conglomerate. As such it can be examined from two perspectives. The first, the layering of assemblages on top of each other, was discussed in the section on hatching density. The second concerns the juxtaposition of assemblages. It is especially important because the effective placement of hatching assemblages is an elementary technical problem. A seamless axial connection of hatchings with uniform directions as in the Libyan sibyl's companion (fig. 6), or an organic coordination of assemblages with different directions as in the arm study (fig. 5) or the cloak of the Philosopher (fig. 3), do not occur automatically. Both imply a high degree of sensitivity and kinetic control. The Libyan sibyl studies in New York (fig. 8)

and their doubles in Florence (fig. 7) differ from the Libyan sibyl's companion in that they attempt to achieve through a greater quantum of movement what the companion achieved through an optimum differentiation of movement. Nevertheless, the "seams" could not be completely concealed: they appear as soon as the hatching system begins to lose density. In figure 8 a sharp seam separates the horizontal hatching strokes of the left part of the dorsal muscle from the assemblages that mark the ribs. It has the same cause as the "scar" that extends from the cheekbone down to the jaw in the head study. In both cases a new assemblage was added on to the existing one without taking its structure into account—as if two pieces of tissue of different texture were stitched together.

These patchwork pieces can become more frequent and unobtrusive the more unthinkingly the hatching is carried out. In the studies in figures 88 and 90 the hatching looks like sweepings of stubble; it does nothing to qualify the surface of the object. One might want to attribute this circumstance to an accidental case of "absent-mindedness" on the part of the draftsman. But this same stubble effect also characterizes the hatching of the *Resurrection* in Windsor (fig. 81)—if a bit softened by the massing of the hatching—as well as that of the highly finished drawing of the *Lamentation* in London, which is signed by Clovio (fig. 87). The stubble effect reflects the kinetic monotony that was apparently typical for the miniaturist's technique.

Hatching seams can also be produced intentionally. They are an effective and economical means of expression, especially when the draftsman wants to depict certain terrain formations. The best proof of this is provided by the terrain hatching in Michelangelo's Tityos drawing (fig. 19), where the horizontal or slightly inclining assemblages, which display a multiplicity of gradations in density and strength, are largely joined together so that the seams produce the broken edges and fissures of a rugged cliff. One could actually expect to find a similar effect in the background hatching of the *Resurrection* in Windsor (fig. 81), because this hatching is also intended to evoke a rocky terrain (a cave). In reality, however, it renders nothing more than an enlarged version of the same scratchy stubble that characterizes the hatchings of the body and the sarcophagus. There exists between them and the contours outlining the entrance to the cave the same accidental relationship as between the hatching and contour of the cliff in Clovio's copy of the *Tityos* (fig. 20). The effects are the same: in figure 20 parts of the plateau surface on which Tityos lies seem to resemble a thin, fringed pasty layer that juts out over the actual "rock," while in figure 81 the exterior of the cave seems to overlap the interior like stage scenery.

In pen-and-ink drawings the results of careless joinings of hatchings have, by their very nature, more persistent effects than in chalk drawings. For this reason pen and ink is better suited for illustrating the various types of hatching seams. The pen-and-ink study in figure 90 is an excellent example of the three usual types of seams. The first type can be found at the gluteus maximus, and is produced because assemblages consisting of zigzag or hooked hatching strokes, which are joined along their axes, are wedged or hooked into each other ("hooked" assemblages). The second type is found mainly in the mid-region and along the lower contour of the thigh, where a couple of parallel assemblages are joined at their axes; these assemblages have hatching strokes whose ends are melted together, thereby producing more or less obvious solder points ("soldered" assemblages). The third type was produced in the same region because hatching assemblages with different directional orientations crash into each other at sharp angles without overlapping (assemblages with sharp angles). Whereas solder points generally remain unobtrusive (only on close observation do most of the apparently long hatching strokes in figures 52 and 55 turn out to consist of soldered short strokes), hooks tend to make the stroke system look like bark (figs. 74, 77: nude seen from the rear; figs. 81, 87, 89). But the most striking defects are the distorted angles. They make the texture bulky and thereby negate any organic or material effect (fig. 3: beard; fig. 55: lower pen-and-ink drawing; fig. 56: right arm; fig. 73).

DISTRIBUTION

Art historians tend to believe that the problem of hatching distribution can be solved as simply as that of the light and shadow problem in paintings. They are mistaken. Sketches like the David in figure 5 or the Madonna in figure 38 are not consciously created as "works of art." The perfect plasticity produced by their hatchings is based on intuition and not on preliminary studies; it cannot be simply taken for granted. The hatching of the youth in figure 75, too, aims to express plasticity. But it appears to be distributed according to different guidelines than that of the David or the Madonna. In figure 75 the hatching assemblages are distributed almost uniformly over the figure and are represented almost equally next to the right and left contours of the body. They act as partners of a modeling light that is distributed separately by

area rather than uniformly. The modeling of the head suggests a different angle of illumination than that of the torso, that of the left leg another angle than that of the right leg. The whole appears as a sum of individual plastic data that is given inner coherence only by the contour.

The parcel-like quality of this hatching is not an isolated case. It is typical of that group of drawings in the "Michelangelo" corpus whose indicators of authorship point to Cellini (including figs. 77–80). Each drawing in this group shares a kind of inductive modeling that is achieved by differently "lighted" parts. In figures 77 (nude seen from the rear) and 79 the figure seems to be broken into individual, more or less sharply outlined areas, each of which was hatched independently and without reference to a common source of illumination. In figure 79 the collar and breast bones, the large chest muscle (m. pectoralis maior), the oblique abdominal muscle (m. transversus abdominis), and the knee were the principal delineators of distinct areas. The hatching between the chest muscle and the beginning of the thigh forms its own area. What is curious about this longitudinal and transverse division of the body is that it is indifferent to skeletal function. The breast bone and spine are treated as functionally indifferent separators rather than as elements that connect and combine the sides of the body. This suggests a conception of the human body based only on its surface appearance. No wonder that, in spite of the extensive hatching, the volume suggested in these drawings seems flat in comparison with the space-defining power even of those Michelangelo drawings that remained unhatched (fig. 1; fig. 4: male nude).

In contrast to the examples with "parceled" hatching the black-chalk drawings in figures 46 and 47 have a hatching distribution that is quite similar to that of the David and Madonna sketches (figs. 5, 38). The assemblages are concentrated along the right contours of the body, as befits an appropriate relationship to the modeling light. But this similarity is deceptive. What are collected here are not curving factors but flat, more or less uniformly structured paths of shadow that strike whole complexes of limbs with a uniform dark shading without taking into account organic details like limbs or muscles. The distribution of the hatching follows a principle of illumination that divides the body into areas that are either illuminated and turned to the light or shaded and turned away from the light. It suggests a "painterly" attitude toward the body that diametrically opposes Michelangelo's haptic approach. This painterly conception was characteristic of the Venetian Sebastiano del Piombo. It is thus no surprise that these two sketches were created with reference to his painting of the *Resurrection of Lazarus* (London, National Gallery).[15]

In spite of all serious differences these examples share a certain equilibrium in their hatched and unhatched areas. And in this regard they differ from an imposing number of sketches that tend to be totally hatched even in their first layers (figs. 100, 105, 107, 111). In these drawings dark and light are mere functions of the density and thickness of the hatching strokes. They "slur" against each other in a softly vibrating sfumato. The ground has surrendered its active role to the hatching; it appears as a passive substrate whose unique function consists in gleaming through the hatching. Where the ground remains unhatched it acts like a clearing that is created by the sudden tearing of a veil of fog.

This expansive hatching—in contrast to that of the "David and Goliath" sketches in figure 123 or Daniele's apostle study in figure 119—is characterized by an astonishingly narrow range of thicknesses. Its delicate texture allows the bone-less, soft body to flow along its breadth and to glow as if from within. This type of hatching has nothing to do with painterly or plastic effects. Instead it expresses a special sensitivity to mysteriously dusky effects. As will become clear in chapter 7, this sensitivity was a strength of Venusti, the artist from Como.

Nothing of the kind can be detected in the hatching of the *Resurrection* in Windsor (fig. 81). Its "atmospheric" or material articulation has as little to do with the Christ figure in figure 107 or the apostle study in figure 119 as its plastic qualification has to with figures 19, 23–24, and 32, or its chiaroscuro with figures 45–47. But the quantitative expansion of its hatching exceeds almost all comparable sketches of the "Michelangelo" corpus. One step further and the surface of the sheet would be as completely buried under the thicket of strokes as in Clovio's highly finished drawing (fig. 87). How are we to account for this?

This question also presents itself in the cases of pen-and-ink drawings (the "St. Anne" in fig. 4; figs. 52–54 and 56) where the hatchings extend over the figures like a coarse, constantly growing wire web. Whatever aesthetic intentions one might attribute to them, there is none that satisfactorily explains them. For every plastic, painterly, or material effect could have been more effectively achieved with somewhat more economy or a more articulated type of movement. In the "St. Anne" the careless way in which expressive elements are flattened—or even covered over—by the hatching, while individual organs or pieces of drapery are isolated without any apparent purpose, makes one wonder. The hatching stands in striking contrast to the contour. St. Anne's right

hand, the feet of Mary, and the Christ Child are drawn with the same expressive, plastically qualifying contour-strokes that characterize the standing nude and make hatching essentially superfluous. Indeed, the volume suggested by the group must have been both stronger and more uniform before the draftsman began his hatching campaign. The volume was frittered away, in part destroyed by the hatching. The spatial connection between St. Anne and Mary was torn asunder at the same time that their draperies seem to be stitched together. The herculean child raises himself from Mary's lap and left leg without any visible support, as if his mother's body were merely background. The draftsman who outlined the group (Michelangelo) was fully entitled to jest: "Who would ever say that it is by my hand?"!

Both in the "St. Anne" and in figures 52–54 a conspicuously large number of hatchings dissolve in amorphous blotches. The reason for this is exaggerated compression, which is in turn attributable to a lack of experience in calculating distances and an attitude toward the paper ground that is typical for a beginner. The beginner perceives the paper ground as expressively neutral. He mistrusts it. He feels the need to shade it as completely as possible, that is, to replace it with an artificial ground that serves as the basis for the "real" modeling. As a consequence he expends far more energy on hatching than the draftsman whose hatchings are attuned to specific purposes from the start. In the case of the drawings used as examples, up to five layers are superimposed on each other (in figure 3 there are three at the most), of which the first (fig. 4: Mary's face; fig. 52: back of the head!) contribute nothing to plastic structuring.[16]

The need for prophylactic shading of the ground typically disappears as the draftsman develops a routine. But for certain draftsmen it can become a regularly used technique. In Clovio's highly finished drawings (fig. 87) the hatching procedure has the character of monochromatic painting that seems to anticipate the future painting with color; the procedure must have had the same meaning in the *Resurrection* sketch in Windsor (fig. 81). There is no other explanation for why its hatching, which is so weakly differentiated in terms of shapes and strength, should be so multilayered and expansive.

Drawings and the Surface of the Sheet

A sheet of paper is something different for the draftsman than a piece of canvas is for the painter: it is not a potential pictorial space but a neutral surface—a piece of fallow land that can be built upon "somewhere," on several places at the same time and also in different directions. On it each drawing establishes its own location and abode. This self-generated "sovereign territory," which is theoretically independent of the borders of the sheet, possesses as such no perceptible characteristics. It counts as an aesthetic factor only when competitors appear on the scene, that is, when a second, third, or more drawings are placed in the vicinity of an already existing one. The placement of subsequent drawings can be determined by respecting either the spatial claims or the axial relationships of the first drawing (figs. 6, 9–11). But it can also be determined without any consideration for the existing drawings. In the first case the result is an overarching order, in the second, chaos. Either way, placement has something to say about the aesthetic approach of the draftsman in question.

Figure 5 can once again serve as an introductory example. As the central position of the arm study indicates, the draftsman did not plan on further use of the sheet surface at the time it was created. It is therefore all the more astonishing that the David is anchored in the "bay" of this arm in such a way that the space seems to have been created especially for him. Separated by the great differences in their sizes and a distance that respects the heteronomy of their existential spaces, the two figures form an ornamental "organism" sui generis. Even the manuscript texts are harmonized with this "organism" by acting as balancing factors: their eccentric location counteracts the unbalanced concentration of shapes on the left half of the sheet.

The Oxford sheet (fig. 6) by the same artist (Michelangelo) confirms the suspicion that such a balanced disposition of elements is intentional rather than accidental. Figure 6 unites no fewer than nine different drawings. Once again the first drawing—the red-chalk study for the Libyan sibyl's companion—was placed on the surface as if it were to stand there alone. The addition of the hand study negated its claim to absolute sovereignty, but not its independence. The hand study is situated at the place from which it can be organically linked with the boy's movement. Taken together, the two studies form something like a closed electrical circuit. Each increases the dynamism of the other. But their inner coherence remained intact even after the seven pen-and-ink sketches were added. Of these, the slaves appeared as a closed group simply because of their placement. They accommodate themselves as if automatically in the "reception zones" created by the red-chalk studies. The sweep of movement that extends from the hand study to the upper right arm of the boy is seconded by the motif of the three small figures that are organized on top of each other like stairs. The

arrangement follows the same playful rhythm as that which determined the arrangement of sketches in figures 35 and 36.

The inner logic of this type of arrangement has such a compelling effect mainly because it simultaneously follows three different principles: the economic principle of efficient use of a surface, the ornamental principle of external coordination, and the "political" principle of respecting another object's autonomy. This type of arrangement has an integral character and in this is distinguished from the logic of arrangement of most *alleged* Michelangelo sheets, in which, at best, coexisting drawings are organized by placing their main axes parallel or at right angles to one another (figs. 46, 55, 72, 76, 127). As a rule this implies neither a recognizable rhythm nor consistent respect of "sovereignty." That drawings collide (figs. 69, 72, 77), are plastered over (fig. 88), or downright overlap (figs. 71, 74) are a matter of course. In figures 69, 71, or 88 the distribution of the drawings is guided solely by the criterion of spatial economy. The relationships between distances and axes seem to be dictated by chance: the greater the number of coexisting partners, the more higgledy-piggledy the effect. Since the later drawings take no account of the "sovereign space" allotted the drawings already in place it is almost impossible to reconstruct the chronological sequence.

In figures 5, 6, 9–11, and 35–36 the drawings do not appear to be distributed on a surface but in a spatial continuum of indeterminable range and depth. They are, so to speak, organized in foreground and background. Overall, the pen-and-ink sketches in figure 6 appear to be situated in a deeper spatial layer than the red-chalk studies. And among themselves their locations have different depths of space, just as the red-chalk studies have both foreground (hand study) and background (study of the boy). Because of the alternation between foreground and background, the large and small objects no longer seem so strikingly different in size.

It is precisely this characteristically ambivalent effect, which lends the sheet surface the character of a sheet space, that distinguishes the inventory of drawings in figure 5 from the apparently so similarly arranged group in figure 75. Although the relation of spatial depth between David and the arm study cannot be exactly determined (sometimes the David seems to be in the foreground, sometimes in the background, depending on whether the viewer concentrates more on its relationship to the chest piece or to the lower arm of the arm study), it is clearly present and awakens the impression that the nude is under the protection of the arm. In figure 75, on the other hand, the nude and the arm study appear to be in one and the same "picture plane." Their relationship to each other is unquestionably a juxtaposition. The bearded head changes nothing in this regard—in spite of its smallness. It seems to form a common silhouette with the lobe-shaped, formulaic hand. The sheet surface remains intact as a surface.

Curiously, this effect of an intact surface can be found even where heteronomous objects are drawn on top of each other. In figure 74 the standing figure to the left of the sketch of the battling horsemen seems to be pasted on like a collage. The "existential space" of the sheet's inventory of drawings has as little depth as that in figures 73, 75–77. The draftsman in question (Cellini) can hardly have viewed his own drawings as the kind of space-displacing volume constructs that we find in Michelangelo's works. For Michelangelo, what was already present on the sheet remained subsequently taboo. To draw over it without erasing it would have required overcoming a deep inhibition, if not adopting a totally different perspective. The spatial continuum would have had to revert to the surface continuum that existed before the sheet was drawn upon. This sensitivity to those invisible boundaries whose violation destroys the autonomy of an object suggests a fundamentally haptic approach. It has as little to do with "intended style" as indifference to such boundaries has to do with a "satiety of style." This indifference implies that the draftsman "thinks" in contour and surface categories, no matter how much he might have sought to achieve plasticity.

Figure 123 is a further example of the haptic approach. To be sure, in comparison to figures 35 and 36 the drawings are distributed more loosely, the distances between drawings are arbitrary and without any detectable rhythm. Only the two lowermost battle groups are connected spatially and ornamentally. Each of the rest of the drawings seems to have its own, separate existential space. The same applies to figure 127, where the results of arbitrary distances are the most striking. The two sketches in the center of the sheet depict Christ expelling the moneychangers. Their remoteness from the rest of the drawings on the sheet heightens their nearness to each other and thus unintentionally suggests a small community of action. The right figure in the background seems to be chasing the left figure in the foreground with a threateningly raised arm. The irony of this chance relationship is matched in figure 119, where the leg study for the apostle acts like his mutely devoted listener.

The manner of placing drawings on a sheet can also help to answer the question: original or copy?—for example, in the case of the two sheets with the Libyan sibyl in New York (fig. 8) and Florence (fig. 7). On the rectos of both sheets are collections of red-chalk studies for the Libyan sibyl of the Sistine ceiling. The collections are different both in content and topographically, but are similar in two regards: in the

unsystematic hodgepodge of figures and in the trios comprised of chest, torso, and hand studies. It is symptomatic that agreement reigns precisely in these points. If one abstracts from the other studies (head, feet, toes), a space of similar coherence as that in figures 6 or 9–11 emerges. The torso study appears to be situated not only next to but also behind the chest study. Because of their axial relationship the torso study echoes the chest study. The hand study—as in figure 6 the element most in the foreground—now has a similar dynamic relationship to the chest study as in figure 6. On the New York sheet (fig. 8) this relationship is canceled by the leg stump of the foot study, which directly bumps into the thigh, and the spatial relationship between the three figures is flattened by the head drawn into the left torso. On the Uffizi sheet (fig. 7) the inner logic is disturbed by the scattering of foot and toes and the absurd position of the foot. In both cases a contradiction exists between the arrangement of the three-part basic group and that of the other limbs. It indicates that neither sheet faithfully rendered the content of the original—in contrast to the two Haman-study sheets in Boston and London (figs. 9, 10), whose inventories are identical in both content and topography. They display the same logic of spatial arrangement, the same virtuosity in the use of surface as the drawings of the Oxford sheet (fig. 6). The Windsor example (fig. 11) shows how little is required to destroy this subtle system.

Original and Copy

Michelangelo drawings were—especially on account of their rarity—among the most copied art objects of the sixteenth century. They were reproduced in engravings, paintings, and reliefs. Even more frequently facsimiles—copies intended to reproduce even the stroke system of an original drawing— were made of them. Facsimile copies accompany the authentic corpus like uncanny shadows. They deceived admirers and collectors and repeatedly, also those connoisseurs who were convinced they were immune to deception. Their success in passing as originals was all the greater at a time when the opportunities for comparison were more limited and the originals, abused as they were from being traced, did not actually appear to be such. Today, in an age where the possibilities for comparison are unlimited, the identification of copies is more readily accomplished. As never before, scholars—to judge from the tone of their statements—feel themselves in a position to distinguish between the genuine drawing and its imitation in each particular case.

It is therefore all the more regrettable that the way in which this occurs continues to resemble a wine tasting. The objects to be tasted are the surviving examples of one and the same object. They almost always occur in multiples—three in the case of the studies for the *Crucified Haman* (figs. 9–11) or those for the *Adam* in the Creation scene on the Sistine ceiling,[17] four in the case of the *Cleopatra* (fig. 13) or the *Tityos* (figs. 19, 20), five in the case of the *Archers* (figs. 21–22). In the case of the *Crucifixion* for Vittoria Colonna there are seven examples (including fig. 33), while in the case of the "modello" for the tomb of Lorenzo the Magnificent there are even twelve.[18] Whatever appeals most to the connoisseur's taste is considered to be the original, or is considered at worst the "best" copy.[19] It is suitable for presentation to the public. The other examples are brought to public attention in the form of a reference to their existence; in rare cases a small reproduction is provided. But only a tiny group of scholars participated actively in the wine tasting itself. Most were content to appropriate the judgments of their predecessors as their own. This circumstance explains, for example, why, of the seven surviving examples of Michelangelo's *Ganymede*, only the incomplete Windsor drawing (fig. 18) appeared to exist. It was the only one that was even considered as a candidate for the original and that had been deemed worthy of being reproduced in the catalogues.[20] Only in 1975 did it become apparent that scholars would have been well advised to extend their curiosity to the other examples. At that time, on the occasion of the anniversary exhibition at the British Museum, the full-length example in the Fogg Museum in Cambridge (fig. 17)—the most worn example and the only one whose contours are actually damaged by tracing marks—was displayed along with the Windsor drawing.[21] The confrontation worked miracles. Of course neither Tolnay nor Hirst could bring himself to nullify the dogma of the Windsor drawing's superiority. But Tolnay did have the previously ignored drawing reproduced in his *Corpus* in place of the familiar one—on the grounds that it was an even better copy[22]—while Hirst suddenly saw two Ganymede originals: the vertically formatted one in Cambridge and an allegedly lost one, formatted horizontally, that had served as a model for the Windsor example. The vertical one was drawn first, followed by the horizontal one.[23] This, of course, implies that Michelangelo considered it important to have the right eagle's wing cut off at the same place on the sheet's margins each time.

It is unlikely that the alleged original of the *Archers*, the magnificently preserved drawing in Windsor (no. 12778; fig. 21), could one day experience a fate similar to that of the

Windsor *Ganymede*. None of the four other examples of this composition (including fig. 22) shows signs of having been abused. The greatest danger is that a critical public will by chance get a look at the verso (unreproduced in Tolnay's *Corpus*)[24] of this connoisseur's favorite, where "D. Giulio Clouio copia di Michiel Angelo" is written. The inscription is by the same hand that composed Clovio's inventory of 1577 and wrote "D. Giulio Clouio" on the verso (fig. 82) of the Windsor *Resurrection* (fig. 81).[25] Seeing it with one's own eyes is altogether different from allowing oneself to be casually assured by scholars that the verso of the "original sheet" bears the misleading annotation of a Clovio fan.[26]

That scholars have made such scant use of the methodological possibilities of the twentieth century is even more amazing because it is easier to determine whether a drawing is an original than to solve the problems of authorship. Contrary to a widely held opinion, such methods presuppose *no* acquaintanceship with an individual style. The only prerequisite is knowing the difference between what happens during free drawing and during copying. Anyone can teach himself this knowledge—for example, by analyzing some attempts at copying.[27] Its quintessence can be expressed in a few propositions.

The first and most important proposition: a copyist copies only what he immediately sees or thinks he sees. He sits opposite a complicated fait accompli consisting of a pattern of strokes—the record of the draftsman's hand movements—whose sequence is largely undiscernible. He needs a solid framework in order to get any grip at all on this motionless conglomeration of marks whose inherent logic is difficult to unravel. He therefore first prepares an unobtrusive and lightly drawn preliminary sketch. To the extent circumstances permit, he traces as much of the contours and most important marks within the outlined parts of the original as show through the paper or which become more visible when the copy is held with the original against the light (fig. 26). This preliminary sketch is subsequently covered over by the conclusive strokes. In the end the preliminary sketch is no longer detectable—unless it was executed in a different medium from the finished copy or was only thinly covered over. Examples of the first type include the sketch for the *Brazen Serpent* in Oxford (fig. 29) and the *Children's Bacchanal* in Windsor (fig. 25). The contours of both drawings were first sketched with charcoal or lead point (more easily erased than red chalk) before the red chalk was applied. It is understandable that scholars, who regard both drawings as originals, overlooked this preliminary sketch. Its black contours are almost completely congruous with the strongly reinforced red contours—a clear indication that these contours are components of a copy structure and not of a regular sketch.[28] The second example is represented by the *Resurrection* sketch in London (fig. 27), or more precisely by the guard placed on his back on the sarcophagus lid. This guard, in spite of its seemingly fleeting shorthand style, is clearly discernible as a man on his back, whereas the corresponding figure in the Frankfurt example does not even have a human-like form (fig. 28). The difference seems to suggest that the London example is the original, but is instead attributable to the fact that the draftsman of the London sheet made a preliminary sketch of the guard's contours with extremely thin strokes that can be easily detected with a magnifying glass, while the Frankfurt draftsman was bold enough to sketch them ad hoc by eye.

The London outline sketch was in fact only apparently drawn quickly. Its components are generally provided with sharp endings. Some—for example, the left contour of the head—have a lightly wavering course. The volumes of the strokes are often abruptly changed in breadth and consistency (contour of the upper thigh). All this, together with the existence of solderings, points to a typical "arcade rhythm," that is, the contrary of a spirited movement.

The example leads to the second proposition: It is impossible for the copyist to reproduce the kinetic conditions under which the original was created. His freedom of movement is restricted by a mnemonic capacity that permits only tiny sections of the original to be stored. He has to dismantle every long stroke unity of the original into some short parts (between which he must pause briefly to make sure he has it right); every salient swelling of the original's strokes must be suggested by additional strengthenings (examples in fig. 8: face contour of the head study; in fig. 14: toes of the right foot; in figs. 16 and 27: Christ's shroud; in fig. 21: the herm's shield). It is impossible for his contours to achieve the elasticity and functional dynamics of the original (for example, figs. 6, 19, 30–32). Composed of short, interrupted threadlike strokes, they are a priori condemned to look punctilious, brittle, and indifferent to function—all the more so, the more irregularly they are reinforced (figs. 14, 16: hands; fig. 21: herm; fig. 27: Christ's right leg; fig. 25: "still life" in the foreground). Their "chronology" fundamentally contradicts that of the original, and is therefore the copyist's most unmistakable betrayer. The rear edge of the sarcophagus lid in figure 27 *appears* to have been drawn before the shorthand figure lying on it because the lines defining the sarcophagus cover *seem* to take no account of the overlapping presence of that figure. In fact, however, it was sketched after the fact.

The continuity of the line defining the sarcophagus lid is actually interrupted on either side of the upper and lower thighs of the reclining figure. The draftsman used the figural contours as convenient points at which to pause rather than drawing the sarcophagus lid as one continuous, uninterrupted line.

The right arm of the rising Christ in figure 16 demonstrates a similar procedure. Its first version consists of two parts. The one part lies inside, the other outside the minutely hatched definitive version of the arm. While the outside version consists of lightly drawn marks of the same structure as those of the "final" version of the hand, the inside version is characterized by conspicuously sharp, wiry sections of contour whose hardness contrasts with the adjacent final contours of the arm. Both parts were drawn—by eye—after the "final" version. Rather than pentimenti drawn in the normal course of attempting to define the arm properly, they betray the hand and method of a copyist recreating the pentimenti of an original drawing.[29]

Figure 33 demonstrates a third case of the reversal of the usual drawing stages. There the background hatching—as Tolnay already noticed—overlaps most of the two angels. Tolnay concluded that the angels had been drawn over the already existing hatching.[30] This conclusion is doubtlessly correct—but only in the case of the (lost) original. It is incorrect with regard to the sheet in the British Museum (fig. 33, which Tolnay equated with the original).[31] On this sheet the pair of angels, not the hatching, was drawn first.[32] The continuity in the horizontal shading marks appears to be interrupted at precisely the points where they intersect with the contours of the angels! The draftsman involuntarily hesitated before he overlapped the contours of the angels with his background hatchings.

A special problem for a copyist is hatching. An original's hatching offers no orientation marks comparable to those which are offered by normal contours, and even less a possibility of being traced. Even the task of exactly reproducing its directions is a very difficult one. Copies after one and the same original never show precisely the same directional system. At most they correspond to each other in the directions of individual, especially loosely hatched areas—grosso modo (figs. 7, 8: hair, right arm; figs. 14–15: hair, shroud, sarcophagus; figs. 27–28: background). In copies generally the areas of hatching lack the compelling clarity that can be seen, for example, in the shading of the studies for the Libyan sibyl in figure 6, the Tityos rock in figure 19, or the clouds in the *Fall of Phaeton* in figures 23 and 24. The hatching assemblages reveal small deviations in direction everywhere—

results of the fact that the copyist was forced to recreate step by step what the author of the original had produced by a continuous hatching movement (fig. 20: rock; figs. 21–22: ground hatching). From the beginning the rise of an integral tectonic effect is prevented by this piecework procedure.

As with the directions of the shading, the general tone and density of the shading can be only roughly reproduced. The copyist must avoid trying to reproduce them on the first attempt; otherwise he runs the risk of irrevocably exaggerating them. He must try to build up the density of the shaded areas successively. As a result, in his copy the quantity of strokes is far greater than in the original, and the original hatching texture is converted into an overdense dim web with no relationship to the original purpose. Compared with the shading of the composition sketches in figures 23, 30–32, and 37 the complicated webs of hatching marks in figures 27–29 seem like excerpts from highly finished drawings gone wrong, while the shading in actual highly finished drawings in figures 13–16, 18, 20–22, 25, and 33, compared to the original equivalents in figures 17, 19, and 24 awaken the impression that they were partially done with a brush instead of chalk.[33]

The multiplication and overconcentration of shading that characterizes most copies goes hand in hand with the tendency toward unfettered enlargement. In the facsimile copies the harmonious balance between shaded and unshaded areas, so typical of Michelangelo's originals (for example, figs. 6, 17, 19, 23–24), is generally replaced by a preponderance of shading. But this overworked tendency would inevitably result in total inundation of the ground if the copyist did not take precaution to define the areas not to be shaded by first marking them. In contrast to provisional contours, these preliminary markings usually remain visible even in the final version (examples: fig. 7: hand study; fig. 8: hand, foot, and toe studies; fig. 14: lower right arm; fig. 16: face; fig. 21: arms of the archers; fig. 27: lower right arm of Christ; fig. 28: left thigh of the crawling guard; and fig. 33: lower right arm and hand of Christ). Their very presence is an indication that the sheet is a copy rather than an original.

All the described indicators must be present in order to be able to answer definitively the question of whether the original itself is included among the surviving examples of a certain composition or not. If only one indicator is neglected, fatal inferences can be drawn. The attribution history of Michelangelo's *Dream*, now located in the Courtauld Institute, provides impressive proof of this. This sheet—like the three other, much better preserved specimens of the composition (Chatsworth, Norfolk, New York)—was considered to be

a copy by Morelli, Berenson, Frey, Popp, Panofsky, and Dussler.[34] Dussler caviled in particular at the hardness of the contour of the youth, the looseness of the drapery folds, and the inferiority of the draftsmanship in the plumage of the genius figure in contrast to the feathers of the vulture in the *Tityos* (fig. 19). And with reason. The contours, or more precisely, their reinforcements, reveal numerous characteristics typical of a copy: they are abruptly begun and interrupted, functionally meaningless cord strokes. The long feathers of the genius's wing even have a protruding sawtooth profile at some points. Dussler and his likeminded predecessors nevertheless committed an error—the same error scholars habitually make even now. They neglected to verify the conclusion drawn from their observations by analyzing the relationship between the Courtauld sheet and the other extant examples of the composition. Otherwise they would of course have had to change their opinions, but they would have been in a position to prove what their opponents only sensed. The three other examples—like the painted and engraved copies—deviate from each other and the Courtauld example at precisely those points where the latter is ambiguous.[35] The discrepancies between the Courtauld example and the other specimens are to some extent of the same type as those between the example of the *Ganymede* in Cambridge (fig. 17), or the *Tityos* and the other *Ganymede* or *Tityos* specimens (including figs. 18 and 20).[36] The discrepancies say nothing other than that the Courtauld *Dream* functioned as the common model for the other three versions of this composition and as such must be identical with the original drawing by Michelangelo. The characteristics that the *Dream* shares with copies are, in fact, the result of a "restoration." They extend over those contours that were most affected by the copyists' interventions. In the "circle of vices" they are only sparingly present. In their place there are everywhere symptoms of kinetic spontaneity—crossed strokes, gaps in the contours, and shifts in the axes.

In problem cases like the *Dream* the proof of a drawing's having or not having served as a model is sometimes the only means whatsoever of answering the question of whether a certain sheet—if any—among a group of like compositions is identical with the original. In all other cases this proof serves to guarantee the answer. It is especially required when analysis of the stroke system leads to contradiction of received opinion—as, for example, in the case of the *Christ in Limbo* (figs. 14–15), the *Archers* (figs. 21–22), or the *Children's Bacchanal* (fig. 25, 26). In all three cases the claim that one of the surviving examples of the composition is the authentic one and served as the immediate model for the other ones is contradicted by a comparative analysis. Comparative analysis makes the following apparent:

1. In the *Christ Descending to Hell* in Frankfurt (fig. 15) precisely those pentimenti are missing that are especially conspicuous in the alleged original (fig. 14). One is the remnant of a first version of the head that is longer by a nose length than the final version and at the same time was situated somewhat farther forward and to the left. The other, lightly hatched out, is an upper left arm that begins somewhat higher than the final form of the upper arm and, in contrast to the latter, appears to be extended horizontally to the side. Both pentimenti are replaced in the Frankfurt example by a couple of isolated and more or less meaningless contour fragments—signs that the Frankfurt draftsman saw something different and less clear at those places in his model than is evident in the London sheet. His procedure, however, is distinguished from that of the London draftsman only by degree. Seen in context, the London draftsman's upper-arm pentimento likewise produces no organically meaningful object. It joins a shaded hump formation (also suggested in figure 15) beyond the definitive lower arm version—a hump formation that can be interpreted neither as an elbow–lower-arm piece nor as a component of the banner. More likely it is the product of an attempt to reproduce unambiguously a model that was ambiguous at this place.

2. Like the London *Christ in Limbo*, the alleged original of the *Archers* (fig. 21) also has neither scratch marks nor other damages to the stroke system, although the identity of the sizes of the figures and the topography of the contours that exists between it and the other four examples of this composition suggests extensive tracing. The relatively few details in which the four other examples deviate from each other do not correspond to those places where figure 21 is unclear. For example, the portion of the thigh that forms the connection between the truncated trunk of the archer farthest in the background and his protruding calf (fig. 21) is just as clearly drawn as the surrounding context—as is the hand which partially covers this portion of the thigh. It is thus impossible for figure 21 to be identical with that piece of the model that provoked a deviating version in three of the four other examples (including fig. 22)—including a different thumb and index finger position of that hand in each example—and its total deletion in the fourth, the Frankfurt example (and the Beatrizet engraving).[37] The same applies to the fingerlike formation that represents the left toe of the archer in the

foreground located next to the herm in the alleged original (fig. 21). No copyist could have overlooked it, and yet in the Uffizi, Städel, and Albertina versions it is conspicuous by its absence, while in the Windsor version (no. 0442; fig. 22), which is signed on the back by Bernardino Cesari (1571–1622), it appears not as a component of the archer's foot but as part of the flames fanned by the breath of the putto.

3. The arrangement of the incomplete Berlin version of the *Children's Bacchanal* (fig. 26) differs from the alleged original (fig. 25) in two ways: first in that it changes certain proportions and axial relations, and second in that it changes objects themselves. The first type of discrepancy includes the greater angle of the tilted head of the female satyr, the reduced angle of the right elbow of the drunk man, and the insufficient distance between the taphole of the barrel and the vessel held beneath it. These discrepancies prove only that the copyist sketched certain parts—as usual—by eye. More informative are the discrepancies of the second type, that is, actual changes in composition. For example, the frontmost of the small cooks holds only one instead of two spoons in his right hand; the putto kneeling before the fire blows into his horn instead of beside it; the right ear of the pig dragged out of the background actually appears as a pig's ear and not as a component of a helmet cap; the right buttock of the boy fallen asleep on the legs of the female satyr looks normal rather than swollen; the swan's-neck handle of the vessel, which is held with both hands by the middle figure of the trio of boys in the foreground, acts as a handle instead of dipping into the barrel with the beak; and the left index finger of the boy sitting farthest to the right in the same trio is extended in the direction of the hand axis rather than bent downward. These discrepancies have nothing to do with a subconscious need for correction, although the places in question largely are improvements over their equivalents in figure 25. For the evidence of other details—for example, the shoulder and neck musculature of the drunk man—indicates that the Berlin copyist was in no position to judge the degree of correctness of what he copied. Even less are the discrepancies the results of misunderstandings. For each of the above mentioned places is in the form in which it appears clear and ambiguous. The Berlin copy must have been copied after another, unknown model—the same model that was apparently used by the creator of the three copper engravings.[38] For the most part these engravings deviate from the Windsor drawing (fig. 25) at the same places as the Berlin copy.

II

The Drawings and Drawing Technique
of Michelangelo

2

Authenticated Drawings and Criteria for Authentication

Authenticated drawings are those whose identity as creations of Michelangelo are attested to by external, non-stylistic facts that can be verified by everyone. This verification must be unambiguous. It cannot permit any alternatives. The mere provenance of a sheet from the Buonarroti collection in no way implies that Michelangelo was the author of the drawing on the sheet. It merely limits the range of alternatives. Nor does the positive statement of an early collector guarantee authenticity. Such a statement can be considered as a factor in authentication at best when the collector was personally acquainted with Michelangelo and his drawing technique. Experts in times past might have had sharper eyes and a less prejudiced relationship to drawings than present-day researchers, but their methods of identification were no better.[1]

The number and type of criteria for authentication depend on historical circumstances—for example, how sheets of drawings were kept by their author, how they were used by his pupils, and how they were received by other contemporaries. In Michelangelo's case the circumstances were relatively favorable. The artist made multiple use of his paper. Sheets he used to write letters, poems, or notes were often also used for drawing, or vice versa. Writing on a sheet is therefore just as important a criterion for authentication as the countless testimonies appraising Michelangelo's drawings, the contemporary commentaries, quotes, and reproductions. Not least, however, the abundance of biographical data and the originality of Michelangelo's works themselves make it possible to identify certain works as authentic works of the unparalleled master.

Generally, among the various criteria that can authenticate a drawing as a work of Michelangelo one or another serves as the determining factor. This makes it possible to divide the corpus of genuine sheets according to the most important factors of authentication. A division of this type is of course contrary to every current method of cataloguing. But it does have the didactic advantage of allowing the reader to see at a glance which drawings are authenticated primarily on what basis. Moreover, it provides the reader with a methodological tool that can be employed at any time to check whether the drawings eliminated from the authentic Michelangelo corpus have been eliminated with or without reason.

In the following discussion, the authenticated drawings are divided into seven categories; within each category, drawings are discussed in chronological order. Nevertheless, the large number of relevant drawings made it impossible to devote a separate commentary to each sheet. Those that seemed dispensable as substrates of a phenomenology of Michelangelo's style of drawing (because they are replaceable by other, similar drawings) and that are irrelevant to the discussions in the third part of this book are therefore discussed briefly in the notes. The commentaries themselves include information only as to authorship, time of creation, function, and subject matter. Their principal purpose is to communicate the results of the author's research. The reader should consult Dussler's *Katalog* (bib. 80), Tolnay's *Corpus* (bib. 319), or the catalogues of the relevant collections (bib. 15–16, 30, 207, 240, 344) for all other information (provenance, paper quality, or previous literature, and so forth).

Direct or Indirect Written Evidence

Direct or indirect written evidence appears on a total of five sheets (the third, chronologically, is mentioned in note 11). In each case the handwriting is cinquecento and appears on what is identified at present as the recto. Its characteristics correspond to various groups of written evidence with certain fixed dates within the authenticated autograph material of the artist (letters, poems, *ricordi*, and the like). In every case, the handwriting is datable after the drawings with which it coexists, but is written in the same medium as the drawings. The handwriting is at either the right or lower edge of the sheet.

LOUVRE NO. 685r

On this sheet (fig. 4) the handwriting is in the form of an ironic question: "Chi dire mai chella fo[sse] dimie mano" ("Who would ever say that it is by my hand")?. The question refers to the heavily hatched pen-and-ink drawing of St. Anne. It expresses the artist's amazement that the "it" by his hand doesn't appear to be.[2] The question addresses a viewer who looks at the drawing more skeptically than today's scholars are accustomed to do.[3] There is a contradiction in function between the contour and the hatching. What the contour had rendered with optimum clarity—as proved by the unhatched areas (hands, feet, Christ child), the hatching (whose pen-and-ink redaction was preceded by a hatching sketched in black chalk!) largely obscures through its expansive, overly thick, little-differentiated latticework-like complexity. Mary seems to be sitting both on St. Anne's lap and next to it. Her left leg seems flat as a board, while the right calf, whose existence seems to be denied by the deep notch-like drapery folds, gives the impression that it is about to fall through the ground that the two women share (before the hatching its spatial effect might have corresponded to that of the right foot of the Doni Madonna). It is hard to imagine that this hatching stems from the same pen that sketched the outline with such clarity. Its immature style[4] marks it as the product of a pupil who tried to test the level of his hatching ability against the master's outline drawing. As has been proven elsewhere,[5] the pupil was Antonio Mini. There is documentary evidence that the master gave him the sheet. For the dating of the recto, see the section "The Coexistence of Two or More Drawings," below.

LOUVRE NO. 714r

On this sheet (fig. 5) the relevant handwriting is, exceptionally, accompanied by Michelangelo's own signature: "Dauicte cholla fromba / e io chollarcho / Michelagniolo" ("David with the slingshot and I, Michelangelo, with the drill"). This remark refers to the work on the colossal marble statue the Florentines had nicknamed "il gigante." It means: As once little David conquered the giant Goliath with the slingshot, so I, Michelangelo, will overpower the giant David block with the sculptor's tool.[6] At the same time, the writing is inextricably related to the two pen-and-ink drawings. The study in the center of the sheet (turned inversely) appears to refer directly to the aforementioned sculpture, the right arm and shoulder-chest area of which it matches.[7] The sketch to the left is obviously a depiction of a "David with the Slingshot." Nevertheless, it bears a greater resemblance to Donatello's sculptures than to Michelangelo's colossus. It presupposes an idea completely different from that expressed by the colossal work; such an idea is documented by written evidence. It resulted from a commission that the artist received on 12 August 1502, eleven months after he had begun the chisel work on the great marble *David* (13 September 1501).[8] The design was meant to satisfy the desire of the client, Pierre de Rohan (1451–1513), for a bronze *David* that was intended to resemble Donatello's bronze *David* for the Medici.[9] In November 1508 the completed sculpture was shipped to France, where in the course of the seventeenth century it disappeared without a trace.[10]

BRITISH MUSEUM NO. 1859-6-25-543r

The two-line note under the tomb sketch of this sheet (fig. 12) has the character of an explication: "La fama tiene gliepitafi agiacere non ua ne inanzi ne indietro / perche son morti e eloro operare e fermo" ("Fame holds epitaphs fixed, it moves neither forward nor backward, for they are dead and their actions stand still").[11] The explanation refers to the shorthand figure in the middle compartment of the intermediate story.[12] It is evidence that a personification of fame was planned for that space, which was supposed to fix the glorious deeds described in the epitaphs and at the same time, by virtue of its own immobility, personify the finality and immutability of the character and achievements of the famous persons buried there. This indicates that the sketch was meant for the tomb of the two persons whose fame, in Michelangelo's eyes, was eternal: Lorenzo de' Medici, the patron and protector of the young Michelangelo, and his brother Giuliano, who was murdered in the Pazzi conspiracy. Michelangelo designed a common tomb for them in the spring of 1521. It was meant to decorate the entrance wall of the Medici Chapel, and was supposed to serve as a retable, as well as a monument—as a counterpart to the opposite altar.[13] The London sketch shows this double function in the superimposition of a profane sarcophagus with its personification of earthly "fame" and a sacral zone with the character of a church facade.

BRITISH MUSEUM NO. 1895-9-15-517

The last example in which proof of authorship is provided by Michelangelo himself is found on this sheet (fig. 23). It is in the form of a message addressed to Tommaso de' Cavalieri: "[Mess]er tomao se questo scizzo non ui piace ditelo a urbino [acci]o che io abbi tempo dauerne facto unaltro doman dassera [co]me ui promess e se ui piace euogliate che io lo finisca [rim]andatemelo" ("Sir Tommaso, if you don't like this sketch, tell Urbino, so that I have time to do another one before tomorrow evening, as I promised you. And if you do like it, and you want me to finish it, then send it back to me").[14] According to this inscription, the London sheet bears a sketch for a planned finished drawing. It was brought to Cavalieri for appraisal by Michelangelo's factotum Francesco Amadori, nicknamed Urbino. Cavalieri had been prepared for the parcel and apparently had also been busy sketching a *Fall of Phaeton* (fig. 66).[15] But he probably felt irritated when he saw the sketch Michelangelo had sent. Instead of completing his own sketch, he gave Urbino his sheet together with Michelangelo's, after having provided the former with a short message: "lo [l'o] ritracto el meglio che o saputo io pero ui rima[n]do il uostro p[er]ch[e] ne son [?] seruo uostro che lo ritraga un altra uolta" (roughly: "I have drawn the Phaeton, as well as *I* could. But I'm sending yours back to you. Because of it I feel myself obliged to you to draw it again").[16] This transaction appears to have taken place immediately before Michelangelo's departure for Florence at the end of June 1533. Subsequently, however, both parties made good their results. On 6 September Cavalieri reported to Michelangelo: "Forse tre giorni fa io ebbi il mio Fetonte assai ben fatto, e allo visto il Papa, il cardinal [Ippolito] de' Medici e ugnuno. Io non so gia per qual causa sia desiderato di vedere" ("Perhaps three days ago I had satisfactorily finished my Phaeton; and the pope, Cardinal de' Medici, and everyone saw it. I have no idea why they wanted to see it").[17] This report and the

following note concerning the cardinal's delight at seeing the *Ganymede* (fig. 17) and the *Tityos* (fig. 19) might have encouraged Michelangelo to become active again. Nevertheless, the artist was reluctant to re-occupy himself with a sketch that was already two months old. Instead he drew a new sketch (fig. 24) on the blank side of a sheet that, according to the evidence of its present verso drawing (fig. 50), had been left behind in Florence by Antonio Mini.[18] Not satisfied with it, he erased it, outlined a better version on the same area, and finished this ad hoc. As he was drawing he apparently had before his eyes Cavalieri's sketch (fig. 66), which had been taken along to Florence. The inspirational effect of Cavalieri's drawing is evident in the fact that the composition is more rigorous and dynamic than the London sketch (fig. 23).[19] When Cavalieri received the drawing after Michelangelo's return to Rome (early November), he might have perceived in it something of what he had himself secretly striven for.

The Relationship of the Content of a Drawing to a Coexisting Autograph Inscription

The second criterion for authentication differs from the first only in that the priorities are reversed. In the case of the first criterion, the inscription offers a commentary, not the drawing; in the second, the drawing provides the illustration of an attendant inscription. This means that drawings in the second category cannot be preliminary sketches. As illustrations, pictorial explanations, or pictograms, they are classified as incidental sketches created in passing. They are executed with the same pen and ink used to compose the related inscriptions, and are located either to the right or below the written passages. The three sheets in question are all in the Archivio Buonarroti, where the bulk of the extant written legacy from Michelangelo's hand is stored.

ARCHIVIO BUONARROTI NO. XIII, FOL. 111

The earliest of these sketches, approximately 12.5 centimeters long, stands next to the sonnet in which the artist cursed the physical discomforts of painting the ceiling of the Sistine Chapel (fig. 39).[20] It acts as a pictorial gloss, making visible images evoked by the poem—the painter's unsteady footing, the neck swollen with goiter, the hunchback that serves as a resting place for the back of the head, the pigeon chest and the fat rump that grew to counterbalance it. The sketch becomes an "image" of the painter who—deformed by his enforced posture, stepping from one foot to the other and continuously looking up and craning his neck at the ceiling—involuntarily comes to view what he is painting as a portent of his own doom. The poem and the sketch were probably created at the time the vault was being painted, that is, between January 1509 and August 1510.[21] Both were addressed to one Giovanni da Pistoja, a friend who also wrote poems and is possibly the same Ser Giovanni di Benedetto da Pistoja who subsequently became chancellor of the Accademia degli Umidi, which was founded in 1540.[22]

ARCHIVIO BUONARROTI, X, FOL. 578v

The sketches of food (fig. 43) were made nine or ten years later. They illustrate a written list of the components of three meals. Each is in the form of a small pictogram that corresponds to the contents of one line. Only the first, however, which renders "two loaves of bread" as two circles, is found directly opposite the words to which it refers. The other pictograms have their own pattern of organization. Their sizes imperceptibly increased as they were drawn, so that something like a spatial sequence emerged from the paratactical top-to-bottom list—the pictorial formula of a cold buffet, so to speak. The writing and sketches are located on the back of a short letter addressed to Michelangelo, which Bernardo Niccolini, treasurer to the archbishop of Florence, had written to the artist on 18 March 1518.[23] The letter contains nothing that would have required its preservation. It was therefore probably used as a sheet for casual notation immediately after it was received.

ARCHIVIO BUONARROTI, XIII, FOL. 33r

The last document of this type is located at the end of a letter written crossways to four epigrams.[24] In the signature ("Vostro miche*lo* almacel de") the last word, "corvi," which refers to the address of the writer, is replaced by the pictogram of a small raven.[25] The letter and epigrams are addressed to Michelangelo's friend Luigi del Riccio, the head of the Strozzi-Ulivieri bank in Rome. The epigrams are part of a larger series of epitaphs proposed by Michelangelo on the death of Luigi's nephew Cecchino Bracci, who had died on 8 January 1544 at the age of fifteen.[26]

Drawings Accompanied by Autograph Measurements Written with the Same Mediums

In addition to some groundplans and elevations, a large number of sketches for marble blocks can be authenticated.[27] Most of these are preserved in the Archivio Buonarroti, but they are—with one exception—of limited relevance to a phenomenology of Michelangelo's drawing style. They can provide ad-

ditional clues about Michelangelo's methods of filling sheets. But they say little about drawing movements, because in most cases the contours are completely or partially drawn with a ruler—a factor that also disqualifies most of the architecture drawings as objects relevant to analysis of the stroke system.

BRITISH MUSEUM NO. 1859-6-25-544r

The three outline sketches on the recto of the British Museum sheet no. 1859-6-25-544 (fig. 40) comprise the exception. They show the rough shape of one and the same sculpture examined from two different viewpoints and thus represent the schematic résumé of a previous sketching process.[28] The purpose of this résumé consisted in providing an optimum calculation of height, width, and depth either of the marble block required for the execution of the figure or its corresponding clay model.[29] The figure itself, in its complicated posture, acts like a pendant to the large terracotta model of a river god in the Casa Buonarroti.[30] In fact, in the course of executing the Medici tombs Michelangelo had produced or had someone produce for him two large-sized models of river gods (presumably for Lorenzo's tomb).[31] This appears to have happened between the fall of 1525 and the summer of 1526.[32] The fragment of Michelangelo's note on the back of the sheets dates precisely from this time: "Uer se e re di francia mor[i] a prigioniero" ("Check whether the king of France has died in captivity"). It is in the same handwriting as the measurements on the recto and is obviously a reaction to the rumor circulating in Florence in the fall of 1525 that Francis I, held prisoner in Spain by Charles V, was dying.[33]

The Coexistence of Drawings with Autograph Writing Written with the Same Mediums

This type of evidence can be used to authenticate the Annunciation sketch (fig. 37) discussed in the excursis II and two pen-and-ink drawings, each of which shows a bony hand in a different position but with similar purposes (figs. 41–42). The latter coexist with fragments of poems and seem to have been created in the middle of their composition, during a break in the writing. Composed with the same pen and ink as the poem fragments, the casualness of their creation marks them as occasional sketches.

ARCHIVIO BUONARROTI, XIII, FOL. 169v

The larger and earlier sketch (17.5 cm; fig. 41) is located on the Archivio Buonarroti sheet no. XIII, fol. 169v. It depicts a hand held horizontally pointing to the right that branches off from the lower arm at an oblique angle. This hand is drawn from the viewpoint of a draftsman sitting at a table viewing his own left hand with his elbow resting on the table surface; he lets his hand "stand model." [34] It is nothing other than a portrait of Michelangelo's own hand—the same "working hand" [35] that appears with such emphatic emphasis in Jacopino del Contes's much-copied portrait of Michelangelo and which says so much about the sitter's latent energies. [36] The sketch was created after the unfinished draft of the poem was written (the last line of which turned out to be an obstacle for the contour of the index fingertip), [37] but before the revised and longer version of the poem (on the present-day recto) was completed. Before the drawing was made the sheet had been turned 90 degrees to the right—either because turning the paper offered more space or because Michelangelo wanted to distance himself temporarily from the thoughts expressed in the poem. [38] These thoughts are concerned with the death of a dear friend. If the dead person—as Girardi assumes—was Michelangelo's favorite brother, Buonarroto, [39] the sheet must have been written and drawn on shortly after 2 July 1528. [40]

COD. VAT. 3211, FOL. 74r

The second sketch of a hand is located on folio 74r of the Codex Vaticanus 3211 (fig. 42). It is only 4.1 cm high and 6.3 cm wide. Once again its subject appears to be Michelangelo's own left hand—but this time seen in a mirror and in a position at a sharp angle to the lower arm. Since it holds a book, one is tempted to assume that the model posed with one. [41] But this assumption is contradicted by the unclear, casual spatial relationship between hand and book. The book was apparently sketched in only as an afterthought (and for this reason comes close to encroaching on the eleventh line of the sonnet). [42] But this hasty addendum transformed the originally "meaningless" sketch into a small demonstration object that showed the author of the Annunciation sketch in figure 100 how the position of the Madonna's right arm could be improved. The improvement was carried out on the corresponding cartonetto (fig. 101). There Michelangelo's sketch is almost literally copied—with the unintentional effect that the hand of the Madonna seems to grow directly out of the upper arm. [43] The cartonetto is related to a painting made by Michelangelo's friend Marcello Venusti around 1550. [44] Michelangelo's draft of a sonnet appears to have been written about the same time. His vigorous handwriting with its fluctuations in size, shape, and direction caused by old age is identical with that of the love sonnet, conceived out of the resignation of an artist who feels his soul nearly arrived at the

other world ("l'alma quasi giunta a l'altra riva"), on the present-day verso of the sheet. [45] Several drafts of this sonnet exist: two of them [46] are accompanied by the draft of an undated letter by the artist to Benedetto Varchi (1503–65) concerning the superiority of painting or sculpture. [47] They must have been written shortly after 14 March 1547, the date of Varchi's request for Michelangelo's position on the paragone problem. [48]

The Coexistence of Two or More Drawings of Similar Medium, Execution, and Style, One of Which Is Authenticated

This situation is represented on the recto of the Louvre sheet no. 685 (fig. 4). There only the contour of the St. Anne group can be certainly identified as autograph. But since the two other ink drawings have the same contour characteristics, they can also be considered authentic. In fact, some rather precise observations can be made regarding their purpose. It is highly probable that the male nude is a sketch (the only one extant) for Michelangelo's lost *Hercules* statue of 1497 (see excursus I). The creation of this sculpture (July or August 1497) supplies a reliable *terminus ante quem* for the dating of the outline drawing of the St. Anne group, which appeared on the sheet before the nude. [49] The small sketch of a curly head appears to have been drawn at least a quarter century later, after the St. Anne group had been hatched in. [50] The ironic head serves the purpose of emphasizing the written exclamation "Chi dire mai . . . " (as quoted above). What the exclamation expresses in words the sketch seems to say with mimicry—the eye turned sharply upward, toward St. Anne, the skeptically raised eyebrows, the long hooknose and the pinched lips. [51] To a certain extent it represents the person who quips: "Who would ever say this is a product of mine?"! [52]

The Identity of What Is Depicted on an Extant Drawing with the Subject of a Drawing Known to Contemporaries and Documented by Contemporary Written and Pictorial Evidence as Stemming from Michelangelo

It affirms that a particular "invenzione" is by Michelangelo, but says nothing about whether an extant related drawing was actually executed by his hand. This question must therefore be carefully examined case by case, because many drawing subjects that have been attributed as "invenzioni" of Michelangelo generally exist in *several* examples. Michelangelo's original drawing *may* exist among them, but does not necessarily have to. The likelihood of its preservation depends not least on how frequently it was traced. Each tracing is a mechanical operation which results in hurting the original drawing. Tracings leave behind scratches, damage the contours, and—in the case of chalk drawings—smudge the shading. Originals that have been traced more than once are therefore preserved, if at all, in worse condition than their copies (for example, fig. 17). On the other hand, a relatively few well-preserved originals owe their freshness to the fact that they either remained untraced (figs. 23, 30–32, 35–38) or were copied by eye (figs. 6, 19, 23, 34, 39). Copies done by eye differ from each other more than copies that were traced.

Almost all the drawings within this category are certified as works of Michelangelo by more than one contemporary document and have been disseminated in engravings, paintings, and other copies, in addition to facsimiles (figs. 14–16, 18, 20–22, 26–29, 33). Most of these testimonies have already been listed by Thode (bib. 294) and Dussler (bib. 80). In the following they are therefore mentioned only insofar as they assist in the process of authentication. Of a total of nineteen drawings—with the exceptions of figures 27–29 and 36 all highly finished ones—twelve are treated in the text; the others are mentioned in notes 53, 74, 93, 129, and 130.[53]

CHRIST DESCENDING TO LIMBO

On 15 July 1532 Sebastiano del Piombo thanked Michelangelo for a drawing that his friend had sent him.[54] "I am very satisfied with it," he writes. "Nevertheless the Christ is, apart from the arms and the head, almost the same as that in S. Pietro in Montorio; but I will get used to it as well as I can" ("satisfami assai. Però el Cristo, da le braze et la testa in fora, è quasi simile a quello de Sancto Pietro Montorio; ma pur io me accomodarò meglio che potrò"). The only drawing in the "Michelangelo" corpus that fits this description is the finished drawing of a Risen Christ descending to limbo, which survives in two facsimile copies (figs. 14–15).[55] It apparently represents the starting point of a sketching process that resulted in Sebastiano's painting of *Christ in Limbo* (Madrid, Prado). From the evidence of several sketches (including figs. 48–49), Sebastiano attempted to eradicate its fatal similarity to the famous *Flagellation of Christ* (which everyone knew had been designed by Michelangelo).[56] There is even less reason to doubt its identity with the "disegnio," because the drawing came to Michelangelo's and Sebastiano's friend Cavalieri approximately six months after the date of the letter (see chapter 5, "The Solution of a 'Homework Task'").[57] Since the drawing was sent from Florence, it must have been created between early May and mid-June of 1532.[58]

THE ARCHERS

In his life of Marcantonio Raimondi (ca. 1480–1527/34) Vasari provides a list of finished drawings by Michelangelo that Antoine Lafréry (1512–77) rendered in the form of copper engravings: "the Phaeton, the Tityos, the Ganymede, the Archers, the Bacchanal, the Dream, as well as the Pietà and the crucifix" (figs. 24, 19, 17, 21–22, 25, 33).[59] These were the same finished drawings that Clovio helped to disseminate by making copies, sometimes several times. Many of Clovio's facsimile copies survive (even if some of them are unrecognized). Today most of them are located in the Royal Collection at Windsor—where the bulk of the Farnese collection (and thus the drawings left behind by Sebastiano, Cavalieri, and Clovio) have been stored since the reign of George III (1738–1820).[60] One of them is spectacular, at least from the perspective of the history of research: Windsor example no. 12778 of the Archers (fig. 21) mentioned in Clovio's inventory of 1577, "il Sagittario di Michelangiolo."[61] For in spite of the verso inscription ("D. Giulio Clouio copia di Michiel Angelo")[62] in the hand of the writer of the inventory,[63] in spite of the manifest traces of kinetically inhibited movement in the stroke system, and in spite of the lack of any indications that it served as a model for the other extant examples, almost all scholars regard and have regarded it as Michelangelo's original![64] The reason behind this curious fact is obvious: to admit the copy status of the drawing would have meant admitting that the *Resurrection* in Windsor (figs. 81–82), which is signed by the same writer ("D.Giulio Clouio"), was an independent creation of Clovio's. An avalanche would have been started.

Clovio's copy of the *Archers* is one of five surviving examples of this famous highly finished composition.[65] It looks as if it was later cut down. But the same edges of the drawing appear to have been cut in the examples in the Uffizi (no. 126s) and the Städelsches Kunstinstitut in Frankfurt (no. 3979). In the cases of the second Windsor example (fig. 22) signed on the verso by Bernardino Cesari and the example in the Albertina (Sc.L.206) the edges are intact, but not identical. In the Albertina copy the right foot of the hovering female figure is represented in profile, whereas in the Cesari copy it is *en face*. The headdress and hip profile of the herm are designed differently in each case. Thus, the edges must have been filled in by the copyists in both cases. This presupposes that they were not to be seen in the original, in other words: that all the copyists saw the original *framed*.[66] Clovio and the authors of the Uffizi and Städel copies tried to cope with this situation by cutting their sheets from the start to the size of the original drawing surface that remained visible (approximately 20 × 30 cm). In this way they were able to trace the contours directly from the original in spite of the frame. But Cesari and the Albertina copyist apparently selected a more complicated method. Their copies appear to be based on separately prepared tracings of the contours (probably on transparency paper).

The *Archers* original was apparently intended for Cavalieri. That is not expressly documented anywhere, but can be deduced from the following facts: First, during 1530–36 the Venetian painter Battista Franco (1498–1561) lived in Rome "for no other reason than to study and imitate the drawings, paintings, and sculptures of Michelangelo" (Vasari).[67] In Rome he must have become acquainted with the *Archers* in addition to the *Ganymede* (fig. 17) and the *Dream*, since he incorporates figures from all three compositions in his painting of the *Battle of Montemurlo* (Florence, Galleria Pitti) painted after July 1537. Second, both the Béatrizet engraving and the two paintings of a Madonna with Child cited after the sleeping Cupid of the *Archers* (Munich and Cambridge) attributed to Jacopino del Conte (1510–98)[68] were created in Rome. Third, in the list of engravings by Lafréry mentioned above the *Archers* is listed among those drawings that were given to Cavalieri. Fourth, in his short biography of Bernadino Cesari, Baglione writes: "B. C. copied some drawings of Michelangelo Buonarroti that belonged to Tommaso de' Cavalieri, to whom they had been presented by Michelangelo himself."[69]

The composition has—like that of the *Dream*—an allegorical character. The bearers of its main action are the nine adult "archers" who represent humanity in their undifferentiated youth and nakedness on the one hand and their different gender on the other.[70] Unarmed, they hurry toward a common goal, a herm that is situated ambiguously in space. With imaginary arrows and bows, they mime the act of shooting with their left hands (that is, they are *left*-handed archers). Nevertheless their activity is inhibited to the extent that they approach this half real, half "imaginary" goal. While the hintermost, female figure floats weightlessly toward the target, the two frontmost figures lie on the ground on their stomachs, incapable of reaching their goal. The driving force of their actions appears to be the fire stoked by two wingless putti and associated with the dionysian symbol of a drinking vessel. Nourished by the arrows needed for attaining the goal,[71] this fire is the symbol of blind, self-consuming passion—of that animalistic drive that has become flesh in the form of the satyr in the background. This satyr, who is the only figure to run aimlessly around, incapable of making conscious use of his weapon, is located diagonally opposite the winged Eros sleeping in the right foreground. He

appears as its counterpart. Actually the Eros is also set apart from the quasi archers. He turns his back to them and has an entirely closed contour. Assigned to the "irreal" reality of the herm by his sketchy appearance, he is ignored by the archers. But he is the only being in the possession of both a bow and a full quiver of arrows—who is therefore the only one with both the power and the means to hit the target. His inactivity appears as the actual reason for the fictitious, awkward, and futile activity of the archers. In all the whole "reads" like the transformation of an earlier poem.[72] The hurrying world—so the quintessence could read—steadfastly fancies that it can reach its goal even without being armed with love, by the sheer force of its striving.[73]

The *Archers* and the *Dream* are related in their contents like pendants that complement each other. The one drawing illustrates the normal state of human affairs, the other its unmasking and overturning—through the sudden awakening by the call of Eros and the individual's self-realization.[74] Both together produce something like an autobiographical confession: a symbolic depiction of how Michelangelo perceived his life before and since his meeting with the beloved Tommaso.

GANYMEDE

A confession expressed with such an expenditure of manual labor could probably blossom only in the glowing initial phase of the friendship. Actually the first present that Michelangelo gave to Tommaso consisted of a *pair* of drawings. Tommaso received them while he was sick and referred to them in his first letter written in late December 1532.[75] "At least two hours a day," he wrote, "I allow myself the pleasure of viewing both your drawings that Pierantonio brought me; the longer I look at them, the more I like them."[76]

Highly pleased at this reaction, on 1 January 1533 Michelangelo sent his friend a letter with an enclosure whose contents he did not mention "for good reason" ("per buon rispecto").[77] Apparently the enclosure was his *Ganymede*—the only drawing addressed to Cavalieri that could awaken ambiguous associations (whoever saw Michelangelo, "il Divino," with the handsome Cavalieri might have been tempted to think of Jupiter and Ganymede).[78] This drawing is currently located in the Fogg Art Museum in Cambridge (fig. 17). Like the *Dream*, it shows traces of heavy wear. No wonder. From the evidence of the size of the figures and the topography of the contours of the other examples (Windsor 13036 [fig. 18]; Uffizi 245F; Louvre 734, 777, and 826; Paris, private collection),[79] all of which have the characteristics of copies, it must have been traced at least six times.[80] The copies deviate from the original wherever the details of the latter appear ambiguous. For example, in both the Uffizi and Louvre 826 copies[81] and in the Windsor copy Ganymede's left hand, which in the Cambridge drawing was drawn in several subsequent versions, is represented by an unshapely claw with a varying number of fingers. And the contour that defines the left side of the thorax in the Windsor copy appears as a component of the eagle's wing in the Uffizi copy.

There is a curious discrepancy in the degree of finish between the upper and lower halves of the composition. This caused five of the six copyists (including the one of fig. 18) to omit the lower half altogether.[82] The discrepancy even led to the unlikely proposition that Michelangelo himself subsequently reduced his composition to the upper half—by copying the Ganymede-eagle group alone on a sheet now lost (Hirst). In reality this discrepancy is connected with the purpose of the drawing. Michelangelo's *Ganymede* is not a coded declaration of love, as has been claimed since Panofsky (who like almost all scholars regarded the horizontal composition as the authentic one).[83] Like the *Tityos* (fig. 19), the *Fall of Phaeton* (fig. 24), and the *Children's Bacchanal* (fig. 25), it was created during a course of instruction in drawing.[84] The instigation for its creation was a drawing in red chalk created by Cavalieri himself (fig. 58). Michelangelo began with this drawing of Cavalieri's, and from it he proceeded to refine what appeared to him in need of development. He made his eagle and dog the same size as they were in Cavalieri's red-chalk drawing and reduced the size of Ganymede by a nuance. He sensed that the right claw of Cavalieri's eagle, which grips at thin air, needed a foothold, and invented the motif of Ganymede's legs caught in the grip of the eagle's talons. He simultaneously gave Ganymede's right arm, which in Cavalieri's composition turns passively around its own axis and defies perspective by bumping into the eagle's wing, a more plausible position. Michelangelo's efforts were entirely directed at making his drawing a "mirror" in which the pupil could see his own thoughts reflected in clarified form. It was precisely for this reason that he incorporated into his own drawing the differing degrees of completeness and non-finito that characterize Cavalieri's red-chalk drawing. Nevertheless, this did not prevent Michelangelo from as carefully improving the sketchy and ill-defined parts as he improved the Ganymede-eagle group. He transformed Cavalieri's stiff, sheeplike animal, which howls from a standing position, into a true sheepdog; without changing its essential characteristics (proportions, short hair, and thin, bent tail), he naturalized both its shape and behavior and emphasized its role as protector by lightly sketching sheep. He lent the landscape itself greater breadth by reducing the details of the topography. At the same time he increased the distance between the landscape

and the Ganymede-eagle group and so increased the latter's upward shift. Finally, in order to pictorialize the future aspect of the event—Ganymede's ascension to Olympus—he added, with some shading, a mist through which one perceives a circular opening.[85]

TITYOS

Of the finished drawings Vasari listed by name in the 1550 and 1568 editions of his *Lives* as examples of Michelangelo's draftsmanship used to instruct Cavalieri in drawing, the *Tityos* is mentioned second to the *Ganymede* in both cases.[86] The original is identical with the recto drawing of Windsor sheet 12771 (fig. 19) and, with the exception of the Windsor *Fall of Phaeton* (fig. 24), it is the only original that survived multiple copying somewhat intact. It was copied many times, although its originality is confirmed first by the fact that the three other "Tityos" compositions (Windsor 0472r [fig. 20]; Uffizi 248F; Windsor 0471)[87] deviate from each other at those details where the pattern of chalk strokes in Windsor 12771 is indistinct,[88] and second because there is an optimal relation between kinetic economy and esthetic purposefulness.

In the absence of a corresponding drawing by Cavalieri it is impossible to say whether the *Tityos* owes its existence to a similar cause as the *Ganymede* (fig. 17).[89] It is certain, however, that the person to whom it was addressed made quite free use of it. On the verso of the sheet (fig. 61) this uncertain recipient traced the outer contours and most important interior marks defining the head, trunk, upper arms, and thighs. He then completed the figure by adding lower arms, lower legs, and provided a raison d'être for the figure's action by adding a sarcophagus—thus creating a Resurrection.[90] The resultant verso figure (for its purpose see chapter 5) is unlikely to buttress the traditional claim of Michelangelo's authorship.[91] In context, the added-on pieces seem to be turned (lower left leg), disproportionate (right shank), or drawn in a distorted perspective (sarcophagus). The elbow of the right arm and the outer contour of the right thigh—places where the draftsman was left without a model because of the intervention of the vulture—exhibit signs of extreme uncertainty: a confusion of strokes or a break accompanied by a sudden decrease in pressure, which can be diagnosed as a severe fracture.

CLEOPATRA

Vasari writes that Michelangelo presented Tommaso de' Cavalieri with "molte carte stupendissime, disegnate di lapis nero e rosso, di teste divine" ("many stupendous sheets with ideal heads, executed in black and red chalk").[92] But of these "many sheets" only one is known by name: the sheet with the *Cleopatra*.[93] It survives in four drawn examples (Casa Buonarroti 2F; British Museum 1887-5-2-120; Louvre 733; Museum Boymanns-van Beuningen I/388) and one painting (formerly Collection Sir Kenneth Clark).[94] Of the drawings the Casa Buonarroti sheet (fig. 13) is generally considered today to be the original.[95] It appears to be identical with the "carta di mano del divino Michelagnolo, dove è una Cleopatra" (Vasari) that Tommaso had presented to Duke Cosimo de' Medici in 1562 together with the drawing of a crying boy by Sofonisba Anguiscola (1528–1625).[96] In any case, the unstained, sharply demarcated strip along the edges of the paper is evidence that the drawing must once have been framed—as was the version of the *Cleopatra* listed among the "disegni di Michelagnolo Buonarroti" in the Medici inventory.[97] But even though there is little reason to argue against identifying the Casa Buonarroti *Cleopatra* with that mentioned in the Medici inventory, there is little basis for claiming that it is by Michelangelo's hand. The Casa Buonarroti sheet bears, as do the other three examples, the characteristics of a copy (minutely reinforced contours consisting of extremely short, thin broken strokes of continually changing consistency; multilayered hatching strokes cut into little morsels and blurred in the face and neck, yet full of inexplicable changes in direction). Accordingly, it cannot be regarded as a model for the other examples, none of which has such a broad and edged ear, such sharply protruding eyeballs, such a conspicuous bump in the clavicle area of the breast contour, and such a rope-shaped serpent. None—except for the Louvre example—has such a strongly accentuated nipple and such widely separated lips in the left corner area of the mouth. Each one of the extant examples seem to presuppose a prototype that looked more anatomically plausible. In fact, both Vasari's and Cavalieri's conduct suggest that they considered it unwise to disabuse the duke of his certainty that he owned Michelangelo's original. Vasari avoided mentioning the *Cleopatra* in connection with the "teste divine" drawn for Cavalieri in his life of Michelangelo. Instead he mentioned the *Cleopatra*—very casually—in the life of Properzia de' Rossi, awakening the impression that the more valuable part of the two-part gift was the "carta di mano di Sofonisba." The same impression is awakened by Cavalieri's accompanying letter of 20 January 1562,[98] which deals principally with Sofonisba's drawing of a boy and the circumstances surrounding its creation.[99] Only the first two sentences are dedicated to the *Cleopatra*. Coming from the mouth of so talented a draftsman as Cavalieri, they sound ambiguous enough to justify the assumption that the Medici *Cleopatra* (fig. 13) is the

product of his own talent for copying ("mando questo diseggno a me tanto caro, ch' io reputo privarmi di uno de' miei figliuli"—"I send you this drawing, which is so dear to me, that I think I am losing one of my children").[100]

THE RISEN CHRIST

The motif, typology, size, and execution of the drawing of the Risen Christ bear a striking similarity to those of Michelangelo's *Christ in Limbo* (figs. 14–15); two examples survive (Windsor 12768 [fig. 16] and Louvre 1505). Their object is the result of a conscious metamorphosis of the Christ descending into limbo into a figure rising from the sarcophagus. But, unlike the *Christ in Limbo*, this metamorphosis, which took into consideration even the unorthodox motif of light coming from the right, was not accomplished with a view to making a painting.[101] The degree of finish, the lack of any indication of a figural or spatial context (in the case of the *Christ in Limbo* the direction and gesture of the right arm evoke the presence of a pair of ancestors), as well as a certain mannerism in the figure's stance,[102] point to a didactic purpose. In fact the figure appears to have been created within the context of a drawing lesson—as the master's critical answer to Cavalieri's attempts to transform Michelangelo's *Christ in Limbo* into a Risen Christ (see chapter 5). Since these attempts (fig. 61) presupposed the existence of the *Tityos* (fig. 19), they cannot be dated before January 1533.[103] Clovio's inventory, which lists "Tre resurectioni inventione di M.ro Michelangiolo fatte da Don Giulio,"[104] testifies to Michelangelo's authorship of the design. One of these is probably identical with the Windsor drawing (fig. 16). It has the same stroke-system features as, among others, Clovio's copies of the *Tityos* and the *Archers* (figs. 20–21) and the examples of Michelangelo's *Christ in Limbo* and *Resurrection* sketch in London (figs. 14, 27).[105] In any case it is certain that Clovio was thoroughly familiar with the subject of the drawing, for he used it as the basis for the figure of Christ in his *Resurrection* in Windsor (fig. 81).[106]

FALL OF PHAETON

The fifth finished drawing created in the course of Cavalieri's instruction in draftsmanship is the *Fall of Phaeton*. Unlike the sheets discussed above, only *one* example of the finished composition (fig. 24) survives.[107] It has the same characteristics of originality as Windsor 12771r does with the *Tityos* (fig. 19), and the still intact stroke-system areas of the Courtauld example of the *Dream* and the Cambridge example of the *Ganymede* (fig. 17). Its primary contours (relics of the sketch located under the finished drawing—clouds, fluttering reins, tufts of grass, stream) consist of relatively long elastic strokes of highly differentiated form and volume. They are interspersed with numerous small gaps, axial shifts, and stroke crossings. The definitive contours, with their rhythmically imposed, bold reinforcing strokes, appear to be just as much factors of elastic mobility as adequate correspondents to the overall even and finely modulated shading. Indicative is how the raised arms, which are part of the lightly sketched first version of the right heliad, were esthetically neutralized. Apparently these arms could not be totally eradicated when the final version of the figure was drawn. The artist therefore had them disappear under a dusky veil of chalk, which the addition of shading and a couple of jagged contours transformed into something like a mist-enshrouded shrub. The drawing appears to have been created in Florence between early September and late October 1533. The claim that Cavalieri "thanked" Michelangelo for it in a letter dated 6 September is based on an arbitrary reading of the text (cf. note 17).

CHILDREN'S BACCHANAL

What is presumably the last finished drawing created by Michelangelo for Cavalieri depicted a *Children's Bacchanal*. Probably made in Florence in October 1533,[108] it seems—like the *Ganymede* (fig. 17), the *Risen Christ* (fig. 16), the *Fall of Phaeton* (fig. 24), and the lost portrait of Cavalieri—to represent the crowning conclusion to the two friends' mutual endeavors in drawing the subject.[109] It was one of the most complete—and surely the richest in action and figures—of all compositions drawn by the artist up to that time, and was consequently accorded considerable fame. Engraved in copper three times while the artist was still alive,[110] and frequently used as a mine for figural motifs,[111] it appears to have been reproduced several times—by Clovio, among others.[112]

Until recently only the Windsor version (fig. 25) was known to scholars. It was accordingly celebrated. "There has never been the slightest reason to doubt the authenticity of this work," Hartt[113] informed the two erstwhile doubters (Panofsky and Tolnay).[114] Certainly, the unfinished facsimile copy in Berlin (fig. 26) published by Tolnay in 1976 could not compete with the quality of the Windsor drawing even if it had been completely finished in all parts. But the question is not how the two examples compare with each other "qualitatively," but how their genesis is related. The answer is clear: neither the Berlin copy nor the three full-size engravings are reproductions of the Windsor sheet (see p. 34). The Windsor sheet is—like Clovio's copy of the *Ar-*

chers (fig. 21)—in a suspiciously good state of preservation, although, like the *Archers*, it does seem to have been ruthlessly cut. The Windsor *Children's Bacchanal* owes its high quality to the same procedure that was used for making the Windsor copy of the *Flagellation of Christ* signed by Clovio and the unsigned Oxford copy of the *Brazen Serpent* (fig. 29).[115]

The pattern of red-chalk strokes itself is—as is evident in the seemingly swiftly sketched still life of fur, sheep's head, and vessel in the foreground)[116]—created by a massing of short strokes typical of all facsimile copies. The consequences of this massing include the characteristic flattening of the pictorial space. This is evident in comparison with the Berlin copy. In spite of its unfinished state, the Berlin copy does a better job of suggesting spatial depth. This is because from the beginning the Berlin copyist tried to contrast the dark tones between the fore- and background by beginning with the fine hatching at two opposite ends of the composition and concentrating the maximum compression mainly on the foreground. In the process he of course made the unfortunate discovery that deepening the dark tones beyond the degree achieved in the background group was possible only at the cost of the light color of the sheet. The final result would have led either to a total "blackening" of the foreground or to a similar flattening of space as in the Windsor drawing. No wonder that the copyist broke off his laborious work even before he had completely shaded the satyr woman—the object of his experiment in shading.

RESURRECTION

Thanks to the fact that Clovio seems to have copied almost every drawing by Michelangelo that came before his eyes,[117] two drawings can be labeled autograph that otherwise would be included in the authentic corpus only on the basis of stylistic analysis. According to the inventory of the miniaturist, one sketch depicted "una resurecione con otto figure imperfette" ("a Resurrection with eight incomplete figures").[118] This subject must be identical with the drawing that survives on the British Museum sheet 1860-6-16-133 (fig. 27) and sheet 3975 of the Städelsches Kunstinstitut (fig. 28).[119] For Clovio cited this composition twice (figs. 84–85).[120] Actually the London example exhibits specific characteristics of his facsimile style. Mutatis mutandis, it relates to the Frankfurt example in much the same way as Clovio's copy of the *Archers* (fig. 21) relates to Cesari's (fig. 22). Its shading is drier and more patched and shows within the bounds of the lower burial shroud changes in direction whose inappropriateness becomes even more conspicuous the more the various areas of shading strive to match as exactly as possible Michelangelo's characteristic slanting strokes. The contours tend to disfigure the subject by flourishing the strokes wherever the Frankfurt copy tends to simplification (for example, in the right arm of the fleeing figure who looks back and of the figure bending forward behind the sarcophagus; in the lightly sketched figure toward the far right; in the right hand of the guard who sits on the side of the sarcophagus; or in the left foot of the figure crawling toward the left). The stroke system is—just like Clovio's own Resurrection sketch (fig. 81)—characterized by innumerable alternations between hard and scratchy thin strokes and flat, granulated broad strokes, by barky reinforcements of the contours (Christ) and small hatching assemblages whose joinings are marked by hooks or solderings (standing shieldbearer; Christ's left thigh; outer walls of the sarcophagus).[121]

As was discussed elsewhere,[122] Michelangelo's original sketch probably referred to the project for repainting the entry wall of the Sistine Chapel, discussion of which took place at the end of 1533. Its unorthodox iconography appears to be a deliberate concession to the heavily damaged Ghirlandaio fresco painted there, in which the Resurrection of Christ is coupled with the background scene of an Ascension.

PLAGUE OF SNAKES AND BRAZEN SERPENT

The subject of the second sketch copied by Clovio is described in his inventory as "Due gruppi di figurine piccole" ("two groups of small figures").[123] It is probably identical with the two scenes from the story of Moses (plague of snakes and worship of the brazen serpent), which, sketched in red chalk, appear on one sheet in the Ashmolean Museum (fig. 29). This sheet, which is listed in the literature as Michelangelo's original,[124] nevertheless also arouses the suspicion of coming from Clovio's workshop. First, the contours of the drawing on the recto were—like Clovio's signed red-chalk copy after a sketch of the *Flagellation of Christ* (Windsor 0418)—first sketched with black chalk. Second, as is characteristic of many copies, the drawing exhibits a contradiction between the spatial structure implied by the arrangement of the figures and their actions on the one hand and the actual spatial structure on the other. The space appears preposterously flattened as a result of undifferentiated treatment of the foreground and background. In addition, the drawing displays an incongruity between the graphical sharpness of the drawing and pictorial clarity (in the crowded areas in particular it is sometimes difficult or even impossible to tell which body parts belong to which figures), which is contrary to the composition sketches done by Michelangelo's own hand (figs. 30–32). Third, although the drawing is more complete, more fully articulated, and has more resemblance to a free sketch than the other three surviving examples (each of which has only one of the two groups), it cannot be considered as their model.[125] Fourth, it is located on a sheet whose present-day verso is occupied by a gigantic study of a thorax obviously of the same origin as the studies in figures 82–83 and 88–90. This thorax study, which is hobbled together with dry-as-brushwood short strokes and confusing small assemblages, betrays, with its crude neck muscle tendons and clavicle excrescences, the naive human anatomy-by-recipe to which the shoulder and clavicle areas of Clovio's drawn and painted figures is so deeply indebted (figs. 83–85, 87).[126]

Since Popp, Michelangelo scholars have insisted that the two scenes were preparatory sketches for two different paintings.[127] But just viewing of the alleged original demonstrates that they are as intimately linked to each other as the individual groups in figure 30. As there, their apparent independence reflects the fact that the overall pictorial concept crystallized around two centers of interest, corresponding to the double-phased nature of the event, resulting in two different compositional groupings. But if the sketch served as a preparation for a single painting, analogous to the *Last Judgment* in its complexity, then it was probably created within the framework of the same gigantic project of painting new frescoes on the entry and altar walls of the Sistine Chapel; the sketches in figures 30–32 and—probably—the lost Resurrection sketch (figs. 27–28) served as preliminary drawings for such a project.[128]

CHRIST ON THE CROSS

The documented production of the 1540s consists of three highly finished drawings created for Vittoria Colonna. One depicted *Christ and the Samaritan Woman at the Well*,[129] the second a *Pietà*.[130] The third, the most famous and the most frequently quoted, was "a drawing of a Christ on the cross, depicted not, as is usual, dead, but as a living figure, with his face raised to the Father, as if speaking 'Eli, Eli'" (Condivi).[131] Today the drawing in the British Museum (fig. 33) is generally equated with the sheet described by Condivi and given to Vittoria Colonna.[132] It is one of a total of seven surviving examples of the same composition (Budapest, Fine Arts Museum, no. 67.35; formerly London, Collection Sir Robert Mond; Norfolk, Collection Mrs. Brakley; Oxford, Ashmolean Museum, Parker no. 352; Paris, Louvre, no. 732; St. Bees, Cumberland, Collection G. McKay).[133] Its identification had, before 1950, already been rejected by most Michelangelo scholars.[134] The following reasons speak against it: First, there is an absence of scratch marks in the contours—alarming because the high degree of congruence between the contours and proportions of the represented figures on this sheet and in the other examples presupposes extensive tracings.[135] Second, there is a lack of kinetic spontaneity symptoms in the stroke system. The contours are composed of short, cut-off, in some places slightly wobbly hair strokes, which over wide stretches appear bundled as thick strands. Where the contours of these strands are reinforced they have the appearance of compact cordlike strokes. In contrast to the shading of the figures in the *Tityos* and *Fall of Phaeton* originals (figs. 19, 24), the shading is rubbed into a dusky continuum with no visible underlying linear structures. Thin-stroked as the shading is, like the examples in Budapest, Oxford, and Paris, it must have appeared as an impenetrable web even before it was rubbed. Third, there is an absence of any indication that the sheet served as a model. The London example cannot have been the model for the other examples. It has no unclear areas at any of the places at which the latter deviate from it or from each other.[136]

In the correspondence between Michelangelo and Vittoria Colonna the "crocifisso" or "Christo" is discussed several times. Unfortunately, the four relevant letters are not dated.[137] Their sequence seems problematic, and their contents are full of riddles. Previous hypotheses concerning the sequence of letters are contradictory and are only partially compatible with the written evidence.[138] Common to all of them is the assumption that all the letters discuss one and the same object (according to some scholars a finished drawing, according to others a painting), and that Vittoria played the role of passive recipient in the whole affair. Apparently neither assumption is correct. The initiative came from Vittoria, who had commissioned Michelangelo to design a crucifix for her (probably to be painted by Venusti) and desired a sketch from the artist. Michelangelo sent her one, but also secretly prepared a highly finished drawing. He intended to surprise Vittoria with it as soon as she returned the sketch for execution. But things turned out differently than he imagined. Vittoria thought Michelangelo's sketch should include two lamenting angels. She told this to Tommaso de' Cavalieri and asked him to arrange things with Michelangelo. But Michelangelo had meanwhile completed his highly finished drawing and saw his plan foiled by his friend's request. Without enthusiasm he sketched the requested angels to either side of the cross in the already fully shaded background. Without enthusiasm he shipped off his present, together with a letter full of irritation in which he told the countess that, because he was in Rome, it had been unnecessary to make Tommaso a go-between concerning the crucifix

drawing;[139] that a major project had prevented him from communicating his sentiments adequately;[140] and that he had planned a surprise for her. But in the meantime his plan (or the drawing) had been destroyed.[141]

Vittoria reacted to this missive with her inborn cleverness. She ignored the content of the letter and Michelangelo's disappointment and used all her diplomatic gifts to restore her friend's feeling of having successfully carried out his intention. She acted as if she could not believe that it was actually Michelangelo himself who had taken such trouble on her account. In her return letter, Vittoria wrote of her great admiration for the crucifixion drawing and of her wish that it be rendered as a painting by the draftsman himself. She assured Michelangelo that if the drawing was by him she had no intention of returning it, but that if it was by another they should discuss who should execute the painting.

The kindness of these lines does not seem to have been sufficient to dissolve completely the artist's distrust. Vittoria therefore afterward felt required to justify her behavior. She wrote further that she trusted in God to grant Michelangelo supernatural grace in drawing this Christ, and that the Crucifixion *sketch* had exceeded her every expectation. Encouraged by the miracle already wrought, she had sought to improve upon the already perfect, and indeed the finished drawing had accomplished that. For having drawn such a beautiful angel on the right, the Archangel Michael would direct Michelangelo to the Lord's right on Judgment Day.

It is doubtful that Michelangelo was happier about the two angels because he would receive a heavenly reward for inserting them after the fact. The documents speak against such a conclusion. Neither Vasari nor Condivi, in their exhaustive descriptions of the drawing, mention these angels. And although they were faithfully reproduced by most copyists (including all engravers), their presence was dispensable to the authors of seven painted copies and one drawn copy.[142]

Moreover, Vittoria's doubts concerning the possibility of executing the painting appear to have become subsequently dissipated. For in her third letter she asked the artist: "Send me the crucifix for a while, even if it is not complete, for I would like to show it to the courtiers of the most worthy Cardinal of Mantua."[143]

The earliest engraving, published in Rome in 1546, provides a reliable *terminus ante quem* for the dating of both the drawing and painting.[144] The fact that today not a single copy of it can be found indicates that it must have been intended for a small circle of the "initiated"—presumably the pious friends of the countess. Such a purpose, of course, forbids chronologically separating the drawing, painting, and related correspondence from the engraving. These documents should therefore be dated around 1545 and not between 1538 and 1542.

APOSTLES FOR A GETHSEMANE SCENE

A sheet in Oxford with small black-chalk sketches of apostles for a Gethsemane scene (fig. 36) form the last member of this group of authenticated drawings. Closely related to the Oxford sketches for the Rondanini Pietà (fig. 35) in style, execution, and manner of placement, they were also externally tied to the latter from the beginning. The identical quality of paper and vertical crease indicate that both sheets originally formed a single sheet.[145] The authentication of the Pietà sketches thereby guarantees the authenticity of the apostle sketches. But they can also be authenticated independently of the Pietà sketches, namely on the basis of a note in a letter by Daniele da Volterra of 17 March 1564, according to which Michelangelo presented Jacopo del Duca with ''certain small drawings of the Annunciation and of Christ praying at the Mount of Olives.''[146] That this refers to the Oxford sketches[147] is based first on the context of the letter and its implications and second on the association of its original partners. The Pietà sketches (fig. 35) were demonstrably used by Jacopo and inspired the burial relief on his bronze ciborium in Naples (Museo Nazionale).[148]

In contrast to the Pietà sketches, the apostle sketches do not refer to any of Michelangelo's own works. They were made for the benefit of Venusti and served to prepare a small painting that was made for the widow of Michelangelo's servant Urbino, probably in 1558.[149] But their connection to this painting is so loose that one is tempted to assign the sketches the status of accidentally preserved relics from the early stages of a rather long sketching process. But two important facts speak against such an interpretation. One is Venusti's cartonetto (fig. 103).[150] Its existence would be superfluous, its lack of squaring inexplicable, if Michelangelo had already fixed the composition himself in a detailed sketch. The second fact is the paradoxical quantitative and topographical relationship between the sketches of single figures and the overall compositional sketch of the Oxford sheet (fig. 36). Of the ten still recognizable sketches only the one on the far right refers to a *group* of figures. Its peripheral position indicates that it was the last one to be created. Nevertheless, it does not have the character of a ''compilation'' developed from the single-figure sketches but of an autonomous attempt to coordinate several possible positions that ran parallel to the exploration of the postures of the individual figures. All this indicates that the sketches served a didactic purpose. With them Michelan-

gelo attempted to demonstrate to Venusti what postures the apostles would have to adopt in order to express the total isolation of Christ. Venusti caught on. Without clutching to the details of what he had been shown he developed his own design for the group from the various sketches (fig. 103). As a starting point for shaping the figure of his left apostle he used Michelangelo's sketch at the upper left edge,[151] as well as that in the middle of the sheet (fig. 36). From the first he borrowed the position of the upper body, from the latter the position of the legs—in each case reversing them, so that the result of his compilation appeared in the same position (facing left) as the left apostle in Michelangelo's group of three. In drawing his right apostle Venusti referred to the sketch at the lower left edge of the Oxford sheet. The only figures he seems to have invented on his own were the middle apostle (Peter) and the two Christ figures (whose hands are quoted from figures in the Pauline frescoes). In his contorted position, this apostle is the echo of the Christ who stands before him and bends forward. Nevertheless, his legs are conceivable only in a bent position, analogous to the leg position of Michelangelo's two sketches for Peter[152]—representing the difficult act of rising from a squatting position.

The Evidence of a Drawing's Function as a Preparatory Sketch or Study for a Certain Michelangelo Work (Sculpture or Painting)

This type of evidence is produced not simply by the fact that drawing *A* exhibits iconographic and formal relationships to painting or sculpture *B*. For such relationships are also exhibited by every copy or forgery made from an already existing sketch or study. What is truly decisive is what drawing *A* says about the creative processes from which *B* emerged. Only where the relationship between *A* and *B* is consistent with the verified work procedures of the artist in question can we consider *A* to be a preparatory sketch or study for *B*, and, consequently, an authenticated drawing.

Michelangelo's working procedures are not only well known, they were also unorthodox for their time. To the amazement of many of his colleagues, the artist cherished an almost manic aversion to the delegation of work to others.[153] Possessed by the desire to permit his ideas to mature and change in each phase of realizing a project, he saw delegation of work as a threat to his creative freedom. What bottega heads like Raphael (1483–1520) or Andrea Sansovino (1467–1529), Rosso Fiorentino (1495–1540), or Baccio Bandinelli (1493–1560) largely had done by their assistants, Michelangelo did himself. With his own hand (and apparently by eye) he transferred his sketches for a fresco to the cartoons. With his own hand he executed the frescoes.[154] By himself (and usually employing only small bozzetti) he chiseled almost all his sculptures. The results of this stubbornness can be seen in the extent of what he left incomplete.[155] They are present almost everywhere—in the ghostlike, limb-doubling of the Rondanini Pietà as well as in the fact that the Sistine Chapel ceiling and the Medici tombs finally became asymmetric, or that the Louvre slaves for the Julius tomb were displaced by the Boboli slaves—each time owing to an evolving of Michelangelo's idea during the execution processes. His method is characterized by constant change, interruption, beginning anew, enlargement of the figure sizes, and an increase in the dynamism of the figures.[156] Even if none of his preliminary drawings survived, this fact would point to a unique gap between the seed of an idea and the completed work and to a development that resembled, instead of a traditional artist's work procedure, a process of successive accumulation of energy.

The drawings that appear to be stages of such a development are not many. Apart from the few already authenticated on the basis of other factors (figs. 5, 12, 23, 35–36), they include seven series of sketches (including fig. 6, 30–32, 35), three sets of studies (including figs. 6–11), three "modelli," and the fragment of a cartoon (fig. 34).[157] Nearly everything else that is discussed in the literature as "undoubtedly" genuine "preliminary drawings" is of a derivational character.[158] One of many examples is the red-chalk drawing on the recto of the Albertina sheet Sc.R.155 (fig. 132). It is considered today to be a preliminary study for the left ignudo above the Persian sibyl and is, according to Hartt, "one of the most perfect and carefully finished of all Michelangelo's nude drawings."[159] In reality it has the characteristics typical of a forgery. First of all, the drawing's relationship to the figure in the fresco is perverse. It exceeds the fresco in volume and dynamism, instead of vice versa. Second, it reflects the plastic structure not of a live model, but of the painted figure. In those parts that correspond in the fresco to the shaded and only roughly structured parts it exhibits especially summary forms—in contrast to the studies in figures 6–11, whose individual body parts appear to be uniformly well modeled, regardless of whether they are shaded areas in the fresco or covered by pieces of drapery. Third, the two subsidiary studies show no evidence of being preparatory sketches. The hands, for example, the main object of the studies (the left hand is especially hard to see in the fresco) are anatomically miscarried, while the inner contour of the lower right arm (largely obscured in the fresco) shows it to be an imaginary,

arbitrary creation. Fourth, the execution in red chalk is based on a basic sketch drawn with a stylus—which points to a contrived working procedure alien to Michelangelo. Fifth, the plastic effect of the red-chalk hatching was heightened by using white highlights—a technique whose use cannot be documented even in the corpus of Michelangelo's highly finished drawings, let alone in his authenticated studies (including figs. 5–11). In view of the relatively long and resolutely drawn single strokes, the enormous number of pentimenti, and the considerable divergence between the stylus and red-chalk contours at some places, it is highly unlikely that these drawings are either facsimile copies or preparatory studies.[160] They should be classified among those drawings after fresco figures that aim at achieving the effect of preliminary studies, a genre with whose fabrication artists like Denis Calvaert (1540–1619) earned an occasional sum during their youths.[161] As Wickhoff already noticed,[162] they clearly betray their "baroque" character in the play of light and shade that contradicts the rigorous plasticity of Michelangelo's forms.[163]

Such forgeries almost always occur as unique items,[164] whereas the authentic preliminary studies were as a rule copied and therefore usually survive in several examples.[165] However little the existence of facsimile copies as such guarantees Michelangelo's authorship of what is copied, it does bear witness to the fame and rarity of what is copied. Copyists and their Michelangelo-obsessed clientele would hardly have had any reason to use the same few sheets over and over again if the large body of authentic sheets so dearly believed today to exist had indeed existed all along.

STUDIES FOR THE LIBYAN SIBYL

The earliest Michelangelo drawings authenticated by evidence of a drawing's function are three sets of studies used for preparation of the Sistine Chapel ceiling. The first set, not discussed here, refers to the figure of Adam in the Creation fresco,[166] the second (figs. 6–8) to the Libyan sibyl and her companion, the third (figs. 9–11) to the crucified Haman. Each consists of a main study and several subsidiary studies distributed partly on additional sheets. Each was, at least partially, already copied in the sixteenth century. The largest and most problematic is a group of ten studies related to the Libyan sibyl. Today these studies are distributed on three approximately equal-sized sheets, of which, however, only the third (fig. 6), containing the studies for the sibyl's companion and for her right hand, can claim to be an original drawing by Michelangelo. The two other sheets (figs. 7, 8) are partially reflecting what formerly constituted the main sheet. That their inventories represent facsimile copies created independently of one another is obvious from the partial discrepancies and the disparate ways in which they are arranged. In the case of the sheet in New York (fig. 8)—which is considered to be Michelangelo's original—the arrangement is especially absurd. One part of this sheet's inventory, consisting of one study for the legs and one for the right knee of the sibyl (missing from the Uffizi copy), appear on the verso—a circumstance that makes a synopsis of the parts belonging together impossible and contradicts any logical working method.[167]

The Uffizi and New York sheets belong to the category of "anthology sheets." They unite copies whose models were distributed on at least *two* original sheets.[168] The main sheet presumably included only the trio of studies of torso, thorax, and hand reproduced by both copyists, whereas the head, legs, knee, foot, and toe studies occupied the recto of at least one additional sheet.

Together with the two original studies of the Oxford sheet (fig. 6) those of the Uffizi and New York sheets offer important clues about the intermediate stage between the preliminary sketches and the preparation of a cartoon. They presuppose a design of the Libyan sibyl spandrel which already included the idea of clothed figures. For their subjects are almost exclusively those members or joints that in the fresco appear either naked or exhibit their organic shape by closely fitting garment pieces. Apparently the work was begun with a provisional outlining of the sibyl's torso (main study).[169] This made the still weak points of the idea conscious and provoked a corresponding series of detailed studies. The first point concerned the functional connection of the left shoulder and the trunk. Even before the definitive outlining and the addition of shading the connection was clarified in a subsidiary sketch surveyed from a slightly changed perspective. On the other hand the special study of the left and right hands seems to have been done only *after* the main study was hatched—to conclude from the fact that its products are closer to the hands of the fresco figure than to those of the main study, and that they were not worked up in the main study. Yet, the right hand located on the Oxford sheet (fig. 6) also presupposes the companion study. The latter might therefore represent a temporally intermediate stage and might have been created following the leg study (which can be considered a continuation of the main study). The cursory hatching of the leg study possibly played the role of a catalyst for the whole shading process. It might have caused that heightening of the concentration that made possible an immediate modeling of the details of the companion study (fig. 6) and its maximum differentiation in the main study.[170]

The design at the base of this group of studies differs from its final painted form in many ways. The torso of the sibyl and the head of its companion appear more stiffly erect in the drawing than in the fresco. The lower arms are less shortened, calves and hands are bent in a more oblique angle from the thighs and lower arms. The arm position of the main study presupposes a horizontally rather than obliquely held book. That means that the synthetic process that followed the analytic study process and was probably completed directly on the cartoon was accomplished hand in hand with a considerable animating of the previous design.

STUDIES FOR THE CRUCIFIED HAMAN

The nine-part set of red-chalk studies related to the crucified Haman was distributed on two sheets. Neither of the originals survives. The primary sheet with the large main study and the subsidiary studies for the lower extremities are recalled in three copies in Boston, London, and Windsor (figs. 9–11),[171] the secondary sheet with the subsidiary studies for the upper parts of the body in one copy in Haarlem (Teylers Museum A16r).[172] These four copies differ from the Oxford studies of the Libyan sibyl (fig. 6) just as fundamentally as the two representatives of the main sheet of the same figure (figs. 7, 8). Their stroke systems exclusively exhibit symptoms of kinetic inhibition. Both the most important areas left free from hatching and the "pentimenti" and "incomplete" contour areas (which must have been copied by eye) are premarked with preliminary contours. The supposition that the Boston copy is derived from the London example (the alleged original) contradicts the fact that the former is elaborately modeled even at those places where the hatching of the latter produced mere planes (for example, at the beginning of the left thigh of the main study), and, vice versa, is missing precisely those pentimenti that are especially obvious in the London example (for example, below the left hip).[173]

As in the case of the Libyan sibyl Michelangelo began with a detailed outlining of the large "main subject" after the composition of the whole spandrel had been conceived. This outline drawing concerned primarily only the trunk and legs of the Haman. Arms and head were fixed only insofar as appeared necessary for presenting the dynamism of the torso. They appeared in detail only in the large subsidiary study of the secondary sheet. Significantly, this study was placed in the *lower* left quarter of the sheet. As a result an optimum synopsis was produced when the secondary study sheet was placed at the head end of the main sheet. The outlining of the main study and large subsidiary study was followed by a provisional rough hatching of a type similar to that of the leg study on the verso of the Libyan sibyl sheet in New York. Traces of it are the simple parallel hatching marks (probably exaggeratedly condensed by the copyist) on the left arm and right calf of the main study. The subsequent fine-meshed shading proceeded from top to bottom and apparently in one motion up to the right calf and the beginning of the left thigh. When it reached the left thigh there apparently was a need to verify the appropriate musculature. This led to a rapidly sketched subsidiary study, which served as a basis for the further fine hatching of the main study. To judge from the three copies, this fine hatching was abruptly interrupted at the two lower legs, probably because the preconditions required for its deployment, namely a final clarification of the shape of the feet and of the lower left leg, first had to be created. The clarification was accomplished in the lower two related studies. Their careful execution rendered further hatching of the main study superfluous.

The same applies to the related studies for the right ear, left hand, and right arm, which were situated on the secondary sheet. These too depicted final solutions to problems of detail that had occurred in the fine hatching of the upper body. Their placement was determined by the same consideration for the future synthesis as that of the upper body study itself and of the related studies of the main sheet (the present position of the study for the right arm, which does not correspond to the synoptic system, is due to incorrect mounting).[174]

The concept on which the Haman studies were based was heightened during the synthesis—as also happened in the case of the set of Libyan sibyl drawings (figs. 6–8). This can be seen most clearly in the altered axial directions and degrees of foreshortening. For example, in the fresco figure, in contrast to the studies, the right leg has a decidedly sharper angle of bending away from the torso, the head is turned by some degrees more to the right and sunk more deeply on the neck, and the left arm and lower leg are even more strongly foreshortened. The figure accordingly makes a tauter, more active, more spatially imposing impression.

The Haman spandrel, along with the Libyan sibyl spandrel and the picture of Adam's creation, are among the latest parts of the ceiling, executed between the spring and August of 1510. The corresponding studies must accordingly have been drawn during the winter months of 1509–10 when conditions were unsuitable for painting.[175] If their preparation was oriented to the future sequence of the fresco segments, they can be dated at the end of this period, that is, in the spring of 1510.

SKETCHES FOR SLAVES OF THE JULIUS TOMB

While Michelangelo was busy with the gigantic fresco that at first gave him so little pleasure, his thoughts must occasionally have drifted to the sculptural ensemble that later became a nightmare: the tomb of Julius II. The visible evidence can be found in the six pen-and-ink sketches located on the same sheet with studies for the Libyan sibyl (fig. 6). As variations on the bound captive theme they can refer only to the Julius tomb project, work on which had been suspended since 1506. The design called for a slave to stand in front of each of the tomb's lower-story pilasters. The "captive" theme seems to have exerted a special fascination for Michelangelo, as the number and the development of the statues executed from 1513 on prove. Perhaps it was this fascination that kept the dream of the sculptural object alive and allowed it to mature secretly into the new, more compact form of the project that was present when the contract was signed on 6 May 1513.[176]

The sketches for the Julius tomb are originals. Their loose, highly articulated stroke combinations, which vary in pressure and are permeated with innumerable traces of spontaneity, point to an uninhibited movement whose rhythm was marked by clear acceleration and deceleration phases. Mutatis mutandis, they resemble the red-chalk stroke systems of the two studies for the Libyan sibyl, which differ from the other parts of the sibyl group (figs. 7, 8) in their high level of defined form, the length and substantial "heaviness" of their strokes, the rhythmic balance of strengthened and unstrengthened contours and hatched and unhatched areas. In addition the hatching is enormously effective in its suggestion of sculptural volume—even though it consists mainly of a few long-stroke assemblages with equal directional orientations and only sporadic strengthenings. It is therefore all the more astonishing that the hatching process must have been accomplished at a very rapid tempo, because most of the shaded areas show clearly discernible spiral or zigzag hatchings.[177]

COMPOSITIONAL SKETCHES FOR THE LAST JUDGMENT

The drawings of the 1520s authenticated by evidence of their function, which include the sketch in figure 12, are related without exception to the project for the Medici tombs.[178] They comprise the most comprehensive extant group of sketches of the Michelangelo corpus and allow us to reconstruct, almost without a gap, the design history of the chapel's architectural and sculptural decoration. Nevertheless, the figures play a relatively subordinate role in these sketches. For our purposes the representatives of the 1530s are therefore more important: the three compositional sketches for the *Last Judgment* (figs. 30–32). They allow a unique view not only into the genesis of this gigantic fresco, but also into Michelangelo's way of conceiving scenes with masses of figures. Their heuristic value is even greater because all three sketches bear the characteristics of having been executed by Michelangelo's own hand: elasticity of the contour components; large number of gaps, crossings, and shifts in axes in the sequences of contour strokes; marked increase in formal and tonal differentiation in the transition from the first to the corresponding subsequent contour strata; and large, loose hatching assemblages with complete or fragmentary spiral or zigzag forms, and soft, spatially structuring directional contrasts and differences in pressure—all signs of that rapid and economical manner of movement typical of someone who is attempting to formulate a still largely unstable, expandable, and changeable pictorial idea.

The first sketch (fig. 30) represents a stage of conceptual fermentation. It breaks down into three figure complexes that are only loosely linked with each other; each one corresponds to a certain part of the Last Judgment drama. The first complex in terms of the subject, located in the lower left corner of the sheet, illustrates the dead awakening and emerging from their graves. Above it, separated by an empty area, the wide-ranging second complex unfolds in a half-moon shape with the ascension of the blessed, the damning action of a thundering Christ next to a beseeching Mary, and the nervous clutch of apostles in attendance at the judgment. The third complex, which is separated from the first and second by a large empty area partially populated with trumpeting angels, shows the onrush of the damned, who are hindered by devils and thrown back by angels.

The asymmetry and inner discontinuity of the composition expresses the vagueness of a still new idea.[179] But at the same time they seem to reflect a degree of artistic uncertainty. This resulted from an external circumstance. As is demonstrated elsewhere,[180] the Casa Buonarroti sketch refers to the *entrance* wall of the Sistine Chapel, that is, opposite the present location of the *Last Judgment* on the altar wall. It is directly connected with the original project, which was meant to fit into the narrative sequence of the frescoes of the long wall and the ceiling, and according to which the *Last Judgment* should have formed the formal and iconographic pendant to a *Fall of the Rebel Angels* fresco intended for the altar wall. The lower third of his composition was accordingly prejudiced by the existence of the main portal of the Sistine Chapel. This had to be accounted for in the painting—as had already been the case with the *Last Judgment* frescoes in

S. Angelo in Formis, Torcello, and Pomposa. Its inclusion, however, proved to be incompatible with an idea intended to achieve the dynamic unity of the resurrection of the dead, judgment of the resurrected, and ascension to heaven or descent to hell of the judged. The door made it impossible to link the three events causally. In the Casa Buonarroti sketch the selection of the saved is an automatic continuation of resurrection from the grave: the damned have no part in the resurrection of the flesh. Their damnation seems assured independent of Christ's action.[181]

The decision to transfer the *Last Judgment* to the altar wall and to abandon the *Fall of the Rebel Angels* was apparently made around the turn of the year 1533–34. In any case, in February 1534 there was already talk of using this wall for a fresco of a "resurrection" (resurrection of the dead equals the Last Judgment).[182] There is no basis for assuming that the fall of the angels–Last Judgment project was already under discussion on 22 September 1533, when Clement VII (1478–1534) and Michelangelo met in San Miniato al Tedesco.[183] For according to Condivi,[184] the pope had first raised a series of other subjects (probably more appropriate to the iconographic status quo of the Sistine Chapel) before he settled on the Last Judgment theme.[185] Actually the Casa Buonarroti sheet can have been used by the artist only *after* his four-month stay in Florence (early July to late October 1533). For to judge from the drawing on its verso (fig. 59), which is by Cavalieri and was created in the first half of that year (cf. chapter 5), it was among the sheets kept in his *Roman* workshop. Michelangelo's sketch must accordingly be dated between November 1533 and February 1534.[186]

The second compositional sketch (fig. 31), located in Windsor, necessarily came after the decision to paint the *Last Judgment* on the altar wall.[187] It shows the solution of the very problem that previously seemed beyond solution: to make the resurrection region the starting point of the ascent into heaven *and* the descent into hell. The decisive insight was apparently the result of an association of ideas. At the place where the artificial obstacle of the Sistine portal appears in the Casa Buonarroti sketch (fig. 30) the artist sketched a "natural" permeable obstacle: a hill dominated by the prince of hell, Minos. This was characterized as the connecting element between the site of the resurrection and the underworld by means of a cavelike entrance guarded by a lurking demon (in the fresco the hill appears to be broken through by a dark tunnel leading down to the hidden embarkation pier of Charon's ferry).[188]

In the same sketch Michelangelo also solved the problem of the transition from resurrection to ascension into heaven that had been left unresolved in figure 30. He gave the site for the resurrection of the flesh the appearance of an immeasurable plain full of animated life with isolated small figures within it getting ready to rise. They are, so to speak, the small drops from whose joining the ascending cloud of saints is ultimately formed: on the one hand the three small figures hurrying in the background at the left side of the plain of resurrection, on the other hand the couple of figures at the right side of the resurrection plain that were separately attempted or further developed in six subsidiary sketches. In the fresco, whose lower left section relates to the Windsor sketch like a monumentalized condensation, this transition was made clear at the same peripheral places and in principle with the same means. In the fresco the small, already ascending pair of figures in the left background correspond to the three small figures gesticulating upward in the sketch's background. The two forceful couples in the right middle ground, one of which already appears to be in the state of ascending, correspond to the figure couple in the sketch's middle ground. They were directly developed from the compositional sketch or its subsidiary sketches.[189]

Of the subsidiary sketches two deserve special attention: the one located above the head of Minos and its similarly formed neighbor. They exemplify the process of conceptual compression that characterizes Michelangelo's working process from sketch to final composition. Both sketches to a certain extent represent distillations of what in the compositional sketch is distributed over *two* groups of figures—the couple of figures already mentioned, and, to the left of it, the combination of two helpers who are trying to get a recumbent third figure to his feet. At the same time this subject was shaped as a paradigm of the struggle between the powers of heaven and hell for the possession of the resurrected. Each couple is assigned a demon who, functioning as adversary of the helper acting from above, attempts to seize the booty by pulling from below.

Like the second, the third compositional sketch (fig. 32) also relates to a "problem region" whose difficulties result from the initial idea (fig. 30). There the damned were assigned the role of rebel angels who break out of their vaguely defined "underworld," storm the boundary wall defined by the Sistine portal toward the side of the saints, and are hindered in their attack by demons and thrown back by the powers of heaven. This idea excluded the notion of a group of escapees hovering freely between the main mass of the damned and the inhabitants of heaven. As a result the left and right halves of the composition became unbalanced. They became all the more so when the locations of the resurrected and the damned had to be leveled when the resurrection and hell area were reconceived (fig. 31). The empty zone between heaven and hell, which became correspondingly larger, could ultimately be neutralized only by means of a compromise. For there was no iconographic desideratum that corresponded to the formal necessity of filling the zone with figures. The compromise finally consisted of (1) placing the heavenly realm of the right half of the fresco deeper than that of the left and expanding it below by a line of martyr saints, and (2) providing a formal equivalent in the ascending group of saints in the form of a freely hovering cohort of storming and repulsed escapees. The expansion of the heavenly realm by a line of martyrs was unavoidable. Without them the motif of the fall of the damned would have created a compositional predominance over both the mass of the blessed and the main mass of the damned. Their presence—which in any case is iconographically difficult to legitimate—would have come into complete conflict with the Dantesque motif of Charon's ferry.

With the above in mind it is obvious that the subject of the London sketch (fig. 32) is, in addition to the group of the fallen damned, the line of martyrs located above them. In Michelangelo's design the one group was coupled inseparably with the other, since only the two together produced the desired compositional balance with the group of the blessed. But it was just this inner cohesion that made the incorporation of the martyr-damned combination in the upper parts of the overall composition such a special artistic problem. Michelangelo attacked this problem ad hoc, and with his typical economy. Of the heavenly main community he sketched only those figures next to Christ—those which could best be used to articulate the spatial relationship between what had already been designed and what had to be designed now. In a simultaneously simple and precise way he thus determined the position that the partial idea assumed in the overall conception.[190]

Of the figures of the heavenly main community none has an approximate correspondence in the fresco; of those of the line of martyrs and of the group of the fallen only a small number do. Even the group formations as such correspond only roughly with their fresco equivalents. Therefore the sketch probably still reflects a relatively early stage in the conceptual process.[191] The differentiation of the anatomical-plastic structure and the spatial construction are thus all the more astonishing; they appear to be the expression of an inner illumination that grew in the course of designing the concept. Although the whole was presumably linked to the lost sketch for the *Fall of the Rebel Angels*, each individual figure proceeded from an embryonic state that was sketched shorthand ad hoc (and is still present in the pentimenti). The sketching of the figural mass was accompanied by a sketching process that investigated the optimal attitudes of certain individual figures separately. The visible products of this additional process are the small sketches scattered over the surface of the sheet. In each case they proceed from a preliminary draft of the main sketch, for whose final version they again form the direct or indirect basis. Together with the main sketch they represent a design process that is coherent in itself, and that as such corresponds to one and the same phase of the preparatory drawing process.[192]

CARTOON FRAGMENT FOR THE CRUCIFIXION OF PETER

Only *one* preparatory drawing for the frescoes of the Pauline Chapel, painted after the *Last Judgment*, has survived—the cartoon fragment in Naples (fig. 34). It is first mentioned in Fulvio Orsini's will of 31 January 1600.[193] The sizes of the figures correspond exactly to those in the fresco of the *Crucifixion of Peter*. Moreover, the perforations following the inner and outer contours attest to the actual use of the cartoon for transferring the design to the wet-plaster fresco or sub-cartoon. Curiously, however, there is no evidence of squaring—an expected component of surviving cinquecento cartoons that were used in the preparation of monumental wall paintings.[194] The preliminary sketches and studies must have been enlarged and transferred by eye, or at most on the basis of a few orientation marks, to fresco size (6.26 × 6.62 meters).[195] Apparently the artist perceived the act of enlargement as an essential component of the designing process. And not without reason. As the great number of contour layers within the cartoon and the relationship of the cartoon to the corresponding fresco attest, his design continued to develop up to the last brushstroke.[196] This development affected just about all aspects of the "disegno," even its pictorial inventory. This was expanded in the fresco ad hoc by two heads (behind the soldier with the helmet). The whole block of figures thereby appears even more compact than in the cartoon, and its movement appears to be even more clearly oriented to the center of the picture.

The attitude of the figures was changed in two important ways even during the process of drawing the cartoon, in addition to some minor modifications (compare the pentimenti at the legs of the lowermost figure and at the right foot of the soldier with the coat of mail).[197] One affected the head of the lowermost figure. This head appeared—to judge from the pentimenti remaining visible in the skullcap—originally in a similar full back view as the head of the soldier with the coat of mail. The second change affected the position of the lance that this soldier grips with his right hand. In the first version

the lance shaft has a pronounced diagonal position, while in the final version it is almost vertical. These were reciprocal changes. In its original diagonal position the lance would have pointed to the head of that elderly chief executioner, who, holding the crossbeam of the cross with his right hand, gives instructions to his subordinates with his left hand. The lance would have functioned as a compositional connector between the marginal group at the lower left edge and the group in the center of the picture. But this function ultimately fell to the lowermost marginal figure after the lance shaft was made vertical. The head of this figure was turned to the right, away from the previous full back view, into lost profile position, its glance directed toward the chief executioner. Apparently the purpose of the two changes was to bind the group more strongly to the periphery of the painting and to intensify the dynamic circular movement implicit in the composition.

After the cartoon was transferred to the plaster the right foot of the soldier wearing the coat of mail, which had already been slightly modified during the drawing of the cartoon, was again changed so that it appears in the fresco almost at a right angle to the axis of the calf and simultaneously turned in profile. This modification was obviously the result of a small error in calculation. During the transfer the artist appears to have set this piece of the cartoon some centimeters too low. Consequently, without the correction the toes of the soldier's right foot would have stood (embarrassingly for the artist!) directly on the lower picture frame.

In contrast to the attitude of the figures, the drapery was hardly modified during the drawing of the cartoon. The deviations between the cartoon and the fresco are all the more numerous. Of course, because the bodies conform to the individual pieces of drapery, these deviations affect only the system of folds, but within that system almost every single fold is modified in some way. Only during the execution of the fresco were the folds employed to articulate the corporeal solidity of figures as well as to bind them together.

If such a small section of the fresco shows so many consequential deviations from the cartoon, then the fresco as a whole may properly be regarded as a new version of the overall design represented by the "disegno."[198] This means that Michelangelo's cartoon had an unorthodox function. Instead of being, as was the usual practice, the enlarged version of a highly polished "modello," the cartoon functioned as a kind of last sketch. Its creation probably did not even presuppose a synthetic elaboration of preparatory sketches and studies, but instead coincided with it. This assumption is especially supported by the fact that the figures—to judge from the transparency of their drapery and the almost complete reformulation of the fold system when the fresco was painted—were first given drapery only in the cartoon itself. To the extent that they were prepared in individual studies at all, the subject of these studies was—as in the case of the authenticated studies of the Sistine Chapel ceiling (figs. 6–11)—exclusively the naked body.

SKETCHES FOR THE PIETA RONDANINI

The series of drawings authenticated by evidence of their function concludes with the five small black-chalk studies on the Ashmolean sheet, Parker 339 (fig. 35). These are identified as sketches for a sculpture by the blocklike solidity of their outlines, and also in part by indications for plinths. The first sketch chronologically is located in the middle of the sheet and depicts two figures carrying a third, viewed frontally. Its hanging middle figure is noticeably larger than the carrying figures on the side. At the same time it rests with both feet on the ground, giving the impression that it is standing under its own power in contradiction to the passivity in the attitude of the torso and arms. This impression is eclipsed in the case of the second, larger sketch (adjacent to the right). The main figure here appears completely passive, carried hanging. Nevertheless, it no longer possesses the enlarged size of its predecessor. It is given equal rank with its bearers and remains the main figure only by virtue of its centrality and the symmetry of the figures placed on either side. This diminishing of the figure's prominence appears to have provided the impetus to the change in idea that is documented in the appearance of the two-figure groups. In them the passive figure again becomes the figure of greatest significance—because it more or less hides the bearing figure, while its complete length hangs visible in the foreground.

The first of the two-figure groups to be drawn was probably that closest to the left edge of the sheet. In the juxtaposition of the two bodies, in the indication of a base, and in the way that the left arm of the carrying figure was originally stretched out, the sketch still bears obvious resonances of the three-figure design, while the multiplicity of pentimenti shows extensive traces of exploratory designing. It is, so to speak, the result of the elimination of the left figure of the three-figure group. The Madonna, now the single carrying figure, assumes a double carrying function while maintaining her position in three-quarter profile. Why this new solution did not suit the draftsman can be deduced from the two final

sketches, in which only a fragment of the total body of the carrier-figure appears. The aesthetic emphasis is placed exclusively on the carried figure, whose corpselike weight becomes visibly more obvious. In what is probably the last sketch to have been drawn, on the right edge of the sheet, the fact that the carrier-figure is almost entirely hidden behind Christ creates a surprising effect: the profane act of lifting a heavy load appears sublimated in an activity of a spiritual kind: the living figure seems to adapt inwardly to the dead one.[199]

The goal of the five-phase exploratory process was accordingly a sculptural two-figure image in which the opposites of life and death were to be pushed to the extremes and which at the same time appear to be transcended in a loving ambivalence of carrying and embracing—an image which almost certainly depicts a Pietà.[200] But as Pietà sketches they can refer only to Michelangelo's last creation, the Rondanini—the only two-figure Pietà of the sixteenth century whose Mary *stands* (erect) and whose Christ *hangs* lengthwise in his mother's arms.[201]

The Rondanini was probably begun between 1552 and the end of 1555.[202] It appears to have emerged directly from the last sketch, but was unable to withstand the self-criticism of the aged master. Once again during the carving the artist went beyond the idea with which he began. Michelangelo, too weak and too certain of his approaching death to begin all over again, attempted to excavate the newly conceived form from the already existing one. He was stopped in this undertaking by his final illness on 15 February 1564. What he was striving to accomplish can only be guessed at: the idea he wished to express was the paradox of God's being dead. It was supposed to become comprehensible by representing the laws of statics and gravity and human behavior themselves paradoxically. Christ, in his final form, appears hanging, without being supported, and standing weightless. His mother appears as the supporter of the dead figure without the exertion of lifting and holding, and as his innerly protective guardian without the outer signs of sorrow and pain. The slim columnlike formation of the group and the erect posture of Mary also make the direction of movement ambivalent. Christ appears to be slipping out of his mother's arms in the direction of the grave and simultaneously to be equipped with a mysterious force of self-resurrection. "Deposition from the cross," "burial," and "resurrection"—all are equally suggested in this singular group.

3

Michelangelo's Way of Drawing

Michelangelo's authenticated drawings are distributed over a period of approximately sixty-five years (ca. 1495–1558), that is, over nearly the entire creative period of the artist's life. They include representatives of all species and functional types of drawings and exemplify the use of pen and ink as well as red and black chalk. They are listed below:

1. five multifigure sketches for fresco paintings (figs. 27–32), of which two (figs. 31–32) are accompanied by subsidiary sketches;
2. one composition sketch and a series of single-figure sketches (figs. 36–37) for two panel paintings;
3. one composition sketch for a highly finished drawing (fig. 23);
4. one presumed sketch for a marble relief (fig. 4: St. Anne with the Virgin and Child);
5. two multipart series of sketches for a freestanding tomb and a wall tomb (including fig. 12);
6. thirteen sketches related to sculptures (fig. 4: Hercules; fig. 5: David; fig. 6: slaves; fig. 35);
7. one set of sketches for determining the dimensions of a figure block (fig. 40);
8. three multipart sets of studies for fresco figures (including figs. 6–11);
9. one detail study for a sculpture (fig. 5: arm);
10. one cartoon fragment (fig. 34);
11. twenty highly finished drawings (including figs. 13–17, 19, 21–22, 24–25, 33), among them three tomb "modelli";
12. seven occasional sketches (including figs. 4: profile head; 39, 41–43).

No one familiar with the criteria for distinguishing a sketch from a study or highly finished drawing would be likely to dispute the representative value of such material. But one could doubt whether it made sense to base stylistic analysis on the *whole* group when large parts of it (two of the five fresco sketches, four-fifths of the highly finished drawings, and more than nine-tenths of all studies) consist only of copies. That these copies can say nothing about Michelangelo's *kinetic* behavior is obvious. But kinetic behavior is only one aspect of a draftsman's activity, even if the central one. Copies are useful with regard to the other aspects—the modes of using and filling a sheet, of setting the dimensions of the drawing, selection of media, and sketching and study processes—provided that they were made to reproduce exactly Michelangelo's original (which generally applies in the cases cited here). To exclude them would mean arbitrarily depriving oneself of a corrective potential that cannot be replaced by any other.

Use of the Sheet

Analysis of the inventories on the recto and verso of the sheets used by Michelangelo between 1500 and 1564 leads to a surprising result. Insofar as these sheets served to accommodate drawings of figures, only one side of the sheet was used. If not used for Michelangelo's writings and architectural or marble-block annotations, the verso remained blank or is occupied by drawings of either dubious or obviously foreign origin (figs. 50, 61, 71). This use of only one side is all the more important because sometimes it seems to suggest a paradox. In the case of the Libyan sibyl sheet in Oxford (fig. 6) the verso would have offered a far better opportunity for deploying the seven sketches of slaves than the recto, which was filled with the red-chalk studies—even if the two pen-and-ink studies there (which are not by Michelangelo) were already present.[1] Obviously the decision not to draw on the verso of a sheet was an efficiency measure. It allowed the artist to find his way more quickly through the heaps of his papers. From 1501 on, when the commissions piled up, became noticeably larger, and demanded correspondingly more extensive sketch and study work, the practice of using only one side of a sheet probably became a habit.[2]

This was only one aspect of Michelangelo's characteristic use of a sheet. The other aspect concerned the objects of depiction. One and the same side of a sheet was always reserved for drawings of the same object typus (figs. 7–11, 29–32, 35–36) and was freed for accommodating other drawings only when the first had done their preparatory service. But in such—rather rare—cases the use of the sheet was usually restricted to a certain length of time—the time during which the sheet was lying on the artist's worktable. The Hercules must have followed soon after the St. Anne group (fig. 4), the David soon after the arm study (fig. 5), the six pen-and-ink sketches of slaves soon after the pair of red-chalk studies (fig. 6). To judge from the authenticated drawings, Michelangelo appears never to have re-used sheets that had been drawn on years before. The only apparent exception confirms the rule. When Michelangelo again saw his originally unhatched contour drawing of St. Anne with the Virgin and Child (fig. 4) hatched in by Antonio Mini, he felt the urge to make a written and visual commentary on his pupil's intervention.

Placement of Drawings on the Surface of a Sheet

The economic and aesthetic logic of this practice for utilizing sheets found its most consistent expression in the way Michelangelo filled a blank sheet. How it operated in individual cases is exemplified by the Oxford sheet with the five Pietà sketches (fig. 35). This sheet has a very unusual, extremely oblong format that appears to be destined for a series of sketches progressing from left to right. In reality it was filled from the middle. Even when he began the sketching process the artist viewed the sheet not as the neutral bearer of a potential series of sketches, but rather as the unlimited existential space for a specific group of three figures to be sketched *here and now*. Within this existential space the middle seemed to be the "most stable" area. The three-figure group itself demanded placement here because of its symmetrical, absolutely centered structure.

What the Oxford sheet demonstrates with special clarity because of its special circumstances is confirmed by all of Michelangelo's sketch and study sheets. The position of the first drawn object is always oriented according to three factors: first according to the axis of the center of the sheet, second according to the orientation of the action to be depicted, and third according to the type or the external perimeter of the depiction. The sketch for the St. Anne group (fig. 4) and the main studies of the Libyan sibyl and the Haman group (figs. 6–10) share the characteristic of being asymmetrical, that is, their figures seem to be oriented to the right or left. Accordingly their main axes deviate noticeably from the center axis of the individual sheets, either to the right (figs. 6–8) or to the left (figs. 4, 9, 10), depending on which side they require more room for action. In contrast to the St. Anne group, however, which had a more central position between the upper and lower edges of the sheet before the sheet was cut than it has today, the two main studies of the Libyan sibyl series (figs. 6–8) always occupied not the center but the upper half of the sheet. Their placement there is nothing more than the expression of their specific extracted character (the leg studies for the Libyan sibyl were therefore—to judge from the verso of the New York sheet—also logically placed in the lower half of the sheet).[3] According to the intensity of his imaginative faculty, the artist instinctively perceived the given sheet surface as a reservation for a thing's totality, and the center of the sheet accordingly was its "navel" area. It was thus inconsequential whether the imaginary totality was a single figure or a composition with many figures. In the latter case it could also determine the placement of a composition sketch, as the example of Windsor sheet no. 12776r (fig. 31) shows. Its recto surface symbolically represents the existential space of the total composition of the *Last Judgment* (more precisely: the lower half of the same). Its lower left quarter thereby automatically appeared as the place appropriate for a sketch of the field for the resurrection of the dead.

On the Oxford sheet (fig. 35), the second sketch chronologically is located to the right next to the first. However obvious this position appears to be in view of the identical themes of the two sketches and the natural inclinations of a righthanded draftsman, the close bond between the two sketches is nonetheless odd. It seems to be the consequence of that elementary sheet-"space"-experience that determined the centrality of the first sketch. The second sketch had to enter into a spatial partnership with the first in one way or another. But it is not a partner of equal standing. As a revision of the first sketch it is more differentiated, more vigorous, and larger. A factual difference in hierarchy contrasts with the spatial partnership. Therefore the close proximity. It results in one sketch appearing to be behind the other. The second sketch leaves the first "behind it" not only in the temporal but also in the spatial sense.

What the Oxford three-figure sketches demonstrate appears to be the normal case in Michelangelo's corpus. Insofar as the subsequent drawings have their main axes parallel to that of the first one, their appearing results in a marked expansion of the sheet's spatial depth (therefore not in the case of fig. 4), whereby each subsequent sketch appears as the element in the foreground when it relates to the first sketch either as a correction (fig. 31: subsidiary sketches of the compositional sketch) or as a small detail excerpted from a larger drawing (figs. 5–8: hand studies; 9–10: leg and foot studies). However, if the second drawing is an intermediate stage between the initial and final version (figs. 7, 8: thorax study; 32: subsidiary sketches), then it appears to be set back from the first—independent of whether it is excerpted from the first as a detail.[4] In both cases the effect of an expanded sense of depth is achieved by the same factors as in figure 35: spatial proximity, different sizes of the figures.

On the Oxford sheet (fig. 35) the appearance of the second three-figure sketch created a sense of imbalance. The area of maximum of space seems to be concentrated in the third quarter of the recto. Michelangelo instinctively corrected this lack of balance by placing the third sketch toward the left edge of the sheet—the point farthest removed from the crowded community of the first two sketches. The new arrival created its own space on account of this distance. Due to its enlarged format it roughly balances the preexisting community of sketches. Nevertheless the sheet thereby lost some of its suggested spatial depth. It was neutralized, so to speak. Only now could a real juxtaposition arise from the arrangement of sketches. Significantly, however, as soon as the fourth sketch

(second from the left) was about to be drawn, an organizing principle took effect that made a total leveling of the depth values impossible. Its visible expression is a rhythm on four different levels: the sizes of the sketches (medium-large, large, small, medium-large, small); distances (close, far, close, far); the locations (low, high, high, low, high), and the gradation of depths (front, back, back, front, back). This fourfold rhythm combines the whole recto inventory to form an organic chain without limiting the objective autonomy of the individual sketches.

Significantly, similar phenomena are found even under completely different conditions of placement. The small sketches on figure 6, which were created over forty years before the Pietà sketches, had to be adapted to the conditions created by the red-chalk studies, and not by the size of the sheet. The principle of rhythmic arrangement in a row is consequently subordinated to the already existing "sovereign areas" of the sheet. But this subordination goes beyond passive avoidance of the red-chalk studies. It also has its active side. The entablature sketch and the uppermost slave sketch have a stabilizing effect on the position of the large red-chalk study in the suggested space of the sheet precisely because they are so close to it. They simultaneously increase the overall spatial dynamism by producing, together with the remaining pen sketches, their own quasi-background plane, against which both red-chalk studies stand out like a bold relief against a spectral rear wall.

Size

The slave and Pietà sketches have—leaving aside all differences of time, occasion, and purpose of their creation—approximately the same, conspicuously small figure size (average 6.5 or 6.8 cm). Except for the sketches that can be attributed to Daniele da Volterra (figs. 123, 127–28), this figure size is not found in any of the unauthenticated groups of sketches generally connected with Michelangelo's name (whose smallest sizes range from 12 to 18 cm, apart from sporadic exceptions such as in figure 71). But it does characterize a number of other authenticated sketches by the master—including the swift outline sketch of the artist painting the ceiling in figure 39 (approx. 8.5 cm from head to foot), the niche figure outlined in the tomb in figure 12 (figures on the side: 5 cm), the separate little figures neighboring the composition sketches in figures 31–32 (average figure size: approx. 5 cm), or the apostles in figure 36. Nowhere is the size of these drawings the result of a mere lack of space: it appears to be the expression of an individual habit. It documents that Michelangelo sketched in an unusually small scale over a period of at least forty-five years.

An intellectual clarification process begins when the artist begins to sketch. As I indicated in chapter 2, in Michelangelo's case it is expressed by a more or less marked progression of the figure sizes. What has matured in the artist's head becomes optically closer, more corporeal, and thereby more voluminous—even as the artist develops the final form of a conception (Sistine Chapel ceiling; Louvre and Boboli slaves; Lorenzo and Giuliano tomb). Thus it seems logical that a single-figure sketch as precisely drawn as the David in figure 5 should be significantly larger than the little figures in figures 6, 12, 31–32, 35–36, and 39, while at the same time it is surpassed (by ca. 8 cm) by the completed Hercules sketch in figure 4. What could be, at worst, casual is the *David's* absolute height of 15.5 cm (first version: 14 cm). But this height has its equivalent in similarly precise sketch figures from a later time: the Christ of the *Resurrection* sketch of 1533 (figs. 27–28: ca. 15 cm) and the Annunciation figures of 1558 (fig. 37: angel, ca. 17 cm). Apparently it represents an upper limit in Michelangelo's sketching range that was only exceeded under exceptional circumstances. The two exceptions are the Hercules in figure 4 (23.5 cm) and the Madonna in figure 38 (25.5 cm), which, on the basis of authenticated drawings, can reasonably be attributed to Michelangelo. The first is from the time when Michelangelo began to acquire routine as a draftsman, the second from the time when this routine declined (as a consequence of motor disturbances). Neither of the two is typical for the main phases of Michelangelo's productivity as a draftsman (ca. 1500–60).

The impression of regularity suggested by the sizes of Michelangelo's sketches is confirmed by the sizes of individual figures in the multifigure, highly finished drawings. For the most part the individual figures are in the uppermost size range of the sketches (ca. 15–25 cm), but their sizes depend in individual cases on the number of figures or the extent of the scene depicted. In the case of the *Ganymede* (fig. 17), of the *Tityos* (fig. 19), of the Colonna crucifix (fig. 33), and of the Colonna Pietà they correspond to the Hercules size (fig. 4); in the case of the *Fall of Phaeton* (fig. 24) to the David size (fig. 5). In the drawing of the *Dream* the total range of Michelangelo's figure sizes is represented: the Hercules size in the figure of the awakening youth, the David size in the figure of the winged genius, and the small size so typical of the bulk of Michelangelo's sketches in the figures constituting the circle of vices surrounding the main figure. Michelangelo departs from this usual range of

figure sizes only in those highly finished drawings whose subject is either a single figure or a detail of a figure—the Christ descending to limbo and the Risen Christ on the one hand (figs. 14–16: ca. 34.5 and 28.5 cm), and the "teste divine" on the other hand (fig. 13). These apparently represent the maximum size.

Significantly, this maximum size corresponds to Michelangelo's sizes in studies. Of these, the study for The Crucified Haman is the largest (known only in copies) surviving figure drawing of the Michelangelo corpus—but only because of its absolute size (ca. 38 cm from the right heel to the skull), and not because of its body size. If its large subsidiary study on the Teyler Museum sheet A16r, the Adam studies, the torso and the leg study for the Libyan sibyl (figs. 7, 8), the study for the Libyca's companion (fig. 6), and the arm study for the marble David (fig. 5) were expanded to the corresponding full figures, these would all have approximately the same length. Only the small details of bodies, the head, hand, knee, foot, and toe studies would result in significantly larger full-length figures. Nevertheless, even they seem to be subjected to a regular progression. Every smaller detail corresponds to a larger size, the smallest (toe studies in figs. 7, 8) to the largest one.[5]

The Media and Their Use

The authenticated Michelangelo drawings of figures were executed with either pen and ink or with black or red chalk. The use of brush and ink wash is evident only in connection with highly finished drawings for tombs and architecture; the use of styluses cannot be proved at all.[6] It is doubtful that the complete absence of silver point and pencil drawings has only to do with the circumstances of survival. The available material suggests instead that Michelangelo—in contrast, say, to Cellini (figs. 72–80)[7]—had a genuine aversion to hard and especially sharp media and as he grew older preferred soft chalk and broad pen points to sharp ones (figs. 30–32, 35–37, 42).[8]

The authenticated pen-and-ink drawings are fewer in number than the chalk drawings. They are distributed over just as long a period of time as the chalk drawings, but after about 1510 almost all of them belong to the species of occasional sketches (figs. 41–43).[9] The authenticated chalk drawings, on the other hand, include all types of drawings except for purely incidental sketches, but examples cannot be found prior to 1510.[10] The two types therefore follow each other chronologically, insofar as they are included among the sketches, studies, and highly finished drawing species relevant to the overall production. But this can scarcely rest on chance. For literary sources also bear witness to its being a historical fact. According to Condivi (who had to have known it from Michelangelo himself) the drawing of a hand that the young Michelangelo drew in order to identify himself to the emissary of Cardinal Raffaello Riario as the creator of the *Sleeping Cupid* was prepared with a pen (instead of chalk) "perciocchè in quel tempo [1496] il lapis non era in uso" ("because at that time chalk was not yet in use").[11] This casually mentioned— and for that reason precisely so important—explanation documents not only the exclusive use of the pen in Michelangelo's youth, it also emphasizes that in Condivi's experience Michelangelo generally executed drawings in chalk.

To conclude from the evidence of what is authenticated and its implications, Michelangelo probably shifted from pen to chalk in the period ca. 1505–10. This shift was presumably prompted by considerations of efficiency. Chalk allowed several contour strata to be superimposed over each other without injuring the intended final effect, thereby significantly shortening the process of exploring and defining ideas. As a comparison between the David sketch or the arm study in figure 5 and the river god of the *Fall of Phaeton* sketch in figure 23 or the study pair in figure 6 demonstrates *ad oculos*, the traces of the very first layers cannot be obscured nearly so easily in pen-and-ink drawings as they can in chalk drawings. They compete everywhere with the subsequent layers and thereby provoke additional corrective measures in the form of special contour strengthenings and a crooked-stroke hatching, the many directional changes of which are caused by a considerable number of changes in Michelangelo's hand position. In order to achieve the clarity of the contour of the river god, the definitive outline of the David would have had to have been isolated from its first layer and redrawn afresh in a separate place—as apparently happened with the Hercules sketch (fig. 4). This indeed presupposes a more detailed and time-consuming exploration process than is exhibited by the highly finished chalk drawings in figures 14–16 or 24, whose final state is directly superimposed over a sketch, without being disturbed in the least by it.

Michelangelo probably felt it necessary to make his preparatory drawing more efficient at the latest when he received the contract for the fresco of the Battle of Cascina (1505) for the Sala dei Cinquecento in the Palazzo della Signoria, Florence. At that time, after many years of experience designing large statues, he had, for the first time, to sketch a mass of large-size figures, most of which required separate studies. The challenge probably provoked a reaction in the manner

Michelangelo employed his drawing media. It led to that thorough mastering of the red-chalk technique manifested in the study sets for the Sistine Chapel ceiling (figs. 6–11).

The Preliminary Idea and Its Realization through Drawing

Michelangelo's artistic career is accompanied by testimonies of contemporary amazement. People were amazed by the sculpture and paintings. But they were equally amazed at how this man was able to draw. Michelangelo appeared to go beyond all known standards. His imagination and his drawing hand seemed to be one and the same. He succeeded on the first attempt in charming things out of pen or chalk that others would have required multiple attempts to formulate. When Cardinal Riario's agent, searching for the genius who created the Cupid, entered Michelangelo's workshop, the artist had nothing to show in the way of sculpture—so he sketched a hand, and the agent knew that he had found the person he was looking for. When the painter Giuliano Bugiardini was unable to get the foreground figures of his *Martyrdom of Saint Catherine* correct and went to Michelangelo for advice, "the latter placed himself with a piece of charcoal at the panel and outlined with a couple of light strokes a row of naked figures—wonderful figures that in all possible shortenings fell, some backward, some forward, mixed with dead and wounded, all made with the skill and excellence unique to Michelangelo" (Vasari).[12] And when a certain young man from Ferrara asked the artist to draw him a standing Hercules as payment for a service delivered, Michelangelo took the sheet offered him, sat down with it, thought for a while, and then drew the desired object in one draft. To Armenini (1533–1609), who reported this episode, the drawing seemed "so well outlined, hatched, and finished that it exceeded any miniature style and greatly amazed everyone who saw created in such a short time what anyone else would have taken as the product of a month's work."[13]

However unbelievable such reports might sound when read with the eyes of believers in the genuineness of the present-day corpus attributed to Michelangelo, their quintessence is confirmed by what is authenticated. For the authenticated works allow one characteristic to be identified that, if the reports are true, is indispensable: the optimal relation between kinetic effort and esthetic efficiency. This relation points to a specialty of Michelangelo's imaginative power. As Condivi and Vasari noted,[14] the artist had a phenomenal memory. His impressions were so sharp and so palpable that they became recallable on paper, so to speak. An example of how this happened concretely can be demonstrated by his composition sketches for the *Last Judgment* (figs. 30–32).

The first of these sketches (fig. 30) reflects the original state of the idea. With its over fifty small figures it is—together with the lost composition sketch for the *Story of the Brazen Serpent* (fig. 29)—one of the idea sketches with the most figures that were ever created. Of these for the most part completely visible, very differently acting small figures, however, more than thirty have outgrown the formulaic primitive stage of definition and are comparable to the slave sketches in figure 6 or the Pietà sketches in figure 35 in the differentiation of their poses and anatomical structure. Related to each other syntactically, they form three unequally large, independent action groups, which together represent a threefold but unified scene—specified in the resurrection of the dead, ascension of the blessed, and casting down of the damned. These separate nodal points, which are separated from each other by empty areas of the sheet, are nothing but the visible expression of those imaginative areas in the artist's mind that had reached the maximum of optical sharpness at the time they were put down on paper. They indicate that at the decisive moment the artist had a grip not only on the limbs of the one or the other single figure, but of whole figure systems simultaneously, and that he was able to organize them into an already largely closed and coherent compositional whole on the first attempt. It goes without saying that this unique capability had been developed through many years of practice; it presumably reached its high point around 1533. Nevertheless, it appears to be a constant fact of Michelangelo's genius. Both the earliest and the latest preliminary sketches (figs. 5–6; 35–37) and occasional sketches (figs. 39, 41–43) prove that between 1500 and 1560 this capability was always sufficient to at least articulate his mental conception of each individual body ad hoc, its attitude determined, its proportions and anatomical organization correct, and its volume and weight at an optimum.[15] The movement from idea to realization was direct and immediate, with few—and sometimes no—intermediate stages.

After the first of the sketches for the *Last Judgment* was drawn Michelangelo was faced with the task of lighting up the vague areas—independent of whether the projected fresco continued to be destined for the entrance wall of the Sistine Chapel or not. Most of his colleagues would have solved this task by repeating the clearly articulated parts of their first sketch on another sheet, refining them, and modifying and expanding them according to a more mature overall compositional idea (figs. 127–30). But Michelangelo did *not* allow

the further development of his idea to be dependent on its first version. Neither of the two following sketches (figs. 31–32) makes explicit reference to the first one at any place.[16] Instead each represents an extraction from an essential concept that has in the meantime been modified both in composition and also in all details. But when these sketches were made, the designing process had already reached a certain acme. The two sketches are not only more differentiated than the Casa Buonarroti sketch (fig. 30); their figure groups also correspond in part to their equivalents in the fresco, up to and including certain details. They mark the transition into that stage of preparatory work that consists in making large-sized studies for single figures.

The London sketch (fig. 32) shows with special clearness with what minimal kinetic expenditure this maturity was achieved. Even its very first layers were, as is evident from some unretouched small figures, more detailed in its figural definition than those of the Casa Buonarroti sketch (fig. 30), which consists largely of abbreviations. They were successively surpassed. In the process the completion of certain parts preceded by far those of the whole—as in the execution of Michelangelo's sculptures. Some small figures, for example, the standing nude who bends forward and looks down in the middle of the lower row of martyrs, or the damned figure, with his face turned from our view, whose posture suggests a storming of heaven, stand out from their surroundings because of a special prominence and fineness of corporeal definition. And their definitive contours are based on no more than two provisional ones at the most. Such perfection was possible because the artist interrupted his work on the group for a short time to clarify the details most in need of clarification. Two subsidiary sketches of both the martyr and the damned figure appear on the left and lower edge of the sheet. In each case the first one consists of a lightly drawn outline sketch, which in the case of the damned figure has been gone over with a couple of quick reinforcing strokes. The second subsidiary sketch consists of a lightly drawn, improved version of this outline sketch and of a secondary version sketched over it with emphasis. The final version of these small figures found in the group ensemble is in each case the immediate successor to the secondary version. It therefore represents the fifth or sixth stage of the sketching process. A shorter path to such a fully developed and simultaneously so unusual result can hardly be imagined.

Compared with the sketches for the *Last Judgment* (figs. 30–32) and the sketch for the *Story of the Brazen Serpent* (fig. 29), the sketches for a *Pietà* in Oxford (fig. 35) drawn twenty years later have a narrow pictorial extent. Still, the task they tried to solve was one of the most difficult the artist ever confronted—namely, to depict visually the temporary "death" of God. In spite of this difficulty the artist trod the path to the profound design, from which the first version of the Rondanini emerged, in a mere five steps. The first step consisted to some extent in the visualization of the conditions requisite to a solution: Christ as absolute center, dead and nonetheless erect (small group of three). The second step resulted in a sharpening of the dialectics of activity and passivity and a condensation of the figure block's energies (large group of three). Each of the three following steps led to a significant reduction of the "prosaic" effects of bearing and hanging. After the fifth and last step (group of two on the right outside) Michelangelo seems to have known what was to be done with the chisel.

As the present-day state of the Rondanini Pietà, the many pentimenti in the cartoon fragment for the *Crucifixion of Peter* (fig. 34), or the relationship of the surviving Sistine studies (figs. 6–11) to the relevant fresco figures prove, in the case of Michelangelo the conclusion of a sketching process on paper never marks a standstill in the imaginative process. It is merely the external expression of the subjective certainty of having grasped his own artistic conception to the extent that seemed necessary for finally formulating it in the study, cartoon, fresco, or sculpture. This certainty was by no means dependent in each case on the existence of a preceding sketching process. It sometimes happened spontaneously—as in the episode of 1496 or on the occasion of the request from the man from Ferrara. But once this certainty was there it enabled the artist to draw every idea ad hoc as a finished drawing. The *Fall of Phaeton* in Windsor (fig. 24) is a classic example. Michelangelo made one cursory sketch that was completely changed in comparison with his first sketch of the subject (fig. 23). Then feeling sure of his aim, he erased the sketch as well as he could, and drew the finished drawing over it, without bothering anymore about what had just been sketched. His finished drawing has nothing to do with a "reproduction" of his underlying sketch—it reflects a completely new idea.

Contours

Michelangelo's unique capacity for expression is not to be grasped only on the level of what is depicted. It is reflected in the elementary drawing structures and especially in the contours. These are composed of strokes with unusually pronounced variability of volume. They function like letters,

contribute to the modeling of form, and in their totality give the contoured object an essentially three-dimensional look—independent of how cursorily or how deliberately they are drawn, how "logical" or "illogical" the volume thickenings are placed, how static or how dynamic the postures of the figures appear. To judge from the steadfastness of this stroke function, Michelangelo's contouring processes must have been guided by haptic data of imagination before they could be reflected at all.

The appropriateness of the kinetic course corresponds to the functionality of the kinetic pressure. Its most general expression is the purposefulness of the strokes; its specific expression is their formal differentiation. Pure formulaic marks are found almost only in the figure abbreviations—usually hidden under the overdrawing—with which the outlining processes were introduced (fig. 5: first layer of the David contour; fig. 27: outline drawing of guard; figs. 30–32, 35–37: first layers) or the planning of sculpture in an architectonic framework was signaled (fig. 12). At the latest in the following stages of contouring they are either completely replaced by individualized stroke shapes (fig. 5: David; figs. 23, 37) or confined in their distribution to the hand and foot areas—the generally most formulatory parts of the figural sketches (fig. 6: slaves; figs. 30, 36, 39–40). But it is characteristic for Michelangelo that the abbreviations for the hands and feet are functionally differentiated from the beginning. In figure 35 there is a striking difference in definition between the formulas used for the "engaged" hands of the carrier figure and those for the passive hands of the dead figure. Similar differences characterize the relationship of the formulas for the weighted and unweighted feet in figures 6 (slaves), 30–32, 35–36, and 39. While unweighted feet usually consist of a mere zigzag stroke, weighted feet ordinarily have a solid, hooflike appearance. They form a kind of base for the load resting on them. It is impossible to find anything similar in the corpus of alleged Michelangelo drawings (the only exceptions are in Daniele's work: figs. 121, 123–30). The foot formula found there remains indifferent to the relevant functions of the extremities and to gravitational considerations—even in advanced sketching stages (figs. 48–49, 76–77).[17]

A special kinetic rhythm stands behind the unusually high level with which form is articulated in the contours of Michelangelo's authenticated drawings. It is characterized by a relationship between controlled and uncontrolled kinetic phases that looks almost like a reversal of the normally practiced one. The highly controlled phases are longer than the uncontrolled ones. As the drawing became more conscious the alternation between the two became more abrupt. Whereas the controlled phases in the outlines of the river god (fig. 40) "softly" and gradually flowed into the uncontrolled phases while still within the marked parts of the pen's course of movement, in the Hercules sketch (fig. 4) they were abruptly replaced by uncontrolled phases (which are here largely identical with the contour gaps produced by hand movements of the artist between individual strokes that result in no mark being left on the surface). It is obvious that the contouring in the second case proceeded more slowly than in the first. Nevertheless, even in the first and all other similar cases the outlining process cannot have really occurred "quickly," still less "furiously." Otherwise the phenomenal purposefulness of Michelangelo's contours would be a miracle.

This purposefulness is linked to the fact that revisions in the overall kinetic expenditure that led to settling on a contour had only a limited role. The impression that some contour parts were drawn several times, suggested in the David sketch (fig. 5) and the majority of the chalk drawings, is a deception. The fact is that, there, two or even several completely outlined figures are superimposed on each other. The contours of each one of these preliminary figures as well as those of the last one are for the most part formed by a single rail of strokes—as are the contours of almost all pen-and-ink drawings (fig. 4: Hercules, profile head; fig. 6: slaves; figs. 39–43). In any case they exhibit a minimum of repetitious strokes. The Annunciation sketch (fig. 37) constitutes one exception. Its numerous pentimenti are also components of the two superimposed figures.[18] This fact is nevertheless—as in the case of the Madonna drawing in figure 38—the result of a motor disturbance caused by old age. Michelangelo's hand shook as he sketched these figures, and in order to keep inappropriately oscillatory movements under control, he needed an accelerated tempo. Thus he was able to minimize the shaking symptoms (the strokes have a slightly whiplike course rather than a sinuous one), but the movement itself could be controlled sufficiently to create form-defining contours only after several attempts.[19]

The repetition of strokes is only the most conspicuous of the types of revisions represented in the drawings by Michelangelo's own hand. The most frequent by far and those actually typical for Michelangelo throughout his life are those inconspicuous lightning-swift corrections that are expressed in shifts in the axis of the stroke. In the case of pen-and-ink drawings they often represent the only forms of revision whatsoever, but in the case of chalk drawings, too, they can determine the overall character of the stroke system (fig. 37:

angel). Because of their dominating role they are one of the most striking witnesses not only to the high degree of mental concentration that Michelangelo applied in drawing his contours, but also to his enormous certainty of form even as he began sketching.

The rarity of reinforcing strokes is evidence of how little revision accounts for in the total expenditure of movement. Even in the *Tityos* (fig. 19) and the figures of the *Fall of Phaeton* in Windsor (fig. 24)—non plus ultras of Michelangelo's finished draftsmanship—a clear alternation between reinforced and unreinforced contour sections can be seen. This alternation has in principle the same function as the variation in volume of the components of Michelangelo's contours. The reinforcements accentuate the important joint and muscle parts and assist in making implied spatial relationships evident. They are usually so completely integrated in the overall composition of the strokes that it is difficult to perceive them as "additions" with the unaided eye. Frequently, the reinforcing strokes differ from normal strokes with increasing and decreasing volumes only in the especially strong and malleable substance of their bodies (fig. 23: river god) and a certain commalike shortness (fig. 37: angel).[20]

The efficiency of Michelangelo's technique of reinforcing contours must have been perceived and admired as early as the sixteenth century. Even then the creators of the many facsimile copies did not neglect to take into account the striking changes in strength and their space-producing effects, when their unhaptic perception forced them to transform the elasticity of Michelangelo's outlines into the rigidity of wire-contours (figs. 7, 11, 20, 22). Most copyists, on the contrary, tended to exaggerate the original reinforcements—with the result that these seem to become independent and to convert Michelangelo's multifunctional and elastic contour "organism" into a linear chiaroscuro ornament (fig. 8: thorax study; figs. 9–10: legs; fig. 13: serpent's body; fig. 16: shroud folds; fig. 27: Christ).

Hatching

In view of the plastic efficiency of Michelangelo's contours it is no surprise that hatching occurs only rarely in the incidental sketches (fig. 41) and rather irregularly in his preparatory sketches. Nevertheless, hatching is to be found in the latter, independently of what importance these had in the process of articulating a particular form or figure. What is noteworthy, besides the purposefulness and economy, is the function of the hatching. That the David (fig. 5) is shaded while the Hercules (fig. 4) is not probably has to do with the numerous revisions of the contours. The definitive outline had to be reinforced here and there for the sake of clarity, and this resulted in a certain weakening of the three-dimensional effect of the figure. The hatching was used as a corrective. It emphatically sets off the definitive contour from the provisional one—as the spirals on the lower left arm show. But at the same time it serves to explicate spatially the figure's movement. Both the spirals on the lower left arm and those on the right calf optically create a dark contrast to its neighboring limb (upper arm or thigh). Both thereby suggest that the limb in question is not parallel to the picture plane but slightly bent to the rear—an impression that the contour alone could not create. The assemblage of rising rectilinear parallels on the head of Goliath has a similar function. It gives the head a three-dimensionality and also clarifies its spatial relationship to David's left leg. Without it this leg would appear to stand merely *next to* Goliath's head. Because of it, it also appears to be *in front of it*.

What this pen-and-ink sketch exemplifies for Michelangelo's early period the chalk drawing in figure 37 exemplifies for his old age.[21] Its shading, although more economical than that of the David, is, if possible, even more strongly evocative of contrasts. Vigorous and multipartite in the case of Mary, very soft and limited to a minimum in the case of the angel, it heightens the antithesis between the heavy corporeality of the future mother of God and the ethereal being of the angel, already implied in the contours. The hatching consists of simple small assemblages of zigzag strokes. In the case of Mary these are distributed over the face, left shoulder, left upper arm, abdomen, and the intermediate areas between the legs and between the left upper arm and torso. They accentuate the dialectic between the spatial layers—the sense of backward and forward, the depth between trunk and knees and between the right hand and the breast, the cautious, scarcely noticeable bending forward of the upper body and the figure's being spatially situated in the narrow confines of an area consisting of a prie-dieu and chair.

Clarifying the planes of spatial recession is also the chief function of the hatching of the London sketch for the *Last Judgment* (fig. 32). Its tectonic lattices, which are led past whole figure complexes, produce the effect of spatially undefinable background areas. They make the difference in depth between the two main groups separated by the cloud bank comprehensible and also emphasize the dynamics of the action—the forward movement of the group of saints from the background to repulse the damned and the backward-and-forward bubbling-up of the interlaced bodies of the defenders

and the fended-off. What the compositional sketch demonstrates on a large scale, its subsidiary sketches show on a small scale. Its hatching assemblages have a largely passive relationship to the area outlined by the contours. Stretching across whole limbs from outline to outline, they heighten not so much the corporeality (this is sufficiently defined by the contours) as the spatial directional contrasts of the body movements.

An especially differentiated shading corresponds to the definitive contours of individual small figures. It no longer appears here in the form of neutral large and flat lattices that indicate only the spatial position of the relevant limb or limb complex as a whole. Instead, it consists of small areas that refer to the organic structure, contributing to the modeling of muscles and joints and making the bodily surfaces swollen or hollow. Indeed, in some places its strokes are curved into convex shapes adapted to the organic rotundity of the limbs (as in the case of the David sketch [fig. 5] or the large hand sketch [fig. 41]). The passive rectilinear lattices are here transformed into an active modeling hatching. In the case of the London *Fall of Phaeton* (fig. 23) the adjacentness and overlapping of the two functional types determines the overall character of the drawing. Thus the outermost heliad on the right is still largely criss-crossed with flat lattices whose dark values suggest the degree of torso-bending and the projection of the arms and the right leg.

The plastic structuring of this heliad's body was achieved by small "stripple hatching" tonally attuned to the contour strengthenings (their equivalent in the David sketch are the squiggly "microhatchings" which largely occur at the same torso parts). This stripple hatching forms the seeds for the actual modulation hatching. The heliad to the right of the river god exemplifies the transition to the modulation hatching. Her neck, left arm, and left thigh, are, for the sake of clarifying the spatial relationships, still overdrawn with simple lattices. The torso, the front extremities, and the tree stump into which the legs are being transformed, however, are equipped with a number of microhatchings that contrast with each other in direction, strength, and size, thereby producing a finely articulated sculptural effect. This effect is dominant in the case of the horses. The shading there is the equal partner of the contours. It explicates (for example, by purposeful curving of the hatching strokes) that three-dimensionality which the contours already suggest in a more implicit manner. The flat lattices are limited to qualifying the space around the horses and form an abstract background foil that engulfs the remnants of the primary sketch, a kind of relief ground whose curious stability creates a contrast to the dynamism of the falling group. Its equivalent in the lowermost zone are the two free-lying lattices to the left of the river god. In their tectonic symmetry they act like a scaffold that carries itself—the abstract symbol of the torpidity that is suffered here and now by the heliads.

In our eyes the degree of articulation of the London *Phaeton* horses may represent an apex not in need of any improvement. In Michelangelo's eyes it was merely the starting point for perfection. Refining it (fig. 24) was not an end in itself for the artist, but the appropriate means for compressing the content.[22] The refinement transformed the object surfaces completely into a smooth, elastically stretched epidermis and thereby also embued it with inner vitality. The figures of the highly finished drawing appear more individual, but at the same time more dynamic than those of the sketch, because their surface itself is the expression of energetic tension and latent powers. Each individual figure contains that non plus ultra of dynamism and three-dimensionality that form the intended artistic goal of all paintings and sculptures by Michelangelo.[23]

The highly finished drawing differs from the sketch also through an increase in spatial depth. It relates to the sketch as a full-round sculptural group relates to a relief, although it shows no more overlappings and foreshortenings than the sketch. The cause of this effect is obvious: In the highly finished drawing the two important functional types of hatching are integrated with one another. The shading models form and simultaneously perform the task which on the sketch level is performed by the abstract flat lattices—because its dark values are intensified and are given preponderance over the areas free from hatching. In the case of the first heliad on the left it is on the whole more expansive and vigorous than in the case of the river god, but simultaneously so articulated in itself that similar dynamic contrasts in depth between the torso and arm, head and hands, front and rear thigh, are produced as in the case of the heliads of the London sketch. Even the external hatching participates in the integration of the two functional types. By the sheer effect of its fine nuancing of density and strength it gains a three-fold concreteness: that of a conglomeration of clouds in the Jupiter region, of a shadow cast on the mist behind the falling group, and of a soft ground fog behind the heliad and river god.

4

What Finally Can Be Attributed to Michelangelo?

An analysis of Michelangelo's authenticated drawings produces a "sieve" of characteristics that covers virtually all aspects of the artist's draftsmanship between 1495 and 1560. It is sufficiently finely meshed to catch every other authentic drawing (its legibility being presupposed) from the gray mass of what is included under the "Michelangelo" label.[1] That the yield is not overwhelming will come as no surprise to anyone who has followed the analytical part of this book up to this point. Nevertheless, it contains a great variety of drawing species and functional types. The relevant pieces are:

1. a partial sketch for a double tomb (black chalk) in the Casa Buonarroti, no. 107 A-r;[2]

2. two apostle sketches that can be associated with the Oxford sketches (fig. 36) for a Gethsemane scene (black chalk) in the British Museum, no. 1885-5-9-1894;[3]

3. a sketch assumed to be for a statue of the Madonna (fig. 38);

4. an extensive set of anatomical studies surviving in copies (Ashmolean Museum, Casa Buonarroti, Louvre, Teyler Museum, Windsor Castle, and Stanza del Borgo, Milan);[4]

5. two red-chalk studies for slaves of the Julius tomb surviving in facsimile copies (Teylers Museum A26, Uffizi 6550 F, Windsor no. 12765rv);[5]

6. a highly finished drawing of a female "testa divina" (black chalk) surviving in three facsimile copies (British Museum, no. 1895-9-15-493r/494, Windsor no. 0432);[6]

7. two sets of practice sketches (pen and ink) in the Archivio Buonarroti, vol. II–III, fol. 3v (fig. 1) and vol. XIII, fol. 145v;[7]

8. six small incidental sketches (five of them in pen and ink, one in black chalk), distributed over five sheets: Archivio Buonarroti, vol. V, 38, fol. 213v; Casa Buonarroti no. 30 F, 57 F-r and 60 F; British Museum Add. MS. 21907, fol. 1rv;[8]

9. a copy made after two figures of Giotto's fresco of the *Ascension of John the Evangelist* (pen and ink), in the Louvre, no. 706r;[9]

10. three drawn copies made after studies by Domenico Ghirlandaio (pen and ink), distributed over two sheets: Louvre no. 685v (fig. 2) and Albertina Sc.R.150rv;[10]

11. a copy (pen and ink) after an unknown original (in the British Museum) (fig. 3).[11]

What is especially remarkable in this group is the quantitative relationship between the specific preparatory drawings (1–3, 5) and the "autonomous" ones (4, 6–11). It corresponds almost exactly to that in the authenticated corpus. As in the authenticated corpus, the sketches and preliminary studies form a decided minority in comparison to the larger number of highly finished drawings (to which in the case in question the large-size, carefully hatched copies 9–11 must also be assigned) as well as occasional sketches. This fact reflects the historical situation known from literary sources. In relation to the entire drawing production the "autonomous" drawings were of course anything but numerous. But they *had* to win the upper hand eventually, if it is true that the artist gave away only tiny portions of his preparatory works and otherwise used to destroy them. The autonomous drawings represent the only type of drawing that consistently escaped destruction. The highly finished drawings and drawn copies satisfied Michelangelo's idea of perfection.[12] The incidental sketches, on the other hand, were ignored. They had the good fortune to be located on writing sheets, that is, on papers that Michelangelo preserved separately and, as far as is known, never destroyed.

The second thing that stands out in the small corpus of what can be attributed to Michelangelo is its distribution over time. All five copies (9–11), as well as the two sets of practice sketches consisting of seventeen parts in all (7), and possibly also part of the anatomical studies (4)—that is, over 50 percent of the products in question—are from Michelangelo's early youth, a period that isn't represented at all in the authenticated corpus.[13] These drawings show Michelangelo's drawing style *in statu nascendi*. Much about them, from the relatively large size of the figures to the many-layered, finely meshed, expansive hatching seem to bear little resemblance to the authenticated drawings, and can only be explained as the expression of a beginner's behavior. It is therefore necessary to discuss in detail at least one of the two sets of sketches (fig. 1) and one of the five copies (fig. 2).

Having read the first two parts of this book, the reader should have no trouble understanding the reasons why the sheets created later (1–3, 5, 6, 8) can be attributed to Michelangelo. Therefore, in the following these reasons will be discussed at length using only *one* example, the London Madonna sketch (fig. 38). This sketch, in its way, has an importance similar to that of Michelangelo's first drawings: It appears to be his last surviving drawing.

A Document of Michelangelo's Early Draftsmanship

The pen-and-ink sketches on what is now termed the verso of the Archivio Buonarroti sheet (fig. 1) are among the most misunderstood creations in the Michelangelo corpus. Contradictory in their appearance, without reference to anything familiar, they appear to resist any attempt at classification. Perhaps only the handwriting located on the two sides of the sheet prevented their authenticity from being questioned.[14] The handwriting does attest to the fact that the sheet belonged to the Buonarroti family at the latest from 1500.

One of the writings (on the present-day recto) is unquestionably by Michelangelo himself.[15] Dated 22 May 1501, it contains the artist's commentary on the draft for a contract for the decoration of the Piccolomini altar. It appears to have been the last entry on the sheet. The sheet began being filled with the writing of the three (recto) or eight (verso) lines of script placed in the upper edge of the sheet. These lines are written in a quattrocento style, but otherwise have neither a uniform handwriting style nor an intelligible content. They consist of a more or less context-less sequence of individual words, proper names, and sentence fragments. The only connecting links in the recto lines appear to be the subjects "I" and "you"; in the verso lines the names of Michelangelo's uncle Francesco Simone (1434–1508) and his favorite brother, Buonarroto, as well as the words "chompagni lanaiuolj" or "banchierj" ("comrade wool dealers" or "bankers"). Scholars seized on these words, associated them with some "family business," understood the solitary "Buonarroto" in the fourth line of the verso and the equally solitary "Buonnarootto [!] dilodovicho" [!] in the fifth line of the verso as signatures of the brother, and presented the whole to the public as a business letter or simply as a "note" from the beloved brother.[16]

Of course such a complicated piece of writing seemingly having to do with an international family business ("infranza . . . flandra") could—so people believed—only come from an adult Buonarroto—the one who had been employed in Lorenzo Strozzi's cloth shop since 1497–98.[17] On the other hand, it was impossible to regard the verso sketches and the poetic one-liners ("lauoglia inuoglia allassa poi ladoglia" and "lamorte e l finduna prigione scura") written with the same pen and ink as the lattermost writing on the sheet. For the one-liners—attributed a priori to Michelangelo—appeared to correspond to an earlier stage of Michelangelo's handwriting development than the document of 1501. There remained no choice but to date the sketches between 1498 and 1501.[18]

But this dating cannot be reconciled with the current attribution of the sketches to Michelangelo. For if the sketches were created around 1500, they cannot be accommodated in Michelangelo's accepted oeuvre of drawings. Nothing like their thin-stroke contours, permeated by solderings, small corrections, and unmotivated changes in the thicknesses of strokes, and with their inconsistencies in perspective, anatomy, and proportions, are to be found either in the St. Anne group and Hercules sketch of 1495–97 (fig. 4) or in the David sketch of 1502 (fig. 5), let alone then in Michelangelo's later authenticated pen-and-ink drawings (figs. 6, 12, 39–43). They exhibit the specific characteristics of a beginner's style. There is only one alternative: either to remove the sketches from the accepted Michelangelo corpus or to date them in his autodidactic early period (ca. 1485–89).

The sketches themselves allow only the second possibility, because their beginner's style exhibits certain constants of Michelangelo's drawing method, including—in addition to the crystalline clarity of the stroke-system structures—principally the high degree of formal articulation in the individual strokes. Whereas these normally tend to extreme shortness and formality in the case of most apprenticeship products (figs. 54–56, 60),[19] here they are precisely the opposite in their striking length and differentiation. With their volumes softly swelling up and down, they already function positively as factors of plastic qualification (for example, at the lower sides of the gluteal muscles and the right calf of the back figure)—a phenomenon that in this context is probably as rare as the existence of quick and unambiguous corrections (for example, below the right hip and at the left thigh and above the left ankle of the figure seen from the rear).

Dating the sketches earlier also helps make sense of the alleged business document. It is actually a simple writing exercise—or more precisely an attempt to imitate an older style of penmanship by imitating certain words or combinations of words such as they might appear in Michelangelo's father's or grandfather's correspondence (fig. 2). This is borne out not only by the nonsensical contents and the sometimes multiple repetitions of the same words and proper names in varying, occasionally halting writing ("Lododouicho," "disimion," "Buonnarooto"), but also by certain properties of the handwriting itself, such as the enormous range of variation of shapes of individual letters or the frequency of botched letters and of oversaturation of individual strokes (excessive dipping

of the pen!).[20] But as a writing exercise the writing fragments could just as well have been written by Michelangelo himself as by his favorite brother. If by the former then it would be the first written document from the pen of the artist—the only one from his grammar school days.

The sketches also belong to the category of exercises. They appear to reflect that beginning phase of the process of learning to draw in which one learns how to draw contours. This was usually learned and practiced by copying contours from the drawings of one's master or from engravings.[21] Since Michelangelo was largely self-taught,[22] he was freer in the selection of his models than any other apprentice. His hand sketch does not look as if it had been copied from a drawn or engraved model. Instead, it appears to be the result of an attempt to sketch from memory his own writing hand held before his eyes. The two adjacent sketches are also beyond the scope of normal practice drawings. Thus the figure seen from the rear is the product of a compilation process—as the unhomogeneous stroke system and the disparate inner structure of the body reveal. The first thing to be drawn—apparently from a model—was the right leg. It is the only body part that is both correctly articulated anatomically and properly proportioned. It was complemented by the drawing of the left calf, which became too thick and appears in an impossible position in terms of perspective, the too broad posterior, and the misshapen torso with its mushroom head, overlapping the writing. The whole can be understood as a playful attempt to "reconstruct" an entire body on the basis of one limb.[23] The sketch of the legs has a similar experimental character. It consists of a highly differentiated "original stock" that makes sense in itself (the left leg) and a supplement simply added on to it (the hastily sketched right leg) that is supposed to suggest the context of the motif. That the "original stock" in both cases, that is, the right leg of the one sketch and the left leg of the other, have closer connections to Pollaiuolo's figures than to those of Ghirlandaio is further evidence for the early dating of the sketches. For Michelangelo had already learned to draw figures by contours before his friend Granacci lent him drawings of his future master for copying.[24]

A notable anecdote is reported in a letter addressed to Vasari shortly after Michelangelo's death.[25] The unknown correspondent[26] wrote that he had once spoken with the artist about how the two famous Greek painters Protogenes and Apelles had sought to surpass each other in the drawing of subtle lines. Michelangelo had responded that neither of the two had to be a painter to do that. "And he took a piece of chalk to hand and began to draw a toe on a sheet of paper; and while he continued drawing without ever lifting the chalk from the paper, he made the contour of a half figure, and then he said: 'If someone were to come now who would make the other half in the right way, I would consider him a better master than they were.'" If Michelangelo subjected himself to such tests on his own initiative when he was still an apprentice, then at the time of this anecdote he would surely have known just who, if anybody, was capable of passing the test.

Michelangelo and the Drawings of His Future Teacher

The verso drawing of the Louvre sheet no. 685 (fig. 2) has had a similar history of faulty scholarship as the Archivio sketches (fig. 1). Because the writing located in the uppermost section of the sheet was badly misdated (see excursus I), this drawing was and is dated in the sixteenth century—in spite of the impossibility of accommodating it there stylistically, iconographically, or even in method of execution.[27] Scholars, neither willing to drop the attribution to Michelangelo nor ready to examine their basis for dating, fled before the contradiction into speculations about the subject depicted (Salome or Judith?), intellectual sophistry, or, if necessary, into simple ultimatums.[28]

Nevertheless, the attribution is correct. The drawing shares with the authenticated corpus some important characteristics such as the length, sensitive application of pressure, formal purposefulness of the contours, and a finely modeled hatching beside whose richness of tectonic contrasts and tonal nuances Mini's hatching system of the St. Anne group (fig. 4) appears inefficient and lifeless. These indications of Michelangelo's authorship are nevertheless coupled with properties that prove the drawing to be the product of a beginner. Several sections of the contours are botched (for example, the chin and neck of the girl, the nose of the severed head, the eagle's beak). The shading, which is permeated by small ink blobs and tends toward harsh black-white contrasts, still consists largely of straight lines (in contrast to the shading of the St. Anne group which is closer to the style of Michelangelo's later shading techniques with curved strokes). In places their assemblages even continue to form harsh angles where they meet. The formation of the drapery folds seems edgy, the representation of the arm and leg sometimes unclear and in a distorted perspective. Finally, the subject itself points to Michelangelo's early period. Both the position and the linear

calligraphy of the drapery-fold style identify the kneeling girl, whose garment is so suggestive of the elegant women's fashion of the late quattrocento, as a derivation from one of those "repoussoir figures" viewed from the back who so frequently populate the foreground of the paintings of Domenico Ghirlandaio and his pupils.[29]

Nevertheless, the drawing does not seem to depend on a painting but on one of its own kind.[30] Some of its most conspicuous characteristics are found both in Ghirlandaio's authentic studies[31] and in certain study-copies of his atelier:[32] (1) the almost uniform distribution of the dark values on *both* sides of the body, producing more of an effect of breadth than of depth; (2) the lack of defining sharpness in the hair, the position of the left arm, the position and structure of the right sleeve, the position of the legs, and the relationship between hanging and slack folds; (3) the tendency of the peripheral areas of drapery that are independent of the body to take on a life of their own; (4) the tendency toward exaggeratedly deep folds of drapery; (5) the ring formations at the back of the head and around the hand. The Louvre drawing accordingly belongs to that period in Michelangelo's development when he was trying to acquire the technique of a master. According to the unanimous opinion of the sources Michelangelo acquired this technique *before* he entered Ghirlandaio's workshop (April 1488).[33] But it occurred by copying Ghirlandaio drawings that had been lent to the boy by his friend Granacci. No wonder that the product of this activity is located on a sheet from his great-grandfather's business papers rather than on a blank piece of paper from Ghirlandaio's workshop.

The theme of the drawing presents a special problem. The kneeling girl forms only one part, the main part, of the drawing. The other part, which immediately followed the first, is the curious union of reversed eagle and vase (also called a lamp) drawn in the same pen and ink.[34] It is placed in a way that points to an intended association of content with the kneeling girl. It appears as the motivation for the abrupt turn of head and the object of the attentive look. The whole is not without a touch of humor, called forth by the nonchalance with which the girl balances the plate that is far too small for its grisly content. Scholars, fixated a priori on a biblical theme, seem to have driven this comic touch, which is heightened by the napkin bobbing on the plate, the overlong nose of the girl, and the plucked impression the eagle makes, from their consciousness.[35] Nevertheless, it must have been intended. The right arm is *not* designed to carry so heavy a load—as his "unburdened" attitude proves. The load, that is, the severed and so curiously flattened head, is an arbitrary addendum which causes a transformation of the content of the object being copied. But as an addendum it must be seen together with the two other additions, the eagle and the vase.[36] The result is a depiction of neither Judith nor Salome but a rebus in which "Judith" or "Salome" or "Holofernes" or "John" form one cipher among other ciphers.[37] It documents the creative need to make the copied object the carrier of a new, self-imposed expression.[38] Apparently the boy Michelangelo already took a rather distanced stance toward his models.

The Last Drawing

The London sketch of the Madonna (fig. 38) was never in danger of being doubted as a work by Michelangelo. For at no time was the possibility of its being viewed objectively darkened by false assumptions. The conformity of its individual style with the authenticated black-chalk sketches (figs. 23, 30–32, 35–37) is evident. In both cases we see the relatively broad and mellow strokes with their increasing and decreasing volume, the large range of stress values, the balanced relation of strokes drawn with minimal and maximum pressure and of shaded and unshaded areas, the heavy volume effect. But strange traits are mixed in with the familiar ones. The forces that otherwise guarantee an astonishing precision even in the smallest-size drawings here, in this 25.5-centimeter drawing, seem threatened by forces of destruction. The contour and hatching structures resemble a leaky conducting system in which the electricity crackles as it branches out.

The difference is alarming. It has nothing to do with a change of aesthetic attitude (as is so often claimed).[39] It is based on a disturbance of motor movement caused by tremor. The course of the contour strokes is anomalously discontinuous, waving, permeated here and there by abrupt breaks and varying pressure. Stroke crossings are to be seen only sporadically, axial relations between the end of one and the beginning of the following stroke not at all. Instead the continuity of the contour compounds is continually broken by marked axial shifts—a phenomenon that in this context indicates not so much a chronic compulsion to correct as the frequency of uncontrolled manual jerks that were transferred to the chalk during the slowing phases of the movement. But this discontinuity does not uniformly determine the stroke system. Along the outer left contour (as seen by the viewer) it appears to be more strongly prominent than in the other contour areas. Here strokes accumulate that have no visible

connection with each other and can be interpreted as components of the figural contour only on the basis of the bundled formation and their successive massing toward the right. They are apparently test strokes. As such they provide evidence about the intensity of the motor disturbance. They indicate that the chalk had to move into the purposeful contour course after several attempts before the shaking was under sufficient control to achieve innerly coherent stroke assemblages.

The actual assemblages look as if magnetic forces had prevented them from breaking apart. These forces are mainly certain reinforcing accents. Totally tuned to the manual jerking rhythm in their commalike shortness, they act, so to speak, as optical guiding marks. In addition, however, they fulfill the same task of three-dimensional definition as all of Michelangelo's contour reinforcements. Occurring mainly at the organically important points of articulation, they lend the figure a peculiarly heavy suppleness and—in combination with the shading—a volume that evokes a sense of massive weight. They thereby prove that Michelangelo continued to have an exceptionally clear conception of the human body.

As in the contours, the artist also tried in shading to counteract the uncontrolled twitchings of his hand by accelerating the tempo. The shading accordingly consists exclusively of more or less fully written-out spiral and zigzag stroke assemblages that are uniformly oriented. In contrast to Michelangelo's normal hatchings, these assemblages are composed of conspicuously short strokes. In this respect they resemble the hatchings of Clovio (figs. 81–83, 87–90) or Condivi (figs. 91–97). But in contrast to them they are characterized by a purposeful regulation of pressure and interval. Clearly differentiated in the main and recurrent phases, they are sometimes light, sometimes dark, sometimes tighter or looser, depending on the requirements of modeling or spatial construction. Their being short-phased is nothing more than the expression of an instinctive effort to adapt the main and recurrent phases of the to-and-fro movement to the rhythm of the manual jerks and in this way to outwit the tremor. In fact the lengths of the individual hatching strokes are subject to the volatile change that indicates the irregular aspect of the jerking rhythm. They were not completely controllable, and occasionally shoot beyond the goal assigned them by the contour (for example, the left thigh of the Madonna). Together with the hooks in the hatching structure they make visible the limits that were placed on the drawing efforts of a hand weak from age.

The Madonna sketch is the most striking but by far not the only representative of Michelangelo's drawing style in old age. The Oxford Pietà and apostle sketches (figs. 35–36) already show traces of a disturbed manual movement. Their contours are abruptly interrupted by larger or smaller jagged parts—and display a certain irregular rhythm. A larger eruption always follows several microscopically small eruptions. These discontinuities are of course minimal in comparison to those of the Madonna sketch. In the case of the Pietà and apostle sketches the involuntary jerks could still largely be caught in time and compensated for by a decisively quick and resolute movement of the chalk. They still had no influence on the habitual small size of the sketches. On the other hand, they seem to have become so strong by the time of the Oxford Annunciation sketch (fig. 37) that the necessity of counteracting them by increasing the tempo forced the artist to enlarge the room for movement considerably. In the case

of the Madonna sketch this room had to be enlarged even more in order to make a legible structure possible at all. The figure size (25.5 cm) thereby again drifted *nolens volens* into the range of those products of his apprenticeship years (fig. 3: 31.5 cm).

To judge from its blocklike statuesque appearance the sketch might have been created with reference to a sculpture.[40] Perhaps Michelangelo considered adorning his own tomb with such a sculpture.[41] Be that as it may—the sketch in any case appears to have some connection with work on the Rondanini Pietà. In the broken posture of the Madonna the presence of a burden heavier than the lively child is perceptible—a burden as oppressive as the thought of a dead man escaping the motherly embrace.

III

Some Victims of the Michelangelo Cult

5

Tommaso de' Cavalieri (ca. 1509/10–1587)

Michelangelo hated to use inflated language. To be sure, he did address the twenty-two-year-old Tommaso as "light of our century, unique in the world"—not to flatter, but because in his eyes Tommaso *was* that light.[1] He might have found it brighter than would have been the case had his own feelings at the time not burned so intently. But his feelings cannot be called unrealistic. For in addition to a noble title and a collection of artworks from antiquity Cavalieri possessed advantages that predestined him to attract the attention of Rome's artists and connoisseurs.[2] The "incomparable beauty of his body" was illuminated by "such endearingness of behavior and such shining intelligence and charm that he deserved and continues to deserve to be loved all the more the better one knows him" (Benedetto Varchi, 1549).[3] The friendship that grew out of the first meeting between the artist and the educated youth in the autumn of 1532 was in fact to become the longest of Michelangelo's life, surviving all his fluctuations of mood. The younger man received the lifelong feeling of being protected by a new fatherly love.

Tommaso was among the first members of the nobility to fulfill Castiglione's requirement that the perfect courtier must also "be able to draw and possess knowledge about the art of painting."[4] He had drawn even *before* their fateful meeting, and by his drawings awakened Michelangelo's special interest. In his earliest extant letter to Michelangelo (December 1532) Cavalieri mentions—in passing—"those works of mine that you have seen with your own eyes and on whose account you show me not a little affection" ("quelle opre mie che con uostri occhi hauete uiste, per le quali mostrate di mostrarmi non poca affectione").[5] They must have revealed a talent that seemed to the master worthy of fostering. And so it came to the instruction in drawing witnessed by Vasari,[6] in the course of which the famous quartet of highly finished drawings by Michelangelo—*Ganymede, Tityos,* the *Fall of Phaeton,* and the *Children's Bacchanal* (figs. 17, 19, 24–25)—was created.

For a long time Michelangelo scholars had a curious relationship to this quartet. They spoke of "presentation sheets" and coded love messages,[7] and thereby suggested that Cavalieri's role was merely that of a passive recipient whose talent and possible own productivity were not worth investigating. In 1964 I argued that the *Fall of Phaeton* version in Venice (fig. 66), which had been previously attributed to Michelangelo without reason, was a work of Cavalieri, and as such proved that master and pupil had worked together in drawing the antique subject.[8] But all this proof did was to start Tolnay thinking about Michelangelo's practice as a drawing instructor.[9] Otherwise it lapsed into *damnatio memoriae.*

The first to break this silence was Frommel. In his little book *Michelangelo und Tommaso dei Cavalieri*, published in 1979, he stated in an aside that the attribution of the drawing in Venice to Cavalieri was "not very convincing."[10] More convincing, apparently, were the conclusions drawn from the attribution, for he recapitulated them in the text of the book.[11] The public was thereby unexpectedly confronted with a "new" Cavalieri awakened from previous passivity to active life—a Cavalieri who discusses the themes to be drawn with his master, who dares to criticize his master's sketches, and who "also makes counterproposals for drawings." Frommel was of course unable to say what the latter looked like, but he did know where to look: "among the numerous drawings of Michelangelo's immediate successors."[12] In other words: anywhere but in the "Michelangelo" corpus.

The Solution of a "Homework Task"; or the Art of Making a Risen Christ out of a Crucified Haman

A black-chalk giant, 42 centimeters high (fig. 59) is found on the verso of the Casa Buonarroti sheet with Michelangelo's small-figure first sketch for the *Last Judgment* (fig. 30). "Magnificent" (Dussler),[13] "bellisimo" (Barocchi),[14] "superb" (Hartt),[15] of "masterful conception" and "sure execution," "qualitatively" equal to the "contemporaneous sheets for Cavalieri" (Dussler), it shows—with its "tragic-massive anatomy grubbed up from the inside out" (Berti)[16]—"the supremacy of Michelangelo's genius in his powers of imagination and construction" (Wilde).[17] In fact this "study after the living model" (Delacre)[18] is constructed with considerable crudeness. It is concerned with neither the laws of anatomy nor of movement. Nevertheless, it cannot have sprung from the "powers of imagination" alone. It is also based on Michelangelo's preliminary study for the Sistine Haman (figs. 9–11), out of which the draftsman attempted to make a Risen Christ by reversing the pose, changing the function of the leg propped against the tree into a standing leg, and turning the thorax to such an extent that the left shoulder and the left arm disappeared.[19] Of the latter all that remains visible, like a growth on the torso, is the pawlike little hand. The attempt attests to boldness, certainly, but also to a lack of distance with regard to the original. The parts that were literally copied (left leg and abdomen) turned out markedly better than the altered ones (right leg and thorax). Moreover, the figure is executed on the same scale as the Haman study (height from tip of the foot of the stretched-out leg to the

skull: 38 and 38.5 cm, respectively), even though the Casa Buonarroti sheet was rather unsuitable for a figure the size of the Hamn study. If this figure were not drawn in this giant format, which is inappropriate to the sketch character of the drawing, the contortions of the body would seem more tolerable, the proportions more harmonious, the signs of painstaking probing of the contours less obtrusive, and the scholars' descriptions would probably be cooler.

In any case the Archivio Buonarroti nude (fig. 60), which is only half as large, does not enjoy the many superlatives, even though it represents an improvement over the giant.[20] It is—as the numerous pentimenti prove—the result of several attempts to give the organism an inner coherence and a plausible movement, principally by harmonizing the positions of the right arm (whose first version immediately follows the giant) and the right leg, as well as the hip contour, with the exaggerated torsion of the torso. Its reduced size and the hastily sketched quality of its appearance can therefore not be interpreted as indicators of its having been produced before the giant. They signal instead that the draftsman in the meantime had become able to assimilate inwardly the model, Michelangelo's study for Haman.[21]

Not much was gained by doing so. Like the old figure, the new one looks like a mutant from a mad scientist's laboratory. Neither the reason for the spread-leg posture and the gesticulating arm nor the sense of exaggerated torsion are apparent. A reformulation was called for. It followed on a sheet in the Ashmolean Museum (fig. 62). With the suggestions of a sarcophagus and of a cover propped against its back wall, the drawing suggests an ambience for the figural action. And the downward-glancing little head and the upward-pointing index finger of the left hand even suggest a motivational context.[22] But the draftsman had achieved this result only after referring back to Michelangelo's *Tityos* (fig. 19), whose form must have seemed especially suitable as a model for a new mutation. On the verso of the Windsor sheet (fig. 61) he had traced the *Tityos* contours while changing the position of the lower arms and the bent leg and complemented the tracing with the outline sketch of a sarcophagus and the cover leaning against it.[23] Afterward he noticed that the mutation suffered from a disturbance of equilibrium, and that the exaggerated downward leaning of the figure appeared senseless. After a vain attempt to cure the second evil independently of the first—by drawing an upward-glancing face into the skull of the traced Tityos head—he took refuge in a subsidiary sketch placed to the right of the tracing. Like its companion's skull-face, this sketch again appears to have followed the giant (fig. 59), but instead of the forcefully contorted torso it has one viewed almost frontally.[24] Whether it immediately or intermediately paved the way to the Oxford drawing (fig. 62) is unimportant. In any case the Oxford drawing has the quality of a synthesis. It unites in itself the legs of the *Tityos* tracing (fig. 61) and—in improved and side-reversed form—the torso along with the hand holding the periclete of the giant (fig. 59) or the Archivio Buonarroti nude (fig. 60).

This synthesis remains artificial, for it reflects an inner contradiction between what the figure actually is doing and what it appears to want to do. The draftsman attempted to correct this contradiction on the spot by repeating the left arm and the right leg in an altered position. The arm correction was a false solution. It led to a mere duplication of the posture of the right arm, which is of course not visible, but which is determined by the position of the hand. A happier idea was to replace the bent right leg with an outstretched one. This put an end to the senseless leg-spreading and paved the way for a final solution to the problem of the figure's pose, which was worked out in a highly finished drawing now in the Uffizi (fig. 63). This drawing shows for the first time the body in a hovering state. The draftsman succeeded at carrying off the trick not least because he found the "correct" models. In shaping the torso, left arm, and head he continued to follow Michelangelo's Haman (fig. 9–11). But the legs and the right arm (including the Paraclete) were, in part literally, quoted from the master's *Christ in Limbo* (fig. 14–15)—a model that up to then had been consulted only in passing, for example, in the completion of the right arm of the *Tityos* tracing (fig. 61) or in the new version of the right leg of the Oxford figure (fig. 62). In order to round out the process, all that was needed was an improved presentation of the sarcophagus. Nevertheless, the draftsman was content with executing it in the same far too small form in which it appears in figures 61 and 62.[25]

That the laborious sketching and construction process ended in a highly finished drawing (fig. 63) depicting the isolated figure of a Risen Christ makes any further question of purpose superfluous.[26] What we have here is a pupil's attempts to solve a "homework task," and not documents of professional preliminary work. But only Cavalieri can be considered as the author of these attempts. He alone had, as owner of the *Tityos* sheet (figs. 19, 61), the opportunity and the right to use its verso for his own purposes. He alone enjoyed, ca. 1532–33, that unconstrained intimacy with the master that explains why the first attempt (fig. 59) coexists with a Michelangelo sketch from the end of 1533 (fig. 30) on the other side (now the recto) of the sheet, the second (fig. 60) with a letter of 19 September 1532 addressed to Michelangelo

on the verso,[27] and the fourth (fig. 62) with a sketch for the reliquary of San Lorenzo sketched by Michelangelo between October 1531 and October 1532, also on the verso of the sheet.[28] In fact no one at that time except Cavalieri could expect the unusual: that the master would react to a pupil's attempts with a drawing of his own.

The result was the highly finished drawing of a Risen Christ by Michelangelo that survives in two facsimile copies (one of them fig. 16). They relate to the drawings discussed above in the same way that Michelangelo's *Ganymede* and *Fall of Phaeton* (figs. 17, 24) relate to the compositions in the Uffizi (fig. 58) and in Venice (fig. 66). A condensation of the same figures that Tommaso had already utilized (figs. 9–11, 14, 19), Michelangelo's highly finished drawing acted as a model solution that enabled the pupil to evaluate his own performance objectively. To what degree it took into account Tommaso's own efforts can be seen in the shape of the sarcophagus and in the way it relates to Christ's legs. Both were linked to the Uffizi drawing (fig. 63). Michelangelo did what has always been the goal of every empathetic teacher. He retrieved the latent potential from what was given so that the pupil could recognize it in drawing as that which he himself had striven for.

The Appropriation of Physiognomy

Among the numerous drawings of heads in the "Michelangelo" corpus that are classified, to use a phrase of Vasari's, as "teste divine," the three examples on the recto and verso of Windsor sheet no. 12764 (fig. 64) and on Ashmolean sheet no. 10 (fig. 65) occupy a special place. There is something androgynous about them, and in two regards. Their subject seems to be neither clearly masculine nor feminine, neither completely idealized nor pictorially "realistic." Their execution arrived at a point where the differences between the species of drawing are obscured and the question "highly finished drawing or study?" appears to be unanswerable.[29]

All three drawings seem to depict the same face—a relatively narrow face with a long, straight nose slightly arched forward at the tip, a sensitive mouth that swings into pronounced dimples, dreamy eyes, and a small but forceful chin parted by a clear cleft. It is more carefully drawn than the headdress, neck, and shoulders and lies in its roughly formed surroundings like a jewel in a setting that is too coarse. Its individuality exceeds the bounds of the "teste divine" framework. Especially in the case of the Windsor drawing (fig. 64) the asymmetry of the eyes and the lips, pursed as if about to whisper, indicate the presence of a living face. Apparently what we have here are attempts at portraiture.

The first, prematurely broken-off attempt is located on the present-day verso of the Windsor sheet. The position of the head corresponds exactly to that of the recto drawing (fig. 64)—with the exception of a scarcely noticeable difference in the tilt of the head. Curiously, however, the contours of its neck and shoulder appear more natural and anatomically correct than on the recto. On the recto, the neck relates to the face like an artificial base. It seems too long and at the same time too thick.[30] The neck of the Oxford head (fig. 65) is similar. Neither its size nor its twistedness conforms to the well-proportioned face. In both cases its unnatural form, in combination with the fantastic headdress, has the unexpected effect of turning the apparently masculine face into an androgynous "testa divina." But this effect was obviously intentional. What appears to be an attempt at portraiture in reference to the face is, in totality, the product of an encounter with Michelangelo's ideal heads, or more precisely, with the *Cleopatra* created for Cavalieri (fig. 13). In one case (fig. 64) it is the rightward-turning view and the perspective of the head, the oblique view of the neck, and the cheek straps of the cap that correspond to the *Cleopatra*. In the other case (fig. 65) it is the size of the figure, the forcefulness of the head-turning (which so contradicts the stoic peacefulness of the face), and the swollen neck musculature. In both cases the excessive length of the neck matches that of the *Cleopatra*.

The Windsor drawings and the Oxford drawing appear to be the only surviving documents of a free exploration of Michelangelo's *Cleopatra*. That they were created by the recipient and owner of this famous *testa* is probable for this reason alone. Nevertheless, two additional reasons speak in favor of Cavalieri's authorship. One is the identity of the faces, the other the varying intensity of the presence of the model. The face of the Windsor drawings (fig. 64) is more subtle, more lively, more realistic than that of the Oxford drawing (fig. 65). Indeed, it appears to be even more correctly reproduced, although its slightly turned face was harder to master than the face in profile. The Oxford face has curious inconsistencies: a distorted perspective that causes the face to look flatter in the lower parts, in contrast to the rotundity of the neck; an excessively protruding left eyelid without a corresponding eye; a swollen cheek; and a bulbously over-accentuated lower jaw. These inconsistencies largely exclude the possibility that the drawing was executed directly from a model. They identify the Oxford face as a pastiche—executed on the basis of the Windsor face. But only a draftsman who can see his model in half-profile but not in profile view, that is, the self-portraitist, needs such a basis.

Paradoxically, the half-closed eyes confirm that the basis of the Oxford face—the Windsor face (fig. 64)—was actually a self-portrait. They are the only parts that appear imprecise, even defective, in spite of multiple revisions. That fact can be explained only as the result of post-facto mutation. The eyelids and pupils appear to have been drawn into the face as an afterthought—to heighten the idealizing effect mentioned above. But this presupposes that the model could be seen only with open eyes during the act of portrayal. It implies that the identity of the drawn face is to be found in the draftsman's mirror.

In spite of their self-portrait character, the drawn faces look like earthly siblings of the ideal figures (Bacchus, Pietà in Saint Peter's, David, Apollo, Dying Slave, Sistine ignudi, and so forth) that Michelangelo drew and carved in his youth. Their model must have corresponded to the artist's ideal of beauty; and for that very reason, the model was most likely Cavalieri,[31] who was about twenty-three when he stepped into Michelangelo's field of vision. Noble birth, wealth, and good connections had shielded him from the iniquities and troubles of life, and presumably had preserved the youthful softness of his features.

According to Vasari, Cavalieri was the only living person who enjoyed the privilege of being portrayed by Michelangelo (with black chalk).[32] His "incomparable beauty" may have contributed to that honor, but it is not an explanation. At other times Michelangelo also came across strikingly handsome youths (for example, Febo di Poggio) without becoming a portraitist. That he did so in this one instance presupposes a unique set of circumstances, which was presumably supplied by Cavalieri's attempts at self-portraiture. On the basis of their relationship to the *Cleopatra*, the drawings were probably done in the year of Cavalieri's drawing instruction (1533) and accordingly under the watchful eyes of the master. In fact, to conclude from a contemporary description,[33] Michelangelo's portrait of Cavalieri shared several conspicuous characteristics with the drawings of the Windsor and Oxford sheets. First, it depicted the portrayed person "vestito all'antica" ("in antique clothing")—that is, idealized. Second, it was executed in black chalk. Third, its execution seems to have had the same contrast between a high degree of finish (face) and sketchiness (bust) as the Windsor and Oxford drawings. For even after praising the "divine" treatment of "those beautiful eyes, mouth and nose . . . seemingly [drawn] by the hand of an angel," the author of this description found himself unable to identify the object the portrayed person holds in his hand—"un ritratto, o medaglia che si sia" ("an image or a medal or something"). Unclearly sketched as it was, this object can scarcely have been selected simply to indicate Tommaso's interests in antiquity. Like every other material attribute in Michelangelo's works it presumably functioned as a *motivans*. But if the object was meant to motivate a lowered gaze such as that in the Windsor and Oxford drawings (which lacks motivation), then Michelangelo's Cavalieri portrait must have followed the same didactic purpose as his *Risen Christ* (fig. 16).

However that may be, one thing is certain: Michelangelo drew the Cavalieri portrait not for himself but for Cavalieri.[34] But he appears to have assimilated the beloved features by this unique act of portrayal to such an extent that he subsequently (in the summer of 1553 or 1534), either consciously or unconsciously, lent them to his marble *Giuliano de' Medici*. The *Giuliano* has the same physiognomic characteristics as the Windsor and Oxford drawings (figs. 64–65), the deep eyes with the heavy lower lids, the girl-like fine mouth with the dimples, the small, energetic chin. With the exception of the *Brutus* bust, it is Michelangelo's only sculptural work stamped with the uniqueness of a living model. Compared to the *Giuliano*, its partner *Lorenzo* seems like the embodiment of an abstract idea.[35]

The Proving Time: Cavalieri and the Last Judgment

Apart from the four months between late June and late October 1533, which he spent in Florence seeing to the completion of the Medici tombs, Michelangelo had the whole year free of urgent obligations. He was at leisure to attune himself to the thoughts and archaeological interests of his friend and to occasionally set a small crown on Cavalieri's attempts at drawing. Michelangelo's *Risen Christ* (fig. 16) and his lost Cavalieri portrait, his *Ganymede* (fig. 17), *Fall of Phaeton* (fig. 24) and *Children's Bacchanal* (fig. 25),[36] but probably also his *Tityos* (fig. 19)—the only one among these jewels that cannot be connected to any surviving preliminary efforts on the part of the pupil—all appear to be the offshoots of a lovingly critical engagement with Cavalieri's drawings, documents of a pedagogical Eros that allowed him to forget time and his own concerns.

Their production broke off abruptly about one month after the commission for the *Last Judgment* (22 September 1533), which demanded the commitment of his whole person. Michelangelo was no longer able to concern himself with his friend's favorite topics. But he made a virtue of this necessity. He gave Tommaso the opportunity to take active part in the accomplishment of the great task. In what form this participation occurred can be seen from those sketches and studies

for the fresco that must have come directly from the artist's workshop, but which, to judge from the style of their figures, composition, and draftsmanship, were not by the master himself.

Among them are the two composition sketches: in Bayonne, Musée Bonnat, no. 1217 (fig. 67), and in the Uffizi, no. 170S (fig. 68). The first—it is claimed—depicts Michelangelo's original idea.[37] Presupposing the correctness of the attribution,[38] it must in fact have been created *before* Michelangelo's Casa Buonarroti sketch (fig. 30), for it shows the traditional "cloud theater" (Aretino)[39]—a topos which the Casa Buonarroti sketch had long since outgrown. But if the Bayonne sketch did precede the Casa Buonarroti sketch, the following points remain inexplicable:

1. why it depicts only the heavenly zone instead of the whole;
2. why its average figure size is approximately 30 percent larger than those of Michelangelo's authenticated *Last Judgment* sketches (figs. 30–32);[40]
3. why some of its figures—in contrast to those of the Casa Buonarroti sketch—already have hatching and contours appropriate to the study stage;
4. why two of the figures (the two frontmost seated figures) are found in the fresco, whereas none has any correspondence in the authenticated sketches.

In contrast to the Bayonne sketch, the Uffizi sketch (fig. 68) must have been drawn *after* Michelangelo's Casa Buonarroti sketch (fig. 30)—regardless of its author. For it presupposes not only the Casa Buonarroti's unorthodox overall compositional scheme, but also its relationship between Christ and Mary or the martyrs of the right side.[41] But if it was created after the Casa Buonarroti sketch, the following—presupposing Michelangelo's authorship[42]—remain mysterious:

1. why it shows such a small number of clearly sketched figures despite the extracted character of the composition;
2. why some of the martyrs already appear in the poses of certain fresco figures, while the Christ-Mary pair still reflect a stage anterior to the Casa Buonarroti sketch (fig. 30);
3. why Christ has a beard, while in the Casa Buonarroti sketch he is beardless as in the fresco itself;
4. why obvious differences in size and a more additive arrangement predominate in the nearly finished martyr group of the foreground than in all authenticated composition sketches by Michelangelo.

The other unauthenticated drawings—Musée Bonnat no. 681 (fig. 70), British Museum no. 1895-9-15-518rv (fig. 32: first and third drawing layer), Casa Buonarroti no. 47F and 69F-rv, Windsor no. 12776rv (fig. 31: torso study; fig. 71)—make the confusion complete. They point only to relationships among themselves, but not to authenticated drawings (an exception is the four studies in fig. 71). The smaller (upside down) of the two erased sketches that together constitute the first drawing campaign in figure 32 (it is nevertheless almost twice as large as the small figures of Michelangelo's composition sketches) depicts a half-standing, half-sitting nude with an outstretched raised right arm and a downward-glancing face. It is obviously meant to be a judging Christ figure.[43] As such he appears to have played a role as intermediary between the Christ of the Bayonne sketch (fig. 67) and that of the Uffizi sketch (fig. 68), to whose size he corresponds.[44] His partner, the giant sitting nude, can only confirm this. For he—as his leg position proves—is formally even more closely connected with these two Christ figures.[45] But if the figures of the first drawing campaign in figure 32 mark the transition from the Bayonne to the Uffizi sketch, then the latter must also have been created even before the authenticated composition sketch that constitutes the second drawing campaign in figure 32 and, although it presupposes the Casa Buonarroti sketch (fig. 30), it must have been created independently of it.[46] This excludes any possibility of locating the genesis of the two Bayonne sketches (figs. 67, 70) and the Uffizi sketch (fig. 68) within the designing process that led from the Casa Buonarroti sketch (fig. 30) via the Windsor (fig. 31) and London sketches (fig. 32) to the fresco.[47]

The twisted torso of the large erased sitting nude (fig. 32), who together with the legs is a mirror image of the Bayonne *Christ* (fig. 67), is not only inclined forward, but also markedly to the right. The first attempts to fix the position of the left arm took no account of this inclination. Only in what appears to be the final arm did the torso receive adequate support. This version of the arm was slapped on to the body haphazardly. It depicts an extremely short upper arm, a lower arm dangling from it, and the indication of a hand flatly lying on the imaginary ground. A similar supporting arm attached to a similar chest-and-shoulder joint is the object of a study on the upper left edge of the Casa Buonarroti sheet no. 69F-verso (fig. 69); it is apparently a study of the critical part of a new, side-reversed version of the London sitting nude.

The head study located at the lower edge of the same Casa Buonarroti sheet (fig. 69) also seems to have proceeded from this sitting nude. To judge from its peripheral position it must, like the supporting arm study, have been created at a time when the sheet was already occupied by the sitting torso,

the two knee studies, and the nude seen from the rear that is freely quoted from a guard in Michelangelo's *Resurrection* sketch (figs. 27–28).[48] It probably immediately preceded the supporting arm study (which had to take preference with an even smaller space). For it also appears to have been conceived for a new version of the sitting nude, but for a new version seen from the same viewpoint. When the thought of reversing the sitting nude occurred, the head study became the basis of a mirror projection whose result is the same-sized head in red chalk on the Casa Buonarroti sheet no. 47F. This red-chalk head, however, never achieved the intended integration with the supporting arm study. Instead it led to the construction of two other heads, again drawn in the same large size. These heads are located on the verso of precisely that London sheet whose recto (fig. 32) includes the initial figure, the large sitting nude! They still have the same anatomically warped modeling with slanting hatching lattices as the head in figure 69. The misconstruction of the eyes has become even more obvious.[49]

The London sheet was accordingly occupied with studies for individual figures of the *Last Judgment* even before Michelangelo had drawn his compositional sketch (fig. 32) on it. Who should be surprised that of these studies not even the two heads created in such a complicated manner have an approximate correspondence in the fresco? What is more amazing is that this lack of correspondence does not likewise apply to the supporting arm and the small torso study in figure 69. The former finds its equivalent motif in the fresco in the largely hidden figure below the outstretched right arm of the so-called John the Baptist (among the group of saints to the right, at the level of Christ's head),[50] the latter in the fully visible figure above Saint Blaise and to the left of Simon of Cyrene.[51] This fact appears unintentionally to support the attribution (just carried ad absurdum) of the whole group of drawings to Michelangelo. Whoever is responsible for the fresco figures should indeed—or so one would think—also be responsible for the corresponding studies.

But the difficulty once again begins with the chronology. The small torso study, to judge from its position on the sheet, was drawn before the supporting arm and head study. For it is linked to the closest apostles in the left and right foreground of the Bayonne sketch (fig. 67)—two figures that are freely cited from the same *Resurrection* sketch (figs. 27–28) by Michelangelo from which the small nude seen from the rear is drawn (they each depict a version of the guard sitting on the edge of the sarcophagus). The two knee studies also seem to be linked to the Bayonne sketch. They correspond to the left knee of the Christ figure, which is in urgent need of fuller study.[52] But if the torso and knee studies were drawn with the intention of better articulating what was sketched on the Bayonne sheet, then they must have been created even *before* the large nude figures of the London sheet (fig. 32) and before the Uffizi sketch (fig. 68), therefore also before Michelangelo's two partial composition sketches (figs. 31 and 32). Presupposing the correctness of the current attribution, we would once again stand before the paradoxical situation of Michelangelo's having begun with the execution of detail studies even before his overall design for the fresco had been fixed![53]

The torso study of the Casa Buonarroti sheet (fig. 69) at first became—like the study of a head added later—the basis for a reversed figure. This version completed to a full figure is the nude seen from the rear in the foreground of the second Bayonne sketch (fig. 70). This nude seen from the rear again has a precise equivalent in Michelangelo's fresco (St. Andrew, i.e., the figure of the martyr with a cross between John the Baptist and Mary), although the sketched group as a whole has nothing to do formally with the fresco. It is impossible that the sketch could be by Michelangelo.[54] Compared with his wide-ranging, precisely formulated, dynamic combinations of small figures (figs. 27–32), it looks like a spatially disparate conglomeration of large, defectively constructed figures. The close connection of its nude seen from the rear to the fresco must therefore have a different reason than that the draftsman and the painter were one and the same person. The same applies to the two frontmost apostles of the first Bayonne sketch (fig. 67); the large sitting nude of the London sheet (fig. 32), which anticipates in reversed position the pose of Saint Lawrence; the supporting arm study of the Casa Buonarroti sheet (fig. 69); and some martyrs of the Uffizi sketch (fig. 68)—all of which have close approximations in the fresco. The most obvious reason for these approximations would be that all these drawn figures played a role in the genesis of the painted figures similar to that which Cavalieri's drawings of the *Risen Christ* (figs. 59–63), the *Ganymede* (fig. 58), the *Fall of Phaeton* (fig. 66), and the *Children's Bacchanal* played in the genesis of the corresponding highly finished drawings by Michelangelo (figs. 16–17, 24–25). The whole group of drawings must accordingly be by Cavalieri. In any case no one but him would have had the opportunity to express his ideas about the future fresco at the same time as the master and in part on the same sheets that Michelangelo himself used.

In fact precisely the earliest drawings of this group (figs. 67–68; fig. 31: large nude sketches) are closely connected with motifs found in Cavalieri's *Fall of Phaeton* (fig. 66), the pupil's first larger composition. The Christ figure and two of the right background figures of the Bayonne sketch (fig. 67) can be identified as derivatives of the Jupiter there. The front-most apostle to the left appears to have been developed from the upside-down figure of Phaeton, the excitedly gesticulating one to the outer right from the river god (or more precisely: from the outermost heliad in the partial sketch on the Teyler Museum sheet A31-recto).[55] Even the Mary of the Uffizi sketch (fig. 68), with her half nervously bowed, half aggressive froglike posture, can scarcely deny her descent from the shrieking group of heliads.[56]

The detail studies on the recto of the Casa Buonarroti sheet no. 69F (Tolnay, bib. 319, no. 91r) and the verso of the Windsor sheet no. 12776 (fig. 71) form a case in themselves. The studies of the latter refer to parts of three neighboring figures of the resurrection region in the *Last Judgment*.[57] It is impossible that these painted figures are based on Cavalieri's sketches, for, without exception, the corresponding embryonic forms are found in a work of Michelangelo's, namely his composition sketch on the recto of the Windsor sheet (fig. 31). The four preliminary studies can accordingly—one would like to think—be only either Michelangelo originals or copies after them. The first possibility is excluded in view of the irrational manner of their distribution over the sheet, which prevents any synthesis of what belongs together. The second possibility, on the other hand, founders because symptoms characteristic of most copies are lacking. The contours betray a cautious, extremely conscious movement, but none that is so inhibited as to be chopped into small pieces. They differ from the contours of their neighbors, the two previously drawn sketches of individual figures, only in the more differentiated character of their course.

The large study of two legs (fig. 71) indicates the way out of this deadend. It is internally disparate. The right and left legs fit together neither in terms of perspective, nor in terms of structure or size. An anatomical connection is lacking. Moreover, the foot of the left, smaller, and more "realistic" leg was drawn into the already existing calf of the overlong, more crudely structured right leg. The left leg must accordingly have been studied separately from the right one and added to it after the fact. However much such an additive procedure contradicts Michelangelo's holistic thinking,[58] it appears to have been typical for Cavalieri. The detail studies of the Windsor and Casa Buonarroti sheets can thus be regarded as attempts by the pupil to verify the structure and posture of figures as they appeared in certain of Michelangelo's sketches (figs. 31–32) through detailed study of the model. They possibly even had the purpose of relieving the master of part of the copious study work for the fresco.[59]

Faced with the torso study on the recto of the Casa Buonarroti sheet no. 69F, Michelangelo scholars have repeatedly searched for a corresponding sitting figure in the fresco and been frustrated at being unable to find it.[60] They would have done better to look closely first at the study. However unambiguously its subject appears as sitting, it is certain that what produces the impression of sitting (the right upper calf) was treated secondarily. The draftsman gave his principal attention to the torso and arms. But the torso is—as Panofsky noticed[61]—fixed in a posture that a sitting person would not assume if he could help it. Bent at the hip and nevertheless unusually long, with a stout, steeply upright thorax and a sunken-in abdomen, it expresses a condition in which activity and passivity can no longer be kept apart. That is—as Brugnoli recognized[62]—in principle the same posture that characterizes the torso of the fresco figure to which the study of legs and the study for the lower right arm in figure 71 refer.[63] Now, if we accept that the legs and arms of this fresco figure had been studied separately, then the corresponding torso must have been studied separately as well. But if a living model was used at all, it would have to have been a sitting model, since the omission of the legs is otherwise inexplicable. The figure represented in the fresco is accordingly identical with the figure referred by the draftsman of the torso study.[64] In fact the arm study associated with the torso study relates to the hand study in figure 71 like a large extract to a small extract. Like the hand study, it must refer to the right arm of the demon who tries to pull down the resurrected dead—studied in the torso and arm studies of the Uffizi sheet and the legs and arm studies of the Windsor sheet (fig. 71)—by the legs. Consequently, the detail drawings distributed on the two sheets together form a closed set.

With the above discussion in mind, the history of the development and execution of the *Last Judgment* concept probably looks somewhat more earthly and more human than the myth of a lonely brooding titan would have it. Apparently the conception began with both of the two unequal friends attempting to put his vision of the whole of the idea on paper (figs. 30 and 67). Even this early step showed how much master and pupil were attuned to each other's imaginations. Both proceeded, each in his own way, from experiences they had gained in their common occupation with the theme of the *Fall of Phaeton* (figs. 23–24, 66). It was only to be expected that Cavalieri would fall behind with his first attempt at an overall composition (fig. 67), which he did in two ways—through the conventionality and the piecemeal character of his overall design. He was forced, in order to keep pace with the master, to appropriate Michelangelo's overall concept expressed in the Casa Buonarroti sketch (fig. 30) and to tailor his later sketches (figs. 68, 70, and others) to it in some way or other. Nevertheless, Cavalieri's own prelimi-

nary conception paled to the extent that he appropriated Michelangelo's (figs. 31–32). It is thus all the more astonishing that his participation outlasted the end of the sketching stage. In fact his participation became—as the studies of the Casa Buonarroti sheet no. 69F (recto) and of the Windsor sheet (fig. 71) attest—part of a regular cooperation. The psychic prerequisites were presumably created by the master. He entrusted his pupil with the execution of certain detail tasks such as the final transformation of individual figural sketches into more fully articulated studies. But this was the least of what Michelangelo did to encourage Cavalieri's talent and self-confidence. His most important pedagogical measure consisted once more in identifying and developing further everything in his adept pupil's efforts that seemed perfectible. And so in the end he gave Cavalieri the unique satisfaction of being able to view the completed fresco through the eyes of a co-creator. For at least ten of the fresco figures—among them such important ones as Lawrence, Andrew (left next to Mary), and Simon of Cyrene—appear to be Cavalieri's ideas that Michelangelo thought through to their final form. No poem or letter, no matter how heartfelt, could better prove how seriously the artist took the efforts of his talented and favorite pupil.

Cavalieri's Figure and Composition Style

If the drawings discussed here were lined up next to each other, they would probably be immediately recognizable as the works of a pupil because of the extreme differences in the sizes of the figures. These differences are irrational. That the first sketch for the *Risen Christ* (fig. 59) was executed more carefully than the second one (fig. 60) is no explanation for its being more than twice as large. Otherwise the relatively carefully contoured and still crudely hatched stepping nude in figure 71 would also have to be twice as large as the outline sketch that coexists with it. But here the ratio is reversed, the outline sketch (approx. 22 cm) is nearly twice as large as the stepping nude (approx. 13 cm). The same discrepancy in size is found even between drawings equivalent in type or purpose, drawings such as the two sketches of nudes which constitute the first layer of the London sheet (fig. 32), or between the torso study on the recto and that on the verso (fig. 69) of Casa Buonarroti no. 69F. What we have here is a typical sign of lack of routine. Whereas the professional artist consciously or unconsciously scales the sizes of his sketches and studies according to an inner norm developed in practice, the beginner is initially forced to determine the size of what is to be drawn on a case by case basis. His "decision" is chiefly influenced by external factors (for example, by the size of the model or of the sheet), while his underdeveloped sense of estimating by eye represents an additional handicap. In the present case the sometimes grotesque differences in size within one and the same composition sketch (fig. 68: martyrs), but above all the many discrepancies in the proportions of the figures (fig. 58: Ganymede's legs) attest to this.

The placement of the figures on the page also appears to be subject to the same arbitrariness as the sizes of the figures. Cavalieri's sketches and studies appear to "swim" on the surface of the sheet, just like Clovio's (figs. 82, 88) or Condivi's (fig. 91). Their axial relationships seem unstable and arbitrary. The two head studies on the verso of London sheet no. 1895-9-15-518 (Tolnay, bib. 319, no. 350v) seem to constitute an exception. Thanks to their simple similarity, their spatial closeness, the identical angle at which the heads are inclined, and their diagonal arrangement, they form an ensemble not dissimilar to Michelangelo's study combinations (figs. 6–11). Significantly, however, the connection is achieved at the cost of their material autonomy. The lower head seems to be penetrating into the domain of the upper one. Moreover, since it is smaller than the upper one, it seems to be in the same plane, not in the foreground—an effect that is underlined by its flatness-accentuating profile position and which produces the impression that its missing skull had been consumed by the upper head.

The inner contradiction signals a certain weakness of the pupil's ability to visualize space. Even the individual figures as such seem flat when measured against the spatial implications of their postures. Their doughy volume is unfolded—as the rump shapes show, for example—as broadness rather than as three-dimensionality. The feet of the small nude in figure 71 seem as parallel to the picture plane as those of a tightrope walker. The left arm of the torso study on the recto of Uffizi sheet no. 69F (Tolnay, bib. 319, no. 91r) seems to be veritably glued to the torso, although its connection to the lower right leg indicates that it is stretching forward. Frequently, errors in perspective also contribute to this kind of flattening effect (compare the relationship between the figures and sarcophagus in figures 61–62 or the legs of the river god in figure 66). No wonder that the combination of figures in the composition sketches (figs. 66–68, 70) can hardly expand the sense of three-dimensionality in spite of the many overlappings. In the case of the *Fall of Phaeton* (fig. 66) the falling figures and terrestrial figures are disposed in one and the same thin plane of space—their collision seems unavoidable. Even a composition like figure 67, which seems to be so

closely related to Michelangelo's spacious *Resurrection* sketch (figs. 27–28), reveals, when examined closely, disparate characteristics. Instead of being enthroned in the middle of the circle of attendants, Christ sits next to its front periphery (in the first version he sat practically in the "corridor"). His badly aimed gesture of damnation appears to hit the heads of the frontmost apostles of the right semicircle.[65]

Such flaws, typical for a pupil, are of course balanced by the efficiency of an abstract organizing principle that treats the compositional elements like the parts of a work of architecture. It expresses itself in a demonstrative schematism of the symmetrical axes system and lends certain sketches (figs. 66–67) something of the rigid logic of quattrocento paintings. Curiously this principle seems to have made a lasting impression on the aging Michelangelo—perhaps precisely because it was so diametrically opposed to his genuine way of conceiving. It influenced the development of the composition both of the *Fall of Phaeton* (figs. 23–24) and of the *Last Judgment* (fig. 30, fresco). When, around 1545, the artist stood before the task of finding the adequate symbolic pictorial form for a mystery that transcends time, it became the determining compositional factor.

In his *Pietà* drawing created for Vittoria Colonna Michelangelo also reached back to one of Cavalieri's Christ figures (Bayonne, Musée Bonnat no. 650 recto; Tolnay, bib. 319, no. 337r)—the same one that had inspired him in 1533 to the figure of the drunken man in his *Children's Bacchanal* (fig. 25). The reference was no accident. What the *Fall of Phaeton* in Venice (fig. 66) and the Bayonne sketch for the *Last Judgment* (fig. 67) show on a large scale this Christ shows on a small one. With its right-angle limb axes and the symmetry of its bent arms it has the effect, in spite of the diagonal projection of the legs, of a plastic ornament braced into the surface—best suited to become the center point of a symbolic depiction without activity. Of course in Cavalieri's case this effect was unintentional. The parallelism, the right angles, and symmetry of the limb axes appear to have been congenital characteristics of the figures drawn by him. They lead to a permanent stasis of the action. The bodies are, so to speak, frozen in their positions and bound to an abstract relief ground. Their actions seem to be ahistorical, fixated in a moment in time that is sealed off from past and future (figs. 58, 66). Whether the Risen Christ in figure 63 moves upward or downward, whether the small nude in figure 71 is walking or standing, whether the attendants in figure 67 are engaged in private conversations or a public event—the viewer can decide only insofar as an answer is suggested by the iconographic context.

Occasionally the momentary quality of the actions is made more potent by a studied wildness of the gestures. Ganymede's arm and leg contortions in figure 58, the contoured torso torsion of the Risen Christ in figure 59, the hysterical gestures of the heliads and river god in the *Fall of Phaeton* (fig. 66) and some apostles in the Bayonne sketch (fig. 67), or Mary's position in figure 68, where she crouches as if to jump, carry a trace of the scurrilous into the already anecdotally colored reality of the picture. However little such affected touches might fit the particular iconographic context, they are comprehensible as substitute formulas for the missing expression of the vitality that informs the master's figures (for a similar phenomenon in the case of Condivi, see chapter 6). At the same time, however, they reveal a special sense for the psychological and for the uniqueness of the individual—a talent that led to accentuation of the physiognomies even in the first sketching stages (fig. 66: group on the ground; fig. 67) and which found its most complete expression in the diverse head studies (figs. 64–65, 69).

Cavalieri's Drawing Style

Harder to comprehend than his peculiar figure and composition style is Cavalieri's style of drawing as such. Not only the whole figures (sizes), but even the individual strokes have a protean character. Almost from drawing to drawing, indeed even within one and the same sketch (fig. 71: large nude), they have opposing characteristics—hard/soft, sharp/dull, thin/wide, gentle/vigorous, doughy/granulated, and so forth. Nevertheless, this fact appears to owe more to the instruments and how they were held than to kinetic causes. The draftsman sometimes used dull and sometimes sharply pointed chalk and changed from one to the other (just as he changed from black to red chalk or vice versa), occasionally in the course of one and the same drawing campaign (figs. 59–63). At the same time he changed the position of his hand while drawing so frequently that precisely those contours and hatching that were drawn with rather dull pieces of chalk are full of especially marked contrasts in hardness (fig. 62: torso and upper right arm; fig. 71: legs study). Both kinds of behavior are characteristic for the beginner. No pupil finds the medium appropriate to his need for expression and the way of holding the medium most propitious to kinetic economy from the start. He must discover them through practice. But in the process those stroke characteristics that are specifically determined by movement will remain constant. Thus, in the present case the individual strokes are for the most part

thread-like and flat. They resemble those of Mini's drawings (figs. 50–56) or of Clovio's (figs. 81–83, 87–90).

Although the individual strokes remain threadlike, there are considerable differences in tonality between them even in the most primitive contour formations (fig. 60; fig. 66: group on the ground; fig. 71: large nude). As the drawing becomes more detailed, these differences become more marked through the addition of forceful strengthening strokes. Superficially, many of these (fig. 71: small nude) astonishingly resemble Michelangelo's contour strengthenings (fig. 23: river god), but in contrast to them they work more to decorate the outline than to enhance the possibilities of spatial definition. The reason for this is obvious: the distribution of lightly drawn and heavily emphasized strokes occurs—as in most of the non-Michelangelo drawings of the "Michelangelo" corpus—independent of haptic notions; it depends only on a need to make the contour lines more precise.

It is a matter of course that the first phases in Cavalieri's sketching processes were determined almost exclusively by formula strokes. Of sometimes scroll-like, sometimes segmented course, as a whole these formulas result in quite clumsy anthropoids with wide torsos, "hanging" rumps, arms consisting of ringlets, and lower legs that come to a point at the bottom and are usually tied off by zigzagged feet abbreviations. But these strokes are astonishingly durable, as in the case of Cellini (figs. 72–80). Over wide stretches the corrections are mere pentimento duplications (fig. 62: torso and left leg). Their massing leads now and then to ornamentally undulated contours that are difficult to justify anatomically (fig. 58: Ganymede's left leg; figs. 59–60: torso contours)—the equivalents of those "arcades" of which the contours of the two knee studies in figure 69 consist. It is no accident that figures like the heliad in figure 66, the Christ figure in figure 68, or the large nude in figure 71 remain stuck in the same primitive stage of development as some of Michelangelo's single-railed outline sketches (fig. 27: cover figure), although almost every single section of contour has been revised—sometimes several times.

To judge from the slow reduction of the formula strokes during the process of figural definition, the draftsman found it difficult to render the details of his ideas according to his intention. Even the drawings of individual figures disintegrate into unequally defined areas (fig. 58: torso, left hand; fig. 60: legs; fig. 63: upper and lower right arm; fig. 32: torso, left arm or legs of the large seated nude). In the case of the composition drawings the imbalance is sometimes so crude that it makes identification of the type of drawing difficult (fig. 66). There can be no talk here of a simultaneous, overall vision characteristic of Michelangelo's contemporaneous authenticated composition sketches (figs. 23, 27–32). Even the seemingly so spontaneously designed *Last Judgment* sketch in figure 67 turns out to be an elaborate compilation on closer inspection. The contours of the attendants always break off at the places where they meet the contours of the neighboring figure in front of them. They thereby indicate that the "overlapped" figures were composed successively from right to left (left group) and from left to right (right group) onto the frontmost figures. This un-Michelangelesque-like procedure nevertheless had the advantage of effectively disguising the narrow scope of what was to some degree clearly present in the initial concept. It could therefore have been a contributing factor of the traditional circle arrangement of the *Last Judgment*.[66]

Cavalieri's training using Michelangelo's drawings is revealed most strikingly in the hatching, whose structure largely consists of simple inclining assemblages of flat lattices. Here and there in the final stages of definition these are joined by rounded hatching combinations (Uffizi no. 69F-r: arm study; Tolnay, bib. 319, no. 91r). If looked at cursorily, the texture differs from those of Michelangelo's hatchings only in certain unharmonious effects typical of a beginner, such as the small deviations in directions (which detract from the overall tectonic effect), the irregularity of the hatching intervals, the frequency of coarse ladder-rung assemblages and of assemblages that are soldered, hooked, or joined at sharp angles. However, the extreme differences in density from assemblage to assemblage, the blotted character of the strongly condensed assemblages, and the large-scale light-dark contrasts produced by the distribution of the hatching point to a sensitivity for "painterly" rather than haptic stimuli. Characteristically, this unmichelangesque technique is reflected most purely in the *Ganymede* (fig. 58)—a work that probably constituted the beginning of Cavalieri's instruction in drawing, if indeed it did not precede it. Michelangelo must

have balked at such an uninhibited development of painterly effects. Even a painter like Sebastiano del Piombo, whose training was totally oriented to the painterly, tried to become "sculptural" after he had come under the influence of the great sculptor (figs. 45–49).

Cavalieri's Development as a Draftsman

The drawings discussed above represent only Cavalieri's early work.[67] They are distributed over a period of about one year. Nonetheless, they indicate an astonishingly clear development both in the handling of media and in capability of expression. The stroke systems, still marked by a crude imbalance between movement expenditure and esthetic efficiency at the stage of the Christ drawings (figs. 59–63), become increasingly simpler and more economical (fig. 70). Already at the stage of the *Fall of Phaeton* (fig. 66) they express relatively coherent conceptions of the human body. The forced, twisted quality of the movement motifs (fig. 58) gives way to a more or less coherent construction and a more or less uniform dynamic. In the case of the *Last Judgment* sketches even the primitive figural outlines (fig. 67: background) are physically more plausible than the complicated giant nude like the Risen Christ of figure 59. The process of formal definition also appears to have become somewhat shorter as time went by. While the highly finished drawing in figure 63 represents a time-consuming elaboration preceded by at least four large-size individual figure sketches, such multipart composition sketches as those in figures 67–68 and 70 were presumably drawn largely ad hoc and without further preparatory work. The difference attests to an unusually quick acquisition of artistic self-confidence. It presupposes not only talent and intensive practice at drawing, but also constant supervision by the well-wishing critical eye of the master.

6

Ascanio Condivi
(1524–1574)

When Ascanio Condivi, at the age of twenty-six or twenty-seven, set out to write his life of Michelangelo, it was probably with a sense of pride in having something in common with his idol.[1] Like Michelangelo, he came from a family that attached great importance to its lineage and the suitably lofty occupations of its members. Like Michelangelo, he had four siblings and a father who failed to make a scholar of his brightest son. As chance would have it, Condivi was approximately the same age as Michelangelo had been when in 1541 he made his first anatomical studies.[2] To be sure, Condivi probably used as models the woodcuts of an edition of Mondino rather than cadavers, and his efforts were on behalf of an older cousin studying medicine, not for his own benefit. But if Condivi had suspected that he would be posthumously confused with Michelangelo—at least as a draftsman—his self-confidence as an artist would hardly have crumbled by the time he was thirty.

Condivi grew up in Ripatransone, a small town in the Marches, where he attended school and received sufficient training as a painter to recommend him to the city fathers as the man to paint the municipal arms on banners for two city wards.[3] Upon reaching adulthood he went to Rome (about 1545).[4] Thanks to the connections of his two educated uncles, Sebastiano and Ceccone Condivi, he gained access to influential circles and enjoyed the favor of Pope Julius III (1550–55)[5] and Cardinals Tiberio Crispi (1498–1566) and Niccolo Ridolfi (1501–50).[6] He was also befriended by the famous anatomist Realdo Colombo (ca. 1516–59)[7] and Cardinal Alessandro Farnese's secretary Annibale Caro (1507–66), whose niece Porzia he married in 1555.[8] By an exceptionally happy coincidence (in his opinion),[9] he made Michelangelo's acquaintance.

It is not known when this meeting took place. What is certain is that it was full of consequences—if of a different kind—for both parties. The aged Michelangelo appears to have been immediately taken with the well-mannered, industrious, and modest youth.[10] For his part, Condivi was spellbound and blinded by the fame and gruff charm of the master. The young man saw Michelangelo as the keeper of all the secrets of art and hung on his every word as though it had been spoken by an oracle. Convinced that Michelangelo's art could be grasped by reducing it to its theoretical fundamentals, Condivi did something that never would have occurred to any previous pupil: he collected the master's utterances and stacked them in his memory like bricks for a monumental edifice.[11] Needless to say, what Condivi absorbed inevitably rubbed off on his own artistic practice. Whether with chalk, brush, or chisel, Condivi was probably more consciously imitative of Michelangelo than any other of Michelangelo's pupils, including Cavalieri. Whatever he created in Michelangelo's shadow was created in the genuine or assumed knowledge of the artist's "secrets." For precisely this reason it is important to know what the work looked like that Condivi left behind in Rome when he returned to Ripatransone in the fall of 1554.[12]

From what is known today, this corpus consisted of a bronze bust of Sulla and one painting. The bust has disappeared without a trace. It was completed in July 1551 and delivered to Lorenzo Ridolfi (1503–76), who lived in Florence and was related to Lionardo Buonarroti's wife, Cassandra (died 1553).[13] Apparently, however, the bust was originally commissioned by Lorenzo's older brother Niccolo Ridolfi—the same cardinal for whom Michelangelo had begun his marble bust of Brutus in 1549–50.[14] The painting survives (fig. 98), but is generally considered a design of the master,[15] for Michelangelo scholars assure us that the cartoon in the British Museum (figs. 95–97) is by the master's hand.[16] If this assurance were reliable, the Condivi file could be closed once and for all.

The So-Called Epiphany Cartoon

Berenson (1903) admitted that it requires "some faith" to see the hand of the great master in the London cartoon (figs. 95–97).[17] But of course he *had* this faith, as did his successors with the exception of Frey, who boldly called the cartoon the "work of an assistant" and was rewarded by the collective silence of his colleagues.[18] This cartoon—or so it is generally argued—is one of the ten "cartoni" found in Michelangelo's house at the Macel de' Corvi on 19 February 1564. Moreover, it is claimed to be identical with the "cartone" mentioned by Vasari (1568; bib. 329, 1:120), a cartoon which the artist supposedly drew in order to help his young friend with the execution of a "panel." Who then should have doubts as to its authenticity?

But things are not as simple as they appear to the faithful. The problems begin with the fact that Michelangelo made no will and thus said nothing about which of his effects belonged to whom. Legally his estate fell to his nephew Lionardo (1519–99), at least insofar as no one else had compelling claims to ownership. As it happens, the ten surviving cartoons were subject to this restriction. When Lionardo arrived in Rome on 22 February 1564,[19] they had already been taken to the governor's house, and the governor at first refused to release them.[20] Only on 21 April did Lionardo, thanks to the

intervention of Duke Cosimo's envoy, at least receive eight of the ten items.[21] The governor had already disposed of two of the cartoons. One was the "large cartoon, on which the figure of Our Lord Jesus Christ and that of the glorious Virgin Mary, his mother, are depicted and sketched" (*Christ's Farewell to His Mother*), which had been given to Cavalieri on 7 April.[22] The other, the cartoon in the British Museum (figs. 95–97), was given to the notary Aloisio della Torre for safekeeping by order of the governor.[23] Both cartoons had been drawn in preparation for a painting.

At this late date it is hardly possible to determine whether the governor's actions were correct. Certainly the legal situation that dictated them was full of entanglements. The cartoon of *Christ's Farewell* was claimed by both Cavalieri and another friend of Michelangelo's, Cardinal Giovanni Morone. Cavalieri based his claim on a promise from the deceased, while the cardinal maintained that the cartoon had been prepared at his request ("a stantia sua").[24] Both claims superseded that of the universal heir, Lionardo, and required careful examination. Presumably the case was similar for the London cartoon.

Curiously, neither Lionardo nor any of Michelangelo's friends appear to have taken any interest in the London cartoon (in contrast to the cartoon of *Christ's Farewell*, in which Daniele da Volterra and Vasari expressed interest, in addition to the cardinal and Cavalieri).[25] At an undetermined date it passed into the possession of Fulvio Orsini (1529–1600), and after his death into the Farnese collection. Orsini, the scholar-librarian of the three Farnese cardinals, Ranuccio, Alessandro, and Odoardo, can of course not have commissioned the painting in question (fig. 98). He is mentioned neither in Condivi's life of Michelangelo nor in any of Condivi's surviving letters.[26] Nor is there any evidence to indicate that he owned the painting in addition to the cartoon. At most, it is possible that he had inherited the cartoon in 1566 from Alessandro Farnese's secretary, Annibale Caro, and that it was Caro who had commissioned the painting from Condivi.[27]

But whoever commissioned the painting would not have had to wait until Michelangelo's death to make his claim on the cartoon. Suppose he had not made himself known by 21 April 1564; what then prevented the governor and his notary from giving the cartoon to Lionardo? But if he had requested it while Michelangelo was still alive, why then was it still in the artist's possession? In contrast to the other "cartoni" left behind, which without exception referred to projects that were not carried out, this one had already served its purpose. Of course, the painting was not completed, but it could have been brought to completion even without the cartoon.

The only escape from this maze appears to be in the assumption that Michelangelo either had or believed he had no right to dispose of the cartoon—regardless of whether the person who commissioned the painting requested it or not. That would necessarily have been the case if the cartoon was Condivi's (who had been absent since 1554) and Michelangelo—as later the notary—served merely as its custodian.[28]

A letter from Daniele da Volterra to Vasari on 17 March 1564 seems to hint at Condivi's authorship.[29] The letter provides a brief and incomplete list of what was still in Michelangelo's house on the day the inventory was taken. Included was a cartoon "that Ascanio painted, if you remember" ("quello que dipigneua Ascanio, se uene ricorda"). The verb *dipigneua* is carelessly read by all researchers except Frey[30] in the sense of "rendered as a painting." But "dipignere un cartone" means—according to the sixteenth-century meaning of the verb ("paint," "draw," "depict," "inscribe," and so on)[31]—first and foremost the act of producing something. When the mere act of rendering in paint was meant, the verb *colorire* was almost always used.[32] In the case in question the context of the letter virtually requires that the relationship between "quello" and "dipigneua" be understood as a relationship between the product and the production process.[33]

Vasari's note of 1568, according to which "Ascanio of Ripatransone . . . spent several years on a panel for which Michelangelo had supplied a cartoon" ("Ascanio dalla Ripatransone . . . pestò parecchi anni intorno a una tavola che Michelagnolo gli aveva dato un cartone") appears to speak against such an interpretation.[34] But Vasari's note includes a few irritating ambiguities, among them the use of the indefinite article in reference to the cartoon ("un cartone"). This usage contrasts with the precise mode of expression the biographer usually employs in similar cases—that is, when he wants to say that the picture painted by B was based on the cartoon drawn by A.[35] It gives the impression that there may have been *several* cartoons for Condivi's painting, or that the cartoon drawn by Michelangelo had disappeared. Also irritating is the offhand way—here, in the middle of Michelangelo's biography—in which his participation is mentioned. This contrasts with Vasari's manner of discussing the cartoons for the *Venus and Cupid* and the *Noli me tangere*,[36] and reduces a work that would be at least as important—if it had indeed been done by Michelangelo—to a negligible quantity not even interesting enough for its subject to be mentioned. The third cause for irritation, however, is Vasari's claim that Condivi spent "several years" on a painting. This comment refers either only to the act of priming and painting

(which, in view of the unfinished state of the painting, must be regarded as a gross exaggeration), or—as hinted at by the suggestive "intorno"—to *both* the execution *and* designing phases. If the latter is true, it would tend to indicate that Condivi spent several years not just on the painting but also on its design and presumably the preparatory sketches and cartoon, thereby refuting the claim that Michelangelo gave Condivi "a cartoon."[37]

Vasari's note is sandwiched between two sweeping judgments of caustic spite. The first: "Ascanio went through great labors, but no fruit was ever seen, either in works or in drawings" ("Ascanio . . . durava gran fatiche, ma mai non se ne veddi il frutto ne in opere ne in disegni").[38] The second: "In the end that high expectation one placed in him went up in smoke. For I remember that Michelangelo was so overcome with pity for his efforts that he came to his [Ascanio's] assistance with his own hand; but it helped little" ("nel fine se n'è ito in fummo quella buona aspettazione che si credeva di lui. che me ricordo che Michelagnolo gli veniva compassione sì dello stento suo, che l'aiutava di sua mano; ma giovò poco").[39] Doubtless, at least one thing in the second statement is true: Condivi did not live up to the expectations that "one" placed in him. His bust of Sulla failed to please.[40] The *Epiphany* was never even completed. But how does this failure square with the presence of Michelangelo's help? Was it this help that failed? Or was its scope never as great as Vasari suggested?

Vasari's reports on recent events tend to be ambiguous and contradictory chiefly when, for certain reasons, he was trying to hide something.[41] He probably knew the man who commissioned Condivi's painting, and if that man was Annibale Caro, he was even a friend.[42] If Vasari had something to hide, it was probably connected to the expectations of Condivi's client. After all, it is highly unlikely that a member of Rome's exacting upper crust would have contracted for a painting with over-life-size figures from a provincial like Condivi without compelling reason. Whoever took such a step probably had cause to assume that Condivi's protector, Michelangelo, would furnish at least the basis for the painting by making a drawing.[43] This expectation might have rested on the assurance of the master himself. But the master often promised more, out of simple courtesy, than time and other projects allowed.[44] If this is what happened in the case of Condivi's painting, then everything falls into place.

Condivi, left in the lurch by Michelangelo at the crucial moment and forced to develop a design on his own, then actually did labor over a panel for several years without achieving a satisfactory result. The client had to be soothed year after year, until finally—after Michelangelo's death—he learned that the artist had indeed left behind "a cartoon" for the painting. In his eyes it was "the cartoon." And in the eyes of the governor, too, it might have been "the cartoon." But the governor must have taken a different view of the matter from the client. The main question was: How could a cartoon that had sat in Michelangelo's house for at least ten years be the same one for which the client claimed to have waited just as long in vain? Even if no one claimed to know who was the actual author of this thing, the governor would have to have determined that it was Condivi's property, not Michelangelo's.

The only written source naming Michelangelo as the author of the surviving *Epiphany* cartoon is found in Fulvio Orsini's will of 1600.[45] But this document is unusable as a pillar of Michelangelo dogma because it was drawn up at a time when the corresponding painting (fig. 98) was also generally accepted as an authentic product of the great master.[46] Orsini's attribution is not an affirmation made from knowledge but from faith—the same faith that stands behind the claims of the present-day Michelangelo scholars. The last word on this issue must be left to the cartoon itself.

The Style of the Epiphany Cartoon

The last word is not very edifying. As in the painting, the oversized figures in the cartoon are repellent. The picture's space collapses under the weight of a mass of figures whose members look like prisoners in an overcrowded dungeon. The three powerful full figures form, as it were, the outer shell of a quarter cylinder that—contrary to all pictorial logic—encloses an empty area at the back stuffed with unnecessary personages.[47]

Curiously, the composition's center of energy is *not* identical with the middle figure of this living cylinder shell. The center is to the left of this figure, in the intermediate zone between the seated woman and her weightily acting, standing neighbor. This intermediate zone, which is emphasized by the symmetrical arrangement of the five extra heads, has no esthetic equivalent on the right side. As a result, the effect of the composition is unbalanced. It lists to one side.[48] This lack of balance reflects a lack of inner coherence. The dense throng of figures, the resoluteness of the gestures and gazes, the violent torsions of the heads and torsos fail to mask the fact that every figure ultimately remains a monad, incapable of demonstrating any coherent action or meaning. True, the heads of the two main figures, which are turned toward each

other, the "speaker's" vouching gesture with his left hand, and the arm movement of the seated middle figure, which pushes away the standing figure on the edge, suggest a loud parley. But this speech finds no resonance in the circle of the other figures. It bounces off their casual attention like empty rhetoric.[49] Contemporaries appear to have perceived this as well. The title *Epiphania*, which first appears in the supplementary protocol to the inventory of Michelangelo's estate,[50] was meant expressly as a provisional designation, as the epithet "so-called" ("nuncupato") indicates. Orsini was baffled by it. He saw in the scene "a Madonna and a Saint Julian and other figures."[51] At the end of the eighteenth century it was the "Madonna with the Apostles."[52] And today scholars continue to puzzle over what really is to be seen in it.[53]

The cartoon has neither squarings nor perforations. It must have been both drawn and transferred to the panel by eye. In fact, the painting deviates from it in numerous places. The lower right arm of the painted "Madonna" is at a noticeably steeper angle than that in the drawing. Instead of hovering in air, it is correctly placed on the upper right thigh. The upper left thigh, whose axis in the cartoon is parallel to the right one, is turned slightly toward the outside in the painting, so that the seated motif is more plausible and the head of the "Christ Child" is less threatened with suffocation. The large dish-shaped fold that inexplicably rests on the right upper thigh of the drawn "Madonna" was replaced by a couple of simple hanging folds, while the tube-shaped fold dangling in isolation between the legs of the drawn "speaker" was replaced with a group of flattened folds in the painting. Each of these deviations represents an effort at improvement and proves that the exploratory process was concluded only on the panel—as in the case of Michelangelo's *Crucifixion of St. Peter*, the genesis of which Condivi probably witnessed with his own eyes.[54]

The execution of the cartoon is as uneven as its composition. A mishmash of completed or half-completed parts are juxtaposed with others that have the quality of raw sketches. In the case of the "boy John" the finished definition breaks off at the shoulder of the right arm and at the left wrist and right ankle and gives way to awkward scribblings. In the case of the "Madonna" important limbs such as the right arm or the left leg are fixed only by rough outlines, while secondary elements such as the fold mentioned above or the piece of cloak hanging on the left arm are already lovingly hatched. The "Joseph" figure has similar disparities. His relatively detailed face contrasts with an unshapely hand meditatively dabbing at his beard. It is as if the draftsman's chalk, hopping from one detail to another, lingering briefly here and longer there, had finally grown weary and delegated the work to the brush.

That work on the cartoon was broken off prematurely is ultimately the result of its having been begun too early. The work began before the draftsman had even halfway thought out how the bodies should look. It consisted mainly in that exploratory labor that normally forms a part of the regular sketching process. The main figure provides ample evidence. Its neck originally grew right out of the left shoulder, the left leg was a good deal too short. Both infelicities were corrected. But the corrections also missed—this time to the other extreme—the golden mean. Setting everything right would have required a third revision of the neck and head and a total revision of the left leg. But drawing over the figures once again would have made what was already drawn illegible. The draftsman appears to have realized his mistakes only when the drawing had already been fixed with an unerasable expenditure of chalk.

The stroke system also testifies to the draftsman's difficulties. Its unsolid, brittle, in many places thicketlike structure is as far removed from the soberly clear tectonics of the stroke system used in Michelangelo's cartoon fragment (fig. 34) as a primeval forest is from a Renaissance park. The contours, consisting of innumerable bundles of strokes placed next to, over, and through each other, are not much more than formal approximations. They deserve the praise scholars have bestowed only if the drawing is reduced to postcard size.[55] Seen from a normal viewing distance, the contours disintegrate into unconnected, individual pieces. An example is the outer contour of the "speaker's" left leg, which appears in two distinctly distinguishable variations, neither of which leads to an anatomically satisfactory conclusion, although each, in its own right, consists of a multiplicity of individual layers. The outer variation suggests a thickly swollen lower leg. It ends at the foot contour, but otherwise has no obvious relation to it. The other variation, which is situated a good bit farther inside, appears to be organically adapted to the foot, but then peters out in the middle of the hatching area of the kneecap. The problem with the leg, which is solved when viewed from afar, in reality remained unresolved—just like the problem with the correct neck position of the "Madonna." The draftsman's idea of the bodies remained nebulous to the end.

The most explicit expression of this nebulous quality is the hatching. In spite of its expansiveness and its high degree of compression, it appears to be the result of a series of noncommittal attempts at shading. Its capacity to suggest three-dimensionality is minimal. Shoulders, arms, and legs look like boneless and jointless landscapes of flesh and cartilage,

the faces like anthropomorphic jellyfish in whose soft hollows the organs seem more to swim than to sit fast. The soft effect results from the sheer quantity of hatching strokes; it has nothing to do with their organization. The individual groups of hatching strokes change direction without rhyme or reason and at the same time are so crudely juxtaposed that they produce a patchwork-quilt texture teeming on all sides with joints, hooks, and sharp angles. Within this texture the few places remaining unshaded look like chance omissions.

The act of drawing proceeded at a remarkably slow pace in spite of the enormous expenditure of kinetic energy. However short they may be,[56] the individual strokes are for the most part wavy, billowed, or otherwise inappropriately bent. Moreover, in many sections of the drawing they are so weak that it appears that the draftsman's fear of making a mistake prevented him from resolutely gripping the chalk. In fact, the continual change of stroke width in general and the unusual frequency of "edge strokes" in particular indicate that the chalk was held too loosely, too timidly, and as a result the chalk turned in the draftsman's hand without his noticing it, thereby resulting in arbitrary applications of pressure. In addition, even when larger surfaces were shaded, almost every stroke was applied individually, and the hatching intervals and directions thus seem irregular even within individual groups of strokes.

All these characteristics indicate that the cartoon is the work of an unpracticed draftsman without proficiency in anatomy or perspective. It is thus impossible to attribute even partial authorship of the cartoon to Michelangelo. The cartoon *must* be Condivi's. And as his only authenticated drawing it provides the basis for recognizing Condivi's drawing style.

The Holy Family in the Ashmolean Museum

The groundless attribution of the *Epiphany* cartoon to Michelangelo produced total disregard for the creativity of the pupil and an artificial inflation of the value of a series of products that, judged on their own merits, would never have been linked with so illustrious a name. The most curious of these products is the small panel in Oxford (fig. 99). Unfinished like the *Epiphany* cartoon and because its execution never got beyond the first underpainting stage, it is something between a painting and a preparatory drawing. This fact alone would be reason enough to awaken special interest among scholars. From time to time obligatory explanations concerning Michelangelo's authorship were offered,[57] but otherwise it was common practice to avoid discussing the panel whenever possible.[58]

The subject depicted on the panel is in fact as obscure as that of the *Epiphany*. Previous titles of convenience include "The Return of the Holy Family from Egypt,"[59] "Medea with Her Two Children and the Pedagogue,"[60] and "Holy Family with the Infant John."[61] Such titles are a vain attempt to obscure the fact that the subject *cannot* even be determined, because a decisive prerequisite—as in the case of the *Epiphany*—is missing: the inner coherence of the scene. The compositional coherence of the figures is limited, as in the *Epiphany*, to a loose grouping that lists to the left. The positions of the figures appear to be derived from the same "anti-contrapposto" basis that also determined the attitudes of the "speaker" and the "boy John" in the *Epiphany*.

Lacking any firm footing, the figures move as if in an airless and gravitationless space, walking clumsily, wobbling, reeling here and there. Their weight does not affect the position of their feet, their standing and walking have no connection to a corresponding location. Broad-footed, narrow-chested, with drooping shoulders and shaved heads, they reflect a conception of the human body that seems to lack any practical foundation.

As in the case of the Epiphany, a cartoon probably preceded the composition on the panel. It may well have been at least equal to the London cartoon (figs. 95–97) in its lack of balance. But certain characteristics of the "painted" figures, such as the missing left leg and the stumplike arm of the male figure, as well as the many pentimenti (the woman's lower leg), indicate that its contours were still largely ambivalent, and that some were not even roughly fixed. And the cartoon itself was already the product of a tortuous sketching process.

Condivi's Sketches

What the products of such a sketching process looked like is demonstrated by those "undoubtedly genuine" sketches that, distributed over a total of six sheets (including figs. 91–94), have always been located in the periphery of the *Epiphany* cartoon and the Oxford panel.[63] We see the familiar spastic movement schema and the familiar defects in construction and proportions. In addition we witness a timidity of proceeding that exceeds by far what is typical for a beginner and which cannot be explained by a simple lack of practice.[64] Even the primitive anthropoid in figure 92 turns out to be, on closer examination, the product of an excessively clumsy movement that was deliberated over stroke for stroke and inhibited by

this deliberation. Insofar as its crumbly contour components have any remnants of uncontrolled movement, they together form a spiral ornament (inner contour of the upper left arm) or rough sawtooth contour pieces (outer contour of the left thigh). The formal expedience of the individual strokes is minimal, and as a consequence the sketches are characterized by that curious emptiness of expression, awareness of which necessarily led to repeated revisions. Although simple in appearance, each one already contains the seeds of the future bramble of strokes (fig. 91).

Following Thode it became common practice to include the *Epiphany* cartoon (figs. 95–97) in the discussion of these sketches,[65] whereas it had not yet occurred to anyone even to mention Michelangelo's cartoon fragment for the *Crucifixion of Peter* (fig. 34) in connection with the authenticated sketches of his later period. This practice expresses the perception of an exceptional situation: that in the case of Condivi, drawings of widely disparate sizes are absolutely identical in style.[66]

Like a normal sketch, the *Epiphany* cartoon was drawn almost exclusively with movements of the wrist and finger joints, that is, from a minimal distance. Its overabundance of contour strokes and hatching is nothing more than the result of an uneconomical way of guiding the chalk that endlessly slowed down the execution. While scribbling on the roughly four-square-meter surface Condivi was unable to distance himself from it, either inwardly or outwardly, sufficiently to activate fully the movement of his arm joint, which would have been required to increase efficiently the radius of his hand movement. The time expended on the cartoon can thus be estimated simply by multiplying the time spent preparing the small sketches. Execution of the cartoon must have taken several times longer than did Michelangelo's own cartoon fragment of the *Crucifixion of Peter* (fig. 34), which is of roughly equal size and has a similarly large number of figures.

Theory and Practice

In his biography of the master Condivi protested against the supposition, apparently widely held in his time, that Michelangelo was unwilling to train pupils. "On the contrary," he writes, "that he did gladly, and I experienced it myself, for he revealed to me every secret that belongs to this art."[67] However justified this rectification might have been, it probably did little to silence the grumblers. For where the reader expects examples of practical instruction he merely finds references to a supposed course of theoretical instruction that is not further specified. Even *between* Condivi's lines he always hears the same melody: that the master influenced his pupil above all through his high professional ethics, his exemplary conduct, and the way he commented on his and other people's artistic practice in aphorisms ("detti") and sought to fix them in precepts ("precetti"). Nowhere is a word to be found about the assignment of tasks or a corrective intervention, let alone about what most Michelangelo scholars consider to have been his chief form of assistance: supplying sketches. Condivi—in contrast to Vasari—even passes over the chief witness to Michelangelo's pedagogical Eros, the famous highly finished drawings for Gherardo Perini (or Antonio Mini)[68] and Tommaso de' Cavalieri. It certainly seems as though Condivi himself never received the direct form of instruction enjoyed by his unnamed predecessors, and perhaps this secretly galled him. Obviously, with increasing age the master felt less inclination to express his sympathies through drawing instruction. Like the instruction Michelangelo might have received from the old Bertoldo (1420–91) in his own youth, the help he offered Ascanio probably consisted of pointers, leaving him to do as he liked, and the candid self-revelation that rings so true in Condivi's biography.

This kind of instruction made demands that an average talent could scarcely live up to. It left the adept only one alternative: either to find himself or to fail. Condivi seems to have at least sensed this when he ran through the list of those who considered themselves to have been Michelangelo's veritable pupils. "But misfortune would have it that he [Michelangelo] fell upon subjects who had either little talent ("poco atti") or, if they were suited, did not stick it out, but instead considered themselves masters after only a couple of months in his training."[69] Condivi probably considered himself among the talented. But he was honest enough to recognize that mere knowledge of "secrets" does not produce a master. In fact no one before him so clearly felt the fatal power exuded by Michelangelo's art and the problems associated with a praxis based on merely knowing its externals.

Condivi saw such great ability and knowledge ("tant'arte e dottrina") in Michelangelo's figures that they were almost beyond imitation, regardless of the painter's talents ("quasi sono inimitabili da qualsivoglia pittore"). He was also of the opinion that nature set an absolute limit on the average talent ("virtù ordinaria"), and that generally only one person in any given field was selected by nature to exceed these limits and serve as an example and norm ("esempio e norma"). As a result, the average talent was destined either to imitate the example set by the best in his field, or else to fail by stray-

ing from the correct path ("quanto più dalla via retta si dilunga").[70]

Three phrases in Condivi's summation deserve particular attention: "beyond imitation," "example and norm," and "correct path." They express awareness of an irresolvable contradiction. The inimitable requires its imitation precisely because it possesses the significance of a "norm" and a "correct path." To refuse to imitate it is just as perverse as the will to imitate is essentially doomed in advance. Seen from this perspective the fact that none of Condivi's works begun under the master's spell was even halfway completed takes on something of a tragic dimension. It appears to be the expression of a shipwreck consciously suffered on the rocks of Michelangelo's greatness.[71]

But the shipwreck was preceded by an unshakable effort to follow the "correct path." Condivi did not make it easy for himself. His *Epiphany*, his Oxford panel, and his sketches have little to do with the compilations in which the imitation of the epigones so often culminates. They set out to follow the spirit, not the letter. For just that reason they lack the eclecticism so typical of a student like Antonio Mini (figs. 50–57), who used what was available as a vast quarry.[72] They are connected with that world of forms whose creation Condivi experienced himself, into which he imperceptibly grew, and in which the secret of perfection out of a seeming nothingness happened to him. Without being actual quotations, its figures exhibit a specific "Pauline" behavior: the torsos are resolutely bent forward and twisted, one arm is laid crosswise, and their looks are penetrating.[73] But in Condivi's case these qualities are a purpose unto themselves. Freed from any overarching context of meaning, they lack precisely what lends Michelangelo's figures such a characteristically "tragic" pathos: an inwardly burdened, heavily suffered corporeal movement. Condivi's figures act as if their task were the demonstration of an abstract doctrine of movement.

We do not know the content of Michelangelo's theory of movement.[74] But it is significant that it was Condivi, and not Vasari, who considered the theory worth pondering and remembering. Condivi claimed that Michelangelo occasionally thought of writing a work that would deal with all types of human movement, a work that would explicate an ingenious theory drawn from his long experience with sculpture and painting ("una ingegnosa teorica, per lungo uso da lui ritrovato"). According to Condivi, Michelangelo found Dürer deficient ("gli por cosa molto debole") because he treated only the measures and variations ("misure e varietà") of the body without saying anything about human actions and gestures— a topic Michelangelo considered more important, and more useful.[75] Condivi was apparently well acquainted with Michelangelo's "ingenious theory," because, after all, the master had "revealed [it] with great love in all its details" ("minutissimamente"). He even hoped one day to be able to publish what had been revealed on the basis of his notes and with the assistance of scholars, so that it would be convenient and useful ("a comodità e utile") to "all those who wish to be creatively active in painting or sculpture."[76] But what for the master was the conceptual residue of decades of artistic practice became for the adept the point of departure for practice and thereby a mere formula. From the awareness that the essence of a human being is completely expressed only in movement came the battle cry: Away with ramrod-straight figures—movement is everything!

Condivi's misunderstanding of Michelangelo's theory of art had its worst effects in his compositions. The inner disparateness of the *Epiphany* (figs. 95–98) and the Oxford panel (fig. 99) cannot be explained by Condivi's artistic limitations alone. Nothing would have been easier than to follow Cavalieri's example (figs. 58, 66–67) and to orient the figural arrangement according to one of those familiar composition schemas that guarantee, if not coherence, then at least the apparent effect of harmony. Apparently that was just the type of thing Condivi wanted to avoid. In his two compositions the accidental quality of the figures' relations to the pictorial space are just as obtrusively irrational as the movements of the individual figures are obtrusively active. These compositions reflect a certain theory—a theory that might be identical with Michelangelo's theory of composition. Condivi did not mention anything about such a theory in his writings. Nevertheless, it can be assumed that it formed merely a component of Michelangelo's theory of movement and tended to the conclusion that even in questions of composition no "valid rule could be given." But when Condivi compared his master's works with those of others, one thing in particular must have struck him: beginning with the Centaur relief up to the Pauline frescoes not one exhibits anything like a compositional schema that would prejudice the relationship of the parts to the whole. Each presupposes—as the multifigure compositional sketches demonstrate ad oculos (figs. 27–32)—an intuitive overall conception, in whose dynamic content the dynamism of the parts was already fully integrated. But it was precisely this ability to envision the coherence of the overall conception that the pupil lacked. Condivi knew what made Michelangelo's compositions appear so overwhelming. He wanted to reproduce this effect from his knowledge. He failed to consider that it was "inimitable" without a lifetime of artistic practice. In the belief that he was following the "right path" he lost his footing and was unable to develop even his own talent for artistic expression.

Marcello Venusti (1512/15–1579) and the Crucifixion Drawings

The group of "late" Crucifixion drawings is known to every student of Michelangelo's work. It consists of six large-size black-chalk compositions of a crucified Christ between Mary and John (figs. 105–07, 109–11), the fragments of a seventh composition (figs. 112–14, 116), and several sketches of single figures (including figs. 104, 108). No one knows the cause and purpose of their existence, the reasons for their preservation, or their first owner.[1] But everyone seems to know in his bones that these drawings depict "perhaps Michelangelo's greatest achievement as a draftsman"[2] and "reveal the almost obsessive mystical devotion of Michelangelo at the end of his life."[3]

The Problems

Early scholars, recently joined by Cimino,[4] dated the Crucifixion drawings to the time of Michelangelo's friendship with Vittoria Colonna (1492–1547), that is, between 1536–38 and 1547.[5] More recently, scholars have dated them in the 1550s, for "stylistic" reasons.[6] In any case, the decisive reason is left unspoken: that both the Crucifix drawn for Vittoria Colonna (fig. 33) and certain figures of the fresco of the *Crucifixion of Peter* completed in December 1549 totally or partially recur in these drawings.[7] The Colonna *Crucifix* determined the first version of the Christ figure in figure 106. It is still present as a model in the final state of the thorax and the left leg, and in the individual versions of the arms and hands. Moreover, the hands of Christ in the Colonna *Crucifix* provided the model for the hands of Christ in figures 107 and 109. The attitude of its torso is repeated in the Christ in figures 105, 108, and 109. The structure, proportions, and feet position of its legs are echoed in all six drawings. The *Crucifixion of Peter*, on the other hand, influenced the configuration of Mary and John.[8] The youth dragging the cross in the right center of the Pauline fresco lent his face and his torso, together with the associated piece of drapery, to the John in figure 111. He lent his legs to the John in 110, the left assistant figure in figure 105, and the male nude in figure 104. The protesting youth in the center of the fresco imparted his right hand to both the figures at the base of the cross in figure 110 and his left hand (reversed) to the Madonna in figure 111 (in large measure also his torso and the position of his arms). The man stepping forward in the right foreground of the Pauline fresco was responsible for the folded arms of the John in figure 107, while a figure in the group of women in the foreground at the right and the figure of the youth warning the others to be quiet (behind the protesting youth) provided the model for John's arms bent in front of the chest and his symmetrical hands in figure 106 (and apparently also for the first version of the John in figure 111). Finally, the dress of some soldiers appears to have served as a model for the apronlike robe of the John in figures 106 and 110, and the right assistant in figure 105; their leather caplike headwear as a model for the left assistant in figure 105 and the Madonna in figure 106.[9]

The problem of the function of these drawings is a harder nut than the dating. Tolnay attempted to crack it. Seizing on an assumption of Robinson's,[10] he reiterated several times his opinion that the six compositions and their satellites were "projects for a group in marble."[11] This was—so he thought—"proven" by the existence of two relevant sketches for marble blocks: the pen-and-ink sketch for the blocks of a three-figure crucifixion in the Archivio Buonarroti (I, 154, Fol. 274) and the black-chalk sketch of a block supposedly for the Christ figure on the verso of Windsor sheet no. 12761. The first is in fact a work of Michelangelo's. But unfortunately the dimensions of the block are incompatible with the proportions of the figures in the Crucifixion drawings.[12] The second sketch, on the other hand, does seem to describe a shape that conforms to the Christ figure of the front side (fig. 107). But unfortunately it has nothing in common with a sketch for a corresponding marble block by Michelangelo, apart from the fact that it consists of strokes (which Tolnay's readers fail to notice, because Tolnay neglected to reproduce the verso of the Windsor sheet in his *Corpus*).[13] Otherwise, it is hard to see how drawings that—in contrast to Michelangelo's Rondanini sketches (fig. 35)—have no indications for plinths and have always been praised as representatives of a "painterly" style, are supposed to be sketches for a sculpture.[14] Some scholars therefore contented themselves with solving the problem of function in a harmless way.[15] They speak of "sketches" or "preliminary studies" and avoid saying for what. But most rid themselves of the problem by asserting that the Crucifixion drawings are a series complete in itself.[16]

But this claim flies in the face of the reality of what is drawn. It seems to be a typical example of repression. Scholars were presumably aware that the only thing the Crucifixion drawings have in common with the authenticated Michelangelo drawings of the "late period" (figs. 35–37) is the use of black chalk, and that otherwise they are characterized by a discrepancy between kinetic effort and aesthetic efficiency that flatly contradicts the character of Michelangelo's authentic sketches. But this awareness was incompatible with the dogma of authorship. It was repressed by turning the discrepancy into something positive and genial; it was ar-gued that Michelangelo intentionally employed a style and means of expression alien to him. The drawings, which teemed with pentimenti and corrections, with inconsistencies in spatial, anatomical, and tonal structure, were transformed into products of mystical visions, into products of a trancelike state. They "came closer than the disciplined earlier studies to achieving the goal of apparent effortlessness" (Clements).[17]

Accordingly they were described not as drawings, but as if they were completed paintings, *nolens volens*. Any objective description would have rendered ridiculous the alleged purposefulness of the above-named discrepancies. It is impossible to declare figure 107 to be a completed work of art without having to ask, on closer observation, whether "Michelangelo" really intended to depict this: a cross swaying to and fro, a Christ with jerking limbs hanging on it, a gaping John, and a Madonna who in effect consists of a tangled clump of wool threads?

The Design Process

The question of determining the chronology of the sheets on the basis of internal, stylistic evidence proved to be the most troublesome of all problems. Brinckmann,[18] Wilde,[19] and Hartt[20] declared it to be beyond solution and thereby relieved others of the task. The conclusions of those who proceeded contrarily seemed to prove them correct, for each scholar came up with a different answer:

W^2 (fig. 106)—L^1 (fig. 111)—W^1 (fig. 107)—L^2
(fig. 109)—O (fig. 105)—P (fig. 110) according to
Baumgart;[21]
W^2—W^1—L^1—P—O—L^2 according to Berenson;[22]
O—W^1/L^1—W^2—P—L^2 according to Goldscheider;[23]
O—P—L^1—L^2 according to Dussler;[24]
W^2—O—L^1—L^2 according to Tolnay's original opinion,
P—W^1—L^1—W^2—O—L^2 according to Tolnay's
intermediate opinion, P—O—W^1—W^2—L^1—L^2
according to Tolnay's latest opinion;[25]
W^1—L^1—W^2—O—L^2 according to the catalogue of the
London exhibition of 1975.[26]

Each of these proposed chronologies reflects the author's personal reading. None is logically grounded.

It is curious that the Oxford drawing (fig. 105) appears four times in second-to-last place, although in many respects it falls outside the framework of the other compositions. It is the only one whose left side, reserved by centuries-old tradition for Mary, is occupied by a naked figure of masculine gender. Its Christ figure is more poorly proportioned, more schematic in the definition of the position of the arm, more discrepant in the position of the legs, and less related to the cross than all other Christ figures. It ostentatiously turns its rump and back to the male figure pressing forward on the left, as though possessed with a zeal to talk to the person (right) who in blind desperation cannot see and hear anything. The drawing reflects—as Goldscheider and Dussler thought—the opposite of a mature design concept.

On the other hand, it does not represent a primordial sketch. The left figure is based on the verso sketch of the Paris fragment (fig. 104). It repeats the latter down to the last detail of the contour's course (right arm, part of the left cheek) and deviates from it only in the position of the head, which, set forward, suggests a bent-forward upper body position. The draftsman seems to have noticed that the deviation was unavoidable only after he had equipped the figure with a head in profile corresponding to the Paris sketch (remnants of the same are still recognizable in the nose, eyes, and forehead profile of the forward-set head) and thereby learned that this head in profile is looking at Christ's back. Of course, the Paris figure cannot have been a component of a complete Crucifixion scene if this was the corresponding recto drawing (fig. 112). Otherwise it must be assumed that the complete scene represented in figure 112, for inexplicable reasons, would have been placed in the right half of the original whole-sheet rather than in the center. But if the verso sketch always stood isolated on the periphery of the sheet (on the right when seen from the verso, on the left when seen from the recto), then its existence and its relationship to the left attendant figure of the Oxford drawing should probably be taken as signs that each of the three Oxford figures was designed separately. Its iconographic and formal discrepancies would thus be explicable as the expression of experimentation. Apparently the draftsman was testing two possible motifs of movement and their implicit relation to the motif of the crucified Christ. Gender and personal identity were thus initially unimportant.

The John of P (fig. 110) relates to the attendant figures of O (fig. 105) like a synthesis. Its arm and leg positions correspond to those of the left figure of O, while his drapery corresponds to that of the right figure. The stooped, hurrying forward of the one figure and the unmoving rigid stance of the other are united in appearance and transformed into a timorously hesitant stepping figure inhibited by spiritual defeat or resignation. But in the company of Mary and Christ, who receive all the emphasis of the chalk, this John stands out as a bodiless phantom. He represents a transitional stage in the drawing process. After the John had been sketched roughly once, the draftsman apparently had the impression that this pose better suited Mary. The draftsman abruptly made the rough form a starting point for the genesis of a Mary by switching its position to the left side of the cross and lengthening the drapery to the feet.[27] He gave one arm a different position, but kept the right hand of the John in the same perspective.

The result of this alteration was developed further—together with the associated Christ—in L¹ (fig. 111). This happened first only by altering minor details, for example, the right front hand of the Mary (which—as in the case of figure 110—is repeated almost literally in the right hand of Christ). Its middle, ring, and small fingers were slightly spread rather than bent. The overall appearance—head, arm, and torso position as well as the system of drapery folds—remained largely unchanged, as presumably the position of the legs did too. Only in a second attempt that proceeded on the basis of a thin covering layer of white lead was the frontal position of the torso and legs replaced by one that is halfway turned toward the cross and the rhetorical gesture of the backward-stretched right arm transformed into a gesture of fervent humility by crossing it with the left arm.

The Mary of W² (fig. 106) looks strikingly similar to this second state of the Mary in L¹. It suggests a slightly modified, highly finished drawing. Since the John also appears very decisively designed, one might be tempted immediately to agree with those scholars who perceived the whole composition W² as the immediate successor of L¹ (fig. 111). Nevertheless, the Christ figure contradicts this perception. It seems to be still completely bound by Michelangelo's Colonna *Crucifix* (fig. 33). And this perception is completely contradicted by the fact that the formal equivalent of the W² John is the *primary* version of the L¹ John (fig. 111)—a version that had been covered over with zinc white highlights at the same time as the first version of the Mary there and then revised (it showed a head in profile turned toward the left and two arms folded across the chest). W² (fig. 106) must have been created *before* L¹ (fig. 111) and, since the latter drawing immediately follows P (fig. 110), even before P (fig. 110).

In fact the Christ figure of W² (fig. 106) was originally an improved new version of figure 105. Its hip swung to the left, the left leg appeared in profile, the arms branched almost horizontally from the torso, the head was tilted toward the left (but the face was turned toward the right, not the left attendant figure). Subsequently this new version was successively revised. In the end the original position of the torso was almost completely reversed and thereby it again almost approximated—presumably unintentionally—the model of the Colonna *Crucifix* (fig. 33) that was present from the very beginning. The result was not very convincing since the strong swinging out of the hip in particular seems incompatible with the impression of passive hanging suggested by the extended diagonal arms. The draftsman therefore made a new start in figure 107. He now omitted the thrusting out of the hip and heightened the effect of passivity of the vertical torso by bringing the arms from their initial position linked to the final version in figure 106 into a steeper position. At the same time he tried to modify Michelangelo's Christ, which continued to be present in the articulation of the torso, in the left leg, and in the position of the hands, by giving the right leg a profile view similar to that which he had tried for the left leg of Christ of O (fig. 105). The draftsman saw that this was a mistake, but he saw this only after the right leg had already been carefully hatched. He cut the gordian knot of this problem by using a thick, additional contour and thereby took the decisive step toward the verticalism of the Christ in figures 109–11.

But the draftsman was at first unable to free himself from the spell of his model (fig. 33). On the recto of Louvre sheet no. 842 (fig. 108) he again returned to the torsion of the torso and horizontal arm position, although both were inconsistent with the rigidly stretched legs. Apparently he momentarily saw in this return the only way to solve the new problem of symmetry that had resulted from the upright torso and vertical legs. Inclining the head to the side created a disturbing effect, however—as the Christ in figure 109 demonstrates. It therefore had to be replaced by a position that corresponded to the axis of the body. Forming the head erected (and with closed lids) was apparently the obvious solution—seen from the standpoint of the draftsman under the spell of the Colonna *Crucifix*. But it was incompatible with the diagonal position of the arms, and its combination with horizontally drawn arms was consequently unavoidable. Result: Christ seems to stand on the cross, or more precisely, to lift himself on his tiptoes with a puffed-out chest and a haughtily raised head.[28]

It is obvious that this was no solution. Nevertheless, it was a new starting point, and so the next phase of the exploratory process (fig. 109) again began with a hurried sketch of what had just been drawn (first version of head and arms in fig. 109). In the subsequent revision the torso and arms were retained and—with a sidelong glance at Michelangelo's *Crucifix* (fig. 33)—modeled in the position taken from the

Louvre figure (fig. 110). The draftsman borrowed the arms from the Colonna Christ. In the attempt to attach them to the torso in a slightly diagonal position, however, he had the bad luck to miss the anatomically correct joining of limbs— the right arm seems to be inserted in Christ's right armpit. The draftsman had the most trouble with the position of the head. An upright head was out of the question after the disaster of figure 108. The attempt to have the head appear bent back and lying on the right shoulder (second head version) had to be given up because the joining with the neck was unsuccessful. In the end the draftsman returned to the solution already tested in O (fig. 105)—the shriveled head looking diagonally downward.

The revision of this Christ, whose upper body continued to appear composed of disparate elements, was redrawn on a special sheet (London, Courtauld Institute; Tolnay, bib. 319, no. 420). It shows the sequence of versions typical for our draftsman: a lightly drawn first version that takes up from the just preceding version (final version in fig. 109) and the actual, heavily drawn corrected version (which for its part is filled with pentimenti). The latter draws the necessary consequences from the unsuccessful heads and arms in figure 108–09. The torso appears strictly frontal, the head bent forward in the precise center axis of the body, the arm position diagonal. The spell of the model was broken, the ambivalence of activity and passivity made way for the expression of death or dying. The Courtauld sketch forms the immediate predecessor to the mature conception of the Christ figure seen in figures 110 and 111.[29]

The Final Drawing

That the previous chronology resembles random combinations in a lottery drawing is obviously the result of there being no unified conception that was developed step by step. From the beginning the development seems to have proceeded on two tracks, separated according to the main figure (Christ) and secondary figures. While the conception of the main figure was developed rather straightforwardly (because it was closely related to Michelangelo's Colonna *Crucifix*), the development of the attendant figures displays a curiously erratic course (because of the many alternatives that the model, Michelangelo's *Crucifixion of Peter*, offered). Thus, as early as the stage of W^2 (fig. 106) there appear two attendant figures that are brought to a finished stage of completion which are completely different from the initial version of O (fig. 105). They were immediately laid aside and only taken up again at the stage of L¹ (fig. 111). In figure 107 two attendants appear in their place, of which at least the left, phantom-like one can be recognized as the product of a spontaneous idea. A third attendant figure, consisting of a conglomeration of scroll-like, contour parts, seems to have immediately preceded the figure on the right (John), by which it is partly covered over. It depicts a figure embracing the cross and thereby reveals itself as the seed of an idea that is developed into a two-sided embracing motif in the following stage (fig. 109). This sudden maturation of a figural *concetto* deviating from the previous iconographic schema was probably possible only because the draftsman was able to refer back to something already available. He created the evangelist in figure 109 by combining the legs of its equivalent in figure 107 with a mirror image of the upper body of the left attendant of figure 105. The Mary, on the other hand, was created by combining an upper body developed from the Mary-phantom of figure 107 with a mirror image of the leg position of the John in figure 106 (in the initial version her forward-placed foot stood like that of this John in profile). It is logical that the motif of embracing was subsequently dropped again (fig. 110): it would of necessity have led to a nonsensical verticalization of the picture format after the diagonal arm position of Christ had already been established. It was therefore no wonder that the attendants in figure 110 again proceed from O (fig. 105), those in figure 111 (second version of Mary, first version of John) from W² (fig. 106).

With L¹ (fig. 111) the exploratory process entered a critical stage. While the Christ figure had apparently arrived at a final stage of development, Mary and John with their phantomlike first versions continue to be provisional figures at different stages of development. Each required further formulation. The results are the recto figures of Louvre fragments nos. 720 and 698 (figs. 112–13). The state of their development is as unequal as that of the attendant figures in figures 107, 110, and 111—with the difference that they exceed the latter in sharpness and detail. Curiously Mary's pose is again immediately connected to the verso sketch (fig. 104). This reference back to a drawing from the beginnings of the exploratory process would be hard to explain were it not for the fact that all compositions with the exception of L² (fig. 109) have a serious weak point: each of the attendant figures seems concerned only with itself. The Louvre Mary (fig. 112) emphatically breaks through this isolation by acting as a "speaker" turning to both Christ and John. Otherwise she was not developed in any way beyond her distant and immediate predecessors. The cloak that is held together over her chest by a brooch and falls

behind over her upper arms is cut to the model of Mary's drapery in figures 106, 110, and 111, where the folds of the right sleeve are already preformed at the elbow and the wrist. The right hand appears as an improved replica of that of the Mary in figure 111 (first version), the drapery led across the lap to the left arm appears to be a derivative of the identical section of drapery of the Mary in figure 106.

Significantly, the Louvre John (fig. 113) proceeds from the same Mary (fig. 106). His slightly forward-stooping posture with crossed arms and bent knees is nothing more than a mirror-image of Mary, with slight modifications in the position of the head, hands, and foot in the back (whose first version nevertheless shows the same profile view as in figure 106). This reference back to a Mary figure seems to express the need for an improved symmetry.

It is evident that the Mary and the John of the Louvre fragments mark a culmination in the articulation of the two attendant figures. But this fact is also attested to by some paintings and engravings of the Crucifixion (including figs. 115, 117) in which precisely these two Louvre figures are reproduced. Nevertheless, to our surprise the Christ of the paintings and engravings is not the same one developed in the Crucifixion drawings (fig. 111). Instead it is sometimes (including fig. 117) Michelangelo's Colonna *Crucifix* (fig. 33), another time (fig. 115) a Christ with a crown of thorns hanging dead on the cross. The latter is based on a drawing (fig. 114) that indeed forms part of the Crucifixion drawings, but is not derived from its last stage. Instead it probably proceeded from the Christ in figure 106 (the head of its Christ collapsed on the chest is related to the secondary version of Christ's head in fig. 106).[30] Is it possible that the final version of Christ aimed at by the development of that figure in the Crucifixion drawings did not exist?

It did and does exist, and even in the form one would expect: as a definitive new formulation of the Christ of figure 111, oriented to create an axially symmetric and frontal composition. The sheet on which it is drawn (fig. 116) is located in the Städelsches Kunstinstitut in Frankfurt.[31] It is—just like the Louvre sheet with the dead Christ (fig. 114) and the Louvre sheets with the attendant figures (figs. 112–13)—an extract from a larger sheet. Like them it comes from the collection of Antoine Coypel (1661–1722). The size of the crucified figure (from toes to skull) corresponds—like the figure in figure 114—to the maximum size of the Christ figures of the Crucifixion drawings (approximately 25 cm), while the sizes of Mary and John correspond to the maximum sizes of the attendant figures there (approximately 23 cm).

The Author of the "Late" Crucifixion Drawings

The fact that the Christ associated with the fully worked-out figures of Mary and John occurs in three different versions seems to have provoked some confusion among scholars, because it appeared to be incompatible with the standard opinion according to which each of the "late" Crucifixion compositions is an autonomous work of art. The Frankfurt version (fig. 116) was declared to be a copy after one of the "late" Crucifixion drawings (the drawing in the Courtauld Institute; Tolnay, bib. 319, no. 420). The Louvre drawings of Mary and John (figs. 112–13) were rejected as components of the Crucifixion group; instead—Tolnay stated—they are supplements to the Colonna *Crucifix* (fig. 33) personally designed by Michelangelo.[32] With them the artist had gone back and "perfected" the crucifix (whose subject is—according to Condivi—Christ's despairing of his loneliness)—apparently without Condivi and Vasari knowing anything about it, and after the version described by them had already been disseminated through engravings and paintings.[33] But he subsequently altered the thus "perfected" version (which too became available for reproduction by engravers and painters)[34]—once again without the knowledge of his biographers—by replacing the living Christ with a dead one. Unfortunately he did not live to see the publication of this "final" version. For its only representative, an engraving by Philipp Soye (fig. 115), dates from 1568.[35] The name of Michelangelo does not appear on it.[36]

One thing is doubtlessly correct about this puzzling repair-work thesis: neither the two attendant figures (figs. 112–13) nor Michelangelo's (fig. 33) or Michelangelo's alleged version of the Christ (figs. 114, 116) can be perceived as members of a simultaneously conceived Golgotha scene. For they function as movable scenery in both the "perfected" (fig. 117) and the "final" composition (fig. 115). And external evidence alone in part identifies them as such. The drawings of Mary and John, as well as the two drawings of Christ that are connected with the Crucifixion drawings (figs. 114, 116), exist on separate sheets, each of which is more or less precisely cut to the size of the particular figure. Of course it would be nice to assign the blame for such an eccentric use of the sheet to the scissors of Coypel or some wicked predecessor, but the suspicion of guilt falls fully on the author himself. The surviving contemporary chalk copies prepared after the Louvre drawings of Mary, John, and Christ (figs. 112–13, 116) also exist on separate sheets. They presuppose that their objects of reference already existed on separate sheets.[37]

The "perfected" and "final" compositions (figs. 117, 115)

are accordingly simple compilations. But as such they prove that not only themselves, but also the late Crucifixion drawings are products of an imitation of Michelangelo.

In fact the collage principle on which they are based is present from the first phases of the sketching process. It is expressed both in the type of citation and the additive assimilation of the citations and in the curious metamorphoses of Mary and John and in the continuous experimentation with shifted limbs (Christ's arms). It is also expressed in the tendency to make the upright and transverse beams of the cross dependent on the body position of the crucified figure and thus to treat them as a continuously changing afterthought (it is significant that in figure 114 there is nothing to be seen of a cross). The collage principle is especially evident in the fact that the development always proceeds only from individual figure to individual figure, and never from whole to whole. Each figure of one composition is interchangeable with the corresponding figure of another composition. Attributing the Crucifixion drawings to Michelangelo ultimately runs into the problem of assigning to this artist just that type of creative process that is typical for epigones.

Most of the many paintings in which the two Louvre figures (figs. 112–13) accompany the Colonna *Crucifix* (fig. 33)[38] are considered works of Michelangelo's friend Marcello Venusti. The best-documented is the qualitatively excellent specimen in the Galleria Doria-Pamphili in Rome (fig. 117).[39]

It is probably also the first and oldest of the many painted versions, since it comes from the estate of Michelangelo's servant Francesco Amadori (Urbino), who died in 1556. According to his widow, Amadori had personally commissioned Venusti for the work (see excursus II). A second example, today located in the Martin D'Assy Collection, once belonged to the Cavalieri family,[40] to judge from the two stamps with coat-of-arms affixed to the verso. It was possibly one of the paintings that Tommaso de' Cavalieri had executed by Venusti, the specialists for "small paintings" (Vasari) whom he encouraged.[41] The relative and absolute sizes of both paintings correspond. The sizes of their Mary and John figures correspond to those of the two Louvre drawings (figs. 112–13). But compared to the Louvre figures the painted attendant figures exhibit several significant modifications. The steep angle of Mary's glance in the drawing, which would have required an implausibly high placement of the crucified figure, is considerably reduced in the painted figure. The drapery-fold combinations hanging between the legs and along the outer contour of the right thigh were lengthened toward the bottom. In the case of John in the painting the lower seam of the cloak crossing over the torso of the drawn figure was placed at the height of the navel instead of at the level of the left elbow, and the lower right arm (which in figure 113 has no visible connection to the upper arm) was lengthened in such a way that its elbow seems to be just covered by the hanging sleeve of the cloak. Each of these alterations indicates that in the execution of the two attendant figures—unlike the execution of the crucified Christ and angels (which were not changed at all from the Michelangelo drawing)—the painter functioned not as a mere copyist but as the completer of his own design. As such he must be identical with the draftsman of the Crucifixion drawings.[42]

Venusti's Drawing Method

The drawings do not stand alone in the corpus of the sacrosanct. They are stylistically and typologically related to another group of black-chalk drawings (including figs. 100–03) which also refer to Venusti's paintings and have already been demonstrated elsewhere to be products of his hand.[43] Together with these they form the only sure foundation to date for determining Venusti's drawing style.

The non-Michelangelo qualities of these drawings are already expressed in the ratios of figure sizes. The figures possess—independent of their importance in the design and development process—a standard size that averages between a minimum of 16.8 cm (sketch of the crucified figure on the verso of figure 105) and a maximum of 27.5 cm (standing Christ in figure 103). This unusually large and simultaneously unusually uniform figure size, however, is directly connected to a sketching procedure that attempted to accomplish finishing on the spot and in a single phase, if possible. From the first sketch on the contours of objects like crosses or reading stands delimited by straight lines were cleanly drawn with the ruler (figs. 105–12)[44]—which in the end usually led to a confusion of geometric forms seconding the confusion of organic forms superimposed on each other (figs. 106–08, 110). The draftsman could have avoided these confusions without further ado by continuing the sketching process on a new sheet at the right moment. But he preferred to delay that moment of transference for as long as possible by covering certain defects with zinc white (whose subsequent oxidation produced the moldlike appearance) and placing the following versions on this artificially created tabula rasa. For the same reason he also seems to have favored an especially light touch. The *Crucifixion* and *Annunciation* sketches are executed with the same extremely sharpened chalks as Ven-

usti's highly finished drawings (figs. 101–03). Like the latter they consist of extremely tender, thin threadlike strokes. Since the pressure on the chalk during the movements of the hand remained relatively constant and strengthenings were usually used only for the details of the final versions, the individual revisions of limbs of one and the same figure often seem absolutely equal. That in the case of the Annunciate Mary in figure 100 it was the lower and not the upper version of the left arm that was drawn first could be deduced—if there were not the corresponding highly finished drawing (fig. 101)—from the disturbing fact alone that its integrity is respected by the upper version, instead of being overdrawn.

The genesis of the figures resembles a protracted act of conjuring. To the extent that it is not a mere quoting, it has the character of a successive summation of formal approximations, as in the cases of Clovio (figs. 82–83, 88) or Condivi (figs. 91–97). The increase in definition from version to version is astonishingly small. Up through the final revisions the contours are determined by formulaic strokes—by the same segment formulas seen in the primitive first outline sketches in figure 107 (Mary and first version of the John) and figure 109 (first version of the left leg of the John).[45] Only in the structure of the individual stroke sequences is something like a maturation of the form level expressed. Whereas the stroke sequences in the first outline sketches show a partially chaotic discontinuity (fig. 107: Mary), the contour strokes of the later versions usually combine to form more or less closed arcades. Seconded by a shading, which was used as early as the first contour versions (fig. 100: angel; fig. 107: Mary) and which accordingly prematurely tends to become overconcentrated, they result in limbs of unusual softness. The bodies are alienated from their skeletons. Slightly bloated, flowing, and ungraspable in their substance, they are outright antipodes of Michelangelo's characteristic figure types.

What appears to be uncorporeally soft and dusky at the figure level nevertheless displays curiously contradictory characteristics at the elementary level of the stroke system. The individual contours and shaded areas are sometimes malleable, sometimes brittle, and in places scratched or roughened. They are composed of elements of varying consistency. Doughy or grainy thin strokes alternate abruptly with sharp and hard ones. This alternation seems to be nothing other than the result of the fact that the chalk was constantly turned during the drawing—probably to avoid dulling the point on one side—and in the process touched the paper periodically with the sharp edge of its dull surface. It has its correspondence in the striking differences in clearness between the sections of contours sketched ad hoc and those quoted from models (fig. 107: relationship between the contour of the left arm and that of Christ's torso); and, on the other hand, that shaded and unshaded areas are often especially sharply demarcated where the hatching has not yet reached the maximum of concentration and expansion, thus generating the effect of harsh lightings created by the tearing apart of a veil of fog (fig. 100: Mary's legs; fig. 109: John).

All these contradictions were of course lessened in the advanced stages of the individual exploratory process. But since this occurred mainly through successive massing or concentration of strokes, they make themselves noticeable even in the highly finished drawing stage—at least under the magnifying glass (thus, for example, the abrupt changes in the stroke consistency are obvious in the angel in figure 101). Their frequency—in connection with the far-reaching uniformity of the movement pressure and the formulaic character of the stroke's courses—therefore points to an astonishing indifference to the expressive possibilities of the individual stroke as such. What ultimately counted for the draftsman was not the individual stroke but the conglomeration of strokes—the contour skein and the hatching web.

This attests to an aesthetic attitude that was diametrically opposed to Michelangelo's. As the typically frontal figures of Venusti attest, this attitude aimed not at evoking the three-dimensional substance of the figure in space, but at their "painterly" qualification. Nevertheless, this basic "painterly" tendency differs from that of Sebastiano (figs. 45–49) in one important point. It seeks less the light-dark *contrasts* than the intermediate tones, the mysteriously dusky, smoky, vibrating charm of a materiality that remains undefined and lets the naked appear as the same quality as the clothed, indeed as the surroundings of the figures. It is not for nothing that unusually expansive and highly concentrated outer hatchings comparable to those of Clovio's *Resurrection* drawing in Windsor (fig. 81) appear as early as in the sketches (figs. 107, 111). Like the inner hatchings, they lack all tectonics. With their curiously unstable, mostly "hanging" layers they form not so much an abstract background foil as a— slightly wavy—veil formation that seems to be located more between than behind the figures and almost seems to penetrate them. Instead of optically expanding the space, they tend to flatten it.

8

Daniele Ricciarelli da Volterra (1509–1566) and the *Expulsion of the Moneychangers*

At the present it appears that there were two Daniele Ricciarellis, both from Volterra. One was a painter and sculptor by profession. He was one of the most renowned and original of the artists who lived in Rome in the second third of the cinquecento.[1] In his relatively short life he employed more apprentices and journeymen than Michelangelo did in his long one.[2] He is the Daniele known to Daniele scholarship. The other Daniele had less success. He was a "pupil" by occupation, but is occasionally considered to have been a "parasite."[3] After becoming acquainted with the aged Michelangelo he apparently suffered a creative blackout. We meet him principally in the Michelangelo literature.

The Daniele Problem

Once again the "Michelangelo" corpus is responsible for this double-birth. Under the heading "drawings from his old age" it includes a conspicuously large number of small-sized black-chalk sketches, which, in addition to being "indubitably authentic," have the fatal characteristic of being related not to Michelangelo's works but to Daniele's. Corresponding to these works are five groups of sketches and the remnant of a sixth. Each group represents, if not a complete sketching process, at least fragments of one. None exhibits any traces of the disturbed movement characteristic of Michelangelo's old age.

The first group is the smallest. It consists of four sketches, to which the copy after a fifth can be added.[4] Two of these sketches (fig. 121 and Tolnay, bib. 319, no. 377) and the copy (fig. 120) depict a man looking upward to the right who is undressing with the help of a boy. The man is standing with his left foot on a pedestal (in figure 121 the indications of a bed with a figure lying on it are associated with this pedestal). The two other sketches, indicated with slight contours (fig. 125: on the left edge of the sheet; Casa Buonarroti no. 19F-v [Tolnay, bib. 319, no. 368v]: to the right of the center of the sheet, drawn over by the tomb sketch) are first sketches for the masculine figure (same leg position). Its final version can be seen on a sheet in the Albertina (fig. 122). All five sketches and this final version are related to a painting that survives only in a copy; the original painting had been painted by Daniele for Giovanni della Casa (1503–56) in 1555–56. It depicts the moment when Aeneas, just about to undress before Dido's bed, receives Mercury's command to depart Carthage.[5]

This first group of sketches is linked to the second by the Casa Buonarroti sketch (Tolnay, bib. 319, no. 368v). The second group is distributed over the recto and verso of Casa Buonarroti no. 19F and over a sheet in the Ashmolean Museum (Parker no. 338) and consists of four complete and two fragmentary sketches of a seated male nude,[6] whose attitude largely corresponds to that of the *John the Baptist in the Desert* painted for Giovanni della Casa (copies in Munich and Rome).[7] The object held by three of the four completely drawn figures in their extended right hand affirms that the sketches were intended for this painting. It can only be the bowl with which John, in the painting, is about to fetch water from the rivulet flowing at his feet.[8]

The third group of drawings consists of eleven sketches. Four of them, each on a tiny sheet fragment, are located in the Pierpont Morgan Library; the other seven are on the recto of a single sheet in the Ashmolean Museum (fig. 123).[9] Their subject is a two-figure group of warriors consisting of one larger figure lying on the ground and defending himself against a smaller figure who is striking him. These drawings are related to the third commission that the scholarly Giovanni della Casa entrusted to Daniele around 1555(?). This commission stipulated—to judge from the text of Vasari's report[10] as well as from the surviving panel in Fontainebleau[11]—the pictorial exemplification of a paragone problem. Daniele was supposed to depict David's beheading of the giant Goliath three times—once in the form of a "modello finito" and twice in the form of a painting. The two painted versions were to be painted on the front and back sides of one and the same wooden panel, and in such a way that they, apparently corresponding to two contrary views of the "modello," would result in two autonomous yet related pictures, understandable independently from each other. Daniele solved this ticklish task in a way that bears shining witness to his spatial imagination. He had the two painted pairs of figures appear as the front and back views of the same group, but had their poses deviate from each other wherever the depicted action would have led to the hiding or obscuring of body parts relevant to the dynamic expression. Just as he stressed the equality of the two Goliath and David figures by the sameness of their size ratios, implements, and robes, so he also emphasized the identicalness of the site of the action by placing the same section of a Philistine tent behind each pair. The result is two interchangeable pictures that are nonetheless independent of each other. Together they appear to demonstrate that painting is just as capable as sculpture of making even the most complicated body comprehensible from any view, as long as it is composed according to pictorial laws. In the confrontation with the "modello finito" the paintings might have given Giovanni and his visitors the feeling that the endless quarrel

about the preeminence of the arts (it had reached its high point around 1546–49) had finally been decided in the sense of a perfect equivalence of painting and sculpture.[12]

The surviving *David and Goliath* sketches provide evidence of the difficulty of the task that Daniele confronted. They treat no less than three different aspects of the group: two contrary "frontal views" and an oblique view. Nevertheless, they are—with the exception of the sketch for the group viewed obliquely (fig. 123)—all conceived to create a pictorial effect. The depth of the total volume of the group always corresponds to the width of an individual figure. Overlappings are minimal; the action of the bodies remains fully visible. For the sake of this visibility the artist went so far as to have David swing his weapon in his right or his left hand, depending on whether his torso appears in frontal, rear, or side view.[13] The sketching process must accordingly have been primarily aimed at the double-sided painting.[14] It was only from its later (undocumented) phases that a terracotta bozzetto was produced. It formed the basis from which both the "modello finito" and the three surviving large-size studies were made (Louvre no. 1512–13, Uffizi no. 14965F). These studies[15] of course do not by any means correspond to the final phases of the development of the design—in contrast to most of the other surviving studies by Daniele. They deviate in detail almost as much from the paintings as from the later sketch versions and thereby attest to the trouble and difficulty of the process which led to the creation of the double-sided painting.

The fourth and largest group of sketches attests to similar difficulties (figs. 127–30). Although it coexists in part with the *David and Goliath* sketches of the Oxford sheet (fig. 123), it is the only group that has not till now been connected with Daniele. Instead it was claimed that it had been created in connection with a lunette fresco on the entrance wall of the Pauline Chapel.[16] But there is no source that mentions anything about a fresco project of the *Expulsion of the Moneychangers* for a lunette in the Pauline Chapel.[17] Moreover, to judge from the architectonic background in figure 128, the sketches presuppose a plan for a rectangular and not a semicircular frame.[18] The lunette fresco thesis functions as an alibi. It diverts attention from the true function of the sketches—the London painting of the *Expulsion of the Moneychangers* (fig. 131). Scholars found it hard to fit this painting into their scheme of things, for it is by neither Michelangelo nor Daniele.

In contrast to the first, third, and fourth group, the fifth group of drawings consists exclusively of sketches of individual figures. Two of these (fig. 126) are located on the recto of the Teyler sheet with the two Aeneas sketches (fig. 121), the other nine on the recto and verso (fig. 125) of Teyler sheet A29.[19] The subject in each case is a standing, draped male figure, composed in statuesque solitude; this figure was in part explicitly characterized as a niche statue. In both motif and typology it corresponds to the two large niche statues (Peter and Paul) in the chapel of Cardinal Giovanni Ricci da Montepulciano (†1574) in San Pietro in Montorio. Daniele had been commissioned to do the statues around 1555.[20]

The lonely remnant of a sixth group can be added to these relatively multipartite groups of sketches: the small sketch of a riderless equestrian monument in the Rijksmuseum in Amsterdam.[21] It is the only drawing of the "Michelangelo" corpus that can be connected to a commission in which both Michelangelo and Daniele were documentably involved. Michelangelo had been asked twice (on 14 November 1559 and 30 October 1560) by Catherine de' Medici (1519–89), the widow of King Henry II of France, who had died in an accident on 10 July 1559, to do the design ("il carico del disegno") for an equestrian monument for the dead king.[22] Nevertheless, he declined—Vasari writes[23]—because of his age and suggested that Daniele be entrusted with the task. Daniele subsequently executed "a small clay model according to the advice and judgment of Michelangelo" ("un modelletto secondo il consiglio e guidizio di M."), which then became the basis for the commission.

The Crisis of Faith and Its Transcendence

The six-partite mass of sketches was created at a time (1555–60) when Daniele's artistic career was at its apex. They reflect six different exploratory processes. Five of them refer to works that contemporaries regarded as creations of Daniele. The sixth refers to a painting (fig. 131) that scholars agree is not by Michelangelo. None of the motifs of their various figures is even approximately identical with their respective final products. Each is characterized by a distance between itself and the final product that presupposes further independent development. Moreover, this mass of sketches was certainly not part of Michelangelo's legacy. But there is considerable likelihood that it formed part of Daniele's estate. For in contrast to Michelangelo, Daniele left behind—according to the inventory conducted on 5 April 1566—mountains of "schizzi," "disegni," and "cartoni."[24] And these were all products of his own hand.

In view of these facts any reader will be hard put to accept that this group was "undoubtedly" created by Michel-

angelo. He will find it even more unlikely in view of the fact that it relates to the equally "undoubtedly" genuine group of Venusti-related sketches (figs. 100, 104–13) as a stylistic and typological contrast program. Large sizes are transformed into tiny ones, the "painterly" becomes sculptural, and the intimate becomes dramatic. Have scholars really never doubted what they today present to their public as a truism?

They have doubted—temporarily and in part. In the 1920s Panofsky was the first to begin combing through the "Michelangelo" corpus for allegedly lost Daniele sketches.[25] He indeed found a series of suspicious sheets, but none that belongs to our presently identified group of sketches. Instead, it fell to Wilde to come across something interesting.[26] He had been struck by the evident connection between the Aeneas sketch in Haarlem (fig. 121) and the copy after Daniele's Aeneas painting then located in Stockholm, and this led him to subject the sketch to scrutiny under the magnifying glass. Wilde found "discrepancies." He found that the figure style was internally disparate, the "treatment of forms and stroke pattern" was unlike Michelangelo's. He removed the sketch from the Michelangelo corpus and attributed it to Daniele. He did the same with the recto sketches of the Haarlem sheet (fig. 126), which relate—as Wilde did not know at the time—to the statues in the Ricci Chapel designed at the same time as the painting. Wilde's attribution, published in 1927, was welcomed by Stechow the following year.[27] But "authenticated," as Stechow thought, it was certainly not. For Wilde had neglected to analyze the remaining sketches that can be connected to works by Daniele, because he—like Panofsky—had assumed in advance that they were genuine products of Michelangelo's hand. In the final analysis his thesis thus seemed more like an unnecessary attempt to drive a wedge between stylistically similar drawings than an act of far-reaching reorganization.

But Wilde's thesis was done in by its association with Panofsky's attempt. This relatively wide-ranging undertaking was continued—under the same questionable presuppositions—by Baumgart in 1934–35.[28] The result was a potpourri of drawings whose stylistic variety is exceeded only by the "Michelangelo" corpus itself, and whose lack of reference to Daniele's paintings and sculptures could not remain hidden from anyone for long.[29] What was to be feared happened; in 1938 Berenson dismissed the previous search for Daniele sketches as premature and in the process singled out Wilde's attribution of the Haarlem sketches for attack—the only attribution that stood on halfway solid ground. Turning the knife, he played up the qualities of the Aeneas sketch (fig. 121) against the defects of the painted version—which he assumed to be the original. "Undoubtedly," he wrote, "the drawing served for the picture."[30] But this did not prove by a long shot that it was by Daniele. On the contrary: "It has all the dynamic ponderousness of the aged Michelangelo, as well as his tricks and mannerisms of notation at that period. Daniele reduced it to something sleek, half elegant, half brutal. Why should he draw so differently from the way he paints? He does not even quite transfer the drawing to his cartoon. Not only is the rest of his composition totally unlike the drawing, but the two principal figures are much more vertical, more 'classical' in the bad sense, than Michelangelo ever is. I know no drawing plausibly ascribed to Daniele that offers a justification for this attribution. What we have here is a note made by Michelangelo for one of his parasites, in this case Daniele da Volterra."

Berenson's ferocious criticism worked miracles. In 1953 Wilde recanted his Daniele attribution and confessed that Berenson had led him back to the true faith.[31] And as if to prove the sincerity of his conversion, in the same breath he acquainted the public with the previously overlooked relationship of the recto sketches of the Haarlem sheet (fig. 126) to Daniele's sculptures for the Ricci Chapel. This unconditional surrender gives one pause because Berenson's criticism was unusually subjective. What connoisseurs in general and Berenson in particular had all along considered as one of the most important indicators of identity between designer and painter or sculptor (the discrepancies between sketch and executed work in formal detail and in dynamic effect) was suddenly declared to be the expression of artistic inferiority and as an indicator that the author of the sketch and that of the executed work were not identical. Daniele was—according to Berenson's logic—not even capable of making proper use of the Haarlem sketch. How then should he ever have been capable of having drawn it himself!?[32]

Thanks to Wilde's capitulation, Berenson's logic became gospel.[33] It determined not only the thinking of Michelangelo scholars, but also—paradoxically—that of Daniele scholars.[34] The latter, accustomed to respecting the articles of faith of their more prestigious partners in all things relating to drawing, immediately made the main argument against heresies of Wilde's stamp their own. The main argument runs, in Berenson's formulation: "I know no drawing plausibly ascribed to Daniele that offers a justification for this attribution."

Berenson's formulation was correct. He and his successors were and are unable to know any sketch by Daniele comparable to the Haarlem sketches, for they know no Daniele sketches.[35] Their knowledge of Daniele's draftsmanship was

and is based on a cartoon fragment and a rather large number of large-size studies (among them figs. 119, 122)—drawings whose subtle, highly detailed contours and highly finished shading withhold any information about the sketching process that led to their execution.[36] But some scholars knew how to make a virtue out of the necessity of this one-sided knowledge. Daniele—said Levie[37]—never really sketched; instead he "designed in a study-like way." All at once—said Dussler[38]—he put his designs on paper in a way "that, while avoiding every sketch-like phase, seeks exclusively to bring out the plastic values, and thereby the drawing structure already largely approximates the appearance in the painting." By accident the "pupil" or "parasite" turned out to be a wonder of nature. And Berenson's argument, the "most important argument" (Dussler) concerning this question, turned into the following elucidation: the Haarlem *sketches* and their related drawings cannot be by Daniele because they do not look like Daniele's *studies*.

The Expulsion of the Moneychangers

The sketches for the *Expulsion of the Moneychangers* (figs. 123, 127–30) appear to be better protected against potential attacks than all the other groups of sketches. To be sure, in 1850 they were treated as products of Venusti.[39] But this long-since forgiven faux-pas can be explained—or so scholars think—simply by the fact that the alleged author of the painting in question (fig. 131) was prematurely equated with the name of the draftsman. Of course only the painting is by "Venusti." Why, they do not know, but scholars trust that it was no misstep to attribute it to him and yet not the related drawings. Nevertheless, as early as 1650 the painting had been attributed to Venusti,[40] but then in 1693 to Luca Cambiaso (1527–85).[41]

The sketches for the *Expulsion of the Moneychangers* form the largest of the six groups of proposed Daniele drawings. Moreover, it is the only group that reflects the final phases of the sketching process in addition to some of the beginning and middle phases. The sketch in figure 130 even appears to represent the cartoon phase. It corresponds—as Wilde recognized[42]—to the figure group of the painting even in size. So it is all the more amazing that it shows no place for the figural action. Did the painter sketch the architectonic environment himself?

Scholars generally preferred to play dumb when confronted with this question. Otherwise they would have had to answer the way Wilde answered: "We do not know the source of his

["Venusti's"] architectural background, but its remarkable design makes it unlikely that it was Venusti's own invention."[43] Wilde's answer is unobjectionable. Neither Michelangelo nor Venusti can be considered as designers of the painted architecture. Its preponderance over the figural components of the picture is alien to both. To be sure, the powerful cupola is reminiscent of Michelangelo's buildings. But the imbalance between the massive heaviness of its pendentive and archivolt zone and the daintiness of its columns are enough to delete every thought of Michelangelo. The pictorial space of the London painting presupposes an artist who viewed architecture as an organizing factor par excellence and who gave the historical site of an action at least as much importance as the actors themselves.

Daniele was such an artist. His authenticated paintings demonstrate this quality ad oculos. The *Senate Speech of Quintus Fabius Maximus* of the large frieze in the Palazzo Massimo (ca. 1538–43), the *Ascension of Mary*, and the *Massacre of the Innocents* in the Rovere Chapel in SS. Trinità de' Monti (ca. 1550–53) are composed according to a similar principle as the London painting.[44] In all cases the scene of the event is a closed stage of moderate depth whose cool monumentality and rigid symmetry give scope to the figures enhancing their dynamic. As in the *Expulsion of the Moneychangers*, in the *Ascension* and the *Massacre of the Innocents* the symmetrical effect of the architecture is largely determined by four columns (in the *Senate Speech* its equivalent is the powerful pair of cupola pillars). As in the *Expulsion*, in the *Massacre of the Innocents* and in the *Senate Speech* it is made more powerful by a centralized architectonic perspective. As in the London painting, stairs or pedestals are used to show the figures their seats, and architectonic elements with "rotation effects" reinforce the dynamism of the figural action. In all these cases even the chiaroscuro effects are aimed at emphasizing the plasticity and symmetry of both the architectural and figure elements.

The figures and architecture of the London painting are—as in Daniele's frescoes—in harmony with one another. The arrangement of the figures is oriented to the roundel in the tile floor marking the middle of the dome. At the same time it refers—through the position of the outermost of the moneychangers—to the invisible side arms of the room indicated by the stairs. The regularly curved silhouette of the group ultimately has its formal correspondence in the lunette and in the altar space with its lunette window, while the torsions of the Christ figure and of the most conspicuous moneychangers reflect the torsion motifs of the "Pillars of Salomon." This compositional linking of figure group and architectonic elements can hardly be explained by assuming that the former was subsequently given a container by a third hand. For whoever knows how to say "B" doesn't need to be told how to say "A." In fact the concept of a circular room is already implied in the mature sketch in figure 130. The architectural indications in figure 128 prove that it was developed simultaneously with the concept for the figural group. Double authorship (group concept by "Michelangelo," architecture concept by an unknown) is therefore out of the question.

We stand like Hercules at the crossroads. Either we cling to the never proven and unprovable thesis that the sketches for the *Expulsion of the Moneychangers* are by Michelangelo; in which case we must also attribute the architectonic overall design to him in spite of its total incompatibility with his historical paintings—or we hold to the justified assumption that the architectural frame was developed by Daniele; in which case we also have to recognize the figural sketches as Daniele's. I prefer to take the second road. For this one alone leads us out of the deadends into which the first one directs us. It explains not only why the sketches for the *Expulsion of the Moneychangers* are associated with four groups of sketches that are related to works by Daniele, it also solves a typological riddle—the question of why the striplike figure compositions have their only parallel not in Michelangelo's oeuvre but in that of Polidoro da Caravaggio (ca. 1495–1543), who was of the same generation and possibly a friend of Daniele. Polidoro's frieze composition of *The Gathering of Manna*, which survives in an etching by Michaeli Grechi, appears to have influenced the ensemble of figures in figure 130 down to the individual action motifs.[45]

To judge from their partial coexistence with the sketches for the *David and Goliath* painting (fig. 123) the *Expulsion* sketches were created either simultaneously with or immediately after the pictures for Giovanni della Casa (1555–56) and the preparatory work for the Ricci Chapel. In those years Daniele appears to have been intensively involved with architectural problems. In 1560 he appears in the sources for the first time as a building expert.[46] In 1563 he was named representative for the aged Michelangelo in the office of chief architect of St. Peter's.[47] This appointment presupposes not only a high opinion of Daniele's architectural abilities, but also implies that Daniele was acquainted with Michelangelo's Roman building plans. Two things are thereby explained in one stroke: (1) that the architecture of the London painting (fig. 131) is composed of motifs derived from Michelangelo's three most important late architectural works—S. Giovanni dei Fiorentini (organization of the presbytery), S. Maria degli Angeli (lunette), and St. Peter's (pendentive zone and cupola drum); and (2) that part of the sketches for the statues of the Ricci Chapel coexist with sketches for the dome of St. Peter's (Teylers Museum A29r). Whether the latter are by Daniele or—as is supposed to be "beyond doubt"[48]—by Michelangelo is a moot point. One way or another their coexistence with sketches for the Ricci Chapel reflects the close cooperation between the two artists, a cooperation that is indirectly reported by the sources of the 1560s.

Attributing the sketches for the *Expulsion of the Moneychangers* to Michelangelo meant that their function remained undetermined. The only certain and extant referent—the London painting (fig. 131)—could not be considered the object at which the sketches aim, and a corresponding monumental painting could not be found either in reality or as a subject mentioned in the sources. The attribution to Daniele also solves this problem insofar as Daniele—in contrast to Michelangelo—produced both cabinet paintings and frescoes. Nevertheless, the London painting was not painted by Daniele himself, nor is there any question of its having been painted by Venusti. Both the garishness of its color scheme, effected by harsh local color contrasts (in the drapery of the figures bright lemon yellow changing into orange, ultramarine, light green, wine red, and tomato red predominate), and the broad facial types with their widely spaced eyes and dimpled corners of their mouths, point to the hand of Giulio Clovio. The painting is the same size and also has figures of approximately the same size and number as Clovio's *Resurrection* painting in Cambridge (fig. 84). It relates to the latter like a pendant.

We know nothing about Clovio's personal relations with Daniele. What is certain is that the miniaturist was thoroughly acquainted with the painting for which the *David and Goliath* sketches (fig. 123) had been created. He quoted from it in his *David and Goliath* miniature, which was painted between 1555 and 1561 and is now in the Wildenstein collection in Paris.[49]

Daniele's Sketching Methods

Michelangelo scholars tend to take little notice that all facts speak against them as long as they have the feeling that their articles of faith are sanctified by a "style." Of course no one ever felt it necessary to analyze this style. But the analysis is worth undertaking. Thanks to the fact that the five groups of sketches have many parts, the style can be analyzed from two perspectives: first, by looking at the style of the *sketches*, and second, by looking at the style of *sketching*. It seems profitable to analyze the style of sketching first.

The five groups of sketches are among the most wide-ranging of the presumed "Michelangelo" corpus. Nevertheless, they seem to reflect the early exploratory stages of a conception less completely than, say, Michelangelo's sketches for the Rondanini Pietà (fig. 35). Their unusually large number of components therefore arouses the suspicion that they are the result of a specific conceptual behavior—especially in view of the fact that the problems of ideation were by and large simpler than those that Michelangelo had to overcome since circa 1533. In fact, the process of formal realization resembles in a sense walking in place. The differences between the first and the corresponding sketches that follow are generally smaller than those between the individual development stages in Michelangelo's *Fall of Phaeton*, *Last Judgment*, or *Pietà* (figs. 23–24, 30–32, 35). In many cases they relate only to a formal degree of clarity (figs. 125–26: apostle sketches; fig. 123: lowermost *David and Goliath* sketches). The relatively small repertoire of types of movement is indicative of this laborious development. Its limitations are expressed above all in the partial interchangeability of the bodily poses of thematically heterogeneous figures (Aeneas in figure 121; apostles at the left and right edges of figures 125 and 124; Christ in figures 128–30; the Davids in figure 123).[50] Both characteristics indicate a certain incapability on the part of the draftsman to distance himself from a form once it had been sketched. Instead of enhancing his imagination, the initial sketch seems to have had a laming effect. From time to time he needed a whole series of new starts in order to jump over his own shadow.

What consequences this laboriousness had when it came to sketching a multifigure action community can be seen in the fact that no less than twelve of the twenty surviving sketches for the *Expulsion of the Moneychangers* served only to explore the Christ figure. Even if only a minimum of sketches had been dedicated to the individual moneychangers, this would mean that the number of sketches of single figures would vastly outnumber the composition sketches. Unlike the case of Michelangelo, the sketches of individual figures functioned as independent "building blocks" whose integration in the figural group seems to have occurred only after a certain level of development was achieved.

The development of the overall idea occurred in two main phases. One is characterized by the left orientation of Christ's action, the other by a right orientation. The first main phase is represented by the composition sketch in figure 128, which is associated with a double arcade, the beginning of the second by the composition sketch on British Museum sheet no. 1860-6-16-2/1r (Tolnay, bib. 319, no. 386v). The Christ figures of both sketches proceeded from separate exploratory processes, one of which is documented by two small figures in the center of figure 127, the other by four small figures on British Museum sheet no. 1860-6-16-2/1v (Tolnay, bib. 319, no. 386r), three in figure 128, two in figure 123, and one in figure 130 (partially overdrawn by the figures of the right half of the composition sketch). Significantly, the laboriously explored right-oriented Christ figure was subsequently retained almost unchanged (figs. 129–30). Its development practically came to a standstill in the first stage while the group as such was further modified.

The same applies to most of the figures of the money-changers. The seated nude seen from the rear, for example, who appears for the first time on British Museum sheet no. 1860-6-16-2/1r, is found almost unchanged again in figure 129 (left sketch) and figure 130. He too must have been designed independently of the group. The development of the whole group proceeded by a process of assimilation and combination. This can be seen in the fact that the figures of the last composition sketch (fig. 130 have very different gestation periods. The basket-carrier on the left already appears in his final attitude in a sketch (fig. 128) that belongs to the first main phase of articulating the overall group composition. He is "older" than the seated nude seen from the rear and the frightened figure behind the seated figure with the barrel, who appear only at the beginning of the second main phase (British Museum no. 1860-6-16-2/1r). These latter two figures are again "older" than the figure at the left edge who first appears in figure 129, and "older" too than the woman with chickens behind the seated male nude, who first appears in the last sketch (fig. 130). But apart from the nude seen from the rear, the frightened man, and the figure at the left edge, none of these "older" figures has retained its original topographical relationship to the Christ figure and the periphery of the group. Each was combined with other, in part "younger" figures in the course of the group's development, and accordingly reoriented to the central figure and to the composition as a whole. Thus, when seen as a whole, the group was not "rejuvenated" in the sense that the figures of the first main phase of group development (fig. 128) were successively replaced by new ones. On the contrary, almost all of them are retained, even if more or less sharply modified, and "new" figures were merely added to them. Even the Christ figure received no fundamentally new pose in the second main phase. He appears only to be viewed in a somewhat modified perspective. The difference corresponds to that be-

tween individual figures within such Daniele paintings as *Moses and the Worship of the Golden Calf* (Dresden) or the *Massacre of the Innocents* (Rome, SS. Trinita de' Monti and Florence, Academy).

This one-sidedly "inductive" composition method manifested in the sketches for the *Expulsion of the Money-changers* appears to have been typical for Daniele. It also determined the creation of his Aeneas picture. In this case too the exploratory process began with individual sketches for the main figure—one of the two extant ones is located on the verso of Casa Buonarroti sheet no. 19 (center of the sheet; Tolnay, bib. 319, no. 368v), the other on the Haarlem sheet (fig. 121: outer left). In its second main phase a likewise separately sketched Ascanius figure was probably associated with the separately sketched Aeneas figure (fig. 120; Tolnay, bib. 319, no. 377). Only in its third phase, when the question of the milieu of the action of the Aeneas-Ascanius pair became pressing, did the bed and Dido appear—again on the Haarlem sheet (fig. 121). Whereas the Aeneas-Ascanius pair appear to have been formulated to the point where they were ready for execution, the bed and Dido remain still in an embryonic state—just like the horse of the Amsterdam equestrian monument sketch (Tolnay, bib. 319, no. 435), which sits upon a genetically "older" and accordingly more specifically articulated base.[51]

Unlike the cases of Condivi or Venusti, the laboriousness, complexity, and slowness of the design process relating to Daniele's works have *nothing* to do with weaknesses in visualizing bodies or space. On the contrary, they go hand in hand with a sure sense of proportion and a mastery of the structures and functions of the human body. And that is precisely an indication of authorship. For the artist who had difficulty formulating in every way was not Michelangelo but Daniele. His overconscientious and slow methods were ridiculed by his colleagues and drove his clients to frustration.[52] Daniele suffered from this[53] and felt himself increasingly isolated in the midst of an up-and-coming generation of fast painters for whom sketching was apparently child's play. But he was unable to change. For—as Vasari stated with regret—"his nature and his ingenuity were simply this way."[54]

Daniele's Style of Drawing

That Michelangelo scholars saw no reason up to now to retreat from their position is understandable in one respect. The sketches under discussion are more closely related to authenticated drawings from Michelangelo's late period (figs. 27–37) than all other non-Michelangelo drawing groups of the "Michelangelo" corpus discussed in this book. They have the appropriate small size and the expected three-dimensionality coupled with the expression of physical weight. They have everything that suggests the born sculptor and painter. There is only one thing they do not possess: the appropriate stroke system. Even their elements are different—smoother, flatter, on the average also thinner—than in Michelangelo's sketches. The variability in volume of the individual drawing stroke is limited, the threadlike character of the stroke is dominant from the beginning. The decisive changes in pressure occur almost exclusively in the sequence of strokes—as sometimes quite abrupt changes of stressed and unstressed strokes. The sketches lack the fine elasticity that in Michelangelo's case contributes so much to the vitalization of what is depicted.

Their stroke systems are comparatively static—as if they were constructed according to the principles of crystalline geometry. The contours are characterized by straight components or components tending to straightness. The figures, whose limb axes tend to form sharp angles, appear to be developed from the same basic stereometric forms as the pedestals, tables, and stools in the *Aeneas* and *Expulsion* sketches (figs. 121, 127–30).[55] It is no accident that their statuesquely closed contours are demonstratively connected with rigid rectangular frame shapes where the purpose of the sketch was a niche statue (fig. 125).

Curiously, the corrections tend to run parallel to the corresponding original strokes—as if their purpose consisted in the mere doubling of the original contour. Primary and secondary rails can be separated only in exceptional cases, because they—as in the cases of Condivi or Venusti (figs. 91–97, 100, 104–13)—usually occur in the same tonal strength. The result is a latent devaluation of the enclosing function of the contour. The contours seem to "dissolve," the bodies to meld with the surrounding space. Significantly, this devaluation is more pronounced when the drawings are shaded. Instead of following the spontaneous impetus of the wrist action, the shading tends to follow the contours of the body or of the limb axes. The denser and more expansive the shading strokes, the more they make the contour unrecognizable as an autonomous figure-defining line, because they integrate it into their own untectonic stroke system. Reinforcements of the contour are too scarce to counteract this devaluation.

The "stylistic" gap between these sketches and Daniele's studies (figs. 119, 122) thus turns out to be an optical illusion. Such a gap can be found wherever the act of making preparatory drawings disintegrates into an act of sketching and an act of working up the results of the sketching process—even in the case of Michelangelo (figs. 23–24). However much Daniele's studies might differ from the authenticated studies and highly finished drawings by Michelangelo—the differences are all along the same line as those between the corresponding sketches. The delicate, "passive" contour molded with the outermost shading boundary and the subtle hatching texture produced by exact parallel layers, which almost completely cover the contoured surfaces and materially and plastically qualify them—both are nothing more than the result of a deliberate realization of what the draftsman's movement already unconsciously strove for during the exploratory process. At the same time, however, it appears to be the expression of a largely invariable, rigid notion of what constitutes an object—and therein probably lies the explanation for the idiosyncratic perfectionism of these studies. Daniele's highly finished studies presuppose a total memorization of the sketching results. Without a laborious and lengthy exploratory process they would be inconceivable. Their sheer existence should make the senselessness of attributing the results of this exploratory work to Michelangelo obvious—or so one would think.

I: The Male Nude on Louvre Sheet No. 685-R and Michelangelo's Hercules Statue

To judge from the relevant literature, Michelangelo's *Hercules* statue and the pen-and-ink drawing of the Louvre sheet (fig. 4) have only two things in common: the masculine gender and a certain enigmatic quality. Otherwise they are supposedly separated by a gap of at least ten years (1492–94/ 1504–06). The lost statue is described in none of the contemporary sources, nor is the extant drawing reflected in any surviving statue. For decades, scholars have been guessing about what the former looked like and for what purpose the latter was made.[1]

The enigma surrounding the Louvre sheet results from an oversight committed at the beginning of modern Michelangelo scholarship. The oversight concerns the long inscription on the current verso of the Louvre sheet (fig. 2). This text is an introduction to a ledger kept by the "merchants and money-changers Donato di Bertino and Bonarroto di Simone." Because it is merely a business document, it never seems to have aroused particular interest. Berenson was perhaps the first scholar to dignify it with a reading. But he read it cursorily and without paying attention to the fourteenth-century character of the handwriting. As a result he committed a fatal error. He confused the banker and statesman "bonarotto di simone," Michelangelo's great-grandfather (1355–1405),[2] with Buonarroto di Lodovico (1477–1528), Michelangelo's favorite brother and an employee of the Strozzi cloth merchants.[3] His exegesis was published in 1903 ("This Buonarroti is, of course, M.'s brother").[4] Frey[5] thereupon determined that, since it was (theoretically) impossible for Michelangelo's brother to have operated an independent business before 1511,[6] the drawings of the Louvre sheet could have been created, at the earliest, in the second decade of the sixteenth century. Frey's successors, irritated that the style of drawing fit this period so poorly, were reluctant to believe him, although they were unable to contradict him. They arbitrarily placed the drawings in the first decade of the 1500s, hoping that Michelangelo's brother could have opened his obscure exchange business even *before* 1511.[7] Only in 1975 was Berenson's error revealed to the public—by Tolnay, who, while preparing the first volume of his *Corpus*, stumbled across a corrective handwritten note by the deceased Giovanni Poggi. In the meantime, of course, the dating derived from the false premise had taken on a life of its own. The generally accepted dating of the drawings to the first decade of the sixteenth century had become a cornerstone of the canonical chronology. Tolnay therefore did not allow himself to be swayed by Poggi's correction. He casually made the correction public (bib. 319, no. 26v) and otherwise acted as though his previous dating of 1505–06 had been correct all along. Joannides, in his review of Tolnay's *Corpus*, had no objections.

The dating founded on Berenson's sand has obviously distorted any objective view of the drawing. The male nude was seen as the contemporary of the *David*, the *Matthew*, the statues of the Piccolomini altar, and the ignudi of the Doni Tondo. Accordingly no attempt was ever made also to see those features that are not related to these works. Otherwise the fact that the body of the nude, although in a more passive state than his presumed playmates, appears heavier, stronger, and more "masculine," would presumably have triggered alarms. For a forcefulness exceeding even that of the most active Michelangelo figures of the first decade, coupled with an expression of contemplative peace, only has the weight of an attribute. Together with the knitted brows expressing *terribilità* and strenuous meditation and the traces of a moustache, it indicates the naked figure is a resting Hercules.[8] The curious head covering, which Valentiner misinterpreted as a turban and other scholars have ignored, is therefore meant as the lion's head helmet, and the stylized object indolently pushed against the thigh by the right hand that Valentiner took to be a cross and on which the figure's lowered gaze seems to rest is meant as the grip of the Herculean club. The standing motif and the figure's behavior identify the drawing as a sketch for a sculpture.

Between 1504 and 1529 Michelangelo's *Hercules* statue found its way into the Palazzo Strozzi in Florence. In 1529 it was sold and transported to France.[9] According to Condivi and most Michelangelo scholars, it must have been begun immediately after Lorenzo de' Medici's death (8 April 1492) and been completed in early October 1494 at the latest (that is, before Michelangelo's flight to Bologna in November).[10] But Condivi's report is—like his description of Michelangelo's youth in general—not very reliable.[11] It offers more riddles than it solves. The first riddle concerns the financial aspect of the enterprise. Condivi claims that Michelangelo's father had no sympathy for, and Lorenzo's heir, Piero de' Medici, no interest in, Michelangelo's artistic ambitions.[12] If that is true, the financial basis for the seventeen-year-old artist's purchasing the marble block for a larger-than-life sculpture and working on it in his father's house remains a mystery. The second riddle concerns the impact the statue had. It is hard to imagine how Michelangelo's many months of labor on a statue that displayed the Medici's "house patron" in monumental size for the first time could have been ignored even

by such curious Florentine chroniclers as the apothecary Landucci (1436–1516), if it is true—as Condivi claims—that it was created in Florence and at a time of growing anti-Medici sentiment.[13] The third riddle concerns the very existence of the statue. According to Condivi the incident of the *Cupid* forgery occurred *after* the *Hercules* statue was finished. But when the agent of the cheated Cardinal Raffaele Riario came to Michelangelo in 1496 (probably in the middle of June) to see something of his work, the artist had—according to Condivi—"nothing to show." He therefore grabbed pen and paper and drew a hand. Thereupon he was asked by his visitor whether he had ever done a sculpture. Michelangelo's answer: indeed, he had done a *Cupid*, among others.[14] Apparently no mention was made of a larger-than-life *Hercules*.

Michelangelo subsequently accompanied the agent to Rome and there created his *Bacchus* on commission from the cardinal, who had meanwhile been placated.[15] After its completion (June 1497), however, something happened that belies Condivi's statements about Piero de' Medici's lack of interest in Michelangelo's art, and which scholars have therefore only reluctantly acknowledged. The artist received—as he himself reported to his father on 19 August 1497—"from Piero de' Medici [who since his expulsion from Florence had lived in Rome] the contract for a *figura!*"[16] Michelangelo had already bought the marble, but had at first neglected to work on it, because Piero had not "adhered to what he promised" (owing to his dissolute way of life, Piero was chronically short of money).[17] Michelangelo finally decided to execute the statue for his own satisfaction. But the already purchased block proved unsuitable, and he was forced to buy a better one for the same price of five ducats.

This relatively low price which corresponded to that for the first block, together with the unsoundness of the first block and the fact that Rome had no marble quarries of its own, indicates that the second block had a similar origin to the first one (and the blocks for Michelangelo's last Pietà sculptures). It was chosen by the artist among those antique spoils offered for sale, the quality of which was always difficult to assess in advance (even while carving the *Pietà* in the cathedral in Florence the artist had trouble with unsuspected veins). This means that the second block (like the first one) was affected by what Condivi describes as a characteristic of the *Hercules* block: it had "been exposed to the water and the wind for many years."

Condivi apparently knew nothing of this Roman episode and the role Piero de' Medici played in it. But then he comes to speak of Piero immediately following his report on the *Hercules*: "While he [Michelangelo] created this statue, a heavy snow fell over Florence. Piero de' Medici . . . , young as he was, wanted to have a snowman made in the middle of his courtyard [of the Palazzo Medici] and remembered Michelangelo. He had him fetched and had him make the snowman and arranged for him to stay in the house as in the time of his father."[18] In Condivi's memory there must have been a connection between the creation of the *Hercules* and Piero's person. What type of connection remained hidden to the biographer. But the fact that one existed is sufficient reason, after what has already been said, to construe Condivi's chronology of the facts as the result either of a misunderstanding on his own part or of misinformation on the part of his informant, the aged Michelangelo. The events obviously occurred differently and in a different sequence from what Condivi and the scholars who swear by him report.[19] That Piero again remembered his former playmate Michelangelo only on the occasion of the great snowfall of January 1494 presupposes that Michelangelo had done nothing since Lorenzo's death to make the latter's son remember him. The commission for the snowman and the artist's return to the palace thus formed not the conclusion of the old relationship, but the beginning of a new one—a relationship that survived Piero's flight from Florence (9 November 1494) and created the precondition necessary for the creation of a resting Hercules. But if this Hercules was created in Rome and in connection with a commission from Piero, Michelangelo could have had no interest in broadcasting the news to the Florentines. For after the republican regime in Florence had already made mere contact with the exile a punishable offense, the acceptance of such an ostentatious commission would have been taken as a double affront. Thus it is not surprising that the artist, in a letter to his father, hid the subject of his sculpture behind the harmless "figura" and never again uttered a written word about his work on it, which probably occupied him until August 1498 (commission for the Pietà in St. Peter's). Nor is it surprising that the Strozzi, after purchasing the statue, made no efforts to enlighten the Florentines as to its background.[20] Around 1550 Vasari was still of the opinion that Michelangelo's *Hercules* had been commissioned by the Strozzi themselves and executed in their palazzo (built between 1489 and 1504).[21]

Correcting the traditional dating of the *Hercules* has its consequences. It makes a difference whether the larger-than-life sculpture was the work of a seventeen-year-old who had previously carved a faun's head and two small reliefs and had at most only an indirect knowledge of the famous antiquities of Rome, or whether it was the work of a twenty-two-year-old who had probably already executed two life-size statues (the *Giovannino* and the *Bacchus*) and knew the Roman

monuments at first hand. In the first case no direct connections to a Roman *Hercules* monument and to Michelangelo's *Bacchus* can be expected, while in the second case they must be expected. Actually, both are present in the male nude (fig. 4). The sturdiness of its body, with the weight concentrated on the left leg, the leftward orientation of the contemplative attitude, the position of the arm with respect to the presumed club—all appear to have been borrowed from that larger-than-life antique bronze statue of a *Hercules* equipped with club and the apples of the Hesperides (fig. 44), which, having been excavated during the reign of Sixtus IV (1471–84) and displayed in the courtyard of the Palazzo dei Conservatori, became one of the city's main points of interest in the closing years of the fifteenth century.[22]

Nevertheless, the right shoulder of the drawn figure appears to be farther forward, to be more obviously related to the forward movement of the lower leg than that of the bronze. The free leg is more strongly bent, its foot tucked more closely to the foot of the engaged leg, the right arm placed more closely to the body, the bending of the head more conspicuously contrasted with the axis of the torso. The contour accordingly appears more closed, the energy potential—in spite of the unobtrusive muscle formation—more powerful and gathered. In these discrepancies from the antique model an independent statuary idea is expressed. It is of the same inner dynamism as that which is objectified in the *Bacchus*. The relationship of the nude in the drawing to the *Bacchus* is that of a robust, grown-up, and sober brother. It suggests a block contour that is similarly closed and a volume that is similarly compact. The taut elasticity of its body construction and the space-producing play of the limb axes resemble an organically metamorphosed *Bacchus*. The drawing accordingly represents a sketch for Michelangelo's *Hercules*. As such, it is the only extant document that provides a reliable clue as to the appearance of the lost statue.

The degree of reliability is indicated by the ratio of measurements. The ratio of the size of the sketch (23.5 cm) to the size of the statue as indicated by Condivi (four "braccia" equal approximately 2.2–2.35 m) is almost exactly one to ten.[23] This simple ratio seems to have been Michelangelo's customary basis for dimensioning his *bozzetti*. It determined both the height of the *David* bozzetto (approximately 49 cm) modeled for preparing the marble *David* (approximately 5 m) in the Casa Buonarroti[24] and that of the bozzetto for the eight-and-a-half "braccia" high marble block (approximately 4.7–4.96 m) from which Michelangelo planned to chisel a Hercules-Cacus group in the fall of 1516 (or later), and which Bandinelli actually did carve in 1525 (this bozzetto measured approximately 48 cm before the raised arm was broken off).[25] In the case of our sketch the 1:10 ratio confirms what the high degree of differentiation of the contours already says in itself: that the sketch marks a relatively final stage of the relevant design process.

In 1540 the Louvre sheet apparently passed into the possession of Benvenuto Cellini.[26] The *Hercules* sketch became the most significant source of inspiration for his most important work of sculpture. The sketch determined the essential features of the surviving sketches (including fig. 79) for the twelve larger-than-life silver statues for which the goldsmith was commissioned by the French king after his arrival in Paris. Cellini presumably viewed the *Hercules* sketch as the ideal means for assimilating the spirit of Michelangelo's marble statue—a statue that he had to assume was the measure by which his own statues of the Olympian gods and goddesses would be judged at the royal court.

II: The Annunciation *Sketch at Oxford and the Legacy of Michelangelo's Servant*

The Oxford drawing (fig. 37) is not exactly a favorite among Michelangelo scholars. It seemed just good enough to be dated repeatedly and to be praised a bit now and again. Until 1966 it was generally considered to be an *Annunciation* scene,[27] but since then its subject matter has been interpreted as the appearance of the Risen Christ before Mary.[28] The reason for its creation and its destination remain obscure, and the only attempt to determine them proved unsuccessful.[29]

The drawing appears to have been drawn with the same black chalk that was later used to write the ricordo located in the upper left corner of the sheet. This ricordo (" . . . ci V[scudi] al pictore perdio . . . / . . . dro a pasquino per mandare a chasteldurante / legnie") presupposes the receipt of Cornelia Colonelli's letter of 13 December 1557, in which the widow of Michelangelo's servant Francesco Amadori (who was nicknamed "Urbino" and who died on 3 January 1556)[30] asked the artist for replicas of two paintings.[31] The duke of Urbino (Guidobaldo della Rovere)—so it is said in the letter—had learned the preceding October that Cornelia's two little children owned two paintings prepared from Michelangelo's drawings ("dua quadri retratti da vostri disegni"). He wanted to buy the paintings at any cost, and in the end, pressed on all sides, she had no choice but to acquiesce.[32] It now turned out that these paintings had been bequeathed to the children by her husband's last will and testament,[33] and as a result their sale had not been lawful. In view of this situation, she

wished that Michelangelo could arrange for Marcello Venusti to prepare two more paintings after the same drawings—cost what it may.[34]

The artist was happy to fulfill the request. For the ricordo describes what had already happened or was just about to happen: payment of ten or (fifteen ([die]ci or [quindi]ci) ducats to the painter,[35] and shipment (of the items paid for) to Casteldurante. It even records the name of the mule driver (Pasquino), who usually acted as messenger whenever Cornelia and Michelangelo exchanged letters or packages.[36] It was written either in the same December (1557) as the letter or at the beginning of the following year. In any case the two *quadri* receive no further mention in the later correspondence between Cornelia and Michelangelo (up to September 1561).[37]

Cornelia's letter is silent on what was depicted on the *quadri*. Certainly *not* depicted were the widow's two young sons (the younger of whom was not even born at the time of Urbino's death). The assertion that they *were*, which has haunted the Michelangelo literature since Thode,[38] and which in Tolnay's case led promptly to the "discovery" of the relevant portrait drawings,[39] rests on an error in translation. A researcher who was either careless or unfamiliar with sixteenth-century idiom had at some time interpreted Cornelia's phrase "dua quadri retratti da vostri disegni" as "two portraits" and thereby led his gullible successors astray. An estate inventory of the then duchess of Urbino, Lucrezia d'Este, conducted in 1592, provides us with the actual subjects depicted.[40] Of the two "Michelangelo" paintings listed in the inventory, one shows "Our Lord on the cross with two angels and Saint John and a Madonna," the other "an Annunciation." Both paintings came from the estate of Guidobaldo della Rovere, who had presented them to his daughter-in-law between 1570 and 1576.[41] After Lucrezia's death (1598) they went to her universal heir, Cardinal Pietro Aldobrandini.[42] Whereas all traces of the *Annunciation* painting were subsequently lost, the painting of the crucified Christ appears twice, in 1626 and 1682, in the inventories of the Aldobrandini collection—each time listed with the correct name of the painter (Venusti).[43] At some point it seems to have arrived at the Galleria Doria-Pamphili, where it is still to be found today, identified by the inventory number 340/164 (fig. 117).[44]

This 51 × 33 cm panel is of course not based on an ad hoc sketch by Michelangelo. It is a painted copy, expanded by the figures of Mary and John, after the crucifix drawing Michelangelo had created for Vittoria Colonna circa 1545 (fig. 33).[45] This drawing, which quickly became famous, was undoubtedly known to Cornelia's husband, as it had been created virtually under his eyes. But Michelangelo's servant may have regarded it as an incomplete, provisional drawing—as Tolnay did four hundred years later.[46] Urbino's simple spirit found the drawing lacking in the conventional touches, so he had them added by Venusti—without noticing that the poignancy and force of Christ's exclamation of doubt ("My God, my God, why hast Thou forsaken me?"), which according to Condivi was of so great consequence to Michelangelo, is compromised by the presence of the figures at the base of the cross. Michelangelo's uncompromising pictorialization of a biblical paradox (Matthew 27:46; Mark 15:34) was transformed into a conventional devotional painting.

This "improvement" is important in determining the origins of the second, the *Annunciation* painting, for it proves that Urbino was not concerned with owning two authentic Michelangelo compositions when he ordered the two paintings. He wanted two devotional paintings, created in the spirit of Michelangelo, but in the way *he* understood it.[47]

Urbino would thus have left it to Michelangelo's friend Venusti to develop the appropriate "michelangelesque" concept in accordance with his wishes. But a total of four *Annunciation* compositions by Venusti are known—two large-size compositions and two others derived from these, both cabinet-size pictures. The former are the 320 × 213 cm painting in St. John Lateran and the lost painting that once stood on the altar of Cardinal Federico Cesi's chapel in Sta. Maria della Pace.[48] Both had been commissioned by Michelangelo's intimate friend Cavalieri, and represented the most modern and most monumental approaches to the subject to be seen in Rome around the middle of the century. They may have been familiar to Urbino for this reason alone. The reduced replica that Venusti prepared from the Lateran *Annunciation* is no longer extant.[49] Its existence, however, is proved by the 40.5 × 54.7 cm cartonetto, which has been located in Florence since 1564 (fig. 102).[50] The supposed replica of the Cesi *Annunciation* (Rome, Galleria Nazionale), the cartonetto of which has also survived (fig. 101),[51] measures 45 × 30 cm, but is slightly cut on the top and sides. Its original dimensions probably corresponded fairly precisely to those of the *Crucifixion* painting (fig. 117). This external congruence of dimensions is matched by an internal one. The angel of the annunciation has the same size as the figures of Christ, Mary, and John; his wingspan corresponds to the length of the crossbar of the cross; the size of the Moses statuette is the same as that of the weeping angels. In addition, the facial profile of the Mary in the *Annunciation* looks like a rejuvenated duplicate of that of the Mary under the cross. The *Annunciation* and *Crucifixion* paintings relate to each other like pendants. One

represents the beginning, the other the end of the Son of God's earthly career. If the latter was painted for Urbino, then so too was the former.[52]

Michelangelo's Oxford drawing confirms this conclusion (fig. 37). It is so intimately connected with the *Annunciation* painting, both typologically (the angel coming from the right) and in motif, that it could be considered a sketch for Venusti's work. Of course it cannot be such a sketch, if only because the *Annunciation* painting is based on sketches (including fig. 100) by Venusti himself that were developed directly from his Lateran *Annunciation*.[53] The close connection between the Oxford drawing and Venusti's painting might therefore express a deliberate relationship.[54] Michelangelo apparently took Cornelia's request as an occasion to conjure up in his mind, once again, Venusti's *Annunciation* panel commissioned by his servant, and to develop a new composition based on the old one. The new composition corrected what probably always disturbed the artist in his friend's work—the unmotivated discrepancy in the size and position of Mary and the angel, the episodic quality of the action, the inexplicable, vague quality of the angel's message. Michelangelo's angel has no wings (like all Michelangelo's angels), is ethereal and of commanding height. Carefully raising the veil over the lower body with his left hand, he allegorically reveals to the future mother of God the secret of what will happen to her. Mary herself acts as though she were recovering from a sudden shock. Her movements are halting. While her right hand pauses—frightened, questioning, doubting—the left appears to be gingerly probing the reality of the miracle, to be thrusting itself forward along the surface of the desk toward the angel's hand.

For the time being, the question of whether Venusti actually cited this sketch when he executed the replacement painting requested by Urbino's widow must be left unanswered. No such painting is known to date. On the other hand, it is documented that Michelangelo subsequently presented his sketch to his friend Jacopo del Duca—together with the sheet containing a series of sketches for the Christ and the sleeping apostles of a Gethsemane scene (fig. 36). These sketches were also intended for one of Venusti's paintings. This gift is mentioned in a letter written by Daniele da Volterra to Vasari on 17 March 1564.[55] In the eyes of the writer, it was one of the most memorable events of the artist's last years and was—as the letter indicates ("se uene ricorda," "as you remember")—also known to Vasari.[56] Obviously, Vasari and Daniele both knew that these "certain small sketches" ("certi disegni piccolj") had been created partly "for those Annunciations" ("dj quelle Nuntiate"), and partly "for the Christ who prays in the garden'' (''del Christo che ora all'orto''). It also appears as if both were in agreement that the sketches and the corresponding paintings belonged together.

Daniele had a concrete reason for reminding Vasari of the gift-giving episode. At the time the letter was written, Michelangelo's nephew and heir Lionardo Buonarroti (1519–99) was in Rome attempting to buy the ''small drawings'' from Jacopo del Duca, so as to please the disappointed duke of Florence (''Ma il nipote per donare qualche cosa al duca glieli leuara''). And he did succeed in pleasing the duke, but not by giving him the genuine articles. After returning to Florence in May 1564, Lionardo gave the duke in their stead two supposed Michelangelo drawings: the cartonetto for the replica of Venusti's Lateran *Annunciation* (fig. 102) and the cartonetto for Venusti's *Gethsemane* painting (fig. 103).[57] The duke regarded both cartonetti as genuine.[58] He was apparently convinced that he had in his hands precisely those drawings that Michelangelo had personally presented to Jacopo del Duca.

It is understandable that Vasari, although he knew better, did not tell the duke the truth. What is astonishing is that he tried to hide even the actual purpose of the two cartonetti from him. In the *Lives* dedicated to the duke, Vasari abruptly describes the *Annunciation* cartonetto (fig. 102), the derivative of the Lateran *Annunciation*, as the latter's preliminary. In the same breath he acts as if the panel, which was over three meters high and located in one of the most important churches in Rome, were a small cabinet piece (Cavalieri supposedly commissioned it from Venusti for no other reason than that Venusti had a talent ''for small pictures''!).[59] This deceiving tactic makes sense only if it is understood as a means to increase the value of the cartonetto in the mind of its owner. It suggests that in Vasari's opinion the real purpose of the cartonetto would not have satisfied the duke's expectations. The duke apparently expected two things: first, that the drawings put before him were genuine, and second, that the purpose of their creation must be lofty.[60] Vasari suggested this loftiness to the duke through his frantic attempt to connect at least one of the two cartonetti directly with Cavalieri and his prestigious ecclesiastical commission. It is the same cartonetto that the duke had framed.[61]

That Vasari considered it necessary to increase the value of the two cartoons artificially to make them acceptable to the duke presupposes their ''low'' purpose. Given the circumstances, this can mean only that they were in truth drawn on commission from Urbino's widow, in which case, however, Michelangelo comes under suspicion of having acted contrary to Cornelia's wishes. This suspicion of course cannot be substantiated—unless a plausible motive existed for the possibility that Michelangelo acted arbitrarily. One did exist. The paintings that the servant had had painted contradicted the artist's ideas. To have them repeated in the same form would moreover have meant that the injustice done Urbino's widow by the duke would be compensated by a mere pair of replicas. On the other hand, Michelangelo was certainly not eager to disappoint Cornelia. On the contrary, he wanted to suggest to her that her money was fetching both what she wanted and something more than she expected. For this reason, no deviation would have been made from the pendant character of or the number of figures in the original paintings. Both were respected. The choice of the Gethsemane scene ensured that a scene of the Passion and of divine sorrow again stood opposite the Annunciation. By depicting Christ twice, the number of figures was harmonized with that of the original painting, the painting of the *Crucifixion*. In the case of the *Annunciation*, this numerical correspondence with the original picture was achieved by keeping the Moses statuette—in spite of the fact that it is basically superfluous, being no more the object pointed at by the angel. Contrary to the original pictures, both substitutes had the form of a horizontal rectangle of probably the same size. As indicated by the cartonetti (figs. 101–02), their figure sizes must have been determined by each other—as in the original pictures. In contrast to the figure sizes of the original pictures, they have grown considerably, just as the paintings themselves are considerably larger. But in contemporary thinking, this increase in size meant an objective increase in value. Whether Michelangelo had personally conceived the Gethsemane picture, or whether the *Annunciation* picture reflected the more famous or the less famous of Venusti's monumental compositions, was probably unimportant to Cornelia. The increase in material value was certainly not.

The *Gethsemane* and the lost *Annunciation* paintings were therefore, in all probability, the answer to Cornelia's request. Which means that at least the Oxford *Annunciation* sketch (fig. 37), but presumably also the Oxford *Gethsemane* sketch (fig. 36), served a different function from that which is usually attributed to them. They apparently document not so much the ordinary process of preparing a work as merely the "prologue" to one. They might have been intended as non-binding suggestions to be handed to Venusti. For that reason they need not have passed into Venusti's possession. Their purpose was fulfilled when the friend had understood Michelangelo's general idea of the two pictures. Thus it becomes readily understandable that two years later they could have been given to a third party not involved in the Cornelia affair—as does the fact that no painting exists in which either sketch is literally copied. Michelangelo respected the artistic independence of his friends—in contrast to some Michelangelo scholars who prefer to deny it.

Notes

1. For the proceedings and circumstances attendant to Michelangelo's death, see Frey, bib. 102, 2:33–48.

2. Ibid., 2:82, 901. The inventory is reproduced in Gotti, bib. 118, 2:148–56; see also Vasari, bib. 329, 4:1848–51.

3. Frey, bib. 102, 2:902.

4. Ibid., 2:33.

5. *Michelangelo*, bib. 186, 1:318.

6. Aretino, bib. 4b, 1:112–13; 2:162.

7. Frey, bib. 102, 1:35–39. Frey doubted that this drawing, "the so minutely finished ear" ("l'orecchia cosi minutamente finita") of which Aretino had admired above all, was really by Michelangelo. He was chastised on this account by Baumgarten (bib. 24, 354n2), but his assertion was not disproved.

8. Frey, bib. 102, sub voce.

9. Vasari, bib. 329, 1:7.

10. Ibid., 1:117.

11. On the question of the authenticity of the "Michelangelo" drawings owned by Vasari, see Ragghianti Collobi, bib. 249, 150–52. Like the sketch for the suspension device, the corrected pupil's drawing, and the *Catherine*, the lost Michelangelo drawing once included in the "Libro" of Vasari's friend Vincenzo Borghini (1515–80) was also a product of the artist's youth—judging from the fact that its owner considered it to be donatellesque (Vasari, bib. 329, 3:226).

12. Vasari, bib. 329, 1:117; cf. chap. 3, n. 23.

13. *Michelangelo*, bib. 186, 1:121.

14. Sebastiano's life and work are described in Hirst, bib. 139.

15. Vasari, bib. 329, 1:118, 122, 126, 240–42; 4:1907–27. See also Perrig, bib. 220 and bib. 221.

16. Vasari, bib. 329, 1:68, 122, 124; Varchi, bib. 327, 16.

17. Vasari, bib. 329, 1:68.

18. Ibid., 3:1123–24.

19. Ibid., 1:68; 3:1124.

20. Frey, bib. 99, 347.

21. Vasari, bib. 329, 1:118, 122.

22. Ibid., 1:122, 260–61, 266; 3:1123; 4:1936–40, 2054.

23. Steinmann and Wittkower, bib. 290, 435, nos. 59–60.

24. Vasari, bib. 329, 1:118, 121–22; 4:1898–99, 1902–03, 1905.

25. See chap. 5.

26. Vasari, bib. 329, 1:118.

27. See Gotti, bib. 118, 2:155–56.

28. Vasari, bib. 329, 4:1905.

29. See Frey, bib. 102, 2:54.

30. Vasari, bib. 329, 1:70; Perrig, bib. 228, 3:8–9.

31. According to Vasari (bib. 329, 4:412), after the death of Pope Clement VII (1534) Alfonso Lombardi had prepared a wax model for the tomb of Clement and Leo X—"on the basis of some Michelangelo sketches" ("sopra alcuni schizzi di Michelagnolo Buonarroti"). Cf. Norberto Gramaccini, *Alfonso Lombardi*, Frankfurt a.M. and Cirencester, 1980, 63–64. Nevertheless, these do not appear to have been ad hoc sketches. They were probably drawn in 1524–26, when

the project of a double tomb for the two Medici popes was first discussed and designed. Bugiardini, on the other hand, received spontaneous, direct assistance—according to Vasari (bib. 329, 1:259–60). It consisted of Michelangelo's tracing in charcoal a line of naked figures on Bugiardini's panel of the *Martyrdom of Saint Catherine*. On Michelangelo's assistance in drawing for Condivi, Venusti, and Daniele, see chap. 6–8.

32. Vasari, bib. 329, 4:1566. See also Wolf, bib. 352, 71, no. 42.

33. Vasari, bib. 329, 1:88–89. See also Perrig, bib. 226, 33–35. The names of Ammannati and Nanni di Bacio Bigio are given by Vasari. That they are correct, seems to be proven by the terracotta relief of the Virgin and Child which is attributed to Ammannati (Perrig, bib. 226, fig. 7). For this relief presupposes the knowledge of the Louvre sheet No. 685 (here fig. 4) which belonged to the sheets given by Michelangelo to Antonio Mini.

34. Vasari, bib. 329, 1:119, 279. See also Perrig, bib. 222, 261–74, and p. 116 above.

35. Vasari begins his report on Michelangelo's last act of destruction (bib. 329, 1:117) with the phrase "come io so che" ("as I know"). He *had* to have known it indeed, because he had been informed about it almost simultaneously by several parties. See note 1 above; and Frey, bib. 102, 2:29.

36. Tolnay, bib. 318: "Only a part of Michelangelo's drawings has survived; in fact he himself gave orders for the destruction of his drawings, 'so that no one might see the hardships endured by him,' as Vasari relates. However, we think Vasari's sentence should be understood as being limited to the lascivious drawings that Michelangelo had executed in his youth and maturity along the lines of Renaissance erotic art, which contrasted with the religiosity of his later years. This modesty in relation to one's own work is rather typical of mannerists like Vasari [but he, apparently, never gave a thought to destroying his own drawings!]. . . . Otherwise it would be impossible to explain how on earth so many studio drawings by Buonarroti have survived."

37. See note 16 above.

38. See note 5 above.

39. Tolnay, bib. 320, 189–226.

40. The fifth volume of Tolnay's Michelangelo opus (bib. 302), published at that time, includes in its catalogue section—in addition to the drawings of the "final period"—a series of addenda to the catalogue sections of the earlier volumes. It therefore reflects Tolnay's opinion as of 1960.

41. Included are the "Michelangelo" drawings of the Teyler Museum published by Knapp (bib. 159a), and those in the Vatican and the Archivio Buonarroti published by Tolnay (bib. 295 and 296).

42. Delacre is ignored in Tolnay's *Corpus* (bib. 319), even though he anticipated a considerable share of the attributions made therein.

43. Bertolotti, bib. 42, 10–19. See also Popp's corrections, bib. 246, 66–67n2.

44. "Vasari implies that it was the concern he felt about the commission (with its intimidating aspect of *paragone* with Raphael) which prevented him [Sebastiano] from carrying it out," thought Hirst (bib. 139, 130–31), without considering what a ridiculous role he thereby assigned to Michelangelo, who allegedly supplied the sketches.

45. Including *Drawings*, bib. 76, no. 38, and, most recently, Tolnay, bib. 319, no. 255r.

46. Vasari, bib. 328, 8:558. For Clovio's *vita* see Bradley, bib. 47. Giulio's drawing and the Windsor drawing are first mentioned together in 1983 by G. Passavant (bib. 210a, 207–09), who could explain their similarity—according to his premises (Windsor drawing by Michelangelo and thus independent of Giulio's) only by positing a common prototype. Both drawings—he believes—depend directly on Martin Schongauer's (ca. 1450–91) engraving of the *Resurrection* (5.2). Unfortunately, however, neither composition bears any resemblance to Schongauer's.

47. Cf. Perrig, bib. 223.

48. Dussler, bib. 80, 7.

49. Dussler himself felt it necessary to register strong doubts expressed by other scholars about Michelangelo's authorship in at least 30 of a total of 243 "indubitable" cases (bib. 80, nos. 5, 55–58, 83, 94, 131, 134, 137, 145, 147, 158–59, 171, 176, 179, 189, 192–93, 196, 199, 208–12, 216, 240, 242).

50. What Dussler (bib. 80) or Hartt (bib. 130) offer the reader in the introductions of their catalogues, and what Hirst offers in his book *Michelangelo and His Drawings* (bib. 139b) can hardly be described as a phenomenology of Michelangelo's drawing style and the development of his draftsmanship.

51. Hartt, bib. 130, nos. 2, 155; Tolnay, bib. 319, nos. 4, 100; Hirst, bib. 139a, 11, 39. See also Perrig, bib. 231.

52. Most recently Goldscheider, bib. 115, no. 40; Hartt, bib. 130, no. 89. For the correct dating see Gilbert, bib. 112.

53. *Drawings*, bib. 77, no. 89.

54. Wilde, bib. 344, no. 29.

55. The pen-and-ink and chalk drawings on the British Museum sheet no. 1887-5-2-116 and on the sheet in the Brinsley-Ford Collection in London, which Tolnay (bib. 319, nos. 52, 94) generally declared to be preliminary studies for the cartoon of the *Battle of Cascina* (1504) or the Christ statue in Sta. Maria sopra Minerva (1514 or 1518–19), are further examples of these many "revivals." In reality, the drawings are by the young Cellini (see Perrig, bib. 229, 4:24–25). See also chap. 5, note 49.

56. Degenhart, bib. 66.

57. Ibid., 303–05 (on the characteristics of the Milanese style).

58. This section, abridged to include only the most necessary information, repeats the contents of Perrig, bib. 227.

CHAPTER 1
Drawing and How It Is Produced

1. Winkler, bib. 348, no. 645.

2. See also Perrig, bib. 227, 91–92n19.

3. According to Dussler, bib. 80, no. 354. Brinckmann (bib. 49,

no. 15) stated that the Madonna sketches had a "shifting and hopping stroke pattern."

4. On Cellini's authorship, see Perrig, bib. 229, 26–37, 50, 83.

5. On Cellini's authorship of the sketches in figure 74, see Perrig, bib. 229, 62–69, 83.

6. See Tolnay, bib. 315, 20.

7. In the initial state Mary was probably kneeling on a stool. The twice-revised lower leg was bent sharply to the left, the left hand was placed in front of the chest. The head was almost en face.

8. On the purpose of this type of quoting, see Perrig, bib. 220.

9. On Cellini's authorship of these drawings (figs. 78–79) see Perrig, bib. 229, 30–37, 77–79, 82–83.

10. See Arnheim, bib. 6, 147, 188–90, 192–93.

11. On Michelangelo's and Daniele's alleged stippling method see Perrig, bib. 227, 92–93n21.

12. On Cellini's authorship of the drawings in figure 75, see Perrig, bib. 229, 31–33, 38–41, 83.

13. On the phenomenology of a beginning draftsman's style see Perrig, bib. 227, 79–87. On the copying of hatchings see ibid., pp. 67–68.

14. On Mini's authorship of the sketches in figure 55, see Perrig, bib. 226, 37–39.

15. Perrig, bib. 221.

16. On Mini's authorship of the hatching of St. Anne and the drawings in figures 52–54 and 56, see Perrig, bib. 227 and bib. 231.

17. On the Adam studies see chap. 2, n. 166.

18. For a list of copies of the "modello" see Perrig, bib. 230, 282 n57.

19. Meder (bib. 184, 487) thought rather too optimistically when he wrote (1923): "The older criticism which would, meaning well, point to the best of the lot as the original is today suspect."

20. It was regarded as the original—with certain reservations—by Berenson (bib. 34, 36, no. 1614), Frey (bib. 101, no. 18), Thode (bib. 294, 2:350–58; 3:no. 539), Rinaldis (bib. 262, 200–01), Panofsky (bib. 200, 51), and Delacre (bib. 69, 249–50, 252, 254, 298); as the "best" copy by Brugnoli (bib. 50, nos. 42–43), Goldscheider (bib. 115, no. 75), Hartt (bib. 130, 395), Joannides (bib. 151, 257), and Gere (bib. 77, no. 124). Woodward's keen-sighted assumption (bib. 353, 24) that it was by Clovio's hand was taken with as little seriousness (except by Wilde, bib. 343a, no. 457 and Dussler, bib. 80, no. 722) as Bradley's groundless equation of the original with the Uffizi example no. 245F (bib. 47, 59n).

21. Cf. Hirst (bib. 138, 253–54) on the history of the reception of this example, which was mentioned in passing by Frey (bib. 101, 11), attributed to Venusti by Berenson (bib. 36, no. 1614), and first published in 1964 by Tolnay (bib. 309, 141 and plate XLI).

22. Tolnay, bib. 319, no. 344. In Tolnay's commentary his earlier description (bib. 302, 3:112) is repeated word for word, even though it was originally written in reference to the incomplete Windsor example.

23. Hirst, bib. 137–38 and bib. 139b, 112.

24. Tolnay, bib. 319, no. 336.

25. Popp (bib. 246, 64) with good reason assumed that the writer was Clovio's pupil and collaborator Claudio Massarelli da Caravaggio.

26. *Drawings*, bib. 77, no. 127: "In spite of the old inscription on the back . . . which can only mean that this drawing was at some time believed to be one of the copies by Clovio . . . , the doubts as to its authenticity are surely ill-founded, as Wilde maintained."

Tolnay—if only temporarily—was one of the few scholars who refused to accept such an argument as legitimate (bib. 302, 3:221–22, no. 121; bib. 305; bib. 306, 289); however, in the end he gave it a new twist (bib. 319, no. 336) by stating that the drawing was both original and copy, a kind of Michelangelo-Clovio co-production. Begun on the outer right by Michelangelo, the whole of the left had been completed by Clovio. Afterward the miniaturist "bragged" in writing on the back of the sheet that he had "executed the whole copy of the drawing" [!] ("e poi nella scritta del verso si vantò d'aver fatto tutta la copia del disegno").

27. This knowledge cannot be gained from the literature. None of the more recent manuals of drawing (Hutter, bib. 142; Koschatzky, bib. 161; Leymarie, bib. 172; Tolnay, bib. 315) concerns itself with the question of the features that identify originals and copies. Meder (bib. 184, 486), who listed some distinguishing characteristics, had no illusions about the practical use of this list. He was still a long way from taking into account the kinetic aspect of the problem.

28. The same congruence between the black-chalk contours of the preliminary sketch and the red-chalk contours of the definitive drawing also characterizes the *Flagellation of Christ* on Windsor 0418. That the preliminary sketch in this case was accurately recognized (most recently by Dussler, bib. 80, no. 705) is probably due to the inscription on the verso of the sheet ("Julio Clouio da M.Angelo Bon.t").

29. Dussler (bib. 80, no. 363) declared them *expressis verbis* to be indicators of an original—without noticing that he thereby also raised Louvre 1505 to the status of an original.

30. Tolnay, bib. 302, 5:195–96, no. 198; Tolnay, bib. 319, no. 411.

31. In Tolnay's version, one way or another the conclusion is wrong. For according to him it was a "pupil" who sketched the angel.

32. The same is applicable to the other versions of this composition.

33. The hopelessness of reproducing an erased fine hatching in chalk so that it corresponds to the original caused some copyists to use an ink wash in order to recreate the effects of chalk shading. Examples of such copies using ink wash facsimile copies are the Colonna crucifix copy in Norfolk (Mrs. Brakley Collection) and the Colonna Pietà copy in Haarlem (Teylers Museum A90); another is the lost "Archers" (?) example that—under the heading "battaglia degli Dei"—figures in Fulvio Orsini's estate inventory of 1600 (Steinmann, bib. 290, 435) and which was incorrectly equated with Michelangelo's original by Steinmann and Wittkower (bib. 290), and Dussler (bib. 80, no. 721).

34. Cf. Dussler, bib. 80, no. 589. Hirst, too, seems to regard it as

a copy. In his *Michelangelo and His Drawings* (bib. 139b) no drawing of this subject is mentioned.

35. The ambiguous places of the Courtauld example include:

1. The head of the female nude seen from the rear who is undressing herself. It is impossible to identify in which direction it is looking. In the New York example (Pierpont Morgan Library iv.7) it appears as a lump seemingly separated from the torso, and with its face turned toward the right as in the Norfolk example (Dussler, bib. 80, fig. 262); in the Chatsworth example (Dussler, bib. 80, fig. 263), on the other hand, it appears as a ball-shaped thing turned to the left.

2. The nodding head of the lowermost figure of the right half of the "circle of vices." It provides no information about the type of headdress or about its spatial relation to the right thigh. In the New York example it appears to be bald and to bend over the right thigh. In the Chatsworth example it is veiled and only its nose protrudes over the thigh (in the Norfolk example the right part of the "circle of vices" fell victim to the cutting of the sheet).

3. The two figures above the sleeping figure. The left one in the foreground is presumably supposed to be pulling a bedsheet over its head from behind, with its arm reaching back, while the right one more in the background seems to lounge like a shapeless mummy. In the Chatsworth example the foreground figure is engaged in an activity that looks like head-scratching, while in the New York example it looks as though it is pressing its head. Its companion in the New York example appears as a hard-to-decipher contour-phantom with a pointed nose directed downward, while in the Chatsworth example it looks like a bent-over, deeply veiled seated figure.

36. See chap. 2, n. 88.

37. In the Frankfurt example (Städelsches Institut no. 3979) and in the mirror-image engraving by Nicolas Beatrizet (Rotili, bib. 268, fig. 21) the calf seems to grow from the head of one of the archers in the background. In the fresco of the Galleria Borghese, which had been painted on the basis of the engraving for the Casino Olgiati (Pergola, bib. 214, 2:181, pl. 180), it is omitted.

38. The two first engravings (Rotili, bib. 268, no. 38) are by Béatrizet (ca. 1515–65). The second (a later proof of the first) is dated 1553. The third engraving, dated 1556 (Rotili, bib. 268, no. 31), is by Enea Vico (1523–67). All three correspond in size (28.2 × 39.5 or 28.5 × 40.6 cm) to the Berlin example, figure 26 (28.8 × 40.1 cm).

CHAPTER 2
Authenticated Drawings and Criteria for Authentication

1. Christina Riebesell has recently disclosed a most illuminating early case of massively wrong attribution concerning the drawings of the Farnese collection in Rome (bib. 261a, 124–31). At the death of its first owner, Cardinal Alessandro Farnese (1520–89), this collection, which was systematized neither by author nor by provenance, contained 638 sheets, most of which (ca. 403) bore drawings by Giulio Clovio. Until 1653 (at the earliest) its stock remained virtually unaltered, apart from a loss of 18 sheets that occurred between 1588 and 1626. But within these sixty-four years the Clovio sheets successively disappeared from the inventory lists and the Giulio Romanos diminished from 17 to 1 piece, whereas the number of the sheets by prominent authors successively grew (in 1653 the original number of the Michelangelos and Raphaels had tripled!). Nobody knowing this fact will ever again be able to put his trust in an attribution without having previously ascertained its historical foundation.

2. Cf. Perrig, bib. 226, 29.

3. In the literature the authenticity of the drawing is always supposed to be self-evident. See Salvini, bib. 270, 136, and Salvini, bib. 271, 38; Keller, bib. 156, 79; Tolnay, bib. 319, no. 26r (inscription not mentioned).

4. See chap. 1, n. 13 above.

5. Perrig, bib. 226, 32–39.

6. Cf. Seymour, bib. 277, 7–8; Liebert, bib. 174, 220–21. For the earlier interpretations see Seymour, bib. 277, 84–85n5, and Clements, bib. 60, 415–20. Einem (bib. 88, 35) and Tolnay (bib. 319, no. 19r) draw from the inscription the conclusion that the marble *David* was meant as "an ideal self-depiction" of Michelangelo. On its political implications see Levine (bib. 170) and Verspohl (bib. 331). According to Wittkower (bib. 350, 104–10) the *David* is the last of Michelangelo's sculptures that was created with extensive use of the drill ("arco").

7. Weinberger (bib. 338, 87–88) doubted that it was created with reference to the marble *David*: "the forearm seems longer and the hand is not in a position to hold the end of the sling." But that the right hand of the executed statue holds the end of a sling is also impossible to see.

8. Gaye, bib. 109, 2:55.

9. Ibid., 2:52, no. IV.

10. For the history of the bronze *David* see Barocchi, bib. 328, 2:217–23; Parronchi, bib. 208, 1:153–55; Règaci Courtois, bib. 258, 250–53. The lost work seems to have been cited (1) in the small painted *David* sculpture that appears as an akroterion figure on the temple in Francesco Granacci's Metropolitan painting of the *Birth of John the Baptist* (Holst, bib. 140, fig. 10); (2) in the youth dressed in loincloth and leather armor in the right niche of the plaster frame surrounding the *Twins of Catania* in Rosso Fiorentino's Gallery of Francois I at the castle at Fontainebleau (Règaci Courtois, bib. 258, 252–53).

Balas (bib. 11) believes she can see the copy after a second, lost sketch of the bronze *David* by Michelangelo on a sheet from the castle museum at Blois that she published. This view, however, is based on long disproved suppositions. It is difficult to see how the drawn object ("a mature, bearded man") is supposed to bear any resemblance to a *David*.

11. The second case of an inscription with explanatory character is

located on British Museum sheet no. 1859-5-14-824r (after 5 February 1518). Tolnay, bib. 319, no. 57r.

12. On its meaning see Weinberger, bib. 338, 394–95; Gilbert, bib. 111, 394–95; Tolnay, bib. 319, no. 189r. For the design of the "Fama" idea in the executed tombs see Perrig, bib. 230, 275.

13. Cf. Perrig, bib. 230, 247, 259–62.

14. Transcription according to Wilde, bib. 344, 91, no. 55.

15. On Cavalieri's authorship of the *Fall of Phaeton* drawing in Venice cf. Perrig, bib. 224; see chap. 5 ("Cavalieri's Figure and Composition Style").

16. Transcription according to Frey, bib. 101, no. 75.

17. *Michelangelo*, bib. 186, 4:49. Throughout the literature (most recently, Tolnay, bib. 319, no. 343r; Frommel, bib. 104, 55; Liebert, bib. 174, 277n14) the phrase "io ebbi il mio Fetonte" is interpreted in the sense of a receipt for Michelangelo's finished drawing (fig. 24)—despite the fact that this interpretation makes little sense in the context of the letter. I myself previously translated the expression (Perrig, bib. 224, 166) as "I *received* my Phaeton"—thinking that "Fetonte" meant Cavalieri's sketch in Venice (fig. 66). This opinion was based on (1) the current but apparently erroneous supposition that the inscription on the sheet in Venice is Michelangelo's (nothing supports such a supposition) and (2) on the assumption that it was precisely *this* sheet that was returned (which is improbable in view of the wording).

18. My previous attribution of this verso drawing to Cavalieri (Perrig, bib. 224, 170), which was based on inadequate familiarity with Cavalieri's drawings, has in the meantime been adopted by Frommel (bib. 104, 116n61); in Tolnay, bib. 319, no. 343v, it is implied in the claim (which relies on Goldscheider, bib. 114, no. 96, and bib. 115, no. 93, and Hartt, bib. 130, no. 369) that the drawing was copied after a "modello di Michelangelo, forse una prima versione" of the "Leah" for the Julius tomb, created around 1542. The attribution is nevertheless untenable. The drawing is a product of Mini—as Berenson (bib. 37, no. 1617; bib. 35, 243, 252, 275), Popp (bib. 242, 20; bib. 243, 75), and Dussler (bib. 80, no. 717) had already assumed. It belongs to a group of stylistically and physiognomically similar head and half-figure drawings (including figs. 50–51 and Tolnay, bib. 319, no. 307v, 308v, 309–10, 314v, 315v, 316v, 320–21, 330r, 331v), all of which are clearly products of a student's coming to terms with Michelangelo's "Perini" sheets (see note 93, this chapter, below). All extrinsic indicators as to time of creation point to the 1520s, all authorship indicators to Mini, whose self-portrait appears to be present in Tolnay, bib. 319, no. 331v. More detailed information on the subject will be found in a forthcoming publication planned by the author.

19. Cf. Perrig, bib. 224, 168–69.

20. Frey, bib. 103, no. IX; Girardi, bib. 113, no. 5.

21. The previous datings (1511–12; including Tolnay bib. 296, 427; bib. 302, 105–112; bib, 319 no. 174; bib. 320, 197–98.) can be regarded as superseded since Gilbert's (bib. 112) correction of Tolnay's chronology of the paintings.

22. Guasti, bib. 124, 158; Gilbert, bib. 112, 159.

23. *Michelangelo*, bib. 186, 1:328; *Michelangelo*, bib. 187, 37–38, no. XXXIII; Tolnay, bib. 319, no. 117.

24. Tolnay, bib. 319, no. 367.

25. A similar joke is found in a letter from Michelangelo to Gherardo Perini in 1522 (*Michelangelo*, bib. 186, 2:343). There the signature consists of an "M" adorned with two angel's wings.

26. Frey, bib. 103, 62–77, 351–60; Girardi, bib. 113, nos. 179–228.

27. Tolnay, bib. 319, nos. 57–58, 441–476r, 478–81, 485v, 486r, 505v.

28. Cf. Wilde, bib. 344, no. 35; Dussler, bib. 80, no. 154; Neufeld, bib. 191, 279–80.

29. Since Berenson (bib. 34, no. 1491) it has been repeatedly claimed—most recently by Tolnay (bib. 319, no. 227r) and Bertelà (bib. 38, no. 307)—that the sketches were prepared for a stonemason. For an opposing view see Neufeld, bib. 191, 279.

30. On this model see Barocchi, bib. 329, 3:950–52; Neufeld, bib. 191, 279–80; Lebrooy, bib. 164, 102–03; Tolnay, bib. 320, 208, no. 36. On the meaning of the projected river gods see Perrig, bib. 230, 272–74.

31. Doni, bib. 75, 3:24.

32. Cf. *Michelangelo*, bib. 186, 171, 173, 214, 227. According to Hartt (bib. 130, no. 252) the London sketches could have been created as early as Michelangelo's three-week stay in Carrara in April 1521 (bib. 187, 106).

33. Wilde, bib. 344, 70.

34. For unexplainable reasons, in the previous literature the sketch has been reproduced either held vertically (Tolnay, bib. 296, fig. 38 and bib. 302, 3:fig. 163; Dussler, bib. 80, fig. 66; Barocchi, bib. 16, pl. CDLXI) or vertically hanging (Hartt, bib. 130, no. 250; Tolnay, bib. 319, no. 225v) or lying on its back and pointing to the left (Gurrieri, bib. 124a, fig. 174). It has been judged accordingly (Hartt, Tolnay, and Guerrieri see in it a study for the left hand of Giuliano). For a contrary view see Perrig, bib. 227, fig. 19.

35. On Michelangelo's habit of holding the hammer with his left hand while sculpting see Gaye, bib. 109, 3:583.

36. On Jacopino's portrait of Michelangelo, located at the Metropolitan Museum since 1977, and its copies, see Steinmann, bib. 287, pl. 8, 10–11, 14; Tolnay, bib. 316, 206n1; Montebello, bib. 189, no. 48. According to Tolnay (bib. 314, 19–20; bib. 316, 206–08) this portrait and Bugiardini's portrait of Michelangelo (Steinmann, bib. 287, pl. 2–6; Parronchi, bib. 209; Redig de Campos, bib. 254) are each supposed to reflect a self-portrait drawing (a blatant contradiction of Vasari's statements, bib. 328, 6:206 and 7:258). The reason: the head drawing in the Louvre (no. 2715), which corresponds to Bugiardini's portrait type and is executed in a fine miniaturist style, stems from Michelangelo himself (according to Parronchi, bib. 208, 1:159; Tolnay, bib. 319, no. 118; Joannides, bib. 153, 682 at no. 118).

37. According to Barocchi (bib. 16, no. 343) it is "certo anteriore."

38. On this poem Frey, bib. 103, 104, 383, no. XCIX; Girardi, bib. 113, 23, 196–98, no. 45.

39. On Buonarroto's life see Gotti, bib. 118, 2:20; Liebert, bib. 174, 50–52.

40. Previous datings: (1) 1520–21 (Hartt, bib. 130, no. 250); (2) ca. 1524 (Tolnay, bib. 302, 3:213, no. 89); (3) ca. 1525 (Barocchi, bib. 16, no. 343); (4) 1525–30 (Dussler, bib. 80, no. 46; Tolnay, bib. 319, no. 225v); (5) 1532 (Wilde, bib. 344, 3, no. 1); (6) 1547 (Frey, bib. 103, 383, no. XCIX).

41. Tolnay (bib. 319, no. 396r) reads from the sketch "un tenero amore per l'oggetto che la mano tiene."

42. According to Girardi (bib. 113, 442, no. 273) the sketch "evidentemente" found its way onto the sheet *before* any of the verses. Nevertheless, because it is located below the center of the sheet and because the last line of the third strophe of the poem in no way accommodates it, it speaks more as evidence for the contrary.

43. On the authorship of the *Annunciation* sketch and cartonetto see chap. 7, n. 43 below.

44. Cf. Perrig, bib. 222, 261–79, and above, Excursus II. Tolnay (bib. 321, 214n4) dated the painting ca. 1547.

45. Frey, bib. 103, no. CXIX; Girardi, bib. 113, no. 272.

46. Girardi, bib. 113, no. 272, IIb.

47. Barocchi, bib. 14, 1:82.

48. Cf. Frey, bib. 103, 372, 473–74.

49. The incorrect dating of the sheet in the first decades of the sixteenth century led to a confusion of contradictory theories as to the drawing's purpose. In these theories the *Madonna with St. Anne* figures as (1) a sketch for Christ's ancestor, the Ozias for the Sistine Chapel ceiling (Berenson, bib. 34 and bib. 37, no. 1579; Steinmann, bib. 286, 602, no. 49, 655–56; Frey, bib. 101, no. 27); (2) a sketch for the Pitti Madonna (Hartt, bib. 130, no. 57; Keller, bib. 156, 78); (3) a sketch for an unknown marble tondo (Tolnay, bib. 302, 1:190, no. 33; Tolnay, bib. 306, 273; Tolnay, bib. 319, no. 26r; Dussler, bib. 80, no. 208; Berti, bib. 40, 406n18; Weinberger, bib. 338, 104); (4) a sketch for the Pietà in St. Peter's, transformed into a study for the Medici Madonna (Popp, bib. 244, 134–39, 174). The contour drawing, however, exhibits symptoms of an early style similar to that of the first two reliefs (ca. 1492). Thus Mary's right foot appears inexplicably to break through the ground level indicated by its left foot and St. Anne's right hand—a phenomenon paralleled in the lowermost zone of the *Battle of the Centaurs*, where individual limbs of the figures sink purposelessly into the ground. In both cases the cause of this incongruity was probably a lack of experience in the projection of limbs. It also caused the distorted perspective of the right foot and left shoulder of the *Madonna of the Stairs*. Indeed, the present drawing relates to this latter relief like an iconographic refinement. The attitudes of St. Anne and Mary are vehicles of a mute dialogue referring to the fate of the child. Whereas Mary's torso leans toward the inside of the picture as if she had been suddenly frightened, the child steps into St. Anne's field of vision (who recalls an aged *Madonna of the Stairs*). He is thereby drawn into her gloomy vision (Mary's lower right arm forms a bridge between the two figures) and simultaneously becomes the subject of the fearful question that appears to be expressed in the abrupt head-turning of the mother.

50. According to Tolnay (bib. 319, no. 26r) it appeared on the sheet *before* the male nude.

51. Only Hartt (bib. 130, no. 57) seems to have grasped its ironical expression. Tolnay, who had earlier described the subject of the sketch as a "caricature profile" (bib. 302, 4:184, no. 53), as did Berti after him (bib. 40, 402), subsequently called it a "faun's head," following Brinckmann (bib. 49, no. 2) and Popp (bib. 244). It reminded him of the faun's head on British Museum sheet 1895-9-15-495 (bib. 319, no. 16)—a drawing that might stem from Cellini, the sometime owner of the Louvre sheet (Perrig, bib. 229, 31–37, 50, 167n362, no. 40; see also chap. 4, n. 8 below).

52. On Michelangelo's "caricature style" see Vasari, bib. 329, 4:2084–89.

53. The earliest documentably authenticated drawing—which is also the only documented highly finished drawing executed in pen and ink—depicted a seated *Prudentia* with three small boys. It survives in a facsimile copy (Uffizi 614E; Barocchi, bib. 15, no. 199 and pl. CCCIX) and three student copies—Chantilly, Musée Condé no. 28rv (Delacre, bib. 69, figs. 81–82); British Museum, Ff. 1–5r (Wilde, bib. 344, no. 89 and pl. CXLI); Milan, Ambrosiana, Cod. Resta, F.261, INF.17. The facsimile is possibly identical with the "figura di penna di Prudenza con due [*sic*] puttini di Michelangiolo fatta da D.n Giulio" mentioned in Clovio's inventory (Steinmann and Wittkower, bib. 290, 434). Ignored by most scholars (including Tolnay), the lost original (or the copy taken for it) was dated by some from the time of the Sistine Chapel (Thode, bib. 294, 2:347 and 3:no. 210), by others in the 1520s (Dussler, bib. 80, no. 500; Wilde, bib. 344, no. 344; Barocchi, bib. 15, no. 199). In reality it was probably a product of Michelangelo's autodidactic early period (ca. 1485–89). The copies share a number of idiosyncratic flaws and therefore cannot be ascribed to the copyists (who worked independently of each other). In particular they include a lack of spatial depth and a flatness of the figures, a number of vague details, the imbalance of the execution, and the lack of proportion between the amount of shading and the degree of figural modeling. Presumably the drawing was made after an antique relief. Evidence for this hypothesis is provided by the following: (1) the extensive background shading—it renders the sheet surface in the vicinity of the figures as a compact wall of indeterminate proximity; (2) the curious vagueness of the parts belonging to the background layers of the picture (left leg of the boy hiding himself, rear part of the cloak of the mask wearer, among others); (3) the missing indications of a ground plane; (4) the "classical" physiognomies, postures, and properties.

54. *Michelangelo*, bib. 186, 3:419.

55. Of the two, the London example (fig. 14) is generally believed to be the original (cf. esp. *Drawings*, bib. 77, no. 47; Tolnay, bib. 319, no. 263r). Its relation to the Frankfurt example (fig. 15)—apparently known to only a few scholars—has never been investigated. Cf. above, pp. 33–34.

56. Perrig, bib. 220 (see also Dussler, bib. 82, no. 1562). According to scholarly statements, the "Cristo" mentioned in Sebastiano's letter cannot be traced (cf. Hirst, bib. 139, 129–30). No wonder: the drawing on figs. 14–15 has already been assigned a subject and a

purpose. Its subject is considered to be a *rising* Christ. The uncritical attitude that stands behind this designation is reflected, for example, in Tolnay's reversal of opinion. Following Popp's example (bib. 243, 75, bib. 244, 172; bib. 245, 10), Tolnay had initially dismissed the drawing as schoolwork (bib. 296, 445n60; bib. 302, 3:188)—on the grounds that the drawing, if interpreted as an "Ascension" (!), would be nonsense. Given this generally acceptable assessment, there remained only *one* way to rehabilitate the drawing: revision of the previous interpretation. This could have been done easily, seeing that Berenson (bib. 34 and bib. 37, no. 1523) had already indirectly pointed to the dubiousness of the Resurrection interpretation and Goldscheider (bib. 114, no. 81; bib. 115, no. 83) had even already named the alternative by name ("certain details . . . remind us of the 'Christ in Limbo'"). But Tolnay preferred to use the backstairs. In 1956 (bib. 302, 5:180, no. 166) he annulled his earlier verdict without so much as expressing doubt about the method that led him to his original interpretation (cf. most recently, bib. 319, no. 263r). The reader is accordingly forced to conclude that Tolnay regarded the Christ in figures 14–15 as a risen Christ, although as such it appeared "contradictory and absurd" (Tolnay, bib. 296).

For Tolnay's thesis regarding the drawing's purpose see Perrig, bib. 228, 24–26n14.

57. Significantly, Michelangelo's Christ is illuminated from the right. The direction of the light corresponds to the direction of Christ's forward foot and appears to be deliberately harmonized with the intended pictorial context. It presupposes the idea of a pair of ancestors (Adam and Eve) who are illuminated from where Christ is coming. Curiously, Sebastiano changed it to the normal illumination from the left—with the result that the light source appears to be in limbo itself, and Christ, instead of stepping from the light into the dark, absurdly seems to be stepping from the dark into the light. The painter probably thought the actual lighting conditions where the painting was to be displayed more important than the contextual meaning of the light. His concern for lighting conditions had in fact caused him to deviate from Michelangelo's model already on an earlier occasion. Sebastiano's *Flagellation of Christ* in S. Pietro in Montorio is illuminated from the right, while Michelangelo's lost drawing for the Christ figure is—as is proven by Sebastiano's composition sketch in the British Museum (Tolnay, bib. 319, no. 73), in which Michelangelo's drawing is quoted—illuminated in the normal way, i.e., from the left.

58. Michelangelo had departed for Florence on 29 April 1532, where he remained until mid-August (Thode, bib. 293, 1:420–23).

Previous datings: (1) 1517–18 (Hartt, bib. 130, no. 183); (2) 1518–20 (Robinson, bib. 264, no. 61); (3) ca. 1532–33 (Wilde, bib. 344, 90; Hirst, bib. 139, 130); (4) ca. 1533 (Goldscheider, bib. 114, no. 81 and bib. 115, no. 83); (5) ca. 1533–34 (Dussler, bib. 80, no. 328); (6) ca. 1534 (Tolnay, bib. 302, 5:180, no. 166 and bib. 319, no. 263r).

59. Vasari, bib. 329, 1:234.

60. Popham and Wilde, bib. 240, 11ff.

61. Steinmann and Wittkower, bib. 290, 434.

62. Similar verso inscriptions are located on the Windsor example

(no. 0472; fig. 20) of the *Tityos* ("Julio Clovio d M Angelo Buonarrotj") and on Windsor sheet 0418 with the *Flagellation of Christ* ("Julio Clouio da M. Angelo Bon.t").

63. See chap. 1, note 25.

64. Cf. *Drawings*, bib. 76, no. 42; *Drawings*, bib. 77, no. 127 Wilde, bib. 347, 152; Hirst, bib. 139b, 111–13; see also above p. 34. Setting aside the "quality," it is another verso inscription that seemed to speak in favor of the originality of the drawing ("andrea quaratesi venne quj a di 12 di ap[r]ile 1530 ed ebbe [struck out: a 10] p[er] ma[n]dare a suo padre a pisa"). Written by an unknown hand, it relates to a money transaction on the part of Michelangelo's friend Andrea Quaratesi (1512–85), the son of the Florentine banker Riniero Quaratesi, and therefore indicates the possibility that the sheet once belonged to Michelangelo. But, as Popp (bib. 243, 75, and bib. 246, 64), Tolnay (bib. 302, 3:221–22, no. 121; bib. 305) and Dussler (bib. 80, no. 721)—explicitly or implicitly—already ascertained, this inscription cannot be considered as an indicator of the authorship of the drawing on the recto. For according to his inventory (Steinmann and Wittkower, bib. 290, 433–34) Clovio possessed several sheets that came from Michelangelo's workshop, ten of which were provided with Michelangelo drawings such as "Un candeliere," "Una finestra," "Due profeti," "Un schizzo di penna di gamba et bracci," "Una porta," etc. Possibly the miniaturist received them en bloc from that same Andrea Quaratesi, whom he may have known during his stay in Florence in 1551–53.

65. In addition there are two partial copies in the Louvre (nos. 811, 818) and a third in the Ambrosiana.

66. Fulvio Orsini's estate inventory of 1600 proves how common the practice of framing drawings was in the sixteenth century (see Nolhac, bib. 192). Each and every one of the twenty "Michelangelo" sheets or cartoons listed there (Steinmann and Wittkower, bib. 290, 434–35) was encased in a walnut frame ("corniciato di noce"). The marks of this framing are distinctly recognizable on the extant sheets and cartoons (figs. 24, 34, 95). Similar marks can also be found on the original of Michelangelo's *Dream* (Tolnay, bib. 319, no. 333) and on Venusti's Annunciation cartonetto in the Uffizi (fig. 102; cf. Excursus, note 61 below). Owners appear to have shown a considerable lack of attention to the peripheral zones of drawings.

67. Vasari, bib. 329, 1:265.

68. Holst, bib. 140, 53 and figs. 56–57.

69. Baglione, bib. 10, 147.

70. Nevertheless, only *one* figure appears to be indubitably feminine—the hovering figure on the left (also distinguished from the other figures by her headdress). Since Panofsky (bib. 206, 225) the literature always refers to two. But the reader is not told where the second is located.

71. According to Panofsky (bib. 206, 226) the boys are working "apparently in order to harden the arrow-heads by dipping them red-hot into a goblet." In reality the (easily combustible) feathers of the arrows, and not their tips, are lying in the fire—as Dussler (bib. 80, no. 721) noticed.

72. "Ogn'ira, ogni miseria e ogni forza / Che d'amor s'arma uince ogni fortuna" ("Every anger, every misery, and every force—

whoever arms himself with love conquers every fate"). Frey (bib. 103, 19 and 315, no. XXVII) and Girardi (bib. 113, 16 and 182, no. 29) dated the poem fragment ca. 1524–26.

73. Cf. Summers, bib. 292, 304–07 (the most solidly grounded of all previous interpretations).

74. As Summers (bib. 292, 215) noted, Benedetto Varchi (1503–65) provides indirect evidence that the drawing of the *Dream* located today in the Courtauld Institute in London (Tolnay, bib. 319, no. 333; Bradford and Braham, bib. 46, no. 30) was made for Cavalieri. In his *Due lezzioni* (Florence, 1549, 50), Varchi calls Cavalieri the "beautiful person or thing who sometimes awakens us from the dream of human life" (quoted from Summers, bib. 292). He thereby alludes to the winged genius whose call causes the awakening youth to perceive the place of his existence as a hollow container of masks and as a source of restlessness and to become conscious of the desolate nightmare-reality of his previous condition. This genius is usually interpreted as an angel (Summers, bib. 292, 215; Liebert, bib. 174, 310), although Michelangelo's innumerable authenticated angels appear without wings and are the size of adults (fig. 37). More recently, he was described as the personification of virtue by Tolnay (bib. 319, no. 333 and bib. 322, no. 79), and as the "Genius of Fame" by Frommel (bib. 104, 66). As Marabottini (bib. 183a, 354) recognized, in reality he represents Eros, the god whose essence is surprise. He appears here in the role of the platonic Daimon who in a sudden revelation reawakens in man the consciousness of the world of ideas and thereby reveals earthly reality to be a world of appearances.

75. *Michelangelo*, bib. 186, 3:445–46.

76. The continually repeated claim that the "doi uostri disegni" refer to *Ganymede* and *Tityos* (figs. 14, 19; Tolnay, bib. 319, no. 344r; Hirst, bib. 138, 257 and bib. 139b, 111–12; Frommel, bib. 104, 15; Liebert, bib. 174, 277n14) was formerly based on the erroneous opinion that the *Ganymede* original was longer than it was wide (see above p. 3) and had therefore been conceived as a pendant to the *Tityos*. This opinion was in turn based on the fiction that both drawings were related to each other like two verses of a love poem (alleged message: Just as Ganymede felt himself carried off by the eagle of Zeus, so did the—fifty-seven-year-old—artist feel himself carried off by the "furor amatorius," while at the same time suffering the tortures of Tityos over his presumptuous love). In Tolnay's case this interpretation became an idée fixe, allowing him to claim out of the blue (bib. 319, nos. 344r and 345r) that Cavalieri himself had referred to the *Ganymede* and *Tityos* as pendants—in a letter dated 6 September 1533 (*Michelangelo*, bib. 186, 4:49).

77. *Michelangelo*, bib. 186, 4:1–3.

78. According to Ramsden (bib. 251, 1:183n4) the enclosure was "a portfolio of drawings, from which Cavalieri was free to choose what he liked." Judith A. Testa, on the other hand, thought (as quoted in Liebert, bib. 174, 271) "that Michelangelo was not referring to the drawing, but, rather, to passions that cannot be named in writing and that were the inspiration for the series of presentation drawings."

79. On the example in the Uffizi, cf. Barocchi, bib. 15, no. 278; on that in the Paris collection, cf. Jaffé, bib. 149.

80. A seventh copy was in the possession of Francisco Pacheco (1564–1654). It was accepted by him as the original (bib. 198, 35)—a view that is shared by De Maio (bib. 70, 121).

81. Barocchi, bib. 15, pl. CCCLXIX; Tolnay, bib. 319, 2:110.

82. The lower half was accordingly considered an arbitrary addition by an unidentified copyist until 1975—in spite of the fact that it appears not only on figure 17 and in Louvre no. 826, but also in the Beatrizet engraving (Rotili, bib. 268, fig. 18) and in several paintings (including one described by Pacheco, bib. 198, 35). Advocates of the contrary opinion (Berenson, bib. 37, no. 1614; Kirschenbaum, bib. 158, 100; Sedlmayr, bib. 275, 260) went unheard.

83. Panofsky, bib. 206, 216.

84. Vasari, bib. 329, 1:118. See also chap. 5.

85. The history of appraisal of the Uffizi drawing (fig. 58) reflects in a nutshell that of the appraisal of the "Michelangelo" corpus as a whole. "Certainly not by Michelangelo," decreed Berenson (bib. 34, no. 1634). The same view was shared by Jacobsen (bib. 145, 258) and also by Frey (bib. 101, no. 18), who assumed Alessandro Allori (1535–1607) to be the author. On the other hand, Thode (bib. 294, 3:no. 216) considered it "beyond doubt that this powerful sketch originates from no one other than Michelangelo. The only question is whether it is an original or a copy. It seems to be the first version of the ideas later developed in another composition for Cavalieri." Delacre (bib. 66, 250–53) was more concerned with the "riddle" of how a Michelangelo could arrive at something so "tame" and "common" as his finished drawing (fig. 18!) after such a "wild" sketch (fig. 58). Wilde simply assumed that the drawing was "perfectly genuine" (bib. 345, 274n2). Dussler (bib. 80, no. 498), however, refuted Wilde with the statement "that the way the drawing is executed does not in the least betray M's hand: the contours are rough and lacking in nuance and the type of modeling is equally alien to the master." Barocchi (bib. 15, no. 277) found Dussler's criticism justified and for her part pointed to "Il chiaroscuro dolciastro e il segno non sempre sicuro." The "tratto spiritoso" and the "garbata delicatezza di certi contorni e del paesaggio" reminded her of Cavalieri's contemporary Francesco Salviati (1510–63). Hartt (bib. 130, 383) excluded the drawing from the "Michelangelo" corpus without comment, while Hirst (bib. 137, 166; bib. 138, 256) reincorporated it—with the comment that "the touch is entirely characteristic of Michelangelo and the pictorial invention is magnificent, worthy of inclusion in any anthology of representations of the subject." Tolnay, too, ultimately reincorporated it into the corpus—but only as a copy (bib. 319, no. 298r). Joannides (bib. 153, 683) found this inadequate. In his eyes the drawing is "a worn and faded original, possibly strengthened along some contours, but approaching Rembrandt in the brutality of conception."

86. Vasari, bib. 329, 1:118.

87. On the Uffizi copy, cf. Barocchi, bib. 15, no. 279; Lecchini Giovannoni, bib. 166, no. 11. On the Windsor copy (no. 0471), cf. Popham and Wilde, bib. 240, no. 458.

88. The most important deviations affect the following parts of

Tityos's body: (1) the eyes and base of the nose; (2) the section of the arm that appears between the vulture's neck and Tityos's thigh; (3) the left thigh (in fig. 20 it appears without a hint of chains, while in the Uffizi and Windsor copies it appears fastened by a cord); (4) the chains of the right calf and the right upper arm. Windsor no. 12771r (fig. 19) is ambiguous at all four places!

89. Cf. n. 76 above.

90. Hartt (bib. 130, no. 184, 353) stood the chronological relationship between recto and verso on its head. According to him, the verso sketch was created ca. 1517–18, i.e., fifteen years before the recto drawing.

91. Cf. most recently Tolnay, bib. 319, no. 345v (and in contrast bib. 296, 445n60, and bib. 302, 3:189: "a kind of pasticcio"); Hirst, bib. 138, 258, bib. 139b, 113, 115, and bib. 139c, no. 43; Poggetto, bib. 236, 79; Liebert, bib. 174, 285. In contrast Perrig, bib. 220, 24–28 (erroneous attribution to Sebastiano del Piombo).

92. Vasari, bib. 329, 1:118.

93. The three other authenticated "teste divine" were created in the 1520s, allegedly for the Florentine aristocrat Gherardo Perini (1480–1564). They have survived exclusively as facsimile copies:

1. "Furia": Florence, Uffizi no. 601E and 18738F; Frankfurt, Städelsches Kunstinstitut no. 3972; Haarlem, Teylers Museum A6r; formerly London, Vaughan Collection; Windsor no. 01365r.
2. Three women's heads in profile (three ages of life): Florence, Uffizi no. 599E–r; Haarlem, Teyler Museum A13r; Montpellier, Musée Fabre no. 73079 (fragment of a copy).
3. So-called Zenobia (Venus with Amor and Mars): Florence, Uffizi no. 598E–r; Windsor no. 0419.

The Uffizi examples (nos. 601E, 599E, and 598E) are apparently identical with the "tre carte" that were once in Perini's possession and after his death passed into the possession of Duke Cosimo's son Don Francesco de' Medici (1541–87) (Vasari, bib. 329, 1:122), and which are listed in the Medici inventory as Michelangelo's originals (Frey, bib. 102, 2:57n). They have therefore been equated with the originals since ca. 1964 (Tolnay, bib. 319, no. 306–08r; Wilde, bib. 347, 151–52; Poggetto, bib. 236, 76; Bertelà, bib. 38, no. 308; Joannides, bib. 153, 683; Hirst, bib. 139a, 555 and bib. 139b, 107–09). In reality all non-stylistic evidence supports Mini's authorship, as will be shown elsewhere. Mini was probably the recipient of the drawings. Perini's role in the affair seems to have been limited to convincing his contemporaries, after Mini's and Michelangelo's departures from Florence (1531 and 1534, respectively), that the products of Mini's assiduous labors were original drawings and personal presents from Michelangelo (see the obtrusive "dedication" and "signature" on Uffizi 601E).

94. On the painting, cf. bib. 43, no. 153. The Louvre sheet is reproduced in Tolnay, bib. 319, 2:100.

95. Cf. Tolnay, bib. 318, no. 92, and bib. 319, no. 327r; Joannides, bib. 153, 683 at no. 306; Hirst, bib. 139b, 116–17, and bib. 139c, no. 48.

It was regarded as a copy first by Berenson (bib. 34, no. 1655); Jacobsen (bib. 145, 326); Steinmann and Pogatscher (bib. 289, 417 and 504), and Thode (bib. 294, 2:341 and 3:no. 12), and more recently by Dussler (bib. 80, no. 409) and Tolnay (bib. 302, 5:169–70, no. 151).

96. Vasari, bib. 329, 1:226.

97. Frey, bib. 102, 2:57n.

98. Vasari, bib. 329, 4:1890–91.

99. Sofonisba presented *Michelangelo*, not Cavalieri, with this drawing (probably before she left for Spain in 1559). Michelangelo, however, presumably gave it to Cavalieri when he saw the embarrassment caused his friend by Cosimo de' Medici's request for a drawing. This embarrassment is revealed by the fact that Cavalieri visited Michelangelo on 14 November 1561 to show him Cosimo's request (Frey, bib. 103, 538).

100. Significantly, the sheet was pasted onto a second, thicker sheet—possibly by Cavalieri himself. The most likely purpose of this mounting was to hide something disturbing—as in the case of the Munich sheet with the Masaccio copy (fig. 53; cf. Perrig, bib. 231, 4, 8) and the Oxford sheet with the sketch for the story of the *Brazen Serpent* (fig. 29; n. 126 below). In any case Barocchi (bib. 15, no. 133) discovered the drawing of a head on the pasted-over verso, which appeared to her to be a typical pupil's product. Tolnay declined to reproduce this drawing in the *Corpus*, although in the case of Louvre 706 he prided himself on having the verso exposed (bib. 319, no. 3v). It was reproduced for the first time in 1988 by Hirst (bib. 139c, 121) after it had been delivered from its wrapper. The reproduction is good enough to reveal the characteristics of Cavalieri's sketching style (see chap. 5).

101. Tolnay considered the drawing to be a preliminary study for a painting (bib. 302, 5:19–20, 99–100, 180, no. 167; bib. 319, no. 265); as did Hartt (bib. 130, no. 125), and Hirst (bib. 139, 130; bib. 139c, no. 41). Cf. Wilde, bib. 344, no. 54, and Dussler, bib. 80, no. 363, for different interpretations; see also Perrig, bib. 228, 24–26n14.

102. Berenson (bib. 34 and bib. 37, no. 1616) had already noted "certain mannerisms." Popp (bib. 243, 75, and bib. 244, 172) and Tolnay (bib. 296, 445n60, and bib. 302, 3:188) considered these clear evidence that the drawing was a pastiche by a student.

103. The current datings vary between 1532 and 1534. Hartt (bib. 130, no. 125) dates it at 1512, Hirst (bib. 139c, no. 41) at 1530.

104. Steinmann and Wittkower, bib. 290, 433. Since the inventory identifies *multi*figure compositions as such, "resurectione" might mean the isolated depiction of the risen Christ.

105. In contrast to their sister copies, all these drawings have very abrupt contrasts in tone, a considerable number of thin-stroke pentimenti, and a brittle hatching with tiny assemblages and abounding directional changes and seams. In addition, they attempt to compensate for lack of clarity in the originals by adding little flourishes. In figure 21, for example, the left foot of the sleeping Amor and the penis area of the herm are each represented by a complicated bunch circlet instead of the simple abbreviations in the Cesari copy (fig. 22). The drapery piece has a mishmash of meaningless folds, the herm pedestal an accumulation of profile fragments whose senseless isolation is further emphasized by the thickness of the stroke.

106. Perrig, bib. 228, 39n6.

107. A second example, since lost, was seen by Frey (bib. 101, no. 58) in the collection of Sir Charles Newton Robinson (who considered it to be the original). It was possibly the facsimile copy mentioned in Clovio's inventory (Steinmann and Wittkower, bib. 290, 433). A painted copy in Vienna by Hans von Aachen (1552–1615), not mentioned in the Michelangelo literature, was recently published by Scheicher (bib. 273, 161).

108. It must have been studied by Raffaello da Montelupo (ca. 1505–66), who had entered the artist's workshop in the late summer of that year, before Michelangelo's return to Rome (late October), since Raffaello copied parts of it with black chalk and pen on an Ashmolean sheet (Parker, bib. 207, no. 410; cf. Wilde, bib. 240, no. 431). His copy was drawn left-handed and in the same beginner's style that also characterizes his drawings after the Medici Madonna (Louvre 715).

Tolnay dated the *Children's Bacchanal* "early 1533" (bib. 319, no. 338) and thereby contradicted his own assertion that it had been created in Florence (Michelangelo spent the entire period from late August 1532 to late June 1533 in Rome).

109. The two compositional sketches on the recto and verso of the Musée Bonnat sheet no. 650 were the starting point of Michelangelo's *Children's Bacchanal*. Berenson (bib. 37, no. 2474B) attributed them to Sebastiano, Dussler (bib. 79, 185, no. 193; bib. 80, no. 370a) and Pallucchini (bib. 199, 82–3) to an anonymous draftsman, and Thode (bib. 294, 3:no. 512d), Venturi (bib. 330, 224–25), Bean (bib. 30, 69), Tolnay (bib. 319, no. 337), and Hirst (bib. 139b, 115) to Michelangelo. In truth the sketches display all the features of Cavalieri's draftsmanship (see chap. 5). The black-chalk sketch on the verso of the Musée Bonnat sheet gave Michelangelo the idea for the terraced, stagelike space, for individual attitudes (the vessel-bearer viewed from the rear on the right became—when reversed—the middle of the three mule drivers!), and for the association of a group of children and adults situated in the foreground. The red-chalk sketch of the recto (burial) gave Michelangelo the idea of the drunken man teased by children.

110. Rotili, bib. 268, nos. 31, 38.

111. Examples: Goldscheider, bib. 115, fig. 17; bib. 167, no. 150; Tolnay, bib. 302, 5:fig. 307; Libertini, bib. 173; Delacre, bib. 69, figs. 63–64.

112. Steinmann and Wittkower, bib. 290, 433.

113. Hartt, bib. 130, no. 361. See also *Drawings*, bib. 77, no. 122; Wilde, bib. 347, 153–56; Tolnay, bib. 319, no. 338; Liebert, bib. 174, 289–91; Hirst, bib. 139b, 73, 111, 115–16, and bib. 139c, no. 47.

114. Panofsky, bib. 205, 180, and bib. 206, 221; Tolnay, bib. 297, 522, bib. 302, 3:221, no. 120, bib. 305, bib. 306, 289. Cf. also Berenson, bib. 37, 1:227.

115. The lightly drawn primary contours of the Berlin copy (fig. 26) correspond to the provisional black chalk sketch of the Windsor drawing. They too are so covered over by the definitive contours that the unassisted eye unavoidably overlooks them.

116. Tolnay (bib. 319, no. 338) describes it as "una sorta di cerchio magico, disegnato sulla terra."

117. Clovio's inventory, which is located in the state archives in Rome (I thank my student Christina Riebesell for a photocopy and transcription), lists, in addition to some copies after parts of frescoes and sculptures, about fifty copies after finished drawings, studies, and sketches by Michelangelo. But it is doubtful that all these drawings were actually made by Michelangelo. When Clovio dictated the information to Massarelli concerning his Windsor copy of the *Flagellation of Christ* (Popham and Wilde, bib. 240, no. 251), he seems to have erred not only in the number of figures ("Un Xpo alla colonna . . . con 3 figure" instead of four), but also in reference to the author of the original ("di Michelangiolo") (cf. note 119 below). The evidence of the Windsor copy indicates that this original (with which Clovio had probably become acquainted in Cavalieri's collection) had the same unmichelangelesque style of figures, composition, and chiaroscuro drawing as Sebastiano's *Flagellation* sketch in the British Museum (Tolnay, bib. 319, no. 73). It is related to the latter like a reformulated final version adapted to the real lighting conditions in S. Pietro in Montorio (cf. n. 57 above). Typically, however, it reveals once more the "difference in style" between the fine-limbed, well-proportioned Christ figure (quoted from a model of Michelangelo's) and the summarily structured, mannered and overlong, "skipping" torturers created by Sebastiano himself (on a similar difference in style in Sebastiano's sketches for the *Resurrection of Lazarus*, cf. Perrig, bib. 221, 176–81).

118. Popp, bib. 246, 66–67n2.

119. Clovio's pupil Massarelli, who drew up the inventory for his aged, nearly blind master (see chap. 1, note 25 above), originally wrote "quattro" (subsequently struck over and replaced with "otto"). This mistake and its erroneous correction can hardly be explained except by the assumption that Clovio himself dictated the information while looking through his pile of sheets.

120. On the miniature (fig. 85) see Levi d'Ancona, bib. 168, 65–70.

Voss's claim (bib. 335, 1:116) that Venusti's *Resurrection* picture in Forlì (fig. 118) was also based on Michelangelo's drawing, which has haunted the literature ever since (most recently Goldscheider, bib. 115, 50n69), appears to be the result of a misunderstanding. Scannelli (bib. 272, 72) had baselessly claimed in 1657 that this picture depended on "a" corresponding drawing by Michelangelo.

121. That the London example is identical with the original is one of the dogmas of Michelangelo scholarship (cf. most recently Tolnay, bib. 319, no. 258, and bib. 322, no. 64; Hirst, bib. 139b, 15). For a contrary opinion see Perrig bib. 228, 36–37n63.

122. Perrig, bib. 228, 17–18.

123. Bertolotti, bib. 42, 13. Inadvertently omitted by Steinmann and Wittkower (bib. 290, 433–34).

124. Most recently Tolnay, bib. 319, no. 266r, and bib. 322, no. 65; Pignatti, bib. 234, no. 21.

125. The three other examples are obviously copies.
1. Uffizi no. 606E: *Brazen Serpent* (pen). Attributed to Giovanni Battista da Sangallo (1496–1552) by Degenhart (bib. 68, 282) and Zentai (bib. 354, 85n25).
2. Uffizi no. 17371F: *Plague of Serpents* (black chalk).

Traditionally attributed to Domenico Gabbiani (1652–1726). For a contrary opinion, see Delacre, bib. 69, 247.

3. Budapest, Fine Arts Museum no. 1959r: *Plague of Serpents* (pen). Attributed to G. B. da Sangallo by Zentai (bib. 354, 79–92).

A copy of the healing scene was formerly in the Hugh Blakers collection (+ 1936). Like figure 29, a pen-and-ink drawing viewed by Thode (bib. 294, 1:251) in the Royal Academy in Düsseldorf united both scenes, but with a reduced number of figures.

Of the three extant copies, at least Uffizi 17371 is marked by an attempt to reproduce the original precisely. The contours are first sketched with extremely thin strokes and consist of short, threadlike strokes with sharp endings that are frequently blended together but which are of changing strength and consistency. Nevertheless, this copy deviates from what is shown in the Oxford drawing (fig. 29) at several points. For example, the head of the figure who is fleeing to the right and throwing his arms up in a self-protective gesture (third figure from the left in the back row) does not turn back, as in fig. 29, but—as in the Budapest copy—faces forward. And the left leg of the cowering figure (frontmost figure viewed from the rear, on the far right) appears without a distinctly drawn thigh, although it is completely visible, while in fig. 29 it is not only overlapped by the right leg of the Israelite standing behind him but also lacking in definition (the same figure's head, whose orientation is in no way indicated in fig. 29, is here, as in the Budapest copy, turned to the left). Finally, the back of the supine figure toward the bottom left, supporting himself on his right arm and left elbow, has a few anatomically well-founded marks that are missing in fig. 29 for no apparent reason. Each of these discrepancies excludes the possibility that the Oxford drawing functioned as a model for Uffizi 17371.

126. The verso was pasted over until 1953. Hartt (bib. 130, no. 142) was the first to reproduce "this very powerful study"—in such a small form as to make invisible its coarse features. He dated the study around 1545 and suspected it was "a study for the impenitent thief." Tolnay, on the other hand, saw it as an anatomical study and dated it around 1530 (bib. 319, no. 266v).

127. Most recently Tolnay (see note 124 above). In contrast, see Perrig, bib. 228, 41n79.

128. Perrig, bib. 228, 19–21.

129. The *Samaritan Woman* is mentioned in a letter from Vittoria written in 1541 (Frey, bib. 103, 534, no. 112); and also by Vasari (bib. 329, 1:121). Two drawn copies (Courtauld Institute and Louvre 766 [Tolnay, bib. 302, 5:figs. 334, 336]) and an engraving by Béatrizet (Rotili, bib. 268, no. 42 and fig. 26) survive. According to Annesley and Hirst (bib. 4a) a preliminary sketch by Michelangelo has also been kept alive: the black chalk drawing (43.6 × 33.7 cm) depicting *Christ and the Samaritan Woman* in the Martin Bodmer Foundation, Geneva. But this drawing relates to Michelangelo's composition in a similar manner as the Christ figures in the "late" Crucifixion drawings (figs. 105–11), its stylisitc siblings, relate to Michelangelo's Colonna Crucifix (fig. 33). It is a derivate, not a preliminary sketch. All the characteristics of its figure and drawing style are Venusti's (see chap. 7).

130. The *Pietà* is mentioned by Vasari (bib. 329, 1:120–21) and discussed at length by Condivi (bib. 62, 188). It survives in several engravings (Rotili, bib. 268, nos. 41, 141) and countless paintings, reliefs, and free imitations. The Isabella Stewart Gardner Museum in Boston and the Teyler Museum (A90) in Haarlem each own a facsimile copy (Davidson, bib. 65, 6–8); there is a second-hand drawing copy in Windsor (no. 0434; Popham and Wilde, bib. 240, no. 464).

Since 1960 the Boston example has generally been presented as the original (most recently Eisler, bib. 89, 42; Tolnay, bib. 319, no. 426; Hirst, bib. 139b, 56, 117), although it (1) is tailored precisely to Venusti's incomplete painting copy in the Galleria Nazionale in Rome; (2) is not identical with the model for the Haarlem example; (3) like the latter, exhibits the characteristics of a copy. Its individual-style components point clearly to Venusti.

131. Vasari, bib. 329, 4:2003.

If the notations "Un x.po in croce Invent.ne di MichelAng.lo" (or "da" or "di Michelangelo") in Clovio's inventory (see note 117 above) invariably apply to the Colonna crucifix, then the miniaturist must have copied it no less than five times. He cited it—with altered head and finger positions—in his drawing of a crucifixion (Uffizi 14753F) and in the small painting of the crucified Christ with Mary Magdalene (Uffizi).

132. Most recently Tolnay, bib. 319, no. 411, and bib. 320, 109, 273, no. 245; *Drawings*, bib. 78, no. 21, Hirst, bib. 139b, 117–18.

133. An eighth example, without angel, is located in the British Museum, Ff. 1–7 (Wilde, bib. 344, no. 93).

134. Most recently by Tolnay, bib. 304, 117n85, and bib. 302, 5:59, 195–96, no. 198.

135. Even in the apparently inexact Louvre example, the overall height of the Christ figure differs from the London example by only 1 mm (26 cm instead of 25.9 cm); the span of the arms differs by 7 mm (25.4 cm instead of 24.7 cm). The width of the upright beam is identical (2.6 cm).

136. The most important discrepancies are: (1) the opening of Christ's mouth; (2) the head of the nail with which Christ's right hand is fastened to the cross; (3) the elbow contour of the left arm. In figure 33 it has a striking protuberance, which also appears in the Budapest example, but merely as a component of a lightly drawn pentimento. In the other examples it is—as is anatomically correct—smoothed out; (4) the contour piece below the right hip (medial gluteal muscle). Uniformly underdefined in figure 33, in the Budapest and Oxford examples it appears correctly differentiated into a soft upper and a powerful lower section; (5) the spaces between the folds of the upper right part of the loincloth; (6) the lower of the two intermediate areas of the calf; (7) the drapery folds of the angel.

137. *Michelangelo*, bib. 186, 4:101–05.

138. Frey (bib. 103, 533–34, nos. 107–09, 111), Pfister (bib. 233, 140–42), Deri (bib. 73, 27–28), Tolnay (bib. 302, 5:195, no. 198), and Rotili (bib. 268, 61) held to the sequence proposed by Ferrero and Müller (bib. 93, 206–09), while Goldscheider (bib. 114, no. 113, and bib. 115, no. 107), Ramsden (bib. 251, 2:240–41), Cimino (bib. 58, 101–02), Gatti (bib. 108, 14–15), Poggi (bib. 186,

4:101–05), and Liebert (bib. 174, 315–20) follow Thode's (bib. 293, 2:402–03, and bib. 294, 2:466). The first relates to the second as A-D-B-C relates to D-A-B-C: that is, neither makes sense.

139. Only Ramsden (bib. 251, no. 202) appears to have understood the expression "accioche io la serua": "Seeing that I am in Rome, I do not think it was necessary . . . to have made him an intermediary between your ladyship and me, your servant, to the end that I might serve you."

140. This more likely refers to the execution of the *Conversion of Paul* begun in November 1542 than to work on the *Last Judgment* finished in late 1541 (as Ramsden [bib. 251, 2:5n2] assumes).

141. "E stato guasto el mio disegnio" has two meanings. "Disegnio" here means both: plan (intent) and drawing.

142. On the painted copies without angels, see Negri Arnoldi, bib. 190, 60 and figs. 3–4; Baudouin, bib. 23, 67–69; Cimino, bib. 58, 1–3 and pl. I–V. On the free copy in the Galleria Doria, no. 494, see Torselli, bib. 323, fig. 100. On the facsimile copy see note 133 above.

143. The following sentence of the letter ("And in case you are not working today, and you find it suitable, you could visit me for a talk") in itself excludes the possibility that Michelangelo could then have been working on the crucifix painting.

144. Passerini, bib. 212, 195–96.

145. Cf. Parker, bib. 207, no. 339.

146. Frey, bib. 102, 2:54.

147. See Perrig, bib. 222, 268–74, on the assertion that the two Uffizi cartonetti (nos. 229–30F; figs. 102–03) were thereby meant (most recently Tolnay, bib. 319, nos. 393, 409; Hirst, bib. 139b, 19, 54–56, and bib. 139c, no. 54).

148. Jacopo's first sketch (black chalk), a direct derivative of the larger of the two three-figure groups in figure 35, is extant (Dussler, bib. 80, no. 593 and fig. 269; Tolnay, bib. 319, no. 426 A–r). At important points he anticipates the final relief design (on the ciborium cf. Barocchi, bib. 329, 4:1784–89). Its figures exhibit the same disproportions between torso and head or arms, the same schematic modeling of the naked limbs that tends to overaccentuate individual parts (shoulder parts), the same unstable footing, indeed in part even the same physiognomical characteristics (spherical heads with conspicuously small noses) as the bronze figures.

Tolnay's thesis that the sketch was "copied" after a lost, multifigure composition by Michelangelo is comprehensible only as a protective assertion. For him to concede that it depended on figure 35 would have immediately invalidated his arbitrary identification of the "disegni piccolj" in Jacopo's possession with Venusti's Uffizi cartonetti (figs. 102–03). Also unsupportable is his claim that the black-chalk drawing in the Stedelijk Museum in Amsterdam, erroneously attributed to Clovio (bib. 319, 3:79), depicts "un altra copia della composizione di Michelangelo," for this drawing relates to Jacopo's first sketch like a new revision with reversed sides and strongly modified details. It has the same figure-style and stroke system characteristics.

149. See excursus II. From the extant examples of Venusti's paint-

ing, the 53 × 76 cm panel in the Galleria Nazionale in Rome (no. 10049) is the most likely candidate as the original. It appears to be identical with the "quadro in tavola bislongo con Nro Sigre nell'horto alto palmi due et un quarto [approx. 50 cm] di Michelangelo" [*sic*], which is listed in the Aldobrandini inventory of 1682 (Pergola, bib. 217, 66, no. 170).

150. On the claim that this cartonetto was drawn by Michelangelo (most recently Tolnay, bib. 318, no. 113; bib. 319, no. 409; bib. 320, 112; Hirst, bib. 139b, 19, 41, 47) cf. Perrig, bib. 222, 261–74.

151. According to Tolnay (bib. 319, no. 404) "forse un pensiero per una 'Pietà' con due figure."

152. Tolnay classified these two sketches as "studies for the figure of Christ" (bib. 302, 5:210, no. 277; bib. 319, no. 404).

153. This aversion became a public nuisance in 1518–19, when the facade of S. Lorenzo was awaiting execution. Cf. Vasari, bib. 329, 1:54–55 and 2:686–89.

154. On his original intention to use the help of experienced fresco painters for painting the ceiling of the Sistine Chapel, see Vasari, bib. 329, 1:37–38.

155. The lack of large-size clay models made it impossible for the clients subsequently to have the unfinished statues completed.

156. Cf. Perrig, bib. 228, 33–35n59 (change of design during the execution of the Sistine Chapel ceiling); Perrig, bib. 219, 71–133 (change of design during the carving of the Pietà); Perrig, bib. 230.

157. The drawings not discussed in the text are listed in notes 166 (studies), 176 ("modello" for the Julius tomb), and 178 (sketches and "modelli" for the Medici tombs) below.

158. Tolnay's list of separate drawings for the Sistine Chapel (bib. 319, nos. 119–73) consists of fifty-five sheets, most of them drawn on both sides. The group is distinguished not only by a colorful potpourri of styles, but also by a phenomenal confusion of media. If the claimed authorship is accepted as correct, Michelangelo would have used about a dozen different inks, at least ten kinds of red and black chalk (as well as white chalk), and silver point and metal point for his sketches and studies of 1508–11.

159. Hartt, bib. 130, no. 105. Most recently Viatte, bib. 332, 65; Tolnay, bib. 319, no. 144r; Hirst, bib. 139, 45, bib. 139b, 30, 61, 67, bib. 139c, no. 13.

160. The sheet was considered a facsimile copy by Dussler (bib. 80, no. 701) and Freedberg (bib. 97, 258), among others. For a contrary view see Jaffé, bib. 148, 394n11.

161. According to Malvasia (bib. 181, 165), one day Calvaert was introduced to Cardinal Ippolito d'Este, who wished to see an example of the artist's drawing ability. After Calvaert had drawn a half-figure Madonna with child, he was allowed to view the cardinal's collection of drawings. He was immediately able to name the authors of the various sheets. "But when he came to a Michelangelo nude for the *Last Judgment* and to two figures from Raphael's *School of Athens*, he declared that these were not originals but copies he had himself prepared after the frescoes, although somewhat altered in accordance with the commission from a certain Pomponio, who had ordered them. And this Pomponio was in fact the same man who, after

having blackened them and here and there furnished them with traces of their having been used, had sold them to the cardinal as originals, as it subsequently turned out." Whether Calvaert, who after all was thirty years old when he came to Rome, really did not know for what purpose he "somewhat altered" the figures (as Malvasia would like his readers to believe), is beside the point. What is certain is that the alleged "Michelangelo" corpus does not lack in counterfeits of the kind described. British Museum sheet 1860-6-15-5 (Tolnay, bib. 319, no. 352)—which currently enjoys the status of being "undoubtedly authentic"—can serve as a representative example. It appears to provide the connoisseur insight into the study process, which, among others, is supposed to have been preparatory to the angel in the *Last Judgment* (right lunette) who hovers at the column of the *Flagellation*. This purpose was served on the one hand by a "typically michelangelesque" hierarchy of main and related studies, on the other hand by a list of various states of figural definition. The "final" state of the angel on the recto appears to have been developed directly from two—illogically placed on the verso—"embryonic states" and an embryonic detail study of the left arm. The primitiveness of these verso "preliminary steps" (beside which the small figures in Michelangelo's sketches in figs. 31–32 look like elements of a highly finished drawing) is a fatal indication of affectation. The lower, larger, "secondary" verso study exhibits no increase in refinement in comparison to the upper "preliminary" study—except that its face looks more human and its left arm ends in a paw (which, for unexplainable reasons, is placed through a ring) instead of a circle. In contrast, its torso is even more unshapely. Moreover, the arm, torso, and head attitudes of both the "secondary" and "preliminary" verso studies are virtually identical with those of the recto study. The existence of the two embryonic figures lacks any motivation, especially in view of the fact that there is a gaping discrepancy between the quality of shape definition in the verso and recto studies—how did the recto study miraculously arise from the two lumpy growths on the verso? Possibly, in this case the connoisseur should reckon with "intermediate stages" in which the crude segment formulas of the contours were successively diminished and the functionless (and therefore superfluous) crude hatching lattices were replaced by modeling hatching.

The recto study itself does not correspond exactly to the fresco figure. The positions of the head, arm, and left-hand are different. The whole figure appears to have been observed from a different angle. These deviations, however, reflect inner contradictions. The right half of the back and buttocks, which is larger than in the fresco, suggests an angle of viewing that is negated by the rest of the body (whose spatial position corresponds to that of the fresco figure). At the same time its lack of structural definition distinguishes it from the left half of the body. The right half of the drawn figure's body reflects the real optical circumstances: from the normal point of observation the right half of the fresco figure's back and buttocks cannot be seen. The right arm of the recto study deviates from the fresco figure only in relation to the position of the upper arm. Instead of being bent back, the upper arm is an elongation of the shoulder axis.

Despite this, it is almost as strongly foreshortened as in the fresco and thus stumplike. The course of its outer contour corresponds to that of the related study to the upper right, but this arm corresponds completely to that of the fresco figure—except for one inconspicuous detail: the inner surface of the hand, which is hidden in the fresco. The inner surface was added on to the hand profile in the same additive way as the right half of the back and buttocks was added on to the left half. It broadens the body part in an equally clumsy way.

162. Wickhoff (bib. 341, CXCII) correctly dated the Albertina sheet to the seventeenth century. In his opinion it was the work of a Fleming.

163. The counterfeit theory is buttressed by the seven-part set of studies on the verso of the sheet. These drawings have obviously confounded scholars—for they are related, even though their style and technique of execution conform completely to the recto set, to the Mary of the Pietà in Viterbo completed by Sebastiano del Piombo in 1516! Although Volpe and Lucco (bib. 334a) passed over them in silence (to the atonishment of Hope [bib. 141a, 637]), other scholars postulated that these drawings were actually intended for the Eve of the *Expulsion from Paradise* in the Sistine Chapel (most recently Hartt, bib. 130, no. 72; Tolnay, bib. 319, no. 144v). Hirst (bib. 139, 44–45) solved the problem by dating the creation of the cartoon, which, according to Vasari (bib. 328, 5:567–68), Michelangelo had given to Sebastiano, as early as possible (1513). Freedberg (bib. 97), on the other hand, declared that the contents of the sheet's recto and verso were simultaneously created copies by Sebastiano after studies by Michelangelo created at different times. None of these theories explains why the six related studies, which encircle the main study, (1) are partially executed with black chalk or pen (and in two different inks), (2) repeat the hand pair of the main study with such a large expenditure of strokes and so little substantive modification, and (3) are partially upside down with reference to the main study.

164. The red-chalk studies on the rectos and versos of the two Haarlem sheets, Teyler Museum A20 and A27, are exceptions (Tolnay, bib. 319, nos. 135–36). Excerpts from them were copied on Windsor sheet 0441 (Popham and Wilde, bib. 240, no. 449).

165. The Oxford sheet with the studies for the Libyan sibyl (fig. 6) is the only exception. A facsimile could not be made because of the pen and ink sketches on it. Nevertheless a pen and ink workshop copy of each of the two red chalk studies exists on Windsor 5435 (Popham and Wilde, bib. 240, no. 785 and fig. 148).

166. This set was apparently concentrated on the recto of a single sheet. It survives in three facsimile copies: (1) British Museum 1926-10-9-1r (red chalk over black chalk); (2) Montauban, Musée Ingres, no. 867.4110 (black chalk); (3) Louvre R.F.70–28961r (red chalk). Since Steinmann (bib. 286, 598, no. 31) most scholars have identified the London example as the original (most recently Tolnay, bib. 319, no. 134r; Olszewski, bib. 196, 20; Joannides, bib. 153, 682). Delacre (bib. 69, 463–64) suspected this example as a fake and defended the originality of the Louvre sheet. His thesis found no adherents, but all the same the consensus was challenged—first by Berenson (bib. 34, no. 1519A), later (among others) by Tolnay (bib. 302,

2:207, no. 6A), most recently by Gere and Turner (bib. 78, no. 7). Joannides responded to the most recent challenge in the language of the church fathers: "This is an aberration," he decreed, "Beautiful drawings are like beautiful women—always on display."

167. Only Oertel (bib. 195) disputes the originality of the New York sheet in globo. On the other hand, Panofsky (bib. 202, 37), Barocchi (bib. 269, no. 24), and Brugnoli (bib. 50, no. 24), and, for a time, Tolnay (bib. 302, 2:61, 204, no. 46, 209, no. 13A) and Gold-scheider (bib. 114, no. 30) put forth the curious thesis that the torso, hand, and foot studies were by Michelangelo, but the rest of what appears on the sheet was drawn by a copyist or "pupil" (on this subject see Hartt, bib. 128, 242, and bib. 130, nos. 87–88; Dussler, bib. 80, no. 339). All other scholars assume that the New York sheet is the original and that it served as model for the Uffizi example (most recently Bean and Stampfle, bib. 31, no. 36; Goldscheider, bib. 115, nos. 30, 39; Tolnay, bib. 319, no. 156; Olszewski, bib. 196, 16–18, 20, 24, 26nn18, 21; Bean, bib. 31a, no. 131; Hirst, bib. 139c, no. 16). But certain divergences in the details speak against its having functioned as the model. One of them concerns the course of the contour of the abdomen of the main study. It can only be explained by assuming that the corresponding section of the original exhibited multiple versions of the contour, and that each copyist perceived a different one as correct. Similar considerations apply to the discrepancies in the contour defining the left shoulder. Here both draftsmen made a more or less clear distinction between first version and correction. But what the one drew as the definitive contour, the other copied as a provisional one, and vice versa. Finally, some areas of shading are also differently formed. In the Uffizi example the shading of the lower posterior has a semicircular notch that is missing in the New York example. But it must have characterized the model, because the Uffizi draftsman marked its extremity with an auxiliary contour that is still clearly visible. On the original it was probably the result of deliberate attention to the "sovereignty area" of the hand study (which must have been created before the shading of the main study).

168. The Uffizi and New York sheets differ from normal "anthology sheets" (examples: Dussler, bib. 80, nos. 392, 424, 520, 615) in both the meticulousness of reproduction and in the fact that the reproduced contents are related and are in part even placed on the sheet in conformance with the original. This formal difference also indicates a difference in the purposes for which they were reproduced. The copyists of the Uffizi and New York sheets certainly did not create their pedantic reproductions for use as a supply of examples in their own workshops.

169. The head study in particular demonstrates that the contours *and* the shading of the main study were not executed at one and the same work session. The head study as it appears in figure 8 can only be interpreted as an intermediate stage that had served as a basis for the definitive contour of the face and shading of the head of the main study.

170. Tolnay's sequence thesis (bib. 319, no. 157r): (1) legs and right knee; (2) thorax study; (3) main study; (4) head study ("questa volta da un modello femminile"); (4) left hand; (5) left foot, toes; (6) Libyan sibyl's companion and right hand. The two last studies were supposedly created only *after* completion of the fresco, ca. 1512–13.

171. The traditional equating of the London example (fig. 10) with the original (most recently Tolnay, bib. 319, no. 163; Olszewski, bib. 196, 20, 26n18; Hirst, bib. 139b, 2, 25, 61, 67–68, bib. 139c, no. 17) meant that its verso drawings (of which neither the Boston nor the Windsor examples show anything) belong to the original Haman drawings set, even though they have no apparent function. According to Hettner (bib. 132, 82) and Hartt (bib. 130, no. 91), the largest and only decipherable one is an intermediate stage between the first version of the recto main study and the torso study of the second sheet. In reality it presupposes acquaintance with the fresco figure—as the left hand and the outer and inner contours of the left shoulder and arm (among others) attest. It thereby reveals itself as an attempt—supported by a quite inadequate understanding of anatomy—to "reconstruct" one of Michelangelo's auxiliary studies. Its like appears always to have served to strengthen the connoisseurs' belief in the originality of the sheet in question.

172. Since Wölfflin (bib. 351, 320) the Haarlem studies have been occasionally regarded as studies after the fresco figure (most recently Tolnay, bib. 319, 2:213, no. 26A). Only Hettner (bib. 132, 74, 84) and Dussler (bib. 80, no. 522) seem to have recognized that they belong in the category of facsimile copies and are therefore neither studies after the frescoes nor originals (as, most recently, Hartt, bib. 130, no. 92, Tolnay, bib. 319, no. 164r, Bambach, bib. 13a, and Hirst, bib. 139b, 2, 25, 70–71, 102, and bib. 139c, no. 18, thought). Anyone will realize this by looking at what Hartt found "quickly contoured" (e.g., the finger abbreviations of the left hand of the torso study) under a magnifying glass.

173. Like the Windsor example (fig. 11)—according to Brinckmann (bib. 49, no. 96) the model of the London example (fig. 10)—the Boston example (fig. 9) is distinguished by a sharper modeling of the surface. In its subsidiary study of the thigh the shading was accomplished with a clear herringbone pattern instead of untectonic flickering; its main study exhibits, instead of a flatly arched section of the right shoulder, a sharply articulated one and a relatively defined instead of formulaic left foot. Moreover it has—in contrast to the London example—indications of a face.

174. Only Hettner (bib. 132, 82–84) has dealt with the question of the genesis of the studies. According to him the main study is the multilayered product of a model study whose subject was first a recumbent and then a standing nude model.

175. Since Gilbert's (bib. 112) correction of Tolnay's chronology of the painting projects (bib. 319, 2:109–12) all other datings have been invalidated.

176. In the literature the sketches are usually dated *after* the conclusion of this contract (most recently Tolnay, bib. 319, no. 157r; Balas, bib. 11a, 668; for opposing views see Jacobsen, bib. 146, 392; Goldscheider, bib. 115, no. 40; Einem, bib. 88, 81)—as if the "designum, modellum seu figura dicte sepulture" (Vasari, bib. 329, 2:629)

mentioned there and intended for execution had been a sudden inspiration whose existence did not presuppose sketching work.

This "designum," moreover, appears to be identical with the severely damaged, washed pen-and-ink finished drawing of the tomb front elevation in Berlin, Kupferstichkabinett no. 15305r (Tolnay, bib. 319, no. 55r). In any case the latter is beyond doubt attributable to Michelangelo, as the inscription on the facsimile copy by Jacomo Rocchetti also located there attests ("questo disegno è di mano di Michelangelo Buonarota havuto da M. Jacomo Rocchetti pittore suo discepolo"; cf. Dussler, bib. 80, no. 374). A second facsimile copy is located in the Nationalmuseum in Stockholm, CC 2655; partial copies deviating in details are located in the Uffizi, no. 608E–r (Tolnay, bib. 319, no. 56r: by Hirst, bib. 139c, no. 20, considered as original) and in the Galleria Corsini in Rome.

177. Joannides (bib. 151, 261, and bib. 152, 682 at nos. 156–57) tried to describe the differences in the stroke system between the Oxford and New York studies for the Libyan sibyl (figs. 6, 8) as an expression of heterogeneous functions.

Tolnay's claim that the Oxford and New York sheets are components of one and the same original "foglio reale" is also wishful thinking (bib. 319, no. 157r). It is contradicted by the different paper and qualities of red chalk alone.

On the two pen and ink studies on the verso of the Oxford sheet, see Perrig, bib. 229, 122n85.

178. They can be divided into two groups. The first consists of sketches for the freestanding tomb planned at the end of 1520. They are distributed on Casa Buonarroti nos. 49A-r, 71A-r, and 88A-r, and on British Museum no. 1859-6-25-545r (Tolnay, bib. 319, nos. 182–83, 181, 184). These sketches have been subject to widely varying interpretations, some of them have been considered sketches for a wall tomb. Nevertheless, analysis of the surviving correspondence (*Michelangelo*, bib. 186, 2:259–60, 264–65, 267–69) indicates that until late December 1520 Michelangelo insisted on his freestanding tomb project despite all objections and counterproposals from Cardinal Giulio de' Medici. He did nothing to prepare drawings for a wall tomb project. His attitude seems to have changed only in January 1521, when he created the second group of sketches, culminating in a "modello" for the Magnifici and Lorenzo tombs, respectively (treated at length in Perrig, bib. 230; see also the excellent study by Wallace, bib. 336a).

179. The pen and ink drawing of a *Last Judgment* in the Courtauld Institute, which was first sketched in black or red chalk and has been attributed to Ferraù Fenzoni, has, since 1964, been classified as a copy after an allegedly lost Michelangelo sketch that antedated the Casa Buonarroti drawing (fig. 30) (Regteren Altena, bib. 257, 177–80; Hall, bib. 125, 89; Tolnay, bib. 319, 3:22; Hirst, bib. 139b, no. 51). In 1988 it was presented as a copy after a "lost modello" based on the Casa Buonarroti drawing (Barnes, bib. 13c). It is nothing of the kind, for the following reasons: (1) At least three of its figures correspond exactly to those of the fresco: (a) the draped, seated figure depicted in left profile and turned toward the center of the picture, who is situated in the mid-region of the community of saints to the

left of Christ, as well as the two-figure group consisting of (b) the figure of a saint kneeling at the edge of a bank of clouds and (c) its companion seen from the rear in the community to the right of Christ (the latter two figures are depicted on the opposite sides in the fresco). The first figure does not even appear in the Casa Buonarroti sketch. The second and third appear there, but in an embryonic stage. (2) Three of the four martyrs of the lowermost row of saints are excerpted from the Uffizi sketch no. 170S (fig. 68)—a drawing that (a) is by Cavalieri and (b) is based on Michelangelo's Casa Buonarroti sketch. (3) The curious mixture of earlier stages (including the compositional system of the Casa Buonarroti sketch) and later stages, of "primitivisms" such as that which flaws figure 30 (St. Michael above the lintel) and fully matured fresco "anticipations" are accompanied by a contradiction between the apparent primeval quality of what is drawn and the constant sharpness and detailedness of the draftsman's manner of formulation. The Courtauld drawing exhibits nothing of those alternations between dusky and clear areas that characterize both Michelangelo's own sketches (figs. 30–32) and the copies drawn after them (figs. 27–29). It is an example par excellence of a *forged* sketch. But the forger's obvious success is based on the fact that he sold both his "preliminary" and "secondary" sketch (New York, Metropolitan Museum; Tolnay, bib. 319, 3:24; Bean, bib. 31a, no. 133). In the secondary sketch the upper half of the "preliminary sketch" is reproduced—in black chalk and on an enlarged scale. Progressive development is indicated by the fact that Christ has a new pose and also a palm branch, Mary a robe, and St. Lawrence a grill.

180. Perrig, bib. 228, 10–13. Hirst (bib. 139c, no. 51) denies this reference of the Casa Buonarroti sketch (fig. 30) to the entrance wall with the argument that "deux figures . . . un élu à gauche, un damné vu de dos à droite, sont cramponnées à la partie basse de cet espace, ce qui serait impossible dans le cas d'une porte mais pourrait s'expliquer s'il y avait à l'origine un vide entre le mur et la table d'autel." But Hirst seems to have overlooked that the (fragmentary) indications of what he calls the "altar-piece" were sketched only after the figure composition had been sketched (hence the two figures on the top of the "altar-piece" seem to penetrate the entablature instead of being situated upon it!), and that the topographical relation of the figures to the rectangle indications therefore says nothing about the meaning of the latter. All that this relation says is that Michelangelo underestimated the area to be left free when he sketched the figure composition.

181. Tolnay (bib. 319, no. 347r) also noticed that Christ's action (in contrast to the Jupiter in figs. 23–24) does not function as the motivating *cause* of the event. All the same he wrote: "lo stretto legame di cause ed effetto tra i singoli elementi crea un' autentica unità di tempo e di spazio."

182. Pastor, bib. 213, 4/2:567n2.

183. Vasari, bib. 329, 3:1156.

184. *Das Leben Michelangelos*, bib. 63, 146.

185. Cf. Perrig, bib. 228, 17–22.

186. Tolnay ultimately abandoned his dating "shortly after Feb-

ruary–March 1534," which he had still advocated in the *Corpus* (bib. 319, no. 347r), and replaced it with September 1533 (bib. 322, no. 71). Apparently in the end he was no longer convinced of his own thesis, which he had upheld for decades, that in February 1534 a fresco of the *Resurrection of Christ* had been planned for the Sistine altar wall (cf. Perrig, bib. 228, 24–26n14; see also Hall, bib. 125).

187. Cf. Perrig, bib. 228, 15.

188. For a divergent interpretation of the hill of hell cf. Steinberg, bib. 283–85.

189. Such correspondences, as well as the fiction of a fresco of a *Resurrection of Christ* planned in February 1534 (see note 186 above) caused Tolnay (bib. 319, no. 351r) to date the sketch between 1538 and 1540 (Hirst, bib. 139c, no. 52: "datation . . . impossible."). He had apparently forgotten that the *cartoons* for the *Last Judgment* had already been created long before Paul III acceded to the papacy on 13 October 1534 (Vasari, bib. 329, 1:72 and 3:1192–96).

190. Except for Frey (bib. 101, no. 79) all scholars dated the London sketch earlier than the Windsor sketch (fig. 31)—most recently Tolnay (bib. 319, nos. 350r, 351r). Thode supplied the reason (bib. 294, 2:8, no. IV): "The group of falling angels," he wrote, are pulled "more toward the depths than on the wall painting, which allows one to conclude that Charon's boat was not yet planned, but rather as in sketch II [fig. 30] the fall was supposed to extend into the lower right corner."

191. According to Tolnay (bib. 302, 5:186, no. 178, and bib. 319, no.350r) it was created ca. 1535–36, i.e., like the Windsor sketch (fig. 31) *after* the cartoon was prepared.

192. Tolnay had once attributed part of the auxiliary sketches, together with the large-size drawings, to a pupil (bib. 301, 145n6). Most recently (bib. 319, no. 350r) he thought they were "probably made immediately after the main group." See chap. 5 for a discussion of the *large* chalk drawings of individual figures as well as their verso studies.

193. Steinmann and Wittkower, bib. 290, 435, no. 59.

194. Armenini (bib. 5, 101) wrote that there were people who declared squaring useless because it made the "dissegno" less effective. The context reveals that he had Michelangelo, in particular, in mind. Michelangelo does not figure in Armenini's list of examples of the representatives of "correct" cartooning (Raphael, Perino del Vaga, Giulio Romano, Daniele da Volterra, Taddeo Zuccaro), although he is otherwise steadfastly described as an example of model artistic behavior.

On the cartoons of individual cinquecento artists, cf. Bacou, bib. 7, 194, 265. On the technical aspects of Michelangelo's cartoon fragment see Bambach, bib. 13b.

195. On the fresco, cf. Steinberg, bib. 282, 42–55; most recently Wallace, bib. 336b.

196. Up to now little attention was paid to the pentimenti of the cartoon. Differences between the cartoon and the fresco were at most noted in reference to the design of the drapery and helmet (most

recently by Hartt, bib. 130, no. 407; Tolnay, bib. 319, no. 384) or the lance of the right soldier (Hirst, bib. 139c, no. 53).

197. On the right thigh of the figure wearing armor the piece of undergarment that appears under the armor of the fresco figure, as well as a vertical strap of some sort, was subsequently marked. The latter was not transferred to the fresco.

198. The same applies to the *Conversion of Paul*. If the head of Paul's horse was painted over by Michelangelo himself, as Tolnay assumes (bib. 302,5:73–74, 142n12; cf. Magi, bib. 180, and Wallace, bib. 336b, 121n9), the initial design must have been partially altered even in the final stages of execution.

199. Since Tolnay (bib. 299, 146) the second sketch from the left has been generally accepted as "undoubtedly" (Dussler, bib. 80, no. 201) the first version, and its neighbor to the left as the last version of the two-figure groups (most recently Einem, bib. 88, 229; Tolnay, bib. 319, no. 433; Liebert, bib. 174, 410–11). It follows from Dussler's reasoning that two criteria were critical for this view: on the one hand the degree of intensity in the explication of the opposites of weighing and carrying, on the other hand the degree of withdrawal of that which is "beautiful, harmonious, and proportioned." The second criterion is a priori inappropriate. Sketches 4.5 to 8.5 cm high cannot be treated as studies or paintings. The first criterion is absurd because it turns the priorities upside down.

Moreover, the traditional sequence of the sketches is not made any more plausible by stating that the first sketch from the left "is closest to" Breker's reconstruction of the first version of the Rondanini Madonna (Dussler, bib. 80): it is "closest" because Baumgart (bib. 25) had assigned it, as the last of the series, to the sculptor Arno Breker. No wonder that "the points of departure of the reconstruction do not correspond exactly to the original" (Frey, bib. 98, 209n2).

200. Isermeyer (bib. 143, 352) and Steinberg (bib. 281, 271) have with good reason challenged the view that the intended subject of the three-figure sketches was a burial (most recently Tolnay, bib. 319, no. 433; Hirst, bib. 139b, 40).

201. This view has already been put forth by Robinson, bib. 263, no. 70.

202. For the reasons, cf. Perrig, bib. 219, 71–82. Einem (bib. 88, 228–29, 283n22), followed by Salvini (bib. 271, 174–75), sticks to his earlier dating of the Rondanini and the Oxford sketches ca. 1547 or 1545 (bib. 84, 85–86, 88; bib. 87, 84). He argues that the second sketch from the left "stylistically" predates the Florentine Pietà.

CHAPTER 3
Michelangelo's Way of Drawing

1. On these studies, and their authorship (Cellini), see Perrig, bib. 229, 122n85.

2. Only Michelangelo's letter to his father of 31 January 1506 (*Michelangelo*, bib. 186, 1:11) provides some (paltry) information about the way he stored his drawings: his father was asked to send

to Rome "quelle carte che io messi in quel sacho" ("those sheets that I put in that sack").

3. Before the (uneven) cutting of Louvre 714 (fig. 5) the study of the arm was situated somewhat higher and more to the left. It thereby had the effect of being the visible excerpt of an invisible three-quarter figure standing along the center axis of the sheet.

4. In figure 32 most of the accessory sketches—in keeping with their genetic intermediate position—have a smaller size than the figures to which they are related in the composition sketch. But their sizes differ according to the same laws of progression as those of the auxiliary sketches in figure 31 which function as successors. The secondary, more heavily drawn auxiliary sketch is also always larger and appears more in the foreground.

5. The sizes of the occasional sketches (figs. 39–43) presumably followed other laws. They are conspicuously small, independent of the object of depiction. The exception: the hand sketch in figure 41 (length approximately 15 cm).

6. This does not exclude the possibility that Michelangelo occasionally drew preliminary contours with a metal point in the pen-and-ink drawings created during his early youth. In the case of the *Prudentia* (cf. chap. 2, n. 53 above) the existence of such an auxiliary contour is indicated by the pen-and-ink copies Uffizi 614E and British Museum Ff.1–5r, whose pen-and-ink contours are preceded by contours drawn which with silver point. These ink contours are suspended at certain illuminated parts of the body (e.g., at the thigh of the boy with the mask) in order to increase the effect of brightness.

7. Cf. Perrig, bib. 229, 15.

8. The contour corrections by the fourteen- to fifteen-year-old Michelangelo in the Ghirlandaio pupil drawing owned by Vasari were drawn with a "penna più grossa" (Vasari, bib. 329, 1:7)—a circumstance that might have contributed in large part to the astounding "differenza delle due maniere."

9. Joannides' opinion (bib. 151, 258) that Michelangelo "seems virtually to have abandoned the pen" only in the late 1520s is based—like all similar statements in the literature—on the mass of sheets questionably attributed to Michelangelo.

10. The earliest chalk drawings that *can be attributed* (on the basis of the authenticated ones) to Michelangelo were probably created in 1506 (cf. chap. 4, n. 5 below).

11. *Condivi*, bib. 62, 61.

12. Vasari, bib. 329, 1:259.

13. Armenini, bib. 5, 75–76: "mi parve cosi ben lineato, ombrato, & finito, che passaua ogni vso di minio, & era un stupor grande à quelli che ciò haueano veduto fare in cosi poco tempo, che altri vi hauerebbe giudicato dentro la fatica di vn mese."

14. *Condivi*, bib. 62, 196; Vasari, bib. 329, 1:124.

15. This ability must have been amazingly highly developed as early as 1492. The way in which individual limbs are swallowed by the ground in the centaur relief would be inexplicable if the artist had conceived the figures individually instead of as a coherent mass and had made their position in the composition primarily dependent on

the given rectangular frame (as Bertoldo had done in his bronze relief of the battle of horsemen).

16. Only individual movement motifs are developed directly from figure 30—including the attitude of the risen figure supporting himself with both arms on the ground in the lowermost part (middle) of figure 31. It corresponds somewhat to the attitude of the small figure at the lowermost left in figure 30.

17. Cf. Perrig, bib. 227, 36–40.

18. The angel was originally depicted standing. On the initial version of Mary see chap. 1, note 7.

19. On the phenomenology of drawing in old age, see Perrig, bib. 227, 85–87.

20. The reinforcing strokes in figure 5 and in the first sketch from the left in figure 35 appear to spring primarily from the need to extrapolate the definitive sketch from the competing provisional ones. Nevertheless, these strokes are found only in those sections of the contours on whose clarity the appearance of the whole especially depended. They form contrasts of the same type as the strengthenings in figures 23–24.

21. The hand sketch in figure 41 can be considered a representative of the 1520s. While its long horizontal hatching assemblage emphasizes the shortening of the back of the hand, the vertical spiral hatchings serve to make the inward turning of the middle finger clear. Without it this finger would appear parallel to the picture plane like the index finger.

22. The opinion that Michelangelo's finished manner is the expression of "mannerism" seems to be widespread. It is reflected in the fact that several anthologies (e.g., Salmi's, Tolnay's, Barocchi's, or Schmidt's) reproduce the London sketch (fig. 23) and the sketch in Venice [by Cavalieri!] (fig. 66), but not the highly finished drawing of the *Fall of Phaeton* (fig. 24). Hartt does reproduce it but in a substantially smaller size than the two preparatory sketches (bib. 130, nos. 358, 353, 357).

23. Michelangelo's ideal of perfection was diametrically opposed to Vasari's. This is revealed in an exemplary manner by the way in which the two artists judged Donatello, who was—Condivi writes (Vasari, bib. 329, 4:1650)—"very much praised by Michelangelo, except for one thing: that he did not have the patience to polish his works; while these had a wonderful effect when seen from afar, they lost their worthiness when viewed up close." In Vasari's eyes (1646–50) this *non-finito* represented just the opposite—a characteristic that couldn't be praised enough!

CHAPTER 4
What Finally Can Be Attributed to Michelangelo?

1. The hastily drawn small black-chalk sketch located under the draft of a madrigal written with a pen on folio 93r of Cod. Vat. Lat. 3211 (Tolnay, bib. 319, no. 353r) might serve as an example of the

drawing genre that is *not* discussed here because it is not sufficiently legible.

2. Tolnay, bib. 319, no. 281. Probably a component of the mass of sketches for the wall tombs of the Medici Chapel created in the spring of 1521 (cf. chap. 2, n. 178). Cf. Neufeld, bib. 191, 276.

3. Tolnay, bib. 319, no. 405.

4. Tolnay, bib. 319, nos. 105–13 (with the exception of no. 110, listed as originals of Michelangelo). On the studies of the Stanza del Borgo attributed to Bartolommeo Passarotti (1529–92) see *Disegni italiani*, bib. 74, no. 59.

To judge from these copies (which are believed to be originals also by Hirst, bib. 139b, 14, and bib 139c, no. 27) the original set of studies was divided into a group of anatomical "notes" sketched hastily with a pen while observing dissections and a smaller group of carefully executed red-chalk drawings that should probably be viewed as subsequent upgradings of the note material.

The sheets listed in Tolnay's *Corpus* are numbered by one cinquecento hand, presumably that of the copyist. These numbers were placed at various places on the sheets—some in the upper right corner, others centered. They suggest that the sheets were not bound, and that they thus do not constitute a "libro" (as is claimed) but a "fascio [bundle] di disegni." Since the reign of George III (1760–1820) the largest part of this "bundle" has been located in the "Michelangelo" files of the Royal Collection in Windsor. It must therefore come from the same Farnese collection from which at least the majority of the rest of the file contents originate. But if the "bundle" was once in the possession of Cardinal Alessandro Farnese (1520–89), then only Giulio Clovio can be considered the author. He is the only copyist of Michelangelo's "notomie" known to this day who bequeathed to the cardinal, his patron, whole "fasci di disegni" with numbered contents, in addition to a large number of unnumbered single sheets (Bertolotti, bib. 42, 11–19; Bradley, bib. 47, 355–59). The drawing style of the copies confirms this conclusion.

5. To judge from the copies (Teylers Museum; Windsor 12765r)-the one study was equipped with indications of proportion. It therefore is considered a "proportion study" (most recently Tolnay, bib. 319, no. 61r; Summers, bib. 292, 384–87). But the incompleteness of the markings, the inexactness of the measuring point intervals, the lack of a constructive scaffolding (cf. Summers, bib. 292, 386–87)—and above all the posture of the nude—speak against this interpretation. This posture is unsuitable for making the quantitative relationships between face length ("testa") and the length of the body or limbs readily apparent. It is that of a chained person. Michelangelo's short description of his *Rebellious Slave* (Louvre)—"figura di marmo ricta . . . che à le mani drieto" (*Michelangelo*, bib. 186, 2:7: "standing marble figure who has its hands behind")—could just as well be connected with this study.

Following Popham and Wilde (bib. 240, no. 421) the study was dated circa 1516, on the basis of its formal relationship to Sebastiano's *Flagellation of Christ* (Panofsky, bib. 204, 222, had even dated it ca. 1530). In reality a similar difference exists between it and Sebastiano's Christ (or the slave sketches in fig. 6!) as that between the first and last painted ignudi of the Sistine Chapel ceiling. The expression of physical dynamism in the study is still one-sidedly concentrated on the upper half of the body and not on the whole body. Actually the nude is closer in motif to the Hercules of 1497 (fig. 4) than to any of the slave sketches of 1510 (fig. 6). It can only refer—as Berenson (bib. 34, no. 1607) and Thode (bib. 294, 1:154 and 3:no. 532) already assumed—to the beginning project of the Julius tomb and must have been created between 1505 and 1508. In those years Michelangelo might have occasionally felt the need to reassure himself about the "correctness" of the body proportions by quickly and summarily measuring them. Roger de Piles (bib. 235, 14–15) and Jombert (bib. 154, 59) still recommended this method to artists in training.

The second red-chalk study must also be assigned the same relationship. The curious position of its arms can only be the expression of being bound, the figure as a whole can only be interpreted as a "slave." Obviously created *before* the "proportion study," it was regarded by Michelangelo as a mere provisorium—to conclude from the summarily sketched hatching reproduced in the two copies (Uffizi 6550F and Windsor 12765v). That may explain why the two studies atypically seem to have been located on the recto and verso of the same sheet. The Windsor sheet makes clear what kind of difficulties this placement made for the copyist. On the Windsor sheet a preliminary sketch in metal point preceded the red-chalk drawing of the verso. It refers only to the contours of the left half of the body and of the head—those parts that were probably not to be seen (because of the recto figure) in a direct tracing from the original (held against the light) and that therefore had to be copied by eye.

6. Of the three examples London 1895-9-15-493r is today considered the original (most recently Tolnay, bib. 319, no. 316r; Gere and Turner, bib. 78, no. 15; Hirst, bib. 139b, 117). If it were the original, its exceptional state of preservation would have to be regarded as a miracle. For the unusually close correspondence in the topography of the contours of all three examples presupposes extensive tracing, and these no original could have endured without damage.

The drawing was engraved by Antonio Tempesta (1555–1630) in 1617—together with the black-chalk drawing of a warrior bust on British Museum sheet 1895-9-15-492 (Wilde, bib. 344, no. 87), which thanks to the inscription on the engraving has acquired its widely accepted (but entirely fantastic) name "Count of Canossa." That it resembles the latter like a pendant (Venus and Mars) is evident, but no reason to regard *both* drawings as inventions of Michelangelo. Michelangelo drew only the Venus. Drawing the Mars to go along with her was a homework assignment, and it was solved in the typical fashion of a pupil. In contrast to the Venus, whose fantastic variety of forms appears to be condensed into an ornamental organism that sparkles with an inner dynamic, the Mars has the effect of a living cabinet of curiosities. There is no functional coherence between its "components." The additive effect is unnecessarily heightened by senseless doubling of similar forms (Mars' eye / bird's eye; Mars' face / warrior's mask; feather wreath / animal tail), by the ubiquity of the important ornaments and the considerable lack of homogeneity of execution. The drawing is—as Popp (bib. 242, 16, 20) and Dussler (bib. 80, no. 567) already recognized—a compilation. From the three copies of the Venus drawing it is also different in that it shows no signs of being a copy—even though it bears close resemblance to Michelangelo's highly finished drawing style. The universal recognition of its character as a copy (most recently Tolnay, bib. 319, 2:95) seems principally to function as an alibi. Suggesting the former existence of a "famous" original, it overlooks the absolute lack of any indicators of Michelangelo's authorship.

7. The second set displays the same beginner's style as the first (fig. 1) and was probably created at a correspondingly early date (see chap. 4: "A Document of Michelangelo's Early Draftsmanship"). Previous datings: (1) 1530–40 (Berenson, bib. 34 and bib. 37, no. 1460); (2) 1525–30 (Tolnay, bib. 302, 2:201–02, no. 40, and bib. 318, no. 94; Dussler, bib. 80, no. 251; Hartt, bib. 130, no. 310); (3) 1508–12 (Tolnay, bib. 319, no. 312v).

8. Tolnay, bib. 319, nos. 278v, 251, 313r, 300, 217rv. Of the two sketches (black chalk) on the verso of the British Museum sheet (Tolnay no. 217) only one has a stroke system characteristic of Michelangelo—the hastily drawn, small outline sketch of a curly head that stares with a wide open mouth at the amateurish leg sketch in front of it (a study for the *Giorno*, according to Tolnay). As its placement indicates, its function is similar to that of the small pen-and-ink sketch of the curly head shown in profile in fig. 4.

9. Tolnay, bib. 319, no. 3r. Cf. also Perrig, bib. 231.

10. Tolnay, bib. 319, no. 26v, 5. Cf. also Perrig, bib. 231.

11. Tolnay, bib. 319, no. 6r. Cf. also Perrig, bib. 231.

12. Cf. chap. 3, n. 23.

13. That the beginner's production of an artist escapes the range of the authenticated is normal. These drawings usually have a private character.

14. In the case of the Archivio sketches vol. XIII, fol. 145v (cf. n. 7 above) there is no such obstacle. Tolnay (bib. 302, 2:200–01, no. 40), Goldscheider (bib. 114, 177, note 13), and Barocchi (bib. 16, no. 368) therefore promptly attributed these to a pupil—completely or partially.

15. Transcribed in Barocchi, bib. 16, 3–4.

16. Most recently Tolnay, bib. 319, no. 15v, and Gurrieri, bib. 124a, 232, no. 167. According to Tolnay the text is a letter addressed to *Michelangelo*.

17. For the life of Buonarroto see Gotti, bib. 118, 2:20, no. 1.

18. Since Tolnay (bib. 302, 1:69) scholars believe this dating can be supported by reference to an alleged conformity of style with the Pietà in St. Peter's and the *Bacchus*.

19. Cf. Perrig, bib. 227, 79–85.

20. Significantly, the writer, probably overwhelmed by fatigue, fell out of character at the end of the eighth line of the verso. The two beginning letters of the last word ("flandra") are not only set apart and separated from the five other letters; they are also in the form of the more modern educated penmanship (in which both Michelangelo's brothers and Michelangelo himself had been instructed).

21. On the training of apprentices in quattrocento Florence, see Dvoràk, bib. 83, 1:124–39; Mesnil, bib. 185; Wackernagel, bib. 336, 336–45.

22. See Vasari, bib. 329, 1:5–7 and 2:64–68. The apprenticeship contract signed between Lodovico Buonarroti and Ghirlandaio on 1 April 1488 foresaw only training in painting. Moreover, it specified payment of the apprentice already in the first year of instruction. Both were exceptional stipulations based on the fact that in Ghirlandaio's eyes Michelangelo required no instruction in drawing.

23. Tolnay (bib. 296, 424, and bib. 302, 1:69) described the drawing as an "écorché" that exposed "the whole network of sinews of the interior" and allowed "its tensions to be felt." Einem (bib. 87a, 365) and Hartt (bib. 130, no. 5) declared it to be a study after a living model. Berti (bib. 39, 395) praised the "sure mastery of anatomy."

24. On Granacci's help, see Vasari, bib. 329, 1:6 and 2:66–67.

25. Frey, bib. 102, 2:64–65.

26. According to Frey either the Daniele pupil Michele degli Alberti or Michelangelo's last servant, Antonio del Franzese.

27. Most recently Hartt, bib. 130, no. 60 (1505–08); Tolnay, bib. 319, no. 26v (ca. 1505).

28. Only Baumgart (bib. 27, 254–55) drew appropriate conclusions from the misinterpretation of the writing. He rejected the verso drawing in the realization that a figure that "can nowhere free itself to a plastic rounding and arching" (*sic*) has nothing to do with the works of the artist created in the first or second decade of the sixteenth century. Carli (bib. 55, no. 112) obviously shared this opinion; nevertheless, he did not allow himself to be led astray by the writing. He upheld Michelangelo's authorship, but dated the drawing around 1485–90.

29. Only Portheim (bib. 247, 142) appears to have noticed the relationship to Ghirlandaio.

30. Tolnay (bib. 319, no. 26v), in contrast: "probabilmente è la copia di un dipinto . . . della prima metà del Quattrocento."

31. On Ghirlandaio's drawings, see most recently Ames-Lewis, bib. 3, 146–60, and bib. 4.

32. For example, in the Uffizi copy after a study for Ghirlandaio's "Epiphany" tondo in the Uffizi (Tolnay, bib. 302, 1:fig. 75).

33. See note 22 to this chapter above.

34. According to Popp (bib. 244, 138) the eagle and the vase were drawn twenty-four or twenty-five years *after* the girl; according to Goldscheider (bib. 114, no. 31, and bib. 115, no. 28), seven or eight years. Neither gives justification.

35. Since Portheim (bib. 247, 142) and Berenson (bib. 34, no. 1579) the girl has been alternately interpreted as being Salome with the head of John the Baptist, as Judith with the head of Holofernes, or as a servant of Judith or Salome.

36. That the eagle and vase do not accidentally stand upside down, but are intended to be interpreted so, is proven by the position of the outer hatching around the eagle's head. This hatching functions to indicate the ground.

37. The content of the rebus probably also included the fragmentary comment "andro qu . . . " placed next to the eagle's neck and upside down. That it is difficult to complete it to read "Andrea Quaratesi" (as Goldscheider, bib. 115, no. 28, would like) is confirmed by the birthdate of this banker's son (13 November 1512).

38. The Ghirlandaio drawing was probably a preliminary study for a female servant in a no longer extant depiction of Mary's or John the Baptist's birth. Ghirlandaio appears to have drawn two such scenes (one each for Mary and John) for Francesco Tornabuoni in Santa Maria sopra Minerva in Rome (Vasari, bib. 328, 3:259–60).

39. Tolnay (bib. 302, 5:230, no. 266), for example, correctly concluded that the Madonna was sketched "with the trembling hand of the aged master." But in the same breath he interpreted the *results* of this trembling hand ("The forms are no longer defined by closed, continuous outlines and by precise modeling, but they are only generally suggested by short repeated outlines and diagonal hatching, which do not follow the roundings of the forms") as the expression of a new artistic intention ("By this approximate suggestion of the forms, the master evoked the lighted aura which seems to envelop the vision")—as if what was caused unconsciously by motor disturbance could simultaneously be intentional and planned in advance. Cf. also Ramsden's critique, bib. 252, 204.

40. According to Tolnay (bib. 319, no. 391) it was created without special purpose. The sculpture was—so he thought—by its very nature inappropriate for expressing such "visions."

41. That must have happened at a time when the artist had the feeling that he had come to a deadend with his Pietà Rondanini, i.e., around 1559–60 (cf. Perrig, bib. 219, 71–82). That the Rondanini (just like the Pietà in the Florence Duomo) had been conceived for his own tomb is revealed by the course of the work on it and its chronology. On the whole problem, see Perrig, bib. 219.

CHAPTER 5
Tommaso de' Cavalieri (ca. 1509/10 –1587)

1. *Michelangelo*, bib. 186, 3:443 (letter of late December 1532).

2. On the person and life of Cavalieri see most recently Perrig, bib. 225; Frommel, bib. 104; Liebert, bib. 174, 270–76.

3. Vasari, bib. 329, 4:1889.

4. Quoted after Kemp, bib. 175, 57.

5. Michelangelo, bib. 186, 3:445.

6. Vasari, bib. 329, 1:118.

7. Tolnay (bib. 302, 3:111) did concede that "these sheets [in the meantime he had increased their number—in bib. 319, nos. 332–45—by a half dozen] were supposed to have served as models, so that Cavalieri with their aid could learn to draw," and that "this immediate purpose may in part explain the strangely cool, objective treatment of the forms." Nevertheless, he interpreted them—as Panofsky had already done (bib. 206, 215–28)—as "subjective confessions of love." "Confessions of love" became the standard exegetical formula, on the basis of which the interpretation of the sheets

has proceeded until today (most recently Liebert, bib. 174, 276–92; Hirst, bib. 139b, 112).

8. Perrig, bib. 224.

9. Tolnay, bib. 317.

10. Frommel, bib. 104, 116, n. 61.

11. Frommel, bib. 104, 62.

12. Frommel, bib. 104, 39.

13. Dussler, bib. 80, no. 55.

14. Barocchi, bib. 15, no. 142, and Salmi, bib. 269, no. 54.

15. Hartt, bib. 130, no. 349.

16. Berti, bib. 40, 468.

17. Popham and Wilde, bib. 240, 252, no. 428.

18. Delacre, bib. 69, 466.

19. The relationship of the nude to the Haman was already noticed by Delacre (bib. 69, 466) and—indirectly—by Tolnay (bib. 296, 448n62, and bib. 302, 3:220, no. 113) and Goldscheider (bib. 114, no. 76). The latter spoke of "a return to older motives" and cited as one among other examples the pen-and-ink sketch in figure 75 that is derived from the Sistine Haman (on Cellini's authorship of this sketch, see Perrig, bib. 229, 38–41). Tolnay had noticed the Haman relationship in the sketch in figure 60 and taken this for the model of the giant (fig. 59). Cf. note 21 below.

20. Gurrieri (bib. 124a, 235, no. 169) sees in it "una rielaborazione più tarda e matura."

21. How difficult it was for scholars to incorporate the two drawings into the accepted canon is revealed by Tolnay's ambivalent attitude. He had at first seen in the giant an anonymous copy after the Archivio sketch (see note 19 above), and later, in bib. 302, 5:184, no. 172, "a copy made by the master himself." Even later (bib. 307, 13), he saw in it "a new version of the same figure." In the end (bib. 319, no. 347v, and bib. 322, no. 71v) he was of the opinion that the giant had been "developed" by Michelangelo from the Archivio sketch. But in the fifty-two years that elapsed between Tolnay's first and last pronouncements he never asked:

1. the reason for the enormous difference in size between the two drawings;
2. the reason for the one-sided concentration of almost all pentimenti in the hip and leg area;
3. the mechanical anatomy and movement of the depicted bodies;
4. the relationship of the two drawings to authenticated Michelangelo sheets.

Even this Tolnay apparently found self-evident: that by dating the Archivio figure—which in his opinion needed no improvement—as the earlier of the two, his chronology suggested that it was in fact the worse.

22. Berenson (bib. 34 and bib. 37, no. 1713; bib. 36, 109) had attributed the drawing, which had been sketched with the right hand, to the left-handed Raffaello da Montelupo. Since then scholars nevertheless felt themselves obliged to discover certain weaknesses in the "undoubted original of the master" (Dussler, bib. 80, no. 199). Dussler thought that the contours had been "in part gone over by

another hand." According to Tolnay (bib. 319, no. 260v) also the shading "non è all'altezza dei disegni migliori di Michelangelo, ma crediamo alla sua autografia."

23. According to Tolnay (bib. 302, 5:175) the tracing has "auto-biographical significance. . . . Since the Tityos is a symbol for the tormented lover, the representation of a Risen Christ in almost the same attitude on the back of the same sheet may be meant as a symbol of the liberation and rebirth of the lover." Liebert (bib. 174, 285) gleans a similar reading from the tracing: it "testifies to the artist's dread of death and the wasting of the mortal body. It reflects his deep unconscious wish for the magical undoing of the suffering that awaited the sinner after death."

24. Frey (bib. 101, no. 219) and Thode (bib. 294, 3:no. 540) had already recognized that the sketch is an attempt to reformulate Christ's attitude (most recently Tolnay, bib. 319, no. 345v). In contrast, its subject was misinterpreted as a guard of the grave by Berenson (bib. 37, no. 1615), Wilde (bib. 240, 253, and bib. 344, 89), Dussler (bib. 80, no. 241), and Hartt (bib. 130, no. 184).

25. The Uffizi drawing and its duplicate, the black-chalk drawing in the Boymans Museum in Rotterdam (I, 20), have since Berenson (bib. 37, no. 1676A) been accepted as copies after an unknown Michelangelo original (most recently Lecchini Giovannoni, bib. 166, no. 13; Tolnay, bib. 319, no. 259 bis), although its compilation character was already recognized by Wilde (bib. 344, 89). This view seems to be—as in other, similar cases (cf. chap. 4, note 6)—the expression of an unconscious denial. The magic formula "copy" is used to drive anything that is considered to be alien for Michelangelo from the conscious mind. In reality it is the two drawings themselves between which an original-copy relationship exists. With its hard-edged, wiry contours the Rotterdam drawing follows the Uffizi sketch down to the misguided details (neck muscles, hands, right foot, small toes of the left foot, among others), complementing, for better or for worse, what is crossed out with special emphasis (sexual organs). Paradoxically, since Tolnay (bib. 302, 3:220, no. 114), it figures in the literature as the "better" copy.

26. On Tolnay's speculations as to purpose, see Perrig, bib. 228, 24–26n14.

27. *Michelangelo*, bib. 186, 3:432.

28. Tolnay, bib. 319, no. 260r.

29. This ambiguous character is reflected in the multiplicity of divergent assessments. Initially both Berenson (bib. 34, no. 1608), seconded by Steinmann (bib. 286, 603, no. 56), and Thode (bib. 294, 1:268–69) had regarded the Windsor head (fig. 64) as a study for the Sistine Chapel ceiling. Subsequently, however, both retreated from this opinion, whose substantiation Jacobsen (bib. 146, 494) had doubted, in favor of a dating around 1533–34 (Thode, bib. 294, 3:no. 533) or between 1517 and 1540 (Berenson, bib. 35, 275n1). Panofsky (bib. 201, no. 6) found this shift of opinion unjustified; for him, dating the sketch in the 1530s was "out of the question." The head was "presumably connected with the lunette pictures of the Sistine Chapel ceiling." Brinckmann (bib. 49, no. 20) even saw a "distinct relationship to the drawings of Leonardo." He dated the

head, also because of the "hatching technique" and the "hardness in the eyes" even earlier—to 1506.

While all these scholars proceeded on the assumption that the drawing was an original by Michelangelo, Popp (bib. 243, 75) thought it was a copy. Clark (bib. 59, 181) went even one step farther. The drawing was satisfactory "neither in construction nor in touch. . . . The nose is flattened out, the construction of the left cheek bone and the relation between the neck and the jaw bone to the left are both misunderstood. Above all, the thin and hesitating outline . . . is quite unlike Michelangelo. This touch seems to be very similar to that of the drawing of the Martyrdom of St. Catherine . . . which . . . served as a model for Bugiardini's picture in Santa Maria Novella, Florence" (Tolnay, bib. 319, no. 365B). This frontal attack on the Michelangelo dogma bounced off the shields of belief. Dussler (bib. 80, no. 715) again took up Popp's thesis of a copy. The other scholars went back to guessing about the time of creation and the purpose. Wilde (bib. 240, no. 434) thought the drawing was an incomplete study for an unknown Madonna created around 1540. The alleged "veil" was "characteristic of almost all Michelangelo's Virgins, and the form of the veil cap is the same as in the two Annunciations painted by Marcello Venusti from Michelangelo's drawings [meaning, among others, fig. 100] about 1550." Goldscheider (bib. 114, no. 84, and bib. 115, no. 90) thought it more likely "a type of Madonna used by him [Michelangelo] in his early period," but for reasons of "technique" dated the drawing about 1533. Tolnay (bib. 302, 5:171, no. 154, and bib. 319, no. 325r), Brugnoli (bib. 50, no. 46), and Hartt (bib. 130, no. 364) followed his example, but replaced the thesis of an "unfinished study" with the assumption that it was a highly finished drawing prepared for Cavalieri.

Jacobsen had assumed that the headdress in the Windsor drawing was a helmet and that the sex of the depicted person was therefore masculine. Thode, Brinckmann, Delacre (bib. 69, 542), Wilde, Dussler, and Gere (bib. 77, no. 130), on the other hand, thought it was feminine, while other scholars classified it as not clearly identifiable, but more likely masculine.

In contrast to the sex of the Windsor head, that of the Oxford head (fig. 65) has been a subject of controversy or "not altogether clear" (bib. 77, no. 112) only since 1971, when Hartt (bib. 130, no. 363) counterposed the previous feminine thesis (most recently Pignatti, bib. 234, no. 20; Tolnay, bib. 319, no. 323) with the thesis that it was masculine. But the time of creation and purpose of this drawing have been debated since Popp (bib. 242, 21). Popp dropped the Sistine study thesis generally accepted up to that point and proposed that the drawing belonged in the 1520s and was a product of Michelangelo's pupil Carlo. She at first found complete agreement from Tolnay, who (bib. 302, 2:209–10, no. 15A) for his part rejected the drawing from Michelangelo's corpus, but in order to attribute it to Bacchiacca (1494–1557). Other scholars, whom Tolnay rejoined in 1960 (bib. 302, 5:170, no. 152), stood fast by their belief in its "undeniable authenticity" (Weinberger, bib. 338, 342n8). Nevertheless, they found themselves prepared to examine again the question of dating and purpose. The result of this examination: two new theories regarding the drawing's purpose and eight new theories as to its date. The former are: (1) presentation drawing (the majority vote); (2) "study from life" (Hartt, bib. 130, no. 259). The dating theses: (1) about 1516 (Wilde, bib. 77, no. 112); (2) before 1520 (Berenson, bib. 37, no. 1552; Weinberger, bib. 338, 342n8; Hirst, bib. 139c, no. 23); (3) about 1520 (Dussler, bib. 80, no. 342); (4) about 1522 (Goldscheider, bib. 115, no. 49); (5) about 1520–25 (Tolnay, bib. 302, vol. 5; Berti, bib. 40, 467n166); (6) about 1525–30 (Tolnay, bib. 319, no. 323); (7) about 1528–30 (Goldscheider, bib. 114, no. 65); and (8) about 1533–34 (Hartt, bib. 130).

30. Berenson (bib. 37, no. 1608), Popham and Wilde (bib. 240, no. 434), and Goldscheider (bib. 114, no. 84, and bib. 115, no. 90) believed they saw in the verso drawing another, weaker hand at work than in the drawing on the recto. Wilde suspected the hand was Cavalieri's and thereby earned the distinction of mentioning Michelangelo's friend as a possible author for the first time in the history of Michelangelo scholarship.

31. Goldscheider (bib. 114, 46n84) had already sensed Cavalieri's characteristics in the Windsor head (fig. 64). He subsequently dropped this hypothesis (bib. 115), but it was picked up by Frommel (bib. 104, 68).

32. Vasari, bib. 329, 1:118. Without cause, Wilde (bib. 344, 97) and Barocchi, in the comments to her edition of Vasari's work (bib. 329, 4:1903–04), doubted the accuracy of Vasari's note. To be sure, a portrait drawing of Cecchino Bracci *is* mentioned in the letter of Luigi del Riccio which they quote, but it was not by Michelangelo. It had been sent to him after Cecchino's death with the request that he have a bust carved after it. But—as the letter also indicates—the artist had not found the drawing to his liking, and he therefore promised to do a drawing of the already buried Cecchino himself.

On the alleged portraits of the children of Michelangelo's servant Urbino see excursus II.

33. Vasari, bib. 329, 4:1905.

34. The verbatim text of Vasari's report on the "carte" prepared for Cavalieri (Vasari, bib. 329, 1:118) excludes the possibility that the portrait passed into the latter's possession only after the fact.

35. Fischel (bib. 94, 122–23) and Groote (bib. 122, 26), among others, had already noticed that the Giuliano, in contrast to the Lorenzo, has portrait-like qualities, but they incorrectly equated these with the features of the historic Giuliano (1478–1516).

36. For Cavalieri's concern with the subject of the *Children's Bacchanal* see chap. 2, n. 109 above.

37. Most recently Einem, bib. 88, 137; Keller, bib. 156, 85; Tolnay, bib. 319, no. 346; Wilde, bib. 347, 160–61; Liebert, bib. 174, 337–38; Hirst, bib. 139b, 50–51, and bib. 139c, no. 51. For a contrasting view see Perrig, bib. 228, 28n26.

38. Berenson (bib. 37, 1:229n1) already found the drawing "so unusual in feeling for Michelangelo, so Raphaelesque in a way, that one may hesitate to accept it as M.'s." Even Tolnay conceded earlier (bib. 302, 5:183, no. 170) that "the attribution to Michelangelo is not sure." Both scholars—and with them Hartt (bib. 130,

no. 370)—put the lid on their doubts with the thesis that the drawing had been worked over at a later date (a thesis correctly rejected by Dussler, bib. 80, no. 246).

39. Vasari, bib. 329, 3:1255. The conventionality of the sketch corresponds to that of Cavalieri's *Fall of Phaeton* (fig. 66). Cf. Jacoby, bib. 147, 156.

40. The Iudex in figure 67 can be drawn into a rectangle of approximately 70 square centimeters, in which a good part of the damned group in figure 30 would find room.

41. In spite of this it was dated *before* figure 30 by Barocchi (bib. 15, no. 141, and bib. 17, no. 1), Forlani Tempesti (bib. 95, no. 26), and Einem (bib. 88, 137).

42. Its correctness was doubted only by Popp (bib. 243, 73: "pasticcio after the fresco") and for a time by Berenson (bib. 34, no. 1399K) and Tolnay (bib. 301, 127). Cf. most recently Tolnay, bib. 319, no. 349; Bertelà, bib. 38, no. 310.

43. Described as a "martyr" in the literature.

44. The heavily erased first version of the right arm seems to have immediately started from the Bayonne Christ (fig. 67).

45. He reminds all scholars since Wilde (bib. 344, 98) either of the Saint Lawrence of the *Last Judgment* or of the ignudo to the right above Joel or of the Delphic Sibyl of Sistine Chapel ceiling (most recently Tolnay, bib. 319, no. 350r). Previously the figure reminded everyone of "one of the elect who tries to pull others upward" (Steinmann, bib. 286, 606, no. 75).

46. More recently scholars take this fact into account to the extent that the Uffizi sketch is generally dated between figures 30 and 32.

47. Scholars seem to have sensed this. The Bayonne and Uffizi sketches are treated extensively only in the catalogues. In discussions of the process of creation of the *Last Judgment* (Wilde, bib. 343; Tolnay, bib. 301 and bib. 302, 5:24–43; Einem, bib. 88, 137–42; Hirst, bib. 139b, 50–52; among others) they are either omitted or discussed only in iconographic terms.

48. This nude seen from the rear appears to be the result of an attempt to reform the slightly oblique Michelangelo figure into a frontally viewed one. The number and form of the pentimenti attest to the draftsman's difficulty in overcoming the foreshortening problem. Some of the pentimenti (e.g., on the left leg) indicate that the draftsman was still under the spell of an oblique body. The misconstruction of the nude is evident mainly in the position of the legs; their being spread contradicts the intended running effect. Panofsky (bib. 204, 241n3) was inclined, "after recent examination . . . , to see [in Casa Buonarroti sheet 69F] an atelier copy within which, however, the small nude seen from the rear of the verso side [fig. 69] might be regarded as by Michelangelo's own hand."

49. To conclude from the relevant statements the four head studies must document one of Michelangelo's many style "revivals" (see introduction). While the head studies in figure 69 and on the verso of the London sheet have always been connected with the *Last Judgment* (most recently Tolnay, bib. 319, nos. 91v, 350v), the head study on Casa Buonarroti sheet 47F, which is equivalent in physi-

ognomy, size, and technique of execution and saddled with the same anatomical defects, was treated by everyone except Hartt (bib. 130, no. 396) as if it had nothing to do with it. Thode (bib. 294, no. 43) dated it in the time of the cartoon for the *Battle of Cascina* (ca. 1504), Steinmann (bib. 286, 602, no. 50), Berenson (bib. 34 and bib. 37, no. 1409D), Barocchi (bib. 15, no. 22), Berti (bib. 40, 428n62), Parronchi (bib. 208, 1:138), and Tolnay (bib. 319, no. 124) connected it with the Sistine Chapel ceiling. Dussler (bib. 80, no. 266) made a plea for its creation in the 1520s, not without the question: "Whether it's original" ("any of M.'s authenticated analoga are missing")?

50. Redig de Campos, bib. 256, pl. XXVIII.

51. Ibid., pl. LIV.

52. Panofsky (bib. 205, 180) had already determined that the knee studies "in the fresco [are] of course not directly documentable, but they can be explained without further ado within this area of activity" (Dussler, bib. 80, no. 274). Tolnay (bib. 302, 5:189, no. 182) at first wanted to see them explained outside this area. But after Hartt (bib. 130, no. 387) noticed that the lower study "clearly" had been intended for the left leg of the figure located above Saint Blaise (Redig de Campos, bib. 256, pl. LIII), Tolnay found—for both studies—a correspondent in the fresco, namely the left leg of Saint Bartholomew (bib. 319, no. 91v).

53. Whether such considerations have ever played a role in the evaluation of figure 69 is doubtful. What is certain is that the drawings were more critically studied in the past than they are today. That they were autograph works by Michelangelo was disputed by Wilde and Panofsky (bib. 204, 241n3, and bib. 205, 180–81), Popp (bib. 245, 13, and bib. 246, 54) and Goldscheider (bib. 114, no. 61), and indirectly (by not mentioning them) by Frey and Thode. Even Delacre (bib. 69, 365) considered them as doubtful. Tolnay (bib. 302, 5:189, no. 182) tried at first to separate the hands by disattributing the right arm study at the top ("weaker in execution, probably not by the master") before he convinced himself and his public that "gli studi sono stati generalmente attribuiti, secondo noi a ragione, a Michelangelo" (bib. 319, no. 91v).

54. According to general opinion, on the other hand, it is "undeniable" that it is by Michelangelo (most recently Tolnay, bib. 319, no. 348r).

55. See also Dussler, bib. 80, no. 246. The only judgment that does justice to the additive character of the Teyler Museum sketch (Tolnay, bib. 319, no. 341r.) which apparently served to prepare the group on the ground in figure 66, is Dussler's (bib. 80, no. 533).

56. See also Dussler, bib. 80, no. 294.

57. Redig de Campos, bib. 256, pl. XCVI.

58. Tolnay regarded the study as "a feeble copy . . . executed after the fresco" (bib. 301, 128n4), before he declared it to be an original of the great master (bib. 302, 5:188–89, no. 181, and bib. 319, no. 91r).

59. That Cavalieri supposedly transformed sketch figures of the master into studies will probably seem unique and therefore unbelievable to most present-day readers. But at least in the seventeenth century such a practice was in no way out of the ordinary. Bellori (bib. 33, 94) reports that after Annibale Carracci (1560–1609) had executed the paintings for the Cappella di San Diego in S. Giacomo degli Spagnuoli in Rome, "he left the whole task to Albani [1578–1660], who on the basis of the master's sketches prepared movement and affect studies after the living model and thereby executed and completed the two large history paintings and the second lunette above it."

60. Following Panofsky (bib. 203) the torso study was repeatedly declared to be a preliminary study for the *Last Judgment* (the arm study coexisting with it referred—so it was thought—to the outstretched right arm of the angel holding the sponge with vinegar; Redig de Campos, bib. 256, pl. XVI), but otherwise it was almost exclusively treated as a model for Sebastiano's *Pietà* in Ubeda or its preliminary study in the Louvre (Tolnay, bib. 319, no. 92). Hirst (bib. 136, 587–88, bib. 139, 128, bib. 139b, 39, 61, 69, 70, and bib. 139c, nos. 49–50) classified both the torso and the arm study simply as "studies for Sebastiano's picture." As late as 1960 Tolnay refrained from discussing it (bib. 302, 5:189, no. 182) and satisfied himself with a reference to Dussler, bib. 79, 188, no. 203, although he had in the meantime abandoned his earlier copy thesis of 1940 (see note 53 above) which he had adopted from Wilde, Panofsky, and Popp (see note 58 above). In 1975 (bib. 319, no. 91r), however, he concluded one of his typical compromises. He assigned the Casa Buonarroti sheet to the "Composizioni per Sebastiano del Piombo" and classified the torso study as a preliminary drawing for the Pietà of Ubeda (commission: summer 1533). The arm study, on the other hand, which was outlined and shaded with the same chalk in the same way, he declared to be a preliminary drawing for the angel holding the sponge with vinegar (which means that the latter, according to Tolnay's chronology of the sketches for the *Last Judgment*—see chap. 2, n. 189—must have been created five to seven years *after* the torso study).

61. Panofsky, bib. 203, 156.

62. Brugnoli, bib. 50, no. 51.

63. Redig de Campos, bib. 256, pl. XCVI.

64. As Brugnoli-Pace (bib. 51, 107–08) demonstrated, the torso was studied not after a living model but after the fragment of a Roman marble group (ibid., pl. XVI/5), which was in turn copied after a Greek bronze depicting the Aeolus offspring Athamas with his son Learchos, whom he had killed in anger.

Brugnoli-Pace further pointed out that the finger indications under the right armpit of the torso study correspond to the right hand of Athamas. They confirm not only that the study refers to the fresco, but also the assumption that its starting point was the small group of figures in Michelangelo's compositional sketch (fig. 31), which for its part was probably also inspired by the Athamas-Learchos group.

65. Cavalieri attempted to correct this impression after the fact by adding a second, strongly downward-turning face to the head of the figure. This corresponds more or less to the head studies on the verso of British Museum sheet 1895-9-15-518 (Tolnay, bib. 319, no. 350v).

66. The motifs of individual movement of this sketch are based on a few clichés. The attitude of Christ, for example, is repeated, slightly modified, no less than three times within the circle of seated attendants.

67. Research into his more mature products presents some difficulties, but is indispensable if such drawings as the *Labors of Hercules* in Windsor (Tolnay, bib. 319, no. 335) are finally to find the esteem they deserve.

CHAPTER 6
Ascanio Condivi (1524–1574)

1. On Condivi's life and work, see Grigioni, bib. 120 (unsurpassed), Settimo, bib. 276, and Patrizi, bib. 213a.

2. Settimo, bib. 276, 25–26.

3. Ibid., 26.

4. Grigioni, bib. 120, 15–16.

5. Ibid., 20; see also Condivi, bib. 62, 23.

6. Condivi described both of them as friends of Michelangelo and as "reverendissimo patron mio" or "mio reverendissimo padrone" (Condivi, bib. 62, 183–84.

7. Condivi, bib. 62, 176.

8. Gualandi, bib. 123, 180; Settimo, bib. 276, 43–44.

9. Condivi, bib. 62, 25.

10. That Condivi felt himself obliged to protect his master against the charge of homosexuality (bib. 62, 192)—twenty years after Michelangelo's having met the young Cavalieri—gives one pause. Had the rumors been revived by his appearance on the scene?

11. Condivi, bib. 62, 25.

12. Grigioni, bib. 120, 20, 55–56; Settimo, bib. 276, 41–42.

13. Grigioni, bib. 120, 54, 73–75.

14. Lorenzo Ridolfi is not mentioned in Condivi's biography of Michelangelo. Niccolò, however, "il mio reverendissimo padrone" (see note 6 above), might have commissioned the work in the expectation that Michelangelo would at least supply the sketches. He possibly intended to found a gallery of "uomini famosi romani." In the literature on the bust of Brutus (most recently Tolnay, bib. 320, 61–63, 212–13) Condivi's Sulla is not mentioned.

15. Michelangelo Buonarroti the Younger, the artist's greatnephew (1568–1647), purchased it and had it restored in the belief that it was an authentic work by his great-uncle—which speaks volumes about his understanding of Michelangelo (Procacci, bib. 248, 178–79). Thode (bib. 294, 2:439–43) and Steinmann (bib. 288, 6) were the first to see in Condivi's painting the "tavola" mentioned by Vasari (bib. 329, 1:120).

16. Most recently, *Drawings*, bib. 77, no. 153; Parronchi, bib. 208, 2:216–17; Tolnay, bib. 319, no. 389; Hirst, bib. 139b, 75, 77–78, and bib. 139c, no. 53.

17. Berenson, bib. 34, no. 1537.

18. Frey, bib. 102, 2:37n.

19. Ibid., 36.

20. Gotti, bib. 118, 2:153. In his letter to Vasari of 17 March 1564 Daniele (Frey, bib. 102, 2:54) writes that the cartoons have "gone to a place where one will have trouble seeing them or getting them back" ("Ma tutti sono iti in luogo, che si durera faticha a uederli non che a riauerlj").

21. Frey, bib. 102, 2:54, 60; Gotti, bib. 118, 2:156. Lionardo appears to have subsequently given one of these eight cartoons—"dov'è designata una Pietà con nove figure non finite" (Gotti, bib. 118, 2:151)—to Daniele. In any case, Daniele's estate inventory of 5 April 1566 (Levie, bib. 169, 218) lists "una pietà di cartone di mano di Michelagnolo."

22. Gotti, bib. 118, 2:155–56.

23. Ibid., 156.

24. His letter of 17 March (see note 20 above) suggests that Daniele himself, who was present at the inventory on 19 February, had probably blocked the immediate delivery of the cartoon to Cavalieri—by pointing to the cardinal's claims.

25. Daniele mentions this cartoon of the *Farewell* three times in his letter and explicitly describes it as the "best" ("il meglio"). He regrets that Vasari would not accept it when Michelangelo wanted to present it to him ("Quanto mal fu non accettare quel Cristo . . . , quando uelo volse dare!"). He suggested to the cardinal that he would make a copy of it (probably meaning a painting) if he were successful in obtaining the cartoon.

For Michelangelo, this cartoon was presumably a provisional work. He had offered it to Vasari because he intended to prepare a new version. But Vasari probably counted on this definitive version and therefore refused the gift. Ultimately all his trouble was for nothing because Michelangelo—as Daniele writes—"never made another one" ("a ogni modo non ci fece mai altro"). His final illness and death prevented him from doing so.

26. Grigioni, bib. 120, 73–75.

27. In addition to Caro, Tiberio Crispi might also have commissioned the work (see note 6 above). Condivi lived near his titular church, S. Agata dei Goti (bib. 62, 177; see also Pemsel, bib. 63, 172n2).

28. Between 1554 and 1564 Condivi spent only one short period in Rome, the winter of 1561–62—as emissary of the town of Ripatransone (Grigioni, bib. 120, 24–25).

29. See note 20 above.

30. Frey, bib. 102, 2:37n.

31. Battaglia, bib. 21, 4:509–12.

32. Examples in Vasari, bib. 329, 1:37, 119, 229, 254, 263–64, 266, 270. Cf. also Battaglia, bib. 21, 3:317.

33. If Daniele had indeed seen a work of Michelangelo in the *Epiphany* cartoon, contextual logic dictates that the phrase should read "quello che [Michelangelo] fece per Ascanio" instead of "quello che dipigneua Ascanio."

34. Vasari, bib. 329, 1:120.

35. See Vasari, bib. 328, 5:568, and the following note.

36. Vasari, bib. 329, 1:122.

37. According to Hartt, it must be wrong in any case. For accord-

ing to him (bib. 130, no. 440) the cartoon was not created around 1550 (according to Settimo, bib. 276, 108, around 1547)—as most recent scholarship would have it—but in 1553, that is, in the year before Condivi's return to Ripatransone. Gombrich (bib. 117a, 176) went even so far as to wish it had been created in "the last years of the master's life," in order to make its dating compatible with his theory that the cartoon and the picture were destined for S. Giovanni dei Fiorentini (which even in 1564 was far from being finished).

38. The selection and placement of words reflect that passage in Condivi's dedication to the pope (bib. 62, 23–24), which reads: "ch'io ho fatto fatiche e spero di dar frutti."

39. Wilde (bib. 344, no. 75) and Dussler (bib. 80, no. 178) relate this remark to the *Epiphany* cartoon (fig. 95), which shows—according to Wilde—Michelangelo's help in the position of "John's" right arm. He thought that it had been changed ad hoc from that of the cartoon version. In reality it reflects the right-arm position of the cartoon's second draft, which is drawn in rough contours.

40. Grigioni, bib. 120, 73–75.

41. See Vasari, bib. 329, 1:226 and my remarks on Michelangelo's *Cleopatra* in chap. 2; furthermore, see excursus II.

42. See Frey, bib. 102, 1:171–73.

43. According to Vasari (bib. 329, 1:240–41) the banker Pierfrancesco Borgherini already assumed as much when in 1516 he commisioned the *Flagellation of Christ* from Sebastiano del Piombo, who was little known in Rome. See also Perrig, bib. 219, 150–52n6.

44. Examples of promises that were—as far as can be determined—not kept: *Michelangelo*, bib. 186, 1:182, 2:376, 3:272, 315. On Michelangelo's aversion to commissions for altarpieces, see *Michelangelo*, bib. 186, 4:299.

45. Steinmann and Wittkower, bib. 290, 435.

46. See note 15 above.

47. Tolnay (bib. 302, 5:214; bib. 319, no. 389; bib. 320, 112–13) and Berti (bib. 40, 489), in his wake, regarded the five heads of the secondary figures as later additions by Condivi because they were "of inferior quality." This assessment was based on Michelangelo's estate inventory, which speaks only of "three large figures and two children." According to their curious argumentation, Condivi must at some time after 19 February 1564 have hurried from Ripatransone to Rome in order to touch up the cartoon with elements he had already painted on the panel.

48. Awareness of this fact was sufficiently alive even during Richter's lifetime as to lead to the assumption that the cartoon had originally included more figures on the left side (Richter, bib. 261, 153). During Tolnay's time, on the other hand, it was brushed aside with the explanation that the cartoon "has an abstract-symmetrical composition made up of three parallel verticals, reminiscent of the works done for Vittoria Colonna" (Tolnay, bib. 302, 5:66).

49. "What do these mute, brutal figures want with their useless weight?" asked Bayersdorfer (bib. 29, 106–07). "Of what is the Evangelist speaking?" asked Berenson (bib. 37, 1:231–32). "Perhaps of the Christ Child Who . . . is . . . making believe that He will not play with the infant John."

50. Gotti, bib. 118, 2:156.

51. See note 45 above.

52. Procacci, bib. 248, 178–79.

53. Most recently, *Drawings*, bib. 77, no. 153; Settimo, bib. 276, 106–10; Tolnay, bib. 319, no. 389; Gombrich, bib. 117a. The only plausible speculation: "some kind of Sacra Conversazione" (Wilde, bib. 344, no. 75), and "Exceptionally enigmatic in subject" (Hirst, bib. 139b, 77).

54. Instead of analyzing the relationship between the cartoon and the painting, scholars have always celebrated the former and wrinkled their noses at the latter. Hartt (bib. 130, no. 440): "The tragic intensity of these heads [the secondary figures in the cartoon] is completely misunderstood in Condivi's inept painting"! Hirst (bib. 139b, 78): These features [i.e. the alleged "indications of improvisation and speed" in the cartoon] must have created problems for Condivi, whose altar-piece . . . has been characterized as appallingly incompetent."

55. Tolnay, bib. 320, 113: "the light and shade are delicately rendered, giving the overall effect of a vision." See also note 66 below. In the available reproductions of the cartoon it is difficult to determine even the number of heads of secondary figures. Richter (bib. 261, 153) counted four heads instead of five; Thode (bib. 294, 2:441) and Berti (bib. 40, 489) counted only three.

56. On average they are at least 75 percent shorter than the strokes in Michelangelo's cartoon fragment (fig. 34).

57. Most recently, Hartt, bib. 128a, 54.

58. Tolnay took up the question only in 1978. Under no. 389 of his *Corpus* (bib. 319) he attributed the panel to an "anonymous successor of Michelangelo" who had been inspired by the *Epiphany* cartoon. Under no. 389bis, on the other hand, he annulled "our previous opinion" and dated the panel "around 1500–1505." The composition had been designed by Michelangelo himself "and then gone over by a less apt hand, perhaps in order to make the strokes drawn by the master more legible." And then again it was possibly "a copy after an original drawing of Buonarroti."

Apparently between nos. 389 and 389bis the Oxford catalogue had come to Tolnay's attention, with its confusing dating of the panel between 1516 and 1530 (Christopher, bib. 57a, 118). Cf. also Johannides, bib. 153, 684 ("I find it impossible to believe it is that early and would maintain my dating of ca. 1516–30, if it is by Michelangelo."

59. First Robinson, bib. 263, 89–90; most recently Tolnay, bib. 319, no. 389bis.

60. Berenson, bib. 34 and bib. 37, no. 1725A.

61. Hartt, bib. 128a, 54.

62. Notwithstanding it can be supposed that the picture treats the seldom depicted theme (not mentioned in *Lexikon*, bib. 171) of the Christ Child learning to walk. Luca Cambiaso (1527–85) rendered it in two washed pen-and-ink drawings (Munich, Staatliche Graphische Sammlung no. 2724–5).

63. Tolnay, bib. 319, no. 401–2r, 427–30; most recently Hirst, bib. 139c, nos. 56–57. The only doubts about Michelangelo's

authorship expressed to date refer to fig. 91 and its verso (Perrig, bib. 219, 123n20 and 130n34), to figure 92 (Tolnay, bib. 302, 5:218), and to figure 94 (Frey, bib. 101, no. 225).

64. Dussler (bib. 80, nos. 3, 351), on the other hand, saw in figure 91 an "exceptionally soft handling of the chalk," and in figure 94 a "palpably light and self-assured sketching process."

65. Most recently, *Drawings*, bib. 77, no. 157; Tolnay, bib. 319, no. 427; Hirst bib. 139c, nos. 56–57.

66. Dussler (bib. 80, no. 178) on figure 95: "The wonderful, soft, and transparent process of the modeling, the fine, shaky contour competes, even on this large scale, with the effects of drawings of a small size."

67. Condivi, bib. 62, 196.

68. See chap. 2, note 93.

69. Condivi, bib. 62, 196.

70. Ibid., 165–66.

71. It is significant that Condivi consistently fails to discuss his own works in his Michelangelo *Vita*.

72. On Mini, see Perrig, bib. 231.

73. Of course, it is undeniable that some of Condivi's figures are derived from *certain* individual Pauline figures. The "Joseph" in the Oxford panel (fig. 99) is based on the chief executioner in the *Crucifixion of Peter*. The missing left leg probably reflects Condivi's helplessness at finding this leg hidden in the fresco. The "speaker" in the *Epiphany* (figs. 95, 98) is derived from the spear-carrier standing in front of the captain's horse in the same picture, or from the angel in the upper right corner of the *Conversion of Paul*. The "boy John" of the *Epiphany* is derived from the upward-gazing shield-bearer in the foreground of the same *Conversion of Paul*. Finally, the seated Madonna, whose posture was not represented in the Pauline material, appears to be influenced by the "Moses" for Julius's tomb—a sculpture that Condivi studied with special avidness, as his careful description of it suggests (bib. 62, 151–52).

74. Lomazzo supplies a rudimentary idea of it (bib. 177, 22–23, and bib. 178, 46). Cf. most recently, Summers, bib. 292, 71–96, 406–17.

75. Condivi, bib. 62, 175–76.

76. Ibid., 177.

CHAPTER 7
Marcello Venusti (1512/15–1579) and the Crucifixion Drawings

1. Pignatti (bib. 234, 73) thinks the Oxford drawing (fig. 105) "bears the artist's [Michelangelo's] authentic signature." He is mistaken. The inscription "di Bona Roti" on the verso [!] is by a collector and represents, like countless others of its type, a mere expression of belief.

2. Goldscheider, bib. 115, 22.

3. *Drawings*, bib. 77, 183.

4. Cimino, bib. 58, 70–77.

5. Most recently Tolnay, bib. 297, 522–23.

6. Most recently Tolnay, bib. 319, nos. 412–22; bib. 78, no. 24; Hirst, bib. 139c, 57–58, and bib. 139c, no. 60.

7. On the history of the creation and after-effect of the Pauline frescos, see Steinberg, bib. 282, 15–21.

8. See Wittkower, bib. 349, 160.

9. The only figure in the Crucifixion drawings that seems to refer back to the *Conversion of Paul* created in 1542–45 is the St. John in figure 106. The shape of the head, profile of the face, and opening of the mouth match the head of the upward-glancing shield-bearer.

10. Robinson, bib. 263, 86, and bib. 264, nos. 72–73.

11. Tolnay, bib. 302, 4:155 and 5:60, 80, 223–25, nos. 253–54, 256; bib. 306, 293; bib. 319, 3:67 and nos. 412r, 413, 416v, 486.

12. Tolnay was aware of this. He never connected the Archivio sketch *expressis verbis* to the Crucifixion drawings, but—with applause from Dussler (bib. 81, 132n12), Barocchi (bib. 16, no. 355), and Hartt (bib. 130, nos. 417–18)—to the composition that survives in Philipp Soye's engraving of 1568 (fig. 115) and is inseparably connected with the Crucifixion drawings. Joannides (bib. 150, 551n50) appears to have been the first to state that the figure silhouettes of this engraving and of the Archivio sketch or the Crucifixion drawings are incompatible. He connects the Archivio sketch to a Calvary group that was possibly planned for the "cappelletta" of the Medici Chapel (On this opinion see Perrig, bib. 230, 275, 286n83).

13. Hartt, bib. 130, no. 422: "A single line seems inadequate to support so sweeping a conclusion."

14. Pope-Hennessy (bib. 238, 39) thought that the Crucifixion drawings did not result in a sculptural group perhaps only "because the image was inherently unsculptural."

15. It is questionable whether Tolnay himself was completely convinced by his marble-group thesis. In any case he sometimes (bib. 312, 30, 34) was of the opinion that part (which part?) of the Crucifixion drawings referred to a wooden crucifix that Michelangelo intended to carve in the summer of 1562—according to the letters of one Lorenzo Marottini and one Cesare Bittino.

16. Popham and Wilde, bib. 240, no. 437, and Wilde, bib. 344, no. 82; Dussler, bib. 80, 27–28 and no. 236, and bib. 81, 132n12; Einem, bib. 88, 230; *Drawings*, bib. 77, no. 183; Hirst, bib. 139b, 57–58, and bib. 139c, no. 60. Tolnay made his contribution to this thesis with the remark (bib. 315, 48): "In the last period (1542–1564) it seems that Michelangelo no longer made studies." This same remark can already be found in Clements, bib. 60, 58.

17. Clements, bib. 60, 58–61. Grassi (bib. 119, 75), who presented figure 105 to his readers as a representative example of Michelangelo's draftsmanship, commented: "Ormai l'insofferenza di Michelangelo per la materia, impossibile di spiritualizzarsi del tutto, diventa tale, che il non-finito di questo disegno appare veramente intenzionale."

18. Brinckmann, bib. 49, no. 75.

19. Wilde, bib. 344, 120.

20. Hartt, bib. 130, no. 421.

21. Baumgart, bib. 26, 135; W = Windsor; L = London; O = Oxford; P = Paris.

22. Berenson, bib. 37, 1:233.

23. Goldscheider, bib. 114, no. 125, 128; bib. 115, nos. 124, 126.

24. Dussler, bib. 80, no. 204, 211, 174–75, 185.

25. Tolnay, bib. 295, 201; Tolnay, bib. 302, 5:80–81, 221–26; Tolnay, bib. 319, nos. 414–19.

26. *Drawings*, bib. 77, nos. 178–83.

27. He apparently had a similar mutation in mind while preparing the Oxford drawing (fig. 105). The short cloak of the right figure, which reaches to the knee, was subsequently lengthened downward.

28. It is probably on account of this embarrassing effect that many scholars attached a slight reservation to their attribution to Michelangelo (Dussler, bib. 80, no. 358: "despite certain weaknesses"). Most recently Tolnay, bib. 302, 5:221, no. 248, and bib. 311, 251n13; Hartt, bib. 130, no. 410.

29. Wittkower (bib. 349, 159–60), who published the drawing and first connected it with the rest of the Crucifixion drawings, considered it to be the last version. Dussler (bib. 80, no. 185), Tolnay (bib. 302, 5:225–26, no. 257, and bib. 319, no. 420), and Hartt (bib. 130, no. 430) shared this opinion. Gere (bib. 77, no. 179), on the contrary, assumed that it could be "a study" for fig. 111. Cf. most recently Bradford and Braham, bib. 46, no. 29.

30. This drawing, whose connection with the Crucifixion drawings was first recognized by Wilde (bib. 344, 120), was regarded by Delacre (bib. 69, 311, 315) as a Michelangelo original, but by Thode (bib. 294, 2:471, no. IX, and 3:no. 504), Wilde, Dussler (bib. 80, no. 677), and Tolnay (bib. 302, 5:266, no. 339, and bib. 319, 3:66) as a copy of a Michelangelo original.

31. Dussler (bib. 80, no. 185) and Tolnay (bib. 302, 5:226, no. 257, and bib. 319, no. 420) categorized it as a copy after the Courtauld sketch. Delacre (bib. 69, 315) considered it to be a Michelangelo original, while Thode (bib. 294, 2:472, no. X, and 3:no. 250) regarded it as a copy of an original.

32. Tolnay, bib. 302, 5:59–60, 195–96, and bib. 319, no. 411; Goldscheider, bib. 115, no. 110; Baudouin, bib. 23, 68.

33. The authentic composition, which survives in seven facsimile copies (see, e.g., fig. 33), was engraved no less than five times (cf. Thode, bib. 294, 2:468). Four of the five engravings date from the sixteenth century and designate Michelangelo as the inventor. This same composition was reproduced at least six times in painting form: a)–c) Cimino, bib. 58, pls. Xiii, XVii, XViii; d) Viterbo, Palazzo Vescovile (De Maio, bib. 70, 441n84); e) Bordeaux, Musée des Beaux-Arts (Collection Campana); f) mentioned in the inventory of the painting collection of Vincenzo Giustiniani of 9 February 1638 (Salerno, bib. 268a, 147, no. 290). The relief copy in the Staatliche Museen in Berlin (no. 327) is probably identical with the "Crocifisso di basso rilievo, che rende l'anima al padre, ritratto da un disegno fatto da Michelagnolo" mentioned by Vasari (bib. 329, 1:250) in the life of Pierino da Vinci (ca. 1530–53).

34. It was apparently engraved only once, in 1573 by Mario Cartaro ("Michel Angelo Bona Rota inventor"). On the painted copies cf. Thode, bib. 294, 2:469; in addition, Baudouin (bib. 23), Borland (bib. 44), Cimino (bib. 58), Gatti (bib. 108). An unpublished painting copy in Paris, private collection (formerly London, Woolf Posner Collection).

35. Already Wilde (bib. 344, no. 82) felt that it could have nothing to do with Michelangelo's intentions. Cf. also *Drawings*, bib. 78, no. 24.

According to Tolnay (bib. 302, 5:60, and bib. 319, no. 411) and Hartt (bib. 130, no. 417) the Crucifixion miniature in the missal of the Cardinal of Armagnac in Avignon, dated 1549, Bibl. Municipale, MS 172, fol. 10 (Tolnay, bib. 302, 5:fig. 338) supplies a *terminus ante quem* for the dating of the composition reproduced in Soye's engraving. In reality it is based on Michelangelo's Colonna crucifix (fig. 33). It relates to the Colonna crucifix in the same way as Clovio's crucifixion drawing and his miniature of the crucified Christ with Mary Magdalene (both in the Uffizi). As in that case the model is crudely altered by changing the position of the head and arm.

36. It first appears in P. Thomassin's engraving of 1649 (Rotili, bib. 268, no. 121)—probably as a means for increasing the value.

37. The draftsmanship of the Louvre copies published by Tolnay (bib. 302, 5:figs. 166, 169) differ in the same way as their models (figs. 112–13). Tolnay (bib. 302, 5:196–97, nos. 199, 201, 258, no. 169) took this as an occasion for separating the hands. He attributed the Mary figure to Clovio, and the other (with John) to an anonymous draftsman.

38. See note 34, this chapter.

39. On this specimen see Pergola, bib. 216, 440, and bib. 217, 85.

40. Borland, bib. 44, 433–44.

41. Cf. Vasari, bib. 329, 1:119, 2788–79. In addition, Perrig, bib. 222, 261–67.

42. The British Museum sheet Fawkener 5211–75 supplies one more proof for Venusti's authorship. Its fragmentary verso drawing (Tolnay, bib. 319, 3:72) shows a pair of legs that corresponds precisely to the legs of the Frankfurt Crucifixion drawing (fig. 116). The lamentation drawing of the recto from the same copyist (Wilde, bib. 344, pl. CXXXVi), however, clearly echoes Venusti's Annunciation in fig. 101 (head and hand position of the Madonna) and his "Adoration of the Shepherds" in S. Silvestro al Quirinale or in the Galleria Nazionale dell' Umbria in Perugia (attitude and drapery of St. John). The sheet probably came from Venusti's Roman workshop.

43. Perrig, bib. 222. There is no need to discuss the since-then published literature (most recently Tolnay, bib. 319, nos. 393–96, 398–99, 409; *Drawings*, bib. 78, no. 22; Hirst, bib. 139b, 53–57, and bib. 139c, nos. 54–55) at this point, since a new argument in favor of Michelangelo's authorship cannot be found.

44. Cf. also the reading stand of the *Annunciation* sketch, British Museum no. 1900-6-11-1r (Tolnay, bib. 319, no. 394r).

45. What Venusti's sketches looked like when their execution was, by exception, broken off in the initial phase is shown by the gigantic outline sketch of an Annunciation Mary on the verso of the British Museum sheet no. 1900-6-11-1 (Tolnay, bib. 319, no. 394v). It apparently represents an intermediate stage between the first and that second version of the Mary figure in fig. 100, which led to the car-

tonetto (fig. 101). Although there is no stylistic difference between it and figure 100 or the recto drawing, until 1979 it was dismissed by all scholars (including Wilde, bib. 344, no. 71) as the product "of a very average pupil's hand" (Dussler, bib. 80, no. 579; most recently Tolnay). J. A. Gere et al., in The New York exhibition catalogue (*Drawings*, bib. 78, 100), recognize the untenability of this arbitrary judgment, but because of the attribution of the recto sees itself forced to deploy ritualistic formulas ("the graphic shorthand seems to us entirely characteristic of Michelangelo himself, as does the masterly economy with which the weight and movement of the figure are suggested in a few rapid strokes").

CHAPTER 8
Daniele Ricciarelli da Volterra (1509–1566) and the Expulsion of the Moneychangers

1. In his *Giuoco della Pittura* (Bologna, 1551) Innocenzio Ringhieri placed Daniele on the same level as such prodigies as Mantegna, Michelangelo, Raphael, Titian, Leonardo, Andrea del Sarto, Giulio Romano, and others (Striker, bib. 291, 172). Armenini (bib. 5, 117) listed Daniele's works, together with those of Michelangelo and Francesco Salviati, as the "most lifelike examples" ("vivissimi essempi") of the depiction of the naked body. Cf. also Vasari, bib. 328, 7:49–71.

2. On Daniele's many pupils cf. Levie, bib. 169, 91.

3. Most recently Hartt, bib. 130, 24, and nos. 463, 474. See also Hirst, bib. 139b, 38–40.

4. Tolnay, bib. 319, nos. 368v, 376–77. The sheet with the copy (British Museum no. 1956-10-13-13; 10.1 × 14 cm) belongs to a group of thirteen sheets acquired in 1956 and labeled "Ricciarelli." The black-chalk drawings on these sheets have not only one and the same individual style, but also the same characteristics of copies: slightly distorted proportions and exaggeratedly accentuated detail strokes, forms; short, abrupt indications of the beginning and end of strokes, somewhat wavy contour strokes; individual hatching strokes organized to form clean ladder-rung assemblages, and so forth. In four cases (no. 1956-10-13-8/10/11/20) the copy character is additionally attested to by a rectangular network that lies *under* the drawing and is respected by its contours. That the copyist was a *pupil* of Daniele is attested to by the fact that all copies appear to have been copied after sketches from the master's mature period. Numbers 1956–10–13–14 presuppose Daniele's involvement with the paintings for Giovanni della Casa of 1555–56, number 1956-10-13-16 . . . 20 with the preparatory works for the *Deposition from the Cross* in SS. Trinita de' Monti of circa 1545. Two drawings in the Ashmolean Museum also appear to be by the same pupil: the black-chalk drawing of a man taking off a stocking, which Parker (bib. 207, no. 210) attributed to Daniele and Gombosi (bib. 117, 116, no. 4) to Moretto da Brescia (ca. 1498–1554) and Levie (bib. 169, 167) treated as apocryphal; and the small red-chalk sketch of a seated nude, which Barocchi (bib. 15, 23) and older Michelangelo scholarship attributed

to Michelangelo and Parker (bib. 207, no. 370), Dussler (bib. 80, no. 601), and Hartt (bib. 130, 391) to a pupil of Michelangelo.

It is logical that the London copies are today considered original sketches by Daniele's hand (most recently Tolnay, bib. 319, 3:42; Barolsky, bib. 19, 93, 99, 114–15) and serve to indicate the attribution of further drawings with copy properties to this artist (cf. Davidson, bib. 65a, 157 and pl. 21). The sketches related to authenticated Daniele works *without* copy characteristics are already "occupied" by the name of Michelangelo.

5. Most recently Barolsky, bib. 19, 98–99.

6. Tolnay, bib. 319, nos. 368–69.

7. On the painting, see most recently Barolsky, bib. 19, 94–97.

8. Robinson (bib. 263, nos. 70–73) interpreted it intuitively in this sense without having known the painting. Cf. also Levie, bib. 169, 177–78; *Drawings*, bib. 77, no. 165.

9. Tolnay, bib. 319, nos. 370–74r.

10. Vasari, bib. 328, 7:61.

11. Barolsky, bib. 19, figs. 66–67.

12. Only Sricchia Santoro (bib. 279, 26) seems to have interpreted the panel in this sense. Freedberg (bib. 96a, 331) still saw in it nothing more than a (double-acting) pictorial realization of Michelangelo's thesis that a painting was better the more it approximated sculpture (cf. Barocchi, bib. 14, 1:82).

13. That such theological speculations as Verspohl (bib. 331, 241n105) assumed behind the position of the hand of Michelangelo's marble *David* could stand behind this interchangeability of the weapon-holding hand may be excluded.

14. In view of the fact that the New York and Oxford sketches have the same miniature sizes and graphic properties and depict the same motifs (one hand of the victor holds the head of the vanquished, while the other is raised for the fatal stroke), the impartial reader will be hard pressed to accept what is contained in the relevant literature, where only the New York sketches are titled *David and Goliath*. For mysterious reasons the Oxford sketches (fig. 123) are titled differently: (1) *Samson's Battle* (Robinson, bib. 263, no. 69; Berenson, bib. 34 and bib. 37, no. 1571; Delacre, bib. 69, 536; Parker, bib. 207, no. 328; Dussler, bib. 80, no. 200, and bib. 81, 137; Bean and Stampfle, bib. 31, no. 37; Tolnay, bib. 302, 5:200, no. 207, 202, no. 211, and bib. 319, no. 374r; Berti, bib. 40, 487); (2) *Hercules and Cacus* (Brinckmann, bib. 49, no. 44; Hartt, bib. 130, no. 473); (3) other battle or death scenes (Thode, bib. 294, 2:377–78, 455, and 3:no. 441; Goldscheider, bib. 114, no. 105, and bib. 115, no. 118; Barocchi, in Salmi, Tolnay, and Barocchi, bib. 269, no. 63). The result of this curious diversity of themes, till now rejected only by Frey (bib. 101, no. 76, 157), Panofsky (bib. 200, 5–6), and Baumgart (bib. 26, 135): "The purpose of these sketches [fig. 123] is unknown, but from their style they probably date from c. 1550–5" (*Drawings*, bib. 77, no. 164)!

15. Barolsky, bib. 19, figs. 68, 70–71. The copy after a fourth study is on British Museum sheet 1956-10-13-14 (Barolsky, bib. 19, fig. 69).

16. Tolnay, bib. 302, 5:78, 212, no. 235, and bib. 319, 3:49–51;

Dussler, bib. 81, 130n4; Hartt, bib. 130, 316; Steinberg, bib. 282, 16.

17. Even Vincenzo Borghini's (1515–80) letter of 1573, addressed to Vasari, which includes detailed proposals for an iconographic program for completion of the chapel, makes no mention of an *Expulsion of the Moneychangers* (Baumgart and Biaggetti, bib. 28, 85–89).

18. This was already the opinion of Gere, in *Drawings*, bib. 77, no. 167, and *Drawings*, bib. 78, no. 23. Cf. also Wilde, bib. 347, 181.

19. Tolnay, bib. 319, nos. 376v, 596.

20. Vasari, bib. 328, 7:551; Barolsky, bib. 19, 101–04.

21. Tolnay, bib. 319, no. 435.

22. Vasari, bib. 329, 4:1947; Gotti, bib. 118, 2:146.

23. Ibid., 1:273.

24. Levie, bib. 169, 216–19.
The "bellissimi disegni" that—according to Baglione (bib. 10, 66)—Daniele made over to his pupil Giacomo Rocca († between 1592 and 1605) must also be added to what is listed in the inventory.

25. Panofsky, bib. 202, bib. 203, 161n22.

26. Wilde, bib. 342, 143–44.

27. Stechow, bib. 280, 83n3.

28. Baumgart, bib. 24, bib. 26, 131n1; Baumgart and Biagetti, bib. 28, 29–30.

29. Included among the drawings distributed over a total of thirty-one sheets that Panofsky and Baumgart attribute to Daniele are: (1) the black-chalk drawing of a horse associated with two male nudes in the Ashmolean Museum, Parker, bib. 207, no. 296v—a product that I attribute to Benvenuto Cellini (Perrig, bib. 229, 85–87); (2) the Annunciation sketch in figure 100—a sheet I give to Marcello Venusti (Perrig, bib. 222, 279–86); (3) the set of studies in figure 69 and the partial sketch for the *Fall of Phaeton* in figure 66 in the Teylers Museum, A31r—probably products of Tommaso de' Cavalieri; (4) the red-chalk studies on the Teyler sheets A20v and A27r (Tolnay, bib. 319, nos. 135v, 136r)—most likely early examples of study forgeries (for a similar example see chap. 2, n. 161 above).

30. Berenson, bib. 37, no. 1470.

31. Wilde, bib. 344, 114n1.

32. Of similar subjectivity, even if it remained without effect in the history of Michelangelo scholarship, was Delacre's criticism, which appeared at the same time as Berenson's (bib. 69, 210, 453n1).

33. Of the nine catalogue numbers that Goldscheider dedicated to characterizing "Daniele's" drawing style in the first edition of his *Michelangelo Drawings* (bib. 114, nos. 184–92) not one was repeated in the second edition (bib. 115)!

34. Levie (bib. 169, 171–72) criticized older Michelangelo scholars for no other reason than because they had maintained "that Daniele had, after the 'Deposition from the Cross,' adapted himself to Michelangelo's style development." This claim was based "on Michelangelesque sketches incorrectly attributed to the artist," and was refuted by the "following conclusion" from an analysis of Daniele's later paintings: "Immediately after completion of the 'Deposition from the Cross' Daniele set out on a new, individual path that ultimately led him to carving." Translated into a logical text: Daniele's later works cannot have borrowed from Michelangelo's style development because the sketches related to Daniele's late works were not by Daniele but by Michelangelo!

35. Cf. above n. 4.
Berenson's attribution to Daniele of the Louvre drawing no. 2716 (bib. 37, no. 1744, fig. 837)—which is apparently by the hand of a miniaturist (according to Monbeig-Goguel, bib. 188a, 41, 46n44, by Guilio Clovio)—documents what kind of nebulous idea Berenson himself had of Daniele's drawing style.

36. See Barolsky, bib. 19, figs. 26, 28–40, 42, 56–60, 68, 70–71, 77, 85, 87, 101–23.
Levie (bib. 169, 160) found it "more advisable to admit to not knowing what Daniele's sketches looked like." Nevertheless, he knew that they must be *different* than figures 120–21, 123–30.

37. Levie, bib. 169, 99n19.

38. Dussler, bib. 80, no. 297.

39. Wilde, bib. 344, 177n76.

40. Manilli, bib. 183, 113.

41. Pergola, bib. 218, 456, no. 275.
Since Ramdohr (bib. 250, 1:296) and Passavant (bib. 211, 113) the name of Venusti was firmly attached to the painting.

42. Wilde, bib. 344, 118.

43. Ibid.

44. On the Massimo frieze and the Rovere frescoes, see most recently Barolsky, bib. 19, 42–48, 82–86.

45. The influence of Polidoro on Daniele, which was already suspected by Longhi, had possibly been transmitted by Michaeli Grechi himself. As a temporary collaborator of Perino del Vaga (1501–47) Grechi in any case might well have been acquainted with Daniele (cf. Davidson, bib. 64).

46. Levie, bib. 169, 215–16.

47. Thode, bib. 293, 1:475–76.

48. Most recently, Tolnay, bib. 319, no. 596.

49. Cf. Levi d'Ancona, bib. 168, fig. 1.

50. On the poverty of figural motifs in Daniele's paintings, cf. Levie, bib. 169, 45, 72, 128n79, 149–50.

51. The attribution of this sketch to Michelangelo extends to a perversion of artistic roles. It implies that the artist (Daniele) who was responsible for the final version of the monument engraved by Nicolas van Aelst (Tolnay, bib. 319, 3:84) viewed the novelty of the "Michelangelo" sketch, namely the abnormal aesthetic preponderance of the excessively decorative base as a defect and replaced it with a better-proportioned solution, namely one like Michelangelo's Marcus Aurelius base.

52. Vasari, bib. 328, 5:610–11 and 7:49–50, 52, 55–57, 59, 70. Daniele scholarship was able to recognize the traces of laboriousness even in his paintings. Cf. Hirst, bib. 135, 505n26; Sricchia Santoro, bib. 279, 18–19.

53. "Io duro troppo fatica a scriuere, si come fo anco a ogni cosa" ("I have too much trouble with writing, so as with everything else") reads the last sentence of a letter to Vasari on 17 March 1564 (Frey, bib. 102, 2:54). See also Armenini, bib. 5, 15.

54. Vasari, bib. 328, 7:56.

55. Keller (bib. 156, 89) on fig. 129: "despite the dramatic event . . . a block-life coherence of the individual figures is strived for. Although it is a sketch for a painting, individual figures act like models for the preparation of marble blocks."

EXCURSUS

1. The various accounts of the supposed appearance of Michelangelo's *Hercules* would produce a hefty book with many illustrations of actual and alleged, legible and illegible *Hercules* figures: Richter, bib. 260, 131; Wickhoff, bib. 340, 410; Frey, bib. 100, 103–10; Thode, bib. 294, 1:16–17; Justi, bib. 155, 4; Liphart-Rathshoff, bib. 175; Tolnay, bib. 298, 120–21, bib. 302, 1:198, bib. 303, 142, bib. 306, 269, bib. 310, and bib. 313; Weinberger, bib. 337, 70, and bib. 338, 43–47; Isermeyer, bib. 143, 312–13; Châtelet-Lange, bib. 56; Harprath, bib. 126, 84, and bib. 127, 310; Parronchi, bib. 208, 2:35–60; Utz, bib. 325; Gaborit, bib. 105; Joannides, bib. 152, and 153a. For the theories concerning the identification of the Louvre nude (fig. 4) see note 8 below.

2. For an account of his life see Gotti, bib. 118, 2:16–17, no. 12. On the affluence of the Buonarrotis in the fourteenth century, see Becker, bib. 32.

3. Ibid. 2:20, no. 1.

4. Berenson, bib. 34, no. 1579.

5. Frey, bib. 101, no. 28.

6. According to Ramsden (bib. 251, 1:88n2 at no. 92) he could not have set up shop until the summer of 1513.

7. Tolnay, bib. 319, no. 26r, and bib. 320, 270, no. 209; Salvini, bib. 271, 34. Demonts (bib. 71, no. 107) and Goldscheider (bib. 114, no. 35) and bib. 115, nos. 28–29), on the other hand, date the drawing ca. 1513.

8. Frey (bib. 101, no. 27), Brinckmann (bib. 49, no. 35), and Tolnay (bib. 319, no. 26r) interpreted the drawing as a sketch for an apostle, whereas Berenson (bib. 34 and bib. 37, no. 1579), Delacre (bib. 69, 416–17), and Monbeig-Goguel (bib. 165, no. 85) interpreted it as a sketch for the marble *David*. Valentiner (bib. 326, 222) interpreted it as a sketch for the Christ of the Piccolomini altar. Tolnay apparently saw in the traces of a moustache the expression of an academic naturalism. The nude is—he wrote with his disarming logic—"copiato forse dal vero, perchè rappresenta un modello con baffi ricurvi."

9. For the fate of the statue see Châtelet-Lange, bib. 56, 455–60; Parronchi, bib. 208, 2:37–41; Joannides, bib. 152, 550–53.

10. Condivi, bib. 62, 47: "Appena aveva finita quest' opera [the centaur relief], ché; Magnifico Lorenzo passò di questa vita. Michelagnolo se ne tornò a casa del padre, e tanto dolor prese della sua morte, che per molti giorni non potette far cosa alcuna. Pur poi a sè tornato e comperato un gran pezzo di marmo, qual molti anni s'era giaciuto all'acqua e al vento, di quello cavò un Ercole, alto braccia quattro, qual poi fu mandato in Francia."

11. The best-known example of Condivi's imprecise narration—probably caused by the failing memory of his chief informant, Michelangelo—is the denial that Michelangelo was an apprentice of Ghirlandaio. This necessarily led to inconsistencies—for example, in the story of the copy of the Schongauer engraving. Vasari (1550) had already told this story (bib. 329, 1:8–9), and indeed in a way that makes it obvious it occurred in Ghirlandaio's workshop. Condivi (Vasari, bib. 329, 2:86–87), on the other hand, transposed it to an indefinite space and time and had Granacci give the youth both the engraving and the brushes and colors necessary for making a colored reproduction. Condivi thereby stripped all motivation and credibility from Ghirlandaio's supposed reaction to the small masterpiece of copying. Ghirlandaio is supposed to have claimed the copy as the product of his workshop, although it allegedly was not even created there; and he did this not for readily understandable reasons of pride, but because he wanted "to devalue the work." See also note 15 below.

12. According to Condivi (bib. 62, 41–42) in 1490, when Michelangelo received the invitation to live in the Palazzo Medici, Lodovico Buonarroti still held fast to the idea that sculpture and stonemasonry were one and the same trade and that its practice by a Buonarroti would bring shame to the family. Only after he saw—writes the biographer, with reference to the events of early 1494 (bib. 62, 49)—how his son "almost constantly associated with [the] high lords" did he become somewhat more friendly to the youth.

As far as Piero de' Medici is concerned, according to Condivi (bib. 62, 49) he treated the young artist like a bauble and placed him on the same level as the Spanish page who excelled as a fast runner.

13. The Medici appear to have regarded Hercules as the symbol of their own power and invincibility at least since the time of Piero's great-grandfather Cosimo (1389–1464). Circa 1460 Cosimo had the famous trilogy of the deeds of Hercules painted for the large hall of the Palazzo Medici in Florence (see Busignani, bib. 54, 56–57, 101–02; Ettlinger, bib. 91, 26–28, 164–65, no. 44). Two deeds of Hercules appear on the chest armor of the terracotta bust in Bargello, created circa 1470, which at least possibly depicts Piero's uncle Giuliano (1453–78) (Ettlinger, bib. 91, 152, no. 22). Antonio Pollaiuolo's bronze group *Hercules and Antaeus* stood in the stanza of Piero's brother Giuliano (1479–1516) (Ettlinger, bib. 91, 147, no. 18). Piero's father, Lorenzo, referred to Hercules in the *Conversationes Camaldulenses*, when he attempted to defend the primacy of the "vita activa" against Alberti (1404–72) (Landino, bib. 162, 35–36). On the Medici's Hercules ideology in the sixteenth century see Ettlinger, bib. 90, bib. 96, bib. 259, bib. 324.

14. Condivi, bib. 62, 61.

15. According to his first letter to his father on 2 July 1496 (*Michelangelo*, bib. 186, 1:1–2), he had arrived in Rome on 25 June and been immediately commanded by the cardinal to view "certain figures" (presumably antique sculptures). Then, together with the cardinal, he bought the block of marble "for a life-size figure," the preparation of which he wanted to begin on 4 July. This letter, and that of 1 July 1497 (*Michelangelo*, bib. 186, 1:3) explicitly contradict Condivi's assertions (bib. 62, 61–66) that the *Bacchus* had been

created under commission from Jacopo Galli and that Michelangelo never made anything for the cardinal.

16. *Michelangelo*, bib. 186, 1:4.

17. For biographical information on Piero see Cleugh, bib. 61, 209–43; on his life in Rome see Villari, bib. 334, 9–11, xvi–xviii.

18. Condivi, bib. 62, 47–49. The snowman episode probably took place at the end of January 1494. According to Landucci (bib. 163, 1:100) "the largest amount of snow that, according to what the oldest people say, anyone remembers" fell on Florence starting 20 January. In Florence such snowfalls were traditionally occasions for high-spirited artistic competitions. As late as 1511, after it had snowed from 13 to 16 January, "all over Florence many beautiful lions of snow and by great masters . . . and many other figures were . . . made, naked, by many masters" (Landucci, bib. 163, 2:190).

19. The unjustified credence enjoyed by Condivi's account is ultimately attributable to Vasari's behavior. In the first edition of his *Lives* (1550), Vasari had quite correctly listed the *Hercules* statue *after* the sleeping *Cupid* and the wooden crucifix, but described it as if it had been created under commission from a member of the Strozzi family (bib. 329, 1:13). When the *Lives* were revised he regarded this information as no longer valid. He deleted the remark that the statue had been executed in the Palazzo Strozzi (where it had presumably stood for some years) and instead used Condivi's information on the purchase of the marble and on the dimensions of the statue. He simultaneously recast the entire passage according to Condivi's chronology and placed it at the time of Lorenzo's death (bib. 329, 1:12–13). His reaction to reading Condivi's account was probably similar to that of Michelangelo scholars. Since this account starts with an exceptionally important event in Michelangelo's biography, the death of his great protector, Vasari involuntarily perceived it as having "internal" credibility.

20. The Strozzis had remained in contact with the exiled Piero de' Medici in spite of official prohibition. In 1508 Filippo Strozzi the Younger (1489–1538) went so far as to marry Piero's fifteen-year-old daughter Clarice (1493–1528)—an ostentatious affront to the Soderini regime for which he had to pay with three years' exile in Naples and a fine of five hundred gold ducats (Villari, bib. 333, 2:139, 548–52). It is unimportant whether it was Clarice who had the statue bought—in memory of her father, who died of drowning in 1503. But what is certain is that Filippo (who joined the opposition to the Medici after Clement VII became pope in November 1523) had his agent Agostino di Francesco Dini (1463–1548) sell the statue shortly after Clarice's death. The purchaser, the Strozzis' friend Giovanni Battista della Palla († 1530), promptly removed it from the reach of his enemies, Clement VII's Medici clan (his future murderers), by shipping it to France that same year (1529), together with those copies after the Medici *Hercules* trilogy by the Pollaiuolo brothers (see note 13 above) that he—according to Vasari (bib. 328, 6:540)—had had prepared by Ridolfo Ghirlandaio (1483–1561).

21. See note 19 above. For the history of the building of the Strozzi Palace (1489–1504), see Bucci, bib. 52, 17–25, and Goldthwaite, bib. 116.

22. On this work in bronze see Weiss, bib. 339, 191.

23. On the problems of making exact measurements of the Florentine *braccio* see Mancusi-Ungaro, bib.182, 23; see also Perrig, bib. 229, 115n110.

24. This bozzetto, which in the sixteenth century was much copied and cited in every possible form, has irritated Michelangelo scholars because of its mirror-like relationship to the marble *David*, provoking lengthy speculation as to its "real" purpose. The most recent speculation comes from Tolnay, who had stumbled across the pen-and-ink Louvre drawing of a frontally standing Hercules with a club, attributed to the young Rubens (1577–1640); he immediately noticed that its motif closely corresponded to that of the bozzetto. He declared the drawing to be a copy of Michelangelo's lost Hercules statue and the Casa Buonarroti bozzetto to be its model (bib. 310 and bib. 313; bib. 312, 14–15, 26; bib. 320, 7, 220, no. 3). In reality the drawing is—as Joannides had already assumed (bib. 152, 553)—a study after the bozzetto that was later arbitrarily completed as a Hercules (and which Rubens had occasion to become acquainted with in October 1600 when he was in Florence and visited the Casa Buonarroti). Its first version, sketched in black chalk, matches the bozzetto in all details—including the missing right arm and the location where it seems to be broken off. This point is important, because it provides the solution of the apparent riddle. It is modeled and softly and "organically" merges into the shoulder and chest area. The bozzetto never even had a right arm. The fact that it is missing points to an "aporie." As is known, Michelangelo came across a block of marble already prepared for a David when he received the commission for his David. This block was lying in the courtyard of the cathedral works. On 2 July 1501 the cathedral building authorities decided to have it erected "so that the experts would see whether it can be further worked on and completed" ("ut videatur per magistros in hoc expertos possit absolvi et finiri") (Seymour, bib. 277, 134–36, doc. 36). They therefore supposed that the future frontal view of Michelangelo's statue might possibly be carved from the still unworked back side of the block. And this possibility must in fact have proved the most practicable, as is indirectly attested to by a document from the year 1501 (Poggi, bib. 236a, doc. 449) which states that Michelangelo, a few days before actually beginning work (13 September), had "removed with one or two chisel strokes a 'nodus' [knot, obstacle] that it [the abbozzo] had on the upper body" ("uno vel duobus ictibus compulisset quoddam nodum quem habebat in pectore"). This "nodus" can hardly have been anything but a projection in the already chiseled front side of the block. It had to be removed so that the block could be made to lie prone (statues of this size could be sculpted only in prone position!). The mirror relationship of the bozzetto and the David is thus the logical consequence of the block's front having been changed. In any case, Michelangelo had to develop his David concept from the already deformed side of the block. The bozzetto depicts the result of this development, which created the absolute prerequisite for making a new front side of the David from the back side of the old one.

25. Tolnay, bib. 320, 202–03. See also Perrig, bib. 229, 175–77.

26. See Perrig, bib. 229, 30–37, 50, and bib. 226.

27. Tolnay, bib. 302, 5:228, no. 264; Salmi, Tolnay, and Barocchi, bib. 269, no. 67; Goldscheider, bib. 115, no. 66; Hartt, bib. 130, no. 435; Keller, bib. 156, 90.

28. The interpretation is Pfeiffer's (bib. 232) and was adjudged "convincing" by Dussler (bib. 82, no. 1576), Gere (*Drawings*, bib. 77, no. 174), and Tolnay (bib. 319, no. 400, and bib. 320, 117). It is based on the following arguments: (1) "The seated figure . . . is a woman of mature years"; (2) "the attitude of the seated woman . . . must be interpreted as one of gazing rather than listening"; (3) "the viewer . . . can ascertain on the right palm of the hovering figure an indication of the nail wound"; (4) "the timid groping of the left hand of the seated woman toward the right hand of the hovering figure. Without reference to the wounds of the Passion this hesitant gesture would have no meaning"; (5) "the figure interpreted here as the Risen Christ lifts his drapery with his left hand, a gesture which can only be understood as the baring of the wound in this side." These arguments can be countered by the following: (1) a sketch like the Oxford drawing gives no clues as to the intended age of the depicted persons. Otherwise Venusti's Annunciation sketches (including fig. 100), indeed even his highly finished drawings (figs. 101–02), would also have to be reinterpreted. In these too Mary is "not a young girl." (2) In the first version the face of the seated woman was drawn nearly en face, i.e., it was tuned exclusively to listening instead of to gazing. (3) To interpret the small crooked line on the inner surface of the right hand of the hovering figure as a wound could be justified within the framework of a multi-layered sketch in black chalk only if there would also be a wound at least on the left hand. In fact there is no wound there or on the feet, much less on the chest. (4) The left hand of the seated woman rests on an object described as a desk. It therefore indicates in the first instance only the type of activity that has been interrupted by the heavenly apparition. (5) What the hovering figure uncovers with its left hand is not so much the breast as the abdomen. In conjunction with the composition's emphasis on the abdomen of the seated woman, this is a clear indication that the intended object of the message is Mary's future motherhood, not Christ's wound in the side. After all, Mary was no Doubting Thomas (on the iconography of the apparition of Christ to Mary see Breckenridge, bib. 48; *Reallexicon*, bib. 253, 5:1350–61; *Lexicon*, bib. 171, 1:667–71; on the iconography of the Annunciation from the right see Denny, bib. 72). There is no evidence for a depiction by Michelangelo of the apparition of the Risen Christ to Mary. The cartoon in Michelangelo's estate inventory (Gotti, bib. 118, 2:151) mentioned by Pfeiffer depicted, according to Daniele, a "Christo che si parte dalla Madre" ("Christ's farewell from his mother"), i.e., an event that took place before the Resurrection and which therefore cannot have involved a transfigured Christ (see chap. 6, n. 24; on the iconography of the subject see Emminghaus, in *Lexicon*, bib. 171, 1:35–37).

29. Perrig, bib. 222.

30. Since Milanesi (bib. 188, 314, 316n1) the date of Urbino's death has been given as 3 December 1555. This dating is attributable to Michelangelo himself, who reports in an undated letter to his nephew (bib. 188, 314) "that yesterday evening on the third of De-

cember about nine o'clock Francesco, called Urbino, departed from this life." Nevertheless, the information is false. Out of simple absentmindedness, the artist had written December when he meant January (which by the Florentine calendar belonged to the old year). The next letter to his nephew, dated 11 January 1556 (bib. 188, 316), makes the correction: "I wrote you last week about the death of Urbino." "Though sick in body, but still healthy in mind and understanding, thank God," Urbino had in fact made his testament on 24 December 1555 (Gotti, bib. 118, 2:137).

31. Gotti, bib. 118, 1:334–35.

32. The transaction was made between 12 and 18 November 1557. See Gualandi, bib. 123, 1:nos. 14–15.

33. In Urbino's extant testament (Gotti, bib. 118, 2:137–40) neither the pictures nor the other chattels of the servant are mentioned.

34. Urbino had left his wife and children 660 gold ducats and named Michelangelo as administrator of this money (Gotti, bib. 118, 2:139).

35. This was apparently the price for a friend. In 1571 Venusti requested a total of 21 gold ducats from Niccolò Gaddi for a small painting of *Christ at the Mount of Olives* (Bottari and Ticozzi, bib. 45, 3:265, no. CIX.

36. Pasquino appears as "mailman" for the first time in April 1557, for the last time in March 1560 (Frey, bib. 99, 354, 375–76.

37. Frey, bib. 99, 360–61, 364–65, 367–70, 386–87.

38. Thode, bib. 294, 309–10.

39. Tolnay, bib. 302, 5:13, 227; bib. 318: no. 103; bib. 319: no. 330r, 331v. In contrast see Wilde, bib. 344, 112, and Dussler, bib. 80, no. 179; see also Perrig, bib. 222, 288n67.

40. Pergola, bib. 215, 343.

41. Gronau, bib. 121, 50.

42. Ibid., 250–51.

43. Pergola, bib. 216, 429, no. 45, and bib. 217, 74, no. 313.

44. Pergola, bib. 216, 440, and bib. 217, 85.

45. See chap. 7.

46. Tolnay, bib. 302, 5:59, and bib. 319, no. 411: "In this composition there are empty spaces at the bottom to the right and left, giving the impression that it is unfinished. It may be supposed that Michelangelo wanted to complete the composition with the figures of the Virgin and St. John." But the empty spaces would suffice only for Lilliputians.

47. The surviving documents provide no evidence whatsoever for the commonly held opinion—also put forth earlier by myself (Perrig, bib. 222, 289)—that the paintings left behind by Urbino had been painted at Michelangelo's instigation. This opinion, which originated with Carlo Promis (cf. Gualandi, bib. 123, 1:51), is based on the sentimental, wishful notion that a "poor" servant can have neither the need nor the means to purchase art on his own. In 1545 Pope Paul III had named Urbino as a "mundator picturarum" (Redig de Campos, bib. 256). In any case his income had permitted him to hire a maid for his wife (*Michelangelo*, bib. 187, 327, no. CCLXXIX). See also note 34 above.

48. See Perrig, bib. 222, 261–79.

49. It cannot be identical with one of the two small pictures in the former Steinmann and Canali collections published by Parroni (bib. 210, 295–96, figs. 8–9); these were copied after the vertical Lateran painting. It is most likely that it is identical with the painting that Passerini (bib. 212, 175) once viewed in the Gonzaga collection in Mantua and which had been reproduced by an unknown engraver in 1720. The dimensions of the engraving (40 × 60 cm) approximately correspond to those of Venusti's Uffizi cartonetto (40.5 × 54.7 cm).

50. This cartonetto was still regarded by Wilde (bib. 346, 370–77) as the product of Michelangelo's own hand. Otherwise, until a short time ago it was generally accepted in the more recent literature as a work of Venusti (including Dussler, bib. 80, no. 486; Tolnay, bib. 302, 5:206–07; Barocchi, bib. 15, no. 197; Perrig, bib. 222, 267–86). Tolnay (bib. 319, no. 393) recently gave it special treatment. He suddenly acted as if the cartonetto could be a copy by Clovio. At the same time he insisted on his assertion that the cartonetto was identical with one of the "disegni piccoli" that Michelangelo had presented to Jacopo del Duca (see Frey, bib. 102, 2:54). For Hirst (bib. 139b, 19, 54, and bib. 139c, no. 54) this alleged identity, which is contradictory to all we know about the use of the words "piccolo," "disegno," "cartone," and "cartonetto" in the sixteenth century, has the value of an article of faith.

51. See Dussler, bib. 80, no. 587; Tolnay, bib. 319, no. 399; Hirst, bib. 139c, no. 55. See also Perrig, bib. 222, 270–86.

52. Wilde (bib. 344, 112) had already assumed that a "replica" after one of Venusti's two monumental Annunciation paintings "was in the possession of Michelangelo's favourite garzone Francesco Urbino." His assumption was ignored—despite the references to sources that accompanied it. Scholars were too deeply in love with their portrait fairy tale.

A question that arises in this connection is whether the panel in the Galleria Nazionale actually reflects the Cesi *Annunciation* (as is always assumed), or whether it is more likely a derivative of the Lateran *Annunciation* designed especially for Urbino. There is nothing to indicate that the sketch in figure 100 and its sibling in the British Museum (Tolnay, bib. 319, nos. 394, 398) could have been sketched with reference to a more monumental version of what appears in figure 101. They differ fundamentally from Venusti's Annunciation sketch (Uffizi 18723F; Tolnay, bib. 319, no. 392), whose widely spaced layout seems to point so clearly to a large-format painting.

53. See chap. 7, n. 43 above.

54. This is indicated first of all by the relation between the two angel figures. In Michelangelo's drawing the wobbly movement of Venusti's angel was transformed into something majestic simply by reducing the angle of the axis of the limbs and making the angel's appearance more vertical. The meaningless combination of the left hand reaching toward the abdomen and the strip of cloth slipping from the shoulder became the mysterious motif of revealing the body, the excitedly pointing hand became a gesture that expresses a simple "So it will be."

55. Frey, bib. 102, 2:54.

56. It might have taken place—as Wilde (bib. 344, 119n1) assumed—during the time Michelangelo and Vasari last met each other in person (28 March–25 April 1560).

57. Frey, bib. 102, 2:82, 83n1.

58. Vasari, bib. 329, 1:119; Frey, bib. 102, 2:57n*. The duke's belief was shared by others, including Portheim (bib. 247, 156–57), Parroni (bib. 210, 287), Delacre (bib. 69, 194–95, 197–99), Wilde (bib. 346, 370–77), and Hirst (bib. 139b, 19, 41, 47, 53–56; bib 139c, no. 54). Tolnay shared it by half. Like the duke, he equated both cartonetti with Michelangelo's "disegni piccoli" (bib. 319, nos. 393, 409), but regarded only the one for *Christ at the Mount of Olives* (fig. 103) as original.

59. Vasari, bib. 329, 1:119, 279. See also Perrig, bib. 222, 261–69.

60. Cavalieri's explanation for the duke, which accompanied the shipment of the Cleopatra (fig. 13) and the Anguiscola drawing, suggests that he too was aware of such an expectation.

61. In the Medici inventory of 1560–67, only the entry concerning the "Annunziata" carries the addendum "ornamento di noce" (Frey, bib. 102, 2:57n*). The fact that it was framed is probably one of the reasons why the Annunciation cartonetto (fig. 102) is better preserved than the *Mount of Olives* cartonetto (fig. 103).

Bibliography

1. Achiardi, Pietro d'. *Sebastiano del Piombo*. Rome: 1908.

2. Ackerman, James S. *The Architecture of Michelangelo*, 2d ed. Harmondsworth: 1970.

3. Ames-Lewis, Francis. *Drawing in Early Renaissance Italy*. New Haven–London: 1981.

4. ———. "Drapery 'Pattern'-Drawings in Ghirlandaio's Workshop and Ghirlandaio's Early Apprenticeship." *Art Bulletin*, 63, 1981, 49–62.

4a. Annesley, Noel, and Hirst, Michael. "'Christ and the Woman of Samaria' by Michelangelo." *Burlington Magazine*, 123, 1981, 608–14.

4b. Aretino, Pietro. *Lettere sull'arte* commentate da F. Pertile, a cura di E. Camesasca. 3 vols. Milan: 1957.

5. Armenini, Giovanni Battista. *De' veri precetti della pittvra*. Ravenna: 1587.

6. Arnheim, Rudolf. *Kunst und Sehen*. Berlin: 1965.

7. Bacou, Roseline. *Cartons d'artistes du XVe au XIXe siècle: LVe exposition du Cabinet des Dessins, Musée du Louvre*. Paris: 1974.

8. Bacou, Roseline, and Viatte, Françoise. *Dessins italiens de la Renaissance: LVIIIe exposition du Cabinet des Dessins, Musée du Louvre*. Paris: 1975.

9. ———. *Michel-Ange au Louvre*. Paris: 1975.

10. Baglione, Giovanni Battista. *Le vite de' pittori scvltori et architetti: Dal Pontificato di Gregorio XIII. del 1572. In fino a'tempi di Papa Vrbano Ottauo nel 1642*. Rome: 1642.

11. Balas, Edith. "Michelangelo Concetti (1505) in the Château de Blois." *Gazette des Beaux-Arts*, 101, 1983, 49–53.

11a. Balas, Edith. "Michelangelo's Florentine *Slaves* and the S. Lorenzo Façade." *Art Bulletin*, 65, 1983, 665–71.

12. Baldini, Umberto. "Die Skulpturen." In *Michelangelo: Bildhauer, Maler, Architekt, Dichter*. Wiesbaden, 1966, 73–148.

13. ———. *Das bildhauerische Gesamtwerk von Michelangelo*. Lucerne, Stuttgart, and Vienna: 1973.

13a. Bambach, Carmen C. "A Note on Michelangelo's Cartoon for the Sistine Ceiling: Haman." *Art Bulletin*, 65, 1983, 661–65.

13b. ———. "Michelangelo's Cartoon for the *Crucifixion of St. Peter* Reconsidered." *Master Drawings*, 25, 1988, 131–42.

13c. Barnes, Bernardine. "A Lost *Modello* for Michelangelo's *Last Judgment*." *Master Drawings*, 26, 1988, 239–48.

14. Barocchi, Paola, ed. *Trattati d'arte del Cinquecento fra Manierismo e controriforma*. 3 vols. Bari: 1960–62.

15. Barocchi, Paola. *Michelangelo e la sua scuola: I disegni di Casa Buonarroti e degli Uffizi*. Florence: 1962.

16. ———. *Michelangelo e la sua scuola: I disegni dell'Archivio Buonarroti*. Florence: 1964.

17. ———. *Mostra di disegni dei fondatori dell'Accademia delle Arti del Disegno*. Florence: 1963.

18. ———. *Michelangelo: Mostra di disegni, manoscritti e documenti*. Florence: 1964.

19. Barolsky, Paul. *Daniele da Volterra: A Catalogue Raisonné*. New York and London: 1979.

20. Bartsch, Adam. *Le Peintre-Graveur.* 21 vols. Vienna: 1803–21.

21. Battaglia, Salvatore. *Grande dizionario della lingua italiana.* Turin: 1961–.

22. Battisti, Eugenio. "Michelangelo o dell'ambiguità iconografica." *Festschrift Luitpold Dussler.* Munich and Berlin: 1972, 209–22.

23. Baudouin, Frans. "Een Michelangelo-motief bij Gillis Mostaert." In *Miscellanea I.Q. van Regteren Altena.* Amsterdam: 1969, 67–69.

24. Baumgarten, Fritz. "Contributi a Michelangelo." *Bollettino d'Arte,* 28, 1934–35, 344–56.

25. ———. "Die 'Pietà' Rondanini: Ein Beitrag zur Erkenntnis des Altersstiles Michelangelos. Mit einer Rekonstruktion von Arno Breker." In *Jahrbuch der preußischen Kunstsammlungen,* 66, 1935, 44–56.

26. ———. "Eine Entwurfszeichnung Michelangelos zur Cappella Paolina." In *Festschrift zum 70. Geburtstag von Adolph Goldschmidt.* Berlin: 1935, 131–36.

27. ———. "Die Jugendzeichnungen Michelangelos bis 1506." In *Marburger Jahrbuch für Kunstwissenschaft,* 10, 1937, 209–62.

28. Baumgart, Fritz, and Biagetti, Biagio. *Gli affreschi di Michelangelo e di L. Sabbatini e F. Zuccari nella Cappella Paolina in Vaticano.* Vatican City: 1934.

29. Bayersdorfer, Adolph. *Leben und Schriften.* Ed. H. Mackowsky, A. Pauly, W. Weigand. Munich: 1902.

30. Bean, Jacob. *Bayonne, Musée Bonnat: Les dessins italiens de la Collection Bonnat.* Paris: 1960.

31. Bean, Jacob, and Stampfle, Felice. *Drawings from New York Collections: I. The Italian Renaissance.* Greenwich, Conn.: 1965.

31a. Bean, Jacob, and Turcic, Lawrence. *15th and 16th Century Italian Drawings in the Metropolitan Museum of Art.* New York: 1982.

32. Becker, Marvin. "An Affluent Ancestor of Michelangelo." *Mediaevalia et Humanistica,* 16, 1964, 105–06.

33. Bellori, Giovanni Pietro. *Le vite de' pittori, scultori et architetti moderni.* Rome: 1672.

34. Berenson, Bernard. *The Drawings of the Florentine Painters classified criticised and studied as documents in the history and appreciation of Tuscan Art.* 2 vols. London: 1903.

35. ———. "Andrea di Michelangiolo e Antonio Mini." *L'Arte,* 38, 1935, 243–83.

36. ———. "I disegni di Raffaello da Montelupo." *Bollettino d'Arte,* 29, 1935–36, 105–20.

37. ———. *The Drawings of the Florentine Painters,* 2d ed. 3 vols. Chicago: 1938.

38. Bertelà, Giovanna Gaeta, et al. *Firenze e la Toscana dei Medici nell'Europa del Cinquecento: Il primato del disegno.* Florence: 1980.

39. Berti, Luciano. *Masaccio.* Milan: 1964.

40. ———. "Die Zeichnungen." In *Michelangelo: Bildhauer, Maler, Architekt, Dichter.* Wiesbaden: 1966, 381–499.

41. Bertini, Aldo. *Michelangelo fino alla Sistina.* Turin: 1942.

42. Bertolotti, A. *Don Giulio Clovio principe dei miniatori: Notizie e documenti inediti.* Modena: 1882.

43. *Between Renaissance and Baroque: European Art, 1520–1600.* Manchester: 1965.

44. Borland, Phyllis. "A Copy by Venusti after Michelangelo." *Burlington Magazine,* 103, 1961, 433–34.

45. Bottari, Giovanni Gaetano, and Ticcozzi, Stefano. *Raccolta di lettere sulla pittura, scultura ed architettura scritta da' piu celebri personaggi dei secoli XV, XVI e XVII.* 8 vols. Milan: 1822–25 (rpt. Hildesheim and New York: 1976).

46. Bradford, William, and Braham, Helen. *Mantegna to Cézanne: Master Drawings from the Courtauld.* London: 1983.

47. Bradley, John W. *The Life and Works of Giorgio Giulio Clovio Miniaturist, 1495–1578.* London: 1891.

48. Breckenridge, James D. "'Et prima vidit': The Iconography of the Appearance of Christ to His Mother." *Art Bulletin,* 39, 1957, 9–32.

49. Brinckmann, A. E. *Michelangelo Zeichnungen.* Munich: 1925.

50. Brugnoli, Maria Vittoria. *Michelangelo (I grandi maestri del disegno).* Milan: 1964.

51. Brugnoli Pace, Maria Vittoria. "Un modello antico e due disegni attribuiti a Michelangelo." In *Essays in the History of Art presented to Rudolf Wittkower.* London: 1967, 106–09.

52. Bucci, Mario. *Palazzi di Firenze, Quartiere di S. Maria Novella.* Florence: 1973.

53. Bush, Virginia. *The Colossal Sculpture of the Cinquecento.* New York and London: 1976.

54. Busignani, Alberto. *Pollaiolo.* Florence: 1969.

55. Carli, Enzo. *Tutta la pittura di Michelangelo,* 4th ed. Milan: 1964.

56. Châtelet-Lange, Liliane. "Michelangelos Herkules in Fontainebleau." *Pantheon,* 30, 1972, 455–68.

57. ———. "Noch einmal zu Michelangelos Herkules." *Pantheon,* 35, 1977, 14–17.

57a. Christopher, Lloyd. *A Catalogue of the Early Italian Paintings of the Ashmolean Museum.* Oxford: 1977.

58. Cimino, Guido. *Il Crocifisso di Michelangelo per Vittoria Colonna.* Rome: 1967.

59. Clark, Kenneth. "Italian Drawings at Burlington House." *Burlington Magazine,* 56, 1930, 175–87.

60. Clements, Robert. *Michelangelo's Theory of Art.* New York: 1961.

61. Cleugh, James. *Die Medici: Macht und Glanz einer europäischen Familie.* Munich and Zurich: 1977.

62. *Michelangelo: La vita raccolta dal suo discepolo Ascanio Condivi.* Ed. P. d'Ancona. Milan: 1928.

63. *Das Leben Michelangelos beschrieben von seinem Schüler Ascanio Condivi.* Translated from the Italian and with commentary by H. Pemsel. Munich: 1898.

64. Davidson, Bernice F. "Introducing Michaeli Grechi Lucchese." *Art Bulletin,* 46, 1964, 550–52.

65. ———. "Drawings by Marcello Venusti." *Master Drawings,* 11, 1973, 3–19.

65a. Davidson, Bernice. "The Birth of John the Baptist and Some Other Drawings by Daniele da Volterra." *Master Drawings*, 21, 1983, 152–59.

66. Degenhart, Bernhard. "Zur Graphologie der Handzeichnung: Die Strichbildunglas stetige Erscheinung innerhalb der italienischen Kunstkreise." *Kunstgeschichtliches Jahrbuch der Bibliotheca Hertziana*, 1, 1937, 223–340.

67. ———. *Europäische Handzeichnungen aus fünf Jahrhunderten*. Berlin and Zurich: 1943.

68. ———. "Dante, Leonardo und Sangallo." *Kunstgeschichtliches Jahrbuch der Bibliotheca Hertziana*, 7, 1955, 101–292.

69. Delacre, Maurice. *Le dessin de Michel-Ange*. Brussels: 1938.

70. De Maio, Romeo. *Michelangelo e la Controriforma*. Rome and Bari: 1978.

71. Demonts, Louis. *Les Dessins de Michel-Ange*. Paris: 1921.

72. Denny, Don. "The Annunciation from the Right from Early Christian Times to the Sixteenth Century." Ph.D. diss., Institute of Fine Arts, New York University, 1965.

73. Deri, Gino. "Una crocefissione di Michelangelo per la Principessa Vittoria Colonna." *Arte figurativa*, 5, no. 4, 1957, 26–28.

74. *Disegni italiani e stranieri del Cinquecento e del Seicento*. Milan: 1969 (Edizioni "Stampa della Stanza del Borgo").

75. Doni, Anton Francesco. *I Marmi del Doni, Accademico peregrino*. Venice: 1552–53.

76. *Drawings by Michelangelo, Raphael and Leonardo and their Contemporaries*. London: 1972.

77. *Drawings by Michelangelo in the Collection of Her Majesty the Queen at Windsor Castle, The Ashmolean Museum, The British Museum and Other English Collections*. London: 1975.

78. *Drawings by Michelangelo from the British Museum*. New York: 1979.

79. Dussler, Luitpold. *Sebastiano del Piombo*. Basel: 1942.

80. ———. *Die Zeichnungen des Michelangelo: Kritischer Katalog*. Berlin: 1959.

81. ———. "Die Spätwerke des Michelangelo." In *Michelangelo Buonarroti*. Würzburg: 1964, 115–55.

82. ———. *Michelangelo-Bibliographie, 1927–1970*. Wiesbaden: 1974.

83. Dvořák, Max. *Geschichte der italienischen Kunst im Zeitalter der Renaissance*. 2 vols. Munich: 1927.

84. Einem, Herbert von. "Bemerkungen zur Florentiner Pietà Michelangelos." *Jahrbuch der Preußischen Kunstsammlungen*, 61, 1940, 77–79.

85. ———. "Michelangelos Jüngstes Gericht und die Bildtradition." *Kunstchronik*, 8, 1955, 89–91.

86. ———. *Michelangelo*. Stuttgart: 1959 (Urban-Bücher No. 42).

87. ———. Review of Ch. de Tolnay, *Michelangelo*, vol. 5. *Zeitschrift für Kunstgeschichte*, 25, 1962, 80–85.

87a. ———. Review of P. Barocchi, *Michelangelo e la sua scuola*. *Zeitschrift für Kunstgeschichte*, 28, 1965, 363–65.

88. ———. *Michelangelo: Bildhauer, Maler, Baumeister*. Berlin: 1973.

89. Eisler, Colin. "An Enigmatic Pietà." In *Tribute to Wolfgang Stechow*. Ed. W. L. Strauss. New York: 1976, 40–43.

90. Ettlinger, Leopold D. "Hercules Florentinus." *Mitteilungen des Kunsthistorischen Institutes in Florenz*, 16, 1972, 119–42.

91. ———. *Antonio and Piero Pollaiuolo*. Oxford and New York: 1978.

92. Fahy, Everett. "Michelangelo and Domenico Ghirlandaio." In *Studies in Late Medieval and Renaissance Painting in Honor of Millard Meiss*. 2 vols. New York: 1977.

93. Ferrero, Ermanno, and Müller, Giuseppe. *Vittoria Colonna marchesa di Pescara: Carteggio*. 2d ed. Turin: 1892.

94. Fischel, Oskar. "Porträts des Giuliano de'Medici, Herzogs von Nemours." *Jahrbuch der Kgl. Preußischen Kunstsammlungen*, 28, 1907, 117–30.

95. Forlani Tempesti, Anna, et al. *Disegni italiani della Collezione Santarelli: Sec. XV–XVIII*. Florence: 1967.

96. Forster, Kurt W. "Metaphors of Rule. Political Ideology and History in the Portraits of Cosimo I de' Medici." *Mitteilungen des Kunsthistorischen Institutes in Florenz*, 15, 1971, 79–89.

97. Freedberg, S. J. "'Drawings for Sebastiano' or 'Drawings by Sebastiano': The Problem Reconsidered." *Art Bulletin*, 45, 1963, 253–58.

97a. ———. *Painting in Italy, 1500 to 1600*. Harmondsworth: 1970.

98. Frey, Dagobert. "Die Pietà Rondanini und Rembrandts 'Drei Kreuze.'" In *Kunstgeschichtliche Studien für Hans Kauffmann*. Berlin: 1956, 208–32.

99. Frey, Karl, ed. *Sammlung ausgewählter Briefe an Michelagniolo Buonarroti*. Berlin: 1899.

100. Frey, Karl. *Michelagniolo Buonarroti: Sein Leben und seine Werke*. Vol. 1: *Michelagniolos Jugendjahre*. Berlin: 1907.

101. ———. *Die Handzeichnungen Michelagniolos Buonarroti*. 3 vols. Berlin: 1909–11.

102. ———. *Der literarische Nachlaß Giorgio Vasaris*. Munich: 1923–30, 2 vols.

103. ———. *Die Dichtungen des Michelagniolo Buonarroti*. 2d ed. Berlin: 1964.

104. Frommel, Christoph Luitpold. *Michelangelo und Tommaso dei Cavalieri*. Amsterdam: 1979.

105. Gaborit, Jean-René. "A propos de l'Hercule de Fontainebleau." *Revue de l'art*, no. 36, 1977, 57–61.

106. Gamba, Carlo. *La pittura di Michelangelo*. Novara: 1945.

107. Garello, Edoardo: *Ritrovato un dipinto autentico di Michelangelo*. Turin: 1966.

108. Gatti, Enzo. *Il Crocefisso di Michelangelo ritrovato*. Modena: 1969.

109. Gaye, Giovanni. *Carteggio inedito d'artisti dei secoli XIV, XV, XVI*. 3 vols. Florence: 1839–40.

110. Gilbert, Creighton E. "Michelangelo's Drawings after Masaccio's Sagra." *Gazette des Beaux-Arts*, 34, 1948, 389–404.

111. ———. "Texts and Contexts of the Medici Chapel." *Art Quarterly*, 34, 1971, 391–408.

112. ———. "On the Absolute Dates of the Parts of the Sistine Ceiling." *Art History*, 3, 1980, 158–81.

113. Girardi, Enzo Noé. *Michelangiolo Buonarroti. Rime*. Bari: 1960.

114. Goldscheider, Ludwig. *Michelangelo Drawings*. London: 1951.

115. ———. *Michelangelo Drawings*. 2d ed. London: 1966.

116. Goldthwaite, R. G. "The Building of the Strozzi Palace: The Construction Industry in Renaissance Florence." *Studies in Medieval and Renaissance History*, 10, 1973, 99–194.

117. Gombosi, György. *Moretto da Brescia*. Basel: 1943.

117a. Gombrich, Ernst H. "Michelangelo's Cartoon in the British Museum." *New Light on Old Masters. Studies in the Art of the Renaissance*. Vol. 4. Oxford, 1986, 171–78 and 187.

118. Gotti, Aurelio. *Vita di Michelangelo Buonarroti*. 2d ed. 2 vols. Florence: 1876.

119. Grassi, Luigi. *Il Disegno Italiano dal Trecento al Seicento*. Rome: 1956.

120. Grigioni, Carlo. *Ascanio Condivi: La vita e le opere*. Ascoli and Piceno: 1908.

121. Gronau, Giorgio. *Documenti artistici urbinati*. Florence: 1935.

122. Groote, Maximilian von. *Die Deutung der Medici-Grabdenkmäler Michelangelos*. Strasbourg: 1927.

123. Gualandi, Michelangelo. *Nuova Raccolta di Lettere sulla Pittura, Scultura ed Architettura scritte da' più celebri personaggi dei Secoli XV. a XIX*. 3 vols. Bologna: 1844–56.

124. Guasti, Cesare, ed. *Le Rime di Michelangelo Buonarroti pittore scultore e architetto*. Florence: 1863.

124a. Gurrieri, Francesco. *Disegni nei manoscritti Laurenziani, Sec. X–XVII*. Florence: 1979.

125. Hall, Marcia B. "Michelangelo's Last Judgment: Resurrection of the Body and Predestination." *Art Bulletin*, 58, 1976, 85–92.

126. Harprath, Richard. *Italienische Zeichnungen des 16. Jahrhunderts aus eigenem Besitz: Kat. der Ausstellung in der Staatlichen Graphischen Sammlung*. Munich: 1977.

127. ———. "Eine neuentdeckte Zeichnung Michelangelos in München zum Herkules von Fontainebleau." *Pantheon*, 35, 1977, 306–11.

128. Hartt, Frederick. Review of Ch. de Tolnay, *Michelangelo*, vols. 2–3. *Art Bulletin*, 32, 1950, 239–50.

128a. ———. *Michelangelo Buonarroti: Gemälde*. Stuttgart, Zurich, and Salzburg: 1965.

129. ———. *Michelangelo: The Complete Sculpture*. London: 1969.

130. ———. *The Drawings of Michelangelo*. London: 1971.

131. Heimeran, Ernst. *Michelangelo und das Porträt*. Munich: 1925.

132. Hettner, Otto. "Zeichnerische Gepflogenheiten bei Michelangelo. Mit einem Anhange über Signorelli und Correggio." *Monatshefte für Kunstwissenschaft*, 2, 1909, 71–87, 134–48.

133. Hirst, Michael. "The Chigi Chapel in S. Maria della Pace." *Journal of the Warburg and Courtauld Institutes*, 24, 1961, 161–85.

134. ———. "Michelangelo Drawings in Florence." Review of P. Barocchi, *Michelangelo e la sua scuola: I disegni di Casa Buonarroti e degli Uffizi*. *Burlington Magazine*, 105, 1963, 166–71.

135. ———. "Daniele da Volterra and the Orsini Chapel: I. The Chronology and the Altar-piece." *Burlington Magazine*, 109, 1967, 498–509.

136. ———. "Sebastiano's Pietà for the Commendador Mayor." *Burlington Magazine*, 114, 1972, 585–95.

137. ———. "A Drawing of 'The Rape of Ganymede' by Michelangelo." *Burlington Magazine*, 117, 1975, 166.

138. ———. "A Drawing of the Rape of Ganymede by Michelangelo." In *Essays presented to Myron P. Gilmore*. Florence: 1978, 2:253–60.

139. ———. *Sebastiano del Piombo*. Oxford: 1981.

139a. ———. Review of Ch. de Tolnay, *Corpus dei disegni di Michelangelo*. *Burlington Magazine*, 125, 1983, 552–56.

139b. ———. *Michelangelo and His Drawings*. New Haven and London, 1989.

139c. ———. *Michel-Ange dessinateur*. Translation by Marie-Geneviève de La Coste-Messelière. Paris, 1989.

140. Holst, Christian von. "Florentiner Gemälde und Zeichnungen aus der Zeit von 1480 bis 1580: Kleine Beobachtungen und Ergänzungen." *Mitteilungen des Kunsthistorischen Institutes in Florenz*, 15, 1971, 1–64.

141. ———. *Francesco Granacci*. Munich: 1974.

141a. Hope, Charles. Review of M. Hirst, *Sebastino del Piombo*, and C. Volpe and M. Lucco, *L'opera completa di Sebastiano del Piombo*. *Burlington Magazine*, 124, 1982, 637–38.

142. Hutter, Heribert. *Die Handzeichnung: Entwicklung, Technik, Eigenart*. Vienna and Munich: 1966.

143. Isermeyer, Christian Adolf. "Das Michelangelo-Jahr 1964 und die Forschungen zu Michelangelo als Maler und Bildhauer von 1959 bis 1965." *Zeitschrift für Kunstgeschichte*, 28, 1965, 307–52.

144. *Italienische Zeichnungen der Renaissance: Zum 500. Geburtsjahr Michelangelos, Kat. der 250. Ausstellung der Graphischen Sammlung Albertina*. Vienna: 1975.

145. Jacobsen, Emil. "Die Handzeichnungen der Uffizien in ihren Beziehungen zu Gemälden, Skulpturen und Gebäuden in Florenz." *Repertorium für Kunstwissenschaft*, 21, 1898, 263–83; 27, 1904, 113–32, 251–60, 322–31, 401–29.

146. ———. "Die Handzeichnungen Michelangelos zu den Sixtina-Fresken: Kritische Bemerkungen zum ersten Anhang von Steinmann, Die Sixtinische Kapelle II." *Repertorium für Kunstwissenschaft*, 30, 1907, 389–98, 490–500.

147. Jacoby, Brigitte. *Studien zur Ikonographie des Phaetonmythos*. Bonn: 1971.

148. Jaffé, Michael. "Rubens as a Collector of Drawings." *Master Drawings*, 2, 1964, 383–97; 4, 1966, 127–48.

149. ———. "Rubens and Joves Eagle." *Paragone*, no. 245, 1970, 23–24.

150. Joannides, Paul. "Michelangelo's Medici Chapel: Some New Suggestions." *Burlington Magazine*, 114, 1972, 541–51.

151. ———. "Michelangelo Drawings at the British Museum." *Burlington Magazine*, 117, 1975, 257–62.

152. ———. "Michelangelo's Lost Hercules." *Burlington Magazine*, 119, 1977, 550–54.

153. ———. Review of Ch. de Tolnay, *Corpus dei disegni di Michelangelo*, 1975–80. *Art Bulletin*, 63, 1981, 679–87.

153a. Joannides, Paul. "A Supplement to Michelangelo's Lost Hercules." *Burlington Magazine*, 123 1981, 20–23.

154. Jombert, Charles-Antoine. *Méthode pour apprendre le Dessein*. Paris: 1755.

155. Justi, Carl. *Michelangelo: Neue Beiträge zur Erklärung seiner Werke*. Berlin: 1909.

156. Keller, Harald. *Michelangelo: Zeichnungen und Dichtungen*. Frankfurt a. M.: 1975 (Insel Taschenbuch No. 147).

157. Kemp, Wolfgang. " . . . um einen wahrhaft bildenden Zeichenunterricht überall einzuführen": *Zeichnen und Zeichenunterricht der Laien, 1500–1870: Ein Handbuch*. Frankfurt a. M.: 1979.

158. Kirschenbaum, Baruch D. "Reflections on Michelangelo's Drawings for Cavaliere." *Gazette des Beaux-Arts*, 38, 1951, 99–110.

159. Kleiner, Gerhard. *Die Begegnungen Michelangelos mit der Antike*. Berlin: 1950.

159a. Knapp, Fritz. *Die Handzeichnungen Michelagniolos Buonarroti: Nachtrag zu den von Karl Frey herausgegebenen drei Bänden, Part 1*. Berlin: 1925.

160. ———. Review of A. E. Brinckmann, *Michelangelo-Zeichnungen*, 1925. *Zeitschrift für bildende Kunst*, 59, 1925. Die Kunstlit., 42.

161. Koschatzky, Walter. *Die Kunst der Zeichnung: Technik, Geschichte, Meisterwerke*. 2d ed. Salzburg and Vienna: 1980.

162. Landino, Cristoforo. *Camaldolensische Gespräche*. Translated from the Latin and with an introduction by E. Wold. Jena: 1927

163. Landucci, Luca. *Ein Florentinisches Tagebuch, 1450–1516 nebst einer anonymen Fortsetzung, 1516–1542*. Translated, with an introduction and commentary, by M. Herzfeld. 2 vols. Jena: 1912–13.

164. Lebrooy, Paul James. *Michelangelo's Models formerly in the Paul von Praun Collection*. Vancouver: 1972.

165. *Le Cabinet d'un Grand Amateur: P.-J. Mariette, 1694–1774*. Paris: 1967.

166. Lecchini Giovannoni, Simona. *Mostra di disegni di Alessandro Allori (Firenze, 1535–1607)*. Florence: 1970.

167. *L'Ecole de Fontainebleau*. Paris: 1972.

168. Levi D'Ancona, Mirella. "Illuminations by Clovio Lost and Found." *Gazette des Beaux-Arts*, 37, no. 2, 1950, 55–76.

169. Levie, Simon H. *Der Maler Daniele da Volterra, 1509–1566*. Cologne: 1962.

170. Levine, Saul. "The Location of Michelangelo's David: The Meeting of January 25, 1504." *Art Bulletin*, 56, 1974, 31–49.

171. *Lexikon der christlichen Ikonographie*. 8 vols. Rome, Freiburg, Basel, and Wien, 1968–76.

172. Leymarie, Jean, Monnier, Geneviève, and Rose, Bernice. *Die Zeichnung: Entwicklungen, Stilformen, Funktion*. Geneva: 1980.

173. Libertini, Guido. "Rilievo cinquecentesco del Museo Communale di Catania." *Bollettino storico Catanese*, 1941, 77–83.

174. Liebert, Robert S. *Michelangelo: A Psychoanalytic Study of His Life and Images*. New Haven and London: 1983.

175. Liphart-Ratshoff, Reinhart von. "L'Ercole di Michelangelo e un disegno del Beccafumi." *Rivista d'Arte*, 15, 1933, 93–104.

176. Loeser, Carlo. "I disegni italiani della Raccolta Malcolm." *Archivio storico dell'arte*, 3, 1897, 341–59.

177. Lomazzo, Giovanni Paolo. *Trattato dell'arte de la pittura*. Milan: 1584.

178. ———. *Idea del Tempio della Pittura*. Milan: 1590.

179. Longhi, Roberto. "Due pannelli di Daniele da Volterra." *Paragone*, no. 179, 1964, 32–37.

180. Magi, Filippo. "Nuovi aspetti michelangioleschi della Paolina." *Ecclesia*, 12, 1953, 584–89.

181. Malvasia, Carlo Cesare. *Felsina Pittrice: Vite dei pittori Bolognesi*. Ed. M. Brascaglia. Bologna: 1971.

182. Mancusi-Ungaro, Harold R. *Michelangelo: The Bruges Madonna and the Piccolomini Altar*. New Haven and London, 1971.

183. Manilli, J. *Villa Borghese fuori di Porta Pinciana*. Rome: 1650.

183a. Marabottini, Alessandro. "Il sogno' di Michelangelo in una copia sconosciuta," *Scritti di storia dell' arte in onore di Lionello Venturi*. Rome: 1956, 1:349–58.

184. Meder, Joseph. *The Mastery of Drawing*. Trans. and revised by W. Ames. New York: 1978.

185. Mesnil, J. *L'éducation des peintres florentins au 15ième siècle*. 1910.

186. *Michelangelo: Il carteggio*. ed. by G. Poggi, P. Barocchi, and R. Ristori. 5 vols. Florence: 1965–83.

187. *Michelangelo: I ricordi*. Ed. L. Bardeschi Ciulich and P. Barocchi. Florence: 1970.

188. Milanesi, Gaetano, ed. *Le lettere di Michelangelo Buonarroti pubblicate coi ricordi ed i contratti artistici*. Florence: 1875.

188a. Monbeig Goguel, Catherine. "Giulio Clovio 'nouveau petit Michel-Ange'. A propos des dessins du Louvre." *Revue de l'art*, no. 80, 1988, 37–47.

189. Montebello, Philippe de. *Notable Acquisitions, 1975–1979. The Metropolitan Museum of Art*. New York: 1979.

190. Negri Arnoldi, Francesco. "Origine e diffusione del Crocifisso barocco con l'immagine del Cristo vivente." *Storia dell'arte*, 20, 1974, 57–80.

191. Neufeld, Günther. "Michelangelo's Times of Day: A Study of Their Genesis." *Art Bulletin*, 48, 1966, 273–84.

192. Nolhac, Pierre de. "Les collections de Fulvio Orsini: Une Galerie de peinture au XVIe siècle." *Gazette des Beaux-Arts*, 29, 1884, 427–36.

193. Oberhuber, Konrad. "Raphael und Michelangelo." *Stil und Überlieferung in der Kunst des Abendlandes*. Berlin, 1967, 2:156–64.

194. Oberhuber, Konrad, and Vitali, Lamberto. *Raffaello: Il cartone per la Scuola di Atene*. Milan: 1972.

195. Oertel, Robert. Review of L. Dussler, *Italienische Meisterzeichnungen* (Munich, 1948) and F. Winzinger, *Deutsche Meisterzeichnungen der Gotik* (Munich, 1949), *Kunstchronik*, 2, 1949, 263.

196. Olszewski, Edward J. "A Design for the Sistine Chapel Ceiling." *Bulletin of the Cleveland Museum of Art*, 63, 1976, 12–26.

197. Ost, Hans. *Das Leonardo-Porträt in der Kgl. Bibliothek Turin und andere Fälschungen des Giuseppe Bossi*. Berlin: 1980.

198. Pacheco, Francisco. *Arte de la pintura, su antiguedad y grandezas*. Seville: 1649.

199. Pallucchini, Rodolfo. *Sebastian Viniziano*. Milan: 1944.

200. Panofsky, Erwin. "Die Michelangelo-Literatur seit 1914." *Wiener Jahrbuch für Kunstgeschichte*, n.s., 1, 1921–22, Die Kunstlit., 1–64.

201. ———. *Handzeichnungen Michelangelos*. Leipzig: 1922.

202. ———. "Bemerkungen zu der Neuherausgabe der Haarlemer Michelangelo-Zeichnungen durch Fr. Knapp." *Repertorium für Kunstwissenschaft*, 48, 1927, 25–58.

203. ———. "Die Pietà von Ubeda—Ein kleiner Beitrag zur Lösung der Sebastiano-Frage." *Festschrift für Julius Schlosser*. Zurich, Leipzig, and Vienna: 1927, 150–61.

204. ———. "Kopie oder Fälschung? Ein Beitrag zur Kritik einiger Zeichnungen aus der Werkstatt Michelangelos." *Zeitschrift für bildende Kunst*, 61, 1927–28, 221–44.

205. ———. "Noch einmal 'Kopie oder Fälschung?'" *Zeitschrift für bildende Kunst*, 62, 1928–29, 179–83.

206. ———. *Studies in Iconology: Humanistic Themes in the Art of the Renaissance*. 2d ed. New York and Evanston: 1962.

207. Parker, K. T. *Catalogue of the Collection of Drawings in the Ashmolean Museum*. 2d ed. Oxford: 1972.

208. Parronchi, Alessandro. *Opere giovanili di Michelangelo*. 3 vols. Florence: 1968–81.

209. ———. "Il più bel ritratto di Michelangelo." *La Nazione*, 16 January 1964.

210. Parroni, Giuseppe. "Michel-Ange ou Venusti?" *Gazette des Beaux-Arts*, 17, 1937, 283–98.

210a. Passavant, Günter. "Reflexe nordischer Graphik bei Raffael, Leonardo, Giulio Romano und Michelangelo." *Mitteilungen des Kunsthistorischen Institutes in Florenz*, 27, 1983, 193–222.

211. Passavant, J. D. *Kunstreise durch England und Belgien*. Frankfurt a.M.: 1833.

212. Passerini, Luigi. *La bibliografia di Michelangelo Buonarroti e gli incisori delle sue opere*. Florence: 1875.

213. Pastor, Ludwig Freiherr von. *Geschichte der Päpste seit dem Ausgang des Mittelalters*, 1886–1933, I–XVI.

213a. Patrizi, G. "Condivi, Ascanio." *Dizionario biografico degli Italiani*. Rome, 1982, 27, 753–56.

214. Pergola, Paola della. *Galleria Borghese: I dipinti*. 2 vols. Rome. 1955–59.

215. ———. "L'inventario del 1592 di Lucrezia d'Este." *Arte Antica e Moderna*, 1959, 342–51.

216. ———. "Gli Inventari Aldobrandini." *Arte Antica e Moderna*, 1960, 425–44.

217. ———. "Gli Inventari Aldobrandini: l'Inventario del 1682." *Arte Antica e Moderna*, 1963, 61–87, 175–91.

218. ———. "L'Inventario Borghese del 1693." *Arte Antica e Moderna*, 1964, 451–67.

219. Perrig, Alexander. *Michelangelo Buonarrotis letzte Pietà-Idee: Ein Beitrag zur Erforschung seines Alterswerkes*. Bern: 1960.

220. ———. "Über eine verkannte Michelangelo-Zeichnung." *Zeitschrift für Kunstgeschichte*, 23, 1960, 19–41.

221. ———. "Bemerkungen zur Genesis von Sebastiano del Piombos Auferweckung Lazari in der National Gallery in London." *Wallraf-Richartz-Jahrbuch*, 22, 1960, 173–94.

222. ———. "Michelangelo und Marcello Venusti: Das Problem der Verkündigungs- und Ölberg-Konzeptionen Michelangelos." *Wallraf-Richartz-Jahrbuch*, 24, 1962, 261–94.

223. ———. "Gedanken zu dem Kritischen Katalog der Michelangelo-Zeichnungen: Luitpold Dussler zum 70. Geburtstag." *Zeitschrift für Kunstgeschichte*, 28, 1965, 353–60.

224. ———. "Bemerkungen zur Freundschaft zwischen Michelangelo und Tommaso de' Cavalieri." *Stil und Überlieferung in der Kunst des Abendlandes*. Berlin: 1967, 2:164–71.

225. ———. "Cavalieri, Tommaso de'." *Dizionario biografico degli Italiani*. Rome: 1979, vol. 22, 678–80.

226. ———. "Authenticity Problems with Michelangelo: The Drawings on the Louvre-Sheet No. 685." *Authentication in the Visual Arts: A Multidisciplined Symposium*. Amsterdam: 1979, 27–56.

227. ———. *Michelangelo-Studien I: Michelangelo und die Zeichnungswissenschaft—Ein methodologischer Versuch*. Bern and Frankfurt a.M.: 1976.

228. ———. *Michelangelo-Studien III: Das Jüngste Gericht und seine Vorgeschichte*. Bern and Frankfurt a.M.: 1976.

229. ———. *Michelangelo-Studien IV: Die 'Michelangelo'-Zeichnungen Benvenuto Cellinis*. Bern and Frankfurt a.M.: 1977.

230. ———. "Die Konzeption der Wandgrabmäler der Medici-Kapelle." *Städel-Jahrbuch*, n.s., 8, 1981, 247–87.

231. ———. "Das Münchener Blatt mit der Kopie nach Masaccios 'Zinsgroschen'-Fresko und die Methoden der Michelangelo-Forschung." *Kritische Berichte*, 10, no. 3, 1982, 3–35.

232. Pfeiffer, Heinrich. "On the Meaning of a Late Michelangelo Drawing." *Art Bulletin*, 48, 1966, 227.

233. Pfister, Kurt. *Vittoria Colonna: Werden und Gestalt der frühbarocken Welt.* Munich: 1950.

234. Pignatti, Terisio. *Italian Drawings in Oxford from the Collections of the Ashmolean Museum and Christ Church.* Oxford: 1977.

235. Piles, Roger de. *Les premiers elemens de la Peinture pratique.* Paris: 1684.

236. Poggetto, Paolo Dal. *I disegni murali di Michelangiolo e della sua scuola nella Sagrestia Nuova di San Lorenzo.* Florence: 1979.

236a. Poggi, Giovanni. *Il Duomo di Firenze.* Berlin: 1909.

237. Pope-Hennessy, John. "The Palestrina Pietà." *Stil und Überlieferung in der Kunst des Abendlandes.* Berlin: 1967, 2:105–14.

238. ———. *Italian High Renaissance and Baroque Sculpture.* 2d ed. London: 1970.

239. Popham, A. E. *Italian Drawings Exhibited at the Royal Academy Burlington House, London, 1930.* London: 1931.

240. Popham, A. E., and Wilde, Johannes. *The Italian Drawings of the XV and XVI Centuries in the Collection of His Majesty the King at Windsor Castle.* London: 1949.

241. Popp, Anny E. *Die Medici-Kapelle Michelangelos.* Munich: 1922.

242. ———. "Garzoni Michelangelos." *Belvedere*, 8, 1925, 6–28.

243. ———. Review of A. E. Brinckmann, *Michelangelo Zeichnungen. Belvedere*, 8, 1925, Forum, 72–75.

244. ———. "Bemerkungen zu einigen Zeichnungen Michelangelos." *Zeitschrift für bildende Kunst*, 35, 1925–26, 134–46, 169–74.

245. ———. "Fälschlich Michelangelo zugeschriebene Zeichnungen." *Zeitschrift für bildende Kunst*, 38, 1927–28, 8–17.

246. ———. "Kopie oder Fälschung." *Zeitschrift für bildende Kunst*, 38, 1928–29, 54–67.

247. Portheim, Friedrich. "Beiträge zu den Werken Michelangelo's." *Repertorium für Kunstwissenschaft*, 12, 1889, 140–58.

248. Procacci, Ugo. *La Casa Buonarroti a Firenze.* Milan: 1967.

249. Ragghianti Collobi, Licia. *Il Libro de' Disegni del Vasari.* Florence: 1974.

250. Ramdohr, Wilhelm Basilius von. *Über Mahlerei und Bildhauerarbeit in Rom für Liebhaber des Schönen in der Kunst.* 3 vols. Leipzig: 1787.

251. Ramsden, E. H., ed. *The Letters of Michelangelo.* Trans. from the original Tuscan. 2 vols. London: 1963.

252. Ramsden, E. H. "Recent Michelangelo Literature." *Burlington Magazine*, 108, 1966, 202–04.

253. *Reallexikon zur Deutschen Kunstgeschichte.* Ed. L. H. Heydenreich and K.-A. Wirth. Stuttgart: 1937–.

254. Redig de Campos, Deoclezio. "Das Porträt Michelangelos mit dem Turban von Giuliano Bugiardini." *Festschrift für Herbert von Einem.* Berlin: 1965, 49–51.

255. ———. "Das Kruzifix Michelangelos für Vittoria Colonna." *Stil und Überlieferung in der Kunst des Abendlandes.* Berlin: 1967, 2:185–87.

256. Redig de Campos, Deoclezio, and Biagetti, Biagio. *Il Giudizio Universale di Michelangelo.* Rome: 1944.

257. Regteren Altena, Johan Quirijn van. "Zu Michelangelo: Zeichnungen, besonders aus den Jahren 1530 bis 1535." *Stil und Überlieferung in der Kunst des Abendlandes.* Berlin: 1967, 2:171–80.

258. Rèpaci Courtois, Gabriella. "A propos du David en bronze de Michel-Ange." *La Revue du Louvre et des Musées de France*, 26, 1976, 250–54.

259. Richelson, Paul William. *Studies in the Personal Imagery of Cosimo I de' Medici, Duke of Florence.* New York and London: 1978.

260. Richter, Jean Paul. "Michelangelo's schlafender Cupido." *Zeitschrift für bildende Kunst*, 12, 1877, 129–34, 170–74.

261. ———. "On some Old Masters at the British Museum." *Art Journal*, 1897, 152–55.

261a. Riebesell, Christina. *Die Sammlung des Kardinal Alessandro Farnese: Ein "studio" für Künstler und Gelehrte.* Weinheim: 1989.

262. Rinaldis, Aldo de. "Transfigurazioni Michelangiolesche." *Rassegna d'arte antica e moderna*, 5, 1918, 200–05.

263. Robinson, J. D. *A Critical Account of the Drawings by Michel Angelo and Raffaello in the University Galleries.* Oxford: 1870.

264. ———. *Descriptive Catalogue of Drawings by the Old Masters, forming the Collection of John Malcolm of Poltalloch, Esq.* London: 1876.

265. Romano, Giovanni, ed. *Gaudenzio Ferrari e la sua scuola: I cartoni cinquecenteschi dell'Accademia Albertina.* Turin: 1982.

266. Rosand, David. "The Elusive Michelangelo." *Art News*, 77, 1978, 48–51.

267. Rosenauer, Artur. "Zum Stil der frühen Werke Domenico Ghirlandajos." *Wiener Jahrbuch für Kunstgeschichte*, 22, 1969, 59–85.

268. Rotili, Mario. *Fortuna di Michelangelo nell'incisione.* Benevento: 1964.

268a. Salerno, Luigi. "The Picture Gallery of Vincenzo Giustiniani." *Burlington Magazine*, 102, 1960, 21–27, 93–104, 135–48.

269. Salmi, Mario, Tolnay, Carlo de, Barocchi, Paola. *Disegni di Michelangelo: 103 disegni in facsimile.* Milan: 1964.

270. Salvini, Roberto. "La 'Battaglia di Cascina'—Saggio di critica

delle varianti." *Studi di storia dell' arte in onore di Valerio Mariani*, Naples: 1971, 131–46.

271. ———. *Michelangelo*. Wiesbaden: 1977.

272. Scannelli, Francesco. *Il Microcosmo della Pittvra*. Cesena: 1657.

273. Scheicher, Elisabeth. *Die Kunst- und Wunderkammern der Habsburger*. Ed. Ch. Brandstätter. Vienna, Munich, and Zurich: 1979.

274. Schmidt, Diether. *Michelangelo Handzeichnungen*. Frankfurt a.M.: 1965 (Insel-Bücherei Nr. 444).

275. Sedlmayr, Hans. *Epochen und Werke*. 2d ed. Mittenwald: 1977.

276. Settimo, Giorgio. *Ascanio Condivi biografo di Michelangelo*. Ascoli Piceno: 1975.

277. Seymour, Charles, Jr. *Michelangelo's David: A Search for Identity*. Pittsburgh: 1967.

278. Shearman, John. "Maniera as an Aesthetic Ideal." *Renaissance Art*. Ed. C. Gilbert. New York, Evanston, and London: 1970, 181–221.

279. Sricchia Santoro, Fiorella. "Daniele da Volterra." *Paragone*, no. 213/33, 1967, 3–34.

280. Stechow, Wolfgang. "Daniele da Volterra als Bildhauer." *Jahrbuch der Preußischen Kunstsammlungen*, 49, 1928, 82–92.

281. Steinberg, Leo. "The Metaphors of Love and Birth in Michelangelo's Pietàs." *Studies in Erotic Art*. Ed. Th. Bowie. New York: 1970, 231–85.

282. ———. *Michelangelo's Last Paintings: The Conversion of St. Paul and the Crucifixion of St. Peter in the Cappella Paolina, Vatican Palace*. London: 1975.

283. ———. "Michelangelo's Last Judgment as Merciful Heresy." *Art in America*, 68, 1975, 49–63.

284. ———. "A Corner of the Last Judgment." *Daedalus*, Spring 1980, 207–73.

285. ———. "The Line of Fate in Michelangelo's Painting." *Critical Inquiry*, 6, 1980, 411–54.

286. Steinmann, Ernst. *Die Sixtinische Kapelle, II: Michelangelo*. Munich: 1905.

287. ———. *Die Porträtdarstellungen des Michelangelo*. Leipzig: 1913.

288. ———. "Cartoni di Michelangelo." *Bollettino d'Arte*, 5, 1925–26, 3–16.

289. Steinmann, Ernst, and Pogatscher, Heinrich. "Dokumente und Forschungen zu Michelangelo." *Repertorium für Kunstwissenschaft*, 29, 1906, 387–424, 485–517.

290. Steinmann, Ernst, and Wittkower, Rudolf. *Michelangelo Bibliographie I: 1510–1926*. Leipzig: 1927.

291. Striker, Cecil L. "Innocenzio Ringhieri's Giuoco della pittura." *Essays in Honor of Walter Friedlaender*. New York: 1965, 165–76.

292. Summers, David. *Michelangelo and the Language of Art*. Princeton: 1981.

293. Thode, Henry. *Michelangelo und das Ende der Renaissance*. 3 vols. Berlin: 1912.

294. ———. *Michelangelo: Kritische Untersuchungen über seine Werke*. 3 vols. Berlin: 1908–13.

295. Tolnay, Karl. "Die Handzeichnungen Michelangelos im Codex Vaticanus." *Repertorium für Kunstwissenschaft*, 48, 1927, 157–205.

296. ———. "Die Handzeichnungen Michelangelos im Archivio Buonarroti." *Münchner Jahrbuch der bildenden Kunst*, n.s., 5, 1928, 377–476.

297. ———. "Michelangelo." Thieme-Becker, *Allgemeines Lexikon der bildenden Künstler*. Leipzig: 1930, 24:515–26.

298. ———. "Michelangelo-Studien (Die Jugendwerke)." *Jahrbuch der Preußischen Kunstsammlungen*, 5, 1933, 95–122.

299. Tolnay, Charles de. "Michelangelo's Rondanini Pietà." *Burlington Magazine*, 65, 1934, 146–57.

300. ———. "Marcello Venusti as Copyist of Michelangelo." *Art in America*, 28, 1940, 169–76.

301. ———. "Le Jugement Dernier de Michel-Ange—Essai d'Interprétation." *Art Quarterly*, 3, 1940, 124–47.

302. ———. *Michelangelo*. 5 vols. Princeton: 1943–60.

303. ———. "Notes Concerning the Youth of Michelangelo: A Reply." *Art Bulletin*, 27, 1945, 139–46.

304. ———. *Werk und Weltbild des Michelangelo*. Zurich: 1949.

305. ———. Letter. *Burlington Magazine*, 94, 1952, 32.

306. ———. "Michelangelo Buonarroti." *Enciclopedia universale dell'arte*. Venice and Rome, 1963, 9:263–306.

307. ———. "Morte e resurrezione in Michelangelo." *Commentari*, 15, 1964, 3–20.

308. ———. "Tod und Auferstehung bei Michelangelo." *Michelangelo Buonarroti*. Würzburg: 1964, 7–50.

309. ———. *The Art and Thought of Michelangelo*. New York: 1964.

310. ———. "L'Hercule de Michel-Ange à Fontainebleau." *Gazette des Beaux-Arts*, 64, 1964, 125–40.

311. ———. "A Forgotten Architectural Project by Michelangelo: The Choir of the Cathedral of Padua." *Festschrift für Herbert von Einem zum 16. Februar 1965*. Berlin: 1965, 247–51.

312. ———. "Der Mensch und Künstler." *Michelangelo: Bildhauer, Maler, Architekt, Dichter*. Wiesbaden: 1966, 7–71.

313. ———. "L'Hercule de Michel-Ange à Fontainebleau." *Stil und Überlieferung in der Kunst des Abendlandes*. Berlin: 1967, 2:126–27.

314. ———. "Alcune recenti scoperte e risultati negli studi Michelangioleschi." *Accademia Nazionale dei Lincei*, 368, 1971, Quad. No.153, Rome: 1971.

315. ———. *History and Technique of Old Master Drawings: A Handbook*. New York: 1972.

316. ———. "Ein unbekanntes Porträt des Michelangelo." *Festschrift Luitpold Dussler*. Munich and Berlin: 1972, 205–08.

317. ———. "Michelangelo lehrt Zeichnen: Bemerkungen über ein

bisher unveröffentlichtes Blatt des Meisters." *Neue Zürcher Zeitung*, 10 March 1974, No. 115, 53.

318. ———. *I disegni di Michelangelo nelle collezioni italiane.* Florence: 1975.

319. ———. *Corpus dei disegni di Michelangelo.* 4 vols. Novara: 1975–80.

320. ———. *Michelangelo: Sculptor, Painter, Architect.* Princeton: 1975.

321. ———. "Una nuova identificazione: un autoritratto ironico di Michelangelo." *Acta Historiae Artium Accademiae Scientiarum Hungaricae*, 24, 1978, 211–14.

322. Tolnay, Charles de, and Squellati Brizio, Paola. *Michelangelo e i Medici.* Florence: 1980.

323. Torselli, Giorgio. *La Galleria Doria.* Rome: 1969.

324. Utz, Hildegard. "The 'Labors of Hercules' and Other Works by Vincenzo de'Rossi." *Art Bulletin*, 103, 1971, 344–66.

325. ———. *Der wiederentdeckte Herkules des Michelangelo.* Munich: 1975.

326. Valentiner, W. R. *Studies of Italian Renaissance Sculpture.* London: 1950.

327. *Orazione funerale di M. Benedetto Varchi fatta, e recitata da Lui pubblicamente nell'essequie di Michelagnolo Buonarroti in Firenze, nella Chiesa di San Lorenzo.* Florence: 1564.

328. Vasari, Giorgio. *Le vite de'più eccellenti pittori scultori ed architettori.* Ed. G. Milanesi. 9 vols. Florence: 1878–85.

329. ———. *La vita di Michelangelo nelle redazioni del 1550 e del 1568.* Ed. P. Barocchi. 4 vols. Milan and Naples: 1962.

330. Venturi, Adolfo. "Disegni inediti di Michelangelo." *L'Arte*, 24, 1921, 224–27.

331. Verspohl, Franz-Joachim. "Michelangelo und Macchiavelli: Der David auf der Piazza della Signoria in Florenz." *Städel-Jahrbuch*, n.s., 8, 1981, 204–46.

332. Viatte, Françoise. "Dessins italiens de l'Albertina de Vienne." *La Revue du Louvre et des musées de France*, 25, 1975.

333. Villari, Pasquale. *Macchiavelli e i suoi tempi.* 2 vols. Milan: 1895.

334. ———. *La storia di Girolamo Savonarola e de'suoi tempi.* 2d ed. Florence: 1930.

334a. Volpe, Carlo, and Lucco, Mario. *L'opera completa di Sebastiano del Piombo*, Milan: 1980.

335. Voss, Hermann. *Die Malerei der Spätrenaissance in Rom und Florenz.* 2 vols. Berlin: 1920.

336. Wackernagel, Martin. *Der Lebensraum des Künstlers in der Florentiner Renaissance.* Leipzig: 1938.

336a. Wallace, William E. "Two Presentation Drawings for Michelangelo's Medici Chapel." *Master Drawings*, 25, 1987, 242–60.

336b. ———. "Narrative and Religious Expression in Michelangelo's Pauline Chapel." *Artibus et Historiae*, 10, no. 19, 1989, 107–21.

337. Weinberger, Martin. Review of Ch. de Tolnay, *Michelangelo*, vol. 1, 1943, in *Art Bulletin*, 28, 1945, 69–71.

338. ———. *Michelangelo the Sculptor.* London and New York: 1967.

339. Weiss, Roberto. *The Renaissance Discovery of Classical Antiquity.* Oxford: 1973.

340. Wickhoff, Franz. "Die Antike im Bildungsgange Michelangelo's." *Mitteilungen des Instituts für Österreichische Geschichtsforschung*, 2, 1882, 408–35.

341. ———. "Die italienischen Handzeichnungen der Albertina. II. Theil. Die römische Schule." *Jahrbuch der Kunsthistorischen Sammlungen des Allerhöchsten Kaiserhauses in Wien*, 13, 1892, CLXXV–CCLXXXIII.

342. Wilde, Johannes. "Zur Kritik der Haarlemer Michelangelo-Zeichnungen." *Belvedere*, 11, 1927, 142–7.

343. ———. "Der ursprüngliche Plan Michelangelos zum Jüngsten Gericht." *Die Graphischen Künste*, n.s., 1, 1936, 7–11.

343a. Wilde, Johannes. "Michelangelo and Leonardo." *Burlington Magazine*, 95, 1953, 65–77.

344. ———. *Italian Drawings in the Department of Prints and Drawings in the British Museum: Michelangelo and His Studio.* London: 1953.

345. ———. "Notes on the Genesis of Michelangelo's Leda." *Fritz Saxl: A Volume of Memorial Essays from his Friends in England.* Edinburgh: 1957, 270–80.

346. ———. "Cartonetti by Michelangelo." *Burlington Magazine*, 101, 1959, 370–81.

347. ———. *Michelangelo: Six Lectures.* Oxford: 1978.

348. Winkler, Friedrich. *Die Zeichnungen Albrecht Dürers.* 4 vols. Berlin: 1936–39.

349. Wittkower, Rudolf. "A Newly Discovered Drawing by Michelangelo." *Burlington Magazine*, 78, 1941, 159–61.

350. ———. *Sculpture: Processes and Principles.* London: 1977.

351. Wölfflin, Heinrich. Review of F. von Marcuard, *Die Zeichnungen Michelangelo's in Haarlem. Repertorium für Kunstwissenschaft*, 24, 1901, 318–20.

352. Wolf, Rosina. *Documenti inediti su Michelangelo.* Rome and Budapest: 1931.

353. Woodward, B. B. *Specimens of the Drawings of ten Masters, from the Royal Collection at Windsor Castle.* London: 1870.

354. Zentai, Roland. "Un dessin de Giovanni Battista Sangallo et les projets de fresques de la Chapelle Médicis." *Bulletin du Musée Hongrois des Beaux-Arts*, 1971, 79–92.

Index

Note: Museum accession numbers appear in italics.

Albani, Francesco: preparing studies on the basis of his master's sketches, 141*n*59
Albizzi, Girolamo degli, 2
Aldobrandini, Pietro, 114
Altoviti, Bindo, 2
Amadori, Francesco, 39, 99, 114, 115; date of death, 150*n*30; income, 150*n*47
Ammannati, Bartolommeo, 3, 120*n*33
Amsterdam
—Rijksmuseum: sketch of an equestrian monument, 104, 108
—Stedelijk Museum: sketch of a Deposition, 130*n*148
Anguiscola, Sofonisba: drawing of a crying boy, 45, 127*n*99
Apelles, 69
Aretino, Pietro, 1, 3
Armenini, Giovanni Battista, 61
Attribution methods, 5–11, 37–56, 104–5, 122*n*1, 126*n*85, 130*n*158, 138*nn*21–22, 139–40*n*29, 140*n*38, 141*n*53, 143*n*58, 145–46*n*45, 146*n*4, 147*n*51; consequences of misattribution, 9
Authentication, criteria for: 37; written evidence, 38, 39; autograph measurements, 40; coexistence of drawings with autographs, 40–41; contemporary written and pictorial evidence, 41–49; evidence of function, 49–56

Bandinelli, Baccio, 49, 113
Bayonne, Musée Bonnat: *no. 650*, 83, 128*n*109; *no. 681* (fig. 70), 80, 81; *no. 682* (fig. 46), 10–11, 24, 27; *no. 1217* (fig. 67), 79–82, 83–85 *passim*
Beginner's style, 10, 17, 23, 25, 28, 69, 70, 83, 84, 91
Berlin, Kupferstichkabinett: Giulio Romano's *Resurrection* drawing (fig. 86), 7; copy after *Children's Bacchanal* (fig. 26), 33–34, 46; *no. 15305r*, 133*n*176
Bertoldo di Giovanni, 92
Bettini, Bartolommeo, 2
Boston, Isabella Stewart Gardner Museum: *B400*, 21, 30, 51–52, 58, 132*n*173; Colonna *Pietà* copy, 129*n*130
Bracci, Cecchino, 40, 140*n*32
Bugiardini, Giuliano, 3; *Martyrdom of St. Catherine*, 61, 119–20*n*31; portrait of Michelangelo, 123*n*36
Buonarroti, Buonarroto, 41, 68, 111
Buonarroti, Cassandra, 87

Buonarroti, Francesco Simone, 68
Buonarroti, Lionardo, 3, 87, 116
Buonarroti, Lodovico, 148*n*12
Buonarroti, Michelangelo: estate, 1, 2, 87, 88; ideal of perfection, 2, 135*n*23; characteristics of draftsmanship, 9, 16, 17, 33, 52, 56–66, 69, 71; stylistic revivals, 10, 11, 140–41*n*49; working hand, 41; working procedures, 49, 51–56, 61–63; media used, 50, 60–61; use of the sheet, 58–59; helping Bugiardini, 61; memory, 61–62; moving from idea to realization, 61–62; writing exercises, 69; drawing exercises, 69, 70; anecdote concerning the completing of a half figure, 69–70; traces of tremor, 71–72; ideal of beauty, 78; theory of movement and composition, 92–93; asked to design an equestrian monument, 104; Cupid forgery, 112; and Piero de' Medici, 112–13; portraits of, 123*n*36; apprenticeship contract, 137*n*22
—Cartoons: *Christ's Farewell*, 3, 87, 142*n*25; *Crucifixion of St. Peter*, 2, 10, 20, 55–56; *Pietà*, 142*n*21; squaring, lacking, 134*n*194
—Drawings: lost, 1–3; fate of, 1–4; given away to friends, 2–3; alleged number of, 3–4, 8–9; "lascivious," 4, 120*n*36; arrangement on the sheets, 29–30, 58–59; as subjects of copies, 30–31, 50; signed, 38; authenticated by written evidence, 38–39; illustrating autograph, 39–40; coexisting with autograph, 40–41; of M.'s "invenzione," 41–49; list of authenticated, 57; figure sizes, 59–60, 72, 135*nn*4–5; formulas, 63; contours, 63–64; kinetic rhythm, 63–64; reinforcements, 64; revisions, 64; hatching, 64–66; attributable to M., 67; penmanship, 69; framed, 125*n*66; storing of sheets, 134–35*n*2; mediums used, 135*n*6. Individual drawings: anatomical studies, 67, 136*n*4; *Annunciation*, 3, 20, 64, 65, 72, 114–17, 121*n*7, 150*n*28, 151*n*54; Apostles (*Gethsemane*), 3, 49, 67, 72, 115–16; *Archers*, 31, 33–34, 42–43; arm study, 9, 22, 25–26, 29, 38; *Brazen Serpent*, 31–32, 47; *Children's Bacchanal*, 31–32, 33–34, 46, 83; *Christ and the Samaritan Woman*, 129*n*129; *Christ in Limbo*, 21, 33–34, 42, 45, 77,

Buonarroti, Michelangelo (continued)
124–25nn56–57; Cleopatra, 44–45, 78;
copies after Ghirlandaio, 67, 70; copy
after Giotto, 67; copy after Schongauer,
148n11; Crucified Haman, 21, 30, 50,
51–52, 58, 76, 77; Crucifix for V. Colonna, 24, 32, 47–48, 94–95, 96–99
passim, 114–15, 145n33; Crucifixion,
95; David, 9, 16, 22–27 passim, 29, 38,
58, 61, 64–65; Dream of Human Life,
33, 43, 122n35, 126n74; Ganymede, 31,
43–44, 126n76; hand for Riario's agent,
61; hand pointing, 22, 23, 25, 40–41,
135n21; hand with book, 40–41; head in
profile, 41, 58; Hercules for the Fer-
rarese, 61; Hercules sketch, 18, 19, 21,
41, 58, 64, 111–14; incidental sketches,
67; Julius tomb, 132–33n176; kneeling
girl, 70; Last Judgment, 52–55, 58–59,
62, 65, 79–82, 133n180; Leda, 2, 4;
legs, 69; Libyan Sibyl, 10, 21–24 passim, 26, 29, 30, 50–51, 52, 58; Madonna, 18, 23, 24, 27, 67, 68, 71–72;
marble blocks, 40, 95; Medici tombs,
38–39, 52, 67, 133n178;
Phaeton, 20–24 passim, 39, 45–46, 63,
65–66; Philosopher, 21, 24, 25, 67; pictogram of a raven, 40; pictograms of food,
40; Pietà or Entombment, 48, 49,
55–56, 58–59, 62–63, 72, 134n199;
Pietà for V. Colonna, 83; portrait of
Cavalieri, 78–79; practice sketches, 67;
proportion study, 136n5; Prudentia,
124n53; rebus, 70–71; Resurrection,
5–7 passim, 32, 46–47, 80; Risen
Christ, 32, 45, 77; river gods, 18–19, 40,
64; St. Anne, 18, 25, 28, 38, 41, 58,
124n49; self-caricature, 39–40; self-
portrait, alleged, 123n36; slave sketches,
10, 21, 29, 52, 58, 59; slave studies, 67,
136n5; "teste divine," 44–45, 67,
127n93, 136–37n6; Tityos, 23, 26, 44,
79, 126n76
—Paintings: Battle of Cascina, 61; Crucified Haman, 52; Crucifixion of St. Peter,
55–56, 91, 94–95; Fall of the Rebel
Angels, 53; Last Judgment, 53, 54;
Leda, 4
—Sculptures: Bacchus, 112; Battle of
Centaurs, 124n49; Brutus, 87; David
(bozzetto), 113, 149n24; David (bronze),
38, 122n10; David (marble), 38,
149n24; Giuliano, 79; Hercules, 41,

111–14, 149nn19–20; Hercules and
Cacus, 113–14; Julius tomb, 52; Ma-
donna of the Stairs, 124n49; Pietà
Rondanini, 56, 72; river god, 40; snow-
man, 113
Buonarroto di Simone, 111

Calvaert, Denis: forgeries, 50, 130–31n161
Cambiaso, Luca, 105
Cambridge (Mass.), Fogg Art Museum:
no. 1955.750 (fig. 17), 31, 43–44;
Resurrection painting (fig. 84), 7, 107
Caro, Annibale, 86–88 passim
Caro, Porzia, 86
Casa, Giovanni della, 102, 103
Casteldurante, 114
Castiglione, Baldassare, 75
Cavalieri, Tommaso de', 2–3, 6, 42, 87, 99,
115, 116; drawing collection, 3, 43; and
Michelangelo, 39, 43, 44–45, 46, 75–85,
127n99; letter to Cosimo de' Medici, 45;
figure and composition style, 82–84, 93;
drawing style, 84–85; development as
draftsman, 85
—Drawings: arrangement on the sheets,
83; Children's Bacchanal, 128n109;
Cleopatra, 44–45, 78, 127n100; Deposition, 128n109; figure sizes, 82–83;
Ganymede, 44, 84, 85, 126n85; head
studies, 83; Last Judgment, 79–82, 84,
85; lost, allegedly, 11; Phaeton, 24, 39,
75–76, 81, 83, 84; Risen Christ, 44, 53,
76–77, 84, 139n25; self-portraits,
77–78; "teste divine," 77–78,
139–40n29; torso studies, 141nn60, 64
Cellini, Benvenuto: 2, 11, 26, 27; hatching
style, 27; inspired by Michelangelo's
Hercules, 114
—Drawings: arm study, 22, 23, 25–26,
29–30; arrangement on a sheet, 29–30;
battle of horsemen, 19, 30; bearded
head, 29–30; lost, allegedly, 11; Madonna, 16–19 passim; male nude, 22,
23, 25–26, 27, 29–30; male nude seen
from the rear, 21, 26, 27; statue
sketches, 30; striding nude, 21, 27;
youth hurrying, 26
Cesari, Bernardino: copy after the Archers,
34, 42–43
Chantilly, Musée Condé: copy after the
Prudentia, 124n53
Chatsworth, Duke of Devonshire: copy
after The Dream, 122n35

Clement VII, 53
Clovio, Giulio: 5–7 passim, 11, 23,
130n148; inventory, 5, 31, 45–47
passim, 125n64, 128nn117, 119; signatures, 5–7 passim, 23, 31, 42, 121n28,
125n62; as copyist of Michelangelo
drawings, 42, 45, 46–47, 124n53,
128n117, 129n131, 136n4
—Drawings: left to Alessandro Farnese,
122n1, 136n4; anatomical, 136n4;
Archers copy, 31; Crucifixion, 145n35;
Flagellation, 121n28; guard for a Resurrection, 21; Lamentation, 22–23, 26, 28;
leg and foot studies, 22, 26; lost, allegedly, 11; Prudentia copy, 124n53; Resurrection, 5–7, 21–23 passim, 26–27,
28, 42, 47; Tityos copy, 23, 26–27, 44
—Miniatures: David and Goliath, 107;
Resurrection, 7
—Paintings: Expulsion of the Moneychangers, 103, 105–6, 107; Resurrec-
tion, 7, 107
Colonelli, Cornelia, 114, 116
Colonna, Vittoria, 47; correspondence with
Michelangelo, 48
Condivi, Ascanio: 3, 61, 99, 144n73; and
Michelangelo, 86–87, 91–93; bust of
Sulla, 87, 88; theory and practice,
91–93; non-finito, 92; figure style, 92;
errors in Michelangelo biography,
112–13, 148n11, 148–49n15
—Cartoon of the Epiphany, 10, 20, 87–90,
91, 92, 144n73; its history, 87–88; its
style, 89–90
—Drawings: anatomical studies, 86; lost,
allegedly, 11; sketches, 91, 92
—Paintings: Epiphany, 87, 88, 89; Holy
Family, 90–91, 144n73
Condivi, Ceccone, 86
Condivi, Sebastiano, 86
Conte, Jacopino del, 41; portrait of Michelangelo, 41, 123n36; quoting from
Michelangelo's Archers, 43
Contour, 17–21; with sawtooth profile, 17,
21; consisting of modulated or thread
strokes, 18; closed or with gaps, 18–19;
axial shifts, 19; pentimento, 19, 20;
single- or multiple-line, 19–21; simple
or strengthened, 21
Copies: characteristics, 17, 20, 23, 31–34,
45–47 passim, 64; how recognized,
30–34; tracing, 31, 42; how produced,
31–33; heuristic potential, 57

Count of Canossa, 136–37n6
Coypel, Antoine, 98, 99
Crispi, Tiberio, 86

Daniele da Volterra, 3, 87; letter of 17
March 1564, 49, 88, 115–16, 142n25,
147n53; "modello" of *David and Goliath*, 103; and Michelangelo, 104, 106–7;
estate, 104, 142n21, 147n24; and modern scholarship, 104–5; sketching methods, 107–8; slowness of working, 108;
drawing style, 108–9; fame, 146n1
—Drawings: related to Daniele's works,
102–4; attributed to, 104–5; sketches
and studies, 109; copied by pupils,
146n4; attributed to Daniele, 147n29.
Individual drawings: *Aeneas and Ascanius*, 23, 102, 104–5, 108; Apostles, 22,
23, 28, 30, 104, 105; *David and Goliath*,
28, 30, 103, 146n14; equestrian monument, 104, 108; *Expulsion of the Moneychangers*, 20, 30, 103, 105–8; *John the
Baptist in the Desert*, 103; leg study, 30;
lost, allegedly, 11
—Paintings: *Assunta*, 106; *David and Goliath*, 103, 107; for Giovanni della Casa,
102–3; *Massacre of the Innocents*, 106,
108; *Moses and the Worship of the Golden Calf*, 108; *Speech of Quintus Fabius
Maximus*, 106
Della Casa, Giovanni, 102, 103
Della Palla, Giovanni Battista, 149n20
Della Torre, Aloisio, 87
Dipignere and *colorire*, 88
Donatello, 135n23; bronze *David*, 38
Donato di Bertino, 111
Drawing behavior: pressure and course,
15–16; direction and shape, 16; rhythm,
16–17; speed and its indicators, 16–17,
19; forms of pausing, 17; organization of
the sheet's surface, 28–30; with chalk or
pen and ink, 61; abbreviations, 63
Drawings: heuristic value of, 9; as pro-
duced by manual movements, 15; origi-
nal and copy, 30–34. See also Contour;
Copies; Hatching; Stroke typology
Drawing styles: local, 10. See also Beginner's style, Hatching
Duca, Jacopo del: as recipient of sketches
by Michelangelo, 3, 49, 115–16;
sketches for *Deposition*, 130n148
Dürer, Albrecht, 15
Dussler, Luitpold: cataloguing method, 7–8

Este, Ippolito, cardinal: drawing collection,
130–31n161
Este, Lucrezia d', 114

Farnese, Alessandro: drawing collection, 3,
122n1, 136n4
Florence
—Archivio Buonarroti: *I/154, fol. 274*, 95;
II/III, fol. 3v (fig. 1), 67, 68–69; *V/38,
fol. 213v*, 67; *VI, fol. 24v* (fig. 60), 76,
77; *X, fol. 578v* (fig. 43), 40; *XIII,
fol. 33r*, 40; *XIII, fol. 111* (fig. 39),
39–40; *XIII, fol. 145v*, 67; *XIII, fol.
169v* (fig. 41), 22, 23, 26, 40–41
—Casa Buonarroti: *no. 107A-r*, 67; *no. 2F*
(fig. 13), 45, 127n100; *no. 19F-r*, 103;
no. 19F-v, 102–3, 108; *no. 30F*, 67;
no. 32F, 21; *no. 44F* (fig. 90), 26, 27;
no. 47F, 80; *no. 57F-r*, 67; *no. 60F*, 67;
no. 61F-v (fig. 49), 20–21, 42; *no. 65F-r*
(fig. 30), 53, 62, 79–80, 82, 133n180;
no. 65F-v (fig. 59), 53, 76–77, 84; *no.
66F* (fig. 48), 20–21, 42; *no. 69F-r*, 80,
81–82, 83, 141n60, 141n64; *no. 69F-v*
(fig. 69), 80, 81, 147n29; *no. 73F-r*
(fig. 78), 21; *David* (bozzetto), 113,
149n24; *Hercules and Cacus* bozzetto,
113–14
—Uffizi: *no. 598E*, 127n93; *no. 599E*,
127n93; *no. 601E*, 127n93; *no. 611E*
(fig. 58), 44, 85, 126n85; *no. 614E*,
124n53; *no. 229F* (fig. 102), 3, 100, 115,
116; *no. 230F* (fig. 103), 3, 49, 100, 116;
no. 6550F, 67, 136n5; *no. 2318F* (fig. 7),
26, 30, 50–51, 58, 132nn167–68; *no.
14965F*, 103; *no. 126S*, 42–43; *no.
17371F*, 128–29n125; *no. 170S* (fig. 68),
79–82, 84; *no. 1450S* (fig. 63), 77,
139n25
Fontainebleau: *David and Goliath* painting,
103, 107
Forgeries, 23, 50, 130–31n161, 131n163,
133n179; 147n29
Francis I, 40
Franco, Battista: quoting from Michelangelo drawings, 43
Frankfurt, Städelsches Kunstinstitut: *no.
3975* (fig. 28), 7, 32, 46; *no. 3976* (fig.
15), 21, 33–34, 42, 45, 124–25n56,
125n57; *no. 3978* (fig. 116), 98, 99;
no. 3979 (copy after *The Archers*),
42–43

Geneva, Martin Bodmer Foundation: draw-
ing of the *Samaritan Woman*, 129n129
Ghirlandaio, Domenico, 148n11
Giovanni di Benedetto da Pistoja, 40
Granacci, Francesco, 2, 69, 70, 148n11
Grechi, Michaeli, 106, 147n45

Haarlem, Teylers Museum: *A16r*, 51,
132n172; *A20v*, 147n29; *A26*, 67,
136n5; *A27r*, 127n93; *A29r*, 104, 107;
A29v (fig. 125), 102, 104; *A31r*,
147n29; *A32r* (fig. 126), 103–5; *A32v*
(fig. 121), 102, 104–5, 108; *A90*, 121n33
Hatching, 21–28; internal and external, 21,
24–25; styles, 21–22; "cross-hatching,"
22; density, 22–23, 26; wiping, 23;
strength, 23; direction, 24–25; shape,
25–26; composition, 26–27; seams, 26–
27; terrain hatching, 26–27; assemblages joined at sharp angles, 27; hooked
and soldered assemblages, 27; distribution, 27–28
Hercules: bronze statue from Forum Boarium, 113; as symbol of Medici power,
148n13. See also Buonarroti, Michelangelo: Drawings, Sculptures

Jacopo del Duca. See Duca, Jacopo del
Julius III, 86

Lafréry, Antoine: engravings after Michelangelo drawings, 42, 43
Landucci, Luca, 112
Lionardo del Sellaio (or del Compagno), 1,
3, 4
Lombardi, Alfonso: 3; tomb of Leo X and
Clement VII, 119–20n31
London
—Brinsley-Ford Collection: studies after
the Christ statue in Sta. Maria sopra
Minerva, 120n55
—British Museum: *no. 1859-5-14-818r*
(fig. 55), 24, 25, 27; *no. 1859-5-14-820*
(fig. 88), 22, 26; *no. 1859-6-25-543r*
(fig. 12), 38–39, 52; *no. 1859-6-25-544r*
(fig. 40), 18–19, 40, 64; *no. 1859-6-25-
562* (fig. 38), 18, 23, 24, 27, 67, 71–72;
no. 1860-6-16-2/1, 107–8; *no. 1860-6-
16-2/2* (figs. 128–29), 103, 105–7,
107–8; *no. 1860-6-16-2/3* (figs. 127,
130), 20, 103, 105–7, 108; *no. 1860-6-
16-5*, 130–31n161; *no. 1860-6-16-133*
(fig. 27), 7, 32, 46–47; *no. 1860-7-14-1*

London (continued)
(fig. 47), 10–11, 24, 27; no. 1885-5-9-
1894, 67; no. 1887-5-2-116, 120n55;
no. 1887-5-2-117r (fig. 80), 26; no. 1895-
9-15-492, 136–37n6; no. 1895-9-15-
493r, 67, 136–37n6; no. 1895-9-15-494,
67; no. 1895-9-15-496r (fig. 74), 19,
30; no. 1895-9-15-497r (fig. 10), 21,
30, 51–52, 58; no. 1895-9-15-497v,
132n171; no. 1895-9-15-498r (fig. 3),
21, 24, 25, 67; no. 1895-9-15-501r
(fig. 14), 21, 33–34, 42, 45, 124–25n56,
125n57; no. 1895-9-15-504 (fig. 33), 24,
32, 47; no. 1895-9-15-509 (fig. 111), 25,
94–98; no. 1895-9-15-510 (fig. 109),
94–98; no. 1895-9-15-516r (fig. 100),
10–11, 18, 20, 41, 100, 115, 147n29,
151n52; no. 1895-9-15-517 (fig. 23), 21,
24, 39, 65–66; no. 1895-9-15-518r
(fig. 32), 53, 54, 62, 65, 80, 81; no. 1895-
9-15-518v, 80, 83; no. 1895-9-15-
518+, 10, 20, 87–90, 91, 92, 144n73;
no. 1895-9-15-654 (fig. 87), 22–23, 26,
28; no. 1900-6-11-1v, 145–46n45;
no. 1926-10-9-1r, 131–32n166;
no. 1946-7-13-114 (fig. 119), 22, 23,
28, 30, 105; no. 1956-10-13-8/-20,
146n4; no. 1956-10-13-13 (fig. 120),
102, 108; Ff.1–5r, 124n53; Add. Ms.
21907, fol. 1, 67, 137n8; Fawkener
5211–75, 145n42
—Courtauld Institute: Christ on the Cross,
97; The Dream, 33, 43, 122n35,
126n74; drawing of a Last Judgment,
133n179
—National Gallery: Expulsion of the
Moneychangers, 103, 105–6, 107
—Seilern Collection: drawing of Aeneas
and Ascanius, 102, 108

Massarelli, Claudio, 121n25, 128nn117, 119
Medici, Catherine de', 104
Medici, Cosimo de', the Elder, 148n13
Medici, Cosimo I de', 1, 3, 45, 116
Medici, Giuliano de', 39
Medici, Ippolito de', 39
Medici, Lorenzo de', the Magnificent, 39,
112, 148n13
Medici, Piero de', 112–13, 148n12
Methods: of cataloguing, 7–8; of stylistic
evaluation, 11; of recognizing original
and copy, 30–34; of authentication, 37;
of dating, 95–96, 111–12, 139–40n29.
See also Attribution methods
Michelangelo. See Buonarroti,
Michelangelo
Mini, Antonio, 2, 4, 25, 39, 92; as owner
of Louvre no. 685 (figs. 2, 4), 38; as
owner of "teste divine," 127n93
—Drawings: Faun's head, 27, 28; lost,
allegedly, 11; Madonna sketches, 24, 25,
27; old woman with boy, 9–11, 28; St.
Peter after Masaccio, 9–11, 25, 28;
"teste divine" copies, 127n93; woman
with mirror, 39, 123n18
Minos, 53
Montelupo, Raffaello: copy after Children's
Bacchanal, 128n108
Morone, Giovanni, 87
Munich, Staatliche Graphische Sammlung:
no. 2191r (fig. 53), 9–11, 25, 28

Nanni di Baccio Bigio, 3
Naples, Museo Nazionale: Crucifixion of
St. Peter (fig. 34), 2, 10, 20, 55, 91
New York
—Metropolitan Museum: no. 24.197.2r
(fig. 8), 22, 26, 30, 50–51, 58,
132nn167–68; no. 24.197.2v, 58; draw-
ing of a Last Judgment, 133n179
—Pierpont Morgan Library: no. I/32a–c,
103, 146n14; no. IV/7 (fig. 101), 20,
40–41, 100, 115, 116; copy after The
Dream, 122n35
Niccolini, Bernardo, 40
Norfolk, Brakley Collection: copy after the
Colonna Crucifix, 121n33; copy after
The Dream, 122n35

Original and copy: how recognized, 30–34;
how currently distinguished, 31
Orsini, Fulvio: 2, 87; inventory, 89,
125n66
Oxford, Ashmolean Museum: Parker no.
210, 146n4; Parker no. 291v (fig.77), 26,
27; Parker no. 296v, 147n29; Parker no.
297r (fig.6), 21–24 passim, 26, 29, 30,
50–51, 52, 58, 59; Parker no. 297v, 58;
Parker no. 309r (fig. 89), 23; Parker no.
311v (fig. 62), 76–77; Parker no. 315
(fig. 65), 77–78, 139n29; Parker no.
318r (fig. 29), 31–32, 47; Parker no.
318v, 47; Parker no. 324, 9–11, 28;
Parker no. 328r (fig. 123), 28, 30, 103,
105–7, 146n14; Parker no. 335 (fig. 92),
91; Parker no. 338, 103; Parker no. 339
(fig. 35), 49, 55–56, 58–59, 62–63, 72,
134n199; Parker no. 340 (fig. 36), 49,
72, 115–17; Parker no. 343r (fig. 105),
94–98; Parker no. 345 (fig. 37), 3, 20,
64, 65, 72, 114–17, 121n7, 150n28,
151n54; Parker no. 370, 146n4; painting of a Holy Family (fig. 99), 90–91,
92, 144n73

Pacheco, Francisco: as owner of a copy
after the Ganymede, 126n80
Paragone, 103
Paris
—Louvre, Cabinet des Dessins: no. 684r
(fig. 52), 27; no. 685r (fig. 4), 18, 19, 21,
25, 28, 38, 41, 58, 64, 111–14, 124n49;
no. 685v, 67, 70–71, 111–12; no. 689v,
16–19 passim; no. 698 (fig. 113), 98, 99,
100; no. 700 (fig. 110), 94–98; no. 706r,
67; no. 714r (fig. 5), 9, 16, 22–24
passim, 25–27 passim, 29, 38, 58, 61,
64–65; no. 716, 141n60; no. 720r (fig.
112), 96, 98, 99; no. 720v (fig. 104), 94,
96, 98; no. 733, 45; no. 842r (fig. 108),
97; no. 843 (fig. 114), 98, 99; no. 1505,
45; nos. 1512–13, 103; no. 2716,
147n35; R.F. 70-1068r, 21, 27;
R.F. 70-1068v (fig. 75), 22, 23, 25–26,
27, 29–30; R.F. 70-28961r, 131–
32n166
—Wildenstein Collection: Clovio's David
and Goliath miniature, 107
Pasquino (mule driver), 114
Perini, Gherardo; as owner of "teste divine" by Michelangelo, 127n93
Polidoro da Caravaggio, 106, 147n45
Protogenes, 69

Quality, 11
Quaratesi, Andrea, 125n64

Raphael, 49
Riario, Raffaele, 112
Ricciarelli. See Daniele da Volterra
Riccio, Luigi del, 40
Ridolfi, Lorenzo, 87
Ridolfi, Niccolò, 87, 142n14
Ripatransone, 86, 87
Rocchetti, Jacomo, 132–33n176
Rohan, Pierre de, 38

Romano, Giulio: 4; *Resurrection* draw-
   ing, 7
Rome
—Galleria Doria-Pamphili: *Crucifixion*
   (fig. 117), 99–100, 114–15
—Galleria Nazionale: *Annunciation*, 115,
   151*n*52; *Gethsemane*, 130*n*149
—Palazzo Massimo: frieze by Daniele, 106
—Pauline Chapel, 103
—San Pietro in Montorio: Ricci Chapel,
   104, 105
Sistine Chapel, 53
—SS. Trinità de' Monti: frescoes in the
   Rovere Chapel, 106
—Vatican Library, *Cod. Vat. 3211: fol. 74r*
   (fig. 42), 40–41; *fol. 93r*, 135–36*n*1
Rosso Fiorentino, 49
Rotterdam, Boymans Museum: *I,20*,
   139*n*25
Rovere, Guidobaldo della, 114
Rubens, Peter Paul: *Hercules* drawing,
   149*n*24
Rustici, Giovanni Francesco, 2

Sansovino, Andrea, 49
Sebastiano del Piombo, 2, 6, 10, 27, 42, 85,
   131*n*163, 141*n*60; estate, 3: hatching
   style, 27–28
—Drawings: *Flagellation*, 128*n*117; lost,
   allegedly, 11; male nudes, 20–21, 42;
   Risen Lazarus, 10–11, 24, 27
—Paintings: *Christ in Limbo*, 125*n*57;
   Flagellation, 125*n*57
Soye, Philipp: *Crucifixion* engraving, 99

Squaring, 134*n*194, 146*n*4
Stockholm, National Gallery: copy after
   Daniele's *Aeneas* painting, 102, 104, 105
Stroke typology: formulaic strokes, 16;
   modulated and thread strokes, 16; stroke
   heads, 17
Strozzi, Clarice, 149*n*20
Strozzi, Filippo, 149*n*20

Tempesta, Antonio: engravings after "teste
   divine," 136–37*n*6

Urbino (Michelangelo's factotum). *See*
   Amadori, Francesco

Varchi, Benedetto, 41
Vasari, Giorgio, 1–2, 3, 4, 42, 44, 45, 87,
   99, 113, 115–16; manner of discussing
   Condivi's work, 88, 142*n*25; deceiving
   tactic, 116
Vasto, Marchese del, 2
Vecchietti, Bernardo, 2
Venice, Academy: *no. 177* (fig. 66): 24, 39,
   75–76, 81, 83, 84
Venusti, Marcello: 3, 10, 28, 41, 105, 106,
   114, 117, 145*n*42; as alleged author of
   the *Resurrection* in Cambridge, 7;
   hatching style, 28; drawing method,
   100–1
—Cartoons: *Annunciation*, 3, 20, 41, 100,
   115, 116; *Gethsemane*, 3, 49, 100, 116
—Drawings: *Annunciation*, 10–11, 18, 20,
   41, 100, 115, 145–46*n*45, 151*n*52;
   Christ and the Samaritan Woman,

129*n*129; Colonna *Pietà* copy, 129*n*130;
   Crucifixion, 24–25, 94–100; figure sizes,
   100; lost, allegedly, 11
—Paintings: *Annunciation*, 115, 116;
   Crucifixion, 99–100, 114–15; *Gethsemane*, 49, 116, 130*n*149, 150*n*35; *Resurrection*, 7
Vienna, Albertina: *no. 497* (fig. 122), 23,
   102, 105; *Sc.L.206*, 42–43; *Sc.R.150*,
   67; *Sc.R.155r* (fig. 132), 23, 50;
   Sc.R.155v, 131*n*163
Windsor Castle, Royal Library: *no. 0418*,
   121*n*28, 128*n*117; *no. 0432*, 67; *no.
   0435r* (fig. 11), 21, 30, 51–52; *no. 0442r*
   (fig. 22), 31, 33–34, 42; *no. 0472r* (fig.
   20), 23, 26–27, 44; *no. 12761r* (fig. 107),
   24–25, 94–98; *no. 12761v*, 95; *no.
   12764* (fig. 64), 77–78, 139–40*n*29; *no.
   12765*, 67, 136*n*5; *no. 12766r* (fig. 24),
   20, 23, 24, 39, 63, 66; *no. 12766v*,
   123*n*18; *no. 12767r* (fig. 81), 5–7, 8, 21,
   22–23, 26–27, 28, 42; *no. 12767v* (fig.
   82), 5–7 passim, 23, 31, 42; *no. 12768*
   (fig. 16), 32, 45, 77; *no. 12771r* (fig. 19),
   23, 26, 44, 79, 126*n*76; *no. 12771v*
   (fig. 61), 44, 76–77; *no. 12775* (fig.
   106), 94–98; *no. 12776r* (fig. 31),
   53–54, 58–59, 80, 81; *no. 12776v* (fig.
   71), 80–83 passim; *no. 12777* (fig. 25),
   31–32, 33–34, 46; *no. 12778r* (fig. 21),
   31, 33–34, 42–43; *no. 12778v*, 125*n*64;
   no. 13036 (fig. 18), 31, 43–44

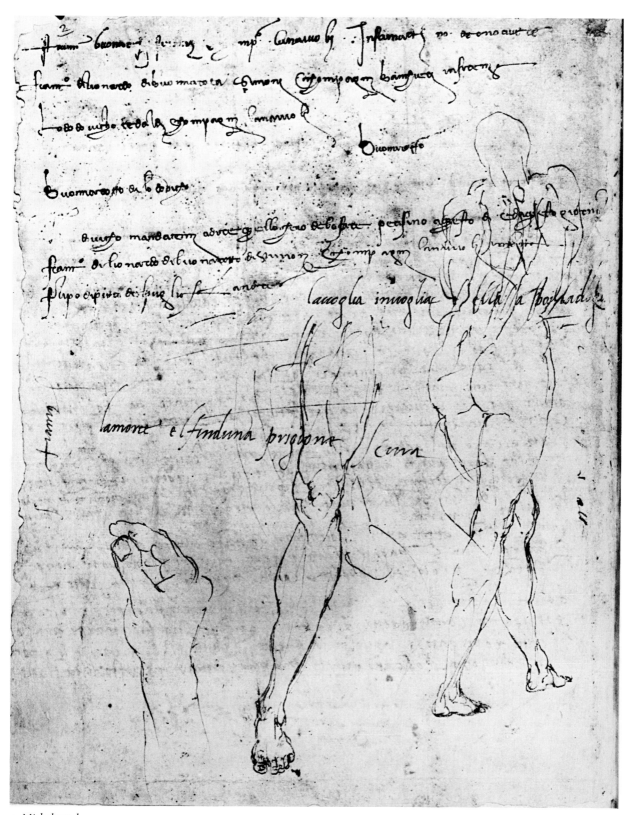

1. Michelangelo
Florence, Archivio Buonarroti, II/III, Fol. 3v: practice sketches, writing exercises; pen and ink; 27.5 × 21.5 cm.

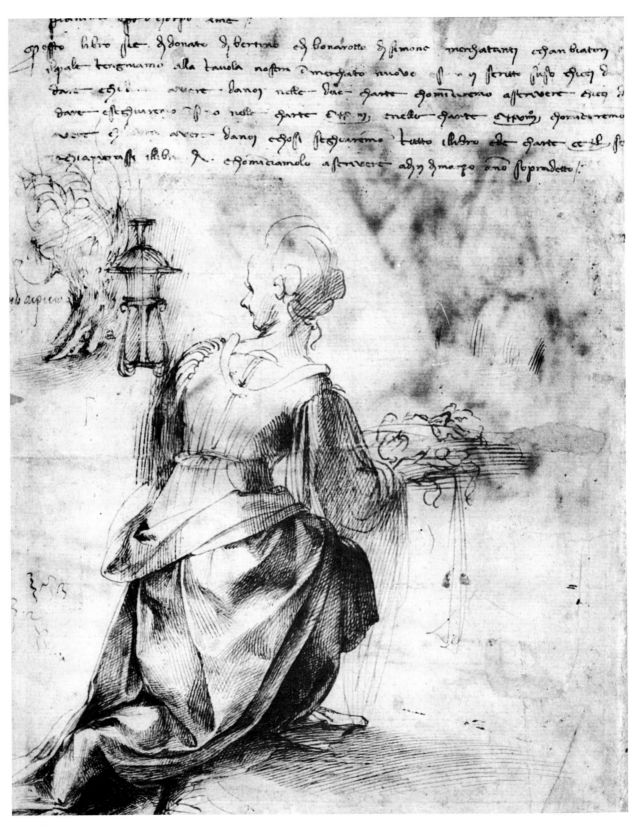

2. *Michelangelo*
Paris, Louvre, no. 685v: preface of a current account ledger, kneeling girl, eagle head, vessel; pen and ink, in part over black chalk (contour of the girl); 32.5 × 26.1 cm; cut (recto: fig. 4).

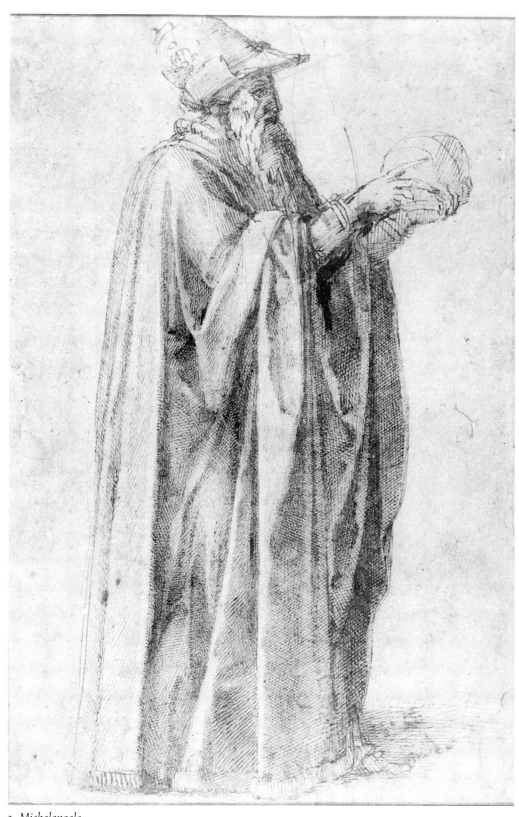

3. Michelangelo
London, British Museum, no. 1895-9-15-498r: draped male figure; pen and ink; 32.8 × 21.2 cm; cut.

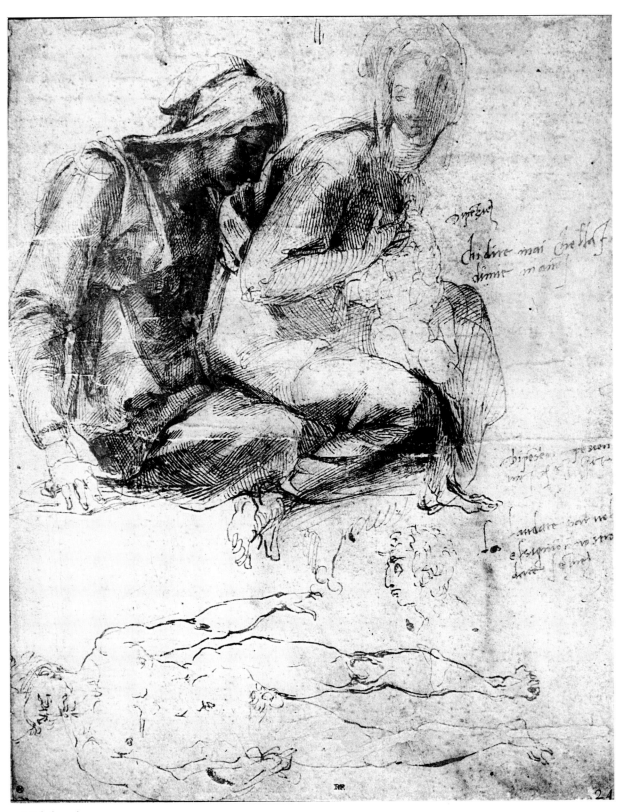

4. *Michelangelo*
Paris, Louvre, no. 685r: St. Anne, male nude, head in profile, manuscript texts; pen and ink, in part over black chalk (hatching of St. Anne); 32.5 × 26.1 cm; cut (verso: fig. 2).

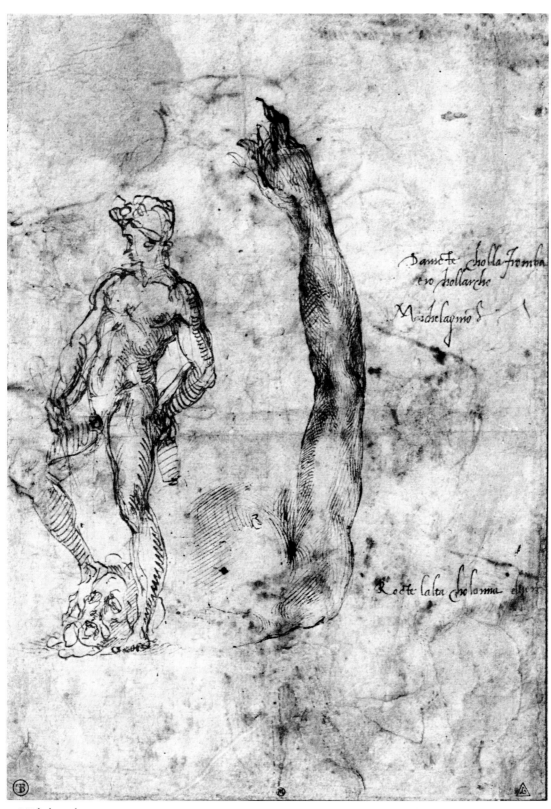

5. Michelangelo
Paris, Louvre, no. 714r: arm study, David sketch, manuscript texts; pen and ink; 26.5 × 18.8 cm; cut.

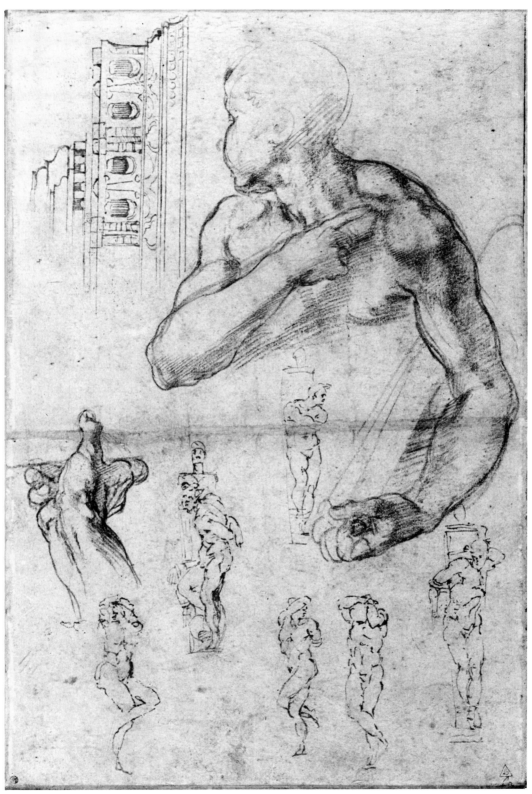

6. *Michelangelo*
Oxford, Ashmolean Museum, Parker no. 297: studies for the Libyan sibyl's companion and for the sibyl's right hand (red chalk); six slaves, entablature piece (pen and ink); 28.8 × 19.4 cm; cut.

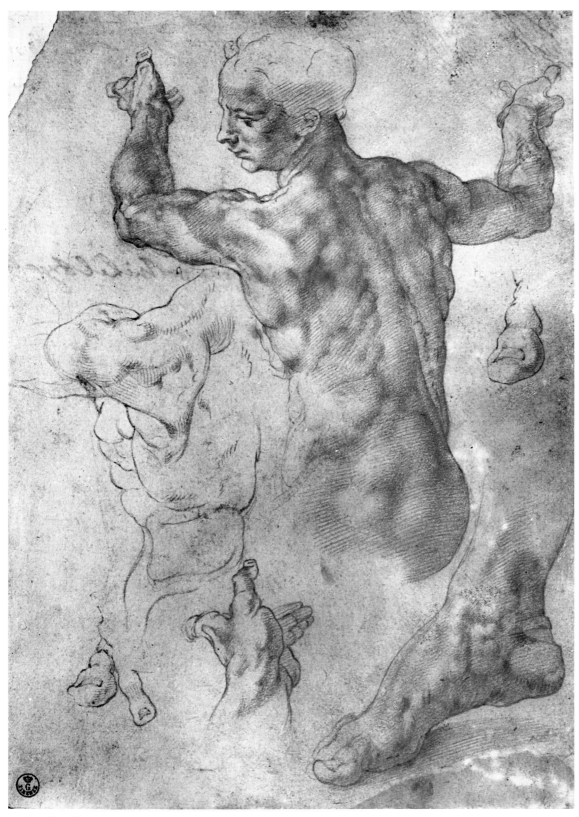

7. *Michelangelo*
Florence, Uffizi, no. 2318F: studies for the Libyan sibyl (copy); red chalk; 28.7 × 21.5 cm; cut.

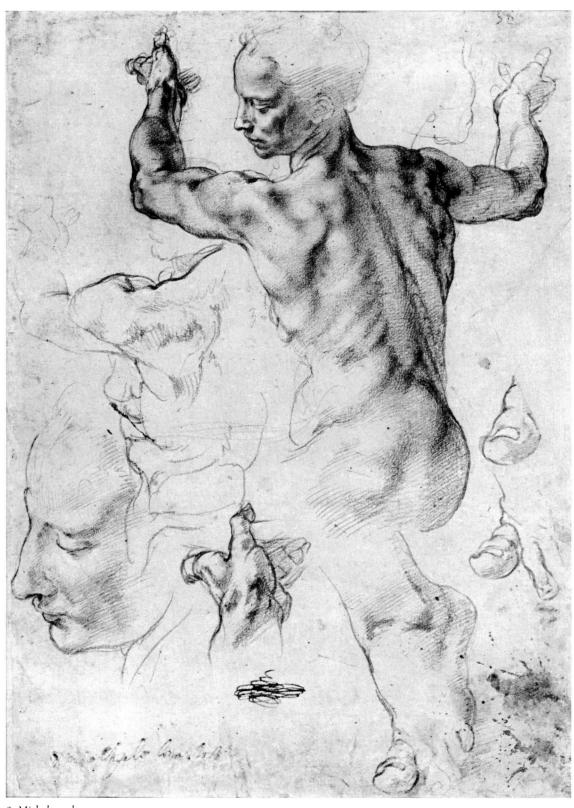

8. Michelangelo
New York, Metropolitan Museum, no. 24.197.2r: studies for the Libyan sibyl (copy); red chalk; 28.8 × 21.3 cm; cut.

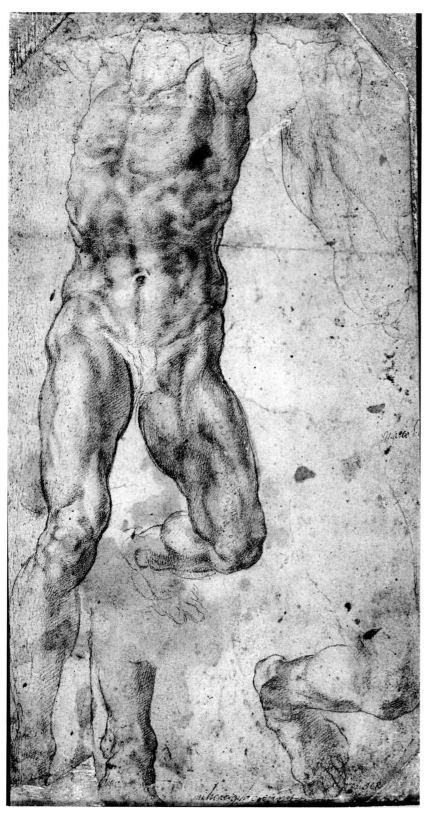

9. *Michelangelo*
Boston, Isabella Stewart Gardner Museum, B400: studies for the crucified Haman (copy);
red chalk; 36.3 × 19 cm; cut.

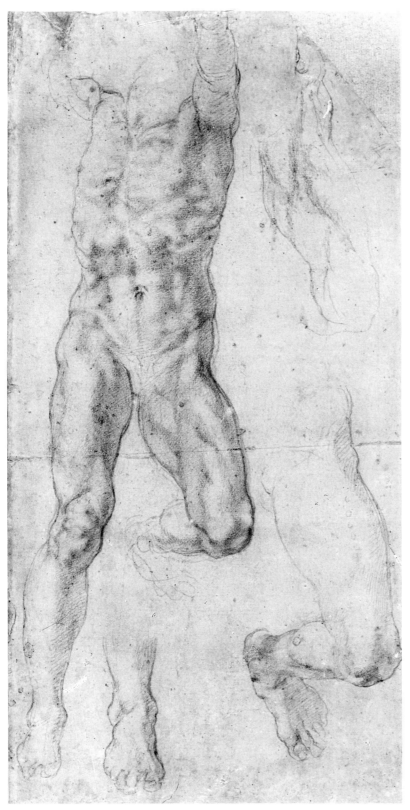

10. Michelangelo
London, British Museum, no. 1895-9-15-497r: studies for the crucified Haman (copy);
red chalk; 40.5 × 20.6 cm; cut.

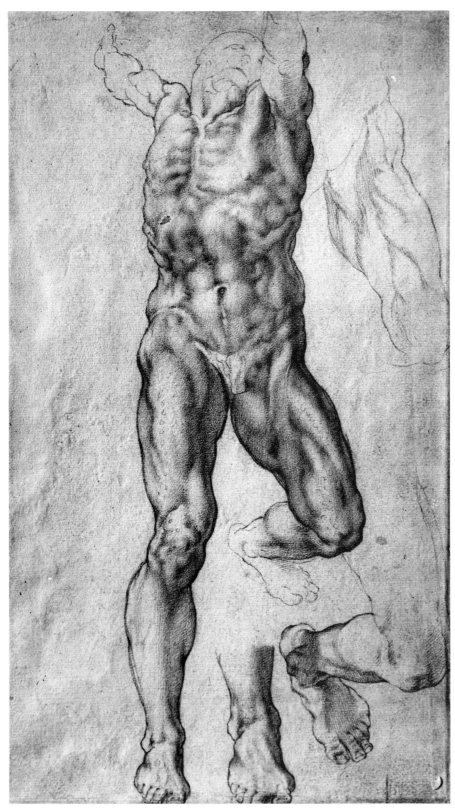

11. Michelangelo
Windsor Castle, Royal Library, no. 0435r: studies for the crucified Haman (copy); red chalk; 39 × 22.2 cm; cut.

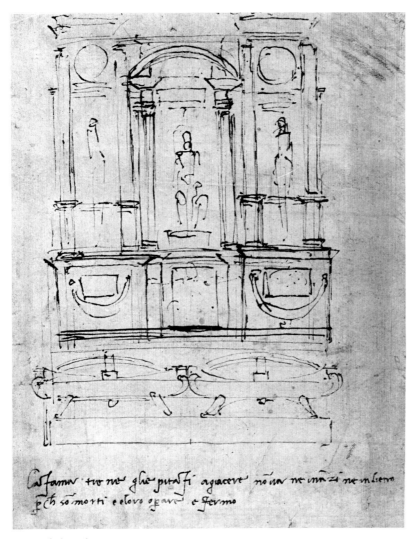

12. Michelangelo

London, British Museum, no. 1859-6-25-543r: sketch of a double tomb for Lorenzo the Magnificent and his brother
Giuliano de' Medici, annotation; pen and ink; 21 × 16 cm; cut.

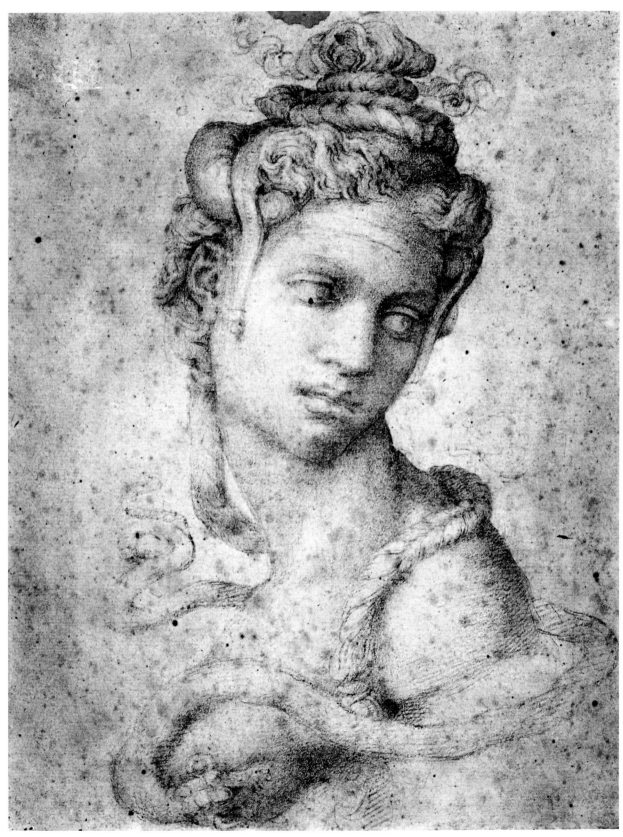

13. *Michelangelo*
Florence, Casa Buonarroti, no. 2F: bust of Cleopatra (copy); black chalk; 23.2 × 18.2 cm; cut.

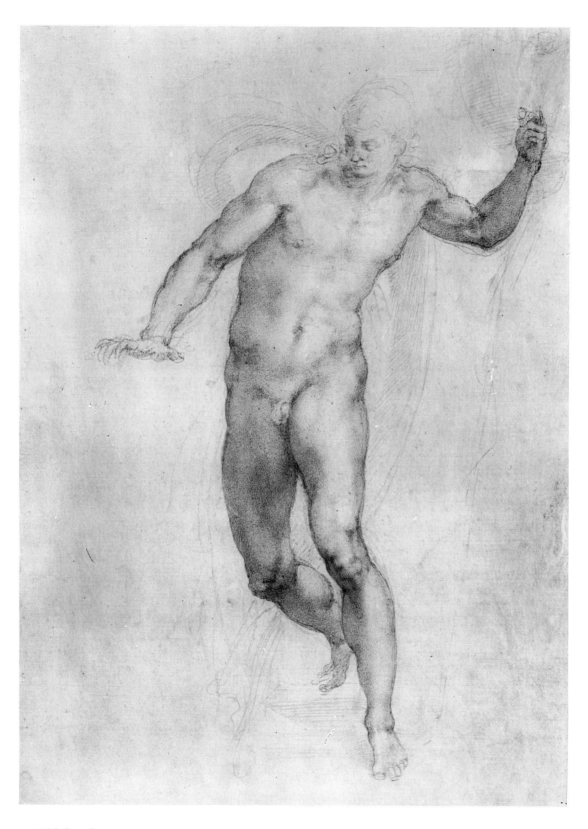

14. Michelangelo
London, British Museum, no. 1895-9-15-501r: Christ Descending to Hell (copy); black chalk; 40.5 × 26.5 cm; cut.

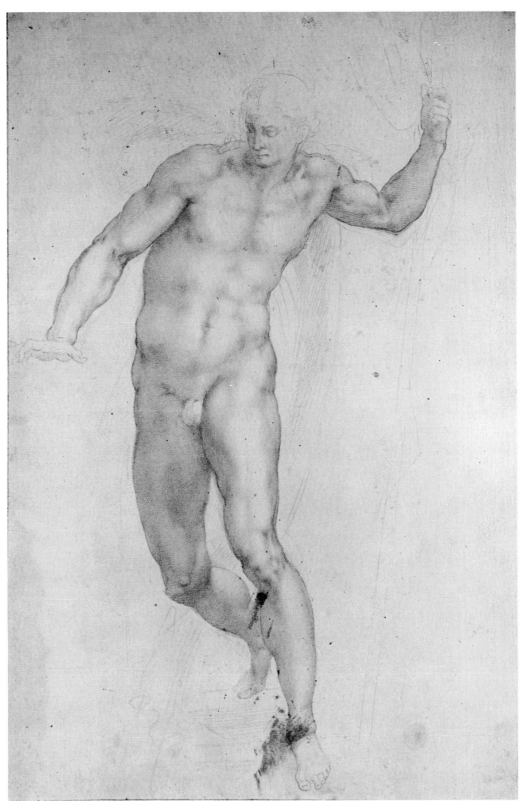

15. *Michelangelo*
Frankfurt, Städelsches Kunstinstitut, no. 3976: Christ Descending to Hell *(copy); black chalk; 37.3 × 22.1 cm; cut.*

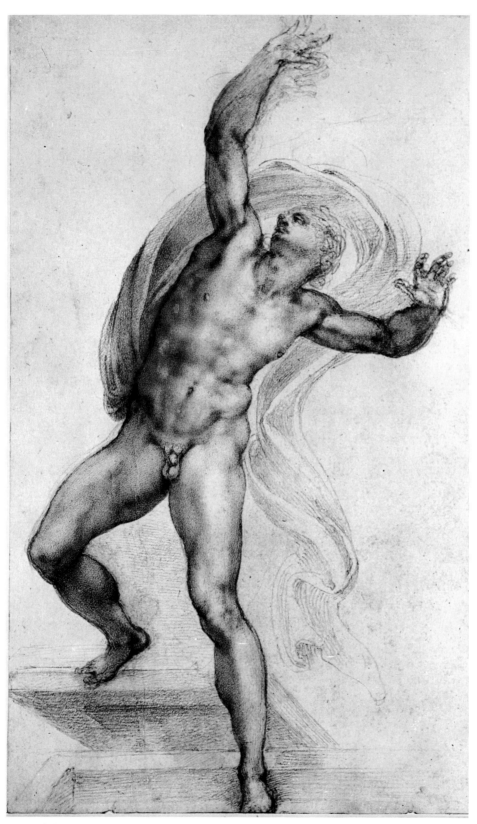

16. Michelangelo
Windsor Castle, Royal Library, no. 12768: Risen Christ *(copy); black chalk; 37.3 × 22.1 cm; cut.*

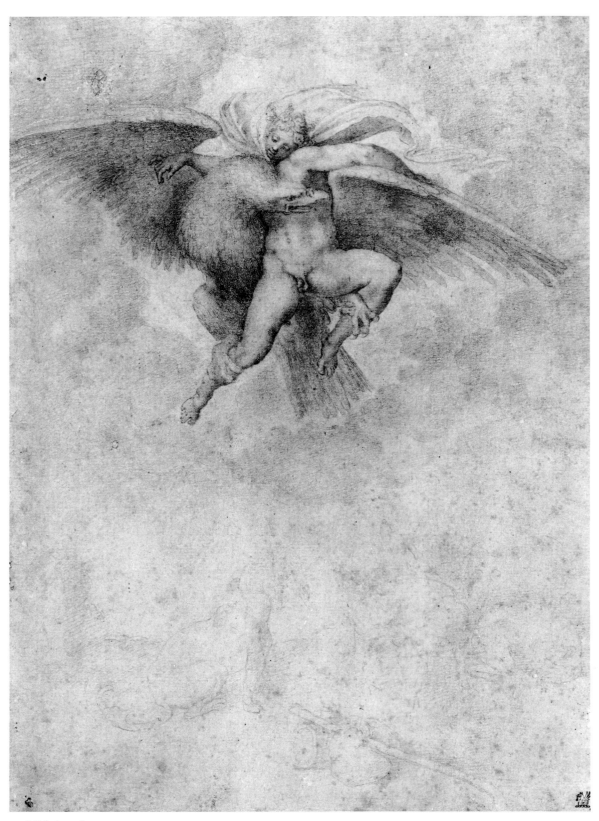

17. Michelangelo
Cambridge, Massachusetts, Fogg Art Museum, no. 1955.750: The Rape of Ganymede; *black chalk; 36.1 × 27.5 cm; cut.*

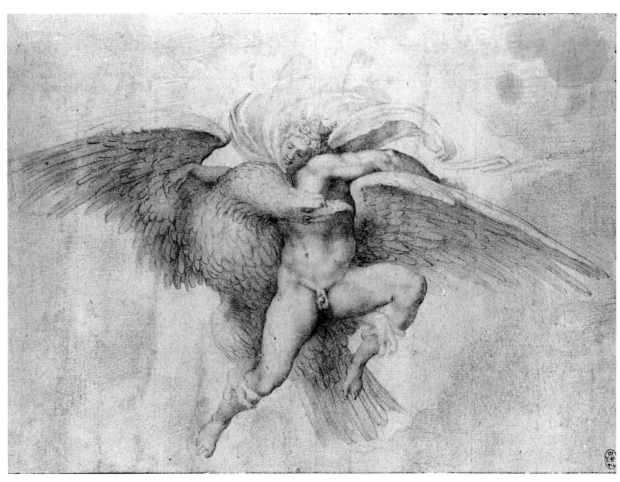

18. Michelangelo
Windsor Castle, Royal Library, no. 13036: The Rape of Ganymede *(copy); black chalk; 19.2 × 26 cm; cut.*

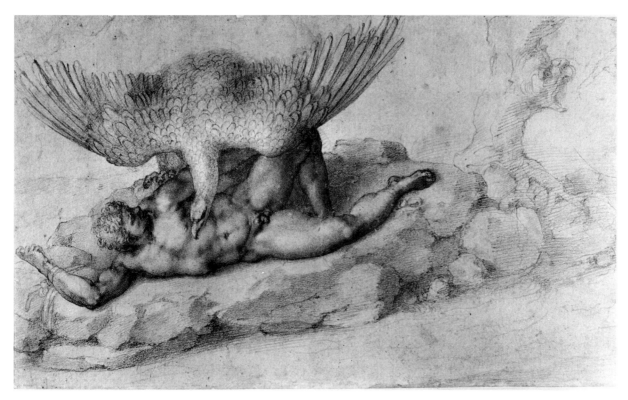

19. Michelangelo
Windsor Castle, Royal Library, no. 12771r: The Punishment of Tityos; *black chalk; 19 × 33 cm; cut (verso: fig. 61).*

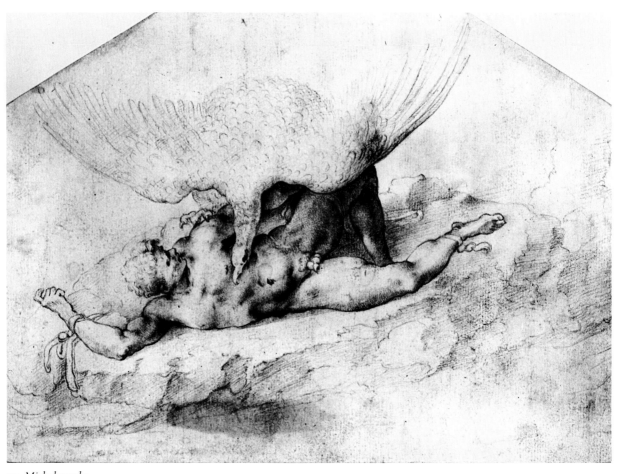

20. Michelangelo
Windsor Castle, Royal Library, no. 0472r: The Punishment of Tityos *(copy, signed on the verso by Clovio); black chalk;*
20.3 × 29 cm; cut.

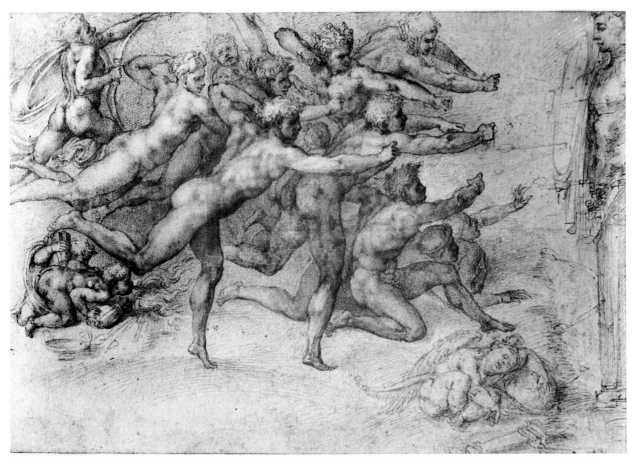

21. Michelangelo
Windsor Castle, Royal Library, no. 12778r: The Archers *(copy, signed on the verso by Clovio); red chalk; 21.9 × 32.3 cm; cut.*

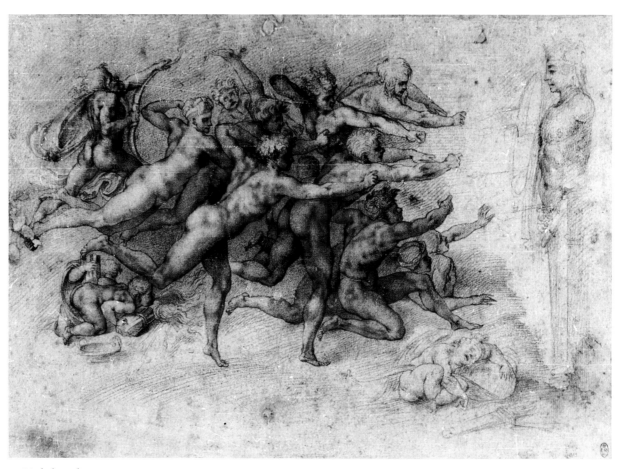

22. *Michelangelo*
Windsor Castle, Royal Library, no. 0442r: The Archers *(copy, signed on the verso by Bernardino Cesari);*
red chalk; 25.7 × 37.2 cm.

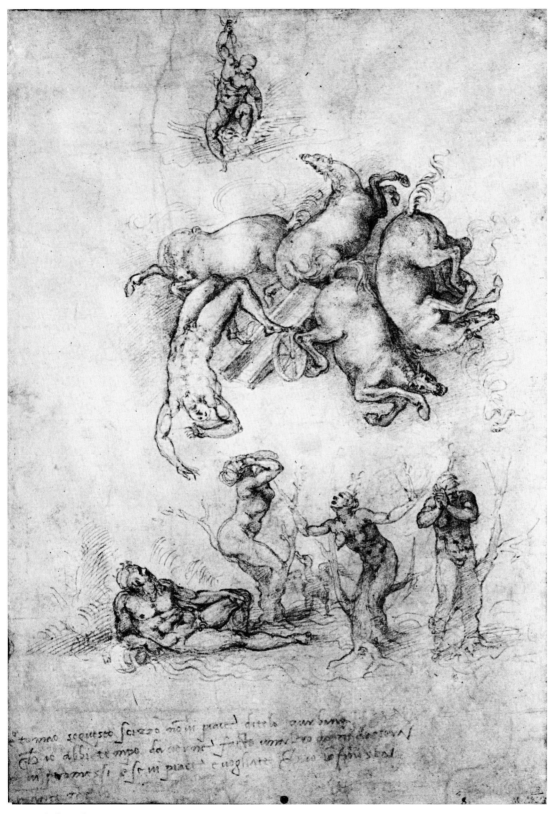

23. Michelangelo
London, British Museum, no. 1895-9-15-517: The Fall of Phaeton, *annotation; black chalk; 31.3 × 21.7 cm; cut.*

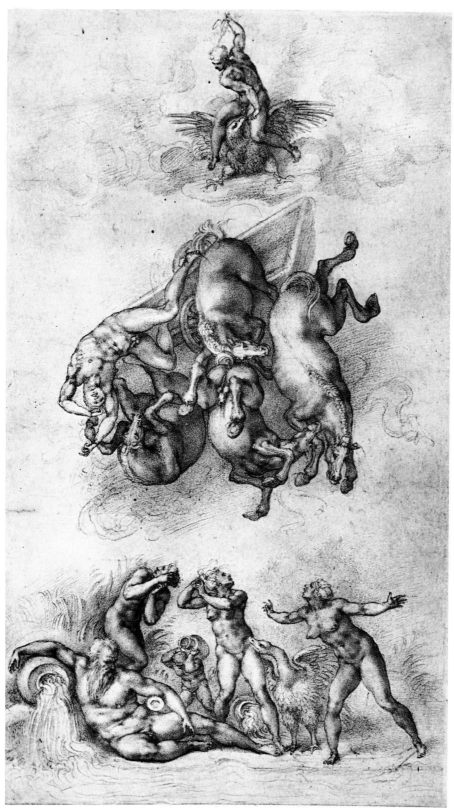

24. *Michelangelo*
Windsor Castle, Royal Library, no. 12766r: The Fall of Phaeton; *black chalk; 41.3 × 23.4 cm; cut (verso: fig. 50).*

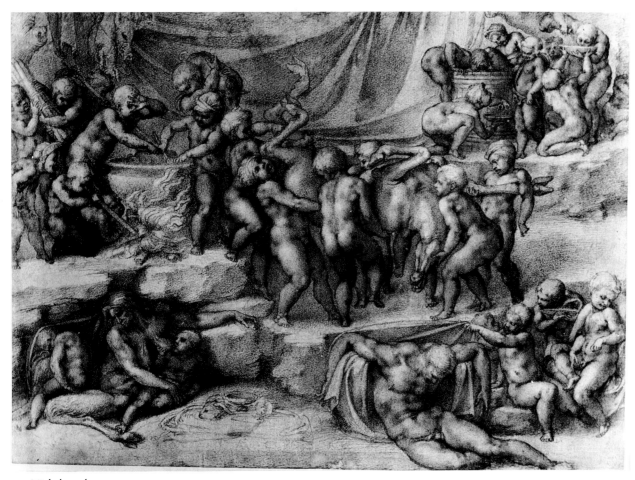

25. *Michelangelo*
Windsor Castle, Royal Library, no. 12777: The Children's Bacchanal *(copy); red chalk over black chalk;*
27.4 × 38.8 cm; cut.

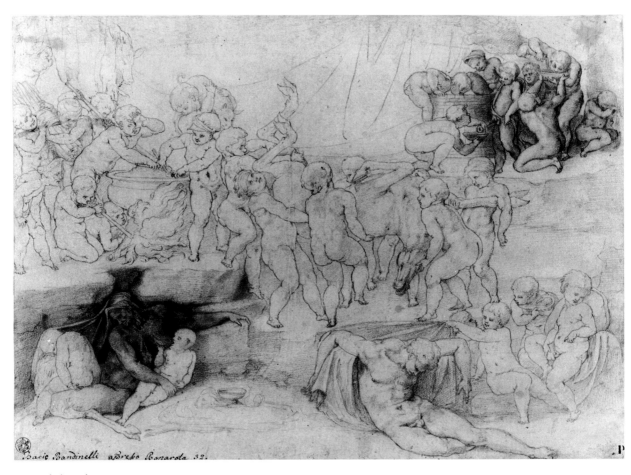

26. Michelangelo
Berlin-Dahlem, Kupferstichkabinett, KdZ no. 17358: The Children's Bacchanal *(copy); red chalk; 28.8 × 40.1 cm; cut.*

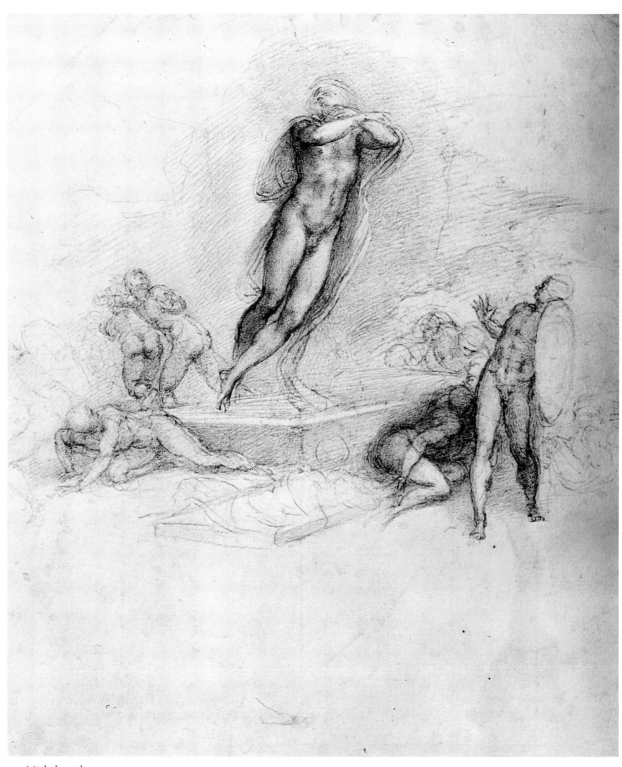

27. *Michelangelo*
London, British Museum, no. 1860-6-16-133: Resurrection of Christ *(copy); black chalk; 32.7 × 28.9 cm; cut.*

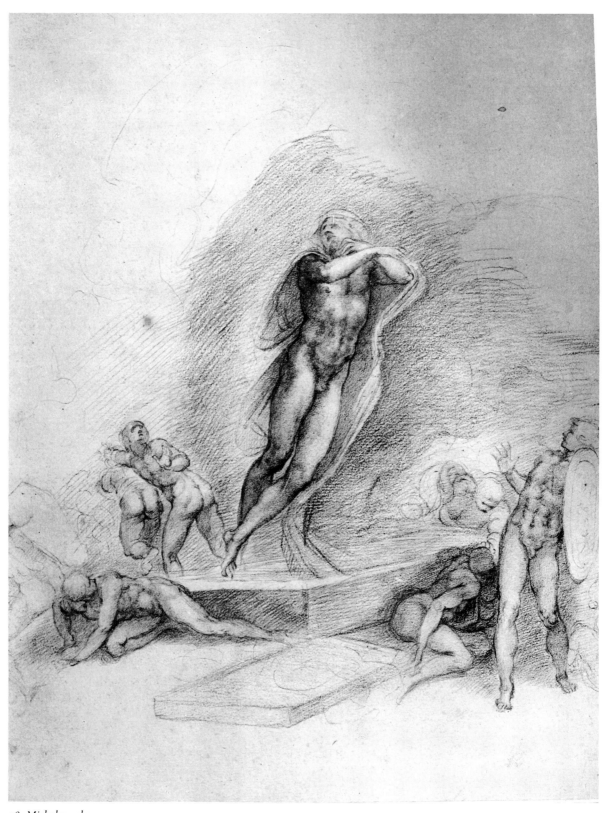

28. Michelangelo
Frankfurt, Städelsches Kunstinstitut, no. 3975: Resurrection of Christ *(copy); black chalk; 32 × 24.4 cm; cut.*

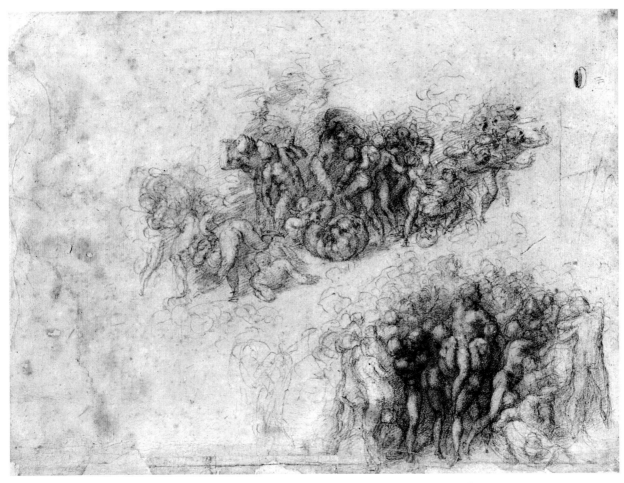

29. *Michelangelo*
Oxford, Ashmolean Museum, Parker no. 318r: Plague of Serpents and Worship of the Brazen Serpent (copy);
red chalk over black chalk; 24.5 × 33.5 cm; cut.

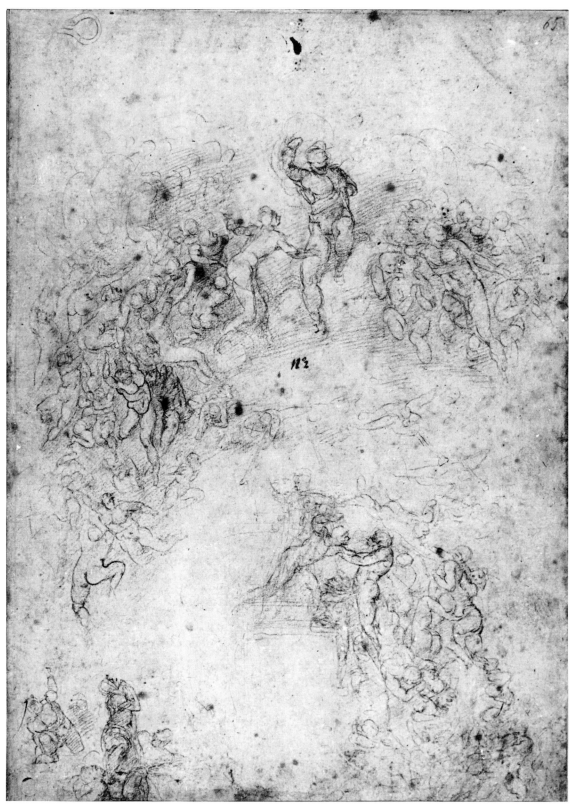

30. *Michelangelo*
Florence, Casa Buonarroti, no. 65F-r: Last Judgment; *black chalk; 41.4 × 30 cm; cut (verso: fig. 59).*

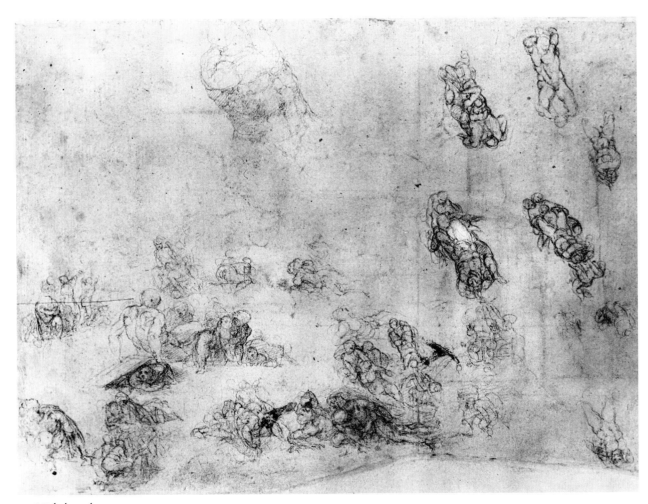

31. Michelangelo
Windsor Castle, Royal Library, no. 12776r: partial sketch for the Last Judgment *with subsidiary sketches, male torso;*
black chalk; 27.7 × 41.9 cm; cut (verso: fig. 71).

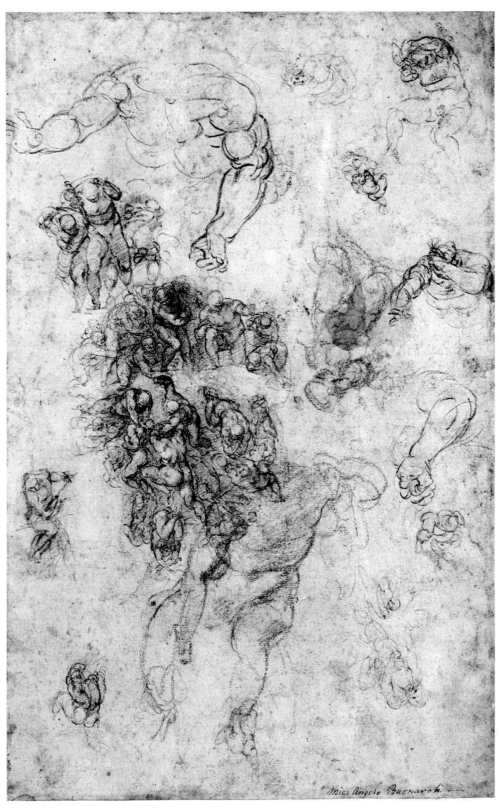

32. Michelangelo
London, British Museum, no. 1895-9-15-518r: partial sketch for the Last Judgment with subsidiary sketches, figure studies; black chalk; 38.2 × 24.7 cm; cut.

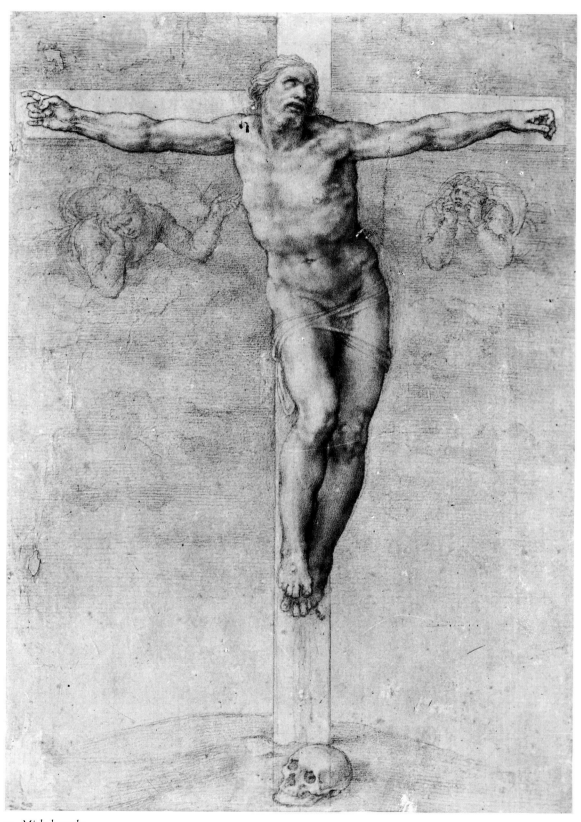

33. Michelangelo
London, British Museum, no. 1895-9-15-504: Christ on the cross between two hovering angels (copy);
37.2 × 27.2 cm; cut.

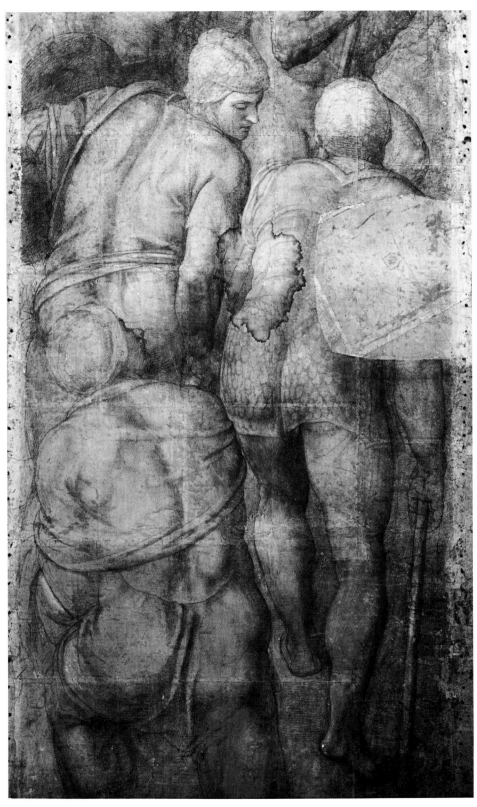

34. Michelangelo
Naples, Museo Nazionale, no. 398: cartoon fragment for the fresco of the Crucifixion of Peter *in the Pauline Chapel; black chalk; 263 × 156 cm; perforated.*

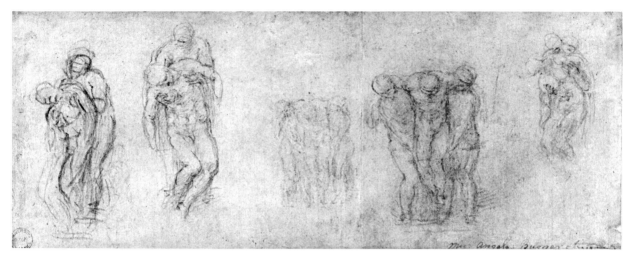

35. Michelangelo
Oxford, Ashmolean Museum, Parker no. 339: five sketches for an Entombment or a Pietà; black chalk; 10.8 × 28.2 cm; cut.

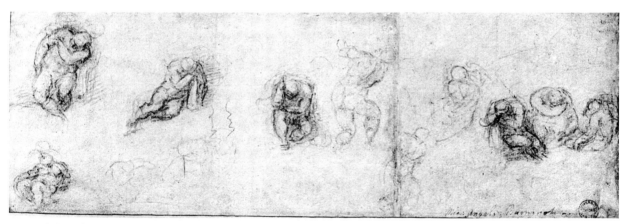

36. Michelangelo
Oxford, Ashmolean Museum, Parker no. 340: sketches for the apostles of a Gethsemane scene; black chalk; 10.8 × 32.7 cm; cut.

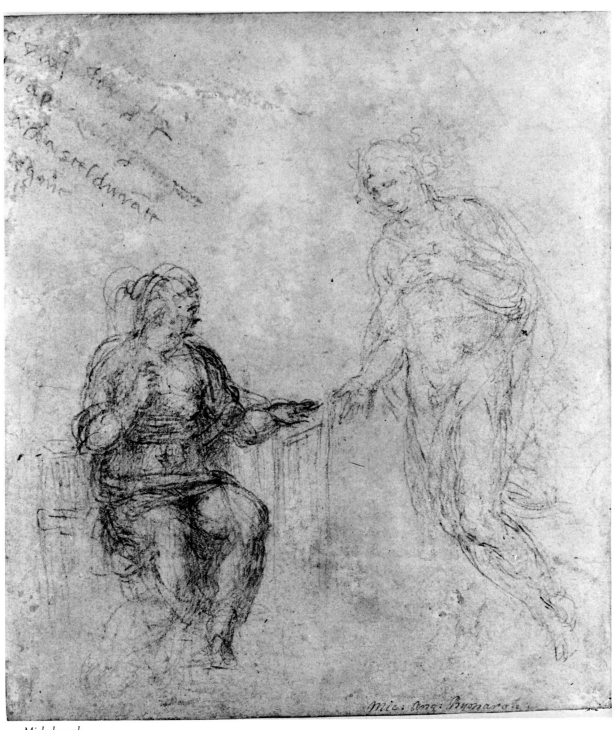

37. Michelangelo
Oxford, Ashmolean Museum, Parker no. 345: Annunciation, manuscript text; black chalk; 22 × 20 cm; cut.

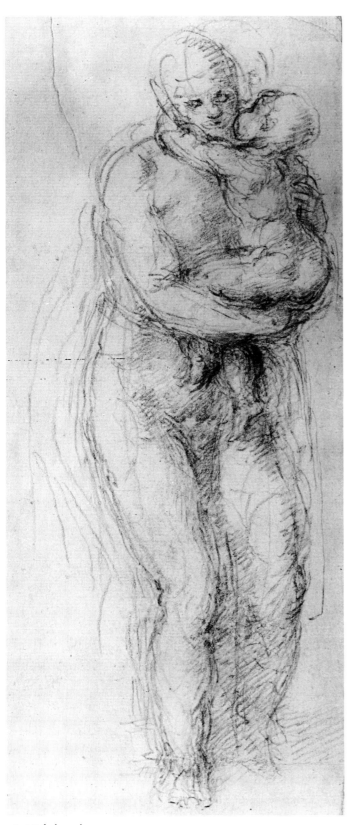

38. Michelangelo
London, British Museum, no. 1859-6-25-562: standing woman with child; black chalk; 26.7 × 11.8 cm; cut.

Io gia facto ingozo isomesto steto
chome fa lacqua agacti ilonbardia
over daltro paese chessi chessisia
cha forza luetre apicha soctolmeto

Labarba alcielo ellamemoria sento
isullo scrignio especto fo darpia
espennel sopraluiso tuctavia
melfa gocciando un richo pavimeto

E lobi entrati miso nella peccia
e fo delcul p chotrapeso groppa
epassi seza ghochi muovo invano

Dimazi misallunga lachoraccia
ep pregarsi adietro siragroppa
e tedomi comarcho soriano

Po fallace escrano
surgie iludicio che lamete porta
ch mal sipra p cerbocana torta

Lamia pictura morta
difedi orma giovanni elmio onore
no sedo iloco bo neio pictore

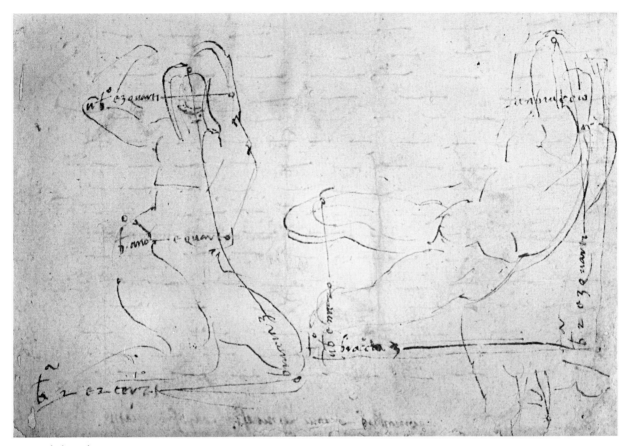

40. Michelangelo
London, British Museum, no. 1859-6-25-544r: block sketches for a river god; pen and ink; 13.8 × 21 cm; cut.

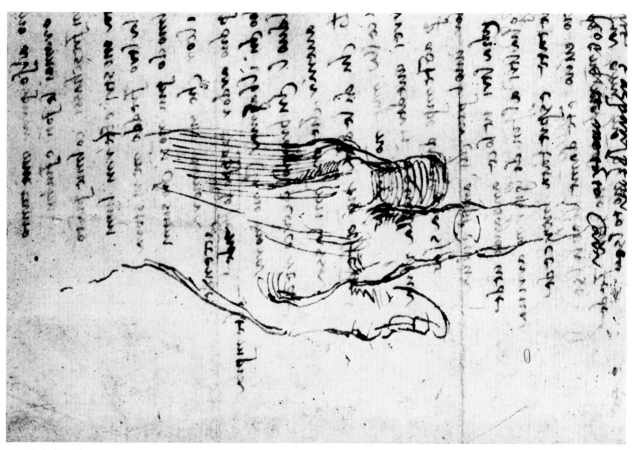

41. Michelangelo
Florence, Archivio Buonarroti, XIII, Fol. 169v: left hand pointing to the right, verse fragments; pen and ink; length of the drawing of a hand approx. 15 cm.

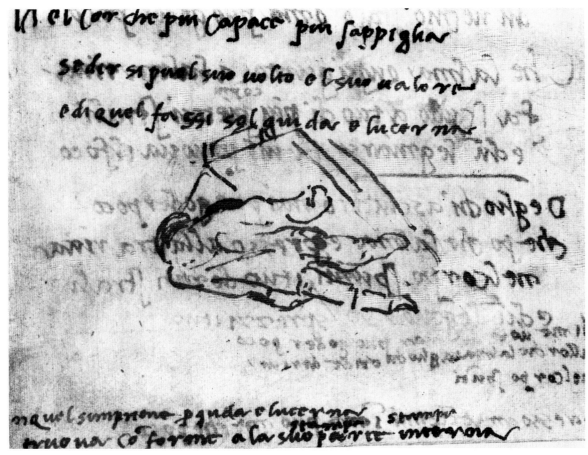

42. *Michelangelo*
Rome, Vatican Library, Cod. Vat. 3211, Fol. 74r: right hand holding a book, verse fragments; pen and ink;
21.2 × 14.4 cm; cut.

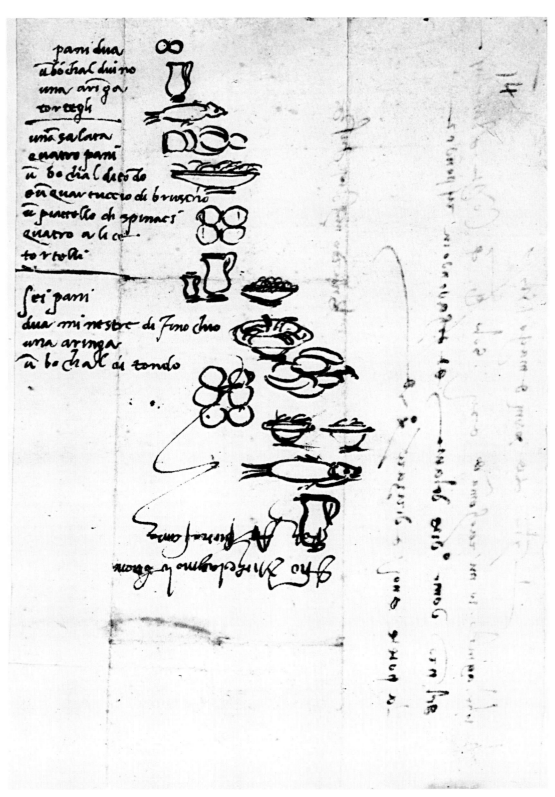

43. Michelangelo
Florence, Archivio Buonarroti, X, Fol. 578v: notes on purchases with accompanying sketches; pen and ink;
21.3 × 14.5 cm; cut.

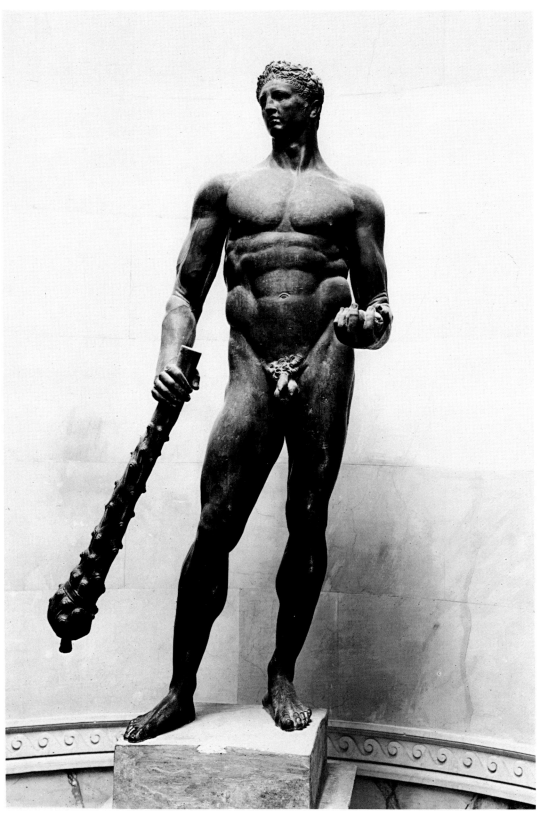

44. *Roman, 2d century A.D.*
Rome, Conservatory Palace: Hercules of the Forum Boarium; *bronze; larger than life.*

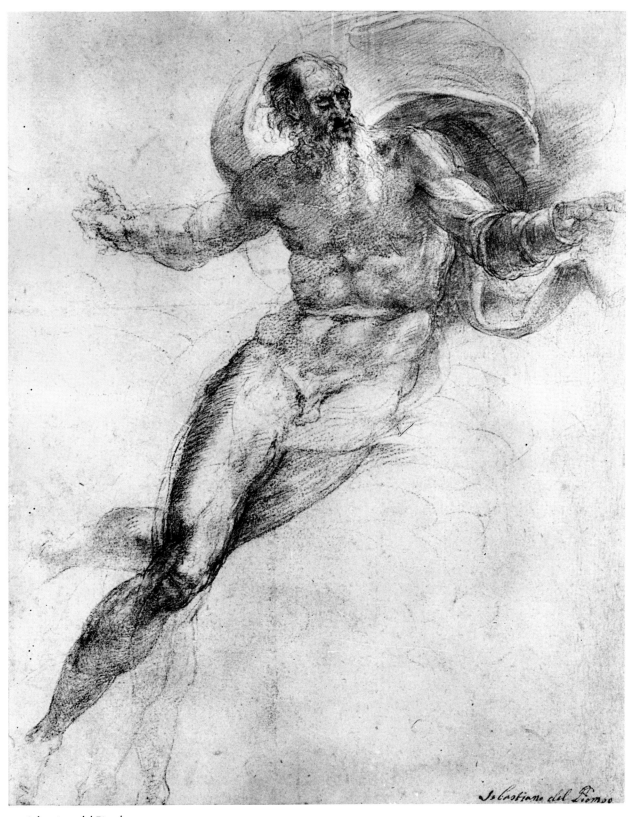

45. Sebastiano del Piombo
Windsor Castle, Royal Library, no. 4815: hovering God the Father; black chalk; 30 × 27.3 cm; cut.

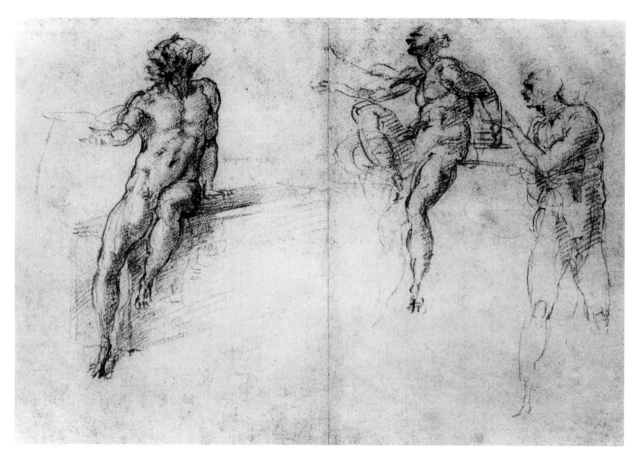

46. Sebastiano del Piombo
Bayonne, Musée Bonnat, no. 682: three sketches for the risen Lazarus; red chalk; 20 × 33 cm; cut.

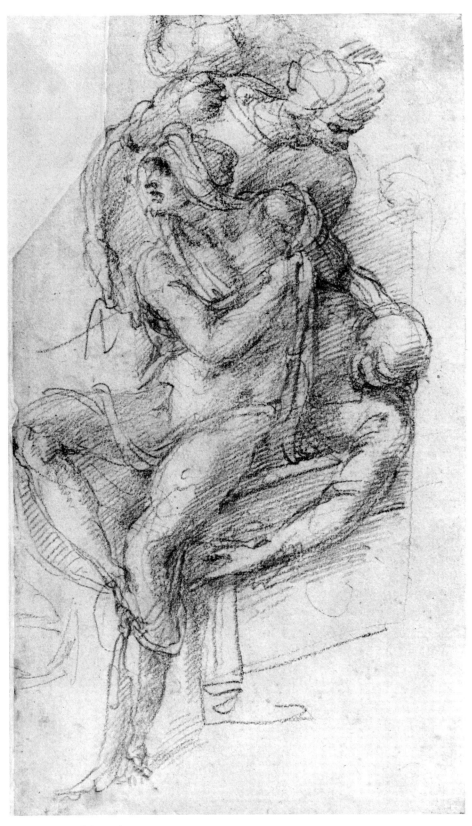

47. Sebastiano del Piombo
London, British Museum, no. 1860-7-14-1: the risen Lazarus with two helpers; red chalk; 25 × 14.5 cm; cut.

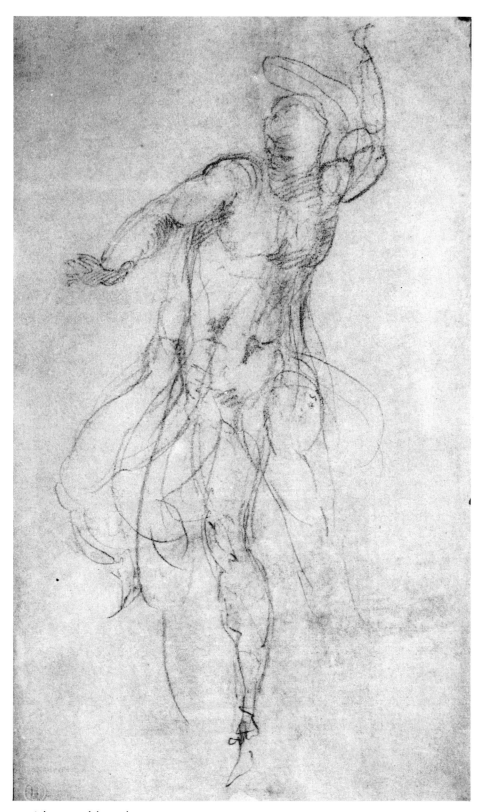

48. Sebastiano del Piombo
Florence, Casa Buonarroti, no. 66F: male nude; black chalk; 32.5 × 19 cm; cut.

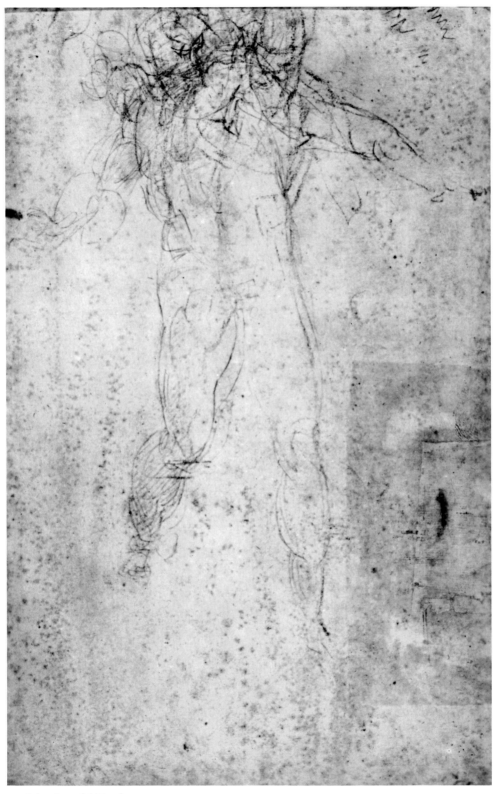

49. Sebastiano del Piombo
Florence, Casa Buonarroti, no. 61F-v: male nude; black chalk; 38 × 25.2 cm; cut.

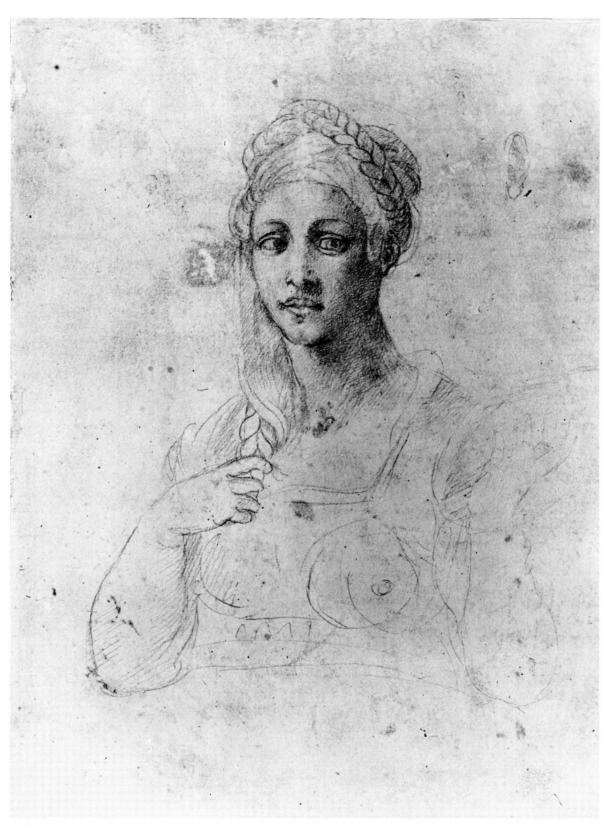

50. Antonio Mini

*Windsor Castle, Royal Library, no. 12766v: half-length portrait of a girl with mirror, left ear; red chalk;
41.3 × 23.4 cm; cut (recto: fig. 24).*

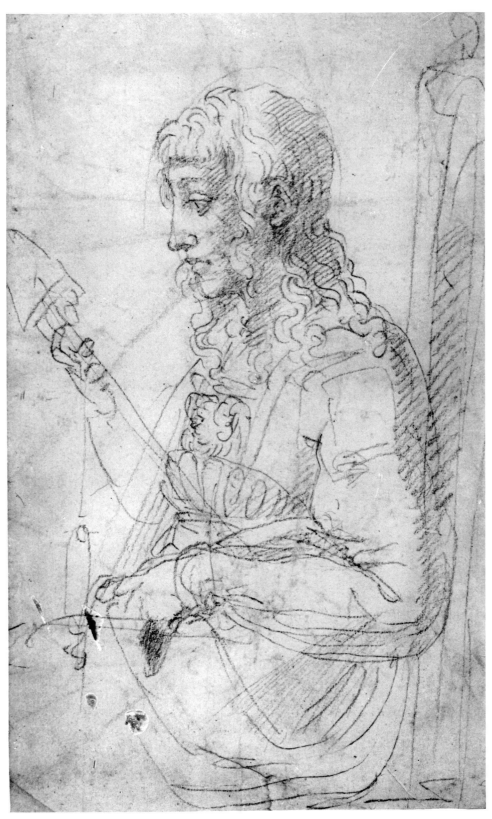

51. Antonio Mini
London, British Museum, no. 1859-6-25-561: girl with distaff; black chalk; 28.5 × 18.2 cm; cut.

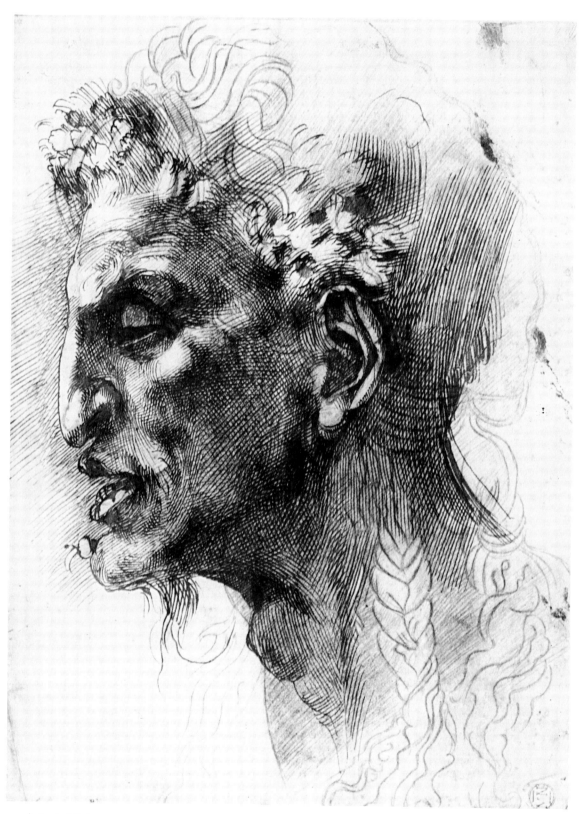

52. Antonio Mini
Paris, Louvre, no. 684r: faun's head; ink over red chalk; 27.5 × 21 cm; cut.

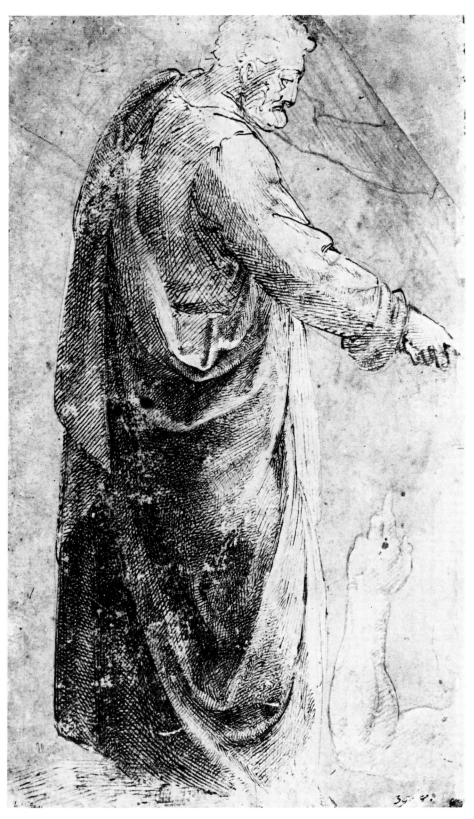

53. Antonio Mini
Munich, Staatliche Graphische Sammlung, no. 2191r: two arm studies, red chalk; St. Peter after Masaccio's
Tribute Money, *ink over red chalk; 31.7 × 19.7 cm; cut.*

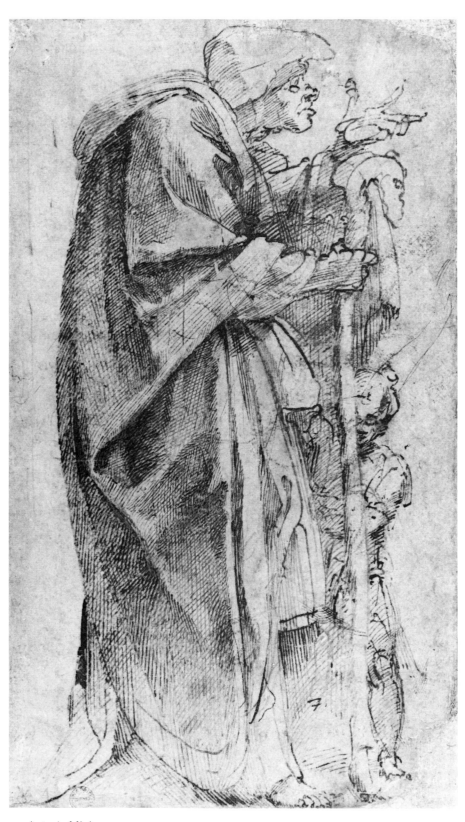

54. *Antonio Mini*
Oxford, Ashmolean Museum, Parker no. 324: draped old woman with cane, accompanied by a boy;
ink over black chalk; 32.9 × 19.2 cm; cut.

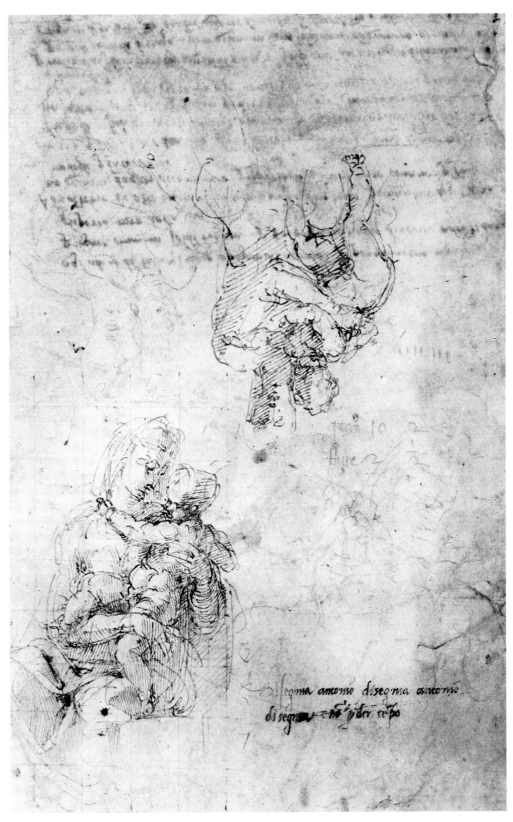

55. Antonio Mini
London, British Museum, no. 1859-5-14-818r: four sketches of a Madonna with child; ink or red chalk (square net in black chalk); manuscript text, pen and ink; 40 × 26.9 cm; cut.

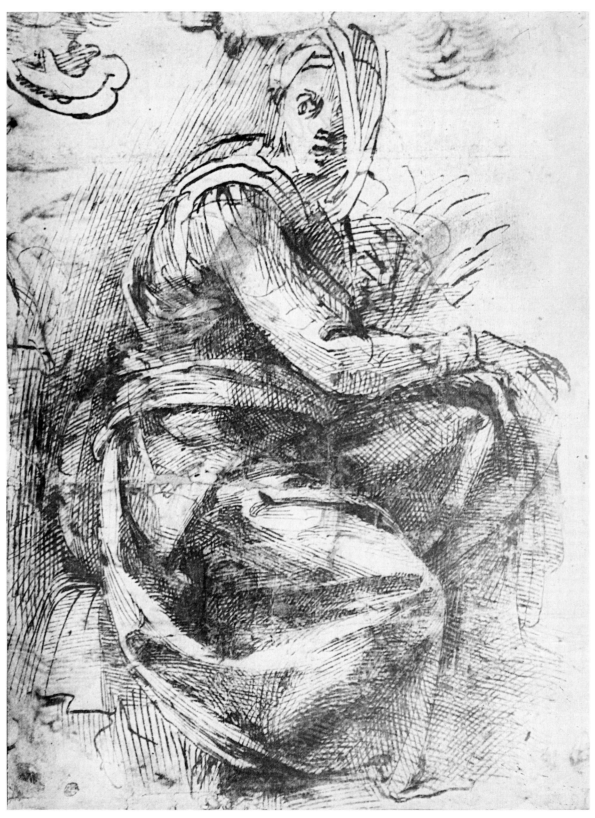

56. *Antonio Mini*
Oxford, Ashmolean Museum, Parker no. 325: seated female draped figure ("Sibyl"); pen and ink;
26.3 × 20 cm; cut.

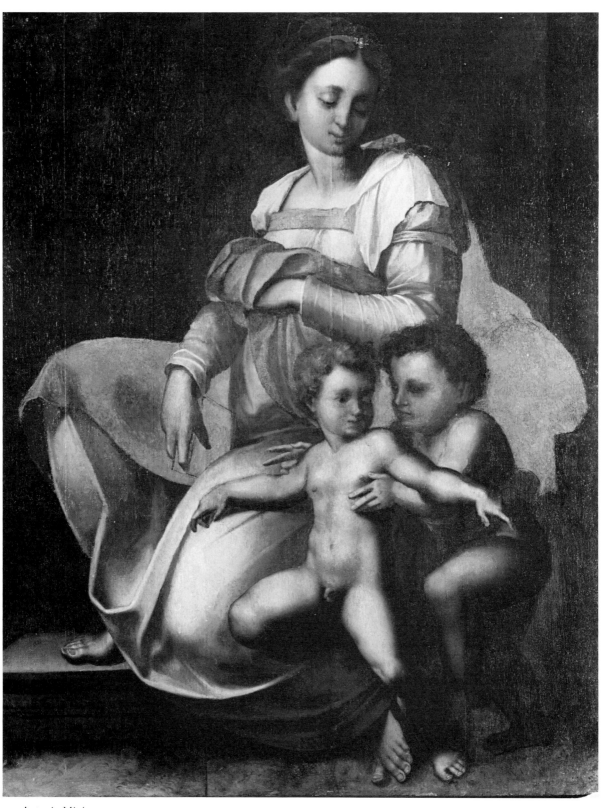

57. Antonio Mini
London, formerly Collection Woolf Posner: seated Madonna with Christ Child and St. John; tempera on wood;
94 × 75 cm.

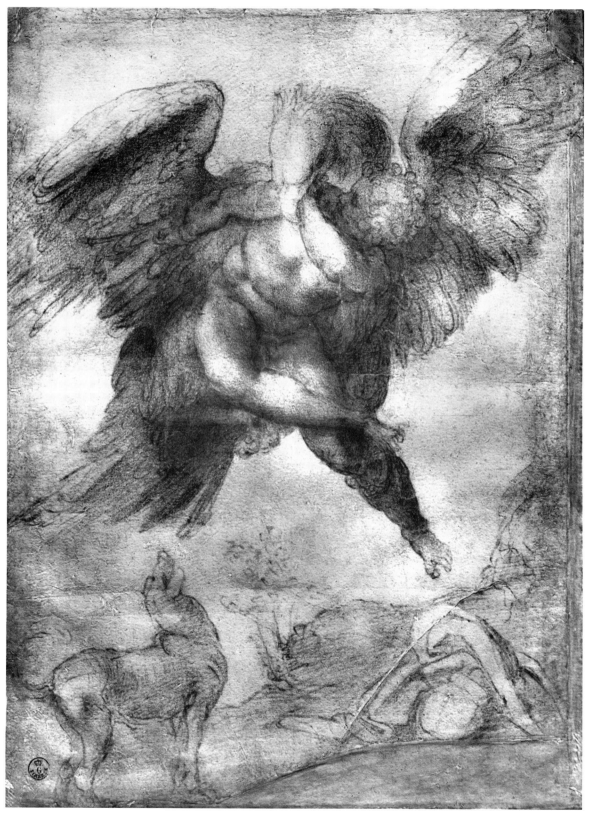

58. Tommaso de' Cavalieri
Florence, Uffizi, no. 611E: The Rape of Ganymede; *red chalk; 31 × 22.5 cm; cut.*

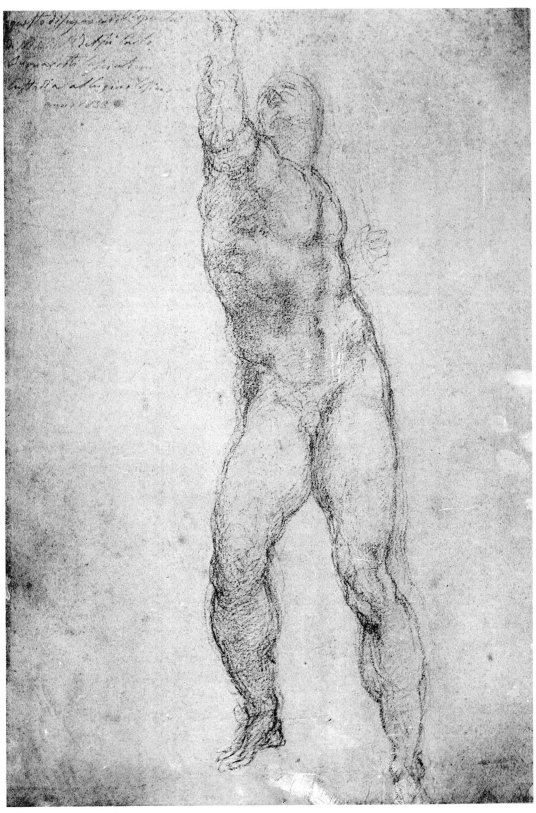

59. *Tommaso de' Cavalieri*
Florence, Casa Buonarroti, no. 65F-v: Risen Christ; black chalk; 41.4 × 30 cm; cut (recto: fig. 30).

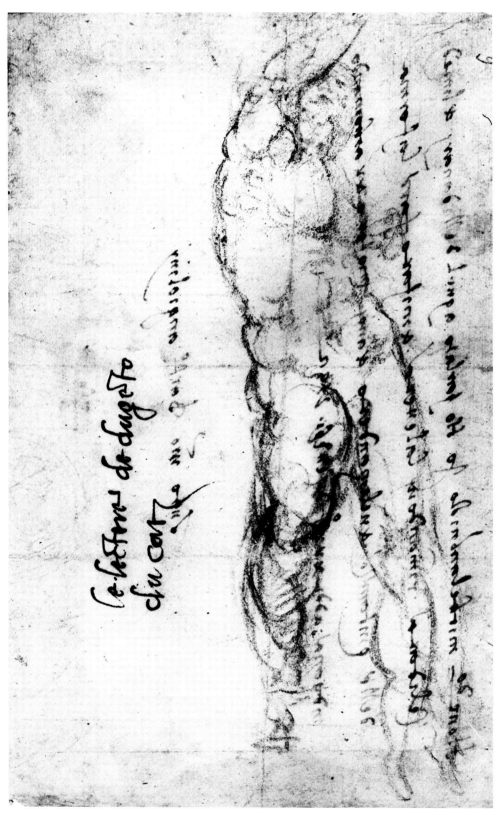

60. *Tommaso de' Cavalieri*
Florence, Archivio Buonarroti, VI, Fol. 24v: Risen Christ, *black chalk; manuscript text, pen and ink;*
21 × 13.8 cm; cut.

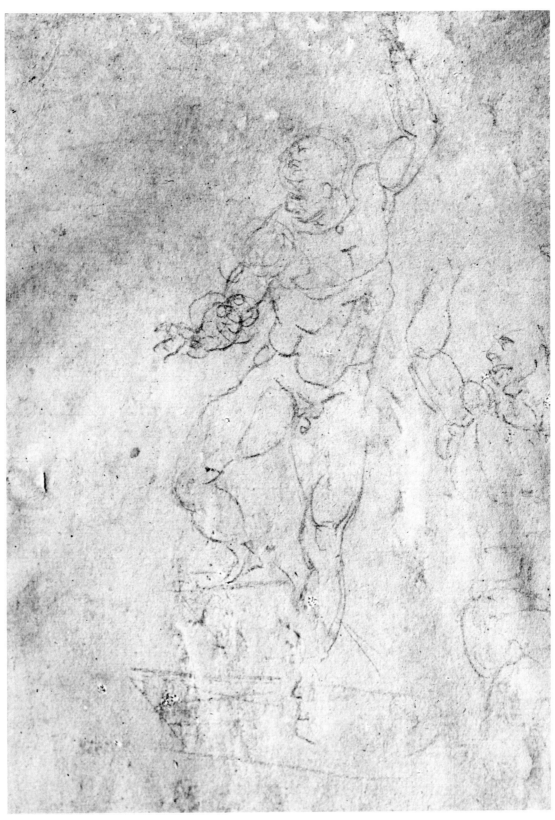

61. Tommaso de' Cavalieri
Windsor Castle, Royal Library, no. 12771v: two sketches of a Risen Christ; black chalk; 33 × 19 cm; cut
(recto: fig. 19).

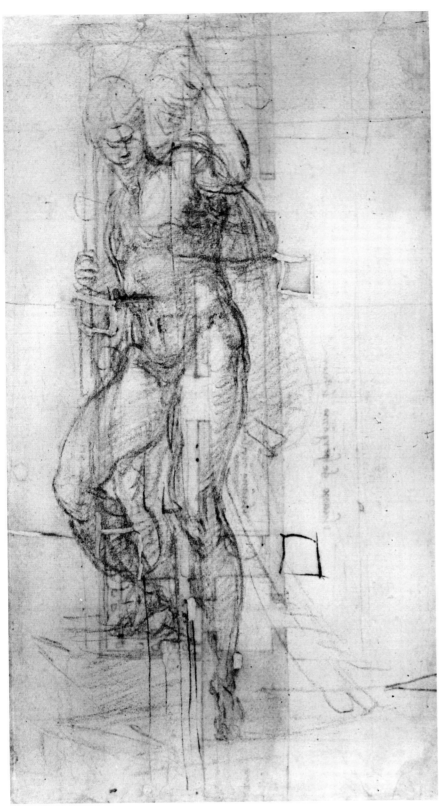

62. *Tommaso de' Cavalieri*
Oxford, Ashmolean Museum, Parker no. 311v: Risen Christ; *black chalk; 27.3 × 15.7 cm; cut.*

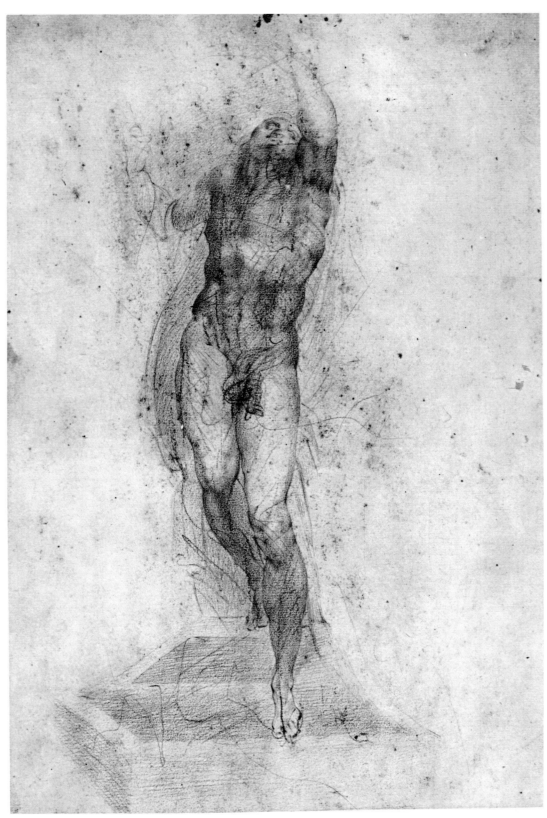

63. *Tommaso de' Cavalieri*
Florence, Uffizi, no. 1450S: Risen Christ; *black chalk; cut.*

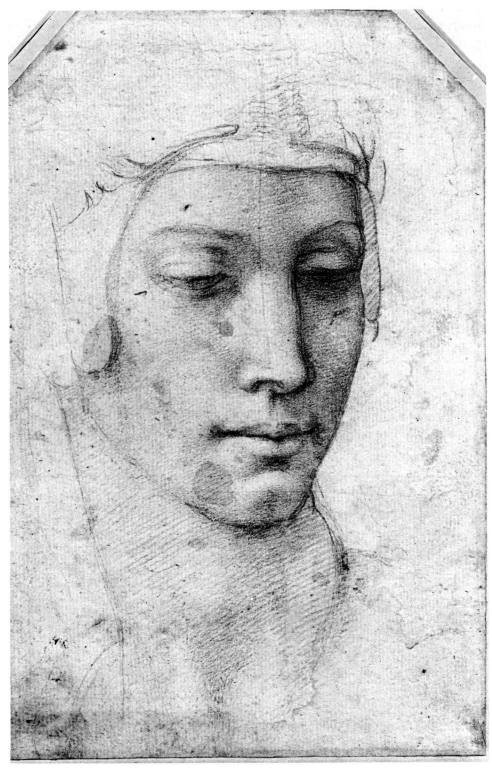

64. *Tommaso de' Cavalieri*
Windsor Castle, Royal Library, no. 12764r: head of a youth with cap; black chalk; 21.2 × 14.2 cm; cut.

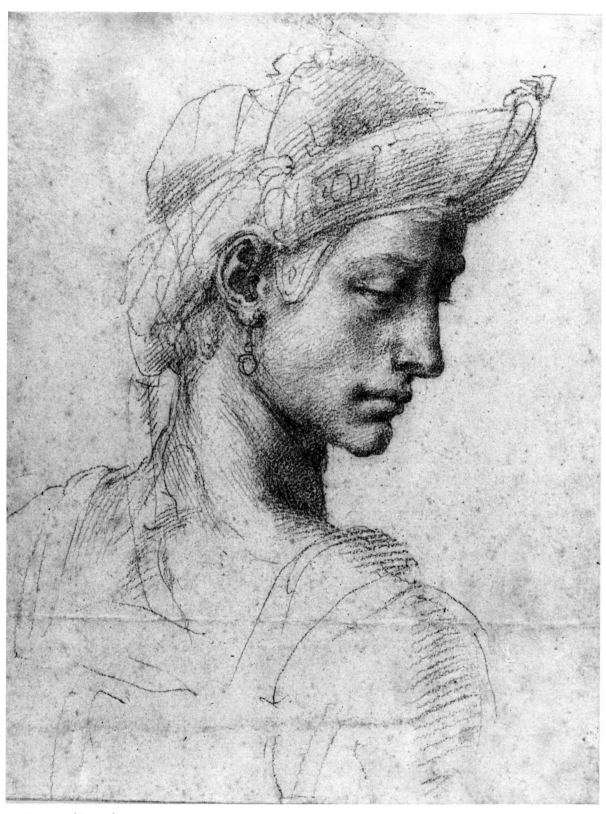

65. Tommaso de' Cavalieri
Oxford, Ashmolean Museum, Parker no. 315: bust of a youth in fantastic dress; red chalk; 20.5 × 16.5 cm; cut.

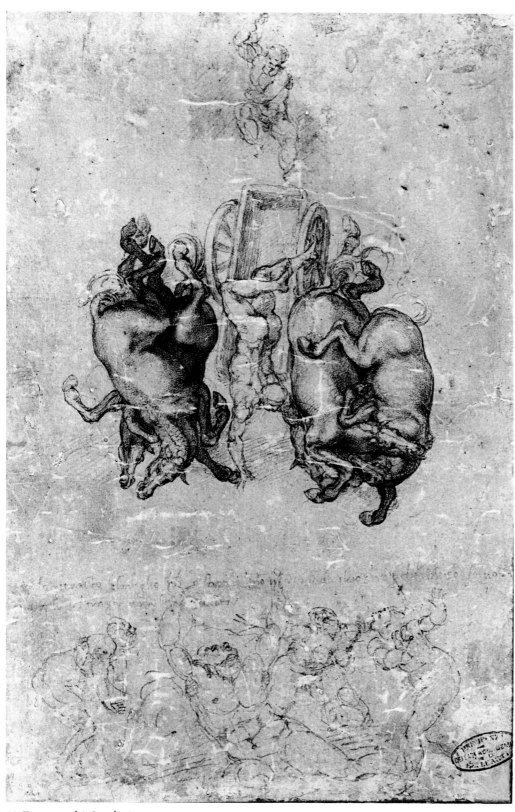

66. *Tommaso de' Cavalieri*
Venice, Academy, no. 177: Fall of Phaeton; *black chalk; 39.4 × 25.5 cm; cut.*

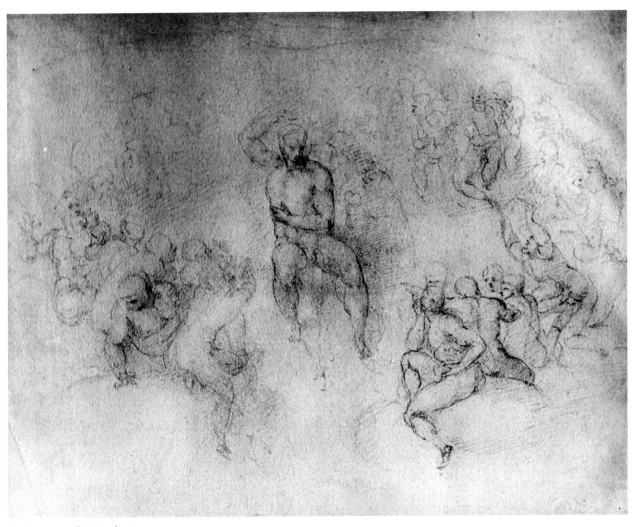

67. Tommaso de' Cavalieri
Bayonne, Musée Bonnat, no. 1217: partial sketch of a Last Judgment; black chalk; 34.4 × 29 cm.

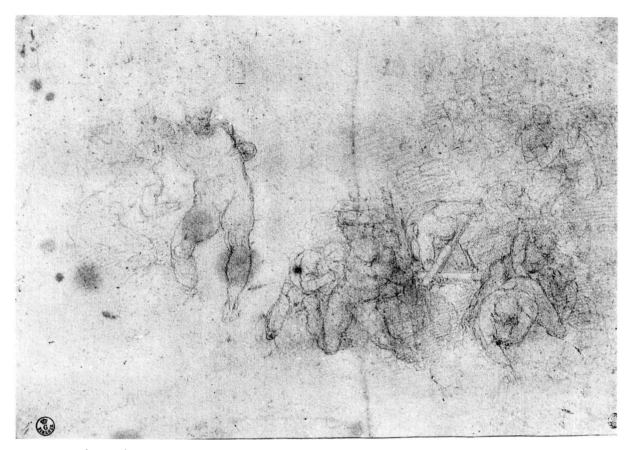

68. Tommaso de' Cavalieri
Florence, Uffizi, no. 170S: partial sketch of a Last Judgment; black chalk; 19 × 28.7 cm; cut.

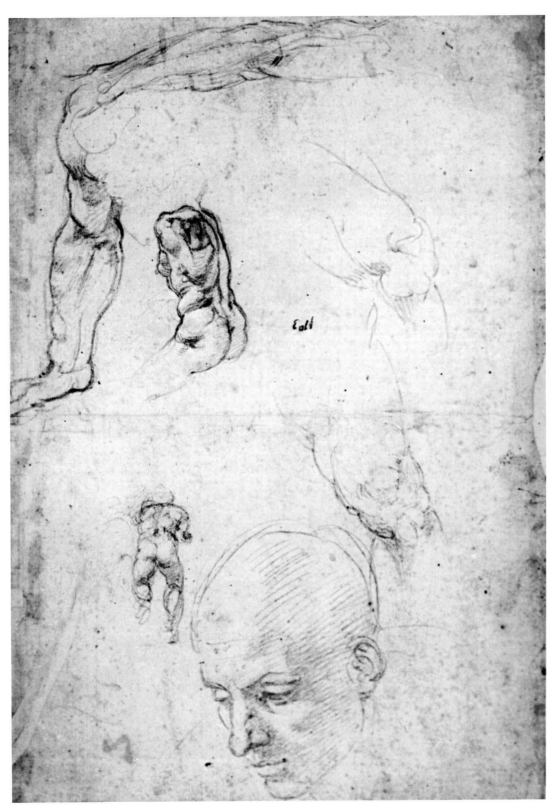

69. *Tommaso de' Cavalieri*
Florence, Casa Buonarroti, no. 69F-v: arm and knee studies, male torso, nude seen from the rear, and head; black chalk; 39.8 × 28.2 cm; cut.

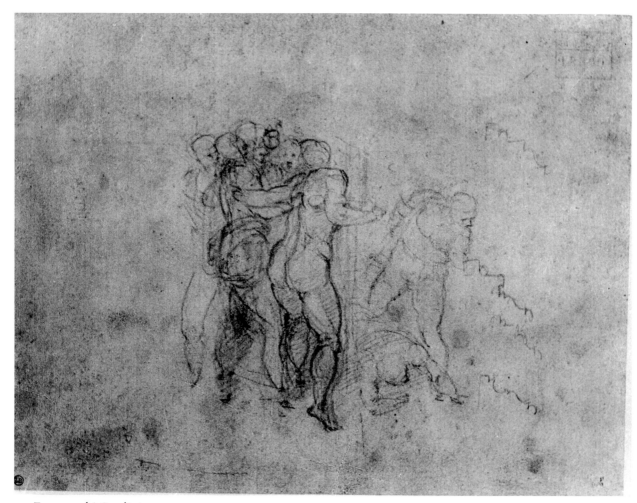

70. Tommaso de' Cavalieri
Bayonne, Musée Bonnat, no. 681: partial sketch of a Last Judgment; black chalk; 17.9 × 23.8 cm.

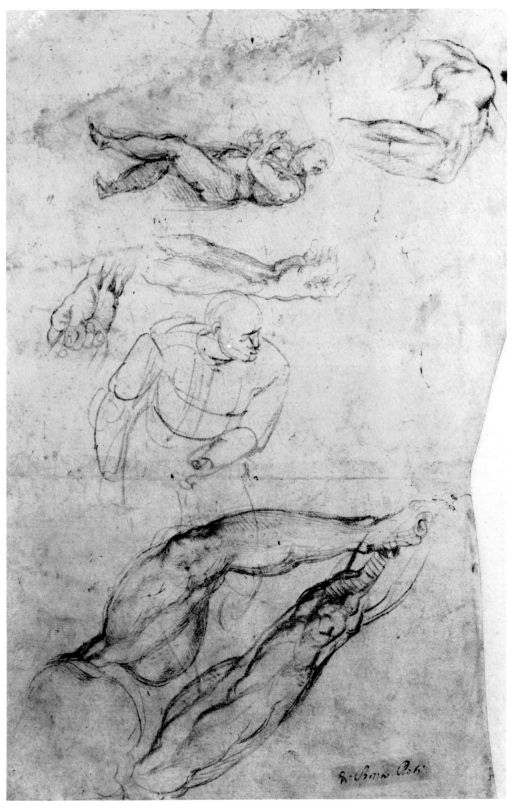

71. *Tommaso de' Cavalieri*
Windsor Castle, Royal Library, no. 12776v: four limb studies, two male nudes; black chalk;
27.7 × 41.9 cm; cut (recto: fig. 31).

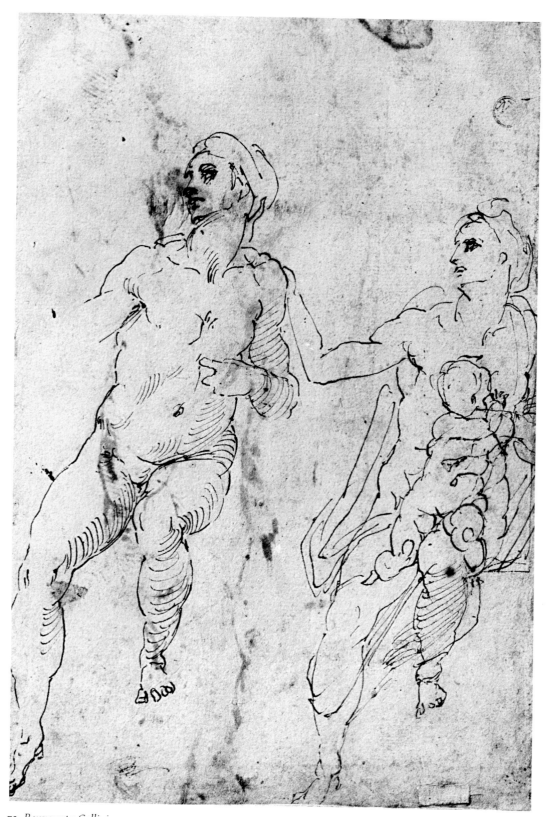

72. *Benvenuto Cellini*

Paris, Louvre, no. 689v: two seated female nudes, one with a suckling child; ink over metal point; 25 × 17 (sheet excerpt) or 37.5 × 19.5 cm (whole sheet).

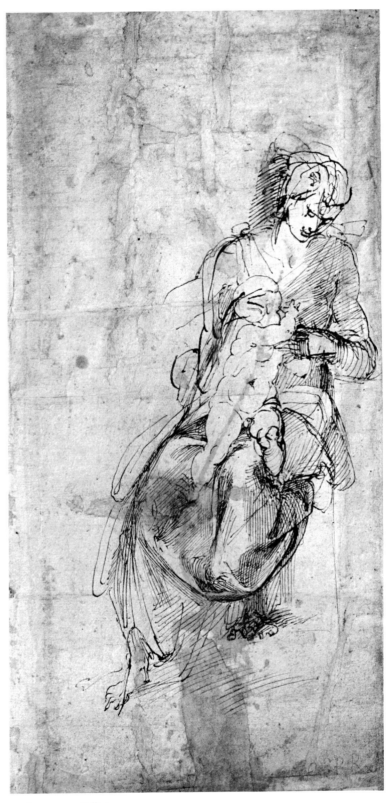

73. Benvenuto Cellini
Vienna, Albertina, Sc.R.152v: seated Madonna with suckling child; pen and ink; 39 × 19.5 cm; cut.

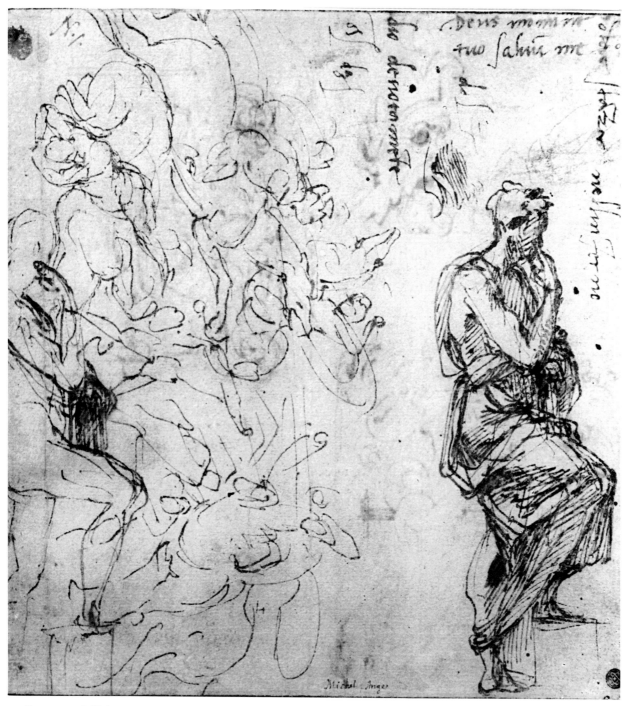

74. *Benvenuto Cellini*
London, British Museum, no. 1895-9-15-496r: sketch of battling horsemen, two statue sketches; pen and ink;
18.6 × 18.3 cm; cut.

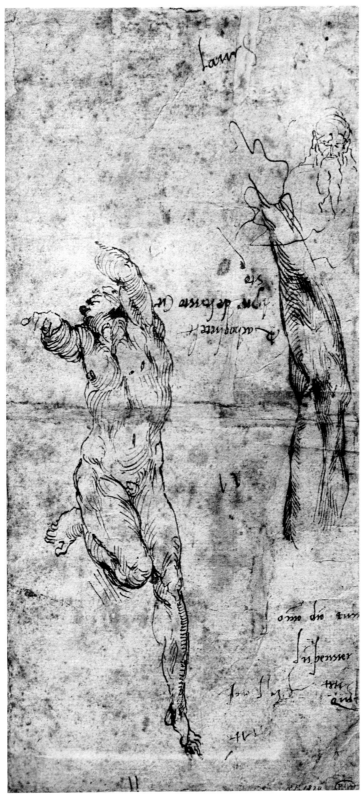

75. *Benvenuto Cellini*
Paris, Louvre, R.F. 70-1068v: male nude, arm study, bearded male head, manuscript texts;
pen and ink; 34 × 16.8 cm; cut (recto: fig. 79).

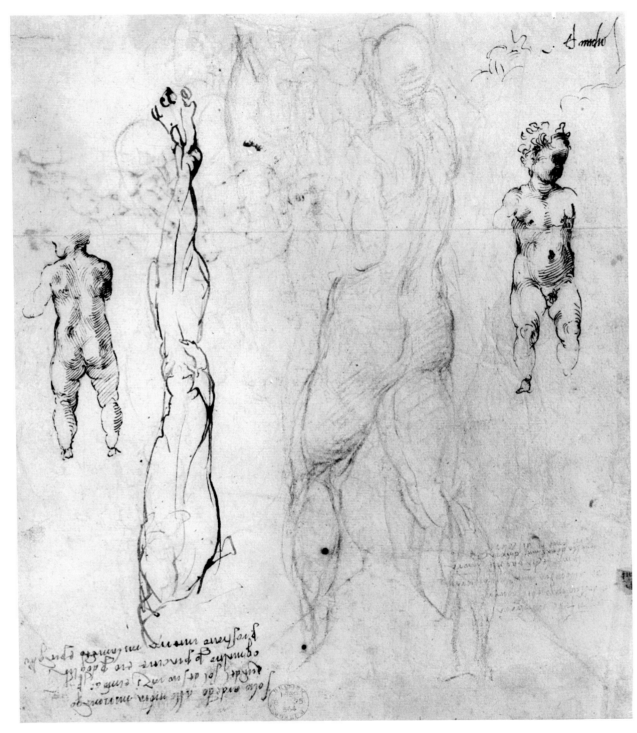

76. Benvenuto Cellini
London, British Museum, no. 1859-6-25-564v: fragmentary group of three male nudes (black chalk), leg study, verse fragment (pen and ink), two standing boys (ink over metal point); 31.5 × 27.8 cm; cut.

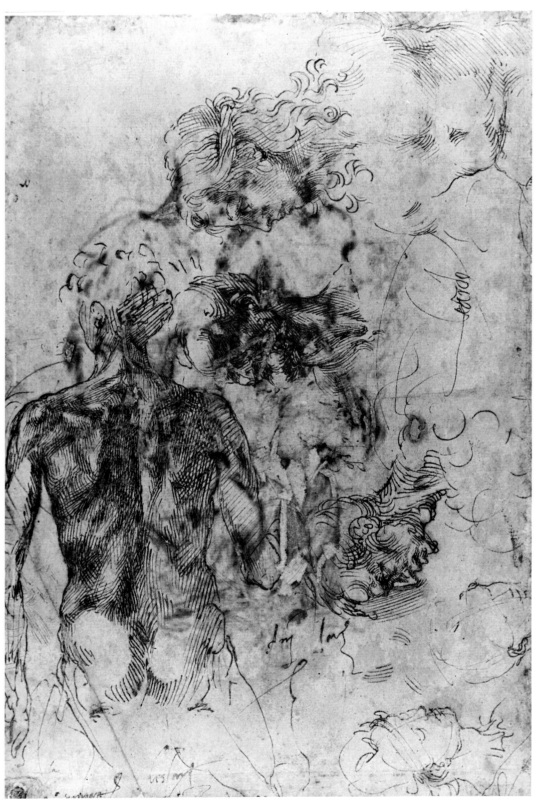

77. *Benvenuto Cellini*
Oxford, Ashmolean Museum, Parker no. 291v: male nude seen from the rear, half-length figure of a youth, four heads, manuscript texts; pen and ink; 25.7 × 17.5 cm; cut.

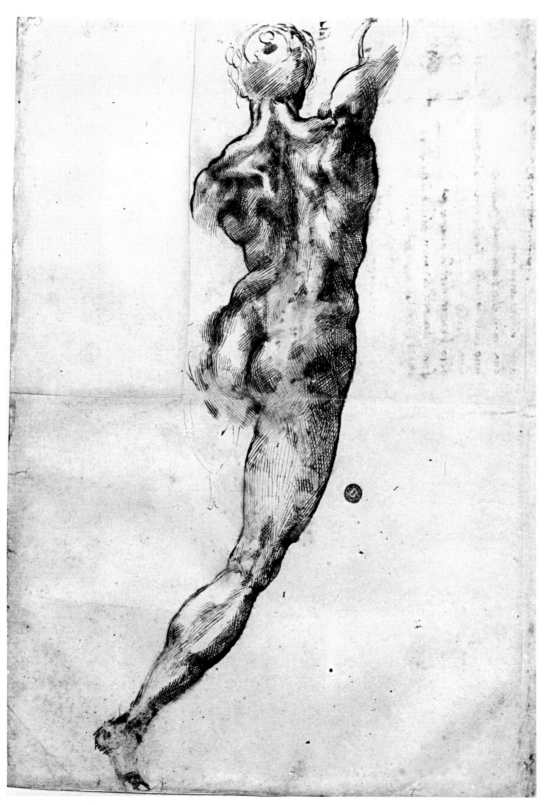

78. Benvenuto Cellini
Florence, Casa Buonarroti, no. 73F-r: male nude seen from the rear; ink over black chalk; 40.8 × 28.4 cm; cut.

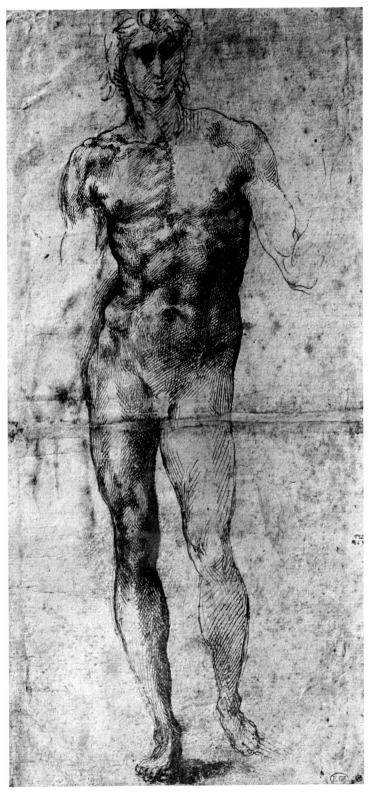

79. *Benvenuto Cellini*
Paris, Louvre, RF 70-1068r: striding nude youth; pen and ink; 34 × 16.8 cm; cut (verso: fig. 75).

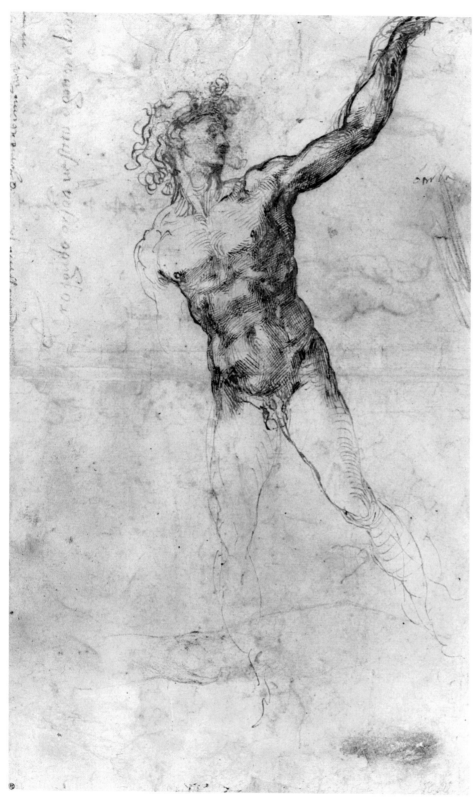

80. *Benvenuto Cellini*
London, British Museum, no. 1887-5-2-117r: youth hurrying to the left (pen and ink), leg study (black chalk),
manuscript texts (pen and ink or black chalk); 37.5 × 23 cm; cut.

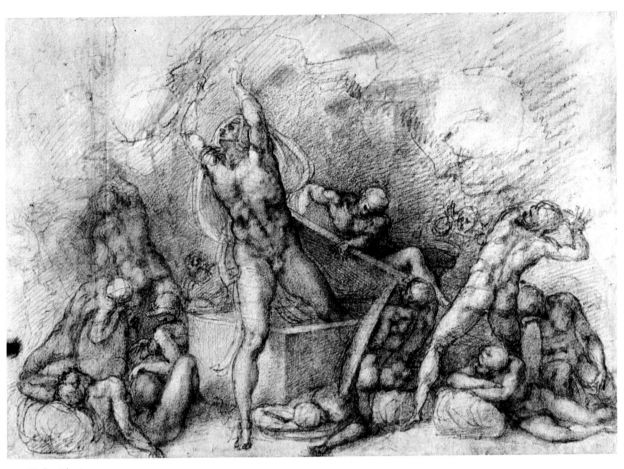

81. *Giulio Clovio*
Windsor Castle, Royal Library, no. 12767r: Resurrection of Christ; *black chalk; 24 × 34.8 cm; cut (verso: fig. 82).*

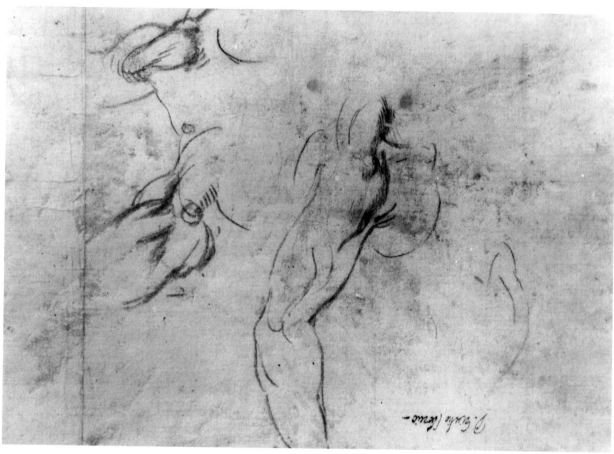

82. Giulio Clovio
Windsor Castle, Royal Library, no. 12767v: study of a right arm with shoulder, two shoulder studies (black chalk),
"D. Giulio Clovio" (pen and ink); 24 × 34.8 cm; cut (recto: fig. 81).

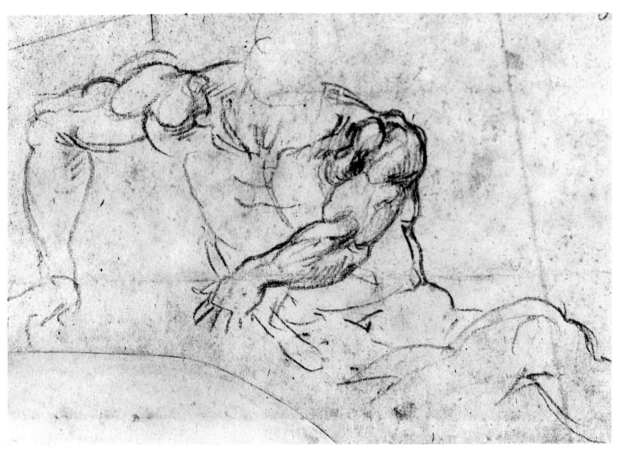

83. Giulio Clovio
Florence, Casa Buonarroti, no. 32F: seated male nude; red chalk; 13.5 × 19.5 cm; cut.

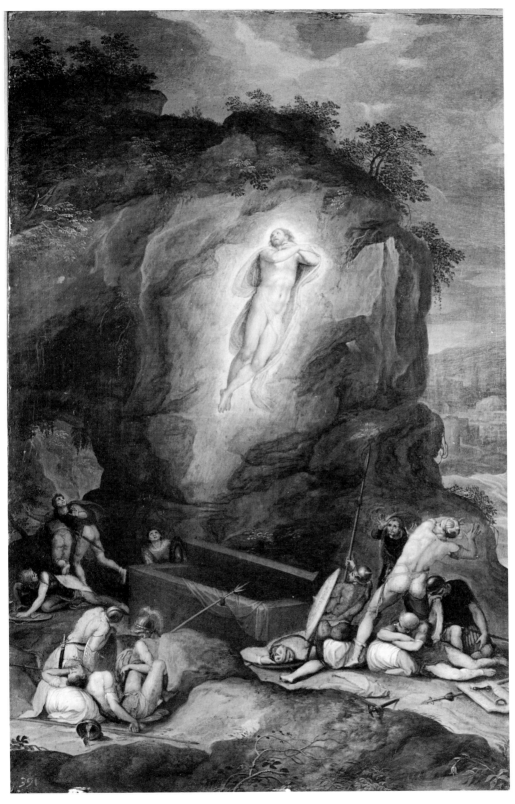

84. *Giulio Clovio*
Cambridge, Massachusetts, Fogg Art Museum, no. 1943.125: Resurrection of Christ; *oil on wood; 60 × 40 cm.*

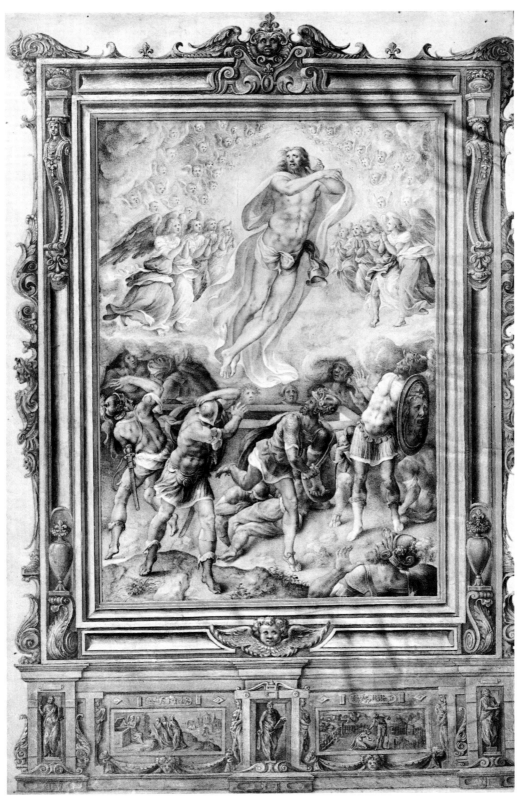

85. Giulio Clovio
New York Public Library, Towneley Lectionary, Fol. 16v: Resurrection of Christ; *miniature.*

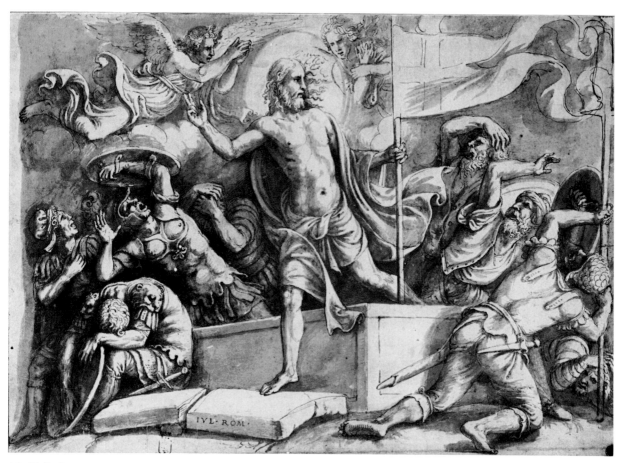

86. Giulio Romano
Berlin-Dahlem, Kupferstichkabinett, KdZ no. 26368: Resurrection of Christ; *pen and ink and brush; washed; cut;*
27.9 × 40.7 cm.

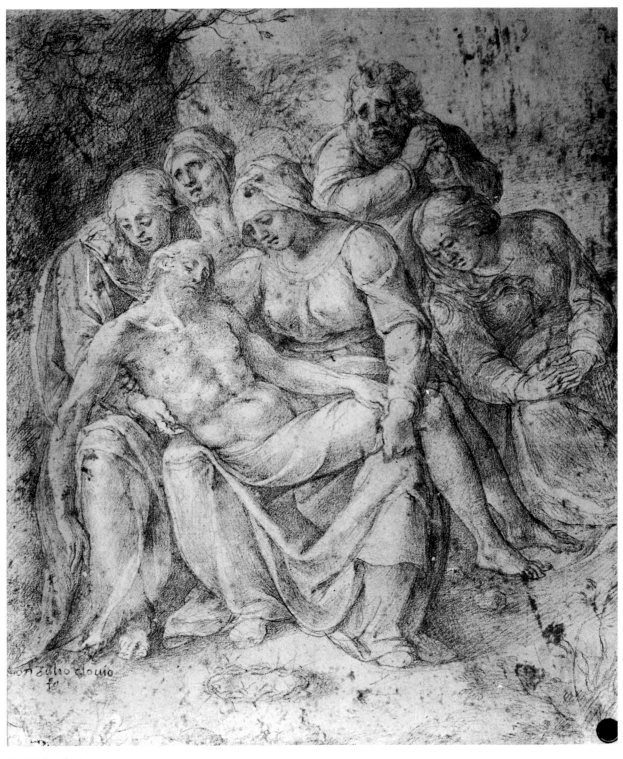

87. Giulio Clovio
London, British Museum, no. 1895-9-15-654: Lamentation of Christ; *signed by Giulio Clovio; black chalk;*
25 × 12 cm; cut.

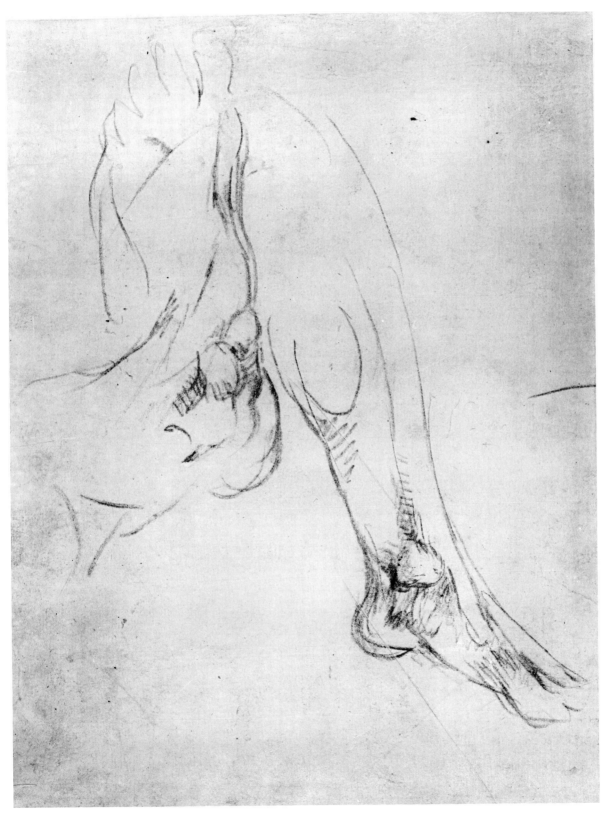

88. Giulio Clovio
London, British Museum, no. 1859-5-14-820: left leg and left foot; red chalk; 21.4 × 16.1 cm; cut.

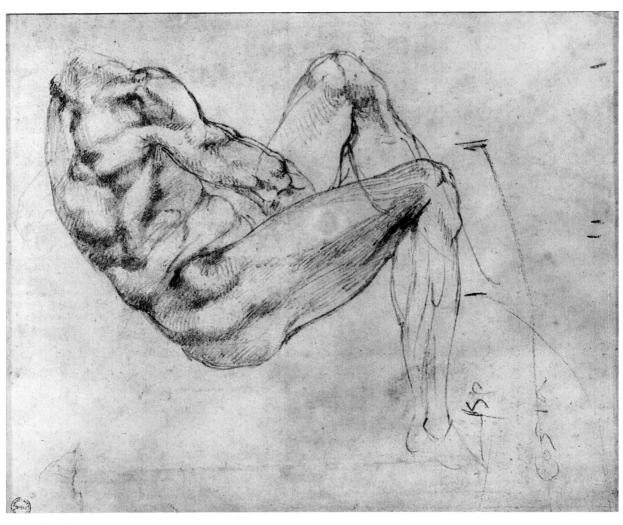

89. Giulio Clovio
Oxford, Ashmolean Museum, Parker no. 309r: reclining male nude, manuscript texts; black chalk; 25.8 × 33.2 cm.

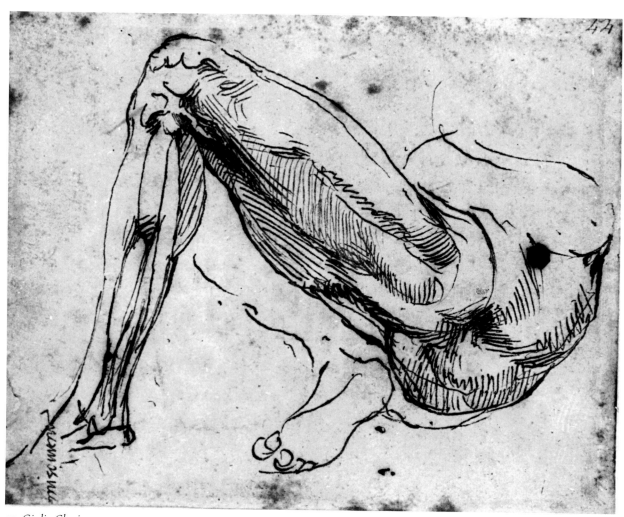

90. *Giulio Clovio*
Florence, Casa Buonarroti, no. 44F: lower half of a reclining nude; pen and ink; 14.5 × 19.3 cm; cut.

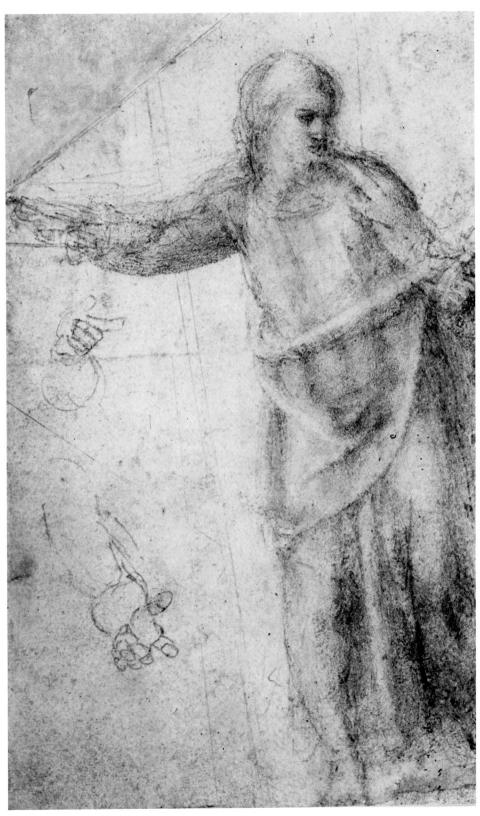

91. *Ascanio Condivi*
Cambridge, Fitzwilliam Museum, no. 3056r: draped male figure, two arm sketches; black chalk;
26.5 × 16.2 cm; cut.

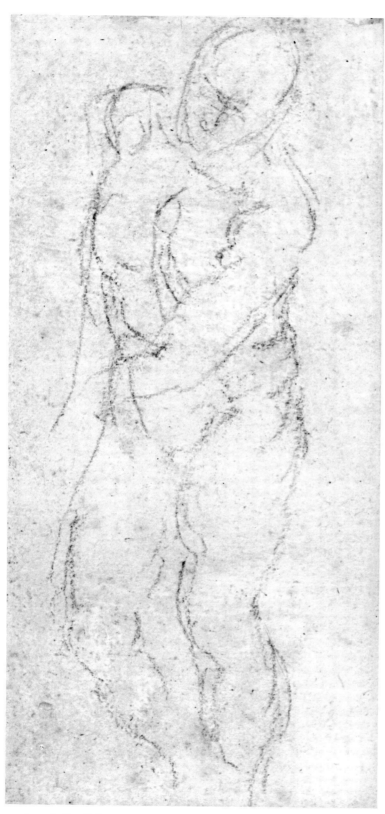

92. Ascanio Condivi
Oxford, Ashmolean Museum, Parker no. 335: striding male nude; black chalk; 18.1 × 8.7 cm; cut.

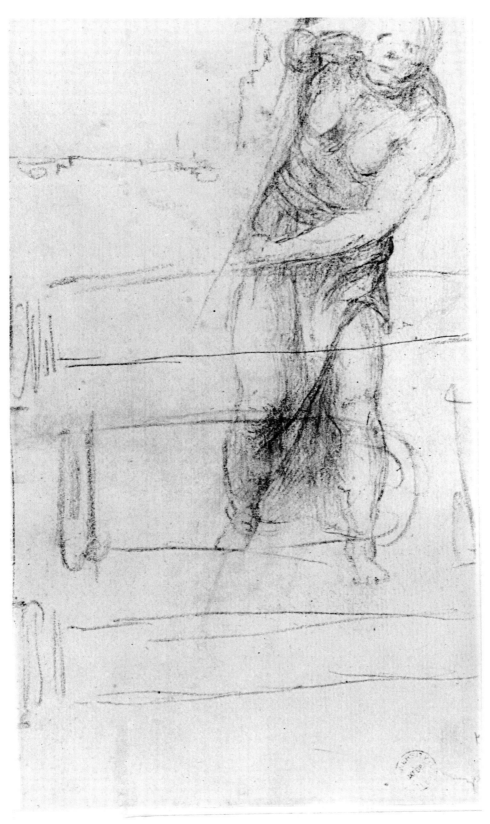

93. Ascanio Condivi
Oxford, Ashmolean Museum, Parker no. 334v: striding draped figure, column niche, ground plan; black chalk;
20 × 12 cm; cut.

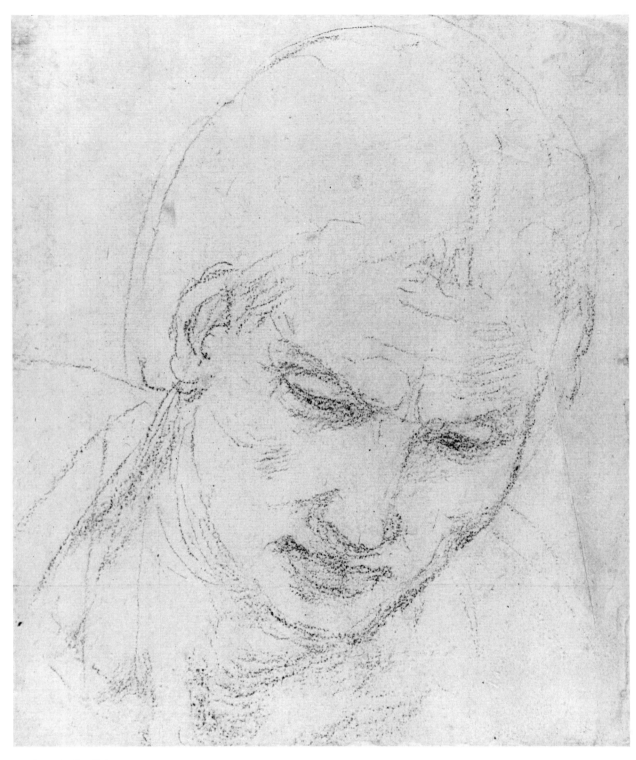

94. Ascanio Condivi
Oxford, Ashmolean Museum, Parker no. 337r: male head; black chalk; 23.8 × 20.1 cm; cut.

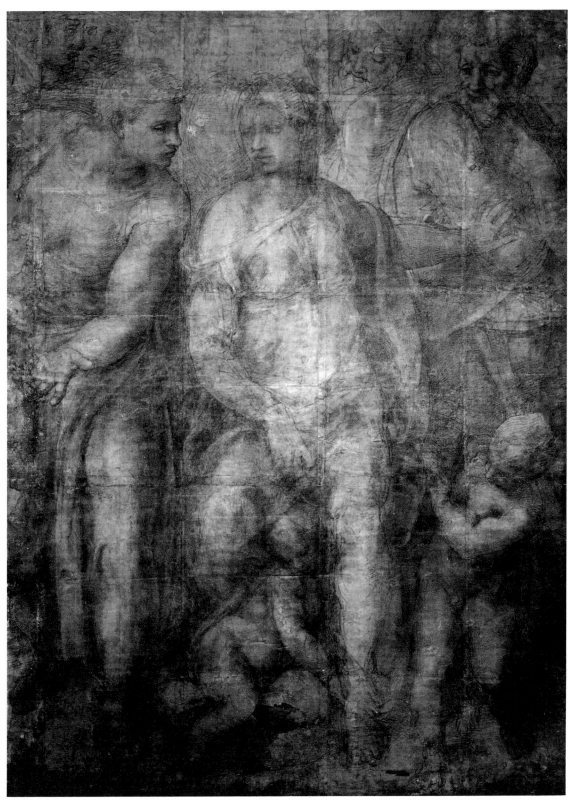

95. *Ascanio Condivi*
London, British Museum, no. 1895-9-15-518+ : "Epiphany"; black chalk; 232.7 × 165.6 cm; cut.

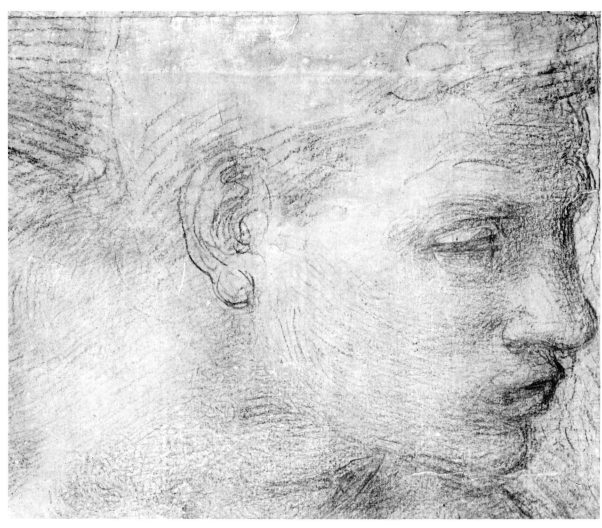

96. Ascanio Condivi
London, British Museum, no. 1895-9-15-518 + : "Epiphany" (detail).

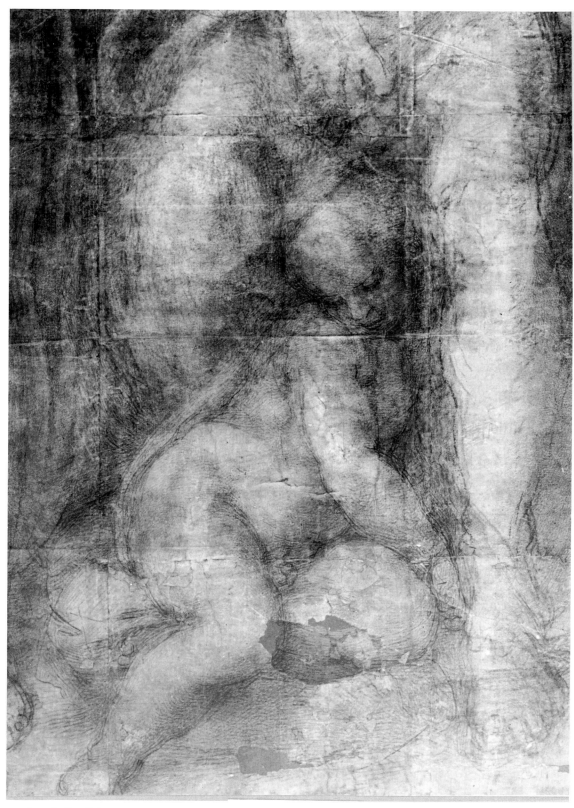

97. Ascanio Condivi
London, British Museum, no. 1895-9-15-518+ : "Epiphany" (detail).

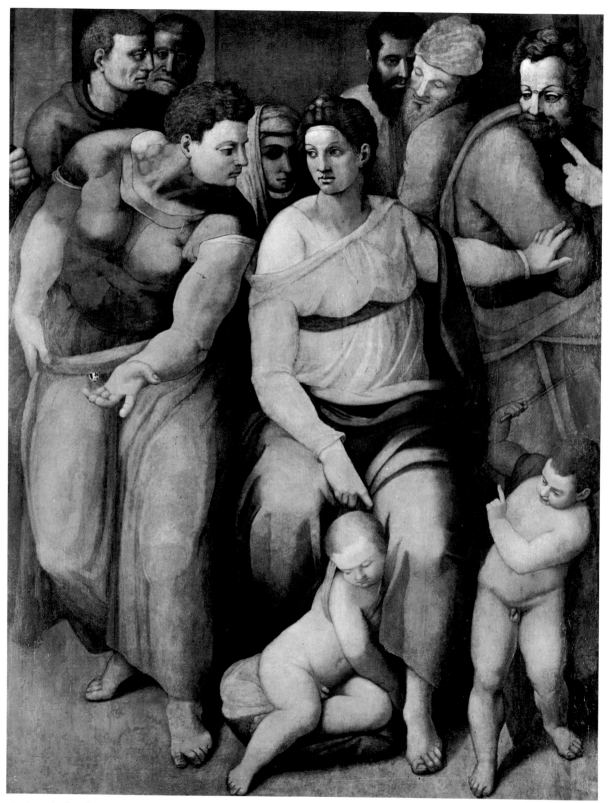

98. Ascanio Condivi
Florence, Casa Buonarroti: "Epiphany"; tempera on wood; 240 × 187 cm.

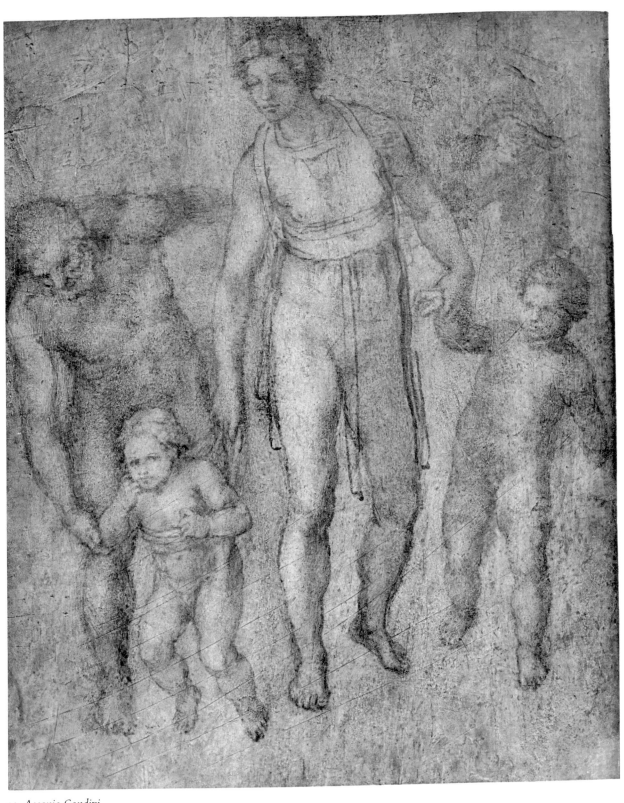

99. *Ascanio Condivi*
Oxford, Ashmolean Museum, no. 278: ambiguous scene; bistre over a green plaster ground on wood; 66 × 53 cm.

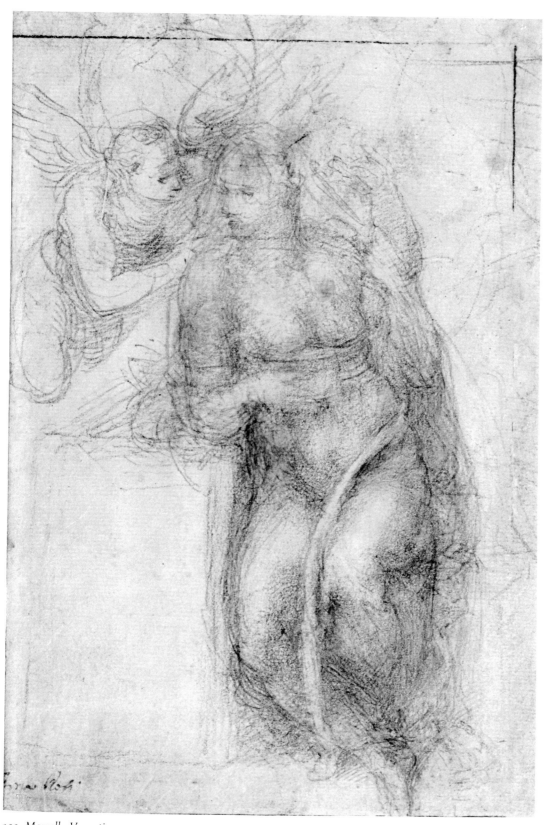

100. *Marcello Venusti*
London, British Museum, no. 1895-9-15-516r: Annunciation; *black chalk; 28.3 × 19.6 cm; cut.*

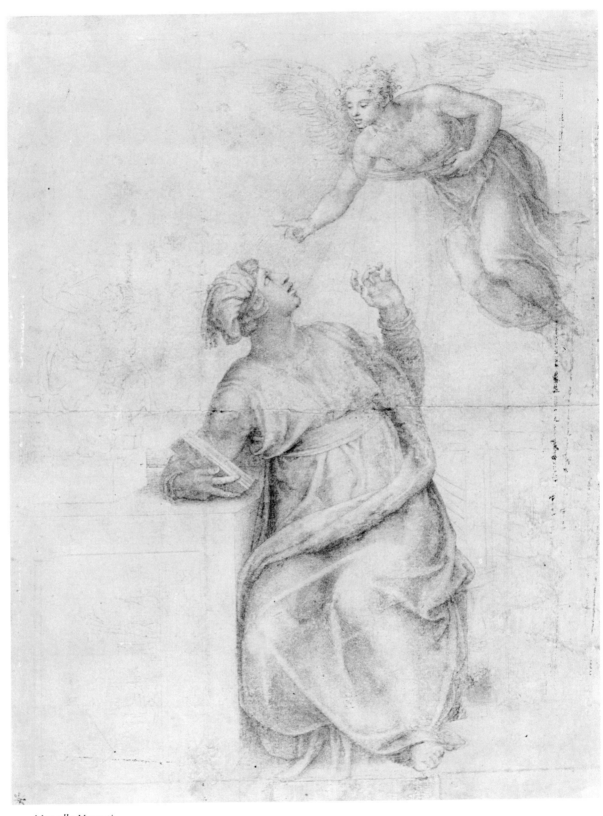

101. Marcello Venusti
New York, Pierpont Morgan Library, no. IV, 7: Annunciation; *black chalk; 38.2 × 29.6 cm; cut.*

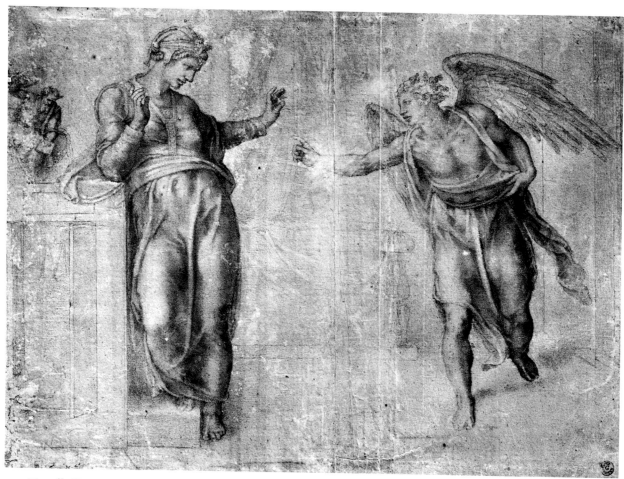

102. *Marcello Venusti*
Florence, Uffizi, no. 229F: Annunciation; *black chalk; 40.5 × 54.7 cm; cut.*

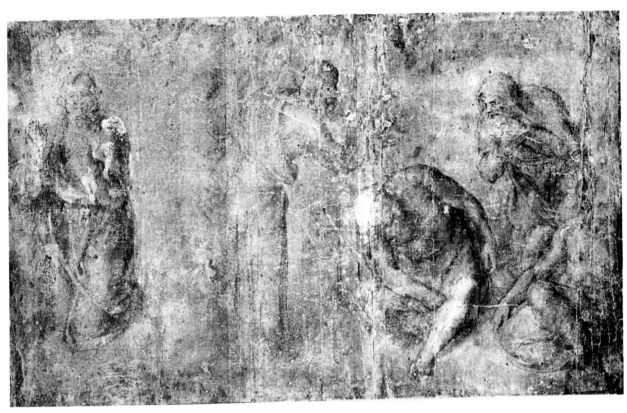

103. *Marcello Venusti*
Florence, Uffizi, no. 230F: Christ in Gethsemane; *black chalk; 36 × 60 cm; cut.*

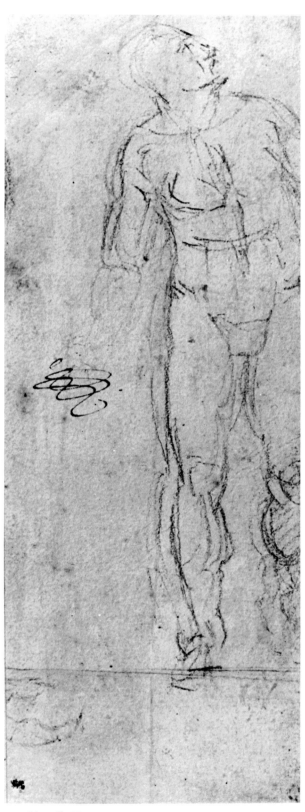

104. Marcello Venusti
Paris, Louvre, no. 720v: male nude looking upward; black chalk; 23 × 11 cm; cut (recto: fig. 112).

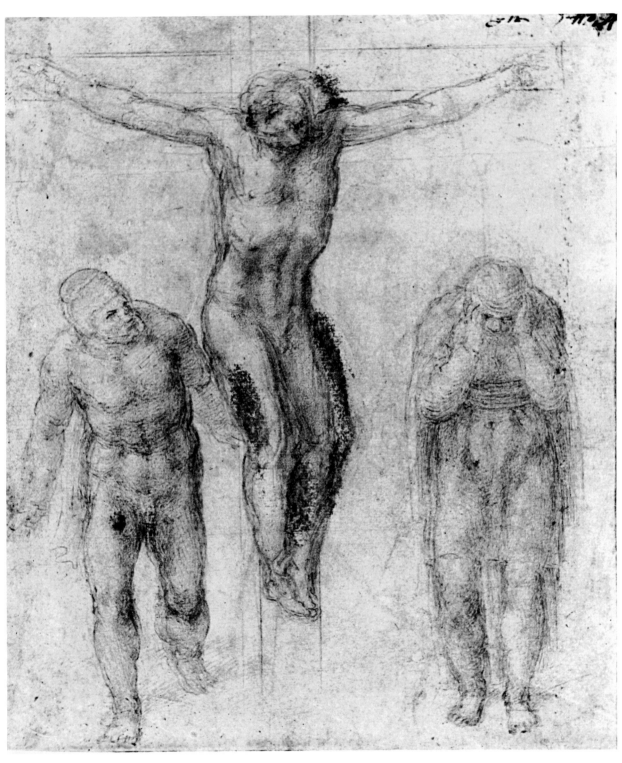

105. Marcello Venusti
*Oxford, Ashmolean Museum, Parker no. 343r: Christ on the cross between two secondary figures; black chalk,
treated in some places with white lead (oxidized); 27.8 × 23.4 cm; cut.*

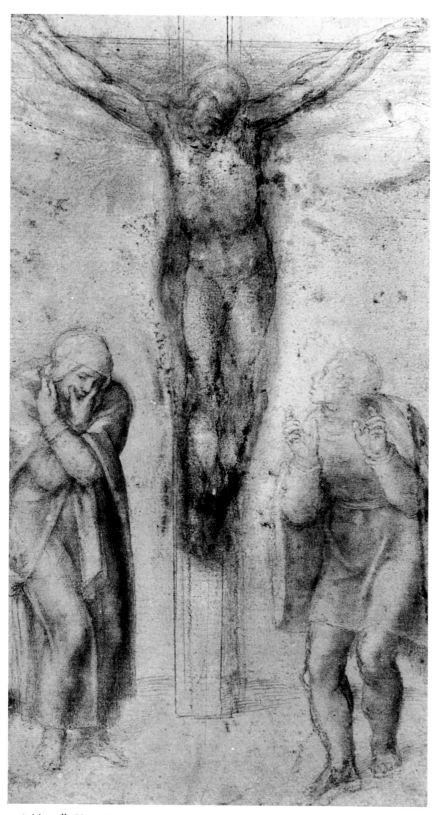

106. Marcello Venusti
Windsor Castle, Royal Library, no. 12775: Christ on the cross between Mary and John; black chalk, treated in
some places with white lead (oxidized); 38.2 × 21 cm; cut.

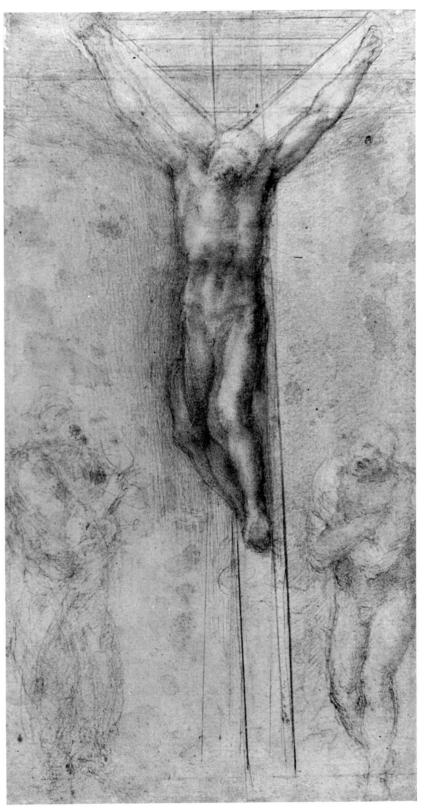

107. *Marcello Venusti*
Windsor Castle, Royal Library, no. 12761r: Christ on the cross between Mary and John; black chalk;
40.5 × 21.8 cm; cut.

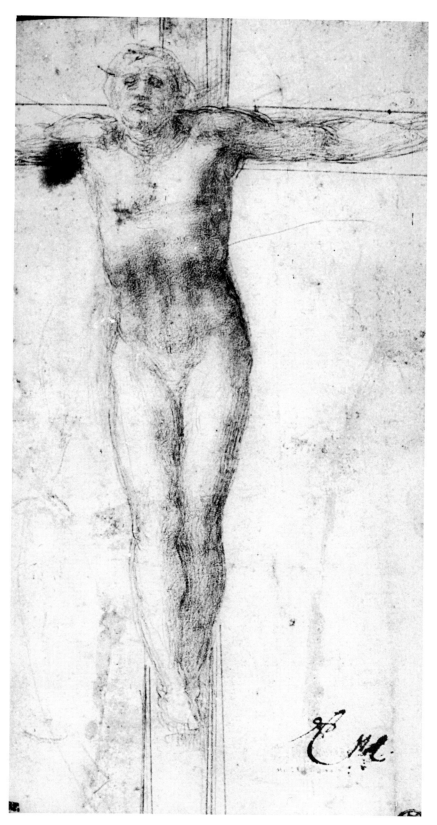

108. Marcello Venusti

Paris, Louvre, no. 842r: Christ on the cross; black chalk; 25.5 × 13.5 cm; cut.

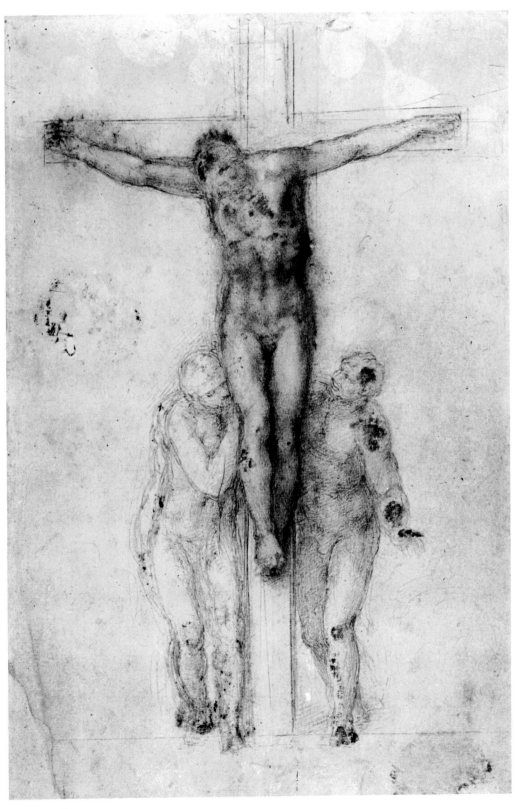

109. Marcello Venusti
London, British Museum, no. 1895-9-15-510: Christ on the cross between Mary and John; black chalk treated in some places with white lead (oxidized); 41.2 × 27.9 cm.

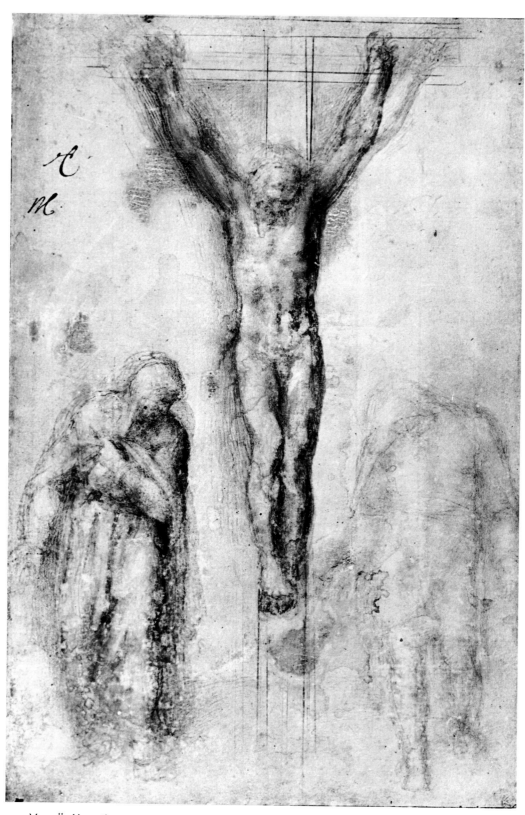

110. *Marcello Venusti*
Paris, Louvre, no. 700: Christ on the cross between Mary and John; black chalk, treated in some places with white
lead (oxidized) and ink; 43.3 × 29 cm; cut.

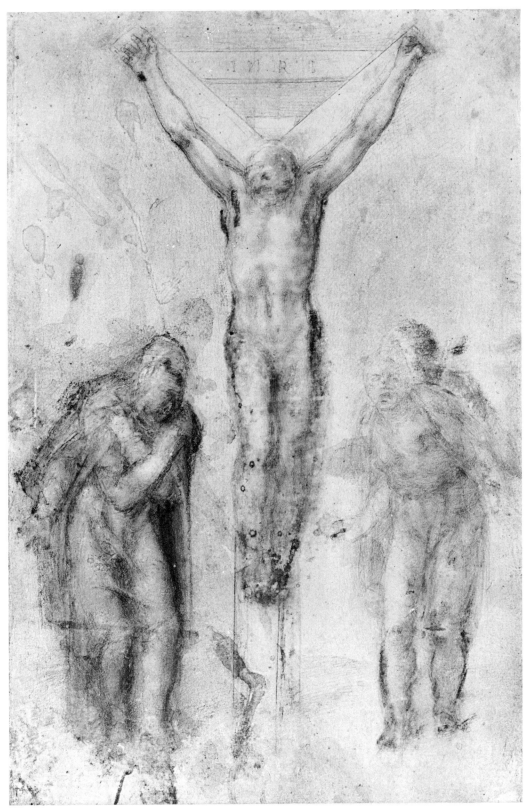

111. Marcello Venusti

London, British Museum, no. 1895-9-15-509: Christ on the cross between Mary and John; black chalk, treated in some places with white lead (oxidized); 41.3 × 28.6 cm; cut.

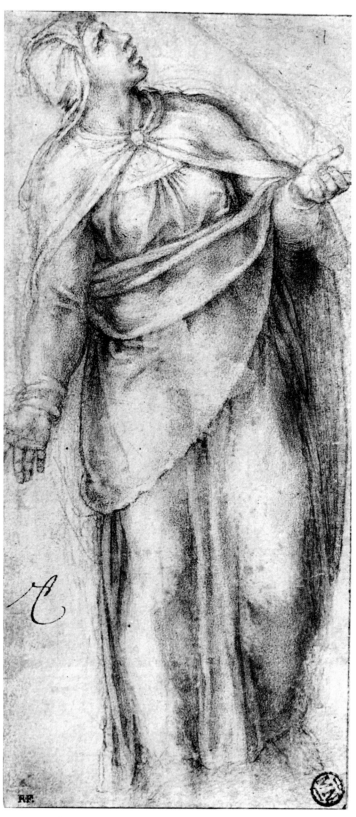

112. *Marcello Venusti*
Paris, Louvre, no. 720r: Mary looking up (at the crucified Christ); black chalk; 23 × 11 cm;
cut (verso: fig. 104).

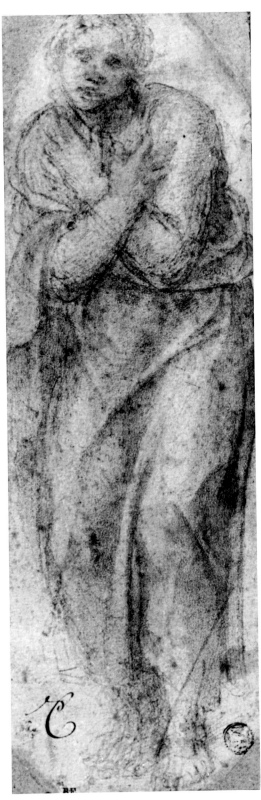

113. *Marcello Venusti*
Paris, Louvre, no. 698: John (under the cross); black chalk; 25 × 8.2 cm; cut.

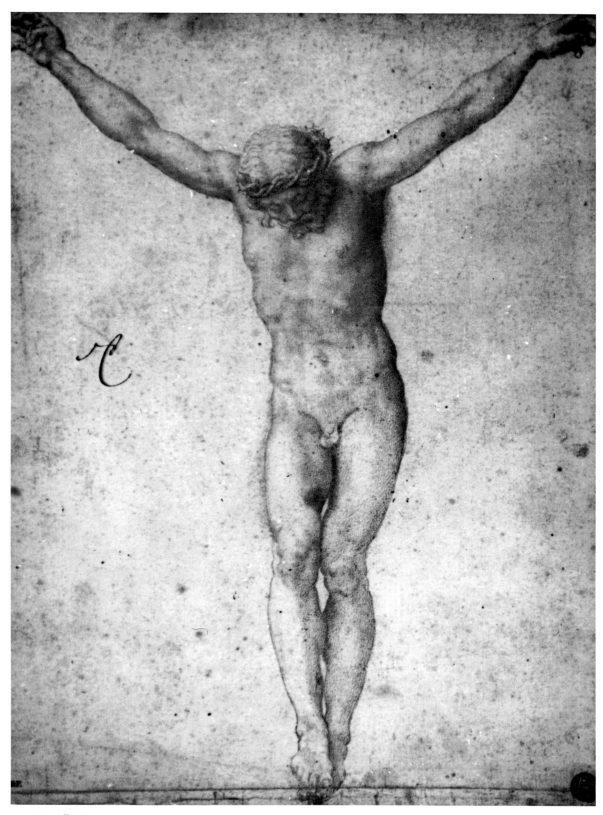

114. Marcello Venusti
Paris, Louvre, no. 843: crucified Christ with crown of thorns (copy); black chalk; 29 × 23 cm; cut.

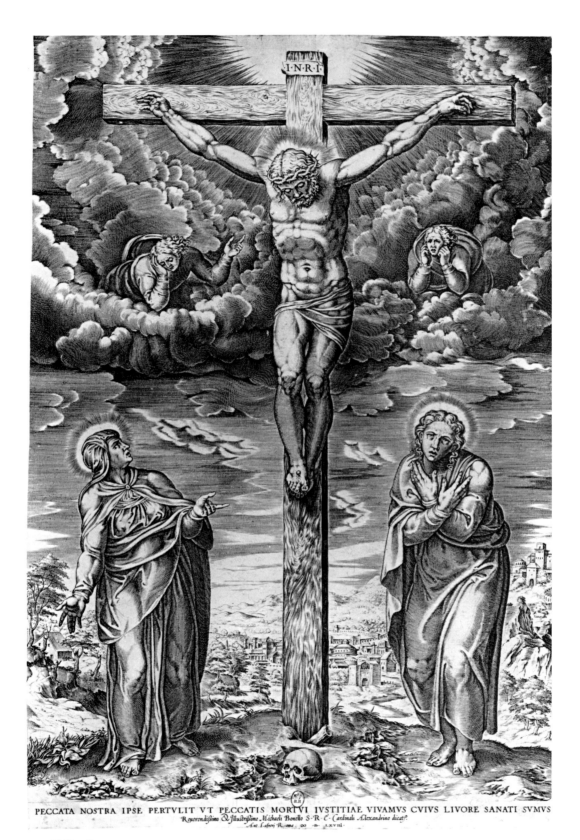

PECCATA NOSTRA IPSE PERTVLIT VT PECCATIS MORTVI IVSTITIAE VIVAMVS CVIVS LIVORE SANATI SVMVS
Reuerendissimo & Illustrissimo Michaeli Bonello S·R·E· Cardinali Alexandrino dicat.
Ant·Lafreri Romae ∞ ⅃ ·LXVIII·

115. *Philipp Soye*
Christ on the cross between Mary and John and two angels; copper engraving, dated 1568.

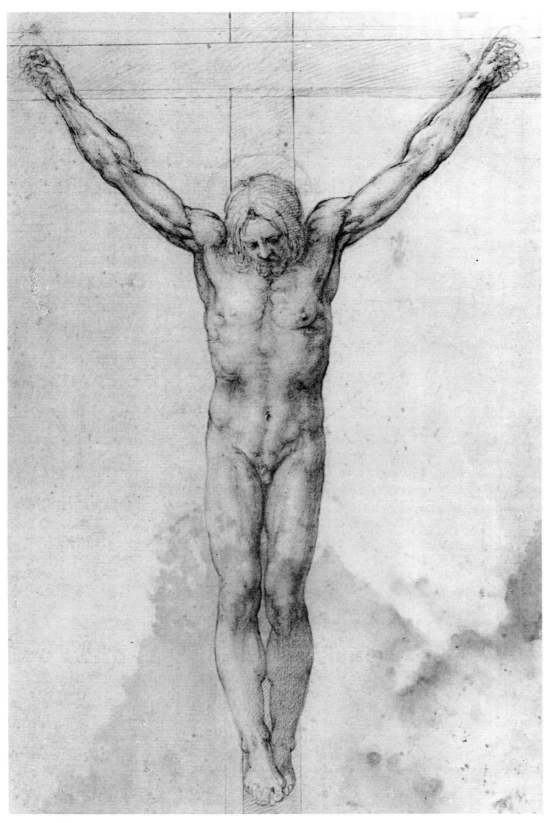

116. Marcello Venusti
Frankfurt, Städelsches Kunstinstitut, no. 3978: Christ on the cross (copy); black chalk; cut.

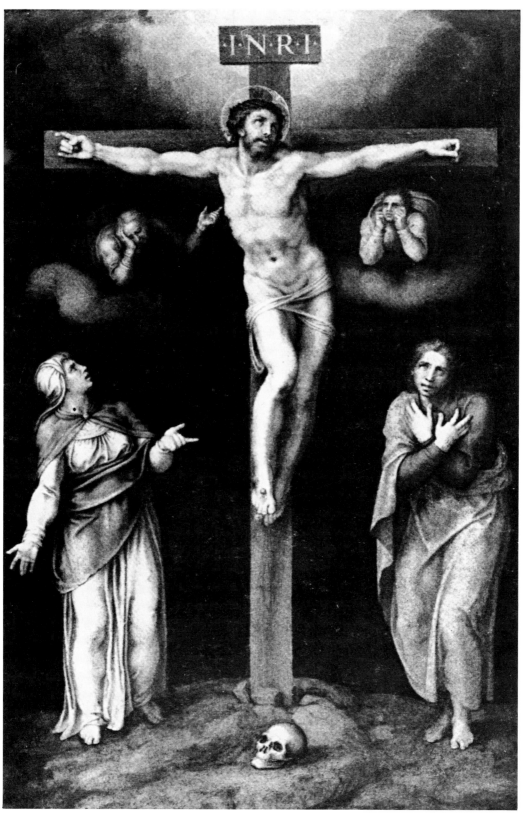

117. *Marcello Venusti*
Rome, Galleria Doria-Pamphili, no. 340: Christ on the cross between Mary and John and two angels; oil on wood;
51 × 33 cm.

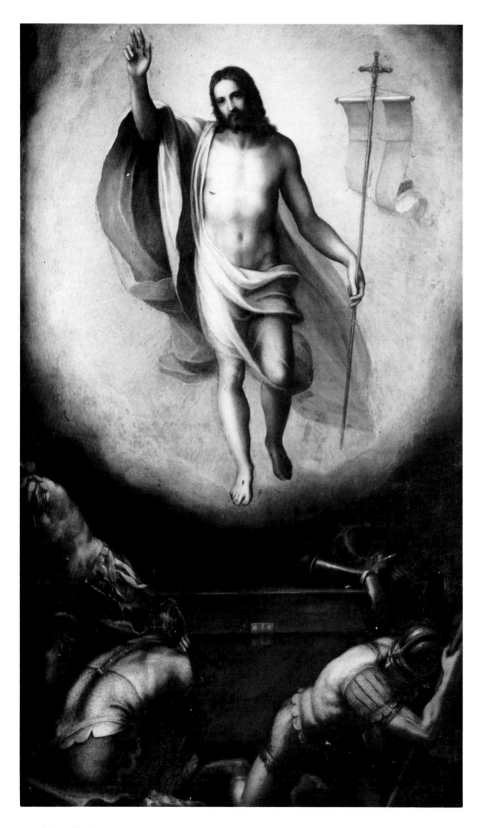

118. Marcello Venusti
Forlì, Pinacoteca: Resurrection of Christ; *oil on wood; 72 × 44 cm; cut.*

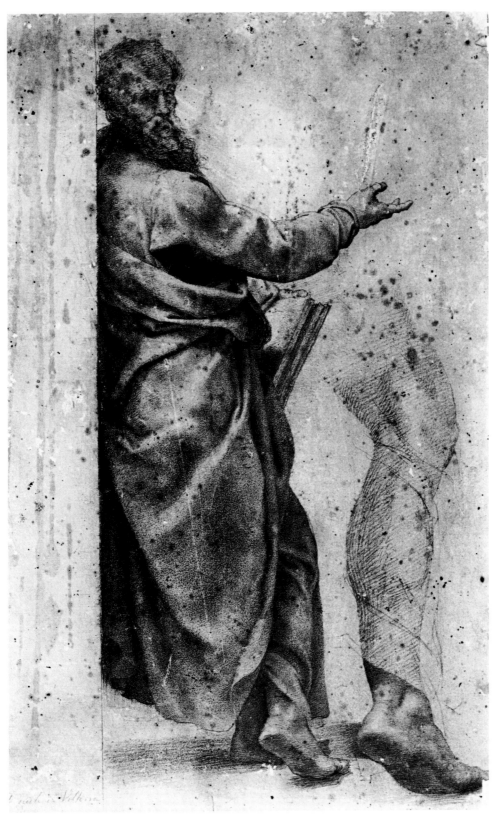

119. Daniele da Volterra
London, British Museum, no. 1946-7-13-114: *draped male figure with book (apostle), left leg; black chalk;*
37.2 × 22.8 cm; cut.

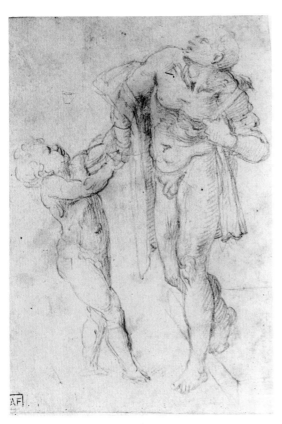

120. *Daniele da Volterra (copy)*
London, British Museum, no. 1956-10-13-13: upward-glancing man being undressed by a naked boy
(Aeneas and Ascanius); black chalk; 14 × 10.1 cm; cut.

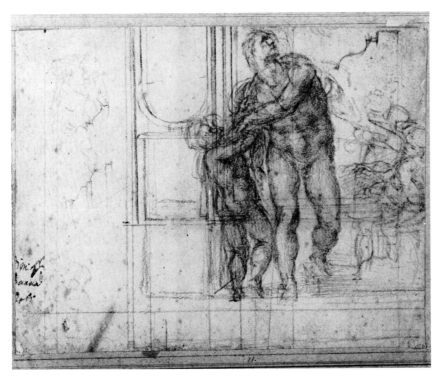

121. *Daniele da Volterra*
Haarlem, Teylers Museum, A32-v: upward-glancing man being undressed by a naked boy in front of a bed occupied
by a figure (Aeneas, Ascanius, and Dido), architectural profiles and frameworks; black chalk; 18 × 13.6 cm; cut
(recto: fig. 126).

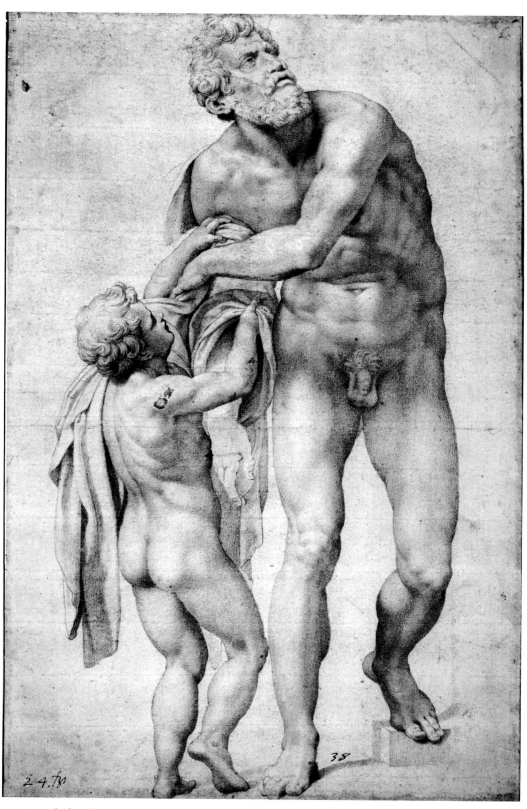

122. *Daniele da Volterra*
Vienna, Albertina, no. 497: upward-glancing man being undressed by a naked boy (Aeneas and Ascanius); black
chalk; 52.1 × 34.6 cm; cut.

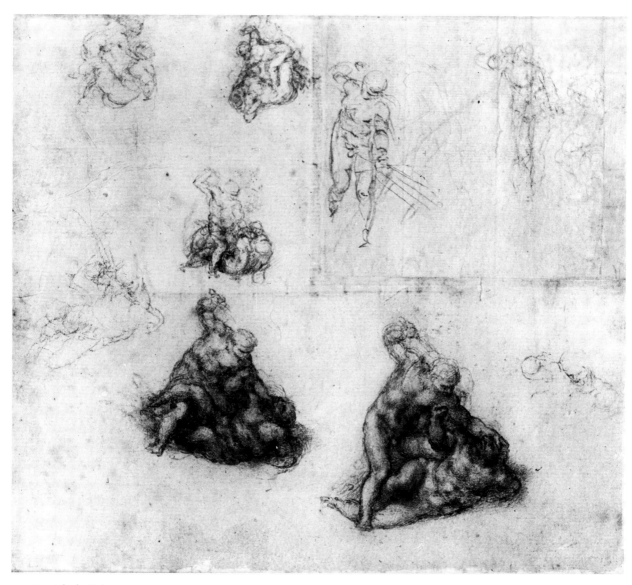

123. Daniele da Volterra
Oxford, Ashmolean Museum, Parker no. 328r: seven sketches for a battle group, four sketches for an Expulsion of the Moneychangers; black chalk; 21 × 24.5 cm; cut.

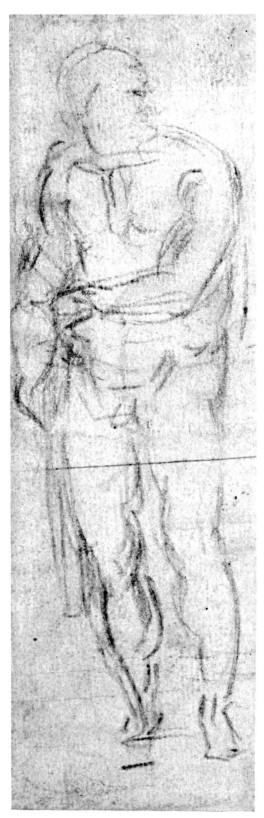

124. Daniele da Volterra
London, British Museum, no. 1895-9-15-513: standing male nude; black chalk; 17 × 5.5 cm; cut.

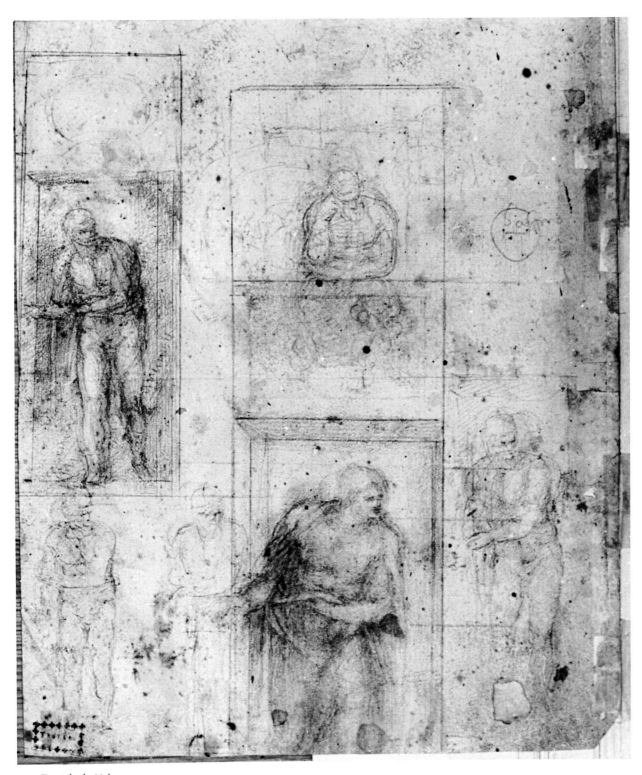

125. Daniele da Volterra
Haarlem, Teylers Museum, A29v: seven figural sketches, niche frames; black chalk; 39.9 × 23.5 cm; cut.

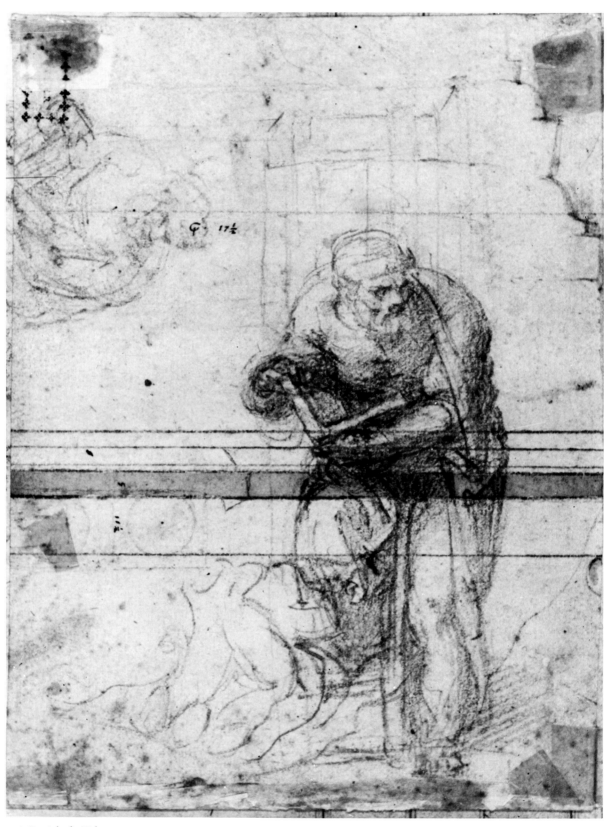

126. *Daniele da Volterra*
Haarlem, Teylers Museum, A32r: two sketches of a standing man with open book (apostle), architectural sketches;
black chalk; 18 × 13.6 cm; cut (verso: fig. 121).

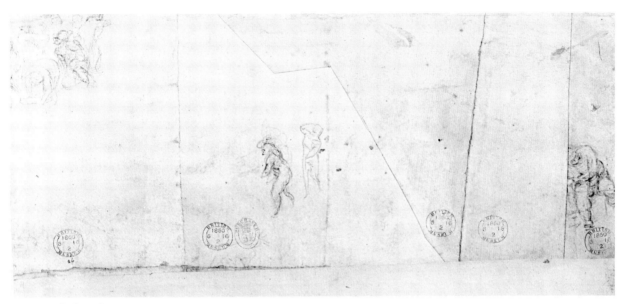

127. Daniele da Volterra
London, British Museum, no. 1860-6-16-2/3v: sketches for an Expulsion of the Moneychangers; *black chalk;*
17.8 × 30.2 cm; cut (recto: fig. 130).

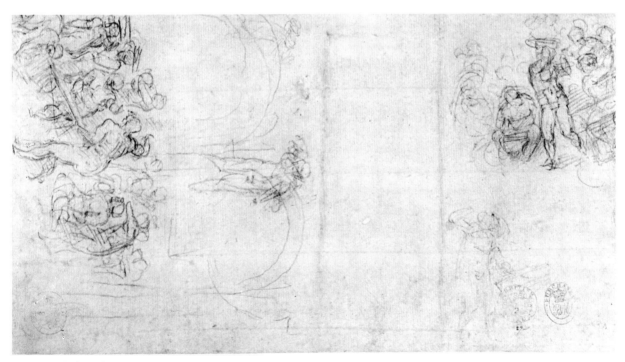

128. Daniele da Volterra
London, British Museum, no. 1860-6-16-2/2v: sketches for an Expulsion of the Moneychangers; *black chalk;*
14.8 × 27.6 cm; cut (recto: fig. 129).

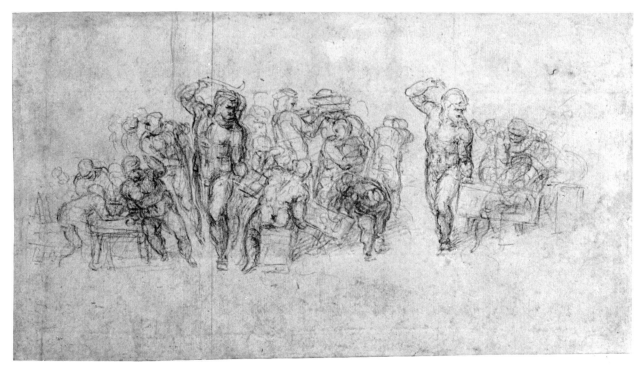

129. *Daniele da Volterra*
London, British Museum, no. 1860-6-16-2/2r: two sketches for an Expulsion of the Moneychangers; *black chalk;*
14.8 × 27.6 cm; cut (verso: fig. 128).

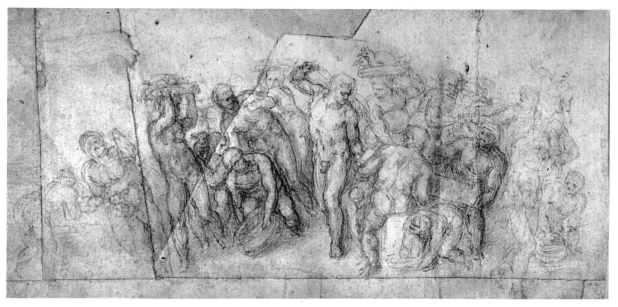

130. *Daniele da Volterra*
London, British Museum, no. 1860-6-16-2/3r: Expulsion of the Moneychangers; *black chalk; 17.8 × 37.2 cm; cut*
(verso: fig. 127).

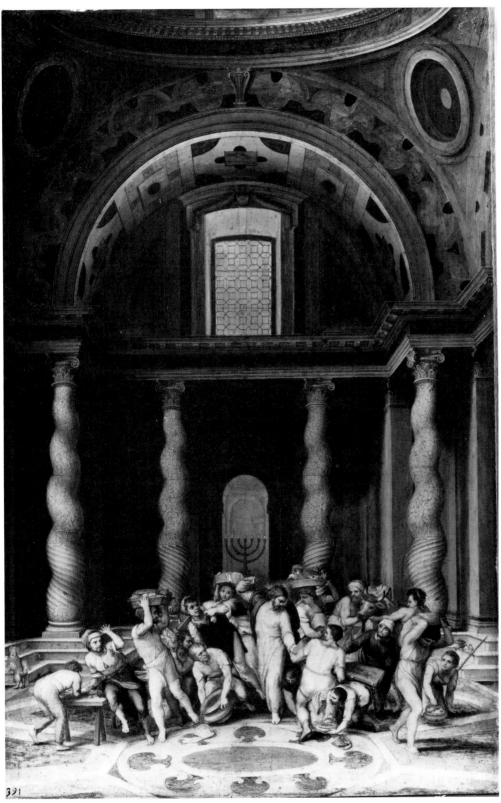

131. Giulio Clovio
Expulsion of the Moneychangers; *London, National Gallery, no. 1194; oil on wood; 60 × 38 cm.*

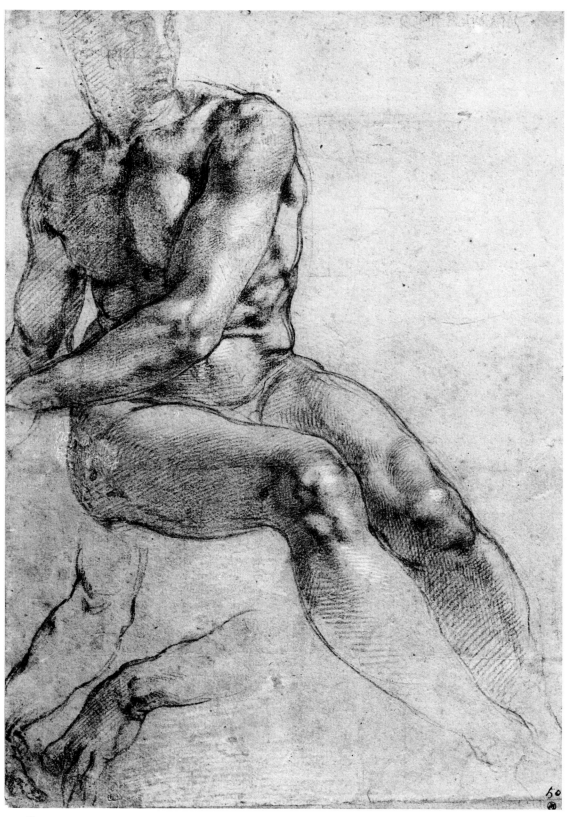

132. *Forgery*

Vienna, Albertina, Sc.R.155r: "studies" for the ignudo to the right above the Persica of the Sistine ceiling; red chalk over metal point, highlighted in white; 27 × 19 cm; cut.

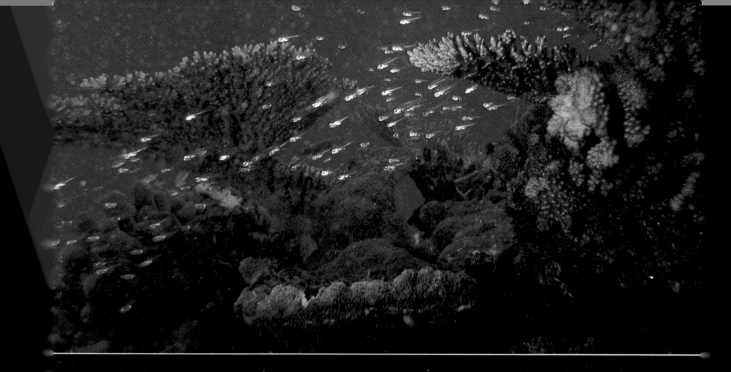

Coral reef aquatic ecosystem

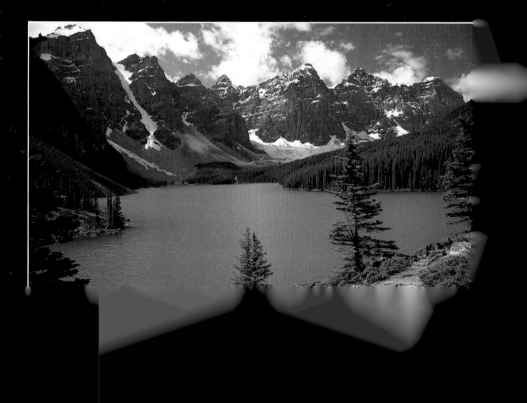

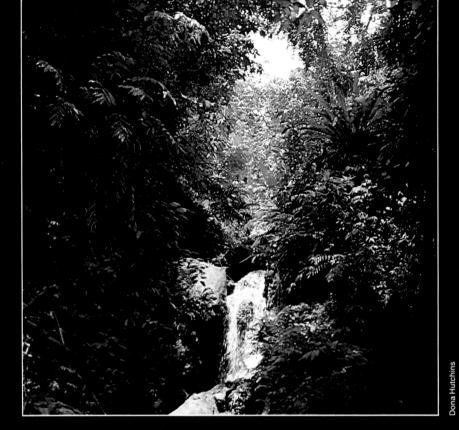

Tropical forest biome

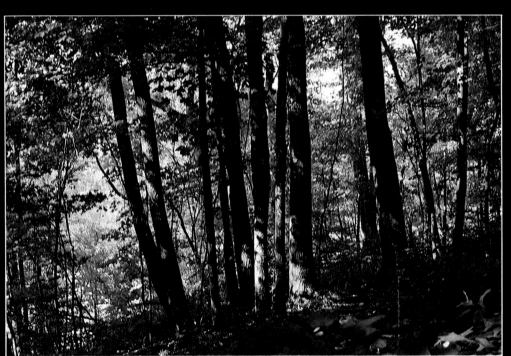

LIVING IN THE ENVIRONMENT
An Introduction to Environmental Science

FIFTH EDITION

■

G. Tyler Miller, Jr.
St. Andrews Presbyterian College

WADSWORTH PUBLISHING COMPANY

Belmont, California
A Division of Wadsworth, Inc.

Science Editor: Jack Carey
Production Editor: Leland Moss
Designer: Julia Scannell
Print Buyer: Barbara Britton
Copy Editor: Noel Deeley
Associate Copy Editor: Jennifer Gordon
Art Editor: Marta Kongsle
Compositor: Graphic Typesetting Service
Illustrators: Joan Carol, Raychel Ciemma, Florence Fujimoto, Darwen and Vally Hennings, Victor Royer, Linda Harris-Sweezey, John and Judith Waller
Photo Research: Stuart Kenter
Cover Photograph: Galen Rowell/Mountain Light

Books in the Wadsworth Biology Series

Biology: The Unity and Diversity of Life, 4th, Starr and Taggart
Energy and Environment: The Four Energy Crises, 2nd, Miller
Replenish the Earth: A Primer in Human Ecology, Miller
Oceanography: An Introduction, 3rd, Ingmanson and Wallace
Environmental Science, Miller

Biology books under the editorship of William A. Jensen, University of California, Berkeley

Biology: The Foundations, 2nd, Wolfe
Biology of the Cell, 2nd, Wolfe
Botany, 2nd, Jensen and Salisbury
Plant Physiology, 2nd, Salisbury and Ross
Plant Physiology Laboratory Manual, Ross
Plants: An Evolutionary Survey, 2nd, Scagel et al.
Nonvascular Plants: An Evolutionary Survey, Scagel et al.
Introduction to Cell Biology, Wolfe

Printed in the United States of America

2 3 4 5 6 7 8 9 10—92 91 90 89 88   48

Library of Congress Cataloging-in-Publication Data
Miller, G. Tyler (George Tyler), 1931–
   Living in the environment.

   Bibliography: p.
   Includes index.
   1. Human ecology.   2. Environmental policy.
I. Title.
GF41.M54   1987   304.2   87-2080
ISBN 0-534-08052-9

The environmental crisis is an outward manifestation of a crisis of mind and spirit. There could be no greater misconception of its meaning than to believe it to be concerned only with endangered wildlife, human-made ugliness, and pollution. These are part of it, but more importantly, the crisis is concerned with the kind of creatures we are and what we must become in order to survive.

Lynton K. Caldwell

This book is dedicated to Mother Earth, who sustains us and all other creatures, to my life partner, spouse, and best friend, Peggy Sue O'Neal, who attempts to work with rather than against the earth, and to my father, G. Tyler Miller, for his love, support, and inspiration.

Preface: To the Instructor

Goals The purposes of this book are to **(1)** cover environmental concepts and information in an accurate, balanced, and interesting way without the use of mathematics, **(2)** enable the teacher to use the material in a flexible manner for one-semester or full-year courses of varying emphases, and **(3)** introduce students to key scientific concepts that govern how nature works (see Chapters 3 through 6), **(4)** consistently use these concepts throughout the course to evaluate problems and options available in dealing with the use of natural resources, population growth, and pollution and environmental degradation, **(5)** expose students to important and controversial environmental issues that affect individuals, countries, and the world now and in the future, **(6)** provide a long-term historical perspective on environmental degradation along with a realistic but hopeful view of how much has been accomplished since 1965 (when the American public first became aware of many environmental problems) and how much more needs to be done (Chapters 2 and 26), and **(7)** show how most environmental problems are interrelated.

A Well-Tested Product The material in this textbook has been used and class-tested by over 1 million students at over two-thirds of the country's colleges and universities. By a very large margin, it has been the most widely used environmental science textbook in the United States since 1975, when the first edition was published.

Two Different Textbooks Available This fifth edition of *Living in the Environment* is the more comprehensive of two related textbooks designed for different types of introductory courses on environmental concepts and problems. The other book, *Environmental Science: An Introduction*, 2nd (Wadsworth, 1988), is a briefer (395-page) version, designed for shorter courses with less emphasis on environmental economics, politics, and ethics.

Flexibility To provide teaching flexibility, this book is divided into six major parts:

- Humans and Nature: An Overview (two chapters)
- Basic Concepts (four chapters)
- Population (three chapters)
- Resources (nine chapters)
- Pollution (five chapters)
- Environment and Society (three chapters)

Once Parts One and Two have been covered, the remainder of the book may be used in any order that meets the needs of the instructor. Major parts, chapters within these parts, and many sections within chapters can be moved around or omitted to accommodate courses with varying lengths and emphases.

Other Major Features The fifth edition, like earlier editions, **(1)** *consistently uses fundamental concepts* (Chapters 3–6) to illustrate the interrelationships of environmental problems and their possible solutions, **(2)** *provides balanced discussions of the opposing views* on major environmental issues, **(3)** *is based on an extensive review of the professional literature* (from more than 10,000 research sources; key readings for each chapter are listed at the end of the text), **(4)** *has received extensive manuscript review* by 175 experts and instructors— probably more reviewers than any textbook ever published (see List of Reviewers, pp. viii–x)—plus unsolicited suggestions from hundreds of students and teachers who have used this material, and **(5)** *uses Guest Essays to expose the reader to various points of view* (see List of Guest Essayists, p. viii).

Major Changes in the Fifth Edition Despite the overwhelming success of this textbook, the publisher and I feel obligated to improve each edition to meet changing needs indicated by the extensive reviews and surveys of users. The major changes in this edition include:

1. Material throughout the book has been updated, rewritten, and in many cases condensed to make this an even better textbook.

2. Throughout the text, important and controversial issues and further insights into environmental problems are highlighted in *Spotlights. Enrichment studies* at the ends of a number of chapters provide more detailed treatment of selected issues.

3. Because there is now greater agreement among instructors on the major topics to be covered in introductory environmental courses, the format of *Living in the Environment* has been reorganized: The enrichment studies placed in a separate section in previous editions have been incorporated into the main text either as chapters (Chapter 21, Solid Waste and Hazardous Waste, and Chapter 23, The Environment and Human Health), chapter sections, or end-of-chapter enrichment studies (see Detailed Table of Contents). The new organization is designed to make the book flow more smoothly and logically from one topic to another; as in previous editions, enrichment material can easily be omitted or used as the instructor chooses.

4. The treatment of pesticides has been expanded to a full chapter (Chapter 22), and new material (mostly as enrichment studies) has been added on the coastal zone (Chapter 5), environmental risk analysis and risk management (Chapter 6), desertification (Chapter 11), indoor air pollution from radioactive radon gas (Chapter 19), and the Great Lakes (Chapter 20).

5. Seven new guest essays have been added to seven used in earlier editions.

6. Color has been added to charts, maps, and drawings, and the number of illustrations and photographs has been increased dramatically from 201 in the fourth edition to 440 in this edition.

7. Three new study aids have been added:
(a) *general objectives*, a list of major questions at the beginning of each chapter, (b) *chapter summa-* ries, and (c) a *student preface* to acquaint students with the book's overall goals and numerous study aids.

As you and your students deal with the crucial and exciting issues discussed in this book, I hope you will take the time to point out errors and suggest improvements for future editions. Please send such information to me, care of Jack Carey, Science Editor, Wadsworth Publishing Company, 10 Davis Drive, Belmont, CA 94002.

Supplementary Materials   Dr. Robert Janiskee at the University of South Carolina has written an excellent instructor's manual for use with this text. It contains sample multiple-choice test questions with answers; suggested projects, field trips, and experiments; and a list of suitable topics for term papers and reports for each chapter. In addition, a series of master sheets for making overhead transparencies of many key diagrams is available from the publisher.

Acknowledgments   I wish to thank the many students and teachers who responded so favorably to the first four editions of *Living in the Environment* and offered suggestions for improvement. I am also deeply indebted to the prominent environmentalists and scholars who wrote guest essays and to the reviewers, who pointed out errors and suggested many important improvements. Any errors and deficiencies remaining are mine, not theirs.

It has also been a pleasure to work with a team of talented people who have helped improve this book. I am particularly indebted to production editor Leland Moss, art editor Marty Kongsle, photo researcher Stuart Kenter, designer Julia Scannell, copy editors Noel Deeley (who made many useful suggestions for improvement) and Jennifer Gordon, and to artists Darwen and Vally Hennings, John and Judith Waller, Linda Harris-Sweezey, Raychel Ciemma, Victor Royer, Joan Carol, and Florence Fujimoto. Above all I wish to thank Jack Carey, science editor at Wadsworth, for his encouragement, help, friendship, and superb reviewing system.

G. Tyler Miller, Jr.

Preface: To the Student

Major Goals I have written this book to show you that learning about environmental concepts and issues is **(1)** fun and interesting, **(2)** need not be difficult, **(3)** does not require use of mathematics or complex chemical and biological information, **(4)** is important and relevant to every aspect of your life, and **(5)** can help you make wiser decisions in vital matters that affect you, your loved ones, and society as a whole. This is not just another college course to be passed for credit. It is an introduction to how nature works, how it has been and is being abused, and what we can do to protect and improve it for ourselves, future generations, and other living things. I am convinced that nothing else deserves more of our energy, time, care, and personal involvement.

I have gone to considerable effort to present opposing views on these complex and highly controversial life-and-death issues in a balanced way. My goal is not to tell you what to think but to provide you with ecological concepts and information which you can use to reach your own conclusions. The more I have studied environmental issues, the more I have realized how complex and interrelated they are. I hope this book will stimulate you to begin a life-long involvement in the important and exciting task of learning how nature works and using this information to help make the world a better place to live now and in the future.

How I Became Involved I feel you are entitled to know how I became involved in environmental concerns and to what degree I try to put what I write about into practice in my own life and lifestyle. In 1966, when what we now know as the environmental movement began in the United States, I heard a scientist give a lecture on the problems of overpopulation and environmental abuse. Afterwards I went to him and said, "If even a fraction of what you have said is true, I will feel ethically obligated to give up my present scientific research on the corrosion of metals and devote the rest of my life to these issues. Frankly, I don't want to believe a word you have said, and I'm going into the literature to try to prove what you have said is either untrue or grossly distorted." After six months of study I was convinced of the seriousness

of the problems, and since then I have been studying, speaking, teaching, and writing about them. I have also attempted to live my life in an ecologically sound way—with varying degrees of success—by treading as lightly as possible on the earth. Working toward this goal has involved making more compromises and trade-offs than I have liked, but I continue the effort (see p. 596 for a summary of my own progress in attempting to work with nature).

Emphasis on Concepts The purpose of useful learning is not to stuff ourselves full of information but to learn and understand a small number of basic concepts or principles with which we can integrate numerous facts into meaningful patterns. In this book a small number of key scientific concepts (presented in Chapters 3 through 6 and summarized in the Epilogue) are used throughout to evaluate environmental problems and options for dealing with them. Since this is not a murder mystery, I suggest you take the time now to read the Prologue (p. xxii) and the Epilogue (p. 603) to get an overview of our planetary problems and the ideas you will be using to tie together the facts concerning these problems presented in this book.

A Realistic but Hopeful National and Global Outlook Our actions are based primarily on our worldview—our beliefs about how the world works. In this book I offer a realistic but hopeful view of the future based primarily on **(1)** how much has been done since 1965 (frankly, much more than I expected at that time), when the public first became aware of many environmental problems, and **(2)** the fact that an increasing number of ordinary citizens are developing a new worldview—based on the necessity of sustaining the earth—and are acting on this belief system in their personal and political lives by leading rather than following conventional political leaders.

Politics is not just voting—it is also how you lead your life. For example, turning off a light, buying an energy-saving appliance or car, not buying an all-electric house (the most resource-wasting type), or doing anything that saves electricity and other forms of energy is an important economic action that reduces the need to build more electric power plants and saves you money in a world where electricity and gasoline are expected to become increasingly expensive. At the same time, it is a political action, sending a strong message to other citizens and to those who hope to win our votes.

Much more needs to be done, but there is hope if enough of us care. The key is to *think globally and act locally*. Most environmental problems and their possible solutions are interrelated and must be considered on a local, national, and global scale—as this book does. Pollution, for example, does not respect national boundaries, as was clearly illustrated by the radiation that drifted over much of the world after being released in the 1986 accident at the Chernobyl nuclear power plant in the Soviet Union.

How This Book Is Organized   To get a better idea of what you will be learning, I suggest that you take a few minutes to look at the brief table of contents and the detailed table of contents. This book has been designed to be flexible enough for use in courses with different lengths and emphases. After the six chapters in Parts One and Two have been studied, the remainder of the book can be covered in essentially any order, so do not be concerned if your instructor skips around and omits material (I do hope, however, that you will go ahead and read it on your own).

This book is written for you. To help you learn more efficiently and effectively, I have provided a number of learning aids, as outlined below.

General Objectives and Chapter Summaries   I believe in the old writing and teaching adage: Tell people where you are going, go there, and then remind them of where they have been. As a result, each chapter begins with a few general questions or learning objectives written in nontechnical language and designed to give you an idea of what you will be learning. After you finish a chapter, you can go back and try to answer these questions to review what you have learned. You will also find a brief summary at the end of each chapter. Reading the summary should not replace reading the entire chapter, because the summary is a review that omits much of the information needed for adequate understanding of the material; it should serve only as a reminder of the main points.

Vocabulary   In each chapter you will be introduced to a number of new terms whose meanings you need to know and understand. To help you identify these key terms, each is printed in boldface when it is introduced. The pages where key terms are defined are shown in boldface in the index, and a glossary of all key terms appears at the end of the book.

Visual Aids   Great emphasis has been placed on developing a variety of diagrams that illustrate complex ideas in a simple manner. Many carefully selected photos give you a better picture of how topics discussed in this book relate to the real world.

Discussion Topics   The questions at the end of each chapter are not designed to test your recall of facts. That is left to your instructor. Instead, these questions are designed to make you think, to apply what you have learned to your personal lifestyle, to take sides on controversial issues, and to back up your conclusions and beliefs.

Further Readings   At the end of this book you will find a list of readings, grouped by chapter, which you can use to increase your knowledge of a particular topic and to prepare reports. Most of these works cite other works that can enhance your knowledge.

Save This Book   This book will be a useful reference long after you have completed this course because you will have to deal with its vital issues throughout your life. So instead of throwing it away or reselling it for about half what you paid for it, I suggest you keep it in your personal library. Learning is a lifelong process and you should be building a collection of books that will be useful to you now and in the future. You may also purchase the latest updated version of this text (published every three years) directly from Wadsworth Publishing Company, 10 Davis Drive, Belmont, CA 94002.

Help Me Improve This Book   Publishing a book is such a complex process that some errors are almost certain to be present. If you find what you believe to be an error, write it down, send it to me, and turn in a copy to your instructor. Hundreds of students have helped me improve this book since it was first published in 1975; please continue this tradition by letting me know what you like and dislike most about the book. Send any errors or suggestions for improvement to Jack Carey, Wadsworth Publishing Company, 10 Davis Drive, Belmont, CA 94002. He will send them on to me. Unfortunately, time does not permit me to answer your letters, but be aware of how much I appreciate learning from you.

And Now   Relax and enjoy yourself as you learn about the challenging issues we all face in preserving the earth's life-support system for ourselves, future generations, and the millions of plants and animals we share the planet with and depend upon for our survival.

G. Tyler Miller, Jr.

Guest Essayists

Hannes Alfvén
Professor of Applied Physics, University of California,
San Diego; Nobel Laureate in Physics (1970)

Leon F. Bouvier
Former Vice President
Population Reference Bureau

Herman E. Daly
Professor of Economics
Louisiana State University

Bill Devall
Professor of Sociology
Humboldt State University

Edward J. Kormondy
Vice President of Academic Affairs
California State University, Los Angeles

Amory B. Lovins
Energy policy consultant

Norman Myers
Consultant in environment and development

William Ophuls
Writer and lecturer on politics and ecology

David Pimentel
Professor of Entomology
Cornell University

Philip R. Pryde
Department of Geography
San Diego State University

Julian L. Simon
Professor of Economics and Business Administration
University of Maryland

Robert Leo Smith
Professor of Wildlife Biology, Division of Forestry
West Virginia University

Gus Speth
President, World Resources Institute

Alvin M. Weinberg
Director, Institute of Energy Analysis

Reviewers

Barbara J. Abraham *Hampton College*
Larry G. Allen *California State University,*
Northridge
James R. Anderson *U.S. Geological Survey*
Kenneth B. Armitage *University of Kansas*
Virgil R. Baker *Arizona State University*

Ian G. Barbour *Carleton College*
Albert J. Beck *California State University, Chico*
R. W. Behan *Northern Arizona University*
Keith L. Bildstein *Winthrop College*
Jeff Bland *University of Puget Sound*
Roger G. Bland *Central Michigan University*

Georg Borgstrom   *Michigan State University*
Arthur C. Borror   *University of New Hampshire*
John H. Bounds   *Sam Houston State University*
Leon F. Bouvier   *Population Reference Bureau*
Michael F. Brewer   *Resources for the Future, Inc.*
Patrick E. Brunelle   *Contra Costa College*
Terrence J. Burgess   *Saddleback College North*
Lynton K. Caldwell   *Indiana University*
Faith Thompson Campbell   *Natural Resources Defense Council, Inc.*
E. Ray Canterbery   *Florida State University*
Ted J. Case   *University of San Diego*
Ann Causey   *Auburn University*
Richard A. Cellarius   *Evergreen State University*
William U. Chandler   *Worldwatch Institute*
R. F. Christman   *University of North Carolina, Chapel Hill*
Preston Cloud   *University of California, Santa Barbara*
Bernard C. Cohen   *University of Pittsburgh*
Richard A. Cooley   *University of California, Santa Cruz*
Dennis J. Corrigan
John D. Cunningham   *Keene State College*
Herman E. Daly   *Louisiana State University*
Raymond F. Dasmann   *University of California, Santa Cruz*
Kingsley Davis   *University of California, Berkeley*
Edward E. DeMartini   *University of California, Santa Barbara*
Thomas R. Detwyler   *University of Michigan*
Lon D. Drake   *University of Iowa*
W. T. Edmonson   *University of Washington*
Thomas Eisner   *Cornell University*
David E. Fairbrothers   *Rutgers University*
Paul P. Feeny   *Cornell University*
Nancy Field   *Bellevue Community College*
Allan Fitzsimmons   *University of Kentucky*
George L. Fouke   *St. Andrews Presbyterian College*
Lowell L. Getz   *University of Illinois at Urbana-Champaign*
Frederick F. Gilbert   *Washington State University*
Jay Glassman   *Los Angeles Valley College*
Harold Goetz   *North Dakota State University*
Jeffery J. Gordon   *Bowling Green State University*
Eville Gorham   *University of Minnesota*
Ernest M. Gould, Jr.   *Harvard University*
Katherine B. Gregg   *West Virginia Wesleyan College*
Paul Grogger   *University of Colorado*
J. L. Guernsey   *Indiana State University*
Ralph Guzman   *University of California, Santa Cruz*
Raymond E. Hampton   *Central Michigan University*

Ted L. Hanes   *California State University, Fullerton*
John P. Harley   *Eastern Kentucky University*
Grant A. Harris   *Washington State University*
Harry S. Hass   *San Jose City College*
Arthur N. Haupt   *Population Reference Bureau*
Denis A. Hayes   *Environmental consultant*
John G. Hewston   *Humboldt State University*
David L. Hicks   *Whitworth College*
Eric Hirst   *Oak Ridge National Laboratory*
C. S. Holling   *University of British Columbia*
Donald Holtgrieve   *California State University, Hayward*
Michael H. Horn   *University of California, Fullerton*
Marilyn Houck   *Pennsylvania State University*
Richard D. Houk   *Winthrop College*
Donald Huisingh   *North Carolina State University*
Marlene K. Hutt   *IBM*
David R. Inglis   *University of Massachusetts*
Robert Janiskee   *University of South Carolina*
Hugo H. John   *University of Connecticut*
David I. Johnson   *Michigan State University*
Agnes Kadar   *Nassau Community College*
Thomas L. Keefe   *Eastern Kentucky University*
Nathan Keyfitz   *Harvard University*
Edward J. Kormondy   *California State University, Los Angeles*
Judith Kunofsky   *Sierra Club*
Theodore Kury   *State University College at Buffalo*
Steve Ladochy   *University of Winnipeg*
Mark B. Lapping   *Kansas State University*
Tom Leege   *Idaho Department of Fish and Game*
William S. Lindsay   *Monterey Peninsula College*
Valerie A. Liston   *University of Minnesota*
Dennis Livingston   *Rensselaer Polytechnic Institute*
James P. Lodge   *Air pollution consultant*
Ruth Logan   *Santa Monica City College*
Robert D. Loring   *DePauw University*
T. Lovering   *University of California, Santa Barbara*
Amory B. Lovins   *Energy consultant*
L. Hunter Lovins   *Energy consultant*
David Lynn
Timothy F. Lyon   *Ball State University*
Melvin G. Marcus   *Arizona State University*
Stuart A. Marks   *St. Andrews Presbyterian College*
Gordon E. Matzke   *Oregon State University*
W. Parker Mauldin   *Rockefeller Foundation*
Vincent E. McKelvey   *U.S. Geological Survey*
A. Steven Messenger   *Northern Illinois University*
L. John Meyers   *Middlesex Community College*
Raymond W. Miller   *Utah State University*
Ralph Morris   *Brock University, St. Catherines, Ont., Canada*

Contents in Brief

Prologue / *xxii*

PART ONE / HUMANS AND
NATURE: AN OVERVIEW / *1*

Chapter 1 Population, Resources, Environmental
  Degradation, and Pollution / *2*
Chapter 2 Human Impact on the Earth / *25*

PART TWO / BASIC CONCEPTS / *43*

Chapter 3 Matter and Energy Resources: Types and
  Concepts / *44*
Chapter 4 Ecosystems: What Are They and How
  Do They Work? / *68*
Chapter 5 Ecosystems: What Are the Major
  Types? / *91*
Chapter 6 Ecosystems: What Can Happen to
  Them? / *115*

PART THREE / POPULATION / *135*

Chapter 7 Population Dynamics / *136*
Chapter 8 Population Control / *152*
Chapter 9 Population Distribution:
  Urbanization / *168*

PART FOUR / RESOURCES / *187*

Chapter 10 Soil Resources / *188*
Chapter 11 Water Resources / *208*
Chapter 12 Food Resources and World
  Hunger / *234*
Chapter 13 Land Resources: Wilderness, Parks,
  Forests, and Rangelands / *262*
Chapter 14 Wild Plant and Animal Resources / *291*

Chapter 15 Nonrenewable Mineral Resources / *317*
Chapter 16 Nonrenewable Energy Resources: Fos-
  sil Fuels / *336*
Chapter 17 Nonrenewable and Perpetual Energy
  Resources: Geothermal and Nuclear
  Energy / *361*
Chapter 18 Perpetual and Renewable Energy
  Resources: Conservation, Sun, Wind,
  Water, and Biomass / *387*

PART FIVE / POLLUTION / *421*

Chapter 19 Air Pollution / *422*
Chapter 20 Water Pollution / *455*
Chapter 21 Solid Waste and Hazardous Waste / *491*
Chapter 22 Pesticides and Pest Control / *517*
Chapter 23 The Environment and Human Health:
  Disease, Food Additives,
  and Noise / *534*

PART SIX / ENVIRONMENT AND
SOCIETY / *557*

Chapter 24 Economics and Environment / *558*
Chapter 25 Politics and Environment / *572*
Chapter 26 Environmental Ethics / *590*

Epilogue / *603*
Appendixes / *A-1*
Further Readings / *A-11*
Glossary / *A-39*
Index / *A-57*

Detailed Contents

Prologue / xxii

**PART ONE / HUMANS AND
NATURE: AN OVERVIEW / 1**

Chapter 1 **Population, Resources,
Environmental Degradation, and
Pollution / 2**

1-1 Human Population Growth / 2
*The J-Shaped Curve of Human Population
Growth / Spotlight An Example of Expo-
nential Growth / Population Growth in the
More Developed and Less Developed Coun-
tries / Life in the Poorest Countries / When
Might World Population Growth Come to a
Halt?*

1-2 Resources and Environmental Deg-
radation / 8
*What Is a Natural Resource? / Nonrenewable
Resources / Renewable and Perpetual
Resources / Are We Running Out of
Resources? / Spotlight Environmental Deg-
radation: Survival, Short-Term Economic
Growth, and the Tragedy of the Commons*

1-3 Pollution / 12
*What Is Pollution? / Types, Sources, and
Effects of Pollutants / Pollution Control /
Spotlight Poland: The World's Most Envi-
ronmentally Polluted Country*

1-4 Relationships Among Population,
Resource Use, Technology,
Environmental Degradation,
and Pollution / 13
*The Roots of Environmental Degradation
and Pollution / Two Types of Overpopulation/
Is Technology the Culprit? / Other Factors*

1-5 What Should Be Done? Neo-Malthusians Versus Cornucopians / 17

*Spotlight Cornucopians Versus Neo-
Malthusians*

*Guest Essay "The Global 2000 and World
Resources Reports," by Gus Speth / 20*

*Guest Essay "There Is No Environmen-
tal, Population, or Resource Crisis," by
Julian L. Simon / 22*

Chapter Summary / 24
Discussion Topics / 24

Chapter 2 **Human Impact on the Earth / 25**

2-1 Hunting-and-Gathering Societies / 25
*Early Hunter-Gatherers / Spotlight Do
Today's Remaining Hunting-and-Gathering
Societies Have the Right to Live Undisturbed
on Their Homelands? / Advanced Hunter-
Gatherers*

2-2 Agricultural Societies: The Agricul-
tural Revolution / 27
*Early Pastoralists and Horticulturists:
Domestication of Wild Animals and Plants /
Early Agriculturists / The Emergence of
Agriculture-Based Urban Societies / Impact
on the Environment / Spotlight Environ-
mental Abuse and the Fall of Civilizations*

2-3 Industrial Societies: The Industrial
Revolution / 30
*Early Industrial Societies / Advanced Indus-
trial Societies / Environmental Impact*

2-4 Brief History of Resource Exploita-
tion, Resource Conservation, and
Environmental Protection in the
United States / 31
*Phase I: Frontier Expansion and Resource
Exploitation (1607–1870) / Phase II: Early
Conservation Warnings (1830–1870) / Phase
III: Beginnings of the Government's Role in
Resource Conservation (1870-1916) / Phase
IV: Preservation Versus Scientific Conserva-
tion (1911–1932) / Phase V: Expanding
FederalRoleinLandManagement(1933–1960)/
Phase VI: Rise of the Environmental Move-
ment (1960–1980) / Phase VII: Continuing
Controversy and Some Retrenchment (1980–
1988) / Spotlight Controversy Over Reagan
Administration Environmental Policies*

2-5 Some Possible Futures: The Next
Cultural Revolution / 37
A Critical Turning Point / Some Hopeful Signs

*Guest Essay "Nuclear War: The Worst
Environmental Threat," by Hannes
Alfvén / **40***

Chapter Summary / 42
Discussion Topics / 42

PART TWO / BASIC CONCEPTS / 43

Chapter 3 **Matter and Energy Resources: Types and Concepts / 44**

3-1 Matter: Forms and Structure / 44
Physical and Chemical Forms of Matter / Elements / Compounds

3-2 Law of Conservation of Matter and Changes in Matter / 47
There Is No "Away" / Physical and Chemical Changes / Nuclear Changes and Radioactivity / Spotlight Effects of Ionizing Radiation on the Human Body / Exposure to Ionizing Radiation

3-3 Energy: Types and Changes / 53
Types of Energy / Energy Resources Used by Humans

3-4 First Law of Energy: You Can't Get Something for Nothing / 55

3-5 Second Law of Energy: You Can't Break Even / 55
Energy Quality / Second Law of Energy / Spotlight How to Spot Energy Fraud / Second Energy Law and Increasing Disorder

3-6 Energy Laws and Energy Resources / 59
Which Energy Resources Should We Develop? / Increasing Energy Efficiency / Spotlight Our Energy Future: Cornucopians Versus Neo-Malthusians / Using Waste Heat / Net Useful Energy: It Takes Energy to Get Energy

3-7 Matter and Energy Laws and Environmental Problems / 65
Every Little Bit of Disorder Counts / Throwaway and Matter-Recycling Societies / Sustainable-Earth Societies

Chapter Summary / 67
Discussion Topics / 67

Chapter 4 **Ecosystems: What Are They and How Do They Work? / 68**

4-1 The Biosphere and Ecosystems / 68
The Earth's Life-Support System / The Realm of Ecology / Components of Ecosystems

4-2 Matter Cycling in Ecosystems: Carbon, Oxygen, Nitrogen, Phosphorus, Sulfur, and Water / 73
Biogeochemical Cycles / Carbon and Oxygen Cycles / Nitrogen Cycle / Phosphorus Cycle / Sulfur Cycle / Water, or Hydrologic, Cycle

4-3 Energy Flow in the Biosphere and Ecosystems / 80
The Sun: Source of Energy for Life / Energy Flow in the Biosphere / Energy Flow in Ecosystems: Food Chains and Food Webs / Food Chains, Food Webs, and the Second Law of Energy / Net Primary Productivity of Plants / Biological Amplification of Chemicals in Food Chains and Webs

4-4 Ecological Niches of Species in Ecosystems / 87
The Niche Concept / Specialist and Generalist Niches / Competition Between Species / Competitive Exclusion Principle

Guest Essay "We Propose and Nature Disposes," by Edward J. Kormondy / 88

Chapter Summary / 90
Discussion Topics / 90

Chapter 5 **Ecosystems: What Are the Major Types? / 91**

5-1 Adaptations and Limits of Species to Environmental Change / 91
Species Adaptations / Tolerance Range and Limiting Factors

5-2 Climate and Major Types of Terrestrial Ecosystems / 94
Weather and Climate / Global Circulation of Air and Water / Climate and Major Types of Ecosystems

5-3 Deserts, Grasslands, and Forests / 97
Deserts / Grasslands / Forests

5-4 Freshwater Aquatic Ecosystems / 102
Limiting Factors of Aquatic Ecosystems / Lakes / Reservoirs and Ponds / Streams and Rivers / Inland Wetlands

5-5 Marine Aquatic Ecosystems / 106
Importance of Oceans / Coastal Zone / Open Sea

Enrichment Study Why Is the Coastal Zone So Important? / 110

Chapter Summary / 114
Discussion Topics / 114

Chapter 6 **Ecosystems: What Can Happen to Them? / 115**

6-1 How Living Systems Maintain Stability / 115
What Is Stability? / Stability and Information Feedback / Time Delays and Synergistic and Antagonistic Effects / Effects of Environmental Stress

6-2 Population Responses to Stress / 117
Changes in Population Size / Biological Evolution and Natural Selection / Spotlight Do Benefits of Genetic Engineering Outweigh the Risks? / Speciation

6-3 Ecosystem Responses to Stress / 122
Responses to Small and Moderate Stress / Responses to Large-Scale Stress: Ecological Succession / Spotlight Ecosystem Interference Is Full of Surprises! / Comparison of Immature and Mature Ecosystems

6-4 Human Impacts on Ecosystems / 126
Humans and Ecosystems / Nuclear War: The Ultimate Ecological Catastrophe / Some Lessons from Ecology

Enrichment Study Risk Analysis and Risk Management / 130

Chapter Summary / 134
Discussion Topics / 134

PART THREE / Population / 135

Chapter 7 Population Dynamics / 136

7-1 Birth Rate, Death Rate, and Net Population Change / 136
Net Population Change / Crude Birth Rates and Death Rates / Life Expectancy and Infant Mortality / Annual Percentage Rates of Population Change / Doubling Time

7-2 Migration / 141
Net Migration Rate / Immigration and Population Growth in the United States

7-3 Fertility / 142
*Replacement-Level Fertility and Total Fertility Rate / Fertility and Marriage Age / Using TFR to Project World Population Stabilization / **Spotlight** Teenage Pregnancy in the United States / U.S. Population Stabilization*

7-4 Age Structure / 146
Age Structure Diagrams / Population Momentum and Age Structure / Making Projections from Age Structure Diagrams

Guest Essay "We Are All Population Actors," by Leon F. Bouvier / 149

Chapter Summary / 150
Discussion Topics / 151

Chapter 8 Population Control / 152

8-1 Should Population Growth Be Controlled? / 152
Is World Population Growth Good or Bad? / Is U.S. Population Growth Good or Bad?

8-2 Controlling Population Growth: Economic Development, Family Planning, and Regulating Migration / 154
*Controlling Births, Deaths, and Migration / Economic Development and the Demographic Transition / Family Planning / **Spotlight** Should Government Funds Be Used to Aid Family Planning in the United States? / Restricting Immigration*

8-3 Methods of Birth Control / 158
*Present Methods / Preventing Pregnancy / Terminating Pregnancy: Abortion / Future Methods of Birth Control / **Spotlight** Should Abortions Be Banned in the United States?*

8-4 Socioeconomic Methods for Controlling Population Growth / 162
Beyond Family Planning / Economic Rewards and Penalties / Changes in Women's Roles

8-5 Efforts at Human Population Control: China and India / 163
Population Policies / India / China / 163

Enrichment Study Computer Modeling and the Limits-to-Growth Debate / 164

Chapter Summary / 166
Discussion Topics / 167

Chapter 9 Population Distribution: Urbanization / 168

9-1 Urbanization, Urban Growth, and the Urban Environment / 168
*The World Situation / **Spotlight** Life in Two of the World's Supercities / The U.S. Situation / **Spotlight** Major Internal U.S. Population Shifts*

9-2 Urban Systems and Natural Ecosystems / 173
Is an Urban System an Ecosystem? / Urban Spatial Structure

9-3 Urban Transportation / 176
*Transportation Options / Motor Vehicles / Mass Transit / Heavy-Rail Mass Transit / **Spotlight** Increased Use of Bicycles / Light-Rail Mass Transit / Bus Mass Transit / Paratransit*

9-4 Coping with Urban Problems / 180
Repairing Existing Cities / Revitalizing Existing Cities / Revitalizing Public Housing Projects / Creating Free-Enterprise Zones / Building New Cities and Towns / Making Cities More Self-Sufficient

9-5 Urban Land-Use Planning and Control / 182
*Methods of Land-Use Planning / **Spotlight** Steps in Ecological Land-Use Planning / Methods of Land-Use Control*

Enrichment Study Preserving Urban Open Space / 184

Chapter Summary / 184
Discussion Topics / 186

PART FOUR / RESOURCES / 187

Chapter 10 Soil Resources / 188

10-1 Soils: Uses, Components, and Profiles / 188
The Base of Life / Soil Layers and Components

10-2 Soil: Formation, Porosity, and Acidity / 190
Formation / Porosity / Acidity

10-3 Major Types of Soil / 193

10-4 Soil Erosion / 196
Natural and Human-Accelerated Soil Erosion / The World Situation / The U.S. Situation

10-5 Soil Conservation / 198
*Soil Management Methods / **Spotlight** The Dust Bowl: Will It Happen Again? / Conservation Tillage / Contour Farming, Terracing, and Strip Cropping / Gully Reclamation and Shelterbelts / Appropriate Land Use / Maintaining Soil Fertility / Achieving More Effective U.S. Soil Conservation*

Guest Essay "Land Degradation and Environmental Resources," *by David Pimentel / 205*

Chapter Summary / 207
Discussion Topics / 207

Chapter 11 **Water Resources** / 208

11-1 Water's Unique Physical Properties / 208

11-2 Supply, Renewal, and Use of Water Resources / 209
Worldwide Supply and Renewal / Surface-Water Runoff / Groundwater / World and U.S. Water Use

11-3 Water Resource Problems / 214
*The Major Problems / Too Little Water / Too Much Water / **Spotlight** Benefits and Risks of Living in Flood-Prone Areas / Water in the Wrong Place / Lack of Sanitary Drinking Water / Irrigation Problems: Salinization and Waterlogging / The U.S. Situation*

11-4 Water Resource Management: Increasing the Usable Supply / 220
*Methods for Managing Water Resources / Dams and Reservoirs / Water Diversion Projects / **Spotlight** Benefits and Costs of Egypt's Aswan Dam / Tapping Groundwater / **Spotlight** Depletion of the Ogallala Aquifer / Desalinization / Towing Icebergs / Cloud Seeding*

11-5 Water Resource Management: Water Conservation / 228
*Importance of Water Conservation / Reducing Irrigation Losses / Wasting Less Water in Industry / Wasting Less Water in Homes / **Spotlight** How to Save Water and Money*

Enrichment Study Desertification / 231

Chapter Summary / 233
Discussion Topics / 233

Chapter 12 **Food Resources and World Hunger** / 234

12-1 World Agricultural Systems: How Is Food Produced? / 234
*Plants and Animals That Feed the World / **Spotlight** Major Components of Advanced Industrialized Agriculture / Major Types of Agriculture / U.S. Energy Use and Industrialized Agriculture*

12-2 Major World Food Problems / 239
*Food Quantity: Population Growth and Food Production / **Spotlight** China's Successful Food Production System / Undernutrition, Malnutrition, and Overnutrition / **Spotlight** Africa: A Continent in Crisis / Food Storage and Distribution / Poverty: The Geography of Hunger / Environmental Effects of Producing More Food*

12-3 Increasing Crop Yields and Using New Types of Foods / 247
*Green Revolutions / Limitations of Green Revolutions / Loss of Genetic Diversity / Do the Poor Benefit? / Unconventional Foods / **Spotlight** Possible Future Green Revolutions/ Vitamin and Protein Supplements and Fabricated Foods*

12-4 Cultivating More Land / 251
Availability of Arable Land / Location, Soil, and Insects as Limiting Factors / Water as a Limiting Factor / Money as a Limiting Factor

12-5 Catching More Fish and Fish Farming / 252
The World's Fisheries / Trends in the World Fish Catch / Fish Farming: Aquaculture / Can the Annual Catch Be Increased Significantly?

12-6 Making Food Production Profitable, Providing Food Aid, and Distributing Land to the Poor / 256
*Government Agricultural Policies / The U.S. Farm Situation / International Relief Aid / Distributing Land to the Poor / **Spotlight** Is Food Relief Helpful or Harmful?*

12-7 Sustainable-Earth Agriculture / 258
*Sustainable-Earth Agriculture in LDCs / Sustainable-Earth Agriculture in MDCs / Reducing Food Waste / **Spotlight** Major Components of Sustainable-Earth Agriculture in LDCs / What Can You Do?*

Chapter Summary / 260
Discussion Topics / 261

Chapter 13 **Land Resources: Wilderness, Parks, Forests, and Rangelands** / 262

13-1 Land Use in the World and the United States / 262
Why Are Nonurban Land Resources Important? / Private and Public U.S. Land Ownership / Public Land Resources

13-2 Wilderness / 265

*Expansion of U.S. Wilderness Areas and Wild and Scenic Rivers / Use and Abuse of Wilderness Areas / Why Preserve Wilderness? / **Spotlight** Major Components of Federal Public Lands / **Spotlight** How Should Public Land Resources Be Used? / How Much Wilderness Is Enough?*

13-3 Parks / 269

*U.S. Parks / Internal Stresses on Parks / **Spotlight** Should Wolves Be Reintroduced in Yellowstone? / External Threats to Parks / What Should Be Done? / **Spotlight** What Should Be Done to Maintain and Improve the National Park System?*

13-4 Importance and Management of Forest Resources / 271

Commercial and Ecological Importance of Forests / Management of Commercial Forests / Tree Harvesting and Regeneration Methods / Protecting Forests from Fires / Protecting Forests from Diseases and Insects / Protecting Forests from Air Pollution

13-5 Status of World and U.S. Forests / 277

*World Forests / The Fuelwood Crisis in LDCs / Tropical Deforestation / Forests in the United States / **Spotlight** Should the United States Stop Importing Beef from Tropical Countries? / Importance and Use of National Forests / Conflicting Demands on National Forests*

13-6 Rangelands / 282

*The World's Rangeland Resources / U.S. Rangeland Resources / Characteristics of Rangeland Vegetation / Rangeland Carrying Capacity and Overgrazing / Rangeland Management / **Spotlight** Should Grazing Fees on Public Rangeland Be Increased? / **Spotlight** Should Poisons Be Used to Kill Coyotes and Other Livestock Predators?*

Guest Essay *"Tropical Forests and Their Species: Going, Going . . . ?" by Norman Myers / 288*

Chapter Summary / 288
Discussion Topics / 290

Chapter 14 **Wild Plant and Animal Resources** / 291

14-1 Why Preserve Wild Plant and Animal Species? / 292

*How Many Species Exist? / Economic and Health Importance / Aesthetic and Recreational Importance / Ecological Importance / **Spotlight** Ecological Importance of the American Alligator / Ethical Importance*

14-2 How Species Become Endangered and Extinct / 295

Extinction Before the Dawn of Agriculture / Extinction of Species Today / Threatened and Endangered Species / Habitat Disturbance and Loss / Commercial Hunting / Predator and Pest Control / Pets, Medical Research, and Zoos / Pollution / Introduction of Alien Species / Characteristics of Extinction-Prone Species

14-3 Protecting Wild Species from Extinction / 301

*The Species Approach: Treaties and Laws / **Spotlight** Bats: Feared, Misunderstood, and Vulnerable / The Species Approach: Wildlife Refuges / **Spotlight** The Snail Darter Controversy / The Species Approach: Gene Banks, Zoos, Botanical Gardens, and Aquariums / The Ecosystem Approach*

14-4 Wildlife Management / 307

*Management Approaches / **Spotlight** Sport Hunting Controversy / Population Regulation by Controlled Hunting / Manipulation of Habitat Vegetation and Water Supplies / Management of Migratory Waterfowl*

14-5 Fishery Management / 310

*Freshwater Fishery Management / Marine Fishery Management / The Whaling Industry / **Spotlight** Near Extinction of the Blue Whale*

Guest Essay *"Funding Wildlife Restoration in the United States," by Robert Leo Smith / 314*

Chapter Summary / 316
Discussion Topics / 316

Chapter 15 **Nonrenewable Mineral Resources** / 317

15-1 Locating and Extracting Mineral Resources / 317

Mineral Resource Abundance and Distribution / Making Mineral Resources Available / Locating Deposits / Extraction

15-2 Environmental Impact of Mining and Processing Mineral Resources / 322

*Overall Impact / Mining Impacts / Processing Impacts / **Spotlight** Should All Surface-Mined Land Be Restored?*

15-3 Will There Be Enough Mineral Resources? / 325

How Much Is There? / How Fast Are Supplies Being Depleted? / Who Has the World's Nonfuel Mineral Resources? / Will There Be Enough?

15-4 Increasing Mineral Resource Supplies: The Supply-Side Approach / 328
Economics and Resource Supply / Finding New Land-Based Mineral Deposits / Spotlight Are Rich Nations Exploiting the Mineral Resource Base of Poor Nations? / Obtaining More Minerals from Seawater and the Ocean Floor / Improved Mining Technology and Mining Low-Grade Deposits / Substitution

15-5 Extending Mineral Resource Supplies: The Conservation Approach / 331
Recycling / Spotlight Should the United States Have a National Beverage Container Deposit Law? / Obstacles to Recycling in the United States / Reusable Containers / The Low-Waste Society: Beyond Recycling and Reuse

Chapter Summary / 335
Discussion Topics / 335

Chapter 16 **Nonrenewable Energy Resources: Fossil Fuels** / 336

16-1 Brief History of Energy Use / 336
Primitive to Modern Times / Energy Use and Problems in Less Developed Countries / The Oil Crisis of the 1970s / The Oil Glut of the 1980s / The Next Oil Crisis / Spotlight Are Low Oil Prices Good or Bad?

16-2 Evaluating Energy Resources / 341
Future Energy Resources / Questions to Ask / Environmental Impact of Energy Alternatives

16-3 Oil / 342
Conventional Crude Oil / How Long Will Supplies of Conventional Crude Oil Last? / Major Advantages and Disadvantages of Oil / Heavy Oils from Oil Shale and Tar Sands

16-4 Natural Gas / 348
Conventional Supplies of Natural Gas / How Long Will Natural Gas Supplies Last? / Unconventional Sources of Natural Gas / Advantages and Disadvantages of Natural Gas

16-5 Coal / 350
Conventional Types of Coal / Distribution of Coal / Health and Environmental Hazards of Coal Mining / Uses of Coal / How Long Will Supplies Last? / Air Pollution from Burning Coal / Burning Coal More Cleanly and Efficiently / Synfuels: Gaseous and Liquid Fuels from Coal / Advantages and Disadvantages of Solid Coal and Synfuels

Guest Essay "Technology Is the Answer (But What Was the Question?)," *by Amory B. Lovins* / 357

Chapter Summary / 360
Discussion Topics / 360

Chapter 17 **Nonrenewable and Perpetual Energy Resources: Geothermal and Nuclear Energy** / 361

17-1 Nonrenewable and Perpetual Geothermal Energy / 361
Nonrenewable Geothermal Energy / Perpetual Geothermal Energy

17-2 Conventional Nonrenewable Nuclear Fission / 364
A Controversial Fading Dream / How Does a Nuclear Fission Reactor Work? / Nuclear Fuel Cycle / Nuclear Reactor Safety / Spotlight Major Safety Features of U.S. Nuclear Power Plants / Spotlight Some Significant Nuclear Accidents and Incidents / Disposal and Storage of Radioactive Wastes / Decommissioning Nuclear Power Plants / Spotlight What Can We Do with High-Level, Long-Lived Radioactive Waste? / Proliferation of Nuclear Weapons / Soaring Costs: The Achilles Heel of Nuclear Power / Advantages and Disadvantages of Conventional Nuclear Fission / Spotlight Does Adding More Nuclear Power Plants Reduce U.S. Dependence on Imported Oil? / Spotlight France's Commitment to Nuclear Power

17-3 Nonrenewable Breeder Nuclear Fission / 381

17-4 Nonrenewable and Perpetual Nuclear Fusion / 382
Controlled Nuclear Fusion / Achieving Controlled Nuclear Fusion / Building a Commercial Nuclear Fusion Reactor

Guest Essay "Nuclear Power: A Faustian Bargain We Should Accept," *by Alvin M. Weinberg* / 384

Chapter Summary / 386
Discussion Topics / 386

Chapter 18 **Perpetual and Renewable Energy Resources: Conservation, Sun, Wind, Water, and Biomass** / 387

18-1 Energy Conservation: Doing More with Less / 387
Reducing Unnecessary Energy Waste: An Offer We Can't Afford to Refuse / Improving Industrial Energy Efficiency / Improving Transportation Energy Efficiency / Improving the Energy Efficiency of Commercial and Residential Buildings / Spotlight The Energy-Efficient House of the Near Future / Developing a Personal Energy Conservation Plan / Energy Efficiency Differences Between Countries

18-2 Direct Perpetual Solar Energy for Producing Heat and Electricity / 393

*Passive Solar Systems for Low-Temperature Heat / Active Solar Systems for Low-Temperature Heat / **Spotlight** How to Save Energy and Money / Advantages and Disadvantages of Solar Energy for Providing Low-Temperature Heat / **Spotlight** Earth-Sheltered Houses / Concentrating Solar Energy to Produce High-Temperature Heat and Electricity / Converting Solar Energy Directly to Electricity: Photovoltaic Cells*

18-3 Indirect Perpetual Solar Energy: Producing Electricity from Falling and Flowing Water / 402

Types of Hydroelectric Power / Present and Future Use / Advantages and Disadvantages / Tidal Power / Wave Power

18-4 Indirect Perpetual Solar Energy: Producing Electricity from Heat Stored in Water / 404

Ocean Thermal Energy Conversion / Advantages and Disadvantages of OTEC / Inland Solar Ponds / Advantages and Disadvantages of Solar Ponds

18-5 Indirect Perpetual Solar Energy: Producing Electricity from Wind / 406

Wind Power: Past and Present / Wind Power in the Future / Advantages and Disadvantages

18-6 Indirect Renewable Solar Energy: Biomass / 408

*Renewable Biomass as a Versatile Fuel / Burning Wood and Wood Wastes / **Spotlight** Solar-Assisted Wood Stove / Energy Plantations / Burning Agricultural and Urban Wastes / Converting Solid Biomass to Liquid and Gaseous Biofuels*

18-7 Developing an Energy Strategy for the United States / 413

Overall Evaluation of U.S. Energy Alternatives / Economics and National Energy Strategy / Free Market Competition / Keeping Energy Prices Artificially Low: The U.S. Strategy / Keeping Energy Prices Artificially High: The Western European Strategy / Why the U.S. Has No Comprehensive Long-Term Energy Strategy / Taking Energy Matters into Your Own Hands

***Enrichment Study** Hydrogen as a Possible Replacement for Oil / 417*

Chapter Summary / 419
Discussion Topics / 420

PART FIVE / POLLUTION / 421

Chapter 19 **Air Pollution** / 422

19-1 Types and Sources of Outdoor and Indoor Air Pollution / 422

*Our Air Resource: The Atmosphere / Major Types of Outdoor Air Pollutants / Sources of Outdoor Air Pollutants / Primary and Secondary Air Pollutants / **Spotlight** Air Pollution in the Past / Indoor Air Pollution*

19-2 Industrial and Photochemical Smog, Urban Heat Islands, and Acid Deposition / 427

Industrial Smog / Photochemical Smog: Cars + Sunlight = Tears / Local Climate, Topography, and Smog / Urban Heat Islands / Acid Deposition

19-3 Effects of Air Pollution on Human Health / 432

*Damage to Human Health / Body Defenses Against Air Pollution / Overloading and Degrading the Body's Defense Mechanisms / **Spotlight** What Should Be Done About Asbestos?*

19-4 Effects of Air Pollution on Plants, Animals, and Materials / 435

Damage to Plants / Damage to Livestock and Fish / Damage to Materials

19-5 Effects of Air Pollution on the Ozone Layer and Global Climate / 438

Chlorofluorocarbons and Ozone Layer Depletion / Some Effects of Ozone Depletion / Protecting the Ozone Layer / Increased Global Warming from the Greenhouse Effect / Some Effects of Global Climate Changes / Dealing with the Threat of Global Warming

19-6 Controlling Air Pollution / 443

*U.S. Air Pollution Legislation / Trends in U.S. Air Quality and Emissions / Methods of Pollution Control / Control of Sulfur Dioxide Emissions from Stationary Sources / **Spotlight** Should Scrubbers Be Required on All U.S. Coal-Burning Power Plants? / Control of Emissions of Nitrogen Oxides from Stationary Sources / Control of SPM Emissions from Stationary Sources / Control of Emissions from Motor Vehicles / What Needs to Be Done*

***Enrichment Study** Is Your Home Contaminated with Radioactive Radon Gas? / 451*

Chapter Summary / 452
Discussion Topics / 454

Chapter 20 **Water Pollution** / 455

20-1 Sources, Types, and Effects of Water Pollution / 455

Point and Nonpoint Sources / Major Water Pollutants and Their Effects / Disease-Causing Agents / Oxygen-Demanding Wastes / Water-Soluble Inorganic Chemicals / Inorganic Plant Nutrients / Organic Chemicals / Sediments / Radioactive Substances / Heat

20-2 Pollution of Rivers, Lakes, and Reservoirs / 461

*Natural Processes Affecting Pollution Levels in Surface Water / Rivers and Degradation of Oxygen-Consuming Wastes / U.S. River Water Quality / River Water Quality in Other Parts of the World / Pollution Problems of Lakes and Reservoirs / **Spotlight** A Setback for the Rhine River / Control of Cultural Eutrophication / Thermal Pollution of Rivers and Lakes / Reduction of Thermal Water Pollution*

20-3 Ocean Pollution / 469

*Are the Oceans Dying? / Ocean Dumping / **Spotlight** The Chesapeake Bay: An Estuary in Trouble / Ocean Oil Pollution / Effects of Oil Pollution / Controlling Ocean Oil Pollution*

20-4 Groundwater Pollution / 474

*Is It Safe to Drink the Water? / Vulnerability of Groundwater to Pollution / Sources of Groundwater Contamination / Control of Groundwater Pollution **Spotlight** What Should Be Done About Leaking Underground Tanks?*

20-5 Water Pollution Control / 477

Control of Nonpoint Source Pollution / Control of Point Source Pollution: Wastewater Treatment / Alternatives to Large-Scale Treatment Plants / Purification of Drinking Water / Land Disposal of Sewage Effluent and Sludge / Individual Waste Management

20-6 U.S. Water Pollution Control Laws / 483

Protecting Drinking Water / U.S. Control Efforts / Future Water Quality Goals

Enrichment Study The Great Lakes / 485

Guest Essay "Economics Versus Ecology in the USSR: The Case of Lake Baikal," by Philip R. Pryde / 487

Chapter Summary / 488
Discussion Topics / 489

Chapter 21 **Solid Waste and Hazardous Waste** / 491

21-1 Solid Waste Production in the United States / 491

What Is Solid Waste and How Much Is Produced? / Strategies for Dealing with Solid Waste

21-2 Disposal of Urban Solid Waste: Dump, Bury, Burn, or Compost? / 493

Littering and Open Dumps / Sanitary Landfills / Incineration / Composting

21-3 Resource Recovery from Solid Waste / 496

The High-Technology Approach / The Low-Technology Approach

21-4 Types, Sources, and Effects of Hazardous Waste / 499

*What Is Hazardous Waste? / How Much Has Been Dumped on the Land in the Past? / How Much Is Produced Today? / **Spotlight** Recycling Paper / **Spotlight** The Love Canal Tragedy*

21-5 Control and Management of Hazardous Waste / 502

*Methods for Dealing with Hazardous Waste / Present Management of Hazardous Waste / Recycling, Reuse, and Industrial Process Redesign / Conversion to Less Hazardous or Nonhazardous Materials / Land Disposal of Hazardous Waste / Federal Legislation and Control of Hazardous Waste / **Spotlight** Illegal Disposal of Hazardous Waste / Individual Action*

Enrichment Study Toxic Metals, PCBs, and Dioxins / 510

Chapter Summary / 514
Discussion Topics / 516

Chapter 22 **Pesticides and Pest Control** / 517

22-1 Pesticides: Types and Uses / 517

Natural Control of Pests in Diverse Ecosystems / Why the Need for Pest Control Has Increased / The Ideal Pest Control Method / First Generation Pesticides / Second Generation Pesticides / Major Types of Insecticides and Herbicides

22-2 The Case for Pesticides / 520

Using Insecticides to Control Disease / Using Insecticides and Herbicides to Increase Food Supplies

22-3 The Case Against Pesticides / 521

*Development of Genetic Resistance / Killing of Natural Pest Enemies / Creation of New Pests / Mobility and Biological Amplification of Persistent Pesticides / Threats to Wildlife / Short-Term Threats to Human Health / **Spotlight** The Kepone and Bhopal Tragedies / Long-Term Threats to Human Health*

22-4 Pesticide Regulation in the United States / 526

Is the Public Adequately Protected? / Export of Banned Pesticides / Has DDT Really Been Banned?

22-5 Alternative Methods of Insect Control / 527

Modifying Cultivation Procedures / Biological Control / Genetic Control by Sterilization / Genetic Control by Breeding Resistant Crops and Animals / Chemical Control Using Natural Sex Attractants and Hormones / Irradiation of Foods / Integrated Pest Management / Changing the Attitudes of Consumers and Farmers

Chapter Summary / 533
Discussion Topics / 533

Chapter 23 **The Environment and Human Health: Disease, Food Additives, and Noise** / 534

23-1 Types of Disease / 534

*Infectious and Noninfectious Diseases / Acute and Chronic Diseases / The Social Ecology of Disease / **Spotlight** Alcohol and Alcoholism in the United States*

23-2 Infectious Diseases: Malaria and Schistosomiasis / 538

Malaria / Schistosomiasis

23-3 Chronic Noninfectious Diseases: Cancer / 541

*Nature and Effects / Incidence of Cancer in the United States / **Spotlight** The Cancer You Are Most Likely to Get / Diagnosis and Treatment / Cancer Risk Factors / Cancer and Smoking / Cancer and Diet / Cancer and the Workplace / **Spotlight** The Prudent Diet / Cancer and Pollution / **Spotlight** Air Pollution Levels in Mines and Factories*

23-4 Food Additives / 548

Use and Types of Food Additives / Natural Versus Synthetic Foods / Consumer Protection: FDA and the GRAS List / Some Controversial Food Additives / The Delaney Clause / What Can the Consumer Do?

23-5 Noise Pollution / 553

Sonic Assault / Measuring and Ranking Noise / Effects of Noise / What Can Be Done?

Chapter Summary / 555
Discussion Topics / 555

PART SIX / ENVIRONMENT AND SOCIETY / 557

Chapter 24 **Economics and Environment** / 558

24-1 Economic Growth, GNP, and the Quality of Life / 558

*Economic Systems / The Economic Growth Debate / Gross National Product: A Misleading Indicator / **Spotlight** Why You Already Have a Debt of $52,000 / Gross National Quality*

24-2 Toward a Sustainable-Earth Economy / 562

***Spotlight** Key Characteristics of a Sustainable-Earth Economy / Problems with Conventional Economic Systems / A Sustainable-Earth or Steady-State Economy / Barriers and Problems*

24-3 Economics and Pollution Control / 564

Internal and External Costs / Approaches to Environmental Improvement

24-4 Cost-Benefit and Cost-Effectiveness Analysis / 566

*Cost-Benefit Analysis / Cost-Effectiveness Analysis / Problems with Cost-Benefit and Cost-Effectiveness Analysis / **Spotlight** How Much Is Your Life Worth? / What Obligation Do We Have to Future Generations?*

24-5 How Much Should Be Spent on Environmental Improvement? / 569

***Guest Essay** "The Steady State Economy in Outline," by Herman E. Daly / 568*

Chapter Summary / 570
Discussion Topics / 571

Chapter 25 **Politics and Environment** / 572

25-1 Politics and Social Change / 572

Is Politics the Art of the Possible? / Ecology and Politics

25-2 Environmental Law / 573

Some Principles of Environmental Law / Problems with Environmental Lawsuits

25-3 U.S. Environmental Legislation / 574

Environmental Legislation / NEPA and Environmental Impact Statements

25-4 Sustainable-Earth Politics / 576

Characteristics of a Sustainable-Earth Political System / Sustainable-Earth Political Tactics

25-5 Toward a Sustainable-Earth Government in the United States / 578

The U.S. Government as a Corrective Feedback System / Lack of Long-Range Planning / Election Reform and Electing Sustainable-Earth Leaders / Congressional Reform / Bureaucratic Reform / All Is Not Lost

25-6 Achieving Global Security and
Cooperation / 582
The Arms Race / Redefining National Security / Paths to Global Peace and Cooperation / **Spotlight** *One Suggestion for Promoting Global Peace and Cooperation*

Enrichment Study How to Influence
Elected Officials / 585

Guest Essay "The Politics of the Ecological Future," *by William Ophuls / 587*

Chapter Summary / 588
Discussion Topics / 589

Chapter 26 **Environmental Ethics** / 590

26-1 Ethics and Morals / 590
What Is Ethical and What Is Moral? / Some Important Questions

26-2 Throwaway Society Ethics / 591
Some Basic Beliefs / Roots of the Throwaway Mentality

26-3 Sustainable-Earth Society
Ethics / 592
Sustainable-Earth Ethics / Shallow and Deep Ecology / **Spotlight** *Four Levels of Environmental Awareness*

26-4 What Can You Do? / 595
Spotlight *Working with Nature: A Personal Progress Report*

Guest Essay "Becoming a Deep Ecologist," *by Bill Devall / 599*

Chapter Summary / 600
Discussion Topics / 602

Epilogue / 603

Appendixes / A-1
1 Periodicals, Environmental and
Resource Organizations, and Federal and International
Agencies / A-1
2 Units of Measurement / A-7
3 Major U.S. Environmental Legislation / A-8
4 Average U.S. Water Use / A-9
5 National Ambient Air Quality Standards for the United States / A-10

Further Readings / A-11

Glossary / A-39

Index / A-57

Prologue

It is time for the annual State of the Earth report. As you know, we live on a relatively small planet hurtling through space at about 107,200 kilometers (66,600 miles) per hour on a fixed course. Although we can never take on any significant amounts of new supplies, our planetary home has a marvelous set of life-support systems that use solar energy to recycle most of the chemicals needed to provide a reasonable number of us and other life forms with adequate water, air, and food. We also have a large but depletable supply of fossil fuels (oil, coal, and natural gas), metals, and other nonrenewable resources that we have learned to extract from the earth's crust and convert to useful materials.

Let me summarize. There are 5 billion people on earth, living in 166 countries. About 1 billion live in 33 *more developed countries,* most of them enjoying good to luxurious living conditions mostly in the Northern Hemisphere. About 80% of the fossil fuels, metals, and other nonrenewable supplies we get from the earth's crust are used by the affluent people in these countries. Unfortunately, conditions have not improved much this year for many of the 4 billion people in the 133 so-called *less developed countries,* located mostly on the continents of Africa, Asia, and Latin America in the Southern Hemisphere. Many are suffering from hunger, malnutrition, inadequate shelter, and lack of clean water. Although we are feeding more people than ever before, more people starved to death or died from malnutrition-related diseases this year than at any time in human history.

As the gap between rich and poor countries continues to widen, many in the poorer countries wonder whether they will be forced to struggle for survival in "never to be developed countries," and they are beginning to demand a fairer share of the planet's nonrenewable and potentially renewable supplies. As a result, during the coming decades the focus of international political and economic confrontation over the earth's resources will shift increasingly from East–West to North–South.

The most important fact molding our lives today is that over the past hundred years we have "gone around the bend" of four curves shaped like the letter J, which represent global increases in population, resource use, pollution of air and water, and environmental degradation of the soil, grasslands, forests, and wildlife populations that form the base of all human economic activity and growth. Although human population growth rates have decreased slightly in recent years, at the current rate our present population of 5 billion will probably grow to about 6.1 billion by the year 2000 and could reach 10.4 billion by the year 2100.

Our global life-support systems are threatened by a combination of *people-overpopulation* in the poorer countries and *consumption-overpopulation* in the rich countries. Each affluent person uses so many resources at a rapid rate that each has an impact on our life-support systems equal to about 25 times that of each poor person. Efforts to conserve and reduce unnecessary waste of our supplies in the rich countries are still grossly inadequate. Pollution control in many of these countries is improving, but there is a long way to go.

Billions of tons of soil, one of our most precious resources, are washed or blown away each year as a result of unwise management for survival in poorer countries and for short-term economic gain in rich countries. Once-productive croplands and grazing lands are being degraded and converted to deserts by overuse and poor management in both rich and poor countries. Tropical forests, containing perhaps one-fifth of all the different kinds of plants and animals on earth, are being chopped down at an alarming rate to provide temporary cropland, grazing land, and firewood for the landless poor and to furnish the rich with choice lumber. If they are not replanted and their rate of removal is not sharply reduced, little will remain of these vital and essentially nonrenewable storehouses of biological diversity by the middle of the next century. In the oceans we ravage one fishery after another. We pollute the seas just as we do many of the world's inland freshwater lakes and rivers and precious deposits of fresh groundwater located beneath the earth's crust.

We are burning up in only a few hundred years the earth's finite supply of fossil fuels, which took hundreds of millions of years to form. This burning releases so much carbon dioxide gas that some scientists fear it will cause a long-term warming of the earth's atmosphere. Such a change could disrupt food supplies for decades and perhaps centuries, reduce dependable supplies of fresh water, and within a hundred years or so raise average sea levels from the gradual melting of Antarctic glaciers, flooding heavily populated coastal cities.

Some experts say we can avoid such a catastrophe by shifting to nuclear power rather than burning coal to produce most of our electricity. There is growing evidence, however, that nuclear power is an uneconomic source of energy, compared to other energy alternatives. Many also believe that nuclear power is ethically unacceptable at any cost because catastrophic accidents may occur, because future generations must store our nuclear wastes safely for thousands of years by methods that experts still can't agree will work, and because the chances of nuclear war are increased by the spread of "peaceful" nuclear knowledge and materials throughout the world.

An increasing number of experts urge that over the next 50 to 75 years we begin a global effort to reduce unnecessary waste of matter, energy, and biological resources and shift from nonrenewable fossil and nuclear fuels to renewable energy in the form of essentially inexhaustible supplies of sunlight, wind, flowing water (hydropower), and vegetation (biomass). Efforts to bring about this shift have started but, compared to fossil fuels and nuclear energy, are still inadequately supported by governments and taxpayers.

Although the interlocking problems of population growth, resource depletion, pollution, and environmental degradation are serious, the single greatest human and environmental threat to the earth's life-support system is war—especially global nuclear war. It is discouraging that so little progress has been made in reducing the extravagant waste of resources and human talent devoted to the arms race. We live in a world where the number of countries with the knowledge to produce nuclear weapons continues to increase; there is one soldier for every 43 people and one doctor for every 1,030 people; 40% of our research and development expenditures and 60% of our physical scientists and engineers are devoted to developing weapons to improve our ability to kill one another—when we already have enough atomic weapons to kill everyone on earth 67 times; and this year we spent 250 times more on military expenditures than on international cooperation for peace and development.

Some thinkers believe that the human species is already doomed. Others see a glorious future based on using human ingenuity to invent technologies and change social institutions to solve the problems we face. Most experts agree that the situation is serious but not hopeless. They believe that if we begin now, we can learn to control the growth of human population, to reduce unnecessary resource consumption and waste and the resulting pollution and environmental degradation, and to live together peacefully on the beautiful and fragile planet that is our home. Our most important and exciting challenge is to engage in individual and group action to sustain—not further degrade—the earth's support systems for present and future generations of human and other forms of life.

1. Two college students spending the weekend at a Colorado ski resort caught the State of the Earth report on television. "I'm sick of hearing about environmental problems, nuclear war, and nuclear power plants," said John, as he ripped the tab from his third can of beer. "It's already too late. My motto is 'Eat, drink, and have a good time while you can.' What's the world done for me?"

"I don't think it's too late at all," observed Susan. "If we can put astronauts on the moon, we can certainly solve our pollution problems. Sure it's going to cost some money, but I'm willing to pay my share. The whole thing is just a matter of money and technology. By the way, John, during Christmas break let's fly to Switzerland. There are too many people here. We always have to wait in line, and all these hideous new ski lodges and condominiums have spoiled the view. Besides, I want to shop for a new ski outfit."

2. In a tenement room in New York City, Larry angrily switched off the television, even though he usually kept it on to drown out noises around him—particularly the rats scratching. A high school dropout, he's given up looking for work. "This ecology crap is just another way for the rich to keep us from getting a piece of the action. What do I care about pollution when my baby sister was bitten by a rat last night, my little brother is a drug addict, my ma's got emphysema, and we haven't had any heat in this firetrap for months. Tell it to my uncle in Florida who's paralyzed from the waist down from some chemical used on the fruit he was picking. Give me a chance to pollute and then I might worry about it."

3. In Calcutta, Mukh Das, his wife Kamala, and their seven children did not hear the broadcast in the abandoned piece of drainage pipe where they lived. Mukh, age 36, watched his emaciated 34-year-old wife patting animal manure into cakes to be dried and used for fuel to cook the little food they had and to provide some heat. He was glad that 7 of their 12 children were still alive to help now that he and Kamala were in their old age. Five of their children had died as infants from malnutrition and diarrhea caused by contaminated water from the single spigot serving hundreds of other poor people like themselves. Mukh felt a chill, and he hoped the children would soon return from begging and gathering manure and scraps of food. Perhaps they had been lucky enough to meet a rich American or European tourist today as they did last week.

4. In a Connecticut suburb, Bill and Kathy Farmington and their three children were discussing the broadcast. David, a college senior, turned away in disgust. "Environmentalists don't understand economics and how the world works. Increased economic growth and improved technology will allow us to protect the environment, feed the poor, and allow most people in the world to live longer and become more affluent. When I get my MBA degree from Harvard, I plan to start my own genetic engineering company to develop better crops and drugs and make millions before I'm 28 years old."

"You're the one who doesn't understand what's going on," said Karen, a college sophomore. "The real problem is that poor people have too many children. Why don't you work on family planning in the slums this summer? I did last year, and I even got college credit for it. This is the problem I plan to work on when I get my sociology degree."

Bill Farmington, chief engineer for Monarch Power Company, looked irritated. "I agree with you, David. I'm all for clean air and water, but we can't stop the economic growth our American way of life is built on. Remember last year when we had a lot of misinformed people and ecofreaks trying to stop us from starting up the new nuclear power plant? In spite of all the talk about energy conservation, Americans are going to use more and more energy, and it's my job to make sure our customers have all the electricity they want.

David, it's getting hot in here. Would you please turn up the air conditioning?"

Kathy Farmington, a real estate agent, slowly shook her head. "I just don't know. We have to do something about pollution and overpopulation. The problem is, I don't know what to do. One scientist says we shouldn't build nuclear plants, another says we should. One says ban pesticides, and another says that if we do, many people will die from diseases and starvation. How can we know what to do when experts disagree? I recognize that the population problem is bad in Asia, Africa, and South America. Remember how horrid it was to see all of those people begging in the streets when we were in Calcutta on our vacation last summer? I just couldn't wait to leave. I'm glad we don't have an overpopulation problem in the United States. At least your father and I have made enough money to raise and educate the three of you."

As Linda, a college freshman, got up, she was thinking that no one in her family had really understood the speech. "Don't you realize that we are all connected with one another and that our primary goal must be to preserve—not degrade or destroy—the life-support systems that keep us and other species alive? Can't you see that everyone on earth is a unique human being, entitled to a fair share of our basic resources? I'm afraid for all of us, too, but I don't think it's too late if enough of us truly care. When I become a public service lawyer, I plan to devote my life to environmental reform."

PART ONE

Humans and Nature: An Overview

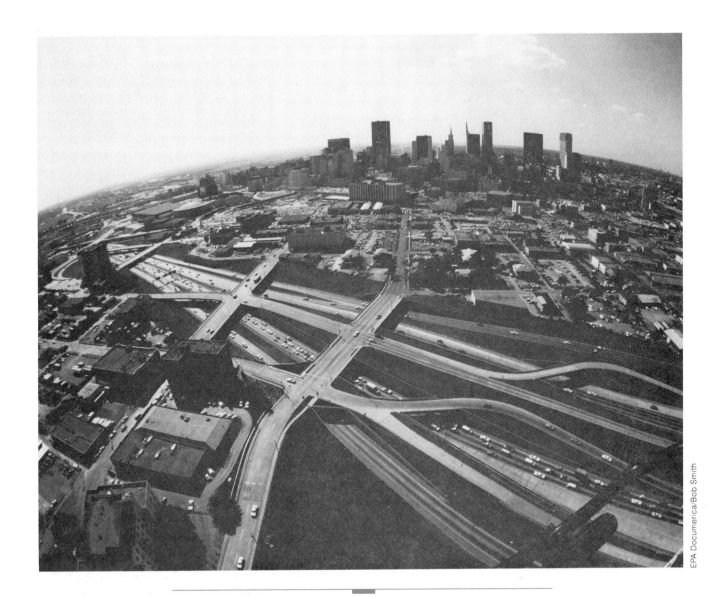

EPA Documerica/Bob Smith

It is only in the most recent, and brief, period of their tenure that human beings have developed in sufficient numbers, and acquired enough power, to become one of the most potentially dangerous organisms that the planet has ever hosted.

John McHale

Human despair or default can reach a point where even the most stirring visions lose their regenerating powers. This point, some will say, has already been reached. Not true. It will be reached only when human beings are no longer capable of calling out to one another, when the words in their poetry break up before their eyes, when their faces are frozen toward their young, and when they fail to make pictures in the mind out of clouds racing across the sky. So long as we can do these things, we are capable of indignation about the things we should be indignant about and we can shape our society in a way that does justice to our hopes.

Norman Cousins

1

Population, Resources, Environmental Degradation, and Pollution

GENERAL OBJECTIVES

1. How rapidly is the human population on earth increasing and when might it stabilize?

2. What are the major types of resources and are they in danger of being depleted?

3. What are the major types and sources of environmental degradation and pollution?

4. What are the relationships among human population size, resource use, technology, environmental degradation, and pollution?

5. What are the two major opposing schools of thought about how to solve environmental problems?

We travel together, passengers on a little spaceship, dependent on its vulnerable resources of air, water, and soil . . . preserved from annihilation only by the care, the work, and the love we give our fragile craft.

Adlai E. Stevenson

We have spent billions to transport a handful of people to the moon, only to learn the importance of protecting the rich diversity of life on the beautiful blue planet that is our home. Technological optimists promise a life of abundance for everyone, but as more people use and abuse the earth's resources, prophets of doom warn that the earth's life-support systems are being destroyed—or at least severely degraded.

This chapter is devoted to an overview of the interrelated problems of population growth, resource use, pollution of the air and water, and environmental degradation of topsoil, forests, grasslands, and fisheries that support human life. Later chapters will discuss these problems and options for dealing with them in greater depth.

1-1 HUMAN POPULATION GROWTH

The J-Shaped Curve of Human Population Growth If we plot the estimated number of people on earth over time, the resulting curve roughly resembles the shape of the letter *J* (Figure 1-1). This increase in the size of the human population is an example of **exponential growth,** which occurs when some factor—such as population size—grows by a constant percentage of the whole during each unit of time (see the Spotlight on p. 3). Although the percentage growth may vary from year to year, the world's population will grow exponentially as long as the number of births exceeds the number of deaths each year. This type of growth starts out slowly. But eventually the size of the population becomes so large that even a small annual percentage increase adds a large number of people.

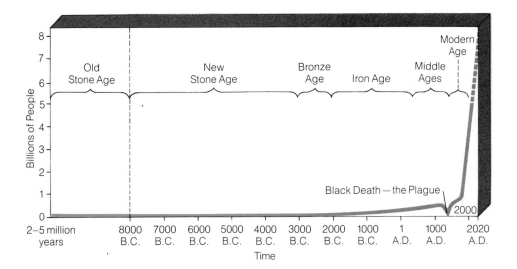

Figure 1-1 J-shaped curve of past exponential world population growth with projections to 2020 A.D. (Data from World Bank and United Nations)

An Example of Exponential Growth

Exponential growth can be illustrated by the following hypothetical example. If you were to repeatedly fold a page of this book in half, the thickness would increase exponentially. A page in this book is about 0.1 millimeter (1/254 inch) thick, so after one fold its thickness would be doubled to 0.2 millimeter. After 12 doublings it would be about 410 millimeters (1.34 feet) thick. If you plotted the increase in thickness for the first 12 doublings, this phase of exponential growth would be on the almost horizontal portion of the J-shaped curve because the thickness being doubled each time is still relatively small. However, assuming it would be physically possible to continue doubling the page, by the 35th fold its thickness would be 3,440 kilometers (2,136 miles)—about equal to the distance from New York City to Los Angeles, California. After 42 doublings this hypothetical mound of paper would reach from the earth to the moon, 386,400 kilometers (240,000 miles) away. Slightly past the 50th doubling the pile would reach the sun, 149 million kilometers (93 million miles) from the earth's surface. This is what it means to go around the bend on a J-shaped curve of exponential growth.

During the first several million years of human history, when people lived in small groups and survived by hunting wild game and gathering wild plants, the earth's population grew exponentially at an extremely slow average rate of about 0.002% a year. This slow or lag phase of exponential growth is represented by the almost horizontal portion of Figure 1-1. Since then, the average growth rate has increased and has led to such a large increase in people that the curve of population growth has rounded the bend of the J and has been heading almost straight up from the horizontal axis. With such exponential growth it has taken an increasingly smaller number of years to add each additional billion people (Figure 1-2).

During 1987, when a deceptively small annual growth rate of 1.7% acted on a base population of 5 billion, about 86.7 million people were added to the earth's population. At this rate it takes less than five days to replace a number of people equal to all Americans killed in all U.S. wars; slightly more than a year to replace the numerical equivalent of the more than 75 million people killed in the world's largest disaster (the bubonic plague epidemic of the fourteenth century); and only about two years to replace the numerical equivalent of the estimated 165 million soldiers who died in all wars fought on this planet during the past 200 years.

The 86.7 million new people added in 1987—amounting to an average addition of 1.7 million a week, 238,000 a day, or 9,900 an hour—and the even larger numbers to be added annually for decades need to be fed, clothed, housed, educated, and kept in good health. Each person will use some resources and will add to global pollution and degradation of the earth's life support systems. Yet this growth is occurring at a time when, according to United Nations estimates, at least half the adults on this planet cannot read or write, one out of six people is hungry or malnourished and does not have adequate housing (Figure 1-3), one out of four lacks clean drinking water, and one out of three does not have access to adequate sewage disposal or effective health care.

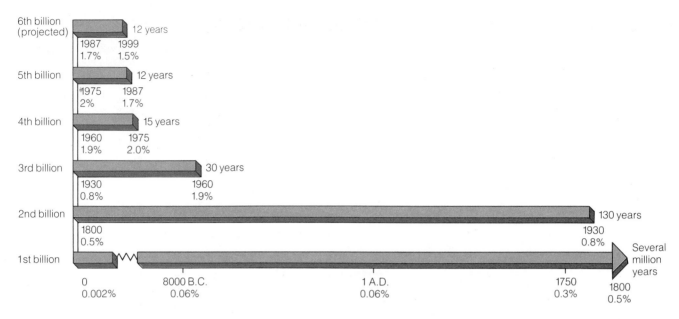

6th billion (projected)		12 years				
	1987 1.7%	1999 1.5%				
5th billion		12 years				
	1975 2%	1987 1.7%				
4th billion		15 years				
	1960 1.9%	1975 2.0%				
3rd billion			30 years			
	1930 0.8%		1960 1.9%			
2nd billion					130 years	
	1800 0.5%				1930 0.8%	
1st billion						Several million years

0 0.002%	8000 B.C. 0.06%	1 A.D. 0.06%	1750 0.3%	1800 0.5%

Figure 1-2 The number of years to add each successive billion people to the earth has decreased dramatically. Percentages indicate annual rates of exponential growth.

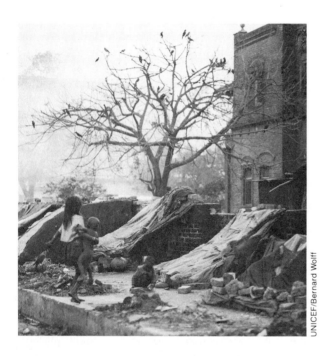

Figure 1-3 One-sixth of the people in the world do not have adequate housing. Lean-to sidewalk shelters like these are homes for many families in Dacca, Bangladesh.

By the year 2000, if the annual growth rate of population drops as projected to 1.5%, there will be 6.16 billion people on earth. Because the population will still be growing exponentially and the population base will have increased by more than 1 billion people, 89 million people will be added in 2000—2 million more than the number added in 1987.

Population Growth in the More Developed and Less Developed Countries The world's 166 countries with populations of 150,000 or more can be divided into two general groups based primarily on the average annual **gross national product** or **GNP** (the total market value of all goods and services produced per year) per person (Figure 1-4): The 33 **more developed countries (MDCs),** consisting of the United States, the Soviet Union, all European countries, Japan, Australia, and New Zealand, have significant industrialization, have a high average GNP per person, and are located primarily in the Northern Hemisphere. The 133 **less developed countries (LDCs)** have low to moderate industrialization, have a very low to moderate average GNP per person, and are located primarily in the Southern Hemisphere in Africa, Asia, and Latin America. At present, 92% of the world's annual population growth is taking place in the LDCs.

Viewed in this way the world is polarized into two major groups: one rich and one poor; one occupying areas of the Northern Hemisphere with mostly favorable climates and fertile soils, the other in areas of the Southern Hemisphere, often with less favorable climates and less fertile soils; one literate, the other largely illiterate; one with many overfed and overweight people, the other with many hungry and malnourished people; one with a low rate of population growth, the other with a very rapid rate.

Although dividing the world into MDCs and LDCs is convenient for dramatizing major differences in *average* living conditions, it is an oversimplification. Some countries designated MDCs are richer and more

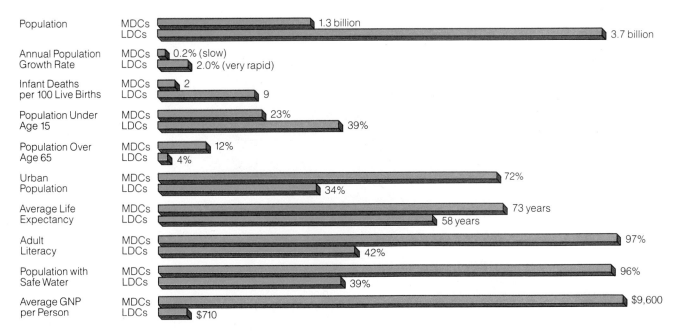

Population	MDCs	1.3 billion
	LDCs	3.7 billion
Annual Population Growth Rate	MDCs	0.2% (slow)
	LDCs	2.0% (very rapid)
Infant Deaths per 100 Live Births	MDCs	2
	LDCs	9
Population Under Age 15	MDCs	23%
	LDCs	39%
Population Over Age 65	MDCs	12%
	LDCs	4%
Urban Population	MDCs	72%
	LDCs	34%
Average Life Expectancy	MDCs	73 years
	LDCs	58 years
Adult Literacy	MDCs	97%
	LDCs	42%
Population with Safe Water	MDCs	96%
	LDCs	39%
Average GNP per Person	MDCs	$9,600
	LDCs	$710

Figure 1-4 Some characteristics of more developed countries (MDCs) and less developed countries (LDCs) in 1986. (Data from United Nations)

industrialized than others; some LDCs are poorer than others; and some poverty is found in the richest countries. In the United States during 1986, for example, 34 million people—one of every seven and almost one of every three Hispanic and black Americans—were classified by the government as living below the poverty level. To sort out some of these differences it is useful to further divide the world's countries into categories based on their degree of industrial development and their average GNP per person (Figure 1-5).

Life in the Poorest Countries Life for the poor people who comprise at least half the population of the 79 LDCs with low and very low average GNPs per person consists of a harsh daily struggle for survival. In typical rural villages or urban slums, groups of malnourished children sit around wood or dung fires eating breakfasts of bread and coffee. The air is filled with the stench of refuse and open sewers. Children and women carry heavy jars or cans of water, often for long distances, from a muddy, microbe-infested river, canal, or village water faucet. At night people sleep on the street in the open, under makeshift canopies, or on dirt floors in crowded single-room shacks, often made from straw, cardboard, rusting metal, or abandoned sections of drainage pipes. Families consisting of a father, mother, and from seven to nine children consider themselves fortunate to have an annual income of $300—an average of 82 cents a day. The parents, who themselves may die by age 45, know that three

or four of their children will probably die from hunger or childhood diseases, such as diarrhea or measles, that rarely kill in affluent countries.

When citizens of affluent countries see such conditions in person or on television, they often try to blot these grim pictures out of their minds. Some consider poor people ignorant for having so many children. To most poor parents, however, having a large number of children, especially boys, makes good sense. It gives them much needed help for work in the fields or begging in the streets and provides a form of social security to help them survive when they reach old age (typically in their forties). For people living near the edge of survival, having too many children may cause problems, but having too few can contribute to premature death.

Although the world is feeding more people than ever before, there are an estimated 750 million desperately poor people—one out of every six people on earth—living mostly in low- and very low income countries. These people do not have enough fertile land or money to grow their own food in rural areas or enough money to buy the food they need in cities. As a result, between 12 million and 20 million die prematurely each year from starvation, malnutrition (lack of sufficient protein and other nutrients needed for good health), or normally nonfatal diseases such as diarrhea brought on by contaminated drinking water, which, for people weakened by malnutrition, becomes deadly.

This means that during your lunch hour 1,400 to 2,300 people died of such causes; by the time you eat

Figure 1-5 Division of world's countries into categories based on their degree of industrial development. (Data from Population Reference Bureau. Map based on a modified Goode's projection, copyright by the University of Chicago, Department of Geography, and used by their permission.)

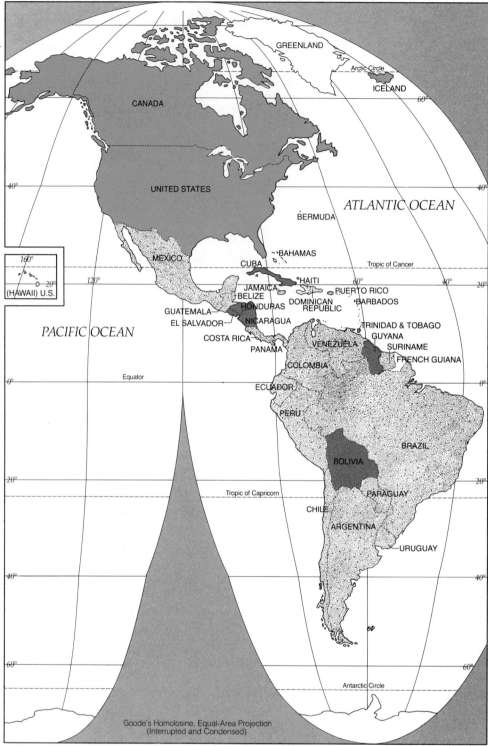

Type	Average GNP per Person (U.S. dollars)	Percent of World Population
Highly industrialized countries	$6,900–$16,250	21%
Moderately developed, high-income, oil-exporting countries	$6,800–$24,000	0.3%
Moderately developed, middle-income countries	$1,000–$6,400	17%

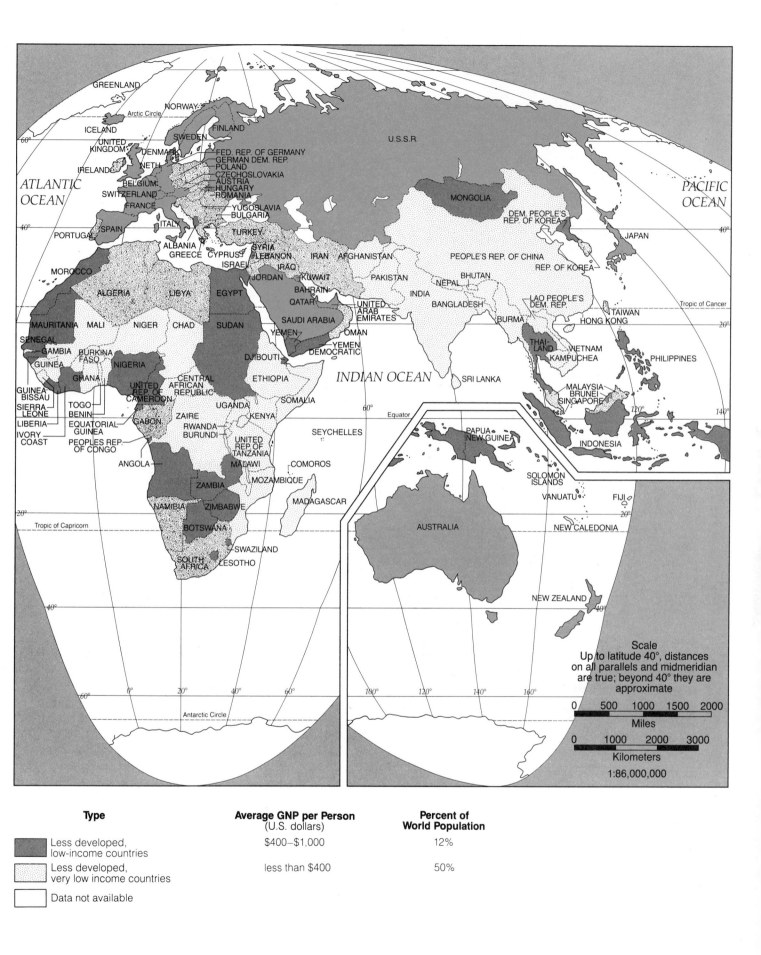

Type	Average GNP per Person (U.S. dollars)	Percent of World Population
▨ Less developed, low-income countries	$400–$1,000	12%
░ Less developed, very low income countries	less than $400	50%
☐ Data not available		

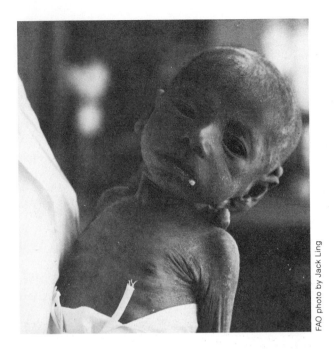

Figure 1-6 This Indonesian child is one of the estimated 750 million people on earth who suffer undernutrition (too little food) and malnutrition resulting from a diet insufficient in protein and other nutrients needed for good health.

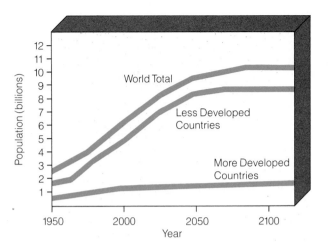

Figure 1-7 Past and projected population size for the more developed countries, less developed countries, and the world, 1950–2120 A.D. (Data from United Nations)

lunch tomorrow 33,000 to 55,000 more will have died; and by this time next week, 231,000 to 385,000. Half are children under the age of 5 (Figure 1-6). This starvation and malnutrition is not classified as famine by most officials because it is spread throughout much of the world (especially rural Africa and Asia) and not confined to one country.

When Might World Population Growth Come to a Halt? If the annual rate of population growth continues to decrease, we eventually will reach a state termed **zero population growth (ZPG),** in which the annual number of births equals the number of deaths (births per year − deaths per year = 0). Some MDCs in Europe have reached or are approaching ZPG, and some, such as West Germany, Hungary, and Denmark, are even experiencing population declines. In most LDCs, however, population growth will continue for many decades (Figure 1-7). Unless there is a global nuclear war or greatly increased famine and disease, UN population experts project that the world is not likely to attain ZPG until around 2100, when it will reach a population of 10.4 billion—twice that in 1986—with most of the growth taking place in the LDCs.

1-2 RESOURCES AND ENVIRONMENTAL DEGRADATION

What Is a Natural Resource? A **natural resource** or **resource** is usually defined as anything obtained from the physical environment to meet human needs. Some resources are available for use directly from the environment. Examples include solar energy, fresh air, rainwater, fresh water in a river or stream, and naturally growing edible plants. Other resources, such as oil, iron, groundwater, fish, and game animals, are not directly available for our use. Whether these and other materials in the environment are considered to be human resources depends on a combination of human ingenuity, economics, and cultural beliefs.

Human ingenuity enables us to develop scientific and technological methods for finding, extracting, and processing many of the earth's natural substances and converting them to usable forms. Groundwater found deep below the earth's surface was not a resource until we developed the technology for drilling a well and installing pumps and other equipment to bring it to the surface. Fish and game animals are not a resource unless we have some way of catching and (in most cases) cooking them. Petroleum was a mysterious fluid until humans learned how to locate it, extract it, and refine it into gasoline, home heating oil, road tar, and other products. Cars, television sets, tractors, and other manufactured objects are available only because humans developed methods for converting an array of once-useless raw materials from the earth's crust into useful forms.

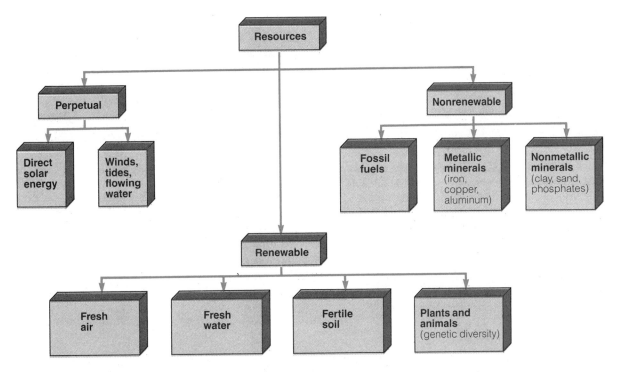

Figure 1-8 Major types of natural resources. This scheme, however, is not fixed; renewable resources can be converted to nonrenewable if used for a prolonged time faster than they are renewed by natural processes.

Economics also determines whether something is classified as a resource or a potential resource. Some known deposits of oil, coal, copper, and other potentially useful materials are located so far beneath the earth's surface or in such low concentrations that they would cost more to find, extract, and process than they are worth. In the future, however, their prices may rise due to their scarcity, or cheaper, more efficient mining and processing technologies may be developed, converting these potential resources to actual resources.

Cultural beliefs can also determine whether something is considered a resource. For example, protein-rich grasshoppers and other insects are considered food resources in some parts of Africa, but are viewed with disgust as sources of food in the United States and in most MDCs. In some cultures, religious beliefs prohibit the use of pork or other types of food resources. The perceived or actual degree of risk involved in using a resource such as nuclear power can also play a role in whether or how widely it is used (see the Enrichment Study at the end of Chapter 6).

Nonrenewable Resources   Resources can be classified as nonrenewable, renewable, and perpetual (Figure 1-8). A **nonrenewable resource** is one that exists

in a fixed amount (stock) in various places in the earth's crust and either is not replenished by natural processes or is replenished more slowly than it is used. Examples include **(1) fossil fuels**—buried deposits of decayed plants and animals that have been converted to materials such as oil, coal, and natural gas by heat and pressure in the earth's crust over hundreds of millions of years; **(2) metallic minerals** such as uranium, iron, and aluminum; and **(3) nonmetallic minerals** such as phosphates and potassium used as plant nutrients in commercial fertilizers.

The easily available deposits of nonrenewable minerals and fossil fuels are usually found in high concentrations near the earth's surface in nonhostile environments; once they are depleted, extraction costs rise. Increasing scarcity can raise the prices paid for such resources, stimulating a search for new deposits or making the mining and processing of lower grade deposits more feasible. Eventually, however, the cost of finding, extracting, and concentrating increasingly lower grade or difficult-to-extract deposits may become so high that these substances are no longer considered resources even though some supplies remain. *Typically, a nonrenewable resource such as oil or copper is considered depleted from an economic standpoint when 80% of its total estimated supply has been removed and used.*

Some nonrenewable resources can be recycled or

reused to stretch supplies—copper, aluminum, iron, and glass, for example—and others, such as fossil fuels, cannot. **Recycling** involves collecting and remelting or reprocessing a resource (aluminum beverage cans), whereas **reuse** involves using a resource over and over in the same form (refillable beverage bottles). But discarded aluminum cans, refillable bottles, and abandoned car hulks can be dispersed so widely that it becomes too costly to collect them for reuse or recycling.

We live in a brief **fossil fuel era** in which deposits of solar energy captured by plants and converted to nonrenewable deposits of crude oil, coal, and natural gas over hundreds of millions of years are being used up in several hundred years. During 1986 these one-time deposits of fossil fuels, which cannot be recycled or reused, provided about 82% of the energy used in the world for electricity, heating, cooling, transportation, and manufacturing. The largest fraction of this energy (36%) was provided by oil. Affordable supplies of oil are projected to last for only a few more decades.

Sometimes a substitute or replacement for a nonrenewable resource that is scarce or too expensive can be found. Although some resource economists argue that we can use human ingenuity to find a substitute for any nonrenewable resource, this is not always the case at a particular time or for a particular purpose. Some materials have such unique properties that they cannot easily be replaced; the would-be replacements are inferior, too costly, or otherwise unsatisfactory. For example, nothing now known can replace steel and concrete in skyscrapers, nuclear power plants, and dams.

Renewable and Perpetual Resources A **renewable resource** is one that can be depleted in the short run if used or contaminated too rapidly but normally will be replaced through natural processes in the long run. Examples include trees in forests, grasses in grasslands, fish and game, fresh surface water in lakes and rivers, most deposits of groundwater, fresh air, and fertile soil.

Classifying something as a renewable resource, however, does not mean that it is inexhaustible and that it will always remain renewable. The highest rate at which a renewable resource can be used without impairing or damaging its ability to be fully renewed is called its **sustained yield.** If this yield is exceeded, the base supply of a renewable resource begins to shrink and can eventually become nonrenewable on a human time scale or in some cases nonexistent—a process known as **environmental degradation** (see Spotlight on p. 11). Considerable evidence indicates that in many parts of the world, especially in LDCs, the sustained yields for potentially renewable resources such as topsoil, groundwater, grasslands, forests, fisheries, and wildlife are being exceeded.

The **biological or genetic diversity** in the world's millions of different types of plants and animals is another key renewable resource in the struggle to provide food and other materials for the world's rapidly growing population. Preserving this genetic diversity, either in the wild or in genetic storage banks set up around the world, can be essential to long-term human welfare.

A **perpetual resource** is one that comes from an essentially inexhaustible source and thus will always be available in a relatively constant supply regardless of whether or how we use it. Solar energy is the most important example of such a resource; it will arrive at the earth at a reasonably constant rate during the remaining lifetime of the sun, estimated as at least 5 billion years. Other perpetual resources, based primarily on the direct input of solar energy and gravitational forces, include wind energy, tidal energy, and flowing water.

Are We Running Out of Resources? Increasing population causes a corresponding rise in resource use, and a rise in the standard of living creates a significant rise in average use of nonrenewable and renewable resources per person. For example, the average U.S. citizen consumes 50 times more steel, 56 times more energy, 170 times more synthetic rubber and newsprint, 250 times more motor fuel, and 300 times more plastic than the average citizen of India.

During the past 100 years and especially since 1950, affluent countries have gone around the bend on a J-shaped curve of increasing average consumption per person of renewable and nonrenewable resources. *With only 24% of the world's population, the MDCs use 80% of the world's processed energy and mineral resources. The United States alone, with only 4.8% of the world's population, produces about 21% of all goods and services, uses about one-third of the world's processed energy and mineral resources, and produces at least one-third of the world's pollution.*

Average resource use per person in affluent countries is projected to rise sharply in coming decades. At the same time, the world's LDCs hope to become more affluent. For even moderate worldwide economic growth to occur between 1975 and 2020, it is projected that the production of food and of common minerals must increase fourfold and fivefold, respectively. Because the gap between the rich and poor countries has been increasing since 1960 (Figure 1-9), an increasing number of leaders and citizens in LDCs fear that rapid resource depletion by the MDCs may not leave enough resources for their countries to ever become MDCs. They are calling for the MDCs to waste less resources and to provide greatly increased assistance and access to trade and markets to help the LDCs become more self-sufficient and have access to a more equitable share of the world's resources.

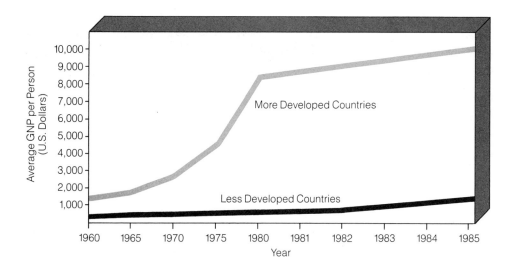

Figure 1-9 The gap in average GNP per person between the more developed and the less developed countries has been widening since 1960, raising fears by many LDCs that they may become never-developed countries. Adjusted for inflation, the average GNP per person in LDCs has actually decreased since 1960. (Data from United Nations)

Spotlight Environmental Degradation: Survival, Short-Term Economic Growth, and the Tragedy of the Commons

Environmental degradation is a broad term referring to processes that deplete or destroy a region's resource base and thus hinder its long-term biological and economic productivity. Examples of major types of environmental degradation include **(1)** covering productive land with water, silt, concrete, asphalt, or buildings to such an extent that agricultural productivity declines and places for wildlife to live are lost, **(2)** cultivating land so intensively without proper soil management that agricultural productivity is reduced by soil erosion and depletion of plant nutrients, **(3)** irrigating cropland without sufficient drainage so that excessive accumulation of water (*waterlogging*) or salts (*salinization*) in the soil decreases agricultural productivity, **(4)** removing trees from large areas without adequate replanting (*deforestation*) so that wildlife habitats are destroyed and timber productivity is decreased by flooding and soil erosion, and **(5)** depleting grass on land grazed by livestock (*overgrazing*) so that soil is eroded to the point where produc-

tive grasslands are converted into nonproductive deserts (*desertification*).

Environmental degradation of grasslands, forests, croplands, fisheries, and wildlife in many areas of LDCs is caused by hundreds of millions of poor people trying to survive in the short term, diminishing the normally renewable resource base on which the future economic productivity and growth of these countries depend. Unless these harmful trends can somehow be reversed, even more people will face harsh lives and premature deaths.

Some environmental degradation occurs when an LDC exports lumber, beef, and other products to MDCs without making adequate attempts to prevent long-term degradation of its forests, croplands, and grazing lands. Short-term economic growth is the major driving force behind this MDC-induced degradation of renewable resources in LDCs. Individuals and large national and multinational corporations maximize short-term profits with little concern

for the future availability or long-term sustainability of renewable resources.

Another situation giving rise to environmental degradation involves common or shared resources. A **commons** is a resource to which a population has free and unmanaged access—in contrast to a private property resource (accessible only to the owner) and a socialized resource (where access is controlled by elected or appointed managers). A phenomenon known as the **tragedy of the commons** occurs when resources such as clean air, clean water in a river or lake, or fish of the sea, are considered common property free to be used by anyone. They are then overharvested (fish) or polluted (air and water) because each user reasons, "If I don't use this resource, someone else will." Individuals continue maximizing their use of such a common resource until the cumulative effect of many people doing the same thing so depletes the supply that it is no longer available to anyone at an affordable price.

Approaches to **resource conservation** include efforts to reduce unnecessary resource waste in order to extend the useful life of nonrenewable resources, to prevent renewable resources from being converted to nonrenewable resources through overuse, and to reduce the environmental impact of resource use.

1-3 POLLUTION

What Is Pollution? Any change in the physical, chemical, or biological characteristics of the air, water, or soil that can affect the health, survival, or activities of humans or other forms of life in an undesirable way is called **pollution.** Pollution does not have to cause physical harm; pollutants such as noise and heat may cause injury but more often cause psychological distress, and aesthetic pollution such as foul odors and unpleasant sights offend the senses.

People, however, may differ in what they consider to be a pollutant, on the basis of their assessment of benefits and risks to their health and economic well-being. For example, visible and invisible chemicals spewed into the air or water from an industrial plant might be harmful to humans and other forms of life living nearby. However, if the installation of expensive pollution controls forces the plant to shut down, workers who would lose their jobs might feel that the risks from polluted air and water are minor weighed against the benefits of profitable employment. The same level of pollution can also affect two people quite differently—some forms of air pollution might be a slight annoyance to a healthy person but life threatening to someone with emphysema or another respiratory disorder.

Such risk-benefit analysis enters into most environmental decisions and leads to economic, political, and ethical trade-offs (see the Enrichment Study in Chapter 6). As the philosopher Georg Hegel pointed out, the nature of tragedy is not the conflict between right and wrong but between right and right.

Types, Sources, and Effects of Pollutants As long as they are not overloaded, natural processes or human-engineered systems (such as sewage treatment plants) can biodegrade or break down some types of pollutants to an acceptable level or form. Depending on their biodegradability, pollutants can be classified as being **rapidly biodegradable** (such as human sewage and livestock wastes), **slowly biodegradable** (such as DDT and other chemical pesticides), and **nonbiodegradable** (such as toxic mercury and lead compounds and some radioactive substances).

Table 1-1	Pollutants Generated by Natural and Human Activities	
	Type of Pollutant	Text Discussion
Class 1: Almost Completely Generated by Human Activities		
	DDT, PCBs, and other chlorinated hydrocarbon compounds	Chapter 22
	Lead in the air (from burning leaded gasoline)	Chapter 21
	Solid wastes and litter	Chapter 21
Class 2: Primarily Generated by Human Activities		
	Radioactive wastes	Chapter 17
	Oil in the oceans	Chapter 20
	Sewage (animal and plant wastes)	Chapter 20
	Phosphates in aquatic systems	Chapter 20
	Waste heat in rivers, lakes, and oceans	Chapter 20
	Photochemical smog in the air (from burning gasoline)	Chapter 19
	Sulfur dioxide in the air (from burning coal and oil)	Chapter 19
	Noise	Chapter 23
Class 3: Primarily Generated by Natural Sources		
	Hydrocarbons in the air	Chapter 19
	Carbon monoxide and carbon dioxide in the air	Chapter 19
	Solid particles in the air	Chapter 19
	Mercury in the ocean	Chapter 21

Polluting substances can enter the environment naturally or through human activities (Table 1-1). Most natural pollution is dispersed over a large area and is often diluted or degraded to harmless levels by natural processes. In contrast, the most serious human pollution problems occur in or near urban and industrial areas, where large amounts of pollutants are concentrated in relatively small volumes of air, water, and soil. Furthermore, many pollutants from human activities are synthetic (human-made) chemicals that are slowly biodegradable or nonbiodegradable.

Often, pollutants released into one part of the environment don't remain there and can affect people and other forms of life at the local, regional, and in some cases the global levels. Sulfur dioxide gas released into the atmosphere by coal-burning industrial and electric power plants in the midwestern United States is converted to acidic droplets and solid particles that fall to the earth's surface and kill some species of trees in mountain forests and fish and other aquatic life in lakes in the northeastern United States and southeastern Canada.

Complicating matters further, pollutants can have both acute and chronic effects on human health. An **acute effect,** such as a burn, illness, or death, occurs shortly after exposure, often in response to fairly high concentrations of a pollutant. A **chronic effect** is a condition that lasts a long time and usually takes a long time to appear, often due to exposure to low concentrations of a pollutant. For example, people exposed to a large dose of radiation may die within a few days. However, people receiving the same total dose in small amounts over a long period may develop various types of cancer 10 to 20 years later or may transmit genetic defects to their children.

During a lifetime an individual is exposed to many different types and concentrations of potentially harmful pollutants. The scientific evidence correlating a particular harmful effect to a particular pollutant is usually statistical or circumstantial—as is most scientific evidence. For example, so far no one has been able to show what specific chemicals in cigarette smoke cause lung cancer; however, smoking and lung cancer are causally linked by an overwhelming amount of statistical evidence from more than 32,000 studies.

Another complication is that certain pollutants acting together can cause a harmful effect greater than the sum of their individual effects. This phenomenon is called a **synergistic effect.** For example, asbestos workers, already at higher-than-average risk of lung cancer, greatly increase that risk if they smoke because of an apparent synergistic effect between tobacco smoke and tiny particles of asbestos inhaled into the lungs. Testing all the possible synergistic interactions among the thousands of possible pollutants in the environment is prohibitively expensive and time-consuming, even for their effects on just one type of plant or animal.

Pollution Control   Some countries, especially MDCs such as the United States, are making progress in controlling some types of pollution; others are not (see Spotlight above). There are two fundamentally different approaches to pollution control. **Input pollution control** prevents potential pollutants from entering the environment or sharply reduces the amount emitted or discharged. In this preventive approach taxes, incentives, or other economic devices are used to make the resource inputs of a process so expensive that these resources will be used more efficiently, thus decreasing the output of waste material.

The other is a "treat-the-disease" or **output pollution control** approach that deals with wastes after they have been produced. The three major methods

Spotlight   Poland: The World's Most Environmentally Polluted Country

In 1985 the Polish Academy of Sciences released a report describing Poland as the most environmentally polluted country in the world, primarily because it spends only 1% of its gross national product on pollution control and environmental protection—a much lower percentage than even most LDCs. Less than half of Poland's 800 cities have sewage treatment plants, and even the capital, Warsaw, is not scheduled to have one until 1990. As a result, 90% of the water in the country's rivers is too polluted to drink and much of the water in its biggest river is too polluted even for industrial use. According to the report, satellite photographs show that the biggest clouds of smoke in Europe hang over Poland, partly because large power and industrial plants have shut down their air pollution control equipment to save power and money.

of output control are **(1)** cleaning up polluted air, water, or land by reducing pollutants to harmless levels or by converting them to harmless or less harmful substances, **(2)** disposing of harmful wastes by burning them, dumping them in the air or water in the hope that they will be diluted to harmless levels, or burying them in the ground and hoping they will remain there, and **(3)** recycling or reusing matter output from human activities.

1-4   RELATIONSHIPS AMONG POPULATION, RESOURCE USE, TECHNOLOGY, ENVIRONMENTAL DEGRADATION, AND POLLUTION

The Roots of Environmental Degradation and Pollution   What causes most environmental degradation and pollution? The obvious answer is people trying either to survive or to make short-term profits. We could conclude that most forms of pollution and environmental degradation tend to increase with population growth, but the real situation is not that simple because pollution and environmental degradation vary with the technological methods and the types of resources people use. According to one simple model,

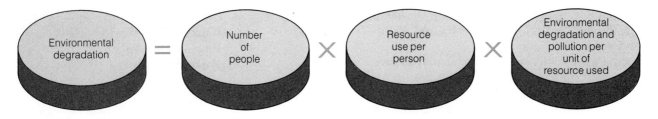

Figure 1-10 Simplified model of how three factors affect overall environmental degradation and pollution or environmental impact.

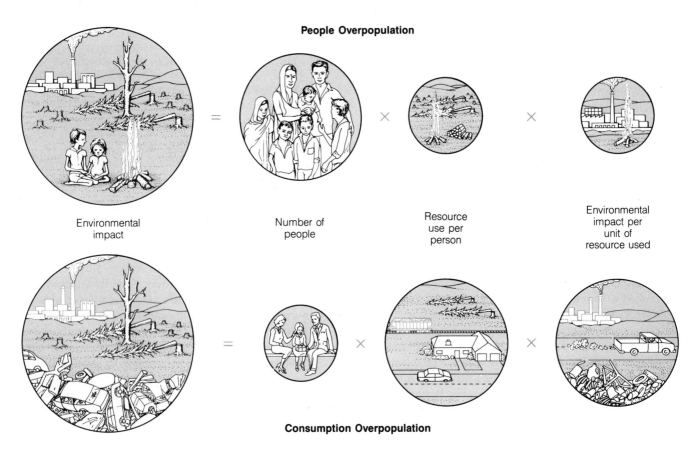

Figure 1-11 Two types of overpopulation based on the relative importance of the factors in the model shown in Figure 1-10.

the total environmental degradation and pollution or environmental impact of population in a given area depends upon three factors: **(1)** the number of people, **(2)** the amount of resources each person uses, and **(3)** the environmental degradation and pollution resulting from each unit of resource used (Figure 1-10).

Two Types of Overpopulation   In general, **overpopulation** occurs when the people in a country, a region, or the world are using nonrenewable and renewable resources to such an extent that the result-

ing degradation or depletion of the resource base and pollution of the air, water, and soil are impairing their life-support systems. Differences in the relative importance of each factor in the model shown in Figure 1-10 have been used to distinguish between two types of overpopulation (Figure 1-11).

The type known as **people overpopulation** exists where there are more people than the available supplies of food, water, and other vital resources can support, or where the rate of population growth so exceeds the rate of economic growth that an increasing number of people are too poor to grow or buy sufficient

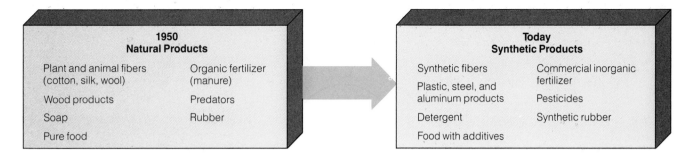

1950 Natural Products		Today Synthetic Products	
Plant and animal fibers (cotton, silk, wool)	Organic fertilizer (manure)	Synthetic fibers	Commercial inorganic fertilizer
Wood products	Predators	Plastic, steel, and aluminum products	Pesticides
Soap	Rubber	Detergent	Synthetic rubber
Pure food		Food with additives	

Figure 1-12 Some synthetic products substituted for natural products in industrialized countries since 1950.

food, fuel, and other vital resources. In this type of overpopulation, population size and the resulting environmental degradation of potentially renewable soil, grasslands, forests, and fisheries tend to be the most important factors determining the total environmental impact. In the world's poorest LDCs, people overpopulation results in premature death for 12 million to 20 million human beings each year and bare subsistence for hundreds of millions more—a situation that many fear will worsen unless population growth is brought under control and improved resource management is used to restore degraded renewable resource bases.

Affluent and technologically advanced countries such as the United States, the Soviet Union, and Japan are said by some to have a second type of overpopulation, known as **consumption overpopulation.** It is based on the fact that without adequate pollution and land use controls, a small number of people using resources at a high rate produces more pollution and environmental degradation than a much larger number of people using resources at a much lower rate. With this type of overpopulation, high rates of resource use per person and the resulting high levels of pollution per person tend to be the most important factors determining overall environmental impact.

In countries said to have consumption overpopulation, relatively few people face starvation. Instead, unless such countries devote a growing fraction of their GNP to pollution and land use control, many people face illness or premature death over the *long-term* from contaminated air and water and increasingly degraded croplands, grazing lands, and forests. Such countries, sometimes referred to as **overdeveloped countries** or **ODCs,** are accused of hastening the depletion of many of the world's vital resources through a throwaway lifestyle based on unnecessary resource waste—thus helping make many of today's LDCs *never-to-be-developed countries* (Figure 1-9).

There is disagreement, however, over whether LDCs are really overpopulated—especially over whether the MDCs should be considered as being overpopulated, as discussed in Section 1-5.

Is Technology the Culprit? Some analysts argue that the most important factor in the model presented in Figure 1-10 is the pollution per unit of resource used. They suggest that the introduction of environmentally harmful technologies since World War II has become the major cause of pollution in industrialized, affluent countries. These countries have shifted much of their production and consumption from natural materials that can be broken down, diluted, or absorbed by natural processes to synthetic products that are either slowly biodegraded or not biodegraded by natural processes (Figure 1-12).

Others argue that this is an oversimplification. While technological developments such as the automobile and phosphate detergents create new environmental problems or aggravate existing ones, other technological developments can help solve various environmental and resource problems. For example, substitutes have been developed for many scarce resources (light bulbs have replaced whale oil in lamps, thus helping protect the world's rapidly diminishing supply of whales from extinction). Unnecessary resource waste has been reduced. For example, more of the branches, trunks, and other woody parts of trees are now used, and more energy is recovered from a ton of coal than in the past. Processes to control and clean up many forms of pollution have been developed.

Most analysts agree that *our problem and challenge is not to eliminate technology but to decide how to use it more carefully and humanely.* One major attempt to use technology wisely is the increased global emphasis on using appropriate technology. **Appropriate technology** is usually small, simple, decentralized, and inexpensive to build and maintain, and it usually utilizes locally available materials and labor. The use of huge tractors to plow fields in a poor rural village in India

Figure 1-13 Environmental problems are caused by a complex, poorly understood mix of interacting factors, as illustrated by this greatly simplified multiple-factor model.

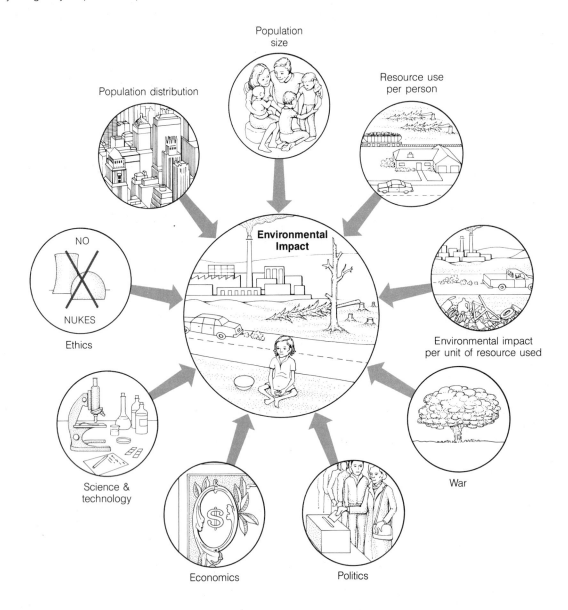

is often cited as an example of inappropriate and destructive technology. In such villages the most plentiful resource is people—willing and needing to work on farms. The tractor deprives these people of their only means of survival and forces them to migrate to already overpopulated cities, looking for nonexistent jobs. The wealthier farmers who remain become dependent on industrialized countries for expensive gasoline and parts and find the tractor too complex to be repaired by untrained local people. Instead of a large tractor, an appropriate technology would be a well-designed metal plow, made and repaired by a local blacksmith and pulled by locally available draft animals such as oxen or water buffaloes. Supporters of appropriate technology recognize that it is not a cure for all our environmental problems but believe

that its increasing use is an encouraging trend that should be nurtured.

Other Factors   The four-factor model shown in Figure 1-10, though useful, is far too simple. The actual situation is much more complex: an interacting mix of problems and contributing factors shown in simplified form in Figure 1-13. For example, pollution and environmental degradation are intensified not only by population size but also by population distribution. The most severe air and water pollution problems usually occur when large numbers of people are concentrated in urban areas. Conversely, spreading people out can have a devastating effect on potentially renewable soil, forest, grassland, and recreational resources.

War also has a devastating environmental impact.

Economic, political, and ethical factors are also involved. We can manipulate the economic system to control pollution, environmental degradation, and resource waste by making it unprofitable (in free-market economies) or illegal (in centrally controlled economies) to engage in such practices. We can use the political process to enact and enforce pollution control and land use control laws. However, such economic and political efforts will not be undertaken until an informed and politically active segment of the population (probably 5% to 10%) in countries with free elections and the leaders in other countries realize that it is both unwise and unethical to abuse the world's life-support systems for short-term economic gain. Finally, as pointed out earlier, science and technology can be applied to pollution control and efficient resource use, but they often lead to products and processes that have detrimental environmental effects.

1-5 WHAT SHOULD BE DONE? NEO-MALTHUSIANS VERSUS CORNUCOPIANS

There are two fundamentally different, opposing schools of thought about what the role of humans in the world should be, how serious the world's present and projected future environmental problems really are, and what should be done to deal with them. **Neo-Malthusians** (called "gloom-and-doom pessimists" by their opponents) believe that if present trends continue, the world will become more crowded and more polluted, leading to greater political and economic instability and increasing the threat of nuclear war as the rich get richer and the poor get poorer. The term *neo-Malthusian* refers to an updated and greatly expanded version of the hypothesis proposed in 1789 by Thomas Robert Malthus, an English clergyman and economist, that human population growing exponentially will eventually outgrow food supplies and will be reduced in size by starvation, disease, and war.

The opposing group, called **cornucopians** (or unrealistic "technological optimists" by their opponents), believes that if present trends continue, economic growth and technological advances based on human ingenuity will produce a less crowded, less polluted world, in which most people will be healthier, will live longer, and will have greater material wealth. The term *cornucopian* comes from *cornucopia*, the horn of plenty, which symbolizes an abundance. The major differences between the two schools of thought are summarized in the Spotlight on pp. 18–19 and are also reflected in the two Guest Essays at the end of this chapter.

This debate between cornucopians (most of whom are economists) and neo-Malthusians (most of whom are environmentalists and conservationists) has been going on for decades. But it is much more than an intellectual debate between people who generally use the same data and general trends to reach quite different conclusions. At a more fundamental level it represents radically different views of how the world works—one's *worldview*—and thus how we should operate in the world.

Cornucopians generally have a **frontier** or **throwaway worldview.** They see the earth as a place of unlimited resources where any type of conservation that hampers short-term economic growth is unnecessary. If we pollute or deplete the resources in one area, we will find resource substitutes, control the pollution through technology, and if necessary obtain additional resources from the moon and asteroids in the "new frontier" of space.

In contrast, neo-Malthusians generally have a **sustainable-earth worldview.*** Seeing the earth as a place with finite room and resources, they believe that ever-increasing production and consumption inevitably put severe stress on the complex, poorly understood natural processes that renew and maintain the air, water, and soil. Some neo-Malthusians have used the term "Spaceship Earth" to help people see the need to protect the earth's life-support systems. However, other neo-Malthusians have criticized this image, believing the spaceship analogy subtly reinforces the arrogant idea that the role of humans is to dominate and control nature; it encourages us to view the earth merely as a machine that we can manipulate at will and to think that we have essentially complete understanding of how nature works.

As we examine major environmental problems and their possible solutions throughout this book, we should be guided by the motto of philosopher and mathematician Alfred North Whitehead (1861–1947): "Seek simplicity and distrust it," and by writer and social critic H. L. Mencken (1880–1956), who warned: "For every problem there is a solution—simple, neat, and wrong."

What is the use of a house if you don't have a decent planet to put it on?
Henry David Thoreau (1817–1862)

---

*Others have used the terms *sustainable society* and *conserver society* to describe this view. I use the word *earth* to make clear that it is the entire earth system, not just the subsystem of humans and their societies, that must be sustained.

Role of Humans on Earth

Cornucopians

Use our ingenuity to develop technologies for *conquering nature* to promote an economy based on ever-increasing production and consumption of material goods.

Neo-Malthusians

Use our ingenuity to develop technologies for *working with nature* to promote kinds of economic growth that sustain rather than deplete and degrade the earth's life-support systems.

Seriousness of Environmental Problems

Exaggerated; can be cured by increased economic growth and technological innovations.

Serious now and could become more serious if many present forms of economic growth and technology are not replaced with forms that place less stress on the environment.

Population Growth and Control

Should not be controlled because people are our most vital source of new technologies that will solve the world's problems.

Should be controlled because adding billions of mostly poor and malnourished people in LDCs (people overpopulation) will not solve the world's problems and will condemn hundreds of millions—perhaps billions—to premature deaths in the future; allowing wasteful types of resource consumption to continue in MDCs (consumption overpopulation) will increase regional and global pollution and environmental degradation.

Economic development will lead to lower birth rates and a stabilized population in LDCs as it has in MDCs since the Industrial Revolution.

Economic development cannot slow population growth in time to avoid greatly increased famine and environmental degradation in the poorer LDCs unless it is coupled with a well-funded, well-planned program for population control.

Many forms of birth control go against some individuals' religious beliefs and are an infringement on people's freedom to have as many children as they want.

People should not be forced to control the number of children they have, but they should have easy access to any form of birth control they find acceptable; people should also be educated to understand that a lower population size in LDCs and MDCs will help reduce resource depletion, pollution, environmental degradation, famine, poverty, social tension, war, and erosion of individual freedom.

Resource Depletion

We will not run out of renewable resources; as resources are degraded, price rises for food, lumber, and other products will lead to better management or a switch to alternatives.

There are no substitutes for potentially renewable resources such as topsoil, grasslands, forests, and fisheries, which are already being overused and converted to nonrenewable resources in many LDCs for survival and in many MDCs for short-term profit.

We will not run out of scarce nonrenewable resources because price rises will stimulate humans to invent ways to mine lower-grade deposits or to find substitutes.

Once a nonrenewable resource is about 80% depleted, it is usually uneconomic to use what's left; substitutes for some widely used resources may not be found or may take too long to develop and phase in without causing severe economic hardship.

Resource Depletion (continued)

MDCs are not overdeveloped countries suffering from consumption overpopulation; in the United States and most MDCs since the 1970s, economic growth has produced industrial products, technology, and knowledge, all of which can be used to control pollution, find new resources, help LDCs grow economically, and increase average life expectancy.

As a result of very high rates of resource use and unnecessary waste, MDCs are causing unacceptable regional and global resource depletion, environmental degradation, and pollution, which can eventually wipe out short-term gains in average life expectancy; when adjusted for inflation, the average GNP per person in LDCs has decreased since 1960—not increased as cornucopians have been promising for decades.

Resource Conservation

Renewable resources should be used and managed efficiently to leave them in reasonable shape for future generations, but not at the expense of short-term economic growth by the present generation.

Renewable resources should be used and managed efficiently for people on earth today, but not at the expense of their future sustainability, on which long-term economic productivity depends.

Reducing unnecessary resource waste, while desirable, is not a high priority because human ingenuity can always find a substitute for any scarce resource.

Reducing unnecessary resource waste should receive the highest priority to stretch supplies that are being depleted and to reduce the environmental impact of resource extraction and use; substitutes may not be found or may be inferior or more costly.

Emphasis on recycling and reusing materials can reduce short-term profits and is unnecessary because we can always find a substitute for any scarce resource.

Recycling and reuse of nonrenewable resources are necessary to stretch supplies, allow more time to find and phase in substitutes (if possible), and to reduce the environmental impact of finding, extracting, and processing primary or virgin resources.

Pollution Control

Pollution control should not be increased at the expense of short-term economic growth, which can provide funds for cleaning up the environment as needed.

Insufficient pollution control leads to short- and long-term damages that will reduce long-term economic productivity; costs of most products and services do not reflect their actual harmful environmental, economic, and health impacts, thus misleading consumers about the impact of their lifestyles.

When pollution control is necessary, emphasis should be on *output control* to clean up pollution that has entered the environment or to burn, dump, or bury waste materials.

Emphasis should be on *input control*; preventing pollution or sharply reducing the amount entering the environment is more effective and less costly than attempting to reduce levels of widely dispersed pollutants after they have entered the environment; some pollutants should be viewed not as wastes but as valuable resources that can be recycled or reused.

Technology

Large, centralized technology, such as large electric power plants, provides more profit for large corporations, enhances a country's short-term economic growth, and provides a more reliable source of energy and other goods and services.

Smaller, decentralized forms of technology use and waste less resources, increase national security by making a country less vulnerable to attack and natural disaster, and give individuals more control over how they obtain goods and services and over the prices they pay.

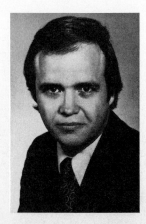

Gus Speth

Gus Speth has been president of the World Resources Institute since 1982. He served as chairman of the President's Council on Environmental Quality (CEQ) between 1979 and 1981, after serving as a member of the council from 1977 to 1979. Before his appointment to CEQ, he was a staff attorney for the Natural Resources Defense Council, a public-interest group he helped found in 1970.

Since 1970 a number of disturbing studies and reports have been issued by the United Nations, the Worldwatch Institute, the World Bank, the World Resources Institute, the International Institute for Environment and Development, the Conservation Foundation, the Organization for Economic Cooperation and Development, and other organizations (see Further Readings for this chapter at the end of this book). These reports have sounded a persistent warning: International efforts to stem the spread of human poverty, hunger, and misery are not achieving their goals; the staggering growth of the human population, coupled with ever increasing human demands, are beginning to cause permanent damage to the earth's resource base.

One such warning was issued in 1980, by the Council on Environmental Quality and the U.S. State Department. Called *The Global 2000 Report to the President*, it was the result of a three-year effort by more than a dozen agencies of the U.S. government to make long-term projections concerning various population, resource, and environmental concerns. Given the obvious limitations of such projections, the report can best be seen as a reconnaissance of the future. And the results of that reconnaissance and a later updating in *World Resources 1986* (to be updated annually), issued jointly by the World Resources Institute and the International Institute for Environment and Development, are disturbing.

The conclusions of these two studies indicate the potential for deepening global problems between now and the end of this century and long thereafter if policies and practices around the world continue as they are today. The next century will begin a much more crowded world, containing more than 6 billion human beings. It *could* be a world where growing numbers of people suffer hunger and privation; where losses of croplands, grasslands, and forests mount while human numbers and needs increase; where per capita supplies of fresh water, timber, and fish are diminished; where deterioration of the earth's air and water accelerates; and where plant and animal species vanish at unprecedented rates.

These findings confront the United States and the other nations of the world with one of the most difficult challenges facing our planet during the coming decades. Disturbing as these findings are, however, it is important to stress what the conclusions of these and other related reports represent: not *predictions* of what will occur, but *projections* of what *could* occur if we do not change our ways. I believe that as the people and governments of the world come to realize the full dimensions of the challenge before us, we *will* take the actions needed to meet it.

The first thing we must do is to get serious about the conservation of resources—renewable and nonrenewable alike. We can no longer take for granted the renewability of our renewable resources. We must realize that the natural systems—the air and water, the forests, the land—that yield food, shelter, and other necessities of life are susceptible to disruption, contamination, and destruction.

In some parts of the world, particularly in the less developed countries, the ability of biological systems to support human populations is being seriously damaged by human demands for grazing land, firewood, and building materials. Nor are these stresses confined to the less developed countries: In recent years, the United States has been losing annually about 3 million acres of rural land—one-third of our prime agricultural land—due to the spread of housing developments, highways, shopping malls, and the like. We are also losing the equivalent, in terms of production capability, of about 3 million more acres a year due to soil degradation, erosion, and salt buildup in irrigated soil.

Achieving the necessary restraint in the use of renewable resources will require new ways of thinking by the peoples and governments of the world. It will require the widespread adoption of a "conserver society" ethic—an approach to resources and environment that, while attuned to the needs of each society, recognizes not only the importance of resources and environment to our own sustenance, well-being, and security, but also our obligation to pass this vital legacy along to future generations.

Fortunately, we are beginning to see signs that people in the United States and in other nations *are* becoming aware of the limits to our resources and the importance of conserving them. Energy problems, for example, are pointing the way to a future in which conservation is the password. As energy supplies go down and prices go up, we are learning that conserving—getting more and more out of each barrel of oil or ton of coal—is the cheapest and safest approach. Learning to conserve nonrenewable resources like oil and coal is the first step toward building a conserver society that values, nurtures, and protects *all* of its resources. Such a society appreciates economy in design and avoidance of waste. It realizes the limits to low-cost resources and to the environment's carrying capacity. It insists that market prices reflect all costs, social as well as private, so that consumers are fully aware in the most direct way of the real costs of consumption.

But the conserver society ethic by itself is not enough. It is unrealistic to expect people living at the margin of existence—people fighting desperately for their own survival—to think about the long-term survival of the planet. When people need to burn wood to keep from freezing, they will cut down trees.

For this reason, an equally important element in an effective strategy to deal with global resource problems must be the *sustainable development* of the less developed nations of the world. Development,

far from being in conflict with resource conservation and environmental protection, is essential to achieving these goals. It is only through sound, sustainable economic development that real progress can be made in alleviating hunger and poverty and in erasing the conditions that contribute so dangerously to the destruction of our planet's carrying capacity.

It is clear that the trends discussed in these reports, especially the growing disparity in income between the rich and poor peoples of the world, greatly heighten the chances for global instability—for exploitation of fears, resentments, and frustrations; for incitement to violence; for conflicts based on resources. While the humanitarian reasons for acting generously to alleviate global poverty and injustice are compelling enough in themselves, we must also recognize the extent to which poverty and resource problems can threaten the security of nations throughout the world.

These growing tensions can only be defused through a much greater emphasis on *equity*—on a fair sharing of the means to development and the products of growth, not only among nations but also within nations. It should be obvious that the interests of all nations of the world, more developed and less developed alike, are inextricably linked. In helping others, we help ourselves, and in providing generous but effective assistance—grants, loans, technical aid—to nations that are in need to help them become more self-sufficient, we can make a national investment that will yield important dividends in the future.

Guest Essay Discussion

1. What specific obligations, if any, do you feel we have to future generations?

2. How would you define *sustainable development* for the less developed countries of the world? If this goal is adopted, what effects might it have on your life and lifestyle?

3. Do you agree that the means to economic development and the products of economic growth must be shared more fairly not only among countries but also within countries? How would you bring about this greater emphasis on equity?

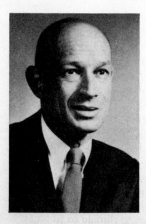

Julian L. Simon

Julian L. Simon is professor of economics and business administration at the University of Maryland. He has effectively presented and defended the cornucopian position in numerous articles and books, including The Ultimate Resource *and* The Resourceful Earth *(see Further Readings).*

This book begins with the proposition that there is an environmental crisis. If this means that the situation of humanity is worse now than in the past, then the idea of a crisis—and all that follows from it—is dead wrong. In almost every respect important to humanity, the trends have been improving not deteriorating.

Our world now supports 5 billion people. In the 19th century the earth could sustain only 1 billion. And 10,000 years ago, only 1 million people could keep themselves alive. People are living more healthily than ever before, too.

One would expect lovers of humanity—people who hate war and worry about famine in Africa—to jump with joy at this extraordinary triumph of the human mind and human organization over the raw forces of nature. Instead they lament that there are so many human beings, and wring their hands about the problems that more people inevitably bring.

The recent extraordinary decrease in the death rate—to my mind, the greatest miracle in history—accounts for the bumper crop of humanity. Recall that it took thousands of years to increase life expectancy at birth from the 20s to the 30s. Then in just the last 200 years, life expectancy in the advanced countries jumped from the mid-30s to the 70s. And starting well after World War II, life expectancy at birth in the poor countries, even the very poorest, has leaped upward (averaging 58 in 1986), due to progress in agriculture, sanitation, and medicine. Life expectancy in China, the world's most populous country, was 64 in 1986, an increase of 20 years since the 1950s. Is this not an astounding triumph?

In the short run, of course, another baby reduces income per person by causing output to be divided among more people. And as the British economist Thomas Malthus argued in 1798, more workers laboring with existing capital results in less output per worker. However, if resources are not fixed, then the Malthusian doctrine of diminishing resources, resurrected by today's neo-Malthusians, does not apply. Given some time to adjust to shortages with known methods and new inventions, free people create additional resources.

It is amazing but true that a resource shortage due to population or income growth usually leaves us better off than if the shortage had never arisen. If firewood had not become scarce in 17th century England, coal would not have been developed. If coal and whale oil shortages hadn't loomed, oil wells would not have been dug.

The prices of food, metals, and other raw materials have been declining by every measure since the beginning of the 19th century and as far back as we know. That is, raw materials have been getting less scarce rather than more scarce throughout history, defying the commonsense notion that if one begins with an inventory of a resource and uses some up, there will be less left. This is despite, and indirectly because of, increasing population.

All statistical studies show that population growth does not result in slower economic growth, though this defies common sense. Nor is a high population density a drag on economic development. Statistical comparison across nations reveals that higher population density is associated with faster rather than slower growth. Drive around on Hong Kong's smooth-flowing highways for an hour or two, and you will realize that a very large concentration of human beings in a very small area does not make impossible comfortable existence and exciting economic expansion, if the system gives individuals the freedom to exercise their talents and pursue economic opportunities. The experience of densely populated Singapore makes clear that Hong King is not unique either.

In 1983 a blue-ribbon panel of scientists summarized their wisdom in *The Resourceful Earth*. Among the findings, in addition to those I have noted above, were:

- Many people are still hungry, but the food supply has been improving since at least World War II, as measured by grain prices, production per consumer, and the famine death rate.
- Land availability will not increasingly constrain world agriculture in coming decades.
- In the U.S., the trend is toward higher-quality cropland, suffering less from erosion than the past.
- The widely published report of increasingly rapid urbanization of U.S. farmland was based on faulty data.
- Trends in world forests are not worrying, though in some places deforestation is troubling.
- There is no statistical evidence for rapid loss of plant and animal wildlife species in the next two decades. An increased rate of extinction cannot be ruled out if tropical deforestation is severe, but no evidence about linkage has yet been demonstrated.
- Water does not pose a problem of physical scarcity or disappearance, although the world and U.S. situations do call for better institutional management through more rational systems of property rights.
- There is no persuasive reason to believe that the world oil price will rise in coming decades. The price may fall well below what it has been.
- Compared to coal, nuclear power is no more expensive and is probably much cheaper, under most circumstances. It is also much cheaper than oil.
- Nuclear power gives every evidence of costing fewer lives per unit of energy produced than does coal or oil.
- Solar energy sources (including wind and wave power) are too dilute to compete economically for much of humankind's energy needs, though for specialized uses and certain climates they can make a valuable contribution.
- Threats of air and water pollution have been vastly overblown. The air and water in the United States have been getting cleaner rather than dirtier.

We do not say that all is well everywhere, and we do not predict that all will be rosy in the future. Children are hungry and sick; people live out lives of physical or intellectual poverty and lack of opportunity; war or some other pollution may do us in. *The Resourceful Earth* does show that for most relevant matters we have examined, aggregate global and U.S. *trends* are improving rather than deteriorating.

In addition, we do not say that a better future happens *automatically* or *without effect*. It will happen because men and women—sometimes as individuals, sometimes as enterprises working for profit, sometimes as voluntary non-profit-making groups, and sometimes as governmental agencies—will address problems with muscle and mind, and will *probably* overcome, as has been usual through history.

We are confident that the nature of the physical world permits continued improvement in humankind's economic lot in the long run, indefinitely. Of course, there are always newly arising local problems, shortages, and pollutions, due to climate or to increased populations and income. Sometimes temporary large-scale problems arise. But the nature of the world's physical conditions and the resilience in a well-functioning economic and social system enable us to overcome such problems, and the solutions usually leave us better off than if the problem had never arisen; that is the great lesson to be learned from human history.

Guest Essay Discussion

1. Do you agree with the author's contention that there is no environmental, population, or resource crisis? Explain. After you have completed this course, come back and answer this question again to see if your views have changed.

2. In effect, the authors of this essay and the one that preceded it have taken the same general trends, projected them into the future, and come to startlingly different conclusions. How can this happen? What criteria can we use to decide who is more likely to be correct?

3. In 1967, Herman Kahn (now deceased), a leading cornucopian and Julian Simon's coeditor for *The Resourceful Earth*, wrote a book using existing trends to project the future from 1967 to 2000. In his projection, the problems of pollution, environmental degradation, and population growth were declared nonproblems and not discussed. Yet shortly thereafter, in the 1970s, these problems became major societal concerns. Environmentalists contend that this demonstrates the tendency of cornucopians to ignore problems or declare them not serious despite clear evidence to the contrary. Do you agree with this analysis? Explain.

CHAPTER SUMMARY

Throughout human history the number of people on earth has been growing *exponentially* at some constant annual percentage. After averaging about 0.002% a year for several million years, the exponential growth rate accelerated and reached an all-time high of 2.06% in 1970, before dropping slightly to 1.7% in 1987 when 86.7 million people were added to the 5 billion people on earth. About 1 billion of these people are in the 33 richer, *more developed countries (MDCs)* with high average GNPs per person and located mostly in the Northern Hemisphere; the remaining 4 billion are in 133 poorer, *less developed countries (LDCs)* with very low to moderate average GNPs per person primarily in the Southern Hemisphere. Another billion people, most in LDCs, are expected to be added between 1986 and 1998, and the world's population is not projected to level off and reach *zero population growth (ZPG)* until 2100, at around 10.2 billion.

Resources obtained from the environment to meet human needs can be classified as *nonrenewable* (with a fixed supply, such as nonrecyclable and nonreusable fossil fuels and potentially recyclable and reusable metals obtained from the earth's crust), *renewable* (such as forests, grasslands, animals, fresh water, fresh air, and fertile soil, which are regenerated by natural processes if not used faster than they are replenished), and *perpetual* (essentially inexhaustible resources such as solar energy and wind). Some resources, such as fresh air, are directly available for use, but most of the earth's natural energy and matter become resources only as a result of *human ingenuity* (using science and technology to find, extract, process, and convert them to usable forms), *economics* (affordable supplies), and *cultural beliefs* (acceptable forms).

Environmental degradation refers to processes that deplete or destroy a region's potentially renewable topsoil, grasslands, forests, and supplies of fresh water, which together act as a resource base for survival and for present and future economic activity. *Pollution* is a change in the physical, chemical, or biological characteristics of the air, water, or soil that can affect the health, survival, or activities of humans or other forms of life in an undesirable way. People, however, disagree over what they consider to be undesirable, what degree of risk they are willing to accept from pollution and environmental degradation, how much they are willing to pay for environmental protection, and to what degree short-term economic gain should be favored over long-term environmental degradation, pollution, and possible economic loss. Pollutants can be classified as *rapidly biodegradable* (animal and crop wastes), *slowly biodegradable* (DDT), and *nonbiodegradable* (mercury and lead). Pollution can be controlled by using *input approaches*, which prevent potential pollutants from entering the environment or sharply reduce the amounts released, and *output approaches*—cleaning up pollution after it has entered the environment; disposing of harmful wastes by burning, dumping, or burying them; and recycling or reusing materials output from human activities rather than discarding them.

Environmental problems are caused by a complex, poorly understood, interrelated set of population, resource use, technological, economic, political, social, and ethical factors; the same factors can also be used to reduce the severity of these problems to acceptable levels. There is sharp disagreement between opposing groups known as *neo-Malthusians* and *cornucopians* over how serious these problems are, what should be done about them, and whether we should use human ingenuity and technology to conquer the earth to sustain economic growth or should develop forms of economic growth that work with nature to sustain rather than degrade and deplete the earth's support systems.

DISCUSSION TOPICS

1. Is the world overpopulated? Why or why not? Is the United States suffering from consumption overpopulation? Why or why not?

2. Explain how zero population growth in the world could allow average per capita income, standard of living, and quality of life to rise and pollution levels and environmental degradation to either rise or fall. Do you favor ZPG for the world? For the United States? Why or why not?

3. Debate the following proposition: The high level of resource use by the United States and other MDCs is beneficial because it allows greater purchases of raw materials from poor countries, providing them with funds to stimulate economic growth, and because increased economic growth in the MDCs can provide funds for higher levels of financial aid to LDCs.

4. Debate the following proposition: The world will never run out of resources because technological innovations will produce substitutes or allow use of lower grades of scarce resources.

5. On the whole, are the resource substitutes shown in Figure 1–12 desirable or undesirable to you? Which ones would you eliminate? Why? How would these changes affect your life and lifestyle?

6. Should economic growth in the United States and in the world be limited? Why or why not? Is all economic growth bad? Which forms do you believe should be limited? Which forms should be encouraged?

7. What forms of existing technology do you believe should be eliminated or sharply curtailed? Why?

8. Assume you have been appointed to a new-technology assessment board. What environmental drawbacks and advantages would you list for the following: (a) intrauterine devices (IUDs) for birth control, (b) snowmobiles, (c) sink garbage disposal units, (d) trash compactors, (e) pocket transistor radios, (f) television sets, (g) electric cars, (h) computers, (i) nuclear power plants, (j) a drug that a woman could take to cause a medically safe abortion, (k) effective sex stimulants, (l) drugs that would retard the aging process, (m) drugs that enable people to get high but are physiologically and psychologically harmless, (n) electrical or chemical methods that would stimulate the brain to remove anxiety, fear, unhappiness, and aggression, (o) genetic engineering (manipulation of human genes) that would produce humans with superior intelligence, strength, and other attributes? In each case, would you recommend that the technology be introduced?

9. What are the major environmental problems facing your hometown and state and what major actions are being taken to reduce or eliminate these problems?

10. Do your own views more closely resemble those of a neo-Malthusian or a cornucopian? Does your lifestyle indicate that in reality you are acting as if you were a cornucopian or a neo-Malthusian? Compare your views with others in your class.

11. List ten changes in your lifestyle that you would be willing to make to protect the environment. Which of these changes, if any, do you believe you will actually make? Compare your list with those drawn up by other members of your class.

2

Human Impact on the Earth

GENERAL OBJECTIVES

1. What major impacts did early and advanced hunter-gatherer societies have on the environment and what was their primary relationship to nature?

2. What major impacts have early agricultural societies and present-day nonindustrialized agricultural societies had on the environment and what is their primary relationship to nature?

3. What major impacts do present-day industrialized societies have on the environment and what is their primary relationship to nature?

4. What are the major phases in the history of resource exploitation, resource conservation, and environmental protection in the United States?

5. What hopeful signs are there that we may be gradually shifting from today's mix of industrialized and nonindustrialized societies to new, sustainable-earth societies?

A continent ages quickly once we come.

Ernest Hemingway

During the two million years humans have lived on earth, they have been able to gain increasing control over their environment through a series of major cultural changes: Human society has changed from **(1)** a small number of people, the hunter-gatherers, who survived for 2 million years by hunting wild game and fish and gathering wild plants to **(2)** a gradually increasing number, the early agriculturalists, who learned to tame and breed wild animals and cultivate wild plants about 10,000 years ago to **(3)** today's rapidly growing population of 5 billion living in a mix of countries ranging from nonindustrialized to highly industrialized. These hunter-gatherer, agricultural, and industrial societies represent the patterns in which groups of humans have cooperated to ensure their survival and enhance their quality of life. The J-shaped curves of increasing population, resource use, pollution, and environmental degradation are the results of these cultural patterns.

2-1 HUNTING-AND-GATHERING SOCIETIES

Early Hunter-Gatherers During 99.9% of the time that humans have lived on earth, they were **hunters and gatherers,** obtaining enough food by gathering edible wild plants and other materials and hunting wild game and fish from the nearby environment. Archeological findings and studies of the few, rapidly decreasing hunter-gatherer tribes that remain today (see Spotlight on p. 26) indicate that hunting, carried out by men, was too unreliable to provide a consistent source of food. Thus, most of the food was provided by women and children, who collected plants, roots, fruits, seeds, berries, nuts, honey, eggs, mollusks, reptiles, amphibians, and insects.

These studies also indicate that early hunter-gatherers and the more advanced ones that followed lived in small groups or tribes, rarely containing more than

Today less than 1% of the earth's inhabitants live by hunting, fishing, and gathering. They live in vast, isolated parts of Africa (the Bushmen of southern Africa and the Pygmies of central Africa), South America (various Indian tribes in Ecuador, Brazil, Chile, and Peru), Australia (the aborigines), the Philippines (the Kalingas), and Alaska, Greenland, and Arctic Canada (the Eskimos). These people have lived for centuries with little or no knowledge of modern civilization, creating little environmental disturbance.

Increasingly, governments of the countries in which these people live are laying claim to their homelands and driving them out so that land can be developed for farming, grazing, timber cutting, mineral removal, building dams and reservoirs, and other projects.

Suddenly these people are displaced from their native lands, forced to live in unfamiliar areas, and exposed to modern civilization. Unable to make a living by the methods they know and exposed to modern technologies they do not understand, most become frightened and confused. Their death rates increase sharply from exposure to modern infectious diseases, alcoholism, depression, and the psychic trauma of losing their traditional values and customs. Once-proud and skilled male hunters and female gatherers and their children often are reduced to begging for scraps of food.

The gradual elimination of these cultures leads to an irreversible loss of their survival knowledge, including information on the thousands of wild plants and animals that can be used for food, medicines, birth control, dyes, and other purposes—information of immense value to modern society. Even more important, this process reduces the earth's rich cultural diversity.

Many observers argue that the world's remaining hunter-gatherer societies have the right of ownership of the land they and their ancestors have lived on for thousands of years and the right to be left alone by modern civilization. These observers ask how we would feel and how we would survive if suddenly a much more technologically advanced and powerful culture from outer space came to earth, displaced us from our native lands, and forced us to live in tropical jungles with none of our present technology available. What do you think?

50 people, who worked together to hunt and gather enough food to survive. If a group became so large that its members could not find enough food within reasonable walking distances, it split up to form other groups, which moved to different areas. Many of these widely scattered groups were nomads, moving with the seasons and migrations of game animals to obtain sufficient food and to allow renewal of plant and animal life in the areas they left behind.

The hunters and gatherers were experts in survival. Their intimate knowledge of nature enabled them to predict the weather, find water even in the desert, locate a wide variety of edible wild plants and animals, and learn which plants and animal parts had medicinal properties. Their material possessions consisted mostly of primitive weapons and tools made by chipping sticks and stones into forms useful for killing animals, fishing, cutting plants, and scraping hides to be used for clothing, shelter, and other purposes.

Studies of today's few remaining hunter-gatherer societies suggest that women and children spent an average of 15 hours a week gathering the food they needed, and men hunted for only about a week out of each month or a few hours each day. The studies also show that these "primitive" people enjoyed a more diverse diet and had more free time and less stress and anxiety than most people in today's LDCs and MDCs.

Although malnutrition and starvation were rare, infant mortality was high, primarily from infectious diseases. This factor, coupled with infanticide (killing the young), led to an average life expectancy of about 30 years and helped keep population size in balance with available food supplies. Population size was also kept down by the natural birth control and spacing of births caused by the suppression of women's ability to ovulate and conceive during the 3 to 4 years they breast-fed each of their children.

Early hunter-gatherers exploited their environment—as do all forms of life—in order to survive. Their environmental impact was small and localized, however, because of their small numbers, their movement from place to place, and their reliance on only their own muscular energy to modify the environment.

Advanced Hunter-Gatherers Archeological evidence indicates that about 300,000 years ago the 1 million hunter-gatherers living in scattered groups primarily in the tropical and subtropical regions of Africa began gradually spreading out over several continents. They developed improved tools and hunting weapons such as spears with sharp-edged stone points mounted on wooden shafts and later the bow and arrow (about 12,000 years ago). They learned to cooperate with members of other groups to hunt herds of reindeer, wooly mammoths, European bison, and other big game; to use fire to flush game from thickets toward hunters lying in wait and to stampede herds of animals into traps or over cliffs; and to burn vegetation to promote the growth of plants that could be gathered for food and that were favored by some of the animal species they hunted.

These practices meant that advanced hunter-gatherers had a greater impact on their environment than early hunter-gatherers, especially in converting forests into grasslands. But because of their relatively small numbers and their dependence on their own muscle power, their environmental impact was still fairly small and localized. Both early and advanced hunter-gatherers were examples of *humans in nature,* who learned to survive by understanding and cooperating with nature and with one another.

2-2 AGRICULTURAL SOCIETIES: THE AGRICULTURAL REVOLUTION

Early Pastoralists and Horticulturists: Domestication of Wild Animals and Plants One of the most significant changes in human history is believed to have begun about 10,000 years ago. During this period people in several parts of the world independently began learning how to domesticate—herd, tame, and breed—wild game for food, clothing, and carrying loads and to domesticate selected wild food plants, planting and growing them close to home instead of gathering them over a large area. Over the next several thousand years the importance of hunting and gathering declined as more and more people became shepherds (pastoralists) and farmers and developed the domesticated crops and livestock animals on which we depend today.

Some anthropologists believe that the first type of plant cultivation, which today we call *horticulture* ("hoe culture"—that is, small-scale vegetable growing, or gardening), originated in tropical forest areas of Burma, Thailand, and eastern India. Evidence indicates that women discovered they could grow some of their favorite wild food plants such as yam, sweet potato, taro, and arrowroot by digging holes with a stick (a primitive hoe) and placing the roots or tubers of these plants in the holes between tree stumps in

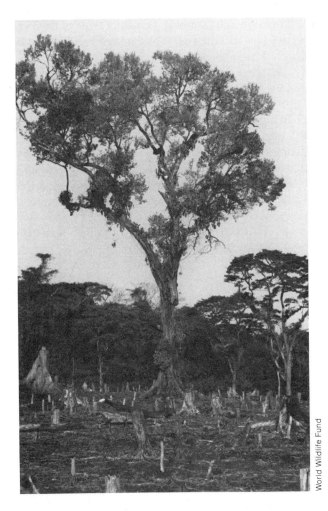

Figure 2-1 Slash-and-burn cultivation in tropical forests was probably the first technique used to grow crops. It is still practiced today, as shown in this cleared patch of rainforest in the Tuxtla Mountains, Veracruz, Mexico.

small patches of forest. They cleared the ground by **slash-and-burn cultivation**—cutting down trees and other vegetation, leaving the cut vegetation on the ground to dry, and then burning it (Figure 2-1). The resulting wood ashes added plant nutrients to the nutrient-poor soils found in most tropical forest areas, which were chosen because they had fewer roots than grassland soils and thus were easier to cultivate with digging sticks.

These early growers also discovered the principle of **shifting cultivation:** A single plot was harvested and replanted for 2 to 5 years, until further cultivation was no longer worthwhile because of a reduction in soil fertility or because the area had been invaded by a dense growth of vegetation from the surrounding forest. A new plot was then cleared to begin a new cycle of cutting, burning, planting, and harvesting for several years. The growers learned that each abandoned patch had to be left fallow (unplanted) for 10 to 30 years to allow a new growth of trees to become established and the soil to be renewed before it could again be used to grow crops.

In other parts of the world—temperate, drier regions of eastern Africa, Turkey, and China—early horticulturists cleared woodlands and learned how to plant and grow seed crops such as grains (wheat, barley, rice), legumes (peas, lentils), and corn. Like the peoples of the tropical rain forests, these growers practiced **subsistence farming,** growing only enough food to feed their families. The dependence of all the early subsistence horticulturists on human muscle power and crude stone or stick tools meant that they could cultivate only small plots; thus, they had relatively little impact on their environment.

Shifting cultivation and subsistence farming are still practiced in tropical areas of Africa, Latin America, and Southeast Asia by 150 million to 200 million people. Some agricultural experts contend that shifting cultivation is the most environmentally sound way of growing crops on a sustainable basis in the nutrient-poor soils of most tropical rain forests, as long as population density and the degree of land clearing both remain low. Otherwise, abandoned areas are replanted too soon and large areas are cleared for logging, grazing, or growing crops—irreversibly eroding and depleting already fragile soils.

Early Agriculturists True *agriculture* (as opposed to horticulture) began around 5000 B.C. with the invention of the metal plow, pulled by domesticated animals and steered by the farmer. The use of animal-pulled plows greatly increased crop productivity by allowing farmers to cultivate larger parcels of cropland and to cultivate fertile grassland soils in spite of their more extensive root systems. In some arid (dry) regions early farmers further increased crop output by diverting water into hand-dug ditches and canals to irrigate crops. With this animal- and irrigation-assisted agriculture, families could provide themselves with sufficient food and sometimes have enough left over for sale or for storage to provide food when flooding, prolonged dry spells, insect infestation, or other natural disasters reduced crop productivity.

The Emergence of Agriculture-Based Urban Societies The gradually increasing ability of a few farmers to produce enough food to feed their families plus a surplus that could be traded and used to feed other people had four important effects: **(1)** Population began to increase because of a larger, more constant supply of food; **(2)** people cleared increasingly larger areas of land and began to control and shape the surface of the earth to suit their needs; **(3)** urban-

ization began as the need for farming decreased and former farmers moved into villages, many of which gradually grew into towns and eventually into cities; and **(4)** specialized occupations and long-distance trade developed as former farmers in villages and towns learned crafts such as weaving, toolmaking, and pottery to produce handmade goods that could be exchanged for food.

Beginning around 3500 B.C., the trade interdependence between rural farmers and urban dwellers resulted in the gradual development of a number of **agriculture-based urban societies** or civilizations (which means "city dwelling") near early agricultural settlements in six major areas of the world (Figure 2-2). The development of the cities that served as the centers of these civilizations between 3500 B.C. and 1000 A.D. is outlined in Figure 2-3.

The trade in food and manufactured goods made possible by the agriculture-based urban societies created wealth and the need for a managerial class to regulate the distribution of goods, services, and land. For example, in Mesopotamia (now Iraq, Iran, Turkey, and Jordan) near the Fertile Crescent along the broad river valleys of the Tigris and the Euphrates rivers (Figure 2-2), priest-rulers of the Babylonian Empire used large labor battalions to construct extensive irrigation canal networks and to build monumental palaces and religious temples. As ownership of land and water rights became a valuable economic resource, conflict increased. Armies and war leaders rose to power and took over large areas of land. A new class of powerless people, the slaves, minorities, and landless peasants, were forced to do the hard, disagreeable work of producing food.

Impact on the Environment The rise of agriculture-based urban societies created an environmental impact far exceeding that of hunting-and-gathering societies and early subsistence farmers. Forests were cut down and grasslands were plowed up to provide vast areas of cropland and grazing land to feed the growing populations of these emerging civilizations and to provide wood for fuel and for buildings to serve the growing number of city dwellers. Such massive land clearing destroyed and altered the habitats of many forms of plant and animal wildlife, endangering their existence and in some cases causing or hastening their extinction.

Poor management of many of the cleared areas led to greatly increased deforestation, soil erosion, and overgrazing of grasslands by huge herds of sheep, goats, and cattle—helping convert once fertile land to desert. The silt that washed off these denuded areas polluted streams, rivers, lakes, and irrigation canals, making them useless. The concentration of large numbers of people and their wastes in cities helped spread

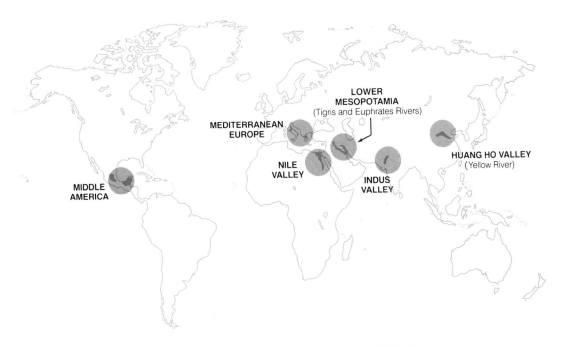

Figure 2-2 General locations of the world's earliest agriculture-based urban civilizations.

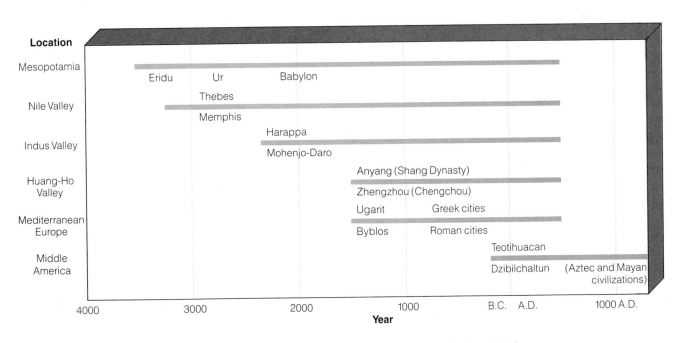

Figure 2-3 Development of the world's earliest cities, which served as centers of ancient agriculture-based urban societies.

infectious human diseases and parasites. The gradual degradation of the vital resource base of soil, water, forests, grazing land, and wildlife was a major factor in the downfall of many great civilizations (see Spotlight on p. 30).

The development and gradual spread of agriculture meant that most of the earth's population shifted from life as hunter-gatherers *in nature* to life as shepherds, farmers, and urban dwellers *against nature*. For the first time human beings saw themselves as distinct and apart from the rest of nature and they created the concepts of "wild" and "wilderness" to apply to animals, plants, and parts of the earth not under their control.

The great civilizations that flourished in the Middle East, North Africa, and the Mediterranean area between 3500 B.C. and 500 A.D. (Figure 2-3) are noted for their many superb achievements in literature, art, science, and government, which we treasure and use today. However, archeological evidence and historical records show that these agriculture-based urban societies prospered economically by degrading their land resource base so severely that they helped bring about their own downfall. The resource legacy these early civilizations left to future generations was so impoverished that much of the land never recovered and remains barren today.

The sites of the great Sumerian and Babylonian civilizations in Mesopotamia near the Fertile Crescent, for example, were covered with productive forests and grasslands as late as 7000 B.C. With each generation, the Tigris and the Euphrates rivers and the elaborate network of irrigation canals that supported these civilizations became filled with more silt as a result of deforestation, overgrazing, and soil erosion. An increasing number of slaves and laborers were needed to keep the irrigation channels free of silt. By 3000 B.C. the situation had become unmanageable and much of this once-productive land had been converted into the barren desert that

makes up much of Iran and Iraq today. This environmental degradation was a significant factor in weakening the Babylonian Empire. It fell because it was unable to resist a succession of invading armies, each of which further increased the environmental devastation of the area.

Some analysts argue that unless we learn from these past environmental lessons and use our knowledge and technology to work with rather than against nature, we will repeat these mistakes on a global scale. What do you think?

2-3   INDUSTRIAL SOCIETIES: THE INDUSTRIAL REVOLUTION

Early Industrial Societies   The next major cultural adaptation, known as the Industrial Revolution, began in England in the mid-eighteenth century, spurred by a period of prolific human inventiveness. The invention of the coal-burning steam engine (1765) was followed by other inventions, such as the steam locomotive (1829), the steamship (1807), and the internal combustion engine (various versions, 1860–1892), which allowed carriers running on fossil fuels to replace horse-drawn vehicles and wind-powered ships. Within a few decades, these innovations transformed agriculture-based urban societies in western Europe and North America into even more urbanized, **early industrial societies.**

These societies and the more advanced ones that followed were based on machines that could harness energy derived from the burning of coal and later oil and natural gas to do tasks that could previously be performed only by means of large amounts of human and animal labor. Thus, these machines greatly increased the average energy resource use per person. The use of fossil-fuel-powered machines in agriculture greatly reduced the number of people needed to produce food and increased the number of former farm-

ers migrating from rural to urban areas. Many found jobs in the growing number of mechanized factories, where they worked long hours for low pay and were usually subjected to noisy, dirty, and hazardous working conditions. (Such exploitation of factory, mine, and mill workers still exists in parts of today's advanced industrialized societies and in many of today's LDCs in the early stages of industrialization.)

Advanced Industrial Societies   After World War I (1914–1918) the greatly increased use of fossil fuels, the development of more efficient machines and techniques for mass production, and advances in science and technology led to the development of today's **advanced industrial societies** in the United States and other MDCs. These societies have provided a number of important benefits for most people living in them: (1) the creation and mass production of many useful and economically affordable products, (2) significant increases in the standard of living in terms of average GNP per person, (3) a sharp increase in average agricultural productivity per person as a result of advanced industrialized agriculture, in which a small number of individual and corporate farmers produce large outputs of food, (4) a sharp rise in average life expectancy as a result of improvements in sanitation, hygiene, nutrition, medicine, and birth control, and (5) a grad-

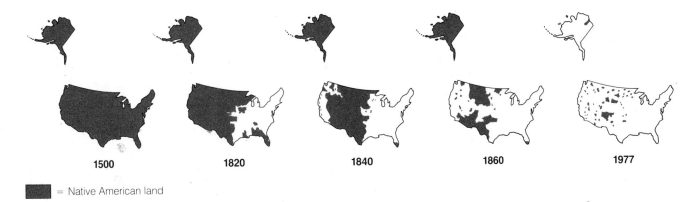

1500   1820   1840   1860   1977

■ = Native American land

Figure 2-4 Progressive loss of land occupied by Native Americans. (Data from U.S. Bureau of Ethnography)

ual decline in the rate of population growth from simultaneous decreases in average birth rates and death rates as a result of improvements in health, birth control, education, average income, and old-age security.

Environmental Impact Along with the many benefits, advanced industrialized societies have intensified many existing environmental problems and created a series of new ones such as air, water, and soil pollution from DDT, radioactive wastes, and a host of hazardous substances. These and other environmental problems now threaten people's well-being not only at the local level but also at the regional level (acid deposition) and the global level (buildup of carbon dioxide in the atmosphere caused by the burning of fossil fuels).

By decreasing the number of people engaged in food production, industrialized agriculture has led to massive shifts of population from rural to urban areas and helped intensify a variety of social, political, economic, and environmental problems. The combination of industrialized agriculture, increased mining, and urbanization has also led to increased degradation of topsoil, forests and grasslands, and wildlife—the same problems that helped lead to the downfall of earlier civilizations. Because of these numerous, interrelated, harmful effects, industrialized societies must now use an increasingly larger fraction of their financial, human, and natural resources for control of pollution and land use to prevent environmental overload and degradation.

The benefits of the Industrial Revolution are so great that very few people would propose that we abandon most of the technological achievements of the past two and a half centuries. However, by enabling humans to have much greater control over nature and decreasing the number of people who live close to the land, the Industrial Revolution encouraged humans to view themselves as apart from and superior to nature.

2-4 BRIEF HISTORY OF RESOURCE EXPLOITATION, RESOURCE CONSERVATION, AND ENVIRONMENTAL PROTECTION IN THE UNITED STATES

Phase I: Frontier Expansion and Resource Exploitation (1607–1870) When European colonists began settling in North America in 1607, they found a vast continent with what appeared to be inexhaustible supplies of timber, fertile soil, water, minerals, and other resources for their own use and for export to Europe. Such abundance, coupled with the frontier view that most of the continent was a hostile wilderness to be conquered, opened up, cleared, and exploited, led to considerable resource waste and little regard for future needs.

By the mid-1800s, 80% of the total land area of the United States was government owned, most acquired in the Louisiana Purchase, the Oregon Compromise, the purchase of Alaska, the Mexican cession, and other acquisitions. All of these transfers of land ownership ignored the rights of members of various Native American tribes, or nations, who had lived on these lands for centuries (Figure 2-4). The government signed and then broke dozens of treaties giving various Indian nations ownership of large tracts of land, as summarized by an old Sioux Indian in 1891: "They made us many promises, more than I can remember, but they never kept but one; they promised to take our land and they took it."

During the mid-1800s several laws were passed to promote the rapid transfer of the vast holdings of public land into private ownership to encourage settlement and economic development of the continent and thus strengthen it against its enemies. By 1900 more than half of this land had been given away or sold at nominal cost to railroad, timber, and mining companies, and land developers, states, schools, universities, technical schools, and homesteaders. Under the Homestead Act of 1862, any person, citizen or not, was permitted to settle on 160 acres, either purchasing the land at a minimum price of $1.25 per acre or acquiring free title after five years of residence and cultivation. By artificially depressing the prices of resources, these land transfers encouraged widespread exploitation, waste, and degradation of the country's forests, grasslands, and minerals.

Phase II: Early Conservation Warnings (1830–1870)

In 1832 George Catlin, a student and painter of American Indian cultures, saw how rapidly the country's wilderness was being exploited through overgrazing, overcutting, and general misuse. He proposed that part of the unspoiled wilderness owned by the government be withdrawn from public use and preserved in the form of a magnificent national park—a plea that went unheeded. Between 1850 and 1870 Horace Greeley, Ralph Waldo Emerson, Henry David Thoreau, Frederick Law Olmsted, Charles W. Eliot, and other early conservationists (Figure 2-5) renewed the cry for wilderness preservation.

Most of the early conservationists, because they were intellectuals whose writings did not reach popular audiences, had relatively little influence on politicians. In 1864, however, George P. Marsh, a scientist and congressman from Vermont, published a book, *Man and Nature* (see Further Readings) that eventually proved to be influential in the debate over conservation versus exploitation. Marsh questioned the prevailing idea of the inexhaustibility of the country's resources, showed how the rise and fall of past civilizations were linked to their use and misuse of their resource base, and set forth basic conservation principles still used today. Many of his ideas for management of publicly owned forests and watersheds were put into effect in the early 1900s by President Theodore Roosevelt, an ardent conservationist.

Phase III: Beginnings of the Government's Role in Resource Conservation (1870–1916)

By 1890 most forests in the eastern United States had already been cut once and conservationists' attention was turning to the widespread cutting going on in the West. In 1900 the United States had a population of 75 million and had become one of the world's great economic powers. With this growth came the slow realization that the country's strength was based on preserving its natural resource base—especially forests. The writ-

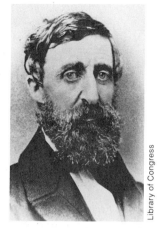
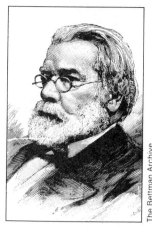

Henry David Thoreau 1817–1862

George P. Marsh 1801–1882

Figure 2-5 Some early American conservationists.

ings and efforts of the early conservationists and those who followed, such as Franklin B. Hough, John Muir, Carl Schurz, Bernard E. Fernow, Frederic Jackson Turner, Gifford Pinchot, and Theodore Roosevelt became more widely appreciated.

In 1872 President Ulysses S. Grant signed an act designating over 8,100 square kilometers (2 million acres) of forest in northeastern Wyoming for preservation as Yellowstone National Park. This action was the world's first instance of large-scale forest preservation in the public interest and marked the beginning of the first wave of resource conservation in the United States.

In 1885 New York became the first state to set up a state forest, preserving a large tract in the Adirondacks with the stipulation that it "shall be kept forever as wild forest lands." In 1891 Congress designated Yellowstone Timberland Reserve—the first federal forest reserve—and authorized the president to set aside additional federal lands to ensure future availability of adequate timber. Between 1891 and 1897, Presidents Benjamin Harrison and Grover Cleveland withdrew millions of acres of public land from timber cutting. Powerful political foes—especially westerners accustomed to using these public lands as they pleased—called these actions undemocratic and un-American.

Effective protection of the national forest reserves did not exist, however, until 1901 when Theodore Roosevelt became president. He transferred administration of the reserves from the Department of the Interior, which had a reputation for lax enforcement, to the Department of Agriculture. In 1905 Congress created the U.S. Forest Service to manage and protect the forest reserves, and Roosevelt appointed Gifford Pinchot as its first chief. Pinchot pioneered efforts to manage these renewable forest resources according to

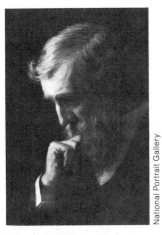

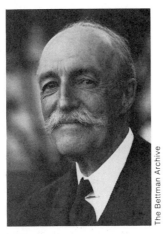

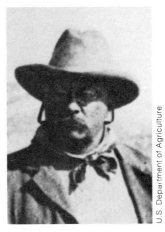

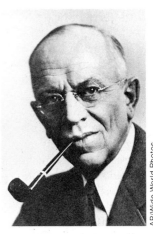

John Muir 1838–1914   Gifford Pinchot 1865–1946   Theodore Roosevelt 1858–1919   Aldo Leopold 1886–1948

the principles of *sustained yield* (Section 1-2) and *multiple use,* by which forests are to be used for a variety of purposes, including timbering, recreation, grazing, wildlife conservation, and water conservation.

The period between 1901 and 1909 when Theodore Roosevelt was president is regarded by many as the country's golden age of conservation. Roosevelt tripled the size of the forest reserves and withdrew from private exploitation 80 million acres of public land rich in coal and 4 million acres rich in oil. He also used the Lacey Act passed by Congress in 1906 to protect several million acres of public land as national monuments, many of which—the Grand Canyon, for instance—would later become part of the National Park System, and he began the National Wildlife Refuge System in 1903 by designating Pelican Island off the east coast of Florida as a federal wildlife refuge. In 1907, Congress, upset over Roosevelt's addition of vast tracts to the forest reserves, amended the Forest Reserve Act of 1891 to prohibit further withdrawals of public forests by the president and to change the name of the reserves to National Forests—implying that these lands should not be preserved from all types of development. On the day before this amendment became law, Roosevelt defiantly reserved another 16 million acres of national forests.

In 1912 Congress created the U.S. National Park System and in 1916 passed legislation declaring that national parks are set aside to conserve and preserve scenery, wildlife, and natural and historic objects for the use, observation, health, and pleasure of people and are to be maintained in a manner that leaves them unimpaired for future generations. The same law established the National Park Service within the Department of the Interior to manage the system, which by then included 16 national parks and 21 national monuments, most of them in the western states. The Park Service's first director, Stephen Mather, recruited a corps of professional park rangers to manage the parks.

Phase IV: Preservation Versus Scientific Conservation (1911–1932) After 1910 the conservation movement split into two schools of thought: preservationists (forerunners of today's neo-Malthusians) and scientific conservationists (forerunners of today's cornucopians; see Section 1-5). **Preservationists,** with their roots in philosophy and aesthetics, emphasized preserving and protecting public lands from mining, timbering, and other forms of development by establishing parks, wilderness areas, and wildlife refuges whose beauty and wealth could be used and enjoyed by present generations and passed on unspoiled to future generations. To preservationists wise use of a resource means using only what is really needed (not merely wanted) and completely using what is taken with little if any waste.

Preservationists were led by California nature writer John Muir, who founded the Sierra Club in 1892, and, after Muir's death in 1914, by forester Aldo Leopold. According to Leopold, the role of the human species should be that of a member, citizen, and protector of nature—not its conqueror. Another ardent and effective supporter of wilderness preservation was Robert Marshall, an officer in the U.S. Forest Service, who together with Aldo Leopold founded the Wilderness Society in 1935. Others, who have led preservationist efforts in more recent years, include David Brower, former head of the Sierra Club and founder of Friends of the Earth, Ernest Swift, and Stewart L. Udall.

Scientific conservationists, with their roots in economics and led mostly by foresters trained in the

European principles of scientific forest management, saw public lands as resources to be used now to enhance economic growth and national strength and to be protected from depletion by being managed for sustained yield and multiple use. The scientific conservationists were led by Theodore Roosevelt, Gifford Pinchot, John Wesley Powell, Charles Van Hise, and others. Roosevelt declared that his goal was not to "lock up" the forests but to consider "how best to combine use with preservation." Pinchot went further, angering preservationists who had been active allies in Roosevelt's conservation efforts, when he stated his principle of the wise use of a resource:

The first great fact about conservation is that it stands for development. There has been a fundamental misconception that conservation means nothing but the husbanding of resources for future generations. There could be no more serious mistake. . . . The first principle of conservation is the use of the natural resources now existing on this continent for the benefit of the people who live here now.

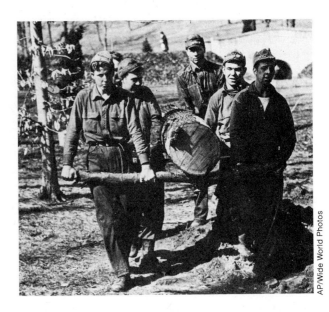

Figure 2-6 CCC crew in 1937, cleaning up woodlands, removing dead trees, pruning live ones.

Phase V: Expanding Federal Role in Land Management (1933–1960) The second wave of national resource conservation began during the early 1930s, as President Franklin D. Roosevelt attempted to get the country out of the Great Depression (1929–1941). To provide jobs for 2 million unemployed young men, he established the Civilian Conservation Corps (CCC), which worked on projects such as planting trees, developing parks and recreation areas, restoring silted waterways, providing flood control, controlling soil erosion, and protecting wildlife (Figure 2-6).

In 1933 the Soil Erosion Service under the Department of Agriculture was created to correct some of the soil erosion problems that contributed to the Depression (Section 10-4). In 1935 it was renamed the Soil Conservation Service (SCS) and Hugh H. Bennett became its first director. Roosevelt also created the Tennessee Valley Authority (TVA) to develop an integrated, regional resource management and economic development program for the severely depressed Appalachian region of the Southeast. The TVA devoted itself primarily to replanting forests to control erosion and building large dams to generate hydroelectric power and control floods. During the 1930s many large dams, such as Hoover Dam on the Colorado River, were built by the federal government in the arid western states.

For many decades public lands, especially in the West, where they were subject to periodic drought, had been heavily overgrazed because of ranchers' ignorance and greed. The Taylor Grazing Act of 1934

placed 80 million acres of public land into grazing districts to be managed jointly by the Grazing Service, established within the Department of the Interior, and committees of local ranchers. The law also established a system of fees for use of federal grazing lands and placed limits on the number of animals that could be grazed.

From the start, however, ranchers resented government interference with their long-established unregulated use of public land. Since 1934 they have led repeated efforts to have these lands removed from government ownership and turned over to private ranching, mining, timber, and development interests. Until 1976, western congressional delegations kept the Grazing Service (which in 1946 became the Bureau of Land Management, or BLM) so poorly funded and staffed, and without enforcement authority, that many ranchers and mining and timber companies openly continued to misuse western public lands.

Between 1940 and 1960 there were relatively few new developments in federal conservation policy. The 1940s and 1950s were dominated by World War II and the economic recovery from the war, and growing prosperity and industrialization led to increasing pollution.

Phase VI: Rise of the Environmental Movement (1960–1980) During the early 1960s a small but growing number of Americans continued efforts to expand the federal government's role in protecting public lands. This led to the third wave of national resource conservation, beginning during the short administration of John F. Kennedy (1961–1963) and expanded under the administration of Lyndon B. Johnson between 1963 and 1969.

In 1962 biologist Rachel Carson published *The Silent Spring* (see Further Readings), a book that described pollution of air, water, and wildlife from the widespread use of persistent pesticides such as DDT. The book helped broaden the concept of resource conservation to include the preservation of the *quality* of the air, water, and soil, which were under assault by a country experiencing rapid economic growth. This marked the beginnings of what is now known as the *environmental movement* in the United States.

Another important factor in the movement was the publication in 1963 of *The Quiet Crisis* (see Further Readings) by Stewart L. Udall, secretary of the interior under Kennedy. This book described past abuse of the country's resource base and called for renewed efforts to conserve resources—echoing and bringing up to date many of the concerns voiced by George P. Marsh in 1864, Paul B. Sears in 1935, and Fairfield Osborn in 1948 (see Further Readings).

The Wilderness Act of 1964 authorizes the government to protect undeveloped tracts of public land from development as part of the National Wilderness System unless Congress decides they are needed for the national good. This act defines **wilderness** as areas where the earth and its community of life have not been seriously disturbed by humans and humans are only temporary visitors. Conservation efforts continued during 1965, when the "Conservation Congress" passed 51 protection measures.

By 1965 a growing segment of the American public had begun to embrace the notion of environmental protection. Between 1965 and 1970 extensive media coverage of pollution and ecology and the popularized writings of biologists such as Paul Ehrlich, Barry Commoner, and Garrett Hardin helped the public become aware of the interlocking relationships between population growth, resource use, and pollution (Section 1-4). As a result, between 1970 and 1980, sometimes called the "environmental decade," more than two dozen separate pieces of legislation (Appendix 3) were passed to protect the air, water, land, and wildlife. Senators Edmund Muskie and Gaylord Nelson were key leaders in seeing that these tough environmental protection laws were passed. In 1970 President Richard M. Nixon used his administrative powers to create the Environmental Protection Agency (EPA), empowered to determine environmental standards and enforce federal environmental laws. William D. Ruckelshaus was appointed its first director.

The accomplishments taking place between 1965 and 1980 represent a fourth wave of national resource conservation, expanding from protection of public land resources to protection of shared air and water resources. During this period citizen-supported environmental organizations such as the Sierra Club, Wilderness Society, National Wildlife Federation, Friends of the Earth, Environmental Defense Fund (EDF), and Natural Resources Defense Council (NRDC) lobbied for better protection and management of public lands. They also began suing the government to secure enforcement of environmental laws. In addition, private organizations such as the Nature Conservancy and the Audubon Society accelerated their efforts to buy and protect unique areas of land threatened by development. Energy shortages in the mid-1970s dramatically demonstrated the need for effective conservation of energy resources, especially oil, and mineral resources that are found, extracted, processed, and converted into manufactured goods by the use of large amounts of fossil fuels.

Between 1977 and 1981 President Jimmy Carter created the Department of Energy to help the country deal with present and future energy shortages, and appointed a number of competent and experienced administrators to key posts in the EPA and the Department of the Interior, drawing heavily on established environmental organizations for such appointees and for advice on policy. He also created the $1.6 billion "Superfund" to clean up toxic waste sites. Just before leaving office, Carter protected 104 million acres of public land (an area larger than California) mostly in Alaska. Thus, he more than tripled the amount of land in the National Wilderness System and doubled the area under the administration of the National Park Service.

Phase VII: Continuing Controversy and Some Retrenchment (1980–1988) The Federal Land Policy and Management Act of 1976 gave the Bureau of Land Management its first real authority to manage the public lands, mostly in the West, under its control. Many of these lands not only are useful for grazing livestock but also contain rich deposits of gold, silver, coal, gas, oil, oil shale, uranium, and other resources. Western ranchers, farmers, miners, off-road motorized vehicle users, and others, who had been doing pretty much as they pleased on BLM lands, discovered that this was no longer possible.

In the late 1970s western ranchers, who had been paying low fees for grazing rights that encouraged overgrazing, launched a political campaign that came to be known as the "sagebrush rebellion." Three

Between 1982 and 1985 several of the country's major environmental groups studied President Reagan's environmental administrative actions and legislative proposals in detail (see Further Readings). Some of their major charges were that the administration

■ Appointed people from industries or legal firms that opposed existing federal environmental and land use legislation and policies to key positions in the EPA, the Interior Department, and the BLM—something like putting the fox in charge of the henhouse

■ Barred established environmental and conservation organizations and leaders from having any input into such appointments and into the administration's environmental policies

■ Made it difficult to enforce existing environmental laws by encouraging drastic budget and staff cuts in environmental programs under the guise of reducing spending—while adding far more to the federal deficit than any president in history

■ Greatly increased energy and mineral development and cutting of timber by private enterprise on public lands, often sold at giveaway prices to large corporations, thus depriving taxpayers of funds that could have been used to reduce the federal deficit or to prevent cuts in environmental programs

■ Gave ranchers excessive influence over how public rangelands should be used and managed

■ Increased the federal budget for nuclear power, which is still not economically feasible even with taxpayer subsidies of over $32 billion and which would never have been developed if it had been forced to compete with other energy alternatives in a free market

■ Drastically cut the budget for energy conservation and the development of renewable energy from the sun and wind, with the rationale that these energy alternatives (unlike nuclear energy) should be developed under free market competition

The Reagan administration countered that

■ It is normal for a newly elected president to appoint key personnel who wish to see the president's policies carried out

■ Drastic budget and staff cuts were necessary to reduce waste and help decrease the mounting national debt

■ Increased energy and mineral exploration and sale of timber on federal lands are necessary to encourage private enterprise, stimulate economic growth, and improve national security by ensuring that the country will have sufficient resources

■ It is better to return decision making about public rangelands to ranchers and to transfer ownership of some public lands to states and private ownership because federal bureaucrats are inept managers

■ The federal government should continue to subsidize nuclear power because it is a safe and proven technology that can provide the country with much-needed electricity in the future

■ The budget for energy conservation and alternative renewable energy sources should be decreased so that these emerging technologies can be developed by private enterprise under free market competition.

What do you think?

leaders in this campaign to have environmental laws weakened were James G. Watt, Robert Burford, and Anne Gorsuch (who later married Burford) who in 1981 were appointed by President Ronald Reagan to head, respectively, the Department of the Interior, the Bureau of Land Management, and the Environmental Protection Agency. The goals of this campaign, like earlier attempts since the 1930s, were to transfer most western public lands (including national forests) from federal ownership to state ownership and then to influence state legislatures to sell or lease the resource-rich lands at low prices to ranching, mining, timber, land development, and other corporate interests. Six western states, led by Nevada, laid claim to federal lands in court, and some western congressional representatives introduced legislation to give public lands to the states. So far the court suits and legislative efforts inspired by the sagebrush rebellion have failed.

Environmentalists and conservationists have helped fight off such efforts for decades. They have argued that resources on public lands owned jointly by all Americans should not be sold or leased to private interests at below average market prices because this provides subsidies and increased profits for a few influential corporations and individuals at the taxpayers' expense. They have also noted that legislatures of the western states have long been dominated by corporations and have some of the country's weakest conservation policies, poorest environmental records, and most corrupt histories in the management of public lands. Indeed, departments and agencies such as the Interior Department, the EPA, and the BLM were set up primarily because most *states* had failed to protect commonly shared land, air, and water resources from exploitation and abuse by private interests.

In 1981 Ronald Reagan, a declared sagebrush rebel, became president. He had won the election by a substantial margin, after campaigning as an advocate of a strong national defense, less federal government control, and reduced government spending to reduce the national debt and help combat the economic recession that followed the sharp rises in oil prices during the 1970s. Since 1981 there has been considerable controversy over his environmental policies (see Spotlight on p. 36).

Because of strong opposition by Congress, public outcry, and legal challenges, many of the Reagan administration's attempts to set back earlier environmental progress were thwarted. Although enforcement had been weakened, the major environmental legislation passed during the 1970s remained intact. Two of Reagan's key environmental appointees, James G. Watt and Anne Gorsuch, were forced to resign before the end of Reagan's first term. Although the full-scale attack on the environmental movement was blunted, most environmentalists and conservationists consider the period between 1981 and 1988 a time of retrenchment in the country's efforts to protect its resource base.

2-5 SOME POSSIBLE FUTURES: THE NEXT CULTURAL REVOLUTION

A Critical Turning Point Our numbers are now so large and our forms of technology so powerful that we are at a critical turning point in human cultural development—a new hinge of history. Today there are increasing signs that we have no more than 50 to 75 years to make the next cultural transition (Figure 2-7)—or an unwanted transition will be forced upon us. As described earlier, the neo-Malthusians and the cornucopians offer us two different ways to adapt for the future. The neo-Malthusian option is to make a change from our present situation to a series of *sustainable-earth societies* spread throughout the world. To make this change, we must learn how to work *with* nature and preserve our life-support system by bringing about a sharp reduction in the rate of population growth (especially in LDCs) and by eliminating unnecessary use and waste of resources (especially in MDCs).

The cornucopian option is to continue and expand our efforts at dominating and working *against* nature with the goal of ever-increasing economic growth. If the assumptions of the cornucopians are correct, this will lead to a superindustrialized world using highly advanced technology to support 10 billion or more people at a high average standard of living. But if the assumptions of the neo-Malthusians are correct, this option will lead to a world in which we have devastated our resource base either through environmental overload or global nuclear war (see the Guest Essay at the end of this chapter). Although this devastation probably would not eradicate the human race, it could lead to a world consisting again of scattered bands of people surviving primarily by hunting and gathering a greatly reduced variety of wild game and plants and using relatively primitive agriculture and other forms of technology like our early ancestors.

Some Hopeful Signs Is the achievement of a less crowded, less polluted world in just a few decades an unattainable goal? Is a society in which most people are healthier and live longer and emphasis is placed on preserving rather than disrupting the long-term sustainability of the earth a hopeless, idealistic dream? Most analysts say the answer to these important questions is no. Present undesirable trends do not necessarily indicate where we are heading. As biologist René Dubos reminds us, "Trend is not destiny."

Today in the MDCs there is widespread awareness of the global problems of population, pollution, and resource depletion. This knowledge is spreading rapidly to the LDCs. In addition to seeing themselves as citizens of a particular country, a growing number of people also consider themselves as *citizens of the earth*, whose primary loyalty is to protect and restore the natural systems that support all life on this planet. Such a worldview transcends all of the world's ideologies, including economic systems based on ever-increasing economic growth at the expense of the long-term survival of humans and other life forms.

During the short period since 1965, most U.S. citizens became aware of and concerned about the environment. On April 22, 1970, the first annual Earth Day in the United States, 20 million people in more than 2,000 communities took to the streets to demand better environmental quality. Today polls show that 70% of Americans are more concerned about the environment today than at any time in the past, and 65% indicate they favor greater protection of the environment even if it costs them 10% more in taxes and cost of living.

More important, such environmental awareness has been translated into action. Today more than 4,000 organizations worldwide are devoted to environmen-

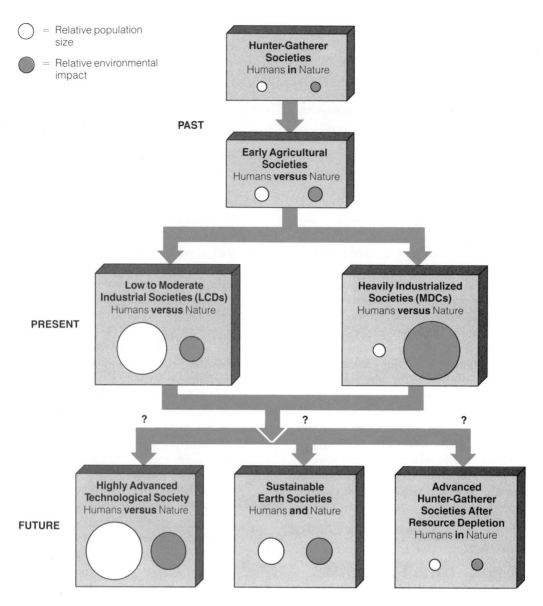

○ = Relative population size

● = Relative environmental impact

Hunter-Gatherer Societies
Humans **in** Nature

PAST

Early Agricultural Societies
Humans **versus** Nature

PRESENT

Low to Moderate Industrial Societies (LCDs)
Humans **versus** Nature

Heavily Industrialized Societies (MDCs)
Humans **versus** Nature

?   ?   ?

FUTURE

Highly Advanced Technological Society
Humans **versus** Nature

Sustainable Earth Societies
Humans **and** Nature

Advanced Hunter-Gatherer Societies After Resource Depletion
Humans **in** Nature

Figure 2-7 Major past cultural changes and some possibilities for the next cultural change.

tal issues. By 1986, environmental protection agencies had been established in 151 of the world's 166 countries—including 112 LDCs, compared to only 11 LDCs in 1972. The U.S. concept of setting aside land for protection in national parks, wilderness areas, and wildlife refuges has been adopted by more than 100 other countries, including many LDCs. By 1986, about 3% of the world's land surface had been set aside for protection from development, overgrazing, and overcutting. The amount of protection actually provided for these designated lands, however, varies widely throughout the world.

Most MDCs have passed laws designed to protect the air, water, land, wildlife, and public health. More than 80 federal protection laws have been enacted in the United States since 1970 (see Appendix 3), and private and government expenditures on pollution control totaled at least $600 billion between 1970 and 1985. By 1985, government and industry in the United States were spending $70 billion a year—an average of $293 a year for each American—to reduce pollution.

These efforts have paid off. Since 1965, as many as 75 U.S. rivers, lakes, and streams have been cleaned up. Restrictions against the dumping of untreated sewage, garbage, and toxic chemicals into lakes, rivers, and oceans have helped stem a serious decline in the quality of the country's surface water. About 3,600 of the country's 4,000 major industrial water polluters are meeting federal cleanup deadlines. Twenty major U.S. cities now have measurably cleaner air than before the passage of the Clean Air Act of 1970, and about 90% of major factories are in compliance with federal air pollution regulations. The overall rate of improvement in air quality, however, slowed down and in some cases deteriorated between 1982 and 1986, presumably because of budget cuts in environmental protection and enforcement since 1981.

Other industrialized countries have also made significant progress in pollution control. Smog in London has decreased sharply since 1952, and the river Thames is returning to life. Japan, once regarded as the most polluted country in the world, has dramatically reduced air pollution in most of its major cities and has upgraded the quality of its waters since passing antipollution laws in 1967. The Japanese environment is still highly degraded, however, partly because the country's small size relative to its large population means that most of the people live in crowded cities, thus creating centers of concentrated pollution.

When energy prices rose in the 1970s, many Americans began to realize that energy conservation is our cheapest, least environmentally harmful energy option and the best and quickest way to reduce excessive dependence on the world's rapidly diminishing supply of oil (Chapters 16 and 18). Since the oil embargo in 1973, the United States has derived 100 times more energy from conservation than from oil, coal, and nuclear power combined. Many Americans are driving more fuel-efficient cars; some now keep their homes cooler in the winter and warmer in the summer than in the 1970s; many homes have been insulated; about 1.1 million U.S. homes obtain some or all of their energy from the sun; about 850,000 have solar hot water heaters; and many industries and businesses have led the way in reducing energy waste.

However, there is still a long way to go. A temporary glut of oil in the 1980s has led some drivers to return to bigger cars with poor gas mileage and has encouraged cutbacks in funds and efforts for energy conservation and development of renewable energy alternatives such as solar and wind energy. Most American-made cars still get much poorer gas mileage than most of those made in Japan and Europe. Most homes and buildings are still underinsulated. Although household appliances that use half the electricity of 1970 models are available, relatively few homes have them. Although using nuclear energy to produce electricity is now considered uneconomic by most financial experts, the government still uses taxpayer dollars to provide massive subsidies for nuclear power research and tax breaks to utilities to offset massive losses from building nuclear plants (see Chapter 17).

With regard to population, the good news is that between 1970 and 1987 the annual growth of the world's population slowed from an all-time high of 2.1% to 1.6% (Section 1-1). Despite this hopeful trend, United Nations population experts project that the world will probably not reach zero population growth until 2100 with a population of 10.4 billion. The rate of population growth in the United States has slowed significantly, with the average number of live children born per woman decreasing from 3.8 in 1957 to 1.8 in 1987. If this trend persists, the United States could reach ZPG by 2020 or sooner, depending on the annual addition of legal and illegal immigrants.

To some the amazing thing is not the lack of progress in dealing with environmental and resource problems in many parts of the world but that so much has been done since 1965. Nevertheless, we cannot afford to settle back and rest on our progress to date. There is a long way to go, as discussed throughout this book. Environmentalists must constantly struggle to see that existing environmental laws (Appendix 3) are enforced and to prevent them from being weakened by developers and mining, timber, energy, and other companies who still struggle against conservationist restraints. Moreover, many serious environmental problems have only recently been identified: leaking hazardous-waste dump sites that can poison wells and groundwater supplies, acid deposition that can kill trees and aquatic life, and rapid depletion of the world's remaining tropical forests.

Environmentalists urge that spending on environmental protection and resource conservation be increased. Although by 1985 environmental damage was costing Western industrialized countries about 4% of their annual gross national product, these countries were spending less than an average of 2% of their GNP (1.6% in the United States) on environmental protection.

The promising developments since 1965, however, indicate that many people are beginning to ask the right questions: What are our responsibilities toward our fellow humans and other life forms? How close are we to overloading the earth's life-support systems? Are we as individuals willing to modify our own lifestyles to reduce resource waste and pollution?

We found our house—the planet—with drinkable, potable water, with good soil to grow food, with clean air to breathe. We at least must leave it in as good a shape as we found it, if not better.

Rev. Jesse Jackson

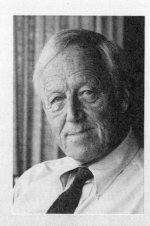

Hannes Alfvén

Hannes Alfvén has been professor of applied physics at the University of California, San Diego, since 1967. Before that he was professor of plasma physics at the Royal Institute of Technology in Stockholm, Sweden. He has been science advisor to the Swedish government and member of the Swedish Atomic Energy Commission. In 1970 he received the Nobel Prize in physics. In recent years Alfvén has used his expert knowledge to warn the world of the grave dangers of nuclear war and nuclear power plants.

The environmentalist movement is now a major factor in the political life of the United States and of the whole world. It started long ago as a protest against the factory around the corner that stinks or fouls the water in the river you used to swim in, or mars the scenic view from your window. About three decades ago it was found that in many cases industry had much more serious effects. It made the spring "silent," its waste killed fish and wildlife and was also dangerous to human beings. The processes by which this damage happens are sometimes very complicated and cannot be understood without careful studies of how nature works and how it is affected by industrial wastes.

This introduced a second phase in the environmentalist movement: It was obvious that unless environmentalists acquired at least the same competence in these problems as the industrialists, their fight against industrial pollution was hopeless. This challenge has given rise to the new interdisciplinary fields of human ecology and environmental science, which are introduced in this book.

A third phase in this movement began with the controversy over nuclear energy. The nuclear industry presented nuclear energy as a perfectly clean, cheap, and inexhaustible supply of energy, a wonderful result of the most sophisticated science and technology: no smoke, no dirty water. When some environmentalists objected, they were denounced as ignoramuses. They would understand that nuclear energy was a savior of humanity if only they studied the matter more closely.

The environmentalists followed this advice. Guided by a few very competent scientists, they learned how radioactivity induces cancer and produces genetic damage, and they discovered that the methods to keep the radioactive substances isolated from the air, water, and soil might work in a technological paradise but are unlikely to work in the real world. Now an increasing number of environmentalists have the same knowledge as the nuclear insiders. They can now judge nuclear energy without the unavoidable bias of those who have devoted a lifetime to the development of nuclear power or have invested $100 billion in this development. The result of this spread of knowledge seems to be catastrophic to the nuclear industry: It is increasingly difficult to claim that the radioactive substances are under control, it is increasingly dubious that nuclear energy is cheap, and it is quite clear that there are several other and better ways of solving our energy problems.

The environmentalists have also learned that the most serious objection to nuclear energy is its coupling to nuclear arms. It is now generally admitted that any country—large or small—that can build nuclear reactors will eventually get a nuclear arms capability. The peaceful atom and the militant atom are Siamese twins. This fact has led the environmentalist movement into its fourth phase, which is likely to be the most difficult but also the most important.

Everybody knows that war is more destructive to the environment—and to the human beings living in it—than anything else. Everybody knows that the destruction caused by nuclear arms is enormous compared with that by conventional arms, and that both the United States and the Soviet Union have enough nuclear arms to destroy the whole world. But most people prefer not to think about such horrible things, much less talk about them. They hope that war is something that takes place somewhere else and that it cannot be a threat to *their* environment. But this hope is false and dangerous in the thermonuclear missile age. It is encouraging that in the 1980s large numbers of concerned citizens in the United States and Europe have taken such matters of life and death into their own hands and have created the widely supported nuclear freeze movement. Hopefully, this will encourage more and more environmentalists to lend their support and knowledge to this important global movement.

Political and military leaders in the United States have attempted to analyze in detail what will happen if a "limited" nuclear war breaks out. Considering that no political or military leadership was able to predict how World War I, World War II, or the Vietnam war would develop, we have little reason to suppose that present predictions—which, moreover, are top military secrets—have very much to do with reality. Many people outside the establishment believe that the first few nuclear bombs released will create such political tension that a number of irrational actions will follow, and that after a few hours the result will be nuclear holocaust. It is not certain that the whole human race would be eliminated, but there would be such destruction of ourselves and our environment that our concern for the stinking factory around the corner, the silent spring, and even the nuclear power plant would seem trivial.

What can the environmentalists do about this? I think the key to the fourth phase of our struggle for a new and better world is the same as in the earlier phases: more knowledge and more concern. We must realize now that our legitimate demand for national security cannot be satisfied through nuclear armament. Instead, the enormous increase in destruction capability results in a global "insecurity" both for the United States and for all nations.

As long as the environmentalists were ignorant, there could be no efficient opposition against nuclear energy. As long as the environmentalists know next to nothing about the global destructive power that the political and military leaders of the world have prepared and are perfecting, there will be no popular movement strong enough to avert the approaching catastrophe. But if enough of us learn about the real situation in the world and act accordingly, there might still be time to stop the "race to oblivion."

Guest Essay Discussion

1. Have you seriously thought about nuclear war as the world's most serious environmental hazard? Why or why not?

2. Do you think or talk about the possibilities of nuclear war? Why or why not? What causes most people to ignore this subject?

3. What is the connection between the peaceful use of nuclear energy in nuclear power plants and the possible spread of nuclear weapons?

4. Should we ban nuclear power plants in the United States? Why or why not? Should the United States ban export of nuclear power plants and technology to other countries? Why or why not?

CHAPTER SUMMARY

Humans have been able to gain increasing control over nature through a series of major *cultural changes*. For several million years a small number of people lived in small, scattered groups of *hunters and gatherers*. Their environmental impact was small and localized because of their small numbers, dependence on their own muscle power, and limited technology. They were examples of *humans in nature* who learned to survive by cooperating with nature and with one another.

About 10,000 years ago people in various parts of the world began learning how to domesticate wild animals and cultivate wild plants. The gradual spread of this major cultural change, known as the *Agricultural Revolution,* resulted in significant population growth, urbanization, trade between farmers and city dwellers, the rise of armies and war leaders as ownership of land and water rights became valuable economic resources, and the rise of a new class of powerless slaves, minorities, and landless peasants who were forced to do hard, disagreeable work. The rise and spread of these *agriculture-based urban societies* led to massive clearing of forests, plowing of grasslands, soil erosion, and diversion of surface waters for irrigation and urban water supplies, and to a growing number of people who viewed themselves as *humans against nature* distinct from and apart from the rest of nature with the goal of conquering and subduing nature for their purposes. The next major cultural change, known as the *Industrial Revolution,* began in England around 1760, when people invented machines that could harness large amounts of energy derived from the burning of coal and later oil, natural gas, and uranium. Since then, the gradual transformation of *early industrialized societies* to the *advanced industrialized societies* in today's MDCs has led to significant increases in average energy use, agricultural productivity, life expectancy, GNP per person, and urbanization, and to a decline in the rate of population growth. As humans have gained increasing control over nature, they have had a greatly increased environmental impact.

The history of resource exploitation, resource conservation, and environmental protection in the United States has taken place in seven phases (some overlapping): **(1)** frontier expansion and resource exploitation (1607–1870), **(2)** early warnings about the need for resource conservation (1830–1870), **(3)** beginnings of the government's role in resource conservation by setting aside and protecting some forests held as public lands (1870–1916), **(4)** a split of resource conservationists into *preservationists* who wanted to protect more publicly owned lands from resource exploitation and *scientific conservationists* who believed that resources on public lands could be used now and also protected for future generations through the concepts of sustained yield and multiple use (1911–1932), **(5)** expanding role of the federal government in the management of public lands by scientific conservation (1933–1960), **(6)** rise of the environmental movement to provide increased scientific conservation and preservation of public forests, grasslands, and soil as well as air and water (1960–1980), and **(7)** continuing controversy and some retrenchment as an administration opposed to many of the environmental reforms of the 1970s gained power but met strong opposition from Congress, environmentalists, conservationists, and the general public (1980–1988).

There are growing signs that over the next 50 to 75 years humans will undergo another major cultural change to one of several possibilities: **(1)** a series of *sustainable-earth societies* based on humans learning to work and cooperate with nature to preserve their resource base, **(2)** a *superindustrialized world* based on major advances in technology that allow humans even greater control over nature, or *(3)* a *small number of humans in scattered bands trying to survive as modern hunter-gatherers* in a world polluted and depleted of resources as a result of either global nuclear war or excessive industrialization without sufficient resource conservation and environmental protection.

There have been some hopeful signs since 1965. There has been a substantial growth in the number of professionals, government agencies, and ordinary citizens in the United States and throughout the world who are devoted to resource conservation and environmental protection. Government and private efforts and greatly increased expenditures on pollution control have led to gradual environmental improvement in some areas, a reduction in the rate of population growth, and some increases in energy conservation. Despite these important and hopeful beginnings, there is a long way to go.

DISCUSSION TOPICS

1. Those wishing to avoid dealing with environmental problems sometimes argue: "People have always polluted and despoiled this planet, so why all the fuss over ecology and pollution? We've survived so far." Identify the core of truth in this position and then discuss its serious deficiencies.

2. Do you believe that the world's remaining hunting-gathering societies should be given title to the land on which they have survived for centuries and have the right to be left alone? Explain. Would you answer yes if it became known that some of their land contained large deposits of oil, coal, uranium or other valuable resources?

3. Make a list of the major benefits and drawbacks of an advanced industrial society such as the United States. Do you feel that the benefits of such a society to its citizens outweigh its drawbacks? Why or why not? What are the alternatives? Do you feel that the benefits of such a society to people in other parts of the world outweigh its drawbacks? Why or why not?

4. Explain how various cultural changes in human societies have led to the environmental and resource problems we face today.

5. Some analysts believe that continued economic growth and technological innovation in today's industrial societies offer the best way to solve the environmental problems we face. Others believe that these problems can only be dealt with by changing from a predominantly industrial society to a sustainable-earth society over the next 50 to 75 years. Which position do you support? Why?

6. Do you believe that a cultural change to a sustainable-earth society is possible over the next 50 to 75 years? What changes, if any, have you already made and what changes do you plan to make in your lifestyle to promote such a society?

PART TWO

Basic Concepts

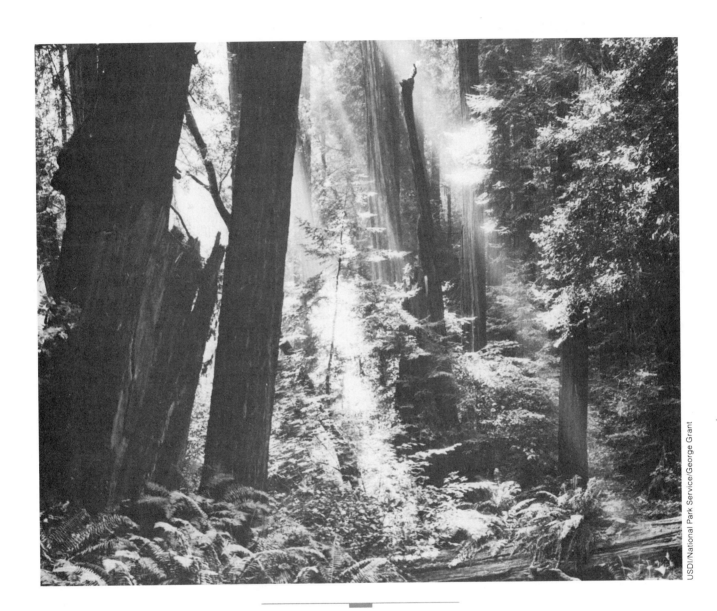

USDI/National Park Service/George Grant

Some Environmental Principles

1. *Everything must go somewhere; or there is no away. (Law of conservation of matter)*

2. *You can't get something for nothing; or there is no free lunch. (First law of energy, or law of conservation of energy)*

3. *You can't even break even; or if you think things are mixed up now, just wait. (Second law of energy)*

4. *Everything is connected to everything else, but how?*

5. *A thing is right when it tends to preserve the integrity, stability, and beauty of the biotic community. It is wrong when it tends otherwise.*

6. *Natural systems can take a lot of stress and abuse, but there are limits.*

7. *In nature you can never do just one thing, so always expect the unexpected; or there are numerous effects, often unpredictable, to everything we do.*

3

Matter and Energy Resources: Types and Concepts

GENERAL OBJECTIVES

1. What are the major physical and chemical forms of matter and what is matter made of?

2. What physical law governs changes of matter from one physical or chemical form to another?

3. What are the three major types of nuclear changes that matter can undergo and how dangerous to humans is the radioactivity released by such changes?

4. What are the major types of energy?

5. What two physical laws govern changes of energy from one form to another?

6. How can the two physical laws governing changes in energy from one form to another be used to help us evaluate present and future sources of energy?

7. What is the relationship of all three physical laws governing changes of matter and energy from one form to another to resource use and environmental disruption?

The laws of thermodynamics control the rise and fall of political systems, the freedom or bondage of nations, the movements of commerce and industry, the origins of wealth and poverty, and the general physical welfare of the human race.

Frederick Soddy, Nobel laureate, chemistry

This book, your hand, the water you drink, and the air you breathe are all samples of *matter*—the stuff all things are made of. The light and heat streaming from a burning lump of coal and the force you must use to lift this book are examples of *energy*—what you and all living things use to move matter around, change its form, or cause a heat transfer between two objects at different temperatures. All transformations of matter and energy from one form to another are governed by certain natural or physical scientific laws, which, unlike the social laws people enact, cannot be broken. This chapter begins our study of basic concepts with a look at the major types of matter and energy and the scientific laws governing all changes of matter and energy from one form to another. These laws are used throughout this book to help you understand many environmental problems and evaluate proposed solutions.

3-1 MATTER: FORMS AND STRUCTURE

Physical and Chemical Forms of Matter Anything that has mass (or weight on the earth's surface) and takes up space is **matter.** All matter found in nature can be viewed as being organized in identifiable patterns, or levels of organization (Figure 3-1). This section is devoted to a discussion of the three lowest levels of organization of matter—subatomic particles, atoms, and molecules—that make up the basic components of all higher levels. Chapter 4 discusses the five higher levels of organization of matter—organ-

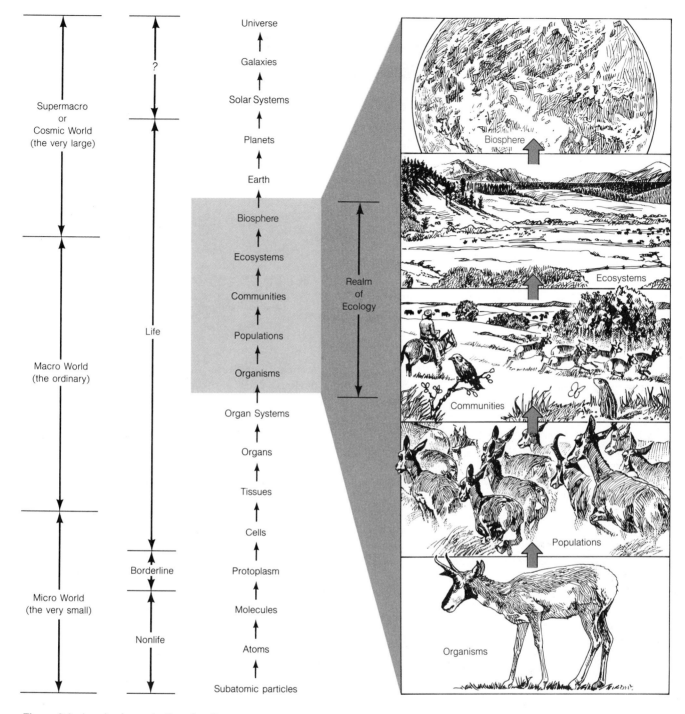

Figure 3-1 Levels of organization of matter.

isms, populations, communities, ecosystems, and the biosphere—that are the major concern of ecology.

Any matter, such as water, can be found in three *physical forms:* solid (ice), liquid (liquid water), and gas (water vapor). All matter also consists of *chemical forms:* elements, compounds, or mixtures of elements and compounds. Any element or compound needed in large or small amounts for the survival, growth, and reproduction of a plant or animal is called a **nutrient.**

Elements Distinctive forms of matter which make up every material substance are known as **elements.** Examples of these basic building blocks of all matter include hydrogen (represented by the symbol H), carbon (C), oxygen (O), nitrogen (N), phosphorus (P), sulfur (S), chlorine (Cl), sodium (Na), and uranium (U).

All elements are composed of an incredibly large number of distinctive types of minute particles called

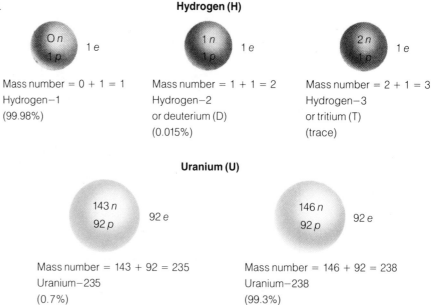

Figure 3-2 Isotopes of hydrogen and uranium.

Hydrogen (H)

0 n
1 p   1 e

Mass number = 0 + 1 = 1
Hydrogen–1
(99.98%)

1 n
1 p   1 e

Mass number = 1 + 1 = 2
Hydrogen–2
or deuterium (D)
(0.015%)

2 n
1 p   1 e

Mass number = 2 + 1 = 3
Hydrogen–3
or tritium (T)
(trace)

Uranium (U)

143 n
92 p   92 e

Mass number = 143 + 92 = 235
Uranium–235
(0.7%)

146 n
92 p   92 e

Mass number = 146 + 92 = 238
Uranium–238
(99.3%)

atoms. Some elements, such as the nitrogen and oxygen gases making up about 99% of the volume of air we breathe, consist of **molecules** formed when two or more atoms of the same element combine in fixed proportions. For example, two atoms of nitrogen (N) can combine to form a nitrogen molecule with the shorthand chemical formula N_2 (read as "N-two"), where the subscript following the symbol for an element indicates the number of atoms of that element in a molecule. Similarly, most of the oxygen gas in the atmosphere exists as O_2 molecules, although a small amount found mostly in the upper atmosphere (stratosphere) exists as ozone molecules with the formula O_3.

All atoms in turn are made up of even smaller **subatomic particles:** protons, neutrons, and electrons. Each atom of an element has a characteristic internal structure consisting of a tiny center, or **nucleus,** containing a certain number of positively charged **protons** (represented by the symbol p) and uncharged **neutrons** *(n)*, and one or more negatively charged **electrons** *(e)* whizzing around somewhere outside the nucleus. Each atom of the same element always has the same number of positively charged protons inside its nucleus and an equal number of negatively charged electrons outside its nucleus so that the atom as a whole has no net electrical charge. For example, each atom of the lightest element, hydrogen (H), has one positively charged proton in its nucleus and one negatively charged electron outside. Each atom of a much heavier element, uranium (U), has 92 protons and 92 electrons (Figure 3-2).

Because an electron has an almost negligible mass (or weight) compared to a proton and a neutron, the approximate mass of an atom is determined by the number of neutrons plus the number of protons in its nucleus. This number is called its **mass number.** Although atoms of the same element must have the same number of protons and electrons, they may have different numbers of uncharged neutrons in their nuclei, and thus different mass numbers. These different forms of the same element with different mass numbers or numbers of neutrons in their nuclei are called **isotopes.** Isotopes of the same element are identified by appending the mass number to the name or symbol of the element: hydrogen-1, or H-1; hydrogen-2, or H-2 (common name, deuterium), and hydrogen-3, or H-3 (common name, tritium) (Figure 3-2). A natural sample of an element contains a mixture of its isotopes in a fixed proportion or percent abundance (Figure 3-2).

Atoms of some elements can lose or gain one or more electrons to form **ions:** atoms or groups of atoms with one or more net positive (+) or negative (−) electrical charges. The charge is shown as a superscript after the symbol for an atom or group of atoms. Examples of positive ions are sodium ions (Na^+) and ammonium ions (NH_4^+). Common negative ions are chloride ions (Cl^-), nitrate ions (NO_3^-), and phosphate ions (PO_4^{3-}).

Compounds Most matter exists as **compounds:** combinations of two or more atoms *(molecular compounds)* or oppositely charged ions *(ionic compounds)* of two or more different elements held together in fixed proportions by chemical bonds. Water, for example, is a molecular compound composed of H_2O (read as "H-two-O") molecules, each consisting of two hydrogen atoms bonded to an oxygen atom. Other molecular compounds you will encounter in this book are nitric oxide (NO); carbon monoxide (CO); carbon dioxide (CO_2); nitrogen dioxide (NO_2); sulfur dioxide (SO_2); ammonia (NH_3); methane (CH_4), the major component of natural gas; and glucose ($C_6H_{12}O_6$), a sugar which most plants and animals break down in their cells to obtain energy. Sodium chloride, or table salt, is an ionic compound consisting of a network of formula units of oppositely charged ions (Na^+Cl^-) held together by the forces of attraction that exist between opposite electric charges.

3-2 LAW OF CONSERVATION OF MATTER AND CHANGES IN MATTER

There Is No "Away" The earth loses some gaseous molecules to space and gains small amounts of matter from space, mostly in the form of meteorites. However, because these overall losses and gains of matter are extremely small compared to earth's total mass, *the earth has essentially all the matter it will ever have.*

Although people talk about consuming or using up material resources, we don't actually consume any matter. We only use some of the earth's resources for a while—taking materials from the earth, carrying them to another part of the globe, processing, using, and then discarding, reusing, or recycling them. In this process we may change various elements and compounds from one physical or chemical form to another, but in every case we neither create from nothing nor destroy to nothingness any measurable amount of matter. This information, based on many thousands of measurements of matter being changed from one physical or chemical form to another, is expressed in the **law of conservation of matter:** When matter is changed from one physical or chemical form to another, no measurable amount of matter is created or destroyed. In other words, in such changes we can't create or destroy any of the atoms involved. All we can do is rearrange them into different patterns.

This law means that there is no "away." *Everything we think we have thrown away is still here with us, in one form or another.* We can collect dust and soot from the smokestacks of industrial plants, but these solid wastes must then go somewhere. We can collect garbage and remove solid grease and sludge from sewage, but these substances must either be burned (perhaps causing air pollution), dumped into rivers, lakes, and oceans (perhaps causing water pollution), or deposited on the land (perhaps causing soil pollution and water pollution). We can certainly make the environment cleaner and convert some potentially harmful chemicals to less harmful or even harmless physical or chemical

forms. But the law of conservation of matter means that we will always be faced with pollution of some sort.

Physical and Chemical Changes Elements and compounds can undergo **physical changes** in which their chemical composition is not changed and **chemical changes,** or **chemical reactions,** in which they are changed into one or more different elements or compounds. Any physical or chemical change either gives off energy or requires energy, usually in the form of heat. Two examples of physical changes are melting and boiling, in which an element or a compound is changed from one physical state to another. For example, when ice is melted or water is boiled, none of the H_2O molecules involved are altered; instead they are organized in different spatial patterns.

A chemical change can be represented in shorthand form by an equation using the chemical formulas for the elements and compounds involved. Formulas of the original starting chemicals, called *reactants*, are placed to the left and formulas of the new chemicals produced, called *products*, are placed to the right; an arrow ($\rightarrow$) is used to indicate that a chemical change has taken place. For example, when coal (which is mostly carbon, or C) burns, it combines with oxygen gas (O_2) in the atmosphere to form the gaseous compound carbon dioxide (CO_2). In this case energy is given off, explaining why coal is a useful fuel. This chemical change can be represented in the following manner:

According to the law of conservation of matter, no atoms are created or destroyed in any chemical change; instead, existing atoms are rearranged in different groupings. Notice that in the chemical equation for the combustion of carbon there are one carbon atom and two oxygen atoms on each side of the equation. A **balanced chemical equation** is one that contains the same number of atoms of each element on each side in accordance with the law of conservation of matter. This balanced equation shows how the burning of coal or any carbon-containing compound such as those in wood, natural gas (CH_4), oil, and gasoline adds carbon dioxide gas to the atmosphere, possibly causing warming of the atmosphere through the greenhouse effect (Section 19-5).

Air contains about 79% nitrogen gas (N_2) and 20% oxygen gas (O_2). When any fuel is burned in air at high temperatures, some of the N_2 and O_2 combine to form molecules of nitric oxide (NO) gas. Without adequate pollution control devices, this oxide of nitrogen spews out of smokestacks, chimneys, and automobile exhaust pipes and is an ingredient in the formation of the type of smog found in cities such as Los Angeles. The equation for the formation of NO from N_2 and O_2 shows that equations are not balanced simply by writing the formulas for the elements and compounds involved:

$$N_2 + O_2 + \textbf{energy} \rightarrow NO \ (unbalanced)$$

This equation is unbalanced because there are two nitrogen atoms on the left and only one on the right and two oxygen atoms on the left and only one on the right. To balance this equation so that it does not violate the law of conservation of matter, the same number of atoms of each element is needed on each side. This is achieved by forming two molecules of NO. This is indicated by placing the number 2 in front of the formula for NO:

element + element + energy $\longrightarrow$ compound

N_2 + O_2 + **energy** $\longrightarrow$ 2NO (*balanced*)

You do not need to know how to balance chemical equations to understand the material in this book. This concept has been shown so that you will understand the shorthand numbers and symbols involved in the small number of other important chemical changes used in this book and to illustrate the meaning of the law of conservation of matter.

Nuclear Changes and Radioactivity   The nuclei of certain isotopes are unstable and can undergo **nuclear changes,** by which they change into one or more different isotopes by altering the number of neutrons and protons in their nuclei. The three major types of nuclear change are natural radioactivity, nuclear fission, and nuclear fusion.

Natural radioactivity is a nuclear change in which

unstable nuclei spontaneously shoot out "chunks" of mass, energy, or both at a fixed rate. An isotope of an atom whose unstable nuclei spontaneously emit fast-moving particles (particulate radiation), high-energy electromagnetic radiation, or both is called a **radioactive isotope,** or **radioisotope.**

Radiation emitted by radioisotopes is called **ionizing radiation** because it has enough energy to dislodge one or more electrons from atoms it hits to form positively charged ions, which can react with and damage living tissue. The two most common types of ionizing particulate radiation are high-speed **alpha particles** (positively charged chunks of matter that consist of two protons and two neutrons) and **beta particles** (negatively charged electrons).

Radio waves, infrared light, and ordinary light are examples of nonionizing electromagnetic radiation, which does not have enough energy to cause ionization of atoms in living tissue. Although X rays are a form of high-energy ionizing radiation that can pass through the body and cause damage, they are not given off by radioisotopes. The most common form of ionizing electromagnetic radiation released from radioisotopes is high-energy **gamma rays,** which are even more penetrating than X rays. Figure 3-3 illustrates the relative penetrating power of alpha, beta, and gamma radiation. Some unstable nuclei emit only one type of ionizing radiation and others emit two types.

The rate at which a particular radioisotope spontaneously emits one or more forms of radiation is usually expressed in terms of its **half-life:** the length of time it takes for half the nuclei in a sample to decay by emitting one or more types of ionizing radiation and, in the process, change into another nonradioactive or radioactive isotope. Each radioisotope has a unique, characteristic half-life. For example, plutonium-239 (an alpha and gamma emitter), which is produced in nuclear fission power plant reactors and by nuclear fission bombs, has a half-life of 24,000 years. This means that half a given sample of plutonium-239 is still radioactive after 24,000 years and one-fourth is still radioactive after two half-lives, or 48,000 years. When inhaled into the lungs, a small speck of plutonium-239 greatly increases one's chances of developing lung cancer within two or three decades. Any exposure to ionizing radiation can cause potential harm to tissue in the human body (see Spotlight on p. 51).

Normally, it takes at least 10 half-lives for a sample of a radioisotope to decay to what is considered a safe level of ionizing radiation. Thus, unless it is cleaned up thoroughly (a difficult and expensive procedure), an area contaminated with plutonium-239 by explosion of an atomic bomb or a severe nuclear power plant accident remains dangerously radioactive for at least $10 \times 24,000$ years or 240,000 years.

Nuclear fission is a nuclear change in which nuclei of certain heavy isotopes with large mass numbers

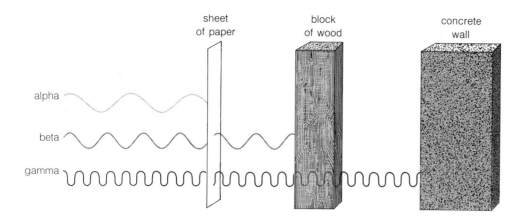

Figure 3-3 The three major types of ionizing radiation emitted by radioactive isotopes vary considerably in their penetrating power.

sheet of paper

block of wood

concrete wall

alpha

beta

gamma

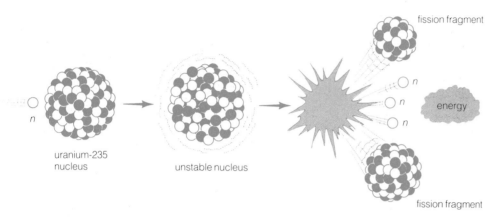

Figure 3-4 Fission of a uranium-235 nucleus by a slow-moving neutron.

fission fragment

energy

uranium-235 nucleus

unstable nucleus

fission fragment

such as uranium-235 are split apart into two lighter nuclei, known as *fission fragments*, when struck by slow- or fast-moving neutrons; this process also releases more neutrons and energy (Figure 3-4). Fissions of uranium-235 nuclei, found in small quantities in uranium ore obtained from the earth's crust, can produce any of over 450 different fission fragments or isotopes, most of them radioactive. The two or three neutrons produced by each fission can be used to fission many additional uranium-235 nuclei if enough are present to provide the **critical mass** needed for efficient capture of these neutrons. These multiple fissions taking place within the critical mass represent a **chain reaction** that releases an enormous amount of energy (Figure 3-5).

In an atomic or nuclear fission bomb, a massive amount of energy is released in a fraction of a second in an *uncontrolled* nuclear fission chain reaction. This is normally done by using an explosive charge to suddenly push a mass of fissionable fuel together from all sides to attain the critical mass needed to capture enough neutrons for a massive chain reaction to take place almost instantly. In the nuclear reactor of a nuclear electric power plant, the rate at which the nuclear fission chain reaction takes place is *controlled* so that, on the average, only one of each two or three neutrons released is used to split another nucleus. In conven-

tional nuclear fission reactors, nuclei of uranium-235 are split apart to produce energy. Another fissionable radioisotope is plutonium-239, which is formed from nonfissionable uranium-238 in breeder nuclear fission reactors, which may be developed in the future to extend supplies of uranium (Section 17-3).

Nuclear fusion is a nuclear change in which two nuclei of isotopes of light elements such as hydrogen are forced together at temperatures of 100 million to 1 billion degrees Celsius (°C) until they fuse to form a heavier nucleus with the release of energy. Because such high temperatures are needed to force the positively charged nuclei (which strongly repel one another) to join together, fusion is much more difficult to initiate than fission. But once initiated, fusion releases far more energy per gram of fuel than fission. Fusion of hydrogen atoms to form helium atoms is what takes place in the sun and other stars.

After World War II, the principle of uncontrolled nuclear fusion was used to develop extremely powerful hydrogen or thermonuclear bombs and missile warheads. These weapons involve the D-T fusion reaction, in which a hydrogen-2 or deuterium (D) nucleus and a hydrogen-3 or tritium (T) nucleus are fused to form a larger helium-4 nucleus, a neutron, and energy (Figure 3-6). Scientists have also tried to develop controlled nuclear fusion, in which the D-T

Figure 3-5 A nuclear chain reaction initiated by one neutron triggering fission in a single uranium-235 nucleus.

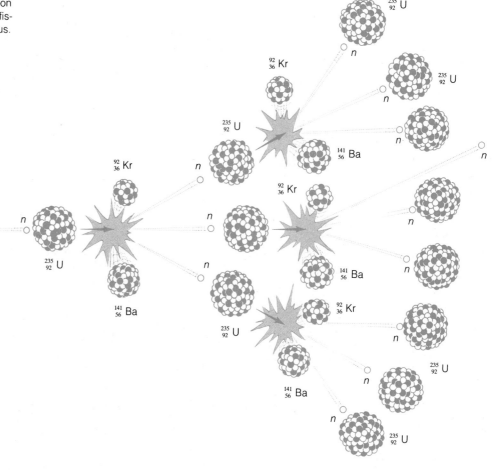

Figure 3-6 The deuterium-tritium (D-T) and deuterium-deuterium (D-D) nuclear fusion reactions, which take place at extremely high temperatures.

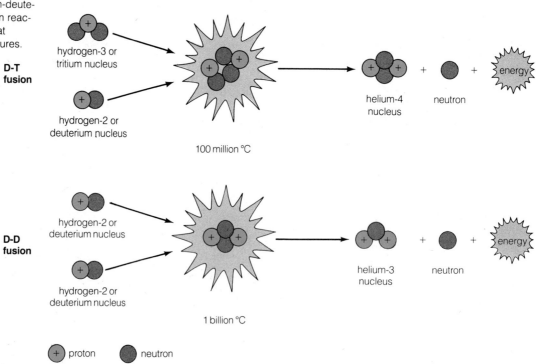

Scientists agree that exposure to any ionizing radiation can damage cells in the human body. The two major types of cellular damage are genetic damage, which alters genes and chromosomes and may show up as a genetic defect in immediate offspring or several generations later, and nongenetic (somatic, or body) damage, which can cause harm during the victim's lifetime. Examples of nongenetic damage include burns, some types of leukemia, miscarriages, cataracts, and bone, thyroid, breast, skin, and lung cancers.

The effects depend on the amount and frequency of exposure, the type of ionizing radiation, its penetrating power (Figure 3-3), and whether it comes from outside or inside the body. From the outside, alpha particles and beta particles can cause burns at high levels of exposure, but neither can penetrate the skin to cause internal damage. However, if a radioactive isotope that emits alpha or beta particles is inhaled or ingested into the body, the particles can cause considerable damage to nearby vulnerable tissues. Gamma rays and high-energy neutrons are so penetrating that they pass through the body easily and inflict internal cellular damage from outside or inside the body.

Some of the radioactive isotopes given off by the explosion of a nuclear fission weapon or by a severe nuclear power plant accident affect the entire body and others concentrate in certain parts of the body. Krypton-85, for example, which has a half-life of 10.7 years, can affect the entire body, triggering such cancers as leukemia in as little as 2 years. In contrast, iodine-131, with a half-life of

Table 3-1	Probable Effects on Humans of Various Doses of Radiation to the Whole Body in a Short Period of Time
Dose (rems)	**Effects**
0–50	No consistent symptoms
50–200	Decreased white blood cells, nausea, vomiting; about 10% die within months at 200 rems
200–400	Loss of blood cells, fever, hemorrhage, hair loss, nausea, vomiting, diarrhea, fatigue, skin blotches; about 20% die within months
400–500	Same symptoms as 200–400 rems but more severe, increased infections due to lack of white blood cells; 50% death rate within months at 450 rems
500–1,000	Severe gastrointestinal damage, cardiovascular collapse, central nervous system damage; doses above 700 rems fatal within a few weeks
10,000	Death in hours
100,000	Death in minutes

only 8 days, concentrates in the thyroid gland, where it can give rise to cancer decades after exposure. Barium-140, with a half-life of 12.8 days, collects in the bones, where it can cause cancer 20 to 30 years later. Most damage occurs in tissues with rapidly dividing cells such as the bone marrow (where blood cells are made), spleen, digestive tract (whose lining must be constantly renewed), reproductive organs, and lymph glands. Rapidly growing tissues of the developing embryo are also extremely sensitive, so pregnant women should avoid exposure to radioactivity and X rays unless they are essential for health or diagnostic purposes.

The two most widely used units for measuring the dose or amount of ionizing radiation in terms of its potential damage to living tissues are the *rem* and the *millirem* (mrem), which is one-thousandth of a rem. Small doses of ionizing radiation over a long period of time cause less damage than the same total dosage given all at once, because our body apparently has some ability to repair itself. Exposure to a large dose of ionizing radiation over a short time, however, can be fatal within a few minutes to a few months later, depending on the dose (Table 3-1). This accounts for many of the immediate and later deaths that occurred after the United States dropped atomic bombs on the Japanese cities of Hiroshima and Nagasaki at the end of World War II and for the 31 deaths within a few months of the 1986 accident at the Chernobyl nuclear power plant in the Soviet Union (Section 17-2).

Table 3-2	Estimating Your Average Annual Radiation Dose from Background Radiation and Human Activities	
Source of Radiation		**Approximate Annual Dose (millirems)**
Natural or Background Radiation		
Cosmic rays from space		
At sea level (average)		40
Add 1 mrem for each 30.5 m (100 ft) you live above sea level		_____
Radioactive minerals in rocks and soil: ranges from about 30 to 200 mrem depending on location		55 (U.S. average)
Radioactivity in the human body from air, water, and food: ranges from about 20 to 400 mrem depending on location and water supply		25 (U.S. average)
Radiation from Human Activities		
Medical and dental X rays and tests; to find your total, add 22 mrem for each chest X ray, 500 mrem for each X ray of the lower gastrointestinal tract; 910 mrem for each whole-mouth dental X ray, and 5 million mrem for radiation treatment of a cancer		80 (U.S. average)
Living or working in a stone or brick structure; add 40 mrem for living and an additional 40 mrem for working in such a structure		_____
Smoking a pack of cigarettes a day; add 40 mrem		_____
Nuclear weapons fallout		4 (U.S. average)
Air travel; add 2 mrem for each 2,400 km (1,500 mi) flown that year		_____
TV or computer screens; add 4 mrem per year for each 2 hr of viewing a day		_____
Occupational exposure; varies with 100,000 mrem per year for uranium ore miner, 600 to 800 mrem for nuclear power plant personnel, 300 to 350 mrem for medical X-ray technicians, 50 to 125 mrem for dental X-ray technicians, and 140 mrem for jet plane crews		0.8 (U.S. average)
Living next door to a normally operating nuclear power plant (boiling water reactor, add 76 mrem; pressurized water reactor, add 4 mrem)		_____
Living within 8 km (5 mi) of a normally operating nuclear power plant; add 0.6 mrem		_____
Normal operation of nuclear power plants, nuclear fuel processing, and nuclear research facilities		0.10 (U.S. average)
Miscellaneous: luminous watch dials, smoke detectors, industrial wastes, etc.		2 (U.S. average)
Your annual total	=	_____mrem
Average annual exposure per person in the United States = 230 mrem (with 130 mrem from background radiation and 100 mrem from human activities)		

reaction is used to produce heat that can be converted into electricity. However, this process is still at the laboratory stage despite almost 35 years of research. If it ever becomes technologically and economically feasible—a big if—it is not projected to be a commercially important source of energy until 2050 or later (Section 17-4).

In all three types of nuclear change, a small amount of the mass of the nucleus of any isotope involved is converted into energy, which is released into the environment. Thus, instead of being governed by the law of conservation of matter, nuclear changes are governed by the **law of conservation of matter and energy:** In any nuclear change the total amount of matter and energy involved remains the same.

Exposure to Ionizing Radiation It is impossible to avoid all exposure to ionizing radiation. All living things are exposed to small amounts of ionizing radiation, known as **natural, or background, ionizing radiation** (Table 3-2). Sources include cosmic rays (a high-energy form of ionizing electromagnetic radiation) from outer space; naturally radioactive isotopes such as radon-222 found in soil and in bricks, stone, and concrete used in construction; and other natural radioactivity that finds its way into our air, water, and food.

We receive additional exposure to ionizing radiation as a result of various human activities, most from dental and medical X rays and diagnostic tests involving the injection or ingestion of radioactive isotopes. These important tools save many thousands of lives each year and prevent human misery. But some observers contend that many X rays and diagnostic tests involving radioactive isotopes are taken primarily to protect doctors and hospitals from liability suits. If your doctor or dentist proposes an X ray or diagnostic test involving radioisotopes, ask why it is necessary, how it will help find what is wrong and influence possible treatment, and what alternative tests are available with less risk.

The smallest amount of human-caused exposure to ionizing radiation in the United States comes from nuclear power plants and other nuclear facilities—assuming that they are operating normally. Nuclear power critics contend that the greater danger from nuclear power is not from small, routine emissions of radioactivity but from the extremely small but real possibility of accidents that could result in the emission of large quantities of ionizing radiation. Such an accident occurred at the Chernobyl nuclear power plant in 1986 (Section 17-2).

Each year Americans are exposed to an average of 230 millirems (0.230 rem) of ionizing radiation, both from natural sources (130 mrem) and human-related sources (100 mrem). According to estimates by the National Academy of Sciences, this exposure over an average lifetime causes about 1% of all fatal cancers and 5% to 6% of all normally encountered genetic defects in the U.S. population.

3-3 ENERGY: TYPES AND CHANGES

Types of Energy Energy is used to grow our food, keep us and other living things alive, move us and other forms of matter from one place to another, change matter from one physical or chemical form to another, and to warm and cool our bodies and the buildings in which we work and live. **Energy** is the ability to do work or to cause a heat transfer between two objects at different temperatures. **Work** is what happens when a force is used to push or pull a sample of matter, such as this book, over some distance. Any physical or chemical change in matter either requires an input of energy from the environment (boiling water and combining nitrogen and oxygen gas) or gives off energy to the environment (water freezing and coal burning).

Everything going on in and around us is based on doing work in which one form of energy is transformed into one or more other forms of energy. Scientists classify most forms of energy as either potential energy or kinetic energy (Figure 3-7). **Kinetic energy** is the energy that matter has because of its motion and mass. Examples include a moving car, a falling rock, a speeding bullet, and the flow of water or charged

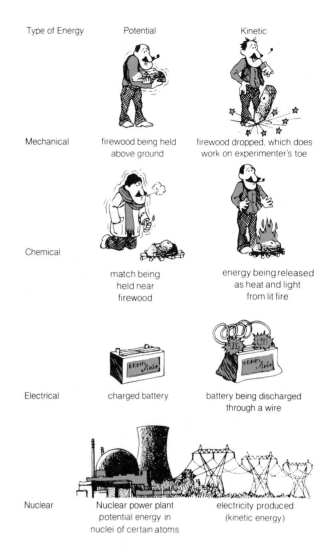

Figure 3-7 Forms of potential energy and kinetic energy.

particles (electrical energy). **Potential energy** is the energy stored by an object as a result of its position or the position of its parts. A rock held in your hand, a stick of dynamite, still water behind a dam, the nuclear energy stored in the nuclei of atoms, the chemical energy stored in the molecules of gasoline, and the carbohydrates, proteins, and fats in food are all examples of potential energy.

Energy Resources Used by Humans The direct input of essentially inexhaustible solar energy alone provides 99% of the thermal energy used to heat the earth and all buildings free of charge. Were it not for this perpetual direct input of various forms of electromagnetic energy from the sun, the average temperature outside would be $-240°C$ ($-400°F$) and life as we know it would not have arisen.

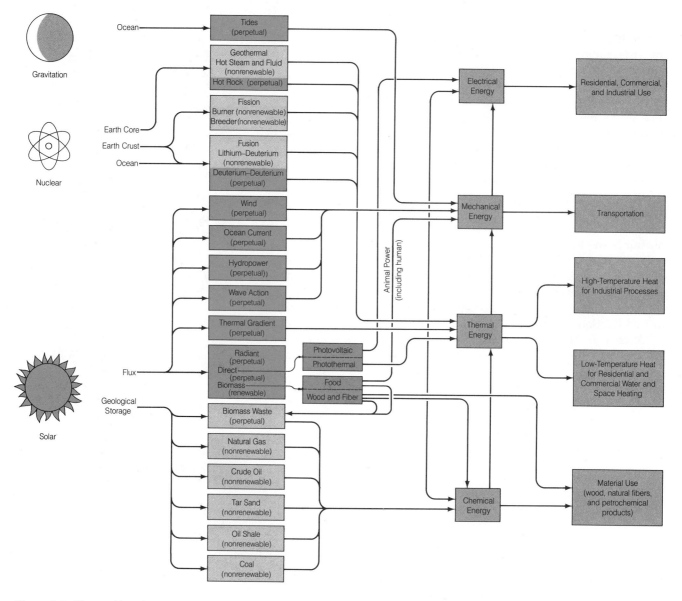

Figure 3-8 The earth's major energy resources and how they can be converted into chemical, thermal, mechanical, and electrical energy for various services. (Adapted from material supplied by Office of Energy Research and Planning, State of Oregon)

Human ingenuity has developed a number of ways to use various forms of perpetual, renewable, and nonrenewable energy resources to supplement the direct input of solar energy and to provide the remaining 1% of the energy we use on earth (Figure 3-8). This supplemental energy is used primarily to provide us with low-temperature heat for heating buildings (space heating) and water, high-temperature heat for industrial processes and producing electricity, and mechanical energy for propelling vehicles. Conserving energy by decreasing the amount unnecessarily wasted in developing and using any of the supplemental energy resources shown in Figure 3-8 is also a major perpetual source of useful energy.

Most people think of solar energy in terms of direct heat from the sun. But broadly defined, **solar energy** includes not only the perpetual *direct* energy from the sun but also a variety of *indirect* forms of energy produced as a result of the direct input. Major indirect forms of solar energy include perpetual wind and falling and flowing water (hydropower), and renewable biomass (solar energy converted to chemical energy in trees and other plants).

We have learned how to capture some of these direct and indirect forms of solar energy. The direct input of energy from the sun is captured and used to heat water and buildings by passive solar energy systems such as double- or triple-paned windows that face toward the sun and active solar energy systems such as specially designed roof-mounted collectors that concentrate the energy and then use pumps to transfer this heat to water or the interior of a building (Chapter 18). We have also developed wind turbines and hydroelectric power plants to convert indirect solar energy in the form of wind and falling or flowing water into electricity.

Direct solar energy has also been converted to chemical energy stored in fossil fuels such as natural gas, coal, crude oil, tar sands, and oil shale. But this form of solar energy stored for us hundreds of millions of years ago is being used up at such a rapid rate that it is *nonrenewable* on a human time scale. About 82% of the supplemental energy used throughout the world (91% in the U.S.) is based on burning oil, natural gas, and coal. Supplies of oil (and perhaps natural gas) may become increasingly scarce and expensive within the next few decades (Chapter 16).

3-4 FIRST LAW OF ENERGY: YOU CAN'T GET SOMETHING FOR NOTHING

To understand what happens when energy is transformed from one form to another in living systems and in devices invented by humans, we must become acquainted with two physical laws that govern all such changes: the first law of energy or thermodynamics and the second law of energy or thermodynamics.

In studying millions of falling objects, physical and chemical changes, and changes of temperature in living and nonliving systems, scientists have observed and measured energy being transformed from one form to another, but they have never been able to detect any creation or destruction of energy. This important information about what we find occurring in nature without fail is summarized in the **law of conservation of energy,** also known as the **first law of energy or thermodynamics:** In any physical or chemical change, movement of matter from one place to another, or change in temperature, energy is neither created nor destroyed but merely converted from one form to another. In other words, the energy gained or lost by any living or nonliving *system*—any collection of matter under study—must equal the energy lost or gained by its *surroundings* or *environment*—everything outside the system.

This law means that we can never get more energy out of an energy transformation process than we put in: *Energy input always equals energy output.* For example, the total amount of chemical energy contained in a gallon of gasoline exactly equals the output of energy in the form of mechanical energy and heat when the gasoline is burned.

This law also means that living things cannot create or destroy energy: *The way that a living plant or animal gets the energy it needs to survive and reproduce is to capture some form of energy from its environment and transform it into other forms of energy.* Green plants obtain the energy they need by converting solar energy to chemical energy stored in sugar molecules such as glucose, which they produce through photosynthesis (Chapter 4); animals get the energy they need by consuming plants or other animals.

The first energy law also means that in terms of energy quantity *it always takes energy to get energy; we can't get something for nothing (or there is no free lunch).* We often hear, for example, that huge amounts of energy are available from both the known and yet-to-be discovered deposits of oil, coal, natural gas, and uranium. However, the first law of thermodynamics tells us that there is really much less *useful* energy available than these estimates indicate because large amounts of energy must be used to find, remove, process, and transport these fuels to the point where they are used, as discussed further in Section 3-7.

3-5 SECOND LAW OF ENERGY: YOU CAN'T BREAK EVEN

Energy Quality   Because the first law of energy states that energy can neither be created nor destroyed, you might think that there will always be enough energy. Yet after filling a car's tank with gasoline and driving around or using a battery until it is dead to power a flashlight, you may have lost something. If it isn't energy, what is it?

The answer involves understanding that energy varies in its *quality* or ability to do useful work—moving matter, changing the physical or chemical form of matter, or altering the temperature of matter. **High-quality energy,** like that in electricity, coal, oil, gasoline, sunlight, wind, nuclei of uranium-235, and high-temperature heat, is concentrated and has great ability to perform useful work. By contrast, **low-quality energy,** like low-temperature heat, is dispersed, or dilute, and has little ability to do useful work. For instance, the total amount of low-temperature heat stored in the Atlantic Ocean is greater than the high-quality chemical energy stored in all the oil deposits in Saudi Arabia. But this low-quality heat is so widely dispersed in the ocean we can't do much with it.

Although sunlight is a form of high-quality energy, it does not melt metals or char our clothes because only a relatively small amount reaches each square meter of the earth's surface per minute or hour during daylight hours—even though the total amount of solar energy reaching the entire earth is enormous. Wind also is a form of high-quality energy, but to perform

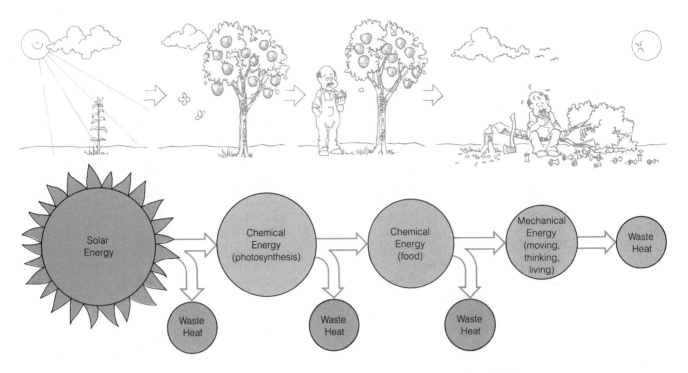

Figure 3-9 The second energy law. When energy is changed from one form to another, some of the initial input of high-quality energy is always degraded, usually to low-quality heat, which is added to the environment.

large amounts of useful work it must flow into a given area at a fairly high rate. Thus, *the overall usefulness of a perpetual energy source such as direct sunlight, flowing water, and wind is determined both by its quality and by its flow rate (flux)—the amount of high-quality energy reaching a given area of the earth per unit of time.*

Unfortunately, many forms of high-quality energy, such as high-temperature heat, electricity, gasoline, hydrogen gas (a useful fuel that can be produced by heating or passing electricity through water), and concentrated sunlight, do not occur naturally. We must use other forms of high-quality energy like fossil, wood, or nuclear fuels to produce, concentrate, and store them, or to upgrade their quality so that they can be used to perform certain tasks.

Second Law of Energy Millions of measurements by scientists have shown that in any transfer of heat energy to useful work, some of the initial energy input is always degraded to lower-quality, less useful energy, usually low-temperature heat that flows into the environment. This summary of what we always find occurring in nature is known as the **second law of energy or thermodynamics.** No one has ever found a violation of this fundamental physical law.

Consider three examples of the second energy law in action. First, when a car is driven, only about 10% of the high-quality chemical energy available in its

gasoline fuel is converted to mechanical energy used to propel the vehicle. The remaining 90% is degraded to low-quality heat that is released into the environment. Second, when electrical energy flows through the filament wires in an incandescent light bulb, it is converted into a mixture of about 5% useful radiant energy, or light, and 95% low-quality heat. *Much of modern civilization is built around the internal combustion engine and the incandescent light, which, respectively, waste 90% and 95% of their initial energy input.* When oil and other forms of energy are abundant and cheap, such waste has little effect on the future availability of energy resources. But as oil and other nonrenewable energy resources become more scarce and expensive, reducing such unnecessary energy loss becomes quite important.

A third example of the degradation of energy quality takes place when a green plant converts solar energy to high-quality chemical energy stored in molecules of glucose and low-quality heat given off to the environment by the plant. When a person eats a plant food such as an apple, its high-quality chemical energy is transformed within the body to high-quality electrical and mechanical energy (used to move the body and perform other life processes) and low-quality heat. In each of these energy conversions some of the initial high-quality energy is degraded into lower-quality heat that flows into the environment (Figure 3-9).

According to the first energy law, we will never

For over 100 years people have been trying without success to develop perpetual-motion machines and chemicals that can be added to gasoline and other fuels to make energy output exceed energy input. Many newspapers and magazines contain misleading advertisements about various get-something-from-nothing engines and fuel additives. The only people who get something for nothing from these schemes are those who sell such devices and "magic" chemicals to consumers who don't understand the implications of the two laws of thermodynamics.

Some scholars who do not know about or understand the implications of these energy laws also develop ideas and proposals that are impossible, or at best highly misleading. For example, Julian Simon, an economist and ardent cornucopian (see his Guest Essay at the end of Chapter 1) has repeatedly stated in his writings (see Further Readings) that energy can be partially recycled. He has used this false idea to imply that we need never worry about running out of affordable supplies of high-quality energy resources.

If someone offers you a way to get more energy out of an energy transformation process than you need to put in, don't waste your money. And don't be fooled by someone who claims that energy can be recycled.

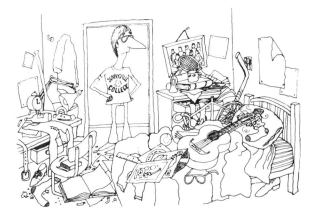

Figure 3-10 The spontaneous tendency toward increasing disorder or entropy of a system and its surroundings.

run out of energy because energy can neither be created nor destroyed. But according to the second energy law, the overall supply of concentrated, high-quality energy available to us from all sources is being continually depleted and in the process converted to low-quality energy. *Not only can we not get something for nothing in terms of energy quantity (the first energy law), we can't break even in terms of energy quality (the second energy law).*

The second energy law also means that *we can never recycle or reuse high-quality energy* to perform useful work (see Spotlight above). Once the high-quality energy in a piece of food, a gallon of gasoline, a lump of coal, or a piece of uranium is released, it is lost. Thus, the actual amount of useful, high-quality energy available from the world's supplies of coal, oil, natural gas, uranium, or any concentrated energy resource is even less than that predicted by the first energy law.

Second Energy Law and Increasing Disorder The second energy law can be stated in various ways. For example, since energy tends to flow or change spontaneously from a concentrated and ordered form to a more dispersed and disordered form, the second energy law also can be stated as follows: Heat always flows spontaneously from hot (high-quality energy) to cold (lower-quality energy). You learned this the first time you touched a hot stove. A cold sample of matter such as air has its heat energy dispersed in the random motion of its molecules. This is why heat energy at a low temperature can do little if any useful work.

By observing the spontaneous processes that are going on around us, we might conclude that a system of matter spontaneously tends toward increasing randomness or disorder, often called **entropy.** A vase falls to the floor and shatters into a more disordered state. Your desk and room seem to spontaneously become more disordered after a few weeks of benign neglect (Figure 3-10). Smoke from a smokestack and exhaust from an automobile disperse spontaneously to a more random or disordered state in the atmosphere, and thus air pollution levels decrease. Similarly, pollutants dumped into a river spread spontaneously throughout the water. Indeed, until we discovered that the atmosphere and water systems could be overloaded, we assumed that such spontaneous dilution was an easy and cheap solution to air and water pollution.

But the hypothesis that *all* systems tend spontaneously toward increasing disorder or entropy is incorrect. Some systems do and some don't. For example, living systems survive only by maintaining highly ordered (low-entropy) systems of molecules and cells. You are a walking, talking contradiction of the idea that systems tend spontaneously toward increasing disorder or entropy.

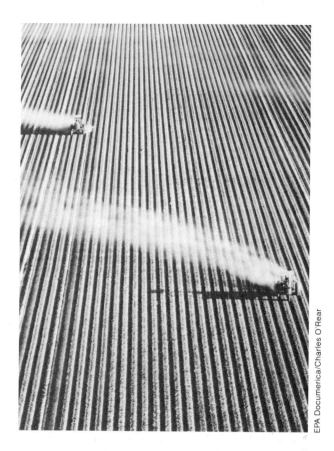

Figure 3-11 Using large inputs of energy, people convert parts of the world into pockets of order such as this crop field in California.

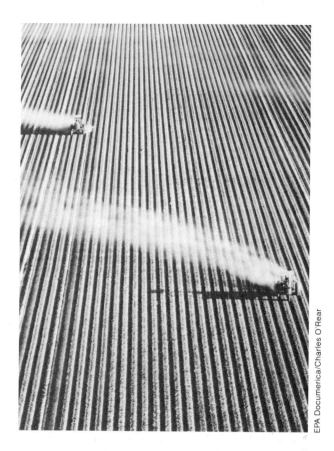

EPA Documerica/Charles O'Rear

Summary of Matter and Energy Laws

Law of conservation of matter: In any physical or chemical change, matter is neither created nor destroyed but only transformed from one form to another.
Or:
We can never really throw matter away.

First law of thermodynamics (law of conservation of energy): In any physical or chemical change, energy is neither created not destroyed but merely changed from one form to another.
Or:
There is no such thing as a free lunch.

Second law of thermodynamics (law of energy degradation): In all conversions of heat to work, some of the energy is always degraded to a more dispersed and less useful form, usually heat given off at low temperature to the surroundings.
Or:
Any system and its surroundings (environment) as a whole spontaneously tends toward increasing randomness, disorder, or entropy.
Or:
If you think things are mixed up now, just wait.

One way out of this seeming dilemma is to look at changes in disorder not just *within* a system but both in the system and in its environment. Look at your own body. To form and preserve its highly ordered arrangement of molecules and its organized network of chemical changes, you must continually obtain matter resources and high-quality energy resources from your surroundings, use these resources, and then return more-disordered, low-quality heat and waste matter to your surroundings. For example, your body continuously gives off heat equal to that of a 100-watt light bulb—explaining why a closed room full of people gets warm.

Planting, growing, processing, and cooking the foods you eat all require additional use of high-quality energy and matter resources that add heat and waste materials to the environment. In addition, enormous amounts of low-quality heat (disorder) and waste matter are added to the environment when concentrated deposits of minerals and fuels are extracted from the earth, processed, and used or burned to heat and cool the buildings you use, to transport you, and to make roads, clothes, shelter, and other items you use.

Measurements show that the total amount of disorder, or entropy, in the form of low-quality heat, added

to the environment to keep you (or any living thing) alive and to provide the items you use is much greater than the order maintained in your body. Thus, *all forms of life are tiny pockets of order maintained by creating a sea of disorder around themselves.* The primary characteristic of any advanced industrial society is an ever-increasing flow of high-quality energy to maintain the order in human bodies and the larger pockets of order we call civilization (Figure 3-11). As a result, today's advanced industrial societies are adding more entropy to the environment than at any other time in human history.

Considering the *system and surroundings as a whole,* experimental measurements always reveal a net increase in entropy with any spontaneous chemical or physical change. Thus, our original hypothesis must be modified to include the surroundings: *Any system and its surroundings as a whole spontaneously tend toward increasing randomness, disorder, or entropy.* In other words, if you think things are mixed up now, just wait. This is another way of stating the second energy law, or second law of thermodynamics. In most apparent violations of this law, the observer has failed to include the greater disorder added to the surroundings when there is an increase in order within the system.

human body
20 to 25%

internal combustion engine
(gasoline) 10%

steam turbine
45%

fuel cell
60%

incandescent light
5%

fluorescent light
22%

3-6 ENERGY LAWS AND ENERGY RESOURCES

Which Energy Resources Should We Develop? The history of energy use since the Industrial Revolution has shown that it takes about 50 years to develop and phase in the widespread use of any new energy resource. Thus, today's energy research and development will largely determine the energy resources available to us 50 years from now. Using large amounts of human ingenuity and limited financial capital to develop the wrong mix of future energy resources could be disastrous for people in both MDCs and LDCs.

Cornucopians and neo-Malthusians tend to disagree over which mix of the energy resources shown in Figure 3–8 should be relied upon for most of the energy used by humans over the next 50 years (see Spotlight on p. 61). The two energy laws are important tools in helping us decide how to reduce unnecessary energy waste and in evaluating the usefulness of various present and future energy resources.

Increasing Energy Efficiency One way to cut energy waste and save money, at least in the long run, is to increase **energy efficiency**—the percentage of the total energy input that does useful work and is not converted into low-quality, essentially useless heat in an energy conversion system. The energy conversion devices we use vary considerably in their energy efficiencies (Figure 3-12). We can reduce waste by using the most efficient processes or devices available and by trying to make them more efficient.

We can save energy and money by buying the most energy-efficient home heating systems, hot water heaters, automobiles, air conditioners, refrigerators, and other household appliances available. The initial cost of the most energy-efficient models is usually higher, but in the long run they save money. Thus, whether an energy conversion device is cost-effective depends on its **lifetime** or **life-cycle cost:** its initial cost plus its lifetime operating cost.

The net efficiency of the entire energy delivery system for a heating system, hot water heater, or car is determined by finding the energy efficiency of each energy conversion step in the system: extracting the fuel, purifying and upgrading it to a useful form, transporting it, and finally using it. Figure 3-13 shows how net energy efficiencies are determined for heating a well-insulated home **(1)** passively with an input

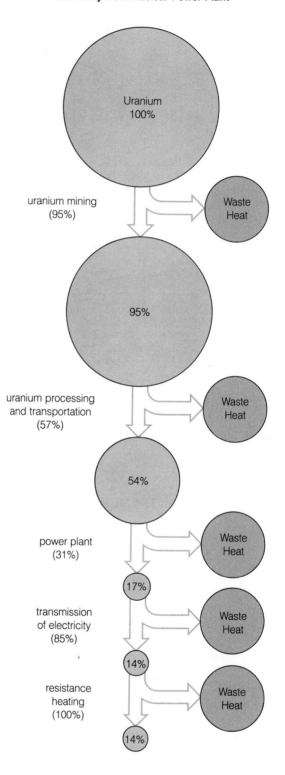

Passive Solar

Electricity from Nuclear Power Plant

Figure 3-13 Comparison of net energy efficiency for two types of space heating. The cumulative net efficiency is obtained by multiplying the percentage shown inside the circle for each step by the energy efficiency for that step (shown in parentheses).

of direct solar energy through south-facing windows and **(2)** with electricity produced at a nuclear power plant and transported by wire to the home and converted to heat (electric resistance heating). This analysis reveals that converting high-quality chemical or nuclear energy in nuclear fuel to high-quality heat at

several thousand degrees, converting this heat to high-quality electricity, and then using the electricity to provide low-quality heat for warming a house to only about 20°C (68°F) is extremely wasteful of high-quality energy. According to energy expert Amory Lovins (see Further Readings), such use of high-quality energy to

Many cornucopians believe that we will always be able to find enough oil or other fossil fuels so that conserving these resources need not be as high a priority as searching the world for the remaining supplies. Cornucopians believe that if oil should become scarce, we should convert solid coal—the world's most abundant fossil fuel—to liquid and gaseous synthetic fuels. They also believe that we should shift to greatly increased use of electricity produced in large, centralized, coal-burning and nuclear fission power plants. After the year 2020 they propose shifting from conventional nuclear fission to breeder nuclear fission, which could synthesize nuclear fuel and thus prolong uranium supplies for at least 1,000 years (Chapter 17). After 2050, if this energy alternative should prove to be technologically, economically, and environmentally acceptable, there would be a gradual shift to almost complete dependence on centralized nuclear fusion power plants.

Neo-Malthusians disagree with this approach. They contend that the quickest, cheapest, and most cost-effective way to meet projected energy needs is *energy conservation*—primarily by improving the energy efficiency of houses, cars, and appliances so that less energy is wasted unnecessarily. They point out that reducing waste saves money and decreases the environmental impact of the use of any energy resource (because less is used to achieve the same amount of work). Conservation also extends supplies of fossil fuels, makes countries such as the United States less dependent on oil imports, and eliminates or sharply reduces the need to build additional electric power plants. Meanwhile, it buys time to phase in a diverse and flexible array of decentralized, mostly perpetual energy resources based on direct sunlight, wind, biomass, and falling and flowing water. Neo-Malthusians also point out that the vulnerability of the United States to nuclear attack would be significantly decreased if we

switched from large, centralized power plants (which can be knocked out by a relatively few missiles) to a widely dispersed array of small-scale energy systems based primarily on locally available energy resources.

In addition, most neo-Malthusians believe that all forms of nuclear power should be phased out because this method for producing electricity is inefficient, uneconomic, unsafe, and unnecessary compared to other available alternatives (Chapter 17). They also view as unacceptable the increased reliance on coal and coal-based synthetic fuels favored by the cornucopians; the massive amounts of carbon dioxide released into the atmosphere when these fuels are burned could bring about undesirable long-term changes in global climate patterns (Section 19-5). What do you think?

---

provide low-quality heat "is like using a chain saw to cut butter." By contrast, it is much less wasteful of high-quality energy to use a passive or active solar heating system to obtain low-quality heat from the environment and, if necessary, raise its temperature slightly to provide space heating.

Lovins argues that high-quality electrical energy should be used only for purposes where energy of that quality is needed, primarily to run lights and motors, refine copper, and produce glass, iron, and steel. Lovins has shown that the United States already has more than enough power plants to produce electricity to meet all such essential needs until 2005—perhaps until 2025—if we eliminated all use of electricity for heating indoor space and water. Critics point out that even though electricity is wasteful of energy when used for certain purposes, people use it to heat homes and hot water because it is convenient.

Figure 3-14 lists the net energy efficiencies for a

variety of space-heating systems. The cheapest and most energy-efficient way to provide heating is to build a superinsulated house that has no need for any type of conventional heating system. Such a house is so heavily insulated and air tight that even in areas where winter temperatures may average −40°C (−40°F), all of its space heating would be provided by a combination of passive solar gain (about 59%), waste heat from appliances (33%), and body heat from its occupants (8%). Passive solar heating is the next most efficient and cheapest in lifetime cost to heat a house, followed by one of the new, 95% efficient, natural gas furnaces. The least efficient and most expensive way to heat a house is with electricity produced by nuclear power plants. For example, in 1986 the average price of obtaining 250,000 kilocalories (1 million British thermal units, or Btus) for heating space or water in the United States was $5.65 using natural gas, $5.95 using fuel oil, and $21.91 using electricity.

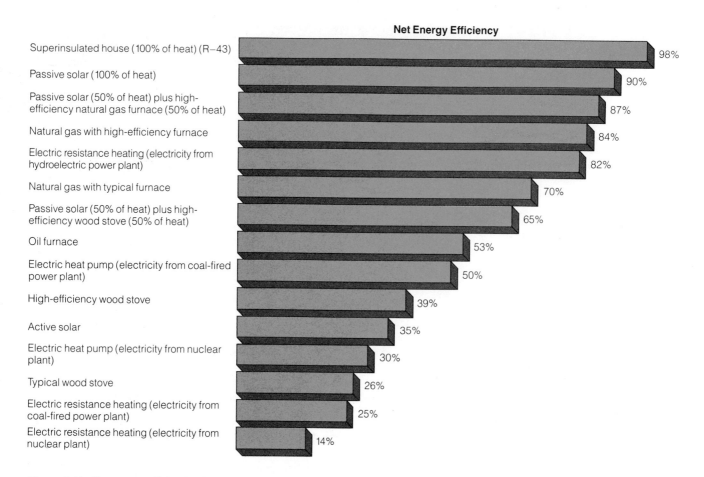

Net Energy Efficiency

Superinsulated house (100% of heat) (R–43)	98%
Passive solar (100% of heat)	90%
Passive solar (50% of heat) plus high-efficiency natural gas furnace (50% of heat)	87%
Natural gas with high-efficiency furnace	84%
Electric resistance heating (electricity from hydroelectric power plant)	82%
Natural gas with typical furnace	70%
Passive solar (50% of heat) plus high-efficiency wood stove (50% of heat)	65%
Oil furnace	53%
Electric heat pump (electricity from coal-fired power plant)	50%
High-efficiency wood stove	39%
Active solar	35%
Electric heat pump (electricity from nuclear plant)	30%
Typical wood stove	26%
Electric resistance heating (electricity from coal-fired power plant)	25%
Electric resistance heating (electricity from nuclear plant)	14%

Figure 3-14 Net energy efficiencies for various space-heating systems.

Figure 3-15 gives a similar net energy efficiency analysis for heating water for washing and bathing. Again the least efficient way is to use electricity produced by nuclear power plants. The most efficient method is to use a tankless, instant water heater fired by natural gas or liquefied petroleum gas. Such heaters fit under a sink and burn fuel only when the hot water faucet is turned on, heating the water instantly as it flows through a small burner chamber and providing hot water only when and as long as it is needed. In contrast, conventional natural gas and electric resistance heaters keep a large tank of water hot all day and night and can run out after a long shower or two. Tankless heaters are widely used in many parts of Europe and are slowly beginning to appear in the United States. A well-insulated, conventional natural gas water heater is also efficient.

Figure 3-16 lists net energy efficiencies for several automobile engine systems. Note that the net energy efficiency for a car powered by a conventional internal combustion engine is only about 10%. In other words, about 90% of the energy in crude oil is wasted by its conversion to gasoline and its subsequent combustion to move a car. An electric engine with batteries recharged by electricity from a hydroelectric power plant has a net efficiency almost three times that of a gasoline-burning internal combustion engine. But this system cannot be widely used in the United States because most hydroelectric resources are found only in certain areas and have already been developed (Section 18-3). In addition, electric cars will not be cost-effective unless scientists can develop more affordable, longer-lasting batteries. The second most efficient system is a car with a gas turbine engine. American, Japanese, and European car makers have prototype gas turbine engines, but they need more development to determine whether they are cost-effective.

Energy waste can also be reduced by development of more energy efficient furnaces, lights, and other devices. Examples include heating systems that heat only the occupants of a building rather than the entire inside space and plastic light pipes and light-emitting devices (diodes) that convert 10 to 20 times more electrical energy to visible light than incandescent or fluorescent bulbs.

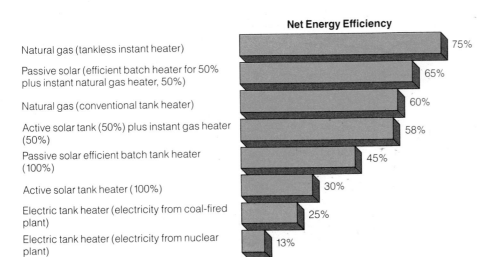

Figure 3-15 Net energy efficiencies for various water-heating systems.

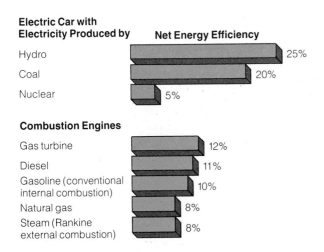

Figure 3-16 Net energy efficiencies for automobiles with various engine systems.

Using Waste Heat Because of the second energy law, high-quality energy cannot be recycled and is eventually degraded to low-temperature heat that flows into the environment. However, the rate at which waste heat flows into the environment can be slowed. For instance, in cold weather an uninsulated, leaky house loses heat almost as fast as it is produced. By contrast, a well-insulated, airtight house can retain most of its heat for five to ten hours, and a well-designed, super-insulated house can retain most of its heat up to four days.

In some office buildings, waste heat from lights, computers, and other machines is collected and distributed to reduce heating bills during cold weather, or exhausted in hot weather to reduce cooling bills. Waste heat from industrial plants and electrical power plants can also be distributed through insulated pipes and used as a district heating system for nearby buildings and homes, greenhouses, and fish ponds, as is done in some parts of Europe.

Waste heat from coal-fired and other industrial boilers can be used to produce electricity at half the cost of buying it from a utility company. The electricity can be used by the plant or sold to the local power company for general use. This combined production of high-temperature heat and electricity, known as **cogeneration,** is widely used in industrial plants throughout Europe. Cogeneration at industrial sites produced 22% of the electricity used in the United States in 1920. By 1986, however, the amount was only about 5%, primarily because most utility companies charge high backup rates when a cogenerating system is out of operation and pay low prices for cogenerated electricity. If all large industrial boilers in the United States used cogeneration, they could produce electricity equivalent to that of 30 to 200 nuclear or coal-fired power plants (depending on the technology used) at about half the cost. This would reduce the average price of electricity and essentially eliminate the need to build any large electric power plants through the year 2020.

Net Useful Energy: It Takes Energy to Get Energy
Because of the two energy laws, energy is always required to produce useful, high-quality energy. The true value of the energy obtainable from a given quantity of an energy resource is its **net useful energy**—the total energy available from the resource minus the amount of energy used (the first law), automatically wasted (the second law), and unnecessarily wasted in finding, processing, concentrating, and transporting

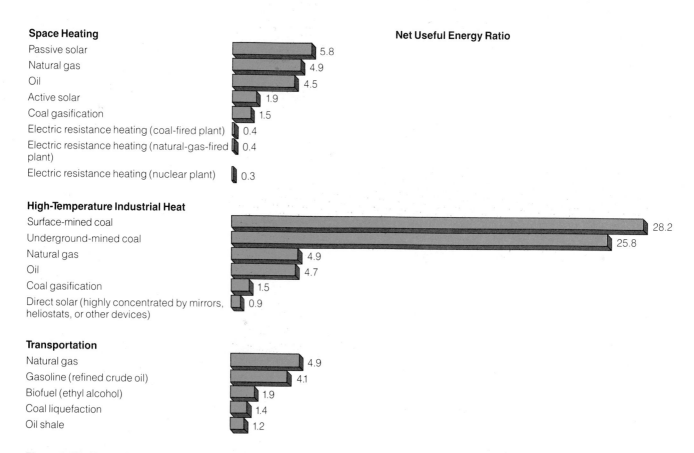

Figure 3-17 Net useful energy ratios for various energy systems. Data from Colorado Energy Research Institute, *Net Energy Analysis*, 1976, and Howard T. Odum and Elisabeth C. Odum, *Energy Basis for Man and Nature*, 3rd. ed., McGraw-Hill, 1981.

it to a user. For example, if it takes nine units of fossil fuel energy to deliver ten units of nuclear, solar, or additional fossil fuel energy (perhaps from a deep well at sea), the net useful energy gain is only one unit.

We can express this as the ratio of useful energy produced to the useful energy used to produce it. In the example above, the net energy ratio would be 10/9, or 1.1. The higher the ratio, the greater the net useful energy yield. When the ratio is less than 1, there is a net energy loss over the lifetime of the system. Figure 3-17 lists estimated net useful energy ratios for various energy alternatives for space heating, high-temperature heat for industrial processes, and gaseous or liquid fuels for vehicles.

Currently, fossil fuels have relatively high net useful energy ratios because they come mainly from rich, accessible deposits. When these sources are depleted, however, the ratios will decline and prices will rise—it will take more money and high-quality fossil fuel to find, process, and deliver new fuel from poorer deposits found deeper in the earth and in remote and hostile

areas like the Arctic—far from where the energy is to be used.

Conventional nuclear fission energy has a low net energy ratio because it takes large amounts of energy to build and operate power plants and take them apart after their 25 to 30 years of useful life, and to safely store the resulting highly radioactive wastes. Large-scale solar energy plants for producing electricity or high-temperature heat for industrial processes also have low net useful energy ratios. This is because the small flow of high-quality solar energy in a particular area must be collected and concentrated to provide the necessary high temperatures. Large amounts of money and high-quality energy are necessary to mine, process, and transport the materials used in vast arrays of solar collectors, focusing mirrors, pipes, and other equipment. On the other hand, passive and active solar energy systems for heating individual buildings and for heating water have relatively high net useful energy ratios because they supply relatively small amounts of heat at moderate temperatures.

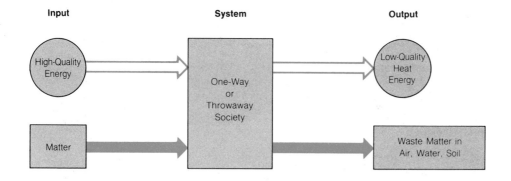

| Input | System | Output |

Figure 3-18 The one-way, or throwaway, society in most industrialized countries is based on maximizing the rates of energy flow and matter flow, resulting in the rapid conversion of the world's resources to trash, pollution, and waste heat.

3-7 MATTER AND ENERGY LAWS AND ENVIRONMENTAL PROBLEMS

Every Little Bit of Disorder Counts The three physical laws governing the use of matter and energy resources can help us understand how to work with rather than against nature, thus reducing the environmental impact of human activities. In this chapter we have seen that because of the law of conservation of matter and the second law of energy, the direct and indirect use of resources by each individual human (or any other living thing) automatically adds some waste heat (entropy) and matter to the environment. Your individual use of matter and energy and addition of waste to the environment may seem small and insignificant. But you are only one of the 1.2 billion individuals in industrialized countries using large quantities of the earth's matter and energy resources at a rapid rate and only one of the 3.8 billion people in the less-developed countries who hope to be able to use a greater share of those resources.

Throwaway and Matter-Recycling Societies Today's advanced industrialized countries are **throwaway societies,** sustaining ever-increasing economic growth by maximizing the rate at which matter and energy resources are used and wasted (Figure 3-18). The physical laws of matter and energy tell us that if more and more people continue to use and unnecessarily waste resources at an increasing rate, sooner or later the capacity of the local, regional, and eventually the global environments to absorb heat and waste matter will be exceeded.

A stopgap solution is to convert from a throwaway society to a **matter-recycling society** so that economic growth can continue without depleting matter resources and without producing excessive pollution

and environmental disruption. But, as we have seen already, there is no free lunch. The two laws of energy tell us that *recycling matter always requires high-quality energy.* However, if a resource is not too widely scattered in its distribution, recycling often requires less high-quality energy than that needed to find, extract, and process virgin or unused resources. Nevertheless, in the long run, a matter-recycling society based on indefinitely increasing economic growth must have an inexhaustible supply of affordable high-quality energy and an environment with an infinite capacity to absorb waste matter and heat. Although experts disagree on how much usable high-quality energy we have, supplies of nonrenewable coal, oil, natural gas, and uranium are clearly finite. There is increasing evidence that affordable supplies of oil, our most widely used supplementary energy resource, may be used up in several decades (Section 16-3).

"Ah," you say, "but don't we have an essentially infinite supply of high-quality solar energy flowing to the earth?" The problem is that the quantity of sunlight reaching a particular small area of the earth's surface each minute or hour is low, and it is nonexistent at night. With a proper collection and storage system, using solar energy to provide hot water and to heat a house to moderate temperatures makes good thermodynamic and economic sense. But to provide the high temperatures needed to melt metals or to produce electricity in a power plant, solar energy may not be cost-effective because it has a very low net useful energy ratio (Figure 3-17).

One promising solar energy technology that may get around this problem is the solar photovoltaic cell, which converts solar energy directly to electricity in one simple, nonpolluting step (Section 18-2). If research can lead to continued improvements in the energy efficiency of such cells and decrease their cost, roofs or walls facing the sun could be covered with these cells to meet all household electricity needs. Mass production and transportation of solar cells would require

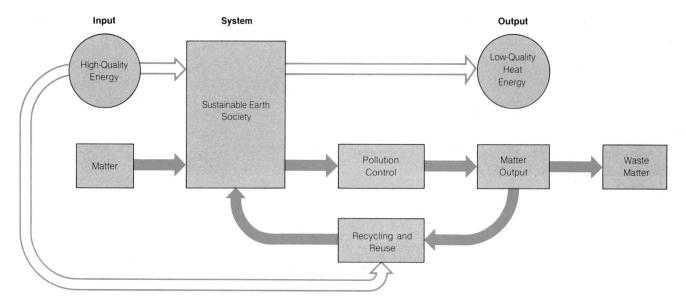

Figure 3-19 A sustainable-earth society, based on energy flow and matter recycling.

energy and matter resources, but most of the matter would come from widely abundant silicon found in sand and other minerals. The excess electricity produced by the cells during daylight can be stored in deep-cycle batteries (like those used in golf carts and marine vessels) for use when the sun isn't shining or sold to the local utility company.

If scientists and engineers can develop methods for mass-producing such cells at an affordable price (which many believe will happen sometime in the 1990s), most of the large, centralized electric power plants throughout the United States and the world might quickly become obsolete. The first country that develops and sells such a technology could rapidly become the dominant economic force in the world—helping explain why Japan is increasing its already extensive research efforts in this area. In the United States, government-supported research in photovoltaic cells was significantly expanded during the late 1970s by President Carter, but since 1980 the Reagan administration has sharply reduced this research.

Even if solar cells or some other breakthrough were to provide an essentially infinite supply of affordable useful energy, the first energy law states that we can't increase the universe's available energy supply and the second energy law states that the more energy we use to transform matter into products and to recycle these products, the more low-quality heat and waste matter we add to the environment. Thus, the more we order or "conquer" the earth, the greater the disorder or entropy we add to the environment. Although experts argue over how close we are to reaching overload limits, the laws of matter and energy indicate that such limits do exist.

Sustainable-Earth Societies The three physical laws governing matter and energy changes tell us not only what we *cannot* do but, more important, what we *can* do. These laws indicate that the best long-term solution is to shift from a throwaway society based on maximizing matter and energy flow and in the process wasting an unnecessarily large portion of the earth's resources, to a **sustainable-earth society** (Figure 3-19). Such a society would go a step further than a matter-recycling society, not only recycling and reusing much of the matter we now discard as trash but also conserving both matter and energy resources by reducing unnecessary waste and by building things that last longer and are easier to recycle, reuse, and repair. Just as important, a sustainable-earth society would cut down on the use of resources by controlling population growth. With such an approach, local, regional, and global limits of the environment to absorb low-quality heat and waste matter would not be exceeded and the depletion of vital resources would be prevented or at least delayed much further into the future.

The matter and energy laws also indicate why in the long run it makes more sense thermodynamically and economically to use input approaches rather than output approaches for controlling pollution (Section 1-3). For example, it is much easier and cheaper in the long run to remove most of the sulfur dioxide from the emissions of a coal-burning power plant before they leave the smokestack than to try to remove the gas once it has been widely dispersed in the atmosphere.

The three basic physical laws of matter and energy show that, like it or not, we are all interdependent on each other and on the other parts of nature for our survival. In the next chapter, we will apply these laws to living systems and look at some biological principles that can help us work with nature.

The second law of thermodynamics holds, I think, the supreme position among laws of nature. . . . If your theory is found to be against the second law of thermodynamics, I can give you no hope.

Arthur S. Eddington

CHAPTER SUMMARY

Matter is found in various *physical forms*—solid, liquid, and gas—and *chemical forms*—elements, compounds, and mixtures of elements and compounds. All matter is composed of uncombined or combined *atoms*, which contain a certain number of *protons, neutrons,* and *electrons*. Atoms of some elements can lose or gain one or more electrons to form positively or negatively charged *ions*. Most matter exists as *compounds:* fixed combinations of two or more atoms (*molecular compounds*) or oppositely charged ions (*ionic compounds*) of two or more different elements.

Elements and compounds can undergo *physical changes* in which their chemical composition is not changed and *chemical changes* in which they are changed into one or more different elements or compounds. According to the *law of conservation of matter,* in any physical or chemical change, matter is neither created nor destroyed but merely changed from one physical or chemical form to another.

The nuclei of certain types of atoms can undergo *nuclear changes* by spontaneously releasing one or more forms of ionizing radiation (*natural radioactivity*), splitting apart when struck by a neutron (*nuclear fission*), or combining with other nuclei at extremely high temperatures and pressures (*nuclear fusion*). Ionizing radiation, released as high-speed alpha or beta particles or high-energy gamma rays from radioactive nuclei and as high-speed neutrons from nuclear fission, can damage living cells. The degree of damage depends on the amount and length of exposure, the type of ionizing radiation, and whether it comes from radioactive materials outside or inside the body.

Energy is the ability to do work or to cause a heat transfer between two objects at different temperatures. Its many forms can be classified as either *potential energy* (stored energy) or *kinetic energy* (energy of motion). The *first law of energy* or *law of conservation of energy* states that in any physical or chemical change, in any movement of matter from one place to another, or in any change in temperature, energy is neither created nor destroyed but merely changed from one form to another. The *second law of energy* states that in any conversion of heat into useful work, some of the initial input of energy is always degraded to lower quality, less useful energy, usually low-temperature heat that flows into the environment. This means that high-quality energy, unlike matter, cannot be recycled or reused. The energy laws can be used to compare efficiencies and net useful energies of various energy alternatives.

On the basis of the law of conservation of matter and the two energy laws, scientists project that sooner or later humans will have to shift from a *throwaway society* based on the flow of both matter and energy resources to a *sustainable-earth society* based on the recycling of matter resources and the flow of energy resources—with greatly increased emphasis on reducing the unnecessary waste of such resources.

DISCUSSION TOPICS

1. Explain why we don't really consume anything, and why we can never really throw any form of matter away.

2. A tree grows and increases its mass. Explain why this isn't a violation of the law of conservation of matter.

3. Criticize the statement "Since beta particles and alpha particles can't penetrate skin, they are not harmful to humans."

4. Criticize the statement "Since we are all exposed continuously to small amounts of ionizing radiation from natural sources, there is no need to worry about the small amounts of ionizing radiation released into the environment as a result of human activities."

5. List six different types of energy that you have used today, and classify each as kinetic or potential energy.

6. Use the second energy law to explain why a barrel of oil can be used only once as a fuel.

7. Criticize the statement "Any spontaneous process results in an increase in the disorder or entropy of the system."

8. Criticize the statement "Life is an ordering process, and since it goes against the natural tendency for increasing disorder, it breaks the second law of thermodynamics."

9. Use the first and second energy laws to explain why the usable supply of energy from fossil and nuclear fuels is usually considerably less than that given by most official estimates.

10. Explain why most energy analysts urge that improving energy efficiency should form the basis of any individual, corporate, or national energy plan. Does it form a significant portion of your personal energy plan or lifestyle? Why or why not?

11. Explain how using a gas-powered chain saw to cut wood for burning in a wood stove could use more energy than that available from burning the wood. Consider materials used to make the chain saw, fuel, periodic repair, and transportation.

12. You are about to build a house. What energy supply (oil, gas, coal, or other) would you use for space heating, cooking food, refrigerating food, and heating water? Consider long-term economic and environmental impact factors.

13. List the energy services (Figure 3–8) you would like to have and note which of these *must* be furnished by electricity.

14. Do you agree with physicist Amory Lovins that the use of an electric resistance system to heat space or water is unnecessary, wasteful of precious high-quality energy resources, uneconomic, and threatens national security by encouraging the building of large coal-fired and nuclear-fueled power plants? Why or why not?

15. a. Use the law of conservation of matter to explain why a matter-recycling society will sooner or later be necessary.

    b. Use the first and second laws of energy to explain why in the long run a sustainable-earth society, not just a matter-recycling society, will be necessary.

4

Ecosystems: What Are They and How Do They Work?

1. What are the major living and nonliving components of ecosystems?

2. What happens to matter resources in an ecosystem?

3. What happens to energy resources in an ecosystem?

4. How can the role of a particular type of organism in an ecosystem be described?

If we love our children, we must love the earth with tender care and pass it on, diverse and beautiful, so that on a warm spring day 10,000 years hence they can feel peace in a sea of grass, can watch a bee visit a flower, can hear a sandpiper call in the sky, and can find joy in being alive.

Hugh H. Iltis

What plants and animals live in a forest or a pond? How do they get the matter and energy resources needed to stay alive? How do these plants and animals interact with one another and with their physical environment? What changes will this forest or pond undergo through time?

Ecology is the science that attempts to answer such questions. In 1866 German biologist Ernst Haeckel coined the term *ecology* from two Greek words: *oikos*, meaning "house" or "place to live," and *logos*, meaning "study of." Literally, then, ecology is the study of living things or organisms in their home. In more formal terms, **ecology** is the study of interactions among organisms and between organisms and the physical and chemical factors making up their environment. This study is usually carried out as the examination of **ecosystems:** forests, deserts, ponds, oceans, or any self-regulating set of plants and animals interacting with one another and with their nonliving environment. This chapter will consider the major nonliving and living components of ecosystems and how they interact. The next two chapters will consider major types of ecosystems, and the changes they can undergo as a result of natural events and human activities.

4-1 THE BIOSPHERE AND ECOSYSTEMS

The Earth's Life-Support System What keeps plants and animals alive on this tiny planet as it hurtles through space at a speed of 66,000 miles per hour? The general answer to this question is that life on earth

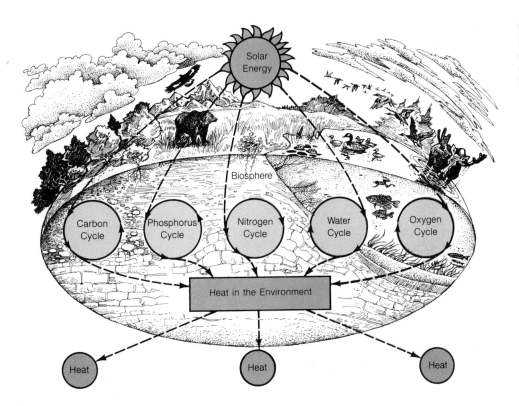

Figure 4-1 Life on earth depends on the cycling of critical chemicals (solid lines) and the one-way flow of energy through the biosphere (dashed lines).

depends on two fundamental processes: *matter cycling* and the *one-way flow of high-quality energy* from the sun, through materials and living things on or near the earth's surface, and into space as low-quality heat (Figure 4-1).

All forms of life depend for their existence on the multitude of materials that compose the **(1)** solid **lithosphere,** consisting of the upper surface or crust of the earth, containing soil and deposits of matter and energy resources, and an inner mantle and core, **(2)** the gaseous **atmosphere** extending above the earth's surface, **(3)** the **hydrosphere,** containing all of the earth's moisture as liquid water, ice, and small amounts of water vapor in the atmosphere, and **(4)** the **biosphere,** consisting of parts of the lithosphere, atmosphere, and hydrosphere in which living organisms can be found (Figures 4-2 and 4-3).

Human life and other forms of life whose existence we can threaten also depend on the **culturesphere:** the use of human ingenuity and knowledge based on past experience to extract, produce, and manage the use of matter, energy, and biological resources to enhance human survival and life quality. A major input of ecology into the culturesphere is that all forms of life on earth are directly or indirectly interconnected. This means that to enhance long-term human survival and life quality, we must not blindly destroy other forms of plant and animal life—we must learn to work with, not against, nature.

The biosphere contains all the water, minerals, oxygen, nitrogen, phosphorus, and other nutrients that living things need. For example, your body consists of about 70% water obtained from the hydrosphere, small amounts of nitrogen and oxygen gases continually breathed in from the atmosphere, and various chemicals whose building blocks come mostly from the lithosphere. If the earth were an apple, the biosphere would be no thicker than the apple's skin. Everything in this "skin of life" is interdependent: air helps purify water and keeps plants and animals alive, water keeps plants and animals alive, plants keep animals alive and help renew the air and soil, and the soil keeps plants and many animals alive and helps purify water. *The goal of ecology is to find out how everything in the biosphere is related.*

The Realm of Ecology Ecology is primarily concerned with interactions among five of the levels of organization of matter shown in Figure 3-1 (page 45): organisms, populations, communities, ecosystems, and the biosphere. An **organism** is any form of life. Although biologists classify the earth's organisms in anywhere from 5 to 20 categories, in this book it is only necessary to classify organisms as plants or animals. Plants range from microscopic, one-celled, floating and drifting plants known as phytoplankton to the largest of all living things—the giant sequoia trees of western North America. Animals range in size from floating and drifting zooplankton (which feed on phytoplankton) to the 14-foot-high, male African elephant and the 100-foot-long blue whale.

Figure 4-2 Our life-support system: the general structure of the earth.

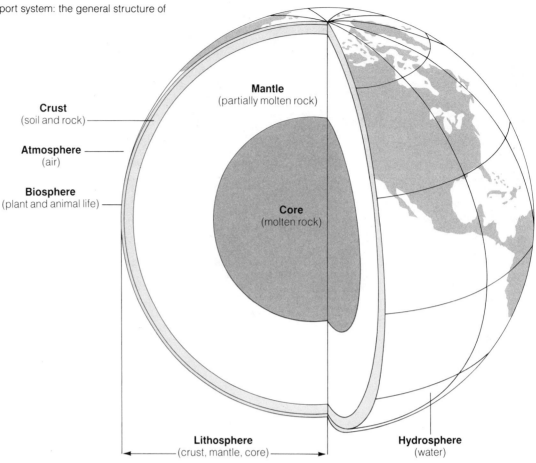

Crust
(soil and rock)

Atmosphere
(air)

Biosphere
(plant and animal life)

Mantle
(partially molten rock)

Core
(molten rock)

Lithosphere
(crust, mantle, core)

Hydrosphere
(water)

All organisms of the same kind constitute a **species.** For those organisms that reproduce sexually, a species can also be defined as all organisms potentially capable of interbreeding. Worldwide, it is estimated that are 5 million to 10 million different plant and animal species. Some biologists put the estimate as high as 50 million species, with 30 million of these being insects. So far about 1.7 million of the earth's species have been described and named, and about 10,000 new species are added to the list each year. One-fourth of these catalogued species are plants and the remainder are animals; 44% of the animals are species of insects.

Each species is composed of smaller units, known as **populations:** groups of individual organisms of the same species that occupy particular areas at given times. All the striped bass in a pond, gray squirrels in a forest, white oak trees in a forest, people in a country, or people in the world constitute particular populations.

Each organism and population has a **habitat:** the place or type of place where it naturally or normally thrives. A **community,** in ecological terms, is made up of all the populations of plant and animal species living and interacting in a given habitat or area at a par-

ticular time. Examples include all the plants and animals found in a forest, a pond, a desert, or an aquarium.

An **ecosystem** is the combination of a community and the chemical and physical factors making up its nonliving environment. An ecosystem can be a tropical rain forest, an ocean, a lake, a desert, a field of corn, a fallen log, a terrarium, or a puddle of water as long as it consists of a self-regulating community of plants and animals interacting with one another and with their nonliving environment. All of the earth's ecosystems together make up the biosphere (Figure 4-3).

The differences among ecosystems found in various parts of the the world are caused by differences in average temperature, average precipitation, and availability of life-sustaining chemicals or nutrients from the soil, water, and air. Although no two are exactly alike, ecosystems can be classified into general types that contain similar types of plants and animals interacting with each other and with their nonliving environment in similar ways. Major land ecosystems such as forests, grasslands, and deserts are called **terrestrial ecosystems** or **biomes.** Ponds, lakes, rivers, oceans, and other major ecosystems found in the hydrosphere

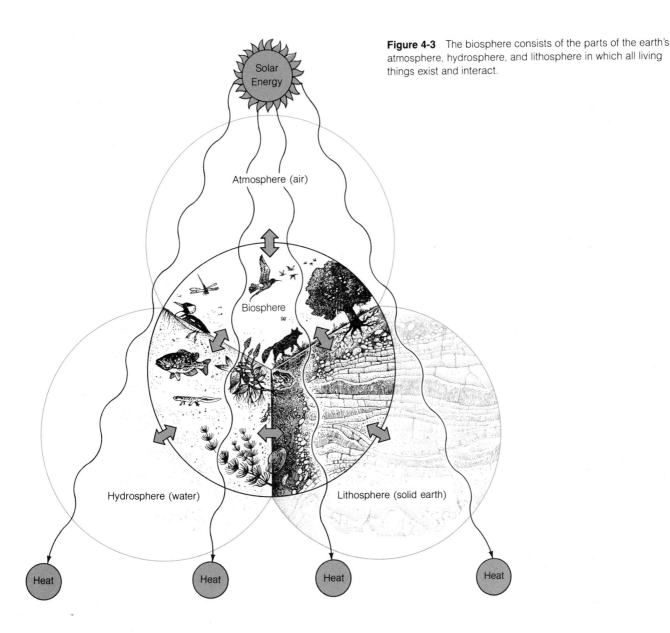

Solar Energy

Atmosphere (air)

Biosphere

Hydrosphere (water)

Lithosphere (solid earth)

Heat

Heat

Heat

Heat

are called **aquatic ecosystems.** The next chapter is devoted to a closer look at key characteristics of the two major types of ecosystems.

Components of Ecosystems Ecosystems consist of various nonliving (abiotic) and living (biotic) components. Figures 4-4 and 4-5 are greatly simplified diagrams showing some key living and nonliving components of ecosystems found in a field and in a freshwater pond.

The nonliving components of an ecosystem include various physical factors (such as sunlight, shade, precipitation, wind, terrain, temperature, and water currents) and chemical factors (all of the elements and compounds in the atmosphere, hydrosphere, and lithosphere that are essential for living organisms). The type, quantity, and variation of these physical and

chemical factors determine the types and numbers of plants and animals that can exist in a particular ecosystem. In turn, the animals and plants in an ecosystem have an impact on their physical and chemical environment. Grasses and trees help form soil, hold it in place, buffer the wind, absorb and hold water, and make the climate cooler. Animals such as birds and bees scatter seeds and pollinate various plants.

The different types of plant and animal organisms that make up the living components of an ecosystem are classified as producers, consumers, and decomposers on the basis of their sources of energy and matter resources. **Producers** are plants that can manufacture their own food. Most are chlorophyll-containing green plants that through photosynthesis capture solar energy and transform it into chemical energy stored in simple sugar molecules, such as glucose ($C_6H_{12}O_6$), and into oxygen gas (O_2) released to the

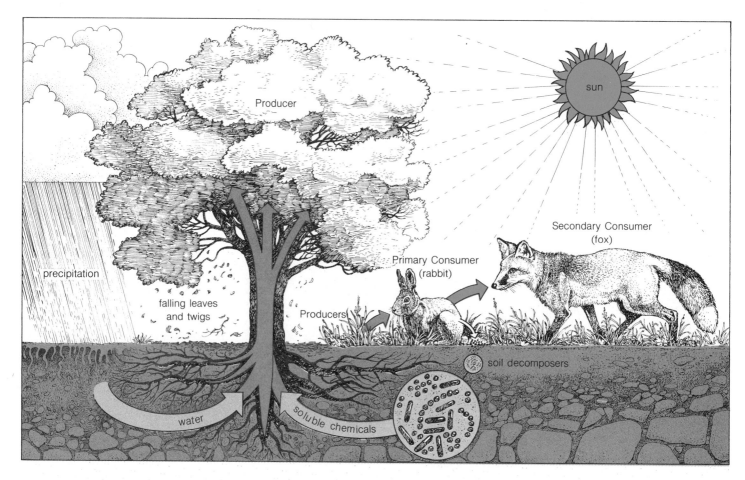

Figure 4-4 The major components of an ecosystem found in a field.

atmosphere for use by animals. The glucose molecules are used by the plant as a source of energy and to produce other, more complex molecules needed for its survival and reproduction.

Since producer plants alone can manufacture food, all animals must rely on them for nourishment and oxygen: *All flesh is grass,* so to speak. Organisms, mostly animals, that feed either directly or indirectly on producers are called **consumers.** Depending on their food sources, consumers fall into four major classes: **(1) herbivores** ("plant eaters"), *primary consumers,* which feed directly on all or part of a plant; **(2) carnivores** ("animal eaters"), *secondary and higher level consumers,* which feed on plant-eating animals; **(3) omnivores** ("plant and meat eaters"), such as pigs, rats, cockroaches, and humans, which can eat both plants and animals; and **(4) decomposers,** microconsumers, such as bacteria, fungi (mostly molds and mushrooms), soil insects, and worms, which obtain nutrients by breaking down complex molecules in the wastes and dead bodies of other organisms into simpler chemicals, some of which are returned to the soil and water for reuse by producers.

In Figure 4-4 the rabbit that feeds on green plants is a primary consumer (herbivore) and the fox that eats the rabbit is a secondary consumer (carnivore). Higher levels of consumers also exist. In Figure 4-5 the fish that feeds on zooplankton (primary consumers) is a secondary consumer and the turtle that feeds on this fish is a tertiary consumer.

Although the life of an individual organism depends on matter flow and energy flow through its body, the community of plants and animals in an ecosystem survives primarily by a combination of matter cycling and energy flow (Figure 4-6). Figure 4-6 also shows that decomposers are responsible for completing the cycle in which vital chemicals in living organisms are broken down and returned to the soil, water, and air in forms reusable as nutrients.

Although the biosphere as a whole cycles almost all the chemical nutrients needed by living organisms, no individual ecosystem completely cycles all the chemicals it needs. More stable ecosystems such as mature forests recycle most nutrients they need; younger, less stable ecosystems such as open fields, however, recycle only a portion of the elements and compounds they need and thus must obtain some nutrients from other ecosystems.

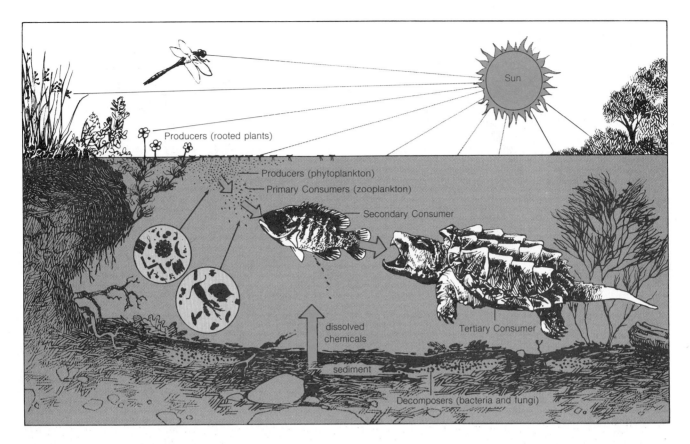

Figure 4-5 The major components of a freshwater pond ecosystem.

4-2 MATTER CYCLING IN ECOSYSTEMS: CARBON, OXYGEN, NITROGEN, PHOSPHORUS, SULFUR, AND WATER

Biogeochemical Cycles Of the earth's 92 naturally occurring elements, only 20 to 30 are constituents of living organisms and thus are cycled through the biosphere. In chemical terms, life can almost be summed up in six words: *carbon, oxygen, hydrogen, nitrogen, phosphorus,* and *sulfur*. These chemicals as elements and compounds make up 97% of the mass of your body and more than 95% of the mass of all living organisms. The remaining 14 to 24 elements needed in some form for the survival and good health of plants and animals are required only in relatively small or trace amounts. The importance of a particular chemical to a living organism varies with the physical and chemical form and location of the chemical. For example, plants obtain most of their carbon in the form of carbon dioxide gas from the atmosphere or water and most of their nitrogen and phosphorus, as nitrate ions

(NO_3^-) and phosphate ions (PO_4^{3-}) from soil water in which compounds containing these ions are dissolved.

Only a small portion of the earth's chemicals exist in forms useful to plants and animals. Fortunately, the essentially fixed supply of elements and compounds needed for life is continuously cycled through the air, water, soil, plants, and animals and converted to useful forms in **biogeochemical** cycles (*bio* meaning "living," *geo* for water, rocks, and soil, and *chemical* for the matter changing from one form to another). These cycles, driven directly or indirectly by incoming energy from the sun, include the carbon, oxygen, nitrogen, phosphorus, sulfur, and hydrologic cycles (Figure 4-1).

Thus, a chemical may be part of an organism at one moment and part of its nonliving environment at another moment. This means that one of the oxygen molecules you just inhaled may be one inhaled previously by you, your grandmother, King Tut thousands of years ago, or a dinosaur millions of years ago. Similarly, some of the carbon atoms in the skin covering your right hand may once have been part of a leaf, a dinosaur hide, or a limestone rock. Without the biogeochemical cycles the entire world would soon be

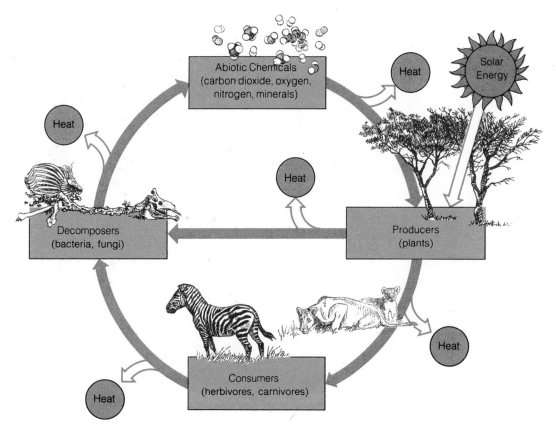

Figure 4-6 Summary of ecosystem structure and function. The major structural components (energy, chemicals, and organisms) of an ecosystem are connected through the functions of energy flow (open arrows) and matter cycling (solid arrows).

knee-deep in plant litter, dead animal bodies, animal wastes, and garbage.

Carbon and Oxygen Cycles Carbon is the basic building block of the large organic molecules necessary for life, including simple sugars or carbohydrates (such as glucose), complex carbohydrates, fats, proteins, and nucleic acids such as DNA. DNA molecules in the cells of plants and animals carry genetic information and chemical instructions for manufacturing various proteins living organisms need.

Most land plants obtain their carbon by absorbing carbon dioxide gas, which makes up 0.03% of the atmosphere, through pores in their leaves. They obtain the oxygen atoms they need from the oxygen in carbon dioxide and from water molecules in soil or bodies of water. The ocean's microscopic floating plants, known collectively as phytoplankton, get their carbon from atmospheric carbon dioxide that has dissolved in ocean water.

Chlorophyll molecules and some other pigments in the cells of green plants absorb solar energy and use it to combine carbon dioxide with water to form glucose along with oxygen gas. This complex process in which radiant energy from the sun is converted into chemical energy stored in plant tissue is called **photosynthesis.** Its 80 to 100 different, interconnected

chemical changes can be be summarized as follows:

Photosynthesis

$$\text{carbon dioxide} + \text{water} + \textbf{solar energy} \rightarrow \text{glucose} + \text{oxygen}$$

$$6\,CO_2 + 6\,H_2O + \textbf{solar energy} \rightarrow C_6H_{12}O_6 + 6\,O_2$$

The glucose molecules are then converted by the plant itself or by animals eating the plant into more complex sugars, starches, proteins, and fats.

Plants and animals transform a portion of glucose and other, more complex, carbon-containing molecules they synthesize (plants) or eat (consumers) back into carbon dioxide and water by the process of **cellular respiration.** The chemical energy released in this complex process drives the physical and chemical changes needed for plants and animals to survive, grow, and reproduce. The almost 100 interconnected chemical changes involved can be summarized as:

Cellular Respiration

$$\text{glucose} + \text{oxygen} \rightarrow \text{carbon dioxide} + \text{water} + \textbf{energy}$$

$$C_6H_{12}O_6 + 6\,O_2 \rightarrow 6\,CO_2 + 6\,H_2O + \textbf{energy}$$

The carbon dioxide released by cellular respiration in all plants and animals is returned to the atmosphere

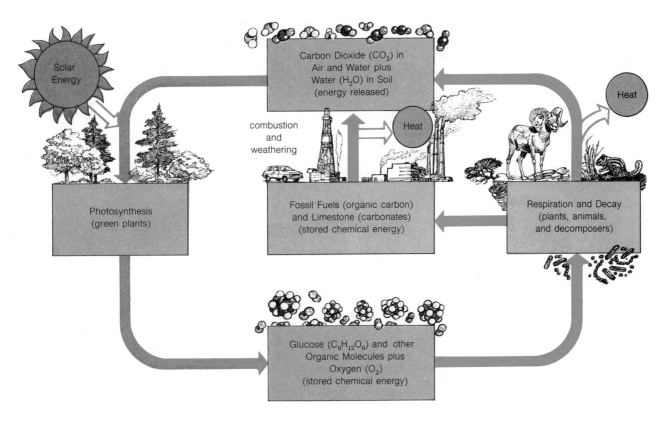

Figure 4-7 Simplified diagram of the carbon and oxygen cycles, showing matter cycling (solid arrows) and one-way energy flow (open arrows).

and water for reuse by producers. Although the overall chemical reaction involved in cellular respiration is the reverse of that for photosynthesis, many of the detailed chemical reactions in the two processes are different.

Photosynthesis and cellular respiration are the basis of the **carbon and oxygen cycles,** shown in greatly simplified form in Figure 4-7, which illustrates some of the ways plants are interdependent. Through these two interconnected cycles, plants produce food and oxygen needed by animals and absorb carbon dioxide given off by animals.

Figure 4-7 also shows that some of the earth's carbon is tied up for long periods in fossil fuels—coal, petroleum, natural gas, peat, oil shale, tar sands, and lignite—formed over millions of years in the lithosphere. The carbon in these mineral deposits remains locked deep in the earth's crust until it is released to the atmosphere as carbon dioxide when fossil fuels are extracted and burned. Some of the earth's carbon is also locked for millions of years in deposits of carbonate rocks below the seafloor, until movements of the earth's crust expose these rocks as part of an island or a continent. The carbon then reenters the cycle very slowly through erosion and other physical and chemical weathering processes that release it as carbon dioxide into the atmosphere.

Humans intervene in the carbon and oxygen cycles in two ways that increase the average amount of carbon dioxide in the atmosphere. First, we remove forests and other vegetation without sufficient replanting so that fewer plants are available worldwide to convert carbon dioxide in the atmosphere to organic nutrients. Second, we burn fossil fuels and wood.

Nitrogen Cycle Living things need nitrogen to manufacture proteins. Thus, the growth of many plants can be limited by a lack of nitrogen available from the soil. Too little nitrogen can also cause malnutrition in humans because many of the body's essential functions require nitrogen-containing molecules such as proteins, DNA, and some vitamins.

The nitrogen gas that makes up about 78% of the volume of the earth's atmosphere is useless to most plants and animals. Fortunately, nitrogen gas is converted into water-soluble ionic compounds containing nitrate ions, which are taken up by plant roots as part of the **nitrogen cycle,** shown in simplified form in Figure 4-8. This *nitrogen fixation*—that is, the conversion of atmospheric nitrogen gas into forms useful to plants—is accomplished by **(1)** soil bacteria, **(2)** rhizobium bacteria living in small swellings called nodules on the roots of alfalfa, clover, peas, beans, and other leguminous plants, **(3)** blue-green algae in water

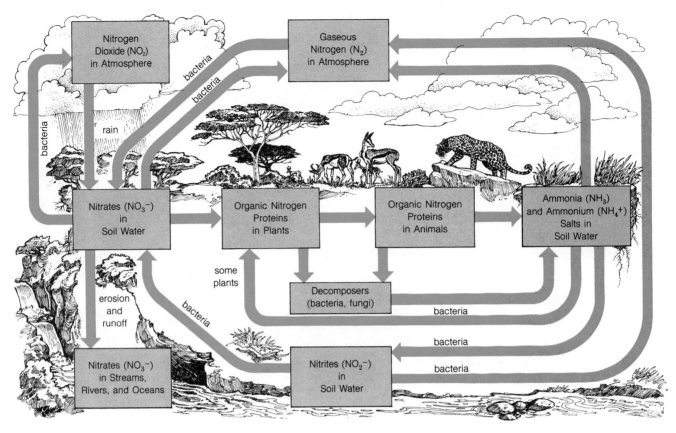

Figure 4-8 The nitrogen cycle (energy flow not shown).

and soil, and **(4)** lightning, which converts nitrogen gas and oxygen gas in the atmosphere to forms that return to the earth as nitrate ions in rainfall and other types of precipitation.

Plants convert nitrates obtained from soil water into large, nitrogen-containing molecules such as proteins and nucleic acids necessary for life and good health. Animals get most of the proteins and other nitrogen-containing molecules they need by eating plants or other animals that have eaten plants. When plants and animals die, decomposers break down the nitrogen-containing molecules into ammonia gas and water-soluble salts containing ammonium ions (NH_4^+). Other specialized groups of bacteria then convert these forms of nitrogen back into nitrate ions in the soil and into nitrogen gas, which is released to the atmosphere to begin the cycle again.

Humans intervene in the nitrogen cycle in several important ways. First, large quantities of NO and NO_2 are added to the atmosphere when fossil fuels are burned in power plants and vehicles. These oxides of nitrogen can react with other chemicals in the atmosphere under the influence of sunlight to form photochemical smog and nitric acid, a major component of acid deposition, commonly known as acid rain (Section 19-2). Second, nitrogen gas and hydrogen gas are

converted by an industrial process into ammonia gas ($N_2 + 3H_2 + $ **energy** $\rightarrow 2NH_3$), which is then converted to ammonium compounds used as commercial fertilizer. Third, mineral deposits of compounds containing nitrate ions are mined and used as commercial fertilizers. Fourth, excess nitrate ions are added to aquatic ecosystems mostly from the runoff of animal wastes from livestock feedlots, the runoff of commercial nitrate fertilizers from cropland, and the discharge of untreated and treated municipal sewage. This excess supply of nitrate plant nutrients can stimulate extremely rapid growth of algae and other aquatic plants, which can deplete the water of dissolved oxygen gas and cause massive fish kills (Section 20-2).

Phosphorus Cycle Phosphorus, mainly in the form of phosphate ions, is an essential nutrient of both plants and animals. It is a major constituent of the genetic material coded in DNA molecules and the main component of bones and teeth. It is also used in some commercial fertilizers.

Various forms of phosphorus are cycled through the lower atmosphere, water, soil, and living organisms by the **phosphorus cycle,** shown in Figure 4-9. The major reservoirs of phosphorus are phosphate

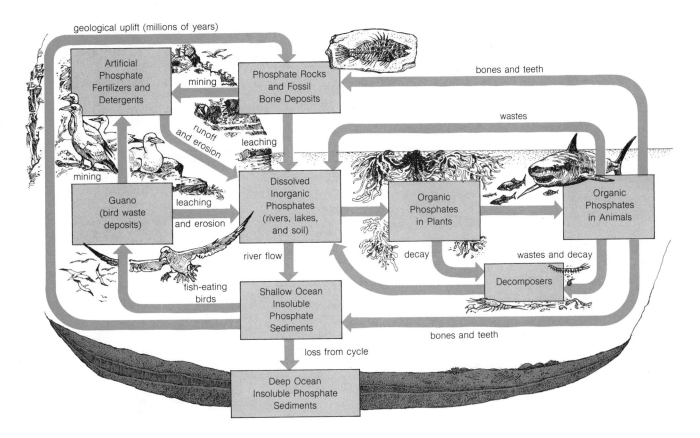

Figure 4-9 The phosphorus cycle (energy flow not shown).

rock deposits on land and in shallow ocean sediments. Some phosphates released by the slow breakdown of phosphate rock deposits are dissolved in soil water and taken up by plant roots. Animals get their phosphorus by eating plants or animals that have eaten plants. Animal wastes and the decay products of dead animals and plants return much of this phosphorus to the soil, rivers, and eventually to the ocean bottom as insoluble forms of phosphate rock. Some phosphate is returned to the land as *guano*—the phosphate-rich manure from fish-eating birds such as pelicans, gannets, and cormorants (Figure 4-10). This return, however, is small compared to the much larger amounts of phosphate eroding from the land to the oceans each year from natural processes and human activities.

Humans intervene in the phosphorus cycle in several ways. First, large quantities of phosphate rock are dug up, mostly from shallow ocean deposits, and used to produce commercial fertilizers and detergents. Second, discharge from sewage treatment plants and runoff of commercial fertilizers can overload aquatic ecosystems with phosphate ions. As in the case of nitrate ions, an excessive supply of phosphate ions can cause explosive growth of blue-green algae and other plants that can disrupt life in aquatic ecosystems.

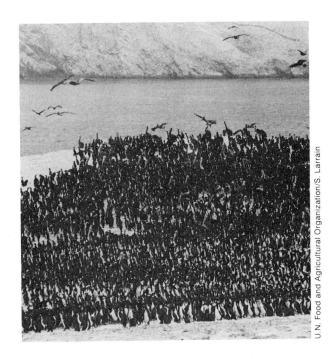

Figure 4-10 "Guano islands" off the coast of Peru are kept as sanctuaries for fish-eating birds, whose droppings (guano) are rich in nitrates and phosphates. The birds return some of these chemicals from the sea to the land as part of the biogeochemical cycles.

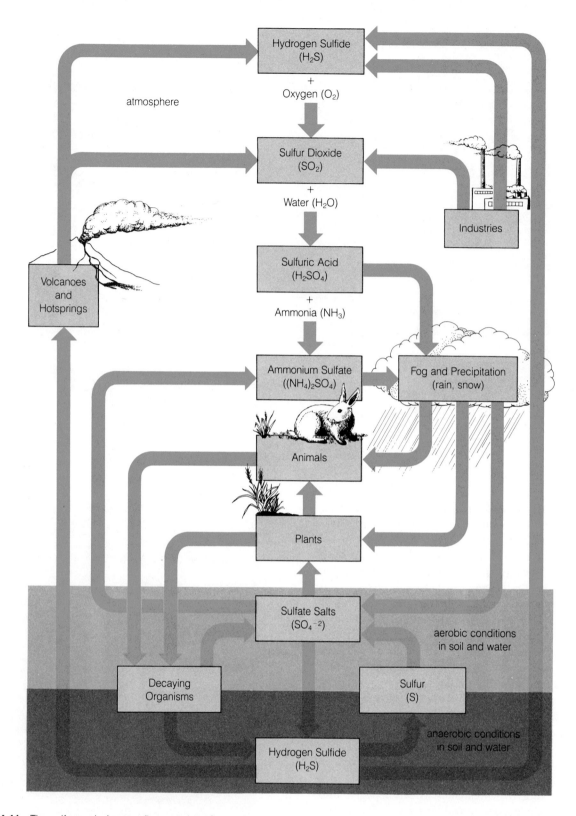

Figure 4-11 The sulfur cycle (energy flow not shown).

Sulfur Cycle Sulfur is transformed to various compounds and circulated through the biosphere in the **sulfur cycle** (Figure 4-11). It enters the atmosphere from natural sources as **(1)** hydrogen sulfide (H$_2$S), a colorless, highly poisonous gas with a rotten-egg smell, from active volcanoes and the decay of organic matter in swamps, bogs, and tidal flats; **(2)** sulfur dioxide (SO$_2$), a colorless, suffocating gas, from active volca-

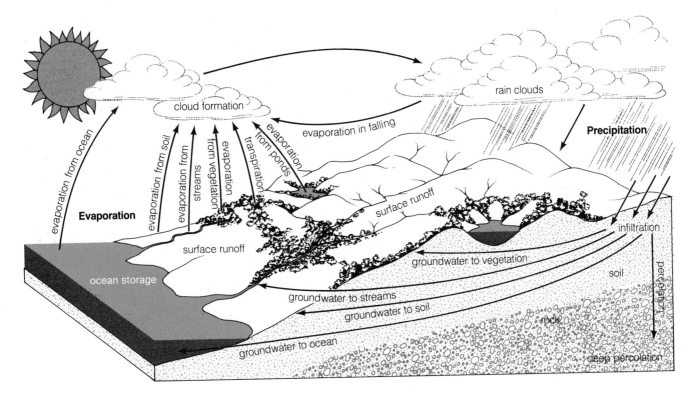

Figure 4-12 The hydrologic cycle. (U.S. Department of Agriculture)

noes; and **(3)** particles of sulfate salts, like ammonium sulfate, from sea spray. Except for occasional volcanic eruptions, these natural additions of sulfur compounds to the atmosphere are widely dispersed and usually are diluted so that they do not exceed the normal levels in clean, dry air.

About one-third of all sulfur compounds and 99% percent of the sulfur dioxide reaching the atmosphere from all sources come from human activities. About two-thirds of the human-related input of sulfur dioxide into the atmosphere results when sulfur-containing coal and oil are burned to produce electric power. The remaining third comes from industrial processes such as petroleum refining and the smelting of sulfur-containing ore compounds of metals such as copper, lead, and zinc to convert them to the free metal.

Water, or Hydrologic, Cycle The **hydrologic, or water, cycle,** which collects, purifies, and distributes the earth's fixed supply of water, is shown in simplified form in Figure 4-12. Solar energy and gravity continuously move water among the ocean, air, land, and living organisms through evaporation, condensation, precipitation, and runoff back to the sea to begin the cycle again.

When incoming solar energy warms water on or near the surfaces of oceans, rivers, lakes, soil, and plant leaves, the water evaporates and enters the atmosphere as water vapor, leaving behind dissolved impurities. Water and various dissolved compounds in the soil are drawn up through the roots of plants into leaves and other surfaces. When warmed by the sun, water in the exposed parts of plants passes through leaf pores in a process called **transpiration** and then evaporates into the atmosphere. This transfer of liquid water in plant tissue and soil to water vapor in the atmosphere through a combination of transpiration and evaporation is called **evapotranspiration.**

Fresh water removed from the oceans and other bodies of water is returned from the atmosphere to the land and bodies of water as **precipitation** in the forms of rain, sleet, hail, and snow. Some of this fresh water becomes locked in glaciers, and some sinks downward or percolates, through the soil, where it may remain for hundreds to thousands of years as groundwater in slow-flowing, slowly renewed, underground reservoirs. When rain falls faster than it can infiltrate downward into the soil, it collects in puddles and ditches and runs off into nearby streams, rivers, and lakes, which carry water back to the oceans, completing the cycle. This runoff of fresh water from the land causes the weathering (slow disintegration) of rock and erosion of soil, which move various chemicals through portions of other biogeochemical cycles.

The hydrologic cycle is influenced by terrestrial organisms in many ways. Plants covering the soil decrease the impact of raindrops and reduce the rate of erosion. Various types of matter in the soil act as sponges to hold water in place for use by plants. When

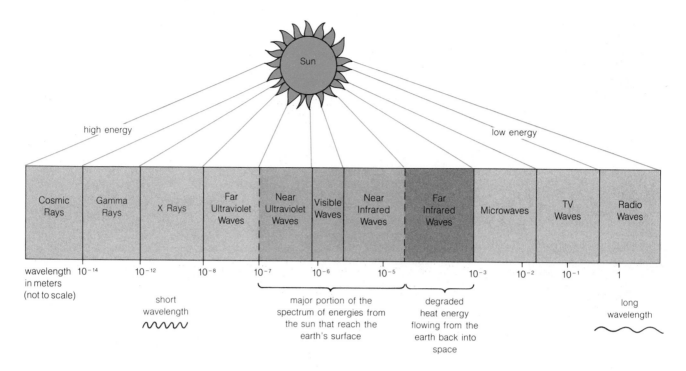

Figure 4-13 The sun radiates a wide range of energies with different wavelengths and energy contents. Since much of this incoming radiant energy is either reflected or absorbed by the atmosphere, little of the harmful shorter-wavelength radiant energy actually reaches the earth's surface.

some of the water obtained by plants from the soil is transpired and evaporated into the atmosphere, the water vapor has a cooling effect on climate.

Humans also intervene in the water cycle. Large quantities of fresh water are withdrawn from rivers and lakes and pumped from underground supplies for irrigation, manufacturing, and domestic uses. In heavily populated or heavily irrigated areas, excessive withdrawals have led to groundwater depletion or intrusion of ocean saltwater into underground water supplies. The clearing of land for agriculture, mining, roads, parking lots, construction, and other activities can increase the rate at which water returns from the land to bodies of water, increase soil erosion, reduce the seepage that recharges groundwater supplies, and increase the risk of flooding.

4-3 ENERGY FLOW IN THE BIOSPHERE AND ECOSYSTEMS

The Sun: Source of Energy for Life The source of the radiant energy that sustains all life on earth is the sun. It lights and warms the earth and provides energy used by green plants to synthesize the compounds that keep them alive and serve as food for almost all other organisms. Solar energy also powers the bio-

geochemical cycles and drives the climate and weather systems that distribute heat and fresh water over the earth's surface.

The sun is a gigantic gaseous fireball composed mostly of hydrogen and helium gases. Temperatures in its inner core reach 30 million degrees Fahrenheit and pressures there are so enormous that the hydrogen nuclei found there are compressed and fused to form helium gas. This thermonuclear, or nuclear fusion, reaction (Section 3-2) taking place at the center of the sun continually releases massive amounts of energy, which pass through a thick zone of hot gases surrounding the inner core and eventually reach the surface. There the energy is radiated into space as a spectrum of heat, light, and other forms of *radiant energy* (Figure 4-13) that travel outward in all directions through space at a speed of 300,000 kilometers (186,000 miles) per hour.

Each type of radiant energy or electromagnetic radiation shown in Figure 4-13 can be viewed as a wave with a different **wavelength:** the distance between the crests of one wave and the next. The longer the wavelength, the lower the energy content of a wave of radiant energy. This explains why the lower-energy, longer-wavelength types of radiant energy shown in the right portion of Figure 4-13 are not harmful to most living organisms, whereas the higher-energy, shorter-wavelength types of radiant energy in the left portion are forms of ionizing radiation harmful to most

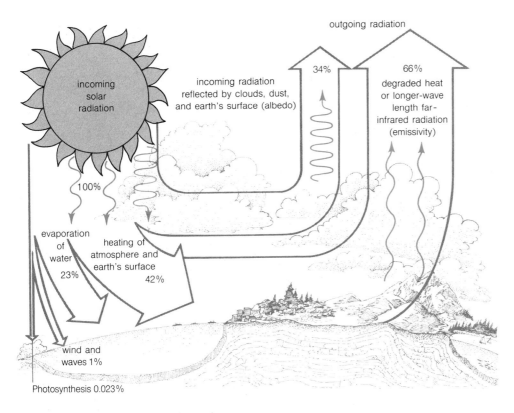

incoming solar radiation

outgoing radiation

incoming radiation reflected by clouds, dust, and earth's surface (albedo)

34%

66% degraded heat or longer-wave length far-infrared radiation (emissivity)

100%

evaporation of water 23%

heating of atmosphere and earth's surface 42%

wind and waves 1%

Photosynthesis 0.023%

Figure 4-14 The flow of energy to and from the earth.

organisms (Section 3-2). Fortunately, most of these harmful forms of radiant energy from the sun are absorbed by molecules of ozone (O_3) in the upper atmosphere and water vapor in the lower atmosphere. Without this screening effect, most life on earth could not exist.

Energy Flow in the Biosphere   Figure 4-14 shows what happens to the solar radiant energy reaching the earth. About 34% of incoming solar radiation is immediately reflected back to space by clouds, chemicals, and dust in the atmosphere and by the earth's surface. Most of the remaining 66% warms the atmosphere and land, evaporates water and cycles it through the biosphere, and generates winds; a tiny fraction (0.023%) is captured by green plants and used to make glucose essential to life.

Most of the incoming solar radiation not reflected away is degraded into longer-wavelength heat, or far-infrared radiation, in accordance with the second law of energy, and flows into space. The amount of energy returning to space as heat is affected by the presence of molecules such as water, carbon dioxide, and ozone and by solid particulate matter in the atmosphere. These substances, acting as gatekeepers, allow short-wavelength radiant energy from the sun to pass through the atmosphere and back into space, but they absorb and reradiate some of the resulting longer-wavelength

heat (far-infrared radiant energy) back toward the earth's surface.

There is growing concern that human activities affect global climate patterns by disrupting the rate at which incoming solar energy flows through the biosphere and returns to space as longer-wavelength heat. For example, according to some scientists, increases in the average levels of carbon dioxide in the earth's atmosphere due primarily to the burning of fossil fuels and land clearing may trap increasing amounts of far-infrared radiation that otherwise would escape into space and raise the average temperature of the atmosphere. Other scientists theorize that particulate matter emitted into the atmosphere from volcanic explosions and human activities such as land clearing and smokestack, chimney, and automobile emissions could reflect significant amounts of sunlight away from the upper atmosphere to lower the average temperature of the atmosphere. These possible effects of human activities on climate are discussed more fully in Section 19-5.

Energy Flow in Ecosystems: Food Chains and Food Webs   In general, the study of the flow of energy and the cycling of matter through an ecosystem is the study of what eats or decomposes what. There is no waste in ecosystems. All organisms, dead or alive, are potential sources of food for other organisms. A cat-

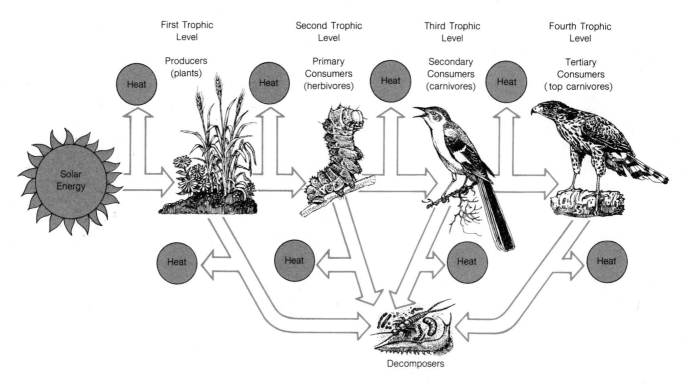

First Trophic Level — Producers (plants)

Second Trophic Level — Primary Consumers (herbivores)

Third Trophic Level — Secondary Consumers (carnivores)

Fourth Trophic Level — Tertiary Consumers (top carnivores)

Solar Energy

Heat

Decomposers

Figure 4-15 A food chain. The arrows show how chemical energy in food flows through various trophic levels, with most of the high-quality chemical energy being degraded to low-quality heat in accordance with the second law of energy.

erpillar eats a leaf; a robin eats the caterpillar; a hawk eats the robin. When the plant, caterpillar, robin, and hawk die, they are in turn consumed by decomposers. A series of organisms, each eating or decomposing the preceding one is called a **food chain** (Figure 4-15), a one-way flow of chemical energy from producers to consumers and eventually to decomposers. Three other common terrestrial food chains are rice → humans; leaves → bacteria (decomposers); and grass → steer → human. Most aquatic food chains, such as phytoplankton → zooplankton → perch → bass → human, involve more energy transfer steps.

All organisms that share the same general types of food in a food chain are said to be at the same **trophic level.** As shown in Figure 4-15, all producers belong to the first trophic level; all primary consumers, whether feeding on living or dead producers, belong to the second trophic level; and so on.

The food chain concept is useful for tracing chemical cycling and energy flow in an ecosystem, but simple food chains like the one shown in Figure 4-15 rarely exist by themselves. Many animals feed on several different types of food at the same trophic level. In addition, omnivores eat several different kinds of plants and animals at several trophic levels. Thus, the organisms in a natural ecosystem are involved in a complex network of many interconnected food chains, called a **food web.** A simplified food web in a terrestrial ecosystem is diagrammed in Figure 4-16, which

shows that trophic levels can be assigned in food webs just as in food chains.

The most obvious form of species interaction in food chains and webs is **predation:** An individual organism of one species, known as the **predator,** captures and feeds on parts or all of an organism of another species, the **prey.** We act as predators whenever we eat any plant or animal food. In most cases a predator species has more than one prey species. Likewise, a single prey species may have several different predators. Each species has certain traits that help it catch prey and/or avoid predators.

Food Chains, Food Webs, and the Second Law of Energy At each transfer from one trophic level to another in a food chain or web, work is done, low-quality heat is given off to the environment, and the availability of high-quality energy to organisms at the next trophic level is reduced. This reduction is the result of the inexorable energy-quality tax imposed by the second law of energy.

The percentage of the available high-quality energy transferred from one trophic level to another varies from 2% to 30% depending on the type of species and the ecosystem in which it is found. However, as an average, only about 10% of the high-quality chemical energy available at one trophic level is transferred and stored in usable form as chemical energy in the bodies

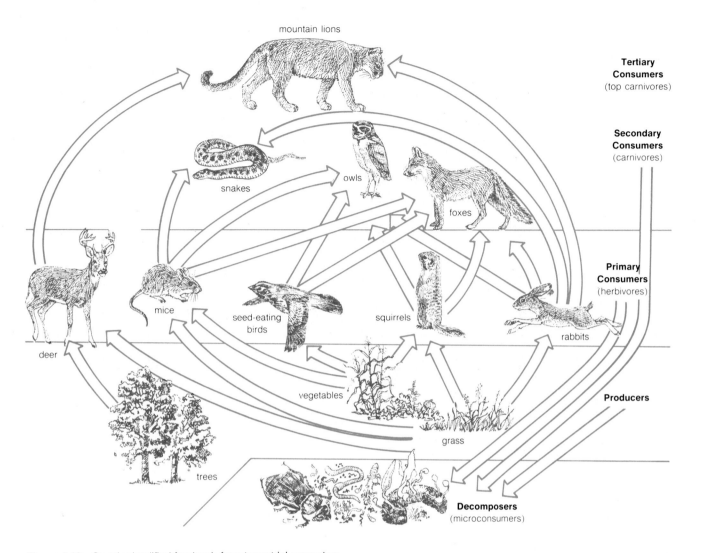

Figure 4-16 Greatly simplified food web for a terrestrial ecosystem.

of the organisms at the next level. The remaining 90% is eventually degraded and lost as low-quality heat to the environment in accordance with the second law of energy.

Figure 4-17 illustrates this loss of usable high-quality energy at each step in a simple food chain. The resulting pyramids of energy and energy loss show that the greater the number of steps in a food chain, the greater the cumulative loss of usable high-quality energy. The pyramid of numbers shows that in moving from lower to higher trophic levels, the total number of organisms that can be supported usually decreases drastically. For example, a million phytoplankton in a small pond may support 10,000 zooplankton, which in turn may support 100 perch, which might feed one human for a month or so. The pyramid of numbers helps explain why in a forest or field we find more plants than plant-eating rabbits and more plant-eating rabbits than rabbit-eating foxes.

An important principle affecting the ultimate population size of an omnivorous species such as humans emerges from a consideration of the loss of available energy at successively higher trophic levels in food chains and webs: *The shorter the food chain, the less the loss of usable energy*. This means that a larger population of humans can be supported if people shorten the food chain by eating grains directly (for example, rice → human) rather than eating animals that fed on the grains (grain → steer → human). For good health such a vegetarian diet must include a variety of plants that provide all the nitrogen-containing molecules needed by the body to form essential proteins.

Net Primary Productivity of Plants   The rate at which the plants in a particular ecosystem produce usable chemical energy or food is called **net primary productivity**. It is equal to the rate at which all the plants in an ecosystem convert solar energy to chem-

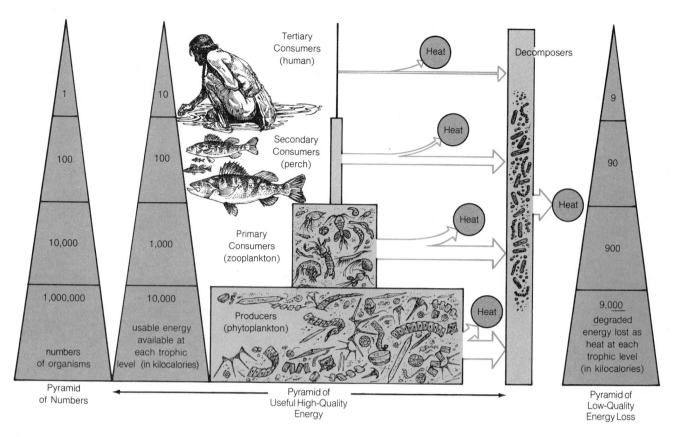

Figure 4-17 Hypothetical energy and number pyramids showing the decrease in usable high-quality energy available at each succeeding trophic level in a food chain.

ical energy stored in plant material through photosynthesis minus the rate at which these plants use some of this chemical energy in cellular respiration to stay alive, grow, and reproduce.

net primary = rate at which − rate at which
productivity plants produce plants use
chemical energy chemical energy

Note that net primary productivity is the rate at which the plants in an ecosystem produce net useful chemical energy—not the total amount of net useful chemical energy produced. Net primary productivity is usually reported as the amount of energy produced by the plant material in a specified area of land over a given time; typical units are kilocalories of energy produced per square meter of land area per year (Appendix 2).

Net primary productivity can be used to evaluate the potential of various ecosystems for producing plant material that forms the base of the food supply for humans and other animals. Farmers attempt to grow the crops that yield the highest net primary productivity in their area of the world. Ecologists have estimated the average annual net primary production per square meter for the major types of terrestrial and

aquatic ecosystems. Figure 4-18 shows that ecosystems with the highest net primary productivities are estuaries (coastal areas where the land meets the sea), swamps and marshes, and tropical rain forests; the lowest are tundra (Arctic grasslands), open ocean, and desert.

You might conclude that we should clear tropical forests to grow crops and that we should harvest plants growing in estuaries, swamps, and marshes to help feed the growing human population. Such a conclusion is incorrect. One reason is that the plants—mostly grasses—in estuaries, swamps, and marshes are not very useful for direct human consumption, although they are extremely important as food sources and spawning areas for fish, shrimp, and other forms of aquatic life that provide protein for humans. In tropical forests most of the nutrients are stored in the trees and other vegetation rather than in the soil. When the trees are cleared, the exposed soil is so infertile that food crops can be grown only for a short time without massive, expensive inputs of commercial fertilizers.

Another reason is that the data in Figure 4-18 do not show how much of each ecosystem is available throughout the world. In contrast, Figure 4-19 shows the *world* net primary productivity for major types of ecosystems. Since the total area of estuaries is small,

Type of Ecosystem

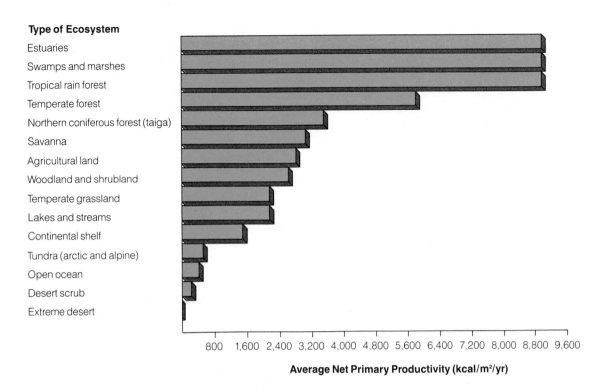

Estuaries
Swamps and marshes
Tropical rain forest
Temperate forest
Northern coniferous forest (taiga)
Savanna
Agricultural land
Woodland and shrubland
Temperate grassland
Lakes and streams
Continental shelf
Tundra (arctic and alpine)
Open ocean
Desert scrub
Extreme desert

800　1,600　2,400　3,200　4,000　4,800　5,600　6,400　7,200　8,000　8,800　9,600

Average Net Primary Productivity (kcal/m²/yr)

Figure 4-18　Estimated average net primary productivity by plants in major types of ecosystems.

Type of Ecosystem

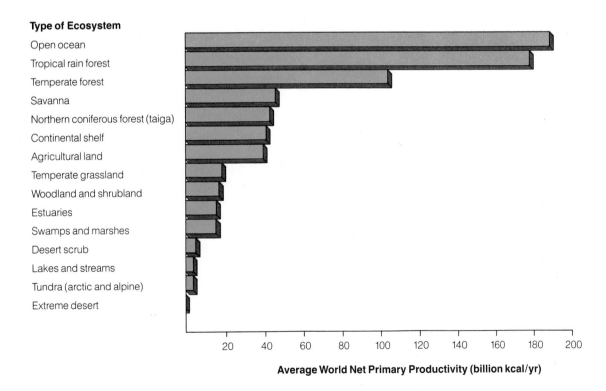

Open ocean
Tropical rain forest
Temperate forest
Savanna
Northern coniferous forest (taiga)
Continental shelf
Agricultural land
Temperate grassland
Woodland and shrubland
Estuaries
Swamps and marshes
Desert scrub
Lakes and streams
Tundra (arctic and alpine)
Extreme desert

20　40　60　80　100　120　140　160　180　200

Average World Net Primary Productivity (billion kcal/yr)

Figure 4-19　Estimated average world net primary productivity by plants in major types of ecosystems.

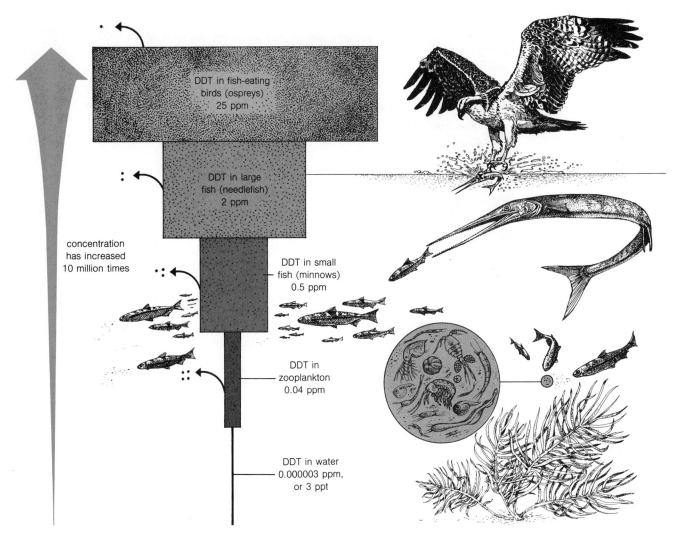

concentration
has increased
10 million times

DDT in fish-eating
birds (ospreys)
25 ppm

DDT in large
fish (needlefish)
2 ppm

DDT in small
fish (minnows)
0.5 ppm

DDT in
zooplankton
0.04 ppm

DDT in water
0.000003 ppm,
or 3 ppt

Figure 4-20 The concentration of DDT in the fatty tissues of organisms was biologically amplified approximately 10 million times in this food chain of an estuary adjacent to Long Island Sound near New York City. Dots represent DDT and arrows show small losses of DDT through respiration and excretion.

it drops way down the list. On the other hand, because about 71% of the world's surface is covered with oceans, the world's open ocean ecosystems head the list. But this can be misleading. The world net primary productivity is high for oceans because they cover so much of the globe—not because they have a high productivity per square meter per year. Moreover, harvesting widely dispersed algae and seaweed from the ocean requires enormous amounts of energy—more than the chemical energy available from the food that would be harvested.

Biological Amplification of Chemicals in Food Chains and Webs A factor affecting the survival of some individual organisms and populations of organisms is **biological amplification:** the phenomenon in which concentrations of certain chemicals soluble in

the fatty tissues of organisms feeding at high trophic levels in a food chain or web are drastically higher than the concentrations of the same chemicals found in organisms feeding at lower trophic levels.

Biological amplification pays a devastating role in certain types of pollution. Many pollutants are either diluted to relatively harmless levels in the air or water or degraded to harmless forms by decomposers and other natural processes, as long as the portion of the environment receiving these chemicals is not overloaded. However, some synthetic chemicals, such as the pesticide DDT, some radioactive materials, and some toxic mercury and lead compounds, become more concentrated in the fatty tissues of organisms at successively higher trophic levels in various food chains and food webs. This accumulation of potentially harmful chemicals is especially pronounced in aquatic food chains and webs because they generally consist of four to six trophic levels rather than the two or three levels of most terrestrial food chains and webs. Figure 4-20 illustrates the biological amplification of DDT in a five-step food chain of an estuary ecosystem adjacent to Long Island Sound near New York City.

Such biological amplification depends on three factors: **(1)** the second law of energy, **(2)** chemicals that are soluble in fat but insoluble in water, and **(3)** chemicals that either are not broken down or are broken down slowly in the environment. DDT, for example, is insoluble in water, soluble in fat, and breaks down slowly in the environment. Thus, if each phytoplankton concentrates one unit of water-insoluble DDT from the water, a small fish eating thousands of phytoplankton will store thousands of units of DDT in its fatty tissue. Then a large fish that eats ten of the smaller fish will receive and store tens of thousands of units of DDT. A bird or human that feeds on several large fish can ingest hundreds of thousands of units of DDT. The high concentrations of DDT or other chemicals can reduce the populations of such species by directly killing the organisms, by reducing their ability to reproduce, or by weakening them so that they are more susceptible to diseases, parasites, and predators. Biological amplification of certain chemicals helps explain why dilution is not always the solution to some forms of pollution.

4-4 ECOLOGICAL NICHES OF SPECIES IN ECOSYSTEMS

The Niche Concept The **ecological niche** (pronounced "nitch") is a description of all the physical, chemical, and biological factors that a species needs to survive, stay healthy, and reproduce in an ecosystem. To describe a species' ecological niche, one must know its *habitat niche* (where it lives); its *food niche* (the species it eats or decomposes and the species it competes with, the species that prey upon it, and where it leaves its wastes for decomposition); its *reproductive niche* (how and when it reproduces), and its *physical and chemical niche* (its temperature, shade, slope, humidity, and other requirements, the chemicals it can and cannot tolerate, and its effect on the nonliving parts of its environment).

A common analogy is that an organism's habitat, which is only part of its niche, refers to its "address" in an ecosystem, while its ecological niche is its "occupation" and "lifestyle." For example, the habitat of a robin includes such areas as woodlands, forests, parks, pasture lands, meadows, orchards, gardens, and yards. But its ecological niche includes additional characteristics such as nesting and roosting in trees; eating insects, earthworms, and fruit; and dispersing fruit and berry seeds in its droppings. Information about

ecological niches helps humans to manage species as sources of food or other resources and to predict the effects of either adding a particular species to an ecosystem or removing a species from an ecosystem. Despite its importance, it is difficult to determine the interacting factors that make up an organism's complete ecological niche.

Specialist and Generalist Niches The niche of an organism can be classified as specialized or generalized, depending primarily on its major sources of food, the extent of its habitat, and the degree of tolerance it has to temperature and other physical and chemical factors. Most species of plants and animals can tolerate only a narrow range of environmental conditions and feed on a limited number of different plants or animals. Thus, such species have a *specialized niche*, which limits them to fairly specific habitats in the biosphere. The giant panda, for example, has a highly specialized niche because it obtains 99% of its food by consuming bamboo plants. The destruction and mass die-off of several species of bamboo in parts of China, where the vulnerable panda is found, has led to its near extinction.

Species with a *generalist niche* are very adaptable, can live on much of the terrestrial portion of the planet, eat a wide variety of foods, tolerate a wide range of environmental conditions, and are usually in much less danger of extinction than species with a specialized niche. Examples include flies, cockroaches, mice, rats, and humans.

Competition Between Species As long as commonly used resources are abundant, different species can share them. However, when two or more species in the same ecosystem attempt to use the same scarce resources, they are said to be engaging in **interspecific competition.** The scarce resource may be food, water, carbon dioxide, sunlight, soil nutrients, shelter, or anything needed for survival.

One species gains an advantage over other competing species in the same ecosystem by producing more young, obtaining more food or solar energy, defending itself more effectively, or being able to tolerate a wider range of temperature, light, water salinity, or concentrations of certain poisons. For example, as species of large-leafed trees grow, they slowly create shade to eliminate or reduce competition from other sun-loving plant species. Some plants use chemical warfare to give themselves a competitive advantage; apple trees do poorly and tomatoes will not grow at all near black walnut trees, which give off a poison through their roots.

Humans spend a lot of time, energy, and money attempting to reduce populations of various species that compete with us for food. Farmers apply insecticides to kill insects and rodenticides to kill rats and other rodents that compete with humans and livestock for grain and other crops. They also apply herbicides to kill weeds, rapidly growing plants that compete with food crops for space, water, and other nutrients. Experience, however, has shown that in the long run this approach usually increases—not decreases—the numbers of pest species. Species such as insects, rats, and weeds, with short generation times and numerous offspring, can gain a competitive advantage by rapid **genetic adaptation** to a new environmental condition. For example, a few members of any large insect population have a built-in genetic resistance to insecticides such as DDT. When DDT is used to reduce the insect population, these members survive and rapidly breed new populations with a larger number of genetically resistant individuals. The more the insect population is exposed to a particular pesticide, the more resistant it becomes. As one observer put it, "I hope that when the insects take over the world, they will remember that we always took them along on our picnics."

Competitive Exclusion Principle   The more similar the ecological niches of two species, the more they will compete for the same food, shelter, space, and other critical resources. According to the **competitive exclusion principle,** no two species in the same ecosystem can occupy exactly the same ecological niche indefinitely. Populations of some animal species can avoid or reduce competition with more dominant species by moving to another area, switching to a less

---

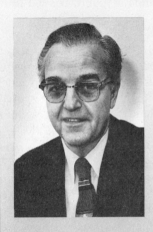

Edward J. Kormondy

Edward J. Kormondy is vice president and professor of biology at California State University at Los Angeles. He has taught at the University of Southern Maine, the University of Michigan, Oberlin College, and Evergreen State College. Among his numerous research articles and books are Concepts of Ecology *and* Readings in Ecology *(both published by Prentice-Hall). A major force in biological education, for several years he was director of the Commission on Undergraduate Education in the Biological Sciences.*

Energy flows—but downhill only; chemical nutrients circulate—but some stagnate; populations stabilize—but some go wild; communities age—but some age faster. These dynamic and relentless processes are as characteristic of ecosystems as are thermonuclear fusion reactions of the sun and other stars.

Thinking one can escape the operation of these and other laws of nature is like thinking one can stop the earth from rotating and revolving or make rain fall up. Yet we have consciously peopled the earth only for hundreds of millions to endure starvation and malnutrition, deliberately dumped wastes only to ensure contamination, purposefully simplified agricultural systems only to cause widespread crop losses from pest invasions. Such actions suggest that we believe that energy and food automatically increase as people multiply, that things stay where they are put, that simplification of ecosystems aids in their management and maintenance. Such actions indicate that we have ignored basic, unbreakable physical laws of ecosystems. We have proposed, but nature has disposed.

We proposed more people, more mouths to be fed, more space to be occupied. Nature disposed by placing an upper limit on the earth's net primary productivity, by using and degrading energy quality at and between all trophic levels, by imposing an upper limit on the total space that is available and which can be occupied. Ultimately, the only way there can be more and more people is for each person to have less and less energy and less and less space. Absolute limits to growth are imposed both by thermodynamics and space. We may argue about what these limits are and when they will be reached, but there are limits and if present trends continue they will be reached. The more timely question then becomes a qualitative one. What quality of life will we have within these limits? What kind of life do you want?

accessible or less readily digestible food source, or hunting for the same food source at different times of the day or in different places. For example, hawks and owls feed on similar prey. Competition is reduced, however, because hawks hunt during the day and owls hunt at night. Where lions and leopards occur together, lions take mostly larger animals as prey and leopards take smaller ones. Two different species of fish-eating birds, the common cormorant and the shag cormorant, look alike, fish in a similar manner, and live on the same cliffs near the ocean. Careful observations, however, reveal that these two species have different ecological niches. The shag cormorant fishes mainly in shallow water for sprats and sand eels and nests on the lower portion of the cliffs. The common cormorant fishes primarily for shrimp and a few fish farther out to sea and lives nearer the top of the cliffs.

This chapter has shown that *the essential feature of the living and nonliving parts of an ecosystem and of the biosphere is interdependence.* The next two chapters show how this interdependence is the key to understanding the earth's major types of terrestrial and aquatic ecosystems (Chapter 5) and how such ecosystems change in response to natural and human stresses (Chapter 6).

We sang the songs that carried in their melodies all the sounds of nature—the running waters, the sighing of winds, and the calls of the animals. Teach these to your children that they may come to love nature as we love it.

Grand Council Fire of American Indians

We proposed exploitative use of resources and indiscriminate disposal of wastes generated by people and technology. Nature disposed, and like a boomerang, the consequences of our acts came back and hit us. On the one hand, finite oil, coal, and mineral resource supplies are significantly depleted—some nearing exhaustion. On the other hand, air, water, and land are contaminated, some beyond restoring. Nature's laws limit each resource; some limits are more confining than others, some more critical than others. The earth is finite, and its resources are therefore finite. Yet another of nature's laws is that fundamental resources—elements and compounds—circulate, some fully and some partially. They don't stay where they are put. They move from the land to the water and the air, just as they move from the air and water to the land. Must not our proposals for using resources and discharging wastes be mindful of ultimate limits and the givens of the earth's chemical cycling processes? What about your own patterns of resource use and waste disposal?

We proposed simplification of our agricultural and to some extent our aquatic food-producing systems to ease the admittedly heavy burden of cultivation and harvest. Nature disposed otherwise, however. Simple systems are youthful ones, and like our own youth, are volatile, unpredictable, and unstable. Young ecosystems do not conserve nutrients, and agricultural systems in such a stage must have their nutrients replaced artificially and expensively by adding commercial fertilizers. Young agricultural systems essentially lack resistance to pests and disease and have to be protected artificially and expensively by

chemical means. These systems are also more subject to the whims of climate and often have to be expensively irrigated. Must not our proposals for managing agricultural systems be mindful of nature's managerial strategy of providing biological diversity to enhance the stability of most complex ecosystems? What of your own lawn?

The take-home lesson is a rather straightforward one: We cannot propose without recognizing how nature disposes. We are shackled by basic ecological laws of energy, chemical cycling, population growth, and community aging processes. We have plenty of freedom within these laws, but like it or not we are bounded by them. You are bounded by them. What do you propose to do yourself?

Guest Essay Discussion

1. Edward Kormondy suggests that the quality of life for individuals is more important than the numbers of people. What is quality of life? What does it mean to you? To other members of your class? To a poor person living on the streets? To a rich person living in a mansion?

2. List the patterns of your life that are in harmony with the laws of energy flow and chemical cycling and those that are not.

3. Can you think of other examples of "we propose" and "nature disposes"?

4. Set up a chart with examples of "we propose" and "nature disposes," but add a third column based on ecological principles titled "we repropose."

CHAPTER SUMMARY

Ecology is the study of the relationships among living organisms and the physical and chemical factors making up their environment. This study is based on examining various types of *ecosystems:* self-regulating communities of plants and animals interacting with one another and with their nonliving chemical environment (the elements and compounds needed by organisms to remain alive and reproduce) and physical environment (solar energy, wind, moisture, and other factors). The major types of living components of ecosystems are *producers* (mostly green plants that are food makers), *herbivores* (primary consumers or plant eaters), *carnivores* (secondary and higher-level consumers that are animal eaters), and *decomposers* (consumers that break down the remains of dead animals and plants or the waste products of living organisms into simpler chemicals for reuse by producers).

Life on earth depends on *matter cycling* and the *one-way flow of high-quality energy* from the sun through the *atmosphere* (the earth's gases), *hydrosphere* (the earth's water), *lithosphere* (the earth's upper layer of solid soil and rock), and *biosphere* (the earth's plants and animals) and back into space as low-quality heat. Human life also depends on the *culturesphere,* in which past knowledge and human ingenuity is used to extract, produce, and use matter and energy resources to enhance human survival and life quality.

The *carbon, oxygen, nitrogen, phosphorus, sulfur, and water cycles* driven by solar energy are the major ways that the key elements and compounds needed for life are recycled within the biosphere in forms usable by plant and animal life. The passage of energy from producers to consumers of plants and animals and eventually to decomposers as part of these chemical cycles in a particular ecosystem can be described in terms of *food chains* and *food webs*. Only about 10% of the total quantity of energy in the food eaten by an organism is useful in keeping it alive. The concentrations of some water-insoluble and fat-soluble chemicals such as DDT can be *biologically amplified* to much higher levels as they pass from one organism to another in a food chain or web.

An *ecological niche* consists of all the physical, chemical, and biological factors that each type of plant or animal in an ecosystem needs to survive, stay healthy, and reproduce. According to the *competitive exclusion principle,* no two types of plants and animals in the same ecosystem can occupy exactly the same ecological niche indefinitely. The key message of ecology is that all forms of life on earth are either directly or indirectly dependent on one another and on their nonliving environment.

DISCUSSION TOPICS

1. Distinguish among *ecosystem, biosphere, population,* and *community,* and give an example of each. Rank them by increasing scale and complexity in terms of their level of organization of matter.

2. Distinguish among *herbivores, carnivores,* and *omnivores,* and give two examples of each.

3. **a.** A bumper sticker asks "Have you thanked a green plant today?" Give two reasons for appreciating a green plant.
   b. Trace back the sources of the materials comprising the sticker and see whether the sticker itself represents a sound application of the slogan.

4. **a.** How would you set up a self-sustaining aquarium for tropical fish?
   b. Suppose you have a balanced aquarium sealed with a transparent glass top. Can life continue in the aquarium indefinitely as long as the sun shines regularly on it?
   c. A friend cleans out your aquarium and removes all the soil and plants, leaving only the fish and water. What will happen?

5. Using the second law of energy, explain why there is such a sharp decrease in high-quality energy along each step of a food chain. Doesn't an energy loss at each step violate the first law of energy? Explain.

6. Using the second law of energy, explain why many people in less developed countries exist primarily on a vegetarian diet.

7. Using the second law of energy, explain why a pound of steak is more expensive than a pound of corn.

8. Why are there fewer lions than mice in an African ecosystem supporting both types of animals?

9. What characteristics must a chemical have before it will be biologically amplified in a food chain or web?

10. Compare the ecological niches of humans in a small town and in a large city; in a more developed country and in a less developed country.

5

Ecosystems: What Are the Major Types?

GENERAL OBJECTIVES

1. What types of adaptations have various species of plants and animals made to different environmental conditions, and how much environmental change can they tolerate?

2. How and why does climate vary in different parts of the world?

3. What are the major types of terrestrial ecosystems (biomes) and how does climate influence the type found in a particular area?

4. What are the major types of aquatic ecosystems and what factors influence the kinds of life they contain?

5. Why is the coastal zone so important?

When we try to pick out anything by itself, we find it hitched to everything else in the universe.

John Muir

Organisms have a variety of characteristics that allow them to live in certain environments and adapt to changes in environmental conditions. Some like it hot and some like it cold. Some like it wet, and others dry. Some thrive in the sunlight, others in the shade or dark. The biosphere, in which all organisms are found, is a mosaic of *terrestrial ecosystems* such as deserts, grasslands, and forests and *aquatic ecosystems* such as lakes, reservoirs, ponds, rivers, and oceans. Each of these ecosystems has a characteristic plant and animal community adapted to certain environmental conditions, such as climate in terrestrial ecosystems and availability of light, dissolved salts, and dissolved oxygen in aquatic ecosystems.

5-1 ADAPTATIONS AND LIMITS OF SPECIES TO ENVIRONMENTAL CHANGE

Species Adaptations All environments change. Weather varies from hour to hour and day to day, seasons come and go, water levels in lakes and rivers rise and fall, forests and grasslands burn and new vegetation sprouts up, and concentrations of various nutrients and pollutants in the atmosphere, water, and soil rise and fall. The earth's incredible diversity of species of plants and animals is testimony to the ability of organisms to adapt to a variety of environmental conditions.

Although terrestrial plants are found in many forms and environments, most have a root system to support them and absorb water containing dissolved nutrients from the soil, green leaves to convert solar energy into chemical energy for their maintenance, growth, and reproduction, and trunks or stems equipped with branches to support their leaves and to channel nutrients and chemical energy to and from their other parts.

Species of terrestrial plants have developed variations in those three basic features to survive a wide range of environmental conditions and get the resources they need. Roots can be spread out near the soil surface to quickly absorb as much water as possible after a brief rain in deserts and other areas where rainfall is infrequent (rye plants and most cacti), shallow in areas where moisture and plant nutrients are concentrated near the surface (hemlocks and most maples), and deep where moisture is located far below the surface (oak, hickory, and mesquite trees). Rootless terrestrial plants such as lichens (consisting of a fungus and an alga living togther and helping one another survive) are attached to rocks, tree trunks, and other surfaces. Lichens are tough enough to survive frozen most of the year and can live as long as 4,500 years. In tropical rain forests rootless epiphytes, or air plants, attach themselves to branches high in trees and get water from the humid air and nutrients from plant and animal matter falling from the heavily populated canopy of leaves above.

Leaves may be large to pick up more sunlight in dense forests or to permit high rates of evapotranspiration in areas where moisture is abundant; they may be small or needlelike with waxy, waterproof coatings to minimize evapotranspiration in areas where moisture is limited. **Evergreen plants** such as pines, spruces, and firs retain some of their leaves or needles throughout the year so that food can be manufactured year round or as soon as climatic conditions become favorable. **Deciduous plants** such as oak and maple retain sufficient moisture by losing all their leaves and becoming dormant during winter when soil moisture may be frozen or during drought when it is unavailable. **Succulent plants** such as desert cacti survive by having no leaves, thus reducing loss of scarce water; they store water and produce the food they need in the thick, fleshy tissue of their green stems and branches. For example, the 30-foot-high saguaro cactus, with shallow roots sprawling over an area up to 90 feet in diameter, can suck up and store all the water it needs each year from just two brief rainfalls.

Stems or trunks may be covered by thick, insulating bark in cold regions, by waxy coatings to reduce water loss in arid regions, and by fine hairs or dead leaves where shade is required to reduce water loss. The stems of leafless succulents such as most cacti are covered by thorns or spines to reflect sunlight and help cool the plant, provide shade, reduce evapotranspiration by breaking up winds and air currents, collect raindrops and dew, and deter animals from making a meal of them.

Some species of terrestrial plants are **perennials,** which continue to flower and produce and set seeds year after year despite seasonal climatic fluctuations.

Others are **annuals,** which die off each year during periods of temperature or moisture stress but leave behind seeds to germinate during the next favorable climatic season. Seeds vary in the conditions necessary for germination. Some have hulls that must be dissolved away; others are eaten by animals and dispersed to new ground through their wastes; still others have hard coverings opened only by floods or fires.

Aquatic plants have also adapted to various environmental conditions. Some live in fresh water (water lilies) and others only in saltwater (eelgrass); some emerge from the water's surface (cattails and bulrushes), others live underwater (water celery and pond weeds). Some aquatic plants found near the shore (cattails and bulrushes) have leaves, stems, and roots; others are rootless and float on the water (phytoplankton and water hyacinths); and others maintain their location in rapidly flowing water by attaching themselves to surfaces such as rocks or stream bottoms (mosses).

Animal species too have a variety of adaptations to environmental conditions. Some are warm-blooded (humans, birds, and bears) and have internally controlled body temperature; others are cold-blooded (reptiles) and have to move in and out of the sun for temperature control. Some live only on land (rabbits and lions), others only in aquatic systems (most fish), and others are amphibians that begin life as aquatic larvae or tadpoles and then become land-dwelling adults (frogs). Fish and other aquatic animals have adapted to living in rivers and other bodies of flowing water by having streamlined bodies that reduce their resistance to water flow or flat bodies that allow them to crawl under rocks and escape the current.

Animals also avoid or minimize environmental stress such as harsh winter cold by increasing the thickness of their fur (foxes and wolves), migrating (some birds fly south for the winter), or hibernating to wait out the stress period in a less active physiological state (chipmunks, bears, and ground squirrels). Desert animals get and conserve water by a number of adaptations. Many live undergound to avoid the hot sun during the day, becoming active only during the night or near dusk or dawn when temperatures are cool. Reptiles and many insects have scales or an exterior covering that helps prevent evaporation of water. Some obtain water from morning dew. Others eat the juicy stems of succulent plants (camels and antelopes), get the liquid they need from the body fluids of prey, or produce water as by-products of digestion (rodents such as kangaroo rats and jerboas, which never drink water).

Tolerance Range and Limiting Factors Despite such adaptations, each species and each individual organism of a species has a particular **range of tolerance** to

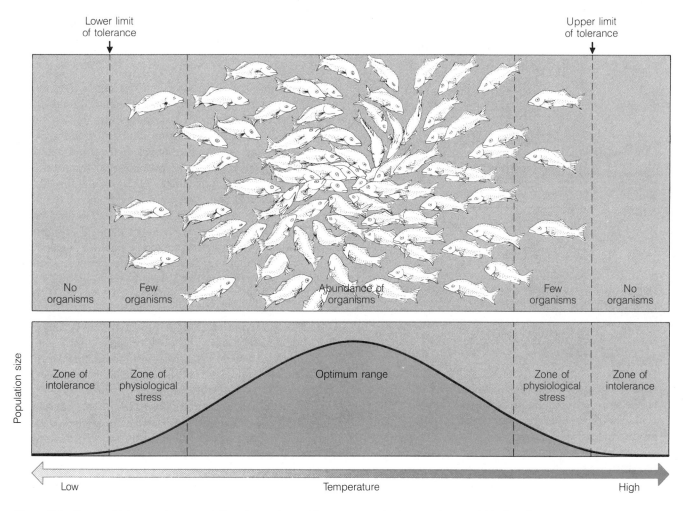

Figure 5-1 Range of tolerance for a population of organisms of the same species to an environmental factor—in this case temperature.

variations in chemical and physical factors in its environment, such as temperature (Figure 5-1). This tolerance range includes an optimum range of values that allow populations of a species to thrive and operate most efficiently and values slightly above or below the optimal level that usually support a smaller population size. Once values exceed the upper or lower limits of tolerance, few if any organisms of a particular species survive.

These observations are summarized in the **law of tolerance:** The existence, abundance, and distribution of a species is determined by whether the levels of one or more physical or chemical factors fall above or below the levels tolerated by the species. Although organisms of the same species share the same range of tolerance to various factors, individual organisms within a large population of a species may have slightly different tolerance ranges because of small differences in their genetic makeup. For example, it may take a little more heat or a little more of a poisonous chemical to kill one frog or one human than another. This is why the tolerance curve shown in Figure 5-1 represents the response of a population composed of many individuals of the same species rather than an individual organism to variations in some environmental factor such as temperature.

Usually the range of tolerance to a particular stress also varies with the physical condition and life cycle of the individuals making up a species. Individuals already weakened by fatigue or disease are usually more sensitive to stresses than healthy ones. For most animal species, tolerance levels are much lower in juveniles (where body defense mechanisms may not be fully developed) than in adults.

Organisms of most species have a better chance of adjusting or acclimating to an environmental change that takes place gradually. For example, we can tolerate a higher water temperature by getting in a tub of fairly hot water and then slowly adding hotter and hotter water. This ability to adapt slowly to new conditions is a useful protective device, but it can also be dangerous. With each change, the organism comes closer to its limit of tolerance until suddenly, without any warning signals, the next small change triggers a

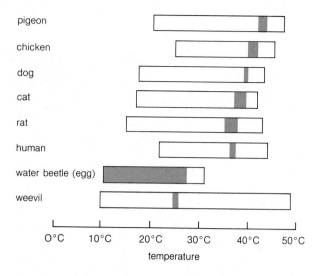

Figure 5-2 Ranges of tolerance for temperature vary among different species. Shaded areas represent the optimum temperature range.

harmful or even fatal effect—much like adding the single straw that breaks an already overloaded camel's back. This **threshold effect** partly explains why so many environmental problems, such as acid deposition, which can kill certain species of trees and aquatic life, or hazardous wastes in groundwater supplies, seem to pop up, even though they have actually been building or accumulating for a long time.

Different species of plants and animals have varying ranges of tolerance for a particular environmental factor such as temperature (Figure 5-2). Those with the widest ranges of tolerance can be found in many different types of environments and generally are less susceptible to extinction than those with narrow tolerance ranges.

Another related ecological principle is the **limiting factor principle:** The single factor that is most deficient in an ecosystem is the one that determines the presence or absence and the population size of a particular plant and animal species. For example, suppose a farmer plants corn in a field containing too little phosphorus. Even if the corn's requirements for water, nitrogen, potassium, and other nutrients are met, the corn will stop growing when it has used up the available phosphorus. In this case, availability of phosphorus is the limiting factor that determines how much corn will grow in the field. Similarly, even with plenty of food and air, you will die in a relatively short time without sufficient water. The human species has increased its numbers and distribution over much of the earth by learning to manipulate various limiting factors and thus occupying a generalist ecological niche (Section 4-4).

5-2 CLIMATE AND MAJOR TYPES OF TERRESTRIAL ECOSYSTEMS

Weather and Climate A major factor determining the types and numbers of plants and animals found in various ecosystems, especially those on land, is climate. **Weather** is the actual moment-to-moment and day-to-day variation in atmospheric conditions such as temperature, barometric pressure, humidity, precipitation, sunshine (solar radiation), cloudiness, and wind direction and speed at a given area. **Climate,** in contrast, is an average of the various day-to-day weather conditions in a region, usually over a 30-year period. Climate is the weather we might expect in a given area at a particular time based on past experience; weather is the atmospheric conditions we actually find.

Global Circulation of Air and Water A major factor affecting the climate of an area is its latitude—distance north or south from the equator. Air in the earth's atmosphere is heated more at the equator (zero latitude), where the sun is almost directly overhead, than at the high-latitude poles, where the sun is lower in the sky and strikes the earth at an angle. Masses of solar-heated equatorial air tend to rise because warm air has a lower density (mass per unit of volume) than cold air. As these warm air masses rise, they spread northward and southward, carrying heat from the equator toward the poles. At the poles the warm air cools, sinks downward because cool air is more dense than warm air, and moves back toward the equator. This general global air circulation pattern leads to warm average temperatures near the equator at zero latitude, cold average temperatures at the high latitudes near the earth's poles, and moderate or temperate average temperatures at the middle latitudes between the two regions. Seasonal variations in these average temperatures in different parts of the world occur primarily because the earth's axis (the imaginary line connecting the North and South poles, around which the earth spins continuously) is tilted in relation to the earth's orbit around the sun (Figure 5-3).

The general tendency for large air masses to move from the equator to the poles and back is modified by the twisting force of the earth's rotation on its axis. This force breaks the general air circulation pattern into three separate belts of moving air, or *prevailing ground winds:* the trade winds, the westerlies, and the polar easterlies (Figure 5-4).

The patterns of air masses and prevailing ground winds influence the distribution of precipitation over the earth's surface. As warm and humid tropical air masses rise and cool, they release some of their water vapor as rain, sleet, snow, or hail in an uneven pattern.

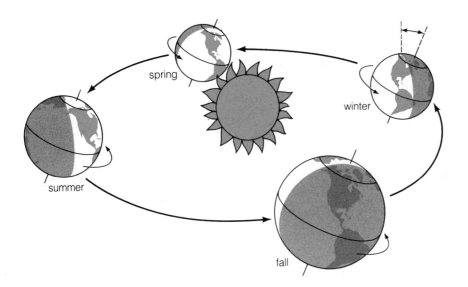

Figure 5-3 The seasons (shown here for the Northern Hemisphere only) are caused by variations in the amount of incoming solar energy as the earth makes its annual rotation around the sun on a tilted axis. Note that the northern end of the earth's axis is tilted toward the sun in summer, making the Northern Hemisphere warmer, and away from it in winter, making it cooler.

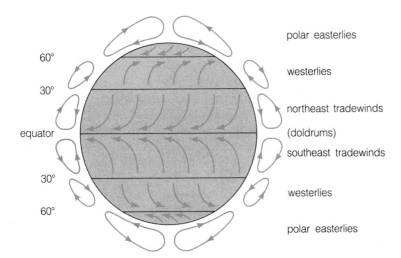

Figure 5-4 Formation of belts of prevailing winds. The twisting motion caused by the earth's rotation on its axis causes the airflow in each hemisphere to break up into three separate belts of prevailing winds.

The earth's rotation, prevailing winds, and variations in water density because of temperature differences also give rise to orderly, well-defined *ocean currents* that distribute warm and cool water throughout the world. Cold, more dense water near the poles sinks beneath the ocean surface and flows toward the equator. There it rises to replace the less dense, warm water that surface currents and prevailing winds are constantly carrying toward the poles. These warm and cold currents affect the climates of coastal areas near their flow. For example, without the warm Gulf Stream, which transports 50 times more water than all the world's rivers, the climate of northwestern Europe would be more like that in the sub-Arctic. With or without major ocean currents, the coastal zones of any continent will always have milder climates than its interior because water loses heat more slowly than land in winter and absorbs heat more slowly than land in summer.

Topographical factors also affect climatic conditions. Because of their higher elevation, mountain highlands tend to be cooler, windier, and wetter than adjacent valleys. For instance, although Mount Kilimanjaro, Africa's highest peak, stands just south of the equator, its summit is perpetually covered with snow. Mountains act as barriers that interrupt the flow of prevailing winds and the movement of storms, primarily because warm air can hold more water vapor than cold air. When prevailing winds blowing in from an ocean reach a mountain range, the moist air, chilled as it rises, drops nearly all of its moisture as rain and snow on the windward slopes. After being essentially "wrung dry," there is little moisture left in the air flowing down the slopes of the lee side and over the land beyond (Figure 5-5). This so-called *rain shadow effect* is the main reason that arid and semiarid deserts lie to the east of the Coast Range and the Cascade and Sierra Nevada ranges of California.

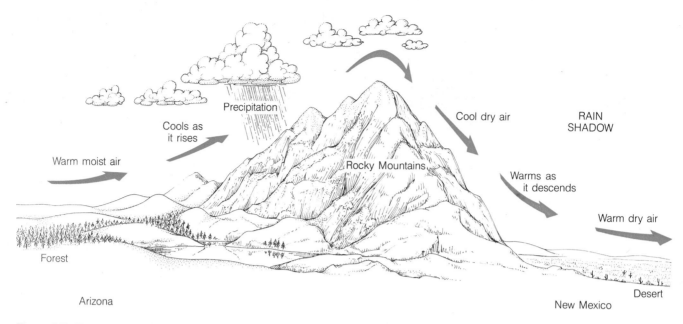

Warm moist air

Cools as
it rises

Precipitation

Rocky Mountains

Cool dry air

RAIN
SHADOW

Warms as
it descends

Warm dry air

Forest

Arizona

Desert

New Mexico

Figure 5-5 Rain shadow effect.

Climate and Major Types of Ecosystems Though the climate of an area is affected by a number of variables, the two most important are its average temperature and average precipitation. Figure 5-7 (pp. 98–99) shows the global distribution of the major types of climate based on average temperature and precipitation in different areas over 30-year periods.

Ecologists find it useful to classify ecosystems according to their general similarities in structure. The three major types of large terrestrial ecosystems, or biomes, are deserts, grasslands, and forests, each with a characteristic set of plants, animals, climatic conditions, and, often, general soil type.

Why is one area of the earth a desert, another a grassland, and another a forest? Why are there different types of deserts, grasslands, and forests? What determines the variations of plant and animal life among these types? In general, the answer to all these questions is differences in climate.

Precipitation is the limiting factor that determines whether the biomes of most of the world's land areas are desert, grassland, or forest. A region will normally be a **desert,** containing little vegetation or widely spaced, mostly low vegetation, if its average amount of precipitation is less than 25 centimeters (10 inches) per year (Figure 5-6). This is true regardless of the average temperature and amount of sunlight and no matter how high the concentrations of plant nutrients in the soil. Many of the world's large deserts are found around latitudes 30 degrees north and south of the equator, where the global climate system tends to produce descending masses of dry air (see map inside the front cover).

Grasslands are found in regions where moderate average precipitation, ranging from 25 to 75 centimeters (10 to 30 inches) a year, is great enough to allow grass to prosper yet so erratic that periodic drought and fire prevent large stands of trees from growing. Undisturbed areas with an average precipitation of 75 centimeters (30 inches) or more a year tend to be covered with **forest,** consisting of various species of trees and smaller forms of vegetation.

The combination of average precipitation and average temperature determine the particular type of desert, grassland, or forest found in a given area. Acting together, these two factors lead to *tropical, temperate* (mid-latitude), and *polar* (high-latitude) deserts, grasslands, and forests (Figure 5-6). The map inside the front cover shows the general distribution of the major types of desert, grassland, and forest biomes throughout the world, and the color landscape photos inside the front and back covers illustrate most of these types. The relationships between climate and vegetation types can be seen by comparing the map of the world's biomes found inside the front cover with the major types of global climate shown in Figure 5-7.

Other factors can also play a role in determining the type of terrestrial ecosystem found in a particular area. For example, the soil type (especially those low in nutrients) can act as a limiting factor, determining the ecosystem type and the types and numbers of plants. And light is often the limiting factor determining the plants and animals in various layers of vegetation in forest ecosystems. Of course, floods, natural and deliberately set fires, and land clearing for human activities may drastically modify the general type of biome found in an area.

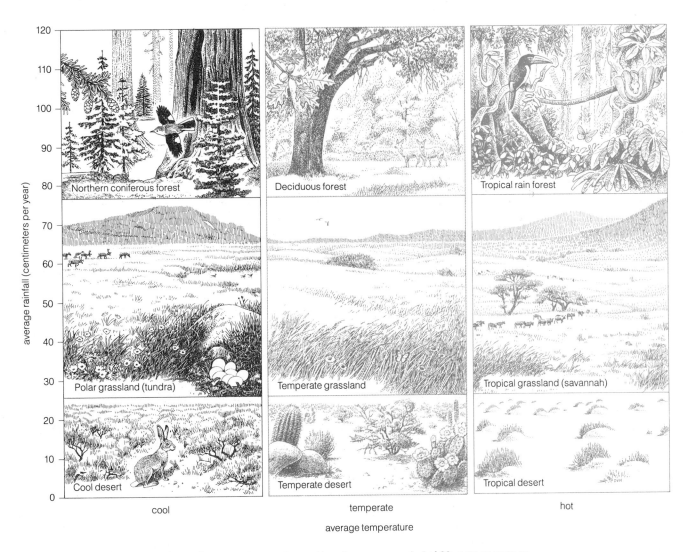

Figure 5-6 Average precipitation and average temperature act together over a period of 30 years or more as limiting factors that determine the type of desert, grassland, or forest ecosystem found in a particular area.

5-3 DESERTS, GRASSLANDS, AND FORESTS

Deserts More than one-third of the earth's land surface is covered with deserts, where average precipitation is low and evaporation rates are high. In combination with low average precipitation, different average temperatures give rise to three types of desert: **(1)** tropical deserts, such as the Sahara, where daytime temperatures are hot year-round and nights are cold because of the lack of sufficient vegetation to moderate temperature declines, **(2)** temperate (mid-latitude) deserts, where daily temperatures are warm most of the year (see photo inside the back cover), and **(3)** cold (high-latitude) deserts, such as the Gobi, where winters are cold and summers are hot.

Tropical deserts, making up about one-fifth of the world's desert area, consist primarily of barren dunes covered with rock or sand. Temperate and cold deserts contain widely scattered thorny bushes and shrubs (acacia, mesquite, sagebrush, greasewood, creosote bush), succulents such as cacti, and small, fast-growing wildflowers that bloom in spring or after a rare, brief, drenching rain. These desert plants get and conserve scarce water by leaving wide spaces between each other, which reduces competition for water.

At night the temperature drops sharply in a desert and a host of small animals such as rodents, reptiles, ground squirrels, jackals, foxes, bats, owls, and insects emerge from hiding and begin to feed. Like desert plants, these animals have developed a number of ways of getting and conserving scarce water (Section 5-1). The nutrient-poor soils, slow growth rate of plants, and lack of water make deserts fragile biomes; vegetation destroyed by human activities such as motorcycling and other off-road driving may take decades to grow back.

Figure 5-7 World climates (Köppen-Geiger classification. Map based on a modified Goode's projection, copyright by the University of Chicago, Department of Geography, and used by their permission.)

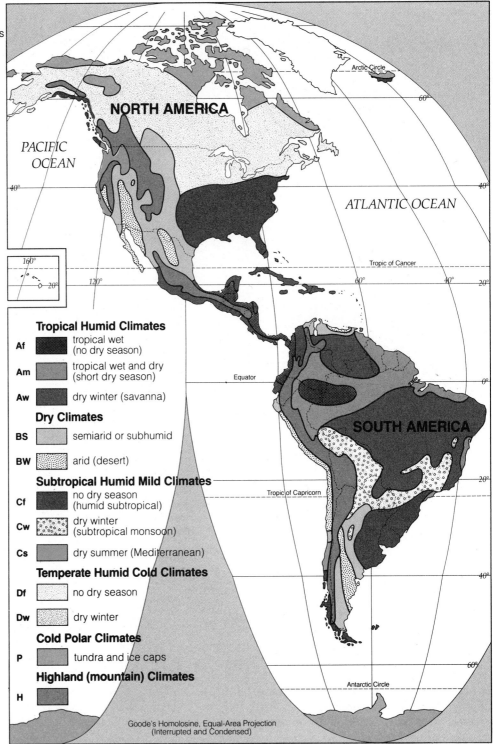

Tropical Humid Climates

Af   tropical wet (no dry season)

Am   tropical wet and dry (short dry season)

Aw   dry winter (savanna)

Dry Climates

BS   semiarid or subhumid

BW   arid (desert)

Subtropical Humid Mild Climates

Cf   no dry season (humid subtropical)

Cw   dry winter (subtropical monsoon)

Cs   dry summer (Mediterranean)

Temperate Humid Cold Climates

Df   no dry season

Dw   dry winter

Cold Polar Climates

P   tundra and ice caps

Highland (mountain) Climates

H

Goode's Homolosine, Equal-Area Projection (Interrupted and Condensed)

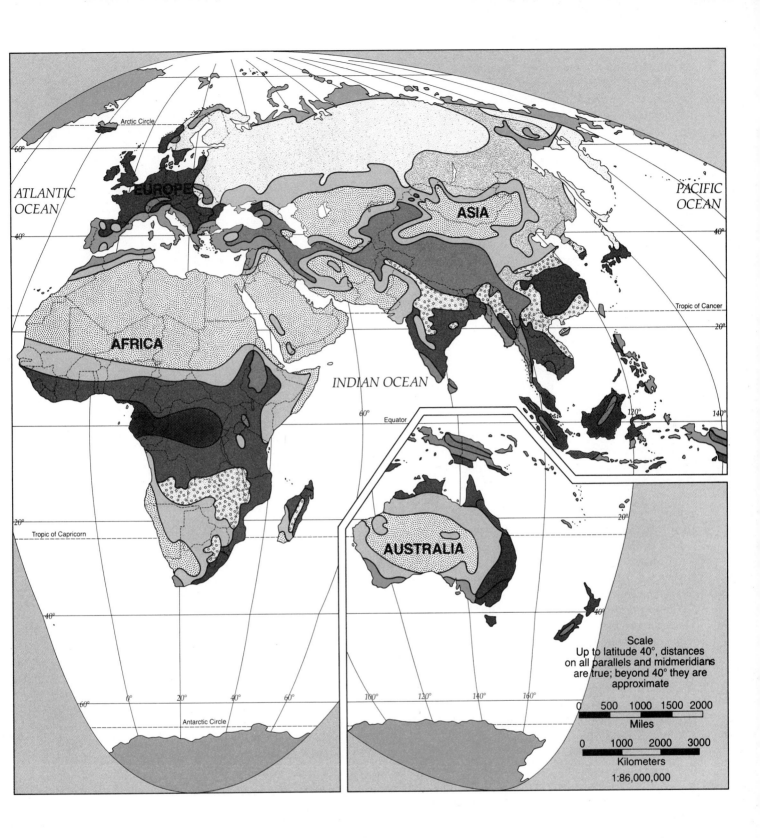

ATLANTIC
OCEAN

PACIFIC
OCEAN

EUROPE

ASIA

Arctic Circle

60°

40°

40°

AFRICA

Tropic of Cancer

20°

INDIAN OCEAN

Equator

60°

120°

140°

20°

20°

Tropic of Capricorn

AUSTRALIA

40°

40°

0°

20°

40°

60°

100°

120°

140°

160°

60°

Antarctic Circle

Scale
Up to latitude 40°, distances
on all parallels and midmeridians
are true; beyond 40° they are
approximate

0   500   1000 1500 2000
Miles

0   1000   2000   3000
Kilometers

1:86,000,000

Grasslands   Grasslands have flat or slightly rolling terrain and cannot support large stands of trees because of high evaporation rates, irregular precipitation and periodic drought, and occasional fires (in tropical and temperate grasslands). *Tropical grasslands,* or *savannas,* are found in areas with high average temperatures, very dry seasons about half of the year, and abundant rain the rest of the year. They are located in a wide belt on either side of the equator between the tropics (see map inside the front cover). Some of these biomes, such as Africa's Serengeti Plain, consist of open plains covered with low or high grasses; others contain grasses along with varying numbers of widely spaced, small, mostly deciduous trees and shrubs, which shed their leaves during the dry season to avoid excessive water loss (see photo inside the back cover). In Africa vast herds of wildebeests, gazelles, zebras, giraffes, antelopes, and other large herbivores graze in different areas of savanna depending on water and soil conditions. Some of these animals and their large predators such as lions, leopards, and cheetahs are disappearing rapidly except in a few protected areas because of ranching, farming, hunting, poaching, and other human activities.

Temperate (mid-latitude) grasslands, located in the large interior areas of continents, have moderate average temperatures, more even distribution of precipitation throughout the year than in tropical grasslands, cold winters with snow covering the ground at times, hot and dry summers, and winds blowing almost continuously. Examples are the tall-grass and low-grass *prairies* of the midwestern and western United States and Canada, the *pampas* of South America, the *veld* of southern Africa, and the *steppes* that stretch from central Europe into Siberia (see map inside the front cover).

Because of their highly fertile soils, all but about 1% of the original tall-grass prairies that once thrived in the midwestern United States and Canada have been cleared for crops such as corn, wheat, and soybeans and for hog farming. The short-grass prairies of the western United States are covered with low perennial grasses and have lower average precipitation and soils too low in some plant nutrients to support taller grasses (see photo inside the back cover). They are widely used to graze unfenced cattle and in some areas to grow wheat and irrigated crops.

Polar (high-latitude) grasslands or Arctic *tundra* in areas just below the arctic region of perpetual ice and snow, have bitter winter cold, icy galelike winds, fairly low average annual precipitation occurring primarily during a brief summer period, and long winter darkness. The wet Arctic tundra is covered with a thick, spongy mat of low-growing plants such as lichens, sedges (grasslike plants often growing in dense tufts in marshy places), mosses, grasses, and low woody shrubs (see photo inside the back cover). Although the ground is frozen in winter, snowfall is rare.

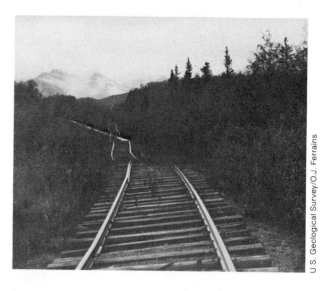

Figure 5-8   Subsidence from thawing of permafrost during construction made this railroad track near Valdez, Alaska, useless.

One effect of the extreme cold is the presence of **permafrost**—water permanently frozen year-round in thick underground layers of soil. During the brief summer when sunlight persists almost around the clock, the surface layer of soil thaws and the biome is turned into a soggy landscape dotted with shallow lakes, marshes, bogs, and ponds. The permafrost below prevents this water from soaking into the ground and the evaporation rate is low. During the thaw hordes of mosquitoes, deerflies, blackflies, and other insects thrive in the shallow surface pools and serve as food for large colonies of migratory birds, especially waterfowl, that fly in from the south.

Most of the tundra's permanent animal residents are small herbivores such as lemmings, hares, voles, and rabbits, which burrow under the ground to escape the cold. Few species are present in large numbers. Musk-oxen are the only large herbivores that live year-round in the tundra; caribou in the North American tundra and reindeer (a similar species found in Eurasian tundra) spend the summer in arctic tundra but migrate south into northern coniferous forests for the rest of the year.

The low rate of decomposition, the shallow soil, and the slow growth rate of plants make the arctic tundra perhaps the earth's most fragile biome. Vegetation destroyed by human activities can take decades to grow back. But fragile as it is, the tundra can be violently inhospitable to human activities: Unless buildings, roads, pipelines, and railroads are built over bedrock, on insulating layers of gravel, or on deep-seated pilings, they melt the upper layer of permafrost and tilt or crack as the land beneath them shifts and settles (Figure 5-8).

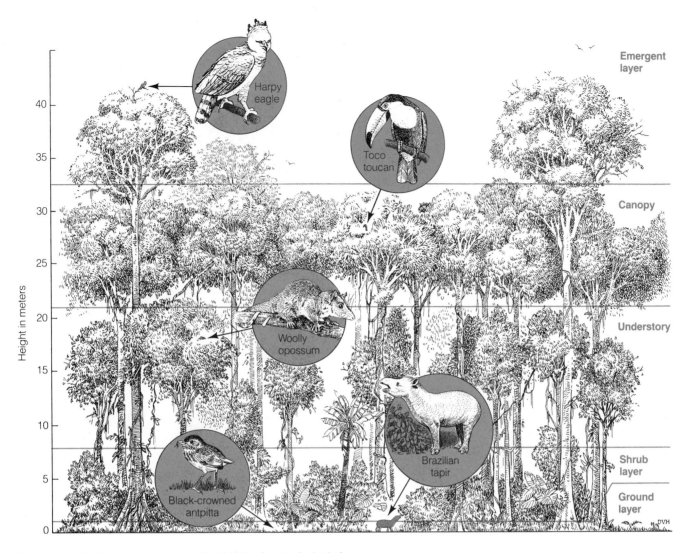

Figure 5-9 Stratification of plant and animal niches in a tropical rain forest.

Height in meters

40
35
30
25
20
15
10
5
0

Harpy eagle

Toco toucan

Woolly opossum

Brazilian tapir

Black-crowned antpitta

Emergent layer

Canopy

Understory

Shrub layer

Ground layer

Forests *Tropical rain forests* are found near the equator in areas with a warm but not hot annual mean temperature of about 27°C (80°F) that varies little either daily or seasonally, high humidity, and heavy rainfall almost daily. Although such forests occupy only 7% of the earth's land surface, they contain 43% of all vegetation in the biosphere and make up almost half of the earth's remaining forests. Their almost unchanging climate means that neither water nor temperature are limiting factors as in other biomes. Because of this lack of major limiting factors, a mature tropical rain forest has a greater diversity of plant and animal species per unit of area than any other biome. More different species of animals can be found in a single tree in such a forest than in an entire forest at higher latitudes.

These diverse forms of plant and animal life occupy a variety of ecological niches in distinct vertical layers (Figure 5-9), with much of the animal life (particularly insects and birds) found in the sunny canopy layer with its abundance of shelter, fruits, and other foods.

Many of the tree trunks and branches in and below the canopy and its understory of shorter trees are covered with a dense tangle of vines, rootless epiphytes or hanging plants, ferns, and other plants (Figure 5-10). This vegetation and the leaves on the lower canopy of smaller trees block out most of the sunlight so that the forest floor is dark, humid, and relatively free of vegetation, except along riverbanks and areas where the big trees have been cleared so that ample sunlight can penetrate to the ground level. Most tall tropical trees have shallow root systems because the abundant rainfall makes it unnecessary for them to penetrate deep into the waterlogged soil; wide trunk bases (buttresses) provide support (Figure 5-10).

The soils lying below these diverse masses of vegetation are mostly thin and deficient in nutrients because decomposition is rapid and complete in the hot, humid climate. Thus, most of the nutrients in this biome are found in the vegetation, not in the upper layers of soil as in most other biomes.

Humans have cleared tropical rain forests to harvest lumber, plant crops, and graze livestock. Once the vegetation is removed, however, the soils rapidly lose the little nutrients they have and cannot grow crops for more than a few years without large-scale use of commercial fertilizers. Furthermore, when vegetation is cleared, the heavy rainfall erodes away most of the thin layer of topsoil so that regeneration of a mature rain forest on large cleared areas is next to impossible.

Temperate (mid-latitude) deciduous forests occur in areas with moderate average temperatures that change significantly during four distinct seasons. They have long summers, not very severe winters, and abundant precipitation spread fairly evenly throughout the year. They are dominated by a few species of broad-leafed deciduous trees such as oak, hickory, maple, poplar, sycamore, and beech (see photo inside the front cover). In most mature deciduous forests, as in tropical forests, the vegetation is found in distinct layers.

The dominant herbivore of most deciduous forests in the eastern United States is the whitetail deer, primarily because most of its natural predators (except humans) have been eliminated. Warblers, robins, and a number of other bird species migrate to these forests during the summer to feed and breed.

Cold (high-latitude) northern coniferous forests, also called *boreal forests* or *taiga*, are found in regions with a subarctic climate where winters are long and dry with only light snowfall, temperatures range from cool to extremely cold, and summers are very brief with mild to warm temperatures. These forests, which form an almost unbroken belt across North America and northern Eurasia (see map inside the front cover), are dominated by a few species of **coniferous** (cone-bearing) evergreen trees such as spruce, fir, larch, and pine (see photo inside the front cover). Their needle-shaped, waxy-coated leaves conserve heat and water during the long, cold, dry winters. Beneath the dense stands of trees a carpet of fallen needles and leaf litter covers the nutrient-poor soil, which remains waterlogged during the brief summers. The surface litter decomposes slowly because of the cold.

Plant species diversity is low in the northern forests because few species can survive the long, cold winters, when soil moisture is frozen. Animals found in the taiga all or part of the year include large herbivores such as mule deer, elk, caribou, and moose; small herbivores such as porcupines, snowshoe hares, squirrels, chipmunks, and other rodents; and medium-to-large carnivores such as grizzly bears, wolverines, foxes, lynxes, martens, and wolves. Insect pests such as the spruce budworm, tussock moth, pine beetle, mosquito, and fly thrive during the warm summer months and are fed upon by birds that fly in from the south for a feast.

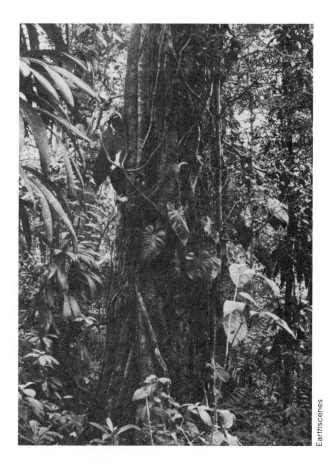

Figure 5-10 Trees in tropical rain forests are covered with vines, ferns, hanging epiphytes or air plants, and other vegetation; they have shallow roots and are supported by wide trunk bases (buttresses).

5-4 FRESHWATER AQUATIC ECOSYSTEMS

Limiting Factors of Aquatic Ecosystems   The main factors affecting the types and numbers of organisms found in aquatic ecosystems are salinity, depth to which sunlight penetrates, amount of dissolved oxygen, and water temperature. **Salinity,** the concentration of dissolved salts (especially sodium chloride) in a body of water, is a limiting factor because different species of aquatic plants and animals have different salinity tolerances. Salinity levels are used to divide aquatic ecosystems into two major classes: **(1)** freshwater ecosystems consisting of inland bodies of standing water (lakes, reservoirs, ponds, and wetlands) and flowing water (streams and rivers) with low salinity, and **(2)** marine or saltwater ecosystems, such as oceans, estuaries (where fresh water from rivers and streams mixes with seawater), coastal wetlands, and coral reefs with high to very high salinity levels.

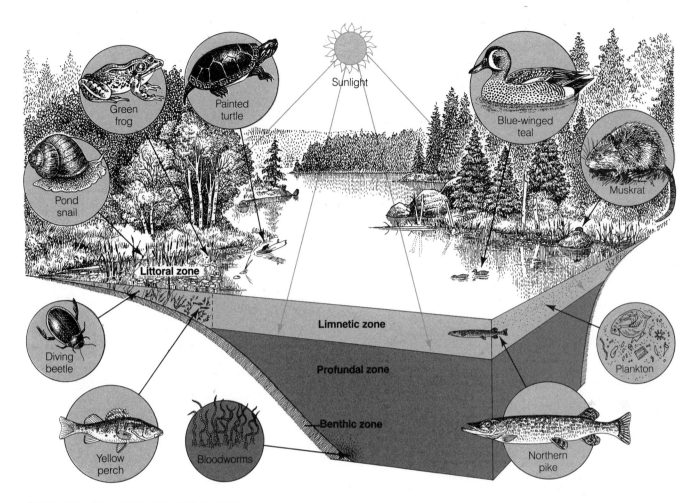

Figure 5-11 Four major zones of life in a lake.

Littoral zone
Limnetic zone
Profundal zone
Benthic zone
Sunlight
Green frog
Painted turtle
Blue-winged teal
Muskrat
Pond snail
Diving beetle
Yellow perch
Bloodworms
Northern pike
Plankton

Lakes Large natural bodies of standing fresh water formed when water from precipitation, land runoff, or groundwater flow fills depressions in the earth created by glaciation (the Great Lakes of North America), earthquakes (Lake Nyasa in East Africa), volcanic activity (Lake Kivu in Africa), and crashes of giant meteorites (Crater Lake in Oregon) are called **lakes.**

Lakes normally consist of four distinct zones (Figure 5-11), which provide a variety of ecological niches for different species of plant and animal life. The **littoral zone,** the shallow, nutrient-rich waters near the shore, contains rooted aquatic plants and an abundance of other forms of aquatic life. The **limnetic zone,** the open water surface layer, receives sufficient sunlight for photosynthesis and contains varying amounts of floating phytoplankton, plant-eating zooplankton, and fish, depending on the availability of plant nutrients. The **profundal zone** of deep water not penetrated by sunlight is inhabited mostly by fish, such as bass and trout, that are adapted to its cooler, darker water and lower levels of dissolved oxygen. The **benthic**

zone at the bottom of the lake is inhabited primarily by large numbers of bacteria, fungi, bloodworms, and other decomposers, which live on dead plant debris, animal remains, and animal wastes that float down from above.

Eutrophication is the process in which lakes receive inputs of plant nutrients (mostly nitrates and phosphates) from the surrounding land basin as a result of natural erosion and runoff. This process gradually fills lakes with sediment over thousands to millions of years. However, near urban or agricultural centers, the input of nutrients can be greatly accelerated as a result of human activities. This **accelerated,** or **cultural, eutrophication** is caused by effluents from sewage treatment plants, runoff of fertilizers and animal wastes, and soil erosion.

Lakes can be classifed into two major types: eutrophic and oligotrophic (Figure 5-12). A lake with a large or excessive supply of plant nutrients is called a **eutrophic lake.** This type of lake is usually shallow and has cloudy, warm water, large populations of phy-

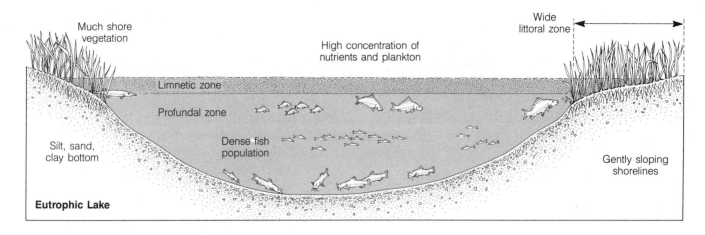

Much shore vegetation

High concentration of nutrients and plankton

Wide littoral zone

Limnetic zone

Profundal zone

Silt, sand, clay bottom

Dense fish population

Gently sloping shorelines

Eutrophic Lake

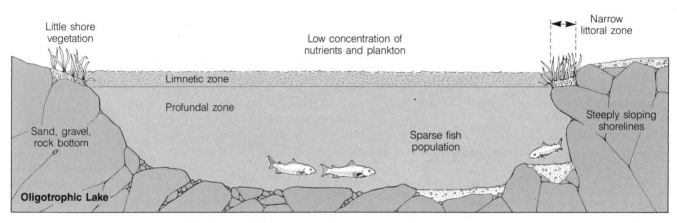

Little shore vegetation

Low concentration of nutrients and plankton

Narrow littoral zone

Limnetic zone

Profundal zone

Sand, gravel, rock bottom

Sparse fish population

Steeply sloping shorelines

Oligotrophic Lake

Figure 5-12 Eutrophic or nutrient-rich lake and oligotrophic or nutrient-poor lake.

toplankton (especially algae) and zooplankton, and diverse populations of fish. A lake with a low supply of plant nutrients is called an **oligotrophic lake.** This type of lake is usually deep and has crystal-clear water, cool to cold temperatures, and relatively small populations of phytoplankton and fish. Many lakes fall somewhere between these two extremes of nutrient enrichment and are called **mesotrophic lakes.**

Most lakes in temperate climate regions, except very shallow eutrophic lakes, become stratified during summer into two distinct layers with different average temperatures (Figure 5-13): the **epilimnion,** an upper layer of warm water with high levels of dissolved oxygen because of its exposure to the atmosphere, and the **hypolimnion,** a lower layer of colder, denser water, usually with a lower concentration of dissolved oxygen. The thin transition zone separating these two layers is called the **thermocline,** in which the temperature drops sharply. Because the thermocline is an effective barrier to the downward transport of dissolved oxygen and nutrients, oxygen can become so depleted in the hypolimnion that there is too little to support the coldwater fish such as trout and whitefish that dwell there. This is especially likely to occur if the hypolimnion has been enriched with sewage and other

plant nutrients as a result of human activities.

Fortunately, thermally stratified lakes undergo a mixing cycle during one or more of the year's seasons. This **turnover** mixes the lake's water from top to bottom, bringing nutrients (mostly nitrates and phosphates) from the bottom to the surface and allowing the bottom layer to replenish its supply of dissolved oxygen by being exposed to the atmosphere. The turnover takes place because the densities of the water in the top and bottom layers of the lake change as their temperatures change during various seasons. Coolwater and cold-water oligotrophic lakes in temperate latitudes, with considerable differences between average summer and winter temperatures, undergo turnovers during the fall and spring. A fairly deep eutrophic lake may undergo a turnover only during winter when its surface water cools.

Reservoirs and Ponds Sometimes incorrectly called lakes, **reservoirs** are fairly large and deep, human-created bodies of standing fresh water, often built behind dams (Figure 5-14). In temperate climate areas they usually have distinct temperature zones like tem-

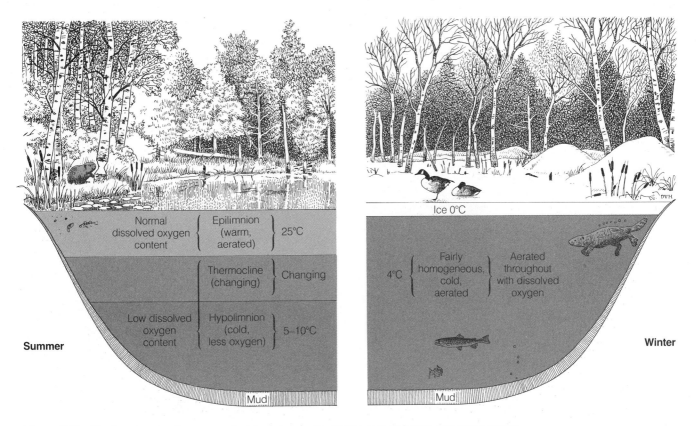

Figure 5-13 The three temperature zones of a lake in temperate climate regions before and after turnover.

perate-zone lakes. Reservoirs are built primarily for water storage; unlike lakes, the volume of water they contain is determined by that being used for hydroelectric power production, irrigation, or domestic consumption.

Ponds are small, shallow, usually human-created impoundments of fresh water used primarily for watering livestock, raising freshwater fish such as catfish, or recreation, especially fishing. Because they are shallow, most ponds consist entirely of a littoral zone covered with rooted plants from shore to shore and do not have distinct temperature zones like reservoirs or lakes. Photosynthesis can take place at all depths during daylight unless the surface water becomes clogged with masses of algae during warm weather.

With ample sunlight and plant nutrients, ponds can support a variety of aquatic life, including warmwater game fishes such as largemouth bass, bluegill, and channel catfish, but maintaining balanced fish populations requires almost continuous management. Because ponds fill up with silt and other matter washing or falling into the water from surrounding land and vegetation, they have short lives unless they are periodically drained and cleaned out.

Streams and Rivers Precipitation that does not infiltrate into the ground or evaporate remains on the earth's surface as surface water. This water becomes runoff that flows into streams and rivers and eventually downhill to the oceans for reuse in the hydrologic cycle (Figure 4-12, p. 79). **Streams** are relatively small, flowing bodies of fresh water that empty into rivers. Most **rivers,** wider and deeper than streams, empty into oceans. The entire land area that delivers the water, sediment, and dissolved substances via streams to a major river, and ultimately to the sea is called a **watershed** or **drainage basin.** Streams and rivers experience considerable annual, seasonal, and even daily variations in water flow.

The downward flow of water from mountain highlands to the sea takes place in three phases (Figure 5-15). In the first phase, narrow headwater or mountain highland streams with cold, clear water rush down steep slopes. As this turbulent water flows and tumbles downward over waterfalls and rapids, it dissolves large amounts of oxygen from the air. Thus, most fish that thrive in this environment are cold-water fish, such as trout, that require a high level of dissolved oxygen.

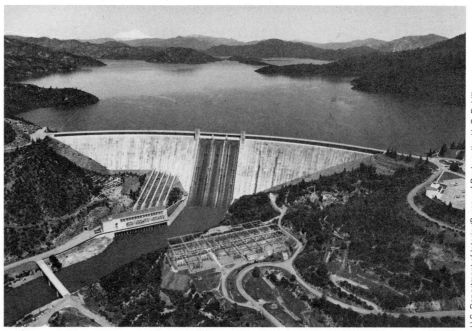

Figure 5-14 Reservoir formed behind Shasta Dam on the Sacramento River north of Redding, California.

U.S. Department of Interior/Bureau of Reclamation/J. C. Dahilig

In the second phase, various headwater streams merge to form wider, deeper, lower-elevation streams that flow down gentler slopes and meander through wider valleys. Here the water is warmer and usually less turbulent and can support a variety of cold-water and warm-water fish species with slightly lower oxygen requirements. Gradually these streams coalesce into wider and deeper rivers that meander across broad flat valleys. The main channels of these rivers support a distinctive variety of fish, whereas their backwaters support fishes similar to those found in lakes. At its mouth a river may divide into many channels as it flows across a **delta**—a built up deposit of river-borne sediments—before reaching the ocean.

Inland Wetlands Land that remains flooded all or part of the year with fresh or salt water is called a **wetland.** Bogs, marshes, swamps, and river-overflow lands that are covered with fresh water and found inland are called **inland wetlands.** Those found near the coast and covered with salt water are known as **coastal wetlands** (see Section 5-5 and Enrichment Study at the end of this chapter).

About 36 million hectares (89 million acres) of inland wetlands are found in the lower 48 states, equivalent in total area to roughly the size of the state of California. Another estimated 71 million hectares (175 million acres) are found in Alaska. These wetlands include a variety of ecosystems: red-maple swamps and black-spruce bogs in the northern states, bottomland hardwood forests in the Southeast, prairie potholes in the Midwest, and wet tundra in Alaska.

These ecosystems provide habitats for a variety of fish and wildlife, including a third of all bird species in the U.S. Species that are heavily dependent on inland wetlands include migratory waterfowl, alligators, freshwater game fish, crayfish, and mammals such as deer, muskrats, mink, bobcats, beaver, and otter. Inland and coastal wetlands comprise nearly 40% of the National Wildlife Refuge System and provide habitats for 35 endangered and threatened species.

In addition to supporting wildlife, inland wetlands serve a variety of other important ecological functions. They store and regulate stream flow, reducing flooding frequency and downstream peak flood levels. They improve water quality by trapping stream sediments and reducing levels of many toxic pollutants through uptake by vegetation and by degradation to less harmful substances. By holding water, they also allow increased infiltration, thus helping recharge groundwater supplies. They are also used to grow important crops such as blueberries, cranberries, and wild rice.

Because people are often unaware of their ecological importance, inland wetlands are dredged or filled in and used as croplands, garbage dumps, and as sites for urban and industrial development. Over half of the country's original wetlands have been destroyed and at least an additional 120,000 hectares (300,000 acres) are destroyed each year.

5-5 MARINE AQUATIC ECOSYSTEMS

Importance of Oceans Oceans play key roles in the survival of life on earth. As the ultimate receptacle for

106 PART TWO Basic Concepts

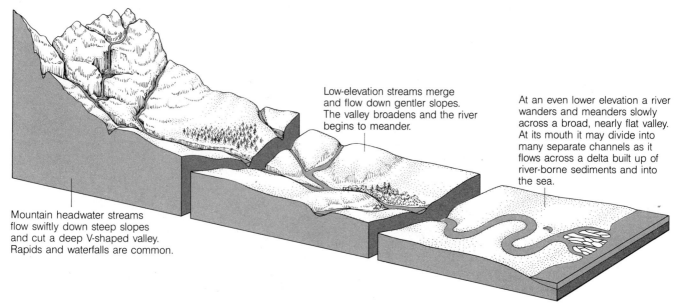

Figure 5-15 Three phases in the flow of water downhill from mountain headwater streams to wider, lower-elevation streams to rivers, which empty into the ocean.

terrestrial water, they dilute many human-produced wastes to less harmful or harmless levels. They also help redistribute solar energy as heat through currents and evaporation as part of the hydrologic cycle, and they play a major role in other major biogeochemical cycles (Section 4-2). In addition, they serve as a gigantic reservoir of dissolved oxygen and carbon dioxide, which, respectively, help to regulate the composition of the air we breathe and the temperature of the atmosphere. Oceans also provide ecological niches for about 250,000 species of marine plants and animals, which provide food for many organisms including humans and serve as a source of iron, sand, gravel, phosphates, oil, natural gas, and many other valuable resources used by humans.

As landlubbers, we tend to think of the earth in terms of land. It is more accurately described, however, as the "water planet" because 71% of its surface is covered by water and 97% of that water is in the oceans. Each of the world's oceans can be divided into two major zones: neritic or coastal and open ocean (Figure 5-16).

Coastal Zone   The **neritic** or **coastal zone** is the relatively warm, nutrient-rich, shallow water zone that extends from the high-tide mark on land to the edge of a shelflike extension of continental landmasses known as the *continental shelf*. This zone includes a number of different habitats. Some coasts have gently sloping **barrier beaches** at the water's edge. If not destroyed by human activities, the two rows of sand dunes on such beaches serve as the first line of defense against the ravages of the sea (Figure 5-17). Other coasts contain steep **rocky shores** pounded by waves; many organisms live in the numerous intertidal pools in the rocks.

Estuaries, found along coastlines where fresh water from rivers mixes with salty oceanic waters, provide aquatic habitats with a lower average salinity than the waters of the open ocean. Extending inland from the estuaries we find **coastal wetlands.** In temperate areas coastal wetlands usually consist of a mix of bays, lagoons, and salt marshes where grasses are the dominant vegetation (see photo inside the front cover); in tropical areas we find mangrove swamps dominated by mangrove trees.

The coastal zones of warm tropical and subtropical oceans often contain **coral reefs** (see photo inside the front cover), consisting mostly of calcium carbonate secreted by photosynthesizing red and green algae and small coral animals. These reefs support at least one-third of all marine fish species as well as numerous other marine organisms. Strings of thin **barrier islands** in some coastal zones (such as portions of North America's Atlantic and Gulf coasts) help protect beaches, estuaries, and wetlands by dissipating the energy of approaching storm waves. Along some steep coastal areas, such as those of Peru, winds blow the surface water away from the shore, allowing cold, nutrient-rich bottom waters, or **upwellings,** to rise to the surface and support large populations of plankton, fish, and fish-eating seabirds (Figure 5-18).

As on land, life in the oceans is unevenly distributed. *The neritic zone, representing less than 10% of the total ocean area, contains 90% of all ocean plant and animal life and is the site of most of the major commercial marine fisheries.* In many heavily populated coastal areas,

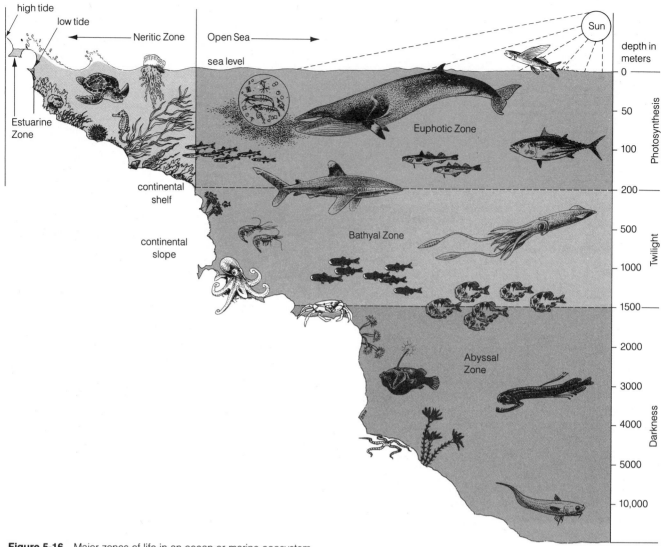

Figure 5-16 Major zones of life in an ocean or marine ecosystem.

human activities are increasingly threatening the abundance of plant and animal life in estuaries and coastal wetlands and destroying some of the important services these ecosystems provide (see the Enrichment Study at the end of this chapter).

Open Sea The sharp increase in the depth of the water at the edge of the continental shelf marks the separation of the neritic zone from the **open sea** (Figure 5-16). This marine zone contains about 90% the total surface area of the ocean but only about 10% of its plant and animal life. The huge open sea has a relatively low average net primary productivity of plant life (Figure 4-18, p. 85) because light is available only at its surface layer and most nutrients are found on the bottom far below.

The open sea is divided into three vertical zones. The surface layer, through which enough sunlight can penetrate for photosynthesis, is called the **euphotic zone.** It supports scattered populations of phytoplankton fed upon by zooplankton, which in turn support commercially important herrings, sardines, anchovies, and other small fish that feed at the surface and their larger predators such as tuna, mackerel, and swordfish.

Below this zone is the **bathyal zone,** a colder, darker layer where there is some penetration by sunlight but not enough to support photosynthesis. Going deeper we find the **abyssal zone,** a layer of deep, pitch-dark, usually near-freezing water and the ocean bottom. About 98% of the ocean's different species (many of them decomposer bacteria) are found in the abyssal zone. Most survive by feeding on dead plants and animals and their waste products, which sink down from the surface waters, and by making daily migrations (usually near dusk) to surface waters to feed. Despite being poor in nutrients and light, the bathyal

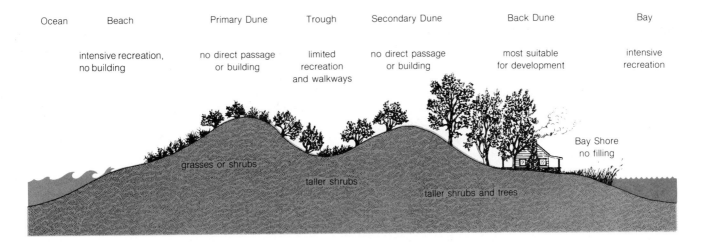

Ocean   Beach   Primary Dune   Trough   Secondary Dune   Back Dune   Bay

intensive recreation,   no direct passage   limited   no direct passage   most suitable   intensive
no building   or building   recreation   or building   for development   recreation
                                              and walkways

Bay Shore
no filling

grasses or shrubs

taller shrubs

taller shrubs and trees

Figure 5-17 Primary and secondary dunes on a barrier beach. Ideally, construction and development should be allowed only behind the second strip of dunes, with walkways to the beach built over the dunes to keep them intact.

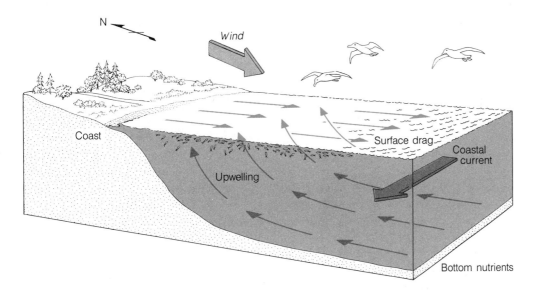

Figure 5-18 An upwelling is caused when deep, cool, nutrient-rich waters are drawn up to replace surface water moved away from the steep coast by wind-driven currents. Such areas support large populations of plankton, fish such as anchovies, and fish-eating seabirds.

and abyssal zones support at least 11% of the known fish species. These species, however, are not a vast untapped source of food because most are tiny, bony, and difficult to capture.

In 1977 a new type of highly productive aquatic ecosystem was discovered deep within the abyssal zone around vents in the ocean floor that spew forth large amounts of very hot, rotten-egg-smelling hydrogen sulfide gas. In this pitch-dark, abnormally warm environment, teeming clouds of specialized bacteria convert hydrogen sulfide into chemical energy without the presence of sunlight through a process called **chemosynthesis.** These bacteria in turn support a variety of abnormally large, strange-looking worms, clams,

blind white crabs, and other animals. This recent discovery reminds us of how little we know about life in the deep ocean.

What has gone wrong, probably, is that we have failed to see ourselves as part of a large and indivisible whole. For too long we have based our lives on a primitive feeling that our "God-given" role was to have "dominion over the fish of the sea and over the fowl of the air and over every living thing that moveth upon the earth." We have failed to understand that the earth does not belong to us, but we to the earth.

Rolf Edberg

Free Services Provided by Estuaries and Coastal Wetlands

Many people view estuaries and coastal wetlands as desolate, mosquito-infested, worthless lands that should be drained, dredged, filled in, built on, or used as depositories for human-generated pollutants and waste materials. Nothing could be further from the truth. These areas provide us and many other species with a number of vital services. They provide food and serve as spawning and nursery grounds for many species of marine fish and shellfish; they are feeding, nesting, and rearing sites for millions of birds and waterfowl. Three-fourths of the commercially important aquatic animal species in the United States spend all or part of their life in estuaries and coastal wetlands. In the United States the $15-billion-a-year commercial and recreational marine fishing industry provides jobs for millions of people.

The coastal areas also dilute and filter out large amounts of waterborne pollutants, helping protect the quality of waters used for swimming, fishing, and wildlife habitats. It is estimated that one acre of tidal estuary substitutes for a $75,000 waste treatment plant and is worth a total of $83,000 when its production of fish for food and recreation is included. In addition, estuaries, wetlands, and the sand dunes of barrier beaches help protect coastal areas by absorbing damaging waves caused by violent storms and hurricanes and serving as giant sponges to absorb floodwaters.

Damage From Hurricanes, Storms, and Beach Erosion

Under natural conditions, the area behind most barrier beaches is protected by two sets of sand dunes held together by sea oats and other grasses and shrubs (Figure 5-17). For more effective flood protection, buildings should be placed behind the secondary dunes; walkways should be built over both dunes to keep them intact. When coastal developers remove the dunes or build behind the first set of dunes, minor hurricanes and sea storms can flood and even sweep away houses and other buildings (Figure 5-19).

Most people call hurricanes and major storms "natural" disasters, not realizing that most of the damage to property and life is really the result of ecologically unsound forms of coastal development. The federal government even

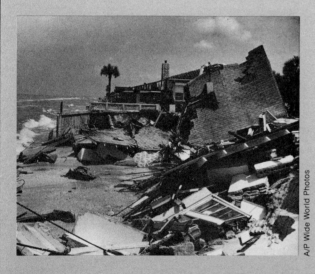
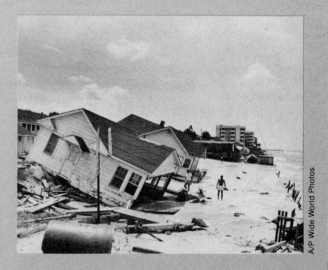

Figure 5-19   Damage to beachfront property wreaked by Hurricane Elena in Florida, 1985.

encourages unsound coastal development by offering coastal home owners inexpensive flood insurance, costing no more than $440 a year. In 1985, federal-flood-insurance policyholders collected $211 million in claims—to rebuild in the very areas devastated by a severe storm or hurricane and wait for the next "natural" disaster.

In addition to the threat of storms and hurricanes, the main problem undermining beachfront development along 80% to 90% of the barrier beaches in the United States is that sea levels have been rising gradually ever since the last ice age ended and the earth began to warm. Although the rise so far is insignificant in many coastal zones, some areas have experienced abnormal increases in the average high-tide mark. For example, most of the beaches of North Carolina and some along the south shore of Long Island are presently moving back at a rate of 0.9 to 1.8 meters (3 to 6 feet) a year; those on the Texas coast are receding even faster. Eighty-six percent of California's coastline is eroding, primarily because of intensive coastal development (Figure 5-20). Many states require that oceanfront structures be elevated and built of concrete, but such structures are still vulnerable to undermin-

ing from beach erosion and to wind and wave damage as the average high-tide mark gradually moves further inland.

A number of devices have been used in attempts to halt or reduce beach erosion (Figure 5-21). *Seawalls* and *stone ripraps* have been built to halt beach erosion, but they actually lead to a dramatic increase in erosion and a much steeper and less usable shoreface because they deflect the waves downward and to the sides against soft sand. *Jetties* to stabilize inlets and *groins* of rock and other materials jutting out perpendicularly from the shore have been built to trap sand as it is carried away by currents.

These barriers temporarily halt some loss of sand in upcurrent beaches, but lead to a dramatic increase in erosion of downcurrent beaches deprived of new sand—sometimes setting off "sand-rustling" controversies between various beach communities. Other areas have rebuilt eroded beaches by pumping in new sand from offshore, but this sand erodes quickly because it steepens the slope of the beach and has finer, more erodable grains. As a result, this extremely costly measure must be repeated every few years. Recognizing that preserving beaches is more important than preserving beachfront property, in 1985 Maine and North Carolina banned construction of new barriers such as seawalls, jetties, and groins.

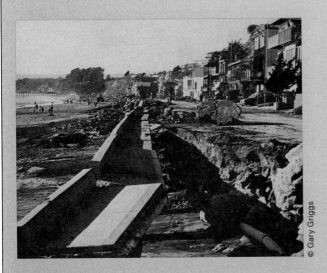

Figure 5-20 Beach erosion at Del Mar, California.

© Gary Griggs

Barrier Islands: The Beaches Are Moving

Along the Atlantic and Gulf coasts, almost 300 natural elongated barrier islands stretch like a broken chain from Maine to Texas. These narrow strips, composed mostly of sand and shells, act as shock absorbers to blunt the force of approaching storm and hurricane waves and thus help protect bay-side wetlands and the mainland shore from erosion and flooding. Today about 70 of these islands, representing over 40% of the country's barrier island shoreline, are highly developed. These include Cape Cod, Massachusetts; Atlantic City, New Jersey; Cape Hatteras, North Carolina; Miami Beach, Florida; Coney Island, New York; and Fenick Island, Maryland (Figure 5-21d). Human structures built on these slender ribbons of sand with water on all sides will sooner or later be damaged or destroyed by flooding and erosion as a result of major storms and hurricanes and by the slow but continual movement of the islands toward the mainland under the influence of currents and winds. As they move, the islands relocate with no net loss of beach, but human structures built near the original high-tide line are gradually undermined.

Use and Protection of Coastal Zones

The fate of the coastal zones in the United States directly or indirectly affects every citizen. About 55% of the U.S. population lives along the coastlines of the Atlantic Ocean, the Pacific Ocean, and the Great Lakes, and two out of three Americans live within 80 kilometers (50 miles) of these shorelines. By the end of this century three out of four will live in or near the coastal zone. Nine

of the country's largest cities, most major ports, about 40% of the manufacturing plants, and two out of three nuclear and coal-fired electric power plants are located in coastal counties. The coasts are also the sites of large numbers of motels, hotels, condominiums, beach cottages, and other human developments.

Because of these multiple uses and stresses, nearly 50% of the estuaries and coastal wetlands in the United States have been destroyed or damaged, primarily by dredging and filling and contamination by wastes. Fortunately, about half of the country's estuaries and coastal wetlands remain undeveloped, but each year additional areas are developed. Some coastal areas have been purchased by federal and state governments and by private conservation agencies, which protect them from development and allow most of

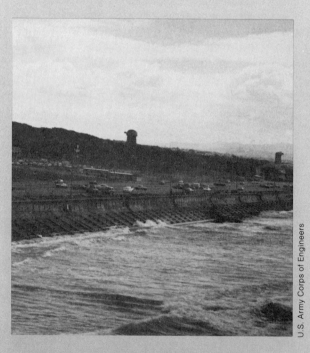

U.S. Army Corps of Engineers

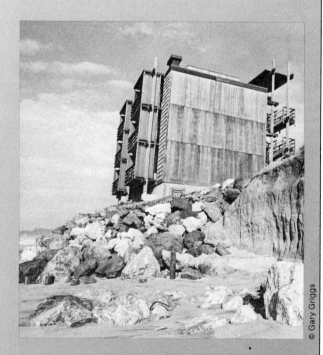

© Gary Griggs

Figure 5-21 (a) Seawalls (along coastline near San Francisco, California); (b) ripraps (at Half Moon Bay, California); (c) jetties (at Santa Cruz, California); and (d) groins (along Fenwick Island, a barrier island off the coast of Maryland). Structures like these, built to reduce beach erosion, are usually unsuccessful.

them to be enjoyed for recreational purposes as parks and wildlife habitats.

The National Coastal Zone Management Acts of 1972 and 1980 provided federal aid to the 37 coastal and Great Lakes states and territories to help them develop voluntary programs for protecting and managing coastlines not under federal protection. By the end of 1986, more than 90% of the country's coastal areas in all but six of the eligible states fell under federally approved state coastal management plans. These plans, however, are voluntary, and many are vague and do not provide sufficient enforcement authority; since 1980 their implementation has also been hindered by federal budget cutbacks. California and North Carolina are considered to have the strongest programs, but developers and others make continuing efforts to weaken such programs.

Protecting the remaining undeveloped coastal ecosystems, while still allowing reasonable use, is a difficult task. A major problem is that more than 70% of the country's shoreline (excluding Alaska) is privately owned, with about 40% of that still officially classified as undeveloped. There are insufficient tax incentives to encourage most private owners to resist lucrative offers from developers and leave these lands undeveloped, restore them, or donate them to government agencies or private conservation organizations. Another difficulty is that even with an ecologically sound management plan, the pressure to use coastal areas primarily for economic purposes is great. Moreover, communities and states sharing a particular estuarine zone often have conflicting goals.

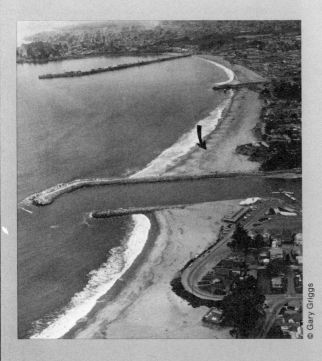

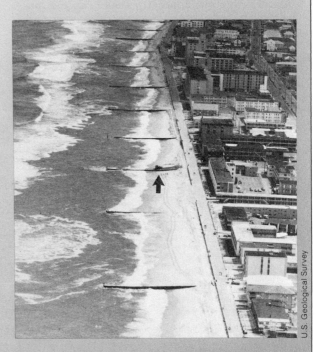

CHAPTER SUMMARY

Organisms have a variety of characteristics that allow them to live in certain environments, obtain sufficient quantities of scarce resources, and adapt to changes in environmental conditions. Despite these characteristics, the existence, abundance, and distribution of an organism is determined by whether one or more physical or chemical factors in its environment fall above or below the levels most individuals in the population of a species can tolerate (*law of tolerance*) and by the single factor that is most deficient in its environment (*limiting factor principle*).

Climate is an average, usually based on 30 years or more of data, of the various day-to-day atmospheric conditions (weather) likely to occur in an area. The two most important factors determining the climate of an area are its *average temperature* and *average precipitation*. Variations in these and other climatic factors in various parts of the world are caused by **(1)** the uneven heating of the equatorial and polar regions of the earth, which causes air masses to circulate between these regions, **(2)** the rotation of the earth around its axis, which creates three major belts of prevailing winds; and **(3)** unequal distribution of land masses, oceans, ocean currents, mountains, and other geological features over the earth's surface.

The major types of terrestrial ecosystems, or biomes, are *deserts, grasslands,* and *forests. Average annual precipitation* determines whether the biome is a desert, grassland, or forest. This factor combined with *average annual temperature* leads to various types of *tropical* (low-latitude), *temperate* (mid-latitude), and *polar* (high-latitude) deserts, grasslands, and forests.

Aquatic ecosystems include **(1)** *freshwater ecosystems* consisting of inland bodies of *standing* water (lakes, reservoirs, ponds, and wetlands) and *flowing* water (streams and rivers) with low salinity, and **(2)** *marine or saltwater ecosystems* consisting of the oceans with high to very high salinity levels. Large and deep aquatic ecosystems such as lakes, reservoirs, and oceans are usually divided into several vertical layers: a *shallow, sunlit, shore zone*, a *sunlit surface layer of open water* where photosynthesis can take place, and a *deeper, colder level of open water and nutrient-rich bottom* where sunlight is absent.

The main limiting factors affecting the types and numbers of organisms found in different aquatic ecosystems and the vertical layers of some of these ecosystems are the concentration of dissolved salts such as sodium chloride (salinity), depth to which sunlight penetrates, amount of dissolved oxygen, and water temperature. Because of ample sunlight and nutrients, the shallow shore zone usually contains the largest numbers of species of aquatic plant and animal life.

Although the coastal zone, consisting of barrier islands, beaches, and highly productive estuaries, wetlands, coral reefs, and upwellings, represents less than 10% of the total ocean area, it contains 90% of all ocean plant and animal life (including most of the commercially important marine fish and shellfish) and helps protect low-lying coastal areas from flooding and other damaging effects of storms and hurricanes. However, these and other important ecological services provided by the coastal zone are being threatened by large-scale human development on scarce, economically valuable land near the coast.

DISCUSSION TOPICS

1. **a.** List three ways that plants obtain scarce water in a desert ecosystem.

   b. List three ways that animals obtain scarce water in a desert ecosystem.

2. How can an area have "bad" weather and a "good" climate?

3. List a probable limiting factor for each of the following ecosystems: **(a)** a desert, **(b)** the surface layer of the open ocean, **(c)** the arctic tundra, **(d)** the floor of a tropical rain forest, and **(e)** the bottom of a deep lake.

4. How does natural eutrophication differ from cultural eutrophication of a lake?

5. What bodies of water, if any, in your area have suffered from cultural eutrophication and what is being done to correct this situation?

6. Why are the oceans so important to life on this planet?

7. Since the deep oceans are vast, self-sustaining ecosystems located far away from human habitats, why not use them as a depository for essentially all of our radioactive and other hazardous wastes?

8. Draw up a list of rules and regulations designed to protect beaches, estuaries, and wetlands while still allowing them to be used for recreation and ecologically sound development.

6

Ecosystems: What Can
Happen to Them?

GENERAL OBJECTIVES

1. How do living systems maintain their stability?

2. How can populations adapt to natural and human-induced stresses to preserve their overall stability?

3. How can ecosystems adapt to small- and large-scale natural and human-induced stresses to preserve their overall stability?

4. What major impacts can human activities have on ecosystems?

5. How are environmental risks determined and how can they be managed?

We cannot command nature except by obeying her.
Sir Francis Bacon

Ecosystems are dynamic, not static. The populations of plants and animals they contain are always changing and adapting in response to major and minor changes in environmental conditions. This ability to adapt and yet sustain themselves is truly a remarkable feature of ecosystems, as we shall see in this chapter.

6-1 HOW LIVING SYSTEMS MAINTAIN STABILITY

What Is Stability? Organisms, populations, communities, and ecosystems all have some ability to withstand or recover from externally imposed changes or stresses. In other words, they have some degree of *stability*. This stability is maintained, however, only by constant change. Although an organism is continually gaining and losing matter and energy, its body maintains a fairly stable structure over its life span. Similarly, in a mature tropical rain forest ecosystem some trees will die, others will take their place. Some species may disappear, and the number of individual species in the forest may change. But unless it is cut, burned, or blown down, you will recognize it as a tropical rain forest 50 years from now.

It is useful to distinguish between two aspects of stability in living systems. **Inertia stability** or **persistence** is the ability of a living system to resist being disturbed or altered. **Resilience stability** is the ability of a living system to restore itself to an original condition if the outside disturbance is not too drastic. Nature is remarkably resilient. For example, human societies survive natural disasters and devastating wars; the genetic structure of insect populations is altered to survive massive doses of deadly pesticides and ionizing radiation; and plants eventually recolonize areas devastated by volcanoes, retreating glaciers, mining,

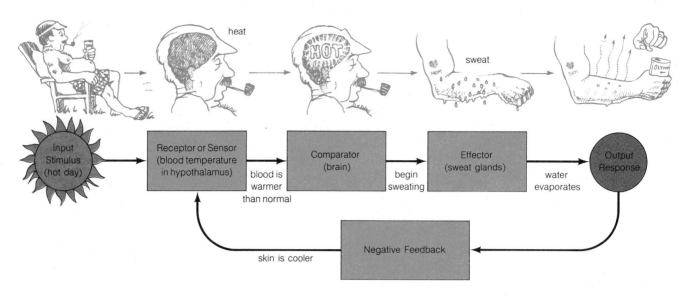

Figure 6-1 Keeping cool on a hot day—a human temperature control system based on negative feedback of information to counteract a change in environmental conditions (arrows show flow of information).

and abandoned farmlands—although such natural restoration usually takes a long time on a human time scale.

Stability and Information Feedback   All living systems from organism to ecosystem to the biosphere have "built-in" means of maintaining internal conditions within some tolerable range when external conditions fluctuate—provided these external stresses are not too severe. Living systems maintain constant internal conditions by means of the flow of information along the network of interconnected parts in the system. **Information feedback** is the process by which information is fed back into a system and causes it to change in order to maintain a particular desired state. The thermostat on a home furnace is an example of control of temperature by information feedback. If the room temperature drops below or rises above the temperature set on the thermostat, this information is fed back into the system to turn the furnace on or off as appropriate.

There are two types of information feedback: negative and positive. The more common is **negative feedback**—a flow of information into a system that enables it to adjust to an environmental change by counteracting the effects of the change. The thermostat-furnace system is an example of temperature control through negative feedback. When room temperature falls too low, more heat is supplied; when room temperature becomes too high, the furnace is turned off.

Similarly, negative feedback keeps human body temperature around 37°C (98.6°F), as shown in Figure 6-1, which diagrams the general self-regulating mech-

anism used by living organisms. An initial input of information (*stimulus*) such as a rise in temperature is detected by sensors in the skin and sent to the brain (*comparator*), which sends a signal (nerve impulse) to sweat glands (*effectors*) in the skin to activate sweating, a cooling mechanism. As sweat evaporates, it takes heat from the skin. When the body is cooled down, this new information (output response) is fed back into the receptors or sensors of the system as *negative feedback*, and the brain then sends a new message to the skin effectors to slow or stop the sweating process. Conversely, if the environment is too cold, a similar negative feedback mechanism stops the sweating, slows blood flow, and causes shivering so that the body will produce more heat.

Positive feedback—also known as *runaway feedback*—occurs when a change in the system in one direction provides information that causes the system to change further in the same direction. For example, suppose the wires on a furnace thermostat were accidentally hooked up backwards. Then when the room got too hot, a positive feedback of information would cause the furnace to turn on and make the room even hotter.

Generally, negative feedback tends to keep a system in a fairly constant or stable state, while positive feedback tends to disrupt a system's stability. Thus, *all living systems are self-regulating systems maintained primarily by negative feedback.*

Time Delays and Synergistic and Antagonistic Effects   Another characteristic of self-regulating systems is **time delay**—the delay between the time a stimulus is received and the time when the system

Table 6-1 Some Effects of Environmental Stress

Organism Level

Physiological and biochemical changes
Psychological disorders
Behavioral changes
Fewer or no offspring
Genetic defects in offspring (mutagenic effects)
Birth defects (teratogenic effects)
Cancers (carcinogenic effects)
Death

Population Level

Population increase or decrease
Change in age structure (old, young, and weak may die)
Survival of strains genetically resistant to a stress
Loss of genetic diversity and adaptability
Extinction

Community–Ecosystem Level

Disruption of energy flow
  Decrease or increase in solar energy input
  Changes in heat output
  Changes in trophic structure in food chains and food webs

Disruption of chemical cycles
  Depletion of essential nutrients
  Excessive addition of nutrients

Simplification
  Reduction in species diversity
  Reduction or elimination of habitats and filled ecological niches
  Less complex food webs
  Possibility of lowered stability
  Possibility of ecosystem collapse

---

makes a corrective action by negative feedback. Different feedback loops in a complex system have different response times. Time delays can protect a system for a while. But a time delay between a cause and its effect often means that corrective action is not effective by the time symptoms of harm appear. A pollutant released into the environment may not affect human health or other organisms for years. For example, workers exposed to a cancer-causing (carcinogenic) chemical or ionizing radiation may not get cancer for 20 or 30 years. By then it is often too late for corrective response through negative feedback, which also has built-in time delays.

You were taught that 1 plus 1 always equals 2. But in complex systems, 1 plus 1 may sometimes be greater than or less than 2 because of synergistic and antagonistic effects. A **synergistic effect** occurs when two or more factors interact so that the net effect is *greater than* that expected from adding together their independent effects (1 plus 1 is greater than 2). For example, separately, either cigarette smoke or tiny particles of asbestos fibers, when inhaled into the lungs over a prolonged period, can cause lung cancer. Acting together, however, they greatly increase one's chance of contracting lung cancer; workers who are exposed to asbestos and who smoke are ten times more likely to contract lung cancer than asbestos workers who do not smoke. Another well-known example is the synergistic interaction between alcohol and sleeping pills. Taken alone, each slows down human body functions, but together the two may be fatal.

An **antagonistic effect** occurs when two or more factors interact so that the net effect is *less than* that of adding their independent effects (1 plus 1 is less than 2). This happens because one factor partially counteracts or cancels the effect of another. For example, by themselves nitrogen dioxide and tiny particles of matter such as soot can harm the lungs when inhaled. When these air pollutants act together, however, the effect on the lungs is less than when each acts alone. The existence of antagonistic effects helps explain why living systems are resilient if not pushed too far.

Effects of Environmental Stress Table 6-1 summarizes what can happen to organisms, populations, and ecosystems if one or more limits of tolerance are exceeded (Section 5-1). The stresses that can cause the changes shown in Table 6-1 may result from natural hazards (such as earthquakes, volcanic eruptions, hurricanes, drought, floods, and fires) or from human activities (industrialization, warfare, transportation, and agriculture). The remainder of this chapter is devoted to a study of how populations and ecosystems respond to such stresses.

6-2 POPULATION RESPONSES TO STRESS

Changes in Population Size Populations of plants and animals that make up ecosystems respond in various ways to changes in environmental conditions such as an excess or shortage of food or other critical nutrients. One way involves changes in the size of the population through feedback mechanisms. The birth rate may increase to allow the population to take advantage of an increase in food or other resources or the death rate may increase to reduce the population to a size that can be supported by available resources. Also, the structure of the population may change. The old, very young, and weak members may die, leaving the population more capable of surviving stresses such as a more severe climate, an increase in predators, or an increase in disease organisms. The major *abiotic* (nonliving) and *biotic* (living) factors that tend to increase or decrease the population size of a given species are summarized in Figure 6-2.

Figure 6-2 Population size is a balance between factors that increase numbers and factors that decrease numbers through negative feedback.

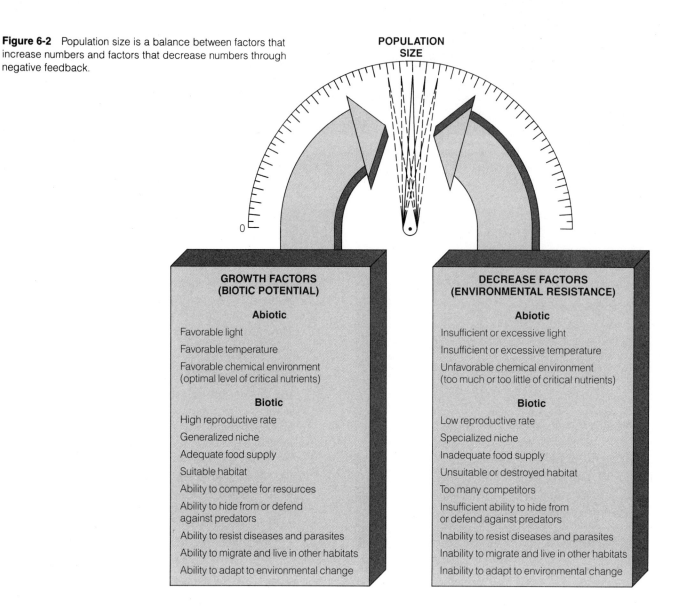

POPULATION SIZE

GROWTH FACTORS (BIOTIC POTENTIAL)

Abiotic

Favorable light

Favorable temperature

Favorable chemical environment (optimal level of critical nutrients)

Biotic

High reproductive rate

Generalized niche

Adequate food supply

Suitable habitat

Ability to compete for resources

Ability to hide from or defend against predators

Ability to resist diseases and parasites

Ability to migrate and live in other habitats

Ability to adapt to environmental change

DECREASE FACTORS (ENVIRONMENTAL RESISTANCE)

Abiotic

Insufficient or excessive light

Insufficient or excessive temperature

Unfavorable chemical environment (too much or too little of critical nutrients)

Biotic

Low reproductive rate

Specialized niche

Inadequate food supply

Unsuitable or destroyed habitat

Too many competitors

Insufficient ability to hide from or defend against predators

Inability to resist diseases and parasites

Inability to migrate and live in other habitats

Inability to adapt to environmental change

The response of the population of a species to a change in resource availability or to environmental stress usually can be represented by two simple curves—a J-shaped curve and an S-shaped curve (Figure 6-3). With unlimited resources and ideal environmental conditions, a species can produce offspring at its maximum rate, called its **biotic potential.** Such growth starts off slowly and then increases rapidly to produce an exponential or J-shaped curve of population growth. Species such as bacteria, insects, and mice, which can produce a large number of offspring in a short time, have high biotic potentials; larger species, such as elephants and humans, which take a much longer time to produce only a few offspring, have low biotic potentials. Since environmental conditions usually are not ideal, a population rarely reproduces at its biotic potential.

The population size of a particular species in a given ecosystem depends on the availability of one or more resources, which can act as limiting factors. The maximum population size of each species that an ecosystem can support *indefinitely* under a given set of environmental conditions is called that ecosystem's **carrying capacity.** All the limiting factors that reduce the growth rate of a population are called the population's **environmental resistance.** It includes factors such as predation, interspecific competition for resources, food shortage, disease, adverse climatic conditions, and lack of suitable habitat. As a population encounters environmental resistance, the J-shaped curve of population growth bends away from its steep incline and eventually levels off at a size that typically fluctuates above and below the ecosystem's carrying capacity. In other words, environmental resistance

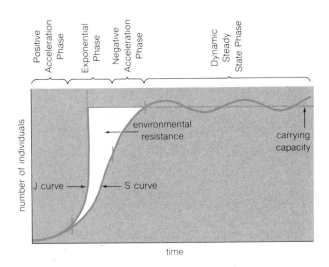

Figure 6-3 The J-shaped curve of population growth of a species is converted to an S-shaped curve when the population encounters environmental resistance and exceeds one or more limiting factors.

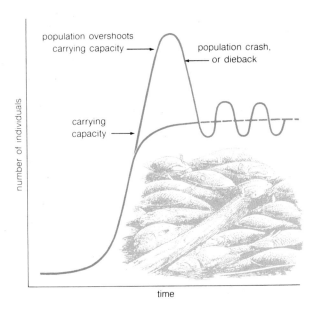

Figure 6-4 A population crash can occur when a population temporarily overshoots its carrying capacity due to time delays, impaired negative feedback controls, or a change in environmental conditions that lowers the carrying capacity of its environment.

lowers the biotic potential of a population and converts a J-shaped curve into an S-shaped curve (Figure 6-3).

Because of a time delay in the application of corrective negative feedback, some populations (especially rapidly reproducing ones such as insects, bacteria, and algae) may surpass the carrying capacity and then undergo a rapid decrease in size, known as a **population crash** (Figure 6-4). Some population crashes involve sharp increases in the death rate; others involve combinations of a rise in the death rate coupled with emigration of large numbers of individuals to other areas. A population crash can also occur when a change in environmental conditions lowers the carrying capacity of an ecosystem.

There have been crashes in the human populations of various countries throughout history. Ireland, for example, experienced a population crash after a fungus infection destroyed the potato crop in 1845. Dependent on the potato for a major portion of their diet, by 1900 half of Ireland's 8 million people had died of starvation or emigrated to other countries. In spite of such local and regional disasters, the overall human population on earth has continued to grow because technological, social, and other cultural changes have extended the earth's carrying capacity for humans. In essence, humans have been able to alter their ecological niche by increasing food production, controlling disease, and using large amounts of energy and mat-

ter resources to make normally uninhabitable areas of the earth inhabitable. Figure 6-5 shows that after each major technological change—except the industrial-scientific revolution we are still experiencing—the population grew rapidly and then leveled off.*

The dashed lines in Figure 6-5 show three projections of future population growth based on our present understanding. No one, of course, knows what the present or future worldwide or regional carrying capacity for the human population is or what the limiting factor or factors might be—food, air, water, or capacity of the environment to absorb pollution and recover from environmental degradation.

Biological Evolution and Natural Selection
Besides responding to changes in population size, a population of a particular species can also adapt to a change in environmental conditions by changing its genetic composition (gene pool). All individuals of a population do not have exactly the same genes; these

---

*The curve shown in Figure 6-5 is plotted by a different mathematical method (a plot of the logarithm of population size versus the logarithm of time) from the method (a plot of population size versus time) used in Figure 1-1 on page 3.

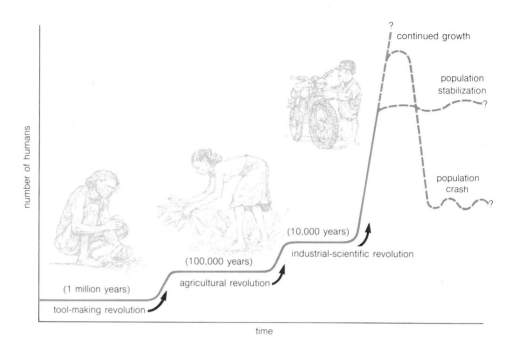

Figure 6-5 Humans have expanded the earth's carrying capacity for their species through technological innovation leading to several major cultural changes. Dashed lines represent possible future changes in human population size: continued growth, population stabilization, and continued growth followed by a crash and stabilization at a much lower level. (These curves are generalized log-log plots not drawn to scale.)

genetic differences (*genotypes*) mean that some individuals in the population have more tolerance to a particular environmental change than others. When subjected to a stress, more of these individuals survive than those without such traits and pass their favorable genetic traits to their offspring. As a result, the gene pool of the population is changed to make it more adaptable to a particular environmental stress. Such a change in the genetic composition of a population is called **biological evolution** or **evolution.**

The process by which some genes and gene combinations in a population are reproduced more than others is called **natural selection.** Charles Darwin, who first proposed this idea in 1858, described natural selection as "survival of the fittest." This has often been misinterpreted to mean survival of the strongest, biggest, or most aggressive. Instead, survival of the fittest means that the most fit genotype in a population is the one that on the average produces the most offspring in a given generation.

Today we have a much better understanding of how natural selection takes place. We now know that hereditary traits of individual organisms are carried in the *genes* and that this information is coded in the sequence of certain groups of atoms in molecules of DNA found in genes. Individuals in a population of a species don't have exactly the same genes because of **mutations** or inheritable changes in the structure of their genes. One way mutations occur is from exposure to various external environmental factors such as ionizing radiation, heat, and certain chemicals that subject DNA molecules to random, spontaneous changes in their chemical makeup. Mutations can also occur internally when a cell divides (asexual reproduction) and when two cells, sperm and egg, fuse (sexual reproduction).

Some of these inheritable mutations are harmful and others are helpful. If a new genetic variation interferes with survival and reproduction, organisms with this trait die prematurely. With each successive generation, more of these harmful genes are eliminated from the *gene pool* of the population. However, if a particular mutation enhances survival and reproduction of an organism, this variation is passed on to greater numbers of offspring in succeeding generations; thus, natural selection has taken place.

Species differ widely in how rapidly they can undergo evolution through natural selection. Some species have many offspring and short generation times; others have few offspring and long generation times. Those that can quickly produce a large number of tiny offspring with short average life spans (weeds, insects, and rodents) can adapt to a change in environmental conditions through natural selection in a relatively short time. Most of the offspring of such species die before reproducing because after birth they are usually left to fend for themselves. However, such a large number of offspring are produced that the chances of a few individuals surviving, reproducing, and passing survival-enhancing genes to the next generation are ensured. For example, in only a few years many species of mosquitoes have become genetically resistant to DDT and other pesticides, and many species of bacteria have become genetically resistant to widely used antibiotics, such as penicillin.

Other species such as elephants, horses, tigers,

For many decades humans have intervened in and shortened natural selection processes by crossbreeding different genetic varieties of plants and animals to develop new varieties with certain desired qualities as human food sources. Today "genetic engineers" have learned how to splice genes and recombine sequences of DNA molecules to produce DNA with new genetic characteristics (recombinant DNA). This new biotechnology, which is just beginning to emerge from the laboratory, may in the near future allow humans greatly increased control over the course of natural selection for the earth's living species.

This increasingly real possibility excites some. They see it as a way to increase crop and livestock yields, and to produce plants and livestock that have greater resistance to diseases, pests, frost, and drought and that provide greater quantities of nutrients such as proteins. They also hope to develop bacteria that can destroy oil spills and degrade toxic wastes and new vaccines, drugs, and therapeutic hormones like insulin. Gene therapy would also be used to eliminate certain genetic diseases and other human genetic afflictions.

Others are horrified by this prospect. Most of these critics recognize that it is essentially impossible to stop the development of genetic engineering, which is already well under way. But they believe that this technology should be kept under strict control. They are particularly concerned that it may be used to reduce the natural genetic diversity among individuals of a single species and the ecological diversity represented by the world's variety of species—both essential to the functioning of ecosystems and the long-term survival of the biosphere. These critics do not believe that humans have enough understanding of how nature works to be trusted with such great control over the genetic characteristics of humans and other species.

Critics also fear that unregulated biotechnology could lead to the development of "superorganisms," which, if released deliberately or accidentally into the environment, could cause many unpredictable, possibly harmful effects. For example, genetically altered bacteria designed to clean up ocean oil spills by degrading the oil might multiply rapidly and eventually degrade the world's remaining oil supplies—including the oil in our cars. The risks of this or other catastrophic events are quite small, but critics contend that biotechnology is a potential source of such enormous profits that without strict controls greed—not ecological wisdom and restraint—will take over.

Genetic biologists answer, however, that it is highly unlikely that the release of genetically engineered species would cause serious and widespread ecological problems. To have a serious effect, such organisms would have to be outstanding competitors and relatively resistant to predation. In addition, they would have to be capable of becoming dominant in ecosystems and in the biosphere, which are already populated with a vast diversity of organisms that act as checks and balances against dominance by any single species (except humans so far).

Some genetic scientists contend that introduction of a well-characterized DNA molecule into the genes of organisms is *safer* than the more random alteration of genetic strains by mutation and natural selection. But other proponents of biotechnology, acknowledging that some genetically engineered organisms might contribute to localized or temporary ecological disasters, join the critics in calling for strict control over this emerging technology. This controversy illustrates the difficulty of balancing the actual or potential benefits of a technology with its actual or potential risks of harm (see the Enrichment Study at the end of this chapter). What do you think?

---

white sharks, and humans have long generation times and a small number in each litter and thus cannot reproduce a large number of offspring rapidly. For such species, adaptation to an environmental stress by natural selection typically takes thousands to millions of years. Instead of having numerous tiny offspring and letting them fend for themselves, such species have a few large offspring and nurse them until they are big and strong enough to survive on their own. This breeding mechanism ensures the species' long-term survival, provided that most or all of the breeding adults and offspring are not killed by disease, accident, predation, starvation, or some other environmental stress before they can reproduce. If that happens, the species becomes extinct and the genetic line ends.

Not only has the human species used its intelligence to develop cultural mechanisms for controlling and adapting to environmental stresses, it has also learned to bring about genetic change in other species at a fast rate—first through crossbreeding and recently through genetic engineering (see Spotlight above).

Speciation   Genetic changes in existing species can occur not only within a single genetic line but also by the splitting of lines of descent into new species through **speciation:** the gradual formation of two or more species from one in response to new environmental conditions. Speciation has led to the estimated 5 to 10 million different species found on earth today. Although in some rapidly producing organisms speciation may take place in thousands or even hundreds of years, in most cases it takes from tens of thousands to millions of years.

Exactly how speciation takes place is not fully understood, partly because it takes place so slowly that biologists have only been able to observe part of the process. In general, most speciation is believed to occur when a population of a particular species becomes distributed over areas with quite different environments for long periods. For example, different populations of the same species may be geographically isolated when floods, hurricanes, earthquakes, or other geological processes break up a single land mass into separate islands (Figure 6-6). Populations also split up when part of the group migrates in search of food (Figure 6-7).

If different populations of a single species are geographically isolated from one another over a great many generations (typically 1,000 to 100,000 generations), they begin to diverge genetically through natural selection in response to their different climates, food sources, soils, and other environmental factors. Eventually, the geographically isolated populations become so genetically different that they are no longer capable of successfully interbreeding should they subsequently come to occupy the same area again. Thus, they have become different species and speciation has taken place.

The incredible genetic diversity created over billions of years within populations of the same species and among different species is nature's "insurance policy" against known and unforeseen disasters. Although many more species than currently exist have appeared and disappeared throughout earth's history, every species here today represents stored genetic information that allows the species to adapt to certain changes in environmental conditions. *This genetic information contained in living species and the cultural information passed from one human generation to the next are the most valuable resources on this planet.*

6-3   Ecosystem Responses to Stress

Responses to Small and Moderate Stress   Ecosystems are so complex and variable that ecologists have little understanding of how they maintain their inertia stability and resilience stability. One major

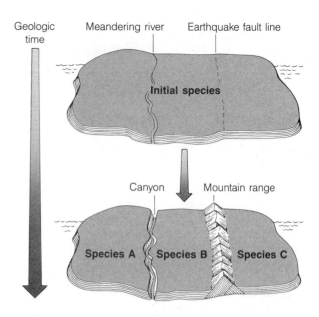

Figure 6-6   Speciation of a single species into three species as a result of prolonged geographic isolation.

problem is the difficulty of conducting controlled experiments. It is virtually impossible to identify and observe even a tiny fraction of the interacting variables found in simple ecosystems. Ecosystems have such complex networks of negative feedback loops, time delays, and synergistic and antagonistic interactions that even the best computer models designed to emulate their functions hardly scratch the surface. In addition, ecologists cannot run long-term experiments in which only one variable in a natural ecosystem is allowed to change. Greatly simplified ecosystems can be set up and observed under laboratory conditions, but it is difficult if not essentially impossible to extrapolate the results of such experiments to more complex, natural ecosystems.

Numerous observations of laboratory and natural ecosystems, however, have led ecologists to the conclusion that one factor affecting the inertia stability or persistence of *some* ecosystems under small or moderate environmental stress is **species diversity**—the number of different species and their relative abundances in a given area. High species diversity tends to increase long-term persistence because with so many different species, ecological niches, and linkages between them, risk is more widely spread. Because it does not "put all its eggs in one basket," an ecosystem with a diversity of species has available more ways of responding to most environmental stresses than much simpler ecosystems, dependent on only one or a few species.

For example, the loss or drastic reduction of one species in a diverse ecosystem with complex food webs usually does not threaten the existence of others because most predators have several alternative food supplies.

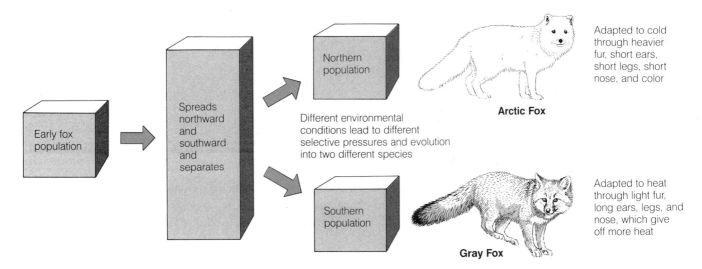

Figure 6-7 Speciation of an early species of fox into two different species as a result of migration of portions of the original fox population into areas with different climates.

In contrast, a highly simplified agricultural ecosystem planted with a single crop (monoculture) such as corn or wheat is highly vulnerable to destruction from a single plant disease or insect. The situation is parallel to that of a city that has a number of diverse economic interests and businesses and is therefore more likely to have long-term persistence than a city that depends primarily on only one business enterprise.

However, some research indicates that there may be exceptions to this intuitively appealing idea. Coastal salt marshes, for example, are not very diverse ecosystems but are persistent if not disturbed too severely, whereas the intertidal ecosystems of rocky seashores have a very high species diversity but can be upset by a single change in their species composition—especially loss of the starfish population.

There are controversies, however, over the interpretation of these and other studies of the relationships between species diversity and ecosystem inertia stability—primarily because of differences in how the terms *diversity* and *stability* are defined for experimental purposes. For example, should species diversity be confined to counts of just the number of different species in an area, or should the relative abundance of each species also be considered? Should the characteristics of the plant and animal species also be considered? Is an ecosystem containing 100 deer and 1,000 rabbits as diverse as one containing 100 deer and 1,000 grasshoppers? Is an ecosystem considered stable as long as its species composition undergoes little change (persistence) or as long as the population sizes of its species remain relatively constant (constancy)?

Does an ecosystem need both high inertia stability and high resilience stability to be considered sta-

ble? Evidence indicates that some ecosystems have one type of stability but not the other. For example, California redwood forests and tropical rain forests have high species diversity and high inertia stability and are thus hard to alter significantly or destroy through natural processes. However, once large tracts of these diverse ecosystems are completely cleared, they have such low resilience stability that they are nearly impossible to restore. On the other hand, grasslands, much lower in species diversity, can burn easily and thus have low inertia stability. But because most of their plant matter is found as roots beneath the ground surface, these ecosystems have high resilience stability that allows them to recover quickly. The grassland can be destroyed only if its roots are plowed up and the soil is used to plant wheat or some other crop.

Clearly, we have a long way to go in understanding how the factors involved in natural ecosystems interact. We don't know for certain that high species diversity always contributes to either the inertia or resilience stability, or both, of a particular ecosystem. But there is considerable evidence that simplifying an ecosystem by the intentional or accidental removal of a species often has unpredictable short- and long-term harmful effects (see Spotlight on p. 124).

Responses to Large-Scale Stress: Ecological Succession Most ecosystems can adapt not only to small and moderate changes in environmental conditions but also to quite severe changes. Sometimes, for example, little vegetation and soil are left as a result of a natural environmental change (retreating glaciers, fires, floods, volcanic eruptions, earthquakes) or a

Malaria once infected nine out of ten people on the island of North Borneo, now known as Brunei. In 1955 the World Health Organization (WHO) began spraying dieldrin (a pesticide similar to DDT) to kill malaria-carrying mosquitoes. The program was so successful that the dreaded disease was almost eliminated from the island. But other, unexpected things happened. The dieldrin killed other insects, including flies and cockroaches inhabiting the houses. The islanders applauded. But then small lizards that also lived in the houses died after gorging themselves on dead insects. Then cats began dying after feeding on the dead lizards. Without cats, rats flourished and began overrunning the villages. Now people were threatened by sylvatic plague carried by the fleas on the rats. The situation was brought under control when WHO parachuted healthy cats onto the island.

On top of everything else, roofs began to fall in. The dieldrin had killed wasps and other insects that fed on a type of caterpillar that either avoided or was not affected by the insecticide. With most of its predators eliminated, the caterpillar population exploded. The larvae munched their way through one of their favorite foods, the leaves used in thatching roofs. In the end, the Borneo episode was a success story; both malaria and the unexpected effects of the spraying program were brought under control. But it shows the unpredictable results of interfering in an ecosystem.

human-induced change (fires, land clearing, surface mining, flooding to create a pond or reservoir, pollution).

After such a large-scale disturbance, life usually begins to recolonize a site in a series of stages. First, a few hardy pioneer species invade the environment and start creating soil or, in aquatic ecosystems, sediment. Eventually these pioneer species change the soil or bottom sediments and other conditions so much that the area is less suitable for them and more suitable for a new group of plants and animals with different ecological niche requirements. Gradually, these new invaders alter the local environment still more by changing the soil, providing shade, and creating a greater variety of ecological niches, paving the way for invasion by a third wave of plants and animals. Each

successive invasion makes the local environment more suitable for future invaders and less suitable for previous communities. This process, in which communities of plant and animal species are replaced over time by a series of different and usually more complex communities, is called **ecological succession.**

If not severely disrupted, ecological succession usually continues until the community becomes much more self-sustaining and stable than the preceding ones and what ecologists call the **climax ecosystem,** or **climax community,** occupies the site. Depending primarily on the climate, climax terrestrial ecosystems may be various types of mature grasslands, forests, or deserts (Figure 5-6, p. 97).

Ecologists recognize two types of ecological succession: primary and secondary. Which type takes place depends on the conditions at a particular site at the beginning of the process. **Primary succession** is the sequential development of communities in a bare or soilless area. Examples of such areas include the rock or mud exposed by a retreating glacier or mudslide, cooled volcanic lava, a new sandbar deposited by a shift in ocean currents, and surface-mined areas from which all topsoil has been removed. On such barren surfaces, primary succession from bare rock to a mature forest may take hundreds to thousands of years.

Figure 6-8 shows the stages of primary succession from bare rock exposed by retreating glaciers to a balsam fir, paper birch, and white spruce climax natural community on Isle Royale in northern Lake Superior. First, retreating glaciers exposed bare rock. Wind, rain, and frost weathered the rock surfaces to form tiny cracks and holes. Water collecting in these depressions slowly dissolved minerals out of the rock's surface. The minerals—the inorganic basis of a pioneer soil layer—supported hardy pioneer plants, such as lichens. Gradually covering the rock surface and secreting a weak acid (carbonic acid), which dissolved additional minerals from the rock, the lichens were replaced by mosses. Decomposer organisms moved in to feed on the dead lichens and mosses and were followed by a few small animals such as ants, mites, and spiders. This first successfully integrated set of plants, animals, and decomposers is called the **pioneer community.**

After several decades the pioneer community had built up enough organic matter in its thin soil to support the roots of small herbs and shrubs. These newcomers slowed the loss of moisture and provided food and cover for new plants, animals, and decomposers. Under these modified conditions, the species in the pioneer community were crowded out and gradually replaced with a different community.

As this new community thrived, it too added organic matter to the slowly thickening upper layers

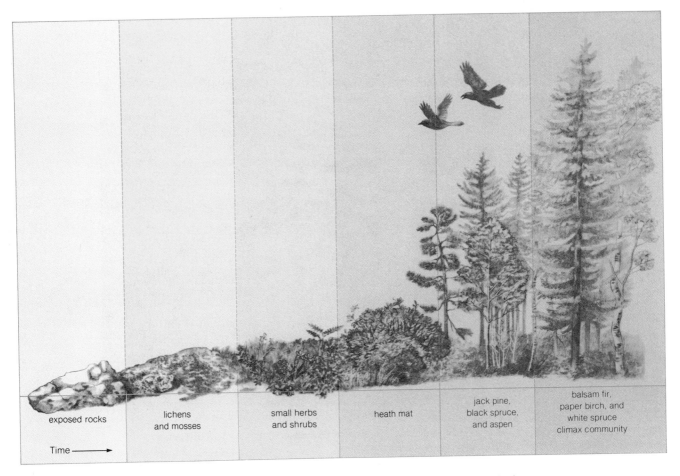

exposed rocks

Time ——→

lichens
and mosses

small herbs
and shrubs

heath mat

jack pine,
black spruce,
and aspen

balsam fir,
paper birch, and
white spruce
climax community

Figure 6-8 Primary ecological succession of plant communities over several hundred years on a patch of exposed rock on Isle Royale in northern Lake Superior. Succession of animal communities is not shown.

of soil, leading to the next stage of succession, a compact layer of vegetation called a *heath mat*. This mat, in turn, provided thicker and richer soil, needed for the successful germination and growth of trees such as jack pine, black spruce, and aspen. Over several decades these trees increased in height and density, crowding out the compact plants of the heath mat. Shade and other new conditions created by these trees allowed the successful germination and growth of balsam fir, paper birch, white spruce, and other shade-tolerant climax species. As these taller trees created a canopy overhead, most of the earlier, shade-intolerant species were eliminated because they could no longer reproduce. After several centuries, what was once bare rock had become a mature, or climax, ecosystem.

The more common type of succession is **secondary succession,** the sequential development of communities in an area in which the natural vegetation has been removed or destroyed, but the soil or bottom sediment is not destroyed. Examples of areas that can undergo secondary succession include abandoned farmlands, burned or cut forests, land stripped of veg-

etation for surface mining, heavily polluted streams, and land that has been flooded naturally or to produce a reservoir or pond. Since some soil or sediment is present, new vegetation can sprout within only a few weeks.

In the central (Piedmont) region of North Carolina, European settlers cleared away the native oak-hickory climax forests and planted the land in crops. Figure 6-9 shows how this abandoned farmland, covered with a thick layer of soil, has undergone secondary succession over a period of about 150 years until the area is again covered with a mature oak-hickory forest. Newly created lakes, reservoirs, and ponds also undergo secondary succession: As they gradually fill up with bottom sediments, they are eventually converted to terrestrial ecosystems, which then undergo terrestrial ecological succession.

Comparison of Immature and Mature Ecosystems Pioneer, or immature, ecosystems and climax, or mature, ecosystems have strikingly different char-

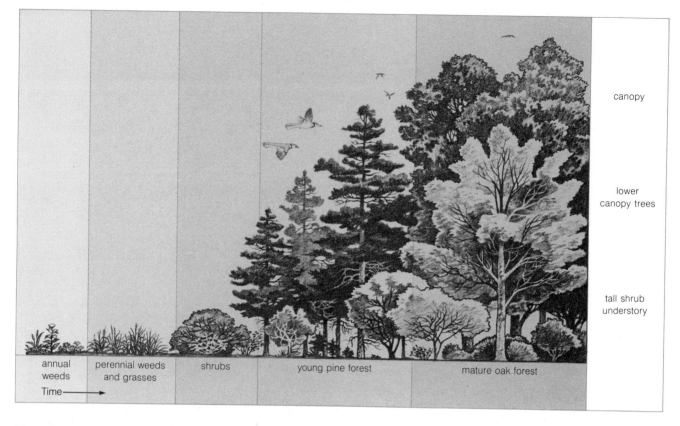

canopy

lower
canopy trees

tall shrub
understory

annual
weeds

Time ——→

perennial weeds
and grasses

shrubs

young pine forest

mature oak forest

Figure 6-9 Secondary ecological succession of plant communities on an abandoned farm field in North Carolina over about 150 years. Succession of animal communities is not shown.

acteristics, as summarized in Table 6-2. Immature communities at the early stages of ecological succession have only a few species (low species diversity) and fairly simple food webs made up mostly of producers fed upon by herbivores and relatively few decomposers. Most of the plants are small annuals that grow close to the ground and expend most of their energy in producing large numbers of small seeds for reproduction rather than in developing large root, stem, and leaf systems. They are partially open systems that receive some matter resources from other ecosystems because they are too simple to hold and recycle many of the nutrients they receive.

In contrast, the community in a mature ecosystem is characterized by high species diversity, relatively stable populations, and complex food webs dominated by decomposers that feed upon the large amount of dead vegetation and animal wastes. Most plants in mature ecosystems are larger perennial herbs and trees that produce a small number of large seeds and expend most of their energy and matter resources in maintaining their large root, trunk, and leaf systems rather than in producing large numbers of new plants. They tend to be closed systems because they have the complexity needed to entrap, hold, and recycle most of their nutrients.

6-4 Human Impacts on Ecosystems

Humans and Ecosystems In modifying ecosystems for our use, we simplify them. For example, we bulldoze and plow grasslands and forests and replace their thousands of interrelated plant and animal species with a greatly simplified, single-crop, or monoculture, ecosystem or with human structures such as buildings, highways, and parking lots.

Modern agriculture is based on deliberately keeping ecosystems in early stages of succession, where net primary productivity of one or a few plant species (such as corn or wheat) is high. But such simplified ecosystems are highly vulnerable. A major problem is the continual invasion of crop fields by unwanted pioneer species, which we call *weeds* if they are plants, *pests* if they are insects or other animals, and *disease* if they are harmful microorganisms such as bacteria, fungi, and viruses. Weeds, pests, or disease can wipe out an entire crop unless it is artificially protected with pesticides such as insecticides (insect-killing chemicals) and herbicides (weed-killing chemicals). When quickly breeding species develop genetic resistance to these chemicals, farmers must use ever-stronger doses or switch to a new product. Persistent, broad-spec-

Table 6-2 Ecosystem Characteristics at Immature and Mature Stages of Ecological Succession

Characteristic	Immature Ecosystem	Mature Ecosystem
Ecosystem Structure		
Plant size	Small	Large
Species diversity	Low	High
Quantity of living matter	Small	Large
Quantity of nonliving matter	Small	Large
Trophic structure	Mostly producers, few decomposers	Mixture of producers, consumers, and decomposers
Ecological niches	Few, mostly generalized	Many, mostly specialized
Community organization (number of interconnecting links)	Low	High
Ecosystem Function		
Plant growth rate	Rapid	Slow
Food chains and webs	Simple, mostly plant → herbivore with few decomposers	Complex, dominated by decomposers
Nutrient chemical cycles	Mostly open	Mostly closed
Efficiency of nutrient recycling	Low	High
Efficiency of energy use	Low	High

trum insect poisons kill not only the pests but also species that prey on the pests. This further simplifies the ecosystem and allows pest populations to expand to even larger sizes.

Thus, in the long run every pesticide increases the rate of natural selection of the pests to the point that the effectiveness of the chemical is eventually doomed to failure. This illustrates biologist Garret Hardin's **first law of ecology:** We can never do merely one thing. There are always numerous effects of any intrusion into nature, many of which are unpredictable.

Cultivation is not the only factor that simplifies ecosystems. Ranchers, who don't want bison or prairie dogs competing with sheep for grass, eradicate these species from grasslands, as well as wolves, coyotes, eagles, and other predators that occasionally kill sheep. Far too often ranchers allow livestock to overgraze grasslands until excessive soil erosion helps convert these ecosystems to simpler and less productive deserts. The cutting of vast areas of diverse tropical rain forests is causing an irreversible loss of many of their plant and animal species. Humans also tend to overfish and overhunt some species to extinction or near extinction, further simplifying ecosystems. The burning of fossil fuels in industrial plants, homes, and vehicles creates atmospheric pollutants that fall to the

earth as acidic compounds, which simplify forest ecosystems by killing trees and simplify aquatic ecosystems by killing fish. To environmentalists these are all signs that we have already gone too far in simplifying the world's ecosystems.

It is becoming increasingly clear that the price we pay for simplifying, maintaining, and protecting such stripped-down ecosystems is high: It includes time, money, increased use of matter and energy resources, loss of genetic diversity, and loss of natural landscape (Table 6-3). There is also the danger that as the human population grows, we will convert too many of the world's mature ecosystems to simple, young, productive, but highly vulnerable forms. The challenge is to maintain a balance between simplified, human ecosystems and the neighboring, more complex, natural ecosystems upon which our simplifed systems depend.

Nuclear War: The Ultimate Ecological Catastrophe

It is generally accepted that the greatest threat to human and other life on this planet is global nuclear war (see the Guest Essay at the end of Chapter 2). The nuclear age began in August 1945, when the United States exploded a single nuclear fission atomic bomb over Hiroshima and another over Nagasaki. Within a few

Table 6-3	Comparison of a Natural Ecosystem and a Simplified Human System	
Natural Ecosystem (marsh, grassland, forest)	Simplified Human System (cornfield, factory, house)
Captures, converts, and stores energy from the sun	Consumes energy from fossil or nuclear fuels
Produces oxygen and consumes carbon dioxide	Consumes oxygen and produces carbon dioxide from the burning of fossil fuels
Creates fertile soil	Depletes or covers fertile soil
Stores, purifies, and releases water gradually	Often uses and contaminates water and releases it rapidly
Provides wildlife habitats	Destroys some wildlife habitats
Filters and detoxifies pollutants and waste products free of charge	Produces pollutants and waste, which must be cleaned up at our expense
Usually capable of self-maintenance and self-renewal	Requires continual maintenance and renewal at great cost

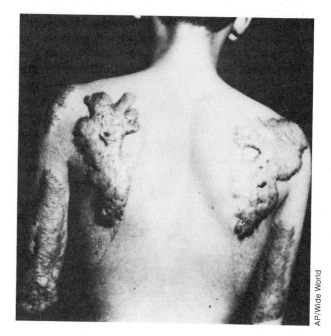

Figure 6-10 Burn scars of a survivor of the atomic explosion at Hiroshima, Japan.

seconds of the blasts, thousands of people in the two Japanese cities were burned to death by the instant release of intense heat and the rapidly expanding fireball that followed or killed when the resulting shock wave (with wind speeds of 200 miles per hour) crushed wooden, brick, and concrete structures within several miles of the detonation point (ground zero). Thousands more, not killed by the fireball and blast, died within 14 days from exposure to high levels of ionizing radiation (Table 3-1, p. 51). In total, an estimated 110,000 to 140,000 people died from these immediate effects. Tens of thousands more were severely injured (Figure 6-10).

By the end of the year another 100,000 had died, mostly from exposure to **radioactive fallout:** dirt and debris sucked up and made radioactive by the blast and falling back to earth near ground zero and on downwind areas hundreds and even thousands of miles away. Air, water, and food supplies were contaminated by fallout for as long as several months. Other people, exposed to nonlethal doses of ionizing radiation, developed cataracts, leukemia, and other forms of lethal cancer years later. Even today—over four decades later—Japanese citizens are dying prematurely from ailments traceable to radiation produced by the two explosions. This shows us what a "small" nuclear bomb can do.

The nuclear fission bomb dropped on Hiroshima was a 21-kiloton weapon (1 kiloton = 1,000 tons). That is, it released energy equivalent to that of the explosion of 21,000 tons of TNT. By 1986 there were approximately 53,100 nuclear warheads in the world's arsenals. Together these nuclear weapons have an explosive power equal to 20 billion tons or 20,000 megatons (1 megaton = 1 million tons) of TNT—equal to that of over 952,000 Hiroshima-type bombs or 6,667 times that of all the explosives detonated during World War II (3 megatons). The total firepower of the nuclear missiles carried on a *single* U.S. Trident submarine is equivalent to that of 19 million tons of TNT—914 Hiroshima bombs or over six times all the explosives detonated in World War II.

In the 1970s some U.S. and Soviet military strategists began talking about the concept of "limited nuclear war," in which combatants would direct nuclear weapons only at military targets rather than launching all-out nuclear attack on both military targets and major cities. According to these strategists, most people in the United States and the Soviet Union could survive a limited nuclear war and the effects on most other countries not involved in the exchange would not be drastic.

Since 1982, however, evaluation of previously overlooked calculations has suggested that even a limited nuclear war could kill 2 to 4 billion people (40% to 80% of the world's population). An estimated 1 billion people, mostly in the Northern Hemisphere, where a nuclear exchange is most likely to take place, would die immediately or within a few weeks as a result of the direct effects of the explosions. Tens of millions more would suffer injuries.

Within the next two years, another 1 to 3 billion might die from starvation caused by disruption of world agricultural production, first in the Northern Hemisphere and later in the Southern Hemisphere. Some models indicate that the mid-latitudes of the Northern Hemisphere, where most of the world's food is grown, would experience what is called the **nuclear winter effect:** Massive amounts of smoke, soot, dust, and other debris, lifted into the atmosphere as a result of the nuclear explosions and subsequent fires, would coalesce into huge smoke clouds. Within two weeks these dense clouds would cover large portions of the Northern Hemisphere and prevent 50% to 90% of all sunlight from reaching these areas. During the weeks or months the clouds persisted, regions under them would be subjected to varying periods of darkness or semidarkness, day and night, and drops in temperature of as much as 40°C, regardless of the season. The resulting sharp drop in food production would cause widespread starvation in the Northern Hemisphere and in African and Asian countries dependent on food imports from countries such as the United States and Canada.

Food production in the Southern Hemisphere would also be affected as the smoke clouds gradually became less dense and spread southward. Although drops in temperature and sunlight would be less severe than in the Northern Hemisphere, even a slight reduction in temperature could be disastrous to agriculture in tropical and subtropical forest areas and could lead to the extinction of numerous plant and animal species. Agriculture in arid or semiarid parts of Africa and Asia might be devastated by the cessation of vital summer monsoon rains. Subtropical grasslands and savannas in Africa and South America might be the least affected of the world's terrestrial ecosystems because their plants are more cold-tolerant and drought-resistant.

The projected nuclear winter effect would not be the only cause of food scarcity. Plagues of rapidly producing insects and rodents—the animal life forms best equipped to survive nuclear war—would damage stored food (and spread disease). In areas where crops could still be grown, farmers would be isolated from supplies of seeds, fertilizer, pesticides, and fuel. People hoping to subsist on seafood would find many surviving aquatic species contaminated with radioactivity, silt, runoff from ruptured tanks of industrial liquids, and oil pouring out of damaged offshore rigs.

All of these projected environmental effects of limited nuclear war are based on calculations and computer models. Some Department of Defense scientists have questioned whether the effects would be quite as great as those projected by these initial studies. Instead of a nuclear winter, they say, some calculations indicate that we would have a **nuclear autumn**—temperatures and light levels would drop but not so severely. However, even these milder effects could still lead to widespread disruption of agricultural productivity for at least one growing season and starvation for at least 1 billion people. For example, even an average temperature drop of only 4°C during a growing season can cut the yields of major crops such as wheat or corn by 50% or more; an average drop of 5°C can wipe out such crops. A one- or two-day nonfreezing cold spell at a sensitive phase of the growing season is enough to destroy rice crops.

In view of even these less drastic projections, a country launching a so-called limited nuclear attack would be killing much of its own population—even if not a single missile were fired in return. While we all hope that such knowledge will deter governments from engaging in nuclear war, many fear that nuclear war is becoming more likely. By 1987, five countries—the United States, the Soviet Union, Great Britain, France, and China—had built and tested nuclear weapons. Although no country has officially joined this nuclear club since 1964, it is projected that by the end of this century sixty countries—one of every three in the world—will have the knowledge and capability to build nuclear weapons. Most of the knowledge and materials enabling these countries to join the nuclear arms club have been provided by the United States, the Soviet Union, France, Italy, and West Germany, which have given or sold commercial nuclear power plants and small, research-oriented nuclear fission reactors to other countries.

Some Lessons from Ecology   It should be clear from the brief discussion of ecological principles in this and the preceding three chapters that ecology forces us to recognize six major features of living systems: *interdependence, diversity, resilience, adaptability, unpredictability,* and *limits.* Ecology's message is not to avoid growing food, building cities, and making other changes that affect the earth's communities of plant and animal life, but to recognize that such human-induced changes have far-reaching and unpredictable consequences. Ecology is a call for wisdom, care, and restraint as we alter the biosphere.

Earth and water, if not too blatantly abused, can be made to produce again and again for the benefit of all. The key is wise stewardship.
Stewart L. Udall

Hazards and Risks

A **hazard** is something that can cause injury, disease, death, economic loss, or environmental deterioration. **Risk** is the probability that something undesirable will happen from deliberate or accidental exposure to a hazard. Risks involve individuals, groups (such as the workers in a factory), or society as a whole. Risks can be local, regional, or global and can last a short or a long time. Expecting or demanding that any activity have zero risk is unrealistic because everything we do involves some degree of risk from one or more types of hazards. **Risk assessment** is the process of determining the short- and long-term adverse consequences to individuals or groups from the use of a particular technology in a particular area.

Calculating the hazardous risk of a particular type of technology is difficult. Probabilities based on past experience are used to estimate risks of older technologies. For new technologies, however, much less accurate statistical probabilities, based on models rather than actual experience, must be calculated. Engineers and systems analysts try to identify everything that could go wrong, the probability of each of these failures occurring, and then the probabilities of various combinations of such events taking place. The more complex the system, the more difficult it is to make realistic calculations based on statistical probabilities. The total reliability of any system is the product of two factors:

$$\frac{\text{system}}{\text{reliability}} = \frac{\text{technology}}{\text{reliability}} \times \frac{\text{human}}{\text{reliability}}$$

With careful design, quality control, maintenance, and monitoring, it is usually possible to obtain a high degree of technology reliability in complex systems such as a nuclear power plant, space shuttle, or early warning system for nuclear attack. However, human reliability is almost always much lower; to be human is to err, and human behavior is highly unpredictable. Workers who carry out maintenance or who monitor safety warning panels in complex systems become bored and inattentive because most of the time nothing goes wrong. They may falsify maintenance records because they believe that the system is safe without their help; they may be distracted by personal problems or illness; they may be told by managers to take shortcuts to enhance short-term profits or to make the managers look more efficient and productive.

For example, assuming that the technology reliability of a system such as a nuclear power plant is 95% (0.95) and the human reliability is 65% (0.65), then overall system reliability is only 62% or 0.62 (0.95 × 0.65 = 0.62). Even if we could increase the technology reliability to 100% (1.0), the overall system reliability would still be only 65% or 0.65 (1.0 × 0.65 = 0.65). This crucial dependence of even the most carefully designed systems on human reliability helps explain the occurrence of such extremely unlikely events as the Three Mile Island and Chernobyl nuclear power plant accidents, the tragic explosion of the space shuttle Challenger, and the far too frequent false alarms given by early warning defense systems upon which the fate of the entire world depends.

One way to improve system reliability is to move more of the potentially fallible elements from the human side to the technical side, making the system more foolproof or "fail-safe." But chance events such as a lightning bolt can knock out automatic control systems, and no machine can replace all the skillful human actions and decisions involved in seeing that a complex system operates properly and safely. Furthermore, the parts in any automated control system are manufactured, assembled, tested, certified, and maintained by fallible human beings, who often are underpaid, have little knowledge of the importance of their work, and are unaware of how their work fits into the overall system.

Risk-Benefit Analysis

The real question we face is whether the short- and long-term benefits from using a particular technology outweigh the short- and long-term risks compared to other alternatives. One method for making such evaluations is **risk-benefit analysis**. It involves calculating the short- and long-term societal benefits and risks involved and then dividing the benefits by the risks to find a **desirability quotient:**

$$\text{desirability quotient} = \frac{\text{societal benefits}}{\text{societal risks}}$$

Ideally, such a quotient would be calculated for each alternative technology available so that individuals, corporations, and governments could compare and make intelligent choices. Assuming that accurate calculations of benefits and risks can be made (often a big *if*), we have several possibilities:

1. $\text{large desirability quotient} = \dfrac{\text{large societal benefits}}{\text{small societal risks}}$

Example: *X rays.* Use of ionizing radiation in the form of X rays to detect bone fractures and other medical problems has a large desirability quotient—provided X rays are not overused merely to protect doctors from liability suits, the dose is no larger than needed, and other less harmful alternatives are not available. Ionizing radiation from X rays is not persistent and can cause mutations only during use, unlike that from a radioactive isotope, which can cause cellular damage for at least ten times the half-life of the isotope (Section 3-2). Other examples with large societal benefits and whose societal risks are relatively small or could be reduced at acceptable cost include mining, most dams, and airplane travel.

2. $\begin{array}{l}\text{very small}\\ \text{desirability}\\ \text{quotient}\end{array} = \dfrac{\text{very small societal benefits}}{\text{very large societal risks}}$

Example: *Nuclear war.* Global nuclear war has essentially no societal benefits (except the short-term profits made by companies making weapons and weapons defense systems) and involves totally unacceptable risks to most of the earth's present human population and to many future generations.

3. $\begin{array}{l}\text{small desirability}\\ \text{quotient}\end{array} = \dfrac{\text{small societal benefits}}{\text{large societal risks}}$

Example: *Thalidomide.* The drug thalidomide was prescribed in the 1950s to prevent morning sickness during pregnancy. The drug was banned several years later when it was learned that many malformed infants were born to women who took the drug during pregnancy (Figure 6-11).

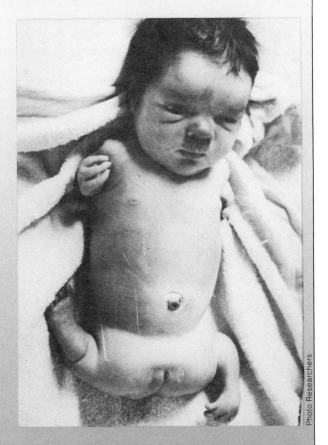

Figure 6-11 A baby whose mother took thalidomide during pregnancy.

4. $\begin{array}{l}\text{small desirability}\\ \text{quotient}\end{array} = \dfrac{\text{large societal benefits}}{\text{much larger societal risks}}$

Example: *Nuclear and coal-burning electric power plants.* Nuclear and coal-burning power plants provide society with electricity—a highly desirable benefit. However, many analysts contend that the short- and long-term societal risks from widespread use of these technologies outweigh the benefit and that there are many other economically acceptable alternatives for producing electricity with less severe societal risks (Chapter 18). The probability of a catastrophic release of ionizing radiation from a nuclear reactor is extremely small, but the immediate and long-lasting harm of such a release and the large population exposed make the overall societal risks very high. For example, if a "worst-case" accident did occur, as many as 100,000 people could die within several months from exposure to high levels of ionizing radiation. Half a million or more other people would have a high risk of developing thyroid disorders and various types of cancer from 5 to 50 years after the accident from exposure to moderate-to-low levels of radiation. There would also be tens to hundreds of billions of dollars in economic damage. Investors in the Three Mile Island facility lost over $1 billion, even though there were no immediate deaths and injuries. The moderately severe nuclear accident at the Chernobyl nuclear power plant in the Soviet Union in 1986 cost an estimated $7 billion to $14 billion, killed 31 people within a few months, and exposed at least 100,000 people to potentially damaging levels of ionizing radiation.

Widespread use of coal-fired plants also poses high short- and long-term societal risks. Air pollutants released by coal-fired electric power plants in the United States are estimated to cause annually about 10,000 premature deaths, 100,000 cases of respiratory illness, and several billion dollars in losses from damage to trees, aquatic life, crops, and buildings. They are also major contributors to possible long-term changes in the global climate due to the greenhouse effect. With much stricter air pollution controls, the short-term societal risks from coal-burning plants could be sharply reduced. But the cost of electricity from such plants would increase, and there is presently no known way to reduce their potential long-term effect on global climate.

5. $\text{uncertain desirability quotient} = \dfrac{\text{small benefits}}{\text{small risks}}$

Example: *Saccharin.* Saccharin is used as an artificial sweetener in many beverages and foods. Studies have shown that saccharin causes cancer in laboratory animals, but the evidence that it causes cancer in humans is slight and controversial. Although saccharin may provide some benefits to diabetics, other artificial sweeteners are available; studies have also

shown that it is of little benefit to people who want to lose weight. Thus, its continued use is primarily a political-economic decision that benefits companies making this product.

6. $\text{uncertain desirability quotient} = \dfrac{\text{large benefits}}{\text{large risks}}$

Example: *Genetic engineering.* Widespread use of recombinant DNA techniques promises a wide range of individual and societal benefits, but without adequate controls the ecological harm of this technology could be too high a price (see Spotlight on p. 121).

Although appearing quite simple and straightforward, calculation of desirability quotients is an extremely difficult and controversial undertaking. For example, many people—especially those who make short-term economic profits from the technologies involved—would disagree with the example calculations just given. Short- and long-term benefits such as kilowatts of electricity produced, time saved, jobs created, and potential profits from use of a particular technology or product are usually fairly easy to estimate. Determining the risks, however, is usually much more difficult. Sufficient data to analyze particular risks are usually not available, either because such information has not been collected in the past or because data are not available for new technologies. Typically, we do not know how many people will be exposed to a particular hazard, how much exposure they might have, whether the hazard will cause damage at any level of exposure or only above a certain threshold level, and how the hazard interacts with other factors, which might enhance or reduce the hazard.

Other problems in calculating societal risks arise because some technologies benefit one group of people (population A), while imposing a risk on another (population B) and because some risk-benefit analysts emphasize short-term risks while others put more weight on long-term risks. There is also the problem of who will carry out a particular risk-benefit analysis. Should it be the corporation or government agency involved in developing or managing the technology or some independent laboratory or panel of scientists? If it involves outside evaluation, who chooses which persons do the study? Also who pays the bill and thus has the potential to influence the outcome by refusing to give the lab or agency future business? Once the study is done, who reviews the results—a government agency, independent scientists, the general public—and what influence will outside criticism have on the final decisions? Clearly, politics, economics, and value judgments that can be biased in either direction are involved at every step of the risk-benefit analysis process.

The difficulty in making risk-benefit assessments does not mean that they should not be made or that they are not useful. But scientists, politicians, and the general public who must evaluate such analyses and make decisions based on them should be aware that at best they can only be expressed as a range of probabilities—not the precise bottom-line numbers that decision makers want.

Risk Management

The process of **risk management** encompasses all of the administrative, political, and economic actions taken to decide how, and if, a particular societal risk is to be reduced to a certain level and at what cost. Risk management involves deciding **(1)** which of the vast number of risks facing society should be evaluated and managed with the limited funds available, **(2)** the sequence or priority in which these risks should be evaluated and managed, **(3)** the reliability of the risk-benefit analysis carried out for each risk, **(4)** how much risk is acceptable, **(5)** how much money it will take to reduce each risk to an acceptable level, **(6)** what level of risk reduction will be attained if insufficient funds are available, as is usually the case, and **(7)** how the risk management plan will be monitored and enforced.

Each step in this process involves value judgments and trade-offs to find some reasonable compromise between conflicting political and economic interests. For example, deciding that a pollutant should be reduced to a level of zero risk would bankrupt almost any company producing the chemical and would not take into account that nature usually provides some degree of pollution control free of charge. On the other hand, it would be wrong for risk managers not

to provide society with a reasonable degree of protection on the grounds that such protection reduces private profits or exceeds rigidly imposed administrative budget cuts. Managing risks is a high-wire juggling act that is almost bound to be criticized from all sides regardless of the final decision.

Risk management involves comparing the estimated *true* risk and harm of a particular technology or product with the risk and harm perceived by the general public. This comparison helps the risk manager develop a management program that is acceptable to the public but that does not cause economic ruin of the companies involved or require prohibitively high expenditures of tax dollars. The public generally perceives that a technology has a greater risk than its actual estimated risk when it **(1)** is a relatively new technology (genetic engineering) rather than a familiar one (dams, automobiles), **(2)** is involuntary (nuclear power plants, nuclear weapons) instead of voluntary (smoking, driving without seat belts), and **(3)** involves a large number of deaths and injuries from a single catastrophic accident (nuclear power plant accident or plane crash) rather than the same number of deaths spread out over a longer time (coal-burning power plants and automobiles). For example, U.S. citizens tolerate 45,000 deaths from automobile accidents each year—equivalent to a fully loaded passenger jet crashing with no survivors every day—because these deaths are distributed in space and time. If they all occurred at one place and at the same time like a plane crash, they would be considered a national catastrophe and would not be tolerated.

Some risk-benefit analysts decry this irrational evaluation of risks by the general public. But other observers contend that when it comes to evaluation of large-scale, complex technologies, the public often is better at looking at the forest than the risk-benefit specialists, who look primarily at the trees. This commonsense wisdom does not usually depend on understanding the details of scientific risk-benefit analysis. Instead, it is based on the average person's understanding that science has limits and that the humans designing, building, running, and monitoring potentially hazardous technological systems and products are fallible just like everyone else.

CHAPTER SUMMARY

When subjected to stress, living systems tend to resist being disturbed (*inertia stability* or *persistence*) and can restore themselves to an original condition (*resilience stability*) if not disturbed too drastically. Organisms, populations, and ecosystems maintain their stability or fairly constant internal conditions primarily through *negative feedback* of information to counteract the effects of environmental stress. Stability is also maintained by *time delays* in negative feedback, by *synergistic effects*, and by *antagonistic effects*.

Populations of a given species can respond to changes in environmental conditions by **(1)** changes in birth rates, death rates, and population structure (fewer old, very young, or weak members; **(2)** gradually increasing the number of individuals with variations in genetic material that make them more likely to survive and reproduce in the altered environment (*evolution through natural selection*); and **(3)** long-term splitting of one genetic line into two or more new species (*speciation*). Species that rapidly produce large numbers of small, usually unprotected, offspring with a relatively short life span (weeds, insects, rodents) can adapt to environmental change fairly rapidly through natural selection. Species that take longer to produce a small number of offspring with longer average life spans and that protect them until adulthood (elephants, tigers, humans) take thousands to millions of years to adapt to environmental change through natural selection.

Existing ecosystems, especially mature ones, are self-sustaining and can adapt to small and moderate changes in environmental conditions through complex negative feedback loops, time delays, and synergistic and antagonistic effects. One factor contributing to inertia stability or persistence of some ecosystems is *species diversity*, which provides numerous alternative ways for such ecosystems to respond to environmental stress.

When severe natural or human-induced environmental changes leave little or no vegetation and soil on a site, the area is gradually recolonized by a series of increasingly complex communities of plant and animal life through *ecological succession*. This resilience stability process begins with an invasion by a hardy, simple, *immature or pioneer community* and, if undisturbed, usually proceeds until the site is occupied by a complex, *mature or climax community*.

Humans greatly simplify natural ecosystems in order to build habitats, grow food, and remove or extract resources. Increasing amounts of money, time, and energy and matter resources are being used to maintain such simplified systems and to protect them from pests, drought, floods, and other disturbances. The challenge is to maintain a balance between simplified human ecosystems and the neighboring, more complex, natural ecosystems upon which the simplifed systems depend.

Risk-benefit analysis involves estimating and comparing the overall short- and long-term benefits and risks to individuals and society of a technology or product to determine its desirability. *Risk management* encompasses all the administrative, political, and economic actions taken to decide how, and if, a particular societal risk is to be reduced to a certain level and at what cost. Both risk-benefit analysis and risk management are important, difficult, and controversial processes that involve many uncertainties, value judgments, and trade-offs.

Ecology teaches us that the forms of life on this planet are characterized by *interdependence, diversity, resilience, adaptability, and limits* and that we should use wisdom, care, and restraint as we alter the biosphere to meet our needs.

DISCUSSION TOPICS

1. Explain how 1 plus 1 does not always equal 2 in an ecosystem.

2. Give two examples of time delays not discussed in this chapter. How can time delays be harmful? How can they be helpful?

3. Someone tells you not to worry about air pollution because the human species through natural selection will develop lungs that can detoxify pollutants. How would you reply?

4. Are humans or insects such as flies and mosquitoes better able to adapt to environmental change? Defend your choice and indicate the major way each of these species can adapt to environmental change.

5. Explain how a species can change local conditions so that the species becomes extinct in a given ecosystem. Could humans do this to themselves? Explain.

6. What is a pioneer community? In what major ways does it differ from a climax community?

7. Describe how introducing or removing a species in a simple ecosystem at an early stage of succession can affect the ecosystem's stability.

8. Explain why a simplified ecosystem such as a cornfield is much more susceptible to harm from insects, plant diseases, and fungi than a more complex, natural ecosystem. Why are natural ecosystems less susceptible?

9. Do you agree or disagree that most of the survivors of a global nuclear war would envy the dead? Why? Would you want to be one of the survivors? Why or why not?

10. Considering the benefits and risks involved, do you believe that **(a)** nuclear power plants should be controlled more rigidly and gradually phased out; **(b)** coal-burning power plants should be controlled more rigidly and gradually phased out; **(c)** genetic engineering using recombinant DNA should be prohibited; **(d)** genetic engineering using recombinant DNA should be very rigidly controlled; **(e)** people not wearing seat belts in vehicles should be heavily fined; **(f)** air bags or other automatic passenger protection systems should be made mandatory on all vehicles; **(g)** smoking should not be allowed in any office, restaurant, or other indoor public place because it involuntarily exposes nonsmokers to harmful air pollutants; **(h)** federal disaster insurance for people choosing to live in areas with high risk of floods, hurricanes, or earthquakes should be prohibited or greatly increased in cost. In each case defend your position.

11. Why are risk-benefit analysis and risk management so important? What are their major limitations? Does this mean that these processes are useless? Why or why not?

PART THREE

Population

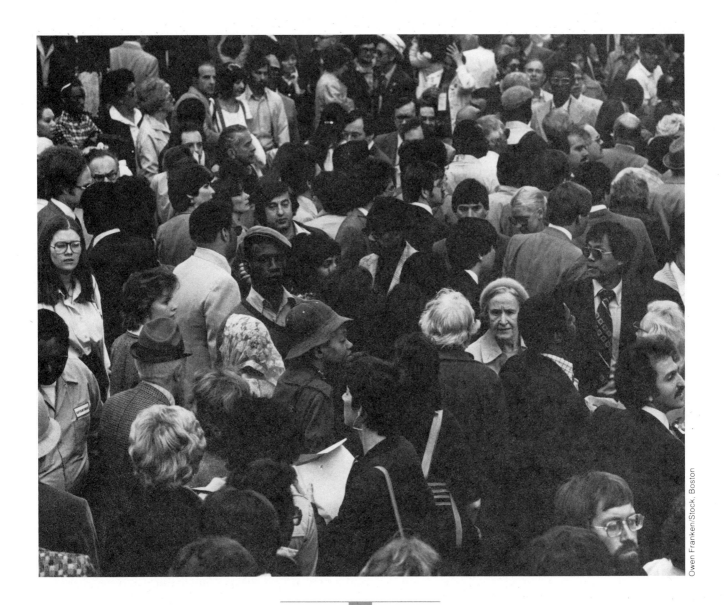

We need that size of population in which human beings can fulfill their potentialities; in my opinion we are already overpopulated from that point of view, not just in places like India and China and Puerto Rico, but also in the United States and in Western Europe.

George Wald, Nobel laureate, biology

7

Population Dynamics

The present extended period of rapid population growth in the world is unique when seen from a long-range perspective; it has never occurred before and is unlikely to occur again.

Jonas Salk and Jonathan Salk

GENERAL OBJECTIVES

1. How are changes in population size affected by birth rates and death rates?

2. How do migration rates affect the population size of a particular country or area?

3. How are changes in population size affected by the average number of children women have during their reproductive years (total fertility rate)?

4. How are changes in population size affected by the percentage of males and females at each age level in the population of the world or a given country (age structure)?

By 1987 the size of the human population was 5 billion and was growing by 86.7 million a year (Figure 1-1, p. 3). Based on present trends, United Nations population experts estimate that world population size will reach 6.2 billion by the year 2000 and 7.8 billion by 2020, and perhaps level off around 2100 at about 10.4 billion—more than twice the number of people on earth in 1987.

What are the major factors causing these dramatic changes in the size of the human population? How can the size and growth rate of the human population be controlled? The first question is discussed in this chapter and the second one in Chapter 8.

7-1 BIRTH RATE, DEATH RATE, AND NET POPULATION CHANGE

Net Population Change Calculating the difference between the total number of live births and the total number of deaths throughout the world during a given period of time (usually a year) yields the **global net population change** over that period:

$$\genfrac{}{}{0pt}{}{\text{global net population}}{\text{change per year}} = \genfrac{}{}{0pt}{}{\text{number of live}}{\text{births per year}} - \genfrac{}{}{0pt}{}{\text{number of}}{\text{deaths per year}}$$

If there are more live births than deaths, the world's population will increase.

There were about 2.6 births for each death throughout the world in 1987. This amounted to a global net population increase of 86.7 million people—or 165 additional people per minute. Words like *million* and *billion* often make little impression on us. But suppose you decide to take one second to say hello to each of the 86.7 million persons added to the world's population during 1987. Talking 24 hours a day, you

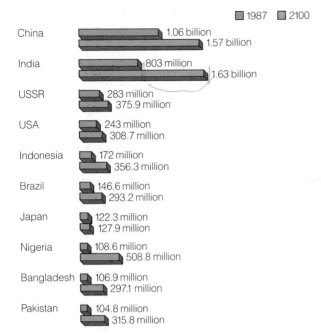

Figure 7-1 The world's ten most populous countries in 1987 with projections of their population size in 2100. (Data from the Population Reference Bureau)

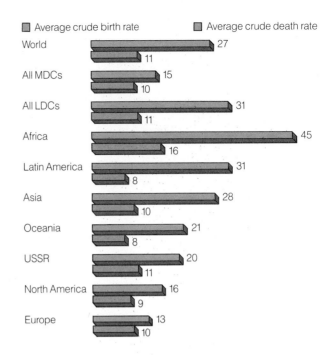

Figure 7-2 Average crude birth rates and crude death rates of various groups of countries in 1987. (Data from the Population Reference Bureau)

would need about 2.7 years to greet them, and during that time 234 million more people would have been added.

About 92% of these 86.7 million people were born in the less developed countries of Africa, Asia, and Latin America, which in 1987 already contained 79% of the world's people. The large difference in population size between LDCs and MDCs is an important factor in the widening gap in average personal income and life quality between countries in the Southern and Northern hemispheres (Section 1-1 and Figure 1-5, pp. 6–7). This difference between LDC and MDC population sizes is projected to increase sharply from 1987 to 2100, when LDCs are expected to have 86% of the world's population (Figure 1-7, p. 8).

Figure 7-1 shows the world's ten most populous countries in 1987 and their projected population size by 2100. Because six of these countries are in Asia, it is not surprising that Asia is by far the most populous continent, containing 58% of the people on earth.

Crude Birth Rates and Death Rates Demographers, or population specialists, normally use the **crude birth rate** and **crude death rate** rather than total live births and deaths to describe population change. The crude rates give the number of live births and deaths per 1,000 persons at the midpoint of a given year (July 1), since this should represent the average population for that year:

$$\text{crude birth rate} = \frac{\text{live births per year}}{\text{midyear population}} \times 1,000$$

$$\text{crude death rate} = \frac{\text{deaths per year}}{\text{midyear population}} \times 1,000$$

Figure 7-2 shows the crude birth rates and death rates for the world and various groups of countries in 1987. *The rapid growth of the world's population over the past 100 years is not the result of a rise in birth rates, as might be assumed; rather, it is due largely to a decline in death rates—especially in the LDCs* (Figure 7-3). The interrelated reasons for this general decline in death rates include better nutrition because of increased food production and better distribution; reduction of the incidence and spread of infectious diseases because of improved personal hygiene and improved sanitation and water supplies; and improvements in medical and public health technology through the use of antibiotics, immunization, and insecticides.

Life Expectancy and Infant Mortality Two useful indicators of the overall health of the people in a country or region are the average life expectancy at birth of its people and the mortality rate of its infants during their first year of life (Figure 7-4). **Life expectancy** is the average number of years a newborn can be expected to live. Increased average life expectancy is a result of better sanitation, nutrition, health care, and living

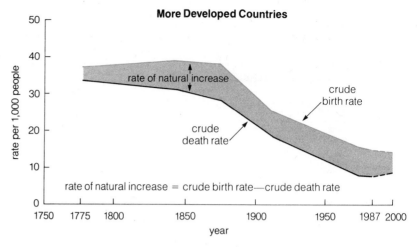

Figure 7-3 Changes in crude birth and death rates for the more developed and less developed countries between 1775 and 1987 and projected rates (dashed lines) to 2000. (Data from the Population Reference Bureau and the United Nations)

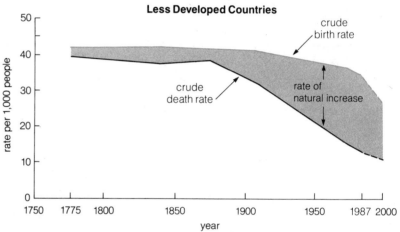

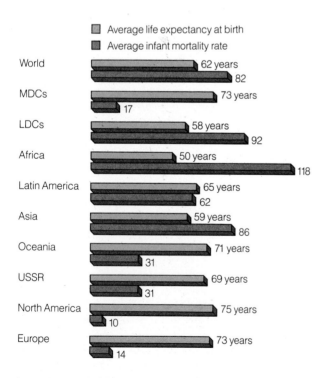

Figure 7-4 Life expectancy at birth and average infant mortality rate for various groups of countries in 1987. (Data from the Population Reference Bureau)

conditions. It is not surprising that people in the world's MDCs have a higher average life expectancy than those in the LDCs. In 1987, average life expectancy at birth ranged from a low of 35 years in Sierra Leone in western Africa to a high of 77 years in Japan, Iceland, and Sweden.

Between 1900 and 1987, average life expectancy at birth increased sharply in the United States from about 42 to 75. Despite this increase, people in eight countries (Japan, Iceland, Sweden, Norway, the Netherlands, Switzerland, Spain, and Canada) had an average life expectancy at birth one to two years higher than people in the United States in 1987.

Average life expectancy is influenced by **infant mortality rate,** the number of deaths of persons under one year of age per 1,000 live births. A high infant mortality rate in a country normally decreases the life expectancy at birth of its population. A high infant mortality rate usually indicates a lack of adequate food, poor nutrition, and a high incidence of infectious diseases (usually from contaminated drinking water). Infant mortality rates differ significantly among groups of countries (Figure 7-4) and among individual countries (Figure 7-5). In 1987, infant mortality rates ranged from a low of 5.5 deaths per 1,000 live births in Japan

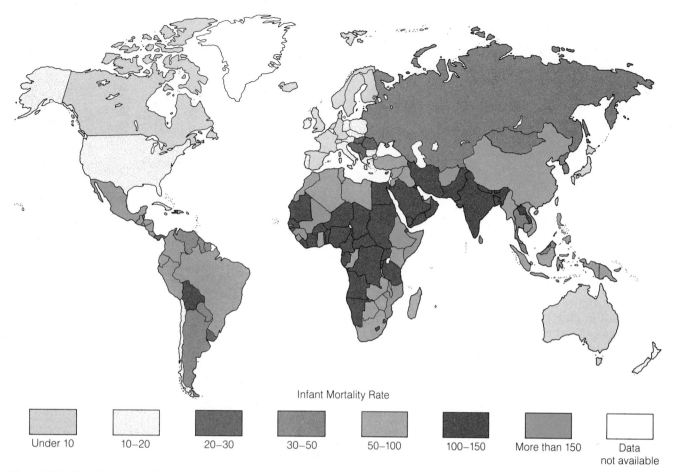

Figure 7-5 Global patterns of infant mortality rate. (Data from the Population Reference Bureau)

to a high of 183 deaths per 1,000 live births in East Timor in Southeast Asia.

There were 19 countries with lower infant mortality rates than the 10.5 deaths per 1,000 live births in the United States—suggesting a need for further improvement in prenatal and infant health care and nutrition in the United States. Every year in the United States 40,000 infants enter the world and then die before their first birthday. Since 1955 the United States has fallen from sixth to a tie for last place among 20 industrialized countries in infant mortality rates.

Annual Percentage Rates of Population Change

The **natural change rate,** also known as the **annual population change rate** (in percent) indicates how fast a population is growing or decreasing. This rate can be calculated using the following formula:

$$\text{natural change or annual population change rate} = \frac{\text{crude birth rate} - \text{crude death rate}}{10}$$

If the crude birth rate in a particular country or collection of countries is higher than the crude death rate,

then the population is growing by a certain percentage each year. If the crude death rate exceeds the crude birth rate, then the population is decreasing by a certain percentage each year.

Using the crude birth and death rates from Figure 7-2, we can calculate that in 1987 the population grew at the following rates:

World   1.6% $\left(\dfrac{27-10}{10}=1.7\right)$

MDCs   0.5% $\left(\dfrac{15-10}{10}=0.5\right)$

LDCs   2.0% $\left(\dfrac{32-11}{10}=2.1\right)$

A population growth rate of 3% or less a year may seem small, but it leads to enormous increases in population size over a 100-year period (Figure 7-6). For example, Nigeria in western Africa, with a population of 108.6 million and a 2.8% growth rate in 1987, is projected to have a population of 274 million by 2020 and eventually 623 million, more people than now live on the entire continent of Africa.

In the late 1970s, a series of newspaper headlines,

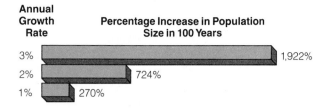

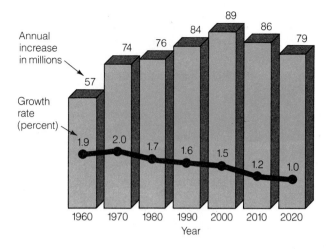

Figure 7-6 Effect of various annual percentage growth rates on population size over 100 years.

Figure 7-7 Actual and projected changes in the annual growth rate and annual increase for the world's population between 1960 and 2020.

such as "Population Time Bomb Fizzles," "Another Non-Crisis," and "Population Growth May Have Turned Historic Corner," falsely implied that world population growth had almost stopped. What actually happened was not a halt in net population growth but a slowing of the annual rate at which the world's population was growing—from a high of 2.0% in 1965 to 1.7% by the mid 1980s (Figure 7-7). Despite this encouraging slowdown in the *annual population growth rate*, the world's *annual net population growth* increased from 57 million in 1960 to 86 million in 1987. It is projected that by the year 2000 the world's annual population growth rate will have dropped to about 1.5%, but annual net population growth will increase to 89 million persons.

Figure 7-8 shows differences in the average annual population change rates in major parts of the world. In 1987 population change rates ranged from a *growth* rate of 3.9% in Kenya in eastern Africa to a *decline* rate of 0.2% in West Germany and Hungary. The world is now divided into two large groups of countries. One, with a population of 2.3 billion, is growing slowly at an average rate of 0.8%—adding about 18.7 million people a year. This group includes Australia, New Zealand, the Soviet Union, China, Japan, Hong Kong, and the countries in North America and Europe. The second group, consisting of the countries in Latin America, Africa, and Asia (excluding China, Japan, and Hong Kong), has a population of 2.7 billion and is growing rapidly at an average rate of 2.5%, adding about 67 million people each year.

Doubling Time Another indication of the rate at which a population is growing is called **doubling time:** the time it takes for a population to double in size if present annual population growth continues unchanged. The approximate doubling time in years can be found by using the *rule of 70*—that is, by dividing the annual percentage growth rate into 70:

$$\text{doubling time (years)} = \frac{70}{\text{annual percent growth rate}}$$

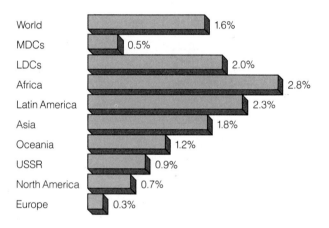

Figure 7-8 Average annual population growth rate in various groups of countries in 1987. (Data from the Population Reference Bureau)

In 1987 the doubling time for the world's population was 41 years (70/1.7 = 41), compared to a doubling time of 128 years for the MDCs and 33 years for the LDCs. Figure 7-9 shows the relationship between annual percent population growth and doubling time and gives the approximate doubling times for the populations of selected countries throughout the world in 1987. Doubling time is only a crude estimate of future population growth because it is based on the often incorrect assumption that a population will have the same growth rate over several decades.

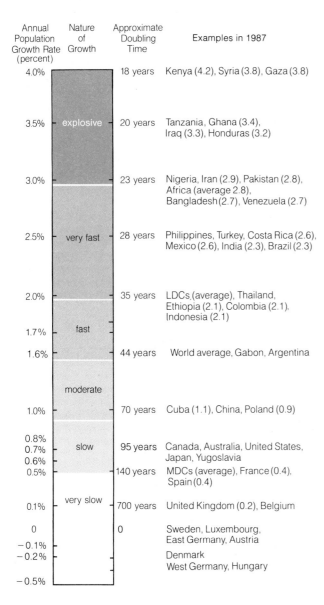

Annual Population Growth Rate (percent)	Nature of Growth	Approximate Doubling Time	Examples in 1987
4.0%	explosive	18 years	Kenya (4.2), Syria (3.8), Gaza (3.8)
3.5%		20 years	Tanzania, Ghana (3.4), Iraq (3.3), Honduras (3.2)
3.0%	very fast	23 years	Nigeria, Iran (2.9), Pakistan (2.8), Africa (average 2.8), Bangladesh (2.7), Venezuela (2.7)
2.5%		28 years	Philippines, Turkey, Costa Rica (2.6), Mexico (2.6), India (2.3), Brazil (2.3)
2.0%	fast	35 years	LDCs (average), Thailand, Ethiopia (2.1), Colombia (2.1), Indonesia (2.1)
1.7% 1.6%	moderate	44 years	World average, Gabon, Argentina
1.0%		70 years	Cuba (1.1), China, Poland (0.9)
0.8% 0.7% 0.6% 0.5%	slow	95 years / 140 years	Canada, Australia, United States, Japan, Yugoslavia / MDCs (average), France (0.4), Spain (0.4)
0.1%	very slow	700 years	United Kingdom (0.2), Belgium
0 −0.1% −0.2% −0.5%		0	Sweden, Luxembourg, East Germany, Austria / Denmark / West Germany, Hungary

Figure 7-9 Relationship between annual population growth rate and doubling time in 1987. (Data from the Population Reference Bureau)

7-2 MIGRATION

Net Migration Rate The rate at which the size of the world's population changes is based only on the difference between crude birth rates and death rates. The annual rate of population change for a particular country, however, is also affected by the net migration or movement of people into (*immigration*) and out of (*emigration*) that country during the year. The **immigration rate** is the number of people migrating into a country each year per 1,000 people in its population. It is usually based only on legal immigrants because of the difficulty in counting illegal immigrants. The **emigration rate** is the number of people migrating out of a country each year per 1,000 people in its population. A country's **net migration rate** per year is the difference between its immigration rate and emigration rate. If more persons immigrate than emigrate, the annual net migration rate is positive. Conversely, if more persons leave than enter, it is negative.

Thus, the annual rate of population change for a country is the difference between its crude birth rate and death rate plus its net migration rate:

$$\begin{array}{l} \text{annual rate} \\ \text{of population} \\ \text{change for a} \\ \text{country} \end{array} = \begin{array}{l} (\text{crude birth rate} - \text{crude death rate}) \\ + \text{net migration rate} \end{array}$$

Migration also takes place within countries, especially from rural to urban areas, as discussed in Chapter 9.

Immigration and Population Growth in the United States The United States, founded by immigrants and their children, has admitted a larger number of immigrants and refugees than any other country in the world. Indeed, the 53.7 million legal immigrants to the United States from various parts of the world between 1820 and 1987 is almost twice the number received by all other countries combined during the same period. Between 1820 and 1960 most legal immigrants to the United States came from Europe, but since then most have come from Asia and Latin America.

The number of legal immigrants entering the U.S. since 1820 has varied during different periods as a result of changes in immigration laws and economic growth (Figure 7-10). Between 1960 and 1987 the number of legal immigrants more than doubled from 250,000 to around 600,000 (Figure 7-10). By 1987, the Census Bureau estimated that the United States also had 4.9 million illegal immigrants, with half in California and additional large populations in Texas, Illinois, New York, and Florida. According to the Census Bureau, 200,000 to 500,000 new illegal immigrants now enter and remain in the United States each year. An estimated 50% to 60% come from Mexico. Thus, in 1987 the total number of legal and illegal immigrants increased the U.S. population by 800,000 to 1,100,000 people.

Excluding legal and illegal immigration, the U.S. population grew at a rate of 0.7% in 1987 with a net increase of about 1.7 million people to its population of 243 million. But if we include the 800,000 to 1,100,000 legal and illegal immigrants, the 1987 growth rate is

Figure 7-10 Legal immigration to the United States: 1820–1987. (Data from the U.S. Immigration and Naturalization Service)

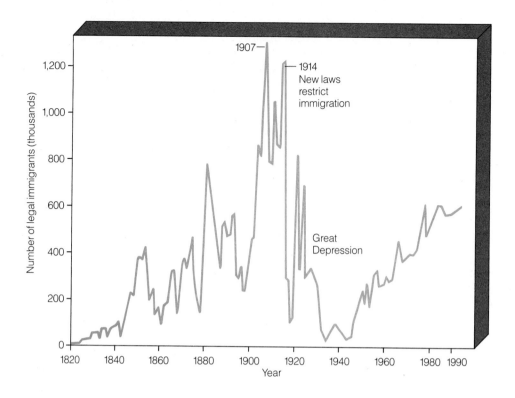

Figure 7-11 Projected changes in the ethnic composition of the U.S. population between 1980 and 2080. (Data from the Population Reference Bureau)

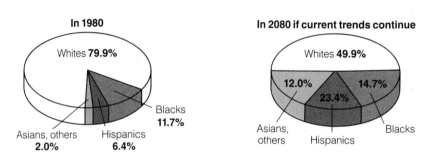

1.0% to 1.2% with a net increase of 2.5 million to 2.8 million—an average increase of about 5 people a minute, 285 an hour, and 6,849 a day. Legal and illegal immigration now accounts for 32% to 39% of the annual population growth in the U.S. This means that the United States is adding the equivalent of another Los Angeles to its population every year and a new California every decade. If birth and death rates and legal and illegal immigration rates continue at present rates, there will be a dramatic change in the ethnic composition of the U.S. population between 1980 and 2020 (Figure 7-11).

7-3 FERTILITY

Replacement-Level Fertility and Total Fertility Rate A key factor affecting the future growth of a population is **fertility**, the average number of live babies born to women in the population during their normal childbearing years (ages 15–44).

Replacement-level fertility is the number of children a couple must have to replace themselves. You might think that two parents would have to have only two children to replace themselves. The actual average replacement-level fertility, however, is slightly higher primarily because some children die before reaching their reproductive years. In MDCs average replacement-level fertility is 2.1 children per couple or woman. In some LDCs, with high infant mortality rates, the replacement level may be as high as 2.5 children per couple.

The most useful measure of fertility for projecting future population change is the **total fertility rate (TFR)**—an estimate of the number of children the average woman will bear during her reproductive years, assuming she lives to age 44. In 1987 the average total fertility rate was 3.6 children per woman for the world as a whole, 2.0 in MDCs, and 4.2 in LDCs—ranging

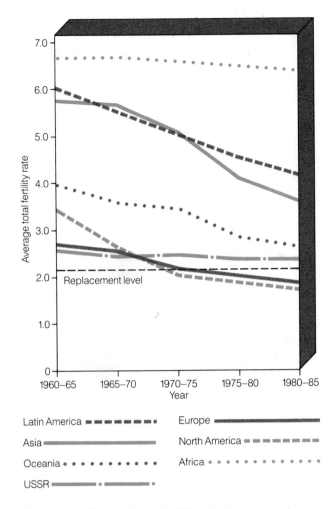

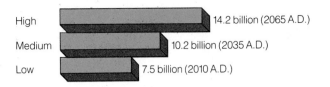

Figure 7-13 Three projections of stabilized world population levels based on different assumptions about the year (shown in parentheses) when the average world total fertility rate drops to replacement level. (Data from the United Nations)

Figure 7-12 Changes in total fertility rates in various regions of the world between 1960 and 1985. (Data from the United Nations)

in Africa, 20–21 in Asia and Latin America, 22 in Oceania, and 23 in Europe. Note that these figures correlate closely with the TFRs for these continents (Figure 7-12).

In the United States the median marriage age for women has increased from 20.3 in 1950 to 23.1 in 1986. During the same period the median marriage age for American men has risen from 22.8 to 25.8. This has helped reduce the TFR in the United States, although it is offset somewhat by the increase in unmarried young women (including teenagers) having children (see the Spotlight on p. 144).

Using TFR to Project World Population Stabilization Many people falsely equate a TFR at or below replacement-level fertility with zero population growth, by which population size remains constant. Although achieving a replacement-level TFR is one of the first steps necessary for achieving ZPG, a population can have a TFR at or below 2.1 and still be growing because the number of women entering their childbearing period is still rising. The larger the number of women under age 15, the longer it takes to reach population stabilization or ZPG after the TFR reaches 2.1 (discussed further in Section 7-4). ZPG occurs at the global level when the world's birth and death rates are equal. For a particular country or group of countries ZPG occurs when the birth rate and death rate are equal and net migration is zero.

Figure 7-13 shows UN projections for world population growth and eventual stabilization based on different assumptions about when the average fertility rate will drop to replacement-level fertility of 2.1. Figure 7-15 projects population size and year of stabilization for different groups of countries, using the medium UN projection (usually taken as the most likely) shown in Figure 7-13.

No one knows whether any of these projections will prove accurate. All are based not only on certain assumptions about TFRs but also on the assumption of adequate supplies of food, energy, and other natural resources. If such supplies are inadequate or if there is global nuclear war, the resulting sharp increase

from a low of 1.3 in West Germany to a high of 8.0 in Kenya. Figure 7-12 shows changes in TFR in major groups of countries between 1960 and 1985. A significant part of the large drop in Asia was the result of massive family-planning efforts by China, as discussed in Section 8-5.

Fertility and Marriage Age One factor that can affect the total fertility rate is the median age of women at first marriage, or, more precisely, the median age at which women give birth to their first child. Studies indicate that significantly lower fertility tends to occur in countries where the median marriage age of women is at least 25, which reduces potential childbearing years (ages 15–44) by ten years. Even more important, this cuts the *prime* reproductive period from ages 20–29 (when most women have children) by about half. Although data are lacking for some countries, the median age at first marriage for women is around 18

Every year 1 million American teenagers become pregnant. About 400,000 will have abortions, accounting for almost one of every three U.S. abortions. In addition to affecting the U.S. average total fertility rate, the increase in such births contributes to an infant mortality rate higher than that of 17 other industrialized countries. Studies show that out-of-wedlock births by teenagers are more likely to end in low birth weight (under 5.5 pounds), mental retardation, or death during the first year of life.

The pregnancy rate among American females of ages 15 through 19 was much higher than that in nearly all other MDCs (Figure 7-14). About 15% of pregnant teenagers become pregnant again within one year; 30% do so within two years. In 1986, teenage pregnancy cost state and federal governments at least $17 billion, double the cost in 1975. It is estimated that each baby born in 1986 as the first child of a teenage mother will cost taxpayers an average of $15,600 over the next 20 years. This helps explain why teenage pregnancy is everyone's problem, not merely that of the mother and her family.

High teenage pregnancy rates in the United States are believed to be due to several factors: sexual activity at an earlier age (partly because a better diet means that the average American girl now reaches puberty at age 12 or 13 compared to 14 or 15 in 1900), lack of effective sex education in the schools, unavailability of contraceptives to teenagers, sexually

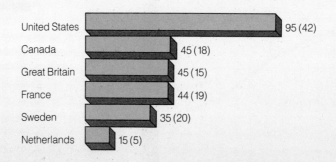

Figure 7-14   Pregnancy rates per 1,000 teenage females in selected MDCs. Figures in parentheses indicate the number of these pregnancies ending in abortion. (Data from the Allan Guttmacher Institute)

suggestive entertainment and advertising, and ambivalent attitudes about sex by most American parents (only about one-fifth of U.S. teenagers learn about the risks of pregnancy and how to prevent it from their parents). Some teenage women become pregnant because they imagine a baby will fill a void in their lives and give them something of their own to love.

Sweden's much lower teenage pregnancy rate (Figure 7-14) can be attributed to the fact that starting at age 7 every Swedish child receives a thorough grounding in basic reproductive biology and by age 10 to 12 has been introduced to the various types of contraceptives. Polls show that 75% of Americans favor sex education in the schools, including information about birth control and school clinics that dispense contraceptives. Yet such education is not widely available and often represents too little too late, primarily because of

strong opposition to sex education by small but highly vocal religious groups who fear that such education will increase sexual activity.

Between 1973 and 1987 high schools in Dallas, Phoenix, Chicago, and St. Paul and 23 other cities opened 75 health clinics, which advise students on contraception and dispense contraceptives. At least 100 more are planned in Los Angeles, Miami, Pittsburgh, and other communities across the U.S. These clinics have led to a sharp drop in teenage dropout rates and birth rates. A panel of doctors, public-health experts, sociologists, and demographers reported that a two-year study found no causal link between availability of such clinics and earlier sexual activity. Indeed, the study found that a majority of teenagers had been sexually active a year before seeking contraceptives. Do you think such clinics should be opened in all high schools?

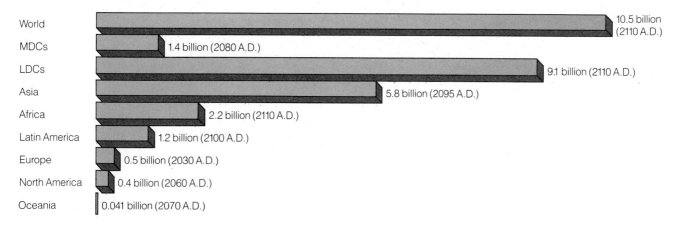

Figure 7-15 United Nations medium projections for stable population size and year of stabilization (shown in parentheses) of various groups of countries.

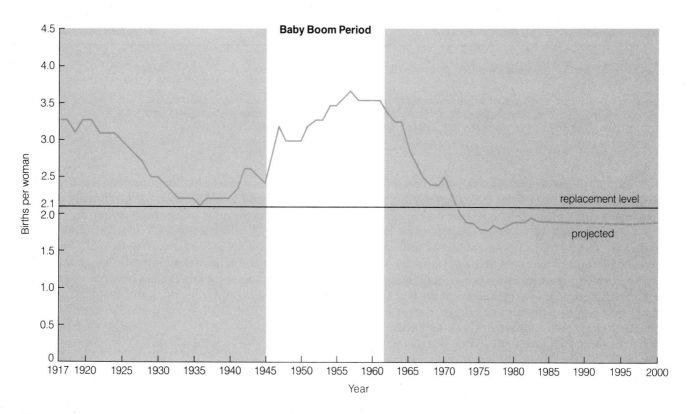

Figure 7-16 Total fertility rate for the United States between 1917 and 1987 and projected rate (dashed line) to 2000. (Data from the Population Reference Bureau and the U.S. Bureau of the Census)

in death rates could lead to population stabilization at a much lower level.

U.S. Population Stabilization Figure 7-16 shows that the total fertility rate in the United States has oscillated wildly. At the peak of the post–World War II baby boom (1945–1963) in 1957, the average TFR reached 3.7 children per woman. Since then the average TFR has generally declined and has been at or below replacement level since 1972. This drop was probably caused by various factors, including reduction in unwanted and mistimed births through widespread use of effective birth control methods, availability of legal abortions, social attitudes in favor of smaller families, greater social acceptance of childless couples, ris-

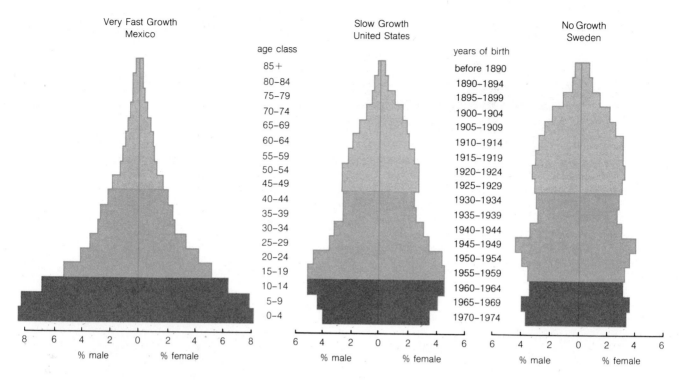

age class	years of birth
85+	before 1890
80–84	1890–1894
75–79	1895–1899
70–74	1900–1904
65–69	1905–1909
60–64	1910–1914
55–59	1915–1919
50–54	1920–1924
45–49	1925–1929
40–44	1930–1934
35–39	1935–1939
30–34	1940–1944
25–29	1945–1949
20–24	1950–1954
15–19	1955–1959
10–14	1960–1964
5–9	1965–1969
0–4	1970–1974

Figure 7-17 Population age structure diagrams for countries with rapid, slow, and zero population growth rates. Dark portions represent preproductive years (0–14), shaded portions represent reproductive years (15–44), and clear portions are postproductive years (45–85+). (Data from the Population Reference Bureau)

ing costs of raising a family ($145,000 to raise one child born in 1985 to age 18), and an increasing number of women working outside the home. For example, by 1987 more than 70% of women of childbearing age worked—up from 40% in 1955—and had a childbearing rate one-third of those not in the labor force.

The United States has not reached ZPG in spite of the dramatic drop in average TFR below the replacement level because of the large number of women still moving through their childbearing years and because of the country's high levels of legal and illegal immigration. In 1986 the Census Bureau made various projections of future U.S. population growth, assuming different average TFRs, life expectancies, and annual net legal immigration rates. The medium projection, assuming an average annual TFR of 1.9 and an annual net legal immigration of 500,000 persons, is that U.S. population will grow from 243 million in 1987 to 309 million in 2050 and then begin to slow down, reaching ZPG by 2080 with a population of 311 million.

Some demographers project a somewhat lower growth on the assumption that the present TFR of 1.8 will be maintained. If this happens, legal and illegal immigration will account for all U.S. population growth by the 2030s. Others project a larger stable population size than 311 million because they believe that an annual net migration rate (including both legal and illegal immigration) of 800,000 to 1.1 million is more likely than the 500,000 figure used by the Census Bureau.

Still others project a higher population size because of a future rise to a TFR above 1.9, primarily from an increase in the nonwhite population (mostly Hispanic and black), which historically has had fertility rates higher than the U.S. average (Figure 7-12). Each of us will play a role in determining which of these and other demographic possibilities becomes a reality (see the Guest Essay at the end of this chapter).

7-4 AGE STRUCTURE

Age Structure Diagrams Why will world population most likely keep growing for at least 100 years, even after the average world TFR has reached or dropped below replacement-level fertility of 2.1? Why do some demographers expect the U.S. birth rate to rise between now and 1994, even though the TFR may stay well below 2.1?

The answer to these questions lies in an understanding of another important factor of population dynamics—the **age structure** of a population: the percentage of the population or the number of people of each sex at each age level in a population. A population age structure diagram is obtained by plotting the percentages of males and females in the total population in three age categories: *preproductive* (ages 0–14),

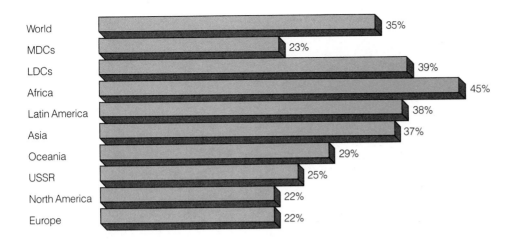

Figure 7-18 Percentage of people under age 15 in various groups of countries in 1987. (Data from the Population Reference Bureau)

World	35%
MDCs	23%
LDCs	39%
Africa	45%
Latin America	38%
Asia	37%
Oceania	29%
USSR	25%
North America	22%
Europe	22%

reproductive (ages 15–44), and *postproductive* (ages 45–85+).

Figure 7-17 shows the age structure diagrams for countries with rapid, slow, and zero growth rates. Mexico and most LDCs with rapidly growing populations have pyramid-shaped age structure diagrams, indicating a high ratio of children under age 15 (an average of 39% in 1987 for all LDCs) to adults over age 65 (4% in 1987). In contrast, the age structure diagram for the U.S., Sweden, and most MDCs undergoing slow or no population growth have a narrower base, indicating a much smaller percentage of population under age 15 (an average of 22% in 1987) and a larger percentage above 65 (11% in 1987). Some MDCs—Sweden, for example, which has achieved ZPG—have roughly equal numbers of people at each age level.

Population Momentum and Age Structure Any country whose population contains a large number of people below age 29, and especially below age 15, has a powerful built-in momentum of population growth. These are the potential parents of the next generation. This momentum exists even if women have only one or two children, simply because there is such a large increase in the number who can have children. Moreover, the population of a country with a large number of people under 29 continues to expand for approximately one average lifetime—roughly 60 to 70 years—after its average TFR has dropped to replacement level.

In 1987 about 33% of the people on this planet were under 15 years of age. In LDCs the number is even higher at 37%, compared to 22% in MDCs (Figure 7-18). This youth-heavy age structure explains why population will continue to grow, especially in LDCs, long after replacement-level fertility rates are reached—unless death rates rise sharply.

Population age structure also explains why it will probably take 50 to 70 years for the United States to reach ZPG, even if fertility rates remain below the replacement level. Although many couples are now having smaller families, the number of births could easily rise for the next several years—not because each woman will have more babies, but because there are more women to have babies. The 37 million women born during the baby boom will affect U.S. population growth through 1994, when women born at the end of the baby boom will turn 30 and move out of their prime reproductive years. As mentioned earlier, U.S. population growth is also maintained by a large annual net migration rate.

Making Projections from Age Structure Diagrams Figure 7-19 shows that the U.S. baby boom caused a bulge in the age structure. This bulge will move through the prime reproductive ages of 20–29 between 1970 and 1994 and through older age groups in later years. This helps explain why the 1960s and 1970s have been called the "youth generation." Similarly, the period between 1975 and 1990 could be called the "age of young adults," the period between 1990 and 2009 the "age of middle-aged adults," and between 2010 and 2058 the "age of senior citizens."

The diagrams in Figure 7-19 can be used to project some of the social and economic changes that may occur in the United States in coming decades. In the 1970s and early 1980s large numbers of "baby boomers" flooded the job market, causing high unemployment rates for teenagers and adults under age 29. This situation probably won't begin to ease until after 1993 when the last of the people born during the baby boom turn 29.

Most baby boomers are having to work harder than the generation that preceded them just to stay even. Many are falling behind and facing financial sacrifice and lowered expectations. Between 1973 and 1983, the real (adjusted for inflation) after-tax income of households headed by a 25- to 34-year-old baby boomer decreased by nearly 19%—even though the portion

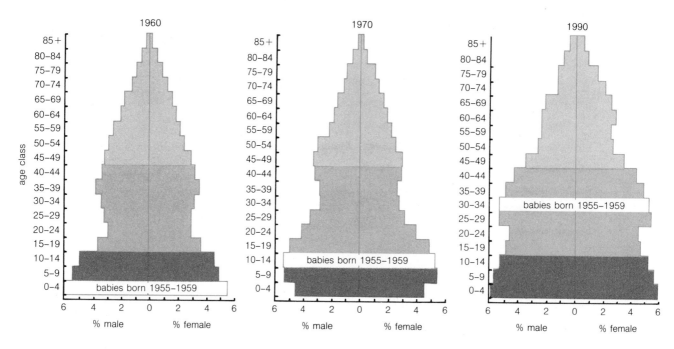

Figure 7-19 Age structure of the U.S. population in 1960, 1970, and 1990 (projection). The population bulge of babies born between 1955 and 1959 is slowly moving up. (Data from the Population Reference Bureau)

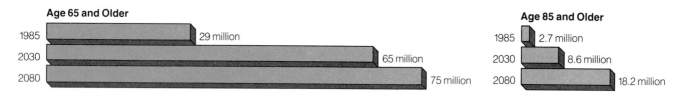

Figure 7-20 Projected growth in the number of people age 65 and older in the United States between 1985 and 2080. (Data from the U.S. Bureau of the Census)

of wives in this group working outside the household more than doubled from 29% to 62% during the same period. In 1983 the average 30-year-old male homeowner spent 44% of his earnings on mortgage payments, compared to only 14% by his counterparts in 1949. This also means that most baby boomers are not able to put very much aside for their retirement. Since the 1970s, for the first time in U.S. history, the economic value of a college degree when adjusted for inflation has declined. It is estimated that between 1980 and 1990, nearly one-quarter of college graduates will be overeducated for the jobs they will be able to get—as secretaries, store clerks, cab drivers, and factory workers.

By 1999 all of the baby boom generation will have reached middle age (35–64). Many of these adults may find little opportunity for professional advancement unless large numbers of their elders decide to retire early. On the other hand, we will probably see more young leaders in government, politics, and private industry.

Between 2012 and 2029 all baby boomers will reach age 65, and many will live at least another 20 years. Assuming that death rates don't rise, the number of people 65 and older will increase dramatically (Figure 7-20). The burden of supporting so many retired people will be on the "baby bust" generation—the much smaller group of people born mostly in the 1970s and 1980s, when average fertility rates were below replacement level. This large increase in retired citizens will put a severe strain on Medicare and the Social Security System. Between 1937 and 1980 the number of workers paying Social Security taxes for each beneficiary dropped from ten to three. By 2030 it is projected that there will be only two workers per beneficiary (Figure 7-21). Thus, many baby boomers may face harsh times after retirement because of lower Social Security benefits, as well as less personal savings.

The baby bust generation should have a much easier time in many respects than the preceding baby boom generation. Much smaller numbers will be competing for education, jobs, and services. Labor short-

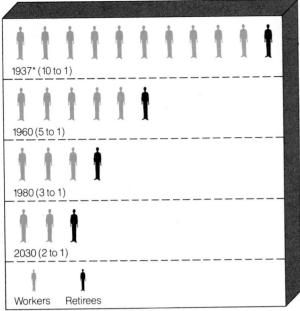

1937* (10 to 1)

1960 (5 to 1)

1980 (3 to 1)

2030 (2 to 1)

Workers   Retirees

*Social Security was established in 1935.

Figure 7-21 Numbers of workers supporting one retired person through the U.S. Social Security System, 1937–2030 (projected). Data from the U.S. Bureau of the Census)

ages should drive up wages for the baby bust generation; in fact, the United States might have to relax current immigration laws to bring in new workers. With a shortage of young adults, the armed forces would be hard-pressed to meet recruiting levels, and there may be pressure to reinstate the draft. On the other hand, the baby bust group may find it hard to get job promotions as they reach middle age because most upper-level positions will be occupied by the much larger baby boom group. They also will probably face much higher income taxes and Social Security taxes (to help pay for retired baby boomers). From these few projections, we see that any bulge or indentation in the age structure of a population creates a number of social and economic changes that ripple through a society for decades.

The population of most less developed countries is doubling every twenty to thirty years. Trying to develop into a modern industrial state under these conditions is like trying to work out the choreography for a new ballet in a crowded subway car.

Garrett Hardin

Guest Essay   We Are All Population Actors

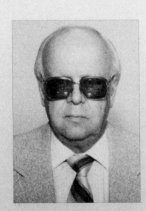

Leon F. Bouvier

Until his retirement in 1986, Leon F. Bouvier served as Director of Demographic Research and Policy Analysis since 1980, and as Vice President of the Population Reference Bureau since 1984. He has written scores of significant articles on population issues, as well as seven books, including Population: Demography and Policy *(with R. Weller, St. Martin's Press, 1981).*

Population size and composition change are affected by shifts in three demographic variables: fertility, migration, mortality. People are born; most people move; people all die once. This is demographic behavior and these are population acts. We decide whether or not to have children and how many to have. We move once, twice, often, or we do not move; sometimes we cross an international border in the process. We all die but once and seldom perform that act willingly. Yet, to a considerable extent the age at which we die is dependent on numerous social as well as biological factors. Thus, we are all population actors.

Any change in the way we play our role determines if our area gains or loses people. It determines what kind of people will live there—young or old, rich or poor, well educated or poorly educated, black, brown, or white, and so on. This is what makes demography so exciting, despite its reliance on numbers. Our actions as population actors help shape the kind of society we live in, now and tomorrow.

Let us see how our demographic behavior and

any shifts that might occur in that behavior affect the United States of the future. Fertility is the major act of demographic behavior. During the 1950s and early 1960s American women were having 3 and 4 children on average. Since 1972, American women have been having an average of only 1.8 children. In other words, Americans have shifted their fertility behavior dramatically in a brief period.

At the same time we have changed our health and exercise habits. Many Americans have given up smoking, reduced their alcoholic intake, exercise more frequently, and pay more attention to what they eat. The result is increased longevity. Our life expectancy is at an all-time peak because many of us are doing something to postpone our moment of death as long as possible. This population act affects not only our own lives but eventually those of others who in the future may be called upon to pay much higher taxes to help support us if we live longer.

We are a nation of movers; on average we can expect to move 13 times in our lives. When possible we select certain places to move to; cities are abandoned while suburbs grow; populations of many southern and western Sunbelt states grow as the populations of many northern and eastern Rustbelt states fall. Even these patterns are subject to radical and quick shifts as our tastes and economic conditions change. In 1982 it seemed as though half of Detroit

was headed for Houston; now the reverse is occurring because the oil glut of the 1980s led to massive layoffs in oil and related businesses.

The size and nature of a society such as the United States is not determined solely by the population acts of its residents. Each year close to 1 million nonresidents decide to move to this country either legally or illegally—a very important population act that affects those individuals and each of us. Over the past two decades some 10 million to 15 million people have taken up residence in the United States, some legally, others illegally. These migration population acts change the composition of our population and help postpone the day when our population may stabilize.

Demographically speaking, we are still a young country when compared to other more developed countries. Our thirteen-year baby boom binge accounts for the fact that in 1985 our median age was 31.5 years while that of most European countries was closer to 40. But we are getting older for three reasons: the large baby boom generation is now approaching middle age; our fertility is so low that the proportion of children in the population is declining; and the proportion of the elderly is increasing in part due to increased longevity. By 2030 when members of the baby boom generation begin becoming senior citizens, about 21% of the population of some

CHAPTER SUMMARY

Four major factors affect the size and the rate of change in size of the human population: difference between birth rates and death rates, migration, fertility, and the number of people at each age level. As long as the *birth rate* is greater than the *death rate,* the world's population size will grow at a rate that depends on the positive difference between these two rates. The population size of the world and of a country tends to increase with increasing *life expectancy* and to decrease with increasing *average infant mortality.*

Population throughout the world is redistributed as people move from one place to another. If more people *immigrate* to than *emigrate* from a particular country during a given period, the population of that area will grow at a rate that depends on the positive difference between the immigration rate and the emigration rate. This factor does not affect world population but does affect population size and rate of growth in various countries.

The population size of the world and of a particular country can level off or stabilize only after the *total fertility rate* or average number of children born to women in the

world during their reproductive years stays at or below an average *replacement-level fertility* of 2.1 children per woman. Once replacement-level fertility is achieved, the length of time required before population size levels off depends primarily on the number of women in their reproductive years (ages 15–44) and the number below age 15 who will be entering their reproductive years. Continued high immigration rates can delay or prevent a country's achievement of zero population growth (ZPG). Normally, the later women marry for the first time or have their first child, the lower the average number of children they have because of a reduction in the number of their potential years for childbearing.

The time necessary for world population or that of a particular country to stabilize after average total fertility rates have reached or fallen below replacement level also depends on the population's *age structure*—the percentage of females and males at each age level. The larger the number and percentage of women in their reproductive years (15–44) and preproductive years (under 15), the longer it will take for population size to reach its peak level (ZPG). Drastic changes in the age structure of a population because of a period of high fertility or low fertility have demographic, social, and economic changes that last a generation or more.

300 million people will consist of those 65 and older, compared to 12% in 1985. We are thus an aging society whose composition is being changed as a result of two major population acts: reduced fertility and increased longevity.

Immigration is another population act affecting the age structure and ethnic makeup of our society. The proportion of our society who are new immigrants or their descendants will increase while that of current residents and their descendants will fall. Indeed, soon after the turn of the century, California, and a little later, Texas will no longer have a white or Anglo majority. Instead each will be made up of a mixture of Anglos, blacks, Hispanics, and Asians, none making up a clear majority of the population. If current rates of fertility, mortality, and migration remain constant, within a century this statement will also be true for the country. Again, demographic behavior is at work. Together low fertility and high immigration are resulting in an ever more heterogeneous nation from an ethnic viewpoint.

Thus, as we prepare to enter the twenty-first century, the United States is getting older and more ethnically diverse. This is not good news nor is it bad news. However, we need to be aware of the shifts already in progress because of our past and present demographic behavior. In this way we as a nation can better prepare ourselves to face the challenges that are bound to follow from such a massive restructuring of the population—all the results of countless individual population acts.

Hopefully, these few examples confirm the fact that demography is useful, exciting, and often unpredictable. Indeed, our demographic behavior could shift drastically at any time. Fertility could rise unexpectedly as it did in the 1950s; new discoveries could extend life expectancy 10 to 25 additional years; new legislation could sharply reduce illegal as well as legal immigration. Our population acts must be constantly monitored if the nation, its policymakers, and each of us are to better plan for the future.

Guest Essay Discussion

1. Do you agree that the present demographic news about the United States is neither good nor bad? If not, which news do you consider good and which bad? Explain.

2. In your own fertility behavior how many children do you plan to have? Why?

3. Do you think the government should discourage illegal immigration? Why? Should legal immigration also be reduced? Why?

DISCUSSION TOPICS

1. Why are falling birth rates not necessarily a reliable indicator of future population growth trends?

2. Suppose modern medicine finds cures for cancer and heart disease. What effects would this have on population growth in MDCs and LDCs? On their population age structures? On their major social problems?

3. Explain the difference between achieving replacement-level fertility and zero population growth (ZPG).

4. What must happen to the total fertility rate if the United States is to attain ZPG in 40 to 60 years? Why will it take so long?

5. Explain why the U.S. population has the potential to grow rapidly again through 1993.

6. Project what your own life may be like at ages 25, 45, and 65 on the basis of the present age structure of the U.S. population or that of the country in which you live. What changes, if any, do such projections make in your career choice and in your plans for marriage and children?

7. Explain why raising the average first marriage age to 25 or higher is an effective means of reducing population growth rates.

8. Criticize each of the following headlines or statements. Be specific.
   a. "Baby Boom Replaced by Bust—U.S. in Danger of Instant ZPG."
   b. "Birth Rates Falling—Prophets of Doom Wrong Again."

9. Explain why it is considered rational by a couple in India to have six or seven children. What possible changes might induce such a couple to think of their behavior as irrational?

10. Do you think the world is more likely to reach the high (14.2 billion), medium (10.2 billion), or low (7.5 billion) population size projected by the United Nations? Explain.

8

Population Control

GENERAL OBJECTIVES

GENERAL OBJECTIVES

1. What are the arguments for and against control of population growth in the world and in the United States?

2. What methods are available for controlling the size of the human population?

3. What success have the world's two most populous countries, China and India, had in trying to control the rate of growth of their populations?

4. How useful are computer models to project future changes in population size, resource availability, and pollution?

Short of thermonuclear war itself, rampant population growth is the gravest issue the world faces over the decades immediately ahead.

Robert S. McNamara

Some consider rapid population growth one of the most serious problems facing the world today. Others believe it is a problem in most LDCs but not in MDCs such as the United States. A small number of analysts contend that population growth is good and should not be discouraged. Whether population growth should be controlled and, if so, how this might be done are complex and highly controversial issues discussed in this chapter.

8-1 SHOULD POPULATION GROWTH BE CONTROLLED?

Is World Population Growth Good or Bad? To some analysts, resource depletion, pollution, and environmental degradation are merely symptoms of an underlying basic problem—the increasing pressure being placed on the natural environment by a growing human population. According to this neo-Malthusian view:

More people → more resource consumption → earlier exhaustion of nonrenewable resources and increased degradation of renewable resources → more pollution → higher production costs for remaining resources because of decreased supplies and increased pollution control expenditure → decreasing average real income per person

The neo-Malthusians challenge the cornucopians, who say that more people create more resources and that people today are better fed and are living longer than ever before, to go out and tell this to the 17 million people who die each year from malnutrition, infection, and preventable disease. Tell it to the 1 billion people who don't have safe drinking water and the 2 billion who have no basic sanitary facilities. Tell it to the one-quarter of the world's families living in makeshift shacks or on the streets.

Neo-Malthusians believe that strong population planning and control programs need to be instituted worldwide on an urgent basis. While they believe that no one should be forced or coerced into not having a wanted child, they also believe it is unethical not to make culturally acceptable forms of birth control available to anyone in the world who wants to use them. They argue that it is unethical not to control population growth as soon as possible because continued rapid population growth can condemn hundreds of millions of people in the next few decades to premature death and reduced freedom in an increasingly crowded world.

A more moderate school of thought, represented in a 1986 National Academy of Sciences study (see Further Readings), contends that global problems such as starvation, poverty, disease, resource depletion, pollution, and environmental degradation are not caused solely by rapid population growth and thus won't be solved solely by population stabilization. Nevertheless, these analysts favor strong population planning and control programs because without them the problems are likely to become much worse.

Most cornucopians do not favor attempting to control population growth because they do not believe that hunger, poverty, pollution, and environmental degradation are caused by population growth or that population planning programs will reduce the severity of these problems. Indeed, many cornucopians think population growth should be stimulated because more people provide more hands and more brains to produce more goods, services, and ideas to spur further economic growth. According to the cornucopian view:

More people → more customers → more business → more profits → more average real income per person

They point out that despite widespread poverty, even the limited economic growth in LDCs means that people in these countries are on average better fed, more healthy, and living longer than ever before. Throughout human history the real prices of fuel, metals, food, and every other natural resource have fallen rather than risen because of human ingenuity. Seeing no reason for this trend to change, the cornucopians envision no limits to economic growth and population growth (see Enrichment Study at the end of this chapter).

Prior to 1984 the United States officially encouraged worldwide population planning and control activities. Until then the United States provided large amounts of financial support for family planning programs and contraceptive and reproductive research to groups such as the International Planned Parenthood Federation and the UN Fund for Population Activities (UNFPA)—the world's two most effective international family planning organizations.

At the 1984 UN International Conference on Population, however, U.S. officials representing the Reagan administration stated that the official position of the United States is that population growth is neither good nor bad. Since 1985 the Reagan administration, spurred by pressure from antiabortion groups, has cut off U.S. contributions to UNFPA, which had been receiving about one-fourth of its annual budget from the United States. The grounds for this action were that UNFPA was providing some grants to China, where the government is alleged to exert intense pressure on women to abort any pregnancies after having one child and to undergo sterilization. China, however, insists that such abuses do not reflect official policy and are being corrected. Furthermore, UNFPA supplies China with funds used only in demographic analyses and training for program managers, not for provision of abortion or other family planning services. Many analysts believe that the U.S. government decision to reduce family planning assistance increases the likelihood that population growth will be slowed by rising death rates rather than falling birth rates.

Is U.S. Population Growth Good or Bad? Some economists argue that the United States (as well as other MDCs) should increase its population to maintain economic growth and power throughout the world. They contend that there are populous countries that are not powerful, but no powerful countries that are not populous.

Other observers disagree. They point out that Japan, with a relatively small population, became one of the world's leading industrial countries since 1945 and, if present trends continue, could be the world's leading economic power by 2000. They contend that economic and military power today does not depend on having large numbers of people, but on being able to develop, produce, and sell increasingly sophisticated technology.

Most environmentalists argue that adding millions to the U.S. population will intensify many environmental and social problems by increasing resource use and pollution. They believe that by establishing an official goal of stabilizing its population, the United States would set a good example for other countries.

8-2 CONTROLLING POPULATION GROWTH: ECONOMIC DEVELOPMENT, FAMILY PLANNING, AND REGULATING MIGRATION

Controlling Births, Deaths, and Migration   A government can alter the size and growth rate of its population by encouraging a change in any of the three basic demographic variables: births, deaths, and migration. Most MDCs now have relatively low birth and death rates, while most LDCs have relatively low death rates but high birth rates (Figure 7-3, p. 138). Governments of most countries in the world achieve some degree of population control by allowing relatively little immigration from other countries and in some cases by encouraging emigration to other countries to reduce population pressures. Only a few countries, chiefly the United States, Canada, and Australia, allow large annual increases in their population from immigration.

Throughout the world decreasing the birth rate is the focus of most efforts to control population growth. By 1986, countries containing 91% of the people living in LDCs had programs to reduce their fertility rates, although the effectiveness and funding of such programs vary widely from country to country. In 1986, countries containing only 3% of the people living in LDCs considered their fertility rates too low.

Two general approaches to decreasing birth rates are *economic development* and *family planning*. Economic development may reduce the number of children a couple desires by bringing about better education, providing more economic security, and reducing the need to consider children a substitute for old age social security. Family planning methods help people regulate the number of children they have and when they have them. Although there is still controversy over which approach is best, there is increasing evidence that a combination of both approaches offers a country the best way to reduce its birth rate and thus its rate of population growth.

Economic Development and the Demographic Transition   After examining birth and death rates in western European countries that became industrialized during the nineteenth century, demographers formed a model of population change and control known as the **demographic transition**. The basic idea of this model is that as western European countries became industrialized, they had declines in death rates followed by declines in birth rates, eventually resulting in decreased population growth. This transition takes place in four distinct phases (Figure 8-1). In the *preindustrial stage*, harsh living conditions lead to high birth rates (to compensate for high infant mortality) and high death rates, resulting in little population growth. The second, or *transitional*, stage begins shortly after industrialization is initiated. In this phase death rates drop, primarily as a result of increased food production and improved sanitation and health. Because birth rates remain high, population growth accelerates and continues at a high rate for a prolonged period (typically about 3% a year). Late in this phase population growth levels off somewhat as industrialization spreads and living conditions improve.

In the *industrial stage*, industrialization is widespread. Crude birth rates drop and eventually begin to approach crude death rates as better-educated and more affluent couples (who have moved to cities to obtain jobs) become aware that children are expensive to raise and that having too many hinders them from taking advantage of job opportunities in an expanding economy. Population growth continues but at a slower and perhaps fluctuating rate, depending on economic conditions. The United States, Japan, the Soviet Union, Canada, Australia, New Zealand, and most of the industrialized western European countries are now in this third phase.

A fourth phase, the *postindustrial stage* takes place when birth rates decline even further to equal death rates, thus reaching ZPG, and then continue to fall so that total population size begins slowly to decrease. By 1986, twelve countries—Austria, Belgium, Denmark, East Germany, Greece, Hungary, Italy, Luxembourg, Norway, Sweden, the United Kingdom and West Germany—had reached or were close to ZPG. Together these countries have a population of 247 million, representing 5% of the world's population. Three of these countries—Austria, Hungary, and West Germany—were experiencing population declines. If West Germany maintains its present total fertility rate of 1.2 and does not allow significant immigration, its population will decrease from 61 million in 1986 to 40 million by 2050. West German leaders are concerned about this projected population decrease and would like to see birth rates rise. They fear that there will be too few workers to support continued economic growth and to pay taxes to support the increasing portion of population over age 65. With a small percentage of its population under age 15, West Germany has built-in momentum for population decline over the next 50 to 70 years. Other MDCs entering the postindustrial stage may become concerned with increasing their birth and fertility rates to reduce their rates of population decline.

Another eight countries with an annual population growth of 0.5% per year or less are approaching ZPG, so that soon about 8% of the world's people will be living in countries with stationary populations. Several countries are not far behind, such as the Soviet Union, the United States, Japan, Canada, Hong Kong, Australia, Poland, Yugoslavia, and China, whose pop-

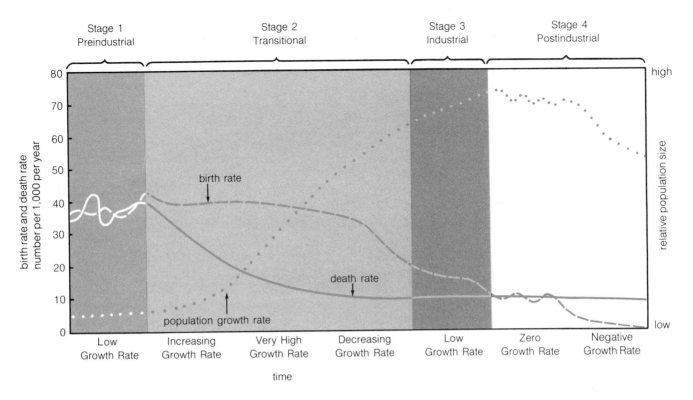

Figure 8-1 Generalized model of the demographic transition.

ulations are expanding between 0.5% and 1% per year.

In most LDCs today death rates have fallen, but not birth rates. In other words, these LDCs are still in the transitional phase halfway up the economic ladder, with fairly high to very high population growth rates. Figure 8-2 compares Sweden, which has entered the postindustrial phase, with Mexico, still in the transitional phase. Mexico, with a population of 82 million in 1987 and a growth rate of 2.5%, is projected to almost double its population by 2020.

Cornucopians believe that today's LDCs will make the demographic transition, becoming MDCs with low population growth rates over the next few decades without increased family planning efforts. However, neo-Malthusians point out that an increase in average annual per capita income occurs only when a country's average annual rate of economic growth exceeds its annual rate of population growth. For example, over the last 100 years, Japan's rate of economic growth has averaged 4% a year while its population growth rate has averaged 1.1% a year. It is the resulting 2.9% average annual growth in per capita income that has made Japan one of the world's wealthiest countries. Similarly, over the past 100 years the rate of economic growth in the United States has averaged 3.3% a year while population has grown at an average rate of 1.5% a year. As a result, the U.S. has averaged a 1.8% annual growth in average per capita income.

Neo-Malthusians fear that the rate of economic growth in many LDCs will not exceed their high rates of population growth. Many LDCs, such as Mexico, could become stuck in the transitional stage of the demographic transition because some of the conditions that allowed today's MDCs to become developed are not available for today's LDCs. For example, even with large and growing populations, many LDCs do not have enough skilled workers to manufacture the high technology products needed for competition in today's economic environment. Most low- and middle-income LDCs also lack the capital and resources needed for rapid economic development, and the amount of money being given or loaned to LDCs—already struggling under tremendous debt burdens—has been decreasing. The LDCs face stiff competition from MDCs and recently modernized LDCs in selling products on which their economic growth depends. In addition, energy experts project that cheap supplies of fossil fuel energy, which enabled today's MDCs to make the demographic transition, will decrease in coming decades and the prices of most other sources of energy will be too high for poor countries.

Family Planning Recent evidence suggests that improved and expanded family planning programs may bring about a more rapid decline in the birth rate and at a lower cost than economic development alone. **Family planning** programs provide educational and

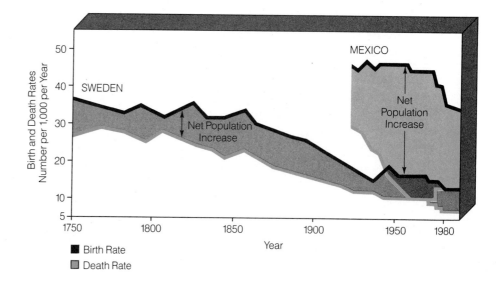

Figure 8-2 Comparison of Sweden, which has undergone the demographic transition, and Mexico, which has not. (Data from Population Reference Bureau)

clinical services that help couples choose how many children to have and when to have them. Such programs vary from culture to culture but usually provide sex education and information on methods of birth-control, distribute contraceptives, and in some case perform abortions and sterilizations, often without charge or at low rates. With the exception of China, family planning programs in most countries have steered clear of trying to convince or coerce couples to have fewer children.

Family planning services were first introduced in LDCs in the 1940s and 1950s by private physicians and women's groups. Since that time, organizations such as the International Planned Parenthood Federation, the Planned Parenthood Federation of America, the United Nations Fund for Population Activities, the U.S. Agency for International Development (AID), the Ford Foundation, and the World Bank have been helping countries carry out family planning by providing technical assistance, funding, or both.

Between 1970 and 1986, birth rates have dropped, sometimes quite rapidly, in more than 30 LDCs. Family planning has been a major factor in reducing birth and fertility rates in highly populated China and Indonesia and in some LDCs with relatively small populations, such as Singapore, Hong Kong, Sri Lanka, Barbados, Taiwan, Cuba, Mauritius, Thailand, Colombia, Costa Rica, South Korea, Fiji, and Jamaica. The common denominators in these successful programs are committed leadership, local implementation and wide availability of contraceptive services. However, only moderate to poor results have been claimed in more populous LDCs like India, Brazil, Bangladesh, Pakistan, and Nigeria, and in 79 less populous LDCs—especially in Africa and Latin America, where population growth rates are usually very high (Figure 7-8, p. 140). Only 3% to 4% of the couples in most African countries use contraception. However,

Brazil, the most populous country in Latin America, has recently launched a program to give all women information on birth control methods and a free supply of birth control pills. Mexico has also stepped up a public education program to publicize the importance of family planning.

The Population Crisis Committee estimates that between 1978 and 1983 family planning programs reduced world population by 130 million and saved at least $175 billion in government expenditures for food, shelter, clothing, education, and health care. Despite these efforts, the delivery of family planning services in much of the less developed world is still woefully inadequate, particularly in rural areas. There are about 800 million women of reproductive age in the world, with 600 million of these women in LDCs. Between 1975 and 1985 nearly half a million women in 61 LDCs were interviewed in the World Fertility Survey and the Contraceptive Prevalence Survey conducted by the United Nations. On the basis of these surveys, the U.N. concludes that about 400 million women in LDCs desire to limit the size and determine the spacing of their children but lack access to family planning services.

Expanding family planning services to reach these women and those who will soon be entering their reproductive years could prevent an estimated 5.8 million births a year and over 130,000 abortions a day and help bring down the world's presently projected ultimate population in the year 2100 from 10.2 billion (the UN medium projection) to 7.5 billion (the UN low projection) by preventing unwanted births. This would mean 2.7 billion fewer people needing food, water, shelter, and health services.

Family planning could be provided in LDCs to all couples who want it for about $8 billion a year. Currently only about $2 billion is being spent; about one-fifth ($400 million) is provided as foreign aid by MDCs

In 1985 the federal government provided about $142 million in grants to 5,000 hospitals, health departments, and community clinics for contraceptive counseling, pregnancy testing, breast exams, and screening for sexually transmitted diseases. These centers serve about 5 million poor women and teenagers each year, most of whom cannot afford private health care. None of these facilities spend any federal money to terminate even a single pregnancy. Instead, they inform women of their options for preventing future pregnancies, terminating an unwanted pregnancy, obtaining prenatal and postnatal health services for themselves and their babies, and putting a baby up for adoption. This program helps prevent pregnancies that would lead to about 282,000 additional births annually

and reduces the number of legal abortions in the United States by about 433,000 a year. For every $1 invested, this program saves taxpayers $2 to $3 the following year in health and welfare costs.

In spite of these benefits, antiabortion activists, many affiliated with religious organizations, are putting great pressure on Congress to eliminate federal funds for any clinic that informs clients that abortion is an alternative to an unwanted pregnancy because they view abortion as murder of an unborn child. Others, mainly Roman Catholic groups, want to go further and cut off funds to such clinics if they inform clients of any "artificial" means of birth control, considering all such methods the wrongful taking of human life. Some groups oppose such clinics because they believe that

making sex and contraception information available promotes promiscuity and leads to soaring pregnancy rates and the spread of sexually transmitted diseases, especially among teenagers.

Supporters of family planning answer that most people seeking these services are already sexually active or plan to become so soon and are going to the clinics to get help in preventing pregnancy and in reducing their chances of contracting disease. Thus, these services help decrease—not increase—pregnancy and the spread of sexually transmitted diseases. Proponents also point out that people who consider abortion murder should be in favor of family planning services that help prevent about 433,000 abortions a year. What do you think?

and private organizations such as the World Bank. If MDCs provided 50% of the $8 billion, it would cost each person in the MDCs an average of only 34 cents a year (compared to the 3 cents now being given) to help reduce world population by 2.7 billion.

But even the present inadequate level of expenditure for family planning is decreasing as a result of the sharp drop of funds provided to international family planning agencies by the United States since 1985. There are also increasing efforts, mostly by antiabortion activists, to have federal assistance to family planning clinics in the U.S. sharply reduced or eliminated (see Spotlight above).

Restricting Immigration   Most countries control their population growth to some extent by limiting immigration. A major exception is the United States, which throughout its history has admitted large numbers of immigrants and refugees (Figure 7-10, p. 142). Today the United States admits between 600,000 and 750,000 legal immigrants each year—about twice as many as all other countries combined. In addition, at least 200,000 illegal immigrants are added each year to the Census Bureau's estimated 4.9 million illegal aliens

already in the country. The Immigration and Naturalization Service (INS), however, puts the estimated number of illegal aliens at 12 million.

In recent years there has been growing pressure to reduce illegal immigration into the United States. Some analysts have also called for establishment of an annual ceiling of no more than 450,000 for all categories of legal immigration, including refugees, to help reduce the intensity of some of the country's social, economic, and environmental problems and reach zero population growth sooner. In polls taken in 1985, half of those surveyed favored lower legal immigration levels, up from 33% in 1965.

In 1986 Congress passed a new immigration law designed to control illegal immigration. Illegal immigrants who entered the U.S. before January 1, 1982 and who can provide evidence that they have lived here continuously since then may become temporary residents. After 18 months in that status they can apply to become permanent residents; five years later, they can apply for citizenship. Illegal immigrants who worked in American agriculture for at least 90 days between May 1, 1985 and May 1, 1986 may also become temporary residents and then apply for citizenship after seven years. The federal government is providing $1 billion a year between 1987 and 1991 to reimburse state and local governments for the cost of supplying public assistance or other benefits to these immigrants. After five years, newly legal immigrants will be eligible for federally funded public assistance.

The immigration bill prohibits the hiring of illegal immigrants. Employers must examine the identity documents of all new employees; those who knowingly employ illegal aliens will be subject to fines of $250 to $10,000 per violation, and repeat offenders can be sentenced to prison for up to six months. The bill also increases the budget for the INS, allowing the Border Patrol staff to be enlarged by 50%, and requires that the service provide a telephone verification system to help employees identify legal immigrants. Critics of the law contend that unless the government introduces a new, tamperproof Social Security card, many illegals may attempt to circumvent the law by obtaining readily available fake documents.

8-3 METHODS OF BIRTH CONTROL

Present Methods Family planning depends primarily on providing couples with information about and access to various methods for preventing unwanted births. The ideal form of birth control would be effective, safe, inexpensive, convenient, free of side effects, and compatible with one's cultural, religious, and sexual attitudes. However, no single method ever has been, and probably no method ever will be, accepted universally because of cultural differences among the world's societies and changes in preferences during different phases of a couple's reproductive years.

About 200 million of the world's 800 million couples of reproductive age use some form of birth control. Available methods either *prevent pregnancy* or *terminate pregnancy before birth* (Table 8-1). These methods vary widely in their typical effectiveness (Figure 8-3) and amount of use throughout the world and the United States (Figure 8-4).

Preventing Pregnancy The most common form of birth control in the world is *sterilization* of females and males, primarily because of its widespread use in three populous countries—China, India, and the United States. Involving relatively simple surgical procedures that can be done under local anesthetic in a doctor's office and having no significant side effects, sterilization is ideal for individuals who are sure they don't want any more children. Sterilization sometimes can be reversed surgically, but reversal procedures presently have a success rate of only 30% to 40% for women and 50% to 60% for men.

Table 8-1 Methods of Birth Control
Pregnancy Prevention by Keeping Sperm and Egg from Uniting
Abstention (no intercourse)
Male Sterilization (vasectomy: tubes carrying sperm to penis are cut and tied)
Female Sterilization (fallopian tubes, which carry eggs from ovary to uterus, are either plugged or cut and tied)
Rhythm Method (periodic abstention; that is, no intercourse during woman's fertile period)
Coitus Interruptus (withdrawal of penis from vagina before ejaculation)
Condom (protective sheath worn over penis; only method that helps prevent sexually transmitted diseases)
Spermicide (sperm-killing chemicals inserted into vagina before intercourse)
Sponge Impregnated with Spermicide (inserted into vagina before intercourse to absorb and kill sperm and partially block cervix)
Diaphragm (flexible, dome-shaped rubber device placed over cervical opening before intercourse and usually used with a spermicide)
Douche (rinsing of vagina with spermicide immediately after intercourse)
Pregnancy Prevention by Suppressing Release of Egg
Breastfeeding (prevents ovulation for up to 29 months after birth)
Oral Contraceptive—"the Pill" (synthetic female hormones taken daily by mouth to prevent ovulation)
Pregnancy Termination
Intrauterine Device—IUD (plastic or plastic and metal device inserted and left in uterus prevents fertilized egg from implanting on uterine wall)
Abortion by Suction Aspiration (suction device used to remove embryo and placenta during the first 12 weeks of pregnancy without stay in hospital)
Abortion by Dilation and Evacuation (fetus is dismembered by forceps and then removed by a suction device between the 13th and 28th weeks of pregnancy; may require overnight hospital stay)
Abortion by induced labor (injection of salt solution into uterus to induce labor; used only after 16 weeks of pregnancy; usually requires overnight hospital stay)
Abortion or "month-after" pill (induces abortion when taken within ten days after a missed period; being tested in France in 1987)

Oral contraceptives are the second most used method for preventing pregnancy in the world and in the United States. New formulations of "the pill" do not increase the risk of any type of cancer and actually decrease the risk of cancer of the ovaries and the lining of the uterus (endometrial cancer) by 40% to 50%. Pill users

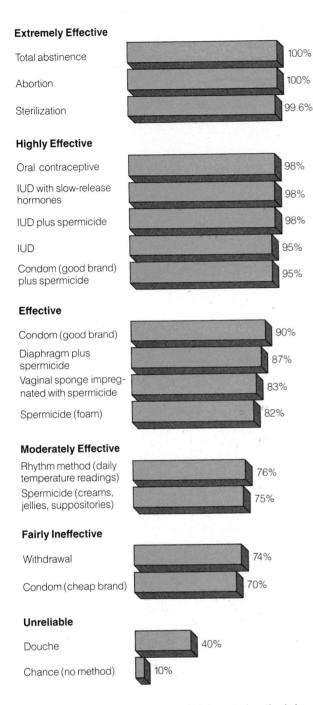

Extremely Effective

Total abstinence — 100%

Abortion — 100%

Sterilization — 99.6%

Highly Effective

Oral contraceptive — 98%

IUD with slow-release hormones — 98%

IUD plus spermicide — 98%

IUD — 95%

Condom (good brand) plus spermicide — 95%

Effective

Condom (good brand) — 90%

Diaphragm plus spermicide — 87%

Vaginal sponge impregnated with spermicide — 83%

Spermicide (foam) — 82%

Moderately Effective

Rhythm method (daily temperature readings) — 76%

Spermicide (creams, jellies, suppositories) — 75%

Fairly Ineffective

Withdrawal — 74%

Condom (cheap brand) — 70%

Unreliable

Douche — 40%

Chance (no method) — 10%

Figure 8-3 Typical effectiveness of birth control methods in the United States.

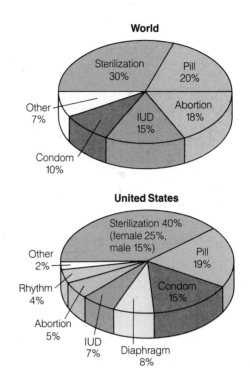

World

Sterilization 30% / Pill 20% / Abortion 18% / IUD 15% / Condom 10% / Other 7%

United States

Sterilization 40% (female 25%, male 15%) / Pill 19% / Condom 15% / Diaphragm 8% / IUD 7% / Abortion 5% / Rhythm 4% / Other 2%

Figure 8-4 Estimated use of various birth control methods in the world and the United States in 1985. (Data from UN Population Division and U.S. National Center for Health Statistics)

also experience a lower than normal incidence of benign breast and ovarian cysts, pelvic infections, iron-deficiency anemia, premenstrual tension, and menstrual cramps. However, women over age 40, women smokers over age 35, and women with diabetes or cardiovascular disease should not use oral contraceptives.

The *intrauterine device* is particularly useful for women who can't take the pill, don't want to undergo sterilization, and don't want to settle for less effective and less convenient methods. The IUD has few health risks for women who have only one sexual partner. However, for childless young women with several sexual partners, the device poses a greater than normal risk of pelvic inflammatory disease (PID), which often leads to sterility. One earlier type of IUD, the Dalkon Shield, caused thousands of cases of PID, sterility, and miscarriages, and it was implicated in the deaths of 20 American women. As a result, the relatively low use of IUDs in the United States is likely to drop further; by 1986 all but one manufacturer had stopped making them, fearing costly liability suits.

Use of *condoms* is increasing, especially in the United States, because in addition to contraception, they offer the best protection against sexually transmitted diseases such as herpes, AIDS, and gonorrhea. Other birth control methods such as diaphragms, spermicides, and spermicide-impregnated sponges are less widely used because they are less effective, messy, inconvenient, and effective only for a limited period of time—usually for just one act of intercourse.

Breastfeeding plays an important role in controlling fertility; women who are lactating (producing milk) usually do not ovulate and thus cannot conceive. However, because the number of nursing women is difficult to count, breastfeeding does not show up in official birth control statistics. Breastfeeding has several other benefits: It helps reduce infant mortality rates because mother's milk provides a baby with anti-

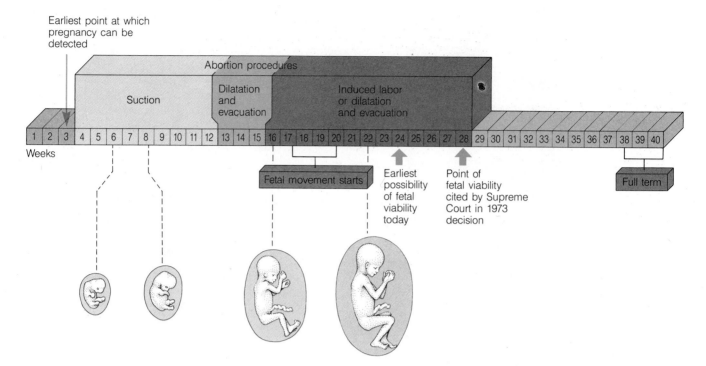

Earliest point at which pregnancy can be detected

Abortion procedures

Suction

Dilatation and evacuation

Induced labor or dilatation and evacuation

Weeks

| 1 | 2 | 3 | 4 | 5 | 6 | 7 | 8 | 9 | 10 | 11 | 12 | 13 | 14 | 15 | 16 | 17 | 18 | 19 | 20 | 21 | 22 | 23 | 24 | 25 | 26 | 27 | 28 | 29 | 30 | 31 | 32 | 33 | 34 | 35 | 36 | 37 | 38 | 39 | 40 |

Fetal movement starts

Earliest possibility of fetal viability today

Point of fetal viability cited by Supreme Court in 1973 decision

Full term

Figure 8-5 Pregnancy and abortion. (Data from Centers for Disease Control)

bodies to help prevent disease and is usually the most nutritious food available for infants in poor families. It also helps a mother's weight return to normal faster. Unfortunately, breastfeeding is declining in many LDCs, primarily because large U.S.-based international companies have promoted the use of infant formulas as an alternative to mother's milk. Buying infant formula when free breast milk is available is an unnecessary expense for a poor family struggling to survive. In addition, formula can lead to increases in infant illnesses and mortality because poor people, lacking fuel, often prepare it with unboiled, contaminated water and use unsterilized bottles.

Terminating Pregnancy: Abortion Only sterilization and oral contraceptives are more widely used for birth control than abortion. Various types of abortion procedures can be performed during each trimester or three-month period of pregnancy (Figure 8-5). Each year an estimated 50 million legal and illegal abortions—an average of 137,000 a day—are performed in the world, most in Latin America, Asia, and Africa. This means that approximately one out of four pregnancies end in abortion. It is estimated that at least half of all abortions could be prevented at little cost by making family planning services readily available to all people.

Three-fourths of the world's people live in countries where abortion is legal at least for health reasons; more than half live in areas where there are few if any restrictions on obtaining a legal abortion during the first trimester (12 weeks) of pregnancy. Even though abortion is legal in most countries, hundreds of millions of women in such countries are either too poor to pay for an abortion or live in rural areas where such services are not available.

Where legal abortion is not available, especially in Latin America, illegal abortion is widespread. An estimated half of all abortions worldwide are performed illegally and are a leading cause of death among women of childbearing age. Often causing infection and internal hemorrhage, an illegal abortion is 50 to 100 times more hazardous than a legal abortion. Perhaps half of all illegal abortions are self-induced: Women commonly swallow dangerous doses of chemicals sold as home remedies; should this method fail, they often attempt to abort themselves with sharpened sticks or wire coat hangers.

In 1973 the U.S. Supreme Court ruled that during the first trimester of pregnancy, abortion cannot be banned or regulated by states. During this period the decision to have an abortion must be left entirely to a woman and her physician, but the procedure must be performed by a licensed physician. About 91% of the approximately 1.5 million legal abortions taking place in the United States each year are performed during the first trimester. During the second trimester of pregnancy, states can establish regulations on abortion to protect the health of women but cannot prevent a woman from obtaining an abortion. About 8% of legal abortions in the United States are performed between weeks 13 and 20 of the second trimester. During the third trimester, when the fetus has the potential to live outside the womb, with or without artificial aid, states can ban abortion except in cases where the woman's life or health is threatened. Only about 1% or 15,000 of the annual abortions in the U.S. take place after the twentieth week of pregnancy near the middle of the second trimester.

Despite the sharp increase in legal abortions since 1973, surveys show that at least one out of four American women who want a legal abortion are unable to obtain it, primarily because 80% of U.S. counties, mostly in rural areas, are without a clinic or hospital that regularly performs abortions. In addition, since 1977, federal law has banned the use of Medicaid funds to pay for abortions, thus making it more difficult for poor women to get abortions.

Since 1980 there have been increased efforts on behalf of the estimated 19% of U.S. adults who believe abortion should be illegal to have the 1973 Supreme Court decision overturned—a position publicly supported by President Reagan. Many antiabortionists also favor a constitutional amendment declaring that life begins at the moment of conception, in effect making abortion, the use of IUDs, and possibly some other forms of birth control acts of criminal homicide (see Spotlight on p. 162). A few antiabortionists have tried to put abortion and family planning clinics out of business by picketing, harassing employees and clients, firebombing, and arson. Between 1982 and 1986, for example, 46 U.S. abortion clinics were firebombed. To cover increased security and liability insurance costs (which have risen up to tenfold), clinics have had to raise their prices and some have gone out of business. Since 1985, antiabortionists have set up 2,000 free clinics, which outwardly look like abortion or family planning clinics; women seeking an abortion or counseling are lured into these clinics and then subjected to scare tactics to jolt them out of considering an abortion. Antiabortion groups are also pressuring the president and Congress to be sure that future appointees to the Supreme Court and other federal courts oppose abortion.

Future Methods of Birth Control Researchers throughout the world are at work trying to develop new and better methods of fertility control (Table 8-2). Despite the importance of population control, annual worldwide expenditures on reproductive research and contraceptive development are minuscule, totaling less than $200 million—an average of 25 cents per person.

In the United States contraceptive research and development by private drug firms has decreased sharply because it typically takes 10 to 15 years and

Table 8-2 Projected New or Improved Technologies for Controlling Fertility

Likely to Be Available by 1990

Improved IUDs

Improved spermicides for women

Vaginal ring (plastic ring, placed in vagina, that releases contraceptive hormones)

Hormone injections that prevent pregnancy for 1–3 months (such as Depo-Provera, approved for use in 90 countries, and Noristerat, approved for use in 40 countries)

Skin implants of slow-release hormones that prevent pregnancy for 3–5 years (such as Norplant, being tested in 14 countries)

Cervical cap (fits over cervix to block sperm; can be left in place for up to three days)

Physician-administered or self-administered drugs that induce abortion when taken within ten days after a missed period (so-called month-after or abortion pills being tested in France)

Could Be Available by 1990

Monthly steroid-based contraceptive pill

New types of drug-releasing IUDs

Antipregnancy vaccine for women

Sperm-suppression contraceptives for men

Simplified male and female sterilization

Reversible female sterilization

Could Be Available by 2000

Antifertility vaccine for men

Antisperm drugs for men

Better ovulation prediction techniques for more effective use of rhythm method

Reversible male sterilization

Drugs for the sterilization of men and women

Source: U.S. Office of Technology Assessment, *World Population and Fertility Planning Technologies: The Next Twenty Years*, Washington, D.C.: Government Printing Office, 1982.

up to $50 million before a new product receives approval by the Food and Drug Administration (FDA). Between 1979 and 1985, federal funding for research decreased by 25% (adjusted for inflation) because of budget cuts and pressure from antiabortion groups. Most population experts fear that unless annual government and private funding for contraceptive research is at least doubled, few if any of the possible new and improved forms of birth control shown in Table 8-2 will be available in the United States.

Highly effective forms of birth control such as Norplant and Depo-Provera, which have been tested and approved for use throughout much of the world, probably won't be available in the United States even with FDA approval. U.S. drug firms consider the

Should Abortions Be Banned in the United States?

Abortion is a highly emotional issue that does not lend itself to compromise or cool debate. On one side are antiabortionists, often calling themselves "pro-lifers," who believe that abortion is an act of murder and should be illegal under all circumstances. On the other side are "pro-choicers," who are not pro-abortion (despite the use of this label by antiabortionists), but who believe that a woman should have the freedom to decide whether or not to have a legal abortion, especially during her first trimester of pregnancy.

The abortion issue is complicated by inconclusive arguments about when life begins. Most scientists agree that science cannot say when life begins and that this is essentially a moral or religious issue. Most ardent antiabortionists are in religious groups holding that life begins at the moment of conception. Other religions make a distinction between an embryo and a "viable" fetus, arguing that until the fetus can survive outside the womb, it is not a true person (Figure 8-5). Members of many religious and secular groups are not in favor of abortion, but at the same time they are not in favor of having the religious views of a minority forced upon them and all Americans. Clearly, the abortion issue will not go away.

financial risks too great because of the threat of liability lawsuits and the high cost of liability insurance. In addition, these companies make much higher profits by selling people 28 pills a month than by selling them four antifertility shots a year or an implant that lasts five years.

8-4 SOCIOECONOMIC METHODS FOR CONTROLLING POPULATION GROWTH

Beyond Family Planning Some population experts argue that family planning, even coupled with economic development, cannot lower birth and fertility rates fast enough because, as surveys show, most couples in LDCs want 3 or 4 children—well above the 2.1 fertility rate needed to bring about eventual population stabilization. These experts call for increased emphasis on socioeconomic methods, especially dis-

couraging births by means of economic rewards and penalties and reducing fertility by increasing rights, education, and work opportunities for women.

Economic Rewards and Penalties Some governments have used various types of economic rewards (incentives) and economic penalties (disincentives) to help reduce fertility. About 20 countries offer small payments to individuals who agree to use contraceptives or to be sterilized and to doctors and family planning workers for each sterilization they perform and each IUD they insert. For example, in India, a person receives about $15 for being sterilized—the equivalent of about two weeks' pay for an agricultural worker. Such payments, however, are most likely to attract people who already have all the children they want. Although payments are not physically coercive, they have been criticized as being psychologically coercive because in some cases the poor feel they have to accept them in order to survive.

Some countries, such as China, also penalize couples who have more than a certain number of children—usually one or two. Penalties may include extra taxes and other costs or not allowing income tax deductions for a couple's third child (used in Singapore, Hong Kong, Ghana, and Malaysia). Families who have more children than the desired limit may also suffer reduced free health care, decreased food allotments, and loss of job choice. Like economic rewards, economic penalties can be psychologically coercive for the poor. Programs that withhold food or increase the cost of raising children are unjust and inhumane, punishing innocent children for actions by their parents.

Experience has shown that economic rewards and penalties designed to reduce fertility work best if they nudge rather than push people to have fewer children, if they reinforce existing customs and trends toward smaller families, if they do not penalize people who produced large families before the programs were established, and if they increase a poor family's income or land ownership.

Changes in Women's Roles In 1985 the world's 2.4 billion women did almost all of the world's domestic work and child care mostly without pay, provided more health care with little or no pay than all of the world's organized health services put together, and did more than half the work associated with growing food, gathering fuelwood, and hauling water. At the same time, women made up about 60% of the world's almost 900 million adults who can neither read nor write, and they suffered the most malnutrition because men and children are fed first where food supplies are limited. Making up one-third of the world's paid labor force in

1985, women were concentrated in the lowest-paid occupations and earned about 75% less than men who did similar work (35% less in the U.S.). They also worked longer, had a lower income, and owned much less of the world's land than men.

Numerous studies have shown that increased education is a strong factor leading women to have fewer children. Educated women are more likely than uneducated women to be employed outside the home rather than to stay home and raise children, marry later (thus reducing the number of their prime reproductive years), and lose fewer infants to death—a major factor in reducing fertility rates.

However, offering more of the world's women the opportunity to become educated and to express their lives in meaningful, paid work and social roles outside the home will require some major social changes. Such changes include eliminating laws and practices that discriminate against women in education and the workplace, providing free or low-cost day-care centers for children of working women, and changing laws that prohibit or make it difficult for women to own land and thus difficult to obtain credit. Making these changes will be difficult because of long-standing political and economic domination by men throughout the world. In addition, competition between men and women for already scarce jobs in many countries should become even more intense by 2000, when another *billion* people will be looking for work.

8-5 EFFORTS AT HUMAN POPULATION CONTROL: CHINA AND INDIA

Population Policies In 1960 only two countries, India and Pakistan, had official policies to reduce their birth rates. By 1986 about 93% of the world's population and 91% of the people in LDCs lived in countries with some type of family planning program. Few governments, however, spend more than 1% of the national budget on family planning services. To get some idea of the results of population control programs, let's look at what has happened in the world's most populous countries, India and the People's Republic of China.

India India started the world's first national family planning program in 1952, when its population was nearly 400 million, with a doubling time of 53 years. In 1987, after 35 years of population control effort, India was the world's second most populous country, with a population of 800 million and a doubling time of 33 years. In 1952 it was adding 5 million persons to its population each year. In 1987 it added 17 million, with only about 25% of Indian couples of childbearing age currently practicing some form of birth control.

The population is projected to more than double to 1.6 billion before leveling off early in the twenty-second century.

In 1987 at least one-third of India's population had an annual per capita income of less than $70 a year, and the overall average per capita income was only $260. To add to the problem, nearly half of India's labor force is unemployed or can find only occasional work. Each *week* 100,000 more people enter the job market, and for most of them jobs do not exist.

Without its long-standing national family planning program, India's numbers would be growing even faster. But the program has yielded disappointing results, partly because of poor planning, bureaucratic inefficiency, low status of women (despite constitutional guarantees of equality), extreme poverty, and lack of sufficient administrative and financial support.

But the roots of the problem are deeper. More than 3 out of every 4 people in India live in 560,000 rural villages, where crude birth rates are still close to 40 per thousand. The overwhelming economic and administrative task of delivering contraceptive services and education to the mostly rural population is complicated by an illiteracy rate of about 71%, with 80% to 90% of the illiterate people being rural women. Although for years the government has provided information about the advantages of small families, Indian women still have an average of 4.3 children, because most couples remain convinced that they need many children as a source of cheap labor and old-age survival insurance. This belief is reinforced by the fact that almost one-third of all Indian children die before age 5. Population control is also hindered by India's diversity: 14 major languages, more than 200 dialects, many social castes, and 11 major religions.

To improve the effectiveness of the program, in 1976 India Gandhi's government instituted a mass sterilization program, primarily for males in the civil service who already had two or more children. The program was supposed to be voluntary, based on financial incentives alone. But officials allegedly used coercion to meet sterilization quotas in a few rural areas. The resulting backlash played a role in Gandhi's election defeat in 1977. In 1978 the government took a new approach, raising the legal minimum age for marriage from 18 to 21 for males and from 15 to 18 for females. After the 1981 census showed that the population growth rate since 1971 was no lower than that of the previous decade, the government vowed to increase family planning efforts and funding with the goal of achieving replacement-level fertility by the year 2000. The success of such efforts remains to be seen.

China Between 1958 and 1962 an estimated 30 million people died from famine in China. Since 1970, however, the People's Republic has made impressive efforts to feed its people and bring its population growth under control. Food production in 1985 was 2.5 times the level of 1960. In 1985 China had enough grain both to export and to feed its population of 1.05 billion. Between 1972 and 1985 China achieved a remarkable drop in its crude birth rate from 32 to 18. By 1985 its average total fertility rate had dropped to replacement level (2.1) and its population was growing at 1% a year, compared to 2.4% for all other LDCs. At this rate China's population grows by about 11 million persons each year. China's leaders have a goal of reaching ZPG by the year 2000 with a population at 1.2 billion, followed by a slow decline to a population between 600 million and 1 billion by 2100. Achieving this goal will be difficult because 28% of the Chinese people are under age 15. As a result, the United Nations

projects that the population of China may be around 1.6 billion by 2100.

To accomplish its sharp drop in fertility, China has established the most extensive and strictest population control program in the world. Its major features include: **(1)** strongly encouraging couples to postpone marriage; **(2)** expanding educational opportunities; **(3)** providing married couples with free, easy access to sterilization, contraceptives, and abortion; **(4)** offering couples who sign pledges to have no more than one child economic rewards such as salary bonuses, extra food, larger old-age pensions, better housing, free medical care and school tuition for their child, and preferential treatment in employment when the child grows up; **(5)** requiring those who break the pledge to return all benefits; **(6)** exerting intense peer pres-

Enrichment Study   Computer Modeling and the Limits-to-Growth Debate

Dynamic Computer Modeling

One method used in recent years to improve our ability to make accurate short-, medium-, and long-range projections is *system dynamics computer modeling.* In constructing any model, we must make certain assumptions about the key variables, trends in these variables, and factors weighting the importance of each variable and trend. In constructing a computer model, analysts attempt to build in the interactions of key variables and the effects of feedback loops, time delays, synergistic interactions, and other properties of complex systems (Section 6-1). The mathematical equations representing the model are then fed into

the computer and used to project future situations and to test the potential effects of various policy changes on achieving or preventing a particular situation. New assumptions and data can easily be introduced to update the model. It is important to note that computer models and any other type of model help us project *what might happen based on certain assumptions*—they do not predict or forecast what *will happen.*

The Forrester-Meadows Computer Model

A number of research teams have used dynamic computer models to project alternative economic and environmental futures for the world and for various geographic regions. In the early 1970s Jay Forrester, Donella Meadows, Dennis Meadows, and their associates developed such a model to project what factor or combination of factors might limit the growth of the human population. The Forrester-Meadows model looked at the dynamic interaction of five major variables: population, pollution, natural resources, industrial output per capita, and food per capita. The projections of this model were published in popular form in 1972 in a book entitled *The Limits to Growth* (see Further Readings). By 1983 more than 3 million

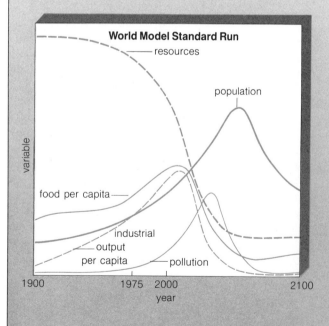

Figure 8-6 The Forrester-Meadows computer model projects that if present trends continue, there could be worldwide depletion of resources and declining industrial growth. Eventually population would decline sharply as death rates rose because of shortages of food and medical services. (*These are projections, not predictions.*) (After Meadows et al., The Limits to Growth, a Potomac Associates book published by Universe Books, New York, 1972. Used by permission.)

sure on women pregnant with a third child to have an abortion; **(7)** requiring one of the parents in a two-child family to be sterilized; **(8)** using mobile units and paramedics to bring sterilization, family planning, health care, and education to rural areas; **(9)** training local people to carry on the family planning program; and **(10)** expecting all leaders to set an example with their own family size.

Most countries cannot or do not want to use the coercive elements (especially items 6 and 7) found in China's program. Other elements of this program, however, could be used in many LDCs. Especially useful is the practice of localizing the program, rather than asking the people to go to distant centers. Perhaps the best lesson that other countries can learn from China's experience is that they should not wait to slow population growth until the choice is between mass starvation and the use of coercive measures. Even at that point, coercion can cause a backlash of public resentment and runs a high risk of failure. China's population control program has been successful so far, but between 1985 and 1987 its birth rate increased from 18 to 21 and its total fertility rate from 2.1 to 2.4.

Population programs aren't simply a matter of promoting smaller families. They also mean guaranteeing that our children are given the fullest opportunities to be educated, to get good health care, and to have access to the jobs and careers they eventually want. It is really a matter of increasing the value of every birth, of expanding the potential of every child to the fullest, and of improving the life of a community.

Pranay Gupte

copies of this book had been printed and it had been translated into 23 different languages.

The Forrester-Meadows dynamic computer model (and others) allows us to ask various "What if?" questions—to ask *what* might happen *if* present trends and policies continue or *if* certain changes are made, as illustrated by the following examples.

Question 1: What if the population and industrial output continue to expand exponentially at 1970 rates? *Answer:* Assuming there are no major changes in the physical, economic, or social relationships that have historically led to these forms of exponential growth, the system will continue to grow exponentially until around 2020, when there will be a global collapse. Nonrenewable resources will be depleted, and there will be a population crash because scarcities of food and medical services will cause death rates to rise. This projection, based on present trends, is known as the "standard run" (Figure 8-6) and is used as a base for comparing the effects of various policies and strategies intended to avert such a collapse.

Question 2: What if, beginning in 2000 A.D., **(a)** everyone had access to birth control, and couples averaged two children; **(b)** world industrial output per capita were stabilized at 1975 levels; **(c)** resource consumption were reduced to one-fourth of 1970 values per unit of production; **(d)** pollution were reduced to one-fourth of 1970 values per unit of production; **(e)** consumption were shifted from material goods toward services such as education and health; **(f)** capital were directed to food production, soil enrichment, and erosion prevention; and **(g)** the productivity of industrial capital used to develop and build factories and machines were greatly increased? *Answer:* Population rise would deplete resources so severely that population size would eventually drop (Figure 8-7).

There has been intense controversy over the validity of the Forrester-Meadows model because its projections challenged the basic cornucopian assump-

Figure 8-7 These projections of the Forrester-Meadows model are based on the assumption that all policies listed in question 2 were instituted in 2000. Population growth leads to severe resource depletion, which begins to reduce population by raising the death rates. (*These are projections, not predictions.*) (After Meadows et al., *The Limits to Growth*, a Potomac Associates book published by Universe Books, New York, 1972. Used by permission.)

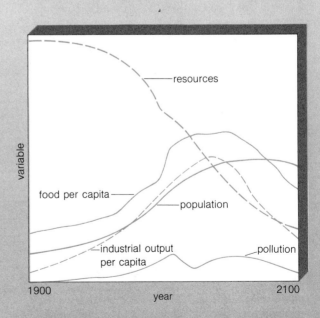

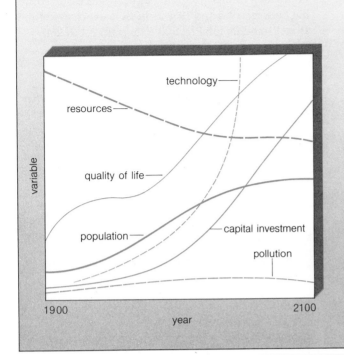

tions upon which today's industrial societies are based—namely that new advances in technology place no physical limits on industrial growth and population growth. The major criticism of the model centers on the role of technology in averting catastrophe. The model assumes major technological advances in finding and recycling resources, increasing food productivity, and controlling pollution. But it doesn't assume that technological innovations will increase exponentially and thus sooner or later solve every problem that might arise.

Figure 8-8 Modified version of the Forrester-Meadows model assumes that technology increases exponentially to provide essentially infinite resources, greatly reduced pollution, greatly increased food yields, and perfect birth control for everyone. Population rises but eventually levels off, resources are not depleted, pollution is kept at low levels, and economic growth and the quality of life keep rising. (*These are projections, not predictions.*) (Modified from Robert Boyd, "World Dynamics: A Note," *Science*, vol. 177, 1972, 516–519.)

CHAPTER SUMMARY

Neo-Malthusians contend that controlling the world's rapid population growth, especially in LDCs, is essential to reduce resource depletion, environmental degradation, and pollution and to give LDCs a better chance of sustainable economic development. Others, contending that resource and environmental problems are not caused solely by rapid population growth, are nevertheless in favor of population control because they believe that without it the severity of these problems will be intensified. Cornucopians are against population control, they believe that more people provide more consumers and more technological innovations, stimulating economic growth, which automatically lowers fertility.

Most governments control population growth to some extent by restricting *immigration* to their countries. A major exception is the United States, which continues to admit significant numbers of legal immigrants and refugees each year. There is growing pressure, however, to reduce the annual level of legal immigrants and to stem the increasing number of illegal immigrants. In 1986 Congress passed a law designed to reduce illegal immigration.

Governments of most LDCs favor reducing birth and fertility rates in their countries through a combination of *economic development* and *family planning*. Cornucopians emphasize economic development, which they believe will allow today's LDCs to become MDCs and reduce their rate of population growth by undergoing a *demographic transition* like that experienced by today's MDCs. Neo-Malthusians fear that many of today's LDCs may not be able to make the demographic transition because they face several important demographic and economic conditions different from those that allowed today's MDCs to become industrialized. They

believe that fertility can be brought down rapidly enough to prevent increased disruption of the world's life support systems only by a combination of economic development, universal availability of family planning, economic rewards and penalties to motivate couples to have fewer children, and improved education and employment opportunities for women.

Effective family planning depends primarily on providing couples with information about and access to various forms of birth control, which either *prevent pregnancy* (sterilization, oral contraceptives, condoms) or *terminate pregnancy before birth* (IUDs and abortion). Two-thirds of the world's population now live in countries where abortions are legal during the first three months of pregnancy. Legal abortion in the United States is under full-scale attack by antiabortionists who believe that it is murder. Most Americans, however, believe that a woman should have the freedom to decide whether or not to have a legal abortion during her first three months of pregnancy.

The world's two most populous countries—India and China—have had quite different degrees of success in bringing down their rates of population growth. Although India has had a national family planning program since 1952, it has had disappointing results because of poor planning, insufficient funding, bureaucratic inefficiency, low status of women, cultural and religious diversity, and extreme poverty—complicated by widespread illiteracy and a high infant death rate. In contrast, China, with the world's largest population, has been able to reduce its crude birth rate from 32 to 18 and achieve replacement-level fertility (2.1) between 1972 and 1985. It also now produces enough food to feed its people with some left over for export. This remarkable drop in fertility has occurred as a result of China's establishment of the world's most extensive and strictest population control

Cornucopians, however, believe that technology *can* grow exponentially. Figure 8-8, for example, shows a modified version of the Forrester-Meadows model, which assumes that technological innovations based on human ingenuity will grow exponentially. In this case, population rises and then levels off, natural resources are not depleted, pollution levels remain very low, and economic growth and quality of life keep rising.

Other Computer Models

Since 1974 almost two dozen other computer models have been developed by interdisciplinary groups throughout the world in attempts to improve upon or challenge the Forrester-Meadows model. At a conference in 1982, developers of these models agreed that their diverse models generally supported the following major conclusions:

(1) Population and physical capital cannot grow forever on a finite planet.

(2) If present policies continue, the already wide gap between rich and poor will increase.

(3) We can change present trends and policies to avert catastrophe and thus supply the basic needs of the world's peoples in the foreseeable future.

(4) No reliable and complete information is available about the degree to which the earth's environment can absorb society's wastes.

(5) Technology can help alleviate but will not solve the problems of population growth, environmental abuse, and income inequality.

(6) Interdependence among the world's peoples and countries is much greater than most people imagine or admit.

Computer simulation models can help us work with large numbers of interacting variables and show how various factors and problems are interrelated. But the projections of such models, like those of any model, are no better than the assumptions used to build each model and the data used to test these assumptions.

program. Despite its effectiveness, this program includes some coercive elements that other countries cannot or do not want to use.

Since the early 1970s over two dozen dynamic computer models have been developed and used to make projections of alternative economic and environmental futures for the world and its major geographic areas. Most of these projections indicate that economic growth and population size cannot continue indefinitely without severe economic and environmental disruption. However, models based on the cornucopian assumption that various forms of new technology will always be developed to solve the world's resource, environmental, and population problems project that there are no physical limits to continued worldwide economic and population growth.

DISCUSSION TOPICS

1. Should world population growth be controlled? Why or why not?

2. How can population growth intensify environmental and social problems even if it is not the root cause of them? Give three examples.

3. How can a high fertility rate be viewed as a result of poverty as well as a cause or intensifier of it?

4. Debate the following resolution: The United States has a serious population problem and should adopt an official policy designed to stabilize its population.

5. Describe the demographic transition hypothesis and give reasons why it may or may not apply to LDCs today.

6. Should federal and state funds be used to provide free or low-cost family planning for the poor in the United States? Explain.

7. Do you believe that each woman should be free to use legalized abortion as a means of birth control or that abortion should be illegal? Give reasons for your position.

8. Should federal and state funds be used to provide free or low-cost abortions for the poor? Explain.

9. Should the number of legal immigrants allowed into the United States each year be sharply reduced? Explain.

10. Should illegal immigration into the United States be sharply decreased? Explain. If so, how would you go about achieving this?

11. Why is the low status of women in terms of education, employment, legal rights, and self-esteem a major factor contributing to high fertility?

12. What are some ways in which women are deliberately and nondeliberately discriminated against in the United States? On your campus?

13. Why has China been more successful than India in reducing its rate of population growth? Do you agree with China's present population control policies? Explain. What alternatives, if any, would you suggest?

14. Explain why you agree or disagree with the following statement: The Forrester-Meadows and other global computer models are useless, misleading, gloom-and-doom approaches to the world's problems.

9

Population Distribution: Urbanization

GENERAL OBJECTIVES

1. What percentages of the people in various parts of the world live in cities or urban areas and how are urban areas projected to grow in the future?

2. What are the major benefits and problems associated with living in an urban area?

3. What effects do urban areas have on rural areas?

4. What are the major advantages and disadvantages of various forms of urban transportation?

5. What are the major ways of dealing with urban problems?

6. What methods are used to decide and regulate how different parcels of land in urban areas are used?

Modern cities are centers of employment, education, and culture. But they are also centers of poverty, delinquency, crime, prostitution, alcoholism, and drug abuse. As a rule, cities offer less space, less daylight, less fresh air, less greenery, and more noise.

Georg Borgstrom

Economic activities, environmental degradation, pollution, and social interactions and problems are affected not only by population growth but also by how population is distributed. Since the Agricultural Revolution about 12,000 years ago, an increasing percentage of the world's people has concentrated in a relatively small part of the earth's surface—in cities and towns. This movement from rural areas to urban areas has advantages and disadvantages, as we shall see in this chapter.

9-1 URBANIZATION, URBAN GROWTH, AND THE URBAN ENVIRONMENT

The World Situation Throughout history people have flooded into cities to find jobs. Those who get good jobs and do well financially often are enthusiastic about living in cities, which provide the greatest variety of goods and services and the most exciting diversity of social and cultural activities. In addition, urban social and cultural activities enrich the lives of people who live far from city boundaries. Thus, it is not surprising that the percentage of the world's people living in cities continues to increase.

A country's **degree of urbanization** is the percentage of its population living in areas with a population of more than 2,500 people. **Urban growth** is the rate of growth of urban populations. Between 1900 and 1985 the percentage of the world's population living in cities increased from 14% to 43% (Figure 9-1). By the year 2000 one-half of the world's population will be living in cities (one-quarter of city dwellers will be homeless), and by 2020 almost two out of three people on earth will be living in cities. The percentage

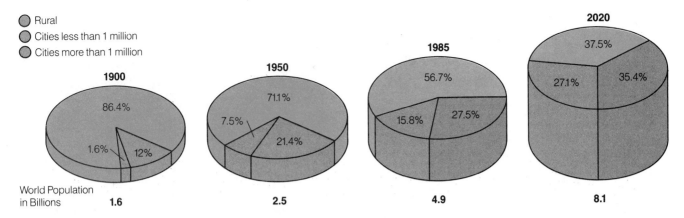

Figure 9-1 Patterns of world urbanization from 1900 to 1985 with projections to 2020. (Data from United Nations and Population Reference Bureau)

Table 9-1 The Ten Largest Urban Areas in the World in 1985 and 2000 (Data from United Nations)

1985		2000	
Urban Area	Population (millions)	Urban Area	Projected Population (millions)
Mexico City	18.1	Mexico City	26.3
Tokyo-Yokohama	17.2	São Paulo	24.0
São Paulo	15.9	Tokyo-Yokohama	17.1
New York-N.E. New Jersey	15.3	Calcutta	16.6
Shanghai	11.8	Greater Bombay	16.0
Calcutta	11.0	New York-N.E. New Jersey	15.5
Greater Buenos Aires	10.9	Seoul	13.5
Rio de Janeiro	10.4	Shanghai	13.5
Seoul	10.2	Rio de Janeiro	13.3
Greater Bombay	10.1	Delhi	13.3

of people living in cities with a population of more than 1 million is also increasing. Accommodating the 4.2 billion additional people projected to be living in urban areas by 2020 will be a monumental task.

Unprecedented urban growth in MDCs and LDCs has given rise to a new concept—the "supercity," an urban area with a population of more than 10 million. In 1985 there were 10 supercities, most of them located in LDCs (Table 9-1). The United Nations projects that by 2000 there will be 25 supercities, most of them in LDCs.

The degree of urbanization varies in different parts of the world (Figure 9-2). From 50% to 75% of the population in North America, Latin America, and Europe live in urban areas, whereas about 70% of the people in Africa and Asia live in rural areas and try to make their living from farming. Although all countries are experiencing urbanization, the rate of urban growth in LDCs surpassed that in MDCs around 1970

and is expected to increase more rapidly in the future (Figure 9-3). LDCs are simultaneously experiencing high rates of natural population increase and rapid internal migration of people from rural to urban areas— each factor contributing about equally to urban growth. In LDCs more than 20 million rural people migrate to cities each year to escape wretched living conditions in the countryside; in the process they overwhelm already inadequate city services.

For most of these migrants, the city becomes a poverty trap, not an oasis of economic opportunity and cultural diversity. Those few fortunate enough to get a job must work long hours for low wages and are usually exposed to dust, hazardous chemicals, excessive noise, and dangerous machinery. With official unemployment levels of 20% to 30%, most of the urban poor are forced to live on the streets or to crowd into slums and shantytowns, made from corrugated iron, plastic sheets, and packing boxes, which ring the out-

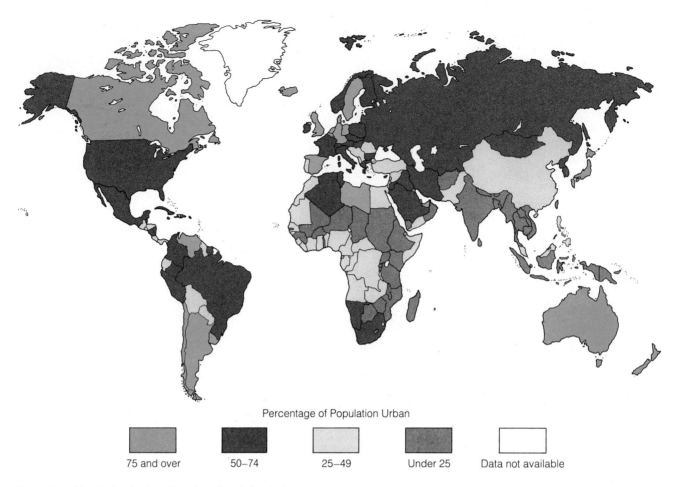

Percentage of Population Urban

| 75 and over | 50–74 | 25–49 | Under 25 | Data not available |

Figure 9-2 World urbanization. (Data from Population Reference Bureau)

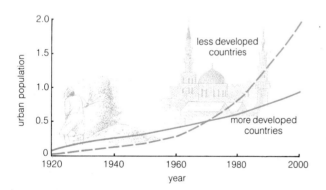

Figure 9-3 Actual and projected urban population growth in MDCs and LDCs between 1920 and 2000. (Data from United Nations)

skirts of most cities in these countries (Figure 9-4). Because many of these settlements spring up illegally on unoccupied land, their occupants live in constant fear of eviction or of having their makeshift shelters destroyed by bulldozers. Many shantytowns are located on land prone to landslides, floods, or tidal waves or in the most polluted districts of inner cities. Fires are common because most residents use kerosene stoves or fuelwood for heating and cooking.

In most large cities in LDCs, shantytown populations double every five to seven years, four or five times the population growth rate of the entire city. Shantytown and "overnight" squatter settlements now hold up to 30% of the population of many urban centers in LDCs. Because it is impossible to get an accurate count of the number of squatters, they are not included in urban population estimates like those given in Table 9-1. Most cities refuse to provide shantytowns and slums with adequate drinking water, sanitation, food, health care, housing, schools, and jobs because of a lack of money and the fear that such improvements will attract even more of the rural poor (see Spotlight on p. 171).

Despite joblessness and squalor, shantytown residents cling to life with resourcefulness, tenacity, and

The world's largest city—Mexico City—with 18.1 million people in 1985, is suffering from severe air pollution, deafening traffic noise, massive unemployment and underemployment, and a soaring crime rate. Slums without running water or electricity are mushrooming almost everywhere (Figure 9-4) and many residents are losing hope. With almost 5 million people having no sewage facilities, tons of human waste are left in gutters and vacant lots every day. About half of the city's garbage is left to rot, attracting armies of rats.

Over 3 million cars, 7,000 diesel buses, and 130,000 factories representing more than half of all Mexican industry spew massive amounts of air pollutants into the atmosphere. Air

pollution is intensified because the city lies in a basin surrounded by mountains. Just breathing the air for one day is estimated to be equivalent to smoking two packs of cigarettes. Overall, the city's air and water pollution are estimated to be responsible for nearly 100,000 premature deaths a year. Even so, Mexico City looks good to 1,000 additional poverty stricken rural peasants who pour into the city every day to swell its slum population of 5 million. These urban problems, already at crisis levels, will be intensified to horrendous levels if the city, as projected, grows to 26.3 million people by the end of this century.

Calcutta, India, with a population of 11 million in 1985, has perhaps the lowest average living

standards in the world. More than 70% of its inhabitants live at or below the poverty line with an income of less than $8 a month or about $32 a month for a family of four. Begging is the only source of income for at least 200,000 Calcuttans, and 600,000 live and die on the streets. People pack into buses like sardines and ride on top of them, hoping not to fall off. The last main sewer was built in 1896, and half of Calcutta's houses have no indoor toilets. There is only one water faucet for each 25 slum dwellings. One out of five buildings is classified as unsafe. One can hardly imagine the problems Calcutta will have if its population swells to 16.6 million by 2000 as projected.

hope. Most of them are convinced that the city offers, possibly for themselves and certainly for their children, the only chance of a better life. On balance, most do have more opportunities and are often better off than the rural poor they left behind. They also tend to have fewer children because there is no room for them and because of better access to family planning programs.

The U.S. Situation   In 1987 more than three out of four (76%) Americans lived in urban areas, and two out of three lived in the country's 28 largest urban regions (Figure 9-5). Since 1800 there have been several major internal population shifts in the United States (see Spotlight on p. 173). The major shift has been from rural to urban areas as the country has industrialized and needed fewer and fewer farmers to produce sufficient food (Figure 9-6). Since 1970, however, many people have moved from large cities to suburbs and to smaller cities and rural areas, primarily because

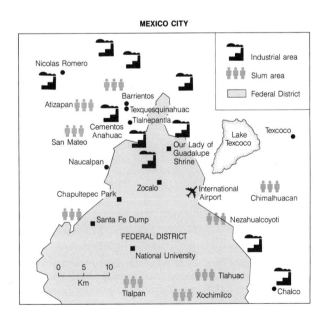

Figure 9-4 Location of major slum or shantytown areas and industrial areas in Mexico City.

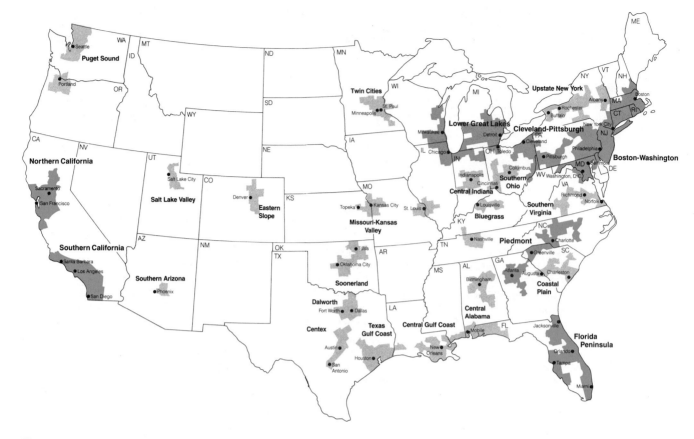

Figure 9-5 Major urban regions in the United States. Largest regions are shown in the darker color. (Data from U.S. Bureau of the Census)

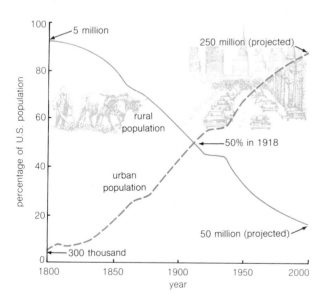

Figure 9-6 Actual and projected percentages of rural and urban populations in the United States between 1800 and 2000. (Data from U.S. Bureau of the Census)

of the creation of large numbers of new jobs in such areas. Since 1980 about 90% of U.S. population increase has occurred in the South and West, much of this the result of migration from the North and East.

Not all U.S. cities are pleasant places in which to live. According to surveys, an increasing number of residents in many central cities in the United States feel isolated, powerless, and entrapped. They are afraid to go out at night and they surround themselves with locks, alarm systems, and other security precautions. Older people are particularly susceptible to these and other strains of urban life. For many young people, street life and peer group pressure in an urban slum tend to reinforce ideas that hard work and traditional employment have few rewards, that crime does indeed pay, and that a person who is not part of mainstream society has no obligations to it.

Many low- and middle-income people living in decaying central cities regard attempts to control pollution as largely irrelevant to their most pressing needs: jobs, housing, health care, and education. However, studies in more than 114 major U.S. cities showed that the urban poor have higher rates of illness and death from diseases associated with air pollution than do persons living in higher-income neighborhoods. The poor in cities also tend to receive poor medical ser-

1. *Rural-to-urban shift:* The percentage of the population living in cities and towns of more than 2,500 increased from 5% to 76% between 1800 and 1987 and is projected to reach 80% to 90% by 2000 (Figure 9-6).

2. *Central-city-to-suburbs shift:* Large numbers of mostly middle- and upper-class citizens have moved from the central city to the suburbs since 1950 to escape some urban problems and to be closer to jobs provided by new factories and businesses located outside central cities. Because of this shift almost one-third of all Americans now live in the suburbs. However, during the 1980s some central cities in the Northeast and Midwest experienced more growth than they did in the 1970s.

3. *Large-city-to-smaller-city shift:* People have been moving away from some cities—especially larger ones—in favor of smaller

towns and cities since 1970. This influx of people to rural counties and small towns and cities has increased the stress on many local governments, hindering their ability to provide schools, houses, sewage disposal, and other services. It is uncertain whether this trend will continue because instead of relocating in rural areas, many U.S. industries are opening new factories in other countries such as Taiwan and Mexico where cheap labor is available and environmental protection laws are weak and poorly enforced.

4. *East-to-West urban shift:* Population and economic and political power have shifted mostly from urban areas in eastern states to urban areas in western states since 1970. Western urban areas such as Phoenix, Arizona; Salt Lake City, Utah; and Riverside-San Bernardino, California, have already experienced phenomenal growth and are pro-

jected to increase their population size by 50% or more between 1986 and 2000.

5. *North-to-South urban shift:* Population and economic and political power have shifted mostly from urban areas in northern states to urban areas in southern states, especially Florida and Texas. The shift to Florida is expected to continue, with most of its major cities, especially West Palm Beach, Orlando, and Fort Lauderdale, projected to grow by 50% to 60% between 1986 and 2000. By the mid-1980s many people who had moved to Texas from northern industrial states in the 1970s were moving back to the North. This reverse migration is a result of massive unemployment in Texas oil industries as a result of a large drop in oil prices and an increase in industrial and business investment in some northern states.

vices. They suffer infestation of their dwellings by rodents and other pests, pay higher heating costs because of poorly insulated buildings, and receive inadequate sanitation and other services. In addition, low- and middle-income workers living in the cities have little choice but to take jobs in factories and sweatshops, where they are often exposed to serious noise and health hazards.

9-2 URBAN SYSTEMS AND NATURAL ECOSYSTEMS

Is an Urban System an Ecosystem? Some ecologists and urbanologists treat cities and urban regions as *ecosystems*. Others argue that an urban system has only some characteristics of a natural ecosystem. In Section 4-1 an ecosystem was defined as a community of plants and animals interacting with one another and with their environment. Technically, a city meets this definition, but there are important differences

between natural ecosystems and artificial urban ecosystems.

Unlike natural ecosystems, cities do not have enough producers—that is, green plants—to support their human inhabitants. Cities have some trees, lawns, and parks, but these are not major sources of food for humans. As one observer remarked, "Cities are places where they cut down the trees and then name the streets after them." This scarcity of vegetation is unfortunate, because urban plants, grasses, and trees absorb air pollutants, give off oxygen, help cool the air as water is evaporated from their leaves, muffle noise, and satisfy important psychological needs of city dwellers.

Cities also lack animals or plants that can be used as food for humans. Thus, urban systems survive only by importing food from external, plant-growing ecosystems. Cities also obtain most of their fresh air, water, minerals, and energy resources from external ecosystems. Instead of being recycled, the solid, liquid, and gaseous wastes of cities are discharged to ecosystems outside their boundaries (Figure 9-7).

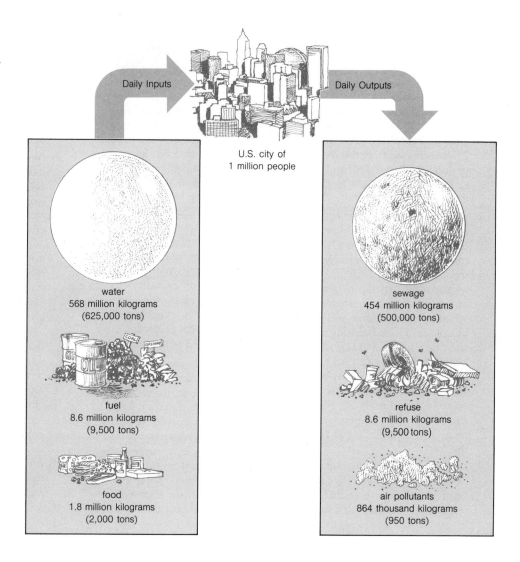

Figure 9-7 Typical daily input and output of matter and energy for a U.S. city of 1 million people.

Daily Inputs

Daily Outputs

U.S. city of 1 million people

water
568 million kilograms
(625,000 tons)

fuel
8.6 million kilograms
(9,500 tons)

food
1.8 million kilograms
(2,000 tons)

sewage
454 million kilograms
(500,000 tons)

refuse
8.6 million kilograms
(9,500 tons)

air pollutants
864 thousand kilograms
(950 tons)

Cities are probably best classified as cultural ecosystems that depend on other ecosystems for their physical survival. Urban systems can be classified as self-sustaining natural ecosystems only if their boundaries are expanded to include the farmlands, forests, mines, watersheds, and other areas throughout the world that provide input materials, and the air, rivers, oceans, and soil that absorb their massive output of wastes. Since the oil embargo of 1973, however, some cities have attempted to become more "natural" or self-sufficient in providing needed resources.

Urban Spatial Structure   Like natural ecosystems, cities have recognizable spatial and physical structures. Three models of urban structure are shown in Figure 9-8. A city resembling the *concentric-circle model* develops outward from its central business district (CBD) in a series of rings. Typically, industries and businesses in the CBD are surrounded by circular zones of housing that usually become more affluent as one moves outward into the suburbs.

A city resembling the *sector model* is a system of pie-shaped wedges, or ribbons, formed when high-, intermediate-, and low-rent commercial, industrial, and housing districts push out from the CBD at the center along major transportation routes. In the *multiple-nuclei model*, a large city develops around a number of independent centers, or nuclei, rather than a single center. Although no city perfectly matches any of them, these simplified models can be used to identify key characteristics.

Major factors determining the spatial character of a city are geographic site, rate of population growth, supply of nearby rural land (especially flat agricultural land) for conversion to urban land, transportation and utility systems, economic and technological level, and cost of energy. If suitable rural land is not available for conversion to urban land, a city tends to grow upward not outward, occupy a relatively small area, and have a high population density. People living in such compact cities tend to walk or use energy-efficient mass transit and tend to live in multistoried apartment buildings with shared walls that have an insulating

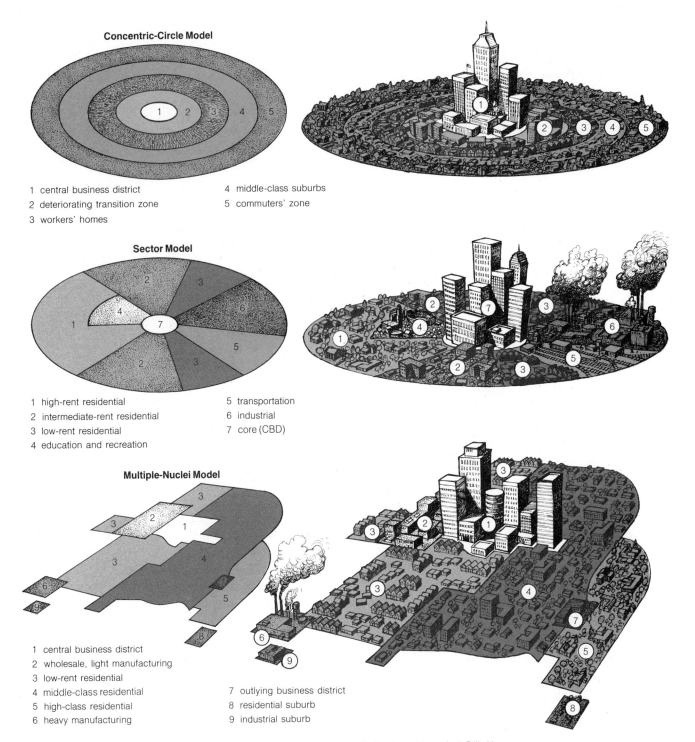

Concentric-Circle Model

1 central business district
2 deteriorating transition zone
3 workers' homes
4 middle-class suburbs
5 commuters' zone

Sector Model

1 high-rent residential
2 intermediate-rent residential
3 low-rent residential
4 education and recreation
5 transportation
6 industrial
7 core (CBD)

Multiple-Nuclei Model

1 central business district
2 wholesale, light manufacturing
3 low-rent residential
4 middle-class residential
5 high-class residential
6 heavy manufacturing
7 outlying business district
8 residential suburb
9 industrial suburb

Figure 9-8 Three models of urban spatial structure. (Modified with permission from Harm J. deBlij, *Human Geography*, New York: John Wiley, 1977)

effect and tend to reduce heating and cooling costs. Because of the lack of suitable rural land, many European cities are compact and tend to be more energy efficient than the dispersed cities found throughout the United States.

A combination of cheap gasoline and a large supply of rural land suitable for urban development tends to result in a dispersed city with a low population density. Most people living in such cities rely on cars with low energy efficiencies for transportation within the central city and to and from its suburbs. Most live in single-family houses whose unshared walls lose and gain heat rapidly unless they are well insulated. Sharp rises in energy prices (especially gasoline) will stim-

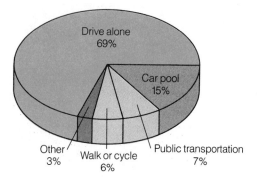

Figure 9-9 How people in the United States get to and from work. (Data from U.S. Bureau of the Census)

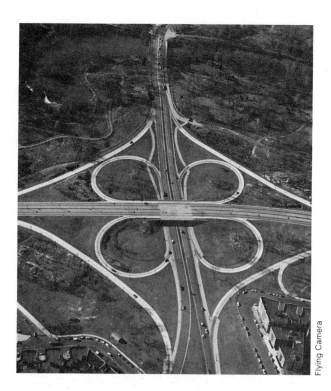

Figure 9-10 Highways and freeways occupy enormous amounts of land and can cause human and ecological disruption.

ulate many suburbanites to move back into the city to cut down on transportation, heating, and cooling costs.

9-3 URBAN TRANSPORTATION

Transportation Options An urban area's transportation system is a major factor affecting its economic activity and quality of life. People in urban areas move from one place to another by three major types of transportation: **(1)** *individual transit* by private automobile, taxi, motorcycle, moped, bicycle (see Spotlight on p. 179), and walking, **(2)** *mass transit* by railroad, subway, trolley, and bus, and **(3)** *paratransit* involving car pools, van pools, jitneys or van taxis traveling along fixed routes, and dial-a-ride systems. Each of these forms of transportation has certain advantages and disadvantages.

Motor Vehicles In 1985 there were approximately 480 million motor vehicles (cars and trucks) in the world, with 700 million projected by the year 2000. Three out of four of the world's motor vehicles are in North America and Europe. With only 4.9% of the world's population, the United States had 35% of the world's motor vehicles (131 million cars and 39 million trucks) in 1985. In the United States the car is now used for about 98% of all urban transportation and 85% of all travel between cities. In 1985 almost two-thirds of all working Americans traveled to and from work alone in their own cars with an average round trip of 37 kilometers (23 miles) a day at an average annual cost of $1,300 per person (Figure 9-9). No wonder British author J. B. Priestly remarked, "In America, the cars have become the people."

The automobile provides many advantages. Above all, it offers people privacy, security, and unparalleled freedom to go where they want to go when they want to go there. In addition, much of the U.S. economy is built around the automobile. One out of every six dollars spent and one out of every six nonfarm jobs are connected to the automobile or related industries such as oil, steel, rubber, plastics, automobile services, and highway construction. This industrial complex accounts for 20% of the annual GNP and provides about 18% of all federal taxes.

In spite of their advantages, cars and trucks have harmful effects on human lives and on air, water, and land resources. By providing almost unlimited mobility, automobiles and highways have been a major factor in urban sprawl, stimulating most U.S. cities to become decentralized and dispersed. The world's cars and trucks also kill an average of 170,000 people, maim 500,000, and injure 10 million each year. This is equivalent to a death about *every 3 minutes* and a disabling injury *every 20 seconds* of every day. In the United States about 25 million motor vehicle accidents each year kill about 45,000 people and injure about 5 million, at a cost of about $60 billion annually in lost income, insurance, and administrative and legal expenses. Since the automobile was introduced, almost 2 million

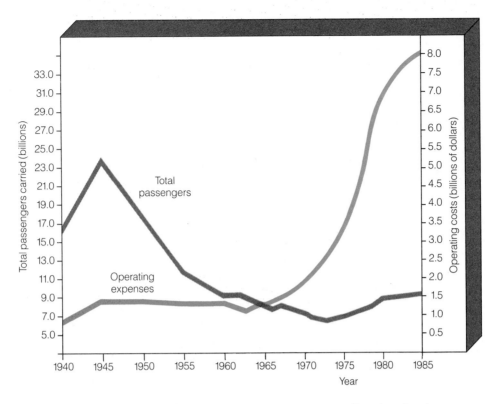

Figure 9-11 U.S. mass transit ridership and operating expenses between 1940 and 1985. (Data from American Public Transit System)

Americans have been killed on the highways—about twice the number of Americans killed in all U.S. wars.

Large areas of land are also utilized by motor vehicles (Figure 9-10). Roads and parking space take up 65% of the total land area in Los Angeles, more than half of Dallas (see photo on page 1), and more than one-third of New York City and the nation's capital. Instead of reducing automobile congestion, the construction of thousands of miles of roads has encouraged more automobiles and travel, causing even more congestion. As economist Robert Samuelson put it, "Cars expand to fill available concrete." In 1907 the average speed of horse-drawn vehicles through the borough of Manhattan was measured at 11.5 miles per hour. Today, crosstown Manhattan traffic—cars and trucks with the potential power of 100 to 300 horses—creeps along at an average speed of 5.2 miles per hour. In Los Angeles traffic on the Hollywood Freeway slows to 20 miles per hour for about 14 hours every day. By 2000 the average speed is projected to drop to about 7 miles per hour.

Mass Transit The number of riders on all forms of mass transit (heavy-rail subways and trains, light-rail trolleys, and buses) in the United States has declined drastically since 1945 (Figure 9-11). This decline generally parallels the increased use of the automobile and the resulting development of increasingly dispersed cities. These interrelated social changes were stimulated by cheap gasoline and the provision of funds from federal gasoline taxes to build highways. At the same time there was relatively little federal support for mass transit.

Since 1960, more than 200 U.S. mass transit companies have gone out of business. Many remaining companies are struggling under greatly increased operating costs (Figure 9-11) and large deficits. Beginning in 1973, Congress allowed some of the money obtained from gasoline taxes to be used for the building and operation of mass transit systems, helping transit ridership to increase somewhat between 1975 and 1985. For 1987, however, the Reagan administration has proposed that federal transit funding be cut by 65% (compared to a 13% cut in highway funding) and plans to eliminate all federal support of Amtrak, the country's major passenger train service.

Mass transit advocates argue that the country needs to increase, not decrease, its support of mass transit and Amtrak to help reduce dependence on imported

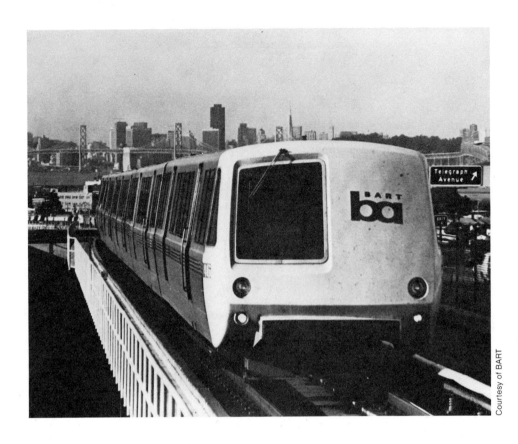

Figure 9-12 Bay Area Rapid Transit (BART) system in San Francisco, California.

Courtesy of BART

oil, unnecessary oil waste, highway congestion, and air pollution. They also argue that mass transit systems stimulate new business development and revitalization in central cities and thus offset the federal, state, and local subsidies usually needed for their construction and operation. In 1986 the American Public Transit Association estimated that every $100 billion spent on mass transit projects results in a $327 million increase in urban business revenues and supports 8,000 jobs.

Heavy-Rail Mass Transit Some analysts see the building of new, fixed heavy-rail mass transit systems and the improvement of existing subway and above-ground urban railroad systems as the key to solving transportation problems in most large cities. Others argue that such systems are useful only where many people live along a narrow corridor, and even then their high construction and operating costs may outweigh their benefits.

Some fixed-rail rapid transit systems have been successful—others have not. Since its opening in 1972, San Francisco's $1.7 billion, computer-controlled Bay Area Rapid Transit (BART) system (Figure 9-12) has

suffered from breakdowns, fires, brake problems, computer failures, massive financial losses, and too few riders. The METRO system of Washington, D.C., is better planned than BART and has the advantage of serving a concentrated urban area. But this efficient mass transit system cost about $90 million a mile to build, compared to $22.5 million a mile for BART. Built entirely at federal expense, METRO has had large annual operating deficits. Since its opening in 1984, Miami's $50 million-a-mile Metrorail system has had a ridership barely one-tenth of what was projected and has suffered large losses. Critics blame many of the problems of large-scale fixed-rail transit systems on overdependence on federal aid and shortsighted planning that overestimated the number of riders and underestimated the costs of building and operating such systems.

Some cities, however, have built successful fixed-rail systems. Since Atlanta's system opened in 1979, it has steadily added riders and opened new stations. Baltimore's state-owned Metro System is also increasing service, routes, and ridership. Pittsburgh has cleaner air and renewed business vitality partly because of its new subway system, opened in 1985.

The leg-powered bicycle won't replace cars in urban areas. But its use could be greatly increased, especially in areas with a warm climate and flat terrain, if cities provided more bike paths and bike lanes and secure parking areas. Using no fossil fuels and requiring few resources to produce, the bicycle is very useful for trips under 8 kilometers (5 miles), which make up about 43% of all urban travel. In traffic, cars and bicycles move at about the same average speed. In Davis, California, a city of 38,000 with a favorable climate and flat terrain, 28,000 bicycles account for about one-fourth of all transportation within the city. City employees are provided with bikes, older residents drive large tricycles, and people haul groceries in trailer buggies attached to the rear of their bikes. The city has constructed 64 kilometers (40 miles) of bicycle lanes and paths and closed some streets to automobiles.

Light-Rail Mass Transit   Other cities—often medium-sized—such as San Diego, California; Buffalo, New York; Portland, Oregon; and Toronto, Canada, have built *fixed light-rail trolley systems*. These are modernized versions of the streetcar systems found in most major U.S. cities in the 1930s and 1940s, before they were purchased and torn up by General Motors and tire, oil, truck, and bus companies to increase sales of motor vehicles. Light-rail systems are much less costly per mile to build than heavy-rail systems. Although the start-up cost for a light-rail system is higher than for a bus system carrying a comparable number of passengers, their operating costs are much lower. Light-rail systems are also cleaner and quieter than buses.

Toronto has the busiest light-rail transit system in North America, with an average 92.2 million fares a year. In the United States the light-rail approach got its biggest boost in recent years from the remarkable success of San Diego's "Tijuana Trolley" running between downtown San Diego and the Mexican border city of Tijuana. This system was funded by California state sales tax revenue and built at a cost per mile almost one-fourth that of San Francisco's BART and one-fifteenth that of Washington's METRO. Since opening in 1981, ridership, averaging 11,000 a day, has exceeded all expectations and fares pay 80% or more of the system's operating costs, compared to an average of 48% for all public transportation. Operating costs are kept low by cutting out red tape, having a nonunion work force (possible because no federal funds were involved), and reducing the number of workers by collecting fares on the honor system. This highly successful system is now being extended.

In Portland fierce citizen opposition blocked a proposed interstate highway and led officials to trade in federal highway funds for mass transit money. As a result, the city's light-rail system, which opened in 1986, cost $14 million a mile compared to an average of $25 million a mile for a new interstate highway. More than a dozen other U.S. cities are building light-rail systems. The biggest barrier to development of new light-rail systems is lack of federal money raised through taxes on gasoline—most of which is used for highway construction.

Bus Mass Transit   Buses are cheaper and more flexible than rail systems. They can be routed to almost any area in widely dispersed cities. They also require less capital and have lower operating costs than most rail systems. But by offering low fares to attract riders, they usually lose money. To make up for losses, bus companies tend to cut service and maintenance and seek federal, state, and local subsidies. At any one time almost half of the city buses in Houston, Texas, are idled by breakdowns, with riders often waiting an hour for service. Philadelphia's aging fleet of buses averages ten accidents a day, often because of improperly done repairs.

Paratransit   Because full-sized buses are cost-effective only when full, they are being supplemented by car pools, van pools, jitneys, and dial-a-ride systems. These paratransit methods attempt to combine the advantages of the door-to-door service of a private automobile or taxi with the economy of a ten-passenger van or minibus. They represent a practical solution to some of the transportation problems of today's dispersed urban areas.

Dial-a-ride systems operate in an increasing number of American cities. Passengers call for a van, minibus, or tax-subsidized taxi, which comes by to pick them up at the doorstep, usually in about 20 to 50 minutes. Efficiency can be increased by the use of two-way radios and computerized routing. Dial-a-ride systems are fairly expensive to operate. But compared with most large-scale mass transit systems, they are a bargain, and each vehicle is usually filled with passengers.

In cities such as Mexico City; Caracas, Venezuela; and Cairo large fleets of *jitneys*—small vans or minibuses that travel relatively fixed routes but stop on demand—carry millions of passengers each day. After laws banning jitney service were repealed in 1979 despite objections by taxi and transit companies, privately owned jitney service has flourished in San Diego, San Francisco, and Los Angeles and may spread to other cities. Analysts argue that deregulation of taxi fares and public transport fares would greatly increase the number of private individuals and companies operating jitneys in major U.S. cities.

9-4 COPING WITH URBAN PROBLEMS

Repairing Existing Cities   As philosopher-longshoreman Eric Hoffer observed, "History shows that the level achieved by a civilization can be measured by the degree to which it performs maintenance." America's older cities have massive maintenance and repair problems—most of them aggravated by neglect. Most of the sewers in New Orleans, some of which were purchased secondhand from Philadelphia in 1896, need replacement. When it rains in Chicago, sewage backs up into basements of about one-fourth of the homes. An estimated 46% of Boston's water supply and 25% of Pittsburgh's is lost through leaky pipes. Forty-five percent of the over 572,000 U.S. bridges evaluated in 1984 were structurally deficient or obsolete and considered safe for cars and light trucks only. Montana led all states with 71% of its bridges deemed safe for cars and light trucks only, followed closely by New York and North Carolina, each with a bridge deficiency rate of 66%.

Maintenance and repair of existing U.S. bridges, roads, mass transit systems, water supply systems, sewers, and sewage treatment plants could cost a staggering $1.2 trillion or more between 1984 and 2000, according to a 1984 study for the Joint Economic Committee of the House and Senate. For example, an estimated 67% of paved roads contain potholes and other defects, which cost the average car owner $210 a year in damages.

The country's massive repair and maintenance bills are coming due at a time when the federal government, to help hold down record budget deficits, is cutting back funds available for building and maintaining public works. To compensate, cities have raised unpopular property taxes and user fees for various services to bring in more revenue. When these taxes and fees are raised, many city residents and corporations move to the suburbs or smaller cities, thus decreasing the tax base needed for maintenance and other city services.

Revitalizing Existing Cities   Billions of dollars have been spent in decaying downtown areas to build new civic centers, museums, office buildings, parking garages, and high-rise luxury hotel and shopping center complexes. The city of Quebec in Canada has built a massive underground mall or "mini-city" serviced by its subway system. U.S. cities such as Baltimore and Pittsburgh have revitalized central-city areas. These projects can do much to revive the economy of cities and can indirectly benefit the poor by providing additional tax revenues. But they are of little direct benefit to the poor because they mainly provide white-collar jobs for suburbanites and shopping and cultural facilities mostly used by tourists and suburbanites.

In most major cities, older neighborhoods are being revitalized by middle- and high-income residents who buy run-down houses at low prices, renovate them, and either live in them or sell them at high prices—a process called "gentrification." This trend benefits the city economically by increasing property values and slowing the flight to the suburbs, but it also displaces low-income residents.

A number of cities have set up *urban homesteading programs* to help middle- and low-income individuals improve and live in abandoned housing. Houses and apartment buildings abandoned by their owners or acquired by a city in lieu of taxes, are resold to individuals or to cooperatives of low-income renters typically for $1 to $100. The new owners must agree to renovate the buildings and live in them for at least three years. In some cases, the city also provides low-interest, long-term loans. This approach has been particularly successful in Wilmington, Delaware, and in Baltimore, Maryland.

Revitalizing Public Housing Projects   During the 1960s and 1970s many blocks of slum dwellings were torn down and replaced with high-rise public housing projects. Although some projects have been successful, many have disrupted families, destroyed protective neighborhood social structures, and eliminated many essential neighborhood stores. In addition, the new rents are often too high for the poor. By 1985 nearly a quarter of the country's 10,000 federally financed public housing projects were losing money, primarily because of local mismanagement, tenant abuse of property, and such shoddy or nonexistent

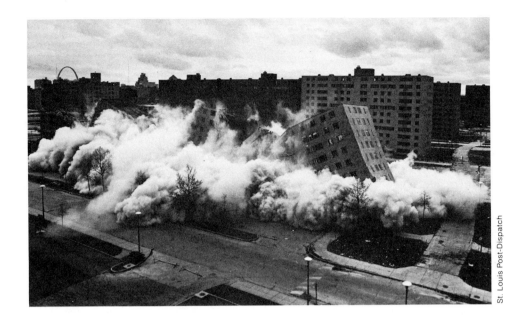

Figure 9-13 Demolition of Pruitt-Igoe public housing complex in St. Louis, Missouri, in 1972. Crime and vandalism so plagued this complex, opened in 1954, that authorities decided it was beyond rehabilitation.

St. Louis Post-Dispatch

maintenance that units could no longer be rented. Some turned into high-rise slums in only a few years and were torn down (Figure 9-13).

The outlook for run-down or abandoned highrise, low-income public housing developments, however, is not totally bleak. Some have been converted to schools and commercial buildings. Just a few years ago tenants at the Kenilworth-Parkside public housing project in Washington, D.C., were plagued by arsonists, thieves, and junkies. In addition, they had endured three years without heat or hot water and the roofs of their apartments were caving in. In 1982, Kimi Gray, a dynamic, unemployed mother of five, persuaded housing authorities to let her and other tenants run the project. By 1986, repairs had been made and utilities restored; crime and welfare dependency dropped substantially, and employment was provided for 140 residents. Moreover, administrative costs were reduced by 60% and rental collections rose 105%.

Creating Free-Enterprise Zones Some analysts call for increased federal aid to help revitalize the cities. Others argue that federal aid is often wasted and is controlled by distant bureaucrats who have little knowledge of the needs of local people. Instead, they propose that state and local tax breaks and other benefits be given to private companies that create new jobs by locating in economically depressed urban areas and that hire the unemployed or disadvantaged. This *free-enterprise zone* concept was the brainchild of a Brit-

ish socialist who proposed it for Hong Kong's slum areas.

Proponents of this approach in the United States point to the example set by Control Data Corporation (CDC), a Minneapolis-based computer firm. Since 1968 CDC has successfully built factories, created jobs, set up career counseling and job training programs, provided day-care centers, and stimulated renewal in blighted areas in Minneapolis, St. Paul, San Antonio, Baltimore, Toledo, and Washington, D.C.—all without federal aid. By 1985 there were free-enterprise zones in at least 440 cities in 19 states. Five other states have passed laws authorizing such zones. This approach, however, can lead to job losses in the suburbs as businesses relocate or expand in inner-city areas. In addition, the tax breaks may result in a loss of state tax revenue.

Building New Cities and Towns In 1898 English planner Ebenezer Howard urged that entirely new towns be built to lure Londoners from the city and provide a more healthful environment for ordinary industrial workers. Since then Great Britain has built 16 new towns and is building 15 more. New towns have also been built in Singapore, Hong Kong, Finland, Sweden, France, the Netherlands, Venezuela, Brazil, and the United States. There are three types: *satellite towns,* located relatively close to an existing large city; *freestanding new towns,* located far from any major city; and *in-town new towns,* located in existing urban areas. Typically, new towns are designed for populations of 20,000 to 100,000.

The most widely acclaimed new town is Tapiola, Finland, a satellite town not far from Helsinki. Designed in 1952, it is being built gradually in seven sections with an ultimate projected population of 80,000. Today many of its 30,000 residents work in Helsinki, but the long-range goal is industrial and commercial independence. Tapiola is divided into several villages separated by greenbelts. Each village has its own architect, selected by competition, and consists of several neighborhoods clustered around a shopping and cultural center. Each neighborhood has a social center and contains a mix of high-rise apartments and single-family houses. Finland has drawn up plans for building six more new towns around Helsinki.

Unfortunately, new towns rarely succeed without massive financial support from the government, and some don't succeed even then, primarily because of poor planning and management. In 1971 the Department of Housing and Urban Development (HUD) provided more than $300 million in federally guaranteed loans for developers to build 13 new towns in the United States. By 1980 HUD had to take title to nine of these projects, which had gone bankrupt. HUD will no longer fund new towns. Private developers of new towns must put up large amounts of money to buy the land and install facilities and must pay heavy taxes and interest charges for decades before they see any profit. In the United States two privately developed new towns—Columbia, Maryland, and Reston, Virginia—have been in constant financial difficulty since they were established almost two decades ago; their situations are gradually improving, however.

Making Cities More Self-Sufficient Some planners have proposed guidelines and models for building compact towns and cities that waste less matter and energy resources and are more self-reliant than conventional municipalities. Such self-sufficient cities would be surrounded by farms, greenbelts, and community gardens. Homes and marketplaces would be close together, and most local transportation would be by bus, bicycle, and foot. Buildings would be cooled and heated by sun and wind, and wastes would be recycled. Food would be grown locally, and there would be few huge factories.

Although no such cities have been started from scratch, some existing cities have begun efforts to become more self-sufficient in certain resources. Erie, Pennsylvania, for example, drilled two producing oil wells between 1978 and 1980, and Palo Alto, California, has rezoned almost 5,000 acres within the city as

open space for agriculture. Fort Collins, Colorado, runs much of its transportation system on methane gas generated from its sewage plant and uses nutrient-rich sludge from the sewage plant to fertilize 600 acres of city-owned land to grow corn, which might be converted to alcohol to fuel city cars. In New York City, Consolidated Edison has drilled into a large city landfill and has retrieved enough methane from decaying garbage to heat tens of thousands of homes. St. Paul, Minnesota, is planning to build the country's first system that will heat all major downtown buildings with waste heat now being dumped into the Mississippi River by an electric utility.

9-5 URBAN LAND-USE PLANNING AND CONTROL

Methods of Land-Use Planning When cities grow haphazardly, sometimes destroying nearby prime farmland, conflicts arise over how land should be used. To deal with such conflicts over land resources, many cities, states, and countries engage in land-use planning. It is a process for deciding the best present and future use for each parcel of land in an area and mapping out suitable locations for houses, industries, businesses, open space, roads, water lines, sewer lines, hospitals, schools, waste treatment plants, and so on.

Three methods used to develop a land-use plan are *extrapolation of existing trends, reaction to crisis,* and *ecological planning.* Planning by extrapolating or projecting existing trends into the future is the most widely used approach but is not very effective in the long run. For a one- or two-year period this method is usually successful, but for longer terms it can be disastrous because of the inability to accurately project interactions between existing trends and to predict new trends and events. Another widely used but usually ineffective approach is to wait until problems reach the crisis stage before developing a plan of action.

The goal of ecological planning (see Spotlight on p. 183) is to strike a balance among the four major types of ecosystems: **(1)** *unmanaged natural ecosystems* (wilderness, deserts, and mountains), **(2)** *managed multiple-use ecosystems* (parks, estuaries, and some managed forests), **(3)** *managed productive ecosystems* (farms, cattle ranches, tree farms, and strip mines), and **(4)** *managed urban ecosystems* (cities and towns). It is particularly important to preserve certain amounts of undeveloped land—open space—within and near urban areas (see Enrichment Study at the end of this chapter).

1. *Making an environmental and social inventory:* Appropriate experts make a comprehensive survey of geological variables (such as soil types and water availability), ecological variables (such as forest types and quality, wildlife habitats, stream quality, and pollution), economic variables (such as housing and industrial development), and health and social variables (such as disease and crime rates, ethnic distribution, and illiteracy).

2. *Determination of goals and their relative importance:* Experts, public officials, and the general public decide on goals and rank them in order of importance.

For example, is the primary goal to encourage or to discourage further economic development and population growth? This is a very important and difficult planning step, which should also set guidelines for settling conflicts over the use of various parcels of land.

3. *Production of individual and composite maps:* Data for each variable obtained in step 1 are plotted on separate transparent plastic maps. The transparencies are superimposed on one another or combined by computer to give three composite maps—one each for geological variables, ecological variables, and socioeconomic variables.

4. *Development of a comprehensive plan:* The three composite maps are combined to form a master composite, which shows the suitability of various areas for different types of land use.

5. *Evaluation of the comprehensive plan:* The comprehensive plan (or series of alternative comprehensive plans) is evaluated by experts, public officials, and the general public, and a final comprehensive plan is drawn up and approved.

6. *Implementation of the comprehensive plan:* The plan is set in motion and monitored by the appropriate governmental, legal, environmental, and social agencies.

In the United States, decisions to grant permits for residential, commercial, industrial, recreational, or any other use of urban land are normally made by the country's 10,000 separate city and county governments. Unfortunately, few of these local governments have the money, staff, and information needed to do comprehensive, long-range, ecological planning. Any type of land-use planning is made more difficult to develop and implement by political conflicts on how land should be used. In addition, land-use planning in one area can be undercut by a lack of planning or by plans with opposite goals in surrounding areas. For example, the Greater New York area has 1,476 governmental jurisdictions, each making land-use decisions that affect other jurisdictions. Another major problem is that elected local officials, hesitant to make controversial decisions that may affect their chances of reelection, are more adept at reacting to crises than engaging in long-term planning.

Methods of Land-Use Control Unless it can be effectively implemented, a land-use plan merely sits on a shelf gathering dust. Major methods for controlling land use include **(1)** direct purchase of land by a public agency or by private interests (such as the Nature Conservancy and the Audubon Society) to ensure that it is used for a prescribed purpose; **(2)** zoning land for a particular use; **(3)** giving tax breaks to landowners who agree to use land only for specified purposes such as agriculture, wilderness, wildlife habitat, or open space; **(4)** purchase by public agencies of land development rights that restrict the way land can be used (for example, to preserve prime farmland near cities from development); **(5)** assigning a limited number of transferable development rights to a given area of land; **(6)** controlling population growth and land development by limiting building permits, sewer hookups, roads, and other services; and **(7)** requiring environmental impact statements for proposed projects and enforcing the correction or cancellation of harmful projects.

The city is not an ecological monstrosity. It is rather the place where both the problems and the opportunities of modern technological civilization are most potent and visible.

Peter Self

Large Open Spaces

Most planners are concerned with preserving open space within and around urban areas. **Urban open space** is any large, medium-size, or small area of land or water in or near an urban area that can be used for recreational, aesthetic, or ecological functions. One of the most ambitious efforts at preserving large open spaces to reduce urban sprawl is London's 10- to 16-kilometer-wide (6 to 10 miles) greenbelt, a zone of undeveloped land around the city, with new towns built outside the belt (Figure 9-14). This example of long-range planning, begun in 1931, has preserved some land-use choices that most cities squandered long ago. But it has failed to halt urban growth; the suburbs have jumped the belt. Some of them are deteriorating, and there is continuing pressure to develop some of the open space.

Medium-Size Open Spaces

Some cities have had the foresight to preserve moderate amounts of open space in the form of municipal parks. Central Park in New York City, Golden Gate Park in San Francisco, and Lake Front Park in Chicago are important examples. Unfortunately, cities that did not plan for such parks early in their development have little or no chance of getting them now.

Since World War II the typical pattern of suburban housing development in the United States has been to bulldoze a patch (or tract) of woods or farmland and build rows of houses, each standard house on a standard lot (Figure 9-15). In recent years a new pattern, known as *cluster development* or *planned unit development* (PUD), has been used with increasing success to preserve medium-size blocks of open space. Houses, townhouses, condominiums, and gar-

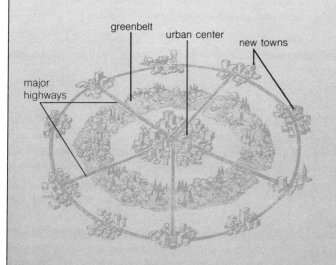

Figure 9-14 Use of a large greenbelt of undeveloped land, surrounded by satellite new towns, to control urban growth.

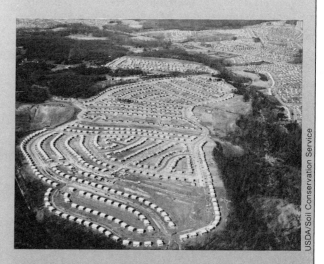

Figure 9-15 A suburban housing tract laid out in conventional row-by-row pattern.

CHAPTER SUMMARY

In both MDCs and LDCs, the percentage of the population living in urban areas (*the degree of urbanization*) has been increasing. The rate of growth of urban areas (*urban growth*) has also been increasing in both MDCs and LDCs but is increasing more rapidly in most LDCs because they are simultaneously experiencing high rates of natural population growth and rapid internal migration of people from rural to urban areas. As a result, many cities in LDCs are flooded with migrants living in squalid conditions in slums and shantytowns.

The world's cities or urban areas are artificial systems that depend on other ecosystems outside their boundaries for survival. They could be classified as self-sustaining natural ecosystems only if their boundaries were expanded to include the farmlands, forests, mines, watersheds, and other areas that provide an input of resources, and to include the air, rivers, oceans, and soil that absorb their massive output of wastes.

Like natural ecosystems, cities have recognizable spatial and physical structures. Three general patterns of urban spatial structure are *concentric-circle cities*, *sector cities*, and *multiple-nuclei cities*. Cities also tend to be either *compact and*

den apartments are built on a relatively small portion of land, with the rest of the area left as open space, either in its natural state or modified for recreation (Figure 9-16).

Small Open Spaces

The most overlooked open spaces are the small strips and odd-shaped patches of unused land that dot urban areas. The Illinois Prairie Path is a walkway and bridle path running from downtown Chicago to its western suburbs along an abandoned trolley line. Other cities have converted abandoned railroad beds and dry creek beds into bicycle, hiking, and jogging paths. San Antonio, Texas, has revitalized a small portion of its downtown area by developing shops, restaurants, and other businesses along the San Antonio River, which runs through a 21-block area of the city. Abandoned lots can be developed as small plazas and

"vest-pocket parks" such as Paley Park in midtown Manhattan, a refreshing refuge for about 3,000 people each day. Research by William H. Whyte, director of the Street Life Project in New York City, has shown that the most widely used small urban plazas and miniparks are located just a few steps from busy streets so that people can easily see and enter them. However, without proper control such areas can become magnets for illegal drug sales and prostitution.

In 1986 the President's Commission on Americans Outdoors proposed the development of a national network of "greenway corridors" near urban areas to allow people to hike, fish, bike, or ride horses. The greenways would consist primarily of interconnected thin strips of land alongside streams, old canal paths, abandoned railways, and electrical power-line rights of way.

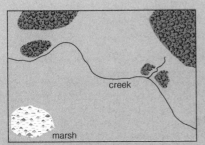

Undeveloped Land

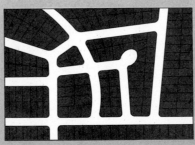

Typical Housing Development

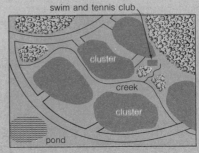

Cluster Housing Development

Figure 9-16 Conventional and cluster development as they would appear if constructed on the same land area.

energy efficient or *dispersed and energy inefficient*, depending on geographic site, rate of population growth, supply of nearby rural land (especially flat agricultural land) for conversion to urban land, transportation and utility systems, economic and technological levels, and the relative cost of energy.

The three major types of transportation used in urban areas are *individual transit*, *mass transit*, and *paratransit*. Most *individual transit*, especially in urban areas in MDCs, is by automobile. The car provides individuals with unparalleled freedom of movement, and automaking and related industries are a major component of economic growth in industrialized countries. However, widespread use of cars and

trucks encourages development of energy-inefficient, dispersed urban areas, kills and injures large numbers of people, requires large amounts of land for roads and parking space, and is responsible for considerable environmental pollution, especially air pollution.

Mass transit is more energy efficient, requires less land, and produces far less pollution than individual motor vehicles. However, *fixed heavy- and light-rail mass transit systems* are too expensive to build and operate in the many dispersed urban areas of the United States. They attract sufficient ridership only where large numbers of people are concentrated along narrow corridors. *Bus systems* are more flexible than rail systems in providing mass transportation within widely dispersed urban areas. They also have cheaper start-up and operating costs since buses can be added as needed. However, because competition from cars reduces ridership, they usually require government subsidies to cover some of their operating costs. *Paratransit systems* involving car pools, van pools, small vans or buses traveling relatively fixed routes (jitneys), and dial-a-ride services are also useful in dispersed urban areas.

Most of America's older cities are in severe need of repairs of roads, bridges, water supply and sewage systems, and other public works. In a time of budget cutting and flight to the suburbs, most local governments are hard-pressed for maintenance funds. On the other hand, some cities have been successful in using private and government funds to stimulate economic activity in decaying downtown areas and to restore and improve rundown or abandoned private and public housing. Another approach to urban problems is to build one or more *new towns* near or within existing cities to stimulate economic activity, improve living conditions, and reduce pressures on crowded urban areas.

Most urban areas use some form of *land-use planning* to decide the best present and future use for each parcel of land in the area. Most land-use planning is based on extrapolating existing trends or reacting to crisis; both methods are ineffective in anticipating and preventing long-term conflicts and problems. *Ecological land-use planning,* in which all major variables are considered and integrated into a model designed to anticipate present and future needs, is a much better method. However, it is not widely used because of political conflicts over valuable pieces of land, inability of officials seeking reelection every few years to be concerned with long-term problems, and lack of cooperative planning between various municipalities in the same general area.

Methods for controlling land use include zoning, direct public or private purchase, buying development rights, giving tax breaks to owners, and controlling urban growth by limiting building permits, sewer hookups, roads, and other services.

DISCUSSION TOPICS

1. Explain how the MDCs are more urbanized, although LDCs have higher rates of urban growth.
2. List the advantages and disadvantages of living in (a) the downtown area of a large city, (b) suburbia, (c) a small town in a rural area, (d) a small town near a large city, and (e) a rural area. Which would you prefer to live in? Why? Which will you probably end up living in? Why?
3. Give advantages and disadvantages of emphasizing rural rather than urban development in LDCs. Why do most LDCs emphasize urban development even though most of their population is rural?
4. Describe how urban systems and natural ecosystems are similar and how they differ.
5. What life-support resources in your community are the most vulnerable to interruption or destruction? What alternate or backup resources, if any, exist?
6. Which, if any, of the models shown in Figure 9-8 best describes the spatial form of the city you live in or near?
7. If you live in a city, try to identify the downwind zones that receive air pollution produced by the city. If you live in a rural area, try to determine which city or cities pollute the air you receive. Consult the local weather bureau for information on prevailing wind patterns and airshed regions.
8. Examine your own dependence on the automobile. What conditions, if any, would encourage you to rely less on the automobile? Would you regularly travel to school or work in a car pool, on a bicycle or moped, or on foot? Explain.
9. What types of mass transit and paratransit systems are available where you live? What systems were available 20 years ago? Has this change been beneficial or harmful? Explain.
10. How is land use decided in your community? What roles do citizens have?
11. Evaluate land use and land-use planning by your college or university.
12. Draw a map identifying small, medium-size, and large open spaces in your area, and label their current uses. Survey class opinion on whether current use is "good" or "bad." Redraw the map to indicate how these spaces could be used more beneficially, and consider presenting this information to local officials.
13. Massive traffic jams hinder you from getting to and from work each day. Government officials say that the only way to relieve congestion is to build a highway through the middle of a beautiful urban park. As a taxpayer, would you support this construction? Explain. What would you suggest to relieve the situation?

PART FOUR

Resources

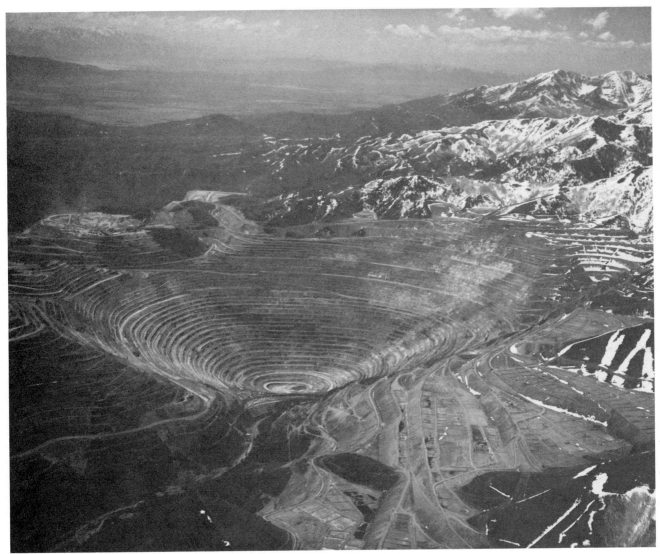

Kennecott Copper Corporation

Our entire society rests upon—and is dependent upon—our water, our land, our forests, and our minerals. How we use these resources influences our health, security, economy, and well-being.

John F. Kennedy

10

Soil Resources

GENERAL OBJECTIVES

1. Why is soil so important and what are its major components?

2. How is soil formed and what key properties make a soil best-suited for growing crops?

3. What are the major differences between grassland, forest, and desert soils?

4. How serious is the problem of soil erosion in the world and in the United States?

5. What are the major methods for reducing unnecessary soil erosion and depletion of plant nutrients in topsoil?

Below that thin layer comprising the delicate organism known as the soil is a planet as lifeless as the moon.

G. Y. Jacks and R. O. Whyte

Despite its importance in providing us with food, fiber, wood, gravel, and many other materials vital to our existence, soil has been one of the most abused resources. Evidence exists that entire civilizations collapsed because they mismanaged the topsoil that supported their populations, treating this potentially renewable resource as though it could not be depleted by overuse. Unless we wish to relearn the harsh lessons of soil abuse, everyone—not just farmers—needs to be concerned with reducing human-accelerated soil erosion.

10-1 SOILS: USES, COMPONENTS, AND PROFILES

The Base of Life Pick up a handful of soil and notice how it feels and looks. The **soil** you hold in your hand is a complex mixture of inorganic minerals (mostly clay, silt, and sand), decaying organic matter, water, air, and living organisms. The earth's thin layer of soil—at most only a meter or two thick—provides nutrients for plants, which directly or indirectly provide the food we and other animals use to stay alive and healthy. Soil also serves as the base for producing the natural fibers, lumber, and paper we use in large quantities.

Soil Layers and Components The components of soils are arranged in a series of layers called **soil horizons** (Figure 10-1). Each horizon has a distinct thickness, color, texture, and composition that varies with different types of soils. A cross-sectional view of the horizons in a soil is called a **soil profile.** Most mature soils have at least three or four of the six possible horizons.

The top *surface-litter layer* (O-horizon) consists mostly of fresh-fallen and partially decomposed leaves,

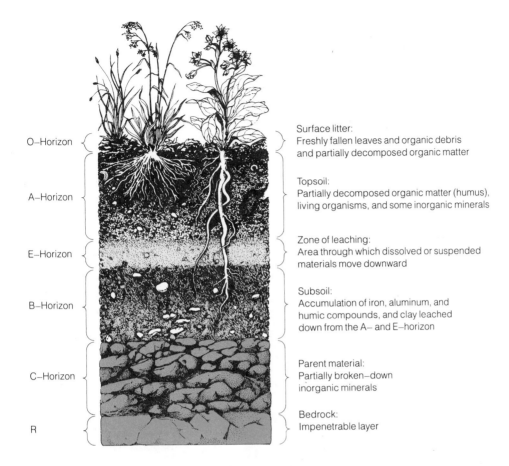

O–Horizon

A–Horizon

E–Horizon

B–Horizon

C–Horizon

R

Surface litter:
Freshly fallen leaves and organic debris
and partially decomposed organic matter

Topsoil:
Partially decomposed organic matter (humus),
living organisms, and some inorganic minerals

Zone of leaching:
Area through which dissolved or suspended
materials move downward

Subsoil:
Accumulation of iron, aluminum, and
humic compounds, and clay leached
down from the A– and E–horizon

Parent material:
Partially broken–down
inorganic minerals

Bedrock:
Impenetrable layer

twigs, animal waste, and other organic debris. It usually has a dark rich color. The underlying *topsoil layer* (A-horizon) is usually a porous mixture of partially decomposed organic matter (humus), living organisms, and some inorganic mineral particles. It is usually darker and looser than deeper layers. Roots of most plants grow in these two upper soil layers (Figure 10-1). Most of a soil's organic matter, which makes up from 1% to 7% of the volume of most soil samples, is found in the first two layers.

The two top layers of most soils are also teeming with bacteria, fungi, molds, earthworms, small insects, and are home to larger, burrowing animals such as moles and gophers—all of which interact in complex food webs (Figure 10-2). Most of these organisms are bacteria and other decomposer microorganisms—billions in every handful of soil. They partially or completely break down some of the complex inorganic and organic compounds in the upper layers of soil into simpler, water-soluble compounds. Soil water carrying these dissolved plant nutrients and other materials is drawn up by roots and transported through stems and into leaves (Figure 10-3).

Other organic compounds are broken down slowly and form a dark-colored mixture of organic matter called **humus.** This partially decomposed, water-insoluble

material remains in the topsoil layer and helps retain water and water-soluble plant nutrients so they can be taken up by plant roots. A fertile soil, useful for growing high yields of crops, has a thick topsoil layer containing a high content of humus.

We can learn a lot about the suitability of a soil for growing crops by noting the color of its topsoil layer. Dark brown or black topsoil contains a large amount of organic matter and is highly fertile. Gray, bright yellow, or red topsoils are low in organic matter and will require fertilizers and perhaps acidity adjustment to increase their fertility.

The inorganic matter in a soil consists of particles of broken-down rock in the form of varying mixtures of sand, silt, clay, and gravel. These materials, making up about 45% of a typical sample of soil, are found mostly in soil layers lying below the surface litter and topsoil.

The spaces, or pores, between the solid organic and inorganic particles in the upper and lower soil layers contain varying amounts of two other key inorganic components: air and water. Air (mostly gaseous oxygen and nitrogen) is obtained from the atmosphere. Oxygen gas, particularly in the topsoil, is used by the cells in plant roots to carry out cellular respiration (Section 4-2). Some of the rain falling on the soil

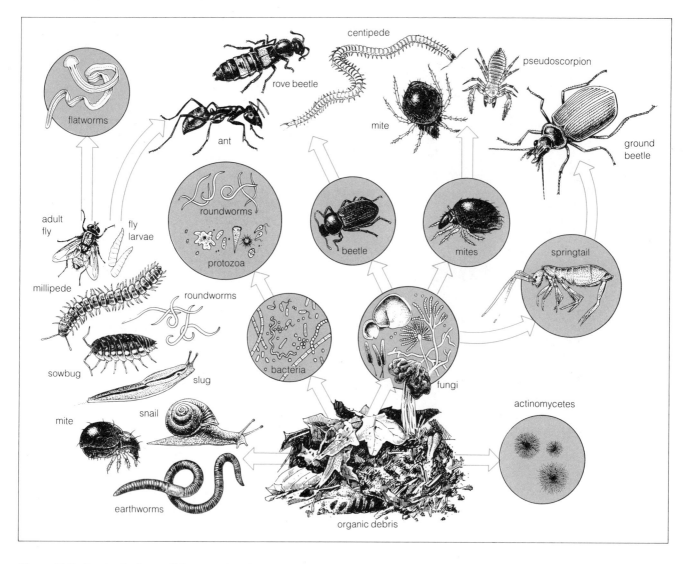

Figure 10-2 Food web of some living organisms found in soil.

surface infiltrates, or percolates through, the soil layers and occupies some of the pores. As this water seeps downward, it dissolves and picks up various soil components in upper layers and carries them to lower layers—a process called **leaching.**

10-2 SOIL: FORMATION, POROSITY, AND ACIDITY

Formation Most soil begins as bedrock, which is gradually broken down through an abrasion process called **weathering** into small bits and pieces that make up most of the soil's inorganic material. Other soils develop from the weathering of sediments that have been deposited on the bedrock by wind, water (alluvial soils), volcanic eruptions, or melting glaciers. In either case, weathering occurs over a long period as a result of various physical and chemical processes. *Physical weathering* involves the breaking down of rock into bits and pieces primarily by exposure to temperature changes and the physical action of moving ice, water, and wind. For example, in the arid climates of desert biomes, repeated exposure to very high temperatures during the day followed by low temperatures at night causes rocks to expand and contract and eventually to crack and shatter. In cold or temperate climates, rock can crack and break as a result of repeated cycles of expansion of water in rock pores and cracks during freezing and contraction when the ice melts. Growing roots can exert enough pressure to enlarge cracks in sold rock, eventually splitting the rock. Plants such as mosses and lichens also penetrate into rock and loosen particles.

Chemical weathering involves chemical attack and dissolution of rock, primarily through exposure to oxygen gas in the atmosphere (oxidation), rainwater

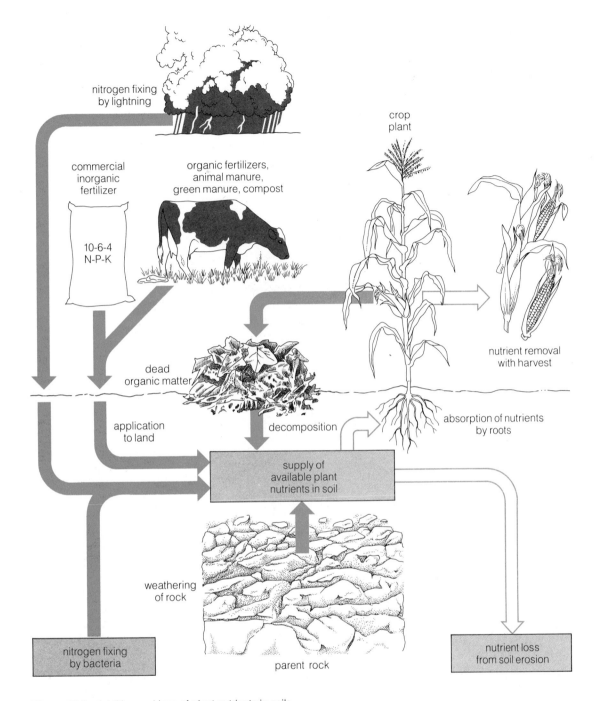

Figure 10-3 Addition and loss of plant nutrients in soils.

(which becomes slightly acidic by dissolving small amounts of carbon dioxide gas from the atmosphere), and acidic secretions of bacteria, fungi, and lichens. In areas where average temperatures are high, these chemical reactions take place relatively rapidly; in colder regions they take place at a slower rate.

The slope of the land also has an important effect on the type of soil and the rate at which it forms. When the slope is steep, the action of wind, flowing water, and gravity tends to erode the soil constantly. This explains why soils on steep slopes often are thin and never accumulate to a depth sufficient to support plant growth. In contrast, valley soils, receiving mineral particles, nutrients, water, and organic matter from adjacent slopes, are often fertile and highly productive if they are not too wet.

Porosity Soils vary in their content of clay (very fine particles), silt (fine particles), sand (coarse particles), and gravel (large particles). The relative amounts of different size particles determine a soil's **porosity**—

Figure 10-4 Soil porosity and texture depend on the percentages of clay, silt, and sand particles in the soil. Loams are the soils best for growing most crops. (Source: USDA Soil Conservation Service.)

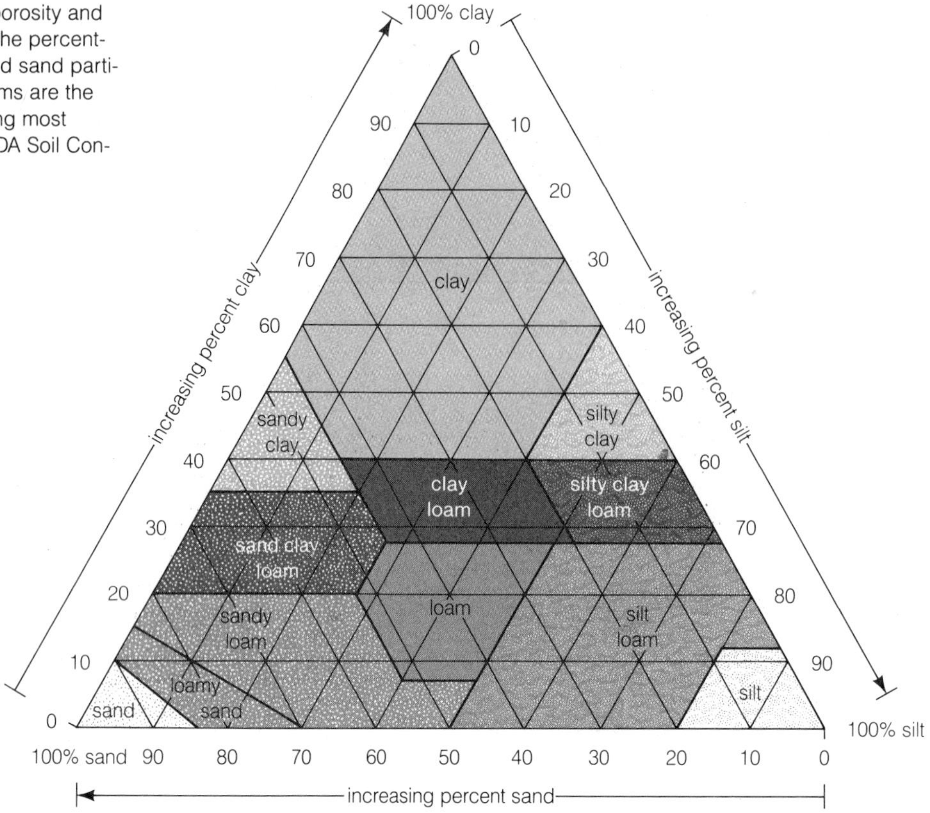

the number of pores it has and the distances between them. Porosity is a major factor controlling the amount of water and air the soil can hold and the rate at which water moves downward through it.

Soils can be classified by their clay, silt, and sand content, a useful indicator of their suitability for agriculture (Figure 10-4). Soils consisting of almost equal amounts of sand and silt and somewhat less clay—known as **loams**—are the best for growing most crops. Of medium porosity, loam has sufficient space to provide ample oxygen for plant root cells and retains enough water for roots to absorb without being waterlogged.

Sandy soils have relatively large pores between particles and the particles have little tendency to adhere to form large clumps. As a result, air and water flow through the particles rapidly. Although sandy soils have good aeration and are easy to work, they retain almost no water and are useful primarily for growing crops without large water requirements, such as peanuts and strawberries. At the other extreme are **clay soils,** in which particles are very small, easily packed together, and when wet can form large clumps—the reason that wet clay is so easy to mold into bricks and pottery. Because of their low porosity, clay soils allow little water infiltration, especially when compacted, and are poorly aerated. They also are hard to cultivate and when compacted may have too little pore space for root growth. Water that does not penetrate drains

poorly so that clay soils are often too waterlogged to grow crops other than onions, potatoes, and celery.

Porosity gives a soil its characteristic texture. To get a general idea of a soil's porosity, take a small amount of topsoil, moisten it, and rub it between your fingers and thumb. Topsoil that contains too much sand for crops will feel gritty and will have little clumping. Topsoil that contains too much clay is sticky when wet and you can easily roll it up into a single clump or group of large clumps. When it dries, it will harden. A loam topsoil best suited for plant growth has a texture between the other two extremes. It has a crumbly, spongy feeling and many of its particles are clumped loosely together.

Acidity The acidity or alkalinity of a soil is another important factor determining which types of crops it can support. Acidity and alkalinity are measures of the relative concentrations of hydrogen ions (H^+) and hydroxide ions (OH^-) in a water solution. A volume of solution containing more hydrogen ions than hydroxide ions is an **acid solution;** a volume of a solution containing more hydroxide ions than hydrogen ions is a **basic,** or **alkaline, solution.** A solution with an equal number of the two types of ions is called a **neutral solution.** Scientists use **pH** as a simple measure of the degree of acidity or alkalinity of a solution. An acid solution has pH less than 7. The lower the pH

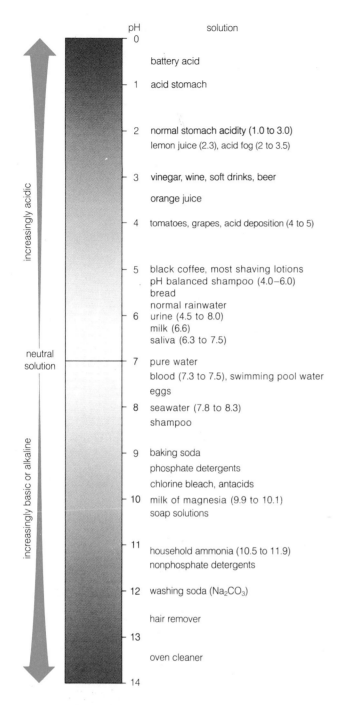

pH   solution

0

battery acid

1   acid stomach

2   normal stomach acidity (1.0 to 3.0)
    lemon juice (2.3), acid fog (2 to 3.5)

3   vinegar, wine, soft drinks, beer

    orange juice

4   tomatoes, grapes, acid deposition (4 to 5)

5   black coffee, most shaving lotions
    pH balanced shampoo (4.0–6.0)
    bread
    normal rainwater
6   urine (4.5 to 8.0)
    milk (6.6)
    saliva (6.3 to 7.5)

7   pure water
    blood (7.3 to 7.5), swimming pool water
    eggs

8   seawater (7.8 to 8.3)
    shampoo

9   baking soda
    phosphate detergents
    chlorine bleach, antacids

10 milk of magnesia (9.9 to 10.1)
    soap solutions

11 household ammonia (10.5 to 11.9)
    nonphosphate detergents

12 washing soda (Na_2CO_3)

    hair remover

13

    oven cleaner

14

increasingly acidic

neutral solution

increasingly basic or alkaline

Figure 10-5 Scale of pH, used to measure acidity and alkalinity of water solutions. Values shown are approximate.

below 7, the greater the acidity of a solution. A solution with a pH of 7 is neutral, and one with a pH greater than 7 is basic, or alkaline. Figure 10-5 shows the general pH values for water solutions containing various substances.

Crops vary widely in the pH ranges they can tolerate. Many common food plants such as wheat, spinach, peas, corn, and tomatoes grow best in slightly acidic soils; potatoes and berries do best in very acidic

soils, and alfalfa and asparagus in neutral soils. When soils are too acidic for the desired crops, the acids can be partially neutralized by adding an alkaline substance such as lime (calcium oxide produced from limestone). But adding lime speeds up the undesirable decomposition of organic matter in the soil, so manure or other organic fertilizer should be added as well. Otherwise, the initial years of good crop yields will be followed by poor yields. Adding organic matter to the soil also helps stabilize pH.

In areas of low rainfall, such as the semiarid valleys in the western and southwestern United States, calcium and other alkaline compounds are not leached away, and soils may be too alkaline (pH above 7.5) for some desired crops. If drainage is good, the alkalinity of these soils can be reduced by leaching the alkaline compounds away with irrigation water. Soil alkalinity can also be reduced by adding sulfur, an abundant and cheap element, which is gradually converted to sulfuric acid (H_2SO_4) by bacteria.

10-3 MAJOR TYPES OF SOIL

Mature soils in different biomes of the world vary widely in color, properties such as porosity and acidity, and depth. These differences can be used to classify soils throughout the world into ten major types or orders (Figure 10-6). Five important soil orders are mollisols, alfisols, spodosols, oxisols, and aridisols. Each of these has a distinct soil profile (Figure 10-7).

Most of the world's crops are grown on grassland mollisols and on alfisols exposed when deciduous forests are cleared. *Mollisols* are middle-aged to young, very fertile soils with a thick, humus-rich, dark brown to black A-horizon. Mollisols underlie grasslands in semiarid dry climates in North America, central Asia, central Europe, northern China, and Argentina.

Alfisols are middle-aged, relatively fertile soils with a brown to gray-brown A-horizon. They are less fertile than mollisols because of their thinner A-horizon and unlike mollisols they have an E-horizon. They underlie deciduous forests in areas with humid, mild climates. The A-horizon is thinner because the relatively high rainfall in alfisol areas leaches many of the nutrients from the O- and A-horizons and deposits them in the underlying E- and B-horizons. Unless key plant nutrients in the A-horizon are replaced by fertilizers, soils of cleared temperate deciduous forests will not grow satisfactory crops after several harvests.

Spodosols are young, acidic soils underlying temperate coniferous forests in humid, cold climates. They have a fairly thick, humus-rich O-horizon overlying a sandy E-horizon; because the E-horizon is highly leached, it is nutrient-poor and almost white in color. The underlying B-layer is fairly rich in humus and iron

Figure 10-6 World distribution of ten major soil orders.(Data from USDA Soil Conservation Service. Map based on a modified Goode's projection, copyright by the University of Chicago, Department of Geography, and used by their permission.)

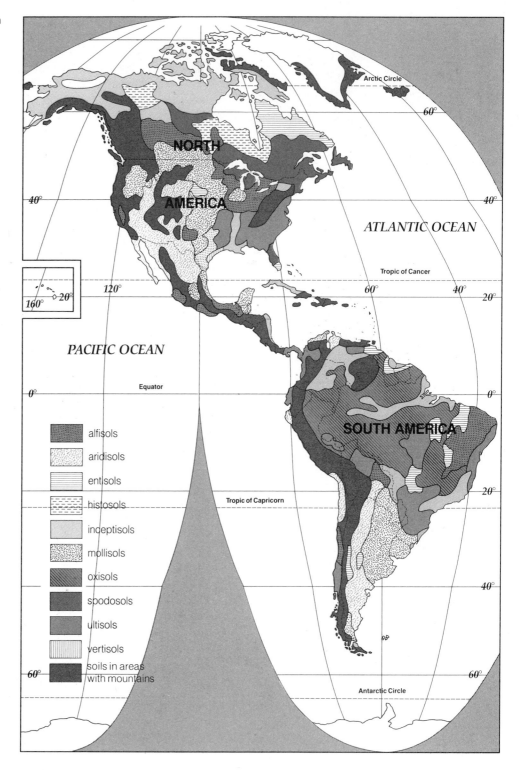

alfisols
aridisols
entisols
histosols
inceptisols
mollisols
oxisols
spodosols
ultisols
vertisols
soils in areas with mountains

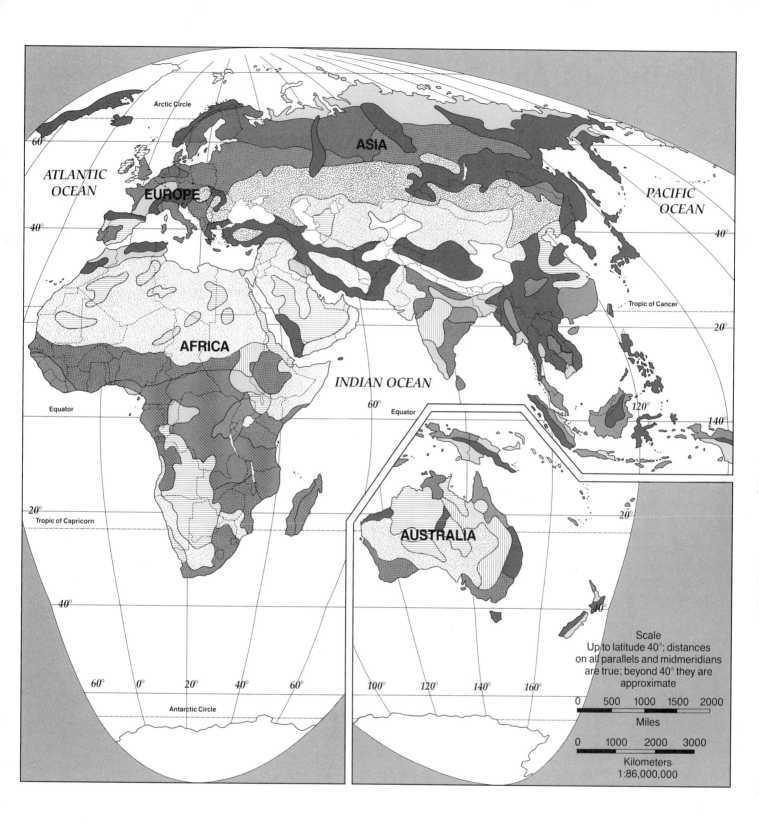

Arctic Circle

ATLANTIC
OCEAN

ASIA

EUROPE

PACIFIC
OCEAN

60°

40°

40°

Tropic of Cancer

20°

AFRICA

INDIAN OCEAN

60°

Equator

Equator

20°

20°

Tropic of Capricorn

AUSTRALIA

120°

140°

40°

40°

40°

Scale
Up to latitude 40°; distances
on all parallels and midmeridians
are true; beyond 40° they are
approximate

60°

0°

20°

40°

60°

100°

120°

140°

160°

0   500   1000   1500   2000

Miles

Antarctic Circle

0   1000   2000   3000

Kilometers
1:86,000,000

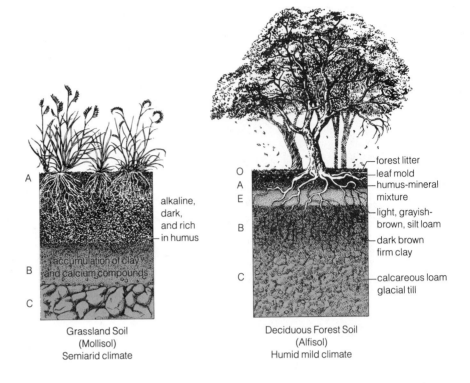

Figure 10-7 Soil profiles for the major soil orders typically found in five different biomes.

Grassland Soil
(Mollisol)
Semiarid climate

A
B
C

alkaline,
dark,
and rich
in humus

accumulation of clay
and calcium compounds

Deciduous Forest Soil
(Alfisol)
Humid mild climate

O
A
E
B
C

forest litter
leaf mold
humus-mineral
mixture
light, grayish-
brown, silt loam
dark brown
firm clay
calcareous loam
glacial till

compounds but low in most plant nutrients. When coniferous forests are cleared, the underlying spodosols are too acidic and too leached of plant nutrients for growing most crops.

Oxisols are highly weathered soils with an acidic, thin A-horizon, containing little organic matter, and a thick, infertile B-horizon high in iron and aluminum compounds. They underlie large areas of tropical rain forests and some subtropical humid forests of Central America, Africa, and Asia, mostly in humid, tropical climates. Although iron and aluminum compounds can be mined from these soils, oxisols are not useful for agriculture. When a large area of tropical rain forest is cleared, the torrential seasonal rains leach most of the remaining nutrients and minerals from the thin A-horizon. Once exposed to air and sun, the iron oxide that remains in some oxisols can form red rock called *laterite* or *ironstone*—so hard it is used for paving highways. Once laterite forms, the land is useless for cultivation. It is estimated that laterite-forming oxisols are found close to the surface on about 7% of the total land area of the tropics, including 2% of tropical America, 11% of tropical Africa, and 15% of sub-Saharan West Africa.

Aridisols are middle-aged soils with little accumulation of organic matter, little development of distinctive soil horizons, and a weakly-developed A-hori-

zon often overlain by rock or a mineral crust called desert pavement. They are found in the hot, arid desert areas of Africa, South America, and western North America. About one-third of the area covered by aridisols is useless for growing crops because of lack of rainfall or irrigation water. In general, land with aridisol soil is better used as grazing land for livestock (rangeland) than for growing crops.

10-4 SOIL EROSION

Natural and Human-Accelerated Soil Erosion Soil does not remain in one place indefinitely. **Soil erosion** is the movement of soil components, especially topsoil, from one place to another. The two main forces causing soil erosion are wind (Figure 10-8) and flowing water (Figure 10-9). Some soil erosion always takes place as a result of these and other natural processes. But the roots of plants generally protect soil from excessive erosion.

Erosion from flowing water is most prevalent on steep slopes that have lost some or all of their natural vegetation cover, but erosion can occur even on moderate slopes if they are cleared or planted with row

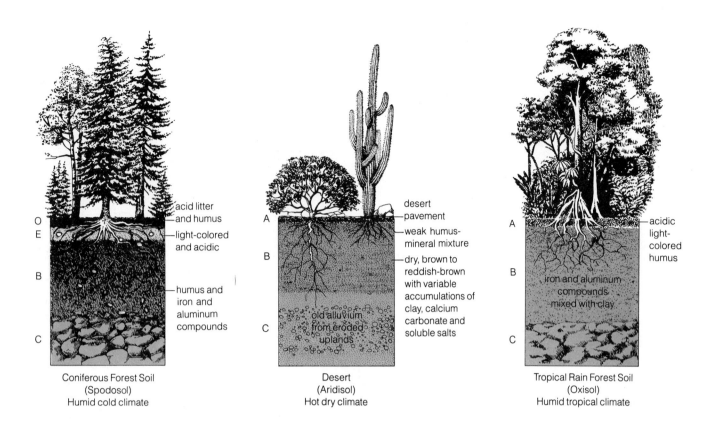

Coniferous Forest Soil
(Spodosol)
Humid cold climate

O — acid litter and humus
E — light-colored and acidic
B — humus and iron and aluminum compounds
C

Desert
(Aridisol)
Hot dry climate

A — desert pavement
— weak humus-mineral mixture
B — dry, brown to reddish-brown with variable accumulations of clay, calcium carbonate and soluble salts
C — old alluvium from eroded uplands

Tropical Rain Forest Soil
(Oxisol)
Humid tropical climate

A — acidic light-colored humus
B — iron and aluminum compounds mixed with clay
C

crops. Wind erosion is particularly severe on flat lands where soil has a sandy texture and on grasslands in windy areas cleared to grow crops or overgrazed by livestock.

If the average rate of topsoil erosion exceeds the rate of topsoil formation on a piece of land, then the topsoil on that land becomes a nonrenewable resource that is being depleted. Topsoil is regenerated at a rate of a few inches every thousand years, but in many areas it is being eroded away as a result of human activities at rates of a few inches per decade or even faster (see the Guest Essay at the end of this chapter). Excessive erosion not only reduces soil fertility—the resulting sediment clogs irrigation ditches, navigable waterways, and reservoirs used to generate electric power and provide drinking water for urban areas.

The World Situation   Today topsoil is eroding faster than it forms on about 35% of the world's croplands—amounting to a net loss of about 23.2 trillion kilograms (25.4 billion tons) per year. The amount of topsoil washing and blowing into the world's rivers, lakes, and oceans each year would fill a train of freight cars long enough to encircle the planet 150 times. At this rate, the world is losing about 7% of its topsoil from potential cropland each decade. This situation, which

is undermining agricultural productivity in many parts of the world, is worsening as cultivation is being extended into areas poorly suited for agriculture.

The ninefold increase in fertilizer use and the near tripling of the world's irrigated cropland between 1950 and 1985 have temporarily masked the effects of soil erosion on crop productivity. Heavy and increasingly expensive applications of commercial inorganic fertilizers can replace some lost soil nutrients and allow more intensive cultivation. However, as we will see in Section 10-5, commercial fertilizer is not a complete substitute for naturally fertile topsoil and merely hides for a time the gradual depletion of this vital resource.

Accelerated erosion from human activities is most widespread in large, populous countries: India, China, the Soviet Union, and the United States. Together these four countries have 52% of the world's cropland, account for over half the world's food production, and contain almost half the world's people. In China, the world's fourth greatest food producer, at least 34% of the land is severely eroded and river siltation is now a nationally recognized threat. Soil erosion and river siltation are also major problems in India, with erosion affecting one-quarter of the country's land area. The Worldwatch Institute estimates that the Soviet Union, which has the world's largest cropland area, may be losing more topsoil than any other country. Increas-

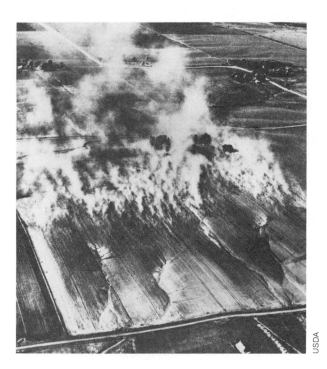

Figure 10-8 Wind blowing soil off Iowa farmland in 1930. If grass had been planted between crops, most of this loss of valuable topsoil could have been prevented.

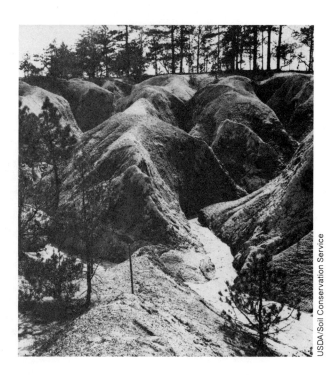

Figure 10-9 Extensive soil erosion and gully formation caused by flowing water. Good farming practices could have prevented the loss of most of this topsoil.

ingly, poor people in many LDCs must either grow crops on marginal land and use cultivation methods that will increase soil erosion or face starvation.

The U.S. Situation According to soil surveys by the Soil Conservation Service, about one-third of the original topsoil on U.S. croplands in use today has already been washed or blown into rivers, lakes, and oceans. Some of the country's richest agricultural lands, such as those in Iowa, have lost about half their topsoil. Enough topsoil erodes away *each day* to fill a line of dump trucks 5,600 kilometers (3,500 miles) long, with the bulk of this coming from less than one-fourth of the country's cropland. The plant nutrient losses from this erosion are worth at least $18 billion a year.

Unless soil conservation efforts are increased, topsoil losses will gradually decrease crop productivity. Over the next 50 years, projected soil erosion may destroy productivity on U.S. cropland acreage equal to the combined areas of the states of New York, New Jersey, Maine, New Hampshire, Massachusetts, and Connecticut. Some analysts, however, estimate that continuation of 1977 rates of soil erosion for one hundred years would reduce national average crop yields by only 5% to 10%, a deficit they believe can easily be made up by advances in agricultural technology.

Others, however, point out that this is misleading because much of the most severe erosion occurs on some of the country's prime farmland. For example, over half of U.S. cropland soil erosion occurs in the corn belt and the northern plains, among the most productive agricultural areas in the world. Without increased use of well-known but little-used soil conservation methods, these fertile Midwest plains are subject to increased erosion from continuous high winds and periodic prolonged drought (see Spotlight on p. 199).

Erosion from U.S. cropland is not the only problem. Improper use and management of forest, range, and pasture lands, as well as activities such as mining and construction, account for at least one-third of the soil eroded from land in the United States. Soil erosion is also caused by motorcycles and other off-road vehicles, which destroy vegetation and create gullies.

10-5 SOIL CONSERVATION

Soil Management Methods The practice of **soil conservation** involves using various management methods to reduce soil erosion and to prevent depletion of soil nutrients. Reducing soil erosion means holding the soil in place. Methods used to accomplish

The Great Plains of the United States stretch through ten states, from Texas through Montana and the Dakotas. The region is normally dry and very windy and periodically experiences long, severe droughts. Before settlers began grazing livestock and planting crops in the 1870s, the extensive root systems of prairie grasses held the rich mollisol in place (Figure 10-7). When the land was planted, these perennial grasses were replaced by annual crops with less extensive root systems. In addition, the land was plowed up after each harvest and left bare part of the year. Overgrazing also destroyed large areas of grass, leaving the ground bare. The stage was set for crop failures during prolonged droughts, followed by severe wind erosion.

The droughts arrived in 1890 and 1910 and again with even greater severity between 1926 and 1934. In 1934, hot, dry windstorms created dust clouds thick enough to cause darkness at midday in some areas (Figure 10-10); the danger of breathing the dust-laden air was revealed by dead rabbits and birds left in its wake. During May 1934 the entire eastern half of the United States was blanketed with a massive dust cloud of rich topsoil blown off the Great Plains from as far as 2,415 kilometers (1,500 miles) away. Ships 320 kilometers (200 miles) out in the Atlantic Ocean received deposits of topsoil. Thus, the Great Plains acquired a tragic new name: the Dust Bowl.

About 89 million acres of cropland were either destroyed (9 million acres) or severely damaged (80 million acres). Thousands of displaced farm families from Oklahoma, Texas, Kansas, and other states migrated westward toward California or to the industrial cities of the Midwest and East. Upon arriving at their destinations, most

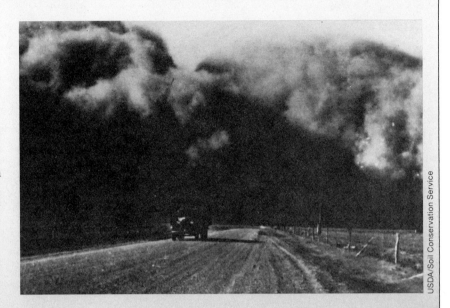

Figure 10-10 Dust storm approaching Prowers County, Colorado, 1934.

found no jobs because the country was in the midst of the Great Depression. The migrants joined massive numbers of unemployed people waiting in line for enough free food to keep themselves and their families alive.

In May 1934 Hugh Bennett of the U.S. Department of Agriculture (USDA) addressed a congressional hearing, pleading for new programs to protect the country's topsoil. Lawmakers in Washington took action when dust blown from the Great Plains began seeping into the hearing room. In 1935 the United States established the Soil Conservation Service (SCS) as part of the USDA. With Bennett as its first head, the SCS began promoting good conservation practices in the Great Plains and later in every state, establishing local soil conservation districts and providing technical assistance to farmers and ranchers.

These efforts, however, did not completely solve the erosion problems of the Great Plains. From both economic and ecological viewpoints, the climate of much of the region makes it better suited for grazing than for farming—a lesson its farmers have relearned several times since the 1930s. For example, because of severe drought and soil erosion in the 1950s, the federal government had to provide emergency relief funds to many Great Plains farmers.

In 1975 the Council of Agricultural Science and Technology warned that severe drought could again create a dust bowl in the Great Plains, pointing out that despite large expenditures for soil erosion control, topsoil losses were 2.5% worse than in the 1930s. So far, these warnings have not been heeded. Great Plains farmers, many of them debt-ridden because of low crop prices, have continued to stave off bankruptcy by maximizing production and minimizing expenditures for soil conservation. What do you think should be done about this situation?

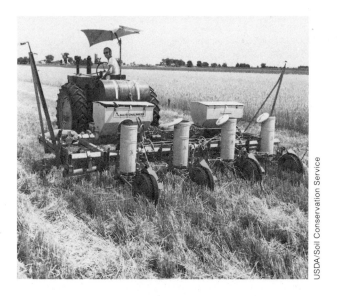

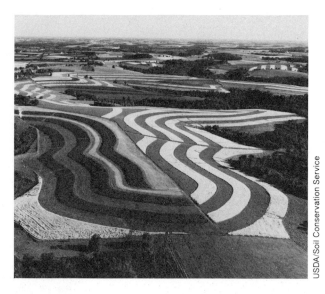

Figure 10-11 No-till farming. A specially designed machine plants seeds and adds fertilizers and weed killers at the same time with almost no disturbance of the soil.

Figure 10-12 On this gently sloping land, contoured rows planted with alternating crops (strip cropping) reduce soil erosion.

this goal include *conservation tillage, contour farming, terracing, strip cropping, gully reclamation, shelterbelts or windbreaks, using land for purposes to which it is suitable,* and *not planting marginal land subject to higher than normal erosion rates.* Replanting cleared land with rapid-growing vegetation is important not only for cropland but for all disturbed land.

Preventing depletion of soil nutrients and restoring nutrients already lost by erosion, leaching, and excessive crop harvesting can be accomplished by *application of organic fertilizers* and *commercial inorganic fertilizers* and by *crop rotation.* These methods, however, should be used along with—not in place of—methods to reduce unnecessary topsoil loss.

Conservation Tillage In conventional, intensive tillage farming, land is plowed, disked several times, and smoothed to make a planting surface. If plowed in the fall so that crops can be planted early in the spring, the soil is left bare during the winter and early spring months.

To lower labor costs, save energy, and reduce soil erosion, an increasing number of U.S. farmers are replacing this approach with **conservation tillage farming,** also known as *minimum-tillage* or *no-till* farming, depending on the degree to which the soil is disturbed. Farmers using this method disturb the soil as little as possible when crops are planted. For the min-

imum-tillage method special subsurface tillers are used to break up and loosen the subsurface soil without turning over the topsoil, the previous crop residues, and any cover vegetation. In the no-till version of this approach, even subsurface tillage is eliminated. Special planters are used to drill a hole in the soil for each plant and inject seeds, fertilizers, and weed killers (herbicides) into unplowed soil (Figure 10-11).

In addition to reducing soil erosion, conservation tillage reduces fuel and tillage costs, water loss from the soil, and soil compaction and increases the number of crops that can be grown during a season (multiple cropping). It also usually allows crops to be planted, treated with herbicide, and harvested when conventional tilled fields would be too muddy to enter. Yields are as high or higher than yields from conventional tillage. Conservation tillage, however, requires increased use of herbicides to control weeds that compete with crops for soil nutrients, and it cannot be used on all soils (especially those in the northern corn belt). Depending on the soil, this approach can be used for three to seven years before more extensive soil cultivation is needed to prevent crop yields from declining.

Increased use of conservation tillage is the most hopeful sign of progress toward reducing soil erosion from U.S. croplands. By 1985 conservation tillage was used on about 35% of the country's croplands and is projected to be used on over half by the year 2000.

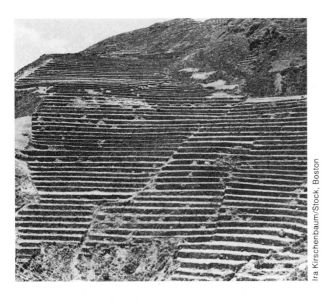

Figure 10-13 These terraces in Pisac, Peru help reduce soil erosion.

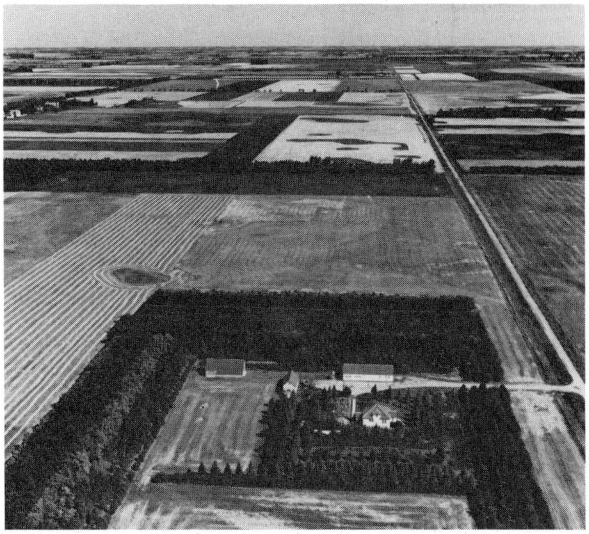

Figure 10-14 Shelterbelts, or windbreaks, reduce erosion on this farm in Trail County, North Dakota.

Ira Kirschenbaum/Stock, Boston

USDA/Soil Conservation Service

The USDA estimates that using conservation tillage on 80% of U.S. cropland would reduce soil erosion by at least half. So far the practice is not widely used in other parts of the world.

Contour Farming, Terracing, and Strip Cropping

Soil erosion can be reduced by 30% to 50% on gently sloping land through the use of **contour farming**—plowing and planting along rather than up and down the sloped contour of the land (Figure 10-12). Each row planted at a right angle to the slope of the land acts as a small dam to help hold soil and slow the runoff of water.

Terracing can be used on steeper slopes. The slope is converted into a series of broad, nearly level terraces with short vertical drops from one to another, following the slope of the land (Figure 10-13). Water running down the permanently vegetated slope is retained and delayed by each terrace. This provides water for crops at all levels and decreases soil erosion by reducing the amount and speed of water runoff. In areas of high rainfall, diversion ditches must be built behind each terrace to permit adequate drainage. Terracing is widely used in China, Japan, the Philippines, the Mediterranean countries, and the Andes in South America.

In **strip cropping,** a wide row of one crop, such as corn or soybeans, is planted; the next row is planted with a crop such as alfalfa, which forms a complete cover and thus reduces soil erosion. The alternating rows of ground cover also reduce water runoff, help prevent the spread of pests and plant diseases from one row to another, and help restore soil fertility, especially when nitrogen-rich legumes such as soybeans are planted in some of the rows. On sloping land, strip cropping can reduce soil losses by up to 75% when combined with either terracing or contour farming (Figure 10-12).

Gully Reclamation and Shelterbelts

On sloping land not covered by vegetation, deep gullies can be created quickly by water runoff (Figure 10-9). Thus, **gully reclamation** is an important form of soil conservation. Small gullies can be seeded with quick-growing plants such as oats, barley, and wheat to reduce erosion. For severe gullies small dams can be built to collect silt and gradually fill in the channels. The soil can then be stabilized by planting rapidly growing shrubs, vines, and trees and providing channels to divert water away from the gully.

Erosion caused by exposure of cultivated lands to high winds can be reduced by **shelterbelts,** or **windbreaks**—long rows of trees planted in a north-to-south direction to partially block wind flow over cropland (Figure 10-14). They are especially effective if land not under cultivation is kept covered with vegetation.

Land Class	Characteristics	Primary Uses	Secondary Uses	Conservation Measures
Land Suitable for Cultivation				
I	Excellent, flat, well-drained land	Agriculture	Recreation Wildlife Pasture	None
II	Good land, has minor limitations such as slight slope, sandy soil, or poor drainage	Agriculture Pasture	Recreation Wildlife	Strip cropping Contour farming
III	Moderately good land with important limitations of soil, slope, or drainage	Agriculture Pasture Watershed	Recreation Wildlife Urban industry	Contour farming Strip cropping Waterways Terraces
IV	Fair land, severe limitations of soil, slope, or drainage	Pasture Orchards Limited agriculture Urban industry	Pasture Wildlife	Farming on a limited basis Contour farming Strip cropping Waterways Terraces
Land Not Suitable for Cultivation				
V	Use for grazing and forestry slightly limited by rockiness; shallow soil, wetness, or slope prevents farming	Grazing Forestry Watershed	Recreation Wildlife	No special precautions if properly grazed or logged; must not be plowed
VI	Moderate limitations for grazing and forestry	Grazing Forestry Watershed Urban industry	Recreation Wildlife	Grazing or logging should be limited at times
VII	Severe limitations for grazing and forestry	Grazing Forestry Watershed Recreation-Aesthetics Wildlife Urban industry		Careful management required when used for grazing or logging
VIII	Unsuitable for grazing and forestry because of steep slope, shallow soil, lack of water, too much water	Recreation-Aesthetics Watershed Wildlife Urban industry		Not to be used for grazing or logging; steep slope and lack of soil present problems

Windbreaks also provide habitats for birds, pest-eating and pollinating insects, and other animals. Unfortunately, many of the windbreaks planted in the upper Great Plains following the Dust Bowl disaster of the 1930s have been destroyed to make way for large irrigation systems and farm machinery.

Appropriate Land Use   To encourage wise land use and reduce soil erosion, the SCS has set up the clas-sification system summarized in Table 10-1 and illustrated in Figure 10-15. Soil type, fertility, slope, drainage, erodibility, and other factors are used to classify a particular land area into one of eight categories of appropriate use. After land has been classified, each community has the responsibility to pass its own land-use and zoning laws to ensure that each parcel of land is used for the purpose to which it is best suited.

An obvious land-use approach to reducing soil erosion is to avoid planting crops on or clearing veg-

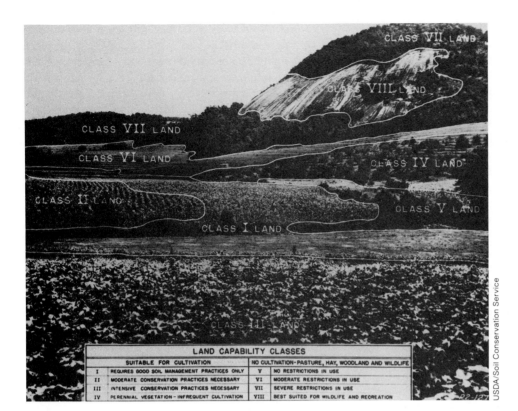

USDA/Soil Conservation Service

Figure 10-15 Classification of land according to capability; see Table 10-1 for description of each class.

LAND CAPABILITY CLASSES

SUITABLE FOR CULTIVATION		NO CULTIVATION - PASTURE, HAY, WOODLAND AND WILDLIFE	
I	REQUIRES GOOD SOIL MANAGEMENT PRACTICES ONLY	V	NO RESTRICTIONS IN USE
II	MODERATE CONSERVATION PRACTICES NECESSARY	VI	MODERATE RESTRICTIONS IN USE
III	INTENSIVE CONSERVATION PRACTICES NECESSARY	VII	SEVERE RESTRICTIONS IN USE
IV	PERENNIAL VEGETATION - INFREQUENT CULTIVATION	VIII	BEST SUITED FOR WILDLIFE AND RECREATION

etation from marginal land (classes V through VIII in Table 10-1), which, because of slope, soil structure, high winds, periodic drought, or other factors, is subject to high rates of erosion.

Maintaining Soil Fertility Organic fertilizers and commercial inorganic fertilizers can be applied to soil to restore and maintain plant nutrients lost from the soil by erosion, leaching, and crop harvesting and to increase crop yields. Three major types of **organic fertilizer** are animal manure, green manure, and compost. **Animal manure** includes the dung and urine of cattle, horses, poultry, and other farm animals. Application of animal manure improves soil structure, increases organic nitrogen content, and stimulates the growth and reproduction of soil bacteria and fungi. It is particularly useful on crops such as corn, cotton, potatoes, cabbage, and tobacco.

Despite its usefulness, the use of animal manure in the United States has decreased. One reason is that separate farms for growing crops and animals (feedlots) have replaced most of the mixed animal- and crop-farming operations in the United States. Although large amounts of animal manure are available at feedlots (normally located near urban areas), it usually costs too much to collect and transport it to distant rural crop-growing areas. In addition, tractors and other forms of motorized farm machinery have largely replaced horses and other draft animals that naturally added manure to the soil.

Green manure is fresh or still-growing green vegetation plowed into the soil to increase the organic matter and humus available to the next crop. It may consist of weeds in an uncultivated field, grasses and clover in a field previously used for pasture, or legumes such as alfalfa or soybeans grown for use as fertilizer to build up soil nitrogen. The effects of green manure on the soil are similar to those of animal manure. **Compost** is a rich natural fertilizer; farmers produce it by piling up alternating layers of carbohydrate-rich plant wastes (such as cuttings and leaves), animal manure, and topsoil, providing a home for microorganisms that aid the decomposition of the plant and animal manure layers.

Today the fertility of most soils, especially in the United States and other industrialized countries, is partially restored and maintained by the application of **commercial inorganic fertilizers.** The most common plant nutrients in these products are nitrogen (as nitrate), phosphorus (as phosphate), and potassium.

The nutrients are designated by numbers; for example, a 6-12-12 fertilizer contains 6% nitrogen, 12% phosphorus, and 12% potassium. Other plant nutrients may also be present. Soil and harvested crops can be chemically analyzed to determine the exact mix of nutrients that should be added. Use of inorganic commercial fertilizers throughout the world increased ninefold between 1950 and 1985 because they are a concentrated source of nutrients that can be easily transported, stored, and applied. By 1985 the additional food they helped produce fed about one out of every three persons in the world.

However, commercial inorganic fertilizers do have disadvantages. They do not add any humus to the soil. If not supplemented by organic fertilizers, continued use of inorganic fertilizers causes the soil to become compacted and less suitable for crop growth and reduces its natural ability to produce nitrogen in forms usable by plants. Inorganic fertilizers also reduce the oxygen content of soil by altering its porosity, so that any added fertilizer is not taken up as efficiently. In addition, most commercial fertilizers do not contain many of the nutrients needed in trace amounts by plants.

Water pollution is another problem related to extensive use of commercial inorganic fertilizers, especially on sloped land near rivers, streams, and lakes. Some of the plant nutrients in inorganic fertilizers are washed by runoff into nearby bodies of water where they can cause excessive growth of algae. Rainwater seeping through soil can leach plant nutrients such as the nitrates in commercial fertilizers into groundwater supplies, where excessive levels of nitrate ions can make drinking water toxic, especially for infants.

A third method for preventing depletion of soil nutrients is **crop rotation.** Crops such as corn, tobacco, and cotton remove large amounts of nutrients (especially nitrogen) from the soil and can deplete the topsoil of nutrients if planted on the same land several years in a row. Through crop rotation, farmers reduce nutrient depletion by planting areas or strips with corn, tobacco, and cotton one year and planting the same areas the next year with legumes, which add nitrogen to the soil, or other crops such as oats, barley, and rye. This method improves soil fertility, reduces erosion by covering land, and reduces pest infestation and plant diseases.

Achieving More Effective U.S. Soil Conservation
Farmers are faced with increased costs for machinery, fuel, fertilizer, seed, pesticides, and interest on loans. These costs, coupled with relatively low crop prices and profit margins, mean that most farmers feel they cannot afford to spend much money, if any, on preventing soil erosion and nutrient depletion. In addition, many do not consider erosion a serious problem because fertilizers and high-yield seeds have increased crop yields, temporarily compensating for the overall loss of natural soil fertility through prolonged erosion.

Government soil conservation programs are available on a voluntary basis, but they often involve restrictions and bureaucratic red tape many farmers don't want to contend with. In addition, farmers who do participate in these programs use about 80% of the funds to combat soil erosion on slightly eroding lands in active production, rather than on highly eroding lands they are not planting. As a result, only about 20% of federally available soil conservation funds are used to reduce erosion on highly erodible marginal cropland, which produces 86% of the country's soil erosion.

In a program enacted in 1985, the federal government pays farmers not to plant crops on highly erodible and marginally productive land. Several other proposals have been made for developing a more effective soil conservation program for U.S. croplands: Nationwide zoning regulations could be enacted to prohibit highly erodible land from being used for cultivation or other activities that would increase erosion. Farmers who use soil conservation measures could be given special tax breaks. Federal soil conservation funds should be concentrated on the most highly erodible land. Only farmers who have federally inspected and approved soil conservation programs in effect should be eligible for government crop insurance, loans, price support payments, or other forms of federal farm aid. A small tax could be placed on all food to support soil conservation.

MDCs could also help establish and finance soil conservation programs for LDCs. With the assistance of the Swedish International Development Authority, Kenya has developed a 25-year national soil management program. By 1984 this program had trained 1,300 agricultural officers and 3,500 technical assistants in soil and water management, had constructed terraces on 100,000 farms, and had brought significant soil conservation improvements to about 35,000 farms. To be successful, such programs must have committed local and national government leadership, community participation, and funding and technical support from MDCs or international agencies supported by MDCs.

Civilization can survive the exhaustion of oil reserves, but not continuing wholesale loss of topsoil.
Lester R. Brown

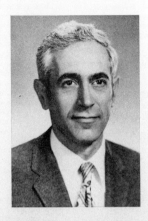

David Pimentel

David Pimentel is professor of insect ecology and agricultural sciences in the College of Agriculture and Life Sciences at Cornell University. He has chaired the Board on Environmental Studies in the National Academy of Sciences (1979–1981); the Panel on Soil and Land Degradation, Office of Technology Assessment (1978–1981); and the Biomass Panel, U.S. Department of Energy (1976–1985). He has published over 300 scientific papers and 9 books on environmental topics including land degradation, agricultural pollution and energy use, biomass energy, and pesticides. He was one of the first ecologists to employ an interdisciplinary, holistic approach in investigating complex environmental problems.

At a time when the world's human population is rapidly expanding and its need for more land to produce food, fiber, and fuelwood is also escalating, valuable land is being degraded through erosion and other means at an alarming rate. Soil degradation is of great concern because soil reformation is extremely slow. Under tropical and temperate agricultural conditions, an average of 500 years (with a range of 220 to 1,000 years) are required for the renewal of 2.5 cm (1 inch)—a renewal rate of about 1 metric ton (t) of topsoil per hectare (ha) of land per year (1t/ha per year). Worldwide annual erosion rates for agricultural land are 18 to 100 times this natural renewal rate.

Erosion rates very in different regions because of topography, rainfall, wind intensity, and the type of agricultural practices used. In China, for example, the average annual soil loss is reported to be more than 40t/ha while the U.S. average is 18t/ha. In states like Iowa and Missouri, however, annual soil erosion averages are greater than 35t/ha. Worldwide degradation of land by erosion and other factors is causing irretrievable loss of an estimated 6 million hectares (15 million acres). In addition, according to the UN Envi-

ronmental Programme, each year crop productivity becomes uneconomic on about 20 million hectares (49 million acres) because soil quality has been severely degraded.

Soil erosion also occurs in forest land but is not as severe as that in the more exposed soil of agricultural land. However, soil erosion in managed forests is a major concern because the soil reformation rate in forests is about two to three times slower than that in agricultural land. To compound this erosion problem, approximately 12 million hectares (30 million acres) of forest are being cleared each year throughout the world. More than half of this is being used to compensate for loss of agricultural land caused by erosion. Average soil erosion per hectare increases when trees are removed and the land is planted with crops.

The status of agriculture and forestry is interrelated in many other ways. Large-scale removal of forests without adequate replanting reduces fuelwood supplies and forces the poor in LDCs to substitute crop residue and manure for fuelwood. When these plant and animal wastes are burned instead of being returned to the land as ground cover and organic fertilizer, erosion is intensified and productivity of the land is decreased. These factors, in turn, increase pressure to convert more forest land into agricultural land—further intensifying soil erosion.

One reason that soil erosion does not receive high priority among many governments and farmers is that it usually occurs at such a slow rate that its cumulative effects may take decades to become apparent. For example, the removal of 1 millimeter (¹⁄₂₅₄ inch) of soil, an amount easily lost during a rain or wind storm, is so small that it goes undetected; but the accumulated soil loss at this rate over a 25-year period would amount to 25 mm (1 inch)—an amount that would take about 500 years to replace by natural processes.

Although reduced soil depth is a serious concern because it is cumulative, other factors associated with erosion also reduce productivity. These are losses of water, organic matter, and soil nutrients. Water is the major limiting factor for all natural and agricultural plants and trees. When some of the vegetation on land is removed, most water is lost to remaining plants because it runs off rapidly and does not penetrate the soil. In addition, soil erosion reduces the water-holding capacity of soil because it removes organic matter and fine soil particles that hold water. When this happens, water infiltration into soil can be reduced as much as 90%.

Organic matter in soil plays an important role in holding water and in decreasing removal of plant nutrients. Thus, it is not surprising that a 50% reduction of soil organic matter on a plot of land has been found to reduce corn yields as much as 25%. When soil erodes, there is also a loss of vital plant nutrients such as nitrogen, phosphorus, potassium, and calcium. With U.S. annual cropland erosion rates of about 18t/ha, estimates are that about half of the 45 million metric tons (49.5 million tons) of commercial fertilizers that are applied annually are replacing soil nutrients lost by erosion. This use of fertilizers substantially adds to the cost of crop production.

Some analysts who are unaware of the numerous and complex effects of soil erosion have falsely concluded that the damages are relatively minor. For example, when economists and modelers assess the effects of erosion based only on reduced average soil depth, they report that an average soil loss in the United States of 18t/ha per year causes an annual reduction in crop productivity of only 0.1% to 0.5%. However, based on an evaluation of all the ecological effects caused by erosion, including a reduction in soil depth, reduced water availability for crops, and reduction in soil organic matter and nutrients, agronomists and ecologists report a 15% to 30% reduction in crop productivity—a key factor in increased levels of costly fertilizer and declining yields on some land despite high levels of fertilization. Because fertilizers are not a substitute for fertile soil, they can only be applied up to certain levels before yields begin to decline.

Reduced agricultural productivity is only one of the effects and costs of soil erosion. In the United States, water runoff is responsible for transporting about 3 billion metric tons (3.3 billion tons) of sediment each year to waterways in the 48 contiguous states. About 60% of these sediments come from agricultural lands. Estimates show that off-site damages to U.S. water storage capacity, wildlife, and navigable waterways cost an estimated $6 billion each year. Dredging sediments from U.S. rivers, harbors, and reservoirs alone costs about $570 million each year. About 25% of new water storage capacity in U.S. reservoirs is built solely to compensate for sediment buildup. When soil sediments that include pesticides and other agricultural chemicals are carried into rivers, lakes, and reservoirs, fish production is adversely affected. These contaminated sediments interfere with fish spawning, increase predation on fish, and destroy fisheries in estuarine and coastal areas.

Increased erosion and water runoff on mountain slopes flood agricultural land in the valleys below, further decreasing agricultural productivity. Eroded land also does not hold water well, further decreasing crop productivity. This effect is magnified in the 80 countries, accounting for nearly 40% of the world's population, that experience frequent droughts. The rapid growth in the world's population, accompanied by the need for more crops and a projected doubling of water needs in the next 20 years, will only intensify water shortages, particularly if soil erosion is not contained.

Thus, soil erosion is one of the world's critical problems and if not slowed will seriously reduce agricultural and forestry production and degrade the quality of aquatic ecosystems. Solutions are not particularly difficult but are often not implemented because erosion occurs so gradually that we fail to acknowledge its cumulative impact until damage is irreversible; many farmers have also been conditioned to believe that losses in soil fertility can be remedied by applying increasingly higher levels of fertilizer.

The principal method of controlling soil erosion and its accompanying runoff of sediment is to maintain adequate vegetative coverage on soils by various methods discussed in Section 10-5. These methods are also cost-effective in preventing erosion, especially when off-site costs of erosion are included. Scientists, policymakers, and agriculturists need to work together to implement soil and water conservation practices before world soils lose most of their productivity.

Guest Essay Discussion

1. Some cornucopians contend that average soil erosion rates in the United States and the world are low and that this problem has been overblown by environmentalists and can easily be solved by improved agricultural technology such as no-till cultivation and increased fertilizer use. Do you agree or disagree with this position? Explain.

2. What specific things do you believe that elected officials should do to decrease soil erosion and the resulting sediment water pollution in the United States?

3. What specific things can individual citizens, homeowners, and home gardeners do to reduce their contribution to soil erosion?

CHAPTER SUMMARY

Soil is a complex mixture of tiny particles of inorganic materials (mostly clay, silt, and sand) and larger pieces of rock, decaying organic matter (humus), water, air, and living organisms (mostly bacteria and other decomposers). These components are arranged in a series of layers, or *horizons*, with a distinct thickness, color, texture, and composition that varies with different types of soils found in grasslands, forests, and deserts.

Most soils are formed from the breakdown, or *weathering*, of underlying bedrock (parent material), but some develop from sediments deposited on bedrock by wind, water, volcanoes, or melting glaciers. A particular soil's *profile*, or series of layers, results from the interaction of parent material, climate, plants and animals, topography, and time.

The proportion of very fine clay particles, fine silt particles, and coarse sand particles determines a soil's *porosity*, the number of pore spaces it has and the relative distances between these spaces. Soils with a high sand content have a high porosity, feel gritty, and have little clumping together of their particles. They drain rapidly and don't hold much water for use by plants. Soils with a high clay content have a low porosity and form large clumps when wet. They have low water infiltration and poor aeration and drainage. Loam soils, with almost equal amounts of sand and silt and somewhat less clay, are the best for growing most crops. They have a medium porosity and hold enough water and air to support good crop growth. The *acidity or alkalinity of a soil* (usually indicated by its *pH*) is also an important factor determining which types of crops it can support. The acidity or alkalinity of soils can be varied by adding various chemicals.

Most of the world's crops are grown on grassland soils (known as *mollisols*) and on soils (known as *alfisols*) exposed when deciduous forests are cleared. Most of the soils that underlie temperate coniferous forests (*spodosols*), tropical rain forests (*oxisols*), and desert (*aridisols*) have too few nutrients for growing most crops unless they are fortified with large inputs of fertilizer.

Soil erosion occurs primarily when rain and wind move soil components, especially topsoil, from one place to another. Throughout much of the world the rate at which soil is being eroded as a result of farming, logging, mining, construction, and overgrazing by livestock greatly exceeds the natural rate of soil regeneration. Thus, in much of the world, including the United States, potentially renewable topsoil is being converted into a nonrenewable resource that is being depleted at alarming rates. In addition to the physical loss of topsoil and the depletion of nutrients from remaining soil, erosion produces massive amounts of sediments that clog navigable waterways, reduce the capacity of reservoirs, and harm fish and other forms of aquatic life.

Soil conservation involves using various management methods to reduce soil erosion—that is, to hold the soil in place—and to prevent depletion of soil nutrients. Methods used to reduce erosion include conservation tillage (where the topsoil is disturbed little if any during planting), contour farming, terracing, strip cropping, gully reclamation, shelterbelts or windbreaks, classifying and using land for appropriate purposes, and not planting marginal land that is subject to higher than normal erosion rates. Replanting cleared land with rapid-growing vegetation is important not only for cropland but for all disturbed land.

Preventing depletion of soil nutrients and restoring nutrients already lost by erosion, leaching, and excessive harvesting can be accomplished by application of organic fertilizers (animal and crop wastes) and commercial inorganic fertilizers and by crop rotation. These methods, however, should be used along with methods to reduce unnecessary topsoil losses.

Preserving soil—the irreplaceable base that provides us with food, fiber, fuelwood, and numerous other materials—must become one of the major priorities for policymakers and ordinary citizens in rich and poor countries.

DISCUSSION TOPICS

1. Why should everyone, not just farmers, be concerned with soil conservation?

2. Explain how a plant can have ample supplies of nitrogen, phosphorus, potassium, and other essential nutrients and still have stunted growth.

3. List the following soils in order of increasing porosity to water: loam, clay, sand, and sandy loam.

4. What are the key properties of a soil that is good for growing most crops?

5. If soil pH is too low for growing a particular crop, what can be done to raise the pH? If the soil pH is too high, what can be done to lower it?

6. Describe briefly the Dust Bowl phenomenon of the 1930s and explain how and where it could happen again. How would you prevent a recurrence?

7. Distinguish among contour farming, terracing, strip cropping, and no-tillage farming, and explain how each can reduce soil erosion.

8. What is crop rotation and how can it be used to help restore soil fertility?

9. Visit rural or relatively undeveloped areas near your campus and classify the lands according to the system shown in Figure 10-15 and Table 10-1. Look for examples of land being used for purposes to which it is not best suited.

10. What are the major advantages and disadvantages of using commercial inorganic fertilizers to help restore and maintain soil fertility? Why should organic fertilizers also be used on land treated with inorganic fertilizers?

11

Water Resources

GENERAL OBJECTIVES

1. How is the existence of life on earth related to the unique physical properties of water?

2. How much usable fresh water is available for human use and how much of this supply are we using?

3. What are the major water resource problems in the world and in the United States?

4. How can the supply of usable fresh water in water-short areas of the world be increased?

5. How can water waste be reduced?

If there is magic on this planet, it is in water.
Loren Eisley

The hydrosphere—the envelope of water that covers about 71% of the earth's surface—is what most clearly distinguishes the earth from other planets. This precious film of water—about 97% salt water and the remainder fresh—helps maintain the earth's climate and dilutes environmental pollutants. Essential to all life, water constitutes from 50% to 97% of the weight of all plants and animals and about 70% of your body. Water is also essential to agriculture, manufacturing, transportation, and countless other human activities.

Because of differences in average annual precipitation, some areas of the world have too little fresh water and others too much. With varying degrees of success, humans have corrected these imbalances by capturing fresh water in reservoirs behind dams, transferring fresh water in rivers and streams from one area to another, tapping underground supplies, and attempting to reduce water use, waste, and contamination.

11-1 WATER'S UNIQUE PHYSICAL PROPERTIES

The physical properties of water are unique compared to those of other molecules, and it is these distinctive properties that make water indispensable to life. Water is the only substance that exists in all three physical states under the climatic conditions of the earth's surface. It is a gas above its normal boiling point of 100°C (212°F), a solid below its freezing or melting point of 0°C (32°F), and a liquid between 0°C and 100°C (32°F and 212°F)—the temperature range required for most life on earth to exist. Without its high boiling and melting points, most of the earth's water would be in the gaseous state and the earth would have no oceans, lakes, rivers, plants, and animals.

Water's very high heat of vaporization means that water molecules absorb large quantities of heat when they are evaporated by solar energy from bodies of water. It also means that large amounts of heat are released when atmospheric water vapor condenses and falls back to the earth as precipitation. This ability to store and release large amounts of heat during physical changes is a major factor in distributing heat throughout the world. This property also means that evaporation of water is an effective cooling process for plants and animals—explaining why you feel cooler when perspiration evaporates from your skin.

Liquid water's extremely high heat capacity—its ability to store large amounts of heat without a large temperature change—prevents large bodies of water from warming or cooling rapidly. This slow cooling and warming helps protect living things from the shock of abrupt temperature changes and helps keep the earth's climate moderate. It also makes water an effective coolant for automobile engines, power plants, and other heat-producing industrial processes.

Liquid water is a superior solvent, able to dissolve large amounts of a variety of compounds. Thus, it carries dissolved nutrients throughout the tissues of plants and animals and flushes waste products out of the tissues. It is a good all-purpose cleanser, removes water-soluble wastes of civilization, and dilutes these wastes to acceptable levels if the water system is not overloaded. But this ability of water to act as a solvent also means that it is easily polluted.

Extremely high surface tension (the force that causes the surface of a liquid to contract) and wetting ability (the capability to coat a solid) are responsible for liquid water's capillarity—the ability to rise from tiny pores in the soil into thin, hollow tubes, called capillaries, in the stems of plants. These properties along with water's solvent ability allow plants to receive nutrients from the soil, thus supporting the growth of plants and the animals that feed upon them.

Liquid water, unlike most substances, expands rather than contracts when it freezes; consequently, ice has a lower density (mass per unit of volume) than liquid water. Thus, ice floats on water, and bodies of water freeze from the top down instead of from the bottom up. Without this property, lakes and rivers in cold climates would freeze solid and most known forms of aquatic life would not exist. Because water expands on freezing, it can also break pipes, crack engine blocks (this is why we use antifreeze), and fracture streets and rocks.

11-2 SUPPLY, RENEWAL, AND USE OF WATER RESOURCES

Worldwide Supply and Renewal The world's fixed supply of water in all forms (vapor, liquid, and solid) is enormous. If we could distribute it equally, there would be enough to provide every person on earth with 292 trillion liters (77 trillion gallons). However, only about 0.003% of the world's water supply is available as fresh water for human use, and this supply is unevenly distributed.

About 97% of the earth's total supply of water is found in the oceans and is too salty for drinking, growing crops, and most industrial purposes except cooling. The remaining 3% is fresh water, but over three-fourths of it is unavailable for use by plants, humans, and other animals because it lies too far under the earth's surface or is locked up in glaciers, polar ice caps, atmosphere, and soil. This leaves 0.5% of the earth's water available as fresh water in rivers, lakes, and economically recoverable underground deposits (groundwater) to a depth of 1,000 meters (1.6 miles). However, when we subtract the portion of this water that is highly polluted or too difficult and expensive to tap, the remaining supply amounts to about 0.003% of the world's water. To put this in measurements that we can comprehend, if the world's water supply were only 100 liters (26 gallons), then our usable supply of fresh water would be only about 0.003 liter (one-half teaspoon) as illustrated in Figure 11-1.

The tiny fraction of usable fresh water still amounts to an average of 879,000 liters (232,000 gallons) for each person on earth. The supply is continually collected, purified, and distributed in the natural hydrologic (water) cycle (Figure 4-12, p. 79). This natural purification process works as long as we don't pollute water faster than it is replenished or add chemicals that cannot be broken down by bacterial action.

Precipitation reaching the earth's surface is returned to the atmosphere through evaporation from land and bodies of water and through evapotranspiration from plant tissue. It infiltrates and percolates downward into the soil (soil moisture) and into deeper underground deposits (groundwater), or runs off rapidly into streams, rivers, lakes, and reservoirs (surface-water runoff) (Figure 11-2). The fresh water we use for drinking, industry, domestic use, irrigating crops, raising livestock, and other human activities comes from two sources—groundwater and surface-water runoff (Figure 11-3).

Surface-Water Runoff Precipitation that does not infiltrate into the ground or return to the atmosphere is known as **surface water** and becomes **runoff**—water that flows into nearby streams, rivers, lakes, wetlands, and reservoirs. The land area that delivers runoff, sediment, and water-soluble substances to a major river and its tributaries is called a **drainage basin** or **watershed.**

Surface water can be withdrawn from streams, rivers, lakes, and reservoirs for human activities, but only part of the total annual runoff is available for use. Some flows in rivers to the sea too rapidly to be cap-

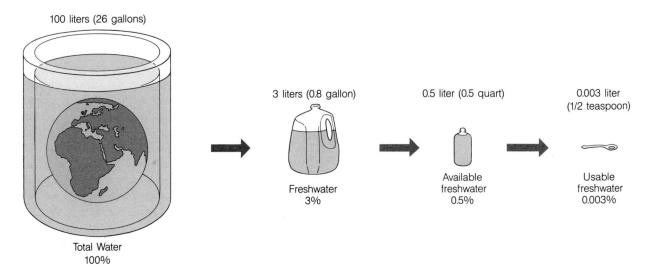

100 liters (26 gallons)

3 liters (0.8 gallon)

0.5 liter (0.5 quart)

0.003 liter
(1/2 teaspoon)

Total Water
100%

Freshwater
3%

Available
freshwater
0.5%

Usable
freshwater
0.003%

Figure 11-1 Only a tiny fraction of the world's water supply is available as fresh water for human use.

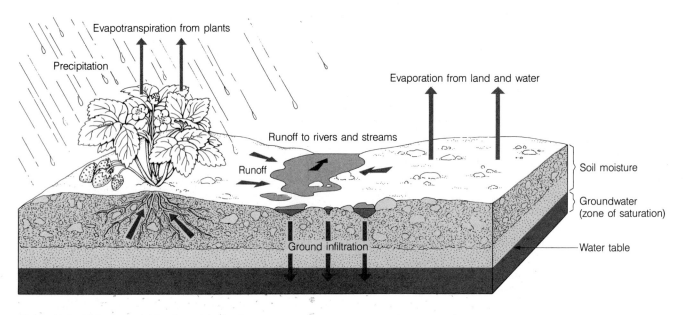

Evapotranspiration from plants

Precipitation

Evaporation from land and water

Runoff to rivers and streams

Runoff

Soil moisture

Groundwater
(zone of saturation)

Ground infiltration

Water table

Figure 11-2 Major routes of local precipitation.

tured, and some must be left in streams for wildlife and to supply downstream areas. In some years the amount of runoff is reduced by drought.

Because of widespread differences in average annual precipitation and evaporation rates, the available supply of usable surface-water runoff varies widely throughout the world. Runoff also varies in quality.

Groundwater Some precipitation seeps or infiltrates into the ground. Some of this infiltrating water accumulates as soil moisture and partially fills pores between soil particles and rocks within the upper soil and rock layers of the earth's crust (Figure 11-2). Most of this water is eventually lost to the atmosphere by direct evaporation or evapotranspiration from leaves after it has been transported into the above-ground portions of plants and from soil.

Under the influence of gravity, some infiltrating water slowly percolates through porous materials deeper into the earth and completely saturates pores and cracks in spongelike, or permeable, layers of sand,

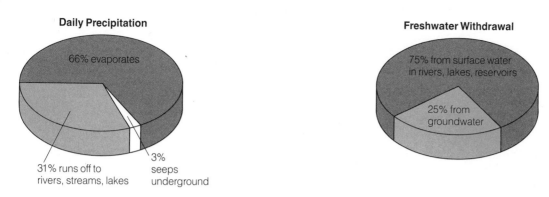

Daily Precipitation

66% evaporates

31% runs off to rivers, streams, lakes

3% seeps underground

Freshwater Withdrawal

75% from surface water in rivers, lakes, reservoirs

25% from groundwater

Figure 11-3 Fate of average daily precipitation and sources of fresh water withdrawn for human activities in the United States.

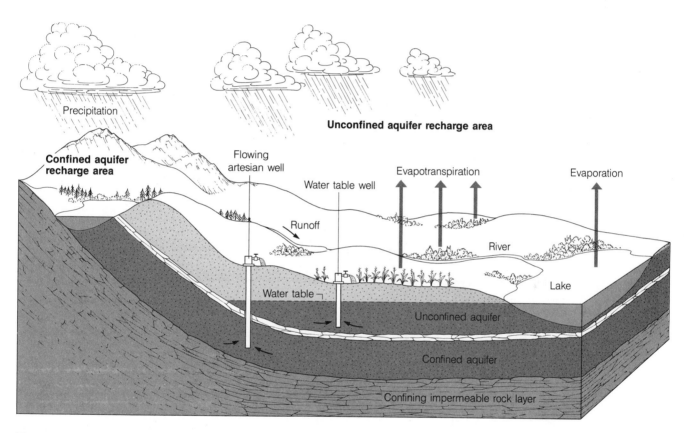

Precipitation

Unconfined aquifer recharge area

Confined aquifer recharge area

Flowing artesian well

Water table well

Evapotranspiration

Evaporation

Runoff

River

Lake

Water table

Unconfined aquifer

Confined aquifer

Confining impermeable rock layer

Figure 11-4 The groundwater system.

gravel, and porous rock such as sandstone. These layers of the earth's crust are termed **aquifers,** and the water in them is called **groundwater** (Figure 11-4).

Aquifers are recharged or replenished naturally by precipitation, which percolates downward through soil and rock in what is called a **recharge area.** The recharge process is usually slow compared to the rapid replenishment of surface water supplies. If the withdrawal rate of an aquifer exceeds its recharge rate, the aquifer is converted from a slowly renewable resource to a nonrenewable resource on a human time scale.

There are two types of aquifers: confined and unconfined. An **unconfined** or **water table aquifer** forms when groundwater collects above a layer of relatively impermeable rock or compacted clay. The top of the water-saturated portion of an unconfined aquifer is called the **water table** (Figures 11-2 and 11-4). Thus, groundwater is that part of underground water below the water table, and soil moisture is that part of underground water above the water table. Shallow, unconfined aquifers are **recharged** by water percolating downward from soils and materials directly above

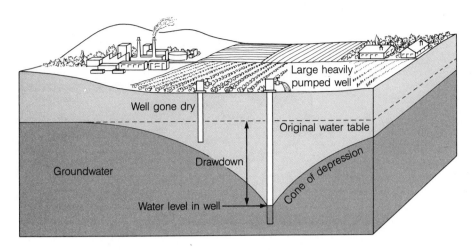

Figure 11-5 Drawdown of water table and cone of depression produced when wells remove groundwater faster than it is recharged.

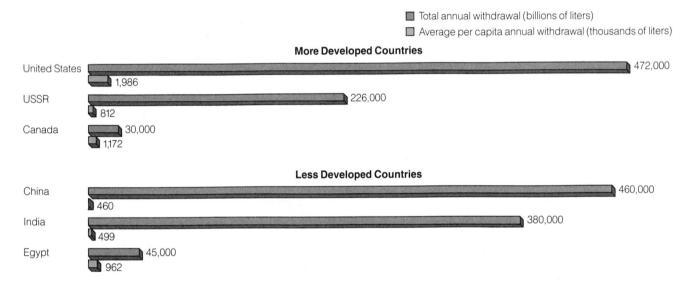

◼ Total annual withdrawal (billions of liters)
◻ Average per capita annual withdrawal (thousands of liters)

More Developed Countries

United States — 472,000
1,986

USSR — 226,000
812

Canada — 30,000
1,172

Less Developed Countries

China — 460,000
460

India — 380,000
499

Egypt — 45,000
962

Figure 11-6 Average total and per capita water withdrawal in selected countries in 1984. (Data from Worldwatch Institute and World Resources Institute)

the aquifer. To obtain water from an unconfined aquifer, a water table well must be drilled below the water table and into the confined aquifer. Because this water is under atmospheric pressure, a pump must be used to bring it to the surface. The elevation of the water table in a particular area rises during prolonged wet periods and falls during prolonged drought. The water table can also fall when water is pumped out by wells faster than the natural rate of recharge, creating a vacated volume known as a cone of depression (Figure 11-5).

A **confined** or **Artesian aquifer** forms when groundwater is sandwiched between two layers of relatively impermeable rock, such as clay or shale (Figure 11-4). This type of aquifer is completely saturated with water under a pressure greater than that of the atmosphere. In some cases the pressure is so great that when a well is drilled into the confined aquifer, water is pushed to the surface without the use of a pump. Such a well is called a flowing Artesian well. With other confined-aquifer wells, known as nonflowing Artesian wells, pumps must be used because pressure is insufficient to force the water to the surface. Confined aquifers cannot be recharged from directly above them; they receive water from areas without overlying impermeable rock layers. Thus, recharge areas for confined aquifers can be hundreds of kilometers away from wells where water is withdrawn, and the rate of

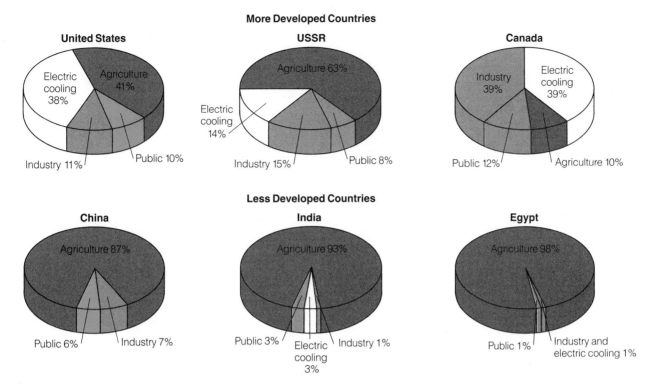

Figure 11-7 Uses of water in selected countries. (Data from Worldwatch Institute and World Resources Institute)

natural recharge is not governed by local precipitation at the point of withdrawal as it is for unconfined aquifers.

World and U.S. Water Use   The two common measures of water use are **withdrawal** and **consumption.** Water is withdrawn when it is taken from a surface or ground source and conveyed to the place of use. Water is consumed when, after withdrawal, it is no longer available for reuse in the local area because of evaporation, storage in the living matter of plants and animals, contamination, and seepage into the ground.

Between 1940 and 1984, total water withdrawals in the world increased fourfold and average withdrawal per person doubled. Total and average per capita annual withdrawals vary considerably among various MDCs and LDCs (Figure 11-6). Almost three-fourths of the water withdrawn each year throughout the world is used for irrigation. The remainder is used for industrial processing, cooling electric power plants, and in homes and businesses (public use). However, uses of withdrawn water vary widely from one country to another depending on the relative amounts of agricultural and industrial production (Figure 11-7).

Worldwide, up to 90% of all water withdrawn is returned to rivers and lakes for reuse and is not consumed. However, about 75% of the water supplied for irrigation is consumed and lost for reuse as surface water in the area from which it is withdrawn. Thus, irrigation, which is projected to double between 1975 and 2000, places the greatest demand on the world's water supplies in terms of both withdrawal and consumption.

Total withdrawal and average per capita withdrawal from U.S. surface and groundwater supplies have been increasing rapidly since 1900 and are projected to increase more between 1985 and 2020 (Figure 11-8). Almost 80% of the water withdrawn in the United States is used for cooling electric power plants and for irrigation. In 1985 average withdrawal for each American was 7,400 liters (1,950 gallons) per day, 1,700 liters (450 gallons) of which was consumed. In the West, average per capita withdrawals are almost twice the level in the East, and average per capita consumption is 10 times higher than in the East. About 340 liters (90 gallons) of the average daily withdrawal is used for domestic purposes (cooking, drinking, washing, watering, and flushing). This is about 3 times the average domestic use per person worldwide and 15 to 20 times that of people in LDCs. Appendix 4 lists examples of the amount of water used for various domestic, agricultural, and industrial purposes.

Along with withdrawal, total water consumption in the United States has grown continuously since 1960, with irrigation accounting for 83% of the total water

Figure 11-8 Total and average per capita water withdrawal and consumption in the United States, 1900–2020 (projected). (Data from U.S. Water Resources Council and U.S. Geological Survey)

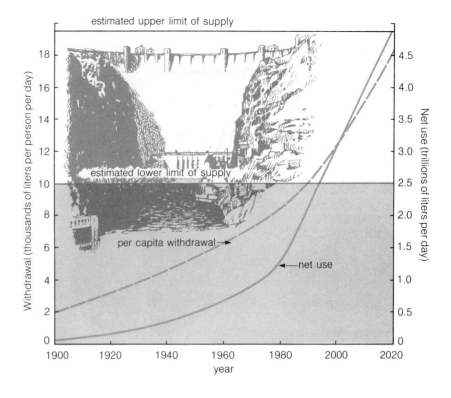

estimated upper limit of supply

estimated lower limit of supply

per capita withdrawal→

←net use

Withdrawal (thousands of liters per person per day)

Net use (trillions of liters per day)

year

Figure 11-9 Percentage of withdrawal consumed for different uses in the United States. (Data from U.S. Geological Survey)

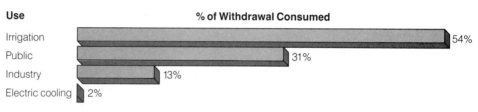

Use   **% of Withdrawal Consumed**

Irrigation — 54%
Public — 31%
Industry — 13%
Electric cooling — 2%

consumed. About 23% of all water withdrawn each year in the U.S. is consumed; the percentage varies with different uses (Figure 11-9).

11-3 WATER RESOURCE PROBLEMS

The Major Problems On a global basis there is plenty of fresh water for everyone. But many parts of the world have serious water supply problems because continents, countries, and areas within countries vary considerably in their average annual precipitation, precipitation patterns, and evaporation rates. There are four basic water supply problems in various parts of the world: too little precipitation, too much precipitation part of the year and too little the rest of the year, adequate precipitation that runs off in major rivers far from agricultural and population centers, and lack of sanitary drinking water. Two related problems arise from the use of water for irrigation: soil buildup

of mineral salts (salinization) and water (waterlogging) to the point where agricultural land becomes unproductive.

Too Little Water At least 80 arid and semiarid countries, accounting for nearly 40% of the world's population, now experience serious periodic droughts and have considerable difficulty in growing enough food to support their populations. Most of these countries are in Asia and Africa (Figure 11-10). During the 1970s, major drought disasters affected an average of 24.4 million people and killed over 23,000 persons a year—a trend continuing in the 1980s. By 1985 more than 154 million people in 21 tropical and subtropical countries in Africa were on the brink of starvation because of the combined effects of rapid population growth, prolonged drought, land misuse, war, and ineffective government policies for water and soil resource management and agricultural development. In many LDCs poor people must spend a good part of their waking

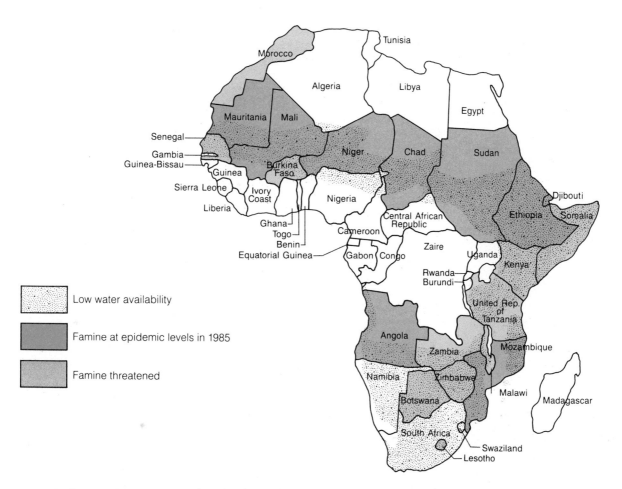

Figure 11-10 African countries suffering from low per capita food production, famine, and poor water availability as a result of rapid population growth, prolonged drought, land misuse, war, and ineffective water and soil resource management. (Data from UN Food and Agricultural Organization)

hours fetching water, often from polluted streams and rivers. To get water, many women and children in LDCs walk 16 to 25 kilometers (10 to 15 miles) a day, carrying back heavy water-filled containers.

Although reduced average annual precipitation usually triggers a drought, rapid population growth and poor land use intensify its effects. In many LDCs large numbers of poor people have no choice but to try to survive on drought-prone land by cutting trees, growing crops at higher, more erosion-prone elevations, cultivating poor soils, and allowing their livestock to overgraze grasslands. The resulting land degradation contributes to the severity of long-term drought by reducing the amount of rainfall absorbed and slowly released by vegetation and soils.

By 2000 only the continent of Asia will be withdrawing more water than is provided by the annual continental stable runoff. But in many areas *within* continents and countries, withdrawal *already* exceeds stable runoff of surface water and groundwater recharge rates.

Too Much Water Other countries get enough precipitation on an annual basis, but receive most of it at one time of the year. In India, for example, 90% of the annual precipitation falls between June and September—the monsoon season. This downpour runs off so rapidly that most of it cannot be captured and used. The massive runoff also leads to periodic flooding.

During the 1970s major flood disasters affected 15.4 million people, killed an average of 4,700 people a year, and caused tens of billions of dollars in property damages—a trend that has continued in the 1980s. Although floods are classified as natural disasters, humans have contributed to the sharp rise in flood deaths and damages since the 1960s. Human activities such as cultivation of marginal lands, deforestation, overgrazing, and mining contribute to the severity of flooding by removing water-absorbing vegetation and soil. Urbanization also increases flooding, even with moderate rainfall, by replacing vegetation with highways, parking lots, shopping centers, office buildings, homes, and numerous other structures. Death tolls

Ever since the Agricultural Revolution, humans have been attracted to low-lying coastal areas and to **floodplains,** flat areas along rivers subject to periodic flooding. Many urban areas and croplands are situated on floodplains and coastlands because these sites are level, have highly fertile topsoil deposited by rivers, are close to supplies of surface water and water transportation routes, and provide recreational opportunities.

The problem is that floodplains and low-lying coastal areas are susceptible to periodic flooding (Figure 11-11). Most of the more than 2,000 U.S. cities (including New Orleans, Louisiana; Phoenix, Arizona; Tallahassee, Florida; and Harrisburg, Pennsylvania) located completely or partially on floodplains suffer flooding on an average of once every 2 to 3 years. Other areas are classified as 18-, 25-, 50-, or 100-year floodplains, according to the average interval between major floods. But this is a statistical average; major floods may occur three times within a month, annually for five consecutive years, or not for several hundred years.

U.S. insurance companies find it too risky to provide homeowners and businesses with flood insurance, but it can be obtained from the federal government at a low cost (about $220 a year for $60,000 of coverage). This has encouraged people to inhabit floodplains and coastal areas and forced taxpayers not living in such areas to subsidize those who do. Since 1925 the U.S. Army Corps of Engineers, the Soil Conservation Service, and the Bureau of Reclamation have spent over $8 billion on flood control projects such as straightening stream channels (channelization), dredging streams, and building dams, reservoirs, levees, and seawalls. Despite these efforts—and because these projects stimulate increased development in flood-prone areas—property damage from floods in the United States has increased from about half a billion dollars a year in the 1960s to an average of about $3 billion a year in the 1980s. Damages are projected to increase to at least $4 billion annually by the year 2000.

There are a number of effective methods for preventing or reducing flood damage: replanting vegetation in disturbed areas to reduce runoff, building ponds in urban areas to retain rainwater and release it slowly to rivers, and diverting rainwater through storm sewers to holding tanks and ponds for use by industry. Even more important is improved management of highly flood-prone areas, especially discouraging their use for certain types of development. Flood area zoning ordinances and building codes should specify the type (for example, requiring first floors to be elevated), density, and location of construction. The government should not provide insurance for construction not meeting these codes. Flood-prone areas should be clearly identified, and sellers of property in these areas should be required to provide prospective buyers with information such as the average flood frequency. Particularly hazardous areas can be purchased by government and converted to parks, parking lots, and other uses less susceptible to flood damage.

Figure 11-11   U.S. land subject to damage from periodic flooding. Numerous local areas subject to periodic flooding are not shown on this generalized map. (Data from U.S. Department of Agriculture)

and damages from flooding have also increased because many poor people in LDCs have little choice but to live on land subject to severe periodic flooding and because many people in LDCs believe that the benefits of living in flood-prone areas outweigh the risks (see Spotlight above).

Water in the Wrong Place   In some countries with sufficient annual precipitation, the largest rivers, carrying much of the runoff, are far from agricultural and population centers where the water is needed. For instance, in Africa, the Zaire River (formerly the Congo) accounts for about 30% of the continent's potentially

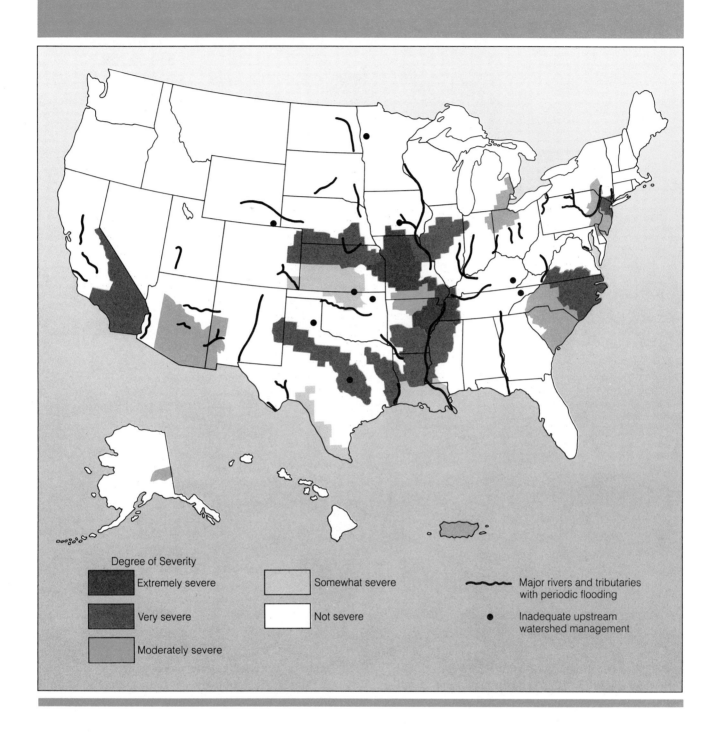

Degree of Severity

■ Extremely severe

▨ Very severe

▨ Moderately severe

☐ Somewhat severe

☐ Not severe

〜 Major rivers and tributaries with periodic flooding

● Inadequate upstream watershed management

usable surface-water supply, but flows largely through rain forest areas far from population centers. Although South America has the largest average annual runoff of any continent, 60% of its runoff flows through the Amazon, the world's largest river, in areas remote from most people.

Lack of Sanitary Drinking Water Although water scarcity, drought, and flooding are serious in some regions, drinking contaminated water is the most common hazard to people in much of the world. In 1980 the World Health Organization (WHO) estimated that in LDCs 70% of the people living in rural areas

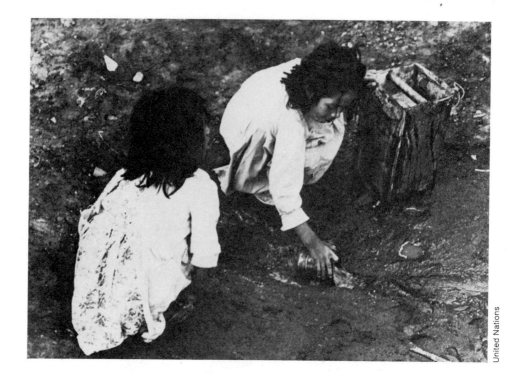

Figure 11-12 About 70% of rural people and 25% of city dwellers in LDCs lack ready access to uncontaminated water. These children in Lima, Peru, are scooping up drinking water from a puddle.

United Nations

Figure 11-13 Salinization and waterlogging of soil on irrigated land without adequate drainage leads to decreased crop yields.

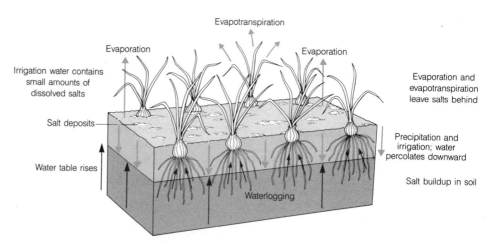

Evapotranspiration

Evaporation

Evaporation

Irrigation water contains small amounts of dissolved salts

Evaporation and evapotranspiration leave salts behind

Salt deposits

Precipitation and irrigation; water percolates downward

Water table rises

Salt buildup in soil

Waterlogging

and 25% of the urban dwellers did not have enough safe water (Figure 11-12). WHO estimated that 25 million people die every year from cholera, dysentery, and other preventable waterborne diseases—an average of 68,500 deaths each day.

The United Nations has proclaimed the 1980s as the International Drinking Water Supply and Sanitation Decade, with the goal of providing all the world's people with clean drinking water and adequate sanitation by 1990. The cost of this ten-year project, which by 1986 was considerably behind its goal, is $300 billion.

Irrigation Problems: Salinization and Waterlogging As irrigation water flows over and through the

ground, it dissolves salts, increasing the salinity of the water. Much of the water in this saline solution is lost to the atmosphere by evaporation, leaving behind high concentrations of salts such as sodium chloride in the topsoil. The accumulation of these salts in soils is called **salinization** (Figure 11-13). Unless the salts are flushed or drained from the soil, their buildup promotes excessive water use, increases capital and operating costs, stunts crop growth, decreases yields, eventually kills crop plants, and makes the land unproductive.

An estimated one-third of the world's irrigated land is now affected by salt buildup, which is particularly serious in Iraq, Pakistan, India, Mexico, Argentina, Mali, North Africa, and the western United States.

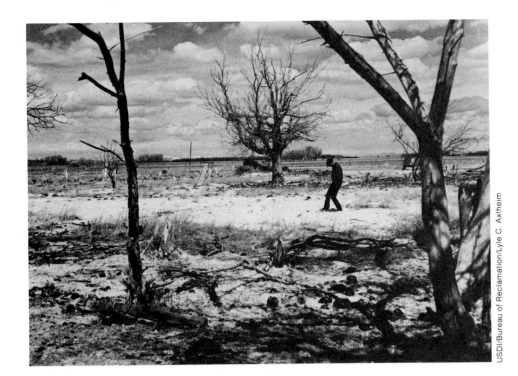

Figure 11-14 Because of poor drainage and severe salinization, white alkaline salts have replaced crops that once grew in heavily irrigated Paradise Valley, Wyoming.

Salinization has already reduced agricultural productivity on 25% to 35% of all irrigated land in 17 U.S. western states (Figure 11-14) and may soon affect half of this land. Worldwide, it is projected that at least 50%, and probably close to 65%, of all presently irrigated land will suffer reduced productivity from excess soil salinity by the year 2000.

One way to reduce salinization is to flush salts out by applying much more irrigation water than is needed for crop growth. But this increases pumping and crop production costs and wastes enormous amounts of precious water in arid and semiarid regions. Pumping groundwater from a central well and applying it by a sprinkler system that pivots around the well maintains downward drainage and is especially effective in preventing salinization (Figure 11-15). However, at least 30% of the water is consumed by evaporation, and eventually groundwater in unconfined aquifers can become too saline for irrigation and other human uses unless expensive drainage systems are installed.

In theory, once topsoil has become heavily salinized, it can be renewed by taking it out of production for two to five years, installing an underground network of perforated drainage pipe, and flushing the soil with large quantities of low-salt water. This scheme, however, is usually prohibitively expensive and only slows the buildup of soil salinity—it does not stop the process. Flushing salts from the soil also increases the salinity of irrigation water delivered to farmers further downstream unless the saline water can be drained into evaporation ponds rather than returned to the river or canal. Drainage ponds, however, can be hazardous to wildlife, especially waterfowl, from the buildup of toxic levels of selenium or other minerals in the water. Another way to reclaim saline soils is to substitute calcium for sodium in the soil minerals by applying large quantities of gypsum (a calcium salt) or by planting a forage grass that promotes the substitution of calcium for sodium.

A problem often accompanying soil salinity is **waterlogging** (Figure 11-13). To keep salts from accumulating and destroying fragile root systems, farmers often apply heavy amounts of irrigation water to wash or leach salts deeper into the soil profile. If drainage isn't provided, water accumulating underground can gradually raise the water table close to the surface, enveloping the roots of plants in saline water. This is a particularly serious problem in areas such as the heavily irrigated San Joaquin Valley in California, where soils contain a clay layer impermeable to water. Worldwide, at least one-tenth of all irrigated land suffers from waterlogging.

The U.S. Situation Overall, the United States has plenty of fresh water, but much of its annual runoff is not in the desired place, occurs at the wrong time, or is contaminated from agricultural and industrial activities. Most of the eastern half of the country usually has ample average annual precipitation, while much of the western half has too little. Many major urban centers in the United States are located in areas that already have inadequate water or are projected to have water shortages by 2000 (Figure 11-16). Because water is such a vital resource, you might find Figure 11-16 useful in evaluating where to live in coming decades.

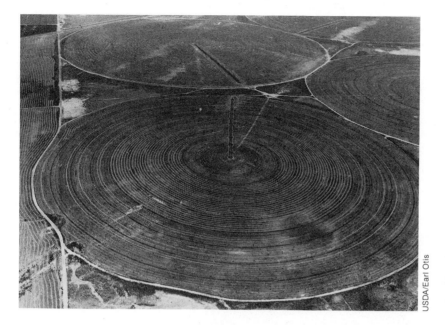

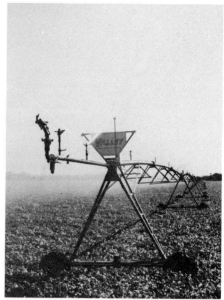

Figure 11-15   Center-pivot irrigation can reduce salinization but wastes 30% of irrigation water.

In the eastern half of the United States, where there is usually no shortage of water, the major problems are flooding, inability to supply enough water to some large urban areas, and increasing pollution of rivers, lakes, and groundwater. For example, 3 million residents of Long Island, New York, must draw all their water from an underground aquifer that is becoming severely contaminated by industrial wastes, leaking septic tanks and landfills, and salt water from the ocean, which is drawn into the aquifer when fresh water is withdrawn.

The major water problem in arid and semiarid areas in the western half of the country is a shortage of runoff due to low average precipitation, high rates of evaporation, prolonged periodic drought, and rapidly declining water tables as farmers and cities deplete groundwater aquifers faster than they are recharged. Present water shortages and conflicts over water supplies will get much worse if more industries and people migrate west as projected and compete with farmers for scarce water.

11-4   WATER RESOURCE MANAGEMENT: INCREASING THE USABLE SUPPLY

Methods for Managing Water Resources   Many areas of the world already face severe water shortages and water resource problems. Within the next 20 to 30 years these problems are expected to intensify and

spread to other areas. Although we can't increase the earth's supply of water, we can manage what we have more effectively to reduce the impact and spread of water resource problems. There are two major approaches to water resource management: Increase the usable supply and decrease unnecessary loss and waste (Table 11-1, p. 222). Most water resource experts believe that any effective plan for water management should rely on a combination of these approaches.

Water problems and available solutions often differ between MDCs and LDCs. LDCs may or may not have enough water, but they rarely have the money needed to develop water storage and distribution systems. Their people must settle where the water is. In MDCs people tend to live where the climate is favorable and then bring in water through sophisticated systems. Some settle in a desert area such as Palm Springs and expect water to be brought to them. Others settle on a floodplain and expect the government to keep flood waters away.

Dams and Reservoirs   Some rainwater and water from melting snow, which would otherwise be lost, can be captured by dams on rivers and stored in large reservoirs behind the dams. This increases the annual supply by collecting fresh surface water during wet periods and storing it for use during dry periods. In addition, dams control the flow of rivers and can reduce the danger of flooding in areas below the dam, provide a controllable supply of water for irrigating land below the dam, generate relatively cheap electricity

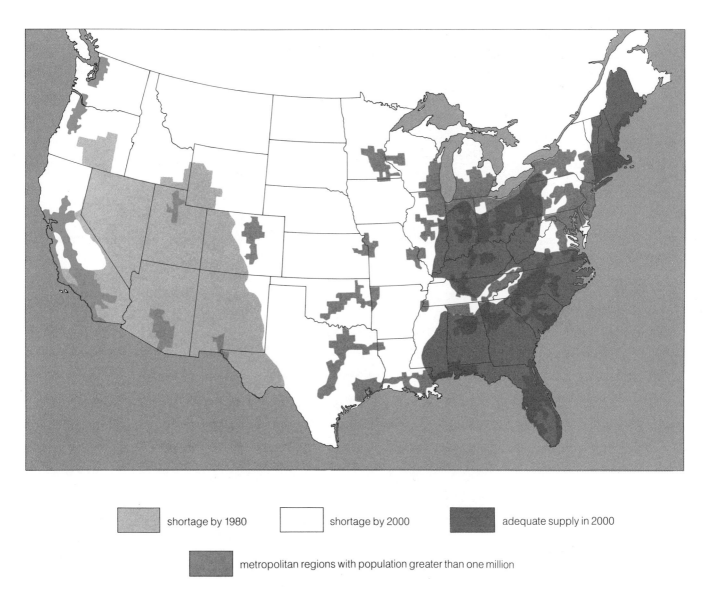

| | shortage by 1980 | | shortage by 2000 | | adequate supply in 2000 |

| | metropolitan regions with population greater than one million |

Figure 11-16 Present and projected water-deficit regions in the United States compared with present metropolitan regions with populations greater than 1 million. (Data from U.S. Water Resources Council and U.S. Geological Survey)

for local and regional residents, and allow people to live on fertile floodplain areas of major rivers below the dam. Large-scale dams also create reservoirs that can be used for swimming, boating, and fishing and thus aid the local economy.

However, the benefits of dams and reservoirs must be weighed against their costs (see Spotlight on p. 223). They are costly to build and reservoirs fill up with silt, becoming useless after 20 to 200 years, depending on local climate and land-use practices. The permanent flooding of land behind dams to form reservoirs displaces people and destroys vast areas of valuable agricultural land, wildlife habitat, white-water rapids, and scenic natural beauty. Construction of the recently completed Tarabela Dam in Pakistan, for example, displaced 85,000 people.

Storage of water behind the dam raises the water table, often waterlogging soil on nearby land, and thereby decreasing crop or forestry productivity. A dam can also decrease rather than increase the available supply of fresh water, especially in semiarid areas, because water that would normally flow in an undammed river evaporates from the reservoir's surface or seeps into the ground below the reservoir. This evaporation also increases the salinity of water by leaving salts behind, decreasing its usefulness for irrigation and intensifying soil salinization.

By interrupting the natural flow of a river, a dam disrupts the migration and spawning of some fish, such as salmon, unless fish ladders (Figure 11-17) are provided. Dams also reduce the flow of nutrients and fresh water into estuaries, decreasing their productiv-

Table 11-1 Major Methods for Managing Water Resources

Increase the Supply	Reduce Unnecessary Loss and Waste
Build dams and reservoirs	Decrease evaporation of irrigation water
Divert water from one region to another	Redesign mining and industrial processes to use less water
Tap more groundwater	Encourage the public to reduce unnecessary water waste and use
Convert salt water to fresh water (desalinization)	Increase the price of water to encourage water conservation
Tow freshwater icebergs from the Antarctic to water-short coastal regions	Purify polluted water for reuse (Chapter 20)
Seed clouds to increase precipitation	

Figure 11-17 Fish ladder on Red Bluff Dam near Sacramento, California, allows king salmon to migrate over dam to upstream spawning grounds on the Colorado River.

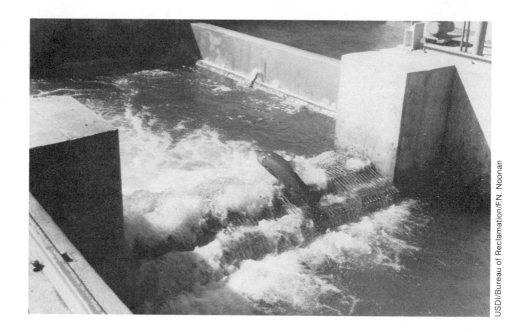

USDI/Bureau of Reclamation/F.N. Noonan

ity. In the opinion of some outdoor sports enthusiasts, a dam replaces more-desirable forms of water recreation (white-water canoeing, kayaking, rafting, stream fishing) with less-desirable, more "artificial" forms (motorboating and sailboating, lake fishing).

Faulty construction, earthquakes, sabotage, or war can cause dams to fail and take a terrible toll in lives and property. In 1972 a dam failure in Buffalo Creek, West Virginia, killed 125 people; another in Rapid City, South Dakota, killed 237 people and caused more than $1 billion in damages. According to a 1986 study by the Federal Emergency Management Agency, the United States has 1,900 unsafe dams in populated areas. The agency reported that the dam safety programs of most states are inadequate because of weak laws and budget cuts.

Water Diversion Projects One of the most common ways to increase a limited supply of fresh water is to transfer water from water-rich areas to water-poor areas. In the United States, major cities such as Los Angeles, Denver, Phoenix, and New York rely on complex, costly diversion systems to supply much of their water.

Two interrelated massive water transfer projects in the United States are the California Water Plan, which transports water from water-rich northern California to arid, heavily populated southern California, and the federally financed $3.9 billion Central Arizona Project, which began pumping water from the Colorado River uphill to Phoenix in 1985 and is projected to deliver water to Tucson by 1991 (Figure 11-18).

For decades northern and southern California have been feuding over this plan. In 1982 voters rejected a

The billion-dollar Aswan Dam on the Nile River in Egypt illustrates what can happen when a large-scale dam and reservoir project is built without adequate consideration of long-term environmental effects and costs. The dam was built in the 1960s to provide flood control and irrigation water for the lower Nile basin and electricity for Cairo and other parts of Egypt. These goals have been partially achieved. Today the dam provides more than 50% of Egypt's electrical power, even though power output is greatly reduced during the winter when water flow is sharply reduced to allow irrigation canals below the dam to be cleaned. The dam saved Egypt's rice and cotton crops during the droughts of 1972 and 1973, and year-round irrigation has increased food production by allowing farmers below the dam to harvest crops three times a year on land that was previously harvested only once a year. Irrigation has also brought about 0.4 million hectares (1 million acres) of desert land under cultivation, although this land has been expensive to reclaim and much of it is of such inferior quality that crop yields are low.

Since operation began in 1964, however, there have been a number of undesirable ecological effects and additional costs not originally anticipated by the Egyptian government. With the dam came an end to the yearly flooding that had fertilized the Nile basin with silt, flushed away mineral salts from the soil and minimized salinization, and swept away snails that can infect humans with schistosomiasis, a debilitating, painful, incurable, and often fatal disease (Section 23-2). As a result, cropland in the Nile basin now has to be treated with commercial fertilizer at a cost of over $100 million a year to make up for plant nutrients once available at no cost. The country's new fertilizer plants use up much of the electrical power produced by the dam. Increased salinization of this once-productive cropland has offset three-fourths of the gain in new, less productive farmland provided by irrigation water from the dam. Since the dam was completed, the incidence of schistosomiasis among farmers wading in irrigation ditches has increased, decreasing agricultural worker productivity and increasing human misery and premature death, often by age 26.

To make matters worse, because of the loss of sediment, the clear river water has eroded its bed and undermined numerous bridges and smaller dams downstream. To remedy this problem, the government proposes to build ten barrier dams between the Aswan Dam and the sea at a cost of $250 million—one-quarter of what the dam cost. In addition, without the Nile's annual discharge of sediment, the sea is eroding the delta and advancing inland, threatening productivity on many acres of rich agricultural land.

Now that nutrient-rich silt no longer reaches the waters at the river's mouth, Egypt's sardine, mackerel, shrimp, and lobster industries have all but disappeared. This has led to losses of approximately 30,000 jobs, millions of dollars annually, and an important source of protein for many Egyptians. Eventually, these losses are supposed to be restored by a new fishing industry based on taking bass, catfish, and carp from the massive reservoir behind the dam. But, so far, fish yields from the reservoir have been low.

The reservoir was expected to be full by 1970 and to have the capacity to meet the water demands of Egypt and the Sudan in a succession of dry years. However, because seepage into the underlying sandstone rock and evaporation have been much higher than projected, the reservoir was only about half full by 1985; most authorities believe that the level may not rise much more in the next 100 years.

Some analysts believe that in the long run the benefits of the Aswan Dam will outweigh its costs. Others consider it an economic, ecological, and hydrological disaster that might have been avoided if the Egyptian government had carried out a proper cost-benefit analysis before construction began. What do you think?

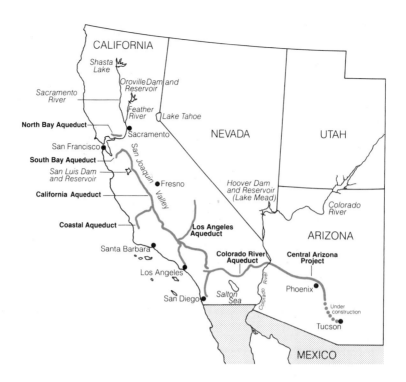

Figure 11-18 California Water Plan and Central Arizona Project for large-scale transfer of water from one area to another.

proposal to expand it by building a $1 billion canal to divert to southern California much of the water that now flows into San Francisco Bay. Opponents of the plan contended that it was a costly and unnecessary boondoggle that would degrade the Sacramento River, threaten fishing, and inhibit the flushing action that helps clean San Francisco Bay of pollutants. They argued that much of the water already sent south is wasted and that if irrigation efficiency was improved by only 10%, abundant water would be available for domestic and industrial uses in southern California. Proponents of the expansion contend that without more water a prolonged drought could bring economic ruin to much of southern California. The issue is far from dead.

Arizona is further complicating California's water problem. When the first portion of the Central Arizona Project was completed in 1985, southern California, especially the arid and booming San Diego region, began losing up to one-fifth of its water supply, which until then had been diverted from the Colorado River by the Colorado River Aqueduct (Figure 11-18). Although Arizona has been legally entitled since 1922 to one-fifth of the Colorado River's annual flow, without the new diversion system, it lacked the ability to use more than half of its share. The surface water diverted from the Colorado will partially replace groundwater overdrafts that have led to falling water tables in many parts of the state during the past 50 years.

The Soviet Union has tentative plans to begin work in the 1990s on building 25 large dams to block the

flow of a number of its rivers that now flow north through Siberia to the Arctic Ocean. This water would then be pumped back over mountains to major population and agricultural centers in the southern portions of the country. This massive project is expected to take 50 years, cost at least $100 billion, flood an area larger than western Europe, and displace tens of thousands of people. Many scientists are concerned that reversing the flow of these rivers would diminish freshwater flow into the Arctic Ocean, increase its salinity, and possibly lead to global climate changes that would affect crop production throughout the world.

Tapping Groundwater   One solution to water supply problems in some areas is heavier reliance on groundwater, which makes up about 95% of the world's supply of fresh water. The quality of groundwater is usually excellent because the porous rock of an aquifer filters the water and removes suspended particles and bacteria. In the United States, total groundwater withdrawals tripled between 1950 and 1985. Two-thirds of this water is used for irrigation, especially in Texas, Arizona, and California. About half of U.S. drinking water (96% in rural areas and 20% in urban areas), 40% of irrigation water, and 23% of all fresh water used is withdrawn from underground aquifers.

This increased use of groundwater gives rise to several problems: **(1) aquifer depletion** or **overdraft** when groundwater is withdrawn faster than it is recharged by precipitation, **(2) subsidence** or sinking of the ground as groundwater is withdrawn, **(3) salt-**

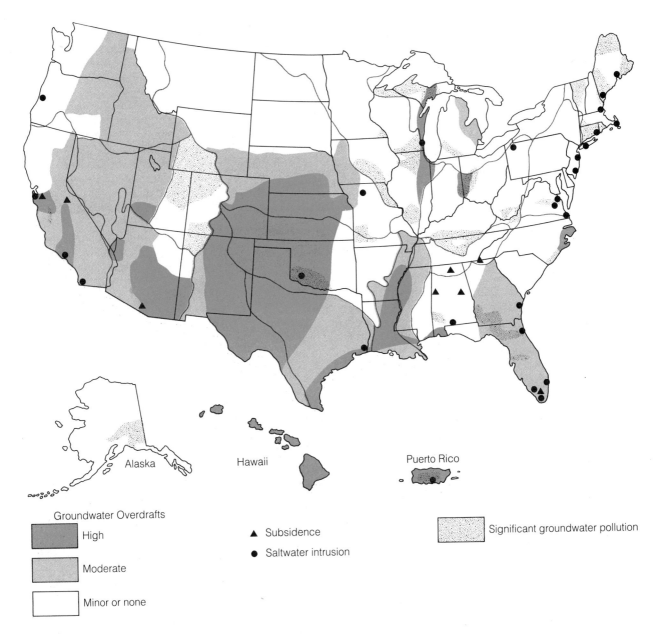

Figure 11-19 Major areas of aquifer depletion, subsidence, saltwater intrusion, and groundwater contamination in the United States. (Data from U.S. Water Resources Council and U.S. Geological Survey)

water intrusion into freshwater aquifers in coastal areas as groundwater is withdrawn faster than it is recharged, and **(4) groundwater contamination** from human activities (Figure 11-19).

Although U.S. groundwater withdrawals amount to only about 10% of the country's overall groundwater supply, much of this water is drawn from large parts of the Southwest and certain smaller areas elsewhere. The major groundwater overdraft problem is in parts of the California-size Ogallala Aquifer extending across the farming belt from northern Nebraska to northwestern Texas (see Spotlight on p. 226). Aquifer depletion is also a serious problem in northern China, Mexico City, and parts of India.

In some areas (but not most of those overlying the Ogallala Aquifer) depleted aquifers can be recharged artificially. Deep groundwater can be pumped up and spread out over the ground to recharge shallow aquifers, or it can be injected directly into an aquifer through a well. But this can deplete deep aquifers and contaminate shallow aquifers because deep groundwater often has a high dissolved-mineral content. Another approach is to recharge aquifers with irrigation water, wastewater, and cooling water from industries and power plants. But much of this water is lost by evaporation, and in many cases it is better and cheaper to reuse cooling water in the industries and power plants themselves. The most effective solu-

The vast Ogallala Aquifer (Figure 11-20) was formed more than 2 million years ago from melting glaciers. The Ogallala's extensive groundwater resources were virtually unknown until the early 1900s and were not tapped for irrigation water until around 1950. Today water withdrawn from this aquifer is used to irrigate one-fifth of all U.S. cropland in an area too dry for rainfall farming. It supports $32 billion of agricultural production a year, mostly wheat, sorghum, cotton, corn, and 40% of the country's grain-fed beef.

Although the aquifer contains a large amount of water, it has an extremely low natural recharge rate because it underlies a region with relatively low average annual precipitation. Today the amount of water being withdrawn is so enormous that overall the aquifer is being depleted eight times faster than its natural recharge rate. Even higher depletion rates, sometimes 100 times the recharge rate, are taking place in parts of the aquifer that lie in Texas, New Mexico, Oklahoma, and Colorado. The entire billion-dollar agricultural economy of the Texas High Plains is built upon an annual overdraft of groundwater from the Ogallala by an amount nearly equal to the annual flow of the Colorado River.

Water resource experts project that at the present rate of depletion much of this aquifer could be dry by 2020, and much sooner in areas where it is only a few meters deep. Long before this happens, however, the high costs of obtaining water from rapidly declining water tables will force many farmers to switch from irrigated farming to dryland farming (planting crops such as winter wheat and cotton that require no irrigation) and to give up the cultivation of profitable but water-thirsty crops such as corn. The amount of irrigated land already is declining in five of the

seven states using this aquifer because of the high and rising cost of pumping water from depths as great as 1,825 meters (6,000 feet). If all farmers in the Ogallala region began using water conservation measures, depletion of the aquifer would be delayed but not prevented in the long run. However, the tragedy of the commons (Section 1-2, p. 11) shows us that most farmers are likely to continue withdrawing as much water as possible from this commonly shared resource to increase short-term profits.

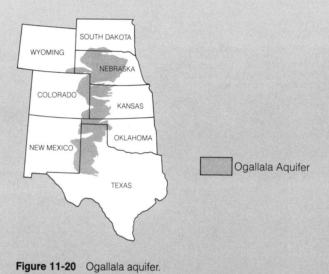

Figure 11-20 Ogallala aquifer.

tion is to reduce the amount of groundwater withdrawn by wasting less irrigation water and by abandoning irrigation in arid and semiarid areas.

Groundwater overdrafts can also cause the land overlying aquifers to sink, or subside (Figure 11-21). Groundwater in an unconfined aquifer fills the pores in the soil above and thus helps support it. When groundwater is withdrawn faster than it is replenished, the soil becomes compacted and subsides. Such subsidence has been a major problem in parts of the southwest and southern California (Figure 11-19). In 1981 a sinkhole formed in Winter Park, Florida, swal-

lowing several cars, a house, two businesses, and part of the municipal swimming pool. Widespread subsidence in the San Joaquin Valley of California has damaged homes, factories, pipelines, highways, and railroad beds. Some cities are sinking at a disastrous rate because of a combination of groundwater overdrafting, petroleum mining, rising sea levels, and the weight of tall buildings. Scientists project that within 100 years Houston, New Orleans, and Long Beach, California will have sunk so much that annual flooding will cause billions of dollars in damage.

Excessive removal of groundwater near coastal

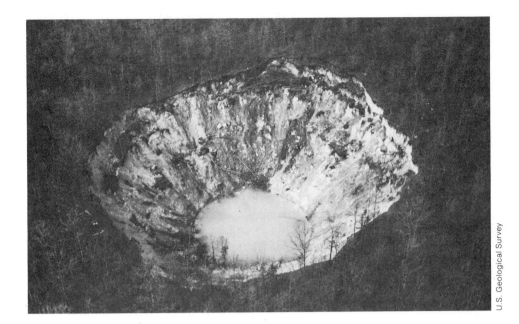

Figure 11-21 Large sinkhole formed in rural Alabama, from withdrawal of groundwater from an unconfined aquifer.

U.S. Geological Survey

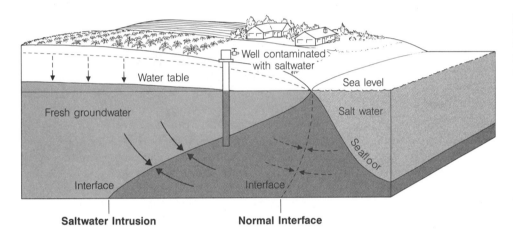

Well contaminated with saltwater

Water table

Sea level

Fresh groundwater

Salt water

Seafloor

Interface

Interface

Saltwater Intrusion

Normal Interface

Figure 11-22 Saltwater intrusion along a coastal region. As the water table is lowered, the normal interface between fresh and saline groundwater moves inland.

areas can lead to saltwater intrusion (Figure 11-22). Such intrusion threatens to contaminate the drinking water of many towns and cities along the Atlantic and Gulf coasts (Figure 11-19). It is especially severe in a number of cities in Florida and southeastern Georgia, where groundwater overdrafting has lowered the water table below sea level. Saltwater intrusion is also a serious problem in the coastal areas of Israel, Syria, and the Arabian Gulf states. Once intrusion occurs, the resulting contamination of groundwater is difficult if not impossible to reverse.

Another growing problem in many MDCs such as the United States is groundwater contamination from agricultural and industrial activities, septic tanks, underground injection wells, and other sources. Because groundwater flow in aquifers is slow and not turbulent, contaminants that reach this water are diluted very little. In addition, organic waste contaminants are not broken down as readily as in rapidly flowing surface waters exposed to the atmosphere because groundwater lacks decomposing bacteria and dissolved oxygen. As a result, it can take hundreds to thousands of years for contaminated groundwater to cleanse itself. Because of its location deep underground, pumping polluted groundwater to the surface, cleaning it up, and returning it to the aquifer is an extremely difficult and expensive process.

Desalinization Removing dissolved salts in ocean water or brackish (slightly salty) groundwater is an appealing way to increase freshwater supplies. Distillation and reverse osmosis are the two most widely used desalinization methods, although salt can also be removed by freezing salt water or by passing electric current through it. Distillation involves heating salt water to evaporate and then condense fresh water, leaving salts behind in sold form. In reverse osmosis, energy is used to force salt water through thin membranes whose pores allow the passage of water molecules but not of the dissolved salts.

The basic problem with all desalinization methods, even reverse osmosis, which requires about one-third the energy input of distillation, is that they require large amounts of energy and therefore are expensive. As a result, most experts project that desalted water will never be cheap enough for widespread use in irrigation, the main use of water throughout the world. Even more energy and money are required to pump desalted water uphill and inland from coastal desalinization plants. In addition, building and operating a vast network of expensive desalinization plants would produce mountains of salt to be disposed of. If the salt were returned to the ocean, it would increase the salt concentration near the coasts and threaten food resources in estuarine and continental shelf waters.

Thus, it is unlikely that desalinization will have a significant impact on future water supplies. However, it can provide fresh water in selected coastal cities in arid regions such as Saudi Arabia, where the cost of obtaining fresh water by any method is high. By 1985 about half of the world's desalinization plants were in Saudi Arabia.

Towing Icebergs   Some scientists believe that it may be economically feasible to use a fleet of tugboats to tow huge, flat, floating Antarctic icebergs to southern California, Australia, Saudi Arabia, and other dry coastal places. But there are a number of unanswered questions and problems: How much would the scheme cost? How can such a massive object be "lassoed," wrapped, and towed? How can most of the iceberg be prevented from melting on its long journey through warm waters? If the towing project is successful, how would the fresh water from the slowly melting iceberg be collected and transmitted to shore? What effects might introducing such a cold mass of water into tropical water have on local weather and marine life? Who owns the icebergs in the Antarctic and how could international conflicts over ownership be resolved?

Cloud Seeding   Several countries, particularly the United States, have been experimenting for years with seeding clouds with chemicals to produce rain over dry regions and snow over mountains to increase run-off in such areas. In principle, cloud seeding involves finding a large, suitable cloud and injecting it with a powdered chemical such as silver iodide from a plane or from ground-mounted burners. The chemical particles serve as nuclei of condensation, causing small water droplets in the cloud to coalesce and form droplets or ice particles large enough to fall to the earth as precipitation.

Since 1977, clouds have been successfully seeded in 23 states, bringing rain to 7% of the U.S. land area; in some places there has been a 10% increase in average annual precipitation. But it is not known whether this represents an increase in total precipitation or merely a shift of precipitation from one area to another. As with all methods of increasing the usable supply of water, there are problems with cloud seeding: It cannot be used effectively in very dry areas, where it is most needed, because rain clouds are rarely available. Large-scale use could change snowfall and rainfall patterns and alter regional or even global climate patterns in unknown and perhaps undesirable ways. Introduction of large quantities of silver iodide into soil and water systems could have harmful effects on humans, wildlife, and agricultural productivity. There are also legal disputes over the ownership of water in clouds. For example, during the 1977 drought in the western United States, the attorney general of Idaho accused officials in neighboring Washington of "cloud rustling" and threatened to file suit in federal court.

11-5   WATER RESOURCE MANAGEMENT: WATER CONSERVATION

Importance of Water Conservation   It is estimated that *30% to 50% of the water used in the United States is unnecessarily wasted.* This explains why many water resource experts consider water conservation the quickest and cheapest way to provide much of the additional water needed in water-short areas.

The major reason for the large amount of water wasted in the United States is that the government, hoping to stimulate economic growth, keeps water prices artificially low by using taxes to build dams and water transfer projects, thus subsidizing the use of water by farmers, industries, and homeowners. In a truly competitive, free-market system, users would know and pay the full direct cost of using a resource. Instead, in U.S. public water systems, subsidies are passed on to taxpayers in the form of higher taxes. Thus, subsidized water users have little incentive to conserve. For example, farmers supplied with irrigation water from federally supported projects pay, on average, less than one-fifth the real cost of supplying it, with taxpayers making up the difference.

Another reason that water waste and pollution in the United States are higher than necessary is that the responsibility for water resource management in a particular water basin is divided among many state and local governments rather than being handled in terms of the entire basin. For example, the Chicago metropolitan area has 349 separate water supply systems and 135 waste treatment plants divided among about 2,000 local units of government over a six-county area. In sharp contrast is the regionalized approach to water management used in England and Wales. The British Water Act of 1973 replaced more than 1,600 separate agencies with 10 regional water authorities based not on political boundaries but on natural watershed boundaries. In this successful ecological approach, each water authority owns, finances, and manages all water supply and waste treatment facilities in its region, including water pollution control, water-based recreation, land drainage and flood control, inland navigation, and inland fisheries. Each water authority is managed by a group of elected local officials and a smaller number of officials appointed by the national government.

Reducing Irrigation Losses   Since irrigation accounts for the largest fraction of water withdrawal, consumption, and waste, more efficient use of even a small amount frees water for other uses. Most irrigation systems distribute water from a groundwater well or surface canal by gravity flow through unlined field ditches. Although this method is cheap, it provides far more water than needed for crop growth and at least 50% of the water is lost by evaporation and seepage.

As available water supplies dwindle and pumping prices rise, farmers find it more profitable to use a number of available techniques for reducing evaporation and using irrigation water more efficiently. For example, many farmers served by the Ogallala Aquifer have switched from gravity-flow canal systems to center-pivot sprinkler systems (Figure 11-15), which reduce water waste from 50% or more to 30%. Some farmers are switching to new, low-energy precision-application (LEPA) sprinkler systems, which spray water downward, closer to crops, rather than high into the air, cutting water waste to between 2% and 5% and energy requirements by 20% to 30%.

Highly water-efficient trickle or drip irrigation systems, developed in Israel in the 1960s, are economically feasible for high-profit fruit, vegetable, and orchard crops. In this approach an extensive network of perforated piping, installed at or below the ground surface, releases a small volume of water and fertilizer close to the roots of plants, minimizing evaporation and seepage. Although drip irrigation accounts for less than 1% of total irrigated area worldwide, it is used on half of the irrigated land in Israel. Its use in the United States is still negligible but is increasing, especially in California and Florida.

Irrigation efficiency can also be improved by using computer-controlled systems to set water flow rates, detect leaks, and adjust the amount of water to soil moisture and weather conditions. Irrigation ditches can be lined with plastic to prevent seepage and waterlogging, and ponds can be constructed to store runoff for later use. Evaporation losses can be reduced by using conservation tillage (Section 10-5), covering ponds with floating alcohol-based liquids, and covering the soil with a mulch. Farmers can switch to new hybrid crop varieties that require less water or that tolerate irrigation with saline water.

Between 1950 and 1985, Israel used many of these techniques to decrease waste of irrigation water from 83% to 5%, while allowing the country's irrigated land to expand by 44%. According to the Worldwatch Institute, using such methods to raise the worldwide efficiency of irrigation by only 10% would save enough water to supply all the world's residential users.

Wasting Less Water in Industry   Many manufacturing processes can use recycled water or be redesigned to use and waste less water. For example, depending on the process used, manufacturing a ton of steel can require as much as 200,000 liters (52,800 gallons) or as little as 5,000 liters (1,320 gallons) of water. An Armco steel mill in Kansas City, Missouri, now reuses each liter of water 16 times before releasing it, after treatment, to the river. To produce a ton of paper, a paper mill in Hadera, Israel, uses about one-tenth the amount of water as most paper mills. Manufacturing a ton of aluminum from recycled scrap rather than virgin resources can reduce water needs by 97%.

More than 80% of all water used in U.S. manufacturing is used in four industries—paper, chemicals, petroleum, and primary metals. Between 1968 and 1985 these four industries increased the amount of water they recycled fourfold. Despite such impressive gains, the potential for water recycling in manufacturing has hardly been tapped because much of the cost of water to industry is subsidized by taxpayers through federally financed water projects. Thus, industries have little incentive to recycle water, which typically accounts for only about 3% of total manufacturing costs, even in industries that use large amounts of water. Only when water and wastewater treatment costs rise does recycling water begin to pay.

Wasting Less Water in Homes   In the United States, leaks in pipes, water mains, toilets, bathtubs, and faucets waste an estimated 20% to 35% of water withdrawn from public supplies. There is little incentive to reduce leaks and waste in many cities, like New York, where there are no residential water meters and users are charged flat rates. In Boulder, Colorado, the introduction of water meters reduced water use by more than one-third. Individuals can develop their own plan for saving water and money (see Spotlight on p. 230).

Each time a typical U.S. toilet—the biggest water user in a home—is flushed it turns about 19 liters (5 gallons) of drinking-quality water into wastewater. This is equivalent in wastefulness to heating a house or water with electricity (Section 3-6). Conventional toilets can be replaced with water-saving models that reduce the water per flush by 30% to 90% or by waterless models. Investments in water-saving toilets, faucets, and appliances usually pay for themselves within a few years by saving money on energy, water, and sewage bills and by reducing the need for more taxes to expand wastewater treatment facilities.

Commercially available systems can also be used to purify and completely recycle wastewater from houses, apartments, and office buildings (Figure 11-23). Such a system, which can be installed in a small shed outside a residence, is serviced for a monthly fee about equal to that charged by most city water and sewer systems.

Born in a water-rich environment, we have never really learned how important water is to us. . . . Where it has been cheap and plentiful, we have ignored it; where it has been rare and precious, we have spent it with shameful and unbecoming haste. . . . Everywhere we have poured filth into it.

William Ashworth

Spotlight How to Save Water and Money

Bathroom (65% of residential water use; 40% for toilet flushing)

- For existing toilets, reduce the amount of water used per flush by putting a tall plastic container weighted with a few stones into each tank, or buy (for about $10) and insert a toilet dam made of plastic and rubber; bricks also work but tend to disintegrate and gum up the water.

- In new houses, install water-saving toilets or, where health codes permit, waterless or composting toilets. Flush only when necessary, using the advice found on a bathroom wall in a drought-stricken area: "If it's yellow, let it mellow—if it's brown, flush it down."

- Take short showers—showers of less than five minutes use less water than a bath. Shower by wetting down, turning off the water while soaping up, and then rinsing off. If you prefer baths, fill the tub well below the overflow drain.

- Use water-saving flow restrictors, which cost less than a dollar and can be easily installed, on all faucets and showerheads.

- Check frequently for toilet, shower, and sink leaks and repair them promptly. A pinhole leak anywhere in a household water system can cost $25 a month in excess water and electricity charges; a fast leak, $50 or more.

- Don't keep water running while brushing teeth, shaving, or washing.

Laundry Room (15%)

- Wash only full loads; use the short cycle and fill the machine to the lowest possible water level.

- When buying a new washer, choose one that uses the least amount of water and fills up to different levels for loads of different sizes.

- Check for leaks frequently and repair all leaks promptly.

Kitchen (10%)

- Use an automatic dishwasher only for full loads; use the short cycle and let dishes air-dry to save energy.

- When washing many dishes by hand, don't let the faucet run. Use one filled dishpan for washing and another for rinsing.

- Keep a jug of water in the refrigerator rather than running water from a tap until it gets cold enough to drink.

- While waiting for faucet water to get hot, catch the cool water in a pan and use it for cooking or to water plants.

- Check for sink and dishwasher leaks frequently and repair them promptly.

- Try not to use a garbage disposal or water-softening system—both are major water users.

Outdoors (10%; higher in arid areas)

- Don't wash your car or wash it less frequently. Wash the car from a bucket of soapy water; use the hose only for rinsing.

- Sweep walks and driveways instead of hosing them off.

- Reduce evaporation losses by watering lawns and gardens in the early morning or in the evening, rather than in the heat of midday or when windy. Better yet, landscape with pebbles, rocks, sand, wood chips, or native plants adapted to local average annual precipitation so that watering is not necessary.

- Use drip irrigation systems and mulch on home gardens to improve irrigation efficiency and reduce evaporation.

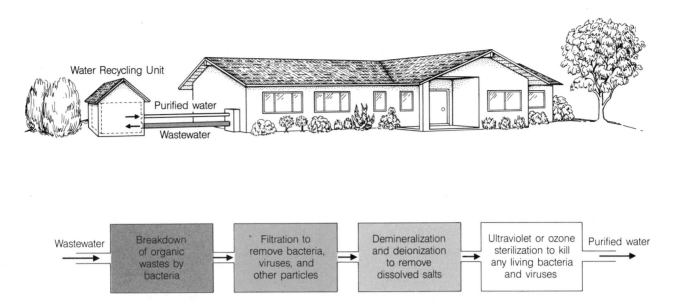

Figure 11-23 Home wastewater purifying and recycling system.

Enrichment Study Desertification

Human activities that degrade soil and water resources have led to the creation of desertlike landscapes in a number of the world's dryland areas—hyperarid, arid, semiarid, and subhumid zones of low and variable rainfall—where deserts should not occur climatically. This conversion of rangeland (uncultivated land used for animal grazing), rain-fed cropland, or irrigated cropland to desertlike land with a drop in agricultural productivity of 10% or more is called **desertification.** Moderate desertification causes a 10% to 25% drop in productivity; severe desertification causes a 25% to 50% drop; and very severe desertification causes a drop of 50% or more and usually the formation of massive gullies and sand dunes.

Prolonged drought and hot temperatures may accelerate the desertification process. But its basic causes are overgrazing of rangeland by concentrating too many livestock on too little land area; improper soil and water resource management that leads to increased erosion, salinization, and waterlogging; cultivation of marginal land with unsuitable terrain or soils; and deforestation and strip mining without adequate replanting.

Desertification does not necessarily mean the creation of barren Sahara-like sand deserts. Instead, it includes a variety of ecological changes that reduce or destroy the ability of land to be used for growing crops or grazing livestock. Destruction of plant cover (followed by soil erosion) is the major desertification

factor for grazing land; soil erosion, for rainfed cropland; and salinization and waterlogging, for irrigated cropland.

Although desertification is not new, it has become worse during the past 50 years as the world's growing population, especially in dryland areas, has greatly increased pressures on rangelands and croplands. It is estimated that about 900 million hectares (2 billion acres)—equivalent to an area ten times the size of Texas—have become desertified during the past 50 years. Moderate to very severe desertification now affects various dryland areas of the southwestern United States, Central America, South America, Africa, Asia, and Australia (Figure 11-24). At least 50 million people, half of them in Africa, have experienced a major loss in their ability to feed themselves. Another 400 million in moderately desertified areas have a reduced capacity to support themselves.

Each year the amount of desertified land grows by about 20 million hectares (49 million acres)—an area equal to that of South Dakota. The actual rate of desertification may be higher, as increasing numbers of people in the earth's drier regions exert even more pressure on the land to meet their needs for food, livestock, and fuelwood. According to the UN Environmental Programme, one-fifth of the world's people now live in areas that may become desertified over the next 20 years.

The spread of desertification can be halted or sharply reduced by improved management of soil resources (Section 10-5), water resources, rangelands (Section 13-6), and forestlands (Section 13-4). It is also economically and technically feasible to reclaim essentially all of irrigated cropland, 70% of rainfed cropland, and 25% of rangeland that have become desertified throughout the world.

The total cost of such prevention and rehabilitation would be about $141 billion. Although this amount may seem staggering, it is only five and one-half times the estimated $26 billion annual loss in agricultural productivity from desertified land. Thus, once this potential productivity is restored, the costs of the program could be recouped in five to ten years.

So far, funds devoted to preventing desertification and restoring desertified lands fall far short of the need because of population growth and economic, cultural, and political forces in dryland areas. Farmers growing food for sale abuse land resources to increase short-term profits and poor farmers abuse these resources to obtain enough food for their short-term survival, even though these practices lead to long-term economic and agricultural losses. LDCs in desertified drylands lack funds and are saddled with large debts to MDCs. Government leaders in many desertified countries emphasize urban and industrial development and buildup of arms at the expense of sound long-term management of croplands, rangelands, and forestlands. Governments gain more political credit by using limited funds on quick, showcase solutions to short-term problems rather than on less glamorous, prolonged efforts to prevent and correct resource abuse. Bankers and international lending institutions also have little interest in funding projects that give moderate returns 10 years down the road.

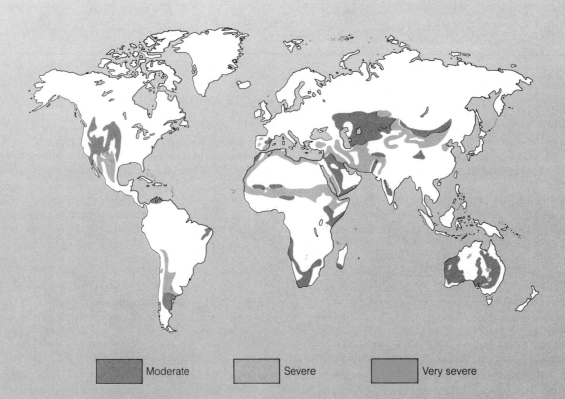

Moderate   Severe   Very severe

Figure 11-24   Desertification of arid lands. (Data from UN Environmental Programme and Harold E. Dregne)

CHAPTER SUMMARY

Life is possible on earth because water has a high boiling and melting point, very high heat of vaporization, extremely high heat capacity, superior ability to dissolve large amounts of a variety of substances, extremely high surface tension and wetting ability, and because it expands rather than contracts when it freezes.

Only about 0.003% of the world's water supply is available as fresh water for human use in the forms of *surface water* and *groundwater*, which are collected, purified, and distributed to various parts of the world in an uneven pattern by the hydrologic cycle. Groundwater is found in *unconfined* and *confined aquifers* that are recharged very slowly compared to the fairly rapid replenishment of surface water in streams, rivers, lakes, wetlands, and reservoirs.

Worldwide, most water withdrawn from surface or ground sources is used and returned to rivers and lakes for reuse. However, about 75% of the water withdrawn for irrigation, the largest use of water throughout the world, is *consumed* through evaporation and seepage and lost for reuse as surface water in the area from which it is withdrawn. Total and average per capita withdrawal and consumption of surface and groundwater for human use have been increasing rapidly and are projected to increase significantly in the future.

The major water resource problems in various parts of the world are **(1)** *water shortages* as a result of low average annual precipitation, prolonged periodic drought, land degradation by human activities that increase the severity of drought, and population growth; **(2)** *periodic flooding* caused by high precipitation during a short period, removal of vegetative cover that absorbs water and reduces flood damage, and imperfect dams and flood control projects; **(3)** *water in the wrong place* in countries where ample annual precipitation flows away in remote rivers far from population and agricultural centers; **(4)** *lack of sanitary drinking water;* and **(5)** *salinization and waterlogging of soil* from improper irrigation.

The usable supply of fresh water in many areas can be increased by *building dams and reservoirs* to catch and store surface-water runoff, *transferring water from water-rich to water-poor regions*, and *tapping groundwater supplies*. Each of these approaches has certain advantages and disadvantages: Increasing use of groundwater has led to depletion of aquifers, subsidence (land sinking), intrusion of saltwater into freshwater aquifers near coastal areas, and aquifer contamination. Desalinization of seawater can also be used to produce fresh water but is too expensive except in areas with acute water shortages.

More fresh water can be made available through *water conservation*—reducing unnecessary waste of water used for irrigation (the largest source of waste) and in industry and homes. The numerous water conservation techniques are not widely used in many countries, including the United States, primarily because water prices are kept artificially low and water resources are managed by a maze of often conflicting political units.

Desertification is the conversion of once-productive rangeland, rainfed cropland, or irrigated cropland in dry parts of the world to nonproductive, desertlike land as a result of human activities such as overgrazing and poor soil and water resource management. Land degradation can be prevented and most desertized land can be reclaimed by use of well-known methods of soil and water resource manage- ment. However, such long-term efforts are not being implemented on a sufficient scale because of growing populations and governments that emphasize short-term survival and economic growth at the expense of long-term resource degradation and economic loss.

DISCUSSION TOPICS

1. Which physical property or properties of water
   a. account for the fact that you exist?
   b. allow lakes to freeze from the top down?
   c. help protect you from the shock of sudden temperature changes?
   d. help regulate the climate?

2. Explain why average annual precipitation is not a measure of the water available for plant or human use.

3. If groundwater is a renewable resource, how can it be "mined" and depleted like a nonrenewable resource?

4. What is the difference between water withdrawal and water consumption? What use of water accounts for the highest overall consumption?

5. How do human activities contribute to drought? How could these effects be reduced?

6. How do human activities contribute to flooding? How could these effects be reduced?

7. In your community:
   a. What are the major sources of the water supply?
   b. How is water use divided among agricultural, industrial, power plant cooling, and public uses? Who are the biggest consumers of water?
   c. What has happened to water prices during the past 20 years?
   d. What water problems are projected?
   e. How is water being wasted?

8. Explain why dams and reservoirs may lead to more flood damage than might occur if they had not been built. Should all proposed large dam and reservoir projects be scrapped? What criteria would you use in determining desirable dam and reservoir projects?

9. How can the following problems be minimized or prevented: **(a)** soil salinity from irrigation? **(b)** saltwater intrusion in coastal areas?

10. Use the first and second laws of energy (Sections 3-4 and 3-5), to explain why desalinized seawater will probably never be an important source of fresh water for irrigation.

11. Should the price of water for all uses in the United States be increased sharply to encourage water conservation? Explain. What effects might this have on the economy, on you, on the poor, on the environment?

12. List ten major ways to conserve water on a personal level. Which, if any, of these practices do you now use or intend to use?

12

Food Resources and World Hunger

GENERAL OBJECTIVES

1. What major types of agricultural systems are used to provide food from domesticated crops and livestock throughout the world?
2. What are the world's major food problems?
3. How can the world's food problems be solved?

Hunger is a curious thing: At first it is with you all the time, working and sleeping and in your dreams, and your belly cries out insistently, and there is a gnawing and a pain as if your very vitals were being devoured, and you must stop it at any cost. . . . Then the pain is no longer sharp, but dull, and this too is with you always.

Kamala Markandaya

The world presently produces more than enough food to feed everyone. Yet, each year 12 million to 20 million people die prematurely from chronic undernutrition (lack of adequate food), malnutrition (lack of sufficient protein, vitamins, and minerals needed for good health), or normally nonfatal diseases worsened by these conditions. This preventable death toll from hunger and hunger-related diseases is equivalent to the number who would die if between 94 and 157 fully loaded jumbo jets crashed *each day*, with no survivors and half of the passengers being children. In addition, hundreds of millions of other individuals suffer from a loss of life quality because they cannot afford to grow or buy enough food. Ironically, while hundreds of millions of people throughout the world are threatened by too little food, many others are threatened by overnutrition or too much food—making best-sellers out of the latest diet books.

Each day natural population growth produces 238,000 more people to feed, clothe, and house, and the world's population is projected to grow from 5 billion to 8 billion between 1985 and 2020. This means that during this 35-year period we must produce as much food as humankind has produced since the dawn of agriculture about 10,000 years ago. Even if enough food is grown, how can it be made available to those who can't afford to buy it, and what are the environmental consequences of growing this much food?

12-1 WORLD AGRICULTURAL SYSTEMS: HOW IS FOOD PRODUCED?

Plants and Animals That Feed the World Although there are an estimated 80,000 edible species of plants, only about 30 types of crops feed the world

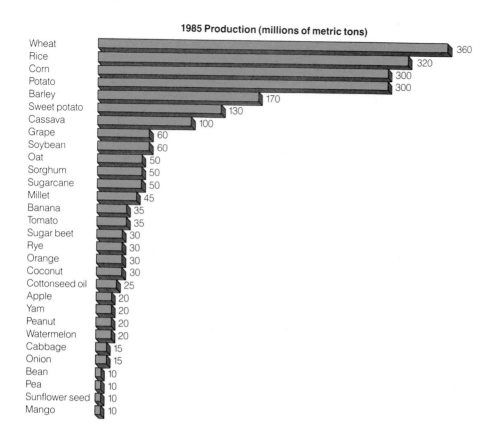

1985 Production (millions of metric tons)

Crop	Production
Wheat	360
Rice	320
Corn	300
Potato	300
Barley	170
Sweet potato	130
Cassava	100
Grape	60
Soybean	60
Oat	50
Sorghum	50
Sugarcane	50
Millet	45
Banana	35
Tomato	35
Sugar beet	30
Rye	30
Orange	30
Coconut	30
Cottonseed oil	25
Apple	20
Yam	20
Peanut	20
Watermelon	20
Cabbage	15
Onion	15
Bean	10
Pea	10
Sunflower seed	10
Mango	10

Figure 12-1 About 30 crops dominate the world's food supply, with the bulk provided by only four crops.

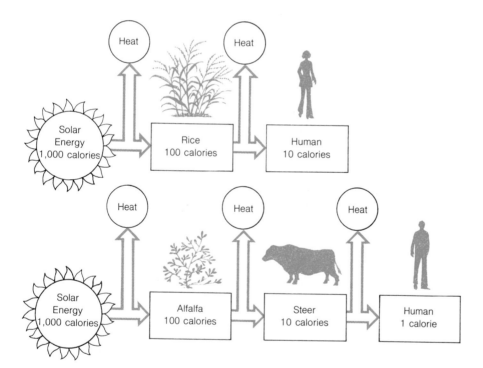

Figure 12-2 Food chain energy losses, caused primarily by the second law of energy, explain why most people in the world survive on a grain diet.

(Figure 12-1). Four crops—wheat, rice, corn, and potato—make up more of the world's total food production than all others combined.

Most of the remainder of the world's food is fish, shellfish, meat, and meat products such as milk, eggs, and cheese. Almost all the meat comes from just nine groups of livestock: cattle, sheep, swine, chickens, turkeys, geese, ducks, goats, and water buffalo. Meat and meat products are too expensive for most people, primarily because of the loss of usable energy resulting from adding the animal link to the food chain (Section 4-3 and Figure 12-2). That is, poor people can get

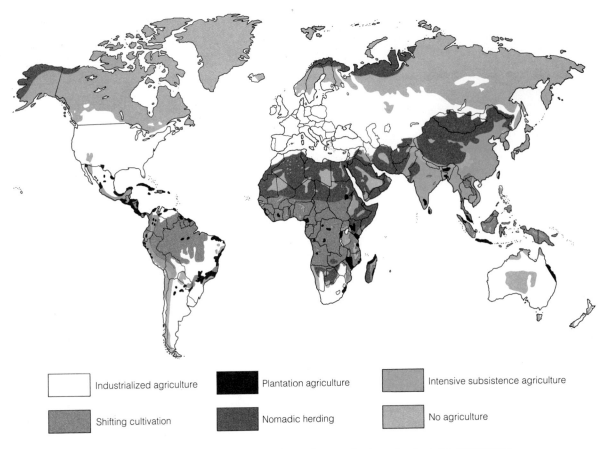

	Industrialized agriculture		Plantation agriculture		Intensive subsistence agriculture
	Shifting cultivation		Nomadic herding		No agriculture

Figure 12-3 The world's four major types of agriculture. Depending on climate and soils, areas within these generalized zones emphasize cultivation of certain crops, dairying, or livestock ranching.

more nourishment—more energy—per unit of money or labor from grain than from meat. However, as their incomes rise, people begin to consume more grain *indirectly*, in the form of meat and meat products from domesticated animals. Because of the greater emphasis on meat-based diets in MDCs, almost half of the world's annual grain production and one-third of the fish catch are fed to livestock.

Major Types of Agriculture Two major types of agricultural systems are used to grow crops and raise livestock throughout the world: subsistence agriculture, practiced by two-thirds of the almost 4 billion people who live in small rural villages in today's LDCs, and industrialized agriculture, widely used in MDCs and spreading slowly to parts of some LDCs.

The goal of **subsistence agriculture** is to supplement solar energy with energy from human labor and draft animals to produce at least enough crops or livestock for survival and at most to have some left over to sell or put aside for hard times. The three types of subsistence agriculture are **(1)** labor-intensive subsistence cultivation of one crop (monoculture) or a small number of crops such as rice, wheat, or other grains; **(2)** land-

intensive subsistence shifting cultivation of a variety of crops (polyculture) in small cleared patches in undeveloped tropical forests; and **(3)** land-intensive subsistence herding (mostly nomadic) of livestock in isolated and sometimes inhospitable areas where crops cannot be grown. About 60% of the world's cultivated land is still farmed by the first two types of subsistence agriculture.

The goal of **industrialized agriculture** (see Spotlight on p. 237) is to supplement solar energy with large amounts of energy derived from fossil fuels (especially oil and natural gas) to produce large quantities of crops and livestock for sale within the country where it is grown and to other countries. Yields per unit of land area are also increased by large inputs of matter resources in the form of commercial inorganic fertilizers, pesticides, and irrigation water.

Industrialized crop production is supplemented by **plantation agriculture,** in which specialized crops such as bananas, coffee, and cacao are grown in some tropical LDCs primarily for sale to MDCs. Industrialized livestock production is supplemented by **livestock ranching,** in which livestock graze on rangeland grass rather than being fed grain in feedlots.

Figure 12-3 shows the generalized distribution of the world's major types of agricultural systems. Figure

1. *Mechanization:* replacing most renewable human and draft animal energy resources with machines such as tractors and combines fueled mostly by non-renewable oil.

2. *Commercial inorganic fertilizers:* using commercially produced, inorganic fertilizers rather than organic fertilizers to increase crop yields and partially restore lost soil fertility (Section 10-5). Between 1950 and 1985, world commercial fertilizer consumption increased ninefold and average per capita fertilizer use increased fivefold. One out of every three persons on earth is now fed with additional food produced by the use of commercial fertilizer.

3. *Irrigation:* building dams and canals and using fossil-fuel-powered pumps to move and apply water to cropland. Currently, 50% of the world's food and 30% of the food grown in the United States is produced on the 15% of the world's cropland that is irrigated.

4. *Agricultural chemicals for disease and pest control:* using specialized synthetic chemicals to reduce animal and crop losses due to pests, diseases, and spoilage, which destroy about 45% of the food produced each year (Chapter 22).

5. *Animal feedlots:* placing hundreds to thousands of some types of domesticated animals in feedlots (Figure 12-4), where they are fed and kept inactive in a small space to encourage rapid weight gain, to develop a specific appearance and quality of meat, and to achieve efficient, factory-like production of meat and animal products. Some types of domesticated animals, such as chickens, are kept in automated feedlots from birth to death, whereas other types, such as beef cattle, are moved there

from pastures and rangelands to be fattened a few weeks before slaughter.

6. *Large-scale, specialized production:* shifting from small, family-owned and -operated farms, where a diversity of crops (polyculture) and livestock are raised, to increasingly larger, specialized, corporate-owned farms and animal feedlots, where only one type of crop or livestock is raised in large numbers. A 1986 study by the Office of Technology Assessment projects that half of the U.S. farmers operating in 1986 will be out of business by 2000, and that 50,000 large corporate farms will then produce 75% of the country's food.

7. *High capital investment:* using large amounts of capital (usually borrowed) to buy fertilizer, pesticides, and large and expensive pieces of equipment for cultivating, harvesting, drying, and storing crops and raising livestock.

8. *Genetic selection and hybridization:* using scientific research to select and develop high-yield, disease-resistant strains of crops and domesticated animals.

9. *Agricultural training and research:* establishing a system of agricultural schools and research centers and using extension services to expose farmers to new developments.

10. *Processed food:* promoting a consumer shift from fresh food totally cooked at home to food factory-processed to retard spoilage, decrease home cooking time, and increase sales appeal and profits.

11. *Storage, processing, distribution, and marketing:* developing storage facilities and extensive transportation, processing, and food marketing networks.

12. *Agribusiness:* increasing control of production, processing, and marketing by a few large multinational companies. Most of the world's grain production and trade is controlled by only five companies. In the United States a handful of companies control the seed, pesticide, fertilizer, farm machinery, and food-processing industries.

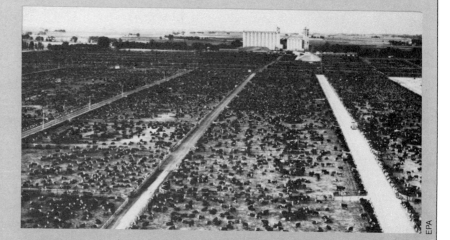

Figure 12-4   Feedlots such as this huge one for cattle near Greely, Colorado, increase production efficiency but concentrate massive amounts of animal wastes, which, without proper controls, can wash into nearby water supplies.

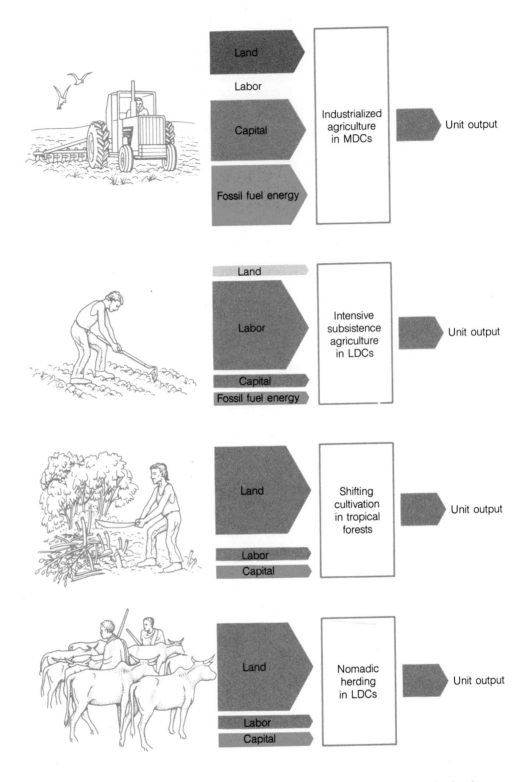

Figure 12-5 Relative inputs of major types of agricultural systems.

12-5 shows the relative inputs of land, human and animal labor, fossil fuel energy, and capital needed to produce one unit of food by modern industrialized agriculture and by the three major forms of subsistence agriculture.

U.S. Energy Use and Industrialized Agriculture The success of industrialized agriculture coupled with a favorable climate and fertile soils has been demonstrated by the dramatic increase in food production in the United States (Figure 12-6). Between 1820 and 1986, the percentage of the total U.S. population working on farms declined from about 72% to 2%, but during the same period total food production approximately doubled, and the output per farmer increased eightfold. Although the number of farmers has declined drastically to about 2 million (with only 650,000 full-time farmers), about 23 million people are involved in the U.S. agricultural system in activities

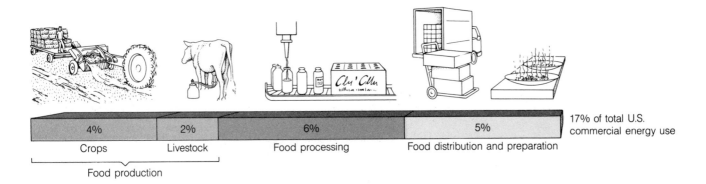

17% of total U.S. commercial energy use

4%	2%	6%	5%
Crops	Livestock	Food processing	Food distribution and preparation

Food production

ranging from growing and processing food to selling it at the supermarket. In terms of total annual sales, the agricultural system is the biggest industry in the United States—bigger than the automobile, steel, and housing industries combined.

The agricultural system consumes about 17% of all commercial energy used in the United States each year (Figure 12-7). Most plant crops in the United States still provide more calories in food energy than the calories of energy (mostly from fossil fuels) used to grow them. But raising animals for food requires much more fossil fuel energy than the animals provide as food calories and protein (Figures 12-8 and 12-9).

The energy efficiency situation is much worse if we look at the entire food system in the United States. Counting fossil fuel energy inputs used to grow, store, process, package, transport, refrigerate, and cook all plant and animal food, *it takes about 10 calories of nonrenewable fossil fuel energy to put 1 calorie of food energy on the table—an energy loss of 9 calories per calorie produced of food energy.*

12-2 MAJOR WORLD FOOD PROBLEMS

Producing a large enough quantity of food to feed the world's population is only one of a number of complex and interrelated agricultural, economic, and environmental food problems. In addition to food quantity, other major problems are food quality, food storage and distribution, poverty (inability to grow or buy sufficient food regardless of availability), economic incentives for growing food, and the harmful environmental effects of agriculture.

Food Quantity: Population Growth and Food Production The good news is that thanks to improved agricultural technologies, practices, policies, and trade, world food production increased by 135% between 1950 and 1985 and kept ahead of the rate of population on all continents except Africa. As a result, average per capita food production increased by more than

Figure 12-8 Energy input needed to produce one unit of food energy in different types of food production.

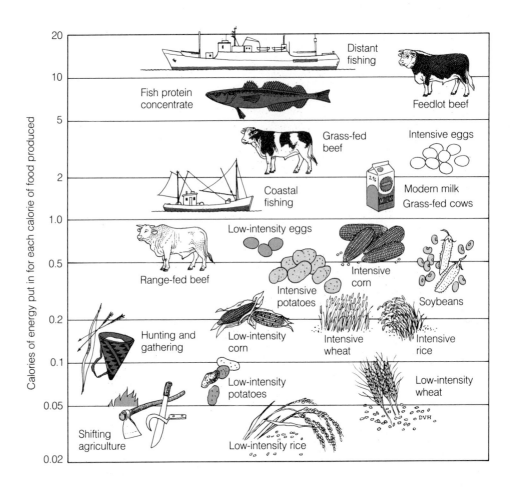

Figure 12-9 Energy inputs needed to produce 1 kilogram (2.2 pounds) of selected plant and animal proteins in the United States.

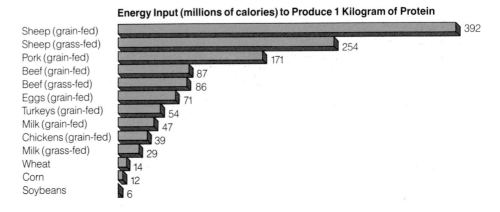

Energy Input (millions of calories) to Produce 1 Kilogram of Protein

Sheep (grain-fed)	392
Sheep (grass-fed)	254
Pork (grain-fed)	171
Beef (grain-fed)	87
Beef (grass-fed)	86
Eggs (grain-fed)	71
Turkeys (grain-fed)	54
Milk (grain-fed)	47
Chickens (grain-fed)	39
Milk (grass-fed)	29
Wheat	14
Corn	12
Soybeans	6

25% even though world population increased by nearly 2 billion. During the same period, food prices adjusted for inflation declined by 25% and the amount of food traded on the world market quadrupled.

This combination of increased production and trade and declining real prices for food helped support a dramatic improvement in the average standard of living for many of the world's people. Perhaps the most spectacular success in food production has taken place in China, which manages to feed its people primarily by labor-intensive subsistence agriculture (see Spotlight on p. 242).

However, the worldwide increase in average per capita food production since 1950 disguises the fact that average food production per person declined between 1950 and 1985 in 43 LDCs containing one out of every seven people on earth (Figure 12-10). The largest declines have occurred in Africa, where average food production per person dropped by 20% between 1960 and 1986 and is projected to drop another 30% during the next 25 years (see Spotlight on p. 242). Furthermore, the rate of increase in world average per capita food production has been steadily declining each decade, rising 15% between 1950 and 1960, rising 7%

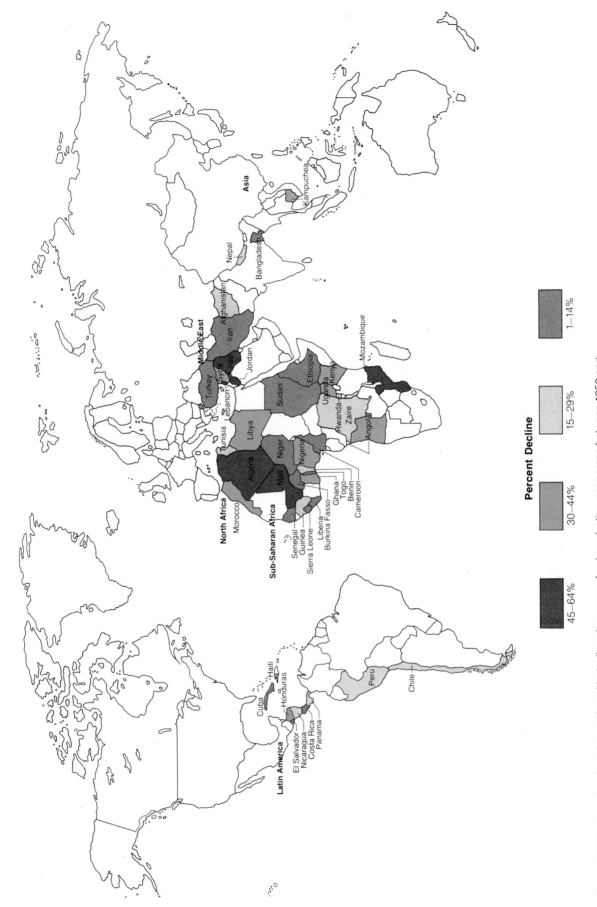

Percent Decline

1–14%	
15–29%	
30–44%	
45–64%	

Figure 12-10   Less developed countries with declines in average food production per person between 1950 and 1985. (Data from U.S. Department of Agriculture)

China has one out of every five persons on earth
and less agricultural land than the United States.
Yet it has been able to grow enough food to feed
its 1 billion people, dramatically raise per capita
food consumption, and largely eliminate malnutrition. Between 1975 and 1985, China almost
doubled its grain production on 8% less cropland, one of the most spectacular increases in
food production in human history.

The key factors in this impressive achievement are expansion of traditional labor-intensive
subsistence agriculture; equitable distribution of
landholdings and food production; shifting in
1978 from a centrally planned, state-controlled
agricultural system to a market-oriented system
left largely in the hands of individual families;
extensive use of human and animal wastes, garbage, and crop residues as organic fertilizer that
permits as many as 12 crops to be grown
annually on some plots of land; and doubling the
production and use of commercial inorganic fertilizer between 1978 and 1985. China and other
LDCs have shown that labor-intensive cultivation
of small plots produces higher yields per unit of
land area than large plots cultivated with expensive industrialized agriculture. Whether China
can continue to feed its population depends on
its ability to control population growth and food
prices and to halt extensive soil erosion and
restore degraded cropland.

between 1960 and 1970, and rising only 4% between
1970 and 1980, a slowing trend that persists in the
1980s.

Undernutrition, Malnutrition, and Overnutrition
Poor people living mostly on one or more plants such
as wheat, rice, or corn often suffer from **undernutrition,** or insufficient caloric intake or food quantity.
Survival and good health require that people must
consume not only enough food but food containing
the proper amounts of protein, carbohydrates, fats,
vitamins, and minerals. People whose diets are insufficient in these nutrients suffer from **malnutrition.**

Severe undernutrition and malnutrition lead to
premature death, especially for children under age five.
Most severely undernourished and malnourished
children, however, do not starve to death. Instead,
about three-fourths of them die because their weak-

The most obvious and tragic breakdown of life-
support systems from environmental degradation, poor environmental management, and
social conflict has been taking place in Africa. Of
Africa's 46 countries, 22 were facing catastrophic
food shortages in 1985 (Figure 11-10, p. 215), and
one out of four Africans was fed with grain
imported from abroad—a dependence that is
likely to increase. This worsening situation is the
result of a number of interacting factors: the fast-
est population growth rate of any continent—1
million more mouths to feed every three weeks; a
17-year drought; poor natural endowment of productive soils in many areas; overgrazing, deforestation, and extensive soil erosion and desertification (Figure 11-24, p. 232); and poor food
distribution systems. Moreover, much of the best
land is used for commercial production of plantation crops such as coffee and cacao, which are
exported to well-fed countries. To prevent urban
unrest, governments often keep food prices so
low that farmers have little economic incentive to
grow more crops. Frequent wars and growing
dependence on food imports, both incurring rapidly rising foreign debts, result in severe underin-
vestment in agriculture and population control.

Most observers believe that the only way
Africa can avoid increased famine, disease, and
war—and a dramatic rise in its already high
death rate—is for its leaders to undertake massive, carefully planned programs of family planning and land restoration. Such a reversal of Africa's decline will require an unprecedented degree
of cooperation among African countries and from
the rest of the world. The African countries have
asked the MDCs to write off one-third of the continent's $175 billion foreign debt. In addition, the
international community must provide massive
financial aid and other support, designed to help
Africa become self-sufficient rather than even
more dependent on MDCs. Political and economic conditions in Africa and the world make it
unlikely that sufficient change will occur. For
example, total foreign aid for Africa declined by
almost 25% between 1980 and 1985.

ened condition makes them vulnerable to normally
minor, nonfatal infections and diseases such as diarrhea, measles, and flu. The World Health Organization estimates that diarrhea kills at least 5 million
children under age 5 a year.

Famine occurs when people in a particular area

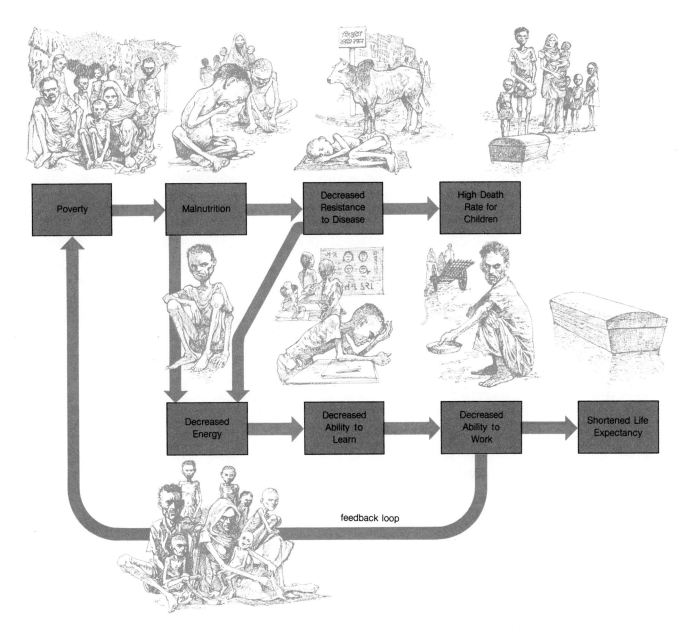

Figure 12-11 Interactions among poverty, malnutrition, and disease form a tragic cycle that perpetuates such conditions in succeeding generations of families.

suffer from widespread lack of access to food as a result of catastrophic events such as drought, flood, earthquake, or war. Because it is so visible and dramatic, famine receives most of the media attention. Yet the overwhelming majority of hunger-related deaths are caused not by famine but by chronic undernutrition and malnutrition among many people in LDCs. Because this condition is "normal" and spread out over much of the world, it is undramatic, often goes unnoticed, and is not widely reported by the media.

Adults suffering from chronic undernutrition and malnutrition are vulnerable to infection and other diseases and are too weak to work productively or think clearly. As a result, their children also tend to be underfed and malnourished. If these children survive

to adulthood, they are locked in a tragic malnutrition-poverty cycle that perpetuates these conditions in each succeeding family generation (Figure 12-11).

Most world hunger is protein hunger because poor people are forced to live on a low-protein, high-starch diet of grain. The two most widespread nutritional-deficiency diseases are marasmus and kwashiorkor. **Marasmus** (from the Greek "to waste away") occurs when a diet is low in both total energy (calories) and protein. Most victims of marasmus are infants in poor families where children are not breast-fed or where there is insufficient food after the children are weaned. A child suffering from marasmus typically has a bloated belly, thin body, shriveled skin, wide eyes, and an old-looking face (Figure 12-12). Diarrhea, dehydration,

Figure 12-12 Most effects of severe marasmus can be corrected. This 2-year-old Venezuelan girl suffered from marasmus but recovered after ten months of treatment and proper nutrition.

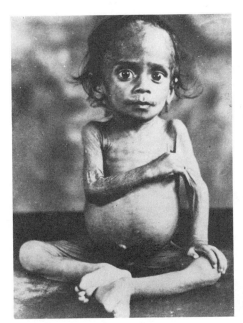 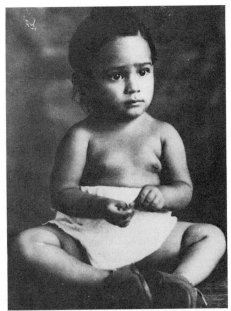

U.N. Food and Agriculture Organization

anemia, muscle deterioration, a ravenous appetite, and possible brain damage are also part of marasmus. If treated in time with a balanced diet, however, most of these effects can be reversed. **Kwashiorkor** (meaning "displaced child" in a West African dialect) occurs in infants and in children 1 to 3 years old when, often because their mothers have a younger child to nurse, they are changed from highly nutritious breast milk to a high-starch grain or sweet potato diet, which is sufficient in calories but deficient in protein. Children with kwashiorkor have swollen tissues because fluids collect under the skin, liver degeneration, permanent stunting of growth, hair loss, diarrhea, skin rash and discoloration, mental apathy, possible mental retardation, and irritability. But if malnutrition is not prolonged, most of the effects can be cured with a balanced diet.

Without a daily intake of small amounts of vitamins that cannot be synthesized in the human body, various vitamin deficiency effects occur (Table 12-1). Although a combination of balanced diets, vitamin-fortified foods, and vitamin supplements have greatly reduced the incidence of vitamin deficiency diseases in MDCs, millions of cases occur each year in LDCs. In many parts of Asia people survive primarily on a diet of polished rice, made by removing the outer hulls. These individuals lack sufficient vitamin B_1, or thiamine (found in rice hulls), and often develop beriberi, which leads to stiffness of the limbs, enlargement of the heart, paralysis, pain, loss of appetite, and eventual deterioration of the nervous system. People who exist primarily on a corn diet have an insufficient intake of vitamin B_5, or niacin, and suffer from pellagra (Figure 12-13). Their skin becomes scaly when exposed to sunlight and they also suffer from diarrhea, inflammation of the mouth, inability to digest food, and severe disturbance of the central nervous system. Each year at least 250,000 children are partially or totally blinded as a result of severe vitamin A deficiency.

Other nutritional-deficiency diseases are caused by the lack of certain minerals, such as iron and iodine. Too little iron can cause anemia, which saps one's energy, makes infection more likely, and increases a woman's chance of dying in childbirth. Iron deficiency anemia affects about 10% of all adult men, a third of all adult women, and more than one-half of the children in tropical regions of Asia, Africa, and Latin America. Too little iodine can cause goiter, an abnormal enlargement of the thyroid gland in the neck (Figure 12-14). It affects as much as 80% of the population in the mountainous areas of Latin America, Asia, and Africa, where soils are deficient in iodine. Every year iodine insufficiency also causes deafness or muteness in an estimated 200 million people in these areas.

This tragic loss of human life and life quality, especially in the world's children, could be prevented at relatively little cost. UNICEF officials estimate that between half and two-thirds of the annual childhood deaths from undernutrition, malnutrition, and associated diseases could be prevented at an average overall cost of only $5 to $10 per child. This program would involve a combination of the following simple measures:

- immunization against childhood diseases such as measles

- encouraging breast-feeding

- counteracting diarrhea with low-cost rehydration therapy in which infants drink a solution of a fistful of sugar and a pinch of salt in water

Table 12-1 Vitamins Required in Human Nutrition

Vitamin	Major Sources	Possible Deficiency Effects
A (retinol)	Fish-liver oils, butter, egg yolks, green leafy and yellow vegetables, milk, fruits	Low resistance to infection, night blindness, scaly skin, acne
D	Fish-liver oils, yeast, liver, fortified milk, egg yolks	Rickets (defective bone formation)
E (α-tocopherol)	Wheat germ oil, cottonseed oil, lettuce, whole grain cereals, egg yolks, soybean oil, beef liver, wheat germ, green leafy vegetables	Sterility? more susceptibility to environmental pollution? more rapid aging?
K	Leafy vegetables, cabbage, cauliflower, vegetable oil, produced by bacteria in the intestines	Hemorrhages, slow clotting of blood
B_1 (thiamine)	Fruits, cereal grains, milk, green vegetables, nuts, rice polishings, liver, brain, heart, kidney	Beriberi, heart failure, mental disturbance
B_2 (riboflavin)	Beef liver, meats, milk, eggs, yeast, leafy vegetables	Sores on lips, retarded growth in young, bloodshot and burning eyes
B_3 (pantothenic acid)	Cereals, beef liver, milk, eggs, yeast, kidney	Retarded growth, emotional instability, digestive disorders
B_5 (niacin or nicotinic acid)	Meats, vegetables, rice, fish, eggs, yeast, whole grains	Stunted growth, pellagra, diarrhea, dementia
B_6 (pyridoxine)	Eggs, liver, yeast, whole grains, milk, fish, legumes	Convulsions in infants, retarded growth, insomnia, eye, nose, and mouth sores
B_{12} (cobalamin)	Meats, eggs, liver, seafood, milk and milk products	Degeneration of spinal cord, anemia
C (ascorbic acid)	Citrus fruits, raw green vegetables (especially tomatoes and green peppers)	Scurvy, low resistance to disease, sterility, hemorrhages, swollen joints
Biotin	Liver, egg white, dried peas and lima beans, produced by bacteria in the intestines	Skin disorders

- preventing blindness by administering large doses of vitamin A twice a year (35 cents per dose)

- providing family planning services to help mothers space births at least two years apart

- increasing female education with emphasis on nutrition, sterilization of drinking water, and improved child care

While 15% of the people in LDCs suffer from undernutrition and malnutrition, about 15% of the people in MDCs suffer from **overnutrition,** which leads to obesity, or excess body fat. Although the causes of obesity are complex and not well understood, experts agree that a major cause is overeating—taking in food containing more energy than the body consumes. In the United States, 10% to 15% of children and 35% to 50% of middle-aged adults are obese, weighing at least 20% more than their normal, desirable weight. These overnourished people exist on diets high in calories, cholesterol-containing saturated fats, salt, sugar, and processed foods, and low in unprocessed fresh vegetables, fruits, and fiber. Partly as a result of these dietary choices, overweight people are at significantly higher than normal risk of diabetes, high blood pressure, stroke, and heart disease. Some elements of this diet are also associated with intestinal cancer, tooth decay, and other health problems.

Food Storage and Distribution Regardless of how much food is produced, much of it will rot or be consumed by pests unless there is a sophisticated system for storing, processing, transporting, and marketing it. Because of inadequate food storage and distribution systems, food production in most LDCs is below its potential and much of the food produced never reaches consumers.

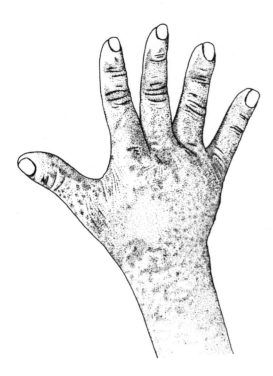

Figure 12-13 Skin lesions from advanced pellagra, caused by a deficiency of vitamin B$_5$, or niacin.

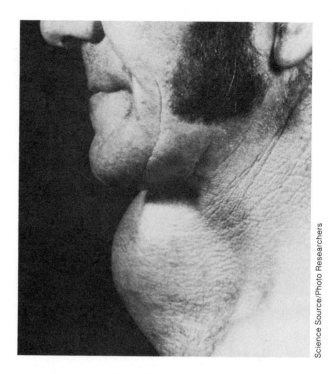

Science Source/Photo Researchers

Figure 12-14 A person with goiter, an enlargement of the thyroid gland, caused by insufficient dietary iodine.

Poverty: The Geography of Hunger If all the food currently produced in the world were divided equally among the earth's people, each person would receive about 2.3 kilograms (5 pounds) of food per day—more than three times the minimum amount needed to stay alive. Actually, the total amount of food produced today is more than enough to feed the 6.1 billion people anticipated by the year 2000, assuming that this food were distributed equally.

The world's supply of food, however, is not now distributed equally among the world's people, nor will it be. *Poverty—not lack of food production—is the chief cause of hunger and malnutrition throughout the world.* The world's desperately poor people do not have access to land where they can grow enough food of the right kind, and they do not have the money to buy enough food of the right kind, no matter how much food is available.

The United Nations Food and Agriculture Organization and the World Bank estimate that there are 450 million to 800 million chronically undernourished and malnourished people, found mostly in the LDCs. About one-third of the world's hungry live in India, even though it is self-sufficient in food production.

Increased worldwide total and average per capita food production often masks widespread differences in food supply and quality between and within countries, and even within a particular family. For instance, although total and per capita food supplies have increased in Latin America, much of this gain has been confined to Argentina and Brazil. In more fertile and urbanized southern Brazil, average daily per capita food supply is high, but in the semiarid, less fertile northeastern interior many people are grossly underfed. In the MDCs too there are pockets of hunger. A 1985 report by a task force of physicians estimated that at least 20 million Americans—about one out of every 12—were hungry, mostly because of cuts in food stamps and other forms of government aid since 1980. Food is also inequitably distributed within families. Among the poor, children (ages 1 to 5), pregnant women, and nursing mothers are most likely to be underfed and malnourished because the largest portion of the family food supply goes to working males.

Without a widespread increase in income and access to land, the number of chronically hungry and malnourished people in the world could double to as many as 1.5 billion by the year 2000. Increasing the world's overall food production does little to solve this fundamental and preventable food problem for the world's poor.

Environmental Effects of Producing More Food Agricultural expert Lester R. Brown says, "The central question is no longer 'Can we produce enough food?' but 'What are the environmental consequences of attempting to do so?'" Industrialized agriculture can feed large numbers of people by using relatively little human labor to produce high yields on a relatively

Table 12-2	Environmental Effects of Food Production
Effect	Text Discussion
Overfishing	Sections 12-5 and 14-5
Overgrazing	Section 13-6
Soil erosion and loss of soil fertility	Sections 10-4 and 10-5
Salinization and waterlogging of irrigated soils	Sections 11-3 and 11-4
Waterborne diseases from irrigation	Section 23-2
Loss of forests (deforestation)	Section 13-5
Endangered wildlife from loss of habitat	Sections 14-3 and 14-4
Loss of genetic diversity	Sections 12-3 and 14-1
Pollution from pesticides	Section 22-3
Water pollution from runoff of fertilizer and animal wastes	Chapter 20
Climate change from land clearing	Section 19-5
Air pollution from use of fossil fuels	Chapter 19
Health dangers from food additives	Section 23-4

small percentage of the world's potential cropland. However, this form of agriculture probably has a greater overall environmental impact on the air, soil, and water than any other system in modern industrialized societies (Table 12-2). Severe environmental degradation also occurs when poor people, struggling for survival, farm highly erodible land on steep mountain slopes, do not allow cleared patches of tropical forests to lie fallow long enough to restore soil fertility, and allow their livestock to overgraze grasslands.

12-3 INCREASING CROP YIELDS AND USING NEW TYPES OF FOODS

Green Revolutions   Most experts agree that the quickest and usually the cheapest way to grow more food is to raise the yield per unit of area of existing cropland. This is done by crossbreeding closely related wild and existing strains of plants to develop new, hybrid varieties that are better adapted to regional climate and soil conditions and can produce higher yields because they are able to make increased use of fertilizer, water, and pesticides. In countries where this method has succeeded in significantly increasing crop yields, the result has been called a **green revolution.**

Between 1950 and 1970 this approach led to dramatic increases in yields for most major crops in the United States and most other industrialized countries (Figure 12-15). In 1967, after 30 years of painstaking genetic research and trials, a modified version of the green revolution began spreading to many LDCs. New, high-yield, fast-growing dwarf varieties of rice and wheat, specially bred for tropical and subtropical climates, were introduced into LDCs such as Mexico, India, Pakistan, the Philippines, and Turkey. The shorter, stronger, and stiffer stalks of the new varieties allow them to support larger heads of grain without toppling over (Figure 12-16). With high, properly timed inputs of fertilizer, water to keep the increased levels of fertilizer from killing the crops, and pesticides, wheat and rice yields from these new varieties can be two to three times higher than those from traditional varieties. With favorable growing conditions, overall yields per unit of land can be increased three to five times because these fast-growing varieties allow farmers to grow two and even three crops per year (multiple cropping) on the same parcel of land.

By the 1970s the new wheat varieties had spread to several parts of the world including China and Bangladesh, and the new rice varieties were adopted in many parts of Southeast and South Asia. Nearly 90% of the increase in world grain output in the 1960s and about 70% in the 1970s came from increased yields, mostly as a result of the second green revolution. It has been the major factor in allowing average per capita food production to remain ahead of population growth in Asia. In the 1980s and 1990s at least 80% of the additional production of grains is expected to result from improved productivity of current cropland through the increased use of high-yield varieties, irrigation, fertilizer, pesticides, and multiple cropping.

Limitations of Green Revolutions   Several factors can limit the spread and long-term success of present and future green revolutions. Without massive doses of fertilizer and water, the new crop varieties produce yields no higher and often lower than those from traditional grains. Thus, areas without sufficient rainfall or irrigation potential cannot benefit from the new varieties; that is why the second green revolution has not spread to many areas.

A second problem is that in some countries, such as India, new varieties have increased overall food production at the expense of protein production. This occurred because the high-yield varieties of rice and wheat displaced legumes, an important source of protein in the Indian diet. In addition, because legumes naturally add nitrogen to the soil, their displacement impoverishes the soil and requires additional inputs of expensive commercial fertilizer.

A third limitation is based on the concept of

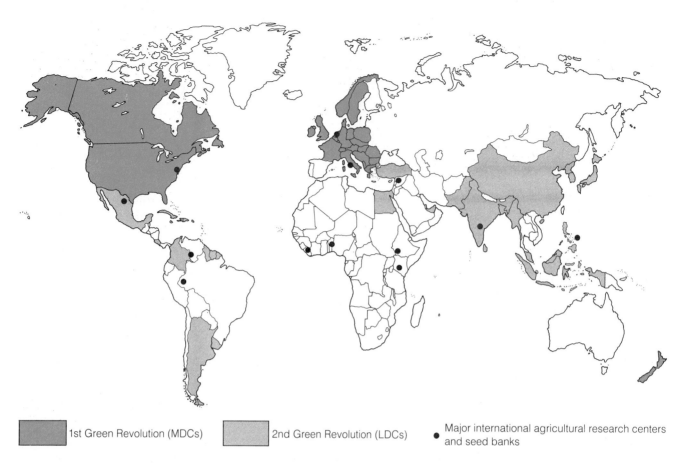

▓ 1st Green Revolution (MDCs)	░ 2nd Green Revolution (LDCs)	● Major international agricultural research centers and seed banks

Figure 12-15 Countries achieving increases in crop yields per unit of land during the first green revolution, from 1950 to 1970 in MDCs, and the second green revolution, from 1967 to 1985 in LDCs with sufficient rainfall or irrigation capacity. Thirteen agricultural research centers and seed banks play a significant role in developing new crop varieties.

diminishing returns, in which a J-shaped curve of exponentially increasing crop productivity levels off and is converted to an S-shaped curve. Increased inputs of fertilizer, water, and pesticides cause yields to increase dramatically at first. But increasingly higher inputs eventually produce little or no increase in productivity, as has happened to yields of sorghum and corn in the United States. Once this point is reached, additional inputs merely add to the cost of crop production without increasing profits. In the 1970s about three-fourths of the gain in U.S. agricultural production came from newly cultivated acreage and only one-fourth from increased yields per unit of cropland.

The diminishing-returns effect, however, typically takes 20 to 30 years to develop; thus, yields in LDCs using existing green revolution varieties are projected to increase for some time. Geneticists also attempt to overcome this built-in biological limitation by developing new and improved varieties (see Spotlight on p. 250).

Loss of Genetic Diversity Another serious potential limitation of the two major green revolutions tak-

ing place in MDCs and some LDCs since 1950 is a loss of genetic diversity needed to develop future green revolutions. When fields of natural varieties are cleared and replaced with monocultures of crossbred varieties, much of the natural genetic diversity essential for developing new hybrids is lost forever. For example, a perennial variety of wild corn that, unlike cultivated corn, replants itself each year was recently discovered. This variety is also resistant to a range of viruses and grows well on wet soils. However, the few thousand plants known to exist were found on a Mexican hillside that was in the process of being plowed up.

Genetic vulnerability was dramatically demonstrated in 1970 when most of the single-variety U.S. corn crop was wiped out by a blight-causing fungus. Seed companies quickly introduced a resistant seed variety and recovery was rapid, but the episode made farmers aware that genetic diversity is an essential form of insurance against disaster. Although monocultures predominate in MDCs, many of the world's 800 million farmers in LDCs plant several varieties of the same crops in their fields to prevent the total loss of a year's work.

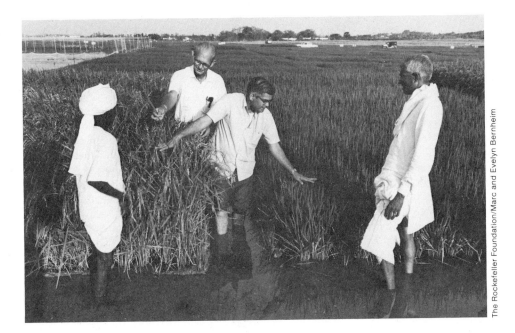

Figure 12-16 Scientists and two Indian farmers compare an older, full-size variety of rice (left) and a new, high-yield dwarf variety, grown in the second green revolution.

The Rockefeller Foundation/Marc and Evelyn Bernheim

To help preserve genetic variety, naturally growing native plants and strains of food crops throughout the world are being collected, preserved, and maintained in 13 genetic storage banks and agricultural research centers located around the world (Figure 12-15).

Do the Poor Benefit? Whether present and future green revolutions help reduce hunger among the world's poor depends on how they are used. In LDCs the major resource available to agriculture is human labor. When green revolution techniques are applied to increase yields of labor-intensive subsistence agriculture in countries with equitable land distribution, the poor benefit, as has occurred in China.

However, when farmers in LDCs are encouraged to couple green revolution techniques with a shift from small-scale, labor-intensive subsistence cultivation to large-scale, fossil-fuel-mechanized agriculture, the rural poor's ability to grow or buy sufficient food is reduced. The problem is that most of the benefits of the green revolution go to large landowners who have money or can obtain credit to buy the seed, fertilizer, irrigation water, pesticides, equipment, and fuel that the new techniques require. Meanwhile, tenant farmers suffer from rising land rents because of increased land value and are often forced off the land; farm laborers are displaced by the increased use of farm machinery. Because small farm owners have difficulty in getting credit to take advantage of the new agricultural technology, they become less competitive and are frequently forced out of business. The net result is that many small landowners, farm laborers, and tenant farmers have been forced to migrate to cities in a desperate attempt to survive.

Coupling green revolution techniques with mechanized, industrialized agriculture also makes LDCs without their own supplies heavily dependent on large, MDC-based multinational companies for expensive supplies of seeds, fertilizer, farm machinery, and oil. This increases the LDCs' national debts, makes their agricultural and economic systems vulnerable to collapse from increases in oil and fertilizer prices, and reduces their rates of economic growth because their capital is diverted to pay for imported oil and other agricultural inputs.

Unconventional Foods Some analysts recommend greatly increased cultivation of various nontraditional plants in LDCs to supplement or replace traditional foods such as wheat, rice, and corn. One little-known crop is the winged bean, a protein-rich legume presently used extensively only in New Guinea and Southeast Asia. Its edible winged pods, leaves, tendrils, and seeds contain as much protein as soybeans, and its edible roots more than four times the protein of potato; it yields so many edible parts that it has been called "a supermarket on a stalk."

Among dozens of other plants that could serve as important food sources are cocoyam, a native plant of West Africa and Central and South America, as nutritious as the potato; quinoa, a grain plant of the Andes that resembles wild rice in taste and whose abundant seeds contain 12% to 19% protein; and the marama bean, a protein-rich legume that grows in the arid Kalahari desert in southern Africa and has a juicy, sweet tuber and good-tasting seeds with more protein than peanuts and more oil than soybeans. The problem is getting farmers to cultivate such crops and convincing consumers to try new foods.

Sustaining existing green revolutions is a never-ending process. The life of a new hybrid wheat variety in the northwestern United States, for example, is about five years. Then, fungi that cause wheat rust become adapted to the hybrid and a new rust-resistant strain must be developed.

In addition to producing new varieties of crops and livestock through crossbreeding, efforts are being made to create new green revolutions much more rapidly by using genetic engineering and other biotechnology. Three major techniques are cloning, in which identical copies of whole plants can be produced from a single cell; cell fusion, in which cells of species that wouldn't normally mate are united to create a completely different species; and recombinant DNA, in which beneficial genes in one plant or animal species are identified, chemically synthesized in the laboratory, and inserted into the seeds or reproductive cells of another species to produce superior offspring. This latter gene-splicing technique can produce an insect-resistant strain of tomatoes in about 4 genera-

tions (or 2 years), whereas it takes up to 12 generations (or about 6 years) by conventional crossbreeding.

Most agricultural biotechnology research so far has centered on bacteria and animals. By 1988 a growth hormone extracted from the pituitary glands of cows, which is expected to increase milk production by as much as 30%, should be on sale in the United States. This could reduce milk prices by as much as 15% and put about 10% of today's U.S. dairy farmers out of business. Geneticists are also working on producing supersized pigs and salmon. Genetically altered bacteria have been developed and are being tested to keep strawberries and potatoes free of frost and thus reduce crop damage and increase yields. However, lawsuits have been filed to prevent the release of genetically engineered bacteria, viruses, and insects into the environment because of fear of possible harmful ecological disruption (see Spotlight on p. 121).

Lured by forecasts that the market for genetically modified seed will grow from $165 million in 1990

to $12.1 billion by 2005, several major U.S. food, chemical, wood products, and oil corporations have begun investing heavily in plant biotechnology research. Goals over the next 20 to 40 years include breeding new high-yield plant strains that have greater resistance to insects and disease; thrive on less fertilizer; make their own nitrogen fertilizer (for example, wheat with the ability of soybean to extract nitrogen from the air and convert it to nitrate fertilizer in its roots); do well in slightly salty soils; withstand periods of drought; and make more efficient use of solar energy during photosynthesis. If even a tiny fraction of this research is successful, the world could experience a new type of agricultural revolution in the early part of the next century based on rapid and enormous increases in crop and animal productivity. Some analysts, however, fear that such breakthroughs will be used primarily to make the rich richer instead of reducing poverty (the leading cause of world hunger) and result in unexpected and harmful ecological effects, as has occurred with previous green revolutions.

Vitamin and Protein Supplements and Fabricated Foods In the United States and most MDCs, enrichment of bread and flour with vitamins and minerals has helped eliminate many nutritional deficiency diseases, and adding small amounts of iodine to table salt has virtually wiped out goiter. Similarly, Japan has essentially eradicated beriberi since World War II by enriching its rice with vitamin B_1. Enriching existing foods is relatively inexpensive and does not require people to change their eating habits. However, such enriched, processed foods are not normally available to rural people in LDCs, where chronic hunger and malnutrition are widespread.

Most LDCs have had low-cost, high-protein meat substitutes, such as Indonesian tempeh made from soybeans, for hundreds of years. Food can also be supplemented with protein by using meal or flour made

from soybeans, cottonseed, peanuts, coconuts, sunflower seeds, rape seeds, and other oil seeds. Soybean meal has been used as a protein supplement for decades, and soybean-based soft drinks are available. Problems arise, however, in purifying some of these meal and flour supplements and making them tasty enough for human consumption.

In MDCs there has been increasing use of imitation bacon, eggs, chicken, ham, and meat extenders, which contain spun vegetable protein (SVP) fibers made primarily from soybean concentrate and wheat gluten. If these products were widely accepted, they could dramatically reduce meat consumption in countries such as the United States. Since SVP contains no cholesterol, it could also reduce the incidence of heart disease. However, to make these processed products look and taste like meat, a number of dyes, flavorings,

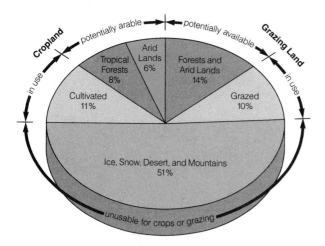

Figure 12-17 Classification of the earth's land. Theoretically, the world's cropland could be doubled in size by clearing tropical forests and irrigating arid lands. But converting this marginal land to cropland would destroy valuable forest resources, cause serious environmental problems, and usually not be cost-effective.

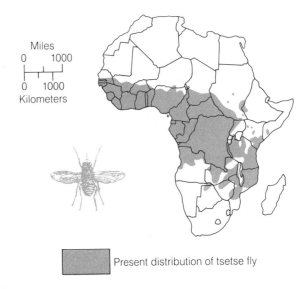

Present distribution of tsetse fly

Figure 12-18 Region of Africa infested by the tsetse fly.

and other food additives must be used, which some fear might increase risks of cancer and other health hazards (Section 23-4).

12-4 CULTIVATING MORE LAND

Availability of Arable Land Before 1950 most increases in world agricultural production resulted from expansion of cultivated land. Since then most increases have resulted from increasing the productivity per unit of area on existing cropland. As a result, the amount of cultivated land per person shrank by more than a third between 1950 and 1985—a trend that is expected to continue.

Some agronomists, however, have suggested that the world's cropland could be more than doubled by clearing tropical forests and irrigating arid lands mostly in Africa, South America, and Australia (Figure 12-17). Others believe such an expansion will not be achieved because most of these arable, or potentially cultivatable, lands are too dry or remote or lack productive soils. Some of the shortcomings of marginal agricultural land can be overcome by massive inputs of water and fertilizers, but doing this is expensive compared to increasing productivity on prime agricultural land already in use. Even if more cropland is developed, much of the increase will be used to offset the projected loss of almost one-third of today's cultivated cropland and rangeland from erosion, overgrazing, waterlogging, salinization, mining, and urbanization.

Location, Soil, and Insects as Limiting Factors About 83% of the world's potential new cropland is in the remote and lightly populated rain forests of the Amazon and Orinoco river basins in South America and in Africa's rain forests (see map inside front cover). Cultivating this land would require massive capital and energy investments in land clearing and in transportation of the harvested crops to populated areas. The resulting deforestation would greatly increase soil erosion and reduce the world's genetic diversity by eliminating vast numbers of the plant and animal species found in these incredibly diverse biomes.

Although the rain forests are blessed with plentiful rainfall and long or continuous growing seasons, the soils often are not suitable for intensive cultivation because much of the plant nutrient supply is tied up in ground litter and vegetation rather than stored in the soil. Nearly 75% of the Amazon basin, roughly one-third of the world's potential cropland, contains highly acidic and infertile soils. In addition, an estimated 5% to 15% of tropical soils (4% of those in the Amazon basin), if cleared, would bake under the tropical sun into brick-hard surfaces called laterites, useless for farming. Some scientists argue that agriculture in the tropics should be limited to plantation cultivation of trees adapted to the existing climates and soils, such as rubber trees, oil palms, and banana trees.

In Africa, potential cropland larger in area than the United States cannot be used for grazing or farming because it is infested by 22 species of the tsetse fly, whose bite can give both humans and livestock incurable sleeping sickness (Figure 12-18). A $120 million eradication program has been proposed but many scientists doubt whether it can succeed.

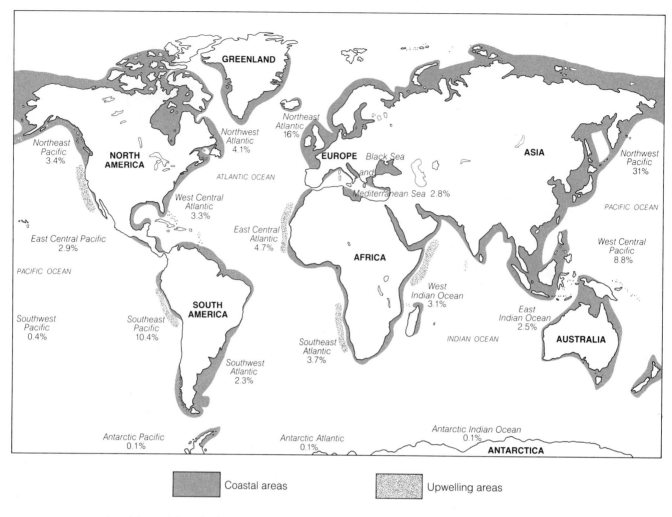

Figure 12-19 Location of the world's major fisheries and distribution of the annual catch. (Data from UN Food and Agriculture Organization)

Water as a Limiting Factor More than half the remaining arable land lies in dry areas (Figure 12-17), where water shortages limit crop growth. This can be overcome with irrigation, but large-scale irrigation in these areas would be very expensive (typically $1,000 to $2,000 per hectare), require large inputs of fossil fuel to pump water long distances, deplete many groundwater supplies, and require constant and expensive maintenance to prevent seepage, salinization, and waterlogging. Unfortunately, Africa, the continent that needs irrigation the most, has the lowest potential for it because of the remote location of its major rivers and unfavorable topography and rainfall patterns.

Money as a Limiting Factor According to agricultural expert Lester Brown, "The people who are talking about cultivating more land are not considering the cost. If you are willing to pay the cost, you can farm the slope of Mount Everest." Thus, the real questions are How much will it cost to increase the total amount of cropland in the world, and how will this cost affect the ability of poor people to pay for the additional food grown on this land?

12-5 CATCHING MORE FISH AND FISH FARMING

The World's Fisheries Fish and shellfish supply about 6% of all human protein consumption and 24% of the animal protein worldwide—considerably more than beef, twice as much as eggs, and three times as much as poultry. Fish and shellfish are the major source of animal protein, iron, and iodine for more than half the world's people, especially in Asia and Africa.

About 91% of the annual commercial catch of fish and shellfish comes from the ocean and 9% from fresh

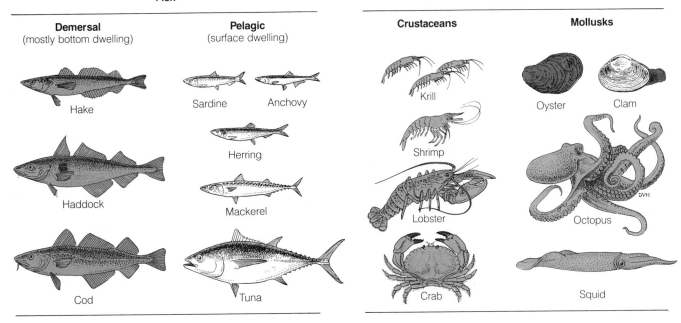

Fish		Shellfish	
Demersal (mostly bottom dwelling)	**Pelagic** (surface dwelling)	**Crustaceans**	**Mollusks**

Figure 12-20 Major types of commercially harvested fish and shellfish.

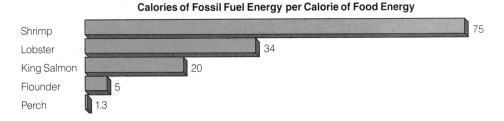

Calories of Fossil Fuel Energy per Calorie of Food Energy

Shrimp 75
Lobster 34
King Salmon 20
Flounder 5
Perch 1.3

Figure 12-21 Energy input needed to produce one unit of food energy for commercially desirable types of fish and shellfish.

water. Figure 12-19 shows the distribution of the world's major commercial marine fisheries. About 99% of the world marine catch is taken within 370 kilometers (200 nautical miles) of the coast; more than half of the catch is taken from the North Pacific and North Atlantic fisheries.

Four main groups of marine species make up the bulk of the annual commercial catch (Figure 12-20). About 70% of the annual marine catch is eaten by humans. The remainder, consisting largely of herringlike fish unacceptable for human consumption, is processed into fish meal, most of which is fed to poultry, pigs, and cattle.

To achieve large catches, modern "distant-water" fishing fleets use sonar (bouncing high-frequency sound waves off solid objects), helicopters, aerial photography, and temperature measurement to locate schools of fish. They use lights and electrodes to attract the fish, and fine nets to "vacuum" the sea. Enormous, floating-fish-factory trawlers follow the fleets

to process and freeze the catch. About 75% of the world's fish catch is taken by such large-scale fishing operations, but small-scale fishing boats account for 40% of the fish consumed by humans.

Using small and large fishing boats to catch fish and shellfish is essentially a hunting-and-gathering procedure taking place over a large area. Because fuel makes up 30% to 40% of the operating costs of fishing boats, energy inputs for each unit of food energy caught for most species are enormous (Figure 12-21). This helps explain why in the United States between 1960 and 1985 the inflation-adjusted real prices rose 70% for edible fish and crustaceans and 40% for mollusks, while the average real price of all food declined.

Trends in the World Fish Catch   Between 1950 and 1970, large-scale distant-water fishing fleets were a major factor in more than tripling the annual catch from 21 million to 70 million metric tons (23 million to

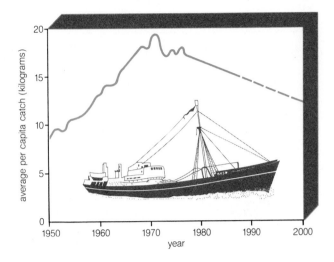

Figure 12-22 Average per capita world fish catch declined in most years since 1970 and is projected to decline further between 1985 and 2000. (Data from United Nations and World-watch Institute)

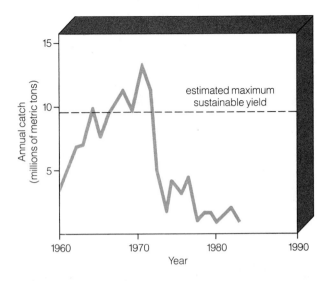

Figure 12-23 Collapse of the Peruvian anchovy catch as a result of a shift in an ocean current and gross overfishing. (Data from UN Food and Agriculture Organization)

77 million tons)—an increase greater than that of any other human food source during the same period. Between 1971 and 1976, however, the annual catch leveled off and rose only slightly to around 76 million metric tons (84 million tons) by 1985. Meanwhile, world population continued to grow, so between 1970 and 1985 the average fish catch per person declined, and is projected to decline even further—back to the 1960 level—by 2000 (Figure 12-22).

This leveling off of the annual catch is due to a combination of natural oceanographic changes, over-fishing, and pollution and destruction of estuaries and offshore areas where most commercial fish and shell-fish are caught. **Overfishing** occurs when so many fish, especially immature ones, are taken that there is not enough breeding stock left for adequate annual renewal. Surveys by the UN Food and Agriculture Organization indicated that by 1985 overfishing was the major factor in depleting stocks of 12 major species of commercially valuable fish to the point where it is no longer profitable to hunt and gather them.

Between 1971 and 1978, for example, the Peruvian anchovy became commercially extinct from a combi-nation of gross overfishing and the shifting away from shore of a cool current that brings nutrients up from the bottom. Since then, the annual yield from this fishery, which previously accounted for 20% of the annual global harvest, has remained at a low level (Figure 12-23). Peruvian fishery officials had not heeded warnings by UN Food and Agriculture Organization biologists that during seven of the eight years between 1964 and 1971, the anchovy harvest had exceeded the estimated sustainable yield.

Fish Farming: Aquaculture If we have trouble catching more fish and shellfish at affordable prices using our present hunting-and-gathering approach, why not raise and harvest fish crops in land-based ponds or fenced-in coastal lagoons and estuaries? This approach, known as **aquaculture,** or fish farming, can produce much higher yields per unit of land area than conventional fishing. It also uses a relatively low amount of fuel and thus is not dependent on the price of oil, which could make most conventional commer-cial fishing prohibitively expensive if oil prices rise sharply as projected some time after 1995.

Aquaculture, which may have originated in China over 4,000 years ago, supplies about 12% of the total world catch and is a major source of protein for the poor in many LDCs. Over half the total is produced in Asia, especially China, India, Japan, South Korea, Indonesia, the Philippines, and Taiwan. In LDCs, aquaculture operations usually involve fertilizing small ponds (usually less than 1 hectare) with animal wastes, fish wastes, or commercial fertilizer to produce phy-toplankton. These are eaten by zooplankton and bot-tom animals, which in turn are eaten by fish such as carp, which grow rapidly and can be easily harvested with nets when they reach a desired size (Figure 12-24). Yields are increased by raising several different types of fish (polyculture) that feed on different sources of food. One problem, however, is that the fish can be killed by pesticide runoff from nearby croplands, as has happened in aquaculture ponds in the Philip-pines, Indonesia, and Malaysia.

Very high yields can be obtained by feeding fish directly with grain or grain by-products supple-

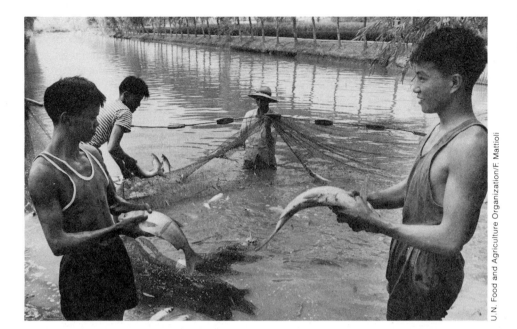

Figure 12-24 Harvesting of silver carp at an aquaculture farm near Chang-Chow, China.

U.N. Food and Agriculture Organization/F. Mattioli

mented with high-quality protein such as soy meal or fish meal from less valuable fish. Nutrient-rich estuaries can also be farmed to produce large yields of desirable marine species such as shrimp, lobster, oysters, and salmon in fenced-off bays, large tanks, or floating cages. In the United States, most of the catfish and crawfish, nearly all rainbow trout, and 40% of the oysters are harvested from fish farms. Aquaculture in MDCs, however, is designed to produce expensive fish and shellfish species for consumption by the affluent. This may be highly profitable, but contributes little to increasing food and protein supplies for the poor.

Can the Annual Catch Be Increased Significantly? Some scientists believe that the world's annual sustainable fish and shellfish catch could be increased to 100 million metric tons (110 million tons) by the year 2000 and perhaps to 200 million metric tons (220 million tons) by 2030 by a combination of methods. First, it is hoped that the signing of the 1982 United Nations Convention on the Law of the Sea by 159 countries will be effective in regulating overfishing in 99% of the world's prime fishing grounds. This treaty recognizes that all coastal countries have the right to control the amount of fishing allowed by their own fishing fleets and by foreign ships within 364 kilometers (200 nautical miles) of their coasts. However, the Law of the Sea will benefit only a small number of LDCs (mostly on the western coasts of Africa and Latin America) because two-thirds of the total value

of the ocean's fish catch has been taken off the coasts of MDCs.

The world fish catch can also be expanded by increasing the harvest of unconventional species such as Antarctic krill and several species of squid. Additional increases could be brought about by a sharp decrease in the one-fifth of the annual catch now wasted, mainly from throwing back potentially useful fish taken along with desired species, lack of adequate refrigerated storage to prevent spoilage, and inefficient processing. Some marine biologists, however, believe that the krill catch will not increase significantly because of bad weather in Antarctic waters, the necessity of processing the catch within three hours if the krill are to be consumed by humans, and the high energy and economic costs of harvesting in distant waters. Some scientists also warn that extensive annual harvesting of krill could lead to declines in the populations of krill eaters, including several species of whale, such as the already threatened blue whale, and several species of fish, seabirds, seals, and penguins. Perhaps the greatest problem is making krill palatable to human consumers.

It is also projected that annual freshwater and saltwater aquaculture production could be increased more than threefold between 1986 and 2000. The Food and Agriculture Organization estimates that only one-tenth of the land suitable for aquaculture, including lowlying, flood-prone land not suitable for crop production, is presently being used. Other fishery experts believe that the world's annual marine fish catch may already be at or near its maximum sustainable yield because of overfishing and pollution of estuaries.

CHAPTER 12 Food Resources and World Hunger **255**

12-6 MAKING FOOD PRODUCTION PROFITABLE, PROVIDING FOOD AID, AND DISTRIBUTING LAND TO THE POOR

Government Agricultural Policies Governments can influence crop and livestock prices, and thus the supply of food, by (1) keeping food prices artificially low, making consumers happy but decreasing profits for farmers; (2) providing farmers with subsidies to keep them in business; or (3) providing no price controls or subsidies and allowing free market competition to determine food prices.

Many governments in LDCs keep food prices in cities deliberately low to prevent political unrest. But this draws more poor people from rural areas to cities, further aggravating urban problems and unemployment. Because prices are too low for them to make a decent living, rural farmers do not produce enough food to feed the country's population. High food export taxes can also discourage farmers from growing food for export because of lack of sufficient profit.

Government price supports, cash subsidies, and import restrictions can be used to stimulate crop and livestock production by guaranteeing farmers a certain minimum yearly return on their investment. For example, despite population problems, the average food supply per person in India has been rising for more than two decades. One reason is the green revolution, but the main reason is removal of government price controls, which were keeping wheat prices at artificially low levels, and their replacement with price supports, which made the price of domestic wheat the same as the import price. With this economic incentive, Indian farmers began producing more wheat.

Government price supports and other subsidies make farmers happy. They are also popular with most consumers because subsidies make food prices seem low. What most consumers don't realize is that they are really paying higher prices for their food indirectly in the form of higher taxes to provide the subsidies. There is no free lunch.

The U.S. Farm Situation If government price supports are too generous and the weather is good, farmers may produce more food than can be sold. Food prices and profits then drop because of the oversupply. Unless even higher government subsidies are provided to prop up farm income by buying unsold crops or paying farmers to idle some of their land, a number of debt-ridden farmers go bankrupt, as has occurred in the United States in the 1980s.

Between 1980 and 1986 several hundred thousand part-time and full-time U.S. farmers quit farming or went bankrupt. Many farm-oriented businesses, including those providing farmers with machinery and other supplies, and general businesses in farming towns also suffered severe economic losses. By 1986 about one-fourth of the country's 650,000 full-time farmers, who produce about 90% of the nation's food, were having trouble paying off their loans.

The farm debt crisis has its roots in the 1960s and 1970s, when the government encouraged farmers to grow food to help fight world hunger and to increase food exports to help offset the mounting bill for imported oil after the 1973 OPEC oil embargo. Most farmers responded by expanding their operations, and many borrowed heavily to buy additional land and equipment. Their heavy borrowing was backed by the rapidly escalating value of their cropland.

During the first half of the 1980s, however, the bottom dropped out for farmers who had borrowed heavily and gambled on increased food demand to keep cropland values and crop prices high. Between 1981 and 1986, the average value per acre of farmland dropped by 27% (by 40% to 50% in some midwestern states), net farm income and exports fluctuated, and tax-supported federal subsidies to farmers increased to buy up surpluses and keep production down to prevent even more farmers from going bankrupt (Figure 12-25). Two major factors contributed to the decrease in land value. First, overproduction reduced crop prices. Second, U.S. food exports declined in most years because of increases in production in many countries as a result of the green revolution, inability of many debt-ridden LDCs to buy the food they needed, and the ability of other countries to sell surplus crops for less because a stronger dollar and federal price supports made U.S. crops more expensive in the world market.

Some agricultural economists see a few rays of hope on the horizon: If interest rates continue to fall and oil prices remain low, farm expenses will be reduced; if the value of the U.S. dollar continues to fall, U.S. farm exports will become more competitive. But the overriding problem is that the U.S. agricultural system is too successful for its own good. There are too many farmers growing too much food. A number of analysts believe that the only way out of this dilemma is to gradually wean U.S. farmers from all federal subsidies and let them respond to market demand—a politically difficult process.

The first step would be to ensure that federal subsidies go only to farmers in economic trouble. Presently, nearly half of all subsidies go to the country's largest, and most successful, farms. In effect, taxpay-

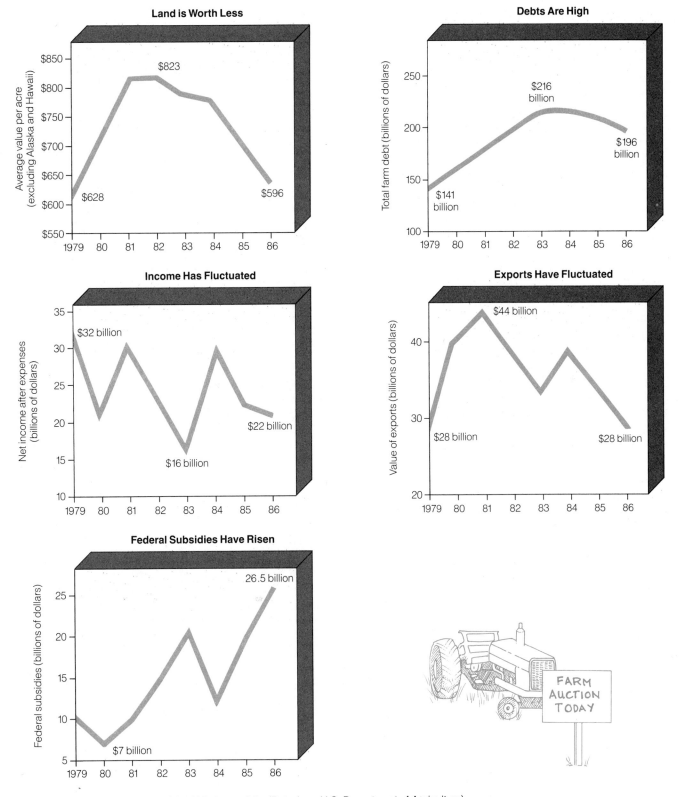

Figure 12-25 Major elements of the U.S. farm crisis. (Data from U.S. Department of Agriculture)

ers are either paying many well-off corporate farmers not to grow food on some of their land (sometimes marginal land they did not intend to farm anyway) or paying them above market prices for the excess food they produce. In 1986 the Crown Prince of Lichtenstein, a Texas landowner, received more than $2 million in federal aid intended for struggling farmers.

By law no farmer is supposed to get more than $50,000 a year in federal subsidies. But many big farmers have gotten around this by dividing the ownership of their acreage among several people, usually relatives, each eligible for the maximum subsidy.

Next the government would phase out farm subsidies over several years. Some of the money saved would be used to help needy farmers pay off part of their debts, provided they practice an approved soil and water conservation program. Once needy farmers' debts were whittled down to a manageable level (no more than 40% of the value of their assets), all federal subsidies would stop. From then on all farmers would respond to the demands of the market so that only those who were good farmers and financial managers would remain in the business. Reducing the debt of presently overextended farmers between 1986 and 1991 would cost taxpayers about $75 billion, less than the $80 billion to $100 billion in farm subsidies projected for the same period.

Phasing out farm subsidies, however, is difficult to accomplish because of the political influence of large corporate farmers, whose profits are higher and risks are lower because of such subsidies. In addition, many small- and medium-sized farmers have become dependent on federal subsidies that now provide one-third to one-half of their income regardless of how much they grow. These farmers and people dependent on them—small-town bankers and businesses, food processors, farm machinery dealers, fertilizer makers, and the like—dominate the economies of their states, which would elect members of Congress opposed to such a program.

International Relief Aid   Since 1945, in terms of total dollars expended per year, the United States has been—and continues to be—the world's largest donor of nonmilitary foreign aid. Aid donated directly to countries (bilateral aid) or to international institutions such as the World Bank for distribution to other countries (multilateral aid) is used primarily for agriculture and rural development, food relief, population planning, health, and economic development projects. In addition to helping other countries, foreign aid stimulates U.S. economic growth and provides Americans with jobs. Seventy cents of every dollar the U.S. gives directly to other countries is used to purchase American goods and services. Despite the humanitarian benefits and economic returns of such aid, the per-

centage of the U.S. gross national product allocated for nonmilitary foreign aid has declined from a high of 1.6% in the 1950s to only 0.25% in 1986—an average of only $34 per American.

Private charity organizations such as CARE and Catholic Relief Services provide at least $2 billion a year of additional foreign aid. In 1985 many of the world's popular musical performers used benefit concerts and record sales to provide aid to nearly bankrupt farmers in the United States and starving people in Ethiopia and other parts of Africa. Some people call for greatly increased food relief aid from government and private sources, while others question the value of such aid (see Spotlight on p. 259).

Distributing Land to the Poor   An important step in reducing world hunger and malnutrition is land reform, by which the landless rural poor in LDCs are given access to land to produce enough food for their survival. Such reform would increase agricultural productivity because small, labor-intensive farms produce more per unit of land area than large, fossil-fuel-intensive farms. Moreover, land reform would reduce the flow of landless poor to overcrowded urban areas and create employment in rural areas.

China and Taiwan have had the most successful land reforms. Supported by financial aid from the United States after World War II, land reform was a key element in ending hunger in Taiwan. Before reform took place, tenant farmers had been paying 50% to 70% of the crops they grew as rent to landowners. To begin its land reform program, the government gave small plots of land to peasant farmers in exchange for a small percentage of the farmers' income over a 10-year period. The government used this money to pay the former landowners for their land. The peasant farmers' incomes typically increased by 81%. The result was a decrease in the infant mortality rate from around 150 in 1945 to 8.9 in 1986. Health care, education, and family planning also improved, and the birth rate declined from 42.1 in 1954 to 20 in 1986. Land reform was followed by greatly increased industrial capacity and increased export of products to MDCs.

This is clear evidence that land reform can reduce hunger and promote economic growth for LDCs. Unfortunately, land reform is difficult to institute in countries where government leaders are unduly influenced by wealthy and powerful landowners.

12-7   SUSTAINABLE-EARTH AGRICULTURE

Sustainable-Earth Agriculture in LDCs   Cornucopians believe that the key to reducing world hunger

Most people view food relief as a humanitarian effort to prevent people from dying prematurely from lack of sufficient food. However, some analysts contend that providing food to starving people in countries where population growth rates are high does more harm than good in the long run, condemning even greater numbers to premature death in the future. Massive food aid can also depress local food prices, decrease food production, stimulate mass migration from farms to already overcrowded cities, and decrease a country's long-term ability to provide food for its people.

Another problem is that much food aid does not reach hunger victims: Transportation networks and storage facilities are inadequate so that some of the food rots or is devoured by pests before it can reach the hungry, and theft by officials who sell the food for personal profit or use it for political gain is rampant. For example, doctors and other volunteers from a French nonprofit, humanitarian group providing medical aid to Ethiopian famine victims charged that much of the famine relief aid provided by donations from U.S. citizens in 1985 was used by Ethiopian officials to suppress a long-standing rebellion in northern parts of the country. The Ethiopian army destroyed many crops, herds, and farms in the north and used food aid to lure thousands of starving people into slave labor camps in the south. Although the food aid saved the lives of many Ethiopians, these observers contend that at least half of all starvation deaths in Ethiopia were caused directly or indirectly by the Ethiopian government.

Critics of food relief are not against foreign aid. Instead, they believe that such aid should be concentrated on efforts to control population growth and on helping LDCs become self-sufficient in growing their own food and in developing resource-efficient forms of economic growth that will help them compete in the world marketplace without excessive dependence on MDCs. They believe that such aid should be provided to countries committed to effective plans for controlling population growth and to equitable distribution of land. What do you think?

is to transfer highly mechanized, industrialized agriculture to LDCs. Neo-Malthusians, however, say that this approach will not end hunger among the poor because it will make LDCs increasingly dependent on MDCs, allow the rich in MDCs and LDCs to get richer at the expense of the poor, and greatly increase pollution and environmental degradation. They believe that the key to reducing world hunger and reducing the harmful environmental impacts of agriculture is for LDCs to become self-sufficient in food production by developing a **sustainable-earth agricultural system** (see Spotlight on p. 260). China, the world's leader in sustainable-earth agriculture, has shown that this approach can essentially eliminate hunger.

Sustainable-Earth Agriculture in MDCs   Some elements of a sustainable-earth agricultural system for LDCs can be readily applied to MDCs. The increased use of no-till and low-till cultivation (Section 10-5) will reduce soil erosion and water pollution. Likewise, increased use of water-conserving forms of irrigation (Section 11-5) will reduce groundwater depletion, river pollution, and erosion, salinization, and waterlogging of soils. Developing government agricultural policies that encourage and reward the use of such strategies should be a major priority.

Rising costs of pesticides, inorganic fertilizers, and fuel, along with decreasing crop yields, have motivated about 35,000 or 5% of the full-time farmers in the U.S. to shift to industrialized organic farming—growing crops and livestock with organic fertilizers and biological pest control. Studies have shown that U.S. organic farms use an average of 40% less energy per unit of food produced and many have 5% to 15% higher yields than conventional industrialized farms. A Department of Agriculture study indicated that a widespread shift to organic farming would increase net farm income, lower farm debts, reduce soil erosion and nutrient depletion, meet domestic food needs, reduce oil imports, and lower the environmental impact of agriculture. However, such a switch would also raise consumer food costs and reduce the amount of food available for export. It would also lead to a sharp reduction in the sales of fertilizers and pesticides; thus, it would be strongly opposed by the politically powerful agricultural chemical industry.

Reducing Food Waste   If the peoples of affluent countries reduced their enormous waste of food, it is often said, more food would be available for export to feed the poor. An estimated 25% of all food produced in the United States is wasted; it rots in the supermarket or refrigerator or is thrown away off the plate. This wasted food, theoretically, could feed more than 60 million people a U.S. meat-based diet and 150 million people a grain-based diet.

It is argued that if cattle in the United States were not fattened in feedlots, enough grain would be available to feed about 400 million people—equal to 69% of Africa's population. Even if feedlots were not eliminated, merely decreasing annual meat consumption in the United States by 10% could release enough grain to feed 60 million people. Similarly, the commercial fertilizers spread on U.S. lawns, golf courses, and cemeteries could, in principle, be used to produce grain for 65 million people each year. Pet foods consumed in the United States, which has the world's highest ratio of pets to people, contain enough protein to feed 21 million people each year.

Many analysts point out, however, that food made available by the reduction of waste would not neces-

sarily go to the poor because they cannot afford to buy it. It is also argued that conserving food in affluent countries would result in less food for the poor by causing temporary food surpluses, followed by price declines, and eventually cuts in food production so that less food would be available for export.

What Can You Do? In addition to becoming more knowledgeable about world food problems and possible solutions to these problems, you can examine your own lifestyle to find ways to reduce the unnecessary waste of food, energy, and matter resources along with the pollution and environmental degradation resulting from the use of these resources. For example, you can use organic cultivation techniques to grow some of your own food in backyard plots, window planters, rooftop gardens, or cooperative community gardens in unused urban spaces. In addition to saving money, you will have a more nutritious diet based on fresh rather than processed convenience foods. Today, almost half of all U.S. households grow some of their own food—an amount worth about $14 billion. Unfortunately, most of it is grown with larger amounts of commercial fertilizers and pesticides per unit of land than are used on most commercial cropland.

There are other ways you can reduce everyday food waste: Put no more food on your plate than you intend to eat, ask for smaller portions in restaurants, recycle garbage in compost piles to produce organic fertilizer for growing your own food, and feed food waste to pets.

To fight hunger on a larger scale, you can become politically involved, supporting state and national leaders whose policies will reduce hunger in the United States and the world and will reduce the harmful environmental effects of agriculture.

The most important fact of all is not that people are dying from hunger, but that people are dying unnecessarily. . . . We have the resources to end it; we have proven solutions for ending it. . . . What is missing is the commitment.

The Hunger Project

CHAPTER SUMMARY

The small number of different types of plants and animals that feed the world are produced by energy-intensive *industrialized agriculture* in MDCs and labor- and land-intensive forms of *subsistence cultivation and herding* in LDCs. The major world food problems are food quantity, food quality, food storage and distribution, poverty, economic incentives for growing food, and the harmful environmental effects of agriculture.

Overall, enough food is produced to feed everyone on earth. However, because food and land are not distributed equitably, there are 450 million to 800 million chronically undernourished and malnourished people in the world, primarily in LDCs. An estimated 12 million to 20 million people, half of them under 5 years old, die prematurely each year from *undernutrition, malnutrition, and diseases related to or worsened by these conditions*. The chief cause of hunger, malnutrition, and preventable deaths from these conditions is *poverty*—not lack of food production.

Since 1950, most increases in food production in MDCs and a number of LDCs are the result of two major *green revolutions*, in which the yield per unit of cropland was increased by planting new, *hybrid crop varieties* that make increased use of fertilizer, water, and pesticides. However, the spread and effectiveness of the green revolutions have been limited by the lack of water, the displacement of protein-rich legumes by low-protein crops, the eventual leveling off of yields regardless of the level of fertilizer and water inputs, and the loss of genetic diversity needed to produce new varieties. *Equitable land distribution* and the use of new crop varieties to increase yields of labor-intensive subsistence agriculture in countries such as China have benefited the poor and essentially eliminated hunger. However, in some LDCs the use of green revolution techniques without accompanying land reform, and with increased cultivation of large plots by energy-intensive industrialized agriculture, has decreased land ownership and jobs for farm laborers and has increased hunger among the rural poor.

Food production can be increased in LDCs by the cultivation of *nontraditional plants* adapted to local growing conditions. It is difficult, however, to get consumers to try new foods. *Adding vitamins and proteins to processed foods* has reduced malnutrition in MDCs. But such foods are normally not available to rural people in LDCs, where chronic hunger and malnutrition are widespread.

Some have suggested that the total amount of cultivated land throughout the world could be doubled, primarily by clearing tropical forests and irrigating arid lands, mostly in Africa, South America, and Australia. Others believe this is unrealistic because most of these potentially cultivatable (arable) lands are too dry or remote or lack productive soils. Massive inputs of fertilizer and irrigation water could be used to overcome these limitations, but in most cases doing this is too expensive compared to increasing productivity on existing cropland.

Fish and shellfish are important sources of animal protein for many of the world's people, especially in Asia and Africa. Some believe that the present annual fish and shellfish catch can be doubled or tripled by increased fishing efforts, increased fish farming (aquaculture), and decreased waste of the annual catch. But other analysts point out that because of *overfishing* and *pollution of estuaries*, there has been only a slight increase in the annual catch since 1971 and the average fish catch per person has declined steadily.

Governments can increase food production by distributing land to the rural poor, making credit available to small farmers, providing farmers with price supports and subsidies, and controlling import and export food prices. MDCs can also provide LDCs with money and technical assistance that enhance their ability to become self-sufficient in food. However, much of today's foreign aid makes LDCs more dependent on MDCs for oil, fertilizer, machinery, and other expensive inputs of industrialized agriculture.

Cornucopians believe the key to reducing world hunger is to transfer energy-intensive industrialized agriculture to LDCs. Neo-Malthusians believe this will merely allow the rich in MDCs and LDCs to get richer at the expense of the poor and will greatly increase pollution and environmental degradation. They believe that LDCs should become self-sufficient by developing a *sustainable-earth agricultural system* that works with nature. Such a system would emphasize land reform, human labor, organic fertilizers, soil and water conservation, polyculture cultivation of perennial crops, and biological control of pests.

Sustainable-earth agricultural techniques applied to the industrialized agriculture of MDCs would include switching to organic fertilizers and biological pest control, increasing soil and water conservation, and reducing unnecessary waste of fertilizer, fossil fuels, and food.

DISCUSSION TOPICS

1. What are the major advantages and disadvantages of labor-intensive subsistence agriculture?

2. What are the major advantages and disadvantages of energy-intensive industrialized agriculture?

3. Explain why most people who die from lack of sufficient quantity or quality of food do not starve to death.

4. Explain why you agree or disagree with the following statement: There really isn't a severe world food problem because we already produce enough food to provide everyone on earth more than three times the minimum amount needed to stay alive.

5. Summarize the advantages and limitations of each of the following proposals for increasing world food supplies and reducing hunger over the next 30 years: (a) cultivating more land by clearing tropical jungles and irrigating arid lands, (b) catching more fish in the open sea, (c) harvesting krill from the ocean, (d) producing fish and shellfish with aquaculture, and (e) increasing the yield per area of cropland.

6. Explain how the green revolution helped eliminate most hunger in China but led to increased hunger in some other LDCs.

7. Should price supports and other subsidies paid to U.S. farmers out of tax revenues be eliminated? Explain. Try to have a farmer discuss this problem with your class.

8. Is food relief helpful or harmful? Explain.

9. What types of foreign aid should the U.S. provide to LDCs and what requirements, if any, should be attached to such aid? Explain.

10. Should tax breaks and subsidies be used to encourage more U.S. farmers to switch to organic farming? Explain.

13

Land Resources: Wilderness, Parks, Forests, and Rangelands

We abuse land because we regard it as a commodity belonging to us. When we see land as a community to which we belong, we may begin to use it with love and respect.

Aldo Leopold

GENERAL OBJECTIVES

1. How is land used in the world and the United States and how should publicly owned lands be managed?

2. Why is wilderness important and how much should be set aside and protected in the United States?

3. Why are U.S. national and state parks important and how can they be protected from overuse and pollution?

4. Why are forests important and how can their renewability be maintained?

5. Why are rangelands important and how can their renewability be maintained?

Many of the three out of four people in MDCs who live in urban areas are unaware or forget that their well-being is linked to the soil, plants, and animals found in the earth's croplands, forests, rangelands, parks, and wilderness areas. Protecting these nonurban land resources from overexploitation and environmental degradation is one of our most important challenges.

13-1 LAND USE IN THE WORLD AND THE UNITED STATES

Why Are Nonurban Land Resources Important? Land in the world and in the United States is used for several major purposes (Figure 13-1). Urban areas containing 43% of the world's population occupy less than 1% of the world's total land area. Urban areas containing 76% of the U.S. population occupy only 2% of the country's total land area. Thus, at first glance it would appear that the world has more than enough nonurban land resources to support today's 5 billion people and perhaps the 10.4 billion projected by the end of the next century.

However, such an assumption does not take into account the vast areas of cropland, forest, rangeland, watersheds, estuaries, and other types of nonurban land, water, and all resources needed to sustain urban areas. Nonurban air, water, and land also serve as receptacles for urban-generated air and water pollutants and solid and toxic wastes.

Private and Public U.S. Land Ownership In the United States 55% of all land is privately owned by individuals and corporations (Figure 13-2). The most

262

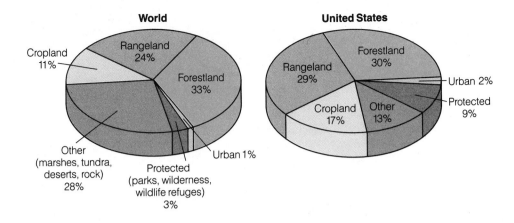

World

- Cropland 11%
- Rangeland 24%
- Forestland 33%
- Other (marshes, tundra, deserts, rock) 28%
- Protected (parks, wilderness, wildlife refuges) 3%
- Urban 1%

United States

- Rangeland 29%
- Forestland 30%
- Cropland 17%
- Other 13%
- Urban 2%
- Protected 9%

Figure 13-1 Land use in the world and the United States. (Data from U.S. Bureau of Commerce, Conservation Foundation, and UN Food and Agriculture Organization)

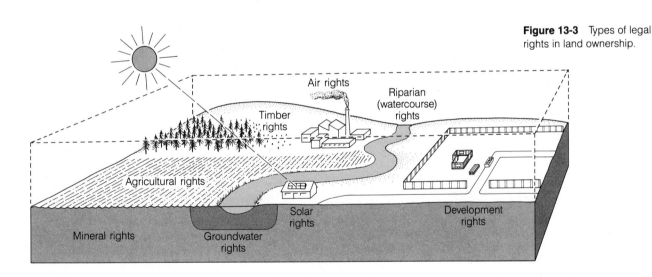

- Federal 35%
- Private 55%
- State and local 7%
- Native American Indians 3%

Figure 13-2 Land ownership in the United States. (Data from Bureau of Land Management)

Figure 13-3 Types of legal rights in land ownership.

Air rights

Riparian (watercourse) rights

Timber rights

Agricultural rights

Solar rights

Development rights

Mineral rights

Groundwater rights

complete form of private ownership is the "fee simple absolute," which gives the titleholder rights over the land and its resources "from the center of the earth to the heavens above." Over a period of time, however, owners of private land may sell to someone else the right to harvest or remove certain resources, such as timber or minerals, or use the land in certain ways (Figure 13-3). The way privately owned land and its resources are taxed generally determines the way it is used. For example, if prime cropland or forestland near an expanding urban area is taxed according to its highest economic value as potential urban land, then its owners will find it hard to resist selling it for urban development. On the other hand, if the land is taxed only on its potential as cropland or forestland, owners have a greater incentive to preserve it for these uses.

About 42% of all U.S. land consists of public lands owned jointly by citizens, and managed for them by federal, state, and local governments. Over one-third (35%) of the country's land is owned jointly by its

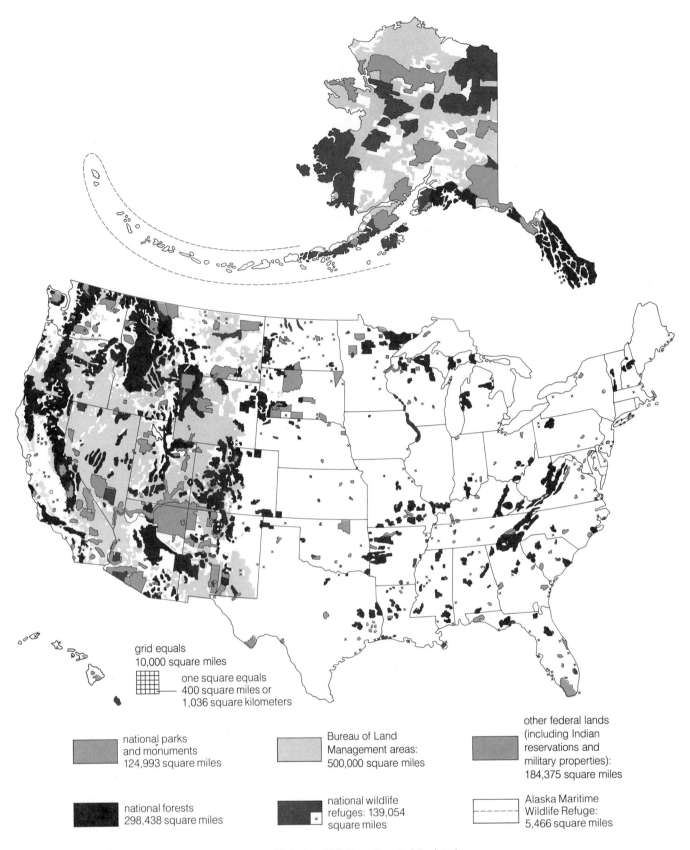

grid equals
10,000 square miles

one square equals
400 square miles or
1,036 square kilometers

national parks
and monuments
124,993 square miles

Bureau of Land
Management areas:
500,000 square miles

other federal lands
(including Indian
reservations and
military properties):
184,375 square miles

national forests
298,438 square miles

national wildlife
refuges: 139,054
square miles

Alaska Maritime
Wildlife Refuge:
5,466 square miles

Figure 13-4 Landholdings of the federal government. (Data from U.S. Department of the Interior,
Geological Survey)

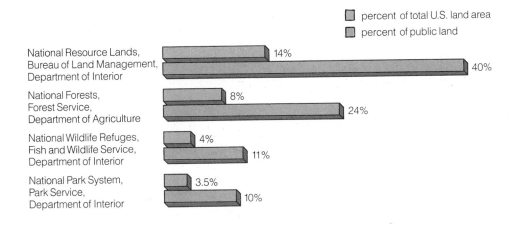

□ percent of total U.S. land area
□ percent of public land

National Resource Lands,
Bureau of Land Management,
Department of Interior — 14% / 40%

National Forests,
Forest Service,
Department of Agriculture — 8% / 24%

National Wildlife Refuges,
Fish and Wildlife Service,
Department of Interior — 4% / 11%

National Park System,
Park Service,
Department of Interior — 3.5% / 10%

Figure 13-5 Percentages of all U.S. land area and of public lands administered by key federal agencies.

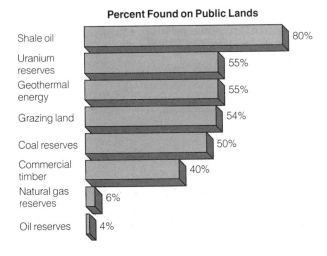

Percent Found on Public Lands

Shale oil — 80%
Uranium reserves — 55%
Geothermal energy — 55%
Grazing land — 54%
Coal reserves — 50%
Commercial timber — 40%
Natural gas reserves — 6%
Oil reserves — 4%

Figure 13-6 Percentages of key resources on U.S. public lands.

citizens and managed for them by the federal government. About 73% of this federally managed land lies in Alaska and 22% is in western states (Figure 13-4). These public lands have been divided by Congress into different units for various purposes (see Spotlight on p. 267) and are administered by several federal agencies (Figure 13-5).

Public Land Resources Federally administered public lands contain a significant portion of the country's timber, grazing land, and energy resources (Figure 13-6) and most of its copper, silver, asbestos, lead, molybdenum, beryllium, phosphate, and potash. Through various laws Congress has allowed private individuals and corporations to use many of these resources. Because of the value of these resources, there has been a long history of conflict between various groups over whether federal public lands should be transferred to private ownership, who should have access to the resources on and under these lands, and

at what price (Section 2-4). These controversies continue today (see Spotlight on p. 268).

13-2 WILDERNESS

Expansion of U.S. Wilderness Areas and Wild and Scenic Rivers Between 1970 and 1986 the amount of land in the National Wilderness Preservation System increased almost tenfold. Alaska, which contains almost two-thirds of all U.S. wilderness area, accounted for most of this increase. Wilderness areas vary from small islands of just a few acres to the 35,000-square-kilometer (8.7 million acres) Wrangell-St. Elias National Park in Alaska. High mountain country is the most common landscape and ecosystem (Figure 13-7), but there are also desert, swamp, and tundra wilderness areas.

In 1968 Congress passed the National Wild and Scenic Rivers Act to prevent further development of

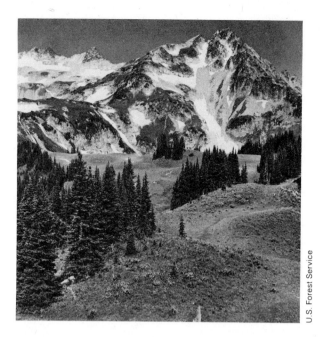

Figure 13-7 Alpine tundra in Glacier Park Wilderness, Washington.

U.S. Forest Service

rivers and river segments with outstanding scenic, recreational, geologic, wildlife, historic, or cultural values. The act recognizes three types of rivers or sections of rivers as suitable for protection: (1) wild river areas that are primitive, unpolluted, free from dams, and generally inaccessible except by trails; (2) scenic river areas that are free of dams, largely undeveloped and primitive, but accessible in places by roads and railroads; and (3) recreational river areas that have been dammed or diverted to some degree, are accessible by road or railroad, and may have some shoreline development. The only activities allowed on these protected areas are camping, swimming, nonmotorized boating, sport hunting, and sport and commercial fishing, with the exception that new mining claims are permitted in scenic and recreational river areas. The system is administered by the Interior and Agriculture departments in cooperation with state agencies.

By 1987, the Wild and Scenic River System protected 75 rivers and river systems, representing about 0.2% of the country's 5.6 million kilometers (3.5 million miles) of rivers. Preservationists have urged Congress to add 1,500 additional eligible river segments to the system by the year 2000. If this goal is achieved, about 2% of the country's unique rivers and river systems would be protected from further development.

Use and Abuse of Wilderness Areas In 1986 an estimated 14 million recreational visits were made to U.S. wilderness areas, about three times the number in 1970. Two-thirds of all recreational use occurs on 10% of the wilderness lands in the lower 48 states, especially in California, North Carolina, and Minnesota. Popular wilderness areas are visited by so many people that fragile vegetation is damaged, soil is eroded from trails and campsites, water is polluted from bathing and dishwashing, litter is scattered along trails, and instead of quiet and solitude users face the congestion they are trying to escape. To protect the most popular areas from damage, government agencies have had to limit the number of people hiking or camping at any one time and designate campsites.

To prevent overuse, historian and wilderness expert Roderick Nash advocates dividing wilderness areas and areas within them into different categories. The accessible and most popular areas would be intensively managed and have trails, bridges, hiker's huts, outhouses, assigned campsites, and extensive ranger patrols. Large, remote wilderness areas would be relatively unmanaged and accessible only to people who qualify for special licenses by demonstrating their wilderness skills. A third category would consist of large, unique areas to be left undisturbed as genetic pools of plant and animal resources, with no human entry allowed.

Why Preserve Wilderness? There are psychological, aesthetic, recreational, economic, ecological, and ethical arguments for preserving wilderness. From a psychological and aesthetic viewpoint, we need wild places where we can experience majestic beauty and natural biological diversity and where we can renew the spirit and enhance mental health by getting away from noise, stress, and large numbers of people. Wilderness preservationist John Muir advised:

Climb the mountains and get their good tidings. Nature's peace will flow into you as the sunshine into the trees. The winds will blow their freshness into you, and the storms their energy, while cares will drop off like autumn leaves.

Even if individuals do not use the wilderness, many want to know it is there, a feeling expressed by novelist Wallace Stegner:

Save a piece of country . . . and it does not matter in the slightest that only a few people every year will go into it. This is precisely its value . . . we simply need that wild country available to us, even if we never do more than drive to its edge and look in. For it can be a means of reassuring ourselves of our sanity as creatures, a part of the geography of hope.

Multiple-Use Lands

National Forests. This system includes 155 individual national forests and 19 national grasslands managed by the Forest Service. Excluding the 15% of this land protected as wilderness areas, this system is managed according to the principles of sustained yield and multiple use. These lands are used for timbering, grazing, agriculture, mining, oil and gas leasing, recreation, sport hunting, sport and commercial fishing, and conservation of watershed, soil, and wildlife resources. Emphasis, however, is on maintaining a forest reserve to furnish renewable timber supplies for the country.

National Resource Lands. These lands consist mostly of grassland, and prairie, desert, scrub forest, and other open spaces located primarily in the western states and Alaska. They are managed by the Bureau of Land Management under the principle of multiple use and, like national forests, are used for a variety of purposes. Emphasis is placed on providing a secure domestic source of energy and strategically important nonenergy minerals and on preserving the renewability of rangelands for livestock-grazing under a permit system. Presently about 10% of these lands are being evaluated for possible designation as wilderness areas.

Moderately-Restricted-Use Lands

National Wildlife Refuge System. This system includes 427 refuges and various ranges managed by the Fish and Wildlife Service. Excluding the 24% of this land protected as wilderness areas, most refuges are used to protect habitats and breeding areas for waterfowl and big-game animals to ensure that adequate stocks are available for hunters. A few are designed to save endangered species from extinction. Although refuges and ranges are not officially managed under the principle of multiple use, sport hunting, sport and commercial fishing, new oil and gas leasing, timbering, and agriculture are permitted as long as the Secretary of the Interior finds such use compatible with the purposes of each unit. New mining claims are not allowed. This system is supplemented by a number of state and privately owned wildlife refuges managed primarily for the benefit of hunters.

Restricted-Use Lands

National Park System. This system consists of 337 units, including 48 major parks (mostly in the West), and 289 national recreation areas, monuments, memorials, battlefields, historic sites, parkways, trails, recreational areas, rivers, seashores, and lakeshores. The units are managed by the National Park Service to preserve natural landscapes and ecosystems, to preserve and interpret the country's historic and cultural heritage, and to provide certain types of recreation. National parks can be used only for camping, hiking, sport and commercial fishing, and motorized and nonmotorized boating. Motor vehicles are permitted only on roads and off-road vehicles are not allowed. In addition to the activities permitted in the parks, National Recreation Areas can be used for sport hunting, new mining claims, and new oil and gas leasing.

About 49% of the land in the National Park System is protected as wilderness areas, and its use is restricted even more. The National Park System is supplemented by a number of state and local parks.

National Wilderness Preservation System. This system includes 275 roadless areas found within the national parks, national wildlife refuges, and national forests, which are managed, respectively, by the National Park Service (44% of wilderness lands), Fish and Wildlife Service (25%), and Forest Service (31%). According to Congress, **wilderness** consists of those areas "where the earth and its community of life are untrammeled by man, where man himself is a visitor who does not remain." Such areas are to be managed and preserved in their essentially untouched condition "for the use and enjoyment of the American people in such a manner as will leave them unimpaired for future use and enjoyment as wilderness." Wilderness areas are open only for recreational activities such as hiking, sport fishing, camping, nonmotorized boating, and in some areas sport hunting and horseback riding. Roads, timber harvesting, grazing, mining, commercial activities, and human-made structures are prohibited, except where such activities occurred before an area's designation as wilderness. Motorized vehicles, boats, and equipment are banned except for emergency uses such as fire control and rescue operations. Exploration and identification of mineral, energy, and other resources is allowed as long as such activities do not involve the use of motorized vehicles or equipment.

Ecosystem-Centered, or Biocentric, Approach

Preservationist View: "Preserve it." Portions of the public land resources should be preserved from development by timber, mining, and other economic interests. Emphasis should be on preserving the biological diversity and sustainability of natural ecosystems. Such areas should be used only for nondestructive forms of outdoor recreation and left as ecological preserves—living laboratories for learning how nature works. The National Wilderness Preservation System, which makes up 11% of all public lands, represents this view.

Human-Centered, or Anthropocentric, Approaches

Short-Term Economic View: "Use It." Public lands should be transferred to private interests and used to provide the highest short-term economic gain for its owners and to promote national economic growth.

Multiple-Use View. Instead of being left untouched or unexploited, public land resources should be used for a variety of purposes, including timbering, mining, grazing, recreation, aesthetics, and wildlife and water conservation, and managed in ways that do not damage or deplete them for future generations. About 60% of all public

land, found in national forests (excluding wilderness) and national resource lands, is officially managed on this basis. However, conservationists contend that far too often multiple-use management ends up being single-use management because of political influence by timber, mining, and ranching interests. The management of 13% of public lands as national wildlife refuges (8%) and national parks (5%) represents a compromise between multiple-use and preservationist views.

In addition to providing recreation for a growing number of Americans, wilderness provides economic benefits by helping support the booming outdoor-gear and tourist industries and providing the salmon industry with increasingly scarce, undisturbed spawning streams. These areas also serve as a repository of resources that could be used later in a true emergency situation, rather than now for short-term economic gain.

Wilderness also has important ecological values. It provides undisturbed habitats for wild animals and a refuge for animals driven from other land; it maintains diverse ecosystems and species, serving as an important ecological reserve protected from environmental degradation; and it provides an ecological laboratory in which we can discover how nature works and measure and observe how much humans have altered the earth. On ethical grounds it is argued that wilderness should be preserved because the plant and animal species it contains have an inherent right to exist without human interference.

How Much Wilderness Is Enough?   Since 1964 the amount of land in the National Wilderness Preservation System has increased significantly, especially from the addition of vast areas in Alaska in the 1970s. Officials of timber, mining, and energy industries and ranchers operating on public lands opposed most of these additions and also oppose any further expan-

sion of the system. They accuse preservationists of wanting to lock up the woods for use as parks by the affluent and physically fit and argue that resources on and under public lands should be used now and in the future to promote economic growth and provide mineral and energy resources to enhance national security. They believe most public lands should continue to be managed under the principle of multiple use, which permits both conservation and development uses.

Since wilderness resource is irreplaceable, preservationists argue that large and diverse areas should be protected as an ecological insurance policy against human abuse of the land and elimination of too much of the earth's natural biological diversity. Preservationists have urged Congress to add more area to the wilderness system, especially in the lower 48 states, where wilderness use is the most intensive and where only 1.7% of the total land area is presently designated as wilderness.

Several reviews of roadless areas by agencies managing public lands concluded that an additional 5% of the total land area in the lower 48 states could qualify for wilderness designation. In the unlikely event that Congress decided to add all these lands to the wilderness system, preservationists note that only 23% of all public lands and 8% of the country's total land area would be classified as wilderness. They contend that the remaining 60% of public lands managed officially or unofficially for multiple use are the country's

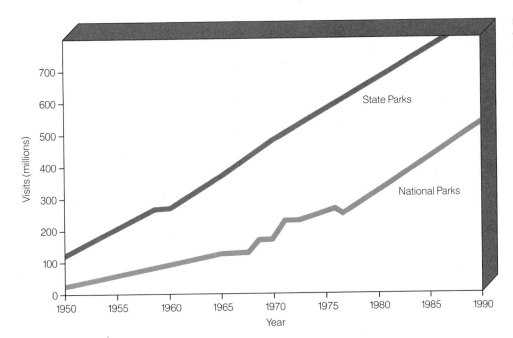

Figure 13-8 Recreational visits to U.S. national and state parks have increased dramatically since 1950.

most resources-rich public lands and should provide ample resources to enhance national security and promote economic growth.

13-3 PARKS

U.S. Parks Years ago the National Park System consisted mostly of large and scenic national parks, created out of federal lands in the West. These parks provide spectacular scenery on a scale not usually found in state and local parks, preserve wildlife that can't coexist with humans, and surround and protect wilderness areas within them. So popular were the U.S. parks that by 1986 approximately 1,000 national parks had been established in 100 other countries.

Today the National Park System is much more diverse. Although its total area is still dominated by large national parks, the largest number of its 337 units are culture-oriented areas such as national historic sites and national battlefields. During the 1970s several urban parks (known as national recreation areas), national seashores, lakeshores, and other units usually located close to heavily populated urban areas were added to bring parks closer to the people. Since they opened in the 1970s, the Golden Gate National Recreation Area near San Francisco and the Gateway National Recreation Area in the Greater New York City area have been two of the most widely used units in the National Park System.

Nature walks, guided tours, and other educational services provided by Park Service employees have provided many Americans with a better understanding of how nature works. Some conservationists urge that this important and effective educational program be expanded to show citizens ways they can work with nature in their own lifestyles. They have proposed that all park facilities be converted to working resource conservation systems, demonstrating energy-efficient, low-polluting methods of heating, cooling, water purification, waste handling, transportation, and matter recycling.

Internal Stresses on Parks Between 1950 and 1986 there was a twelvefold increase in recreational visits to National Park System units and a sevenfold increase in visits to state parks (Figure 13-8). Because they are more numerous and located closer to most urban areas (especially in the East, where there are few national parks), state parks are used more intensively than national parks. Recreational use of state and national parks and other public lands is projected to increase even more in the future, putting additional stress on many already overburdened parks.

Under the onslaught of people during the peak summer season, the most popular national parks are often overcrowded with cars and trailers and plagued by noise, traffic jams, litter, vandalism, deteriorating trails, polluted water, drugs, and crime. Theft of tim-

During the 1920s the federal government launched a successful program to kill all the wolves in Yellowstone National Park because they were considered too great a threat to populations of elk, deer, and other large herbivores. Wolves were also killed by ranchers and federal officials in most other areas of the lower 48 states to protect livestock. Although some 5,000 wolves still live in Alaska, the lower 48 states now contain only about 1,200 wolves in Minnesota and 50 in Wisconsin and Michigan.

Since 1930 when the wolf was exterminated from Yellowstone, the elk population has exploded. The herd, which now numbers 25,000, is depleting vegetation and eating other species out of house and home. To prevent further decline in other plant and animal species, officials are considering three alternatives: controlling the elk population by reintroducing wolves into Yellowstone, authorizing hunters to kill off excess elk, or not interfering at all and allowing large diebacks of elk as they exceed the carrying capacity of the land.

Conservationists favor returning the wolf to Yellowstone, in keeping with the goal of national parks to preserve natural ecosystems. They oppose increased hunting, which would be an unnatural form of control, and waiting for diebacks would endanger many other plant and animal species native to Yellowstone. Sheep and cattle ranchers, however, vehemently oppose reintroducing wolves, fearing that some of them will leave the park to prey on livestock. Conservationists respond that only 0.2% of the 12,000 farms in Minnesota wolf country lose even one animal per year to wolves. Also, under the proposed plan, wolves could be easily tracked because they would wear radio collars, and they could be shot if found on ranchlands. What do you think?

---

ber, petrified wood chips, and cacti from national parks is a growing problem. Park Service rangers, now trained more in law enforcement than resource conservation and management, must wear guns and spend an increasing amount of their time acting as park police officers.

In addition to the stresses brought by human visitors, some parks face degradation by growing populations of certain native animal species. Park Service officials are trying to decide whether some forms of wildlife in national parks should be managed to reduce excessive population growth and resulting vegetation damage or left to regulate themselves (see Spotlight above).

External Threats to Parks   The greatest danger to many parks today is from external threats, such as mining, timber harvesting, grazing, coal-burning power plants, water diversion, and urban development in nearby areas. A 1980 survey by the National Park Service revealed that scenic resources were threatened in more than 60% of the national parks, while visibility, air and water quality, and wildlife were endangered in about 40% of the parks.

The haze over the mountains along the Blue Ridge Parkway in North Carolina and Virginia is no longer blue but gray from air pollution, and many trees at the highest elevations have been damaged or killed by prolonged exposure to air pollutants. At Grand Canyon National Park visitors often cannot see the canyon's opposite rim because of smog, and the noise from helicopters carrying sightseers into the canyon ruins the wilderness experience for others backpacking in the canyon.

Underground rivers in Kentucky's Mammoth Cave National Park carry sewage from nearby communities. The amount and diversity of plant and animal life found in the Everglades National Park in the southern tip of Florida have dropped sharply because much of the water that once flowed southward into this swampland wildlife preserve has been diverted and used for irrigation and urban development.

Planned geothermal energy development may take the steam out of geysers in Yellowstone and Lassen (northeastern California) national parks. Mineral and energy companies have put increasing pressure on the government to allow mining even within some parklands, such as the popular Glen Canyon National Recreation Area in southern Utah and northern Arizona. Similar harmful environmental impacts affect many state and local parks.

What Should Be Done?   Since 1980 there has been considerable controversy between the Reagan administration and conservationists over how to reduce stresses on the National Park System (see Spotlight on p. 271). To maintain, improve, and expand the country's priceless state and national parks, Americans must be willing to pay higher entry and use fees, higher taxes, or both. The alternative is to allow these vital

Reagan Administration

Increase funding for maintenance and repair of existing parks.

Eliminate funding for purchase of additional parkland.

Transfer ownership of some national park units such as the Gateway and Golden Gate National Recreation Areas, and other recently created urban parks to states and localities.

Increase mining, energy development, and other income-producing resource development on public land near national parks.

Allow private enterprise to develop and run luxury hotels, restaurants, and other commercial facilities in parks to bring in more revenue.

Turn more of the management of camping, recreational, and educational activities in parks to private concessionaires.

Sharply increase automobile entrance fees to the point where they provide at least 10% of park operating costs.

Encourage private donations for park restoration (such as the highly successful, privately financed restoration of the Statue of Liberty) and increased use of volunteer workers in park system units.

Conservationists

Agree.

More land should be added to accommodate increasing use, prevent choice parcels from being developed. Additions near existing parks can also be used to reduce external environmental threats.

Disagree. With declining federal and state funding, states and localities are in no position to keep them up.

Strictly regulate such activities to reduce pollution threats to parks.

Reduce congestion, crime, and pollution in national parks by prohibiting addition of any new commercial facilities and removing most existing commercial facilities to private or federally owned areas outside parks, as has been done for Acadia National Park in Maine.

Sharply increase usage fees paid by park concessionaires to return more of the high profits they make to taxpayers; place concessionaires under much stricter control to ensure they provide adequate services at fair prices.

Agree, but would go further and ban motor vehicles from heavily used parks to reduce congestion, noise, crime, and pollution. Visitors would be shuttled by bus to and from satellite parking lots, as is done in parts of Yosemite. Inside the park, visitors could travel by foot, bicycle, or shuttle bus.

Agree, but this should not be used as an excuse to reduce the Park Service budget.

---

resources to become increasingly overcrowded and degraded and pass them on to future generations in an impaired state.

13-4 IMPORTANCE AND MANAGEMENT OF FOREST RESOURCES

Commercial and Ecological Importance of Forests Potentially renewable forest resources cover about one-third of the earth's surface (Figure 13-1 and map inside the front cover). About 69% of the world's total forest area is **closed forest**, where the land surface has an almost complete cover of trees. The remainder is less densely wooded **open forest**, where trees provide varying degrees of partial cover.

About two-thirds of all the world's closed forest has commercially exploitable timber resources; the timber harvested from such forests each year has a market value of at least $150 billion. Worldwide, about one-half of the annual timber harvest is used as fuel for heating and cooking, one-third goes to sawlogs for construction and wood products such as veneer, plywood, and particleboard, and one-sixth is converted to wood pulp used primarily for paper products. The percentage of the world's annual timber harvest used for fuelwood and industrial purposes (sawlogs and wood pulp), however, varies in different regions of the world, with an average of 80% used for fuelwood in LDCs and about 20% in MDCs.

In addition to their commercial value, forests have vital ecological functions that are often unrecognized and unappreciated. They help control climate by influencing wind, temperature, humidity, and rainfall. They add oxygen to the atmosphere and assist in the global recycling of water, carbon, and nitrogen (Section 4-2). Forested watersheds act like giant sponges that absorb, hold, and gradually release water, thus recharging springs, streams, and groundwater aquifers. By regulating the downstream flow of water, forests help control soil erosion, the amount of sediment washing into rivers and reservoirs, and the severity of flooding. Forests provide habitats for organisms that make up much of the earth's genetic diversity. They also help absorb noise and some air pollutants, cool and humidify the air, and nourish the human spirit by providing solitude and beauty.

Too often, economists evaluate forests only on the short-term market value of their products, without considering the value of their long-term ecological benefits. It is estimated, for example, that a typical tree provides $196,250 worth of ecological benefits in a 50-year lifespan; sold as timber, it provides only about $590. In its 50 years the tree produces $31,250 worth of oxygen, $62,500 in air pollution reduction, $31,250 in soil fertility and erosion control, $37,500 in water recycling and humidity control, $31,250 in wildlife habitat, and $2,500 worth of protein. While such a calculation is a general estimate, not reflecting actual market values that can be redeemed, it illustrates dramatically how vital forests are to humans and other forms of life.

Management of Commercial Forests The cultivation and management of forests to produce a renewable supply of timber is called **silviculture**. Just as food production evolved from hunting and gathering to intensively managed cultivated fields and livestock production, forestry is slowly evolving from cutting and gathering natural tree growths to increasingly intensive management of commercial forests.

Moderate forest management involves harvesting timber from existing commercially exploitable forests, usually consisting of uneven-aged stands of several tree species; natural or artificial methods are used to regenerate commercially valuable species, and forests are protected from damage during the regeneration period. **Intensive forest management** typically involves clearing an area of all vegetation, planting it with even-aged stands (Figure 13-9), and then fertil-

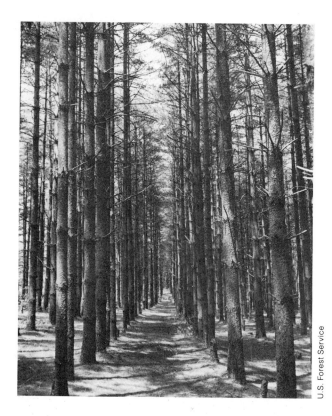

Figure 13-9 Monoculture tree plantation of white pine near Asheville, North Carolina.

izing and spraying the resulting tree plantation with pesticides. Once the trees reach maturity, the entire stand is harvested and the area is replanted. Genetic crossbreeding and genetic engineering techniques can improve both the quality and quantity of wood produced from such plantations.

By 1985 about 58% of the world's commercially exploitable closed forest area was under some form of forest management. About 10% was managed intensively as tree plantations, mostly in Europe, the United States, the USSR, India, and China (China alone contains one-third of the world's total tree plantation area). Worldwide, it is projected that the area of tree plantations will double between 1985 and 2000 and then continue to rise sharply.

There is controversy, however, over how much of the world's commercially exploitable forestland should be managed intensively. Most foresters and resource managers favor intensive forest management. They see it not only as a way to increase short-term profits but also as the best way to increase the amount of timber produced per unit of area to meet the increasing worldwide demand for wood. They believe that careful use of the principle of sustained yield allows intensively managed forest resources to be harvested and regenerated in a manner and at a rate that conserves these potentially renewable resources.

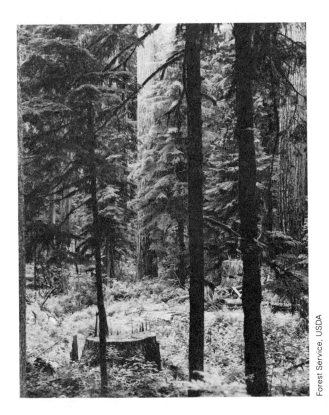

Figure 13-10 Selective cutting of Douglas fir in Mt. Baker National Forest, Washington.

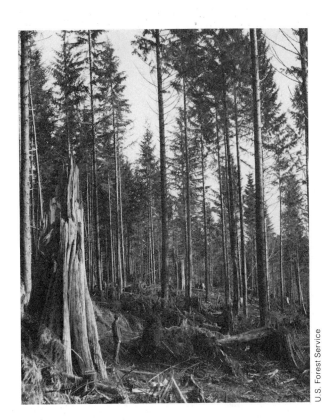

Figure 13-11 Shelterwood cutting of hemlock. Residual stand after first cut in an experimental forest in Grays Harbor County, Washington.

Other foresters and a number of ecologists, however, are concerned that overemphasis on intensive forest management will lead to a severe reduction in the diversity of plant and animal life in the world's commercial forestlands. Replacement of diverse tree species and vegetation with single-species stands of commercial trees could leave large areas of forest highly vulnerable to destruction by pests and diseases. These analysts are not against intensive management altogether but believe that no more than one-fourth of the world's commercially exploitable forestland should be managed in this way. They agree, however, that intensive management is usually the best and quickest way to reforest degraded land and reduce soil erosion and desertification.

Tree Harvesting and Regeneration Methods Harvesting and regeneration are the most crucial parts of any forest management program. It is at this stage that the forester can do the most to improve or to damage the forest for a long time. Trees are harvested and regenerated by five main methods: selective cutting, shelterwood cutting, seed tree cutting, clearcutting, and whole-tree harvesting.

In **selective cutting,** intermediate-aged or mature trees in an uneven-aged forest stand are cut either singly or in small groups at intervals (Figure 13-10). This encourages the growth of younger trees and produces a stand with trees of different species, ages, and sizes; over time the stand will regenerate itself. This harvesting method is favored by those wishing to use forests for both timber production and recreation; if the harvest is too limited, however, there may not be enough timber produced to make the process economically feasible. In addition, the need to reopen roads and trails periodically for selective harvests can cause erosion of certain soils. A similar method of cutting, not considered a sound forestry practice, is called *high grading.* Here the most valuable commercial tree species are cut without regard for the quality or distribution of remaining trees.

Some tree species, known as *shade-intolerant species,* do best when grown in full sunlight in forest openings or in large, cleared and seeded areas. Even-aged stands of such species (Figure 13-9) are usually harvested by shelterwood cutting, seed tree cutting, or clearcutting. **Shelterwood cutting** involves the removal of all mature trees in an area in a series of cuts over one or more decades. In the first harvest, unwanted tree species and dying, defective, and diseased trees are removed, leaving properly spaced, healthy, well-formed trees as seed stock (Figure 13-11). In the next stage, 10 or more years later, the

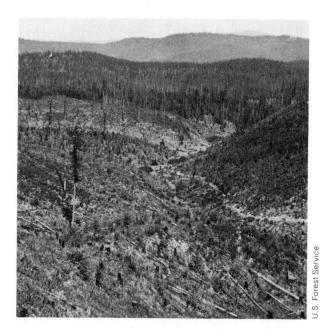

Figure 13-12 Clearcutting of white pine in St. Joe National Forest, Montana.

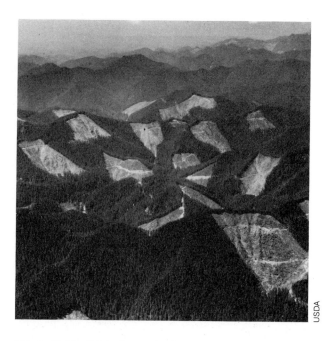

Figure 13-13 Patch clearcutting in Kootenai National Forest, Montana.

stand is cut further so that seedlings can receive adequate sunlight and heat and can become established under the shelter of a partial canopy of remaining trees. Later, a third harvest removes the remaining mature canopy trees, allowing the new stand to develop in the open as an even-aged forest. This method leads to very little erosion. Without careful planning and supervision, however, loggers may take too many trees in the initial cut, especially the most commercially valuable trees.

Seed tree cutting harvests nearly all trees on a site in one cut, with a few of the better commercially valuable trees left uniformly distributed on each acre as a source of seed to regenerate the forest. Allowing a variety of species to grow at one time, seed tree cutting is a form of multiple-use management. However, it is not used for many species because if the remaining seed trees are lost to wind and ice, the site will be left without a sufficient seed source for reforestation.

In **clearcutting,** all trees are removed from a given area in a single cutting to establish a new, even-aged stand, usually of fast-growing, shade-intolerant species (Figure 13-12). The clearcut area may consist of a whole stand, a group, a strip, or a series of patches (Figure 13-13). After clearing, the site is reforested naturally from seed released by the harvest or, increasingly, by planting genetically superior seedlings raised in a nursery. Timber companies prefer clearcutting because it increases the volume of timber harvested

per acre, reduces road building, and shortens the time needed to establish a new stand of trees. Clearcut openings and the fringes along uncut areas also improve the forage and habitat for some herbivores, such as deer and elk, and some shrubland birds.

Conservationists and ecologically oriented foresters recognize that clearcutting can be useful for some species if properly done. Their concern is that the size of the clearcut areas is too often determined by the economics of logging rather than by consideration of forest regeneration, and the method is sometimes used on species that could be harvested by less ecologically destructive methods. Excessive use of clearcutting on steeply sloped land can lead to severe erosion and sediment water pollution. In addition, it creates ugly scars (Figures 13-12 and 13-13) that take years to heal, reduces the recreational value of the forest for years, destroys habitats for many wildlife species, and replaces a genetically diverse stand of trees with a vulnerable monoculture. Careful harvesting and monitoring of individual clear cuts is vital to ensure that negative impacts are kept to acceptable levels.

Whole-tree harvesting is a variation of clearcutting in which a machine cuts each tree at ground level and transports it to a chipping machine, where massive blades reduce the entire tree to small chips in about one minute (Figure 13-14). Some whole-tree harvesting machines pull up the entire tree so that roots are also utilized. This approach, which is used primarily to harvest stands for use as pulpwood or

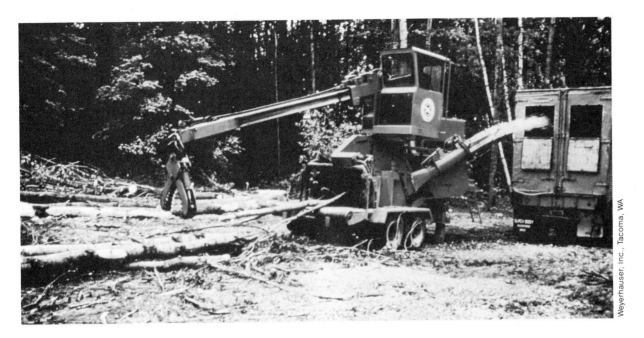

Figure 13-14 Whole-tree harvesting. Tree is fed into chipper, which deposits chips into truck at left.

fuelwood, can increase the yield of a temperate forest by 300% by using all wood materials in a stand, including defective trees and dead standing timber. Many foresters and ecologists, however, oppose this method because the periodic removal of all tree materials eventually removes most soil nutrients. Research is under way to determine the rates of nutrient depletion in various regions and to determine how cutting methods could be modified to reduce the ecological impact of whole-tree harvesting.

Protecting Forests from Fires   About 85% of all forest fires in the United States are started by humans, either accidentally or deliberately. Although fires started by people or lightning are the best-known threats to forests, they account for less than 1% of the annual damage to commercial forests in the United States.

It is important to distinguish between two types of forest fires: ground fires and crown fires. **Crown fires** are extremely hot fires that can destroy all vegetation, kill wildlife, and accelerate erosion (Figure 13-15). They tend to occur in forests where all fire has been prevented for several decades, allowing accumulations of dead wood and ground litter that burn intensely enough to ignite tree tops.

Ground fires are low-level fires that burn only undergrowth (Figure 13-16). They usually do not harm mature trees, and most wildlife can escape them. In areas where excessive ground litter has not accumulated, periodic ground fires reduce the buildup of undergrowth and ground litter and help prevent more-destructive crown fires. They also help release and recycle valuable plant nutrients tied up in litter and undergrowth, increase the activity of nitrogen-fixing bacteria, help control diseases and insects, and provide the intense heat needed for the germination of seeds of some conifers, such as giant sequoia and jack pine. Some wildlife species, such as deer, moose, elk, muskrat, woodcock, and quail, depend on periodic ground fires to maintain their habitats and to provide food from vegetation that sprouts after such fires.

Fire protection of forest resources consists of three phases: prevention, presuppression, and suppression. **Forest fire prevention** is primarily an educational and regulatory process. Examples include the highly successful Smokey-the-Bear educational campaign and regulatory actions like requiring campfire permits or closing portions of forests to use during high risk periods.

Forest fire presuppression involves techniques to prevent a fire's spreading once it has started. Examples include roadside clearing, cutting and maintaining fire roads and cleared strips, and using mechanical methods or deliberately set and carefully controlled ground fires to remove flammable underbrush. Carefully regulated prescribed ground fires are an important tool in the management of some forests, especially those dominated by conifers such as giant sequoia

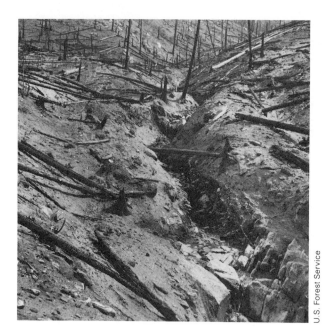

Figure 13-15 Highly destructive effects of a crown fire in Hunts Gulch, Idaho.

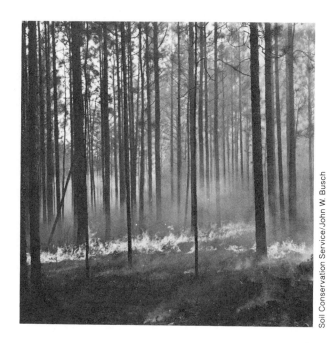

Figure 13-16 Ground fire in a California forest. (USDA Soil Conservation Service)

and Douglas fir. Presuppression includes airplane patrols, satellite surveillance, automated lightning detectors, and lookout towers for early detection of fires. Training fire-fighting personnel in techniques for rapid suppression once a fire begins is also an important aspect of presuppression.

A few decades ago fire fighters accomplished **forest fire suppression** mainly by clearing strips (fire lines) with axes and shovels. Today forest fire fighters use bulldozers to clear fire lines, airplanes and helicopters to drop water and fire-suppressing chemicals, helicopters to carry fire fighters to remote fires within minutes of detection, and an array of sophisticated communications equipment.

Protecting Forests from Diseases and Insects Diseases and insects cause much more loss of commercial timber than fires do, both in the United States (16%) and throughout the world. Parasitic fungi cause most tree-damaging diseases, such as chestnut blight, white pine blister rust, and Dutch elm disease. One way to control tree diseases is to ban imported timber that might bring in new types of parasites. For example, Dutch elm disease probably came to the United States on a shipment of elm logs from Europe. Other methods include developing disease-resistant species, reducing air pollution, which makes trees more susceptible to disease, and identifying and removing dead, infected, and susceptible trees.

Insect pests that cause considerable damage to trees

include the gypsy moth, spruce budworm, pine weevil, larch sawfly, and several species of pinebark beetles. Pest control methods include isolating and removing infested trees, encouraging natural insect control by preserving forest diversity, introducing other insects that prey on pest species (biological control), using sexual attractants (pheromones) to lure insects to traps, releasing sterilized male insects to reduce the population growth of pest species, and pesticide spraying (Section 22-5).

Protecting Forests from Air Pollution Air pollution is a rapidly growing new threat to many of the world's forests. One of the most serious air pollution problems affecting forests is **acid deposition,** commonly called acid rain. It occurs when sulfur dioxide and nitrogen oxide air pollutants, released by the burning of fossil fuels in power plants and cars, are transformed chemically in the atmosphere to sulfuric and nitric acids and dry acidic particulate matter that fall to the earth in rain, snow, or fog (Section 19-2). Another air pollutant that causes severe tree damage is ozone. Trees downwind of coal-burning power plants and industrial areas and trees at high altitudes are exposed to the largest concentrations of damaging air pollutants.

The main solution to this problem is to use air pollution control devices on coal-burning power and industrial plants and on cars to reduce emissions of sulfur and nitrogen oxides (Section 19-6).

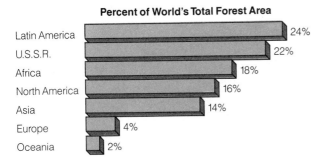

Percent of World's Total Forest Area

Latin America	24%
U.S.S.R.	22%
Africa	18%
North America	16%
Asia	14%
Europe	4%
Oceania	2%

Figure 13-17 Percentage of the world's forests in various groups of countries. (Data from UN Food and Agriculture Organization)

13-5 STATUS OF WORLD AND U.S. FORESTS

World Forests The world's forest resources are divided unevenly among regions (Figure 13-17 and map inside the front cover) because of variations in climate, land use, total land area, population size and density, and past forest exploitation. Almost two-thirds of the world's forests are found in only seven countries: the USSR (22%), Brazil (13%), Canada (11%), the United States (7%), Zaire (4%), China (4%), and Indonesia (3%).

Since the Agricultural Revolution began, it is estimated that human activities have reduced the earth's original forested area by at least one-third and by one-half in the LDCs. In most MDCs the amount of forested area has remained the same and in some cases increased since 1900, primarily because urbanization and industrialized agriculture reduced the need to convert forestland to agricultural land. Overall, however, the world is losing about 1% of its forested land each year as forests—especially tropical forests—in LDCs are cleared for farming and grazing and cut for fuelwood and lumber without adequate reforestation.

The Fuelwood Crisis in LDCs About 70% of the people in LDCs, most of whom live in rural areas, depend on free or cheap wood as their principal fuel for heating and cooking. By 1985 about 1.5 billion people—almost one out of every three persons on earth—in 63 LDCs were unable to obtain enough fuelwood to meet their minimum needs or were forced to meet their needs by consuming wood faster than it was being replenished (Figure 13-18). The UN Food and Agriculture Organization projects that by the end of this century 3 billion people in these LDCs plus 14

others will either face acute fuelwood scarcity (500 million people) or will be depleting remaining supplies to meet their needs (2.5 billion people).

Fuelwood scarcity has several harmful consequences. It places an additional burden on the poor, especially women, who must walk long distances, carry heavy loads, and spend a large amount of their potentially productive time in collecting fuelwood. Deforestation is also accelerated, especially in areas near villages and cities where commercial markets for fuelwood and charcoal (produced as a fuel from fuelwood) exist. Deforestation in turn increases soil erosion, flooding, and desertification, and reduces agricultural production. Food production is also decreased when families who cannot obtain enough fuelwood burn dried animal dung and crop residues, thus preventing vital natural fertilizers from reaching the soil.

LDCs can reduce the severity of the fuelwood crisis by planting more trees to increase the supply and by burning wood more efficiently or switching to other fuels such as charcoal and kerosene to reduce consumption. Experience so far, however, has shown that these measures are difficult to implement in rural areas where they are most needed.

Governments of countries such as China, South Korea, and Nepal have been successful in instituting massive tree-planting programs at the village level. Villagers are provided seed or seedlings by government foresters and encouraged to plant fast-growing fuelwood trees and shrubs in fields along with crops (agroforestry), in plantations, and in unused patches of land around homes and along roads and waterways. But most LDCs suffering from fuelwood shortages have inadequate forestry policies and budgets and lack trained foresters. As a result, they are planting 10 to 20 times less than what is needed to offset forest losses and meet increased demands for fuelwood and other forest products.

Several countries have instituted programs to encourage rural people to switch from energy-wasting open fires to more-efficient cookstoves and to other fuels. Although mud stoves can be made by villagers for several dollars, they do not last long and do not provide light like open fires. Even more important, the rural poor cannot afford to make such stoves and to buy alternative fuels.

Tropical Deforestation Lying on each side of the equator is an immense area of tropical rain and evergreen forests, known collectively as **tropical moist forests,** stretching across Central America, South America, Africa, and Asia (see map inside the front cover). Occupying an area roughly equal to that of the continental United States, these forests are home to at least half of the earth's species of plants and animals.

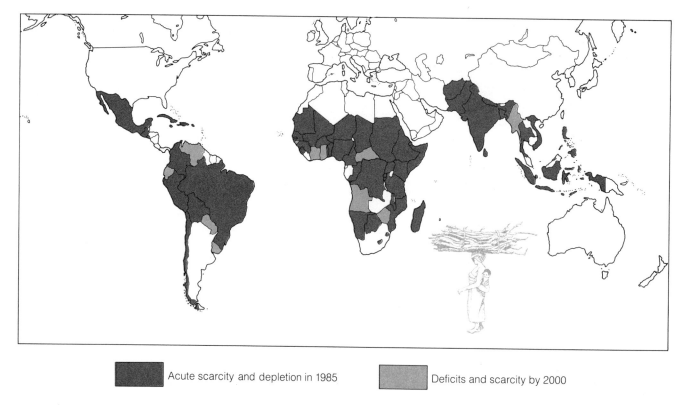

Acute scarcity and depletion in 1985	Deficits and scarcity by 2000

Figure 13-18 Countries experiencing fuelwood scarcity and deficits, 1985 and 2000. (Data from UN Food and Agriculture Organization)

They are by far the earth's most diverse biome—and they are being depleted and degraded faster than any other biome. About one-third of the world's original expanse of these forests has already been cleared and used to grow crops, graze livestock, and provide timber and fuelwood. Africa has lost 52% of its tropical forests, Asia 42%, Central America 37%, and South America 36%.

There is controversy over the rate at which these forests are presently being cleared and degraded because of insufficient data and the tendency of some governments to understate the problem for political reasons. However, on the evidence of surveys made by remote-sensing satellites and other available data, it is estimated that each year tropical forests equal in area to the state of Maine are being completely cleared, and other tropical forests equal in area to state of Virginia are being degraded. This amounts to complete clearing of at least 80,000 square kilometers (31,000 square miles) and degradation of at least 100,000 square kilometers (39,000 square miles) of tropical moist forests per year. Each minute an average of 15 hectares (38 acres) of tropical moist forest are completely cleared and another 19 hectares (47 acres) are disturbed and degraded. Some experts estimate that the rate of removal and degradation is almost two times higher.

About 99% of all tropical deforestation is taking place in 42 LDCs, with Brazil, Indonesia, Colombia, and Mexico accounting for 47% (Figure 13-19). If present rates continue, all remaining tropical forests will be gone or seriously disturbed by 2035.

Why is this happening? There are four direct causes of tropical deforestation and degradation (Figure 13-20): **(1)** poor people clearing land to grow food, **(2)** poor people gathering fuelwood faster than it is regenerated (especially in Africa and Asia), **(3)** commercial logging by international companies (especially in the Pacific Islands, West and Central Africa, and parts of Latin America), and **(4)** ranchers clearing land (primarily in Central America and Brazil's portion of the Amazon basin) to graze cattle and produce low-cost beef mostly for export to MDCs (see Spotlight on p. 280). Indirect causes of deforestation are rapid population growth, poverty, which forces landless people to settle and cultivate unowned forestland, land ownership patterns that favor the wealthy and drive the poor to cultivate forests, and failure of governments to require international timber companies to regenerate cleared areas.

Why should we be concerned? Ecologists warn that loss and degradation of these incredibly diverse biomes could cause the premature extinction of 1 mil-

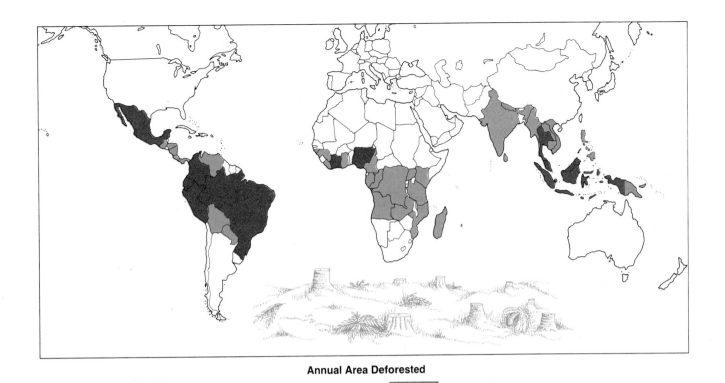

Annual Area Deforested

High (200,000 – 1,480,000 hectares)　　Moderate (10,000 – 199,000 hectares)

Figure 13-19 Countries experiencing large annual destruction of tropical forests, 1981–1985. (Data from UN Food and Agriculture Organization)

lion species—10% to 20% of the earth's total—by the beginning of the next century (see Guest Essay at the end of this chapter). Many of these species may be important in the development of hybrid and genetically engineered food plants needed to support future green revolutions, new medicines to fight disease, and a host of other products important to both MDCs and LDCs. Tropical forests directly affect the survival and life quality of about one of every four persons on earth. They are home to 150 million to 200 million people, who survive by shifting cultivation, and they protect watershed and regulate water flow for other farmers, who grow food for over 1 billion people.

What can be done? In 1985 the World Resources Institute and the World Bank proposed that MDCs fund a five-year $5.3 billion plan to help tropical LDCs protect and renew tropical forests. This plan called for setting aside 14% of the world's tropical forests as reserves and parks to protect them from development, massive planting of fuelwood and multipurpose trees carried out primarily by villagers, establishment of industrial tree plantations in areas where soils are best suited for this type of forest management, rehabilitation of tropical watersheds to reduce flooding and sedimentation, and strengthening of forestry research and training in tropical LDCs. In addi-

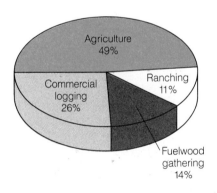

Figure 13-20 Major direct causes of deforestation and degradation of tropical forests. (Data from Norman Myers)

tion, conservationists believe that commercial timber companies should be required to reforest lands they harvest in LDCs. If such a program is carried out, it could represent a turning point in preventing the irreversible loss of most of the world's tropical forests.

Forests in the United States　Since the first colonists arrived at Jamestown in 1607, the United States has lost about 45% of its original forested area. Since 1920, however, the country's total forested area has remained

During the past 25 years almost 40% of Central America's tropical moist forests have been cleared and converted to pastureland. During the 1970s about 40% of the low-cost, grass-fed beef raised on this land was exported to the United States. Because this range-fed beef is lean and tough, it is sold primarily to fast-food chains for hamburger meat and to food-processing companies for use in pet foods, baby foods, luncheon meats, chili, stews, and frozen dinners.

Each quarter-pound hamburger made from meat imported from Central America or any country converting tropical forests to pastureland means the loss of about 5 square meters (55 square feet) of tropical forest—roughly the size of a small kitchen—containing thousands of different plant and animal species. Thus, as tropical forest

expert Norman Myers (see Guest Essay at the end of this chapter) points out, Americans eating hamburgers from fast-food outlets that import beef from tropical countries "indirectly have their hands on the chain saws and bulldozers that are clearing many tropical forests."

After five to ten years of grazing, these tropical pastures become so degraded and weed infested that they are no longer useful for cattle production. Ranchers then clear another large area of undisturbed tropical forest and repeat the process. If allowed to continue, this cheap and ecologically destructive "shifting ranching" will destroy or severely degrade most of Central America's remaining tropical forests.

By 1985 only 19% of the beef produced in Central America was exported to the United States due to a drop in U.S. beef consumption

and declining production caused by pasture degradation and escalating warfare in El Salvador and Nicaragua. Although this drop decreases the rate of tropical deforestation, some conservationists believe that the United States should phase out imports of all meat produced on cleared tropical forestland. Although this would reduce the profits of large ranchers and hurt Central American economies to some degree, it is argued that the long-term ecological and economic benefits of maintaining tropical forests far outweigh any short-term economic losses. The basic question is whether importing beef from tropical countries to cut the cost of a fast-food hamburger by a nickel is worth the destruction and degradation of the planet's greatest storehouse of biological diversity. What do you think?

about the same, covering about one-third of all U.S. land area (Figure 13-21).

About two-thirds of the country's forests are classified as commercial forestland, suitable for growing potentially renewable crops of economically valuable tree species and not protected from commercial logging as part of parks, wilderness, or other protected areas. Most of the sharp increase in U.S. annual timber harvests between 1920 and 1985 has resulted from the use of modern forestry management to increase the average annual growth of wood per unit of area in commercial forestland by about 3.5 times.

The annual harvest of commercial timber comes mostly from the 14% of the country's commercial forestland owned by timber companies, the 18% found in national forests, and another 10% on other federal and state public lands. Most of the 58% of U.S. commercial forestland owned by individuals and families consists of fragmented and small sites managed poorly in terms of timber production.

Importance and Use of National Forests   National forests (Figure 13-4)—covering an area roughly equal to that of the state of California—are unmatched among

federal lands in their importance for wildlife conservation, recreation, and commercial timber production. They contain 84% of the wilderness areas in the lower 48 states. They are home to over 3,000 species of fish and wildlife, including half of the country's big-game animals. Some of these lands are also key to the survival and recovery of many threatened and endangered species, particularly those requiring large undisturbed areas, such as the grizzly bear and the gray wolf. More than 3 million cattle and sheep graze on national forest lands each year. National forests receive more recreational visits than any other federal public lands, accounting for 43% of all recreational visits to federal public lands in 1985. By comparison, the heavily used National Park System accounted for only 20%.

Almost half of national forest lands are open to commercial logging, providing about 15% of the country's total annual timber harvest—enough wood to build about 1 million homes a year. Each year private timber companies bid for rights to cut a certain amount of timber from areas designated by the Forest Service. Forest Service funds provided by taxpayers are used to build and maintain roads to timber harvest areas and to reforest harvested areas. In addition to man-

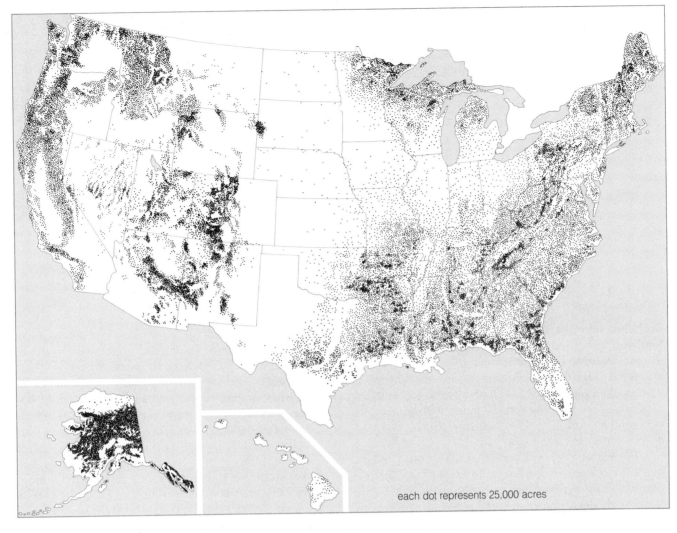

each dot represents 25,000 acres

Figure 13-21 Forest lands in the United States. (Data from Council on Environmental Quality)

aging this vast system, the Forest Service provides technical assistance for the management of private forest and range lands throughout the country.

Conflicting Demands on National Forests Unlike the National Park Service and the Fish and Wildlife Service, the Forest Service is required by law to manage its lands under the principle of multiple use, with no particular use receiving more emphasis than any other. Until 1950, demands on national forests were low and conflicts between competing uses were relatively rare. Since 1950, however, there have been greatly increased demands on the forests for timber sales (Figure 13-22), development of domestic mineral and energy resources, recreational use, wilderness protection, and wildlife conservation.

Since the 1950s, environmentalists have accused the Forest Service of emphasizing commercial logging at the expense of other uses, pointing to the doubling of timber sales and harvesting between the early 1950s and 1960 and the continuation of high levels of harvesting since then. In 1974 outrage by conservationists over extensive and often improperly managed clearcutting in national forests during the 1960s and early 1970s led to passage of the National Forest Management Act. The law set certain limitations and restrictions on timber harvesting methods and required the Forest Service to prepare comprehensive forest management plans for each national forest region, with public participation in this process.

The National Forest Management Act and other environmental laws passed in the 1970s (Appendix 3) resulted in some improvement in management of the National Forest System for recreational use and wildlife, water, and soil resource conservation. However, conservationists charge that commercial logging is still by far the dominant use in terms of management decisions and budget allocation. In 1985, for example, 30% of the Forest Service budget was used for timber sales

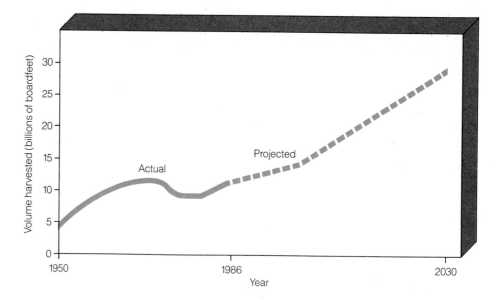

Figure 13-22 Timber harvested in national forests, 1950–1986, and projected harvests to 2030. (Data from U.S. Forest Service)

(including reforestation and road building and maintenance), compared to only 9% for recreation and 6% for soil, water, and wildlife conservation. They also point to administration-supported Forest Service management plans calling for timber sale volumes to double and for building 580,000 miles of new roads between 1986 and 2030. (The entire interstate highway system comprises just 40,000 miles.)

The Forest Service asserts that it can meet the higher timber production levels proposed by the Reagan administration and the timber industry only by temporarily departing from sustained-yield management to cut deeply into the old-growth timber of the Pacific Northwest, where timber companies have already cut most of the mature timber on their own lands. The companies contend that the towering stands of 200- to 400-year-old Douglas fir and other commercially important trees in the country's remaining virgin forests should be cut down and replaced with more productive young stands of one or two faster-growing species to prevent timber shortages and higher prices for houses and wood products.

Conservationists strongly oppose substantial cutting of old-growth timber from national forests. They argue that such a policy would further violate the principle of balanced multiple use. Replacing unique, irreplaceable, and biologically diverse stands of trees with greatly simplified stands would eliminate habitats for a variety of plant and animal life, reduce the ability of such forests to conserve water and prevent soil erosion, and reduce recreational opportunities in some of the country's most diverse and aesthetically appealing forests. Conservationists also challenge the need to increase timber harvests in these and other national forests to avoid timber shortages and higher prices. They note that by 1985 timber bought but not harvested from national forests by the timber industry

was equal to 40 billion board feet—almost four times the average annual volume cut from these forests.

Conservationists have also accused the Forest Service of poor management: By losing money on 22% to 42% of its annual timber sales between 1980 and 1985, the Forest Service has provided timber companies with tax-supported subsidies. Forestry industry representatives argue that such subsidies help taxpayers by keeping lumber prices down. But conservationists note that each year taxpayers already provide the lumber industry with tax breaks almost equal to the cost of managing the entire National Forest System. As long as timber companies can increase profits by cutting timber from public lands at low cost, they will continue to pressure elected officials to increase the amount of timber cut from national forests.

Conservationists propose four ways to reduce exploitation of publicly owned timber resources and provide true multiple use of national forests as required by law: **(1)** Annual timber harvest levels should be cut in half to about 5 billion board feet rather than being increased; **(2)** Between 15% and 25% of remaining old-growth timber in each national forest should remain uncut; **(3)** Congress should require that no timber from national forests be sold at a loss; and **(4)** A much larger portion of the Forest Service budget should be devoted to improving the management and increasing the timber output of commercial forestland owned by individuals and families.

13-6 RANGELANDS

The World's Rangeland Resources Land on which the vegetation is predominantly grasses, grasslike plants, or shrubs such as sagebrush is called **range-**

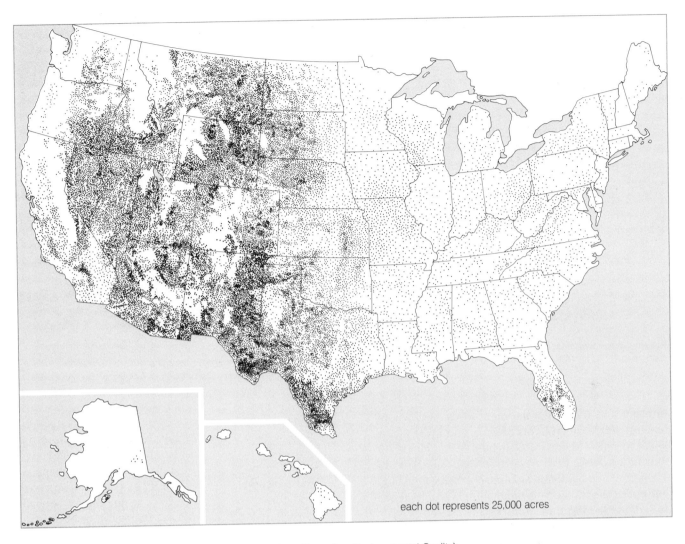

each dot represents 25,000 acres

Figure 13-23 Rangelands in the United States. (Data from Council on Environmental Quality)

land. Rangelands include most of the world's tropical grasslands (savanna) and uncultivated temperate grasslands (see map inside the front cover). Humans cannot digest the cellulose that makes up most rangeland vegetation. But the world's 3 billion domesticated **ruminant animals**—mostly cattle, sheep, goats, and buffalo—have four-chambered stomachs that digest cellulose and produce protein-rich meat, milk, butter, and cheese for human consumption. These livestock animals also provide manure for fertilizing soil and useful nonedible goods such as wool, leather, and tallow (used to make soap and candles). Nonruminant livestock animals such as pigs and chickens cannot feed on rangeland vegetation.

Presently only about 40% of the world's rangelands are used for grazing by domesticated ruminant animals because of rangeland degradation, conversion of the best rangeland to irrigated cropland, and increased use of intensive livestock production in both MDCs and LDCs. By 1985 about three-fourths of the

world's domestic ruminants were intensively managed and fed mostly on hay grown in pastures, sown forage crops like alfalfa, crop residues, or grain in feedlots. Throughout the world an increasing number of the ruminant livestock still raised on rangeland feed on marginal land with low productivity. Much of this land is further degraded by overgrazing.

U.S. Rangeland Resources About 29% of the total land area of the United States consists of rangelands, located mostly in the arid and semiarid western half of the country (Figure 13-23). About two-thirds of these rangelands are privately owned. The remaining 34% is publicly owned land, most of it managed by the Bureau of Land Management and the Forest Service.

Today rangeland grazing plays a small but still important role in U.S. cattle and sheep production. Beef production, for example, involves raising calves to maturity on western rangeland or on planted pas-

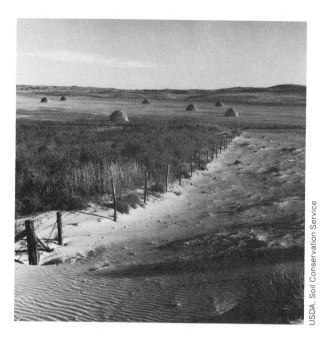

Figure 13-24 Lightly grazed and severely overgrazed rangeland near Atkinson, Nebraska.

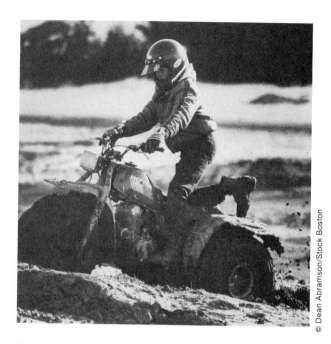

Figure 13-25 Motorcycles and other off-road vehicles harm vegetation and wildlife on public lands.

tureland and then shipping them to feedlots where they are fed large amounts of grain and protein-rich feeds to fatten them for slaughter Although three-fourths of public and privately owned rangeland is actively grazed by domestic animals at some time during each year, range vegetation supplies only about 16% of the food in these animals' life cycles.

The Bureau of Land Management and the Forest Service issue permits allowing about 2% of the country's private ranchers to graze their herds on public land at very low grazing fees. In 1985 about 2 million cattle and 2.3 million sheep, amounting to less than 4% of U.S. herds of these animals, grazed on these lands. The public rangelands are managed under the principle of multiple use and are used for other purposes, such as mining, energy resource development, recreation, and conservation of soil, water, and wildlife.

Characteristics of Rangeland Vegetation Many rangeland weeds and bushes have a single main taproot and can thus be easily uprooted. By contrast, rangeland grass plants have a fibrous taproot system with multiple branches that make the plants very difficult to uproot. This explains why these grasses help prevent soil erosion.

For most plants, when the leaf tip has been eaten, no further leaf growth occurs. In contrast, each leaf of rangeland grass grows from its base, not its tip. Thus, even when the upper half of the stem and leaves

of rangeland grass have been eaten by livestock or wild herbivores such as deer, antelope, and elk, it can grow back to its original length in a short time. However, the lower half of the plant, known as the **metabolic reserve,** must remain if the plant is to survive and grow new leaves. As long as only the upper half is eaten, rangeland grass is a renewable resource that can be grazed again and again.

Rangeland Carrying Capacity and Overgrazing Each type of rangeland has a limited carrying capacity—the maximum number of wild and domesticated herbivores that a given area can support without risk of degradation from consumption of the metabolic reserve. **Overgrazing** can kill the root system of grass so that little if any grass is left (Figure 13-24). Then invader species of weeds and shrubs unpalatable to livestock take over, or all vegetation disappears, leaving the land barren and vulnerable to erosion. Severe overgrazing coupled with drought can convert potentially productive rangeland to desert (see Enrichment Study at the end of Chapter 11). Restoring overgrazed lands is difficult and expensive. During the 5- to 13-year period required for restoration, the number of animals grazing per unit of land area must be decreased or even reduced to zero. Dune buggies, motorcycles, and other off-road vehicles can also degrade vegetation on rangeland and other public lands (Figure 13-25).

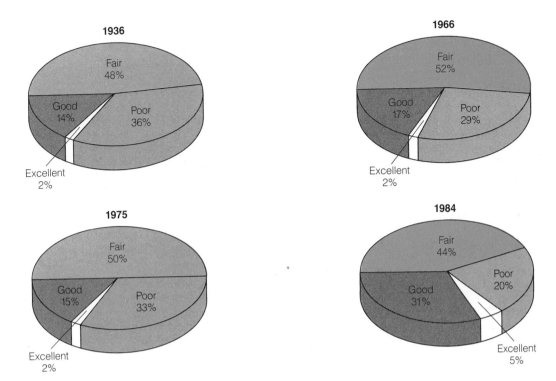

Figure 13-26 Quality of public rangeland, 1936–1984. (Data from U.S. Bureau of Land Management and U.S. Forest Service)

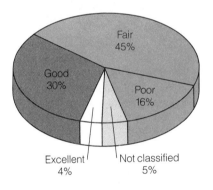

Figure 13-27 Quality of private U.S. rangeland, 1982. (Data from U.S. Department of Agriculture)

Since the passage of the Taylor Grazing Act of 1934, the number of animals using public rangeland has declined by almost one-third and there has been a general improvement in range condition (Figure 13-26). However, assessments reveal that despite over 50 years of management, the share of public rangelands in fair or poor condition has never fallen below 60%. Overgrazing continues on a large portion of public rangeland primarily because grazing fees on this land are low and ranchers pressure the federal government to keep grazing allotments as high as possible (see Spotlight on p. 286).

Throughout the world most rangelands used extensively for livestock show many signs of overgrazing. In the United States unrestricted grazing on the arid and semiarid private and public rangelands of the West in the late 1800s and early 1900s resulted in extensive and severe range deterioration. Today there is still much severe damage to private rangelands in the far-western states (Figure 13-27).

Rangeland Management The most important method of managing rangeland is to control the number and kinds—the stocking rate—of animals grazing on a given area to ensure that its carrying capacity is not exceeded. This is often difficult in practice because carrying capacity varies with climate, seasons of the year, slope, soil type, types of forage, and past land use. Despite these difficulties, examination of the range and knowledge of the amount of vegetation required to support different types of animals can be used to prevent overgrazing. For example, a rangeland manager should know that five sheep consume the same amount of vegetation as one steer.

Controlling the distribution of grazing animals over rangeland is another important way to prevent overgrazing. Ranchers can control distribution by building

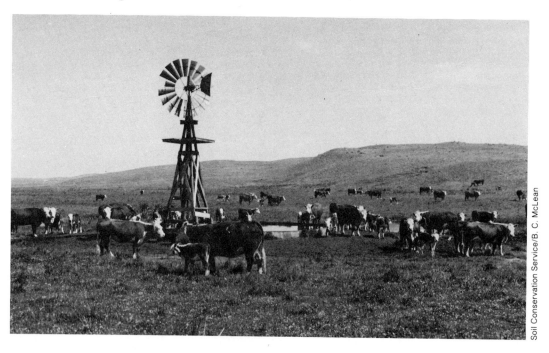

Figure 13-28 Livestock tend to concentrate and overgraze around water sources unless techniques are used to distribute the animals to other areas.

Soil Conservation Service/B. C. McLean

Spotlight   Should Grazing Fees on Public Rangeland Be Increased?

In 1986, U.S. ranchers paid the federal government $1.35 per month per head of cattle to graze livestock on public rangeland. Similar fees for grazing cattle on private rangeland amounted to about $6.25 per month per head. Thus, in 1986 U.S. taxpayers provided subsidies of at least $30 million to ranchers with federal grazing permits. Ranchers defend the low permit price by citing the poor quality of forage on federal land.

Conservationists, however, contend that the primary reason for poor forage is that the low grazing fees lead ranchers to exert political pressure to allow as much grazing as possible. The high grazing levels prevent forage from recovering. Conservationists propose that the government raise grazing fees to reduce overgrazing and give taxpayers a better return on these publicly owned resources.

In response the Bureau of Land Management and the Forest Service proposed that the grazing fee for 1987 be raised to $3.50, but western ranchers lobbied the Reagan administration and obtained a one-year extension of the 1986 fee. They contend that the higher fee would force many of them out of business. During the past ten years their production costs have risen sharply while meat prices have risen only slightly.

Instead of raising grazing fees, Earl Sandvig, former administrator of grazing programs for the Forest Service, has suggested replacing the grazing permit system with the sale of grazing rights by competitive bids, as is done for timber cutting contracts in national forests. Ranchers with permits, however, vehemently oppose this approach because grazing allotments on public land raise the value of their livestock animals by $1,000 to $1,500 per head. Thus, an allotment to graze 500 cattle on public land can be worth $500,000 to $750,000 to the rancher. The permit value is commonly considered the rancher's private property and is included in the market price and loan value of the rancher's property. Ranchers who are not able to get permits believe that the permit system gives politically "well-connected" ranchers an unfair economic advantage; most small ranchers favor open bidding for public grazing rights. What do you think?

fences to prevent animals from grazing on degraded rangeland, rotating livestock from one area to another, providing supplemental feeding at selected sites, and strategically locating water holes (Figure 13-28) and supplies of salt. Livestock need both salt and water, but not together. Placing salt blocks in ungrazed areas away from water sources prevents livestock from congregating and overgrazing near water sources.

A more expensive and less widely used method of rangeland management is to suppress growth of undesirable vegetation with herbicides, mechanical removal, or controlled burning. Growth of desirable vegetation can be encouraged by artificial seeding and fertilization, but this is expensive relative to the economic return on livestock. Reseeding is worth the cost,

however, to prevent desertification of badly degraded public rangeland.

Many ranchers still promote the use of poisons, trapping, and shooting to control herbivores such as jackrabbits and prairie dogs, which compete with livestock for forage, and to kill off predatory species such as coyotes, which sometimes kill livestock, especially sheep. However, experience has shown that this approach usually provides only temporary relief, is rarely worth the cost, and sometimes can make matters worse (see Spotlight below).

Forests precede civilizations, deserts follow them.
François-René de Chateaubriand

Spotlight   Should Poisons Be Used to Kill Coyotes and Other Livestock Predators?

Between 1940 and 1972 a highly controversial program was waged by western ranchers and the U.S. Department of the Interior against livestock predators, especially the coyote. Because coyotes are too numerous and cautious to be hunted effectively, emphasis was placed on lacing livestock carcasses with poison, using poisoned-bait traps set with explosive charges, and placing collars containing poison on sheep. One of the most popular poisons was sodium fluoroacetate—known as compound 1080—28 grams (1 ounce) of which is enough to kill 200 humans or 20,000 coyotes.

A 1972 report by the Advisory Committee on Predator Control recommended that all poisoning of predators by the federal government be halted and that all poisons in use be banned because they could accidentally kill nontarget animals, including dogs, endangered species, and human beings. At that time

President Richard Nixon issued an executive order banning predator poisoning on government lands or by federal employees anywhere. Shortly thereafter the Environmental Protection Agency banned use of several of the poisons, including 1080, even on private land.

In 1985, under pressure from ranchers, western congressional representatives, and the Reagan administration, the EPA decided to allow the use of 1080 in livestock collars. Ranchers, however, wanted to inject the poison into carcasses of sheep or horses for use as bait. Conservation groups opposed any use of 1080 because it can kill nontarget species such as golden eagles, which eat parts of predators killed by the poison. They also noted evidence that extermination or drastic reduction of the coyote population in a given area can reduce rangeland productivity, causing much larger economic losses than those from sheep killed by coyotes. In the

absence of the coyotes, populations of small herbivores, especially rabbits, that coyotes feed on grow unchecked and compete with livestock for rangeland vegetation.

Conservationists suggest that fences, guard dogs, and predator repellants be used to keep predators away. For example, guard dogs have eliminated predation on some Oregon ranches that had suffered heavy lamb losses. In 1986 Department of Agriculture researchers reported that predation can be essentially eliminated by penning young lambs and heifers together for 30 days and then allowing them to graze together on the same range. During the 30-day penning period the cows and sheep develop a strong need to intermingle. Cows butt and kick at predators to keep them away, thus protecting the sheep. The two species coexist nicely on the same range because cattle eat mainly grasses and sheep prefer broadleafed plants. What do you think?

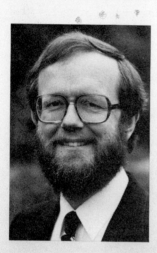

Norman Myers

Norman Myers is an international consultant in environment and development with emphasis on conservation of wildlife species and tropical forests. He has served as a consultant for many development agencies and research bodies including the U.S. National Academy of Sciences, the World Bank, the Organization for Economic Cooperation and Development (OECD), various UN agencies, and the World Resources Institute. Among his recent publications (see Further Readings) are The Sinking Ark *(1979),* Conversion of Tropical Moist Forests *(1980),* A Wealth of Wild Species *(1983),* The Primary Source *(1984), and* The Gaia Atlas of Planet Management *(1985).*

Tropical forests still cover an area roughly equivalent to the continental United States. Bioclimatic data suggest they could have once covered an area at least two-thirds larger. So we have already lost a lot of them, mostly in the recent past. Worse, remote-sensing surveys reveal that we are now destroying the forests at a rate of at least 1% a year, and we are grossly degrading them at a rate of at least another 1% a year—and both of these rates are accelerating. Unless we act now to halt this loss, within just another few decades at most, there could be little left, except perhaps a block in central Africa and another in western Amazonia. Even these remnants may not survive the combined pressures of population growth and land hunger beyond the middle of the next century.

This means that we are imposing one of the most broad-scale and impoverishing impacts on the biosphere that it has ever suffered throughout its 4 billion years of existence. Tropical forests constitute the greatest celebration of nature to appear on the face of the planet since the first flickerings of life. They are exceptionally complex ecologically, and they are remarkably rich biotically. Although they now account for only 7% of the earth's land surface, they still are home for half, and perhaps three-quarters or more, of all the earth's species of plant and animal life. Thus, elimination of these forests is by far the leading factor in the mass extinction of species that appears likely over the next few decades.

Already we may be losing several species every day because of clearing and degradation of tropical forests. The time will surely come, and come soon, when we shall be losing many thousands every year. The implications are profound, whether they be scientific, aesthetic, ethical—or simply economic. In the field of medicine alone, we benefit from myriad drugs and pharmaceuticals derived from tropical forest plants. The commercial value of these products worldwide can be reckoned at $20 billion each year.

By way of example, the rosy periwinkle from Madagascar's tropical forests has produced two potent drugs against Hodgkin's disease, leukemia, and other blood cancers. Madagascar harbors—or rather it used to harbor—at least 8,000 plant species,

CHAPTER SUMMARY

Vast areas of cropland, forest, rangeland, watersheds, estuaries, and other types of nonurban land, water, and air resources are needed to sustain urban areas. Over one-third of all U.S. land consists of public lands owned jointly by all citizens and managed for them by the federal government. Most of these public lands have been divided into several categories: **(1)** National Forests, **(2)** National Resource Lands, **(3)** National Wildlife Refuge System, **(4)** National Park System, and **(5)** National Wilderness Preservation System.

Between 1970 and 1986 the amount of land in the National Wilderness Preservation System increased almost tenfold, with Alaska accounting for most of this increase. A number of wild and scenic rivers and river systems have also been protected from development. Wilderness areas provide not only wild places where one can experience natural beauty and solitude, but also recreational experiences, economic benefits for the outdoor-gear and tourist industries, and undisturbed habitats for wildlife; in addition, they serve as an ecological laboratory for studying how nature works. It is also argued that wilderness areas should be preserved

of which more than 7,000 could be found nowhere else. Today Madagascar has lost 93% of its virgin tropical forest. The U.S. National Cancer Institute estimates that there could be another 10 plants in tropical forests with potential against various cancers—provided pharmacologists can get to them before they are eliminated by chain saws and bulldozers.

We benefit in still other ways from tropical forests. Elimination of these forests disrupts certain critical environmental services, notably their famous "sponge effect" by which they soak up rainfall during the wet season and then release it in regular amounts throughout the dry season. When tree cover is removed and this watershed function is impaired, the result is a yearly regime of floods followed by droughts, which destroys property and reduces agricultural production. There is also concern that if tropical deforestation becomes wide enough, it could trigger local, regional, or even global changes in climate. Such climatic upheavals would affect the lives of billions of people, if not the whole of humankind.

All this raises important questions about our role in the biosphere and our relations with the natural world around us. As we proceed on our disruptive way in tropical forests, we—that is, political leaders and the general public alike—give scarcely a moment's thought to what we are doing. We are deciding the fate of the world's tropical forests unwittingly, yet effectively and increasingly. The resulting shift in evolution's course, stemming from the elimination of tropical forests, will rank as one of the greatest biological upheavals since the dawn of life. It will equal, in scale and significance, the development of aerobic respiration, the emergence of flowering plants, and the arrival of limbed animals, taking place over eons of time. But whereas these were enriching disruptions in the course of life on this planet, the loss of biotic diversity associated with tropical forest destruction will be almost entirely an impoverishing phenomenon brought about entirely by human actions. And it will all have occurred within the twinkling of a geologic eye.

In short, our intervention in tropical forests should be viewed as one of the most challenging problems that humankind has ever encountered. After all, we are the first species ever to be able to look upon nature's work and to decide whether we should consciously eliminate it or leave much of it untouched.

So the decline of tropical forest constitutes one of the great sleeper issues of our time. Yet we can still save much of these forests, and the species they contain. Should we not consider ourselves fortunate that we alone among all generations are being given the chance to preserve tropical forests as the most exuberant expression of nature in the biosphere—and thereby to support the right to life of a large number of our fellow species and their capacity to undergo further evolution without human interference?

Guest Essay Discussion

1. What obligation, if any, do you as an individual have to preserve a significant proportion of the world's remaining tropical forests?

2. Should MDCs provide most of the funds to preserve some of the remaining tropical forests in LDCs? Explain.

3. What can you do to help preserve some of the world's tropical forests? Which, if any, of these actions do you actually plan to carry out?

because the plant and animal species have an inherent right to exist without human interference. Conservationists believe that the U.S. wilderness system should be increased, especially in the lower 48 states, whereas representatives of timber, mining, energy, and other resource industries oppose any expansion of the system.

The National Park System now consists of 337 units, including large national parks and culture-oriented areas such as national historic sites and national battlefields. The twelvefold increase in recreational visits to National Park System units between 1950 and 1986 has led to overcrowd-ing, noise, litter, polluted water, and crime in the most heavily used units. Air and water pollution from nearby mining, timber harvesting, coal-burning power plants, and urban areas pose an even more serious threat to many national parks. Conservationists and the Reagan administration agree that more funds need to be provided for repairing and maintaining existing parks, but disagree over whether new units should be added to provide for present and projected recreational use.

Forests, which cover about one-third of the earth's surface, provide timber for heating, cooking, construction, and paper products. Forests also provide vital ecological functions by helping control climate, adding oxygen to the atmosphere, providing habitats for wildlife, absorbing noise and some air pollutants, and holding and releasing water gradually—thus helping reduce soil erosion, the severity of flooding, and the amount of sediment washing into rivers and reservoirs.

About 58% of the world's commercially exploitable forests are under some form of cultivation and management (*silviculture*). Commercial timber companies want to greatly increase the amount of timber harvested through *intensive management*, in which an area is cleared of all vegetation and planted with an even-aged stand of a fast-growing tree species. Conservationists argue that natural diversity and multiple-use functions should be preserved by using *moderate management* of many existing forests, consisting of uneven-aged trees. In this case only certain commercially valuable species would be removed. Trees are harvested and regenerated by five main methods: *selective cutting, shelterwood cutting, seed tree cutting, clearcutting,* and *whole-tree harvesting.* Each method has certain advantages and disadvantages.

Forests must also be protected from damage by extremely destructive *crown fires* and less destructive *ground fires*. They must also be protected from diseases and insects, which cause much more loss of commercial timber than fires do, and from air pollution.

Since the Agricultural Revolution began about 10,000 years ago, human activities have reduced the world's original forested area by at least one-third, by one-half in the LDCs, and by about 45% in the United States. The world's remaining forests, especially tropical moist forests, are being cut and degraded at a rapid rate by poor people clearing land for fuelwood and to grow food, ranchers to graze cattle and produce low-cost beef mostly for export to MDCs, and by commercial logging companies to provide timber used mostly in MDCs.

In the United States commercial timber companies want to increase the amount of timber harvested from the national forests, which presently provide about 15% of the country's annual timber harvest. Conservationists, however, argue that present overemphasis on commercial harvesting of timber from national forests violates the law requiring that they be harvested at a rate and in a manner that allows them to be used for a variety of purposes (sustained yield and multiple-use management). They believe present timber harvest levels in national forests should be cut in half, some older diverse forests should remain uncut, and no timber in these forests should be sold at a loss to taxpayers.

Presently about 40% of the world's rangelands are used for grazing by domesticated animals. *Overgrazing* by livestock can kill the root system of rangeland grass so that little if any grass is left. Throughout the world most rangelands used extensively for livestock show signs of overgrazing. Presently almost two-thirds of public rangeland in the United States is in poor to fair quality as a result of overgrazing. Rangeland management involves controlling the number and kinds of animals grazing on a given area by using fences, rotating livestock from one area to another, providing supplemental feeding at selected sites, and strategically locating water holes and supplies of salt.

DISCUSSION TOPICS

1. Should more wilderness areas and wild and scenic rivers be preserved in the United States? Explain.

2. Discuss the pros and cons of each of the following suggestions for the use of national parks:
   a. Entrance, activity, and private concessionaire fees should be increased to the point where they pay for 25% of the costs of operating the National Park System.
   b. All private vehicles should be kept out.
   c. Campgrounds, lodges, and other commercial facilities in parks should be moved to nearby areas outside the parks.

3. Should the annual budget for both restoration of existing national parks and purchase of additional parkland be increased? Explain.

4. What would probably be the main characteristics of trees that should be (a) clearcut, (b) selectively cut, and (c) shelterwood cut or seed-tree cut?

5. Should a large fraction of the world's existing uneven-aged mixed forests be converted into even-aged tree plantations? Explain.

6. Explain how eating a hamburger from most fast-food chains indirectly contributes to the destruction of the world's tropical forests.

7. What difference, if any, could the loss of most of the world's tropical forests have on your life?

8. Should tax dollars continue to be used for building and maintaining roads into areas of national forests harvested by private companies and for reforesting such areas, or should some or all of these expenses be borne by the companies who profit from such harvests? Explain.

9. Argue for or against: (a) selling commercially valuable U.S. national forests to private interests, (b) transferring national forests to state governments, (c) leasing commercially valuable national forests to private corporations on a long-term basis.

10. Should many of the old-growth forests on public lands, primarily in the western United States, be logged? Explain.

11. Should fees for grazing on federally owned lands be eliminated and replaced with a competitive bidding system? Why or why not? Why would such a change be politically difficult?

12. Should the poisoning and hunting of livestock predators be allowed on federal rangelands? Why or why not? Try to have both a rancher and a wildlife scientist present to your class their viewpoints on this controversial issue.

13. Should trail bikes, dune buggies, snowmobiles, and other off-road vehicles be banned from all national forests, parks, and wilderness areas? Why or why not?

14

Wild Plant and Animal Resources

GENERAL OBJECTIVES

1. Why are wild species of plants and animals important?

2. What natural and cultural factors cause wild species to become endangered and extinct?

3. How can wild species be protected from premature extinction as a result of human activities?

4. How can populations of desirable animal game species be managed to ensure their availability for sport hunting without endangering their long-term survival?

5. How can populations of desirable species of freshwater and marine fish be managed to ensure their availability for sport and commercial fishing without endangering their long-term survival?

Love the animals, love the plants, love everything. If you love everything, you will perceive the divine mystery in things. Once you perceive it, you will begin to comprehend it better every day. And you will come at last to love the whole world with an all-embracing love.

Fyodor Dostoyevski, The Brothers Karamazov

In the 1850s Alexander Wilson, a prominent ornithologist, watched a single migrating flock of passenger pigeons darken the sky for more than four hours. He estimated that this flock of more than 2 billion birds was 384 kilometers (240 miles) long and 1.6 kilometers (1 mile) wide.

By 1914 the passenger pigeon (Figure 14-1) had disappeared forever. How could the species that was once the most numerous bird in North America become extinct in only a few decades? The major reasons for the extinction of this species were commercial hunting and loss of habitat and food supplies as forests were cleared for farms and cities. Passenger pigeons made excellent eating and good fertilizer. They were easy to kill because they flew in gigantic flocks and nested in long, narrow colonies. People used to capture one pigeon alive and tie it to a perch called a stool; soon a curious flock alighted beside this "stool pigeon" and were shot or trapped by nets that might contain more than 1,000 birds. Beginning around 1858, massive killing of passenger pigeons became a big business. Shotguns, fire, traps, artillery, and even dynamite were used. Some live birds served as targets in shooting galleries. In 1878 one professional pigeon trapper made $60,000 by killing 3 million birds at their nesting grounds near Petoskey, Michigan.

By the early 1880s intensive commercial hunting ceased because the species had been reduced to only several thousand. At this point recovery was essentially impossible and the population continued to decline because passenger pigeons laid only one egg per nest and were susceptible to death from infectious disease and from severe storms during their annual fall migration to Central and South America. By 1896 the last massive breeding

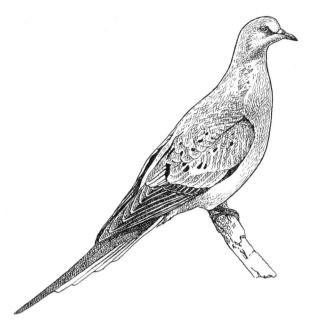

Figure 14-1 The extinct passenger pigeon. The last known passenger pigeon died in the Cincinnati Zoo in 1914.

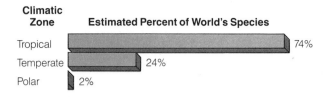

Climatic Zone	Estimated Percent of World's Species
Tropical	74%
Temperate	24%
Polar	2%

Figure 14-2 Percentage of world's wild species found in major climatic zones. (Data from the International Union for Conservation of Nature and Natural Resources and the World Resources Institute)

colony had vanished. In 1914 the last known passenger pigeon on earth died in the Cincinnati Zoo.

Does it really matter that a wild species such as the passenger pigeon became extinct and that the existence of numerous wild plant and animal species, such as the persistent trillium and the whooping crane, is threatened—primarily by human activities?

14-1 WHY PRESERVE WILD PLANT AND ANIMAL SPECIES?

How Many Species Exist? To date, scientists have identified about 1.7 million different species of plants and animals, with insects making up about three-fourths of the total. Species are continually being added to the list as new lands and waters are explored, and the total number of species inhabiting the earth is believed to be somewhere between 5 million and 30 million, mostly insects. Almost three-fourths of the world's known and unknown plant and animal species are believed to live only in areas with tropical climates (Figure 14-2), and 40% to 50% of the world's species live in endangered tropical moist forests (Section 13-5). There are economic, health, aesthetic, recreational, ecological, and ethical arguments against hastening the extinction of any wild species.

Economic and Health Importance Certain wild species, known as **wildlife resources,** are important because of their actual or potential economic value to people. Wildlife resources that provide sport in the form of hunting or fishing are known as **game species.**

Wildlife resources provide people with a wide variety of direct economic benefits as sources of food, spices, flavoring agents, scents, soap, cooking oils, lubricating oils, waxes, dyes, natural insecticides, paper, fuel, fibers, leathers, furs, natural rubber, medicines, and other important materials. Most of the plants that supply 90% of the world's food today were domesticated from wild plants in the tropics. Other wild species not presently classified as wildlife resources may be needed by agricultural scientists to develop new crop strains that have higher yields and increased resistance to diseases, pests, heat, and drought.

Pollination by insects is essential for many food and nonfood plant species. Predatory insects, parasites, and disease-causing bacteria and viruses are increasingly used for the biological control of various weeds and insect pests, thus helping reduce losses of crops and trees. Drinking coffee, adding a low-calorie sweetener to the coffee, eating a banana, enjoying a chocolate bar, chewing gum, applying lipstick, using perfume or after-shave lotion, shampooing hair, swinging a tennis racket, or putting on jogging shoes—all of these activities of our everyday lives involve products derived from tropical forests.

About 40% of the prescription and nonprescription drugs used throughout the world have active ingredients extracted from plants and animals. Annual sales of drugs based on naturally derived chemicals amount to at least $40 billion worldwide and $20 billion in the United States. Aspirin, probably the world's most widely used drug, was developed according to a chemical "blueprint" supplied by a compound extracted from the leaves of tropical willow trees. Quinine, used to treat malaria, is derived from the cinchona tree. Penicillin is produced by a fungus, and certain species of bacteria produce other lifesaving antibiotics such as tetracycline and streptomycin. A key steroid ingredient in today's widely used contraceptive pills is derived from a compound found in a wild Mexican yam. A chemical that causes leaves to change color in the fall is being studied as a possible

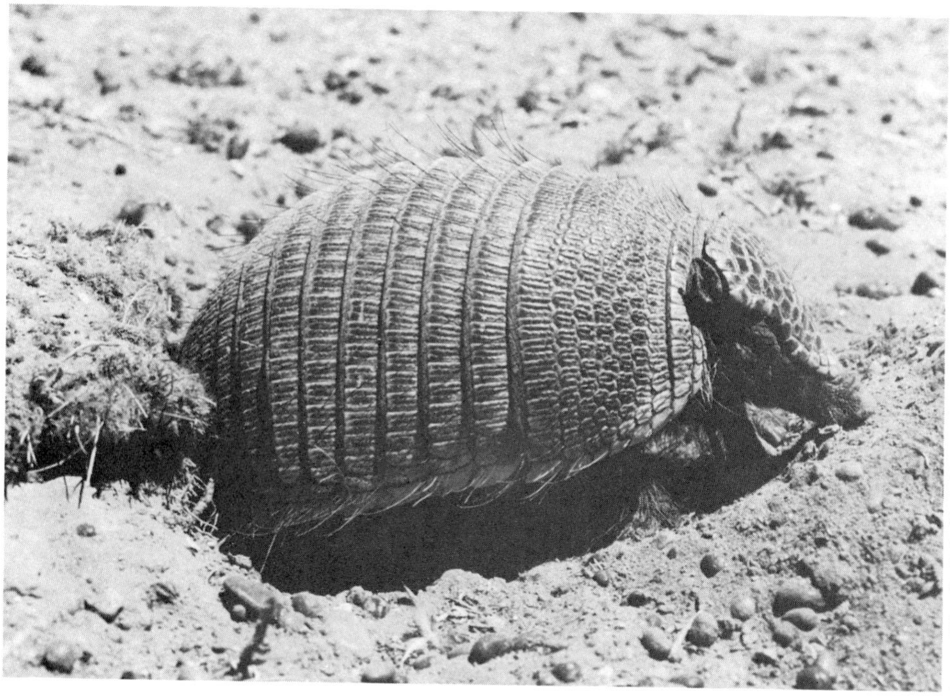

Figure 14-3 The nine-banded armadillo is used in research to find a cure for leprosy.

Jen and Des Bartlett, Photo Researchers, Inc.

cure for colon cancer. Chemicals extracted from seaweeds that grow along the northern California coast have been 99% effective in destroying the two types of herpes viruses that cause cold sores and sexually transmitted infections in laboratory animals; they may soon be tested in humans.

Many animal species are used to test drugs and vaccines and to increase our understanding of human health and disease. The nine-banded armadillo (Figure 14-3), for example, is being used to study leprosy and prepare a vaccine for this disease. The Florida manatee, an endangered mammal, is being used to help understand hemophilia. Many new drugs will come from presently unclassified plant and animal species, most located in tropical forests and the ocean. For example, an estimated 10% of the world's marine species contain anticancer chemicals.

Despite their present and future economic and health importance to humans, scientists know very little about most of the earth's 1.7 million identified species and nothing about the millions of undiscovered species. Less than 1% of the earth's identified plant species have been thoroughly studied to determine their possible usefulness. Loss of this biological and genetic diversity reduces our ability to respond to new problems and opportunities—like throwing away gifts without removing their wrappings.

Aesthetic and Recreational Importance   Many wild species are a source of beauty, wonder, joy, and recreational pleasure for large numbers of people. Observing leaves change color in autumn, smelling the aroma of wildflowers, watching an eagle soar overhead or a porpoise glide through the water are pleasurable experiences that cannot be measured in dollars.

The aesthetic and recreational importance of certain well-known species such as the bald eagle and the blue whale helps protect them from extinction. Unfortunately, people attach little aesthetic and recreational value to most lesser-known plant and animal species. Furthermore, such concerns often disappear when people are hungry and poor.

Ecological Importance   The millions of species inhabiting the earth depend on one another for a number of services. Because of this complex and little-understood web of interdependence, the most important contributions of wild species may be their roles in maintaining the health and integrity of the world's ecosystems (see Spotlight on p. 294). Ecosystem services of wild plant and animal species include provision of food from the soil and the sea, production and maintenance of oxygen and other gases in the atmosphere, filtration and detoxification of poisonous substances, moderation of the earth's climate, regulation of freshwater supplies, decomposition of wastes, recycling of nutrients essential to agriculture, production and maintenance of fertile soil, control of the majority of potential crop pests and disease carriers, maintenance of a vast storehouse of genetic material that is the source of all future adaptations to environmental change, and storage of solar energy as chemical energy in food, wood, and fossil fuels.

People tend to divide plants and animals into "good" and "bad" species and to assume that we have a duty to wipe out the villains. Consider the American alligator, which is hunted for its hide in its marsh and swamp habitat (Figure 14-4). Between 1950 and 1960, Louisiana lost 90% of its alligators; the alligator population in the Florida Everglades also was threatened.

Many people might say, "So what?" But they are overlooking the key role the alligator plays in subtropical wetland ecosystems such as the Everglades. Alligators dig deep depressions, or "gator holes," which collect fresh water during dry spells and provide a sanctuary for aquatic life as well as fresh water and food for birds and other animals. Large alligator nesting mounds also serve as nest sites for birds such as herons and egrets. As alligators move from gator holes to nesting mounds, they help keep waterways open. In addition, by eating large numbers of gar, a fish which preys on other fish, alligators help maintain populations of game fish such as bass and bream.

In 1968 the U.S. government placed the American alligator on the endangered species list. Protected from hunters, by 1975 the alligator population had made a comeback in many areas. Indeed, it had reestablished its population too successfully in some places. People began finding alligators in their backyards and swimming pools. Although the American alligator still remains on the endangered species list in some areas, it has been downgraded from endangered to threatened in Louisiana, Texas, and Florida and in some areas of Georgia and South Carolina. Limited hunting is now allowed in some areas to keep its population from growing too large.

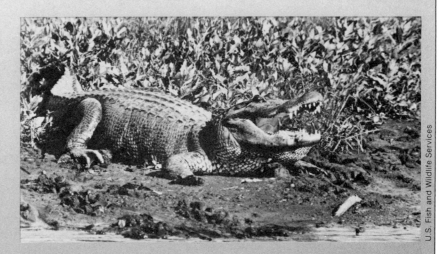

U.S. Fish and Wildlife Services

Figure 14-4 In 1968 the American alligator was classified as an endangered species in the United States. After being protected, its populations in various areas have increased to the point where it has been reclassified as a threatened species.

Because we know little about the workings of even the simplest ecosystems, we cannot be sure which species play crucial roles today, which ones have genes crucial for our survival and the survival of other species, and how many species can be removed before an ecosystem will collapse or suffer serious damage. Conservationist Aldo Leopold suggested that "the first rule of intelligent tinkering is to keep all the parts."

Ethical Importance So far this discussion of wild species has considered their actual or potential usefulness as resources for humans. This viewpoint is based on the common, human-centered, or *anthropocentric*, belief that humans are the most important species on the planet. But many people hold the *biocentric* belief that humans are no more important than any other species on earth. Thus, it is ethically and mor-

ally wrong for humans to hasten the extinction of any species. Many Native Americans, who occupied North America long before the arrival of white settlers, had such a belief, as summarized in the Hopi Indian philosophy of the Sacred Circle of Life:

In the Circle of Life every being is no more, or less, than any other. We are all Sisters and Brothers. Life is shared with the bird, deer, insects, plants, mountains, clouds, stars, sun. To be in harmony with the natural world, one must live within the cycles of life.

Some ethical theorists go further, arguing that each individual wild creature has an inherent right to survive without human interference, just as each human being has the inherent right to survive. In practice, most advocates of an ethical position argue that only a species—not each individual organism—has an

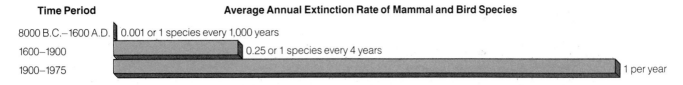

Time Period	Average Annual Extinction Rate of Mammal and Bird Species
8000 B.C.–1600 A.D.	0.001 or 1 species every 1,000 years
1600–1900	0.25 or 1 species every 4 years
1900–1975	1 per year

Figure 14-5 Estimated average annual extinction rate of mammal and bird species between 8000 B.C. and 1975 A.D. (Data from E. O. Wilson and Norman Myers)

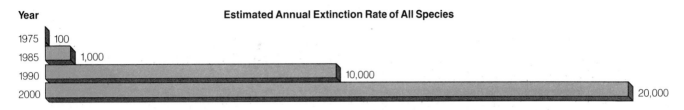

Year	Estimated Annual Extinction Rate of All Species
1975	100
1985	1,000
1990	10,000
2000	20,000

Figure 14-6 Estimated annual extinction rate of all species between 1975 and 2000. (Data from E. O. Wilson and Norman Myers)

inherent right to survive, regardless of whether it has any present or potential future use for humans.

One factor hindering ethical concern for preserving wild species, especially in MDCs, is that most people are urban dwellers, cut off from the natural world of plants and animals. Decades ago conservationist Aldo Leopold pointed out the important connection between direct experience with wild species and ethical concern about those species: "We can be ethical only in relation to something we can see, feel, understand, love, or otherwise have faith in." Thus, until we take time to *experience* wild nature and become emotionally—not just intellectually—involved in understanding its workings and marveling at its beauty, preservation of most wild species will not occur.

14-2 HOW SPECIES BECOME ENDANGERED AND EXTINCT

Extinction Before the Dawn of Agriculture The species found on earth today are the result of two biological processes taking place since life emerged on earth several billion years ago. One is the formation of new species from existing ones through natural selection in response to changes in environmental conditions (Section 6-2). The other is **extinction:** A species ceases to exist because its members cannot adapt and reproduce under new environmental conditions. At least 90% of the half a billion or so different species estimated to have lived on earth have either become extinct or have evolved into a form sufficiently different to be identified as a new species. Over the 3.6 billion years since life is believed to have begun, new

species have formed at a higher rate than the extinction rate; hence the present accumulation of at least 5 billion—perhaps 30 billion—different species.

Fossil remains and other evidence indicate that over the past 500 million years there have been five catastrophic extinctions of life, primarily of numerous species of animals. None of these mass animal extinctions have been adequately explained, but current hypotheses include long-term changes in climate, volcanic eruptions, and impacts from large asteroids. It is known, however, that none of the extinctions occurred abruptly—for example, the disappearance of dinosaurs about 65 million years ago was spread over 2 million years. Each major extinction was followed by the slow emergence of a diversity of new animal species over several million years. We also know that humans caused none of these catastrophes.

Extinction of Species Today Since agriculture began about 10,000 years ago, the rate of species extinction has increased at an alarming rate, especially since 1900 as human settlements have expanded worldwide. The rate is now accelerating rapidly. Rough estimates indicate that between 8000 B.C. and 1975 A.D., the average extinction rate of mammal and bird species increased about 1,000-fold (Figure 14-5).

If the extinction of species of plants and insects are included, the estimated extinction rate in 1975 was 100 species a year—*an average of 1 species every 3 days* (Figure 14-6). Biologist Edward O. Wilson estimated the extinction rate by 1985 had increased tenfold to 1,000 species per year—*an average of three species per day.* Wilson and several other biologists and conservation experts such as Norman Myers (see Guest Essay at the end of Chapter 13) warn that if deforestation (especially of tropical moist forests), desertification, and destruction of wetlands and coral reefs continue at their present rates, then at least 500,000 and perhaps 1 million species will become extinct as a result of human activities between 1975 and 2000. Using the lower estimate, this amounts to an average extinction rate by the year 2000 of 20,000 species per year or *one species every 30 minutes*—a 200-fold increase in the extinction rate in only 25 years. Most of these species will be plants and insects that have yet to be classified as species, much less evaluated for their use to humans and for their roles in ecosystems. Although animal extinctions receive the most publicity, plant extinctions are more important ecologically because most animal species depend directly or indirectly on plants for food. It is estimated that about 10% of the world's plant species are already threatened with extinction and 15% to 25% of all plant species face extinction by the year 2000.

Some analysts contend that the projected species extinction rate for the year 2000 is only a wild guess and that it may greatly overstate the situation. But even if the average extinction rate is only 1,000 per year by the end of this century, the total loss will still rival the great mass extinctions of the past. However, there are important differences between the present mass extinction and those in the past. First, the present mass extinction is being caused by humans. Second, it is taking place in only a few decades rather than over several million years. Third, plant species are disappearing as rapidly as animal species, thus threatening many animal species that otherwise would not become extinct.

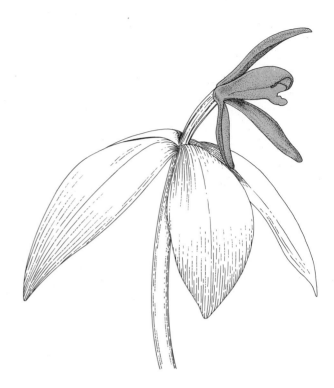

Figure 14-7 The endangered small whorled pegonia. By 1985 only about 3,200 plants of this orchid species existed in 13 states from Maine to northern Georgia.

Threatened and Endangered Species An **endangered species** is one having so few individual survivors that the species could soon become extinct in all or most of its natural range. Examples in the United States are the whooping crane, the California condor, and an orchid called the small whorled pegonia (Figure 14-7). **Threatened species,** such as the grizzly bear and the bald eagle in the United States, are still abundant in their range but are declining in numbers and likely to become endangered in the foreseeable future.

Habitat Disturbance and Loss The greatest threat to wild plant and animal species is destruction or alteration of habitat: the area in which species seek food, find shelter, and breed. As the human population grows, urban settlements, draining and filling of wetlands, clearing forests, and production of food, minerals, energy, and other resources destroy or disrupt

habitats for many wild species. Disturbance and loss of habitat has been a major factor in the extinction of some of America's most magnificent bird species such as the ivory-billed woodpecker and the near extinction of the whooping crane and the critically endangered California condor (Figures 14-8 and 14-9).

Many rare and threatened species exist in unique and vulnerable habitats, such as single trees in tropical forests or small islands. For example, 99% of the known animal species and 95% of flowering plants on the isolated chain of islands that make up Hawaii are found no place else. The loss of species in Hawaii as a result of deforestation and urbanization has been staggering—accounting for half of the 300 extinctions of plants and animals in the United States since 1850 and almost half of the birds classified as endangered in 1986.

Commercial Hunting There are three major types of hunting: **commercial hunting,** in which animals are killed for profit from sale of their furs or other parts; **subsistence hunting,** the killing of animals to provide enough food for survival; and **sport hunting,** the killing of animals for recreation. Although subsistence hunting was once a major cause of extinction of some

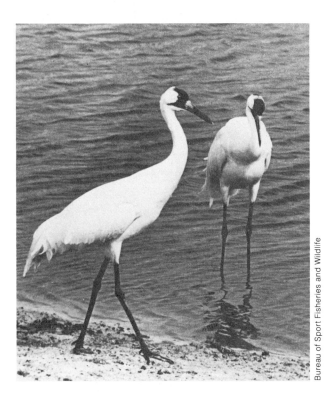

Figure 14-8 The whooping crane is an endangered species in the United States. Since being protected, its population in the wild increased from about 29 to 138 individuals by 1986.

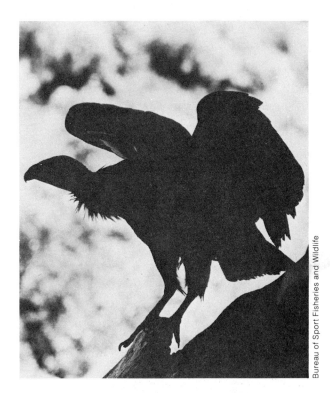

Figure 14-9 The critically endangered California condor is no longer found in the wild.

species, it has now declined sharply in most areas. Sport hunting is now closely regulated in most countries; game species are endangered only when protective regulations don't exist or are not enforced.

On a worldwide basis, commercial hunting threatens a number of large animal species. The jaguar, tiger, snow leopard, and cheetah are hunted for their furs. Alligators are hunted commercially for their skins, elephants for their ivory tusks (accounting for the slaughter of about 90,000 elephants a year), and rhinoceros for their horns.

The black market value of rhinoceros horn—a mass of compact hair—is $20 a gram ($600 an ounce). An entire horn cut from a dead rhino may weigh 1.2 kilograms (40 ounces) and be worth $24,000. It is used to make handles for ornamental knives in North Yemen and ground into a powder and used for medicinal purposes, especially reducing fever, in parts of Asia. It is also thought by many Asians to be an aphrodisiac, or sexual stimulant, even though it consists of a substance (keratin) which can be obtained by eating hair trimmings and fingernails. Although 60 countries have agreed not to import or export rhino horn, illegal traffic goes on because of its high market value.

Between 1970 and 1986 the number of black rhinos

in Africa dropped from 65,000 to about 5,000, and only about 100 white rhinos were left by 1986 (Figure 14-10). In Asia there were only an estimated 1,700 Indian, 750 Sumatran, and 50 Javan rhinos remaining by 1986. If poaching continues at present rates, all species of rhino will be extinct within a decade.

Commercial hunting in the United States was an important factor in the extermination of the American passenger pigeon and the near extermination of the snowy egret and the American bison. In the late 1800s the snowy egret (Figure 14-11), which inhabits coastal regions of the southeastern United States, was hunted almost to extinction because its white plume feathers were used to adorn women's hats. In 1886 the newly formed Audubon Society began a campaign against this slaughter. Texas and Florida passed laws protecting plumed birds, but the laws were mostly ignored. Then in 1900 Congress passed the Lacey Act, which banned interstate traffic in illegally killed wildlife. This cut off the supply and these beautiful birds began thriving again in parks, preserves, and refuge areas established for the protection of wildlife.

Before white settlers came to North America, an estimated 60 million to 125 million American bison, commonly called buffalo, roamed the plains, prairies,

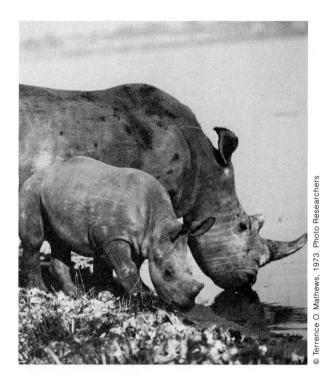

Figure 14-10 Only about 100 critically endangered African white rhinos remain.

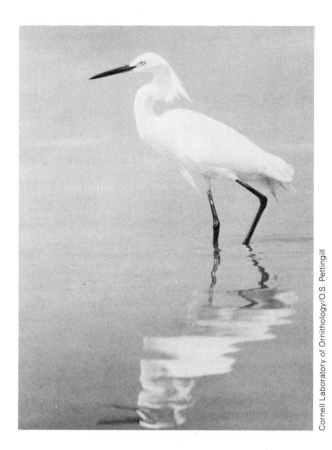

Figure 14-11 The snowy egret was hunted to near extinction in the late 1800s because its feathers were used to adorn women's hats. After being protected, today it is no longer endangered or threatened.

and woodlands of much of the continent (Figure 14-12). Between 1850 and 1906, however, the once massive range of the American bison was reduced to a tiny area, and the species was nearly driven to extinction.

As railroads spread westward in the late 1860s, they hired professional bison hunters to provide the construction crews with meat. As farmers settled the plains, they shot bison because they destroyed crops. Ranchers killed them because they competed with cattle for grass and knocked over fences. An army of commercial hunters also shot them for their hides and for their tongues, which were considered a delicacy. After the Civil War the U.S. Army killed millions of bison to subdue the Plains Indians and take over their lands by killing off this major source of their food.

By 1889 only 85 American bison were left. In the early 1900s the remaining bison were protected by law on public and private lands scattered throughout the West. Today their numbers have increased to about 65,000. Some are now crossbred with cattle to produce hybrids called beefalo, which grow faster and are easier to raise than cattle and require no grain feed.

Predator and Pest Control Extinction or near extinction can also occur because of attempts to exterminate pest and predator species that compete with

humans and livestock for food and with humans for game species. The Carolina parakeet was exterminated in the United States around 1914 because it fed on fruit crops. Its disappearance was hastened because when one member of a flock was shot, the rest of the birds hovered over its body, making themselves easy targets.

Carnivore predators that sometimes kill livestock and game are shot, trapped, or poisoned. Ranchers, hunters, and government employees involved in predator control programs have sharply reduced populations of large predators such as the timber wolf, the mountain lion, and the grizzly bear over most of the continental United States. Campaigns to protect rangeland for grazing livestock by poisoning prairie dogs and pocket gophers have eliminated these rodents' natural predator, the black-footed ferret (Figure 14-13), from the wild.

Pets, Medical Research, and Zoos Worldwide, more than 6 million live wild birds are sold each year, most of them ending up as pets in countries such as the

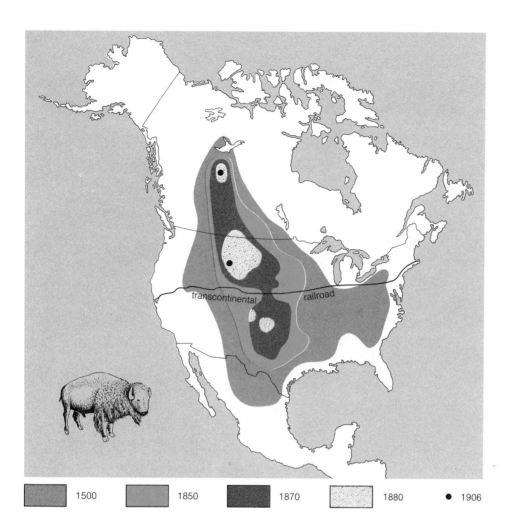

Figure 14-12 Severe shrinkage in the range of the American bison between 1500 and 1906.

transcontinental railroad

| 1500 | 1850 | 1870 | 1880 | ● 1906 |

United States, Great Britain, and West Germany. Large numbers of these animals die during shipment, and after purchase many others are killed or abandoned by their owners. As a direct result of this trade, at least nine bird species are now listed as threatened or endangered but continue to be smuggled illegally into the United States and Europe. For example, bird collectors may pay as much as $10,000 for a threatened hyacinth macaw illegally smuggled out of Brazil.

Some species of exotic plants, especially orchids and cacti, are also endangered because they are gathered, often illegally, and sold to collectors and used to decorate houses, offices, and landscapes. A single rare orchid may be sold for $5,000 to a collector. Nearly one-third of the cactus species native to the United States, especially in Texas and Arizona, are thought to be endangered because they are collected and sold for use as potted plants.

About 71 million animals—mice, rats, dogs, cats, primates, birds, frogs, guinea pigs, rabbits, and hamsters—are used each year in the United States for toxicity testing, biomedical and behavioral research, and drug development. Although most test animal spe-

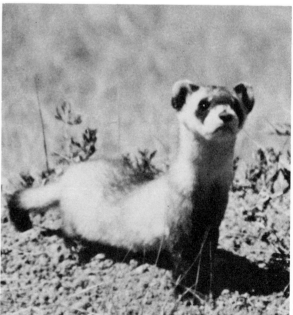

Figure 14-13 The highly endangered black-footed ferret no longer is found in the wild in the United States.

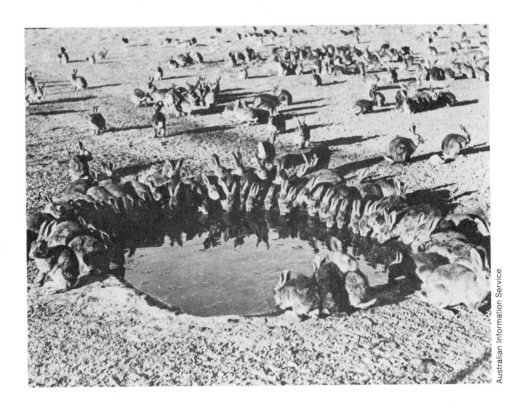

Figure 14-14 European wild rabbits around a waterhole in Australia.

cies are not endangered, medical research coupled with habitat loss is a serious threat to endangered wild primates such as the chimpanzee and the orangutan.

Under pressure from animal rights groups, scientists are trying to find alternative testing methods that do not subject animals to suffering or—better yet—do not use animals at all. Promising alternatives include the use of cell and tissue cultures, simulated tissues and body fluids, bacteria, and computer-generated mathematical models that enable scientists to estimate the toxicity of new compounds from knowledge of chemical structure and properties.

Public zoos, botanical gardens, and aquariums are under constant pressure to exhibit rare and unusual animals such as the orangutan. For each exotic animal or plant that reaches a zoo or botanical garden alive, many others die during capture or shipment. Since 1967, reputable zoos and aquariums have agreed not to purchase endangered species, although there are still some abuses.

Pollution Chemical pollution is a relatively new but growing threat to wildlife. Industrial wastes, mine acids, and excess heat from electric power plants have wiped out some species of fish, such as the humpbacked chub, in local areas. The Canadian aurora trout now appears to be extinct as a result of pollution of its freshwater habitat from acid deposition. Slowly biodegradable pesticides, especially DDT and dieldrin, have been magnified in food chains and have caused reproduc-

tive failure and eggshell thinning of important birds of prey, such as the peregrine falcon, eastern and California brown pelicans, osprey, and bald eagle. Banning persistent pesticides in North America and Europe has allowed most species to recover. Yet those chemicals are still exported in large quantities by U.S. companies for use in LDCs.

Introduction of Alien Species When an alien species is introduced into a new geographical area, it may be able to establish itself without seriously affecting the population size of native species. In other cases, however, an alien species can cause a population decrease or even extinction of one or more existing species by preying on them, outcompeting with them for food, or destroying their habitat. It can also cause a population explosion of existing species by killing off their natural predators. Island species are particularly vulnerable because many have evolved in ecosystems with few if any natural herbivore or carnivore predators.

In 1859 a farmer in southern Australia imported a dozen pairs of wild European rabbits as a game animal. Within six years these 24 rabbits had mushroomed to 22 million and by 1907 had reached every corner of the country. By the 1930s their population had reached an estimated 750 million. They competed with sheep for grass and cut the sheep population in half. They also devoured food crops, gnawed young trees, fouled waterholes (Figure 14-14), and acceler-

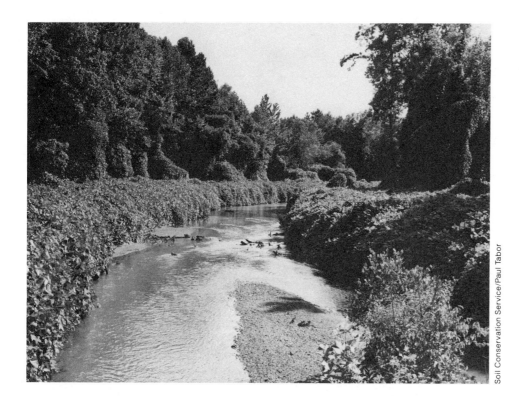

Figure 14-15 Kudzu covering stream banks and a patch of forest in Georgia. So far no one has devised a way to stop the spread of this prolific and hardy, alien plant throughout the southeastern United States.

Soil Conservation Service/Paul Tabor

ated soil erosion in many places. In the early 1950s about 90% of the rabbit population was killed by the human introduction of a virus disease. There is concern, however, that members of the remaining population may eventually develop immunity to this viral disease through natural selection and again become the scourge of Australian farmers and ranchers.

The kudzu vine was deliberately imported into the southeastern United States from Africa to help control soil erosion. It does control erosion, but its growth is so prolific that it has also covered hills, trees, houses, roads, stream banks (Figure 14-15), and even entire patches of forest. People have dug it up, cut it up, burned it, and tried to kill it with herbicides, all without success. Table 14-1 lists examples of other accidental and deliberate introductions of alien species into the United States.

Not all introductions of alien species have had harmful effects. Prized game species such as the ring-necked pheasant and the German brown trout have been deliberately introduced into the United States with great success. However, between 1950 and 1980, populations of the ring-necked pheasant fell by 96% in Ohio, 85% in North Dakota, 70% in Colorado, and more than 60% in five others states primarily as a result of loss of habitat.

Characteristics of Extinction-Prone Species Some species have certain natural characteristics that make them more susceptible to extinction by human activ-

ities and natural disasters than other species (Table 14-2). Each species has a critical population density and size, below which survival may be impossible because males and females have a hard time finding one another. Once this point is reached, population size continues to decline even if the species is protected because its death rate exceeds its birth rate. The remaining small population is also highly vulnerable to extinction from fires, floods, and other catastrophic events. Some species such as bats are susceptible for a combination of reasons (see Spotlight on p. 304).

14-3 PROTECTING WILD SPECIES FROM EXTINCTION

The Species Approach: Treaties and Laws Organizations such as the International Union for the Conservation of Nature and Natural Resources (IUCN), the International Council for Bird Preservation (ICBP), and the World Wildlife Fund (WWF) have identified threatened and endangered species and led efforts to protect them. The IUCN, for example, regularly compiles lists of threatened and endangered species and publishes them in *The Red Data Book*.

Several international treaties and conventions now protect wild species, but most involve only two or a small number of countries. One of the most far-reaching treaties is the 1975 Convention on International

Table 14-1 Damage Caused by Plants and Animals Imported into the United States

Name	Origin	Mode of Transport	Type of Damage
Mammals			
European wild boar	Russia	Intentionally imported (1912), escaped captivity	Destruction of habitat by rooting; crop damage
Nutria (cat-sized rodent)	Argentina	Intentionally imported, escaped captivity (1940)	Alteration of marsh ecology; damage to levees and earth dams; crop destruction
Birds			
European starling	Europe	Intentionally released (1890)	Competition with native songbirds; crop damage, transmission of swine diseases; airport interference
House sparrow	England	Intentionally released by Brooklyn Institute (1853)	Crop damage; displacement of native songbirds
Fish			
Carp	Germany	Intentionally released (1877)	Displacement of native fish; uprooting of water plants with loss of waterfowl populations
Sea lamprey	North Atlantic Ocean	Entered via Welland Canal (1829)	Destruction of lake trout, lake whitefish, and sturgeon in Great Lakes
Walking catfish	Thailand	Imported into Florida	Destruction of bass, bluegill, and other fish
Insects			
Argentine fire ant	Argentina	Probably entered via coffee shipments from Brazil (1918)	Crop damage; destruction of native ant species
Camphor scale insect	Japan	Accidentally imported on nursery stock (1920s)	Damage to nearly 200 species of plants in Louisiana, Texas, and Alabama
Japanese beetle	Japan	Accidentally imported on irises or azaleas (1911)	Defoliation of more than 250 species of trees and other plants, including many of commercial importance
Plants			
Water hyacinth	Central America	Intentionally introduced (1884)	Clogging waterways; shading out other aquatic vegetation
Chestnut blight (a fungus)	Asia	Accidentally imported on nursery plants (1900)	Destruction of nearly all eastern American chestnut trees; disturbance of forest ecology
Dutch elm disease, *Cerastomella ulmi* (a fungus, the disease agent)	Europe	Accidentally imported on infected elm timber used for veneers (1930)	Destruction of millions of elms; disturbance of forest ecology

From *Biological Conservation* by David W. Ehrenfeld. Copyright © 1970 by Holt, Rinehart and Winston, Inc. Modified and reprinted by permission.

Trade in Endangered Species, developed after ten years of work by the IUCN and administered by the UN Environment Program (UNEP). This treaty, now signed by 87 countries, bans hunting or capturing of 700 endangered and threatened species. Although enforcement varies, the treaty has reduced illegal trade of such species. However, Singapore, a major international center for distributing wildlife and wildlife products, and several other countries involved in wildlife trade have not signed this agreement. Even when illegal-wildlife smugglers are caught, the penalties are usually too low to hurt overall profits. In 1979 a Hong Kong fur dealer apprehended for illegally importing 319 Ethiopian cheetah skins valued at $160,000 was fined only $1,540.

Although a number of countries officially offer protection to endangered or threatened species, the most strictly enforced protection is provided by the United States, the Soviet Union, and Canada. Since 1903 several pieces of legislation have been passed in the United States to protect endangered species. One of these, the Endangered Species Act of 1973 (including amendments in 1982 and 1987), is one of the toughest environmental laws enacted by any country. It authorizes the National Marine Fisheries Service of the Department of Commerce to identify and list

Table 14-2 Characteristics of Extinction-Prone Species

Characteristic	Examples
Low reproductive rate	Blue whale, polar bear, California condor, Andean condor, passenger pigeon, giant panda, whooping crane
Specialized feeding habits	Everglades kite (apple snail of southern Florida), blue whale (krill in polar upwelling areas), black-footed ferret (prairie dogs and pocket gophers), giant panda (bamboo)
Feed at high trophic levels	Bengal tiger, bald eagle, Andean condor, timber wolf
Large size	Bengal tiger, African lion, elephant, Javan rhinoceros, blue whale, American bison, giant panda, grizzly bear
Limited or specialized nesting or breeding areas	Kirtland's warbler (nests only in 6- to 15-year-old jack pine trees), whooping crane (depends on marshes for food and nesting), orangutan (now found only on islands of Sumatra and Borneo), green sea turtle (lays eggs on only a few beaches), bald eagle (preferred habitat of forested shorelines), nightingale wren (nests and breeds only on Barro Colorado Island, Panama)
Found in only one place or region	Woodland caribou, elephant seal, Cooke's kokio, and many unique island species
Fixed migratory patterns	Blue whale, Kirtland's warbler, Bachman's warbler, whooping crane
Preys on livestock or humans	Timber wolf, some crocodiles
Certain behavioral patterns	Passenger pigeon and white-crowned pigeon (nests in large colonies), redheaded woodpecker (flies in front of cars), Carolina parakeet (when one bird is shot, rest of flock hovers over body), Key deer (forages for cigarette butts along highways—it's a "nicotine addict")

endangered and threatened marine species, and the Fish and Wildlife Service to identify all other plant and animal species endangered or threatened in the United States and abroad. Any decision by either agency to add or remove a species from the list must be based solely on biological grounds without economic considerations. By 1987, the federal list of endangered and threatened animals and plants protected under this act contained 928 species, including 385 found in the United States.

The Endangered Species Act also authorizes the departments of Commerce and Interior to design and conduct programs for the recovery of endangered and threatened species, to assist states and other countries in conserving such species, and to determine, protect, and, when necessary, purchase critical habitats in the United States to enhance the survival of such species. The act prohibits interstate and international commercial trade of endangered or threatened plant or animal species (with certain exceptions) or products made from such species, and it prohibits the killing, hunting, collecting, or injuring of any protected animal species. It also directs federal agencies not to carry out, fund, or authorize projects that would jeopardize endangered or threatened species or destroy or mod-

ify their habitats. This last provision has been highly controversial (see Spotlight on p. 305).

Conservationists complain that the Endangered Species Act is not being carried out as intended by Congress primarily because of budget cuts and lack of staff. At current rates it will take the Fish and Wildlife Service 29 years to evaluate the 4,000 other species on the waiting list for possible protection. A dozen or so species have already disappeared while awaiting classification and many others are expected to become extinct before they can be protected. Conservationists also note that relatively few plants have been given protection, despite their ecological importance as the base of food webs, because much less is known about plants than animals (thus lengthening the review process for plants).

Listing a species is only the first step. Once a species is listed, the FWS is supposed to prepare a plan to enhance its recovery. Of the 385 listed U.S. species, only 58% had approved recovery plans by 1986 and only about half of these plans were being actively implemented. Less than 25 endangered species with recovery plans were making progress toward recovery, and 35, including the California condor and the black-footed ferret, were very close to extinction. Since

One or more of the world's nearly 1,000 different species of bat are found everywhere except in the most extreme polar and desert regions and a few isolated islands. Despite their variety and distribution, bats are especially susceptible to extinction because of several factors. They reproduce very slowly compared to other mammals and nest in huge colonies in highly accessible places such as caves, where humans can easily destroy them by blocking the entrances. They are highly specialized feeders; some bats feed only on certain types of nectar, others on certain types of fruit, and others on various night-flying insects.

In addition, they are killed in large numbers by humans because of misinformed fears based on "vampire" movies and folklore and the equally misinformed belief that they are dangerous creatures that attack and infect humans and livestock with rabies and other diseases and destroy fruit crops. Some countries have begun massive bat eradication programs, and

others are considering such programs. A number of species have been driven to extinction and others are threatened in Australia, Southeast Asia, and the South Pacific.

The vast majority of bat species, however, are not only harmless to humans, livestock, and crops but also of great ecological and economic importance to humans. Actually, less than half of one percent of bats contract rabies and these individuals rarely become aggressive and transmit rabies to wildlife or humans. The few people who are bitten by a bat are those who foolishly pick up a sick bat, which bites in self-defense, as almost any sick wild animal would. In all of Asia, Europe, Australia, and the Pacific Islands, only two people have been suspected of dying from bat-transmitted rabies and no humans in these areas are known to have died of any other bat-transmitted disease.

Seed dispersal and pollination of tropical trees and shrubs by bats

are crucial for the survival of tropical rain forests. In Thailand, for example, a cave-dwelling, nectar-eating bat species is the only known pollinator of durian trees, whose fruit crops are worth roughly $90 million per year. Many people are unaware that bananas, guavas, mangoes, avocados, dates, figs, and many other economically important tropical fruits are heavily dependent on nectar-eating and fruit-eating bats for pollination and seeding. Studies have shown that fruit-eating bats consume only fruit that is already too ripe to harvest (and worthless to farmers).

Insectivorous bats are the major predators of night-flying insects and help control such insect populations, including many that damage human crops. In parts of Asia families earn a living by periodically scraping bat droppings, or guano, from bat caves and selling it for fertilizer. Hopefully, we will come to see bats as allies—not enemies—before we destroy them and lose their benefits.

1973, when the Endangered Species Act was enacted, only three species—all birds native to small islands in the Pacific Ocean—have recovered enough to be removed from the lists of endangered and threatened species.

The Species Approach: Wildlife Refuges In 1903 President Theodore Roosevelt established the first federal wildlife refuge at Pelican Island on the east coast of Florida to protect the endangered brown pelican (Figure 14-16). By 1986 the National Wildlife Refuge System contained 434 refuges, with one or more in every state except West Virginia. About 88% of the area encompassed by this system is in Alaska. Although more than three-fourths of the refuges are wetlands for protection of migratory waterfowl, many other species are also protected in such refuges. Most of the

species on the U.S. endangered list have habitats in the refuge system. In addition, some refuges have been set aside for specific endangered species and have helped species such as the key deer and the brown pelican of southern Florida and the trumpeter swan to recover.

Unlike other public land systems, Congress has not established guidelines (such as multiple use or sustained yield) for management of the National Wildlife Refuge System. As a result, the FWS has allowed a number of refuges to be used for a variety of purposes, including hunting (250 of the 434 refuges in 1985), trapping, timber cutting, grazing, farming, oil and gas development, mining, and recreational activities. Since 1980 the Reagan administration has encouraged expansion of such commercial activities to offset the costs of operating refuges.

The Snail Darter Controversy

In 1975 conservationists filed suit against the Tennessee Valley Authority to stop construction of the $137 million Tellico Dam on the Little Tennessee River in Tennessee because the area to be flooded by the resulting reservoir threatened the only known breeding habitat of an endangered fish species, the snail darter—a three-inch-long minnow. Although the dam was 90% completed, construction was halted by the court action for several years.

In 1978 Congress amended the Endangered Species Act to permit a seven-member review committee to grant an exemption if it believed that the economic benefits of a project would outweigh the potential harmful ecological effects. At their first meeting, the review committee denied the request to exempt the Tellico Dam project on the grounds that it was an economically unsound, "pork barrel" project. Despite this decision, powerful influence by members of Congress from Tennessee and others afraid of losing present and future projects in their states prevailed, and in 1979 Congress passed special legislation exempting the Tellico Dam from the Endangered Species Act. The dam's reservoir is now full of water. The snail darters that once dwelled there were transplanted to nearby rivers.

In 1981 snail darter populations were found in several remote tributaries of the Little Tennessee River, and in 1983 their status was downgraded by the FWS from endangered to threatened. The important question raised by this incident is to what degree, if any, economic considerations should influence the protection of endangered and threatened species. What do you think?

Conservationists charge that some of these commercial uses are getting out of hand, are not always controlled properly, and can interfere with wildlife protection. They are especially opposed to oil and gas development on refuges and to the 1984 directive by the head of the FWS to open as many refuges as possible to hunting.

A major problem is that the government lacked the money or foresight to acquire rights to any gas, oil, coal, or other minerals that may exist under 80% of the country's refuges. Some companies owning mineral rights under refuge lands claim they have the legal right to do as they please in extracting these resources.

Pollution is also a problem in a number of refuges. A 1986 study by the FWS revealed that perhaps one in five refuges is contaminated with toxic chemicals. Most of this pollution comes from old military and private toxic dump sites and from runoff from nearby agricultural land. A 1983 survey by the FWS showed that 86% of the federal refuges were experiencing water quality problems and 67% were facing air quality and visibility problems.

Several other countries have also established areas to protect individual species from extinction. Examples include the tiny Addo Elephant National Park in South Africa, ten reserves in China for the giant panda, and more than a dozen reserves in India, which have enabled its endangered tiger population to rise from 1,800 in 1972 to around 4,000 today.

The Species Approach: Gene Banks, Zoos, Botanical Gardens, and Aquariums Plant gene banks (collections of varieties of plants) of most known and many potential varieties of agricultural crops and other plants now exist throughout the world, and scientists have urged that many more be established. Despite their importance, gene banks have significant disadvantages and need to be supplemented by preservation of a variety of representative ecosystems throughout the world. Storage is not possible for many species such as potatoes, fruit trees, orchids, and many tropical plant species. Many seeds rot and must periodically be replaced. Accidents such as power failures, fires, and unintentional disposal of seeds can cause irrecoverable losses. Furthermore, stored species do not continue to evolve and thus become less fit for being reintroduced into their native habitats, which may have undergone various environmental changes in the interim.

Zoos, botanical gardens, and aquariums are increasingly being used as a last ditch effort to preserve a representative number of individuals of critically endangered species that would otherwise become extinct. When it is judged that an animal species will not survive on its own, eggs may be collected and hatched in captivity (known as egg pulling), or captive breeding programs may be established in zoos or private research centers. Other techniques include artificial insemination of species that don't breed well in captivity and using adults of one related species to serve as foster parents to hatch collected eggs and raise offspring of another species.

In some but not all cases, captive breeding and egg-pulling programs allow a population to increase sufficiently that the species can be successfully reintroduced into the wild. For example, captive breeding programs at zoos in Phoenix, San Diego, and Los Angeles have been used to save the nearly extinct Arabian oryx antelope (Figure 14-17), which is now being returned in small numbers to the wild.

Primarily because of hunting and loss of habitat, the number of whooping cranes in the wild had declined to only 15 in 1941, bringing the species to the brink of extinction. By 1967, however, protection of its habitat had raised the number to about 44. Between 1967 and 1986 the FWS increased the number to about 138 by a combination of habitat preservation, capturing wild birds and using artificial insemination to breed them in captivity, and removing eggs from nests in the wild and hatching them in captivity. The newly hatched chicks are raised by closely related but much more abundant wild sandhill cranes. Wildlife scientists hope to be able to increase the number of whooping cranes to the point where the species can be moved from the endangered to the threatened category by 2000 and removed entirely from the list by 2020.

Captive breeding can help save some critically endangered species, but it has several disadvantages. It is expensive, and zoos and botanical gardens have room for relatively few of the critically endangered species and the large number of individuals (a minimum of 100 and ideally 250 to 500 for an animal species) needed for each species to avoid extinction through accident, disease, or loss of genetic variability through inbreeding. Presently, for example, the world's zoos contain only 20 endangered species with populations of 100 or more individual animals. Thus, just as physicians must make difficult decisions about which individuals receive transplants of scarce organs from donors, wildlife experts must decide which species should be saved.

The Ecosystem Approach   Most wildlife biologists argue that the major threat to most wildlife species today—namely, the destruction of habitat—cannot be halted by concentrating on preserving individual species. Instead, they believe that the most effective way to prevent the loss of wild species is to establish and maintain a worldwide system of reserves, parks, and other protected areas that would represent at least 10% of the world's land area. These areas would be selected to represent at least five examples of each of the world's 193 major ecosystem types or biogeographical realms. Ideally each reserve would be large enough to sustain viable populations of most of its existing species.

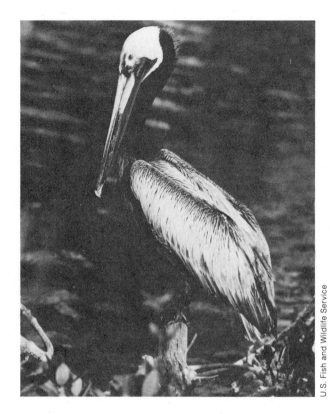

Figure 14-16   The first federal wildlife refuge was established at Pelican Island in Florida in 1903 to protect the brown pelican from extinction. Although its numbers have increased, it is still an endangered species.

Such a global network of ecological reserves would help protect the earth's existing biological and genetic diversity, help prevent species from becoming endangered by human activities, reduce the need for human intervention to prevent extinction, provide sufficient natural habitats for reintroducing endangered species now in zoos and other artificial habitats, provide scientists with opportunities for research, and cost less to run than management of endangered and threatened species one by one. Protecting at least 10% of the earth's land area from development would also help maintain the environmental services needed to sustain the remaining 90%.

By 1985, there were more than 3,500 major protected areas throughout the world, totaling 4.3 million square kilometers (1.6 million square miles). Although this is an important beginning, it represents less than 3% of the earth's land area, and many of the world's different ecosystem types have not been included or consist of too little protected area. Furthermore, many of the protected areas are too small to protect their populations of wild species.

In 1980 the IUCN, the UNEP, and the WWF published a long-range plan for conserving the world's biological resources. The three major goals of this World

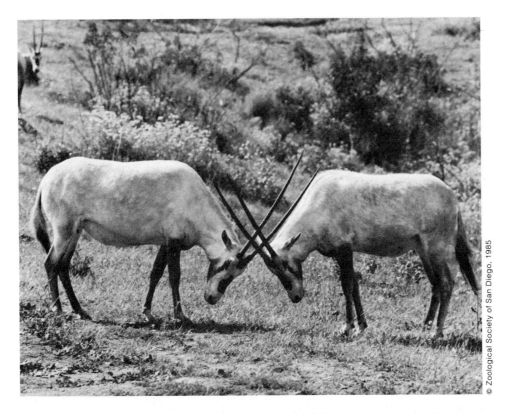

Figure 14-17 The Arabian oryx barely escaped extinction in 1969 after being overhunted in the deserts of the Middle East. Captive breeding programs in zoos in Arizona and California have saved this antelope species from extinction.

Conservation Strategy are to **(1)** maintain essential ecological processes and life-support systems on which human survival and economic activities depend, **(2)** preserve genetic diversity, and **(3)** ensure that any use of species and ecosystems is sustainable.

By 1985 some 40 countries had started or completed national conservation strategies, including Australia, Belize, Italy, Malaysia, Nepal, Norway, Senegal, and the United Kingdom. If this program is supported adequately by the MDCs, it offers a glimmer of hope for preserving the world's biological and genetic diversity and thus enhancing the long-range sustainability of the resource base on which human survival and economic activities depend.

14-4 WILDLIFE MANAGEMENT

Management Approaches The science and art of **wildlife management** involves manipulating populations of wild species and their habitats for human benefit, the welfare of other species, and the preservation of endangered and threatened species. The first step in the process of wildlife management is to decide which species or groups of species are to be managed in a particular area.

A wildlife manager can use one of three basic approaches to meeting these often conflicting goals: **(1)** protect relatively undisturbed areas from human activity, **(2)** manipulate the population size and habitat to maintain a diversity of species in an area, or **(3)** manipulate population size and habitat of an area to favor a single species, usually either a game species or an endangered species.

Once management goals have been decided upon, the wildlife manager must develop a management plan. Ideally, such a plan should be based on an understanding of the population dynamics and the cover, food, water, space, and other habitat requirements of each species to be managed. Often, however, such information is not available or reliable and is usually quite difficult, expensive, and time-consuming to obtain.

This helps explain why wildlife management is as much an art as a science. In practice, it involves considerable guesswork, trial and error, and adaptation of plans to political pressures from conflicting groups, unexpected short- and long-term consequences of interfering in nature's processes, and lack of sufficient

Spotlight Sport Hunting Controversy

Sport hunters, hunting groups, and state game officials contend that Americans should be free to hunt as long as they obey state and local game regulations and don't damage wildlife resources. Wildlife managers point out that since humans have eliminated most natural predators of deer and a number of other large game animals, carefully regulated sport hunting can keep the populations of game species within the carrying capacity of the available habitat and prevent excessive destruction of vegetation and loss of other species.

Conservation groups like the Sierra Club and Defenders of Wildlife also consider hunting an acceptable management tool to keep num-

bers in line with habitat capacity. Defenders of sport hunting point out that fees from hunting licenses and taxes on sport firearms and ammunition have provided more than $1.5 billion since 1937 for the acquisition, restoration, and maintenance of wildlife habitat areas and for wildlife research (see Guest Essay at the end of this chapter).

On the other hand, some individuals and conservation groups such as the Humane Society oppose sport hunting on the grounds that it inflicts needless cruelty on animals. The Humane Society has filed suit to block all hunting in national wildlife refuges on the grounds that state game commissions often set hunting limits to cater to hunters'

demands, not to keep wildlife in balance. The Humane Society also points out that sport hunting tends to reduce the genetic quality of remaining wildlife populations because hunters usually go after the strongest and healthiest individuals. In contrast, natural predators tend to improve population quality by eliminating weak and sick individuals. Antihunting groups contend that populations of wild animal species, including deer, are eventually controlled by lack of food and other natural factors. These groups recommend that in areas where vegetation is being destroyed wildlife officials should reintroduce natural predators, not hunters. What do you think?

funds. The two major approaches used to manage desired species are population regulation and manipulation of habitat vegetation.

Population Regulation by Controlled Hunting
Wildlife managers usually use population management to manipulate the numbers, genders, and age distributions of populations of wild game species. Game animals that reproduce rapidly, such as deer, rabbits, squirrels, quail, and ducks, sometimes exceed the carrying capacity of their habitat. For example, a deer population can more than double every two years. As the number of deer exceeds the carrying capacity of their range, vegetation is destroyed, habitat deteriorates, and many animals die of starvation.

In the United States, populations of game animals are managed by laws that (1) specify certain times of the year for the hunting of a particular species with various types of equipment such as bows and arrows, muzzle-loading guns, shotguns, or rifles, (2) restrict the length of hunting seasons, (3) regulate the num-

ber of hunters permitted in an area, and (4) limit the size, number, and sex of animals allowed to be killed. Some individuals and conservation groups, however, are opposed to sport hunting (see Spotlight above).

Wildlife managers also attempt to control or eliminate wild species considered pests by farmers, ranchers, loggers, hunters, hikers, and other groups. Methods for controlling animal pests include (1) killing by hunting, trapping, and poisoning, (2) using fences or other devices to prevent them from reaching certain areas, (3) moving them to another location, and (4) using chemicals to control their fertility and thus reduce their population size.

Manipulation of Habitat Vegetation and Water Supplies
Wildlife managers can encourage growth of plant species that are the preferred food and cover for an animal species whose population is to be managed. They do this primarily by controlling the stage of ecological succession (Section 6-3) of vegetation in various areas.

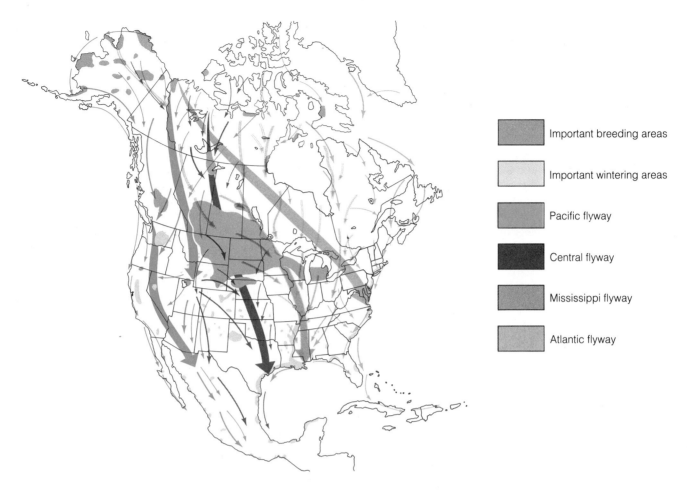

Figure 14-18 Major breeding and wintering areas and fall migration flyway routes used by migratory waterfowl in North America.

Legend:
- Important breeding areas
- Important wintering areas
- Pacific flyway
- Central flyway
- Mississippi flyway
- Atlantic flyway

Grizzly bear, wolf, caribou, and bighorn sheep are examples of **wilderness species**, which flourish only in relatively undisturbed, climax vegetational communities, such as large areas of mature forest, tundra, grassland, and desert. Their survival depends to a large degree on the establishment of large state and national wilderness areas and wildlife refuges. Wild turkey, marten, and gray squirrel are examples of **late-successional species,** whose habitats require establishment and protection of moderate-sized mature forest refuges.

Midsuccessional species such as elk, moose, deer, grouse, and snowshoe hare are found around abandoned croplands and partially open areas created in forests by logging of small stands of timber, controlled burning, or applying herbicides. The removal of old vegetation promotes the growth of vegetation favored as food by midsuccessional mammal and bird species. It also increases the amount of edge habitat, where two communities such as a forest and a field come together. This zone allows animals to feed on vegetation in the fields and quickly escape to cover in the nearby forest.

Early-successional species such as rabbit, quail, ring-necked pheasant, and dove find food and cover in the weedy pioneer plants that invade an area that has been cleared of vegetation for human activities and then abandoned.

Management of Migratory Waterfowl Migratory waterfowl such as ducks, geese, and swans require some special management approaches. Many of these species nest in Canada during the summer and migrate to the United States and Central America along generally fixed routes called *flyways* during the fall hunting season (Figure 14-18). Thus, international agreements are needed to prevent destruction of their winter and summer habitats and to prevent overhunting. In addition, it is necessary to provide protected stop-overs along flyways, where migrating birds can rest and feed. In 1934 Congress passed the Migratory Bird Hunting Stamp Act, which required waterfowl hunters to purchase a special hunting permit, called a duck stamp, each year. The sale of these permits has brought in $300 million, which has been used for waterfowl research and for acquisition, maintenance, and development of waterfowl refuges.

To develop new waterfowl habitats and improve existing ones, game managers can **(1)** periodically drain ponds to keep them from becoming clogged with vegetation, **(2)** create channels and openings in dense marsh vegetation to allow birds to feed and move about, and **(3)** construct artificial ponds, nesting islands, and nesting sites.

14-5   FISHERY MANAGEMENT

Freshwater Fishery Management   The goals of **freshwater fish management** are to encourage the growth of populations of desirable commercial and sport fish species and to reduce or eliminate populations of less desirable species. Several techniques are used. Laws and regulations determine the timing and length of the fishing season for various species, establish the minimum fish size that can be taken, set catch quotas, and require that commercial fish nets have a large enough mesh to ensure that young fish are not harvested. Natural and artificial habitats can be established, protected, and maintained by providing hiding places, removing debris, preventing excessive growth of aquatic plants to prevent oxygen depletion, and using small dams to control water flow. Habitats and desirable species can be protected from buildup of sediment and other forms of pollution. Predators, parasites, and diseases can be controlled by habitat improvement, breeding genetically resistant fish varieties, and using antibiotics and disinfectants. Hatcheries are used to restock ponds, lakes, and streams with species such as trout and salmon.

Marine Fishery Management   The history of the world's commercial fishing and whaling industry is an excellent example of the tragedy of the commons—the abuse and overuse of a potentially renewable resource—in this case, ocean fish and mammals—that is not owned by anyone and is available for use by everyone. Users of the marine fisheries tend to maximize their catch for short-term economic gain at the expense of long-term economic collapse from overfishing. As a result, many species of commercially valuable fish and whales found in international and coastal waters have been overfished to the point of **commercial extinction;** that is, they are so rare that it no longer pays to hunt them.

Several techniques can be used to manage marine fisheries and prevent commercial extinction. Annual quotas can be established for heavily used species, and regulations governing fishing gear and net size can be established and enforced. International and national laws have been used to extend the offshore fishing zone of coastal countries to 322 kilometers (200 nautical miles). Foreign fishing vessels are now allowed to take certain quotas of fish within such zones only with government permission. Food and game fish species, such as the striped bass along the Pacific and Atlantic coasts of the United States, can be introduced. Desirable species can be attracted by constructing artificial reefs from boulders, building rubble, and automobile tires.

The Whaling Industry   Whales, mammals ranging in size from the 0.9-meter (3-foot) porpoise to the giant 15- to 30-meter (50- to 100-foot) blue whale, can be divided into two major groups (Figure 14-19). **Toothed whales,** such as the porpoise, sperm whale, and killer whale, feed mostly on squid, octopus, and other marine animals. **Baleen whales,** such as the blue, gray, humpback, and finback, feed on plankton, krill, and 200 other small marine organisms by using horny plates in their jaws to filter the organisms from seawater.

The pattern of the whaling industry has been to hunt the most commercially valuable species until it becomes too scarce to be of commercial value and then turn to another species (see Spotlight on p. 311). In 1900 an estimated 4.4 million whales swam the ocean. Today only about 1 million remain, with only a few species such as the sperm whale and the minke whale making up most of the total.

Today 40 whaling and nonwhaling countries belong to the International Whaling Commission (IWC), established in 1946 out of concern over the sharp decline in stocks of many whale species from overfishing. The commission was empowered to regulate the annual harvest by setting hunting quotas to ensure a sustainable supply of all commercially important species. However, most fishery experts agree that the annual quotas set by the IWC were so high that during its first 20 years of existence it presided over serious depletion of nearly all the world's whale populations.

The discovery in the 1960s that the blue whale was in danger of extinction led to an international "Save the Whales" movement. In the late 1960s conservationist and other groups began pressuring the IWC to ban all commercial whaling. Greenpeace, the largest worldwide environmentalist group (1.5 million members), has used bold, commandolike tactics to embarrass whaling countries, stop pirate whalers who ignore the quotas, and gain worldwide publicity and support for whale protection. In 1972 the IWC discussed a ban on commercial whaling, and since then the United States and several other former whaling countries have urged that such a ban be imposed.

It was not until 1982, however, that the commission voted to phase out all commercial whaling by the end of 1986. According to IWC rules, member countries that file formal protests to commission rulings do not have to abide by them. In 1982, Japan, the Soviet Union, and Norway, the three major whaling countries, filed formal protests against the ban and announced their intentions to continue commercial whaling operations.

In the 1970s the U.S. Congress had passed two laws authorizing the president to ban imports of fish products from countries violating international fishery conventions and to cut in half the number of fish a country violating IWC rulings could take from U.S. waters. If an offending country did not comply within a year, it could lose all U.S. fishing privileges. To avoid such sanctions, which would result in even greater economic losses than from ending whaling, Japan, Norway, and the Soviet Union agreed to stop commercial whaling by the end of 1988.

Nevertheless, a loophole allows any IWC country to continue killing whales for "research purposes," if most of the meat is consumed domestically. In 1986, Iceland and South Korea increased their whale catch for research purposes in an apparent attempt to get around the ban on commercial whaling. Iceland then sold almost half of the whale meat to Japan. However, under threat of U.S. fishing sanctions both countries have agreed not to sell whale meat obtained as a result of scientific whaling to other countries and to use it only for domestic consumption. Iceland, however, has announced its intention to increase the number of whales taken for scientific purposes and to use the meat for domestic use, much of it as feed for mink farms. Although at least 6,000 whales were killed in 1986—when such killing was supposed to stop—the end of commercial whaling may be in sight.

Spotlight   Near Extinction of the Blue Whale

Blue whales are the world's largest animals and when fully matured can weigh as much as 25 full-grown African elephants. These baleen whales spend about eight months a year in Antarctic waters, where they feed on abundant krill; then they migrate to warm tropical waters where their young are born. This graceful, playful, gentle species has been hunted to near extinction for its oil, meat, and bone. The sharp decline in its population can be attributed to a ruthless, greedy whaling industry as well as to three natural characteristics of the blue whale. First, they are large and thus easy to spot. Second, they can be caught in large numbers because they congregate in their Antarctic feeding grounds. Third, they multiply very slowly, taking up to 25 years to mature sexually and having one offspring every 2 to 5 years. Once the total population has been reduced below a certain level, mates may no longer be able to find each other, and natural death rates will exceed natural birth rates until extinction occurs. Within the next few decades, blue whales could become extinct, even though they are now protected by law.

It is the responsibility of all who are alive today to accept the trusteeship of wildlife and to hand on to posterity, as a source of wonder and interest, knowledge, and enjoyment, the entire wealth of diverse animals and plants. This generation has no right by selfishness, wanton or intentional destruction, or neglect to rob future generations of this rich heritage. Extermination of other creatures is a disgrace to humankind.

World Wildlife Charter

Figure 14-19 Relative sizes of the major species of whale.

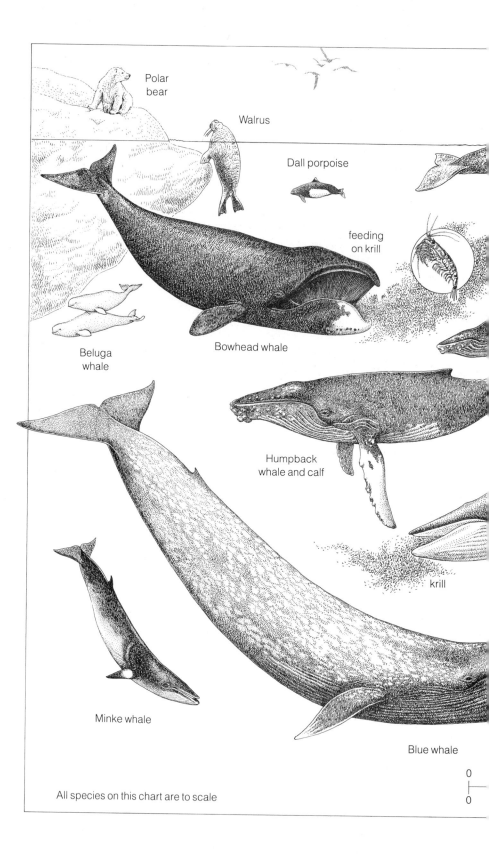

Polar bear

Walrus

Dall porpoise

feeding on krill

Beluga whale

Bowhead whale

Humpback whale and calf

krill

Minke whale

Blue whale

All species on this chart are to scale

0
0

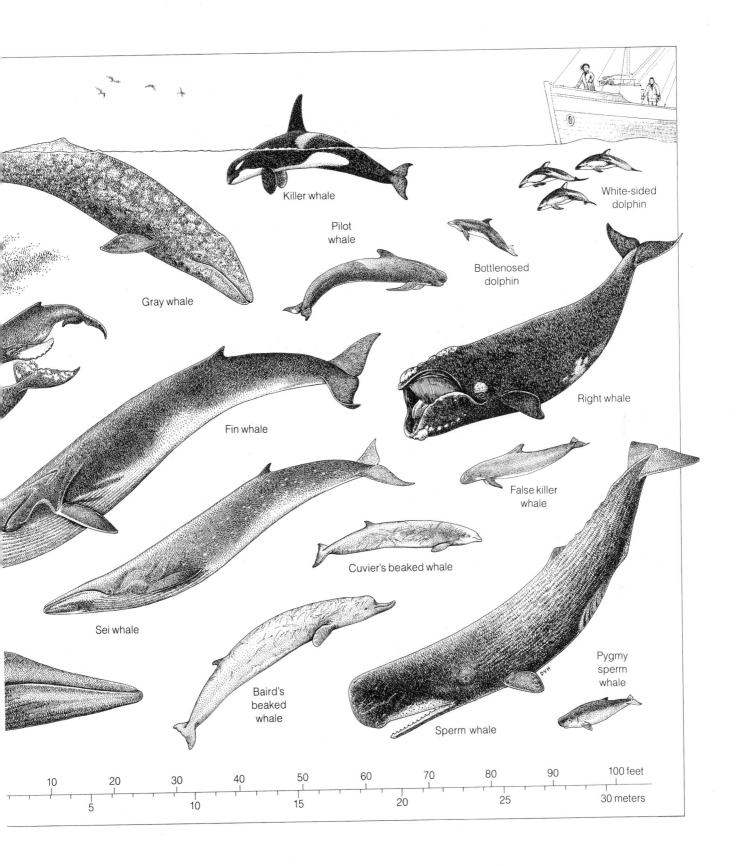

Killer whale

White-sided dolphin

Pilot whale

Bottlenosed dolphin

Gray whale

Right whale

Fin whale

False killer whale

Cuvier's beaked whale

Sei whale

Pygmy sperm whale

Baird's beaked whale

Sperm whale

10	20	30	40	50	60	70	80	90	100 feet
5		10		15		20		25	30 meters

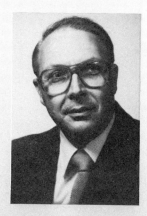

Robert Leo Smith

Robert Leo Smith is professor of wildlife ecology at West Virginia University. In addition to numerous research articles and papers on forest and wildlife management, he is author of three ecology texts (see Further Readings for Chapter 4): Ecology and Field Biology, *3rd ed. (1980),* Elements of Ecology, *2nd ed. (1986), and* Ecology of Man: An Ecosystem Approach, *2nd ed. (1976). He has also served as a consultant to government agencies on wildlife habitat assessment and other environmental issues.*

If you were to ask people, both hunters and non-hunters, how it is we have an abundance of white-tailed deer and wild turkey when they were threatened or endangered species just 50 years ago, few would know why. The answer is the Federal Aid in Wildlife Restoration Act of 1937, better known as the Pittman-Robertson or P-R Act. Born out of the depression and dust bowl of the 1930s, this one piece of legislation is most responsible for pulling many forms of North American wildlife from the brink of extinction and for providing the foundation of modern scientific wildlife management.

U.S. animal and bird wildlife was in a desperate situation in the 1930s. Populations of wild game species such as white-tailed deer, pronghorn antelope, bighorn sheep, wild turkey, and wood duck had been drastically reduced by years of uncontrolled hunting and habitat destruction.

Alarmed that game animals might disappear, a group of people who liked to hunt organized and began lobbying for wildlife conservation measures. One of the group's prominent leaders was Jay N. "Ding" Darling, a nationally syndicated cartoonist for the *Des Moines Register.* His cartoons hit hard at commercial hunters and greedy sport hunters and exploiters of natural resources. His leadership in promoting wildlife conservation prompted President Franklin D. Roosevelt to appoint him as director of the Bureau of Biological Survey, forerunner of today's U.S. Fish and Wildlife Service.

In 1936 Darling advocated a national wildlife policy that would declare the survival of game animals and birds in the national interest and would place wildlife management by states and the federal government on a scientific basis. This was a bold step forward because in the 1930s most wildlife management officials were political appointees with no special training or expertise and often with little interest in their job.

To provide for trained wildlife biologists, Darling proposed that wildlife research units be established at land-grant universities. These units would provide graduate-level training for wildlife scientists and conduct much-needed research. To finance such a program and aid states in undertaking projects to restore wildlife populations, Darling proposed a federal excise tax on the sale of sporting firearms and ammunition. It would be a "user-pay" program in which hunters paid the bill for the conservation and management of wildlife.

In 1937, a bill to this effect, sponsored by conservationists Senator Key Pittman of Nevada and Representative (later Senator) Willis Robertson of Virginia, was passed and signed into law. The P-R Act had three major provisions. It provided states with a portion of the tax revenues from firearm and ammunition sales on a matching basis (75% federal and 25% state) based on each state's size and number of licensed hunters. It prohibited use of these federal revenues for any purpose other than wildlife conservation. And no state could receive funds provided by P-R tax revenues unless it passed a law requiring all income from the sale of state hunting license fees to be used for support of its state fish and wildlife department.

Since 1937 the P-R law has provided more than $1.5 billion to the states for wildlife conservation, to which has been added over $500 million in state matching funds. Nearly half the money distributed to states has been used to develop, maintain, and operate wildlife management areas which benefit most forms of wildlife. The remainder has been used for wildlife research and surveys (25%), land acquisition (13%), and hunter safety and education (9%).

Funds provided by the P-R law have helped restore populations of many birds and animals. Although emphasis has been on game species, in recent years about 12% to 13% of the revenues (a smaller percentage in earlier years) have been spent on the conservation of nongame species. The act has also enabled states to purchase over 16,200 square kilometers (4 million acres) of upland and wetland wildlife habitats used by game and nongame species. Perhaps the most important and least visible result from the P-R Act has been development of the science of wildlife management, which has helped in the restoration of many game and nongame species of wildlife.

The success of the P-R Act led to the passage of the Dingell-Johnson or D-J Act in 1950, cosponsored by Representative John Dingell of Michigan and Senator Edwin Johnson of Colorado. Similar to P-R funding, it provides money for restoration and conservation of fish species with a sport or recreational value through a federal excise tax on fishing equipment including rods, reels, lines, and artificial lures, baits, and flies. The money is apportioned to each state on the basis of its geographical area and number of paid fishing licenses. This law has been especially useful in restoring and maintaining species favored by anglers, such as bass, trout, catfish, and other pan fish. In 1984 Congress passed an amendment to the D-J Act that established a trust fund for fish restoration and more than tripled the amount of money available under the D-J Act, primarily by imposing taxes on additional types of domestic and imported fishing equipment and pleasure boats and yachts.

Attempts to pass federal legislation that would place an excise tax on bird seed, binoculars, certain camera equipment, and other items associated with wildlife-related recreation and to use the resulting revenues for restoration and conservation of nongame wild species have failed. In 1980, however, Congress enacted the Fish and Wildlife Conservation Act, also known as the Nongame Act. It authorizes funding by means of general appropriations from the treasury to encourage states to prepare and carry out plans for the conservation of nongame wildlife species. However, between 1980 and 1987 this program has not been funded because the Reagan administration has not requested any appropriations for this purpose.

Antihunting factions have opposed excise taxes on hunting and fishing equipment under the P-R and D-J acts on the grounds that they sacrifice wildlife in order to increase revenues for state wildlife and fishery departments and increase profits for the sporting equipment industry. However, these critics fail to recognize that for several decades sport hunting and fishing has promoted and financed the restoration of much of the country's wildlife. It is because of these laws that we still have an abundance of wildlife, from bears and deer to bobwhite quail and songbirds. In 1985 revenues collected under the P-R and D-J acts also accounted for 21% of the U.S. Fish and Wildlife Service budget.

In spite of such funding and a wealth of knowledge available on the management of wildlife resources, many species of wildlife face a precarious future because of problems money cannot solve. This results from the relentless destruction and fragmentation of wildlife habitat by an expanding human population—leaving many forms of wildlife without a place to live.

Guest Essay Discussion

1. What do you believe would be the condition of game and nongame wildlife in the United States if Congress had not passed the P-R and D-J acts?

2. Do you agree or disagree with the claim by antihunting factions that these acts have sacrificed wildlife to increase profits for the sporting equipment industry? Explain.

3. Should the Nongame Act passed in 1980 be funded? Explain. Should this act be funded from general appropriations (as is presently the case) or by an excise tax on certain wildlife-related recreational items? Explain.

CHAPTER SUMMARY

Wildlife resources provide people with a variety of economic benefits as sources of food, fuel, paper, fibers, leather, medicines, natural insecticides, and biological control of various weeds and insect pests. Many wild species are also a source of beauty and recreational pleasure. Their most important contribution, however, may be their roles in maintaining the health and integrity of the world's ecosystems. In addition to their actual or potential usefulness as resources for humans (*anthropocentrism*), some people hold the *biocentric* belief that it is ethically and morally wrong for humans to hasten the extinction of any species because humans are no more important than any other species on earth. This belief, however, will not be widespread until we take the time to experience wild nature directly and become emotionally—not just intellectually—involved in understanding its workings and marveling at its beauty.

Despite the importance of wild species, we know very little about most of the earth's 1.7 million identified species and nothing about the millions of undiscovered species. By clearing and degrading diverse tropical forests and other ecosystems we are wiping out numerous species—like throwing away gifts without removing their wrappings.

At least 90% of the half a billion or so different species estimated to have lived on earth have become extinct or have evolved into a new species. Mass extinctions in the distant past have resulted from unknown natural causes. However, since agriculture began about 10,000 years ago, the rate of species extinction as a result of human activities increased a millionfold from about one species every 1,000 years to 1,000 per year by 1985. The rate is projected to increase twentyfold to 20,000 species per year by the end of this century. Species that may soon become extinct are classified as *endangered species* and those likely to become endangered are classified as *threatened species*.

The major human-related factors that can lead to a species becoming threatened, endangered, or extinct are (1) habitat elimination and disturbance; (2) commercial hunting; (3) pest and predator control for protection of livestock, crops, and game; (4) collecting specimens as pets, for medical research, and for zoos; (5) pollution; and (6) accidental or deliberate introduction of a competing or predatory species into an ecosystem. Some species have natural characteristics that make them more susceptible to extinction by human activities and natural disasters than other species. Examples include low reproductive rates, large size, limited or specialized nesting or breeding areas, specialized feeding habits, fixed migratory patterns, and certain behavioral patterns.

Three main strategies are used to protect endangered and threatened wild species and to prevent other wild species from becoming endangered: (1) establishing treaties, passing laws, and setting aside refuges; (2) using gene banks, zoos, research centers, botanical gardens, and aquariums to preserve a small number of individuals of wild species; and (3) preserving and protecting a variety of unique and representative ecosystems throughout the world. Each approach has certain advantages and disadvantages. Most wildlife biologists believe that the major threat to most wild species—namely, the destruction of habitat—can only be halted by establishing and maintaining a worldwide system of reserves, parks, and other protected areas.

Wildlife management involves manipulating populations of wild species and their habitats for human benefit, the welfare of other species, and the preservation of endangered and threatened species. Three approaches are used to meet these often conflicting goals: (1) protect relatively undisturbed areas from human activity; (2) manipulate the pop- ulation size and habitat to maintain a diversity of species in an area; or (3) manipulate population size and habitat of an area to favor a single species. Populations of game animals in the United States are managed by laws that govern how and when certain species can be hunted for sport. Similar laws and regulations are used to manage populations of desirable commercial and sport freshwater and marine fish species. However, many commercially important species of fish and whales have been exploited for short-term economic gain to the point where they are so rare that it no longer pays to hunt them (*commercial extinction*).

DISCUSSION TOPICS

1. Discuss your reaction to the statement: "Who cares that the passenger pigeon is extinct and the blue whale, whooping crane, and other plant and animal species face extinction because of human activities? They are important only to bird watchers, Sierra Clubbers, and other ecofreaks." Be honest about your reaction and present arguments for your position.

2. Why should an urban dweller be concerned about preservation of wild species and wildlife habitat?

3. Do you agree that since most of the species that have existed on earth have become extinct by natural processes, we should not be concerned about extinction of wild species because of human activities? Explain.

4. Some argue that all species have an inherent right to exist regardless of whether they are useful to humans and that they should at least be preserved in a natural habitat somewhere on earth. Do you agree with this position? Explain. Would you apply this idea to (a) anopheles mosquitoes, which transmit malaria, (b) tigers that roam along the Indian-Nepalese border and killed at least 105 persons between 1978 and 1983, (c) bacteria that cause smallpox or other infectious diseases, (d) rats that compete with humans for many food sources, and (e) rattlesnakes.

5. Should all coyotes and eagles be exterminated from lands where sheep graze? Explain. What are the alternatives?

6. Use Table 14-2 to predict a species that may soon be endangered. What, if anything, is being done for this species? What pressures is it being subjected to? Try to work up a plan for protecting it.

7. List ten items that you consume or use that lead to destruction of wild species and wildlife habitats in the United States and other parts of the world.

8. Are you for or against sport hunting? Explain.

9. Should sport hunting be allowed on federal wildlife refuges? Explain.

10. Between 1981 and 1986, federal funds available for protecting and managing wildlife on publicly owned lands have been sharply decreased by Congress under pressure from President Reagan in order to reduce the rate of growth of massive federal deficits. Do you agree or disagree with this trend? Explain.

11. Make a survey of your campus and local community to identify examples of habitat destruction or degradation that have had a harmful effect on populations of various wild plant and animal species. Develop a plan for correcting this situation and present it to appropriate college and local officials.

15

Nonrenewable Mineral Resources

GENERAL OBJECTIVES

1. What methods are used to locate and extract nonrenewable minerals from the earth's crust?

2. What are some of the harmful environmental consequences of mining, processing, and using nonrenewable minerals?

3. Are we likely to run out of affordable supplies of any essential nonrenewable nonfuel minerals in the world and in the United States in the foreseeable future?

4. How can present known supplies of key mineral resources be increased?

5. How can present and potential supplies of key mineral resources be extended through resource conservation?

We seem to believe we can get everything we need from the supermarket and corner drugstore. We don't understand that everything has a source in the land or sea, and that we must respect these sources.

Thor Heyerdahl

What do cars, spoons, beverage cans, coins, electrical wiring, bricks, and sidewalks have in common? Few people stop to think that these products and thousands of others they use every day are made from nonrenewable raw materials extracted from the earth's solid crust—the upper layer of the lithosphere (Figure 4-2, p. 70). Nonrenewable nonfuel resources are discussed in this chapter and nonrenewable fuel resources such as coal, oil, natural gas, and uranium are discussed in Chapters 16 and 17.

15-1 LOCATING AND EXTRACTING MINERAL RESOURCES

Mineral Resource Abundance and Distribution Human ingenuity has found ways to locate and extract more than 100 nonrenewable nonfuel minerals and to transform them into most of the everyday items we use and then discard, reuse, or recycle (Figure 15-1). Any naturally occurring concentration of a free element or compound of two or more elements in solid form is called a **mineral deposit.** Nonrenewable nonfuel raw materials are classified as **metallic minerals,** containing iron, copper, aluminum or other metal elements; and **nonmetallic minerals,** such as sand, stone, and phosphates (used as commercial inorganic fertilizers) composed of nonmetal elements and compounds. Although a few minerals, such as gold and silver, occur as free elements, most are found as various compounds of only ten elements which make up 99.3% of the earth's crust (Figure 15-2). The earth's remaining elements are found only in trace amounts.

Elements in the earth's crust, however, are not distributed uniformly. Geochemical processes occurring over hundreds of millions of years during the

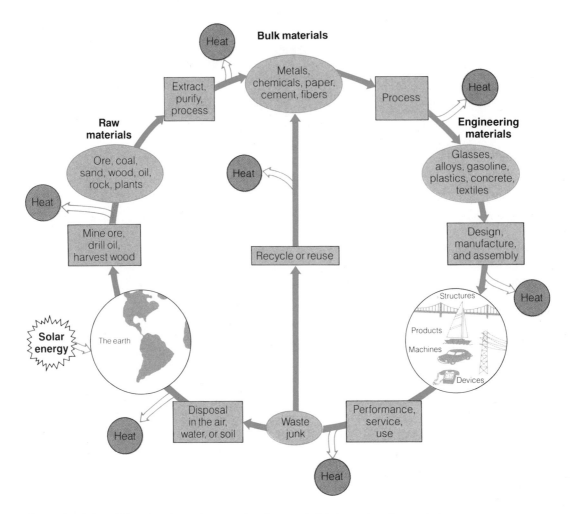

Figure 15-1 Generalized view of the extraction and processing of raw materials to produce the products we use and then discard, recycle, or reuse.

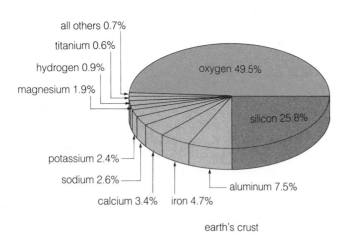

Figure 15-2 Percentage by weight of elements in the earth's crust.

earth's early history selectively dissolved, transported, and deposited elements and their compounds unevenly. As a result, there is a tremendous difference between the average crustal abundances of elements shown in Figure 15-2 and the amount of an element actually found at a single location. Although rich deposits of a particular mineral such as iron or copper may exist at some locations, little or none is found in most places (Figure 15-3).

A mineral deposit with a high enough concentration of at least one metallic mineral to permit the metal to be extracted and sold at a profit is called an **ore** or **ore deposit.** An ore that contains a relatively large concentration of a desired metallic element is called a **high-grade ore** and one with a relatively low concentration is known as a **low-grade ore.**

Making Mineral Resources Available Use of a mineral resource involves several major steps. First,

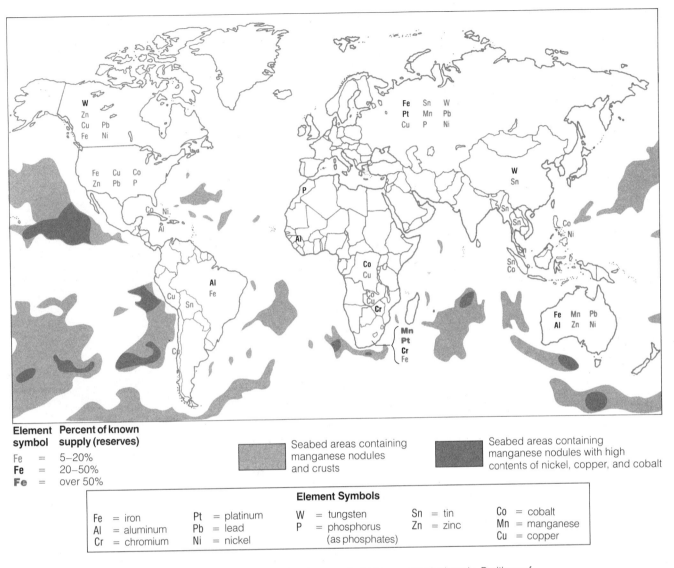

Element symbol	Percent of known supply (reserves)
Fe	=	5–20%
Fe	=	20–50%
Fe	=	over 50%

Seabed areas containing manganese nodules and crusts

Seabed areas containing manganese nodules with high contents of nickel, copper, and cobalt

Element Symbols

Fe = iron	Pt = platinum	W = tungsten	Sn = tin	Co = cobalt
Al = aluminum	Pb = lead	P = phosphorus	Zn = zinc	Mn = manganese
Cr = chromium	Ni = nickel	(as phosphates)		Cu = copper

Figure 15-3 Geographic distribution of major known supplies (reserves) of 13 key nonfuel minerals. Positions of symbols do not indicate location of deposits within countries. (Data from U.S. Bureau of Mines)

a deposit containing enough of the desired mineral to make it profitable to remove must be located. Second, some form of mining is used to extract the mineral from the deposit. Third, the mineral is processed to remove impurities and in some cases (especially metallic ores) converted to a different chemical form by *smelting* or other chemical processes. For example, aluminum is found in the earth's crust in ore form as aluminum oxide (Al_2O_3). After the ore is purified and melted, electrical current is passed through the molten oxide to convert it to aluminum metal (Al) and oxygen gas (O_2). Most smelters and other mineral-processing plants are located near mines because it is too costly to transport the huge volume of ore-bearing rock very far. Finally, the desired form of the mineral is used directly (for example, crushed stone may be applied to roads) or manufactured into various prod-

ucts (aluminum metal is converted to aluminum foil, cans, or cookware).

Locating Deposits Finding concentrated deposits of useful minerals is difficult and expensive because they are very unevenly distributed on earth. Typically the task involves a combination of geological knowledge about crustal movements and mineral formation, the use of various instruments and measurements, and luck. Photos taken from airplanes or images relayed by satellites can sometimes reveal geological features such as mounds or rock formations usually associated with deposits of certain minerals. Instruments can also be mounted on aircraft and satellites to detect concentrated deposits of minerals that affect the earth's magnetic field or modify the earth's gravity

Figure 15-4 A giant shovel used for strip-mining coal. The cars behind the shovel look like toys.

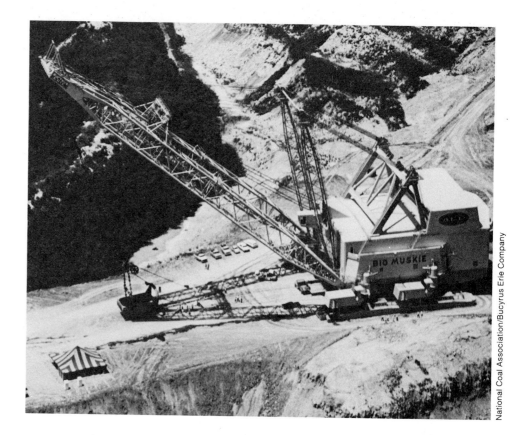

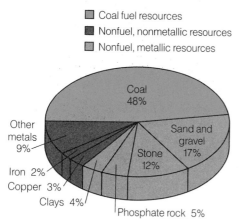

■ Coal fuel resources
■ Nonfuel, nonmetallic resources
■ Nonfuel, metallic resources

Coal 48%

Sand and gravel 17%

Other metals 9%

Stone 12%

Iron 2%
Copper 3%
Clays 4%

Phosphate rock 5%

Figure 15-5 Percentage of surface-mined U.S. land used to extract various mineral resources.

field. Then, at promising sites samples are extracted from test holes, tunnels, or trenches and analyzed for their mineral content.

Extraction Once an economically acceptable mineral deposit has been located, it is removed by surface or subsurface mining, depending on the location of the deposit in the earth's crust. Mineral deposits located near the earth's surface are removed by **surface mining.** Mechanized equipment removes the overlying layer of soil and rock—known as **overburden**—and vegetation so that the underlying mineral deposit can be extracted with large power shovels (Figure 15-4). You can get some idea of such equipment by imagining a shovel 32 stories high, with a metal boom and attached bucket as long as a football field, capable of gouging out 152 cubic meters (5,366 cubic feet) of land every 55 seconds and dropping this 295,000-kilogram (325-ton) load a distance of a city block away. This is an accurate description of Big Muskie, a $25 million power shovel used for surface mining of coal in the United States.

Surface mining extracts about 90% of the metallic and nonmetallic minerals and almost two-thirds of the coal used in the United States. Almost half of the land disturbed by surface mining in the United States has been mined for coal; the remainder has been mined for nonmetallic (38%) and metallic (14%) minerals (Figure 15-5).

Several different types of surface mining are used, depending on the type of mineral and local topography. **Open-pit surface mining** involves using large machinery to dig a hole in the earth's surface and remove a mineral deposit, primarily stone, sand, gravel, iron, and copper. Sand and gravel are removed from

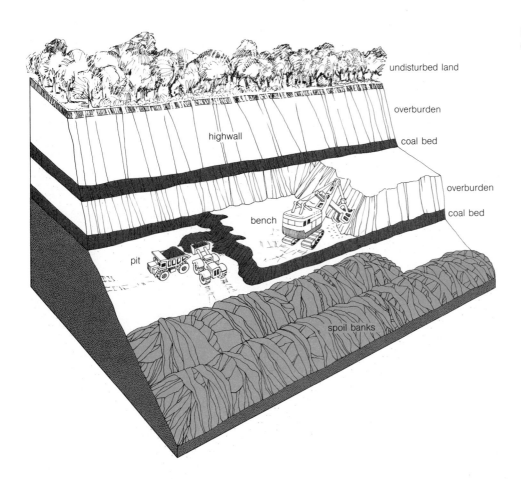

Figure 15-6 Area strip mining of coal.

undisturbed land

overburden

highwall

coal bed

overburden

coal bed

bench

pit

spoil banks

thousands of small pits in many parts of the country. Building rocks such as limestone, granite, and marble are taken from larger pits called quarries. In Minnesota's Mesabi Range near Lake Superior and in some western states, copper (see photo on p. 187) and iron ores are removed from huge open-pit mines.

Area strip mining is carried out on flat or rolling terrain. Bulldozers and power shovels strip away the overburden and dig a trench to remove the mineral deposit (Figure 15-6). Then another, parallel trench is dug and its overburden is placed in the adjacent trench from which the mineral deposit has already been removed. When no attempt is made to restore the area, the result is a wavelike series of highly erodible hills of rubble known as spoil banks (Figure 15-7). This technique is used primarily for mining coal in many western and midwestern states, and phosphate rock—especially in Florida, North Carolina, and Idaho.

Contour strip mining is used in hilly or mountainous terrain. A power shovel cuts a series of shelves or terraces into the side of a hill or mountain, dumping the overburden from each new terrace onto the one below. If the land is not restored, the result is an ugly wall of dirt in front of a highly erodible, steep bank of soil and rock (Figure 15-8). In the United States contour strip mining is used primarily for extracting coal in the mountainous Appalachian region. In areas where the overburden is too thick to be removed economically, coal and some other minerals may be removed by huge drills, called augers, which burrow horizontally into a mountain deposit.

When a mineral deposit lies so deep in the ground that it is too expensive to remove by surface mining, it is extracted by **subsurface mining.** For solid materials such as coal and some metallic ores, this is usually done by digging a deep, vertical shaft, blasting subsurface tunnels and rooms to get to the deposit, and hauling the coal or ore to the surface. In the **room-and-pillar method** as much as half the coal is left in place as pillars to prevent the mine from collapsing. Underground deposits of coal and some ores are also removed by the **longwall method;** a narrow tunnel is created and then supported by movable metal pillars. After a cutting machine has removed the coal or ore from a portion of a mineral seam, the roof supports are moved forward, allowing the earth behind them to collapse. As a result, no tunnels are left after the mining operation has been completed.

Subsurface techniques are also necessary for the extraction of crude oil and natural gas. Wells are drilled into underground rock reservoirs, allowing the pressurized oil or gas to rise to the surface, or a gas or hot water is injected into the well to force remaining oil to the surface (Sections 16-3 and 16-4).

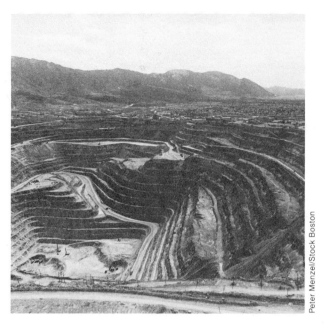

Figure 15-7 Effects of area strip mining of coal near Butte, Montana. Although restoration of newly strip-mined areas is now required, many previously mined areas have not been restored.

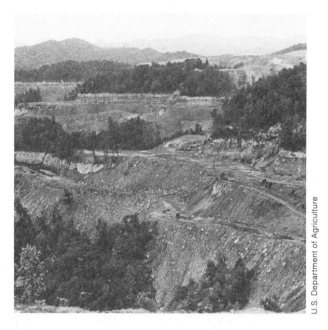

Figure 15-8 Severely eroded hillsides on Bolt Mountain, West Virginia, as a result of contour strip mining of coal without proper restoration.

15-2 ENVIRONMENTAL IMPACT OF MINING AND PROCESSING MINERAL RESOURCES

Overall Impact The mining, processing, and use of any nonfuel or fuel mineral resource causes some form of land disturbance along with air and water pollution (Figure 15-9). Most land disturbed by mining can be restored to some degree, and some forms of air and water pollution can be controlled (Chapters 19 and 20). But these efforts are expensive and they also require energy, which, in being produced and used, can again pollute the environment.

Mining Impacts The harmful environmental effects of mining depend on the specific type of mineral extracted, the size of the deposit, the method used (surface or subsurface), and the local topography and climate. For each unit of mineral produced, subsurface mining disturbs less than one-tenth as much land as surface mining and generally produces less waste material. But subsurface mining is more dangerous and expensive than surface mining. Roofs and walls of underground mines occasionally collapse, some-

times trapping and killing miners. Explosions of dust and natural gas in mines can also kill and injure miners. Miners can also contract lung diseases as a result of prolonged inhalation of coal dust and other types of dust. Sometimes the surfaces above extensively mined areas cave in or subside, causing roads and houses to crack and buckle, railroad tracks to bend, sewer lines to crack, and gas mains to break and possibly explode.

Compared to other uses of land such as agriculture and urbanization, surface mining uses a relatively small amount of the earth's surface. For example, between 1930 and 1985 only about 0.25% of the total land area of the United States has been surface-mined or used to dispose of wastes (spoils) from such mining. Nevertheless, surface mining has a severe environmental impact because the land is stripped bare of vegetation and is not always restored (see Spotlight on p. 325). The exposed soil and mining wastes are subject to erosion by wind and water and can pollute the atmosphere and nearby aquatic ecosystems.

Ideally, restoration of surface-mined land includes filling in and regrading to restore the original contour, replacing topsoil (which can be saved and placed on top of regraded mining rubble), and reestablishing vegetation to anchor the soil. Restoration costs typi-

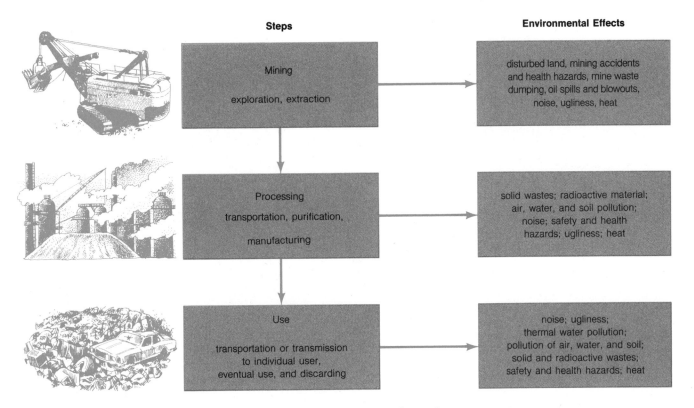

Steps	Environmental Effects
Mining exploration, extraction	disturbed land, mining accidents and health hazards, mine waste dumping, oil spills and blowouts, noise, ugliness, heat
Processing transportation, purification, manufacturing	solid wastes; radioactive material; air, water, and soil pollution; noise; safety and health hazards; ugliness; heat
Use transportation or transmission to individual user, eventual use, and discarding	noise; ugliness; thermal water pollution; pollution of air, water, and soil; solid and radioactive wastes; safety and health hazards; heat

Figure 15-9 Some harmful environmental effects of resource extraction, processing, and use.

cally range from $2,500 to $12,500 per hectare ($1,000 to $5,000 per acre).

The success of restoration efforts is highly dependent on average precipitation, slope of the land, and how well federal and state surface mining regulations are enforced. Restoration is simpler and more effective in areas with more than ten inches of rainfall per year and with flat or slightly rolling topography (Figure 15-10). In the arid and semiarid regions of the western United States, which contain about three-fourths of the country's surface-minable coal, full restoration is usually not possible. For many large open-pit mines and quarries, especially in arid and semiarid regions, there is little hope of restoration. It has been suggested, however, that large and medium-size pit mines could be lined with concrete and used as sites for underground parking garages or storage of petroleum, chemicals, or other supplies.

Another environmental problem of subsurface and surface mining, but more frequent with subsurface mining, is runoff of acids, eroded soil (silt), and toxic substances into nearby surface and ground waters (Figure 15-11). Rainwater seeping through surface-mine spoils and through abandoned subsurface mines, especially coal mines rich in sulfur compounds, causes chemical reactions that produce sulfuric acid. This acid

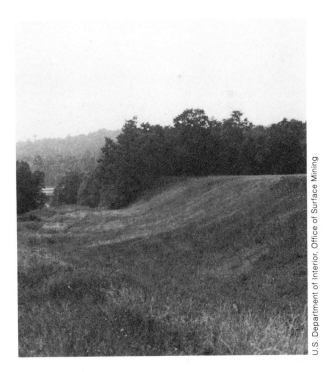

Figure 15-10 With the land regraded to its original contour and grass planted to hold the soil in place, there is little evidence that this was once a coal surface mining site in West Virginia.

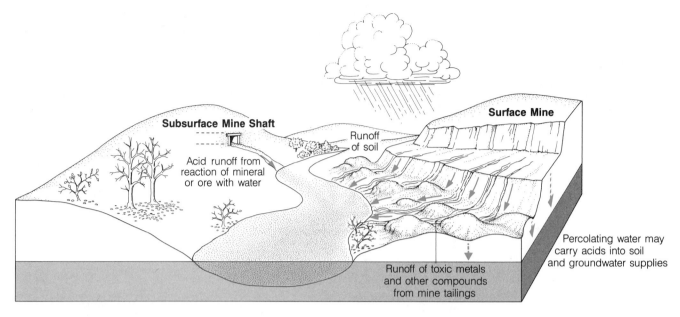

Figure 15-11 Degradation and pollution of a stream and groundwater by runoff of acids and toxic chemicals from surface and subsurface mining operations.

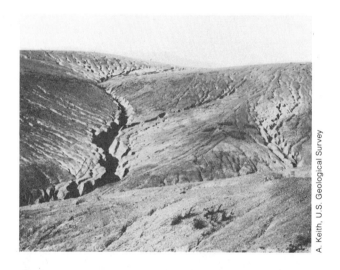

Figure 15-12 Sulfur dioxide and other fumes from a copper smelter in Tennessee killed the luxurious forest that once flourished on this land.

and the toxic compounds leached from mine spoils can run off into nearby rivers and streams, contaminating water supplies and killing aquatic life. These pollutants can also percolate downward and contaminate groundwater.

Processing Impacts Processing extracted mineral deposits to remove impurities produces large quantities of rock and other waste materials called **tailings,** which are stored on the ground in piles or dumped into ponds. Wind blows particles of dust and toxic metals from piles of tailings into the atmosphere; water leaches toxic substances into nearby surface or groundwater supplies. Although some mining companies have made considerable investments to reduce contamination from tailings, there is still a long way to go in requiring and monitoring such efforts.

Without adequate pollution control equipment, mineral-smelting plants emit massive quantities of air pollutants, especially sulfur dioxide, soot, and tiny particles of toxic elements and compounds (such as arsenic, cadmium, and lead) found as impurities in many ores. For example, decades of uncontrolled sulfur dioxide emissions from copper-smelting operations near Copperhill and Ducktown, Tennessee, killed all vegetation for miles around and acidified the soil to such an extent that it took years for even partial recovery (Figure 15-12).

Smelting plants also cause water pollution and produce liquid and solid hazardous wastes that must be disposed of safely or converted into less harmful substances. In addition, workers in some smelting industries have an increased risk of cancer. The lung cancer death rate for arsenic smelter workers is almost three times the expected rate, that for cadmium smelter workers is more than twice the expected rate, and lead smelter workers have higher than normal incidences of lung and stomach cancer.

Environmental protection laws enacted during the 1970s (Appendix 3) have reduced air and water pol-

By 1985 about 52,000 square kilometers (13 million acres) of land in the United States had been disrupted by surface mining of all types. Only about 64% of the land area disturbed by coal mining, 26% by nonmetals, and 8% by metals have been restored. It is projected that by 2000 an additional 60,000 square kilometers (15 million acres) will be disrupted by surface mining.

U.S. mining companies are now required by the Surface Mining Control and Reclamation Act of 1977 and by various state laws to reclaim all land surface-mined for coal.

However, much of the land mined in the past has not been restored, and there are no laws requiring that land used for surface mining of other minerals be restored.

Environmentalists believe that all land surface-mined for any type of mineral in the past, present, and future should be restored unless the damage is so great that restoration is essentially impossible. They propose that funds for such restoration be provided by a combination of a one-time restoration tax on the appropriate mining industries and an ongoing tax on each unit of min-

eral they produce in the future. Of course, mining industries oppose this plan, contending it would raise prices for consumers. In addition, it would make U.S. companies uncompetitive in the international market against countries with less-strict environmental regulations. Environmentalists counter that consumers are already paying higher prices indirectly in the form of health damage and environmental degradation. What do you think should be done?

lution from mineral industries in the United States. However, environmentalists contend that existing legislation is not always enforced and that the levels of many pollutants inside and outside processing plants should be reduced further.

15-3   WILL THERE BE ENOUGH MINERAL RESOURCES?

How Much Is There?   Estimating how much of a particular nonrenewable mineral resource exists on earth and how much of it can be located and extracted at an affordable price is a complex and controversial process. The term **total resources** refers to the total amount of a particular mineral that exists on earth. It is difficult, however, to make reliable estimates of the total available amount of a particular resource because the entire world has not been explored for each resource.

The U.S. Geological Survey estimates actual and potential supplies of a mineral resource by dividing the estimated total resources into two broad categories: identified and undiscovered (Figure 15-13). **Identified resources** are specific bodies of a particular mineral-bearing material whose location, quantity, and quality are known or have been inferred from geological evidence and measurements. **Undiscovered resources** are potential supplies of a particular mineral resource believed to exist on the basis of broad geo-

logical knowledge and theory, although specific locations, quality, and amounts are unknown.

These two categories are then subdivided into reserves and resources depending on the estimated costs of mining them and the degree of certainty of their existence. **Reserves** or **economic resources** are identified resources that can be extracted profitably at present prices with current mining technology. **Resources** are identified and unidentified resources that cannot be recovered profitably with present prices and technology but may be converted to reserves when prices rise or mining technology improves.

Most published estimates of the available supply of a particular nonrenewable mineral refer to reserves—not resources or total resources. The actual supply that becomes available is normally higher than estimated because some of the resources will be converted to reserves by discoveries of new supplies, improved mining technology, and shortage-caused price increases, which permit profitable mining of low-grade deposits. However, a large portion of potentially recoverable resources will not become available because finding and extracting them will take more money and energy than they are worth.

How Fast Are Supplies Being Depleted?   The future availability of a mineral resource depends not only on its actual or potential supply but also on how rapidly this supply is being depleted to the point where what remains is too costly to extract and process for use.

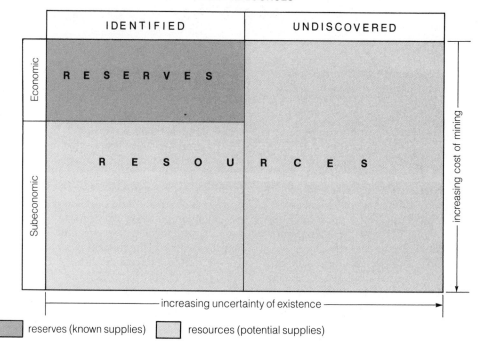

Figure 15-13 General classification of mineral resources by the U.S. Geological Survey.

TOTAL RESOURCES

	IDENTIFIED	UNDISCOVERED
Economic	RESERVES	
Subeconomic	RESOURCES	

— increasing cost of mining →

← increasing uncertainty of existence →

☐ reserves (known supplies)   ☐ resources (potential supplies)

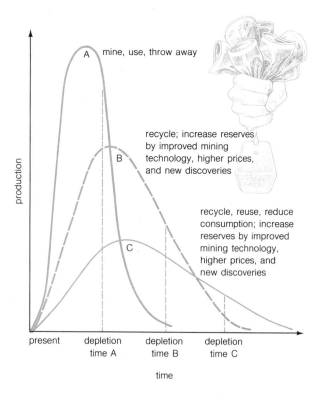

A mine, use, throw away

B recycle; increase reserves by improved mining technology, higher prices, and new discoveries

C recycle, reuse, reduce consumption; increase reserves by improved mining technology, higher prices, and new discoveries

production

present   depletion time A   depletion time B   depletion time C

time

Figure 15-14 Depletion curves for a nonrenewable resource, based on three different sets of assumptions. Dashed vertical lines show when 80% depletion occurs.

Depletion time is the period required to use a certain fraction—usually 80%—of the known reserves or estimated resources of a mineral, at an assumed rate of use.

We can plot a series of projections of different depletion times in the form of depletion curves by making different assumptions about the resource supply and its rate of use. For example, one estimate of depletion time might be based on the assumption that the resource is not recycled or reused and that there will be no increase in its estimated reserves (curve A, Figure 15-14). A longer depletion time estimate can be obtained if we assume that recycling will extend the life of existing reserves and that improved mining technology, price rises, and new discoveries will expand present reserves by some factor, say 2 (curve B).

We can project a still longer depletion time by assuming that present reserves will be expanded even more, perhaps five or ten times, by new discoveries and through recycling, reuse, and reduced consumption (curve C). Of course, finding a substitute for a resource cancels all these curves and requires a new set of depletion curves for the new resource. Figure 15-14 illustrates why there is so much controversy over projected supplies of nonrenewable nonfuel and fuel resources. One can get optimistic or pessimistic projections of the depletion time of a particular resource by making different sets of assumptions.

Table 15-1 U.S. Import Dependence for Selected Key Nonfuel Minerals in 1985

Mineral	Percentage Imported	Major Suppliers	Key Uses
Columbium	100	Brazil, Canada, Thailand	High-strength alloys for construction, jet engines, machine tools
Industrial diamonds	100	South Africa, United Kingdom, Soviet Union	Machinery, mineral services, abrasives, stone and ceramic products
Manganese	99	South Africa, Gabon, France	Alloys for impact-resistant steel, dry-cell batteries, chemicals
Aluminum ore	96	Jamaica, Guinea, Suriname	Aluminum production, building materials, abrasives
Cobalt	95	Zaire, Zambia, Canada	Alloys for tool bits, aircraft engines, high-strength steel
Tantalum	94	Thailand, Malaysia, Brazil	Nuclear reactors, aircraft parts, surgical instruments
Platinum	91	South Africa, United Kingdom, Soviet Union	Oil refining, chemical processing, telecommunications, medical and dental equipment
Graphite	90+	Mexico, China, Brazil	Foundry operations, lubricants, brake linings
Chromium	82	South Africa, Zimbabwe, Soviet Union	Alloys for springs, tools, engines, bearings
Tin	79	Thailand, Malaysia, Indonesia	Cans and containers, electrical products, construction, transportation
Rutile	61	Australia, Sierra Leone, South Africa	Paint, plastics, paper, welding-rod coatings
Vanadium	41	South Africa, Canada, Finland	Iron and steel alloys, titanium alloys, sulfuric acid production

Source: U.S. Bureau of Mines, U.S. Office of Technology Assessment

Who Has the World's Nonfuel Mineral Resources?

Five MDCs—the Soviet Union, the United States, Canada, Australia, and South Africa—supply the world with most of the 20 minerals that make up 98% of all nonfuel minerals consumed in the world (Figure 15-3, p. 319). The major exceptions include copper in South America, tin and tungsten in Southeast Asia, aluminum ore in the Caribbean, and cobalt in Zaire.

The United States and the Soviet Union are the world's two largest producers and consumers of raw and processed nonfuel mineral resources. Unlike other countries, the Soviet Union has long been essentially self-sufficient for almost all of its mineral needs. In 1985 the United States, with almost 5% of the world's population, produced 11% and consumed 13% of the world's nonfuel mineral resources. Despite its rich resource base, the United States imports all or a large percentage of many key nonfuel minerals (Table 15-1), in some cases because the U.S. rate of con-

sumption exceeds domestic production and in other cases because higher-grade ores found in other countries are cheaper to extract than more plentiful lower-grade U.S. reserves. Japan and many western European countries are even more dependent on imports of vital nonfuel minerals.

Currently, the United States stockpiles 93 **strategic materials** vital to industry and defense, 80 of them nonfuel minerals, to cushion against supply interruptions and sharp price rises. The stockpiles are supposed to be large enough to last through a three-year war, but most supplies are well below this level. Although OPEC has been able to raise oil prices, other **cartels** or groups of resource-rich countries banding together to control supplies and raise prices are not considered a serious threat to supplies of minerals.

Unlike oil, which is consumed directly, nonfuel mineral raw materials contribute such a small percentage to the cost of finished products that increases in their prices have relatively small effects. So far no cartel, single country, or company has been successful in controlling the supply and price of any nonfuel mineral except industrial diamonds, which have been rigidly controlled for 50 years by De Beers Consolidated Mines of South Africa.

Nevertheless, the political future of South Africa is particularly important to the United States, especially for supplies of chromium, manganese, and platinum, which are considered essential to national defense and are produced in only small amounts from domestic supplies. In 1984 the United States imported 51% of its chromium, 50% of its platinum, and 35% of its manganese from South Africa. The major alternative supplier of these three strategic minerals is the Soviet Union. Politically unstable Zaire in Africa is the major supplier of cobalt (typically providing 50% to 60% of all U.S. consumption), a fourth mineral resource vital to defense. By 1985 the U.S. had stockpiled enough of these four minerals to weather a 14-month cutoff in imports.

According to the U.S. Bureau of Mines and the U.S. Geological Survey, the United States has adequate domestic reserves of most key minerals—except chromium, cobalt, platinum, tin, gold, and palladium—for at least the next several decades. However, the Geological Survey estimates that present reserves of most key minerals will not satisfy U.S. needs for more than 100 years without increased recycling, conservation, and substitutes.

Will There Be Enough?   There is considerable controversy between cornucopians and neo-Malthusians over whether enough affordable supplies of key nonfuel minerals can be found, extracted, and processed to meet the projected future needs of the world's MDCs and LDCs. Cornucopians believe that supplies can be increased as needed if sufficient economic incentives are provided to increase mineral exploration, mine lower-grade ores, and find substitutes for scarce resources.

Neo-Malthusians agree that supplies can be increased but believe that rising energy and pollution control costs may limit the use of many key resources long before their potentially recoverable supplies run out. Instead of placing emphasis on locating and extracting new supplies (the supply-side approach), they favor greatly increased emphasis on recycling and reusing nonrenewable mineral resources and reducing unnecessary waste of such resources (the conservation approach). Even if enough minerals can be produced, many LDCs fear that most of these resources will be used to sustain increasingly greater economic growth by the MDCs, so that many LDCs will never become developed (see Spotlight on p. 329).

15-4   INCREASING MINERAL RESOURCE SUPPLIES: THE SUPPLY-SIDE APPROACH

Economics and Resource Supply   Although geologic processes determine how much of a mineral resource is available, economics determines what portion of the supply will actually be used. According to standard economic theory, a competitive free market should control the supply and demand of goods and services: If a resource becomes scarce, prices rise; if there is an oversupply, they fall. Cornucopians contend that rising prices based on increased demand will stimulate new discoveries and development of more efficient mining technology, making it profitable to mine ores of increasingly lower grades.

However, a number of economists argue that this idea often does not apply to the supply and demand of nonfuel mineral resources in most MDCs, which use the bulk of these materials. For example, in the United States (and in many other industrial countries) both industry and government have gained so much control over supply, demand, and prices of mineral raw materials and products that a competitive free market doesn't exist. In addition, costs of nonfuel mineral resources account for only a small percentage of the total costs of most goods. As a result, resource scarcities do not cause a large enough rise in the final price of products to encourage consumers to reduce demand soon enough to avoid depletion. Indeed, artificially low prices increase demand and encourage faster resource depletion.

Finding New Land-Based Mineral Deposits   There is little doubt that geological exploration—guided by better geological knowledge, satellite surveys, and other techniques—will extend present reserves of most minerals. According to geologists, rich deposits will probably be found in unexplored areas in LDCs; but in the MDCs and many LDCs the most easily accessible high-grade deposits have already been discovered. Remaining deposits are more difficult and more expensive to find and mine and usually are less concentrated.

Exploration for new resources, therefore, requires large capital investment and is a risky financial venture. It is difficult for someone who is not a geologist to understand the extreme difficulty of finding an economically exploitable mineral deposit, even in a favorable region. Typically, if geologic theory identifies 10,000 sites where a deposit of a particular resource might be found, only 1,000 sites are worth costly exploration; only 100 warrant even more costly drilling, trenching, or tunneling; and only 1 out of the 10,000 is likely to

The one-quarter of the world's population living in the MDCs uses 80% of the world's annual production of nonfuel minerals. Even though the LDCs are expected to have 79% of the world's population in 2000, their projected use at current rates of the world's resources is only 23%— slightly more than the 20% they currently use. Some analysts have charged that MDCs exploit LDCs that have substantial deposits of key nonfuel minerals by controlling international trade so that these LDCs are forced to sell resources at prices far below their value. LDCs back this charge by pointing out that the average per capita cost of raw materials in the United States is less than $150, only slightly higher than at the beginning of the century and lower when adjusted for inflation.

MDCs counter that when they buy raw materials from LDCs, they provide funds that the LDCs need for their own economic development. LDCs agree that selling their resources at any price helps stimulate their economic development, but they contend that being coerced into selling at such low prices primarily stimulates economic growth and resource waste in MDCs and depletes supplies of key resources the LDCs will need for their own future economic growth.

To correct this situation, LDCs have called for a new international economic order, in which a larger and fairer share of the world's wealth would be shifted from MDCs to LDCs. This proposal calls for a substantial increase in aid from industrialized countries to LDCs, including relieving LDCs of some of their massive indebtedness to MDCs, removal of trade barriers that restrict LDCs from selling some of their products to MDCs, increasing the prices paid for raw materials exported from LDCs to MDCs, and providing LDCs with greater influence in the decision making of international lending institutions, such as the World Bank and the International Monetary Fund. What do you think?

be a producing mine. Even if large new supplies are found, no mineral supply can stand up to continued exponential growth in its use. For example, a 1-billion-year supply of a resource would be exhausted in only 584 years if the level at which it was used increased at 3% a year.

Obtaining More Minerals from Seawater and the Ocean Floor   The oceans contain vast, untapped supplies of key mineral and energy resources. Potential ocean resources are found in three areas: seawater, sediments and deposits on the shallow continental shelf and slope, and sediments and nodules on the deep ocean floor. The huge quantity of seawater appears to be an inexhaustible source of minerals, but most of the 90 chemical elements found there occur in such low concentrations that it takes more energy and money to recover them than they are presently worth. For example, to get a mere 0.003% of the annual U.S. consumption of zinc from the ocean would require processing a volume of seawater equivalent to the combined annual flows of the Delaware and Hudson rivers. Only magnesium, bromine, and common table salt (sodium chloride) are abundant enough in seawater to be extracted profitably at present prices with current technology.

Offshore deposits and sediments in shallow waters are already important sources of crude oil, natural gas, sand, gravel, and ten other minerals. Extraction of these resources is limited less by supply or mining technology than by the increasing costs of the energy needed to find and remove them and the harmful effects of oil leaks and spills and extensive mining on marine food resources and wild species.

There is considerable interest in locating and removing manganese-rich rocks, or nodules, found in large quantities on the deep ocean floor at a few sites (Figure 15-3). These potato-sized nodules (Figure 15-15) contain 30% to 40% manganese (used in certain steel alloys) and small amounts of other strategically important metals such as nickel and cobalt. It is proposed that a device—much like a giant vacuum cleaner—be developed to suck these nodules up from muds of the deep ocean floor and deliver them through a three-mile-long pipe to a ship above the mining site. Environmentalists recognize that such seabed mining would probably cause less harm than mining on land. They are concerned, however, that vacuuming nodules off the seabed and stirring up deep ocean sediments could destroy seafloor organisms and have unknown effects on poorly understood deep-sea food webs; surface waters might also be polluted by the discharge of sediments from mining ships and rigs.

Economic uncertainties make it unclear whether these nodules will be extracted in the near future. There is no guarantee that metal prices will be high enough to permit a reasonable profit on such a large and risky investment, especially since ample and much cheaper supplies of these metals are expected to be available for many decades. An even greater threat is posed by international legal and political squabbles over ownership of the nodules because most large deposits are located in international waters.

Improved Mining Technology and Mining Low-Grade Deposits Cornucopians talk of improved mining technology that will allow us to drill deeper into the earth to obtain more minerals. However, the likelihood of obtaining materials from greater depths is slim because of the extreme heat and pressure at such depths and the enormous costs of locating and extracting such resources.

Cornucopians also assume that we can increase supplies of any mineral by mining increasingly lower grades of ore. They point to the fact that advances in mining technology during the past few decades have allowed the mining of low-grade deposits of some minerals—copper, for example—without significant cost increases. Neo-Malthusians point out, however, that as increasingly lower-grade deposits are mined, we eventually run into geological, energy, water, and environmental factors that place limits on the amounts of minerals that can be extracted and processed—long before actual supplies of these minerals are exhausted.

In terms of geological abundance, only iron, aluminum, magnesium, manganese, chromium, and titanium occur in large deposits ranging continuously from high grade to low grade. Another problem is that the ability to mine and process increasingly poorer grades of ore depends on an inexhaustible source of cheap energy. Indeed, the ability to locate and process lower-grade ores between 1935 and 1975 was based primarily on the availability of abundant supplies of cheap oil and natural gas. But most energy experts agree that in the future energy will neither be unlimited nor cheap. Thus, eventually we will reach a point where the cost of energy needed to mine and process a given quantity of metal from lower-grade ore is greater than the value of the metal produced.

Available supplies of fresh water may also limit the supply of some mineral resources because large amounts of water are needed to extract and process most minerals. Many areas with major mineral deposits are poorly supplied with water. Finally, exploitation of increasingly lower grades of ore may be limited by the environmental impact of the catastrophic increase in waste material produced during mining and processing. Mining and processing low-grade ores may lead to such an increase in disturbed land and pollu-

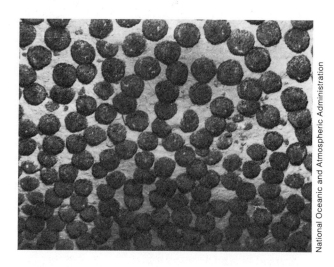

Figure 15-15 Manganese nodules found on the ocean floor.

tion of air and water that the costs of land reclamation and pollution control will eventually exceed the value of the minerals produced.

Substitution Cornucopians believe that even if supplies of key minerals become very expensive or scarce, human ingenuity will find substitutes. They argue that either plastics, high-strength glass fibers and ceramic materials made mostly from silicon (the second most abundant element in the earth's crust), or four of the most abundant metals (aluminum, iron, magnesium, and titanium) can be substituted for most scarce metals. For example, in automobiles, plastics are increasingly substituted for copper, lead, tin, and zinc. Aluminum and titanium are also replacing steel in cars and other products. Glass fibers, beginning to replace copper wires in telephone cables, weigh less, carry more information and electrical signals, and cost half as much as copper wire. Ceramic composites may soon replace important metal alloys containing elements such as cobalt and chromium, whose future supplies may be limited.

Although substitutes can probably be found for many scarce resources, there are problems. Finding substitutes and phasing them into complex manufacturing processes is costly and requires long lead times. During the transition period there could be serious economic hardships as prices of the increasingly scarce resource rise catastrophically. And finding suitable substitutes for some key materials may be extremely difficult if not impossible. Some substitutes may be inferior to the minerals they replace, and some may themselves become scarce and prohibitively expensive because of greatly increased demand.

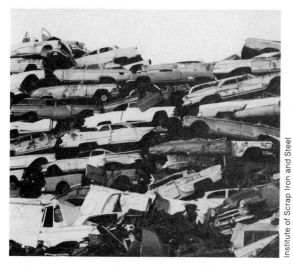
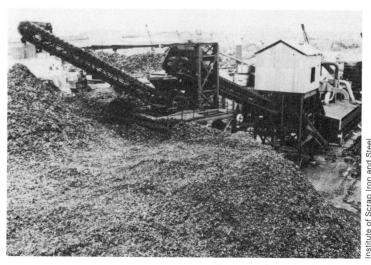

Figure 15-16 Each junk automobile will yield about 909 kilograms (1 ton) of iron and steel scrap, which can be recycled into new products.

15-5 EXTENDING MINERAL RESOURCE SUPPLIES: THE CONSERVATION APPROACH

Recycling Recycling involves collecting used resource materials such as scrap iron and aluminum and remelting and reprocessing them to produce new products. Recycling items containing iron and aluminum, which account for 94% of all metals used, as well as other nonrenewable mineral resources has a number of advantages. It extends the supply of the mineral by reducing the amount of virgin materials which must be extracted from the earth's crust to meet demand. It also usually saves energy, causes less pollution and land disruption than use of virgin resources, and cuts waste disposal costs and prolongs the life of landfills by reducing the volume of solid wastes. For example, using scrap iron (Figure 15-16) instead of iron ore to produce steel conserves virgin iron ore and coal, requires 65% less energy and 40% less water, and produces 85% less air pollution and 76% less water pollution. Recycling aluminum produces 95% less air pollution and 97% less water pollution, and requires 92% less energy than mining and processing virgin aluminum ore.

Despite these advantages, only about one-fourth of the world's iron and aluminum is recovered for recycling. Recycling rates vary in different countries, with about one-half of these two materials recycled in the Netherlands and about one-third in Japan and the United States. It is encouraging that 52% of new aluminum beverage cans used in the United States were recycled in 1986 at more than 5,000 recycling centers set up by the aluminum industry, other private interests, and local governments. People who returned the cans received slightly more than a penny per can for their efforts. But almost half of the aluminum cans produced each year are still thrown away, each equivalent to wasting half a beverage can of gasoline.

Beverage container deposit laws can be used to decrease litter and encourage recycling of nonrefillable glass and metal containers and in some cases plastic containers, which now make up 25% of the total. Consumers pay a deposit (usually a nickel) on each beverage container they purchase; deposits are refunded when containers are turned in for recycling to retailers, redemption centers, or reverse vending machines, which return cash when consumers put in empty beverage cans and bottles. By 1986, container deposit laws had been adopted in Sweden, Norway, the Netherlands, the Soviet Union, parts of Canada, and in ten states (about one-fourth of the U.S. population).

Such laws work. Experience in the United States has shown that a whopping 90% of cans and bottles are turned in for refund, litter is decreased by 70% or more, expensive landfills don't fill up as quickly, energy and mineral resources are saved, and jobs are created. Environmentalists, noting that 61% of Americans live in states with no laws to encourage recycling of beverage containers, believe a nationwide deposit law should be instituted (see Spotlight on p. 332).

In recent years. Americans have heard many slogans: "Waste is a resource out of place," "Urban waste is urban ore," "Trash is cash," "Landfills are urban mines," and "Trash cans are really resource containers." The state of New Jersey and cities such as Chicago and New York have set recycling goals of 25% by 1991. Other cities, such as Berkeley, California, and

A well-funded lobby of steel, aluminum, and glass companies, metalworkers' unions, supermarket chains, and most major brewers and soft drink bottlers has vigorously opposed passage of a national beverage container deposit law as well as such laws in individual states. Merchants don't like to have returned bottles and cans piling up in their stores. Labor unions are afraid that some workers in bottle and can manufacturing industries will lose their jobs. Beverage makers fear the extra nickel deposit per container will hurt sales. Some consumers think returning containers is just too much trouble. They would rather toss their cans and bottles away and let someone else worry about them—out of sight out of mind.

"Keep America Beautiful" and other expensive ad campaigns financed by these groups have helped prevent passage of container deposit laws in a number of states. These industries favor litter-recycling laws, which levy a tax on industries whose products pose a potential threat as litter or landfill clutter. Revenues from the tax are used to establish and maintain statewide recycling centers. By 1986 seven states, containing about 14% of the U.S. population, had this type of law.

Environmentalists point out that surveys indicate that litter taxes are not nearly as effective as beverage container deposit laws. EPA and General Accounting Office studies estimate that a national container deposit law would have a number of desirable effects, including saving consumers at least $1 billion annually. Roadside beverage container litter would be reduced by 60% to 70%, saving taxpayers money now used for cleanup. Urban solid waste would be reduced by at least 1%, saving taxpayers $25 million to $50 million a year in waste disposal costs. Mining and processing of virgin aluminum ore would be decreased by 53% to 74% and the use of iron ore by 45% to 83%. Air, water, and solid waste pollution from the beverage industry would drop by 44% to 86%, and the energy saved would be equivalent to that needed to provide the annual electrical needs for 2 million to 7.7 million homes. There would also be a net increase of 80,000 to 100,000 jobs—collecting and refilling beverage containers is more labor-intensive than producing new ones. Surveys have shown that such a law is supported by 73% of the Americans polled. What do you think?

Portland, Oregon, aim at recycling 50% of their waste materials and now recycle about 22%. Nevertheless, only about 10% of all potentially recoverable waste material in the United States is now recycled—compared to 40% to 60% in densely populated countries such as Japan and the Netherlands, which import most of their fuel and nonfuel minerals. Recycling rates are also high in some LDCs such as Mexico, India, and China, where small armies of poor people go through urban garbage disposal sites by hand. They remove paper and sell it to paper mills, metal scraps to metal-processing factories, bones to glue factories, and rags to furniture factories for use in upholstery.

Obstacles to Recycling in the United States   Several factors have hindered recycling efforts in the United States. One is the failure of many U.S. metals industries to modernize. Since 1950, countries such as Japan and West Germany built new steel plants based on modern processes that use large amounts of scrap steel, much of it bought from the United States. During the same period the U.S. steel industry did not reinvest much of its profits in modernizing and replacing older plants and continued to rely heavily on older processes that require virgin iron ore. As a result, the industry has now lost much of its business to foreign competitors and no longer has the capital to modernize—illustrating how overemphasis on short-term economic gain can lead to long-term economic pain, decline, and loss of jobs for thousands of Americans.

Despite increased awareness of the need for recycling, most Americans have been conditioned by advertising and example to a throwaway lifestyle designed to increase short-term economic growth regardless of the long-term environmental and economic costs (Figure 15-17). Waste collection and disposal costs account for a major portion of local tax revenue expenditures. Consumers pay for these costs indirectly in the form of higher taxes rather than directly by a waste disposal tax placed on all recoverable items. As a result, consumers have no easily identifiable economic incentive to recycle and conserve recoverable resources.

Growth of the recycling or secondary-materials industry in the United States is hindered by tax breaks,

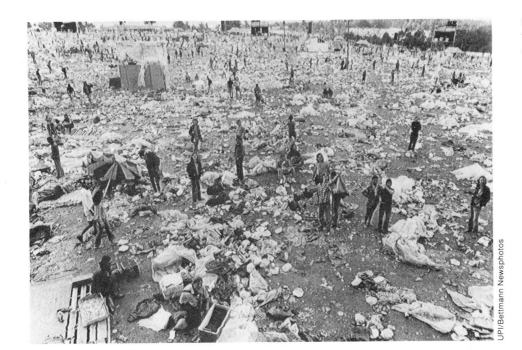

UPI/Bettmann Newsphotos

Figure 15-17 Evidence of the throwaway mentality at the site of an outdoor rock concert.

depletion allowances, and other tax-supported federal subsidies of primary mining and energy industries, designed to encourage them to get virgin resources out of the ground as fast as possible. In contrast, recycling industries receive relatively few tax breaks and other subsidies. Recycling is also discouraged by higher railroad and truck shipping rates for most scrap materials (especially glass and paper) than for virgin materials. The lack of large, steady markets for recycled materials makes recycling industries risky, "boom-and-bust" financial ventures that don't attract large amounts of investment capital.

With economic and political incentives to encourage recycling, the United States could easily recycle half and perhaps two-thirds of the matter resources it uses each year. Such a shift could be accomplished over a ten-year period through the following measures: **(1)** including waste disposal costs in the price of all items, **(2)** providing favorable federal and state subsidies for secondary-materials industries, **(3)** decreasing subsidies for primary-materials industries, **(4)** encouraging federal, state, and local governments to require the highest feasible percentage of recycled materials in all products they purchase, thus guaranteeing a sufficient market to encourage investment, and **(5)** using advertising and education to discourage the throwaway mentality.

Reusable Containers   Reuse involves employing the same product over and over again in its original form, as in the case of beverage bottles that can be collected, washed, and refilled by bottling companies. Reuse extends resource supplies and reduces energy use and

pollution even more than recycling. For example, it takes three times more energy to crush and remelt a glass bottle to make a new one than it does to clean and refill it. It also takes far less energy to clean and refill a bottle than it does to melt a recycled aluminum can and make a new one. If reusable bottles replaced the 80 billion throwaway beverage cans produced annually in the United States, enough energy would be saved to provide electricity for 13 million people.

Instead, about 85% of all U.S. beverage containers are nonreusable bottles and cans, which are either thrown away or recycled. Environmentalists strongly support a national beverage container deposit bill as a step in the right direction, but they would like to go further and ban all nonreusable beverage containers as has been done in Denmark.

The Low-Waste Society: Beyond Recycling and Reuse   In addition to increased recycling and reuse of nonfuel mineral resources, environmentalists also call for increased resource conservation, especially in MDCs, to reduce unnecessary waste of matter and energy resources. They call for the United States and other MDCs to shift from a high-waste society (Figure 3-18, p. 65) to a sustainable-earth society—a low-waste society based on recycling, reuse, and resource conservation (Figure 3-19, p. 66).

Reducing unnecessary waste of nonrenewable mineral resources can extend supplies even more dramatically than recycling and reuse. Furthermore, recycling and reuse require energy. Thus, at some point the supply of energy resources and the environmental impacts associated with their use can limit resource

Table 15-2 Three Systems for Handling Discarded Materials

Item	For a High-Waste Throwaway System	For a Moderate-Waste Resource Recovery and Recycling System	For a Low-Waste Sustainable-Earth System
Glass bottles	Dump or bury	Grind and remelt; remanufacture; convert to building materials	Ban all nonreturnable bottles and reuse (not remelt and recycle) bottles
Bimetallic "tin" cans	Dump or bury	Sort, remelt	Limit or ban production; use returnable bottles
Aluminum cans	Dump or bury	Sort, remelt	Limit or ban production; use returnable bottles
Cars	Dump	Sort, remelt	Sort, remelt; tax cars lasting less than 15 years, weighing more than 818 kilograms (1,800 pounds), and getting less than 13 kilometers per liter (30 miles per gallon)
Metal objects	Dump or bury	Sort, remelt	Sort, remelt; tax items lasting less than 10 years
Tires	Dump, burn, or bury	Grind and revulcanize or use in road construction; incinerate to generate heat and electricity	Recap usable tires; tax all tires not usable for at least 64,400 kilometers (40,000 miles)
Paper	Dump, burn, or bury	Incinerate to generate heat	Compost or recycle; tax all throwaway items; eliminate overpackaging
Plastics	Dump, burn, or bury	Incinerate to generate heat or electricity	Limit production; use returnable glass bottles instead of plastic containers; tax throwaway items and packaging
Garden wastes	Dump, burn, or bury	Incinerate to generate heat or electricity	Compost; return to soil as fertilizer; use as animal feed

recycling and reuse. Table 15-2 compares the present throwaway resource system used in the United States, a resource recovery and recycling system, and a sustainable-earth or low-waste resource system.

Manufacturers can conserve resources by using less resource per product. For example, the trend toward smaller and lighter cars saves nonfuel mineral resources and also saves energy by increasing gas mileage. Solid-state electronic devices and microwave transmissions have significantly reduced materials requirements. The transistor, for example, requires about one-millionth the material needed to make the vacuum tube it replaces. Optical fibers drastically reduce the demand for copper and aluminum wire.

Another approach is to produce products that last longer. The economies of the United States and most industrial countries are built on the principle of planned obsolescence. Product lives are designed to be much shorter than they could be so that people will buy more things to stimulate the economy and raise short-term profits. Many consumers can empathize with Willy Loman, the main character in Arthur Miller's play *Death of a Salesman*: "Once in my life I would like to own something outright before it's broken! I'm always in a race with the junkyard."

In addition to lasting longer, products could be designed so that they could be repaired easily. Presently many items are intentionally designed to make repair impossible or prohibitively expensive, even

though the broken or worn part may represent only a small percentage of the value of the product. The modular design of computers and other electronic devices allows certain circuits to be easily and quickly replaced without replacing the entire item. This is a step in the right direction. Another step is to develop remanufacturing industries, which would disassemble, repair or improve, and reassemble used and broken items. New products could be designed to facilitate remanufacturing.

Some argue that a shift away from a production-disposal, high-waste society to a service-repair, low-waste society will result in a loss of jobs and economic decline. Actually, the reverse is true. The loss of profits and jobs in increasingly automated, machine-intensive production will be more than offset by the increase in profits and jobs in labor-intensive service, repair, and recycling businesses. Such a shift may also have social rewards—service, repair, and recycling jobs involve many more human interactions than do highly automated production jobs. The challenge is to learn how to have satisfying, rewarding, and healthy lives while using and wasting less of our irreplaceable nonrenewable-resource capital.

Solid wastes are only raw materials we're too stupid to use.

Arthur C. Clarke

CHAPTER SUMMARY

Human ingenuity has found ways to locate and extract more than 100 nonrenewable nonfuel minerals from *mineral deposits* in the earth's crust. Use of a mineral resource involves several steps: locating a rich-enough deposit, extracting the mineral by some form of mining, processing the mineral to remove impurities and to convert it to the desired chemical form, and using the mineral directly or manufactured into various products.

Mineral deposits located near the earth's surface are removed by *open-pit surface mining, area strip mining,* or *contour strip mining,* depending on the type of mineral and local topography. A mineral deposit that lies deep in the ground is extracted by *subsurface mining,* which—though more dangerous and expensive than surface mining—disturbs far less land. Surface-mined land can be restored in most cases, except arid and semiarid land, but is expensive.

Estimating how much of a particular nonrenewable resource exists on earth and how much of it can be located and extracted at an affordable price is a complex and controversial process. Supplies of a mineral resource are divided into *identified resources* and *undiscovered resources.* These two categories are then subdivided into *reserves* (identified resources that can be extracted profitably at present prices with current mining technology) and *resources* (identified and unidentified resources that cannot be recovered profitably with present prices and technology). Most published estimates of a particular nonrenewable mineral refer to reserves.

When 80% of the reserves or estimated resources of a mineral have been extracted and used, the resource is said to be depleted because removing the remaining 20% is usually not profitable. The amount available and thus the depletion time can be increased by an increase in the estimated reserves when costs rise to the point that resources are converted to reserves by recycling, reuse, and reduced consumption.

According to official estimates, the United States has adequate domestic reserves of most key minerals—except chromium, cobalt, platinum, tin, gold, and palladium. Cornucopians believe that world supplies of key minerals can be increased as needed by increasing mineral exploration, improving mining technology, mining lower-grade (less concentrated) ores, and finding substitutes for scarce resources.

Neo-Malthusians agree that supplies can be increased but believe that rising energy and pollution control costs may limit the use of many key resources long before their potentially recoverable supplies run out. Even if enough minerals can be found and produced, many LDCs fear that most of these resources will be used to sustain increasingly greater economic growth by the MDCs, so that many LDCs will never become developed. To extend supplies environmentalists favor greatly increased recycling and reusing of nonrenewable mineral resources and reducing unnecessary waste of such resources. Recycling, reuse, and reducing wasteful consumption also require less energy resources and produce less land degradation and air and water pollution than use of virgin resources.

Despite these advantages, only about 10% of the recyclable nonrenewable mineral resources in the United States are recycled, compared to recycling rates of 40% in countries such as the Netherlands and Japan, which must depend on other countries for most of their supplies. Factors hindering recycling in the United States include (1) failure of U.S. industries to install new processes that make use of recycled iron, steel, paper, and other materials; (2) a throwaway lifestyle designed to increase short-term economic growth; (3) tax breaks, depletion allowances, and other tax-supported federal subsidies designed to encourage mining industries to get virgin resource out of the ground as fast as possible; (4) lack of similar incentives for recycling and reuse of materials; and (5) lack of large, steady markets for recycled materials. Environmentalists call for the United States to shift from a high-waste, throwaway society to a sustainable-earth, low-waste society by reversing these factors.

DISCUSSION TOPICS

1. Why should an urban dweller be concerned about the environmental impact from increasing surface mining of land for mineral resources?

2. Debate the following resolution: The United States is an overdeveloped country that uses and unnecessarily wastes too many of the world's resources relative to its population size.

3. What resources are mined in your local area? What mining methods are used? Do local, state, or federal laws require restoration of the landscape after mining is completed? If so, how well are these laws enforced?

4. Summarize the neo-Malthusian and cornucopian views on availability of nonrenewable mineral resources. Which, if either, of these schools of thought do you support? Why?

5. Explain the differences between reserves and resources.

6. Debate each of the following propositions:
   a. The competitive free market will control the supply and demand of mineral resources.
   b. New discoveries will provide all the raw materials we need.
   c. The ocean will provide all the mineral resources we need.
   d. We will not run out of key mineral resources because we can always mine lower-grade deposits.
   e. When a mineral resource becomes scarce, we can always find a substitute.
   f. When a nonrenewable resource becomes scarce, all we have to do is recycle it.

7. Use the second law of energy (thermodynamics) to show why the following options are normally not profitable:
   a. extracting most minerals dissolved in seawater
   b. recycling minerals that are widely dispersed
   c. mining increasingly low-grade deposits of minerals
   d. using inexhaustible solar energy to mine minerals
   e. continuing to mine, use, and recycle minerals at increasing rates

8. Explain why you support or oppose the following:
   a. eliminating all tax breaks and depletion allowances for extraction of virgin resources by mining industries
   b. passing a national beverage container deposit bill
   c. requiring that all beverage containers be reusable

9. Compare the throwaway, recycling, and sustainable-earth (or low-waste) approaches to waste disposal and resource recovery and conservation for (a) glass bottles, (b) "tin" cans, (c) aluminum cans, (d) plastics, and (e) leaves, grass, and food wastes (see Table 15-2).

10. Why is it difficult to get accurate estimates of mineral resource supplies?

16

Nonrenewable Energy Resources: Fossil Fuels

GENERAL OBJECTIVES

1. How have humans used various sources of energy throughout history?

2. What criteria can we use to evaluate present and future energy resource alternatives?

3. What are the major uses, advantages, and disadvantages of oil as an energy resource?

4. What are the major uses, advantages, and disadvantages of natural gas as an energy resource?

5. What are the major uses, advantages, and disadvantages of coal as an energy resource?

We are an interdependent world and if we ever needed a lesson in that we got it in the oil crisis of the 1970s.

Robert S. McNamara

Useful high-quality energy is the lifeblood of human societies—driving virtually all activities that shape individual lifestyles and national and world economic systems. Today about 82% of the world's commercial energy, used to supplement the 99% of all of the earth's energy provided by the sun, is obtained from *nonrenewable* and rapidly decreasing supplies of oil, natural gas, and coal. Once the concentrated, high-quality energy in these fuels is used, it is gone forever on a human time scale.

This chapter examines the history of energy use in the world and the United States, criteria for evaluating present and future energy alternatives, and advantages and disadvantages of using nonrenewable fossil fuels. The two chapters that follow evaluate nonrenewable nuclear and geothermal energy (Chapter 17) and perpetual and renewable energy resources (Chapter 18).

16-1 BRIEF HISTORY OF ENERGY USE

Primitive to Modern Times In each phase of cultural history (Chapter 2) human ingenuity has increased the average amount of energy used per person to supplement the direct input of solar energy (Figure 16-1). In the 1700s, when the Industrial Revolution began, most of the energy used by the United States and other industrializing countries came from perpetual and renewable sources (domesticated animal labor, wood, flowing water, and wind), mostly from locally available supplies.

By 1850 wood provided about 91% of the commercial energy used in industrializing European countries and the United States (Figure 16-2). By 1900 coal replaced wood as the major energy resource in such countries, primarily because of new coal-mining technology and because coal was a more concentrated (higher-quality) source of energy.

Since 1910 oil and natural gas have replaced coal for many uses because they burn cleaner and are easier and cheaper to transport than coal and because oil, unlike coal, can be refined to produce liquid fuels for vehicles. By 1984 about 82% of the commercial energy used throughout the world and 91% of that used in the United States was provided primarily by the burning of three nonrenewable fossil fuels—oil, coal, and natural gas—and a small amount by the nuclear fission of nonrenewable uranium atoms to produce electricity (Figures 16-2 and 16-3). The remaining 18% of the world's energy and 9% of that in the United States was provided by *perpetual* and *renewable* direct and indirect solar energy resources—mostly biomass (wood, dung, and crop residues) and hydropower.

Thus, between 1700 and 1984, today's MDCs shifted from a decentralized energy system based on locally available renewable and perpetual resources to a centralized energy system based on nonrenewable fossil fuels (especially oil and natural gas) increasingly produced in one part of the world and transported to and used in another part. This shift fueled the rapid economic development of the MDCs, especially since 1950. At the same time, this fossil-fuel age has made most MDCs dependent on a finite resource base that is being rapidly exhausted. It has also meant that countries, communities, and individuals, who once obtained most of the energy they needed from local resources, are now dependent on large national and multinational energy companies, government policies, and other countries for most of their energy and the prices they must pay.

Energy Use and Problems in Less Developed Countries   Most increases in energy consumption per person since 1900 have taken place in MDCs, and the gap in average energy use per person between the MDCs and LDCs has widened (Figure 16-4). At one extreme, in 1984 the United States, with about 5% of the world's population, accounted for 25% of the world's commercial energy consumption. At the other extreme, India, with about 15% of the world's people, used only about 1.5% of the world's commercial energy. In 1986 the 241 million Americans used more energy for air conditioning alone than the 1.05 billion Chinese used for all purposes.

The most important source of energy for LDCs is potentially renewable biomass—especially fuelwood

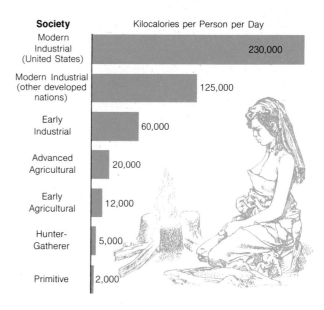

Figure 16-1   Average direct and indirect daily energy use per person at various stages of human cultural development.

—which serves as the main source of energy for roughly half the world's population. This information fails to show up in summaries of world commercial energy use, which are distorted by the massive energy consumption in MDCs and the fact that much fuelwood is gathered by rural people and thus not sold commercially.

While the one-fourth of the world's population in MDCs worries about future shortages of oil, half the world's population already faces a fuelwood shortage energy crisis because of widespread deforestation by logging companies, farmers, and poor people stripping land of firewood for short-term survival. Without adequate replanting, deforestation gradually converts this vital renewable energy resource to a nonrenewable one. About one of every six people on earth also faces a food shortage energy crisis on a daily basis. This shortage results not so much from insufficient food production worldwide but from poverty, which prevents these people from growing or buying sufficient food for good health.

The Oil Crisis of the 1970s   By 1940 the depletion of many low-cost domestic oil deposits made it cheaper for the United States to import much of its oil. During 1973 the United States imported about 30% of its oil (Figure 16-5), with almost half of this coming from the 13 countries in the Organization of Petroleum Export-

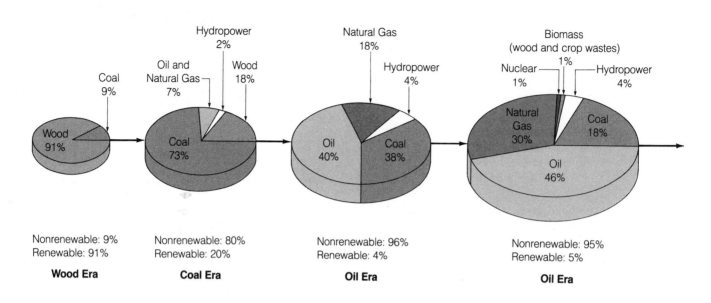

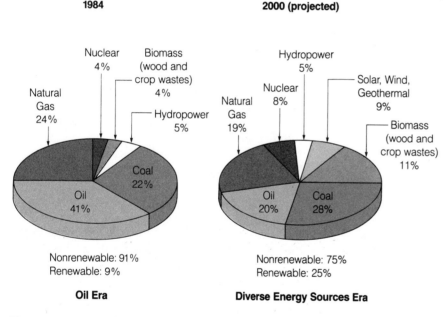

Figure 16-2 Changes in consumption of commercial nonrenewable (shaded) and renewable (unshaded) energy resources in the United States between 1850 and 1984 with a projection for the year 2000. Relative circle size indicates the total amount of energy used. (Sources: U.S. Department of Energy and Center for Renewable Resources; National Audubon Society for 2000 A.D. projection)

ing Countries (OPEC).* Other MDCs, such as Japan and most western European countries, are even more dependent on imported oil than the United States because their domestic supplies are scant or non-existent.

---

*OPEC was formed in 1960 at the urging of Venezuela. Today its 13 member countries are Algeria, Ecuador, Gabon, Indonesia, Iran, Iraq, Kuwait, Libya, Nigeria, Qatar, Saudi Arabia, United Arab Emirates, and Venezuela.

By 1973 the OPEC countries, with 57% of the world's proven oil reserves (compared to only 4% for the United States), accounted for 56% of the world's oil production and about 84% of all oil exports. Saudi Arabia, with the largest and most accessible oil reserves, can produce oil cheaper than any other country at costs ranging from 20 cents a barrel from old fields to no more than $3 from newer fields. By comparison, it costs Norway and Great Britain from $5 to $9 a barrel

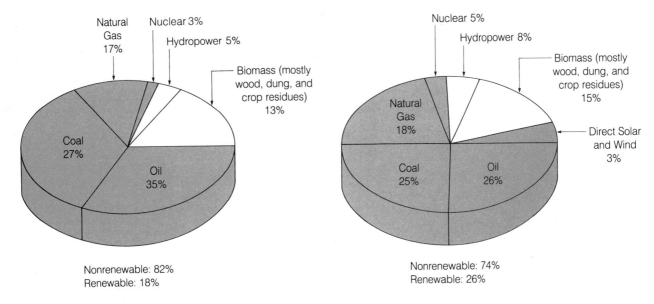

1984

Natural Gas 17%
Nuclear 3%
Hydropower 5%
Biomass (mostly wood, dung, and crop residues) 13%
Coal 27%
Oil 35%

Nonrenewable: 82%
Renewable: 18%

2000 (projected)

Nuclear 5%
Hydropower 8%
Biomass (mostly wood, dung, and crop residues) 15%
Natural Gas 18%
Direct Solar and Wind 3%
Coal 25%
Oil 26%

Nonrenewable: 74%
Renewable: 26%

Figure 16-3 World consumption of commercial nonrenewable (shaded) and renewable (nonshaded) energy by source in 1984 with projections for 2000. (Sources: U.S. Department of Energy and Worldwatch Institute)

to produce oil from the North Sea. Mexico's production cost is $5 to $7 a barrel, and in the United States costs range from $5 a barrel in old fields to $12 a barrel from offshore wells.

This dependence of most MDCs on OPEC countries for imported oil set the stage for the first phase of the oil crisis of the 1970s. On October 18, 1973, during the 18-day "Yom Kippur War" against Israel by Egypt and Syria, the Arab members of OPEC reduced oil exports to Western industrial countries and prohibited all shipments of their oil to the United States because of its support of Israel. The embargo lasted until March 1974 and caused a fivefold increase in the average world price of crude oil (Figure 16-6), contributing to double-digit inflation in the United States and many other countries, high interest rates, soaring international debt, and a global economic recession. Americans accustomed to cheap and plentiful fuel waited for hours to buy gasoline and turned down the thermostats in homes and offices.

Despite the sharp price increase, U.S. dependence on imported oil increased from 30% to 48% between 1973 and 1977, with the percentage of oil imported from OPEC increasing from 48% to 67% during the same period. The increased dependence resulted primarily from the government's failure to lift oil price controls that kept prices artificially low and discouraged energy conservation. This false message to consumers set the stage for the second phase of the oil crisis, when available world oil supplies again

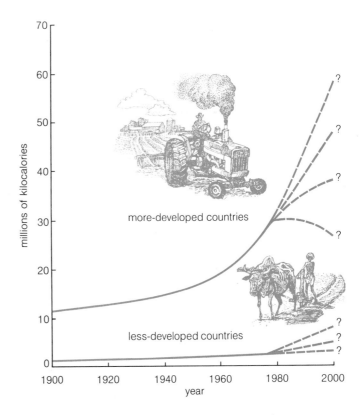

Figure 16-4 Average annual energy consumption per person in the MDCs and LDCs between 1900 and 1984 and four projections (dashed lines) to 2000. (Sources: U.S. Department of Energy and International Energy Agency)

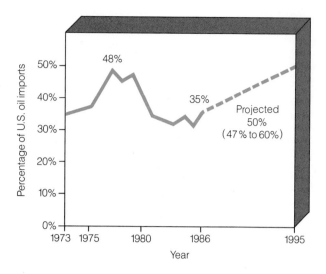

Figure 16-5 Percentage of U.S. oil imported between 1973 and 1986 with projections to 1995. (Data from U.S. Department of Energy and Spears and Associates, Tulsa, Okla.)

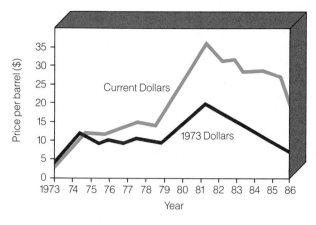

Figure 16-6 Average world crude oil prices between 1973 and 1986. (Data from Department of Energy and Department of Commerce)

decreased in 1979 after the revolution in Iran shut down most of that country's production. Gasoline waiting lines became even longer, and by 1981 the average world price of crude oil rose to about $35 a barrel.

The oil crisis of the 1970s was not due to an actual physical shortage of oil. Instead, it resulted from the significant control held by OPEC over the world's supply, distribution, and price of oil. This situation arose from several factors: **(1)** the rapid and significant economic growth of MDCs during the 1960s, stimulated primarily by low oil prices, often held down by government price controls; **(2)** the greatly increased use of oil worldwide with little concern until 1979 for reducing unnecessary use and waste; and **(3)** the heavy dependence of most MDCs on oil imports from OPEC nations, which have most of the world's proven and unproven oil reserves and the capability to produce oil at much lower prices than most MDCs.

The Oil Glut of the 1980s   Between 1979 and 1982 a combination of energy conservation (the biggest factor), substitution of other energy sources for oil, increased oil production by non-OPEC countries (such as Mexico and Great Britain), and several years of worldwide economic recession led to a 10% drop in world oil consumption. By 1982 these factors and disagreements among OPEC countries that prevented them from reducing production enough to sustain high prices led to an oversupply of oil. As a result, the average price of crude oil dropped from $35 a barrel in 1981 to slightly below $15 a barrel in 1986. This meant that inflation-adjusted crude oil prices in 1986 were about the same as those in 1974. As a result, between 1978 and 1986, OPEC's share of the world oil

market dropped from 48% to about 27%. This oil glut has had good and bad effects (see Spotlight on p. 341).

The Next Oil Crisis   Although the oil glut of the 1980s has had some good short-term effects, it could lead to long-term economic disaster for the United States and other oil-importing countries in the next 10 or 20 years. Most energy analysts believe that the oil glut of the 1980s is only temporary and project significant increases in the price of oil—perhaps rising to at least $32 a barrel and perhaps as high as $98 a barrel—sometime between 1990 and 2015, when world oil use is projected to increase to the point where demand exceeds supply. When this happens, the OPEC countries, with 57% of the world's proven oil reserves and 23% of the estimated undiscovered supplies, are projected to increase their share of the world's oil market from 27% in 1986 to 60% in the 1990s, again dominating world oil markets and prices.

Because of falling domestic production since 1970, the Department of Energy and most major oil companies project that by 1995 the United States could be dependent on imported oil for 60% of its oil consumption—much higher than in 1977 (Figure 16-5). This situation would drain the already debt-ridden United States of vast amounts of money, leading to severe inflation and widespread economic recession, perhaps even a major depression. The Congressional Research Service warns that an increase in the price of oil to between $50 and $98 a barrel could reduce the U.S. GNP by as much as 29%, cut jobs by as much as 28%, and increase the likelihood of war as the world's MDCs competed for greater control over oil supplies to avoid total economic collapse.

The sharp drop in oil prices between 1982 and 1986 (Figure 16-6) had a number of benefits for MDCs such as the United States and for LDCs heavily dependent on imported oil: stimulation of economic growth (except in the oil industry), creation of new jobs (except in the oil industry), and reduction of the rate of inflation.

At the same time, the price drop had a number of undesirable effects: **(1)** a sharp decrease in the search for new oil in the United States and most other countries; **(2)** economic chaos in many oil-producing countries, especially those with large international debts such as Mexico, and in major oil-producing states such as Texas, Oklahoma, and Louisiana; **(3)** loss of many jobs in the oil and related industries; **(4)** failure or near failure of many U.S. banks with massive outstanding loans to oil companies and oil-producing LDCs such as Mexico, which had a $97 billion debt by 1986; and **(5)** reduction in the rate of improvements in energy efficiency and decreased development of energy alternatives to replace oil within 50 to 60 years, when the world is projected to begin facing true physical shortages of affordable oil.

When world oil prices drop below $15 a barrel, countries with relatively high oil-producing costs, such as Norway, Great Britain, Mexico, Canada, and the United States, find little profit in producing and selling oil from newer wells, located mostly in inaccessible and hostile areas such as the North Sea, the Gulf Coast, and northern Alaska. When prices reach $10 a barrel or lower, oil companies lose money from such wells and oil exploration and production drops sharply. This slowdown along with decreasing efforts to reduce unnecessary energy waste can make the United States—the world's largest importer of oil—and other oil-importing MDCs vulnerable to sharp rises in oil prices in the future.

Thus, without greatly increased efforts to reduce energy waste and develop alternatives to oil, the short-term economic bonanza of cheap oil in the 1980s could turn into long-term economic disaster in the 1990s or the first decade of the next century. Unfortunately, since 1981 the United States has done little to prepare for a future oil crisis. As low oil and gasoline prices lulled most consumers and elected officials into a false sense of security, polls showed that less than 5% of the American public listed energy as an important national problem.

16-2   EVALUATING ENERGY RESOURCES

Future Energy Resources   There is considerable controversy over which mix of energy alternatives should be developed to provide most of the energy we need in the future. As we near the end of the world's affordable supplies of oil and perhaps of natural gas, some energy experts call for increased use of nonrenewable coal—the world's most abundant fossil fuel—to produce electricity and high-temperature heat for industrial processes and as a source of synthetic gas and liquid fuels (synfuels) for use in home heating and motor vehicles. Others call for greatly increased dependence on nonrenewable nuclear fission to produce electricity and eventually on almost inexhaustible nuclear fusion, when and if it can be developed (Section 3-2 and Chapter 17).

Conservationists believe that either alternative is the wrong way to go; both coal and nuclear power would keep us dependent on centralized, nonrenewable energy resources that are undesirable from long-term economic, social, environmental, and national security viewpoints. Instead, conservationists call for an energy strategy based on greatly increased energy efficiency to extend remaining fossil fuel supplies long enough to phase in a variety of renewable and perpetual energy sources based primarily on locally available supplies (Figures 16-2 and 16-3 and Chapter 18).

Questions to Ask   To determine which mix of energy alternatives might provide energy for the future, it is necessary to think and plan in three time frames that cover the 50-year period normally needed to develop and phase in new energy resources: the short term (1988 to 1998), the intermediate term (1998 to 2008), and the long term (2008 to 2038).

First we must decide how much we need, or want, of various kinds of energy, such as low-temperature heat, high-temperature heat, electricity, and liquid fuels for transportation (see Figure 3-8, p. 54, and the Guest

Figure 16-7 Oil and natural gas are usually found together beneath a dome of impermeable cap rock.

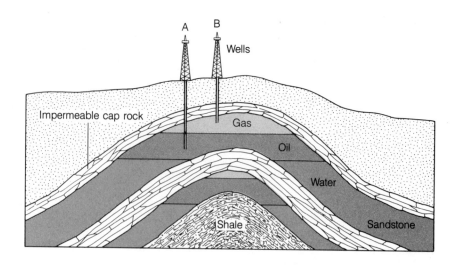

Essay at the end of this chapter). The next step is to project the mix of energy alternatives—including improving energy efficiency—that provide the necessary energy services at the lowest cost and most acceptable environmental impacts. Thus, for each energy alternative, we need to know **(1)** the total estimated supply available in each time frame, **(2)** the estimated net useful energy yield (Section 3-6), **(3)** the projected costs of development and lifetime use, and **(4)** the potential environmental impacts.

Environmental Impact of Energy Alternatives Energy policy is environmental policy because the use of most energy resources has a number of adverse environmental impacts. Energy use is directly or indirectly responsible for most land disruption, air pollution, and water pollution. For example, nearly 80% of all U.S. air pollution is caused by fuel combustion in cars, furnaces, industries, and power plants. In 1984, coal and nuclear power plants used about 45% of all the water withdrawn from surface and subsurface sources. This water, used for cooling, was far greater than the proportion used by all U.S. agriculture for irrigation.

Choosing any single energy option or mix involves making trade-offs between several different potential environmental impacts based on risk-benefit analysis (see Case Study at the end of Chapter 6). The major environmental impacts for each energy alternative are discussed in the remainder of this chapter and in the two chapters that follow. Most analysts believe that the two greatest global threats from present energy use are **(1)** possible changes in global climate from carbon dioxide emitted when any fossil fuel—especially coal and synthetic gaseous and liquid fuels produced from coal—is burned, and **(2)** potential large-scale release of long-lived radioactive materials into

the environment from one or more nuclear power plant accidents or inadequate storage of radioactive wastes.

16-3   OIL

Conventional Crude Oil   A gooey liquid, **crude oil** or **petroleum** is made up mostly of hydrocarbon compounds (90% to 95% of its weight) and small quantities of compounds containing oxygen, sulfur, and nitrogen. Typically, deposits of crude oil and natural gas are trapped together deep underground, beneath a dome of impermeable cap rock and above a lower dome of sedimentary rock such as shale, with the natural gas lying above the crude oil (Figure 16-7). Normally the crude oil is dispersed throughout pores and cracks of the underground rock formation, much like water filling a sponge. Crude oil is also found beneath the seafloor.

If there is enough pressure from water and natural gas under the dome of rock, some of the crude oil will be pushed to the surface when the well is drilled. However, such wells, called gushers, are relatively rare. **Primary oil recovery** involves pumping out all of the oil in gushers and other deposits that will flow by gravity into the hole. When this oil has been removed, water can be injected into the well to force out some of the remaining crude oil. This is known as **secondary oil recovery.** Usually, primary and secondary recovery remove only about one-third of the crude oil in a well.

Two barrels of a thicker oil, called **heavy oil,** are left in a typical well for each barrel removed by primary and secondary recovery. As oil prices rise, it may become economical to remove about 10% of the heavy oil by **enhanced oil recovery.** For example, steam can be forced into the well to soften the heavy oil so that

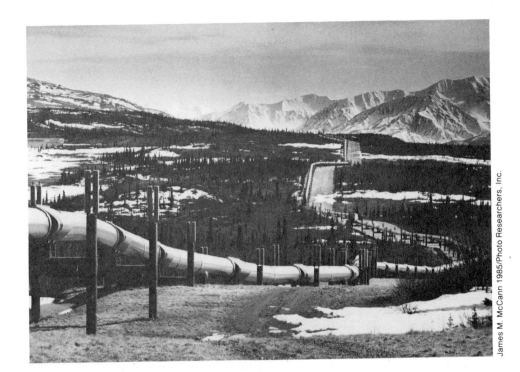

Figure 16-8 More than half of the Trans-Alaskan oil pipeline is located in arctic tundra and is built above ground and held in place by supports buried deep in the permafrost. Fins on top of these supports radiate heat away and reduce permafrost melting.

James M. McCann 1985/Photo Researchers, Inc.

it can be pumped to the surface; or some of the heavy oil can be ignited to increase the flow rate of the surrounding oil so that it can be pumped to the surface. But enhanced oil recovery processes are expensive and require the energy equivalent of one-third of a barrel of oil to pump each barrel to the surface, thus reducing the net useful energy yield. Additional energy is needed to increase the flow rate and remove impurities, especially sulfur and nitrogen compounds, before the heavy oil can be sent via pipeline to an oil refinery. Recoverable heavy oil from known U.S. crude oil reserves could supply U.S. oil needs for only about seven years at 1984 usage rates.

Throughout the United States some 357,000 kilometers (223,000 miles) of pipelines transport crude oil from wells to refineries. The largest and most expensive is the $9 billion 1275-kilometer (800-mile) Trans-Alaska Pipeline, which transports crude oil from North America's largest oil field in northern Alaska to the port of Valdez in southern Alaska (see Figure 16-15 on p. 350), where the oil is loaded on tankers for shipment mostly to West Coast ports. This pipeline crosses three mountain ranges, 34 major rivers and streams, several zones of intense earthquake activity, and large areas of arctic tundra underlain by permafrost (Figure 16-8).

At the refinery crude oil is distilled to separate it into component chemicals, which boil at different temperatures and are removed from various levels of giant distillation columns (Figure 16-9). Some of these chemicals, known as **petrochemicals,** are sent to petrochemical plants for use as raw materials in the manufacture of most industrial chemicals, fertilizers, pesticides, plastics, synthetic fibers, paints, medicines, and numerous other products. Production of these vital petrochemicals requires 3% of the world's fossil fuel production and 7% of U.S. production. This use of oil explains why the prices of a wide range of products based on petrochemicals correspondingly rise after crude oil prices rise.

How Long Will Supplies of Conventional Crude Oil Last? Figure 16-10 shows the uneven distribution of the world's proven reserves of crude oil, natural gas, and coal. OPEC is expected to have long-term control over world oil supplies and prices because most of the world's oil reserves are in the Middle East, whereas most oil consumption takes place in North America, western Europe, and Japan. Saudi Arabia alone has 25% of the world's proven oil reserves. Figure 16-11 shows the locations of the major crude oil and natural gas fields in the United States. Most are in Texas, Louisiana, and Oklahoma and in the continental shelf of the Pacific, Atlantic, Gulf, and Alaskan coasts.

Experts disagree over how long identified and unidentified crude oil resources will last. Cornucopians argue that higher prices will stimulate the location and extraction of unidentified crude oil resources, as

Figure 16-9 Refining of crude oil: Major components are removed at various levels, depending on their boiling points, in a giant distillation column.

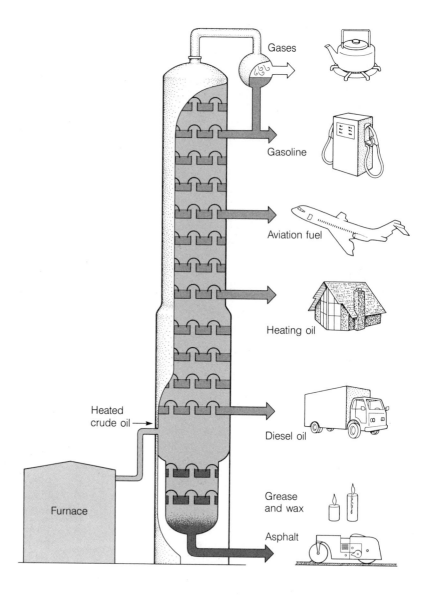

well as the extraction and upgrading of heavy oils from oil shale and tar sands and from oil too thick to pump out of existing oil wells. They point out that global proven oil reserves increased almost ninefold between 1950 and 1973.

Neo-Malthusians, however, argue that cornucopians misunderstand the arithmetic and consequences of exponential growth in the use of any nonrenewable resource. They point out that between 1973 and 1986, global proven oil reserves increased by only 5%, despite much higher oil prices and greatly increased exploration between 1973 and 1980. According to estimates by the U.S. Department of Energy and the American Petroleum Institute, the world's known reserves of crude oil will be 80% depleted by 2013 if annual oil consumption remains at the 1984 rate and by 2006 if the annual depletion rate increases by a modest 2%.

Consider the following implications of the world's present exponential growth in oil use: Assuming the 1984 rate of crude oil consumption is maintained, **(1)**

Saudi Arabia, with the world's largest known crude oil reserves, could supply the world's total needs for only ten years if it were the world's only source; **(2)** Mexico, with the world's sixth largest crude oil reserves, could supply the world's needs for only about three years; **(3)** each year the world consumes oil roughly equivalent to the entire proven reserves of Venezuela or Libya; **(4)** the estimated crude oil reserves under Alaska's North Slope—the largest deposit ever found in North America—would meet world demand for only six months or U.S. demand for two to four years; and **(5)** if drilling off the east coast of the United States meets the most optimistic estimates, which is quite unlikely, the resulting additions to new crude oil reserves would satisfy world oil needs for one week or U.S. needs for less than three months. Thus, cornucopians who argue that new discoveries will solve world oil supply problems must somehow figure out how to discover the equivalent of a new Saudi Arabian deposit *every ten years* merely to maintain the world's 1984 level of oil use.

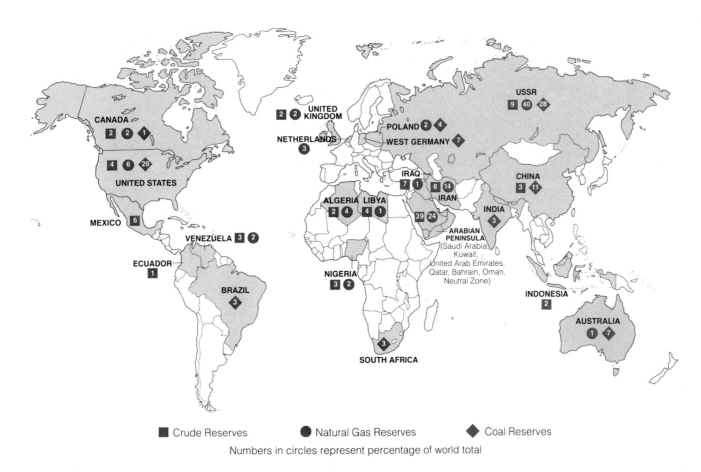

■ Crude Reserves   ● Natural Gas Reserves   ◆ Coal Reserves

Numbers in circles represent percentage of world total

Figure 16-10   Major locations of the world's known reserves of crude oil, natural gas, and coal.

The ultimately recoverable supply of crude oil based on undiscovered deposits (most believed to be in the Middle East) is estimated at more than three times today's proven reserves. Even if *all* estimated supplies of crude oil are discovered and developed— which most oil experts consider unlikely—and sold at a price of $50 to $95 a barrel, this reserve would be 80% depleted by 2076 at 1984 usage rates and by 2037 if oil usage increased by 2% a year. Thus, relatively little of the world's crude oil is likely to remain by the 2059 bicentennial of the world's first oil well.

Although the Soviet Union is presently the world's largest producer, the United States uses more of the world's oil (25%) than any other country. U.S. oil exploration has been more intensive than in any other country, but domestic oil production peaked in 1970 and has declined since then despite increased exploration. In 1979 the United States produced 79% of the oil it consumed but by 1995 is projected to produce only 40%. Any major new discoveries are likely to be in deep water or in remote areas with frigid climates, where production costs are very high and net useful energy yields are low. Because of unsuccessful exploratory drilling, in 1985 the U.S. Geological Survey reduced its estimate of undiscovered oil off the coasts

of the United States by 55%. Officials also expect production from Alaska's North Slope fields, which provided almost one-fourth of U.S. oil production in recent years, to begin falling by 1990.

Oil production by the Soviet Union—presently the world's second largest oil producer—may also decline because it is heavily dependent on old fields with declining yields and is plagued by difficulties in opening up new fields in frigid areas of Siberia far from population centers. Since the Soviet Union now produces one-fifth of the world's oil, any significant decline in its oil production will have a major effect on world supply and price. Oil production in the North Sea is also projected to peak before 1990 and then to decline steadily during the 1990s. This analysis indicates why most energy experts expect oil prices to rise sharply sometime between 1995 and 2010.

Major Advantages and Disadvantages of Oil   Oil has several important advantages that account for its widespread use. It has been and still is relatively cheap (Figure 16-6), can be transported easily within and between countries, and is a versatile fuel that can be burned to propel vehicles, provide low-temperature

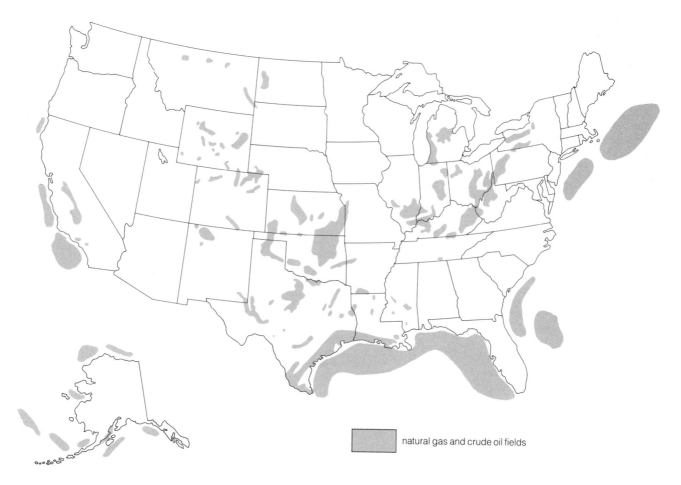

natural gas and crude oil fields

Figure 16-11   Major deposits of natural gas and crude oil in the United States. (Source: Council on Environmental Quality)

heating of water and buildings, and provide high-temperature heat for industrial processes and production of electricity. It also has a high net useful energy yield (Figure 3-17, p. 64).

However, oil also has some disadvantages. Affordable supplies may be depleted in 40 to 80 years. Its burning releases carbon dioxide gas, which could alter global climate, and air pollutants such as sulfur oxides and nitrogen oxides. Its use can also cause water pollution from oil spills and contamination of underground water by the brine solution injected into oil wells. Finally, with the increasing use of less accessible and more remote deposits, the net useful energy yield of oil will decrease.

Heavy Oils from Oil Shale and Tar Sands   Some places on earth contain rich underground deposits containing heavy oil ranging from thick oil that won't flow like conventional crude oil to tar. The two major sources of such heavy oil are deposits of oil shale and tar sands.

Oil shale is a fine-grained rock (Figure 16-12), which contains varying amounts of a solid, waxy mix-

ture of hydrocarbon compounds called **kerogen** disseminated throughout the rock. After being removed by surface or subsurface mining, shale rock is crushed and heated to a high temperature in a large vessel (retort) to vaporize the solid kerogen (Figure 16-13). The kerogen vapor is condensed, forming a slow-flowing, dark brown heavy oil called **shale oil.** Before shale oil can be sent by pipeline to a refinery, it must be processed to increase its flow rate and heat content and to remove sulfur, nitrogen, and other impurities.

The world's largest known deposits of oil-bearing shale are in Colorado, Utah, and Wyoming. Because 80% are on public lands, oil companies must obtain leases from the federal government to exploit these resources. Significant oil shale deposits are also found in Canada, China, and the Soviet Union. It is estimated that the potentially recoverable heavy oil from oil shale in the United States can supply the country with crude oil for 44 years if consumption remains at 1984 levels, and for 32 years if consumption rises by 2% a year.

It takes the energy equivalent of about one-third of a barrel of conventional crude oil to mine, retort, and purify one barrel of shale oil, thus sharply reduc-

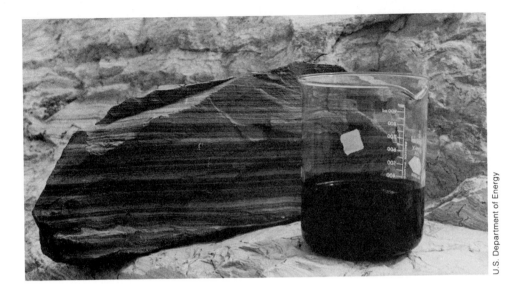

Figure 16-12 Sample of oil shale rock and the shale oil extracted from it. Oil shale projects have now been canceled in the United States because of excessive cost.

U.S. Department of Energy

ing its net useful energy yield compared to conventional oil (Figure 3-17, p. 64). As a result, the price of extracting and processing this oil is high. Until conventional oil prices rise sharply, shale oil is not an economically feasible source of oil without government subsidies or new technology.

Environmental problems may also limit shale oil production. Shale oil processing requires large amounts of water, scarce in the semiarid areas where the richest deposits are found. When the oil is processed and burned, carbon dioxide is released into the atmosphere; without adequate air pollution controls nitrogen oxides and several possibly cancer-causing substances are also released. There would be significant land disruption from the mining and disposal of large volumes of shale rock, which breaks up and expands when heated. Various salts, cancer-causing substances, and toxic metal compounds could be leached from the processed shale rock into nearby water supplies.

One way to avoid some of these environmental problems is to extract oil from shale rock underground—known as *in situ processing* (Figure 16–13). After the shale rock is broken up with explosives or water under high pressure, it is retorted and distilled underground by pumping in air and setting the deposit on fire. As the oil shale vapor is driven through the mine, it comes in contact with cooler shale rock, condenses, and drips to the bottom of the fractured area, where it can be pumped to the surface. However, experimental projects have shown that with present technology it is difficult to fracture the shale evenly enough to allow uniform combustion. In addition, groundwater often seeps into the retort area and extinguishes the fire. Sulfur dioxide emissions per barrel of shale oil are also higher than those from surface retorting.

By 1987, no oil shale extraction and processing technology had reached the commercial stage in the United States. Moreover, most pilot projects were abandoned because both surface mining and in situ methods proved too expensive even with large government subsidies, which were canceled in 1986.

Tar sands (or oil sands) are deposits of a mixture of fine clay, sand, water, and variable amounts of **bitumen,** a black, high-sulfur, tarlike heavy oil. Typically, tar sand is removed by surface mining and heated with steam at high pressure to make the bitumen fluid enough to float to the top. The bitumen is removed and then purified and upgraded to synthetic crude oil before being refined (Figure 16-14). The tar sand is mined with gigantic bucket-wheel excavators half a block long and as high as a ten-story building. So far it is not technically or economically feasible to remove deeper deposits by underground mining or by in situ extraction.

The world's largest known deposits of tar sands lie in a cold, desolate area in northern Alberta, Canada. Other fairly large deposits are in Venezuela, Colombia, and the Soviet Union. There are smaller deposits in the United States, about 90% of these in Utah.

For several years two plants have been supplying about 15% of Canada's oil demand and most of the demand in its northwestern provinces of Alberta and Saskatchewan by extracting and processing heavy oil from tar sands at a cost of between $15 and $25 a barrel. Economically recoverable deposits of heavy oil from tar sands could supply Canada's projected oil needs for about 36 years at the 1984 consumption rate but would supply total world oil needs at the same rate for only about 2 years. The U.S. Office of Technology Assessment estimated that U.S. deposits of tar sands would become economically feasible sources of

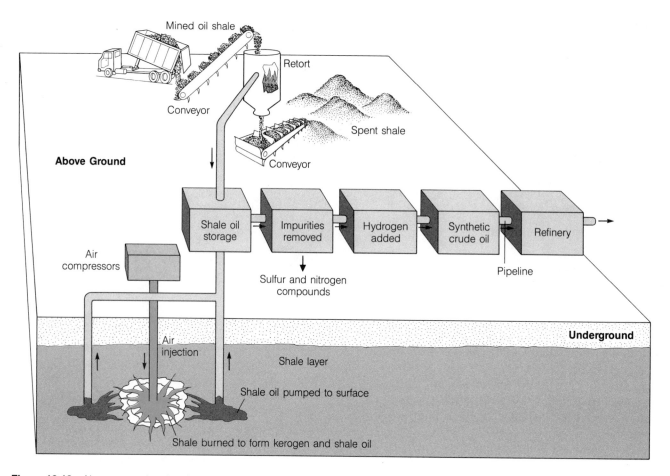

Figure 16-13 Above-ground and underground (in situ) methods for producing synthetic crude oil from oil shale.

synthetic crude oil only with an average world crude oil price of $48 to $62 a barrel. If developed, these deposits would supply all U.S. oil needs at 1984 usage rates for only about three months.

Although large-scale production of synthetic crude oil from tar sands may meet a significant fraction of Canada's oil needs, producing this oil is beset with problems. The net useful energy yield is low because it takes the energy equivalent of one-third of a barrel of conventional oil to produce the steam and electricity needed to extract and process one barrel of bitumen. More energy is needed to remove sulfur impurities and to upgrade the bitumen to synthetic crude oil before it can be sent to an oil refinery. Tar sands are so abrasive that the teeth on the excavator buckets used to scoop it out of the ground are worn out every four to eight hours. Blades on bulldozers and scrapers also last less than half their usual lifetime. In addition, the gooey sands stick to almost everything, clog extraction equipment and vehicles, and slowly dissolve natural rubber in tires, conveyor belts, and machinery parts. Other problems include the need for large quantities of water for processing and the release of air and water pollutants similar to those produced when oil shale is processed and burned.

16-4 NATURAL GAS

Conventional Supplies of Natural Gas In its underground, gaseous state **natural gas** consists of 50% to 90% methane (CH_4) gas and smaller amounts of heavier gaseous hydrocarbon compounds such as propane (C_3H_8) and butane (C_4H_{10}). Although most natural gas used so far lies above deposits of crude oil, it is also found by itself in other underground deposits.

When a natural gas deposit is tapped, propane and butane gases are liquefied and removed as **liquefied petroleum gas (LPG or LP-gas).** The remaining gas (mostly methane) is then dried, cleaned of hydrogen sulfide and other impurities, and pumped into pressurized pipelines for distribution over land. LPG is stored in pressurized tanks for use mostly in rural areas not served by natural gas pipelines. Very low temperature can be used to convert natural gas to **liquefied natural gas (LNG),** which can be transported by sea in specially designed, refrigerated tanker ships. However, LNG is so volatile and flammable that an explosion in a tanker could create a massive fireball that would burn everything within its volume and

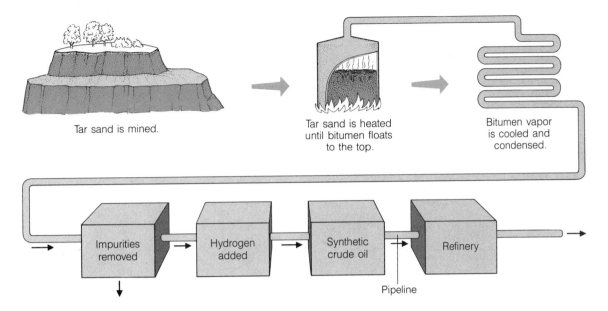

Tar sand is mined.

Tar sand is heated
until bitumen floats
to the top.

Bitumen vapor
is cooled and
condensed.

Impurities
removed

Hydrogen
added

Synthetic
crude oil

Refinery

Pipeline

Figure 16-14 Generalized summary of production of synthetic crude oil from tar sands.

generate radiant energy that would start fires and cause third-degree burns as far as 3.2 kilometers (2 miles) away.

Before the 1970s, natural gas was not traded heavily internationally because most countries lacked the facilities to process and transport it either by pipeline or in liquid form by tanker. Indeed, in many major oil-exporting countries, such as those in the Middle East, the lack of gas pipelines has resulted in the burning off of at least half of the natural gas found at oil well sites—a massive waste of the cleanest and hottest-burning fossil fuel.

Since 1979 several countries have built or are planning to build pipelines for exporting natural gas. Canadian natural gas is now exported to the United States by pipeline, and more pipelines are planned. California, for example, relies on Canada for as much as 40% of its natural gas consumption. Algeria and the Soviet Union use pipelines to supply many eastern and western European countries with natural gas and are planning additional pipelines.

Most of the present U.S. reserves of natural gas are located with the country's deposits of crude oil (Figure 16-11, p. 346). America's largest known deposits of natural gas lie in Alaska's Prudhoe Bay, thousands of kilometers from natural gas consumers in the lower 48 states. Geologists estimate that up to eight times as much natural gas awaits discovery in Alaska's North Slope area. In 1977 the U.S. Congress and the Canadian government approved pipeline construction to bring this natural gas to San Francisco and Chicago (Figure 16-15) at a cost of $43 billion—the most expensive privately financed construction project in history.

How Long Will Natural Gas Supplies Last?
Conventional supplies of natural gas are projected to last somewhat longer than those of crude oil. Between 1973 and 1984, proven reserves of natural gas doubled, whereas those of petroleum and coal have not risen. Much of this increase came from large discoveries in the Soviet Union, which now has 40% of the world's proven reserves (Figure 16-10). Other countries with large proven natural gas reserves include Iran (14%), the United States (6%), Qatar (4%), Algeria (4%), Saudi Arabia (3%), and Nigeria (3%).

Additional discoveries of natural gas are expected, especially in LDCs, as a result of intensified exploration and improved methods of locating deposits. Although known reserves in the United States are projected to last only until 1993 at 1984 usage rates, additional U.S. supplies are expected to be found. However, in 1985 the U.S. Geological Survey reduced its estimate of offshore deposits of undiscovered gas likely to be found by 48% as a result of unsuccessful exploratory drilling.

The world's identified reserves of natural gas are projected to last until 2033 at 1984 usage rates and to 2018 if usage increases by 2% a year. The supply that would be found and recovered at much higher prices would last about 200 years at 1984 usage rates and 80 years if usage increased by 2% a year.

Unconventional Sources of Natural Gas As the price of natural gas from conventional sources rises, some analysts believe it may become economical to drill deeper into the earth and extract and process nat-

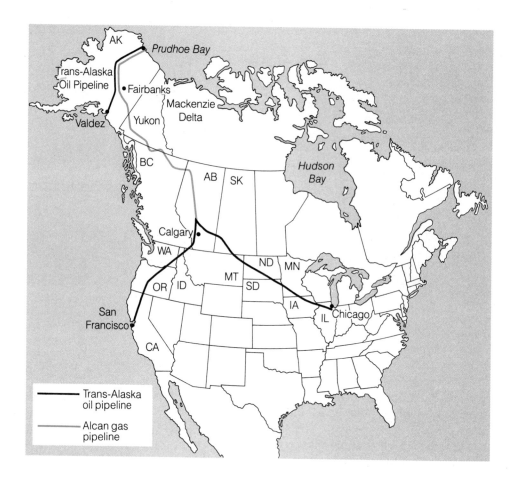

Figure 16-15 Alaskan oil is transported to the lower United States by the Trans-Alaskan oil pipeline. The Alcan pipeline presently under construction will be used to transport natural gas from Alaska. Since 1979 the Trans-Alaskan pipeline has been used to bring oil from northern Alaska to southern Alaska, where it is shipped by tanker mostly to West Coast ports.

ural gas from unconventional sources. These include concrete-hard, deep geologic formations of tight sands, deep geopressurized zones containing deposits of hot water under such high pressure that large quantities of natural gas are dissolved in the water, coal seams, and deposits of Devonian shale rock.

Energy experts agree that there are large deposits of natural gas in such sources but disagree over whether the gas can be recovered at affordable prices. If a reasonable amount of this natural gas could be recovered, world supplies would be extended for several hundred to a thousand years, allowing natural gas to become the most widely used fuel for space heating, industrial processes, producing electricity, and transportation.

Advantages and Disadvantages of Natural Gas

Two major advantages of conventional natural gas are its ability to burn hotter and cleaner than any other fossil fuel and its relatively low price. It is also a versatile fuel, transported easily over land by pipeline, and has a high net useful energy yield (Figure 3-17, p. 64). But affordable supplies of conventional natural gas may be depleted in 40 to 100 years, especially if its use increases sharply as projected. Net useful energy yields are expected to decrease as less accessible and

more remote deposits are used; the useful energy yield is reduced by about one-fourth when natural gas is converted to LNG. Its burning produces carbon dioxide, although the amounts per unit of energy produced are lower than those from other fossil fuels (Figure 16-20, p. 354). Natural gas is also difficult, expensive, and dangerous to transport by tanker as volatile, unstable LNG.

Natural gas from unconventional sources has the same advantages and disadvantages as conventional natural gas except that it is more difficult and expensive to recover and process—thus its net useful energy yield is lower. Furthermore, the deep-drilling technology needed to remove this resource is not fully developed.

16-5 COAL

Conventional Types of Coal

Natural **coal** is a solid formed in several stages as the remains of plants are subjected to intense heat and pressure over millions of years. It is mostly carbon (40% to 98%) with varying amounts of water (2% to 50%) and small amounts of nitrogen (0.2% to 1.2%) and sulfur (0.6% to 4%). The

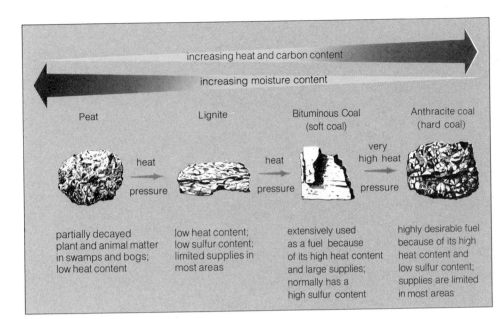

Figure 16-16 Stages in the formation of different types of coal over millions of years.

increasing heat and carbon content

increasing moisture content

| Peat | Lignite | Bituminous Coal (soft coal) | Anthracite coal (hard coal) |

heat   heat   very high heat

pressure   pressure   pressure

partially decayed plant and animal matter in swamps and bogs; low heat content

low heat content; low sulfur content; limited supplies in most areas

extensively used as a fuel because of its high heat content and large supplies; normally has a high sulfur content

highly desirable fuel because of its high heat content and low sulfur content; supplies are limited in most areas

higher the sulfur and nitrogen content of coal, the higher the emissions of sulfur dioxide and nitrogen oxides (also produced by reaction of the N_2 and O_2 in air at high temperatures) into the atmosphere when coal is burned without adequate air pollution control devices.

There are several major kinds of coal, each with a different carbon content, moisture content, sulfur content, and fuel value (heat content), depending on how much the original plant material was modified by heat and the weight of overlying materials (Figure 16-16). **Anthracite,** or hard coal, usually has a low to moderate sulfur content, a very low moisture content (2%), and a high heat content. It burns cleaner with less smoke than other types, but it is not as common and is usually more expensive. **Bituminous coal,** or soft coal, with a moderate to high heat content, is much more abundant but usually has a high sulfur content (2% to 4%). **Subbituminous coal** and **lignite** are generally low in sulfur but also in heat. **Peat,** which is not a true coal, has a low heat content and a high moisture content (70% to 95%) and is burned for fuel in areas such as Ireland where supplies are plentiful.

Distribution of Coal   Coal is the world's most abundant fossil fuel and is widely distributed geographically (Figure 16-10). About 68% of the world's proven coal reserves and 85% of the estimated undiscovered coal deposits are located in three countries: the United States (29% of proven reserves), the USSR (28%), and China (11%). These countries also account for about 60% of present total world coal production.

Major U.S. coal fields are located primarily in 17 states (Figure 16-17). Anthracite, the most desirable form of coal, makes up only about 2% of U.S. coal reserves. About 45% of U.S. coal reserves—containing mostly high-sulfur, bituminous coal with a relatively high heat content—are found east of the Mississippi River in the Appalachian region, particularly in Kentucky, West Virginia, Pennsylvania, Ohio, and Illinois. Because most of this coal has such a high sulfur content, the percentage of all U.S. coal extracted from fields east of the Mississippi River fell from about 93% to 64% between 1970 and 1985.

About 55% of U.S. coal reserves are found west of the Mississippi River. Most of these deposits consist of low-sulfur (typically 0.6%), subbituminous and lignite coals, which can be surface-mined more safely and cheaply than the underground deposits of bituminous coal found east of the Mississippi. Because about 70% of western coal reserves are under federally owned lands, major increases in the development of these resources will depend primarily on the actions of government agencies and to a lesser degree of private groups, including Native American tribes, holding the remaining western coal reserves and water rights.

The heaviest concentration of coal-burning industrial and electric power plants is located east of the Mississippi—far from western deposits. When long-distance transportation costs are added, the average cost of coal surface-mined in the West and delivered by rail to the East is comparable to that of producing coal by more expensive underground mining in the East and delivering it over shorter distances.

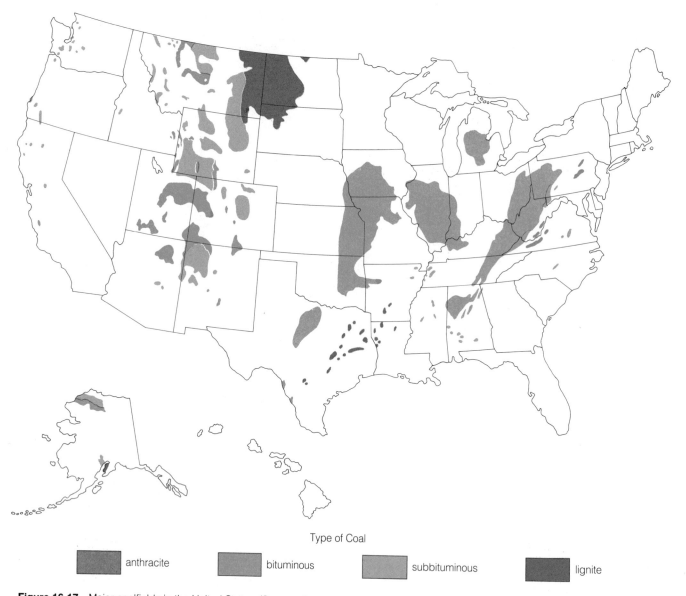

Type of Coal

| anthracite | bituminous | subbituminous | lignite |

Figure 16-17 Major coalfields in the United States. (Source: Council on Environmental Quality)

Health and Environmental Hazards of Coal Mining Underground mining of coal is the second most hazardous occupation in the world (after commercial fishing) because of injuries and deaths from cave-ins and from explosions caused by a single spark igniting underground air laden with coal dust or methane gas. Between 1900 and 1985 underground mining in the United States killed more than 100,000 miners, permanently disabled at least 1 million, and caused at least 250,000 retired miners to spend their last years gasping for breath from **black lung disease** caused by breathing coal dust and other particulate matter over a prolonged period (Figure 16-18). This progressive, debilitating disease is a form of emphysema that overwhelms the natural cleansing mechanism of the lungs and increases a miner's susceptibility to other respiratory diseases. For the victim, even

the slightest movement is difficult and death is slow and painful. Past failures to enact and enforce stricter mine safety laws now cost U.S. taxpayers over $1 billion a year in federal disability benefits paid to coal miners with black lung disease.

U.S. mine safety laws require ventilating systems, methane detectors, water sprayers, lined walls to reduce dust, and protective face masks. But one-third of all underground mines in the United States still have conditions that subject miners to a high risk of black lung disease. Although U.S. coal mining is safer than in most other countries, worker safety could be improved significantly by stricter enforcement of existing laws and by enactment of tougher new laws.

Two major environmental problems resulting from the underground mining of coal are acid mine drainage and subsidence. **Acid mine drainage** occurs when

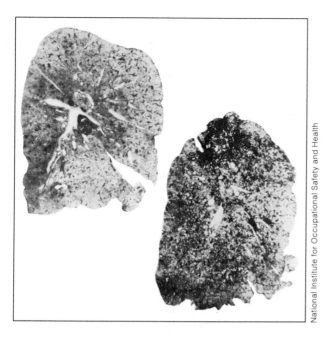

Figure 16-18 Comparison of the lungs of a nonsmoking non-miner (left) and a nonsmoking coal miner, who died from black lung disease, a severe form of emphysema.

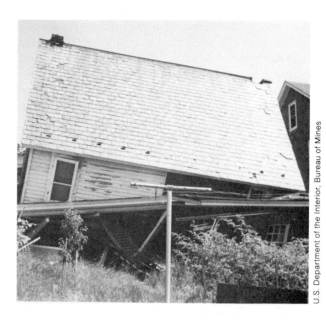

Figure 16-19 Subsidence from an abandoned and inadequately supported underground coal mine caused this home to collapse.

surface water enters an abandoned underground mine and dissolves and carries sulfuric acid and toxic metal compounds into nearby streams and rivers. These chemicals, formed when air and water react with sulfur compounds (such as iron sulfide or pyrite) in rocks or soil in the mine, kill and damage aquatic plant and animal life, make the water rusty-colored and unfit for drinking and swimming, and cause millions of dollars of corrosion damage to metal bridges, canal locks, barges, and ships. In the United States over 11,000 kilometers (7,000 miles) of streams (90% of which are in Appalachia) are severely affected by drainage of acids from underground coal mines. Acid mine drainage can be controlled by filling sinkholes and rerouting gulleys to prevent surface water from entering abandoned mines. It can also be reduced by treating the water draining from mines with crushed limestone to neutralize the acidity, but in practice this does not always work well.

Subsidence occurs when a mine shaft partially collapses during or after mining, creating a depression in the surface of the earth above the mine (Figure 16-19). In the United States over 800,000 hectares (2 million acres) of land, much of it in central Appalachia, has subsided as a result of underground coal mining.

Virtually all coal mined west of the Mississippi River and half that produced in Appalachia is removed by some form of surface mining (Section 15-2). Surface mining now accounts for about two-thirds of the coal extracted in the United States, because it is cheaper per ton of coal removed, more efficient (removing 80%

to 90% of the coal in a deposit compared to 40% to 50% with underground mining), more profitable, less labor-intensive, and safer than underground mining. But without adequate land restoration, surface mining can have a devastating impact on land (Section 15-2). It can destroy the natural vegetation and habitats for many types of wildlife. Soil erosion from unrestored surface-mined land is up to 1,000 times that from the same area under natural conditions. Minerals and salts, which leach out of unrestored land when rainwater and melting snow percolate through overburden deposits, can also kill aquatic life, pollute streams, and contaminate groundwater because many aquifers are located near or in coal seams.

More than 1 million acres of American land disturbed by surface mining have long ago been abandoned by coal companies and not restored. To help control land disturbance from surface mining of coal, the Surface Mining Control and Reclamation Act of 1977 was enacted. According to this act, **(1)** surface-mined land must be restored to its approximate original contour and if requested by the owner also re-vegetated so that it can be used for its original purposes; **(2)** surface mining is banned on some prime agricultural lands in the West, and farmers and ranchers can veto mining under their lands even though they do not own the mineral rights; **(3)** mining companies must minimize the effects of their activities on local watersheds and water quality by using the best available technology, and they must prevent acid from entering local streams and groundwater; **(4)** money from a $4.1 billion fund, financed by a fee on each ton of coal mined, is to be used to restore surface-mined land not reclaimed before 1977; **(5)** responsibility for its enforcement is delegated to the states, but the Department of the Interior has enforcement power where states fail to act and on federally owned lands.

If strictly interpreted, enforced, and adequately funded, this law could help protect valuable ecosystems. Since the law was passed, however, there has been growing pressure from the coal industry (much of which is owned by major oil companies) to weaken it or declare it unconstitutional. In the early 1980s the Reagan administration withdrew federal regulations designed to protect prime farmland from surface mining. The administration also cut federal inspection and enforcement staff by 70%, thus reducing the effectiveness of the federal government in enforcing the act. To cite only one of numerous examples of enforcement laxity, in 1983 Utah state officials were carrying out fewer than half the inspections required by law.

Uses of Coal   Burning coal has been and is expected to remain the cheapest way to produce electricity in countries with large supplies of coal—about 60% of the coal extracted in the world and 70% in the United States is burned in boilers to produce steam to generate electrical power. However, according to Amory Lovins (see Guest Essay at the end of this chapter), essential uses of electricity in the United States amount to only about 8% of annual energy needs, mostly for running lights and motors, refining copper, and some industrial processes. Thus, he says, no new power plants of any type need to be built until 2005—perhaps until 2025, if electricity is used only for such purposes. On the other hand, supporters of coal-fired and nuclear electric power plants point out that even though electricity is wasteful of energy for certain purposes, people use it to heat their homes and water because it is convenient.

The remaining 40% of the coal extracted each year is burned in boilers to produce steam used in various manufacturing processes, heated in airtight ovens to produce coke, a hard mass of almost pure carbon, for use in converting iron ore to iron and steel, and exported to other countries. A major by-product of coke production is coal tar, used for roofing, road surfacing, and manufacture of various drugs, dyes, and other products.

How Long Will Supplies Last?   Based on known reserves, coal is the most abundant conventional fossil fuel in the world and in the United States. Identified world reserves should last for about 276 years at 1984 usage rates and 86 years if usage increases by 2% a year. The world's estimated ultimately recoverable

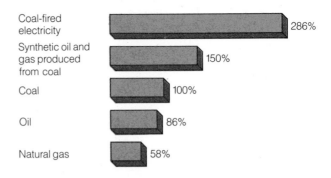

Figure 16-20   Emissions of carbon dioxide per unit of energy produced by burning fossil fuels as percentages of those from burning coal.

supply of coal would last about 900 years at 1984 usage rates and 149 years if usage increased by 2% a year.

Identified coal reserves in the United States are projected to last about 300 years at 1984 usage rates. Unidentified U.S. coal resources could extend these supplies at such high rates for perhaps 100 years, at a much higher average cost.

Air Pollution from Burning Coal   Without effective air pollution control devices, burning coal emits sulfur dioxide, particulate matter (mostly fly ash), cancer-causing substances, and small amounts of radioactive materials (found in coal deposits) into the atmosphere. Air pollution from coal-burning power and industrial plants can be sharply reduced by the pollution control devices (Chapter 19) required by federal law on all U.S. coal-fired plants built since 1978. Although removal of particulate matter and sulfur dioxide reduces air pollution, it produces large quantities of solid waste that must be handled in a way that does not pollute water supplies and soil (Chapter 21). Everything must go somewhere.

Coal-fired plants built before 1978 are not required to meet the new air pollution control standards. As a result, it is estimated that average air pollution control on all coal-burning plants in the United States is only about 50% effective. This means that existing coal-fired boilers are responsible for 70% of the country's sulfur dioxide emissions and 20% to 25% of nitrogen oxide emissions. Both of these pollutants contribute to acid deposition that damages many forests and aquatic ecosystems. They also cause an estimated 5,000 premature deaths, 50,000 cases of respiratory disease, and several billion dollars in property damage each year.

Requiring all older coal-burning plants to have air pollution control devices that remove 95% of sulfur dioxide as well as other harmful emissions would reduce deaths from burning coal to about 500 per year. This improvement in consumer health would increase

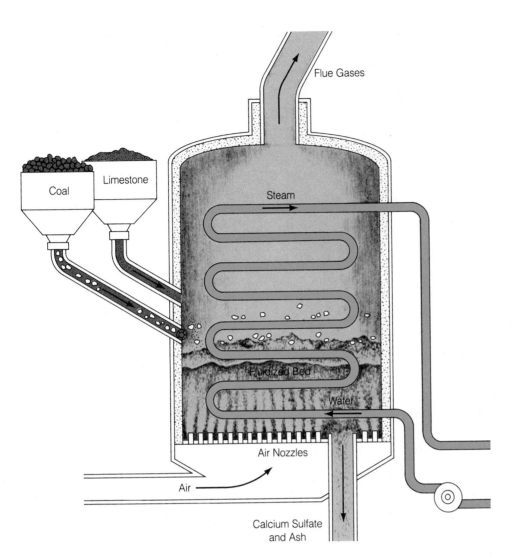

Figure 16-21 Fluidized-bed combustion of coal.

Flue Gases

Coal

Limestone

Steam

Fluidized Bed

Water

Air Nozzles

Air

Calcium Sulfate and Ash

the cost of electricity, but coal-burning plants would still produce electricity more cheaply than nuclear plants.

To many analysts the major disadvantage of coal is that it produces more carbon dioxide per weight when burned than oil or natural gas—especially when it is burned to produce electricity or burned in the form of synthetic natural gas or oil (Figure 16-20). Presently there is no technologically and economically feasible method for preventing this carbon dioxide from reaching the atmosphere.

Burning Coal More Cleanly and Efficiently One method for burning coal more cleanly and efficiently is to burn a mixture of finely powdered coal and water. The finely crushed coal particles can be mixed with water to produce a molasses-like mixture that can be stored in tanks and burned in existing oil burners without too many modifications. Although the grinding-and-mixing process adds to the cost, coal-water

mixtures can be burned more cheaply than oil to produce electricity because coal is still cheaper than oil, even with the low oil prices of the mid-1980s. By 1986 coal-water mixtures were being used in a few small-scale, experimental electricity plants in the United States and Canada.

Another promising method for burning coal more efficiently, cleanly, and cheaply than in conventional coal boilers is **fluidized-bed combustion** (Figure 16-21). In FBC a stream of hot air is blown through a series of small jets into a boiler to suspend a mixture of powdered coal and crushed limestone. When this mixture is red hot, the powdered coal is burned very efficiently and the limestone ($CaCO_3$) is converted to calcium oxide (CaO), which reacts with the sulfur dioxide released from the coal to form dry, solid calcium sulfate ($CaSO_4$). This removes 90% to 98% of the sulfur dioxide gas produced during combustion and emits considerably less nitrogen oxides than present federal air pollution standards permit. FBC boilers also can burn a variety of fuels (including rice hulls, heavy

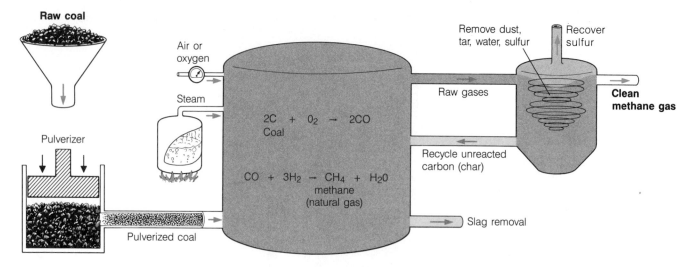

Raw coal

Pulverizer

Pulverized coal

Air or oxygen

Steam

2C + O₂ → 2CO
Coal

CO + 3H₂ → CH₄ + H₂O
methane
(natural gas)

Remove dust, tar, water, sulfur

Recover sulfur

Raw gases

Clean methane gas

Recycle unreacted carbon (char)

Slag removal

Figure 16–22 Coal gasification. Generalized view of one method for converting solid coal into synthetic natural gas.

oils, wood and wood wastes, urban and industrial trash, sewage sludge, and high-sulfur coal) and can be retrofitted to conventional boilers.

Successful small-scale FBC plants have been built in Great Britain, Sweden, Finland, the Soviet Union, West Germany, and China. In the United States, 20 small-scale FBC plants burning coal or wood were in operation by 1986 and are projected to begin replacing conventional coal boilers by the 1990s.

Synfuels: Gaseous and Liquid Fuels from Coal
Techniques for producing gaseous and liquid fuels, called **synfuels,** from coal have been available for many years. These processes were developed by Germany during World War II, when the country was faced with a blockade and insufficient domestic supplies. **Coal gasification** involves converting coal to a gas that can be burned more cleanly as a fuel and, unlike coal, can be transported through a pipeline. In one process, coal is converted to coke, which is heated with steam to produce a gaseous mixture of carbon monoxide and hydrogen, known as producer gas. However, because producer gas has a low heating value, it is uneconomical to transport by pipeline. It is of commercial interest only when it can be burned at an industrial site for heating or producing electricity.

A second and more useful process converts coal to **synthetic natural gas (SNG),** which, like natural gas, has a high heating value and can be transported by pipeline. One way of producing SNG is to burn powdered coal in air to produce carbon monoxide, which is then combined with hydrogen gas in the presence of a catalyst (to speed up the rate of the reaction) to form methane and water vapor (Figure 16-22).

Coal liquefaction involves converting coal to a liquid hydrocarbon fuel such as methanol or synthetic gasoline. A number of different liquefaction processes have been developed. In South Africa a commercial plant has been converting synthetic natural gas made from coal to gasoline and other motor fuels for more than 25 years and now supplies 10% of the country's liquid fuel needs. When two new plants are completed the three plants together are expected to meet 50% of South Africa's current oil needs.

Advantages and Disadvantages of Solid Coal and Synfuels   Coal is the most abundant conventional fossil fuel in the world and in the United States and has a high net useful energy yield for producing high-temperature heat for industrial processes and for the generation of electricity (Figure 3-17, p. 64). In countries with adequate coal supplies, burning solid coal is the cheapest way to produce high-temperature heat and electricity compared to oil, natural gas, and nuclear energy. For these reasons, some energy analysts suggest that coal use be increased to help make a transition from dependence on oil and natural gas to dependence on energy conservation and a mix of renewable and perpetual energy resources over the next 50 to 75 years.

But solid coal has several major disadvantages that may limit its use except in LDCs such as China and India, with large coal supplies and less stringent air pollution control standards. When burned, coal releases more carbon dioxide than other fossil fuels. It is also dangerous to mine, expensive to move from one place to another, and is not useful in solid form as a transportation fuel.

Converting solid coal to gaseous or liquid synfuels allows it to become a more versatile fuel that can be burned more readily to heat homes and power vehicles. Synfuels are easier and often cheaper to transport than solid coal (and, when burned, produce much less air pollution). Indeed, synfuels can usually be burned without expensive pollution control devices.

It is much more expensive, however, to build a synfuel plant than an equivalent coal-fired power plant fully equipped with air pollution control devices. Other major problems of synfuels include their low net useful energy yield (Figure 3-17, p. 64); accelerated depletion of world coal supplies because 30% to 40% of the energy content of coal is lost in the conversion process; large water requirements for processing; release of large amounts of carbon dioxide per unit of weight when processed and burned; increased air pollution from polycyclic aromatic hydrocarbons (PAHs), many of which cause cancer; and greater land disruption from surface mining because of increased use of coal per unit of energy produced. Some of these problems (except carbon dioxide emissions, high costs, and low net energy yields) could be avoided or reduced by using an in situ method to convert coal to SNG underground in the coal seam itself. But despite potential advantages and years of experimentation, in situ coal gasification is still not competitive with conventional coal mining and above-ground coal gasification.

The major factor holding back large-scale production of synfuels in the United States is their high cost compared to conventional oil and natural gas—equivalent to buying oil in 1985 at $90 a barrel. In 1980 Congress set up the U.S. synthetic Fuels Corporation to provide up to $88 billion in grants to oil companies to promote the development of a synfuels industry. By 1984, however, oil companies found it too expensive to continue such experimental projects, even with large government subsidies, and most were abandoned. In 1986 Congress disbanded the U.S. Synthetic Fuels Corporation. Most analysts expect synfuels to play only a minor role as an energy resource until oil prices rise substantially sometime after 2000.

Oil and natural gas will play an important but diminishing role for some time, but how long is less clear. Coal will likely grow in importance, but how much we should burn considering the serious side effects of its use is a tough question.

Daniel Deudney and Christopher Flavin

Guest Essay   Technology Is the Answer (But What Was the Question?)

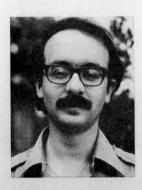

Amory B. Lovins

Physicist and energy consultant Amory B. Lovins is recognized as one of the world's leading experts on energy strategy. Since 1981 he has worked for Friends of the Earth, a U.S. nonprofit environmental conservation lobbying group. He is now director of research at the Rocky Mountain Institute. He has served as a consultant to several United Nations agencies, the U.S. Department of Energy, the Congressional Office of Technology Assessment, the U.S. Solar Energy Research Institute, and the governments of California, Montana, and Alaska. He is active in energy affairs in about 15 countries, and, in addition to many technical papers, has published nine books, including the widely

discussed Soft Energy Paths *(New York: Harper Colophon, 1979) and the nontechnical version of this work with coauthor L. Hunter Lovins,* Energy Unbound: Your Invitation to Energy Abundance *(San Francisco: Friends of the Earth, 1986).*

The answers you get depend on the questions you ask. But sometimes it seems so important to resolve a crisis that we forget to ask what problem we're trying to solve.

It is fashionable to suppose that we're running out of energy, and that the solution is obviously to get lots more of it. But asking how to get more energy begs the question of how much we need. That depends not on how much we used in the past but on what we want to do in the future and how much energy it will take to do those things. How much energy it takes to make steel, run a sewing machine, or keep you comfortable in your house depends on how cleverly we use energy, and the more it costs, the smarter we seem to get. It is now cheaper, for example, to double the efficiency of most industrial electric motors than to get more electricity to run the old ones. (Just this one saving can more than replace the entire U.S. nuclear power program.) We know how to make lights five times as efficient as those presently in use and how to make household appliances that give us the same work as now, using one-fifth as much energy (saving money in the process). The Volkswagen Corporation has made a good-sized, safe car averaging about 34 to 42 kilometers per liter (80 to 100 miles per gallon). We know today how to make new buildings and many old ones so heat-tight (but still well ventilated) that they need essentially no energy to maintain comfort year-round, even in severe climates. These energy-saving measures are uniformly cheaper than going out and getting more energy. Detailed studies in over a dozen countries have shown that supplying energy services in the cheapest way—by wringing more work from the energy we already have—would let us increase our standard of living while using several times less total energy (and electricity) than we do now.

But the old view of the energy problem embodied a worse mistake than forgetting to ask how much energy we needed: It sought more energy, in any form, from any source, at any price—as if all kinds of energy were alike. This is like saying, "All kinds of food are alike; we're running short of potatoes and turnips and cheese, but that's OK, we can substitute sirloin steak and oysters Rockefeller." Some of us have to be more discriminating than that. Just as there are different kinds of food, so there are many different forms of energy, whose different prices and qualities suit them to different uses. There is, after all, no *demand for energy* as such; nobody wants raw kilowatt-hours or barrels of sticky black goo. People instead want energy *services:* comfort, light, mobility, ability to bake bread, ability to make cement. We ought therefore to start at that end of the energy problem: to ask, "What are the many different tasks we want energy *for,* and what is the amount, type, and source of energy that will do each task *in the cheapest way*?"

Electricity is a particularly special, high-quality, expensive form of energy. An average kilowatt-hour delivered in the United States in 1986 was priced at about 8 cents, equivalent to buying the heat content of oil costing $128 per barrel—over eight times the world price during the summer of 1986. A power station ordered in 1984 and completed in 1994 will deliver electricity costing, in 1984 dollars, at least 10 cents per kilowatt-hour, equivalent on a heat basis to buying oil at about $160 per barrel.

Such costly energy might be worthwhile if it could be used for the premium tasks that require it, such as lights, motors, electronics, and smelters. But those special uses, only 8% of all delivered U.S. energy needs, are already met twice over by today's power stations. Two-fifths of our electricity is already spilling over into uneconomic, low-grade uses such as water heating, space heating, and air conditioning. Yet no matter how efficiently we use electricity (even with heat pumps), we can never get our money's worth on these applications. Electricity is far too expensive to be worthwhile for the 58% of the delivered energy that is needed in the form of heat in the United States and for the 34% needed to run nonrail vehicles. But these tasks are all that additional electricity could be used for without wasting energy and money, because today's power stations already supply the real electric needs twice over.

Thus, *supplying more electricity is irrelevant to the energy problem that we have.* Even though electricity accounts for two-thirds of the federal energy research and development budget and for about half of national energy investment, it is the wrong kind of energy to meet our needs economically. Arguing about what kind of new power station to build—coal, nuclear, solar—is like shopping for the best buy in Chippendales to burn in your stove. *It is the wrong question.*

Indeed, *any* kind of new power station is so uneconomical that if you have just built one, you will save the country money by writing it off and never operating it. Why? Because its additional electricity can be used only for low-temperature heating and cooling (the premium, "electricity-specific" uses being already filled up); but to do low-temperature heating and cooling, it is worth paying only what it costs to do the job in the cheapest way. That means weather-stripping, insulation, heat exchangers, greenhouses, window shades and shutters and overhangs, trees, and so on. These measures generally cost about half a penny per kilowatt-hour, whereas the running costs *alone* for a new nuclear plant will be nearly 2 cents per kilowatt-hour, so it is cheaper not to run it. In fact, under our crazy U.S. tax laws, the extra saving from not having to pay the plant's future subsidies is probably so big that society can also recover the capital cost of having built the plant!

If we want more electricity, we should get it from the cheapest sources first. In approximate order of increasing price, these include:

1. Eliminating pure waste of electricity, such as lighting empty offices. Each kilowatt-hour saved can be resold without having to generate it anew.
2. Displacing with good architecture, and with passive and some active solar techniques, the electricity now used for water heating and space heating and cooling. Some U.S. utilities now give zero-interest weatherization loans, which you need not

start repaying for ten years or until you sell your house—because it saves them millions of dollars to get electricity that way compared with building new power plants.

3. Making lights, motors, appliances, smelters, and the like cost-effectively efficient.

Just these three measures can quadruple U.S. electrical efficiency, making it possible to run today's economy, with no changes in lifestyles, using no thermal power plants, whether old or new, and whether fueled with oil, gas, coal, or uranium. We would need only the present hydroelectric capacity, readily available small-scale hydroelectric projects, and a modest amount of wind power. But if we still wanted more electricity, the next cheapest sources would include:

4. Industrial cogeneration, combined-heat-and-power plants, low-temperature heat engines run by industrial waste heat or by solar ponds, filling empty turbine bays in existing big dams, modern wind machines or small-scale hydroelectric turbines in good sites, and perhaps even some recent developments in solar cells with waste heat recovery (Chapter 18).

It is only after we had clearly exhausted all these cheaper opportunities that we would even consider:

5. Building a new central power station of any kind— the slowest and costliest known way to get more electricity (or to save oil).

To emphasize the importance of starting with energy *end uses* rather than energy *sources*, consider a sad little story from France, involving a "spaghetti chart" (or energy flowchart)—a device energy planners often use to show how energy flows from primary sources via conversion processes to final forms and uses. (An example is shown in Figure 3-8, p. 54). In the mid-1970s the energy conservation planners in the French government started, wisely, on the right-hand side of the spaghetti chart. They found that their biggest single need for energy was to heat buildings, and that even with good heat pumps, electricity would be the most uneconomic way to do this. So they had a fight with their nationalized utility; they won; and electric heating was supposed to be discouraged or even phased out because it was so wasteful of money and fuel.

But meanwhile, down the street, the energy supply planners (who were far more numerous and influential in the French government) were starting on the left-hand side of the spaghetti chart. They said: "Look at all that nasty imported oil coming into our country! We must replace that oil. Oil is energy. . . . We need some other source of energy. Voila! Reactors can give us energy; we'll build nuclear reactors all over the country." But they paid little attention to what would happen to that extra energy, and no attention to relative prices.

Thus, the two sides of the French energy establishment went on with their respective solutions to two different, indeed contradictory, French energy problems: *more energy of any kind*, versus *the right kind to do each task cheapest*. It was only in 1979 that these conflicting perceptions collided. The supply planners suddenly realized that the only way they would be able to *sell* all that nuclear electricity would be for electric heating, which they had just agreed not to do.

Every industrial nation is in this embarrassing position (especially if we include in "heating" air conditioning, which just means heating the outdoors instead of the indoors). Which end of the spaghetti chart we start on, or *what we think the energy problem is,* is not an academic abstraction: It *determines what we buy.* It is the most fundamental source of disagreement about energy policy. People starting on the left side of the spaghetti chart think the problem boils down to whether to build coal or nuclear power stations (or both), while people starting on the right realize that *no* kind of new power station can be an economic way to meet the needs for low- and high-temperature heat and for vehicular liquid fuels that are 92% of our energy problem.

So if we want to provide our energy services at a price we can afford, let's get straight what question our technologies are supposed to provide the answer to. Before we argue about the meatballs, let's untangle the strands of spaghetti, see where they're supposed to lead, and find out what we really need the energy *for!*

Guest Essay Discussion

1. List the energy services you would like to have, and note which of these must be furnished by electricity.

2. The author argues that building more nuclear, coal, or other electrical power plants to supply electricity for the United States is unnecessary and wasteful. Summarize the reasons for this conclusion and give your reasons for agreeing or disagreeing with this viewpoint.

3. Do you agree or disagree that increasing the supply of energy, instead of concentrating on improving energy efficiency, is the wrong answer to U.S. energy problems? Explain.

CHAPTER SUMMARY

Each major cultural shift has involved using human ingenuity to increase the average amount of energy used directly and indirectly per person. Today's MDCs, where most of the world's commercial energy is consumed, depend on nonrenewable oil, coal, and natural gas for 82% of their energy. People in LDCs depend primarily on renewable biomass (mostly increasingly scarce wood) to meet most of their energy needs.

Temporary oil shortages in the 1970s due to the OPEC oil embargo and the Iranian revolution led most MDCs to conserve energy, replace some uses of oil, and increase oil production in some non-OPEC nations. The resulting decrease in oil demand led to an oil glut, greatly reduced prices, and reduced control by OPEC over oil prices in the 1980s. Sometime during the 1990s or first decade of the next century, oil prices and OPEC control over these prices are expected to increase sharply—thus increasing the need for the world to phase in substitutes for oil over the next 50 years.

The major factors determining the degree of use of any energy alternative is its (1) estimated short-, intermediate-, and long-term supplies, (2) net useful energy yield, (3) cost, and (4) environmental impact. *Conventional crude oil* can be easily transported throughout the world, is a relatively cheap and versatile fuel, and has a high net useful energy yield. However, affordable supplies may be depleted in 40 to 80 years, burning oil releases carbon dioxide into the atmosphere which could alter global climate, and the use of oil has a moderate environmental impact. *Unconventional heavy oils* obtained from *oil shale* and *tar sands* located in a few mostly semiarid places could extend supplies of oil but are costly, have low net useful energy yields, produce carbon dioxide, require large quantities of water for processing, and have a higher environmental impact than conventional oil.

Conventional natural gas burns hotter and cleaner than any other fossil fuel, is versatile and relatively cheap, and has a high net useful energy yield. But affordable supplies may be depleted in 40 to 100 years and burning of natural gas produces carbon dioxide. Various *unconventional sources of natural gas* could extend supplies for several hundred to a thousand years but are presently much too costly to locate and extract and have a lower net useful energy yield than conventional natural gas.

Coal is the world's most abundant conventional fossil fuel, has a high net useful energy for producing electricity and high-temperature heat for industrial processes, and is the cheapest way to produce these forms of energy in countries with adequate coal supplies. However, it is (1) an extremely dirty, hazardous, and environmentally harmful fuel to mine and burn without adequate and costly air pollution control devices, improved mine safety, and reclamation of strip-mined land, (2) releases more carbon dioxide per unit of energy produced than any other fossil fuel, and (3) cannot conveniently be used to fuel vehicles and heat homes unless converted to gaseous fuels (*coal gasification*) or liquid fuels (*coal liquefaction*). Although gaseous and liquid fuels produced from coal burn more cleanly, are more versatile, and can be transported more conveniently than solid coal, they have low net energy yields, large water requirements for processing, release large quantities of carbon dioxide, and lead to greatly increased land disruption from surface mining because they increase the use of coal per unit of energy produced.

DISCUSSION TOPICS

1. Try to trace your own direct and indirect energy consumption each day to see why it probably averages 230,000 kilocalories (Figure 16-1).

2. Why has the United States in recent decades shifted from a heavy dependence on coal to oil and natural gas even though coal is the country's most abundant fossil fuel?

3. Explain why you agree or disagree with the following statements:
    a. We can get all the oil we need by extracting and processing heavy oil left in known oil wells.
    b. We can get all the oil we need by extracting and processing heavy oil from oil shale deposits.
    c. We can get all the oil we need by extracting heavy oil from tar sands.
    d. We can get all the natural gas we need from unconventional sources.

4. Why is surface-mined coal gradually replacing coal from deep mines in the United States? Do you believe that this is a desirable or undesirable trend? Why? What are the alternatives?

5. Should present U.S. mine safety and surface mining laws be strengthened or weakened, or should the enforcement of existing laws be greatly improved? Defend your choice.

6. Coal-fired power plants in the United States cause an estimated 10,000 deaths a year, primarily from atmospheric emissions of sulfur oxides, nitrogen oxides, and particulate matter. These plants also cause extensive damage to many buildings and some forests and aquatic systems. Should air pollution emission standards for *all* new and existing coal-burning plants be tightened significantly, even if this raises the price of electricity sharply and makes it cheaper to produce electricity by using conventional nuclear fission? Explain.

7. Should all coal-burning power and industrial plants in the United States be required to convert to fluidized-bed combustion? Explain. What are the alternatives?

8. Do you favor a U.S. energy strategy based on greatly increased use of coal-burning plants to produce electricity between 1988 and 2020? Explain. What are the alternatives?

17

Nonrenewable and Perpetual Energy Resources:
Geothermal and Nuclear Energy

GENERAL OBJECTIVES

1. What are the major types of geothermal energy and what are their uses, advantages, and disadvantages?

2. What are the advantages and disadvantages of using conventional nuclear fission to produce electricity?

3. What are the advantages and disadvantages of using breeder nuclear fission to produce electricity?

4. If and when it is developed, what are the advantages and disadvantages of using nuclear fusion to produce electricity?

We nuclear people have made a Faustian compact with society; we offer an inexhaustible energy source tainted with potential side effects that if not controlled, could spell disaster.

Alvin M. Weinberg

Geothermal energy—heat from the earth's interior—and nuclear energy—heat from the fission of nuclei of certain isotopes (Section 3-2)—are used to produce limited amounts of electricity in various parts of the world. Some people urge that the world greatly increase its dependence on energy from nuclear fission to produce electricity because it is a safe, technically well-developed, economically acceptable energy resource that does not produce carbon dioxide and has less environmental impact than coal. Others consider expanded use of this energy resource, as well as its present use, to be unnecessary, uneconomic, unsafe, and unethical compared to other alternatives.

17-1 NONRENEWABLE AND PERPETUAL GEOTHERMAL ENERGY

Nonrenewable Geothermal Energy The molten core of the earth is intensely hot. Some of its heat, or **geothermal energy,** is transferred over thousands to millions of years to normally nonrenewable underground deposits of dry steam (steam with no water droplets), wet steam (a mixture of steam and water droplets), and hot water lying relatively close to the earth's surface. Geothermal wells can be drilled like oil and natural gas wells to bring this dry steam, wet steam, or hot water to the earth's surface for heating buildings, industrial processing, or driving a turbine to produce electricity.

Although nonrenewable on a human time scale, most high-grade geothermal deposits are projected to last from 100 to 200 years. Currently about 20 countries are tapping geothermal deposits, providing space

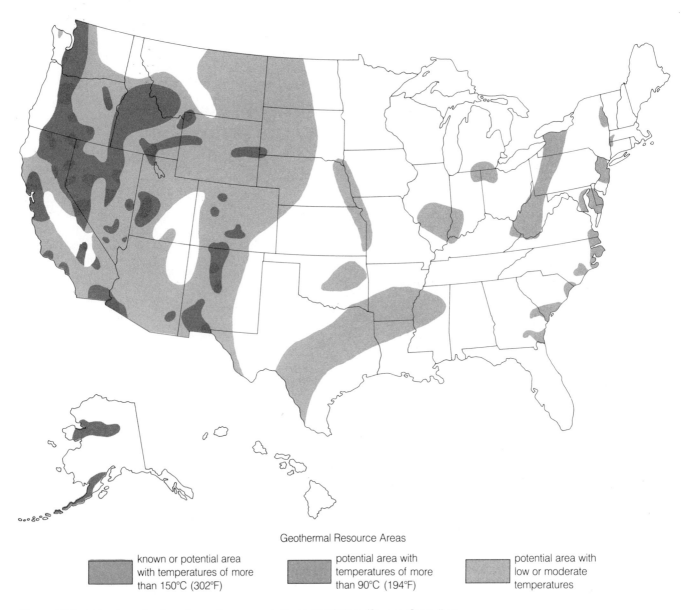

Geothermal Resource Areas

| known or potential area with temperatures of more than 150°C (302°F) | potential area with temperatures of more than 90°C (194°F) | potential area with low or moderate temperatures |

Figure 17-1 Major deposits of geothermal resources in the United States. (Source: Council on Environmental Quality)

heating for over 2 million homes in cold climates and enough electricity for over 1.5 million homes. Figure 17-1 shows that most accessible, high-temperature geothermal deposits in the United States lie in the western states, especially California and the Rocky Mountain states. Hawaii also has a number of possible sites.

Dry steam deposits are the preferred geothermal resource, but also the rarest. These deposits are tapped easily and economically: A hole is drilled into the underground reservoir, releasing the superheated steam through a pipe; solid material is filtered out, and the steam travels through insulated pipes directly to a turbine-generator system to produce electricity. A large dry steam well near Larderello, Italy, has been

producing electricity since 1904 and is a major source of power for Italy's electric railroads. Two other major dry steam sites are the Matsukawa field in Japan, and the Geysers steam field about 145 kilometers (90 miles) north of San Francisco. The Geysers field has been producing electricity since 1960 and by 1987 was supplying more than 2% of California's electricity—enough to meet all electrical needs of a city the size of San Francisco—at less than half the cost of a new coal or nuclear plant. New units can be added every 2 to 3 years (compared to 6 years for a coal plant and 12 years for a nuclear plant), and by 2000 this field may supply 25% of the state's electricity.

Underground *wet steam deposits* are more common but harder and more expensive to convert to electric-

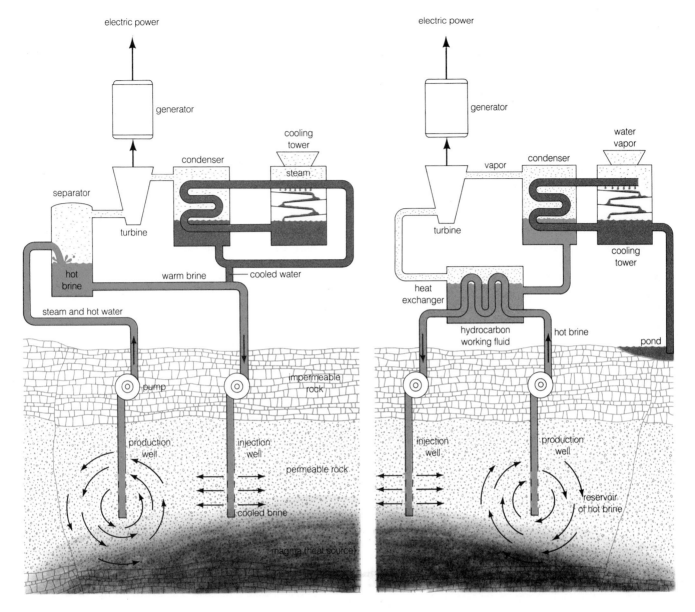

Figure 17-2 Direct-flash (left) and binary-cycle methods for extracting and using geothermal energy to produce electricity.

ity. These deposits contain water under such high pressure that its temperature is far above the boiling point of water at normal atmospheric pressure. When this superheated water is brought to the surface, some of it flashes into steam because of the sharp decrease in pressure. The mixture of steam and water is spun at a high speed (centrifuged) to separate out the steam, which is used to spin a turbine to produce electricity (Figure 17-2). The largest wet steam geothermal electric power plant in the world is in Wairaki, New Zealand. Other wet steam power plants operate in Mexico, Japan, and the Soviet Union. Four small-scale demonstration plants built in the United States since 1980 are producing electricity, but drilling problems and metal corrosion from the salty water have reduced

yields so much that the cost of this energy is equivalent to paying $40 a barrel for oil.

Hot water deposits are more common than dry steam and wet steam deposits. Almost all the homes, buildings, and food-producing greenhouses in Reykjavik, Iceland, a city with a population of about 85,000, are heated by hot water drawn from deep hot water geothermal deposits under the city. At 180 locations in the United States, mostly in western states, hot water deposits have been used for years to heat homes and farm buildings and to dry crops.

The hot salty water (brine) pumped up from such wells can also be used to produce electricity in a binary-cycle system (Figure 17-2). A demonstration binary-cycle system went into operation in 1984 in Herber in

California's Imperial Valley. The main problem is that the brine corrodes metal parts and clogs pipes. An underground binary-cycle system is also being tested: Heat from the hot water vaporizes a liquid, which is brought to the surface to spin the turbine. Not only does this approach avoid corrosion and wastewater problems, it leaves water and steam in the well for continual reheating rather than depleting the resource.

A fourth potential source of nonrenewable geothermal energy is *geopressurized zones*, consisting of high-temperature, high-pressure reservoirs of water (often saturated with natural gas because of the high pressure), usually trapped deep under ocean beds of shale or clay. Such deposits could yield three types of energy: electrical (from high-temperature water), mechanical or hydraulic (from the high pressure), and chemical (from the natural gas). Still in the exploratory phase, geopressurized zones could be tapped by very deep drilling; but with present drilling technology they would provide energy at a cost equivalent to two to three times the price of conventional oil.

Major advantages of nonrenewable geothermal energy include a 100- to 200-year supply of energy for areas near deposits, moderate cost, moderate net useful energy yields for large and easily accessible deposits, and no emissions of carbon dioxide. Two disadvantages are the few easily accessible deposits and the impossibility of using this type of energy directly to power vehicles. Without adequate pollution control there is moderate to high air pollution from hydrogen sulfide, ammonia, and radioactive materials, as well as moderate to high water pollution from dissolved solids (salinity) and runoff of various toxic compounds of elements such as boron and mercury. Noise, odor, and local climate changes can also be problems. Most experts, however, consider the environmental effects of geothermal energy to be less or no greater than those of fossil fuel and nuclear power plants.

Perpetual Geothermal Energy Three potentially perpetual geothermal energy sources are deposits of *molten rock (magma)* at temperatures around 1000°C (1832°F) found near the earth's surface; *hot dry-rock zones*, where molten rock has penetrated the earth's crust and heats subsurface rock to high temperatures; and low- to moderate-temperature *warm rock deposits*, useful for preheating water and geothermal heat pumps for space heating and air conditioning.

The U.S. Geological Survey estimates that bodies of molten rock located no more than 9.6 kilometers (6 miles) below the earth's surface in the continental United States could supply 800 to 8,000 times all commercial energy the country consumed in 1984. But extracting energy from magma is complicated and expensive. Presently scientists at the Sandia National Laboratory plan to test the technological feasibility of

extracting heat from magma at an affordable price at two promising sites in California.

Warm and hot rock deposits lying deep underground are potentially the largest and most widely distributed geothermal resource in the United States and most countries, but they are expensive to locate, tap, and use. By 1984, researchers in the United States and the United Kingdom had drilled several test wells and successfully extracted heat from dry-rock deposits by fracturing the hot rock with hydraulic pressure to create a reservoir, pumping water in, and bringing the resulting steam to the surface to run turbines for creating electricity. In 1986 a fairly large demonstration hot dry-rock plant in New Mexico supported by the U.S. Department of Energy and the government of Japan produced enough electricity and heat for a town of about 2,000 people.

17-2 CONVENTIONAL NONRENEWABLE NUCLEAR FISSION

A Controversial Fading Dream The debate between energy experts over whether nuclear fission power should be a major energy alternative for producing electricity throughout the world and in the United States is intense. Physicist Bernard L. Cohen (see Further Readings) says, "Nuclear power is perceived to be *thousands of times* more dangerous than it is. . . . I am personally convinced that citizens of the distant future will look upon it as one of God's greatest gifts to humanity." Phil Bray, head of General Electric's nuclear reactor division in San Jose, California, says, "I could take a reactor, lose every pump, break every valve, blow every electrical unit, melt the core, and eventually bust the containment building, and we still think no one beyond the site boundary would be hurt." Physicist and strong advocate of nuclear power Alvin M. Weinberg believes that nuclear power can be safe, but he emphasizes that the widespread use of this energy resource is the greatest single long-term risk ever approached by humankind, one that should be accepted only after intensive public education and debate (see his Guest Essay at the end of this chapter).

In contrast, according to Nobel Prize-winning physicist Hannes Alfvén:

Nuclear fission energy is safe only if a number of critical devices work as they should, if a number of people in key positions follow all their instructions, if there is no sabotage, no hijacking of the transport, if no reactor fuel processing plant or repository anywhere in the world is situated in a region of riots or guerrilla activity, and no revolution or war—even a "conventional one"—takes place in these regions. . . . No acts of God can be permitted.

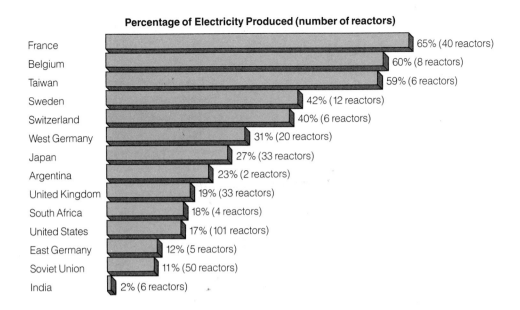

Percentage of Electricity Produced (number of reactors)

France — 65% (40 reactors)
Belgium — 60% (8 reactors)
Taiwan — 59% (6 reactors)
Sweden — 42% (12 reactors)
Switzerland — 40% (6 reactors)
West Germany — 31% (20 reactors)
Japan — 27% (33 reactors)
Argentina — 23% (2 reactors)
United Kingdom — 19% (33 reactors)
South Africa — 18% (4 reactors)
United States — 17% (101 reactors)
East Germany — 12% (5 reactors)
Soviet Union — 11% (50 reactors)
India — 2% (6 reactors)

Figure 17-3 Use of nuclear fission reactors to produce electricity in various countries in 1986. (Sources of data: Atomic Industrial Forum and International Atomic Energy Agency)

Upon his retirement in 1982, the late Admiral Hyman G. Rickover, father of the U.S. nuclear submarine program and its director for more than 30 years, told members of Congress: "The most important thing we could do is have an international meeting where we first outlaw nuclear weapons, then nuclear reactors." According to energy cost analyst Charles Komanoff, "The fundamental problem facing nuclear power, especially in the United States, is that it's just too expensive."

Originally nuclear power was heralded as a clean, cheap, and safe source of energy that with 1,800 projected plants could provide as much as 21% of the world's commercial energy and 25% of U.S. commercial energy by the year 2000. But, by 1986, after 35 years of development, 374 commercial nuclear reactors in 26 countries were providing only 15% of the world's electricity—amounting to about 3% of the world's commercial energy. Five countries—the United States, France, West Germany, Japan, and the Soviet Union—had 72% of the world's nuclear generating capacity by 1986.

By this time, however, some countries depended on nuclear power for 40% or more of their electricity, and some of these countries expect to increase their dependence on nuclear power as most of the 157 reactors still under construction throughout the world are put into operation (Figure 17-3). Industrialized countries like Japan and France, which have few fossil fuel resources, consider increased dependence on nuclear power a necessity to reduce their dependence on increasingly expensive imported oil.

Primarily because of concerns over safety, some MDCs such as Denmark, Luxembourg, Austria, and Norway have chosen not to develop this energy source, and Sweden plans to close its ten operating reactors by 2010. Since the Chernobyl nuclear accident in 1986, most LDCs have scaled back or eliminated their plans to build nuclear power plants. As a result, nuclear power's share of the world's electricity will very likely be lower in the year 2000 than it was in 1986.

The United States, which has abundant coal and a variety of other energy alternatives, can decide to what degree it wants to use nuclear power with less urgency than MDCs with limited energy alternatives. Projected future use of nuclear fission for producing electricity in the United States has decreased sharply since 1975. No new plants have been ordered since 1978 and 114 previous orders have been canceled. By 1986, a total of 101 commercial nuclear reactors in 32 states (mostly in the eastern half of the United States) supplied 16% of the country's electricity and about 4% of its total commercial energy (Figure 17-4). If the 27 reactors still under construction are completed, nuclear power could supply 20% of the country's electricity and 5% of its commercial energy by 1995—far below the 25% of commercial energy predicted in the 1960s. After 1995 U.S. nuclear capacity will decline as aging plants are decommissioned and no new ones are constructed.

How Does a Nuclear Fission Reactor Work? When the nuclei of certain atoms such as uranium-235 and plutonium-239 are split apart by neutrons, energy is released and converted mostly to high-temperature heat in a nuclear fission chain reaction (Figure 3-5, p. 50). The rate at which this process occurs can be controlled in the nuclear fission reactor in a nuclear power plant, where the high-temperature heat released is used to spin a turbine connected to a generator that produces electrical energy.

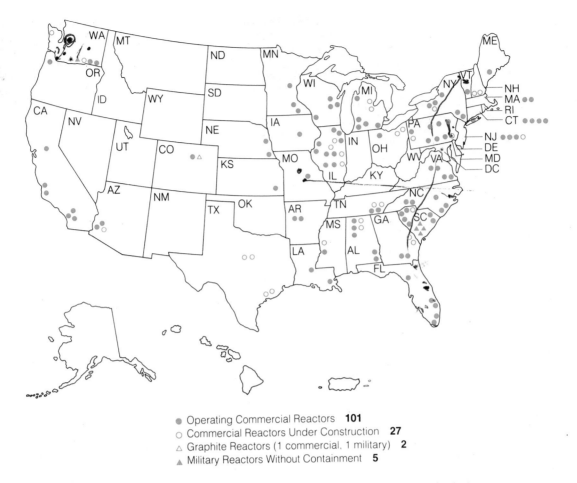

● Operating Commercial Reactors **101**
○ Commercial Reactors Under Construction **27**
△ Graphite Reactors (1 commercial, 1 military) **2**
▲ Military Reactors Without Containment **5**

Figure 17-4 Commercial and military-weapons nuclear fission reactors in operation or under construction in the United States in 1986. (Sources: Atomic Industrial Forum and U.S. Department of Energy)

Although there are about ten different types of nuclear reactors in operation throughout the world, almost three-fourths (62% in the United States) are **light-water reactors (LWRs).** Key parts of an LWR are the core, fuel assemblies, fuel rods, control rods, moderator, and coolant (Figure 17-5). The core of an LWR typically contains about 180 fuel assemblies, each of which contains about 200 long, thin fuel rods made of nonradioactive zirconium alloy or stainless steel (Figure 17-6). Each fuel rod is packed with eraser-sized pellets of uranium oxide (UO_2) fuel consisting of 3% fissionable uranium-235 and 97% nonfissionable uranium-238 (Figure 17-7). The uranium-235 in each fuel rod can produce energy equal to that from about three railroad cars of coal.

Interspersed between the fuel assemblies are control rods made of materials that capture neutrons. These rods are moved in and out of the reactor to regulate the rate of fission and thus the amount of power the reactor produces. To stop the fission process—because of an accident, to make repairs, or to remove spent fuel assemblies—all the control rods must be inserted.

All reactors circulate or place some type of mate-

rial, known as a moderator, between the fuel rods and fuel assemblies to slow the neutrons emitted by the fission process and thus sustain the chain reaction. Most of the world's reactors (73%) use ordinary water, called light water, as a moderator. The moderator in about 20% of the world's reactors (50% of those in the Soviet Union, including the ill-fated Chernobyl reactor) is solid graphite, a form of carbon; in 7% it is heavy water, in which the hydrogen atoms are hydrogen-2 or deuterium instead of hydrogen-1 as in light water. There are two graphite-moderated reactors in the United States. One is a commercial reactor at Platteville, Colorado, near Denver; the other at Hanford, Washington, produces plutonium-239 for use in nuclear weapons. All reactors also have a coolant circulating through the reactor core, removing generated heat to prevent fuel rods and other materials from melting and to produce electricity. Most water- and graphite-moderated reactors use water as a coolant; a few, however, use heavy water or some unreactive gas such as helium or argon.

A typical LWR has an energy efficiency of only 25% to 30%, compared to 40% for a coal-burning plant.

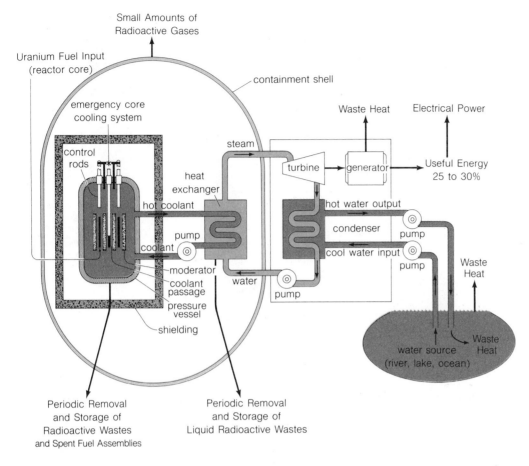

Figure 17-5 Light-water-moderated and -cooled nuclear power plant with a pressurized water reactor.

Although more expensive to build and operate, graphite-moderated, gas-cooled reactors, widely used in the United Kingdom, are more energy-efficient (38%) because they operate at a higher temperature.

Nuclear Fuel Cycle Nuclear power plants, each with one or more reactors, are only one part of the *nuclear fuel cycle* necessary for using nuclear energy to produce electricity (Figure 17-8). *In evaluating the safety and economics of nuclear power, it is necessary to look at the entire cycle—not just the nuclear plant itself.*

The nuclear fuel cycle for an LWR begins with the mining of uranium ore. In mills located near the mines, the ore is crushed, ground, and treated with a solvent to extract uranium oxide (U_3O_8), which is then concentrated. The resulting material, called "yellowcake," contains 70% to 90% uranium oxide with about 99.3% of the uranium in the form of nonfissionable uranium-238 and 0.7% as fissionable uranium-235.

The most serious health threat from this phase of the nuclear fuel cycle is inhalation of radioactive radon-222 gas produced by the decay of uranium-238. In

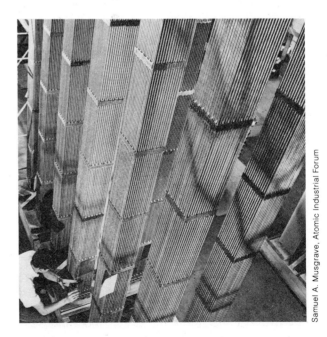

Figure 17-6 Bundles of fuel rods filled with pellets of enriched uranium-235 oxide serve as the fuel core for a conventional nuclear fission reactor.

Figure 17-7 Fuel pellets of enriched uranium-235 oxide.

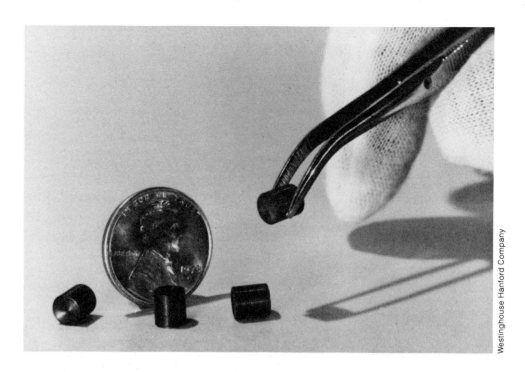

Westinghouse Hanford Company

poorly ventilated uranium mines miners have six times the normal average death rate from lung cancer from exposure to radon-222 gas, which can also cause leukemia and thyroid abnormalities. Since 1970 improved ventilation has reduced average radon levels in U.S. uranium mines about twentyfold but has increased radon levels outside the mines.

The uranium mining and milling process also produces debris, or tailings, which emit radioactive radon-222 gas for hundreds of thousands of years. At least 181 billion kilograms (200 million tons) of these wastes have been left piled on the ground near uranium mills (especially in Rocky Mountain states), dumped in municipal landfills, and used for construction of roads and an estimated 8,200 homes and buildings. For over two decades occupants of 5,000 such homes and buildings in Grand Junction, Colorado, were exposed to ionizing radiation equivalent to 3,650 chest X rays per year; the leukemia rate in Grand Junction is two times higher than in the rest of Colorado. A federal project is now under way to dig up and replace the foundations and other parts of these buildings.

There is considerable controversy over how past, present, and future mill tailings should be cleaned up and who should pay the cleanup costs. Cleanup of all the country's abandoned mill tailings sites may cost from $2 billion to $4 billion; by 1986 only $145 million had been appropriated and cleanup by the Department of Energy had begun at only three sites. Cleanup at active sites has not begun at all. Under industry-backed legislation presently being considered in Congress, utility customers and taxpayers would pay 85% of all cleanup costs for present and future sites, thus providing massive subsidies to milling companies, which make the profits but would pay only 15% of cleanup costs.

Yellowcake is shipped to a conversion plant, where it is converted to gaseous uranium hexafluoride (UF_6). This gas is sent to a government-owned gaseous diffusion enrichment plant, where its concentration of fissionable uranium-235 is increased from 0.7% to about 3% for use as fuel in an LWR (the concentration of uranium-235 in bomb-grade material is at least 85%). This enrichment process requires large amounts of energy, thus contributing the low net useful energy yield for nuclear power (Figure 3-17, p. 64). The enriched uranium hexafluoride then goes to a fuel fabrication plant, where it is converted to uranium dioxide (UO_2), encapsulated in pellets, and placed in fuel rods, which are put together in bundles or fuel assemblies for shipping to commercial nuclear power plants.

After about three years in a reactor, the concentration of fissionable uranium-235 in a fuel rod becomes too low for the chain reaction to proceed, or the rod becomes severely damaged from ionizing radiation. Thus, each year about one-third of the spent fuel elements in a reactor are removed and stored in large, concrete-lined pools of water at the plant site for several years. After they have cooled and lost some of their radioactivity, they can be sealed in heavily shielded, crash-proof casks and transported to other storage pools away from the reactor or to a permanent nuclear waste repository or dump. Because neither of these options exist in the United States, spent fuel is stored at plant sites, where adequate storage space is rapidly running out.

Figure 17-8 The nuclear fuel cycle.

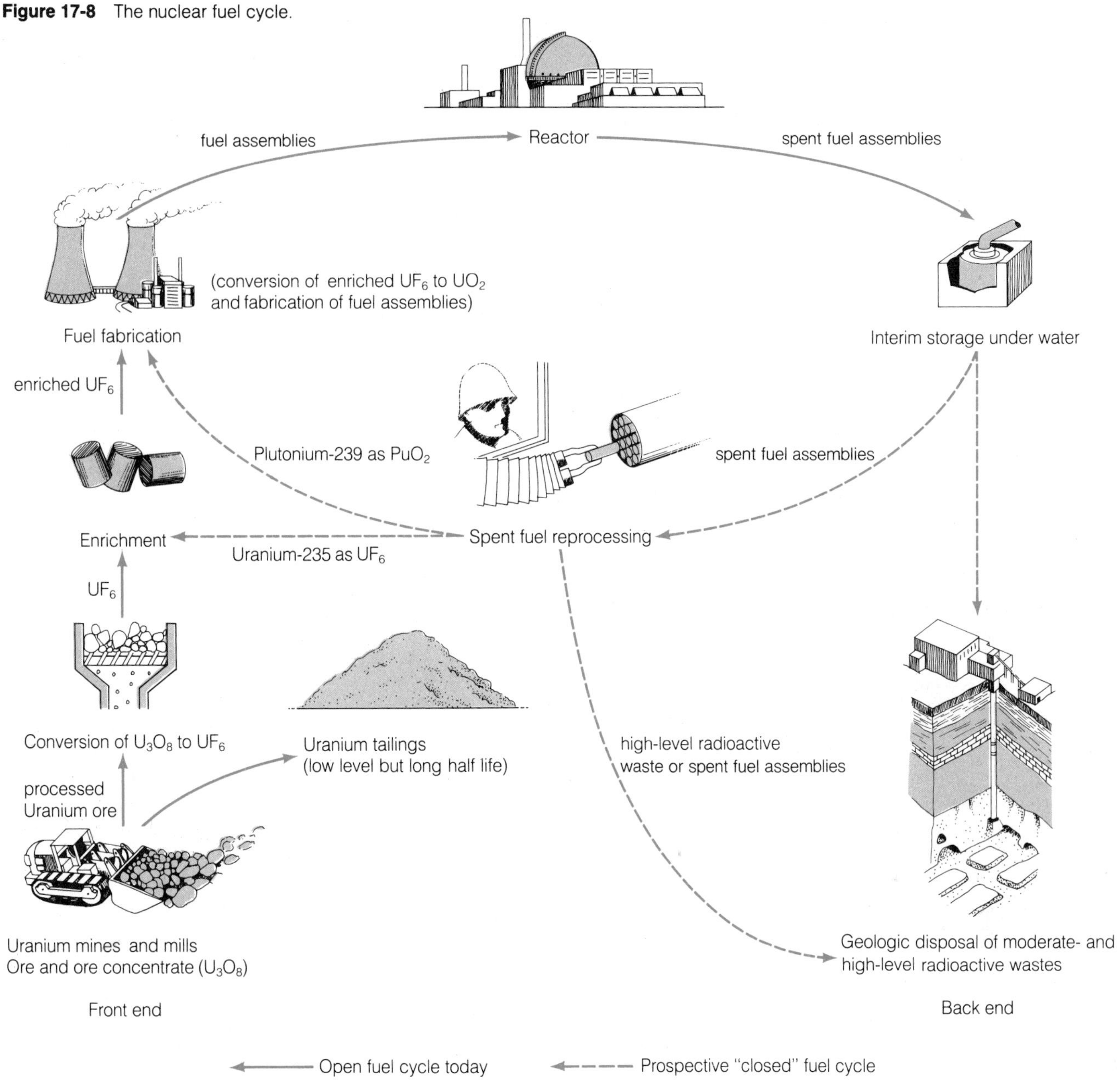

fuel assemblies → Reactor — spent fuel assemblies

(conversion of enriched UF_6 to UO_2 and fabrication of fuel assemblies)

Fuel fabrication

Interim storage under water

enriched UF_6

Plutonium-239 as PuO_2

spent fuel assemblies

Enrichment ← Spent fuel reprocessing ←

Uranium-235 as UF_6

UF_6

Conversion of U_3O_8 to UF_6

Uranium tailings (low level but long half life)

high-level radioactive waste or spent fuel assemblies

processed Uranium ore

Uranium mines and mills
Ore and ore concentrate (U_3O_8)

Geologic disposal of moderate- and high-level radioactive wastes

Front end

Back end

←——— Open fuel cycle today   ←---- Prospective "closed" fuel cycle

A third option is to transport spent fuel to a fuel-reprocessing plant, where remaining fissionable uranium-235 and plutonium-239 (produced as a by-product of the fission process) are removed and sent to a fuel fabrication plant for use in a conventional nuclear fission reactor or a breeder nuclear fission reactor. Three small commercial fuel-reprocessing plants are in operation (two in France and one in West Germany) and a large one is under construction in Great Britain. The United States has delayed development of commercial nuclear-fuel-reprocessing plants because such facilities would handle and ship nuclear fuel in a form that could be used to make nuclear weapons, and because of technical difficulties and high construction and operating costs.

Nuclear Reactor Safety Fission converts some fuel to radioactive fragments, and under intense neutron bombardment the metals in the fuel rods and other metal parts in the core are converted to radioactive isotopes. Because these radioactive fission products produce lots of heat, they continue to heat the fuel even after a reactor has been shut down. Thus, water or some other coolant must be circulated through the core to prevent a **meltdown** of the fuel rods and the reactor core. Such an event could result in the catastrophic release of massive quantities of highly radioactive materials into the environment. For this reason, commercial reactors in the United States (and, indeed, most countries) have a number of safety features (see Spotlight on p. 370).

1. A reactor cannot blow up like an atomic bomb because neither the fissionable uranium-235 fuel nor the fissionable plutonium-239 produced in the reactor when neutrons bombard nonfissionable uranium-238 is present in sufficient concentration to allow the necessary critical mass to form and explode.

2. The reactor vessel has 20-centimeter (8-inch) thick walls and is also surrounded by concrete and steel shields several feet thick to absorb neutrons and ionizing radiation emitted from the reactor core (Figure 17-5).

3. Control rods are automatically inserted into the core to stop fission under certain emergency conditions.

4. The shielded reactor vessel is set inside a steel-reinforced concrete containment building designed to prevent radioactive gases and materials from reaching the atmosphere as a result of most conceivable accidents except a complete core meltdown or a massive chemical explosion. Externally the building is designed to withstand tornadoes, direct collisions from light aircraft, artillery shells, and earthquakes.

5. Large filter systems (somewhat like giant vacuum cleaners) and chemical sprayers inside the containment building remove radioactive dust from the air and further reduce the chances of radioactivity reaching the environment. Several water spray and fan systems also operate inside the containment building to condense steam released from a ruptured reactor vessel and to prevent pressure from rising beyond the holding power of containment building walls.

6. If a coolant water pipeline breaks, an emergency core-cooling system is designed to flood the core automatically with tons of water within one minute to prevent meltdown of the reactor core. To guard against failure of electric power needed to drive the massive pumps in this system, two separate power lines service the plant and these are backed up by several diesel generators.

7. During plant construction, metal welds are subjected to X-ray inspection. When the plant goes into operation, an automatic system detects pipe leaks. Other metal parts are also checked periodically by visual and ultrasonic inspections for signs of leaks or cracking from corrosion.

8. Each major component of the safety system has an automatic backup system to replace it in the event of a failure. Although this elaborate multiple-backup strategy is not perfect, it is designed to reduce the probability of a serious accident to a very low level.

9. Over 300 major safety improvements required by the Nuclear Regulatory Commission (NRC) since the 1979 Three Mile Island accident have made U.S. nuclear plants much safer, and plant operator training has been improved. The NRC requires that state and local officials, the utility company, or both establish an NRC-approved plan for evacuation of all residents within a 16-kilometer (10-mile) radius of each plant; in 1987 the NRC considered reducing the evacuation zone to only 1.6 kilometers (1 mile).

Although a complete reactor core meltdown is extremely unlikely, it is possible. For example, the core might lose its cooling water through a break in one of the pipes that conduct cooling water and steam to and from the reactor core. If the emergency core-cooling system also failed, the loss of coolant would allow the reactor core to overheat and eventually melt down through its thick concrete slab into the earth. Depending on the geological characteristics of the underlying soil and rock, the melted core might sink 6 to 30 meters (20 to 100 feet) and gradually dissipate its heat, or it might burn itself more deeply into the earth's crust and contaminate groundwater with radioactive materials.

Another possibility is that a powerful gas or steam explosion inside the reactor containment vessel could split the containment building open and spew highly radioactive materials high into the atmosphere. The resulting cloud of radioactive materials, which would be at the mercy of the winds and weather, could kill and injure hundreds to tens of thousands of people and contaminate large areas with radioactive isotopes for hundreds to thousands of years. Such an explosion could result from a partial loss of cooling caused by a leak in the cooling system or a turbine failure. In a graphite-moderated reactor the explosion would also ignite the graphite, which would burn like a giant pile of coal, releasing more radioactive fission products into the lower atmosphere surrounding the site. A series of operator errors led to such a catastrophic explosion and graphite fire at the Soviet Union's Chernobyl nuclear reactor in 1986 (see Spotlight on pp. 371–73).

Winter 1957 Perhaps the worst nuclear disaster in history occurred in the Soviet Union in the southern Ural Mountains around the city of Kyshtym, believed then to be the center of plutonium production for Soviet nuclear weapons. Though the cause of the accident and the number of people killed and injured remain a secret, a massive amount of radiation was released—allegedly from an explosion of large quantities of radioactive wastes carelessly stored in shallow trenches. Today the area is deserted, hundreds of square miles have been sealed off, a river has been diverted around the area, and the names of about 30 towns and villages in the region have disappeared from Soviet maps.

October 7, 1957 The water-cooled, graphite-moderated Windscale facility for producing plutonium for nuclear weapons north of Liverpool,

England, underwent an explosion and caught fire as the Chernobyl plant did 19 years later. By the time the fire was put out, 200 square miles of countryside had been contaminated with radioactive material. An estimated 33 people died prematurely from cancers traced to effects of the accident.

March 22, 1975 The flame from a candle used by a maintenance worker to test for air leaks at the Brown's Ferry commercial nuclear reactor near Decatur, Alabama, set off a fire that knocked out five emergency core-cooling systems. Although the reactor's cooling water dropped to a dangerous level, backup systems prevented any radioactive material from escaping into the environment. At the same plant, in 1978, a worker's rubber boot fell into a reactor and led to an unsuccessful $2.8 million search.

Such incidents, based on unpredictable human errors, are fairly common in most nuclear plants.

March 28, 1979 In what is considered the worst accident in the history of U.S. commercial nuclear power, one of the two reactors at the Three Mile Island (TMI) nuclear plant near Harrisburg, Pennsylvania, lost its coolant water because of a series of mechanical failures (involving a main and an auxiliary water pump, a stuck valve, and several other pieces of equipment) and human operator errors not foreseen in safety studies (Figure 17-9). The reactor's core became partially uncovered, underwent a partial core meltdown, and small but unknown amounts of ionizing radiation escaped into the atmosphere. Investigators found that had a stuck valve stayed opened for just another 30 to 60 minutes, there would have been

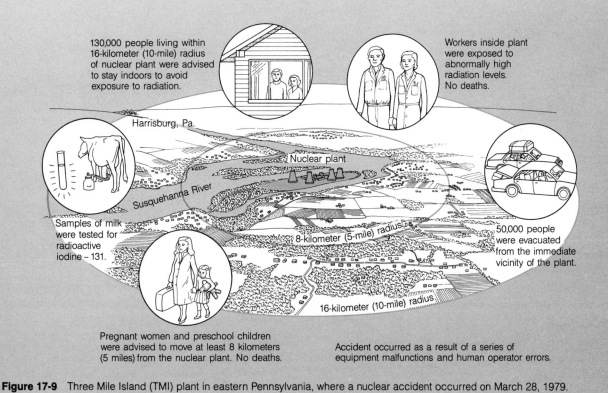

130,000 people living within 16-kilometer (10-mile) radius of nuclear plant were advised to stay indoors to avoid exposure to radiation.

Workers inside plant were exposed to abnormally high radiation levels. No deaths.

Harrisburg, Pa.

Nuclear plant

Susquehanna River

Samples of milk were tested for radioactive iodine – 131.

8-kilometer (5-mile) radius

50,000 people were evacuated from the immediate vicinity of the plant.

16-kilometer (10-mile) radius

Pregnant women and preschool children were advised to move at least 8 kilometers (5 miles) from the nuclear plant. No deaths.

Accident occurred as a result of a series of equipment malfunctions and human operator errors.

Figure 17-9 Three Mile Island (TMI) plant in eastern Pennsylvania, where a nuclear accident occurred on March 28, 1979.

a complete meltdown. Although no one is known to have died as a result of the accident, the long-term health effects on workers and nearby residents is still being debated because data published on the amount of radiation released during the accident are contradictory and incomplete. The cleanup of the damaged TMI reactor, which will probably cost $1 billion to $1.5 billion (compared to the $700 million construction cost of the reactor), threatens the utility with bankruptcy and may not be completed until 1990 or later. Confusing and misleading statements about the seriousness of the accident issued by Metropolitan Edison, which owns the plant, and by the Nuclear Regulatory Commission seriously eroded public confidence in the safety of nuclear power.

March 8, 1981 At a problem-ridden nuclear power plant in Tsurage,

Japan, radioactive wastewater leaked from a tank for several hours. Workers sent to mop it up were exposed to ionizing radiation. For six weeks the incident was kept secret, until radioactivity was detected in a nearby bay.

June 9, 1985 Despite new safety standards and improved operator training since the TMI accident, 16 equipment failures and a human operator who punched the wrong button led to a partial loss of cooling water in a reactor at the Davis-Besse nuclear plant near Toledo, Ohio. Fortunately, the problem, similar to that at TMI, was corrected in time by auxiliary cooling pumps, and no ionizing radiation was released to the environment. Nuclear power critics contend that TMI and hundreds of other serious incidents like this one have not led to a complete meltdown primarily because of luck. Nuclear industry officials claim that

the fact that a meltdown has not occurred demonstrates that the multiple-backup safety systems work.

April 26, 1986 Two gas explosions inside one of the four graphite-moderated, water-cooled reactors at the Soviet Chernobyl nuclear power plant north of Kiev blew the roof off the reactor building and set the graphite core on fire. The accident occurred when engineers deliberately turned off most of the reactor's key automatic safety and warning systems to keep them from interfering with an unauthorized safety experiment they were conducting (Figure 17-10). The explosions and the resulting fire spewed highly radioactive materials into the atmosphere, where they were carried by winds over parts of the Soviet Union and much of Europe (Figure 17-11). Potentially health-threatening radioactive materials were deposited more than 2,000 kilome-

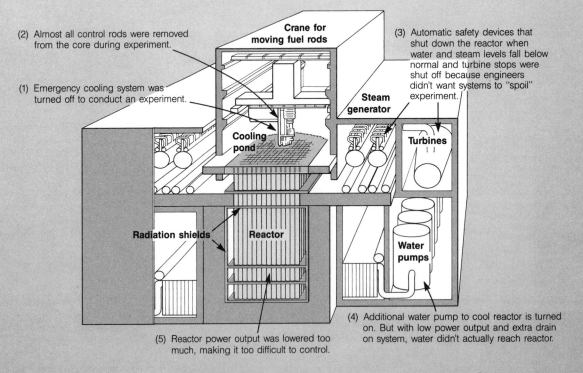

(2) Almost all control rods were removed from the core during experiment.

(1) Emergency cooling system was turned off to conduct an experiment.

Crane for moving fuel rods

(3) Automatic safety devices that shut down the reactor when water and steam levels fall below normal and turbine stops were shut off because engineers didn't want systems to "spoil" experiment.

Steam generator

Cooling pond

Turbines

Radiation shields

Reactor

Water pumps

(4) Additional water pump to cool reactor is turned on. But with low power output and extra drain on system, water didn't actually reach reactor.

(5) Reactor power output was lowered too much, making it too difficult to control.

Figure 17-10 Major events leading to the Chernobyl nuclear power plant accident on April 26, 1986 in the Soviet Union.

ters (1,250 miles) from the plant in over 20 countries. During the ten days that it took firefighters to get the intensely hot graphite fire under control, more radioactive materials were released into the nearby area. Radiation levels rose quickly around the plant and during the ten days following the explosion 135,000 people living within 30 kilometers (18 miles) of the plant were evacuated by an armada of 1,100 buses. These people have been resettled in other villages and probably will not be allowed to return to their homes for at least four years. Five months after the accident 31 plant workers and firefighters had died from exposure to high levels of ionizing radiation, 200 others were suffering from acute radiation sickness (many of whom will die prematurely from cancer), and a land area of 2,590 square kilometers (1,000 square miles) around the reactor was contaminated with radioactive fallout. All nearby forests will have to be cut down and the topsoil removed and buried. Some farmland in the area may have to be abandoned for many decades. Soviet and western medical experts estimate that at least 5,000 and perhaps 100,000 additional people in the Soviet Union will die prematurely over the next 70 years from cancer caused by exposure to ionizing radiation. Thousands of others will be afflicted with thyroid tumors, cataracts, and sterility. One-half to three times as many additional premature deaths are likely outside the Soviet Union. Estimated damages run from $3 billion to $5 billion, but taking into account long-term health effects, damages may be as high as $14 billion. Some American nuclear experts contend that had the reactor been designed with the key safety features of reactors in the United States and most of the rest of the world, no radioactive materials would have been released. In 1987 the United States shut down a Chernobyl-type military reactor at Hanford, Washington, to make safety improvements after a study documented 54 serious safety violations at the facility during 1985 and 1986.

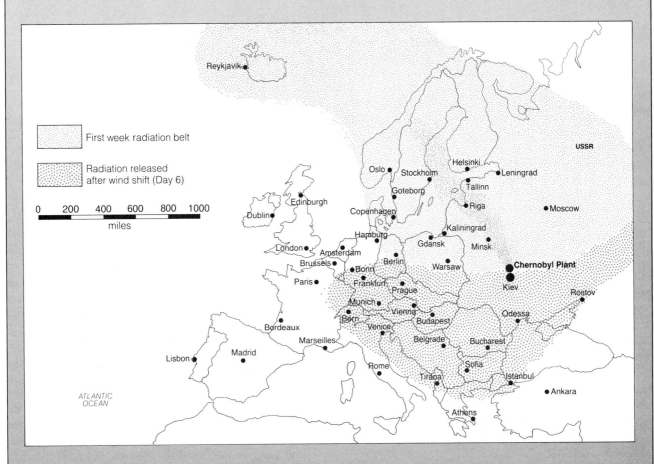

Figure 17-11 Spread of radioactive fallout over parts of the Soviet Union and much of eastern and western Europe after the Chernobyl accident. (Data from National Oceanic and Atmospheric Administration)

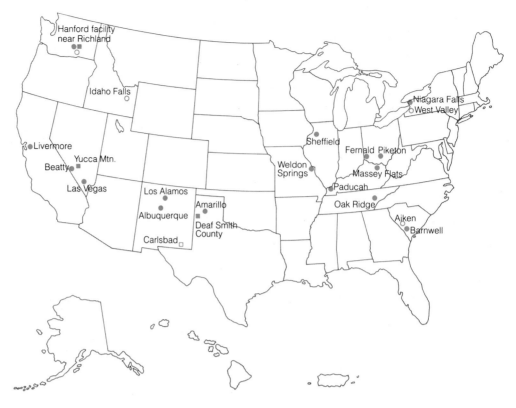

○ Temporary storage of high-level military waste
● Low-level military and commercial waste
□ Permanent storage of military high-level waste (under construction)
■ Possible site of first permanent storage facility for high-level commercial waste

Figure 17-12 U.S. sites for storage of low-level and high-level radioactive wastes from nuclear weapon production and commercial nuclear power plants.

An exhaustive study of the TMI accident concluded:

The principal deficiencies in commercial reactor safety today are not hardware problems, they are management problems . . . problems that cannot be solved by the addition of a few pipes or valves . . . or, for that matter, by a resident federal inspector.

Although operator training was improved after the 1979 TMI accident, it only takes one case of human error to cause an accident (see the Enrichment Study at the end of Chapter 6). In 1981 a federal inspector entered the control room at Commonwealth Edison's reactor near Morris, Illinois, and found two operators asleep; an inspector for Florida Light and Power found a reactor operating at full power with no one in the control room. Since 1981 at least four other incidents of snoozing on duty have been reported.

Thirty years after the first nuclear power plant began operating in the United States, there is still no officially accepted study of just how safe or unsafe these plants are and no study of the safety of the entire nuclear fuel cycle. Despite the uncertainty and controversy over reactor safety, in 1985 the NRC estimated that there is a 45% chance of a complete core meltdown at a U.S. reactor sometime during the next 20 years and a 12% chance of two such meltdowns. They estimate that such an accident would cause up to 100,000 deaths in the first year, 600,000 injuries, 400,000 ultimate cancer deaths, and $300 billion in damages.

Most people and businesses suffering injuries or property damage from a major nuclear accident would receive little if any financial reimbursement. Since the beginnings of nuclear power in the 1950s, insurance companies have been unwilling to underwrite more than a small fraction of the estimated risks. Because having to bear the costs of liability would have prevented the U.S. nuclear industry from ever being developed, federal law in effect since 1957 limits insurance liability from a nuclear accident in the United States to a maximum of only $640 million. Of this amount, $160 million is to be paid by insurance carried

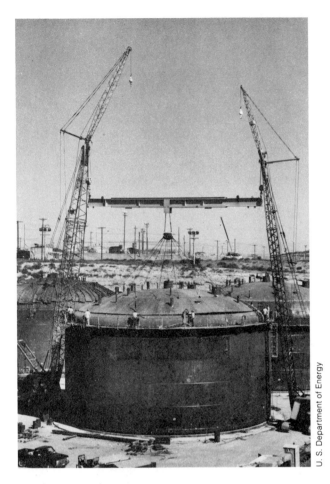

Figure 17-13 Construction of double-walled steel tanks for storing high-level liquid radioactive wastes at the federal government's Hanford nuclear weapon production facility near Richland, Washington. Each tank holds 4 million liters (1 million gallons) and will be covered with seven feet of earth.

have been pushing the NRC to reduce the evacuation area around U.S. reactors to only 1.6 kilometers (1 mile), contending that new safety studies show that less radiation would escape in the event of an accident than previously thought. Reducing the size of the evacuation zone would also limit the ability of state and local governments to block the licensing of new plants by refusing to participate in emergency planning they considered inadequate and ineffective. In 1987 the NRC was considering adopting a regulation that would give the NRC the power to override refusal of state authorities to accept evacuation plans they considered inadequate.

Disposal and Storage of Radioactive Wastes Each part of the nuclear fuel cycle for military and commercial nuclear reactors produces a mixture of solid, liquid, and gaseous, low-level to high-level radioactive wastes that must be stored for about ten times their half-lives until their radioactivity has dropped to extremely low levels. Most low-level radioactive wastes have relatively short half-lives measured in decades or hundreds of years, whereas high-level wastes have half-lives of thousands of years.

From the 1940s to 1970 most low-level radioactive waste was dumped into the ocean in steel drums. Since 1970 low-level wastes have been buried at 13 government facilities for defense-related wastes and 3 sites run by private firms under state and federal regulations (Figure 17-12). Materials are transported to the sites in steel drums. Several drums are then placed in a large container, which is buried in trenches and covered with several feet of dirt.

High-level radioactive wastes consist mostly of spent fuel rods from commercial nuclear power plants and an assortment of wastes from nuclear weapons facilities. By 1987 about 49,000 highly radioactive spent fuel assemblies from U.S. nuclear power plants were stored temporarily in deep pools of water at nuclear plant sites, pending the development of a method for long-term storage or disposal. But space at reactor sites is running out, and 4,000 more spent assemblies are added each year. According to the EPA, spent fuel rods must be stored safely for 10,000 years before they decay to acceptable levels of radioactivity.

High-level liquid wastes from nuclear weapons production, equal in volume to about 200 Olympic-size swimming pools, are also awaiting permanent storage. These wastes, which remain lethal for centuries, are presently stored in underground tanks at the government's Idaho Falls (Idaho), Barnwell (South Carolina), and Hanford (Washington) facilities (Figure 17-13). These tanks must be continuously monitored for corrosion and leaks. Nearly 2 million liters (530,000 gallons) of highly radioactive wastes have already leaked from older, single-shell tanks built between 1943

by the utility company on each plant, and the rest is to be paid by the federal government—the taxpayers. Repeated attempts to have this law repealed or to raise liability limits have failed.

There is also concern over whether nuclear accident evacuation zones and plans in the United States are adequate. After the TMI accident a 16-kilometer (10-mile) evacuation zone was adopted around all U.S. commercial reactors. In 1986 nuclear critics called for an extension of evacuation zones to at least the 30-kilometer (18-mile) zone Soviet officials found necessary after the Chernobyl nuclear accident. These critics point out that areas around many U.S. reactors are up to ten times more densely populated than those around most Soviet reactors and many urban areas near U.S. reactors would be almost impossible to evacuate. In the case of a nuclear accident most Americans would get into their cars and clog up evacuation routes, a situation that didn't occur in the Soviet Union because few people had cars.

The U.S. nuclear industry and utilities, however,

and 1965 at the Hanford and Savannah River storage sites. However, a National Academy of Sciences study concluded that these leaks have not caused any significant radiation hazard to public health. Storage tanks constructed after 1968 have a double shell; if the inner wall corrodes, the liquid will spill into the space between the two walls, where it can be detected in time to be pumped into another tank.

In 1986 once-secret documents revealed that ionizing radiation had been deliberately and accidentally released from the Hanford nuclear waste dump over a 40-year period with no reporting of these incidents to local residents. A 1986 EPA report revealed 14,000 incidents of publicly unreported radioactive waste leaks at the Savannah River Weapons Plant, where nuclear waste storage tanks stand near shallow waters that drain into the Savannah River and above the Tuscaloosa aquifer, a major source of drinking water for parts of South Carolina, Georgia, Alabama, and northern Florida.

After 30 years of research and debate there is still no widely agreed upon scientific solution to how high-level radioactive wastes can be stored safely for the 10,000 years presently required by EPA regulations (see Spotlight on p. 377). Regardless of the storage method, most U.S. citizens strongly oppose the location of a nuclear waste disposal facility anywhere near them. Under present federal law a state or an Indian tribe can oppose the location of a high-level federal nuclear waste repository on its land. This refusal can be overridden only by Congress within 90 days. By 1985 at least 22 states had enacted laws banning radioactive waste disposal.

In 1983 the Department of Energy began building the first underground repository in the United States, to be used only for long-term storage of thousands of tons of high-level radioactive wastes produced by the nuclear weapons program. This $1 billion structure is being built in a salt bed deep under federal land about 40 kilometers (25 miles) east of Carlsbad, New Mexico. Shortly after construction began, it was discovered that water had already entered the underground storage chambers through the ventilation shaft. If water ever penetrates the waste, some experts fear that some of the highly toxic radioactive plutonium-239 could be carried fairly rapidly to the nearby Pecos River. Other experts believe the site is safe.

In 1982 Congress passed the Nuclear Waste Policy Act, which established a timetable for the Department of Energy to choose a site and build the country's first deep underground repository for long-term storage of high-level radioactive wastes from *commercial* nuclear reactors. In 1985 the Department of Energy announced that it planned to build the first repository, at a cost of $6 billion to $10 billion, based on the design shown in Figure 17-14. It is to be built at one of three sites: a compacted volcanic ash formation in Yucca Mountain, Nevada, northwest of Las Vegas; a volcanic basalt formation under the Hanford federal nuclear weapons facility in southeastern Washington; or a salt deposit in Deaf Smith County, Texas, west of Amarillo (Figure 17-12). After each site is tested for five years, the president of the United States is to decide in 1991 which site will be used. Because the first repository will be filled quickly with wastes already awaiting storage, a second site is supposed to be selected in the eastern United States, where most reactors are located, after the first site has opened.

The Department of Energy currently estimates that the costs of building and running the two sites will be from $21 billion to $35 billion, which is being paid for by a 0.1 cent per kilowatt-hour charge added to all electricity bills since 1983. The U.S. General Accounting Office, however, estimates that the cost may be as high as $114 billion. The first site was supposed to be ready by 1998, but in 1987 the DOE announced that it would be delayed to at least 2003; most observers believe it will be delayed to 2008 or later. By 1986 intense opposition from citizens and elected officials in states where the potential sites are to be located and from geologists identifying possible geological and water-contamination problems with each of the three sites had given many members of Congress second thoughts about the entire project.

Citizens in cities and states along the proposed routes for transporting the highly radioactive wastes to each of the possible western repository sites are also concerned. If all waste is transported by truck, there will be about 6,405 shipments every year passing through parts of 45 states—an average of 17 shipments a day for 30 years. If all waste is transported by rail, there will be about 830 shipments annually. A study by the NRC concluded that a serious accident involving a truck or train passing through a heavily urbanized area could result in damages of $2 billion to $3 billion, only part of which would be covered by the insurance liability limits set by federal law on any type of nuclear accident.

Decommissioning Nuclear Power Plants   The useful operating life for a nuclear power plant is between 30 and 40 years. Since the core and many other parts contain large quantities of radioactive materials, the plant cannot simply be abandoned or demolished by a wrecking ball like coal-fired and other power plants. The *decommissioning process* is the final step of the nuclear fuel cycle. Worldwide more than 20 commercial reac-

The long-term safe storage or disposal of high-level radioactive wastes is believed to be technically possible. However, it is essentially impossible to establish that any method will work over the thousands of years required before the wastes decay to safe levels. Some of the proposed methods and their possible drawbacks:

1. *Bury it deep underground.* The currently favored method is to concentrate the waste, convert it to a dry solid, fuse it with glass or a ceramic material, seal it in a metal canister, and bury it permanently in deep underground salt, granite, or other stable geological formations that are earthquake-resistant and waterproof (Figure 17-14). Some geologists question this approach, arguing that extensive drilling and tunneling can destabilize such rock structures and that present geological knowledge is not sufficient to predict the paths of groundwater flows that could contaminate groundwater drinking supplies with radioactive wastes.

2. *Shoot it into space or into the sun.* Even if technically feasible, costs would be very high and a launch accident of a rocket or space vehicle could disperse high-level radioactive wastes over a wide area of the earth's surface.

3. *Bury it under the Antarctic ice sheets or the Greenland ice caps.* The long-term stability of the ice sheets is unknown, and they could be destabilized by heat from the wastes; retrieval would be difficult or impossible if the method failed.

4. *Dump it into downward-descending, deep ocean bottom sediments.* The long-term stability and motion of these sediments are unknown, and wastes could eventually be spewed out somewhere else by volcanic activity; waste containers might leak and contaminate the ocean before being carried down; retrieval would probably be impossible if the method failed.

5. *Change it into harmless or less harmful isotopes.* Presently there is no known way to do this; even if it should become technically feasible, costs would probably be extremely high and new toxic materials and lower-level radioactive wastes created would also require safe disposal.

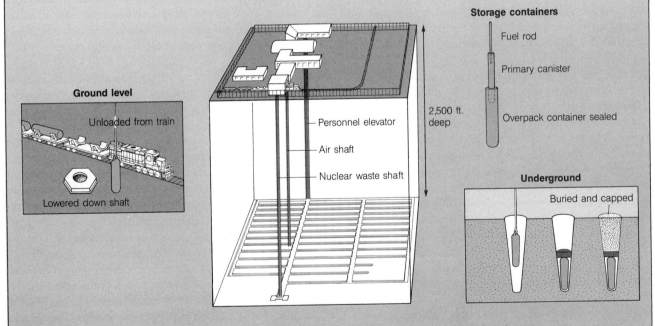

Figure 17-14 Proposed general design for deep underground permanent storage of high-level radioactive wastes from commercial nuclear power plants in the United States. (U.S. Department of Energy)

tors (4 in the United States) had been shut down and were awaiting decommissioning by 1986. Another 225 large commercial units (67 in the United States) will be retired between 2000 and 2010.

Three ways to decommission a nuclear reactor have been proposed: entombment, dismantlement, and mothballing prior to dismantlement. Each method would involve shutting down the plant, removing the spent fuel from the reactor core, draining all liquids, flushing all pipes, and sending all radioactive materials to appropriate waste storage sites. *Entombment* would involve covering the reactor with reinforced concrete and erecting barriers to keep out intruders. Although once viewed as the easiest way out, research has indicated that some remaining radioactive materials would still be dangerous long after the concrete tomb had crumbled. *Dismantlement* would involve decontaminating and taking the reactor apart immediately after shutdown and shipping all radioactive debris to a radioactive waste-burial facility. It is considered the least expensive method. With *mothballing*, a barrier and 24-hour security guard system would be set up to prevent public access, allowing the plant to undergo radioactive decay for 50 to 100 years before dismantling. Dismantling just one large reactor would require a 1,400-truck caravan to carry away the contaminated steel and concrete.

Presently most U.S. utilities favor immediate dismantlement, whereas utilities in France, Canada, and West Germany are planning to mothball their reactors for several decades before dismantlement. Dismantlement of the first commercial nuclear reactor in the United States near Shippingport, Pennsylvania, began in 1986. This five-year project, involving a small reactor, is expected to cost at least $100 million. Utility companies estimate that dismantlement of a typical reactor 10 to 20 times larger and containing several hundred times as much radioactivity as the Shippingport reactor should cost about $170 million, but most analysts consider this figure much too low and put the cost at $1 billion to $3 billion per reactor. Adding dismantlement costs to the already high price of producing electricity by nuclear fission has led some analysts to believe that nuclear power will never become economically feasible compared to other alternatives.

Proliferation of Nuclear Weapons Since the late 1950s the United States has been giving away and selling to other countries various forms of nuclear technology. By 1987 at least 14 other countries had entered the international market as sellers of nuclear technology. For decades the U.S. government has denied that the information, components, and materials used in the nuclear fuel cycle could be used to make nuclear weapons. In 1981, however, a Los Alamos National Laboratory report admitted: "There is no technical demarcation between the military and civilian reactor and there never was one."

Between 4 and 9 kilograms (9 to 20 pounds) of either plutonium-239 or uranium-233, a mass about the size of an orange, and 11 to 25 kilograms (24 to 55 pounds) of uranium-235 are needed to make a small atomic bomb capable of blowing up a large building or a city block and contaminating a much larger area with radioactive materials for centuries. Although difficult, it is believed that a handful of trained people could make such a "blockbuster" nuclear bomb if they could get enough fissionable bomb-grade material. A crude 10-kiloton nuclear weapon placed properly and detonated during working hours could topple the World Trade Center in New York City, easily killing more people than those killed by the 20,000-kiloton atomic bomb the United States dropped on Hiroshima, Japan, in 1945.

Spent reactor fuel is so highly radioactive that theft is unlikely, but separated plutonium-239 is easily handled. Although bomb-grade plutonium-239 is heavily guarded, it could be stolen from nuclear weapons facilities, especially by employees. Each year about 3% of the approximately 126,000 people working with U.S. nuclear weapons are relieved of duty because of drug use, mental instability, or other security risks. By 1978 at least 320 kilograms (700 pounds) of plutonium-239 was missing from commercial and government-operated reactors and storage sites in the United States— enough to make 32 to 70 atomic bombs, each capable of blowing up a city block. No one knows whether this missing plutonium was stolen or whether it represents sloppy measuring and bookkeeping techniques.

Concentrated bomb-grade plutonium fuel could also be stolen from a commercial fuel-reprocessing plant, stolen from more than 150 research and test reactors operating in 30 countries, or hijacked from shipments to six experimental breeder nuclear fission power plants already in operation in parts of Europe. Bomb-grade fuel might also be manufactured by using one of the simpler and cheaper technologies for isotope separation presently being developed to concentrate 3% uranium-235 to weapons-grade material.

Actually, those who would steal plutonium-239 need not bother to make atomic bombs. They could simply use a conventional explosive charge to disperse the plutonium into the atmosphere from atop any tall building. Dispersed in this manner, 1 kilogram (2.2 pounds) of plutonium oxide powder could theoretically contaminate 7.7 square kilometers (3 square

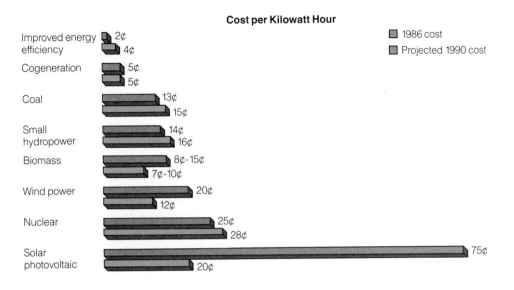

Cost per Kilowatt Hour

- Improved energy efficiency: 2¢ (1986 cost), 4¢ (Projected 1990 cost)
- Cogeneration: 5¢ (1986 cost), 5¢ (Projected 1990 cost)
- Coal: 13¢ (1986 cost), 15¢ (Projected 1990 cost)
- Small hydropower: 14¢ (1986 cost), 16¢ (Projected 1990 cost)
- Biomass: 8¢-15¢ (1986 cost), 7¢-10¢ (Projected 1990 cost)
- Wind power: 20¢ (1986 cost), 12¢ (Projected 1990 cost)
- Nuclear: 25¢ (1986 cost), 28¢ (Projected 1990 cost)
- Solar photovoltaic: 75¢ (1986 cost), 20¢ (Projected 1990 cost)

■ 1986 cost
■ Projected 1990 cost

Figure 17-15 Costs of electricity generated by improving energy efficiency and by various types of new power plants (including costs of construction, fuel, and operation) in the United States in 1983, with projections to 1990. (Sources of data: Charles Komanoff and Worldwatch Institute, January 1984)

miles) with radioactivity. This radiation, which would remain at dangerous levels for at least 100,000 years, could cause lung cancers among those who inhaled contaminated air or dust in such areas.

One suggestion for reducing the possibility of diversion of plutonium fuel from the nuclear fuel cycle is to contaminate it with other substances that render it more dangerous to handle and unfit as weapons material. But so far no acceptable "spiking agent" has emerged that could not be removed by reprocessing or isotope separation.

Soaring Costs: The Achilles Heel of Nuclear Power The largest cutback in commercial nuclear power has taken place in the United States, primarily because of economics. After 35 years of development and a $154 billion investment, including $44 billion in government subsidies, the 101 nuclear power reactors in operation in the United States produced no more of the country's commercial energy than that provided by wood and crop wastes with hardly any government subsidies.

After Hiroshima and Nagasaki, scientists who developed the bomb and elected officials were determined to show the world that the peaceful uses of atomic energy would outweigh the immense harm it had done. Utility companies were skeptical but began ordering nuclear power plants in the late 1950s for four main reasons. First, the Atomic Energy Commission and builders of nuclear reactors projected that nuclear power would produce electricity at such a low cost that it would be "too cheap to meter." Second, the nuclear industry projected that the reactors would have an 80% capacity factor—a measure of the time a reactor is able to produce electricity at its full power potential. Third, the first round of commercial reactors was built with the government paying approximately one-fourth of the cost; these reactors were provided to utilities at a fixed cost with no cost overruns allowed. Fourth, Congress passed legislation that protected the nuclear industry and utilities from significant liability to the general public in case of accident. It was an offer utility company officials could not resist. Today many wished they had.

Since the construction of the first batch of nuclear power plants, it has become increasingly clear that nuclear power is an extraordinarily expensive way to produce electricity, even when it is heavily subsidized to partially protect it from free market competition. Construction costs for nuclear power plants in the United States in terms of dollars per kilowatt of electricity have risen more than tenfold since 1960, and this does not even include the costs of storing radioactive wastes and decommissioning plants. By 1986, producing electricity in a new nuclear plant in the United States had a total cost significantly higher than those of coal, cogeneration, and improved energy efficiency (Figure 17-15). By 1990 nuclear power is expected to be even less competitive with other methods for producing electricity in the United States.

Operating costs have also been higher than projected because in 1983 U.S. reactors operated an average of only 56% of their capacity—far below the 80% capacity factor projected by proponents of nuclear power in the 1950s. In contrast, reactors in West Germany operated at an average of 71% of their capacity.

Reasons for this difference include the lack of standardization of U.S. plant design and poorer design, construction quality, and management than in West Germany.

Banks and other lending institutions have become quite skeptical about financing new U.S. nuclear power plants after the Three Mile Island accident showed that utility companies could lose $1 billion or more in equipment in an hour, plus $1 billion to $1.5 billion in cleanup costs, even without any known serious public health effects.

A 1984 report by the Office of Technology Assessment concluded that nuclear power in the United States is not likely to be expanded in this century beyond the reactors already under construction. Nuclear industry officials believe that this bleak outlook for the future of U.S. nuclear power could change if **(1)** electricity demand were to rise sharply in the 1980s and 1990s (many utilities still push for costly and energy-wasting electric resistance heating to keep demand up); **(2)** costs and time needed to build a nuclear plant were cut significantly by standardizing design and by reducing paperwork, tests, and citizen involvement in the federal licensing process (industry proposals supported by the Reagan administration); **(3)** the federal government and lending institutions could be convinced to finance the development of new and inherently much safer reactor designs to replace existing reactors after their useful life; and **(4)** public confidence in the safety of nuclear power were restored (see Spotlight).

Several governments with major nuclear power programs—especially Japan, France (see Spotlight on p. 381), the United Kingdom, West Germany, and the Soviet Union—remain strongly committed to using nuclear power to produce a significant amount of their electricity by the end of the century. But public opposition to nuclear power is growing in these and other countries, costs have been much higher than projected (except in France), and plans have been scaled back sharply. By 1987 over two-thirds of the people in most European countries were opposed to the construction of any additional nuclear power plants in their countries and half of the people favored shutting down existing plants.

Advantages and Disadvantages of Conventional Nuclear Fission Using conventional nuclear fission to produce electricity has a number of advantages. Nuclear plants do not release carbon dioxide, particulate matter, sulfur dioxide, or nitrogen oxides into the atmosphere like coal-fired plants. Water pollution and disruption of land are low to moderate if the entire nuclear fuel cycle operates normally. Because of mul-

Since the Three Mile Island accident the U.S. nuclear industry and utility companies have financed a $40 million advertising campaign by the Committee for Energy Awareness to improve the industry's image, resell nuclear power to the American public, and downgrade the use of solar and other alternatives to nuclear power. These magazine and television ads do not let readers know they are paid for by the nuclear industry and many repeatedly use the misleading argument that nuclear power is needed in the United States to reduce dependence on imported oil.

In fact, since the oil embargo of 1973, the reduction of oil use and oil imports has come not from increased use of nuclear power but mostly from improvements in energy efficiency, increased use of wood as a fuel in homes and businesses, and increased use of coal to produce electricity. Since 1979 only about 5% of the electricity in the United States has been produced by burning oil; thus, phasing in the 27 nuclear power plants still under construction in 1986 will not save the country any significant amount of domestic or imported oil.

tiple safety systems, a catastrophic accident is extremely unlikely.

There are also some disadvantages. Construction and operating costs in the United States and most countries are high and rapidly rising, even with massive government and consumer subsidies. Electricity can be produced by many other, less controversial methods at a cost equal to or lower than that of nuclear power. Although large-scale accidents are unlikely, a combination of mechanical and human errors, sabotage, or shipping accidents could again result in the release of deadly radioactive materials into the environment. The net useful energy yield of nuclear-generated electricity is low (Figure 3-17, p. 64). There is considerable disagreement over how high-level radioactive wastes should be stored; some scientists doubt that an acceptably safe method can ever be developed. Military and commercial nuclear energy programs commit future generations to safely storing radioactive wastes for thousands of years. Furthermore, the

France has the world's most ambitious and cost-efficient plan for using nuclear energy. By 1986 it had 40 reactors, providing 65% of its electricity, and 15 more under construction, with the goal of generating 75% of its electricity by 1990. France builds its reactors in less than 6 years—compared to 12 years in the United States. The plant construction cost per kilowatt of electricity in France is about half that in Japan and most European countries and one-third that in the United States. Furthermore, France has the lowest electricity prices in Europe and exports electricity to some of its European neighbors.

The major factor responsible for France's ability to build plants cheaper and quicker than most countries is rigid centralized government control. All plants are built to standardized designs with the overall responsibility for design, construction, and operation of all nuclear plants in the hands of a single government-run national utility company. There is little opportunity for public criticism of the program and most citizens accept the deeply embedded tradition of government secrecy. The nuclear program survives largely through government subsidies and an increasing national debt (already the third largest in the world), rather than through open-market economic competition with coal and other energy alternatives.

Since 1984, however, the demand for electricity projected by France's nuclear planners has not kept up with the rapid expansion of supply (see Guest Essay at the end of Chapter 16). Because of a massive national debt and a glut of electricity, France reduced its orders for new reactors from six in 1980 to one in 1986 and 1987. The French Planning Ministry concluded that the only reason for not halting all orders for new reactors for several years is to preserve jobs at the government-run company that designs, constructs, and operates all French nuclear plants. In 1986, polls revealed that 52% of the French public—which for years had supported nuclear power by a large majority—were opposed to construction of any additional nuclear plants in France.

existence of nuclear power technology helps spread knowledge and materials that could be used to make nuclear weapons.

17-3 NONRENEWABLE BREEDER NUCLEAR FISSION

At present rates of use the world's supply of uranium should last for at least 100 years and perhaps 200 years. However, some scientists believe that if there is a sharp rise in the use of nuclear fission to produce electricity after the year 2000, breeder nuclear fission reactors can be developed to avoid rapid depletion of the world's supply of uranium fuel (see Guest Essay at the end of this chapter). Widespread use of breeder reactors could increase the present estimated lifetime of the world's affordable uranium supplies for at least 1,000 years and perhaps several thousand years.

A **breeder nuclear fission reactor** produces within itself new fissionable fuel in the form of plutonium-239 from nonfissionable uranium-238, an isotope that is in plentiful supply (see Figure 3-2, p. 46). Radioactive waste and spent fuel elements from conventional fission reactors are taken to a fuel-reprocessing plant, where the plutonium-239 is separated and purified for use as fuel in a breeder reactor. In the breeder reactor fast neutrons are used to fission nuclei of plutonium-239, and convert the nonfissionable uranium-238 into enough fissionable plutonium-239 to start up another breeder reactor after 30 to 50 years. Because these devices use fast-moving neutrons for fissioning, they are often called *fast breeder reactors*.

A breeder reactor looks something like the reactor in Figure 17-5, except that its core contains a different fuel mixture and its two heat-exchanger loops contain liquid sodium instead of water. Under normal operation a breeder reactor is considered to be much safer than a conventional fission reactor. But in the unlikely event that all its safety systems failed and the reactor lost its sodium coolant, there would be a runaway fission chain reaction, and perhaps a small nuclear explosion with the force of several hundred pounds of TNT. Such an explosion could blast open the containment building, releasing a cloud of highly radioactive gases and particulate matter. A more common problem, which could lead to temporary shutdowns but poses no significant health hazards, is the leakage of molten sodium, which ignites on exposure to air and reacts violently with water. Because the breeder requires little if any mining of uranium, it would have a much smaller environmental impact on the land than conventional fission.

Since 1966 several small- and intermediate-scale experimental breeder reactors have been built in the United States, the United Kingdom, the Soviet Union, West Germany, and France. In 1986 France put into operation a full-sized commercial breeder reactor, the Superphénix, which cost three times the original estimate to build and produces electricity at a cost per kilowatt over twice that of conventional fission reactors. Tentative plans to build full-sized commercial breeders in West Germany, the Soviet Union, and the United Kingdom may be canceled because of the excessive cost of France's reactor, an excess of electric generating capacity, and because studies indicate that breeders will not be competitive economically with conventional fission reactors for at least 50 years.

In 1983, after 13 years of political and scientific debate and a government expenditure of $1.7 billion for planning, the proposed Clinch River intermediate demonstration breeder reactor in Tennessee was canceled. It would have cost 5 to 12 times the original estimate, and it was based on designs outdated by other demonstration breeders in France and the United Kingdom. Moreover, many people fear that the worldwide proliferation of nuclear weapons will be enhanced by the use of plutonium-239 as a fuel in breeder reactors. Numerous studies have shown that the United States will not need breeder reactors until at least 2025, given the slowdown in the building of conventional nuclear fission reactors.

17-4 NONRENEWABLE AND PERPETUAL NUCLEAR FUSION

Controlled Nuclear Fusion In the distant future—probably no sooner than 2050, if ever—scientists in the United States, the Soviet Union, Japan, and a con-

sortium of European nations hope to use *controlled nuclear fusion* to provide an essentially inexhaustible source of energy for producing electricity. Present research is focused on the fusion of two isotopes of hydrogen, deuterium (D) and tritium (T) (see Figure 3-6, p. 50) because this nuclear reaction has the lowest ignition temperature, about 100 million degrees.

Deuterium is found in about 150 out of every million molecules of water (150 ppm) and can be separated from ordinary hydrogen atoms fairly easily. Thus, the world's oceans provide an almost inexhaustible supply of this isotope. Although there is no significant natural source of tritium, an extremely small but sufficient quantity can be extracted from seawater. The two isotopes can be used as an initial charge in a fusion reactor, with neutrons emitted in the D-T fusion reaction used to bombard a surrounding blanket of lithium to breed additional tritium fuel. The scarcity of lithium will eventually limit the use of *nonrenewable* D-T fusion, but the earth's estimated supply could last for several thousand years, depending on rate of use.

Another possibility is the D-D fusion reaction, in which the nuclei of two deuterium (D) atoms would be fused together to form a helium nucleus (Figure 3-6, p. 50). But this reaction requires an ignition temperature about ten times higher than that for D-T fusion and thus is not being pursued at this time. If controlled D-D nuclear fusion were developed, deuterium in the ocean could supply the world with energy at many times present consumption rates for 100 billion years—making this type of nuclear fusion an essentially *perpetual* source of energy. Few scientists, however, expect D-D fusion to become a major source of energy until 2100, if ever.

Achieving Controlled Nuclear Fusion The development of controlled nuclear fusion to produce thermal energy that can be converted into electricity is still at the laboratory stage after 35 years of research. To bring about a self-sustaining, controlled nuclear fusion reaction, the D-T fuel must be heated to about 100 million degrees and then squeezed together long enough and at a high enough density to ensure that sufficient numbers of the nuclei collide and fuse. No physical walls can be used to confine the hot fuel, known as *plasma*, not only because any known material would be vaporized but also because the walls would contaminate the fuel and instantly cool it below its ignition temperature.

Two approaches are being used in attempts to bring about controlled nuclear fusion: magnetic contain-

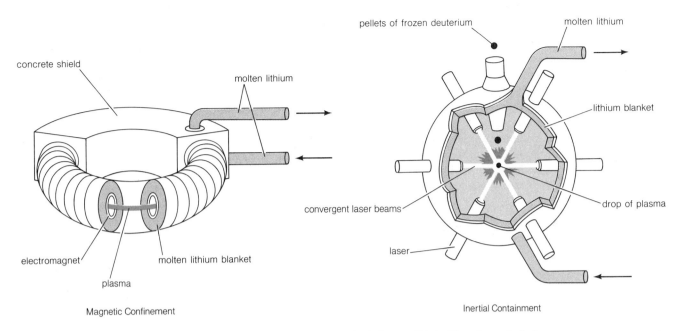

concrete shield

molten lithium

electromagnet

plasma

molten lithium blanket

Magnetic Confinement

pellets of frozen deuterium

molten lithium

lithium blanket

convergent laser beams

drop of plasma

laser

Inertial Containment

Figure 17-16 Magnetic containment and laser inertial confinement methods for possible ignition of a controlled nuclear fusion reaction.

ment and inertial confinement (Figure 17-16). *Magnetic containment* involves using powerful electromagnetic fields to confine and force the fuel nuclei together within a vacuum. In one promising approach, electromagnetic fields squeeze the fuel into the shape of a large toroid or doughnut (Figure 17-16, left). Such a reactor is known as a *tokamak* (after the Russian words for "toroidal magnetic chamber"), a design pioneered by Soviet physicists, including famed Soviet dissident Andrei Sakharov.

A second approach to nuclear fusion is *inertial confinement*, in which a marble-sized, perfectly symmetrical pellet crammed with deuterium and tritium is bombarded from all sides with powerful laser beams, beams of charged particles (light ions), or beams of subatomic particles called muons. The beams would drive the fuel inward, compressing and heating it to the point where the fuel nuclei fuse. Charged particle beams carry enough energy for fusion but spread out too much to focus this energy on the fuel pellets because the like-charged particles repel one another. Lasers can be better focused but so far are not powerful enough to bring about fusion. In 1986 some promising preliminary results were obtained in a third approach known as *muon-catalyzed fusion*, which could allow fusion to take place at even as low as room temperature.

By early 1987 none of the several test reactors using either approach throughout the world had been able

to reach the *break-even point*, where the energy pumped into the reactor equals the energy it produces. When, and if, the energy break-even point is reached in the laboratory, the next, even more difficult step will be to achieve the *burning point*, where the D-T nuclear fusion reaction becomes self-sustaining and releases more energy than is put in.

Building a Commercial Nuclear Fusion Reactor
Assuming that the burning point can be reached, the next step is to build a small demonstration fusion reactor and then scale it up to commercial size. This task is considered one of the most difficult engineering problems ever undertaken. For example, the electromagnets, cooled to practically the lowest temperature possible on earth, would be located only a few meters from the plasma, at the highest temperature produced on earth. Protecting the extremely sensitive electromagnets from heat and radiation damage would be like trying to preserve an ice cube next to a blazing fire, only much harder. Moreover helium, which would be used to cool the magnets, is a rare element, and supply problems might limit the long-term use of nuclear fusion. New developments in superconductivity, however, might overcome some of these problems.

Another engineering problem is the necessity of

maintaining a near perfect vacuum in the interior section of the reactor containing the plasma. More mind-boggling still, the inner walls of the reactor surrounding the lithium blanket must resist constant baths of highly reactive liquid lithium at a temperature of 1,000°C (1,800°F) and steady bombardment by fast-moving neutrons released when deuterium and tritium fuse. Since neutron bombardment eventually destroys or alters the composition of all presently known reactor wall materials, the walls would have to be replaced about every five years, at such enormous cost that some scientists doubt whether fusion will ever be economically feasible. Scientists and engineers hope to overcome some of these problems by developing special new alloys, but some of their elements may be unaffordably scarce.

There are still other problems. The neutron bombardment of the walls and other structural materials near the reactor core would convert many of the chemical elements into radioactive materials. As a result, repairs would have to be made by automatic devices, still to be developed, since no human worker

---

Guest Essay   Nuclear Power: A Faustian Bargain We Should Accept

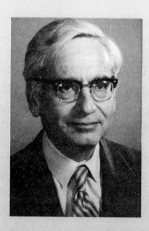

Alvin M. Weinberg

Alvin M. Weinberg was a member of the group of scientists that developed the first experimental fission reactors at the University of Chicago in 1941. Since then he has been a leading figure in the development of commercial nuclear power. From 1948 to 1973 he served as director of the Oak Ridge National Laboratory. In 1974 he was director of the Office of Energy Research and Development in the Federal Energy Administration (now the Department of Energy). Since 1975 he has been the director of the Institute for Energy Analysis of the Oak Ridge Associated Universities. He has written numerous articles and books on nuclear energy (see Further Readings) and has received many awards for his contributions to the development of nuclear energy.

There are two basically different views of the world's future. The one most popular in recent years holds that the earth's resources are limited. According to this neo-Malthusian view, nothing except drastic reduction in population, affluence, and certain types of technology can prevent severe environmental degradation. The other view, held by cornucopians, holds that as scarce materials are exhausted, there will always be new, more expensive ones to take their place. According to this view, Spaceship Earth has practically infinite supplies of resources, but it will cost more and more to stay where we are in terms of resource use as we use up those that are readily available.

The cornucopian view seems to me to be the more reasonable, especially since all of our past experience has shown that as one resource becomes scarce, another takes its place. We do not use whale oil for lighting any more, yet we have better lighting than our ancestors who burned this oil in lamps. In the long run humankind will have to depend on the most abundant and almost infinitely abundant elements in the earth's crust: iron, sodium, carbon, nitrogen, aluminum, oxygen, silicon, and a few others. Glass, cement, and plastics will perform many more functions than they do now. Our average standard of living will be diminished, but probably no more than by a factor of 2.

Thus, in contrast to what seems to be the prevailing mood, I retain a certain basic optimism about the future. My optimism, however, is predicated on certain assumptions:

1. Technology can indeed deal with the effluents of this future society. Here I think I am on firm ground, for, on the whole, where technology has been given the task and been given the necessary time and funding, it has come through with very important improvements such as improvements in air pollution emissions emitted by cars.

could withstand the radiation. There is also concern over the high-level magnetic and electrical fields near the reactor, which might be hazardous to power plant employees.

The estimated cost of a commercial fusion reactor based on presently known approaches is at least two to four times that of a comparable breeder fission reactor and at least four to eight times that of a comparable conventional fission reactor.

If everything goes as planned—which may prove to be one of the biggest ifs in scientific and engineering history—the first U.S. commercial fusion reactor could be completed between 2010 and 2025. If this happens, then between 2050 and 2150 nuclear fusion might produce as much as 18% of U.S. annual commercial energy needs.

The United States, the country that led the world into the age of nuclear power, may well lead it out.

Lester R. Brown

2. Phosphorus, though essentially infinite in supply in the earth's crust at various locations, has no substitute. Will we be able to so revolutionize agriculture that we can eventually use the "infinite" supply of phosphorus at acceptable cost? This technological and economic question is presently unresolved, although I cannot believe it to be unresolvable.

3. All of this presupposes that we have at our disposal an inexhaustible, relatively cheap source of energy. As I and others now see the technological possibilities, there is only one energy resource we can count on—and this is *nuclear fission*, based on *breeder reactors* to extend the world's supply of fissionable uranium far into the future. This is not to say that nuclear fusion, geothermal energy, or solar energy will never be economically available. We simply do not know now that any of these will ever be available in sufficient quantity and at affordable prices, whereas we know that conventional nuclear fission and breeder reactors are already technologically feasible, and standardized, improved, and inherently safer reactor designs already being tested or on the drawing boards should bring costs down in the future.

In opting for nuclear fission breeders—and we hardly have a choice in the matter—we assume a moral and technological burden of serious proportion. A properly operating nuclear reactor and its subsystems are environmentally a very benign energy source. The issue hangs around the words "properly operating." Can we ensure that henceforth we shall be able to maintain the degree of intellectual responsibility, social commitment, and stability necessary to maintain this energy form so as not to cause serious harm? This is basically a moral and social question, though it does have strong technological components.

It is a Faustian bargain (a pact with the devil) that we strike: in return for this essentially inexhaustible energy source, which we must have if we are to maintain ourselves at anything like our present numbers and our present state of affluence, we must commit ourselves and generations to come—essentially forever—to exercise the vigilance and discipline necessary to keep our nuclear fires well behaved. As a nuclear technologist who has devoted his career to this quest for an essentially infinite energy source, I believe the bargain is a good one, and it may even be an inevitable one. It is essential that the full dimension and implication of this Faustian bargain be recognized, especially by the young people who will have to live with the choices that are being made on this vital issue.

Guest Essay Discussion

1. Do you agree that the resources of the earth are practically infinite?

2. The author bases his optimism on three assumptions. Do you believe that these assumptions are reasonable? Explain. Are there any other assumptions that should be added?

3. Do you agree that we should accept the Faustian bargain of conventional and breeder nuclear fission? Explain.

4. Do you agree with the author that "we hardly have any choice" in opting for nuclear fission breeders? Explain.

CHAPTER SUMMARY

Heat from the earth's core, or *geothermal energy*, is transferred to *nonrenewable* underground deposits of *dry steam, wet steam*, and *hot water* at various places. When these deposits are close enough to the earth's surface, their heat can be extracted and used for space heating and to produce electricity or high-temperature heat. They can provide a 100 to 200 year supply of energy for areas near the deposits at a moderate cost and a moderate net useful energy yield with no emissions of carbon dioxide. However, there is not an abundance of easily accessible deposits, the energy cannot be used to power vehicles, and without pollution control its use results in moderate to high air and water pollution.

There are also vast, essentially *perpetual* sources of geothermal energy in the form of *molten rock, dry hot rock*, and *warm rock* deposits. However, these deposits lie so deep under the earth's crust that with present technology they are too costly to develop on a large scale.

During the 1950s and 1960s using *nonrenewable conventional nuclear fission* to produce electricity in nuclear reactors was projected to provide almost one-fourth of all the commercial energy used in the world by the year 2000 at a cost that was supposed to be "too cheap to meter." However, by 1986, after 35 years of development, nuclear fission was providing only 3% of the world's commercial energy at very high and increasing costs. Major *advantages* of using conventional nuclear fission to produce electricity are **(1)** nuclear reactors do not release air pollutants such as carbon dioxide, particulate matter, and sulfur and nitrogen oxides like coal-fired plants; and **(2)** water pollution and disruption of land are low to moderate if the entire nuclear fuel cycle operates normally.

Major *disadvantages* are **(1)** construction and operating costs of nuclear plants have been much higher than projected, even with massive government and consumer subsidies; **(2)** conventional nuclear power plants can be used only to produce electricity; **(3)** although large-scale accidents are extremely unlikely, some have already occurred as a result of a combination of mechanical and human errors, and these have eroded public confidence; **(4)** the net useful energy yield of nuclear power is low; **(5)** safe methods for storing high-level radioactive waste for hundreds to thousands of years have not been developed; **(6)** nuclear power commits future generations to safely storing radioactive wastes for hundreds to thousands of years; and **(7)** its use spreads knowledge and materials that could be used to make nuclear weapons.

Some experts project that *nonrenewable breeder nuclear fission* could be used to greatly extend the world's supply of uranium fuel. However, plants built so far indicate that it produces electricity at a cost over twice that of conventional nuclear fission. It also has essentially the same safety and waste problems as conventional nuclear fission and increases the possibility of its plutonium fuel being diverted to produce nuclear weapons.

Other experts hope that *nuclear fusion* will eventually be able to provide the world with an essentially inexhaustible supply of energy. However, after 35 years of research this technology is still at the laboratory stage and no one has been able to get more energy out of the process than must be put in to initiate the fusion reaction. Even if this problem is overcome, the scaling of a laboratory reactor up to a full-scale commercial reactor would probably be the most difficult engineering feat ever undertaken. In addition, the cost of producing energy in this way could be enormous compared to other already available alternatives. Even if everything goes right, nuclear fusion is not expected to be a significant source of commercial energy until sometime between 2050 and 2150.

DISCUSSION TOPICS

1. Explain why you agree or disagree with the following statements:
   a. Dry steam, wet steam, and hot water geothermal deposits can provide most of the electricity the United States needs by the year 2010.
   b. Molten rock (magma) geothermal deposits should be able to supply the United States with all the electricity and high-temperature heat it needs by 2025.
   c. Although geothermal energy may not be a major source of energy for the United States over the next few decades, it can supply a significant fraction of energy needs in selected areas where high-quality deposits are found.

2. What method should be used for the long-term storage of high-level nuclear wastes? Defend your choice.

3. Do you favor a U.S. energy strategy based on greatly increased use of conventional nuclear fission reactors to produce electricity between 1988 and 2020? Explain.

4. Explain why you agree or disagree with each of the following proposals made by President Ronald Reagan, utility companies, and the nuclear power industry:
   a. Licensing time of new nuclear power plants in the United States should be halved (from an average of 12 to 6 years) so that these facilities can be built more economically and compete more effectively with coal and other renewable energy alternatives.
   b. A major program for developing the nuclear breeder fission reactor should be developed and funded by the federal government to conserve uranium resources and eventually keep the United States from being dependent on other countries for uranium supplies.

5. Do you believe that the United States and other industrialized countries should try to reduce the risk of nuclear war by pledging not to sell or give any additional nuclear power plants or any forms of nuclear technology to other countries? Explain.

18

Perpetual and Renewable Energy Resources: Conservation, Sun, Wind, Water, and Biomass

GENERAL OBJECTIVES

1. What are the advantages and disadvantages of energy conservation as a perpetual source of energy?

2. What are the advantages and disadvantages of capturing and using some of the earth's direct input of perpetual solar energy for heating buildings and water and for producing electricity?

3. What are the advantages and disadvantages of using perpetual indirect solar energy stored in falling and flowing water (hydropower) for producing electricity?

4. What are the advantages and disadvantages of using perpetual indirect solar energy in the form of heat stored in water for producing electricity and heating buildings and water?

5. What are the advantages and disadvantages of using perpetual indirect solar energy stored in winds to produce electricity?

6. What are the advantages and disadvantages of using renewable indirect solar energy stored in plants and organic waste (biomass) for heating buildings and water and for converting biomass to transportation fuels (biofuels)?

7. What are the best present and future energy options for the United States and what should be the country's long-term energy strategy?

8. What are the advantages and disadvantages of producing and using hydrogen gas and fuel cells to produce electricity, heat buildings and water, and propel vehicles when oil runs out?

Throughout most of human history, people have relied on renewable resources—sun, wind, water, and land. They got by well enough, and so could we.

Warren Johnson

Saving energy by using it more efficiently has been the largest source of energy in MDCs such as the United States since 1978, and it is also the largest potential future source of energy. Gradually increasing reliance on perpetual and renewable energy from the sun, wind, water, and biomass (mostly wood) since 1978 is another important energy success story in the United States and many other parts of the world.

Some experts project that the contribution of energy from the sun, wind, water, and biomass to global energy use will increase significantly by the year 2000 and then expand even more rapidly. Others believe that these forms of perpetual and renewable energy will grow at a much slower rate because of uncertain costs, loss of momentum during the temporary oil glut of the 1980s, and sharp cutbacks in federal funds and tax breaks for their development.

18-1 ENERGY CONSERVATION: DOING MORE WITH LESS

Reducing Unnecessary Energy Waste: An Offer We Can't Afford to Refuse Our greatest energy resource now and in the future is **energy conservation,** the reduction or elimination of unnecessary energy use and waste. There are three general methods of energy conservation: **(1)** We can reduce energy consumption at essentially no cost by changing energy-wasting habits. Examples include walking or riding a bicycle for short trips, wearing a sweater indoors in cold weather to allow a lower thermostat setting, and turning off unneeded lights. **(2)** We can use less energy to do the same amount of work. This requires small, ultimately money-saving investments such as installing more building insulation, keeping car engines tuned, and switching to more energy-efficient cars, houses, heating and cooling systems, appliances, and industrial processes. **(3)** We can use less energy to do more work. Industry and government can make long-term investments in developing new devices that waste less energy than existing ones. Examples include more efficient solar cells for conversion of solar energy directly to electricity, new aerodynamic vehicle designs that reduce fuel consumption, and efficient heating and cooling systems, appliances, and vehicle engines.

Using energy conservation to obtain more useful energy has more advantages than any other energy alternative. It is the largest and cheapest essentially unlimited source of energy (Figure 17-15, p. 379). The first two conservation methods do not require development of new forms of technology, and conservation in general provides more jobs and promotes more economic growth per unit of energy gained than other energy resources. It also has a high net useful energy yield, reduces the environmental impacts of all other energy resources by reducing overall energy use and waste, adds no carbon dioxide to the atmosphere, extends domestic and world supplies of nonrenewable fossil fuels, buys time for phasing in new perpetual and renewable energy resources, and reduces dependence on imported oil and other energy resources. In addition, the first two methods of energy conservation can be implemented in a very short time, usually days or weeks—compared with 6 to 12 years for building new coal, nuclear, and hydroelectric power plants.

Energy conservation also has fewer serious disadvantages than any other present or foreseeable energy alternative. One disadvantage is that improving energy efficiency by replacing houses, industrial equipment, and cars as they wear out with more energy-efficient ones takes a fairly long time—30 to 50 years for buildings and industrial equipment and 10 to 12 years for cars. Although most energy conservation measures improve average life quality, certain ones require lifestyle changes that some people do not like. For example, improved automobile gas mileage depends mainly on smaller, lighter, and less powerful cars, which some drivers don't like. These cars also provide occupants with less protection in accidents as long as consumers do not insist that all cars be equipped with air bags and other safety devices.

Between 1975 and 1985, conservation measures in the United States reduced total consumption of all major types of commercial energy, provided much more new energy (by reducing waste) than all other alternatives combined, and cut national energy bills by about $150 billion a year, with $90 billion a year coming from design and engineering changes that improved fuel economy in cars and trucks. On the average, American houses in 1985 used 25% less space-heating energy per square foot than they did in 1975; many new, energy-efficient

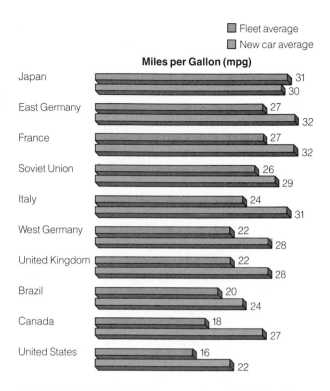

Figure 18-1 Automobile fuel economy for selected countries in 1982.

houses used 75% less. In 1985 new U.S. autos averaged about 26 miles per gallon, nearly double that of new cars in 1973. New refrigerators are now about 72% more efficient than they were in 1972.

Despite these important improvements, massive amounts of energy are still unnecessarily wasted in the United States. Average gas mileage for new cars and for the entire fleet of cars is below that in other MDCs (Figure 18-1). Most U.S. houses and buildings are still underinsulated and leaky and most new houses and buildings do not take advantage of available energy-efficient construction techniques (Figure 18-2). Even with its low energy efficiency, electric heating is installed in over half the new homes in the United States (as well as in many European countries).

Studies have shown that fully implementing methods 1 and 2 of energy conservation would decrease average energy use per person in the United States by 50% between 1986 and 2000, saving about $200 billion a year, enough to pay off the entire national debt and at the same time stimulate the economy. Continuing these improvements and funding crash research programs to implement method 3 energy conservation measures could reduce average energy use per person in the United States by 80% to 90% between 1986 and 2020.

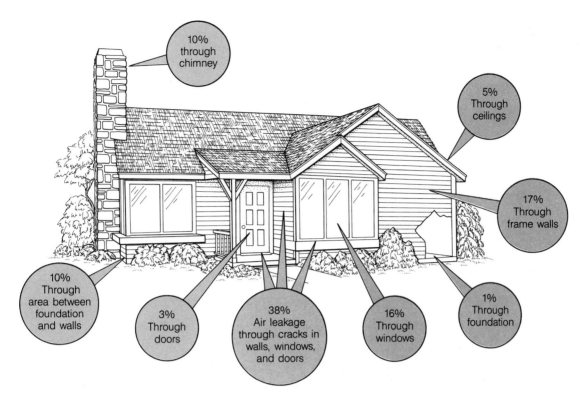

Figure 18-2 Typical new ranch-style homes built throughout the United States not only are heated with energy-wasting electricity but also are full of leaks through which up to 85% of heat is lost.

Improving Industrial Energy Efficiency Industrial processes consume more commercial energy than transportation, residences, and commercial buildings (Figure 18-3). U.S. industry has led the way in instituting energy conservation measures to save money since 1973 and has the greatest long-term potential to switch to new energy-saving processes.

An important way most U.S. industries can save energy and money in a relatively short time is to install *cogeneration units,* which use excess high-temperature steam and high-temperature heat to produce electricity, which can be used by the industry or sold to utility companies. By 1985 industrial cogeneration in the United States provided electricity equivalent to the output of fifteen 1,000-megawatt power plants. New projects, with an additional output of electricity equal to that of 17 large power plants, were under construction or planned in 1985. The U.S. Office of Technology Assessment estimates that cogeneration has the potential to provide electricity equal to that from 200 large power plants by the year 2000.

Japan has the highest overall industrial energy efficiency in the world. France, Italy, Spain, and West Germany also have relatively high industrial energy efficiencies.

Industry accounts for close to half the worldwide use of electricity. Aluminum production is one of the most energy-intensive processes, requiring 1% of the world's commercial energy. Method 3 improvements in energy efficiency in the aluminum industry include a new process that reduces electricity use by 25% and another, using recycled aluminum, that reduces electricity use by 90%. Despite the potential energy savings, the average world aluminum-recycling rate is only 28%; this could easily be doubled or tripled.

Electric industrial motors consume almost two-thirds of the electricity used in industry worldwide and 80% in the United States. Phasing in new motor designs that require 30% to 50% less electricity could reduce overall electricity use in the United States by at least 10%, enough to eliminate the need for two-thirds of the existing U.S. nuclear power plants.

Improving Transportation Energy Efficiency Transporting people and goods accounts for one-fourth of the commercial energy use in the world and the United States (Figure 18-3)—and a much higher percentage of oil use. About one-tenth of the oil consumed in the world each day is used by American motorists on their way to and from work, two-thirds of them driving alone. Thus, the largest savings in oil

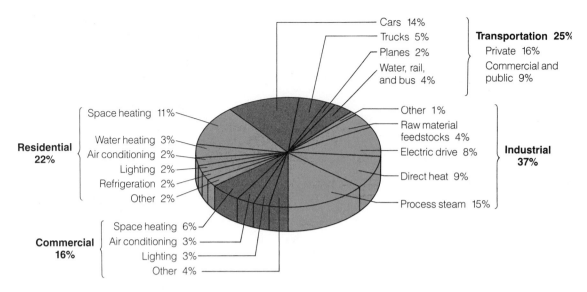

Cars 14%
Trucks 5%
Planes 2%
Water, rail, and bus 4%

Transportation 25%
Private 16%
Commercial and public 9%

Space heating 11%
Water heating 3%
Air conditioning 2%
Lighting 2%
Refrigeration 2%
Other 2%

Residential 22%

Other 1%
Raw material feedstocks 4%
Electric drive 8%
Direct heat 9%
Process steam 15%

Industrial 37%

Space heating 6%
Air conditioning 3%
Lighting 3%
Other 4%

Commercial 16%

Figure 18-3 Distribution of commercial energy use in the United States among various sectors in 1984. (Data from U.S. Department of Energy)

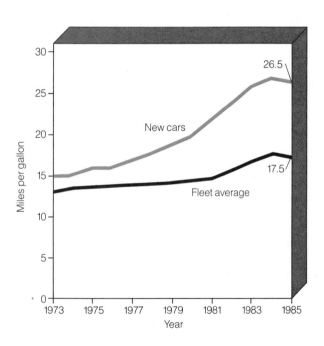

Figure 18-4 Increase in the average fuel efficiency of new cars and the entire fleet of cars in the United States between 1973 and 1985. (Data from U.S. Department of Energy and the Environmental Protection Agency)

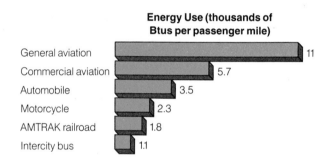

Energy Use (thousands of Btus per passenger mile)

General aviation — 11
Commercial aviation — 5.7
Automobile — 3.5
Motorcycle — 2.3
AMTRAK railroad — 1.8
Intercity bus — 1.1

Figure 18-5 Energy efficiency of various modes of domestic transportation.

can come from improved vehicle fuel economy (Figure 18-4), greater use of mass transit (Figure 18-5), and more efficient hauling of freight.

In 1985 Japan had the highest average fuel economy for new and existing cars, and Canada and the United States had the lowest. The U.S. Office of Technology Assessment estimates that new cars produced in the United States could easily reach an average of 45 mpg by 2000. But so far Congress has not required U.S. car manufacturers to go beyond the 27.5 mpg set for 1985. Experts estimate that with adequate laws average fuel economy levels of 30 mpg for entire fleets could be achieved everywhere by the end of the century and levels of 50 mpg shortly thereafter. Based on prototype models already in operation, the fuel economy for new cars and light trucks could easily be increased to between 60 and 100 mpg through reduced weight, more energy-efficient engines and drive trains, and reduced aerodynamic and rolling resistance.

Lowering and enforcing speed limits also saves energy, money, and lives. According to a 1985 study by the National Academy of Sciences, the national 55-mph speed limit in the United States saves 2,000 to 4,000 lives and prevents 4,500 serious injuries annually, reduces fuel use by 2%, and saves consumers about $65 million a year, primarily from reduction of medical and insurance costs.

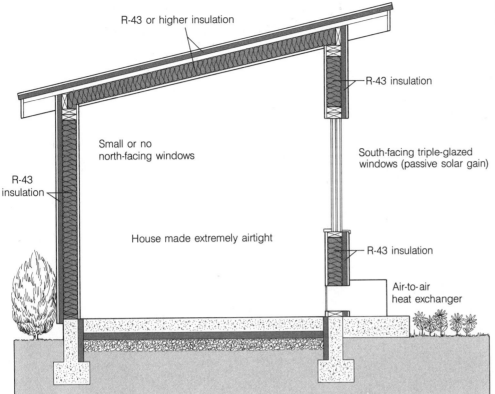

Figure 18-6 Major features of a superinsulated house.

R-43 or higher insulation

R-43 insulation

Small or no north-facing windows

South-facing triple-glazed windows (passive solar gain)

R-43 insulation

R-43 insulation

House made extremely airtight

Air-to-air heat exchanger

Other measures that would conserve the world's diminishing supply of oil include shifting more freight from trucks and airplanes to trains, increasing the efficiency of transport trucks by improving aerodynamic design and using turbocharged diesel engines and radial tires, and not allowing trucks to return empty after reaching their destination.

Improving the Energy Efficiency of Commercial and Residential Buildings Most commercial and residential buildings in the United States consume between 50% and 90% more energy than they would if they were designed to use energy more efficiently. A monument to energy waste is the 110-story, twin-towered World Trade Center in Manhattan, which uses as much electricity as a city of 100,000 persons. Not a single window in its walls of glass can be opened to take advantage of natural warming and cooling; its heating and cooling systems work around the clock, even when no one is in the building.

By contrast, Atlanta's 18-story Georgia Power Company building uses 60% less energy than conventional office buildings. Energy-saving features include an extension of each floor over the one below to create an overhang that allows heating by the low winter sun while blocking out the higher summer sun to reduce air conditioning costs, a computer programmed to turn off all lights at 6 P.M. unless instructed otherwise,

energy-efficient lights that focus on desks rather than illuminating entire rooms, and an adjoining three-story building where employees can work at unusual hours so that the larger structure does not have to be heated or cooled during periods of low use.

Building a **superinsulated house** is the most effective way to improve the efficiency of residential space heating and to save on lifetime costs, especially in cold climates (Figure 18-6). Such a house obtains heat directly from the sun through double- or triple-pane windows facing the sun and has massive amounts of insulation to protect against heat loss. An air-to-air heat exchanger prevents buildup of humidity and indoor air pollution.

Even in Saskatchewan, Canada, where winter temperatures may average $-40°C$ ($-40°F$), a well-designed, superinsulated house can get all its space heating without a conventional backup system from a combination of direct solar gain (typically 59%), waste heat from appliances (33%), and the body heat of the occupants (8%). Such houses retain most of this heat input for at least 100 hours, and inside temperatures probably never fall below 10°C (50°F) even in extremely cold weather. The number of such houses is growing rapidly as consumers, architects, and builders become familiar with their advantages and construction techniques.

Adding an additional $5,000 to $10,000 to the cost of a new house for energy-saving measures can save

The energy-efficient house of the near future will be controlled by microprocessors, each programmed to do a different job and to respond to individual schedules and preferences as well as to the natural flow of solar energy and breezes. They will control the thermostat, open and close windows and insulated shutters, operate fans to control temperature and air distribution, and control the security system.

Windows will have a coating like the light-sensitive glass in some sunglasses, automatically becoming opaque to keep the sunlight out when the house gets too hot. Glass with high insulating values (R-10 to R-15)* will be available so that a house can have as many windows as the owner wants in any climate

without much heat loss. Thinner insulation material will allow roofs to be insulated to R-100 and walls to R-40, far higher than today's best superinsulated houses (Figure 18-6).

By 1987, small-scale cogeneration units that run on natural or LP gas were available; they can supply a home with all its space heat, hot water, and electricity needs. The units are no larger than a refrigerator, make less noise than a dishwasher, and except for an occasional change of oil filters and spark plugs are nearly maintenance free. In most cases, this home-sized power and heating plant will pay for itself in four to five years.

Homeowners can also get all the electricity they need from rolls of solar cells attached like shingles

to a roof or applied to window glass as a coating (already developed by Arco). More people in rural and suburban areas will be drilling wells and using greatly improved heat pumps to extract geothermal heat from warm underground water. Presently most heat pumps used for space heating and air conditioning last only about five years and in moderately cold climates must be supplemented by expensive and energy-wasting electric-resistance heaters when temperatures fall below $-7°C$ (20°F). As the technology improves, however, heat pumps should become more energy-efficient and economical.

*The higher the R-value of a material, the greater its insulating ability.

---

the homeowner $50,000 to $100,000 over a 40-year period by cutting lifetime heating and cooling bills by 50% to 100%. Combining presently known conservation measures with emerging technology could greatly increase the energy efficiency of new houses in the not-too-distant future (see Spotlight above).

Many energy-saving features can be added to existing homes, a process called *retrofitting*. For example, simply increasing insulation in ceilings can drastically reduce heating and cooling loads, with a typical financial payback period of two to ten years. Caulking and weatherstripping around windows, doors, pipes, vents, ducts, and wires saves energy and money quickly (Figure 18-2). Switching to new gas furnaces with energy efficiencies of 90% to 95%, compared to 60% to 65% for most conventional gas furnaces, also saves energy and money on a lifetime-cost basis.

Legal approaches can also be used to increase energy conservation in homes and buildings. Building codes could be changed to require that all new houses use 80% less energy than conventional houses of the same size, as has been done in Davis, California. Laws can require that any existing house be insulated and weatherproofed to certain standards before it can be sold, as is now done in Portland, Oregon.

Using the most energy-efficient appliances avail-

able can also save homeowners energy and money.* About one-third of the electricity generated in the United States and other industrial countries is used to power household appliances. Many American homes have 20 to 50 light bulbs, and burning one 100-watt light bulb just six hours a day each year consumes energy equivalent to fifteen 55-gallon barrels of oil. Socket-type fluorescent light bulbs that use one-fourth as much electricity as conventional bulbs are now available. Although they are expensive, they last 13 times longer than conventional bulbs and return three times more than the original purchase price through reduced electricity bills. Switching to these bulbs would save one-third of the electric energy now produced by all U.S. coal-fired plants or eliminate the need for all electricity produced by the country's 101 nuclear power plants.

Developing a Personal Energy Conservation Plan
Individuals can develop their own plans for saving energy and money (see Spotlight on p. 397). Four basic

*Each year the American Council for an Energy-Efficient Economy publishes a list of the most energy-efficient appliances. For a copy, send $2 to the council at 1001 Connecticut Ave. N.W., Suite 530, Washington, D.C. 20036.

Table 18-1 Energy Use and Conservation in the United States and Sweden

Use or Method	United States	Sweden
Average per capita use	230,000 kcal/day	150,000 kcal/day
Transportation energy use	High	One-fourth of U.S.
Country size	Large	Small
Cities	Dispersed	Compact
Mass transit use	Low	High
Average car fuel economy	Poor	Good
Gasoline taxes	Low	High to encourage conservation
Tariffs on oil imports	Low	High to encourage conservation
Industrial energy efficiency	Fairly low	High
Nationwide energy-conserving building codes	No	Yes
Municipally owned district heating systems	None	30% of population
Emphasis on electricity for space heating	High (one-half of new homes)	High (one-half of new homes)
Domestic hot water	Most kept hot 24 hours a day in large tanks	Most supplied as needed by instant tankless heaters
Refrigerators	Mostly large, frost-free	Mostly smaller, non-frost-free using about one-third the electricity of U.S. models
Long-range national energy plan	No	Yes
Government emphasis and expenditures on energy conservation and renewable energy	Low	High
Government emphasis and expenditures on nuclear power	High	Low (to be phased out)

guidelines should be used: **(1)** Don't use electricity to heat space or water; **(2)** insulate new or existing houses heavily and caulk and weatherstrip to reduce air infiltration and heat loss; **(3)** get as much heat and cooling as possible from natural sources—especially sun, wind, underground geothermal energy, and trees for windbreaks and natural shading; **(4)** buy the most energy-efficient homes, cars, and appliances available and evaluate them only in terms of lifetime cost.

Energy Efficiency Differences Between Countries Japan, Sweden, and most industrialized western European countries with average standards of living at least equal to that in the United States use only one-third to two-thirds as much energy per person as Americans. This is due to a combination of factors including greater emphasis on energy conservation and fewer passenger miles traveled per person (mainly because cities are more compact in these countries). However, energy use patterns in countries vary, and approaches that save energy in one country can't always be used in others. Table 18-1 compares energy practices between the United States and Sweden.

18-2 DIRECT PERPETUAL SOLAR ENERGY FOR PRODUCING HEAT AND ELECTRICITY

Passive Solar Systems for Low-Temperature Heat A **passive solar system** captures sunlight directly within a structure and converts it to heat (Figure 18-7). Its major design features include **(1)** large areas of south-facing double- or triple-paned glass or a south-facing greenhouse or solarium to collect solar energy; **(2)** walls and floors of concrete, adobe, brick, stone, or tile,

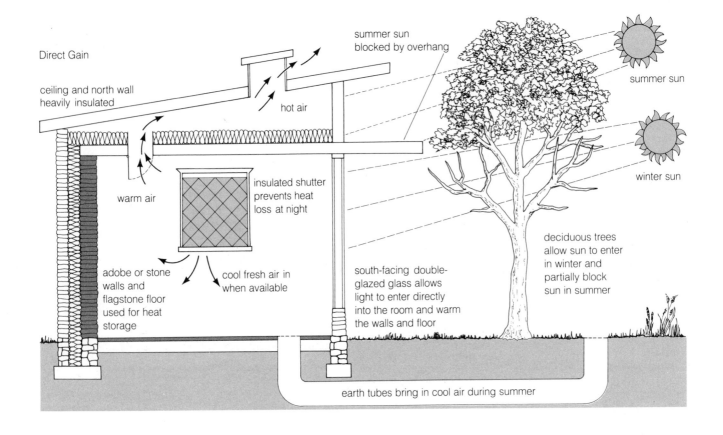

Direct Gain

ceiling and north wall heavily insulated

hot air

summer sun blocked by overhang

summer sun

winter sun

warm air

insulated shutter prevents heat loss at night

deciduous trees allow sun to enter in winter and partially block sun in summer

adobe or stone walls and flagstone floor used for heat storage

cool fresh air in when available

south-facing double-glazed glass allows light to enter directly into the room and warm the walls and floor

earth tubes bring in cool air during summer

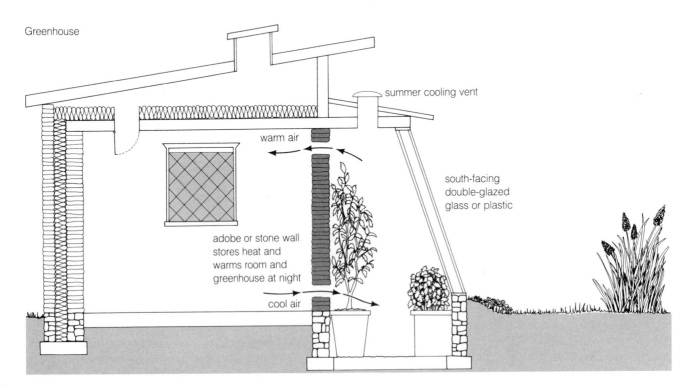

Greenhouse

summer cooling vent

warm air

south-facing double-glazed glass or plastic

adobe or stone wall stores heat and warms room and greenhouse at night

cool air

Figure 18-7 Three examples of passive solar design.

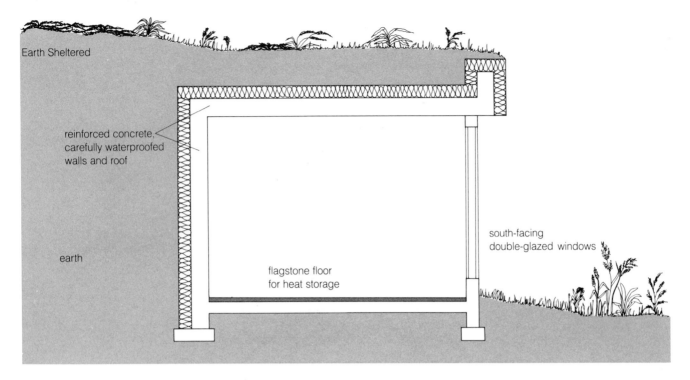

Earth Sheltered

reinforced concrete,
carefully waterproofed
walls and roof

earth

flagstone floor
for heat storage

south-facing
double-glazed windows

Figure 18-7 (Continued) Three examples of passive solar design.

water-filled glass or plastic columns or black-painted barrels, or panels or cabinets containing chemicals to store collected solar energy and release it slowly throughout the day and night; **(3)** few or no north-facing windows, thus decreasing heat loss; **(4)** movable insulated shutters or curtains on windows to reduce heat loss at night; and **(5)** heavy insulation. A series of roof-mounted passive solar water heaters (Figure 18-8) can also be used to provide hot water for a house at an installed cost of $3500 to $4000 in the United States and $1000 in Israel and Japan.

Houses with passive solar systems often have an open design to allow the collected and stored heat to be distributed by natural airflow or fans. An air-to-air heat exchanger is used to provide fresh air without significant heat loss or gain and to prevent buildup of moisture and indoor air pollutants. When necessary, a small backup heating system is also used. A passive solar system can be even more efficient in an earth-sheltered house (see Spotlight on p. 399 and Figure 18-7). A well-designed passive solar system is the simplest, cheapest (on a lifetime-cost basis), most energy-efficient (Figure 3-14, p. 62), most maintenance-free, and least environmentally harmful way to provide 50% to 100% of the space heating of a home or small building, with an added construction cost of only 5% to 10%.

In hot climates the most difficult problem with passively designed buildings is to keep them cool in summer. Passive cooling can be provided by using

deciduous trees, window overhangs, or awnings on the south side to block the high summer sun and using windows and fans to take advantage of breezes and keep air moving. Earth tubes, buried 3 to 6 meters (10 to 20 feet) underground, where the temperature remains around 13°C (55°F) all year long in cold northern climates and about 19°C (67°F) in warm southern climates, can also be used to bring in cool and partially dehumidified air (Figure 18-7).

In areas with dry climates such as the southwestern United States, evaporative coolers can be used to remove interior heat by evaporating water. In hot and humid areas a small dehumidifier or a solar-assisted geothermal heat pump may be needed to reduce humidity to acceptable levels. Solar-powered air conditioners have been developed but so far are too expensive for residential use. According to some experts, climate-sensitive, passive solar cooling and natural ventilation should make it possible to construct all but the largest buildings without air conditioning in most parts of the world.

Active Solar Systems for Low-Temperature Heat

An **active solar system** uses a series of specially designed collectors to concentrate solar energy, pumps to store it as heat in large insulated tanks of water or rock, and thermostat-controlled fans to distribute the stored heat as needed, usually through conventional heating ducts. A series of active solar collectors for

Active Solar Hot Water Heating System

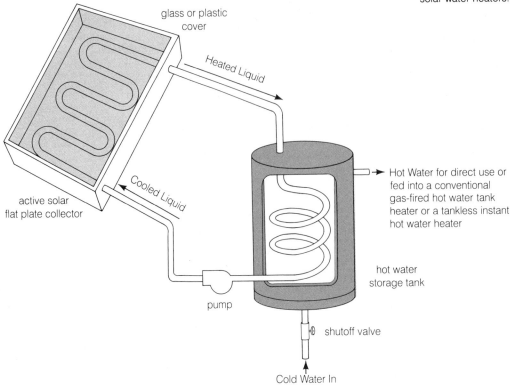

Figure 18-8 Active and passive solar water heaters.

Passive Solar Hot Water Heating System

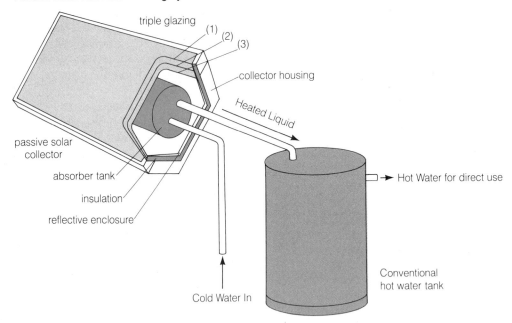

space heating and heating water are usually mounted on a roof with an unobstructed southern exposure.

A typical flat-plate solar collector used in an active system consists of a coil of copper pipe attached to a blackened metal base and covered with two layers of glass separated by an insulating layer of air and encased in an aluminum frame (Figure 18-8). Radiant energy from the sun passes through the transparent glass cover, is absorbed by the blackened surface, transferred as heat to water, an antifreeze solution, or air pumped through the copper pipe, and transferred to an insulated water or rock heat storage system. In

Transportation (50% of average personal energy use)

- Walk or ride a bike for short trips (100% savings).
- Use a car pool or mass transit as much as possible (50% or more).
- Use a bus or train for long trips (50% to 75%).
- Buy an energy-efficient car (30% to 70%).
- Consolidate trips to accomplish several purposes (up to 50%).
- Keep engine tuned and replace air filter regularly (20% to 50%).
- Obey speed limits (20% or more).
- Accelerate and brake gently and don't warm up the engine for more than a minute (15% to 20%).
- Use steel-belted radial tires and keep tire pressure at the recommended level (2% to 5%).

Home Space Heating (25%)

- Build a superinsulated or highly energy-efficient house (50% to 100% savings).
- Dress more warmly, humidify air, and use fans to distribute heat so that thermostat setting can be lowered without loss of comfort (saves 3% for each °F decrease).
- Install the most energy-efficient heating system available (15% to 50%).
- Install an electronic ignition system in furnace, have furnace cleaned and tuned once a year, and clean or replace intake filters every two weeks (15% to 35%).
- Do not heat closets and unused rooms (variable savings).
- Insulate ceilings and walls (20% to 50%).
- Caulk and weatherstrip cracks (10% to 30%).
- Install storm windows and doors or insulated drapes or shutters (5% to 25%).

Hot Water Heating (9%)

- Install the most energy-efficient system available, such as active solar, instant tankless, or high-efficiency-gas water heaters (15% to 60%).
- Turn down thermostat on water heater (5% to 25%).
- Insulate hot water pipes and water heater (10% to 15%).

- Use less hot water by taking two- to five-minute showers instead of baths, washing dishes and clothes only with full loads, washing clothes with warm or cold water, repairing leaky faucets, installing flow reducers on faucets and shower-heads, and not letting water run while bathing, shaving, brushing teeth, or washing dishes (10% to 25%).

Cooking, Refrigeration, and Other Appliances (9%)

- Buy the most energy-efficient stove, refrigerator, and other appliances available—ideally, powered by natural or LP gas, not electricity (25% to 60%).
- Install electronic ignition systems on all gas stoves and other appliances (10% to 30%).
- Use a chest freezer rather than an upright model to prevent unnecessary loss of cool air when door is opened, and keep it almost full (variable).
- Do not locate refrigerator or freezer near a stove or other source of heat and keep condenser coils on back clean (variable).
- Don't use oven for space heating (very expensive).

Cooling, Air Conditioning, and Lighting (7%)

- Buy the most energy-efficient air conditioning system available (30% to 50%).
- Increase thermostat setting (3% to 5% for each °F).
- Close off and do not air condition closets and unused rooms (variable).
- Use small floor fans and whole-house window or attic fans to eliminate or reduce air conditioning needs (variable).
- Close windows and drapes on sunny days and open them on cool days and at night (variable).
- Close bathroom doors and use an exhaust fan or open window to prevent transfer of heat and humid air to rest of house (variable).
- Try to schedule heat- and moisture-producing activities such as bathing, ironing, and washing during the coolest part of the day (variable).
- Cover pots while cooking (variable).
- Use fluorescent and other energy-saving bulbs wherever possible (15% to 25%).
- Use natural lighting whenever possible (variable).
- Turn off lights and appliances when not in use and reduce lighting levels by using dimmers and lower wattage (variable).

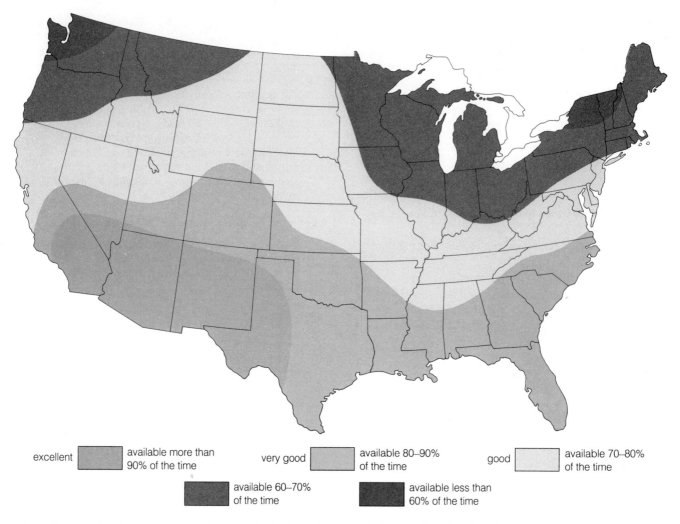

excellent | available more than 90% of the time   very good | available 80–90% of the time   good | available 70–80% of the time

available 60–70% of the time   available less than 60% of the time

Figure 18-9 Availability of solar energy during the day in the continental United States. (Data from U.S. Department of Energy and the National Wildlife Federation)

middle and high latitudes a small backup heating system is needed during prolonged cold or cloudy periods (Figure 18-9).

Active systems are more expensive than passive systems on a lifetime basis because they require more materials to build, need more maintenance, and eventually deteriorate and must be replaced. However, retrofitting an existing house with an active solar system is often easier than adding a passive system. About one-third of the existing buildings in the United States have enough southern exposure and sufficient rooftop or other space for active solar retrofitting that should pay for itself in energy savings in three to seven years.

Most solar experts agree that passive solar design is a more effective and cheaper way to heat homes, whereas active systems are usually better for heating large apartment and commercial buildings, which have large rooftops for mounting the solar collectors. Active solar collectors can also be used exclusively for pro-

viding hot water. By 1986 over 1 million active solar hot water systems had been installed in the United States, especially in California, Florida, and southwestern states with ample sunshine. The main barrier to their widespread use in the United States is a high initial cost of $3,500 to $5,000.

In Israel, which gets 50% of its hot water from the sun, and Japan, where 12% of residences have solar water heaters, mass production and marketing have brought the cost down to about $1,000. Mass production of new designs using thin-film plastic instead of glass and nationwide marketing by large firms could bring costs in the United States down to $750.

Advantages and Disadvantages of Solar Energy for Providing Low-Temperature Heat Using active or passive systems to collect solar energy for low-temperature heating of buildings and water has a number

An increasing number of people in the United States are building passively heated and cooled earth-sheltered houses (Figure 18-7) and commercial buildings partially or completely underground. Most designs cost about 15% more to build initially than a comparable above-ground structure, primarily because of the large amount of concrete needed to bear the heavy load of earth and the need for careful waterproofing to prevent leaks which would be difficult and expensive to repair. However, a new design using preinsulated curved wooden panels that form underground arches has reduced the cost to that of a comparable above-ground structure.

Even with higher initial costs, earth-sheltered homes are cheaper than conventional above-ground houses of the same size on a lifetime-cost basis because of reduced heating and cooling requirements, elimination of exterior maintenance and painting, and reduced fire insurance rates. Earth-sheltered structures also provide more privacy, quiet, and security from break-ins, fires, hurricanes, tornadoes, earthquakes, and storms than conventional above-ground buildings. The interior of an earth-sheltered house can look like that of any ordinary house, and south-facing solar-collecting windows, an attached greenhouse, and skylights can provide more daylight than is found in most conventional dwellings.

of advantages. The energy supply is free and readily available on sunny days. The technology is well developed and can be installed quickly. A passive solar system is the cheapest way to provide space heating for a home in most places on a lifetime-cost basis. An active solar system is cost-effective in most places for providing hot water for homes and buildings and space heating for fairly large buildings on a lifetime-cost basis. Net useful energy yield is moderate to high, carbon dioxide is not added to the atmosphere, and environmental impacts from air pollution, water pollution, and land disturbance are low because the systems themselves produce no pollutants during operation and do not take up valuable land.

However, there are disadvantages. The energy supply is not available at night and on cloudy days, so that heat storage systems and small conventional backup heating systems are necessary except in super-insulated houses. Although lifetime costs are highly favorable, high initial costs discourage buyers not used to considering lifetime costs or buyers who move every few years to change jobs. State and local laws must also be in place to guarantee that others cannot build structures that block a user's access to sunlight—legislation often opposed by builders of high-density developments. Most passive solar systems in use today require that owners open and close windows and shades to regulate heat flow and distribution—tasks that in the near future might be done by cheap microprocessors.

Concentrating Solar Energy to Produce High-Temperature Heat and Electricity   In experimental systems huge arrays of computer-controlled mirrors track the sun and focus sunlight on a central heat collection point, usually atop a tall tower. This highly concentrated sunlight can produce temperatures high enough for industrial processes or for making high-pressure steam to run turbines and produce electricity.

The world's largest *solar furnace*, the Odeillo Furnace, has been in operation high in the Pyrenees Mountains in southern France since 1970 (Figure 18-10). This system, which produces temperatures up to 2,000°C (5,000°F), is used in the manufacture of pure metals and other substances; the excess heat is used to produce steam and generate electricity fed into the public utility grid. Smaller units are being tested in France, Italy, Spain, and Japan.

Several private and government-financed experimental *solar power towers*, which produce electricity, have been built in the United States. One, known as Solar One, is located in the Mojave Desert in southern California and produces enough electricity to meet the needs of 3,000 homes (Figure 18-11). The main use of such relatively small plants will be to provide reserve power to meet daytime peak electricity loads, especially in California and southwestern states with high electrical load peaks in the summer because of air conditioning demands.

Many observers believe that these systems will make little contribution to overall energy supplies because they have a low net useful energy yield, are costly to build (four to six times the cost of expensive new nuclear power plants on a per kilowatt basis), and produce electricity at a cost several times that of hydroelectric, wind, coal-burning, and conventional nuclear fission power plants. Their environmental impact on air and water is low but land disruption is high because of the large area required for solar collection. They are also usually built in sunny, arid, ecologically fragile desert biomes, where sufficient water may not be available for use in cooling towers to recondense spent steam.

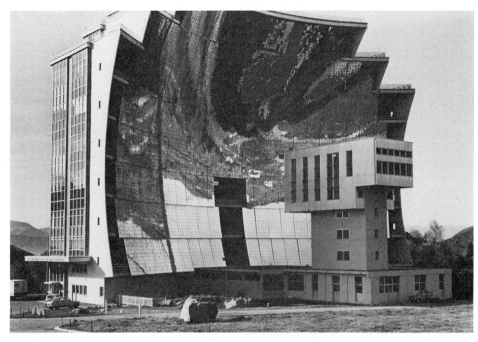

Figure 18-10 Solar furnace located near Odeillo in the Pyrenees Mountains of southern France.

Peter Menzel/Stock, Boston

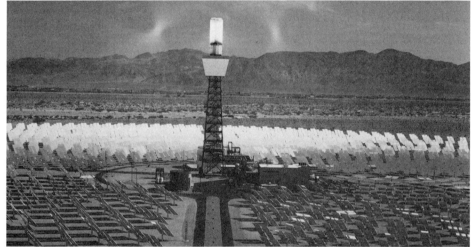

Figure 18-11 Solar One power tower used to generate electricity in the Mojave Desert near Barstow, California.

Sandia National Laboratories, Livermore, CA

Converting Solar Energy Directly to Electricity: Photovoltaic Cells The earth's direct input of solar energy can be converted by **photovoltaic cells,** commonly called *solar cells* or *photovoltaics*, directly into electrical energy in one simple step. A solar cell consists of a thin wafer of purified silicon (which can be made from inexpensive, abundant sand) to which trace amounts of other substances (such as gallium arsenide or cadmium sulfide) have been added so that the wafer emits electrons and produces a small amount of electrical current when struck by sunlight (Figure 18-12).

Since 1958, expensive solar cells have been used to power space satellites and to provide electricity for at least 12,000 homes worldwide (6,000 in the United States), located mostly in isolated areas where the cost of running electrical lines to individual dwellings is extremely high. Some scientists have also proposed putting billions of solar cells on large orbiting satellites and beaming the energy back to earth in the form of microwaves, but such schemes are extremely costly.

Because the amount of electricity produced by a single solar cell is very small, many cells must be wired together in a solar panel to provide a generating capacity of 30 to 100 watts. A number of these panels are then wired together and mounted on a roof or on a rack that tracks the sun to produce electricity for a home or building. Massive banks of such cells can be used to produce electricity at a small power plant.

The resulting electricity is in the form of direct current (DC), not the alternating current (AC) com-

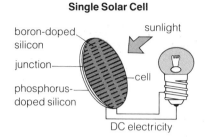

Single Solar Cell

boron-doped
silicon

sunlight

junction

cell

phosphorus-
doped silicon

DC electricity

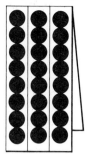

Panel of Solar Cells

Figure 18-12 Use of photovoltaic (solar) cells to provide DC electricity for a home; any surplus can be sold to the local power company.

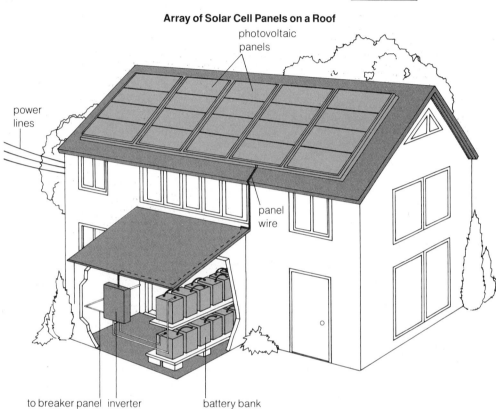

Array of Solar Cell Panels on a Roof

photovoltaic
panels

power
lines

panel
wire

to breaker panel   inverter   battery bank
(inside house)   (converts DC to AC)   (located in shed outside of house
due to explosive nature of battery gases)

monly used in households. One option is to use the electricity directly to power lights and appliances that run on DC like those in recreational vehicles. Any excess energy produced during daylight can be sold to the local utility company or stored for use at night and on cloudy days in long-lasting rechargeable DC batteries like those used in boats and golf carts. Another alternative is to use an electronic inverter to convert direct current to alternating current. In the future, DC electricity produced by solar cells could also be used to decompose water to produce hydrogen gas, which can be stored in a pressurized tank and burned in fuel cells to provide space heat, hot water, and electricity and to run cars (see Enrichment Study at the end of this chapter).

U.S. Department of Energy and solar cell researchers and manufacturers in the United States and Japan project that development of more energy-efficient cells and cost-effective mass-production techniques should allow solar cells to produce electricity at a competitive price almost everywhere by the mid-1990s or shortly after the turn of the century. This goal came closer to reality in 1986 when a group of electrical engineers at Stanford University developed solar cells with an energy efficiency of 27.5%—not much below the efficiency of nuclear and coal-fired power plants.

If cost-effective solar cells can be mass-produced, their use could spread rapidly in MDCs for buildings and houses and in LDCs, where electricity in rural areas is either unavailable or supplied by expensive diesel generators. Since 1981 the U.S. federal research and development budget for solar cells has been cut sharply while Japanese government expenditures in this area have tripled. Some analysts argue that federal and private research efforts on photovoltaics in the United States should be greatly increased. Otherwise the U.S. might one day find its capital being drained to pay for imports of massive numbers of photovoltaic cells from Japan and other Far Eastern countries and lose out on a major global economic market.

Solar cells have a number of important advantages. If used according to projections, they could be providing 20% to 30% of the world's electricity by 2050, thus eliminating the need to build large-scale power plants of any type and allowing the phaseout of many existing nuclear and coal-fired power plants. They are reliable and quiet, have no moving parts, can be installed quickly and easily, need little maintenance (occasional washing to prevent dirt from blocking the sun's rays), and should last 20 to 30 years if encased in glass or plastic. Most are made from silicon, the second most abundant element in the earth's crust. They do not produce carbon dioxide, air and water pollution during operation is low, air pollution from manufacture is low, and land disturbance is very low for roof-mounted systems.

However, there are some drawbacks. Present costs of solar cell systems are high but are projected to become competitive in 7 to 15 years. The net useful energy yield is moderate to low. Depending on design, the widespread use of solar cells may be limited eventually by supplies of expensive or rare elements such as gallium and cadmium used to produce types of cells presently considered to be the most efficient. Their widespread use could also cause economic disruption from the bankruptcy of utilities with unneeded large-scale power plants. Without effective control, solar cell manufacture produces moderate water pollution from hazardous chemical wastes.

18-3 INDIRECT PERPETUAL SOLAR ENERGY: PRODUCING ELECTRICITY FROM FALLING AND FLOWING WATER

Types of Hydroelectric Power Since the 1800s the kinetic energy in the falling and flowing water of rivers and streams has been used to produce electricity in small- and large-scale *hydroelectric plants. Large-scale hydropower* projects tap into the kinetic energy of falling water. High dams are built across large rivers to create large reservoirs. The stored water is then allowed to flow at controlled rates, spinning turbines and producing electricity as it falls downward to the river below the dam. Although based indirectly on the perpetual solar energy that drives the hydrologic cycle, all large hydroelectric dams have finite lives because the reservoirs usually fill with silt and become useless in 30 to 300 years, depending on the rate of natural and human-accelerated soil erosion from land above the dam.

Small-scale hydropower projects tap into the kinetic energy of flowing water. A low dam is built across a small river or stream with no reservoir or only a small one behind the dam, and natural water flow is used to generate electricity. However, electricity production can vary with seasonal changes in stream flow and under drought conditions.

Falling water can also be used to produce electricity in *pumped-storage hydropower systems*, primarily to provide supplemental power during times of peak electrical demand. When electricity demand is low, usually at night, electricity from a conventional power plant is used to pump water uphill from a lake or reservoir to a specially built reservoir at a higher elevation, usually on a mountain. When a power company temporarily needs more electricity than its conventional plants can produce, water in the upper reservoir is released and passed through turbines to generate electricity as it returns to the lower reservoir.

Present and Future Use In 1984 hydropower supplied about one-fourth of the world's electricity—twice that from nuclear power—and almost 7% of the world's total commercial energy. Countries or areas with mountainous regions have the greatest hydropower potential. Hydropower supplies Norway and several countries in Africa with essentially all their electricity, Switzerland 74%, and Austria 67%. Canada gets over 70% of its electricity from hydropower and exports electricity to the United States. In 1985, LDCs got about 42% of their electricity from hydropower, and their total hydropower capacity is expected to double by 1990.

Since its completion in 1983, Brazil's giant Itaipu Dam on the Parana River along the Brazil-Paraguay border has been the world's largest hydroelectric project, producing electricity equivalent to that from almost thirteen 1,000-megawatt coal-fired or nuclear plants. China, with one-tenth of the world's hydropower potential, is likely to become the world's largest producer of hydroelectricity. Work has begun on a hydropower dam across the Yangtze River that will be capable of producing electricity equal to that from 25 large nuclear or coal-fired power plants. This project, however, will force 2 million people to leave their homes. The Worldwatch Institute estimates that projects under construction or in the planning stages will double the worldwide output of electricity from hydropower between 1980 and 2000.

The United States is the world's largest producer

of electricity from hydropower. Hydropower produced at almost 1,600 sites provided 14% of the electricity and about 5% of the total commercial energy used by the United States in 1984. About 46% of this electricity is produced at sites owned and managed by the federal government.

U.S. hydroelectric power plants produce electricity cheaper than any other source. One reason is that most large-scale projects were built from the 1930s to the 1950s, when costs were low. In addition, hydroelectric energy efficiency is high (83% to 93%), plants produce full power 95% of the time (compared to 55% for nuclear plants and 65% for coal plants), and they have life spans two to ten times those of coal and nuclear plants. As a result, regions such as the Pacific Northwest, where most of the electricity can be produced by hydropower, enjoy the lowest electric rates in the country.

Despite these important advantages, it is projected that by 2000 hydroelectric power will be supplying only about 5% of the commercial energy used in the United States—the same percentage as in 1985. High construction costs for new large-scale dams is one factor hindering further development. In addition, most suitable sites have already been used, are located in areas far from where electricity is needed so that transmission costs are high, or are located on rivers protected from development by the Wild and Scenic Rivers Act of 1968 or by state laws.

In 1983 the U.S. Army Corps of Engineers identified 1,407 abandoned small and medium size hydroelectric dams that could be retrofitted to supply electricity equal to that from 19 large nuclear or coal power plants, as well as 541 presently undeveloped small to medium hydropower sites, which could supply electricity equivalent to that of 26 large nuclear or coal plants. Rehabilitating existing dams does not require any new technology and has little environmental impact. Once rebuilt, such units have a long life, need minimal operating crews, require little maintenance, and produce electricity at a cost no higher than that of coal and nuclear power.

By 1986 nearly 200 retrofitted small hydroelectric sites were generating power equivalent to that from two large-scale coal or nuclear power plants. Since then, however, development of new projects has fallen sharply because of low oil prices, loss of federal tax credits, and growing opposition by local residents and environmentalists. These groups contend that by reducing stream flow, hydroelectric projects threaten recreational activities and animal life, disrupt scenic rivers, destroy wetlands, and restrict fish movement. Environmentalists also argue that most of the electricity produced by these projects can be obtained at a lower cost and with less environmental disruption by industrial cogeneration, energy conservation, and importing more hydroelectricity from Canada.

Advantages and Disadvantages Hydropower has a number of advantages. Many LDCs have large, untapped potential sites, although many are remote from points of use. Hydropower has a moderate to high net useful energy yield and fairly low operating and maintenance costs. Plants rarely need to be shut down, and they produce no emissions of carbon dioxide or other air pollutants during operation. Large dams provide some degree of flood control and a regulated flow of irrigation water for areas below the dam.

There are drawbacks, however. Construction costs for new systems are high, and there is a lack of suitable sites for large-scale projects in the United States and Europe. Large-scale projects flood large areas of land to form reservoirs, decrease the natural fertilization of prime agricultural land in river valleys below the dam, and lead to a decline in fishing below the dam (Section 11-4). Without proper land-use control, large-scale projects can also result in greatly increased soil erosion and sediment water pollution near the reservoir above the dam, reducing the effective life of the reservoir. Small-scale projects can disrupt river flows, valleys, and wetlands and restrict fish movement.

Tidal Power Another potential source of energy for producing electricity from flowing water is the daily oscillation of ocean water levels as a result of gravitational attraction among the earth, moon, and sun. Twice a day a large volume of water flows in and out of inland bays or other bodies of water near the coast to produce high and low tides. If a bay has an opening narrow enough to be obstructed by a dam with gates that can be opened and closed, and if there is a large difference in water height between high and low tides, the kinetic energy in the daily tidal flows can be used to spin turbines to produce electricity.

Unfortunately, suitable sites occur only at about two dozen places in the world. Since 1968 a small, 160-megawatt commercial tidal power plant has been in operation on the north coast of France near St. Malo on the Rance River, which has tides up to 13.5 meters (44 feet), and another small plant is in operation in the Soviet Union. Although operating costs are fairly low, the French project cost about 2.5 times more than a conventional hydroelectric power plant station with the same output built further up the Rance River.

Since 1984, Canada has been operating a 20-megawatt experimental tidal power plant at Anapolis Royal, Nova Scotia, on the Bay of Fundy, which has the largest tidal fluctuation in the world—16 meters (52 feet). If this project is successful, the plant may be expanded in the future. Two possible locations for experimental tidal power stations in the United States are the Cook Inlet in Alaska and Passamaquoddy Bay on the Maine coast.

Advantages of tidal energy for producing electricity include a free source of energy (tides), low operating costs, moderate net useful energy yield, low air pollution and no addition of carbon dioxide to the atmosphere, and little land disturbance. However, most analysts expect tidal power to make only a small contribution to world electricity supplies because of the lack of suitable sites, high construction costs, irregular output that varies daily, and extensive seawater corrosion and possible storm damage to dams and power plants.

Wave Power   The kinetic energy in ocean waves, created primarily by wind, is another potential source of energy for producing electricity from moving water. Scientists in Japan, Norway, and France are exploring ways to harness this form of hydropower. So far none of these experiments has led to the production of electricity at an affordable price. In addition, sites with sufficient wave heights are limited, electrical output varies with differences in wave height, construction and operating costs are high, net useful energy yield is low, and equipment is damaged or destroyed by saltwater corrosion and severe storms. In 1986 the United Kingdom abandoned its research on ocean wave power, and most analysts expect this alternative to make little contribution to world electricity production.

18-4   INDIRECT PERPETUAL SOLAR ENERGY: PRODUCING ELECTRICITY FROM HEAT STORED IN WATER

Ocean Thermal Energy Conversion   Ocean water stores immense amounts of heat from the sun. Experiments are under way to use the large temperature differences between the cold bottom waters and the sun-warmed surface waters of tropical oceans to produce electricity. This would be done by a gigantic floating **ocean thermal energy conversion (OTEC)** power plant anchored in suitable tropical ocean areas no more than 80 kilometers (50 miles) offshore (Figure 18-13). Some 62 countries, mostly LDCs in South America and Africa, have suitable sites for such plants. Favorable U.S. locations include portions of the Gulf of Mexico and offshore areas near southern California and the islands of Puerto Rico, Hawaii, and Guam.

In a typical plant, warm surface water would be pumped through a large heat exchanger and used to evaporate and pressurize a low-boiling fluid such as liquid ammonia. The pressurized ammonia gas would drive turbines to generate electricity. Then, cold bottom water as deep as 900 meters (3,000 feet) below the plant would be pumped to the surface through massive pipes 30 meters (100 feet) in diameter and used

to cool and condense the ammonia back to the liquid state to begin the cycle again.

The pumps in a 250-megawatt plant would have to be capable of pumping more water each second than the average flow rate of the Mississippi River; the electricity used by these pumps would reduce the net useful energy yield for the system by one-third. A large cable would transmit the electricity to shore. Other possibilities include using the electricity produced to desalinate ocean water, extract minerals and chemicals from the sea, or decompose water to produce hydrogen gas, which could be piped or transported to shore for use as a fuel. Japan and the United States have been conducting experiments to evaluate the technological and economic feasibility of using this energy resource to produce electricity.

Advantages and Disadvantages of OTEC   OTEC has several advantages. The source of energy is free and perpetual at suitable sites, and there is no need for a costly energy storage and backup system. No air pollution is produced during operation, and the floating power plants require no land area. Nutrients brought up when water is pumped from the ocean bottom might be used to nourish schools of fish and shellfish. Advocates believe that with enough research and development funding, large-scale OTEC plants could be built to produce electricity equivalent to that from ten 1,000-megawatt coal or nuclear power plants by the year 2000.

However, many energy analysts believe that large-scale extraction of energy from ocean thermal gradients may never compete economically with other energy alternatives because of high construction costs (two to three times those of comparable coal-fired plants), high operating and maintenance costs as a result of seawater corrosion of metal parts and fouling of heat exchangers by algae and barnacles, a low net useful energy yield (energy efficiency is only about 3%), the limited number of suitable sites, the potential for severe damage from hurricanes and typhoons, the release of dissolved carbon dioxide gas into the atmosphere when large volumes of deep ocean water are pumped to the surface, and possible disruption of aquatic life.

Inland Solar Ponds   A **solar pond** is a solar energy collector consisting of at least 0.5 hectare (1 acre) of relatively shallow saline water or of fresh water enclosed in plastic bags. Saline solar ponds can be used to produce electricity and are usually located near inland saline seas or lakes, near deserts with ample sunlight. The bottom layer of water in such ponds remains on the bottom when heated because it has a higher salinity and density (mass per unit volume) than the top

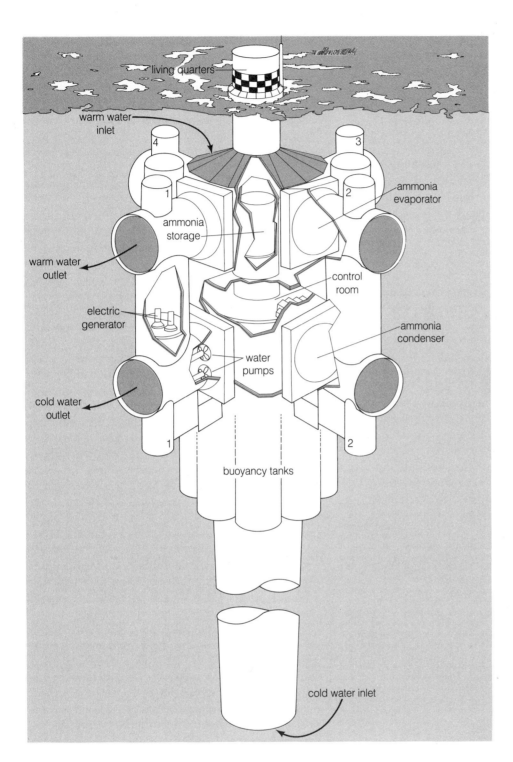

Figure 18-13 Possible design of a large-scale ocean thermal electric plant (OTEC) for generating electricity from the temperature gradient in a tropical area of ocean.

living quarters

warm water inlet

4

3

1

2

ammonia evaporator

ammonia storage

warm water outlet

control room

electric generator

ammonia condenser

water pumps

cold water outlet

1

2

buoyancy tanks

cold water inlet

layer. Heat accumulated during daylight in the bottom layer can be used to produce electricity in a manner similar to that used to tap into the temperature difference between bottom and surface waters in a tropical ocean (Figure 18-13).

An experimental saline water solar pond power plant on the Israeli side of the Dead Sea has been operating successfully for several years. By 2000, Israel plans to build a cluster of plants around the Dead Sea to provide most of the electricity it needs for air con-

ditioning and desalinating water. By 1986, more than a dozen experimental saline water solar ponds had been built in the United States, mostly in desert areas near the Salton Sea in California and the Great Salt Lake in Utah.

Freshwater solar ponds can be used as a source of hot water and space heating. A very shallow hole is dug, lined with concrete, and covered with insulation. A series of large, black plastic bags, each filled with several inches of water, is placed in the hole and covered with fiberglass-reinforced, transparent panels to allow sunlight penetration and to prevent most of the heat stored in the water during daylight from being lost to the atmosphere. A computer-controlled monitoring system determines when water in the bags reaches its peak temperature (typically 140°F to 160°F) in the afternoon and turns on pumps to transfer the hot water to large, insulated tanks for distribution as hot water or for space heating. The world's largest freshwater solar pond went into operation at Fort Benning, Georgia, in 1985. This $4 million 11-acre pond provides hot water for 6,500 troops and is expected to save up to $10 million over a 20-year period.

Advantages and Disadvantages of Solar Ponds Saline and freshwater solar ponds have the same major advantages as OTEC systems. In addition, they have a moderate net useful energy yield, moderate construction and operating costs, and fairly low maintenance. Freshwater solar ponds can be built in almost any sunny area and may be particularly useful for supplying hot water and space heating for large buildings and small housing developments. Enthusiasts project that with adequate research and development support, solar ponds could supply 3% to 4% of U.S. commercial energy by the year 2000.

However, saline solar ponds are feasible only in areas with ample sunlight, usually ecologically fragile deserts. Operating costs can be high because of extensive saltwater corrosion of pipes and heat exchangers. Unless lined, the ponds can become ineffective when various compounds leach from bottom sediment, darken the water, and reduce sunlight transmission. Freshwater solar ponds require large land areas and are too expensive for providing hot water and space heating for individual homes.

18-5 INDIRECT PERPETUAL SOLAR ENERGY: PRODUCING ELECTRICITY FROM WIND

Wind Power: Past and Present Since the 1600s, prevailing winds, produced indirectly by solar energy, have been harnessed to propel ships, grind grain, pump water, and power many small industrial shops. In the 1800s settlers in the American West used wind to pump groundwater for farms and ranches; in the 1930s and 1940s, small farms beyond the reach of electric utility lines obtained electricity from small wind turbines. By the 1950s, cheap hydropower, fossil fuels, and rural electrification had replaced most wind turbines.

Since the 1970s an array of small to large, modern *wind turbines*, usually consisting of a blade or other device that spins and a generator mounted on a tower, have been developed. Experience has shown that these machines can produce electricity at a reasonable cost for use by small communities and large utility companies in areas with average wind speeds of at least 10 miles per hour and ideally from 14 to 24 miles per hour. Many parts of the continental United States have such winds. Hawaii and parts of Alaska also have very favorable winds.

Small (10 to 100 kilowatt) and intermediate-size (200 to 1,000 kilowatt) wind turbines are the most widely used because they are easier to mass-produce, are less vulnerable to stress and breakdown, and can produce more power in light winds and thus remain in operation longer than large turbines. They are also easier to locate close to the ultimate users, thus reducing electricity transmission costs and energy loss.

Use of wind power in the United States has grown more rapidly since 1981 than any other new source of electricity. Starting near zero in 1981, nearly 13,000 wind machines with a total generating capacity equal to a 1,000-megawatt coal or nuclear plant were in operation by the end of 1985—enough to meet the electricity needs of 200,000 homes. Most of these were installed by small private companies in California, where 90% of all U.S. wind power electricity is produced, in **wind farms** consisting of clusters of 50 to 100 small to medium-size wind turbines in windy mountain passes (Figure 18-14). Wind farms can be put into operation within two years and are connected to existing utility lines. More wind development has taken place in California than the rest of the world because of favorable wind conditions not far from urban areas, high prices paid by utilities for electricity produced by private companies, and very favorable state and federal tax credits (which by 1986 were phased out).

The California Energy Commission projects that wind power produced by private companies and utility companies will be the state's second least expensive source of electricity by 1990—right behind hydropower—and will produce 8% of the state's electricity by 2000. However, some of this projected capacity may not be realized because of the elimination of federal and state tax credits.

A smaller number of wind farms, producing a total of about 100 megawatts of electricity, had been installed in other parts of the United States by 1985, especially in the Pacific Northwest, the northern Great Plains, the Northeast, and Hawaii (which experiences northeast tradewinds with 20 to 24 mph speeds 70% of the time). By 1985 the island of Hawaii obtained about 7% of its electricity from wind and expects to obtain this amount for the entire state by 2000. Other countries planning to make increasing use of wind energy include Denmark (with over 2,000 machines installed by 1985), Canada, Argentina, the United Kingdom, Sweden,

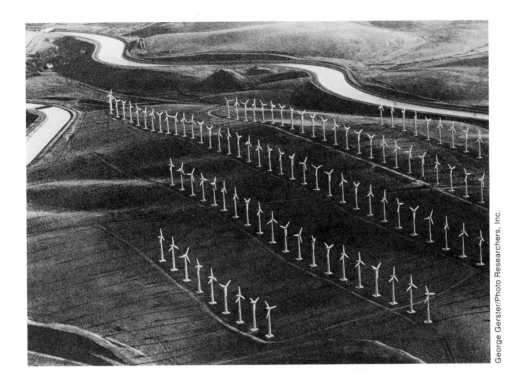

Figure 18-14 A California wind farm consisting of an array of modern wind turbines in a windy mountain pass.

George Gerster/Photo Researchers, Inc.

West Germany, Australia, the Netherlands, and the Soviet Union.

A 1980 study by the Solar Energy Research Institute indicated that 3.8 million homes and hundreds of thousands of farms in the United States are located in areas with sufficient wind speeds to make economical use of small wind generators to provide all or most of their electricity. However, a small, 5-kilowatt wind turbine costs $8,000 to $20,000 installed and often needs repairs requiring parts not readily available. Homeowners would have to add an expensive battery, pumped-storage, flywheel or other system to store energy for use when the wind dies down. A cheaper alternative is to use the power company as a backup and sell it surplus electricity, which utilities are presently required by federal law to buy (although prices vary and many utilities throw up roadblocks). Presently, it makes more sense economically to build wind farms to serve entire communities or groups of homeowners than for most individual homeowners to install wind power systems.

Wind Power in the Future Wind power experts project that with a vigorous development program, wind energy could provide at least 5% and perhaps as much as 10% to 19% of the projected demand for electricity in the United States and as much as 13% of the world's electricity by the end of the century. Many analysts believe that a key to increasing the use of wind power in the United States is reinstatement (for at least five years) of federal and state tax credits, which

reduced the high initial cost of wind installations by 40% to 70%. This would help increase demand and allow small and financially insecure U.S. wind turbine companies to invest in mass production and marketing techniques needed to bring the price down to the point where tax credits would no longer be needed.

Advantages and Disadvantages Wind power has numerous important advantages. It is a perpetual source of energy at favorable sites, and large wind farms with low material requirements can be built within two years. Wind power systems have a moderate net useful energy yield, do not emit carbon dioxide or other air pollutants during operation, and have no cooling water requirements. Their manufacture and use produce little water pollution. The moderate amount of land occupied by wind farms can be used at the same time for grazing and other purposes. Wind farms are projected to have an economic advantage over coal and nuclear power plants in the United States and the world by the 1990s (Figure 17-15, p. 379). This projection, however, assumes that the wind industry can use tax credits to increase demand and can obtain adequate financing to allow construction of mass-production facilities.

Wind power has some disadvantages. It can only be used in areas with sufficient winds and requires backup electricity from a utility company or from a fairly expensive energy storage system when the wind dies down. Present systems have moderate to high initial costs, high operating costs, and operate at full

Figure 18-15 Major types of biomass fuel.

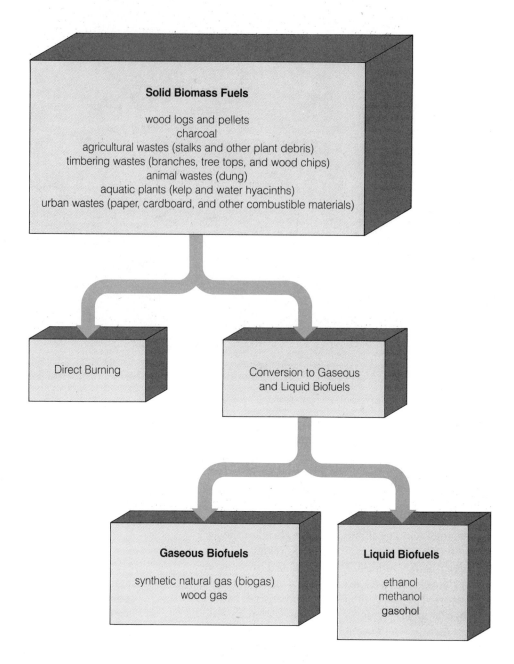

capacity only about 23% of time because of variations in wind availability and speed. The industry expects to achieve 35% capacity with improved designs, but this is still well below the 55% capacity of nuclear power plants and the 65% capacity of coal-fired plants.

Widespread use of wind turbines in the heavily populated Northeast, where the best sites are along heavily used coasts and highly visible mountain ridges, could cause unacceptable visual pollution. Some wind experts have proposed that this problem could be overcome by building large floating wind farms (such as one in operation in Denmark) off the eastern coast to make use of strong offshore winds to produce electricity or hydrogen gas for transmission to shore. Excessive noise and interference with local television reception have been problems with large turbines but can be overcome with improved design and isolated

locations. Large wind farms might also interfere with flight patterns of migratory birds in certain areas.

18-6 INDIRECT RENEWABLE SOLAR ENERGY: BIOMASS

Renewable Biomass as a Versatile Fuel Produced by solar energy through the process of photosynthesis, **biomass fuel** is organic plant matter that can be burned directly as a solid fuel or converted to a more convenient, gaseous or liquid **biofuel** by processes such as distillation and pyrolysis (heating in the absence of air) (Figure 18-15). In 1984, biomass, mostly from the direct burning of wood and animal

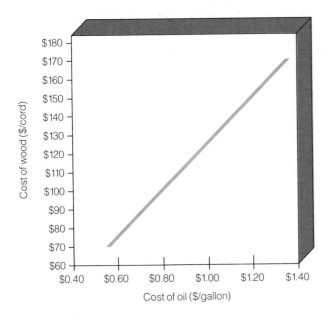

Figure 18-16 Break-even prices for heating with wood instead of oil.

wastes to heat buildings and cook food, supplied about 11% of the world's commercial energy (4% to 5% in Canada and the United States). By 2000, biomass (including biofuels) is projected to provide 15% of the world's commercial energy and 11% to 20% of the commercial energy in the United States.

All biomass fuels have several advantages in common. They can be used to provide a variety of solid, liquid, and gaseous fuels for space heating, water heating, producing electricity, and propelling vehicles. Biomass is a renewable energy resource as long as trees and plants are not harvested faster than they grow back. Although burning a biomass fuel releases carbon dioxide into the atmosphere, living plants also remove carbon dioxide from the atmosphere through photosynthesis. Thus, there is no net increase in atmospheric levels of carbon dioxide as long as the rate of removal and burning of trees and plants does not exceed their rate of replenishment. Burning of biomass fuels adds much less sulfur dioxide and nitrogen oxides to the atmosphere per unit of energy produced than the uncontrolled burning of coal and thus requires fewer pollution controls.

Biomass fuels also share some disadvantages. Without effective land-use controls and replanting, extensive removal of trees and plants can deplete soil nutrients and cause excessive soil erosion, water pollution, flooding, and loss of wildlife habitat. Biomass resources also have a high moisture content (15% to 95%), which reduces their net useful energy. The added weight makes collection and transport expensive. Each type of biomass fuel has additional specific advantages and disadvantages.

Burning Wood and Wood Wastes In 1985 wood was the primary source of energy for cooking and heating for one-half of the world's population and for 80% in LDCs. However, in 1985 about 1.1 billion people were either unable to find or too poor to buy enough fuelwood to meet minimum needs. The United Nations projects that by the year 2000 about 2.5 billion people will live in areas with inadequate fuelwood supplies.

In MDCs with adequate forest reserves, the burning of wood and wood wastes to heat homes and to produce steam and electricity in industrial boilers has increased rapidly because of price rises in heating oil and electricity. Sweden leads the world in using wood as an energy source, mostly for district heating plants. In 1985 the forest products industry (mostly paper companies and lumber mills) accounted for almost two-thirds of U.S. wood energy consumption, with homes and small businesses burning the rest.

By 1985, one in every nine single-family homes (one in six in nonmetropolitan areas) in the United States relied entirely on wood for heating—about the same percentage that relied on oil for heating. The percentage of homes heating with wood in different regions of the U.S. varies, with the greatest use found in New England, where wood is plentiful and expensive oil is the primary heating fuel.

Burning wood and wood wastes has several specific advantages in addition to those associated with all biomass fuels. Wood has a moderate to high net useful energy yield when collected and burned directly and efficiently near its source. Three-fourths of the wood fuel used in U.S. residences is cut or collected by people, mostly in rural areas, who have access to wood at little or no cost. Figure 18-16 shows the prices at which a homeowner breaks even or saves money by heating with wood rather than oil. Solar-assisted water stoves can also be used to combine some of the advantages of wood and direct solar energy (see Spotlight on p. 410).

But wood fuel has several disadvantages. Because wood has a low energy content per unit of weight and a high water content, it is expensive to harvest, transport, store, and burn. As a result, in urban areas where wood must be hauled long distances, it can cost homeowners more per unit of energy produced than oil and electricity. A considerable number of accidents occur as a result of using wood as a fuel. In 1980 there were an estimated 123,000 chain saw accidents that required medical attention and 22,000 house fires and 350 deaths caused by wood stoves in the United States.

Residential wood burning also leads to greatly increased outdoor and indoor air pollution, causing as many as 820 cancer deaths a year in the United States, according to the EPA. The estimated 12 million wood stoves in the United States account for over 15% of the nation's emissions of solid particulate matter. They also emit large quantities of carbon monoxide

One way to avoid most of the problems associated with a conventional wood stove and significantly increase the energy efficiency of a wood heating system is to use a solar-assisted water stove (Figure 18-17). Several roof-mounted active solar collectors are used to heat water stored in a large, well-insulated 250- to 1,000-gallon steel tank (depending on the size of the space to be heated), which has a built-in firebox. Wood, paper, coal, or any combustible material is burned in the firebox in very cold weather and at night to supplement the stored solar energy.

The system is placed outdoors in an open lean-to or small shed, thus eliminating the indoor smoke and soot associated with conventional wood stoves and further increasing the safety of the system. A catalytic converter can be added to reduce outdoor air pollution. A pump connected to the storage tank circulates the heated water through underground insulated pipes to a heat exchanger (much like the radiator in a car) before the water is returned to the tank. The exchanger transfers heat in the water to air, which is blown by a fan through ducts in the building to be heated. With a conventional thermostat to control indoor temperature, the system eliminates the uneven heating provided by a conventional wood stove.

A separate copper coil placed in the firebox and a second pump allow the stove to meet all hot water needs. Additional coils and pumps can be used to heat a swimming pool, hot tub, sauna, or greenhouse. A thermostat-controlled oil or gas burner can also be attached to the tank as a backup. Maintenance is simple: occasionally checking a water-level gauge and turning a valve to add water to the tank to replace water lost by slow evaporation (a minor chore that could be automated) and adding a bottle of rust inhibitor once a year.

The installed cost for a 500-gallon system with four solar collectors—sufficient to provide all the hot water and space heating for a typical 1,800-square-foot house—is about $5,000 to $6,000 (less if the system is installed by the user). Such a system should pay for itself in several years and then lead to considerable annual savings.

Details of Stove

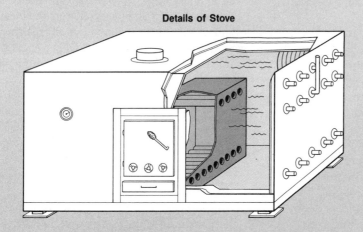

Figure 18-17 Solar-assisted water stove. (Modified by permission from Carolina Water Stoves, P.O. Box 266, Dobson, N.C. 27017)

and polycyclic organic matter (unburnt residues containing cancer-causing substances).

This air pollution can be reduced 75% by a $100 to $250 catalytic combustor (a honeycombed ceramic chamber containing a chemical that speeds up the burning of emission products), which must be replaced after 10,000 operating hours at a cost of about $75. These units also make it more economical to burn wood by increasing the energy efficiency of a typical airtight wood stove from about 55% to as high as 75%, and they reduce the need for chimney cleaning and the chance of chimney fires.

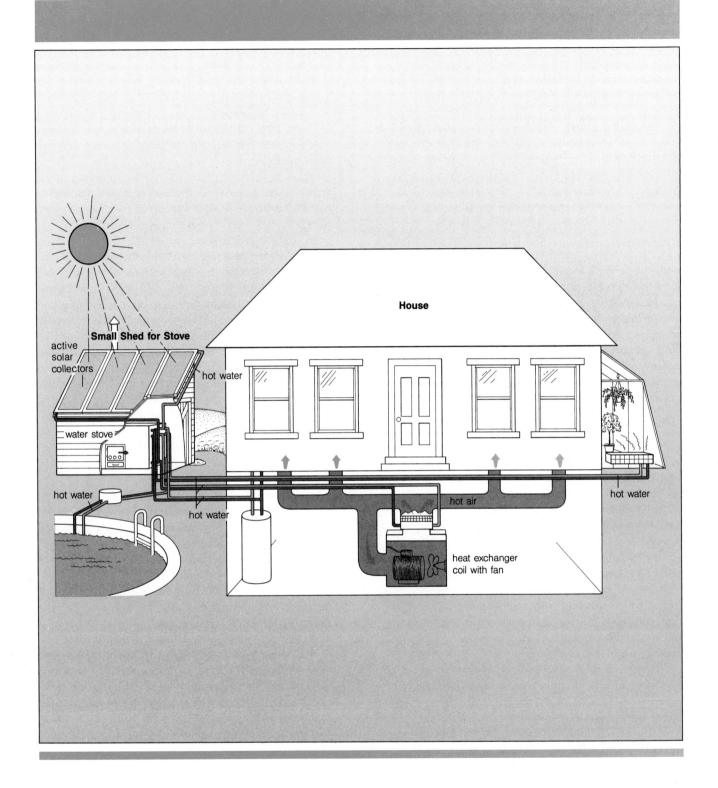

active
solar
collectors

Small Shed for Stove

hot water

water stove

hot water

hot water

House

hot air

heat exchanger
coil with fan

hot water

By 1985, Oregon, Colorado, and Montana had passed laws requiring such devices and in some cases forbidding wood burning when particulate matter in the atmosphere reaches certain levels; at least 20 other states were considering such laws. In some cities—

London, for example—wood fires have been banned to reduce air pollution. In 1987 the EPA proposed that all wood stoves manufactured after 1988 be required to meet certain air pollution emission standards designed to reduce emissions by 70%.

Energy Plantations Another approach to obtaining plentiful amounts of biomass fuel is to establish large *biomass-energy plantations,* where trees, grasses, or other crops would be grown and harvested by automated methods and then burned directly or converted to liquid or gaseous biofuels. Ideal energy crops would be fast-growing, high-yield perennials that reproduce themselves from cuttings—less expensive than seeding.

Another possibility in some areas is to plant energy farms with some of the 2,000 varieties of euphorbia plants, which store energy in hydrocarbon compounds (like those found in oil) rather than as carbohydrates. After harvesting of the plants, the oil-like material would be extracted, refined to produce gasoline, or burned directly in diesel engines. The unused woody plant residues could be converted to alcohol fuel. Such plants could be grown on semiarid, currently unproductive land, although lack of water might limit the amount produced.

However, energy plantations usually require heavy use of herbicides and pesticides, occupy large land areas, can compete with food crops for prime farmland, and are likely to have low or negative net useful energy yields like conventional crops. In addition, the economic feasibility of this approach has not been determined.

Burning Agricultural and Urban Wastes In agricultural areas, crop residues (the inedible, unharvested portions of food crops) and animal manure can be collected and burned or converted to biofuels. Hawaii, which plans to produce 90% of its electricity from renewable energy by 2005, was burning enough bagasse (a residue from sugarcane) in 1983 to produce almost 8% of its electricity. In most areas, however, plant residues are widely dispersed and require large amounts of energy to collect, dry, and transport—unless collected along with harvested crops. In addition, ecologists argue that it makes more sense to use these valuable nutrients to feed livestock, retard soil erosion, and fertilize the soil.

Japan and many European companies have built a number of cogeneration plants, in which collected urban waste (much of it consisting of paper, cardboard, and plastics) is burned to produce high-temperature steam and electricity, mostly for use by industry or local power companies (Section 21-3). Burning such wastes reduces the volume of urban waste by 90%, extending the lives of existing landfills and reducing the need for new ones. But some analysts argue that more electricity is saved by composting or recycling paper and other organic wastes instead of burning them.

Converting Solid Biomass to Liquid and Gaseous Biofuels Plants, organic wastes, sewage, and other forms of solid biomass can be converted by bacteria and various chemical processes into gaseous and liquid biofuels such as *biogas* (a gaseous mixture containing about 60% methane and 40% carbon dioxide), *liquid methanol* (methyl, or wood, alcohol), and *liquid ethanol* (ethyl, or grain, alcohol), and other liquid fuels.

In China, bacteria in millions of devices called biogas digesters convert organic plant and animal wastes into methane fuel for heating and cooking. After the biogas has been removed, the remaining solid residue can be used as fertilizer on food crops or, if contaminated, on nonedible crops such as trees. When they work, biogas digesters are highly efficient; however, they are somewhat slow, unpredictable, and vulnerable to low temperatures, acidity imbalances, and contamination by heavy metals, synthetic detergents, and other industrial effluents. Because of these problems, few MDCs use biogas digesters on a large scale and their use in LDCs such as India and China is declining.

Methane containing biogas is also produced by the underground decomposition of organic matter in the absence of air (anaerobic digestion) in the estimated 20,000 landfill sites around the United States. The gas can be collected simply by inserting pipes into landfills. By 1985, some 40 landfill gas recovery systems (mostly in California) were operating in the United States, 40 others were under construction, and an estimated 2,000 to 3,000 large landfills have the potential for large-scale methane recovery.

Methane is also being produced in some places through the anaerobic digestion of sludge produced at sewage treatment plants. In 1976 a company called Calorific Recovery by Anaerobic Processes (CRAP) began providing Chicagoans with methane made from cattle manure collected from animal feedlots. Converting to methane all the manure that U.S. livestock produce each year could provide nearly 5% of the country's total natural gas consumption at 1985 levels. But collecting and transporting manure for long distances would require a large energy input. Recycling this manure to the land to replace artificial fertilizer, which requires large amounts of natural gas to produce, would probably save more natural gas.

Anticipating the depletion of crude oil supplies, the world must find a liquid fuel substitute for gasoline and diesel fuel. Some analysts see the biofuels methanol and ethanol as the answer to this problem, since both alcohols can be burned directly as fuel without requiring additives to boost octane ratings.

Presently most of the emphasis is on ethanol as an automotive fuel. Ethanol can be produced from a variety of sugar and grain crops (sugarcane, sugar beets, sorghum, and corn) by the well-established process of fermentation and distillation used in the alcoholic beverage business. Pure ethanol can be burned in today's cars with little engine modification. Gasoline can also be mixed with 10% to 23% ethanol to make **gasohol,** now known as super unleaded or ethanol-enriched gasoline, which burns in conventional gasoline engines.

By 1984, ethanol accounted for 43% of automotive fuel consumption in Brazil, where more than 1.2 million of the country's 10 million cars ran on pure ethanol and the remaining 8.8 million used an unleaded gasoline mixture containing 23% ethanol produced from sugarcane. This ambitious program helped Brazil cut its oil imports in half between 1978 and 1984. The country plans to triple its production of ethanol fuel by 1993, but this may be delayed by the temporary oil glut of the 1980s, which has reduced conventional gasoline prices.

By 1986, super unleaded gasoline containing 90% gasoline and 10% ethanol accounted for 7% of gasoline sales in the United States. Most is produced from corn in 150 ethanol production facilities built between 1980 and 1985. Ethanol-enriched gasoline is presently exempt from the federal gasoline tax and from varying amounts of state gasoline taxes in at least 30 states in order to stimulate the development of this industry. Despite these and other tax benefits (amounting to almost $1 a gallon), ethanol-enriched gasoline costs between $1.15 and $1.50 a gallon. Until gasoline prices rise again, the use of this form of unleaded gasoline could level off. Sales, however, could increase when leaded gasoline is banned in the United States after 1988. New, energy-efficient distilleries are reducing the costs of producing ethanol, and soon this fuel may be able to compete with other forms of unleaded gasoline without federal tax breaks (scheduled to expire in 1992).

The distillation process used to produce ethanol also produces large volumes of a toxic waste material known as "swill," which if allowed to flow into waterways would kill algae, fish, and plants. Another problem is that the net useful energy yield for producing ethanol for use as a fuel is moderate for recently completed distilleries using modern technology and powered by coal, wood, or solar energy, low if the tractor fuel used in growing grain for conversion to ethanol is included, and zero or negative when produced in older oil- or natural-gas-fueled distilleries.

Another alcohol—methanol—can be produced from wood, wood wastes, agricultural wastes, sewage sludge, garbage, coal, and natural gas. High concentrations of methanol corrode conventional engines, but in a properly modified engine methanol burns cleanly without any problems. The use of pure meth-anol as a fuel, however, will not be economically feasible until gasoline prices reach about $3 or $4 a gallon—already a reality in many European countries, where gasoline taxes are high. *Diesohol*, a mixture of diesel fuel with 15% to 20% methanol by volume, is being tested and could lower emissions of nitrogen oxide pollutants, a drawback of regular diesel fuel.

18-7 DEVELOPING AN ENERGY STRATEGY FOR THE UNITED STATES

Overall Evaluation of U.S. Energy Alternatives Table 18-2 summarizes the major advantages and disadvantages of the energy alternatives discussed in this and the two preceding chapters, with emphasis on their potential in the United States. Energy experts argue over these and other futuristic projections, and new data may affect some information in this table. But it does provide a useful framework for making decisions based on presently available information. Four major conclusions can be drawn:

1. The best short-term, intermediate, and long-term alternative for the United States and other countries is to reduce unnecessary energy waste by reducing energy consumption and improving the efficiency of energy use.

2. Total systems for future energy alternatives in the world and in the United States will probably have low to moderate net useful energy yields and moderate to high development costs. Since enough financial capital may not be available to develop all alternative energy systems, projects must be carefully chosen so that capital will not be depleted on systems that yield too little net useful energy or prove to be unacceptable economically or environmentally.

3. Instead of depending primarily on one nonrenewable energy resource like oil, the world and the United States probably must shift to much greater dependence on improving energy efficiency and a mix of perpetual and renewable energy sources over the 50 years it typically takes to develop and phase in new energy resources.

4. As improvements in energy efficiency are made and dependence on perpetual and renewable energy resources is increased, commercial energy production will become more localized and variable, depending on local climatic conditions and availability of usable energy resources.

Energy Resource	Estimated Availability			Estimated Net Useful Energy of Entire System	Projected Cost of Entire System	Actual or Potential Overall Environmental Impact of Entire System
	Short Term (1988–1998)	Intermediate Term (1998–2008)	Long Term (2008–2038)			
Nonrenewable Resources						
Fossil fuels						
Petroleum	High (with imports	Moderate with imports)	Low	High but decreasing	High for new domestic supplies	Moderate
Natural gas	High (with imports)	Moderate (with imports)	Low to moderate	High but decreasing	High for new domestic supplies	Low
Coal	High	High	High	High but decreasing	Moderate but increasing	Very high
Oil shale	Low	Low to moderate	Low to moderate	Low to moderate	Very high	High
Tar sands	Low	Fair? (imports only)	Poor to fair (imports only)	Low	Very high	Moderate to high
Biomass (urban wastes for incineration)	Low	Low	Low	Low to moderate	High	Moderate to high
Synthetic natural gas (SNG) from coal	Low	Low to moderate	Low to moderate	Low to moderate	High	High (increases use of coal)
Synthetic oil and alcohols from coal and organic wastes	Low	Low	Low	Low to moderate	High	High (increases use of coal)
Nuclear energy						
Conventional fission (uranium)	Low to moderate	Low to moderate	Low to moderate	Low to moderate	Very high	Very high
Breeder fission (uranium and thorium)	None	None to low (if developed)	Moderate	Unknown, but probably moderate	Very high	Very high
Fusion (deuterium and tritium)	None	None	None to low (if developed)	Unknown	Very high	Unknown (probably moderate)
Geothermal energy (trapped pockets)	Poor	Poor	Poor	Low to moderate	Moderate to high	Moderate to high
Perpetual and Renewable Resources						
Conservation (improving energy efficiency)	High	High	High	Very high	Low	Decreases impact of other sources

Economics and National Energy Strategy   Cost is the major factor in determining which commercial energy resources are widely used by consumers. Governments throughout the world use three major economic and political strategies to stimulate or dampen the short- and long-term use of a partic- ular energy resource: **(1)** *not attempting to control prices,* so that its use depends on open, free market compe- tition (assuming all other alternatives also compete in the same way), **(2)** *keeping prices artificially low* to encourage its use and development, and **(3)** *keeping prices artificially high* to discourage its use and devel-

Energy Resource	Estimated Availability			Estimated Net Useful Energy of Entire System	Projected Cost of Entire System	Actual or Potential Overall Environmental Impact of Entire System
	Short Term (1988–1998)	Intermediate Term (1998–2008)	Long Term (2008–2038)			
Perpetual and Renewable Resources (continued)						
Water power (hydroelectricity)						
New large-scale dams and plants	Low	Low	Very low	Moderate to high	Moderate to very high	Low to moderate
Reopening abandoned small-scale plants	Moderate	Moderate	Low	Moderate to high	Moderate	Low
Tidal energy	None	Very low	Very low	Unknown (moderate)	High	Low to moderate
Ocean thermal gradients	None	Low	Low to moderate (if developed)	Unknown (probably low to moderate)	Probably high	Unknown (probably moderate)
Solar energy						
Low-temperature heating (for homes and water)	Moderate	Moderate to high	High	Moderate to high	Moderate to high	Low
High-temperature heating	Low	Moderate	Moderate to high	Moderate	Very high initially (but probably declining fairly rapidly)	Low to moderate
Photovoltaic production of electricity	Low to moderate	Moderate	High	Moderate	High initially but declining fairly rapidly	Low
Wind energy						
Home and neighborhood turbines	Low	Moderate	Moderate to high	Moderate	Moderate to high	Low
Large-scale power plants	None	Very low	Probably low	Low	High	Low to moderate?
Geothermal energy (low heat flow)	Very low	Very low	Low to moderate	Low	High	Moderate to high
Biomass (burning of wood, crop, food, and animal wastes)	Moderate	Moderate	Moderate to high	Moderate	Moderate	Moderate to high
Biofuels (alcohols and natural gas from plants and organic wastes)	Low to moderate?	Moderate	Moderate to high	Low to moderate	Moderate to high	Moderate to high
Hydrogen gas (from coal or water)	None	Low	Moderate	Unknown	Unknown	Variable

opment. Each approach has certain advantages and disadvantages. Although effective short-, intermediate-, and long-term energy strategies for a particular country should involve a delicately balanced mixture of these approaches, most countries place primary emphasis on one.

Free Market Competition   Leaving it to the marketplace without any government interference is appealing in principle. However, it rarely exists in practice because business leaders are in favor of it for everyone but their own company. Most energy industry executives work hard to achieve control of supply, demand, and prices for their particular energy resource while urging free market competition for any competing energy resources. They try to influence elected officials and help elect those who will give their business the most favorable tax breaks and other government subsidies. This distorts and unbalances the marketplace.

An equally serious problem with the open marketplace is its emphasis on today's prices to enhance short-term economic gain. This greatly inhibits the long-term development of new energy resources, which can rarely compete effectively in their initial development stages without government-supported research and development and economic subsidies.

Keeping Energy Prices Artificially Low: The U.S. Strategy Many governments provide tax breaks and other subsidies, underwrite expensive long-term research and development, and use price controls to maintain artificially low prices for a particular energy resource. This is the main approach in the United States (and in the Soviet Union, where all resources and means of production—and thus prices—are controlled by the central government).

This approach encourages the development and use of energy resources receiving favorable treatment, helps protect consumers (especially the poor) from sharp price increases, can help reduce inflation, and often helps the reelection chances of leaders in democratic societies. At the same time, however, this approach encourages waste and rapid depletion of an energy resource (such as oil) by making its price lower than it should be relative to long-term supply. This strategy discourages development of new energy alternatives not receiving at least the same level of subsidies and price control. Once energy industries such as the fossil fuel and nuclear power industries receive government subsidies, they usually have the power to maintain this support long after it becomes unnecessary, and they often fight efforts to provide equal or higher subsidies for development of new energy alternatives.

In 1984 federal tax breaks and other subsidies for development of energy conservation and perpetual energy resources in the United States amounted to $1.7 billion; the tax breaks were eliminated a year later. In contrast, during 1984 the nuclear power industry received $15.6 billion, the oil industry $8.6 billion, the natural gas industry $4.6 billion, and the coal industry $3.4 billion in federal tax breaks and subsidies. Although energy is the lifeblood of the U.S. economy, 49% of the $4.9 billion research and development budget for the Department of Energy (DOE) in 1987 was allocated to military weapons programs. Meanwhile, allocations for nondefense energy research and development dropped from 65% to 35% of the DOE budget between 1971 and 1987.

About 61% of the remaining nondefense research and development portion of the 1987 DOE budget was allocated to the continued development of nuclear fission and fusion to produce electricity. But energy conservation, the country's largest potential source of energy, received only 5% of this portion of the budget, an amount equivalent to about one-fourth of the cost of a single B-1 bomber. Grants to states and localities for insulation and weatherization of low-income dwellings were virtually eliminated, and direct and indirect solar energy received only 5% of the nondefense research and development budget.

Keeping Energy Prices Artificially High: The Western European Strategy Governments keep the price of a particular energy resource artificially high by withdrawing existing tax breaks and other subsidies or by adding taxes on its use. This approach encourages improvements in energy efficiency, reduces dependence on imported energy, and decreases use of an energy resource (like oil) whose future supply will be limited.

However, such price increases can increase inflation, dampen economic growth, and put a heavy economic burden on the poor unless some of the energy tax revenues are used to help low-income families offset increased energy prices and to stimulate labor-intensive forms of economic growth such as energy conservation. High gasoline and oil import taxes have been imposed by many European governments. This is one factor accounting for much lower average energy use per person and greater energy efficiency in these countries than in the United States.

One popular myth is that higher energy prices would wipe out jobs. Actually, *low* energy prices increase unemployment because farmers and industries find it cheaper to substitute machines run on cheap energy for human labor. On the other hand, *raising* energy prices stimulates employment because building solar collectors, adding insulation, and carrying out other forms of energy conservation are labor-intensive activities.

Why the U.S. Has No Comprehensive Long-Term Energy Strategy After the 1973 oil embargo, Congress was prodded to pass a number of laws (see Appendix 3) to deal with the country's energy problems. Most energy experts agree, however, that these laws do not represent a comprehensive energy strategy. Indeed, elementary political analysis reveals why the United States has not and will probably never be able to develop a coherent energy policy.

One reason is the complexity of energy issues as revealed in this chapter and the two preceding ones. But the major problem is that the American political process produces laws—not policies—and is not designed to deal with long-term problems (Chapter 25). Each law reflects political pressures of the moment and a maze of compromises between competing pressure groups representing industry, environmentalists, and consumers. In addition, once a law has been passed, it is difficult to repeal or modify drastically until any undesirable long-term consequences reach crisis proportions.

Taking Energy Matters into Your Own Hands

While elected officials, energy company executives, and environmentalists argue over the key components of a coherent national energy strategy, many individuals have gotten fed up and taken energy matters into their own hands. With or without tax credits, they are insulating, weatherizing, and making other improvements to conserve energy and save money. Some are building new, passively heated and cooled solar homes; others are adding passive solar heating to existing homes.

Similarly, local governments in a growing number of cities are developing their own successful programs to improve energy efficiency and to rely more on locally available energy resources. Each of these individual and local initiatives are crucial political and economic actions. Increased and amplified, they can help shape a sane national energy strategy with or without help from federal and state governments.

In the long run, humanity has no choice but to rely on renewable energy. No matter how abundant they seem today, eventually coal and uranium will run out. The choice before us is practical: We simply cannot afford to make more than one energy transition within the next generation.

Daniel Deudney and Christopher Flavin

Enrichment Study   Hydrogen as a Possible Replacement for Oil

Some scientists have suggested the use of hydrogen gas (H_2) to fuel cars, heat homes, and provide hot water when oil and natural gas run out. Although hydrogen gas does not occur in significant quantities in nature, it can be produced by chemical processes from nonrenewable coal or natural gas or by using heat, electricity, or perhaps sunlight to decompose fresh water or some of the world's massive supply of seawater (Figure 18-18).

Hydrogen gas can be burned in a reaction with oxygen in a power plant, a specially designed automobile engine, or in a fuel cell that converts the chemical energy produced by the reaction into direct-current electricity (Figure 18-19). Hydrogen burns

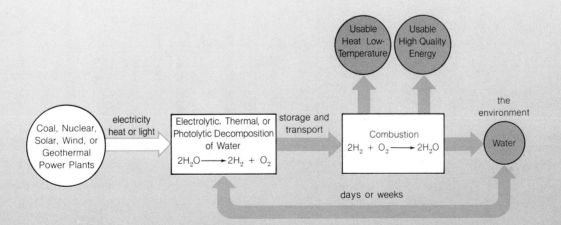

Figure 18-18   The hydrogen energy cycle. Hydrogen gas must be produced by using electricity, heat, or solar energy to decompose water, thus leading to a negative net useful energy yield.

cleanly in pure oxygen, yielding only water vapor and no air pollutants. In addition, hydrogen can be combined with various metals to produce solid compounds that can be heated to release hydrogen on demand in a small automobile fuel-generating system.

A demonstration fuel cell power plant has been in operation in lower Manhattan since 1983. The plant operates with an energy efficiency close to 90%. However, present costs of producing electricity in this way are quite high and it remains to be seen how long present fuel cells will last. Some efforts are also being devoted to developing a fuel cell unit about the size of a garden shed that could provide enough electricity for about 40 homes.

The major problem with using hydrogen as a fuel is that only trace amounts of the gas occur in nature. Thus, it must be produced with energy from another source such as nuclear fission, direct solar, or wind. Depending on the source of energy used to decompose water, this raises the cost. Because of the first and second energy laws, hydrogen production by any method will require more energy to produce it than is released when it is burned. Thus, its net useful energy yield will always be negative so that its wide-spread use depends on an ample and affordable supply of some other type of energy. Another problem is that hydrogen gas is highly explosive; an explosion of a hydrogen tanker or storage tank could lead to massive destruction and loss of life. However, most analysts believe we could learn how to handle it safely, as we have for highly explosive gasoline and natural gas.

Although burning hydrogen does not add carbon dioxide to the atmosphere, carbon dioxide would be added if electricity from coal-burning or other fossil-fuel-burning power plants were used to decompose water. No carbon dioxide would be added if direct or indirect solar energy or nuclear power were used. Scientists are trying to develop special cells that use ordinary light or solar energy to split water molecules into hydrogen and oxygen gases with reasonable efficiency. But even if affordable materials are used and reasonable efficiencies are obtained, it may be difficult and expensive to develop large-scale commercial cells for producing hydrogen gas. According to the most optimistic projections, affordable commercial cells for using solar energy to produce hydrogen will not be available until after 2000.

Figure 18-19 Fuel cell in which hydrogen gas is converted into DC electricity.

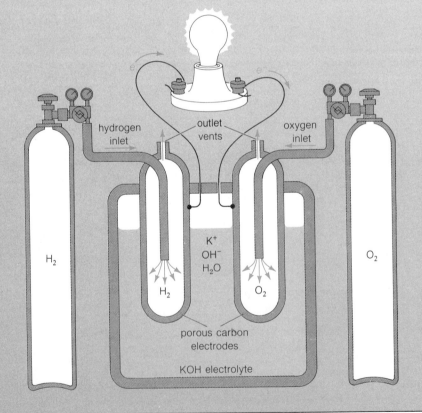

CHAPTER SUMMARY

Energy conservation involves reducing energy consumption by **(1)** changing energy-wasting habits at no cost, **(2)** increasing energy efficiency by known energy-saving techniques and existing energy-efficient devices, and **(3)** developing new energy-efficient devices and industrial processes. It is the largest and cheapest source of energy available and reduces the environmental impact from using energy of any type. Despite important improvements in energy efficiency since 1973, the United States and Canada still remain the two most energy-inefficient MDCs in the world, primarily because of outdated regulations and policies and failure of most consumers to consider lifetime costs when buying a new car, house, or appliance.

Direct solar energy can be used to provide *low-temperature heat* for space heating and heating water. A *passive solar system* in a superinsulated or well-insulated and weatherized house is the cheapest and most energy-efficient way to heat a residence on a lifetime cost basis with a very low environmental impact. An *active solar system* is a cost-effective way of providing hot water for a residence on a lifetime cost basis but with present technology is cost-effective primarily for space heating of large apartment and commercial buildings.

Direct solar energy can also be concentrated to produce *high-temperature heat* for industrial processes and for producing electricity in solar power plants. However, with present technology costs are very high. Direct solar energy can also be converted directly to electricity in *photovoltaic cells*. Environmental impact is low; costs, though still high, may become competitive within the next decade.

Falling and flowing water can be used to produce electricity in large and small *hydroelectric plants*. New large and small hydroelectric projects can greatly increase electricity production in many MDCs with moderate to high costs and moderate to low environmental impact. New large-scale hydroelectric projects in the United States are limited because of a lack of suitable and environmentally acceptable sites. However, many previously abandoned small hydroelectric plants could be reopened at moderate cost with relatively low environmental impact. Producing electricity by tapping into the energy in twice-daily ocean tides (*tidal power*) and ocean waves (*wave power*) is expected to make little contribution to world energy resources because of limited suitable sites and high costs.

Electricity can also be produced from solar energy stored as heat in seawater at tropical ocean sites and in inland solar ponds containing either salt water or fresh water. Suitable sites for large, floating *ocean thermal electric power plants* are limited and technological problems, low energy yields, and high costs may severely limit the use of this energy resource. *Solar ponds* on inland saltwater seas and lakes can provide electricity at a few limited sites, but costs appear high. Building freshwater inland solar ponds may be a quick and effective way to provide low-temperature heat for providing hot water and space heating for large buildings and groups of houses, but costs are still being evaluated.

Electricity primarily for use by local utilities can be produced by large numbers of modern *wind turbines* in wind farms at numerous suitable sites in the United States and the world. Environmental impact is low and installation time is short (one to two years). Costs are still fairly high but may drop with improved design and mass production of wind turbines.

Energy can be obtained from a number of *biomass fuels*. *Wood* is a widely used fuel for cooking, space heating, and water heating throughout the world, especially in LDCs. However, fuelwood supplies are decreasing in many LDCs as forests are being stripped of trees without adequate replanting. In rural areas with ample forests and adequate replanting, burning wood and wood wastes can be a cost-effective way for the forest products industry to cogenerate steam and electricity and for individuals to heat residences. However, burning wood to heat houses produces unacceptable levels of indoor and outdoor air pollution without the addition relatively inexpensive air pollution control devices.

In the future, large quantities of fast-growing plants and trees grown on *biomass-energy plantations* may become another useful source of biomass fuel. However, costs are unknown and environmental impact from increased soil erosion could be high without careful controls. Many cities in Europe and an increasing number in the United States are burning *agricultural and urban wastes*, usually to cogenerate steam and electricity for use by nearby industries, homes (district space heating), and local utility companies. Some analysts argue, however, that more energy would be saved by recycling or composting such organic wastes. Useful but limited amounts of methane-rich *biogas fuel* can be produced by bacterial decomposition of plants, organic wastes buried in large landfills, manure collected from animal feedlots, and sludge from sewage treatment plants.

Ethanol, produced from a variety of sugar and grain crops, is being used in automobiles in Brazil and is mixed with gasoline to produce super unleaded gasoline in the United States. However, prices are quite high and must be supported with government tax breaks. Another liquid biofuel, methanol, can be produced from wood, agricultural wastes, sludge from sewage treatment plants, garbage, coal, and natural gas. With present technology, however, it is far too expensive and can be burned only in modified automobile engines.

Some believe that *hydrogen gas* may be used to fuel cars, heat homes and produce electricity when oil runs out sometime in the next century. Although hydrogen is a very clean-burning fuel, it is rare in nature and must be produced by decomposition of water. The resulting negative net useful energy yield means that its widespread use depends on having a large and affordable supply of energy available from some other source—perhaps from special cells powered by solar energy presently under study in the laboratory.

In the United States energy conservation is the largest potential source of energy. Future U.S. energy alternatives to replace oil will probably have low to moderate net useful energy yields and moderate to high development costs. The United States will probably depend on obtaining low to moderate amounts of energy from a variety of locally available energy resources.

Governments can stimulate or dampen the use of a particular energy resource by not attempting to control prices (free market competition), by keeping prices artificially high, or by keeping prices artificially low. Each approach has certain advantages and disadvantages. Because of the complexity of energy problems and the nature of the American political system, it is difficult, if not essentially impossible, for elected federal officials to develop a coherent national energy plan. As a result, many individuals and local communities are developing their own plans to save energy and money and to make increased use of locally available sources of energy.

DISCUSSION TOPICS

1. What are the ten most important things an individual can do to save energy in the home and in transportation? Which, if any, of these do you do? Which, if any, do you plan to do? When?

2. Make an energy use study of your school, and use the findings to develop an energy conservation program.

3. Describe the major differences between active and passive solar energy for heating homes and water. What are the major advantages and disadvantages of each approach?

4. Should the United States institute a crash program to develop solar photovoltaic cells? Explain.

5. Criticize each of the following statements:

   a. The United States can meet essentially all of its future electricity needs by developing solar power plants.

   b. The United States can meet essentially all of its future electricity needs by using direct solar energy to produce electricity in photovoltaic cells.

   c. The United States can meet essentially all of its future electricity needs by building new, large hydroelectric plants.

   d. The United States can meet essentially all of its future electricity needs by building ocean thermal electric power plants.

   e. The United States can meet essentially all of its future electricity needs by building a vast array of wind farms.

   f. The United States can meet essentially all of its future electricity needs by building power plants fueled by biomass resources.

6. Give your reasons for agreeing or disagreeing with the following propositions, which have been suggested by various energy analysts:

   a. The United States should cut average per capita energy use by at least 50% between 1988 and 2000.

   b. A mandatory energy conservation program should form the basis of any U.S. energy policy.

   c. To solve world and U.S. energy supply problems, all we need do is recycle some or most of the energy we use.

   d. Federal subsidies for all energy alternatives should be eliminated so that all choices can compete in a true free-enterprise market system.

   e. All government tax breaks and other subsidies for conventional fuels (oil, natural gas, coal), synthetic natural gas and oil, and nuclear power should be removed and limited subsidies granted for the development of energy conservation, and solar, wind, and biomass energy alternatives.

   f. Development of solar and wind energy should be left up to private enterprise without help from the federal government, but nuclear energy should continue to receive federal support.

   g. To solve present and future U.S. energy problems, all we need to do is find more domestic supplies of oil and natural gas and increase our dependence on nuclear power.

   h. The United States should not worry about heavy dependence on foreign oil imports because they improve international relations and prevent the U.S. from depleting domestic supplies.

   i. A heavy federal tax should be placed on gasoline and imported oil used in the United States.

   j. Between 2000 and 2020 the U.S. should phase out all nuclear power plants.

7. Explain how a government policy of keeping heating oil, gasoline, and electricity prices artificially low by providing subsidies to fossil fuel and nuclear industries and not imposing higher taxes on gasoline and imported oil can (a) discourage exploration for domestic supplies of fossil fuels, (b) increase or at least not significantly decrease dependence on imported oil, (c) lead to higher than necessary unemployment, (d) discourage the development of direct and indirect sources of solar energy, and (e) discourage improvements in energy efficiency.

PART FIVE

Pollution

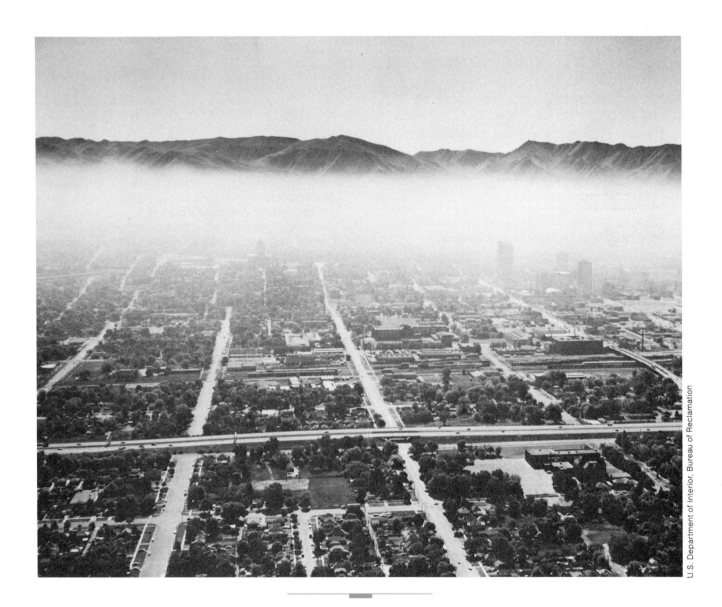

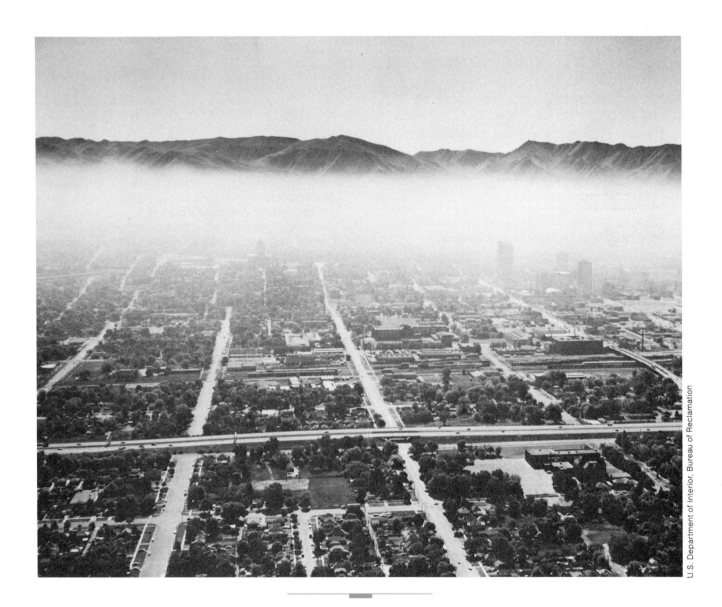
U.S. Department of Interior, Bureau of Reclamation

Humans of flesh and bone will not be much impressed by the fact that a few of their contemporaries can explore the moon, program their dreams, or use robots as slaves, if the planet Earth has become unfit for everyday life. They will not long continue to be interested in space acrobatics if they have to watch them with their feet deep in garbage and their eyes half-blinded by smog.

René Dubos

19

Air Pollution

Tomorrow morning when you get up take a nice deep breath. It will make you feel rotten.

Citizens for Clean Air, Inc. (New York)

GENERAL OBJECTIVES

1. What are the major types and sources of air pollutants?
2. What are industrial smog, photochemical smog, an urban heat island, and acid deposition?
3. What undesirable effects can air pollutants have on humans?
4. What undesirable effects can air pollutants have on other species and on materials?
5. What undesirable effects can certain air pollutants have on the ozone layer and global climate?
6. What legal and technological methods can be used to reduce air pollution?

To stay alive we must inhale about 20,000 liters (21,200 quarts) of air each day. Along with the nitrogen and oxygen gases that make up 99% of the atmosphere, each breath also contains small amounts of other gases, minute droplets of various liquids, and tiny particles of a variety of solids. Some of these chemicals come from natural sources, but most come from cars, trucks, power plants, factories, cigarettes, and other sources related to human activities in urban areas. Repeated exposure to even trace amounts of many of these chemicals, known as air pollutants, can damage lung tissue, plants, buildings, metals, and other materials.

19-1 TYPES AND SOURCES OF OUTDOOR AND INDOOR AIR POLLUTION

Our Air Resource: The Atmosphere The atmosphere, a gaseous envelope surrounding the earth, is divided into several zones (Figure 19-1). About 95% of the mass of the air is found in the innermost layer of the atmosphere known as the **troposphere,** extending only 8 to 12 kilometers (5 to 7 miles) above the earth's surface. If the earth were an apple, our vital air supply would be no thicker than the apple's skin.

About 95% of the volume of clean, dry air consists of two gases: nitrogen (78%) and oxygen (21%). The remaining 1% consists of small amounts of other gases such as argon and carbon dioxide. Air also holds water vapor in amounts varying from 0.01% at the frigid poles to 5% in the humid tropics.

Major Types of Outdoor Air Pollutants As clean air moves across the earth's surface, it picks up addi-

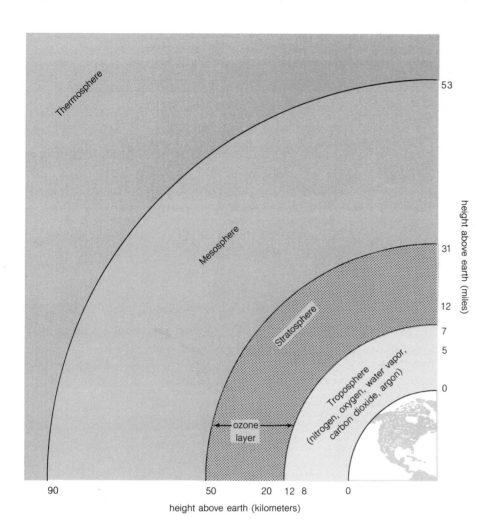

Figure 19-1 Structure of the earth's atmosphere (not drawn to scale). About 95% of the air is in the troposphere.

Thermosphere

Mesosphere

Stratosphere

53

31

12

7

5

0

height above earth (miles)

ozone layer

Troposphere (nitrogen, oxygen, water vapor, carbon dioxide, argon)

90   50   20 12 8   0

height above earth (kilometers)

tional loads of chemicals produced by natural events and human activities. Once in the troposphere, potential air pollutants mix vertically and horizontally and often react chemically with each other or with natural components of the atmosphere. When the concentration of a normal component of air or of a new chemical added to or formed in the air builds up to the point of causing harm to humans, other animals, vegetation, or materials such as metals and stone, that chemical is classified as an **air pollutant.** Worldwide, each year air pollution causes at least 150,000 premature deaths (53,000 in the U.S.), causes or aggravates debilitating respiratory diseases for tens of millions of people, and results in at least $100 billion in damages to crops, trees, buildings, and other objects.

Although there are hundreds of potential air pollutants, most air pollution results from six major classes of substances (Table 19-1). About 90% of all air pollution problems are caused by five groups of pollutants: carbon monoxide, nitrogen oxides, sulfur oxides, volatile organic compounds (mostly hydrocarbons), and suspended particulate matter (Figure 19-2).

The length of time particulate matter remains in the air depends on the relative size of the particles (Figure 19-3) and on the climate. Large particles, with diameters greater than 10 micrometers (about 0.000039 inch) normally remain in the troposphere only a day or two before being brought to earth by gravity or precipitation. Medium-sized particles, with diameters between 1 and 10 micrometers, are lighter and tend to remain suspended in the air for several days. Fine particles, with diameters less than 1 micrometer, may remain suspended in the troposphere for one to two weeks and in the stratosphere for one to five years—long enough to be transported all over the world. These particles are the most hazardous to human health because they are small enough to penetrate the lung's natural defenses; they can also bring with them droplets or other particles of toxic or cancer-causing pollutants that become attached to their surfaces.

Sources of Outdoor Air Pollutants Natural sources of air pollutants include forest fires started by lightning, pollen dispersal, wind erosion of soil, volcanic eruptions, evaporation of volatile organic compounds

Table 19-1 Major Types of Air Pollutants

Class of Pollutants	Major Members of the Class
Carbon oxides (CO_x)	Carbon monoxide (CO), carbon dioxide (CO_2)
Sulfur oxides (SO_x)	Sulfur dioxide (SO_2), sulfur trioxide (SO_3)
Nitrogen oxides (NO_x)	Nitric oxide (NO), nitrogen dioxide (NO_2), nitrous oxide (N_2O)
Volatile organic compounds (VOCs) Hydrocarbons (HCs)—gaseous and liquid compounds containing carbon and hydrogen	Methane (CH_4), butane (C_4H_{10}), ethylene (C_2H_4), benzene (C_6H_6), benzopyrene ($C_{20}H_{12}$)
Other organic compounds	Formaldehyde (CH_2O), chloroform ($CHCl_3$), methylene chloride (CH_2Cl_2), ethylene dichloride ($C_2H_2Cl_2$), trichloroethylene (C_2HCl_3), vinyl chloride (C_2H_3Cl), carbon tetrachloride (CCl_4), ethylene oxide (C_2H_4O)
Suspended particulate matter (SPM) Solid particles	Dust (soil), soot (carbon), asbestos, lead (Pb), cadmium (Cd), chromium (Cr), arsenic (As), beryllium (Be), nitrate (NO_3^-) and sulfate (SO_4^{2-}) salts
Liquid droplets	Sulfuric acid (H_2SO_4), nitric acid (HNO_3), oil, pesticides such as DDT
Photochemical oxidants formed in the atmosphere by the reaction of oxygen, nitrogen oxides, and VOCs under the influence of sunlight	Ozone (O_3), PANs (peroxyacyl nitrates), formaldehyde (CH_2O), acetaldehyde (C_2H_4O), hydrogen peroxide (H_2O_2), hydroxy radical (HO)

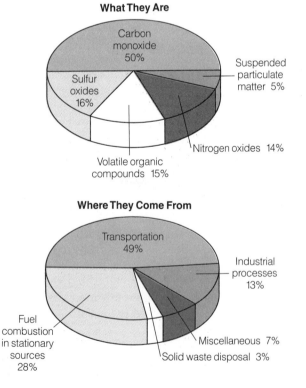

Figure 19-2 Emissions of major air pollutants in the United States. (Data from Environmental Protection Agency)

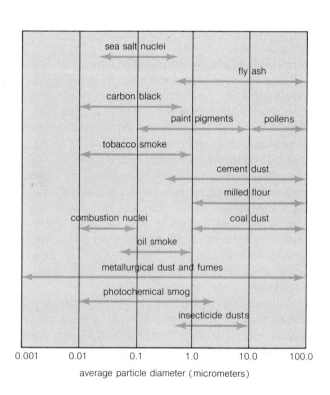

Figure 19-3 Suspended particulate matter is found in a wide variety of types and sizes.

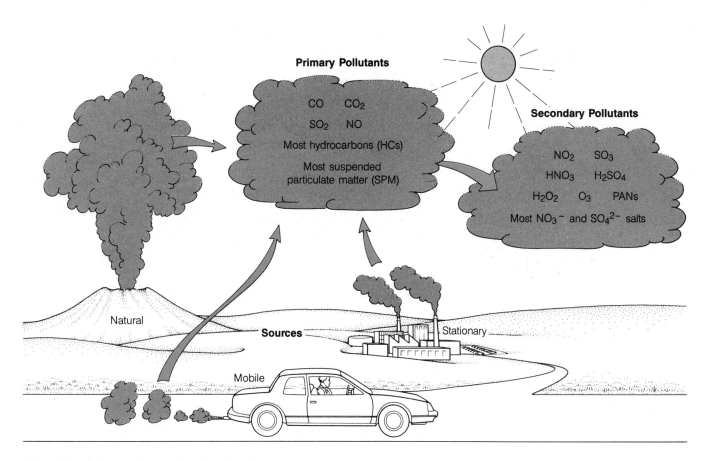

Figure 19-4 Primary and secondary air pollutants.

from leaves (mostly terpene hydrocarbons responsible for the odors of pines and other plants), bacterial decomposition of organic matter, sea spray (sulfate particles), and natural radioactivity (radon-222 gas from deposits of uranium, phosphate, and granite). But emissions from natural sources are dispersed throughout the world and rarely reach concentrations high enough to cause serious damage. Exceptions include massive injections of sulfur dioxide and SPM from volcanic eruptions and buildup of radon-222 gas inside buildings.

Most potential pollutants are added to the troposphere as a result of human activities (see Spotlight p. 426): mainly the burning of fossil fuels in power and industrial plants (stationary sources) and in motor vehicles (mobile sources), the sources of 90% of the air pollutants in the United States (Figure 19-2).

The air pollution capital of the world may be Cubato, near São Paulo in Brazil. The air in this heavily industrialized city contains twice the level of SPM considered lethal by the World Health Organization. Essentially no birds or insects remain, most trees are blackened stumps, more babies are born deformed there than anywhere in Latin America, air pollution monitoring machines break down from contamination, and the mayor refuses to live in the city.

Primary and Secondary Air Pollutants   Air pollutants can be classified as either primary or secondary (Figure 19-4). A **primary air pollutant** is a harmful chemical that directly enters the air as a result of natural events or human activities. For example, carbon monoxide and carbon dioxide are primary pollutants formed when any carbon-containing substance such as coal, oil, natural gas, or wood is burned completely ($C + O_2 \rightarrow CO_2$) or partially ($2C + O_2 \rightarrow 2CO$). In the United States 71% of all carbon monoxide emissions come from motor vehicles. Another primary pollutant, sulfur dioxide (SO_2), is emitted into the air by volcanic eruptions and the burning of oil and coal, which contain sulfur impurities ($S + O_2 \rightarrow SO_2$). In the U.S. 83% of all SO_2 emissions come from coal and oil-burning electric power plants (68%) and industrial plants (15%).

A **secondary air pollutant** is a harmful chemical that forms in the air because of a chemical reaction between two or more air components. For example, the primary pollutant sulfur dioxide reacts with oxygen gas in the atmosphere to form the secondary pollutant sulfur trioxide ($2SO_2 + O_2 \rightarrow 2SO_3$). The sulfur trioxide can then react with water vapor in air to form droplets of sulfuric acid ($SO_3 + H_2O \rightarrow H_2SO_4$), another secondary air pollutant.

Humans probably first experienced harm from air pollution when they built fires in poorly ventilated caves. As cities grew during the Agricultural Revolution, air pollution from the burning of wood and later of coal became an increasingly serious problem. In 1273 A.D. King Edward I of England banned the burning of coal and reinstated wood as the primary fuel in order to reduce air pollution. In 1911, at least 1,150 Londoners died from the effects of coal smoke. The author of a report on this disaster coined the word *smog* for the mixture of smoke and fog that often hung over London. An even worse London air pollution incident killed 4,000 people in 1952, and further disasters in 1956, 1957, and 1962 killed a total of about 2,500 people. As a result, London

has taken strong measures against air pollution and has much cleaner air today.

In the United States the Industrial Revolution brought air pollution as coal-burning industries and homes filled the air with soot and fumes. In the 1940s air in industrial centers like Pittsburgh and St. Louis became so thick with smoke that automobile drivers sometimes had to use their headlights at midday. The rapid rise of the automobile, especially since 1940, brought new forms of pollution such as photochemical smog, which causes the eyes to sting and water, and toxic lead compounds from the burning of leaded gasoline.

The first known U.S. air pollution disaster occurred in 1948, when fog laden with sulfur dioxide fumes and suspended particu-

late matter stagnated over the town of Donora in Pennsylvania's Monongahela Valley for five days. About 6,000 of the town's 14,000 inhabitants fell ill and 20 of them died. This killer fog resulted from a combination of mountainous terrain surrounding the valley and stable weather conditions that trapped and concentrated deadly pollutants emitted by the community's steel mill, zinc smelter, and sulfuric acid plant. In 1963, high concentrations of air pollutants accumulated in the air over New York City, killing about 300 people and injuring thousands. Other episodes during the 1960s in New York, Los Angeles, and other large cities led to much stronger air pollution control programs in the 1970s.

Indoor Air Pollution   High concentrations of air pollutants can also build up indoors, where people spend 85% to 90% of their time, and in other enclosed spaces such as underground mines, where air is slowly replenished. Indoor air today is generally much cleaner than that found decades ago, when most houses and other buildings were heated with leaky coal-burning furnaces, but there is still cause for concern. In recent years, scientists have found that the air inside some homes, schools, and office buildings is more polluted and dangerous than outdoor air on a smoggy day (Figure 19-5). Indeed, in 1985 the EPA reported that toxic chemicals found in almost every home—including those released by soil under foundations, furniture, drapes, carpets, particle board, paneling, paint thinner, fingernail polish, air fresheners, cigarettes, and many other commonly used products—are three times more likely to cause some type of cancer than outdoor air pollutants. Other air pollutants found in buildings produce dizziness, headaches, coughing, sneezing, burning eyes, and flulike symptoms in many people.

Air pollutants can accumulate in any building. But levels tend to be higher in energy-efficient, relatively airtight houses that do not use air-to-air heat exchangers to bring in sufficient fresh air and in the more than 5 million mobile homes found in the United States. Mobile homes have a smaller volume of air and lower air-exchange rates than conventional homes; they also consist of a larger proportion of plywood, particle board, and other materials containing volatile organic compounds such as formaldehyde.

According to the EPA and public health officials, one of the most serious indoor air pollution threats is from radon-222, a colorless, odorless, radioactive gas that decays into solid particles of other radioactive elements that can be inhaled into the lungs. Exposure to these radioactive particles over 20 or 30 years can cause lung cancer. The EPA and several scientists estimate that at least one of every nine American homes (perhaps as many as one of every four) may harbor harmful or potentially harmful levels of this gas (see Enrichment Study at the end of this chapter).

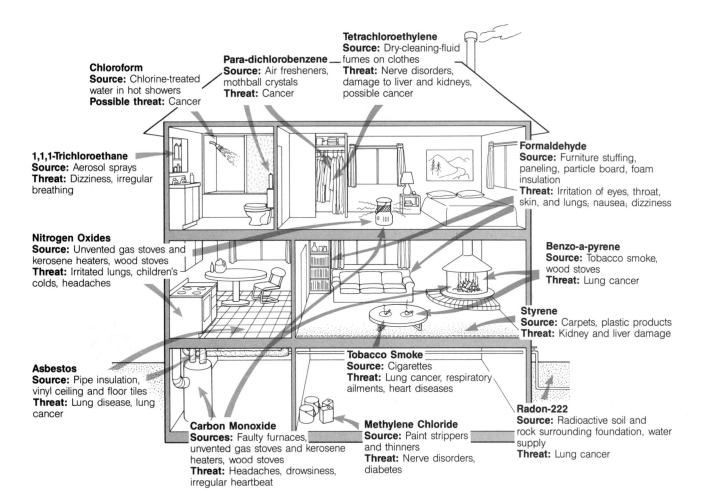

Chloroform
Source: Chlorine-treated water in hot showers
Possible threat: Cancer

Para-dichlorobenzene
Source: Air fresheners, mothball crystals
Threat: Cancer

Tetrachloroethylene
Source: Dry-cleaning-fluid fumes on clothes
Threat: Nerve disorders, damage to liver and kidneys, possible cancer

1,1,1-Trichloroethane
Source: Aerosol sprays
Threat: Dizziness, irregular breathing

Formaldehyde
Source: Furniture stuffing, paneling, particle board, foam insulation
Threat: Irritation of eyes, throat, skin, and lungs; nausea; dizziness

Nitrogen Oxides
Source: Unvented gas stoves and kerosene heaters, wood stoves
Threat: Irritated lungs, children's colds, headaches

Benzo-a-pyrene
Source: Tobacco smoke, wood stoves
Threat: Lung cancer

Styrene
Source: Carpets, plastic products
Threat: Kidney and liver damage

Asbestos
Source: Pipe insulation, vinyl ceiling and floor tiles
Threat: Lung disease, lung cancer

Tobacco Smoke
Source: Cigarettes
Threat: Lung cancer, respiratory ailments, heart diseases

Radon-222
Source: Radioactive soil and rock surrounding foundation, water supply
Threat: Lung cancer

Carbon Monoxide
Sources: Faulty furnaces, unvented gas stoves and kerosene heaters, wood stoves
Threat: Headaches, drowsiness, irregular heartbeat

Methylene Chloride
Source: Paint strippers and thinners
Threat: Nerve disorders, diabetes

Figure 19-5 Some major indoor air pollutants.

Despite the seriousness of indoor air pollution, Congress, the EPA, and state legislatures have been reluctant to establish mandatory indoor air quality standards. Part of the problem with monitoring and controlling indoor air pollution is that there are over a hundred million homes and buildings involved. In addition, many home and building owners would resent having their indoor air tested and being required to reduce excessive pollution levels, even if their indoor air was making them sick or threatening them and other family members with premature death.

One way to control indoor pollution is to install air-to-air heat exchangers, which maintain a flow of fresh air without causing major heating or cooling losses, at prices ranging from $500 to $1,500. A 1984 study showed that indoor levels of formaldehyde and several other toxic gases can also be sharply reduced by house plants such as the spider plant (the most effective), golden pathos, and syngonium. For houses with serious radon gas problems, special venting systems usually have to be installed below the foundations (see Enrichment Study at the end of this chapter).

19-2 INDUSTRIAL AND PHOTOCHEMICAL SMOG, URBAN HEAT ISLANDS, AND ACID DEPOSITION

Industrial Smog Various groups of air pollutants found in the air over cities can be classified as either industrial smog or photochemical smog. Although both types of smog are found to some degree in most urban areas, one type often predominates during at least part of the year as a result of differences in climate and major sources of air pollution.

Industrial smog consists mostly of a mixture of sulfur dioxide and suspended particulate matter, including a variety of solid particles and droplets of sulfuric acid formed from some of the sulfur dioxide. These substances form a grayish haze, explaining why cities where this type of smog predominates are sometimes called *gray-air cities*. This type of air pollution tends to predominate during the winter (especially in the early morning) in older, heavily industrialized cit-

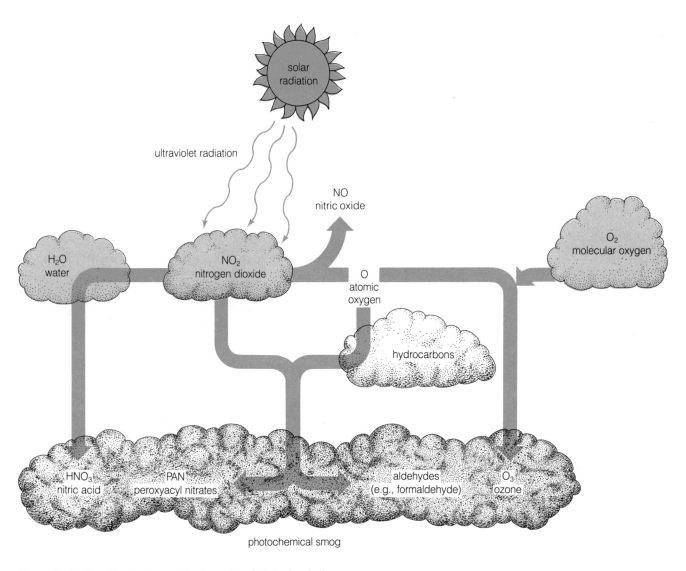

Figure 19-6 Simplified scheme of the formation of photochemical smog.

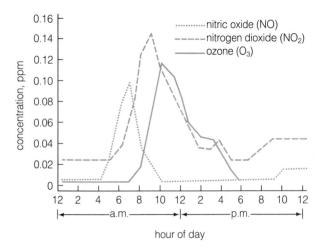

Figure 19-7 Typical variation of atmospheric concentrations of nitric oxide, nitrogen dioxide, and ozone on a sunny day in Los Angeles, California. (Source: National Air Pollution Control Administration)

ies like London, Chicago, Philadelphia, St. Louis, and Pittsburgh, which typically have cold, wet winters and depend heavily on coal and oil for heating, manufacturing, and producing electric power.

Photochemical Smog: Cars + Sunlight = Tears A mixture of primary pollutants such as carbon monoxide, nitric oxide, and hydrocarbons and secondary pollutants such as nitrogen dioxide, nitric acid, ozone, hydrogen peroxide, PANs, and formaldehyde produced when some of the primary pollutants interact under the influence of sunlight is called **photochemical smog** (Figure 19-6). Cities in which photochemical smog predominates usually have sunny, warm, dry climates. They are generally newer cities with few polluting industries and where large numbers of motor vehicles are the major source of air pollution. Examples include Los Angeles; Denver; Salt Lake City (see

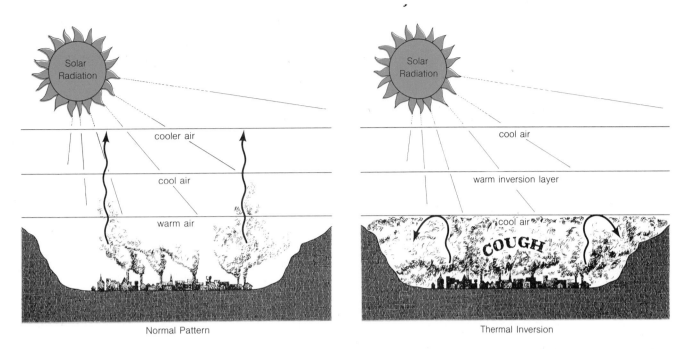

Figure 19-8 Thermal inversion traps pollutants in a layer of cool air that cannot rise to carry the pollutants away.

photo on p. 421); Sydney, Australia; Mexico City; and Buenos Aires, Argentina. The worst episodes from this type of smog tend to occur in summer months between noon and 4 P.M.

The first step in the formation of photochemical smog occurs during the early morning traffic rush hours when NO from automobiles builds up and reacts with O_2 to produce NO_2, a yellowish brown gas with a pungent, choking odor (Figure 19-7). This gas produces a characteristic brownish haze, explaining why cities such as Los Angeles where photochemical smog predominates are sometimes called *brown-air cities.* Then as the sun rises, its ultraviolet rays cause a rapid conversion of the NO_2 back to NO and a highly reactive atom of oxygen (NO_2 + ultraviolet radiation → NO + O). Some of these oxygen atoms react with O_2 in the air to produce ozone gas (O_2 + O → O_3), with peak levels occurring about 10 A.M. Other highly reactive chemicals formed include hydrogen peroxide and hydroxy radicals, with peak concentrations occurring between 10:00 A.M. and 4:00 P.M., depending on atmospheric conditions and components. During the morning hours volatile organic hydrocarbons also evaporate into the atmosphere, mostly from spilled and partially burned gasoline and industrial solvents.

These chemicals interact to form the other components of photochemical smog. The mere traces of ozone, PANs, and aldehydes that build up to their peak levels around noon and in the early afternoon on a sunny day can irritate people's eyes and respiratory tracts. Ozone levels usually drop in the late afternoon and early evening as it reacts with NO generated by afternoon rush-hour traffic. During the summer months most industrial smog cities also experience photochemical smog.

Local Climate, Topography, and Smog The frequency and severity of industrial and photochemical smog in an urban area depend on local climate and topography, density of population and industry, and major fuels used in industry and for heating and transportation. In areas with high average annual precipitation, rain and snow help cleanse the air of pollutants. Winds also help sweep pollutants away and bring in fresh air. However, hills and mountains tend to reduce the flow of air in valleys below and allow pollutant levels to build up at ground level. Buildings in cities also slow wind speed and impede dilution and removal of pollutants.

Air also moves vertically from the ground to higher portions of the atmosphere. During the day the sun warms the earth, and the escaping heat also warms the air nearest the earth's surface. Normally this heated air expands and rises during the day, diluting low-lying pollutants and carrying them higher into the troposphere. Air from surrounding high-pressure areas then moves down into the low-pressure area created when the hot air rises (Figure 19-8, left). This continual mixing of the air helps keep pollutants from reaching dangerous levels in the air near the ground.

But sometimes a layer of dense, cool air is trapped beneath a layer of less dense, warm air in an urban basin or valley. This is called a **temperature or thermal**

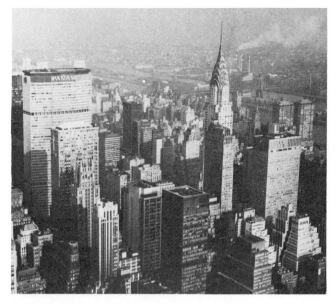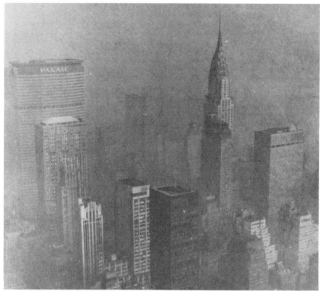

Figure 19-9 Two faces of New York City. The almost clear view was photographed on a Saturday afternoon (November 26, 1966). The effect of more cars in the city and a thermal inversion is shown in the right-hand photograph, taken the previous day.

inversion (Figure 19-8, right, and Figure 19-9). In effect, a warm-air lid covers the region and prevents pollutants from escaping in upward-flowing air currents. Usually these inversions last for only a few hours, but sometimes they last for several days when a high-pressure air mass stalls over an area. When this happens, air pollutants at ground level accumulate to harmful and even lethal levels. Most air pollution disasters—such as those in London and in Donora, Pennsylvania—occurred during lengthy thermal inversions during fall or winter in industrial smog areas.

Thermal inversions occur more often and last longer over towns or cities located in valleys surrounded by mountains, on the leeward sides of mountain ranges, and near coasts. Put several million people and automobiles together in an area with a sunny climate, light winds, mountains on three sides, and the ocean on the other, and you have the ideal conditions for photochemical smog worsened by frequent thermal inversions. This describes the Los Angeles basin, which experiences almost daily inversions, many of which are prolonged during the summer months.

Urban Heat Islands In accordance with the second energy law (Section 3-5), when energy is converted from one form to another, low-quality heat is added to the atmosphere. In the United States, energy use is so high that the average continuous heat load per person injected into the atmosphere is equivalent to that from a hundred light bulbs.

The effect of all this atmospheric heating is evident in large cities and urban areas, which are typically like huge islands of heat surrounded by cooler suburban and rural areas, a climatic effect known as the **urban heat island** (Figure 19-10). This dome of heat helps trap pollutants, especially SPM, and creates a **dust dome** above urban areas. As a result, concentrations of SPM over urban-industrial areas may be a thousand times higher than those over rural areas. If wind speeds increase, this dust dome elongates downwind to form a *dust plume* that spreads the city's pollutants to rural areas and other urban areas tens to hundreds of miles away. As urban areas grow and merge into vast urban regions, the heat and dust domes from a number of cities can combine to form regional heat islands, which affect regional climates and prevent polluted air from being effectively diluted and cleansed.

Acid Deposition One way to decrease ground-level air pollution from sulfur dioxide, SPM, and nitrogen oxides when coal and oil are burned in electric power plants, metal smelters, and other industrial plants is to discharge these emissions from smokestacks tall enough to pierce the thermal inversion layer (Figure 19-8, right). Use of tall smokestacks in the United States,

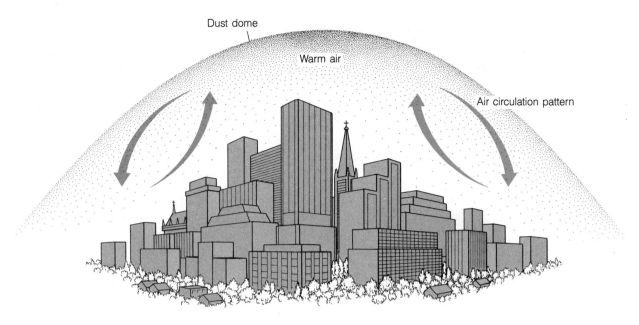

Figure 19-10 An urban heat island causes air circulation patterns that can create a dust dome over the city.

Canada, and western Europe has led to considerable reduction of ground-level pollution in many urban areas.

This approach, however, leads to increased levels of these pollutants and various secondary pollutants in downwind rural and urban areas. As emissions of sulfur dioxide and nitric oxide are transported over long distances by wind currents, they are chemically transformed into a variety of secondary pollutants such as nitrogen dioxide, droplets of sulfuric and nitric acids, and solid particles of sulfate and nitrate salts.

These chemicals then fall or are washed out of the atmosphere onto downwind land and bodies of water. *Wet deposition* occurs when some of the suspended droplets of sulfuric acid and nitric acid return to the earth as acid rain, snow, sleet, hail, fog, or dew. *Dry deposition* occurs when solid particles of sulfate and nitrate salts and gases such as sulfur dioxide fall or are washed out of the atmosphere. These substances can then react with water in soil and bodies of water to form sulfuric and nitric acids. The combined wet and dry deposition of acids or acid-forming substances onto the surface of the earth is known as **acid deposition** (Figure 19-11). This phenomenon is commonly called *acid rain*, but this is a misleading term because these acids and acid-forming substances are deposited not only in rain but also in snow, sleet, fog, and dew and as dry particles and gas.

The relative levels of acidity and basicity of water solutions of substances are commonly expressed in terms of pH (Figure 10-5, p. 193). The lower the pH value, the higher the acidity, with each whole-number decrease in pH representing a tenfold increase in acidity. Natural precipitation has an average pH value of 5.1 (with a range of 5.0 to 5.6 depending on location), caused when carbon dioxide and traces of natural sulfur and nitrogen compounds and organic acids in the atmosphere dissolve in atmospheric water. This slight acidity of natural precipitation helps water deposited on soil to dissolve minerals for use by plants and animals. It also deposits some sulfur and nitrogen used as plant nutrients.

However, deposition of acids and acid-forming substances with higher levels of acidity (pH values of 5.0 and less) than those in natural precipitation can damage materials, leach certain nutrients from soil, and kill fish, aquatic plants, and microorganisms in lakes and streams. Acid deposition, in combination with other air pollutants such as ozone, sulfur dioxide, and nitrogen oxides, can damage trees, crops, and other plants. It can also affect human health.

Acid deposition as a result of human activities is already a serious problem in western and central Europe, Scandinavia, the northeastern United States, southeastern Canada, and southeastern China and is expected to become a problem in other areas. Much of the acid-producing chemicals generated in one country are exported to others by prevailing winds.

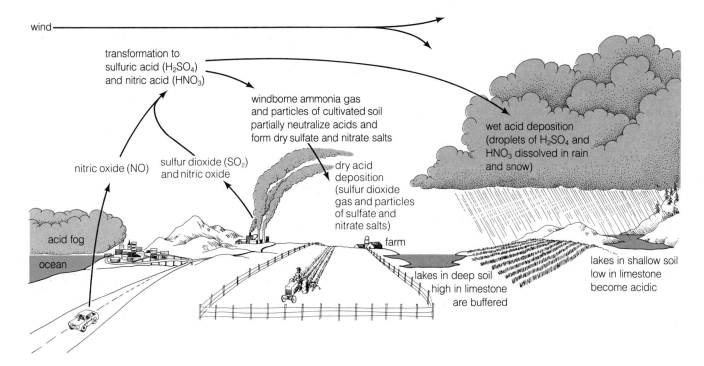

Figure 19-11 Acid deposition.

For example, over three-fourths of the acid deposition found in Norway, Switzerland, Austria, Sweden, the Netherlands, and Finland is blown there from industrialized areas of western and eastern Europe; more than half of the acid deposition in Canada comes from the United States (Figure 19-12).

Almost half of all SO_2 emissions and about one-fourth of NO emissions in the U.S. come from the heavy concentration of coal- and oil-burning power and industrial plants in seven central and upper Midwest states—Ohio, Indiana, Pennsylvania, Illinois, Missouri, West Virginia, and Tennessee. Much of the emission from these states making up the country's industrial heartland is blown northeastward by prevailing winds, accounting for most of the moderate to very high levels of acid deposition in the northeastern U.S. and southeastern Canada, where 86% of all Canadians and 50% of all Americans live. There is also rising concern over acid deposition in the West, especially from sulfur and nitrogen oxides released by smelters on both sides of the Mexico-U.S. border and by large amounts of NO released primarily from automobiles in California.

Once acid deposition reaches the ground, its acidity can be increased or decreased up to tenfold as it passes through local soils before running off into nearby lakes and streams or percolating into groundwater. Soils in some areas contain limestone ($CaCO_3$) and other alkaline (basic) substances that can react with

and neutralize the acids, thus reducing their harmful effects on vegetation and aquatic life. But poor, thin soils, such as those overlying granite and some types of sandstone, are already acidic and have little buffering capacity to neutralize additional acids. Such soils are found in much of Scandinavia, parts of Canada and the United States (Figure 19-12), and large portions of Brazil, southern India, Southeast Asia, and eastern China. Acid runoff in these areas can kill many forms of aquatic life in nearby lakes and streams.

19-3 EFFECTS OF AIR POLLUTION ON HUMAN HEALTH

Damage to Human Health Air pollutants have numerous harmful effects on human health. The types and severity of these effects depend on the particular chemicals involved, their concentration in the air, and exposure time. Evidence suggests that air pollution emitted by burning fossil fuels contributes to the premature death of at least 53,000 Americans each year—more than the total number of Americans killed during the nine-year Vietnam War. Groups particularly sensitive to air pollution include the elderly, especially those with lung and heart disorders; infants, whose respiratory systems are not fully developed; active children, who breathe more than most adults; and

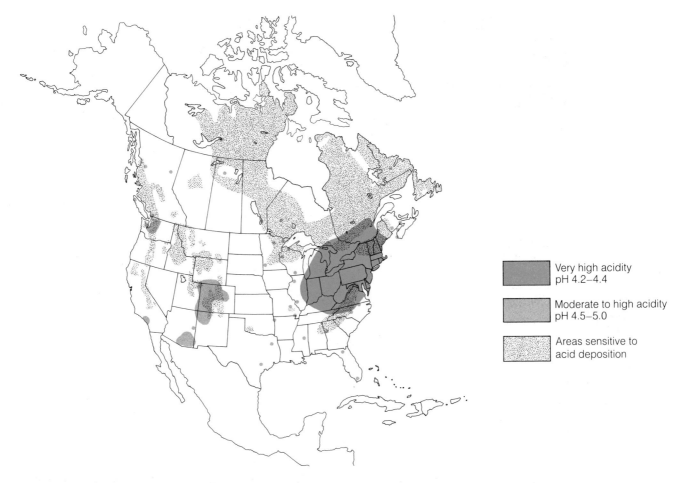

Figure 19-12 Average acidity of precipitation and areas with soils sensitive to acid deposition in North America in 1982. (Data from Environmental Protection Agency)

people with frequent colds or chronic nasal congestion, who breathe through the mouth and thus bypass the filtering mechanism of the nose.

Although tens of thousands of statistical studies provide massive evidence that air pollution harms and sometimes kills people, it is quite difficult to establish that a specific pollutant causes a particular disease or death. Reasons for this include the large number and variety of air pollutants people are exposed to over decades, synergistic interactions between various pollutants that can lead to more harm than that of one acting alone, and the multiple causes and lengthy incubation times of diseases such as emphysema, chronic bronchitis, lung cancer, and heart disease.

Largely because of these difficulties and a misunderstanding of the nature of science, many people are misled when they hear statements such as "Science has not proven absolutely that smoking (or any air pollutant) has killed anyone." Like "Cats are not elephants," such a statement is true but meaningless. *Instead of establishing absolute truth or proof, science estab-*

lishes only a degree of probability or confidence in the validity of an idea, usually based on statistical or circumstantial evidence.

Body Defenses Against Air Pollution Fortunately, the human respiratory system has a number of defense mechanisms that help protect us from air pollution (Figure 19-13). When we inhale air, hairs in the nose filter out large particles, and when pollutants irritate the nose, sneezing expels the air in the upper respiratory tract. The linings of the nose, the trachea (windpipe), the bronchi (the two main branches of the trachea), and thousands of minute ducts, or bronchioles, which carry air throughout the lungs, are covered with a sticky mucus that captures small particles and dissolves some gaseous pollutants. Most of the upper respiratory tract is lined with hundreds of thousands of tiny mucus-coated hairs, called *cilia*, which continually wave back and forth, transporting mucus and the pollutants it traps to the mouth, where it is either

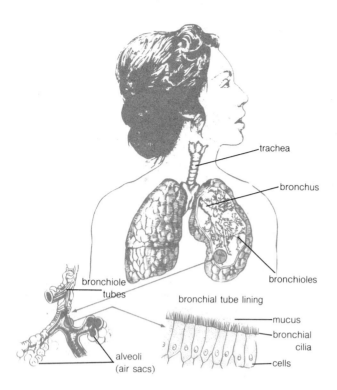

Figure 19-13 The human respiratory system.

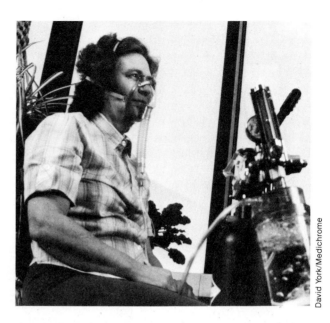

Figure 19-14 People who suffer emphysema may have so much difficulty in breathing that they must breathe pure oxygen, carrying the equipment everywhere they go.

swallowed or expelled. If the lungs become irritated, mucus flows more freely to help remove the irritants and stimulates coughing, which expels the dirty air and some of the contaminated mucus.

Overloading and Degrading the Body's Defense Mechanisms   Despite their effectiveness, our natural defenses against air pollution can be overloaded or impaired. For example, exposure to high levels of an air pollutant or more prolonged exposure to lower concentrations can saturate the mucus so that it can't dissolve any more gases. When this happens, gases penetrate deeper into the respiratory tract and cause persistent irritation and coughing.

Chronic exposure to chemicals in cigarette smoke and other air pollutants such as ozone, sulfur dioxide, nitrogen dioxide, and some types of particulate matter apparently destroy, stiffen, or slow the cilia and thus make them less effective in removing harmful substances. As a result, bacteria and tiny particles penetrate the alveoli, or air sacs, increasing the chances of respiratory infections and lung cancer.

Years of smoking and exposure to air pollutants can trigger so much mucus flow that air passages become blocked, causing coughing. As muscles surrounding the bronchial tubes weaken from prolonged coughing, more mucus accumulates, and breathing becomes progressively more difficult. If this condition persists, it indicates **chronic bronchitis**—a persistent

inflammation of the mucous membranes of the trachea and bronchi that now affects one out of every five American men between the ages of 40 and 60.

Emphysema occurs when such a large number of the lung's alveoli become damaged that a person is unable to expel most of the air from the lung. It begins when prolonged irritation of the lungs by chronic exposure to cigarette smoke and other air pollutants causes the bronchioles to close. Some of the trapped air then expands and fuses clusters of alveoli together, and they lose their ability to expand and contract and may even tear. This reduces the surface area available for transferring oxygen to the blood, so that walking or the slightest exertion causes acute shortness of breath (Figure 19-14). Eventually the victim may die of suffocation or heart failure.

Emphysema kills far more people than lung cancer and is the fastest-rising cause of death in the United States. It is incurable and basically untreatable. Although chronic smoking and exposure to air pollutants can cause emphysema in anyone, about one-fourth of the population is highly susceptible because of a hereditary condition characterized by the absence of a protein that gives the air sacs their elasticity. Anyone with this condition, which can be tested for, should seriously consider not smoking and not living or working in a highly polluted area.

Lung cancer is the abnormal, runaway growth of cells in the mucous membranes of the bronchial passages. Smoking is considered the leading cause, but

Unless completely sealed into a product, asbestos can easily crumble into a dust of tiny fibers small enough to become suspended in the air and inhaled into the lungs, where they remain for many years. Considerable evidence indicates that exposure to even a small amount of asbestos can cause lung cancer or mesothelioma (a cancer of the chest and abdominal lining) 15 to 40 years later. The EPA estimates that exposure to asbestos causes 3,000 to 12,000 cancer cases a year in the U.S., almost all of which are fatal. About 65,000 Americans currently suffer from asbestosis.

Between 1900 and 1986, over 28 million metric tons (31 million tons) of asbestos were used in the United States for hundreds of purposes. Much of it was sprayed on ceilings and other parts of schools and public and private buildings for fireproofing, sound deadening, and insulation, until these uses were banned in 1974.

In 1986 the EPA proposed a ban on the use of asbestos in roofing felt, flooring felt and vinyl tile, cement pipe and fittings used in sewage lines, and heat-resistant clothing used to protect firefighters—all products for which substitute materials are available. Together these uses account for about half of U.S. asbestos use. The EPA proposed that other uses, especially in automobile brake and clutch linings, where there are no ready substitutes, be phased out over a ten-year period unless a use is considered essential and no effective substitute can be found.

EPA officials estimate that the proposed ban would prevent at least 1,900 cancer deaths, primarily among asbestos workers, over the next 15 years. Higher costs for products made with asbestos substitutes would cost each consumer on the average a total of $10 during this period. Representatives of the asbestos industry oppose the EPA proposal, saying that with proper precautions their products can be safely used and that the costs of the ban outweigh the benefits.

Meanwhile some of the asbestos sprayed on ceilings and walls in 30,000 schools nationwide is crumbling—a potential threat to 15 million students and 1.4 million employees. Under current EPA guidelines schools are required only to inspect for asbestos and inform parents and employees of hazards. Cleanup costs are estimated at $2 billion to $3 billion, and financially strapped schools cannot afford such expenditures without increased local taxes or help from state and federal governments.

By 1986 only $100 million of the $600 million authorized by Congress in 1984 for cleanup of asbestos in schools had been appropriated. Some analysts argue that the benefits of such cleanup are not worth the costs except in clear cases where ceilings and walls are deteriorating and releasing asbestos fibers. What do you think should be done?

---

lung cancer has also been linked to inhalation of other air pollutants, including particles of radioactive polonium (produced by the decay of radon gas) and plutonium-239, benzopyrene found in cigarette and other types of smoke, and particulate matter—especially particles of asbestos, beryllium, arsenic, chromium, and nickel. Some air pollutants increase the risk of lung cancer by impairing the action of the cilia so that other, carcinogenic pollutants are not effectively removed.

Miners, mill workers, construction workers, and others whose occupations subject them to chronic exposure to high levels of suspended particulate matter can eventually develop lung disease, which is usually named for the types of particulate matter involved. These diseases, which scar lung tissue, include *black lung* from prolonged inhalation of coal dust, *brown lung* from cotton dust, *asbestosis* from asbestos fibers (see Spotlight above), and *silicosis* from quartz dust generated during mining. Victims usually experience coughing and shortness of breath and eventually may develop pneumonia, chronic bronchitis, emphysema, or lung cancer.

19-4   EFFECTS OF AIR POLLUTION ON PLANTS, ANIMALS, AND MATERIALS

Damage to Plants   Some forms of air pollution, such as sulfur dioxide, ozone, nitrogen oxides, and PANs, cause direct damage to leaves of crop plants and trees (Figure 19-15) when these gases enter leaf pores (stomata). Chronic exposure of leaves and needles to air pollutants can break down the waxy coating that helps prevent excessive water loss and damage from diseases, pests, drought, and frost. Such exposure can also inhibit photosynthesis and plant growth, reduce nutrient uptake, and cause leaves or needles to turn

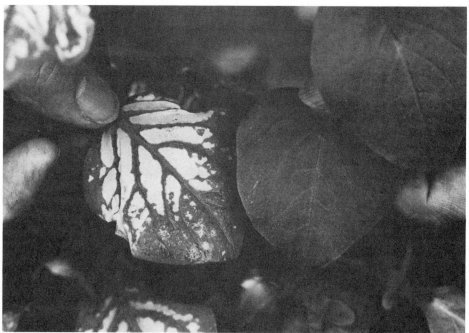

Figure 19-15 Leaves exposed to sulfur dioxide can take on a bleached look due to destruction of chlorophyll. The leaf on the right is healthy.

U.S. Department of Agriculture

yellow or brown and drop off. Coniferous trees are highly vulnerable to the effects of pollution because of their long life spans and the year-round exposure of their needles to polluted air.

In addition to causing direct leaf damage, acid deposition can leach vital plant nutrients such as calcium from the soil and kill essential soil microorganisms. It also releases aluminum ions, which are normally bound to soil particles, into soil water, where they damage fine root filaments and reduce the uptake of water and nutrients from the soil (Figure 19-16). Prolonged exposure to high levels of air pollutants can kill all trees and vegetation in an area.

The effects of exposure of trees to multiple air pollutants may not be visible for decades, when suddenly large numbers begin dying off because of soil nutrient depletion and increased susceptibility to pests, diseases, and drought (Figure 19-17). This is what is happening to many forests in parts of Europe. For example, 8% of the trees in West German forests were found to be dead or damaged in 1982. One year later the figure was 34% and by 1985 the toll stood at 52%. In addition to a $10 billion loss of commercially important trees, these diebacks have eliminated habitats for many types of wildlife. Similar damage is occurring to forestlands in at least 15 other European countries, with Luxembourg, the Netherlands, Austria, Switzerland, and Czechoslovakia having from a quarter to half of their total forest area damaged by 1985.

So far similar diebacks from exposure to multiple

air pollutants in the United States have occurred primarily to stands on higher-elevation slopes facing moving air masses—especially slopes shrouded in pollution-laden clouds or fog much of the time (Figure 19-17). Measurements taken in 15 eastern states have shown a 40% reduction in growth between 1960 and 1984 for 34 tree species found at high elevations. Some tree species at lower elevations are also beginning to show subtle signs of ill health. U.S. Forest Service surveys revealed that commercially important species of pines in the Southeast grew 20% to 30% less between 1972 and 1982 than they did between 1961 and 1972. Many scientists fear that elected officials will continue to delay implementing more stringent controls on all major forms of air pollution until it is too late to prevent a severe loss of valuable forest resources in the United States and Canada like that taking place in much of Europe.

Damage to Livestock and Fish   Little is known about the harmful effects of polluted air on the health of other animals, except commercially valuable livestock and fish. Cattle grazing on grass contaminated with fluoride released from factories that process phosphate deposits for commercial inorganic fertilizers suffer from *fluorosis*, a condition that reduces their milk production, attacks their bones, and causes lameness, severe emaciation, and eventually death (Figure 19-18).

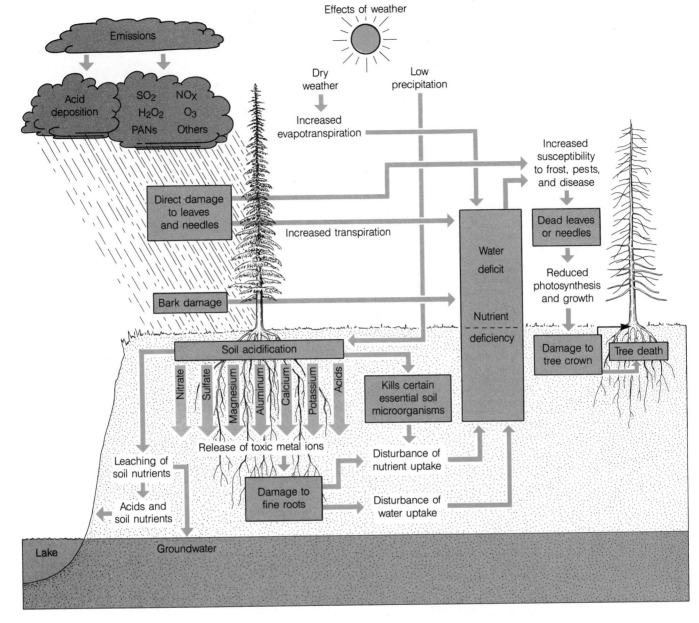

Figure 19-16 Harmful effects of air pollutants on trees.

Acid deposition has a severe impact on aquatic life of freshwater lakes in areas where surrounding soils have little acid-buffering capacity. Much of this damage to aquatic life in the Northern Hemisphere is a result of *acid shock*, which occurs when large amounts of highly acidic water (along with aluminum) suddenly run off into lakes from spring snowmelt or when heavy rains follow a period of drought.

About 4,000 of Sweden's 40,000 acid-sensitive lakes contain no fish because of excess acidity, 18,000 are partly acidified, and the remainder are at risk if emissions of SO$_2$ and NO from other parts of Europe are not sharply curbed. The country also has 90,000 kilometers (56,250 miles) of acidified streams. At least 1,000 acid-sensitive lakes in the eastern United States, especially in New England, are highly acidic (pH below 5.0) and have suffered sharp declines in fish populations. Another 3,000 are moderately acidified. In Ontario, Canada, at least 1,600 lakes are fishless because of excess acidity. Aquatic life in 48,000 more is threatened unless the U.S. and Canada can agree upon and implement a joint program to sharply reduce acid deposition and other air pollutants that remain in the atmosphere long enough to be carried long distances.

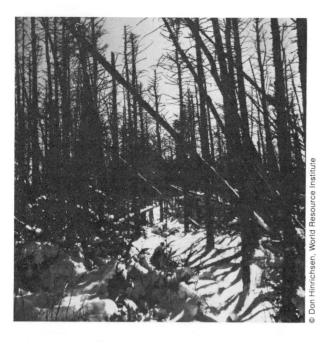

Figure 19-17 This dead coniferous forest on Mount Mitchell, North Carolina, is believed to be the result of long-term exposure to multiple air pollutants.

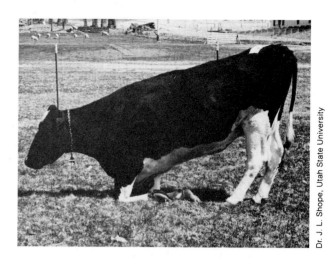

Figure 19-18 Cows exposed to fluorides become emaciated and suffer bone damage.

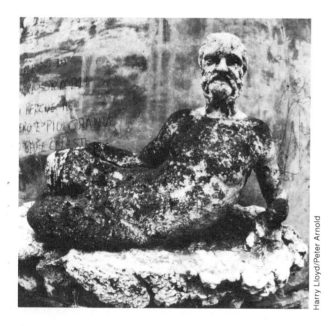

Figure 19-19 This marble monument in Rome has been damaged by exposure to acidic air pollutants.

Damage to Materials Each year air pollutants cause tens of millions of dollars in damage to various materials (Table 19-2). Atmospheric fallout of soot and grit on statues, buildings, cars, and clothing requires costly cleaning. Irreplaceable marble statues, historic buildings, and stained-glass windows throughout the world

are pitted and discolored by air pollutants (Figure 19-19).

Unless they are painted or maintained properly, metals such as iron and steel used in railroad tracks and to support bridges and expressways are corroded and weakened by air pollutants. Such corrosion is believed to be a contributing factor to the 1967 collapse of a steel highway bridge between West Virginia and Ohio, which killed 46 people. Various air pollutants also damage leather, rubber, paper, paint, and fabrics such as cotton, rayon, and nylon (Table 19-2).

19-5 EFFECTS OF AIR POLLUTION ON THE OZONE LAYER AND GLOBAL CLIMATE

Chlorofluorocarbons and Ozone Layer Depletion
In the lower atmosphere, ozone is a pollutant that in trace amounts can damage plants and human health. In the stratosphere, however, ozone protects life on earth by screening out more than 99% of the sun's harmful ultraviolet (UV) radiation. Many scientists are concerned that the average concentration of ozone in the stratosphere is being decreased by **chlorofluorocarbons (CFCs),** often called by the trade name Freon, a group of nontoxic, nonflammable, and cheaply produced chemicals. Since 1955 these chemicals have been widely used as propellants in aerosol spray cans, coolants in refrigerators and air conditioners, industrial

Table 19-2 Harmful Effects of Air Pollution on Materials

Material	Effects	Principal Air Pollutants
Stone and concrete	Surface erosion, discoloration, soiling	Sulfur dioxide, sulfuric acid, nitric acid, solid particulates
Metals	Corrosion, tarnishing, loss of strength	Sulfur dioxide, sulfuric acid, nitric acid, solid particulates, hydrogen sulfide
Ceramics and glass	Surface erosion	Hydrogen fluoride, solid particulates
Paints	Surface erosion, discoloration, soiling	Sulfur dioxide, hydrogen sulfide, ozone, solid particulates
Paper	Embrittlement, discoloration	Sulfur dioxide
Rubber	Cracking, loss of strength	Ozone
Leather	Surface deterioration, loss of strength	Sulfur dioxide
Textile fabrics	Deterioration, fading, soiling	Sulfur dioxide, nitrogen dioxide, ozone, solid particulates

solvents, and Styrofoam and other plastic foams for insulating houses, keeping coffee and fast-food hamburgers warm, and as packing to prevent damage to eggs and shipped items.

Spray cans, discarded or leaking refrigeration and air conditioning equipment, and burning of plastic foam products release these highly unreactive gases into the atmosphere, where they remain up to 110 years. Over several decades they gradually move up to the stratosphere, where under the influence of high-energy UV radiation they break down, releasing chlorine atoms, which speed up the breakdown of ozone into oxygen gas. About 95% of the CFCs released into the atmosphere between 1955 and 1987 are still making their way up to the stratosphere. Since 1978 the use of CFCs in aerosol spray cans has been banned in the U.S., Canada, and most Scandinavian countries, but worldwide nonaerosol uses have risen sharply along with aerosol use in western Europe.

The general consensus, based on theoretical models of chemical reactions taking place in the stratosphere, is that continuing CFC emissions at 1987 levels will reduce average levels of ozone in the stratosphere by 3% to 5% over the next 100 years, although the U. S. National Aeronautics and Space Administration projects a 10% depletion of the ozone layer by 2050. A gradual decrease already believed to be taking place cannot be established by direct measurements because average ozone concentrations can fluctuate by 2% to 4% from year to year because of variations in solar output and large-scale volcanic eruptions.

Ozone depletion may be occurring more rapidly and more extensively than these projections. Satellite images have revealed that each autumn since 1983 a "hole"—that is, a thinning—in the ozone layer has appeared in the stratosphere over the South Pole each September and October; the hole, covering an area the size of the United States, contains 40% less ozone than normal. A smaller hole has been observed over the North Pole. It is not known whether this loss of ozone during part of each year is caused by CFCs, large volcanic eruptions such as Mexico's El Chinchonal in 1982, natural climatic processes such as cyclic changes in solar output, or some combination of these factors.

Some Effects of Ozone Depletion   Less ozone in the stratosphere would allow more UV radiation to reach the earth's surface. The EPA estimates that a 5% ozone depletion would cause an additional 940,000 cases annually of nonmelanoma skin cancer (disfiguring but usually not fatal if treated in time) and 30,000 more cases annually of often-fatal melanoma skin cancer. In addition, humans would be subject to increases in eye cataracts, severe sunburn, and suppression of the immune system.

There would also be a 10% increase in eye-burning photochemical smog. Acid deposition would increase near areas where sulfur dioxide and nitrogen oxides are produced because of an estimated 80% increase in hydrogen peroxide (which speeds up the

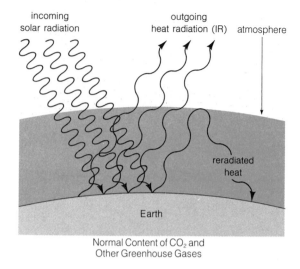

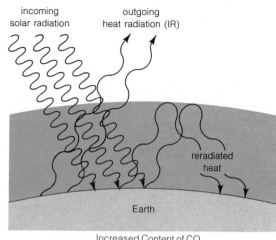

Normal Content of CO_2 and
Other Greenhouse Gases

Increased Content of CO_2
and Other Greenhouse Gases

Figure 19-20 The greenhouse effect.

formation of sulfuric and nitric acids in the atmosphere) for each 1% drop in stratospheric ozone. Other effects include eye cancer in cattle, damage to many species of terrestrial plants (including important food crops such as corn, rice, and wheat), damage to aquatic plant species essential to ocean food chains, and a loss of perhaps $2 billion a year from degradation of plastics and other polymer materials.

Protecting the Ozone Layer Theoretically, the ozone problem is easier to resolve than almost any global pollution issue. CFCs, the primary offender, can be controlled by an international agreement between the major CFC producers and users—the United States, the USSR, and the Scandinavian and West European countries. CFCs are not necessary for the functioning of society, and substitutes are either available or can be found.

However, models indicate that just to keep atmospheric CFCs at 1987 levels would require an immediate 85% drop in total CFC emissions throughout the world. Analysts believe that the first step toward this goal should be a total ban on the use of CFCs in aerosol spray cans, egg crates, fast-food containers, and insulation—all nonessential uses for which cost-effective substitutes are available. The next step would be to phase out all other uses of CFCs over a ten-year period. Although substitutes are available for CFC coolants in refrigeration and air conditioning, testing and phasing them in may take ten years and they could cost five to ten times more than CFCs. But compared to the potential economic and health consequences of ozone depletion, such cost increases would be minor.

An effective international agreement, however, is

unlikely because each country tends to be interested in continuing its use of CFCs for short-term economic gain—the tragedy of the commons. Also, when confronted with long-range problems based on necessarily uncertain scientific models, politicians tend to say, "Let's have more studies before taking any action." But CFCs remain in the atmosphere for up to 110 years; waiting until measurements confirm a decline of a few percent will be too late to prevent catastrophic and irreversible changes that will last for at least a century.

Increased Global Warming from the Greenhouse Effect The average temperature of the earth's atmosphere is maintained by a system in which the amount of energy the earth absorbs from the sun primarily as visible and ultraviolet radiation is balanced by the amount radiated back into space as degraded infrared radiation or heat (Figure 4-14, p. 81). Carbon dioxide, water vapor, and trace amounts of other gases such as ozone in the troposphere, methane, nitrous oxide, and CFCs play a key role in this temperature regulation process.

These gases, known as **greenhouse gases,** acting somewhat like a pane of glass in a greenhouse, let in visible light from the sun but prevent some of the resulting infrared radiation or heat from escaping and reradiate it back toward the earth's surface (Figure 19-20). The resulting heat buildup raises the temperature of the air in the lower atmosphere, a warming action commonly called the **greenhouse effect.** If there were no greenhouse gases in the atmosphere, the earth would be a cold and lifeless planet with an average atmospheric temperature of $-18°C$ (0.4°F).

A buildup of one or several greenhouse gases in

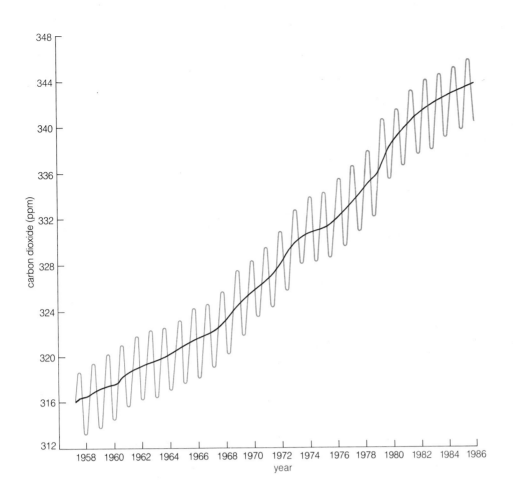

Figure 19-21 Rising concentration of carbon dioxide in the atmosphere as recorded at Mauna Loa Observatory in Hawaii. Seasonal variations occur because carbon dioxide is removed from the air by plants during the summer growing season and is returned by the decay of fallen leaves in winter.

the atmosphere would slow down the escape of heat into space and lead to an increase in the average temperature of the earth's atmosphere. This additional heat could affect global climate and food-growing patterns. Buildup of suspended particulate matter in the atmosphere from natural and human activities might enhance this global warming or cause atmospheric cooling.

Between 1860 and 1986 the average global levels of carbon dioxide in the atmosphere have increased 26% from 275 ppm to 346 ppm (Figure 19-21). This rise is attributed primarily to the burning of fossil fuels throughout the world. Deforestation, especially the wholesale clearing and burning of tropical forests, is also believed to contribute to increased CO_2 levels by drastically reducing the number of plants that absorb carbon dioxide during photosynthesis.

According to the latest climate models, a doubling of the preindustrial CO_2 level of around 275 ppm to 550 ppm would raise the average atmospheric temperature by about 4°C (7°F), with temperatures near the poles rising two to three times this amount. Although seeming small, such a change would make the earth warmer than at any time in human history

and have profound effects on the earth's climate. The earth's average temperature was only 5°C (9°F) colder when vast ice sheets reached the areas we now call New York City and Chicago over 20,000 years ago during the last Ice Age. Even a 1°C or 2°C rise can cause a larger number of violent storms, many more unbearably hot days in summer, and prolonged droughts in many areas.

Depending on the rate of use of fossil fuels, especially coal and oil, CO_2 levels of 550 ppm could be reached sometime between 2040 and 2100. However, a global warming of that magnitude could occur much earlier—between 2010 and 2050—if levels of other greenhouse gases produced by human activities continue to increase at present rates. These include ozone in the lower atmosphere from photochemical smog, methane produced in the digestive tracts of cattle, wetlands, biomass, burning, and in the soils of rice paddies, nitrous oxide from fertilization of soils and concentration of animal wastes in feedlots, and CFCs. CFCs alone can contribute about 20% to global warming; thus, banning them would not only help protect the ozone layer but also slow the rate of global warming.

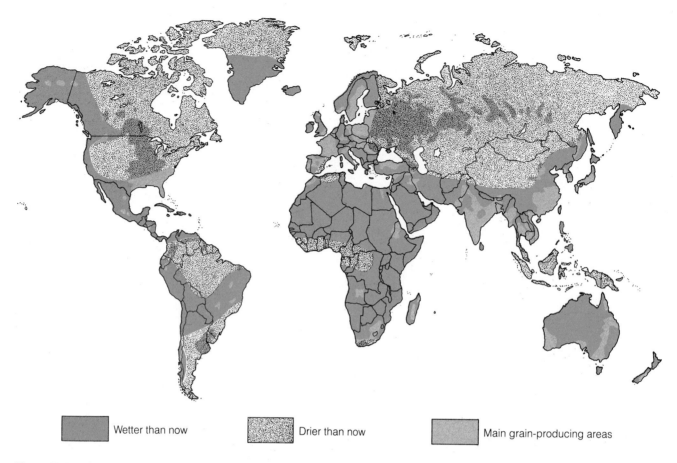

Wetter than now   Drier than now   Main grain-producing areas

Figure 19-22 One of many possible ways the world's climate could change as a result of the greenhouse effect. (Data from National Center for Atmospheric Research)

Some Effects of Global Climate Changes At first glance a warmer average climate might seem desirable, resulting in lower heating bills in middle and higher latitudes and longer growing seasons in some areas. Crop yields might also increase because more CO_2 in the atmosphere can increase the rate of photosynthesis. Other factors, however, could offset potential gains in crop yields. Damage from insect pests could increase because the warmer temperatures would enhance insect breeding. There would also be significant changes in worldwide precipitation and temperature patterns so that crop production in some areas would decline while that in other areas might increase (Figure 19-22). Global cooling would cause similar effects.

Since water expands when heated, an increase in average global temperature will raise average sea levels. Warmer temperatures will also cause partial melting of mountain glaciers and parts of the West Antarctic ice sheet, transferring water from the land to the sea. Present models indicate that raising the average atmospheric temperature by 4°C (7°F) would raise average global sea level by about 0.6 meters (2 feet) as

a result of these processes. This would flood large areas of agricultural lowlands and deltas in Bangladesh, India, and China, where much of the world's rice is grown.

In the United States such a rise would flood major portions of Louisiana and Florida, as well as buildings, roads, tanks storing hazardous chemicals, and other structures along the Gulf and Atlantic coasts, and cause intrusion of saltwater into groundwater supplies. A significant melting of the West Antarctic ice sheet would lead to even larger rises in sea level but would probably be a gradual process, taking 1,000 years or more.

The projection in Figure 19-22 is only one of many possibilities. However, it is clear that any significant change in world climate resulting from warming or cooling will disrupt world food production for many years, lead to a sharp rise in food prices, cause considerable economic damage, and require investments of hundreds of billions of dollars in fertilizers, new water transfer and irrigation projects, and dike systems to prevent flooding.

Dealing with the Threat of Global Warming

Basically there are two ways to deal with global warming: slow it down and adjust to its effects. We can slow down the rate of global warming by banning emissions of greenhouse gases such as CFCs and by sharply reducing the use of fossil fuels, especially coal, which emits the most CO_2 per unit of energy produced. For example, if fossil fuel use grows by 4% a year, CO_2 levels are projected to reach 550 ppm by 2030; if the annual growth rate is only 1%, this level would not be reached until 2100. However, maintaining a 1% worldwide fossil fuel growth rate would mean no growth in MDCs to allow for needed growth in LDCs.

We could achieve significant reductions in fossil fuel use by relying more on a combination of energy conservation and perpetual energy (Chapter 18), or by increased use of nuclear power (Chapter 17). Another approach is to use scrubbers to remove carbon dioxide from the smokestack emissions of coal-burning power and industrial plants and from vehicle exhausts. But present methods remove only about 30% of the CO_2 and are prohibitively expensive. Planting trees worldwide would also slow global warming by increasing the uptake of CO_2 from the atmosphere, as well as reducing other harmful effects of deforestation.

However, many observers doubt that countries will be able to agree to sharply reduce fossil fuel use and deforestation in time to prevent significant global warming. In addition to the tragedy of the commons effect, there is considerable scientific uncertainty over the precise timing of the effects of global warming on various countries. Countries likely to end up with a more favorable climate would resist severe restrictions, while countries likely to suffer from reduced food-growing capacity may favor taking immediate action. Sharply restricting fossil fuel use, no matter how desirable from a long-term environmental and economic viewpoint, would cause major short-term economic and social disruptions that most countries would find unacceptable.

Thus, some analysts suggest that while attempting to reduce fossil fuel use, we should also begin to prepare for the effects of long-term global warming. Efforts should include increased research into the breeding of plants that need less water and plants that can thrive in water too salty for ordinary crops and improved irrigation methods should be widely used so that less water is wasted (Section 11-5). Dikes should be erected to protect coastal areas from flooding, as the Dutch have done for hundreds of years, and zoning ordinances should prohibit new construction on low-lying coastal areas. Large supplies of key foods stored throughout the world would be insurance against climate changes that could shift the world's major food-growing regions and disrupt food production.

19-6 CONTROLLING AIR POLLUTION

U.S. Air Pollution Legislation Air pollution or any other type of pollution can be controlled by laws to establish desired standards and technology to achieve the standards. In the United States, little progress was made until Congress passed the Clean Air Acts of 1970 and 1977, which gave the federal government considerable power to control air pollution. These laws required the EPA to establish **national ambient air quality standards (NAAQS)** for seven major pollutants found in almost all parts of the country: SPM, sulfur oxides, carbon monoxide, nitrogen oxides, ozone, volatile organic compounds (mostly hydrocarbons), and lead. Each NAAQS (listed in Appendix 5) specifies the maximum allowable level, averaged over a specific time period, for a certain pollutant in outdoor (ambient) air.

The EPA was required to set two types of NAAQS without taking into consideration the cost of meeting them. *Primary ambient air quality standards* were set to protect human health, with a margin of safety for the elderly, infants, and other vulnerable persons, and deadlines were set for their attainment. *Secondary ambient air quality standards* were set to maintain visibility and to protect crops, buildings, and water supplies; no deadlines were set for their attainment.

Each of the 247 air quality control regions (AQCRs) established by the EPA across the country was supposed to meet all primary standards by 1982 with some extensions possible to 1987. All areas not meeting deadlines for one or more primary standards are designated as *nonattainment regions.* In such regions no permits for construction of new plants or expansion of existing ones are allowed unless the state can demonstrate that these facilities will not jeopardize the region's progress toward attainment of the primary standards. To meet this requirement, any new plant or significant expansion of an existing one must have pollution control equipment that will lead to the lowest rate of emissions achieved by any similar plant anywhere in the country regardless of cost. There must also be a drop in the total emissions in the area. To meet this second requirement, a company can buy and close down an existing plant or buy equipment to reduce emissions from an existing plant. Another option is to buy emissions credits from another company in the area that has reduced its emissions below that required in its permit.

The EPA established a policy of *prevention of significant deterioration (PSD)* to prevent a decrease in air quality in regions where the air is cleaner than that required by the primary and secondary NAAQS for SPM and sulfur dioxide. Otherwise, industries would move into these areas and gradually degrade air quality to the national standards for these two major pollutants.

Regions of the country are divided into three classes in terms of the allowed increase in these two types of air pollutants. Very little, if any, increase is allowed in Class I areas, which include national parks, wilderness areas, and other largely undeveloped areas mostly in the West. Moderate degradation of air quality is allowed in Class II areas and slightly more in Class III areas. In no case, however, can pollutant concentrations in any PSD region exceed the primary and secondary NAAQSs for these two pollutants. Any new stationary emission source approved in any PSD area must use the best available technology for controlling emissions of SO_2 and SPM regardless of cost. Once the total allowed increase in emissions of these two pollutants in any PSD area is reached, no further permits are issued.

The Clean Air Acts of 1970 and 1977 required each state to develop an EPA-approved state implementation plan (SIP) showing how it would achieve federal standards fully by 1982, with extensions possible until 1987. Congress gave the EPA the power to halt the construction of major new plants or expansions of existing ones and to cut off federal funds for construction of highways for any state not submitting an acceptable plan.

The Clean Air laws also required the EPA to set uniform national maximum emission standards, known as *new source performance standards (NSPS)*, on an industry-by-industry basis for newly built plants or major expansions of existing plants. Unlike NAAQS, costs and energy requirements can be considered in setting these standards.

The EPA is also required to identify and set national emission standards for stationary sources emitting hazardous air pollutants that "may cause, or contribute to, an increase in mortality or an increase in serious, irreversible, or incapacitating illness." Scientists have identified at least 600 potentially hazardous air pollutants. However, by 1986 the EPA had either established or proposed national emission standards for only eight hazardous substances: asbestos, arsenic, beryllium, mercury, vinyl chloride, benzene, sulfuric acid, and radioactive isotopes.

For motor vehicles Congress set a timetable for achieving certain percentage reductions in emissions of carbon monoxide, hydrocarbons, and nitrogen oxides. For autos and light trucks there was to be a 96% reduction in hydrocarbon and carbon monoxide emissions and a 76% reduction in nitrogen oxides from 1970 levels by 1982. Although significant progress has been made, a series of legally allowed extensions pushed the deadlines for complete attainment of most of these goals to 1988 or later.

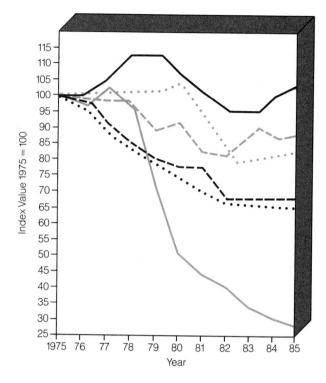

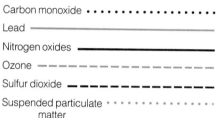

Carbon monoxide · · · · · · · · · · · · · · · · · ·
Lead ——————————————
Nitrogen oxides ▬▬▬▬▬▬▬▬▬▬▬
Ozone – – – – – – – – – – –
Sulfur dioxide ▬ ▬ ▬ ▬ ▬ ▬ ▬ ▬ ▬ ▬
Suspended particulate · · · · · · · · · · · · · ·
    matter

Figure 19-23 Trends in U.S. ambient air quality for six pollutants, 1975–1985. (Data from Environmental Protection Agency)

Trends in U.S. Air Quality and Emissions Between 1975 and 1985 the average ambient concentrations of most major pollutants, except nitrogen oxides, dropped as a result of air pollution control laws, economic recession, and higher energy prices (Figure 19-23). Lead made the sharpest drop because of the gradual phaseout of leaded gasoline. Between 1982 and 1985, however, ambient levels of major pollutants other than lead either remained the same or climbed slightly. Environmentalists allege that these increases are the result of budget cutbacks and efforts by the Reagan administration to relax enforcement of air pollution control regulations.

Averages of air pollutants in several hundred EPA measuring stations across the country do not reveal the severity of air pollution in different major urban areas. The EPA uses a pollution standards index (PSI)

Table 19-3 U.S. Pollutant Standard Index (PSI) Values (Data from the Environmental Protection Agency)

PSI Index Value	Air Quality Level	Pollutant Levels (micrograms per cubic meter)					Health Effect Description	General Health Effects	Suggested Action
		SPM (24 hour)	SO$_2$ (24 hour)	CO (8 hour)	O$_3$ (1 hour)	NO$_2$ (1 hour)			
500	Significant harm	1,000	2,620	57.5	1,200	3,750		Premature death of ill and elderly. Healthy people will experience adverse symptoms that affect their normal activity.	All persons should remain indoors, keeping windows and doors closed. All persons should minimize physical exertion and avoid traffic.
400	Emergency	875	2,100	46.0	1,000	3,000	Hazardous (300 and above)	Premature onset of certain diseases. Significant aggravation of symptoms in the ill; decreased exercise tolerance in healthy persons.	Elderly and persons with existing diseases should stay indoors and avoid physical exertion. General population should avoid activity.
300	Warning	625	1,600	34.0	800	2,260	Very Unhealthful (200–299)	Significant aggravation of symptoms and decreased tolerance in persons with heart or lung disease with widespread symptoms in the healthy population.	Elderly and persons with existing heart or lung disease should stay indoors and reduce physical activity.
200	Alert	375	800	17.0	400	1,130	Unhealthful (100–199)	Mild aggravation of symptoms in susceptible persons with irritation symptoms in the healthy population.	Persons with existing heart or respiratory ailments should reduce physical exertion and outdoor activity.
100	NAAQS	260	365	10.0	240	—	Moderate		
50	50% of NAAQS	75*	80*	5.0	120	—	Moderate		
0		0	0	0	0	—	Good		

*Annual primary NAAQS.

to indicate how frequently and to what degree the air quality in a particular city exceeds one or more of the primary health standards. Table 19-3 lists the PSI values of major pollutants and their degrees of danger to human health. Between 1976 and 1983 there was a sharp drop in the number of days in which the air was classified as hazardous, very unhealthful, or unhealthful in most major urban areas. New York, Chicago, and Cleveland showed considerable improvement, while Los Angeles, Houston, and Dallas-Fort Worth showed relatively little improvement.

Methods of Pollution Control Once a pollution control standard has been adopted, two general approaches can be used to prevent levels from exceeding it: *input control*, which prevents or reduces the severity of the problem, and *output control*, which treats

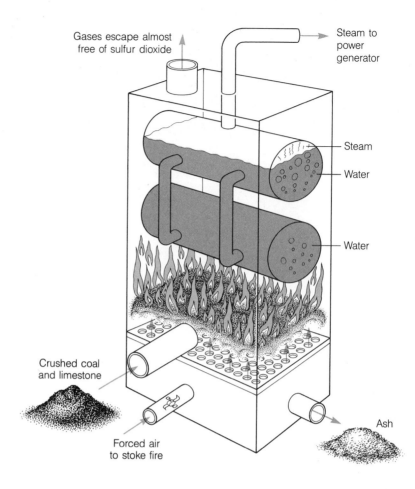

Figure 19-24 Limestone injection multiple burning (LIMB). Crushed limestone is injected into a boiler burning powdered coal at a lower temperature than normal burners. The limestone combines with sulfur dioxide to produce a solid material (gypsum).

Gases escape almost free of sulfur dioxide

Steam to power generator

Steam

Water

Water

Crushed coal and limestone

Forced air to stoke fire

Ash

the symptoms. Output control methods, especially those that attempt to remove the pollutant once it has entered the environment, tend to be expensive and difficult; input methods are usually easier and cheaper in the long run.

There are five major input control methods for reducing the total amount of pollution of any type from reaching the environment:

1. Control population growth (Chapter 8).
2. Reduce unnecessary waste of metals, paper, and other matter resources through increased recycling and reuse; design products so that they last longer and are easy to repair (Section 15-5).
3. Reduce energy use (Section 18-1).
4. Use energy more efficiently (Section 18-1).
5. Switch from fossil fuels to energy from the sun, wind, and water (Chapter 18).

These are the most effective and least costly ways to reduce air, water, and soil pollution and the only cost-effective methods for reducing the rate of buildup of carbon dioxide in the atmosphere. However, they are rarely given serious consideration in national and international strategies for pollution control.

Control of Sulfur Dioxide Emissions from Stationary Sources In addition to the input control methods just mentioned, the following approaches can lower sulfur dioxide emissions or reduce their effects:

SO_2 Input Control Methods

1. *Burn low-sulfur coal.* Especially useful for new plants located near deposits of such coal; major U.S. supplies are located west of the Mississippi (Figure 16-17, p. 352), far from major eastern power plants and industrial centers to which the coal would have to be transported at high cost and use of much energy; boilers in a number of older power plants cannot burn low-sulfur coal without expensive modifications.

2. *Remove sulfur from coal.* Fairly inexpensive; existing methods remove only 20% to 50% of the sulfur but can be combined with methods to reduce emissions to meet national air pollution standards; produces large quantities of high-sulfur ash, which can contaminate groundwater; about 10% of the energy content of the coal is lost in the process.

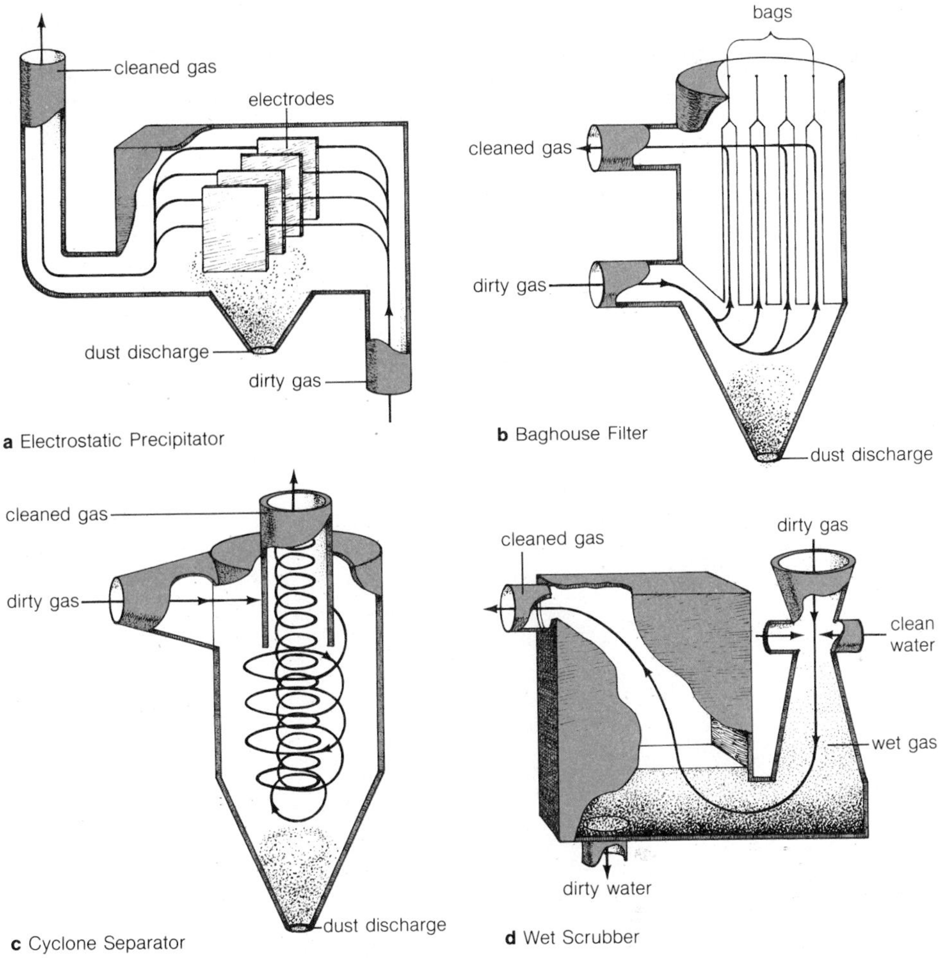

cleaned gas
electrodes
dust discharge
dirty gas

a Electrostatic Precipitator

bags
cleaned gas
dirty gas
dust discharge

b Baghouse Filter

cleaned gas
dirty gas
dust discharge

c Cyclone Separator

cleaned gas
dirty gas
clean water
wet gas
dirty water

d Wet Scrubber

Figure 19-25 Four commonly used methods for removing particulates from the exhaust gases of electric power and industrial plants. The wet scrubber is also used to reduce sulfur dioxide emissions.

3. *Convert coal to a gas or liquid fuel.* Low net energy yield; too expensive at present coal and oil prices (Section 16-5).

4. *Remove sulfur during combustion by fluidized-bed combustion (FBC)* (Figure 16-21, p. 355). Removes up to 90% of the sulfur dioxide produced during combustion; should be commercially available for small to medium-size plants in the 1990s; less costly to build and operate than scrubbers for new plants, but fairly costly to add to existing plants because a new boiler is required.

5. *Remove sulfur during combustion by limestone injection multiple burning (LIMB)* (Figure 19-24). Still in the development and testing stage and a number of technical problems remain to be solved to reduce high operating and maintenance costs; reduces SO_2 emissions by 50% to 60%; does not remove as much SO_2 as scrubbers or FBC but is far less costly to install than either of these methods; can cost-effectively be retrofitted into existing power and industrial plants; produces more fine particles than other methods, making particulate control more difficult and expensive.

SO_2 Output Control Methods

1. *Use tall smokestacks* (200 to 1,250 feet high). Can decrease pollution near power or industrial plants but increases pollution levels in downwind areas; favored by industry because it is cheaper than other approaches and passes costs of dealing with harmful effects to taxpayers at large or to another country rather than to the pollution producers; opposed by environmentalists because it does not decrease emissions of SO_2 and NO, the major contributors to acid deposition.

2. *Remove pollutants after combustion by using flue gas desulfurization (FGD), or scrubbing.* Wet or dry limestone is sprayed into exhaust gases and combines with SO_2 to produce a solid or wet sludge, which can be used as a roadbed filler or for other construction purposes (Figure 19-25d); removes up to 95% of SO_2 and 99.9% of solid particulate matter (but not fine particles); can be used in new plants and retrofitted to most existing large plants; reduces pollution in both local and distant areas; very expensive; so bulky that many small

The 1977 Clean Air Act required all U.S. coal-burning power plants built since 1978 to use scrubbers to remove from 70% to 90% of the sulfur dioxide from smokestack emissions, depending on the sulfur content of the coal being burned. Utility companies have vigorously opposed this requirement, claiming that scrubbers are too costly to build and keep in good operating order, that they are unreliable, that they discourage use of easily mined western low-sulfur coal reserves, and that they could raise the cost of electricity to consumers by as much as 50%.

The EPA argues that scrubber technology is well developed, is used in about 1,000 plants worldwide, and has worked well and remained in operation 90% of the time in Japan and for U.S. utilities that bought and maintained high-quality equipment. The EPA claims scrubbers increase the consumer's cost of electricity by only 5% to 20%—far less than the costs of the harmful effects of sulfur emissions on health, crops, forests, and materials.

Most coal-burning power plants coming on line in the U.S. during the 1980s will have flue gas scrubbers. But utilities are not required to install scrubbers or other SO_2 emission control devices on existing plants, most remodeled plants, and oil-burning plants converted to burn coal. These older plants typically emit seven times as much sulfur dioxide a year as a new plant with a scrubber. To avoid building costly scrubber-equipped plants, some utilities have kept older power plants in operation longer than their normal life spans or renovated them, pro-longing pollution from their smokestacks. As a result, only about 12% of the country's 1,800 coal-burning power plants were equipped with scrubbers by 1986.

Executives of utilities and industrial plants continue to oppose more stringent control of sulfur dioxide emissions, especially on existing plants. Environmentalists, however, urge that by 1995 *all* new and existing coal- and oil-burning electric power and industrial plants be required to reduce sulfur dioxide emissions by 90% and emissions of nitrogen oxides by at least 50% by whatever method or combination of methods can achieve this goal. They also believe that all existing tall smokestacks should be either shut down or reduced in size to no more than 30.5 meters (100 feet). What do you think?

plants do not have enough space to install the equipment; produces large quantities of solid or wet sludge (depending on the method used) as a waste product; opposed by industry because of high costs, part of which must be borne directly by polluting industry rather than indirectly by taxpayers (see Spotlight above).

3. *Add a tax on each unit emitted.* Encourages development of more efficient and cost-effective methods of emissions control; opposed by industry because it costs more than tall smokestacks and requires polluters to bear part of the costs of control.

4. *Add lime or ground limestone to acidified soil and lakes to neutralize acidity.* Favored by industry over the installation of emission control devices because it shifts costs of pollution control to taxpayers at large; expensive ($100 to $150 per acre) and must be repeated periodically; is a temporary treatment, not a cure, for acid deposition.

Control of Emissions of Nitrogen Oxides from Stationary Sources   So far relatively little emphasis has been placed on reducing emissions of nitrogen oxides from stationary sources because control of emissions of sulfur dioxide and particulates has been considered more important. Now it is clear that nitrogen oxides are a major contributor to acid deposition and that they increase tropospheric levels of ozone and other photochemical oxidants that can damage crops, trees, and materials. The following approaches can be used to lower emissions of nitrogen oxides from stationary sources:

NO_x Input Control Methods

1. *Remove nitrogen oxides during fluidized-bed combustion (FBC).* Removes 50% to 75% of the nitrogen oxides. See SO_2 control methods for advantages and disadvantages.

2. *Remove during combustion by limestone injection multiple burning (LIMB).* Removes 50% to 60% of

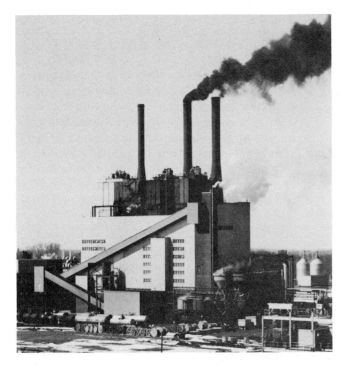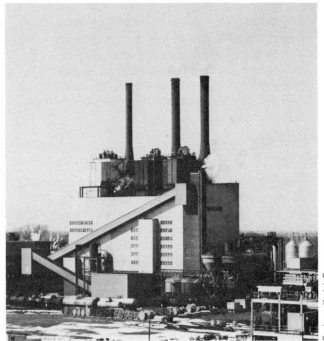

Figure 19-26 The effectiveness of an electrostatic precipitator in reducing particulate emissions is shown by this stack, with the precipitator turned off (left) and with the precipitator operating.

Eastman Kodak Company

nitrogen oxides. See SO_2 control methods for advantages and disadvantages.

3. *Reduce by lowering combustion temperatures.* Removes 50% to 60% of nitrogen oxides; well-established technology; can be used in new plants or retrofitted to existing plants.

NO$_x$ Output Control Methods

1. *Use tall smokestacks.* See SO_2 control methods.

2. *Add a tax for each unit emitted.* See SO_2 control methods.

3. *Remove after combustion through reburning.* Exhaust gases from the primary combustion zone are reburned at a lower temperature in a burner fueled by natural gas or low-sulfur oil; removes 50% or more of nitrogen oxides and up to 90% when combined with input methods; still under development for large plants.

4. *Remove after burning by reacting with isocyanic acid (HCNO).* Still in the laboratory stage and will not be available for at least ten years; removes up to 99% of nitrogen oxides.

Control of SPM Emissions from Stationary Sources The following approaches can be used to lower emissions of particulate matter from stationary sources:

SPM Input Control Method

1. *Convert coal to a gas or liquid.* See SO_2 control methods.

SPM Output Control Methods

1. *Use tall smokestacks.* See SO_2 control methods.

2. *Add a tax on each unit emitted.* See SO_2 control methods.

3. *Remove particulates from stack exhaust gases.* The most widely used method in electric power and industrial plants. Several methods are in use: **(a)** electrostatic precipitators (Figures 19-25a and 19-26), which remove up to 99.55% of the total mass of particulate matter (but not most fine particles) by means of an electrostatic field that charges the particles so that they can be attracted to a series of electrodes and removed from

exhaust gas; **(b)** baghouse filters (Figure 19-25b), which can remove up to 99.9% of the particles (including most fine particles) as exhaust gas passes through fiber bags in a large housing; **(c)** cyclone separators (Figure 19-25c), which remove 50% to 90% of the large particles (but very few medium-sized and fine particles) by swirling exhaust gas through a funnel-shaped chamber in which particles collect through centrifugal force; and **(d)** wet scrubbers (Figure 19-25d), which remove up to 99.5% of the particles (but not most fine particles). Except for baghouse filters, none of these methods removes many of the more hazardous fine particles; all produce hazardous solid waste or sludge that must be disposed of safely; except for cyclone separators, all methods are expensive and none prevents particles formed as secondary pollutants in the atmosphere.

Control of Emissions from Motor Vehicles The following approaches can be used to lower emissions of carbon monoxide, nitrogen oxides, SPM, and lead from motor vehicles:

Motor Vehicle Input Control Methods

1. *Rely more on mass transit and paratransit.*

2. *Shift to less-polluting automobile engines* such as steam or electric engines. Presently these engines do not match the internal combustion engine in terms of performance, fuel economy, durability, and cost. Electric cars would increase use of electricity produced by coal-burning or nuclear power plants and trade one set of environmental hazards for another.

3. *Shift to less-polluting fuels* such as natural gas, alcohols, and hydrogen gas. Supplies of natural gas are limited; alcohol is still too costly but may become competitive when oil prices rise (Section 18-6); hydrogen gas has a negative net useful energy yield and requires much improved production technology (Enrichment Study, Chapter 18).

4. *Improve fuel efficiency.* A quick and cost-effective approach. Present U.S. fuel-efficiency standards should be greatly increased from 26.5 mpg in 1986 to 40 mpg by 2000.

5. *Modify the internal combustion engine to reduce emissions.* Burning gasoline using a lean, or more air-rich, mixture reduces CO and hydrocarbons but increases NO emissions but can be combined with output control to reduce overall emissions; a new lean-burn engine that reduces emissions of nitrogen oxides by 75% to 90% may be available in about ten years.

Motor Vehicle Output Control Methods

1. *Use emission control devices.* Most widely used approach; positive crankcase ventilation (PCV) recycles hydrocarbons released from the crankcase back into the engine for combustion; exhaust gases are recirculated back through the engine to cool combustion temperature and reduce NO emissions; three-way catalytic converters change carbon monoxide and hydrocarbons in exhaust gas into CO_2 and water vapor and NO into N_2; platinum and palladium catalysts used in catalytic converters to speed up these reactions are easily deactivated by lead in gasoline, but this problem will decrease as leaded gasoline is phased out; engines must be kept well tuned for converters to work effectively; three-way catalytic converters now under development can decrease pollutants by 90% to 95% and should be available within a few years.

2. *Require car inspections twice a year and increase fines* to ensure that emission control devices are not tampered with (presently, 22% of U.S. cars and light trucks have been so tampered with) and are in good working order.

What Needs to Be Done Since 1981, when the 1977 Clean Air Act was up for revision, industry officials and the Reagan administration have pushed hard to ease federal auto emission standards, relax industrial cleanup goals, allow more pollution in Class I PSD regions, and extend nationwide EPA deadlines for meeting primary air pollution standards. They claim that the benefits of existing air pollution control laws are not worth their high costs, that these laws threaten economic growth, and that they are implemented too inflexibly by the EPA.

Environmentalists, on the other hand, have proposed stricter limits on all polluting emissions, a ban on CFCs, and enactment of standards for key indoor air pollutants in homes, factories, and office buildings. They point to thousands of studies indicating that reducing the continuing serious harm to plants, materials and humans will require a simultaneous reduction of emissions of all major pollutants from stationary and mobile sources to much lower levels than those allowed under present standards. Such a comprehensive approach is made necessary by the multiple interactions of multiple pollutants and should replace the present "one-pollutant-at-a-time" approach.

Environmentalists accuse the EPA of too frequently granting industries and cities extensions for meeting standards and of reducing efforts to enforce the existing laws. They point out that these laws have not led to the wave of plant closings and high unemployment predicted by industry and have created numerous jobs in the air pollution control industry.

Environmentalists recognize that the costs of implementing a much stricter and more comprehensive air pollution control program will be high. But, they argue, the long-term costs of not doing so could be astronomical: massive damage to humans, livestock, crops, materials, forests, soils, and lakes. By the end of 1986, environmentalists and key congressional allies had prevented the gutting of the 1970 and 1977 Clean Air Acts but had been unable to persuade Congress to pass any new legislation strengthening air pollution control.

At the international level, countries—especially MDCs—need to develop agreements to ban CFCs, reduce emissions of SO_2 and NO to control acid deposition, and reduce emissions of CO_2 to delay global warming. An important start was made when the Soviet Union and 20 European countries agreed to reduce their annual emissions of sulfur dioxide by 30% to 50% by 1995 from 1980 levels. In 1987 the countries producing and using most of the world's CFCs were attempting to reach agreement on a partial ban of these substances. Meaningful reductions in atmospheric carbon dioxide inputs could be accomplished by just three countries—China, the Soviet Union, and the United States—the world's three largest users of coal.

There is the very real possibility that the human race—through ignorance or indifference or both—is irreversibly altering the ability of the atmosphere to support life.
Sherwood Rowland

Enrichment Study   Is Your Home Contaminated with Radioactive Radon Gas?

Where Does Radon Gas Come From?

Radon-222 is an invisible, odorless, naturally occurring radioactive gas produced by the radioactive decay of radium-226, a by-product of the decay of uranium-238 (Section 3-2). Small amounts (about 1 ppm) of radon-producing uranium-238 are found in most soil and rock. But it is much more highly concentrated in underground deposits of uranium, phosphate, and granite rock. Figure 19-27 shows the general locations of such rock deposits in the lower 48 states. When radon gas from such deposits percolates upward to the soil and is released outdoors, it disperses quickly in the atmosphere and decays to harmless levels. However, when the gas is released inside mines or seeps into buildings or water in underground wells over such deposits, it can build up to high levels.

Threats to Health

Radon-222 gas itself is not a threat because when inhaled it is promptly exhaled or carried away from the lungs by the blood. The problem is that radon gas quickly decays, producing tiny solid particles of radioactive polonium-214 and polonium-218, which can build up to high levels in any enclosed space. These particles can then adhere to minute airborne particles of dust and smoke, which are inhaled into the lungs.

Although the polonium decays to harmless levels in several hours, the alpha particles it emits expose a small area of nearby lung tissue to a large amount of radiation. Statistical evidence indicates that repeated inhalation of polonium particles over 20 years or more can produce enough radiation to cause lung cancer, especially in smokers because the particles tend to adhere to tobacco tar deposits in the lungs and upper respiratory tract. Uranium miners who smoke are ten times more likely to develop lung cancer than miners who don't smoke.

Until recently it was assumed that radon posed a threat primarily to uranium miners. In 1984, however, a worker at a nuclear power plant near Boyertown, Pennsylvania, set off radiation alarms when he entered the plant for work. Tests at his home found radon levels 675 times those allowed in uranium mines. During the year that he, his wife, and their two sons had lived in the house, they were exposed to a risk of lung cancer equal to that from smoking 220 packs of cigarettes a day or having 455,000 chest X rays a year.

How Serious Is the Problem?

Between 1984 and 1986 potentially harmful radon levels were found in over 20,000 homes and buildings in 30 states and may turn up in all 50. So far the worst radon hot spots have been found in Pennsylvania, Tennessee, and Wyoming.

On the basis of preliminary data from a nationwide survey of indoor radon levels to be completed by 1988, the EPA estimates that at least 1 million U.S. homes have radon levels above the safety standards for uranium mines; another 4 million to 7 million may have levels high enough for homeowners to take corrective action. Some scientists involved in private radon testing believe that as many as 18 million houses—one of every four in the country—may contain unsafe amounts of radon.

The EPA also estimates that as many as 5 million people, mostly in parts of Maine, New Hampshire, and Massachusetts, may be exposed to radon in water from underground wells located over rock with a high radon content. Drinking water high in radon probably isn't dangerous, but showering or washing clothes probably is. As the hot water splashes out of faucets,

showers, and washing machines, up to half the dissolved radon is released into the indoor air. The EPA estimates that over a 20- to 30-year period people showering or washing clothes with radon-contaminated water have the same risk of getting lung cancer as if they smoked a pack of cigarettes a day.

According to the EPA, prolonged exposure to high levels of radon may be responsible for 5,000 to 20,000 of the 130,000 lung cancer deaths each year in the United States; 100 to 1,000 of these premature deaths may be related to radon released from hot

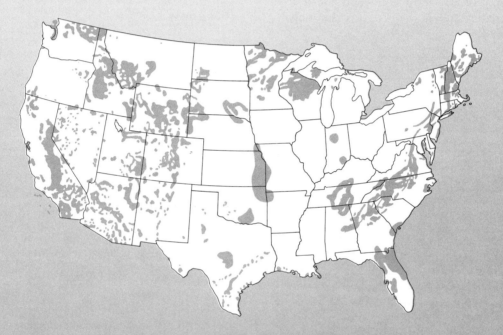

Figure 19-27   Areas with potentially high radon levels. (Data from Environmental Protection Agency)

CHAPTER SUMMARY

Air pollution occurs when the concentration of a normal component of the air or a new chemical added to or formed in the air builds up to the point of causing harm to humans, other animals, vegetation, or materials. About 90% of all outdoor air pollution problems are caused by carbon monoxide, nitrogen oxides, sulfur oxides, volatile organic compounds and suspended particulate matter. Some air pollutants are *primary pollutants* added directly to the air, and others are *secondary pollutants* formed in the air.

Although there are natural sources of some outdoor air pollutants, most are a result of the burning of fossil fuels at *stationary sources* (power and industrial plants) or *mobile sources* (motor vehicles). Although the most serious outdoor air pollution occurs in cities where large numbers of cars and factories are concentrated, some air pollutants can be spread by winds to other cities and to rural areas. High concentrations of certain air pollutants such as tobacco smoke, radioactive radon gas, and formaldehyde can also build up indoors, especially in airtight houses.

Cities that have cold, wet winters and depend heavily

water used for showers and for washing clothes. It is generally agreed that radon is the leading cause of lung cancer among nonsmokers who live in houses with high levels of radon for 20 years or more.

What Can Be Done?

The first step is to find out whether the buildings you live and work in and the water you drink (especially if it comes from an underground well) have high radon levels. Radon detectors are available free or at a low cost from health or environmental agencies in some states (check with local officials). Otherwise, they can be purchased for between $15 and $50 (depending on the type of detector and the number purchased) from private testing firms.

Radiation levels are measured in picocuries per liter of air (pCi/L), with one pCi/L representing the radioactive decay of about two radon atoms in a quart of air. Estimates of what constitutes a potentially hazardous level vary from anything above 2 pCi/L to 8 pCi/L. The EPA recommends taking measures to reduce radon in any house with levels above 4 pCi/L, which roughly carries the same lung cancer risk as about 300 chest X rays a year.

If unacceptable levels are detected, the EPA recommends several ways to reduce radon levels and health risks. The first is to stop all indoor smoking since smoking produces airborne particles that radioactive polonium particles can adhere to and that can be inhaled by smokers and nonsmokers. Ventilation fans (costing about $300) or heat exchangers ($500 to $1,500) can be installed to remove radon and most other indoor pollutants, if infiltration levels are not too high. However, if infiltration rates are high, officials say you could blow a tornado through a house and still have too much radon.

The most effective solution is to prevent entry of radon by installing an interconnected series of plastic pipes over a bed of gravel under the basement floor or foundation slab. A small fan attached to the pipes withdraws 90% to 99% of radon-contaminated air from underneath the house and vents it outdoors at a place where it can't be drawn back into the house. Such a system costs about $1,000 if a layer of crushed stone is already under the slab. Otherwise, costs could run $5,000 or more to remove the slab, put in a layer of crushed stone, and cover it with a new slab. To remove radon from contaminated well water, a special type of activated carbon filter can be added to holding tanks at a cost of about $1,000.

Some scientists argue that the threat of indoor exposure to radon is being exaggerated, especially in buildings where no smoking occurs. Others, however, believe the threat may be underestimated. A 1979 study by the Swedish government determined that up to 40% of all lung cancer cases it examined were related to radon exposure. In Sweden no house can be built until the lot has been tested for radon. If the reading is high, the builder must follow government-mandated construction procedures to ensure that the house won't be contaminated with radon from soil or water supplies.

Environmentalists urge enactment of a similar program for all new construction in the United States. Meanwhile, anyone wishing to install a radon prevention or removal system should have it done by a qualified contractor and approved by a certified inspector. Before purchasing a lot to build a new house, individuals should have the soil tested for radon. Similarly, no one should purchase an existing house unless it has been tested for radon by certified personnel, just as houses must now be tested for termites.

on coal and oil for heating, manufacturing, and producing electrical power often suffer from *industrial smog,* consisting mostly of a mixture of sulfur dioxide and suspended particulate matter. Cities with sunny, warm, dry climates, large numbers of motor vehicles, and few polluting industries often suffer from *photochemical smog,* a mixture of primary pollutants such as carbon monoxide, nitric oxide, and hydrocarbons and secondary pollutants such as nitrogen dioxide, nitric acid, ozone, hydrogen peroxide, PANs, and formaldehyde formed when some of the primary pollutants interact under the influence of sunlight.

Air pollutants can build up to dangerous levels when a layer of dense, cool air is trapped beneath a layer of less dense, warm air. Such *temperature or thermal inversions,* which prevent pollutants from escaping in upward-flowing air currents, tend to occur more frequently over towns or cities located in valleys surrounded by mountains, on the leeward side of a mountain range, or near a coast. Because of concentrated energy use, increased heat absorption by buildings, and reduced wind flow, most cities tend to be hotter than nearby rural areas. This effect, known as an *urban heat island,* creates a heat and dust dome over an urban area.

Some of the sulfur dioxide and nitric oxide emitted by tall smokestacks and other sources can be transported long distances, in the process forming a variety of secondary pollutants such as droplets of sulfuric and nitric acids and solid particles of sulfate and nitrate salts. *Acid deposition* occurs when these liquid acid droplets (wet deposition) and solid acid-forming particles (dry deposition) fall or are washed out of the atmosphere onto the earth's surface.

The human respiratory system has a number of defenses that filter, dilute, or expel air pollutants. However, these defenses can be overwhelmed by exposure to high levels of one or more air pollutants or exposure to low or moderate concentrations of some air pollutants over a long period. Effects include watery eyes, coughing, heart disease, and respiratory diseases such as chronic bronchitis, emphysema, and lung cancer.

Prolonged exposure to multiple air pollutants such as ozone and acid deposition can damage leaves of trees and other plants and kill large numbers of trees, as is occurring in much of Europe, by leaching plant nutrients from the soil, killing essential soil microorganisms, damaging roots, and increasing susceptibility to drought, pests, and disease. Air pollutants such as fluorides can cause severe damage to cows, and acid deposition can kill most or all life in freshwater lakes and streams. Air pollutants also severely damage statues, buildings, metals, rubber, paint, paper, fabrics, and other materials—causing huge economic losses.

There is growing concern that a group of widely used chemicals known as chlorofluorocarbons (CFCs), which remain in the atmosphere for over 100 years, will gradually rise into the stratosphere. There they can deplete levels of ozone that now protect humans and most forms of life on earth by filtering out the sun's harmful ultraviolet radiation. Attempts are being made to get countries to limit or ban the production and use of these chemicals. There is also concern that human activities such as fossil fuel burning and deforestation may lead to a gradual warming of the earth's atmosphere as a result of an enhanced *greenhouse effect,* caused by increased atmospheric levels of carbon dioxide and other gases that prevent some heat from escaping back into space. Such a change in global climate would disrupt food production and cause flooding of low-lying areas. This potentially serious long-range problem can be dealt with by reducing emissions of greenhouse gases and making long-term preparations for a change in climate.

Air pollution control laws enacted in the 1970s set standards for the maximum allowable levels of key air pollutants in outdoor air. Meeting these standards involves using pollution control methods to prevent all or most of a pollutant from being formed (*input control*) or reducing the amount emitted to the atmosphere (*output control*). As a result of the legislation, levels of most major outdoor air pollutants in the U.S. have either decreased or not risen significantly since the laws were enacted. However, considerably more needs to be done to reduce levels of numerous hazardous outdoor pollutants, CFCs, greenhouse gases, and indoor pollutants.

DISCUSSION TOPICS

1. Distinguish between photochemical smog and industrial smog in terms of major pollutants and sources, major human health effects, time when worst episodes occur, and methods of control.

2. Rising oil and natural gas prices and environmental concerns over nuclear power plants could force the U.S. to depend more on coal, its most plentiful fossil fuel, for electric power. Comment on this in terms of air pollution. Would you favor a return to coal instead of increased use of nuclear power? Explain.

3. Evaluate the pros and cons of the statement "Since we have not proven absolutely that anyone has died or suffered serious disease from nitrogen oxides, automobile manufacturers should not be required to meet the federal air pollution standards."

4. Why is air pollution from fine particulate matter one of our more serious problems? What should be done about this problem?

5. Should all uses of CFCs be banned in the U.S., including their use in refrigeration and air conditioning units? Explain.

6. Should MDCs set up a world food bank to store several years' supply of food to reduce the harmful effects of a loss in food production from a change in climate? How would you decide who gets this food in times of need?

7. What are industries in your area doing to control air pollution emissions?

8. How do levels of major pollutants in your area compare with the NAAQs shown in in Appendix 5? What trends in these levels have taken place during the past ten years?

9. What topographical and climate factors either enhance or help decrease air pollution in your community?

10. Do you favor or oppose requiring a 50% reduction in emissions of sulfur dioxide and nitrogen oxides by fossil-fuel-burning electric power and industrial plants and a 50% reduction in emissions of nitrogen oxides by motor vehicles in the U.S. between 1988 and 1998? Explain.

11. Should smoking of cigarettes or other tobacco products be banned in all indoor public places such as restaurants, offices, and buses? Explain.

12. Should all tall smokestacks be banned? Explain.

13. Should all asbestos be removed from U.S. schools? Explain.

14. Do buildings in your college or university contain asbestos?

15. Should standards be set and enforced for most major indoor air pollutants? Explain.

20

Water Pollution

GENERAL OBJECTIVES

1. What are the major types, sources, and effects of water pollutants?

2. What are the major pollution problems of rivers and lakes?

3. What are the major pollution problems of the world's oceans?

4. What are the major pollution problems of groundwater?

5. What technological and legal methods can be used to reduce water pollution?

Brush your teeth with the best toothpaste,
Then rinse your mouth with industrial waste.

Tom Lehrer

Water pollution is any physical or chemical change in surface water or groundwater that can adversely affect living organisms. The level of purity required for water depends on its use. Water too polluted to drink may be satisfactory for washing steel, producing electricity at a hydroelectric power plant, or cooling the steam and hot water produced by a nuclear or coal-fired power plant. Water too polluted for swimming may not be too polluted for boating or fishing.

Water pollution, like air pollution, is a local, regional, and global environmental problem. For example, one of the world's most polluted rivers is the New River, which flows from Mexicali, Mexico, into southern California's Imperial Valley before emptying into the Salton Sea. Because of weak and poorly enforced water pollution control laws in Mexico, this river transports the urban wastes and inadequately treated sewage of 1 million people into the United States. Large quantities of bacteria and viruses that can cause scores of diseases pass through towns and agricultural areas in California before reaching the Salton Sea, where many people boat, fish, and swim. The river also contains large quantities of highly toxic industrial wastes produced mostly by American companies that have built plants in Mexico to avoid the stricter and more costly U.S. water pollution control standards. Since the late 1960s the United States and Mexico have signed four agreements pledging to clean up this river. But these promises have been broken and today the river is more polluted than ever.

20-1 SOURCES, TYPES, AND EFFECTS OF WATER POLLUTION

Point and Nonpoint Sources For purposes of control and regulation it is convenient to distinguish between point sources and nonpoint sources of water

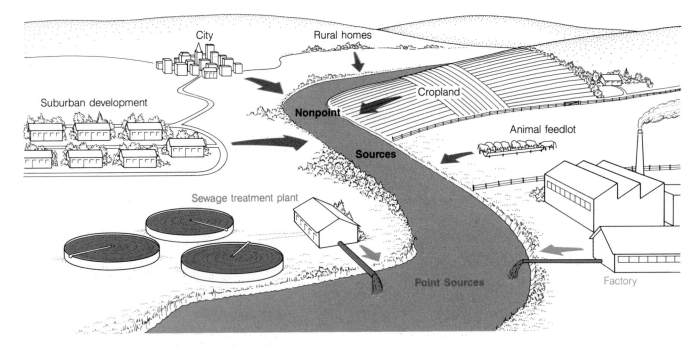

Figure 20-1 Point and nonpoint sources of water pollution.

pollution from human activities. **Point sources** are those that discharge pollutants, usually through pipes, ditches, and sewers, into bodies of water at specific locations (Figure 20-1). Examples include factories, sewage treatment plants (which remove some but not all pollutants), electric power plants, active and abandoned underground coal mines, oil tankers, and offshore oil wells. So far most water pollution control efforts have concentrated on reducing discharges to surface water from industrial and municipal point sources because they are easy to identify.

In contrast, **nonpoint sources** of water pollution are scattered widely and discharge pollutants over a large area (Figure 20-1). Examples include runoff into surface water and seepage into groundwater from croplands, livestock feedlots, logged forests, urban and suburban lands, construction areas, parking lots, and roadways. While point sources usually produce regular, year-round discharges, significant pollution from most nonpoint sources usually occurs only during major storms or when snow melts. Relatively little progress has been made in the control of nonpoint water pollution because of the difficulty and expense of identifying and controlling discharges from so many diffuse sources.

Major Water Pollutants and Their Effects For convenience, biological, chemical, and physical forms of water pollution can be broken down into eight major types:

1. disease-causing agents (bacteria, viruses, protozoa, and parasites)

2. oxygen-demanding wastes (domestic sewage, animal manure, and other biodegradable organic wastes that deplete water of dissolved oxygen)

3. water-soluble inorganic chemicals (acids, salts, toxic metals and their compounds)

4. inorganic plant nutrients (water-soluble nitrate and phosphate salts)

5. organic chemicals (insoluble and water-soluble oil, gasoline, plastics, pesticides, cleaning solvents, and many others)

6. sediment or suspended matter (insoluble particles of soil, silt, and other inorganic and organic materials that can remain suspended in water)

7. radioactive substances

8. heat

Disease-Causing Agents Bacteria, viruses, protozoa (unicellular animals), and parasites such as worms can transmit typhoid fever, cholera, dysentery, infectious hepatitis, and other diseases to humans (Table 20-1). These pathogens enter water primarily through the feces and urine of infected persons and other animals. Major sources include overloaded or malfunctioning septic tanks and cesspools (big holes into which household liquid wastes are emptied), unchlorinated sewage from malfunctioning sewage treatment plants

Table 20-1	Common Diseases Transmitted to Humans Through Contaminated Drinking Water	
Type of Organism	Disease	Effects
Bacteria	Typhoid fever	Diarrhea, severe vomiting, enlarged spleen, inflamed intestine; often fatal if untreated
	Cholera	Diarrhea, severe vomiting, dehydration; often fatal if untreated
	Bacterial dysentery	Diarrhea; rarely fatal except in infants without proper treatment
	Enteritis	Severe stomach pain, nausea, vomiting; rarely fatal
Viruses	Infectious hepatitis	Fever, severe headache, loss of appetite, abdominal pain, jaundice, enlarged liver; rarely fatal but may cause permanent liver damage
	Polio	High fever, severe headache, sore throat, stiff neck, deep muscle pain, severe weakness, tremors, paralysis in legs, arms, and body; can be fatal
Protozoa	Amoebic dysentery	Severe diarrhea, headache, abdominal pain, chills, fever; if not treated can cause liver abscess, bowel perforation, and death
Parasites	Schistosomiasis	Abdominal pain, skin rash, anemia, chronic fatigue, and chronic general ill health (Section 23-2)

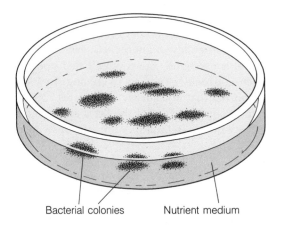

Bacterial colonies   Nutrient medium

Figure 20-2 Testing for coliform bacteria levels in water. Each bacterium present in a 100-milliliter sample of filtered water produces a dark green, shiny colony of millions of bacteria when allowed to grow in a nutrient medium for 24 hours at a constant temperature.

or overloaded combination sewage-and-storm drains, and untreated discharges from meat-processing plants and boats.

In most LDCs, where public water supplies are not well protected or treated, this type of water pollution is a major cause of sickness and death. The World Health Organization estimates that together water contamination and water shortages in LDCs kill 25,000 people each day.

In the United States and other MDCs the purification of drinking water has led to a sharp drop in the incidence of waterborne diseases. But between 1975 and 1986 there were still 90,000 reported cases of diseases resulting from bacteriological contamination of U.S. drinking water. The U.S. Center for Disease Con-

trol believes this is only a fraction of the actual cases, most of which are unreported gastrointestinal illnesses. More than 100 different viruses, many of which may survive for several months, have been identified in human feces. Many of these viruses are a danger in drinking water in LDCs and MDCs because chlorination, the most common way to disinfect water, isn't very effective against them.

Detecting *specific* disease-causing agents in water is a difficult, time-consuming, and costly process. Instead, water used for drinking or swimming is routinely analyzed for the presence of **coliform bacteria**, found in great numbers in the intestines and thus in the feces of humans and other animals. Most coliform bacteria themselves are not harmful. But the presence of large numbers of these bacteria in water indicates recent contamination by untreated feces, which are likely to contain more dangerous bacteria and viruses.

To test for coliform bacteria, technicians filter a 100-milliliter (0.4 cup) sample of water through a special membrane that has pores too small for bacteria to pass through. A medium containing the nutrients that each coliform bacterium needs to grow and form a colony of bacteria is added to a glass dish containing the filter. After the dish has been incubated at a constant temperature for 24 hours, technicians count the number of bacterial colonies (Figure 20-2). Usually, several samples are taken, and the water is considered safe to drink by EPA standards if the arithmetic mean of all samples does not exceed one coliform bacterial colony per 100 milliliters of water, with no single sample having a count higher than four colonies per 100 milliliters. When this level is exceeded, a municipal water treatment plant must either add more chlorine to the water or use an alternative source for drinking water.

The EPA-recommended maximum level for swimming water is 200 colonies per 100 milliliters, but some cities and states allow higher levels. When the allowable level is exceeded, the contaminated pool, river, or beach is usually closed to swimming. In 1985 the EPA reported that in a survey of 40 states 73% of the rivers and streams, 78% of the lakes and reservoirs, and 82% of the coastal waters were safe for swimming.

Oxygen-Demanding Wastes If enough oxygen is dissolved in the water, some organic waste materials can be biodegraded by aerobic (oxygen-consuming) decomposers, primarily bacteria and fungi. Major sources of these **oxygen-demanding wastes** in surface waters are natural land runoff, malfunctioning sewage treatment plants, overflowing sewer-storm drains, general urban runoff, animal feedlot runoff, and oil-refining, food-processing, leather-tanning, textile-making, and paper-making plants.

When surface waters are overloaded with biodegradable wastes, the resulting population explosion of aerobic decomposers can so reduce the supply of dissolved oxygen that aquatic organisms, especially fish and shellfish, die from suffocation. Complete oxygen depletion kills all forms of aquatic life except anaerobic bacteria, which do not require oxygen to break down organic material. The decomposition of organic wastes by these anaerobic decomposers produces toxic and foul-smelling substances such as hydrogen sulfide (recognized by its rotten-egg smell), ammonia, and methane (swamp gas), which bubble to the surface. Sport and commercial fishing, real estate development, and recreation are reduced or eliminated on and near such bodies of anaerobic surface water.

One of the most useful indicators of the ability of a body of surface water to support fish and most other forms of aquatic life is its **dissolved oxygen (DO)** content: the amount of oxygen gas dissolved in a given quantity of water at a particular temperature and atmospheric pressure. Figure 20-3 shows the correlation between water quality and its parts per million of dissolved oxygen. The quantity of oxygen-consuming wastes in water is usually determined by measuring the **biological oxygen demand (BOD):** the amount of dissolved oxygen needed by aerobic decomposers to break down the organic materials in a given volume of water over a five-day incubation period at 20°C (68°F).

Certain chemicals other than organic wastes also react with oxygen dissolved in water. The **chemical oxygen demand (COD)** is a more complete and accurate measurement of the total depletion of dissolved oxygen in water. Water is considered heavily polluted when its BOD or COD causes the dissolved oxygen content to fall below 4.5 ppm and gravely polluted if the DO level falls below 4 ppm.

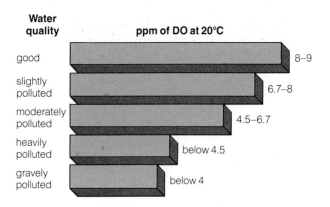

Figure 20-3 Water quality and dissolved oxygen (DO) content.

Water-Soluble Inorganic Chemicals A large number of water-soluble acids, salts, toxic metals, and other inorganic chemicals reach surface water and groundwater from a diverse array of point and nonpoint sources. Acids can enter water from underground coal mines, numerous industries, and as acid deposition (Figure 19-11, p. 432). Salts of sodium, calcium, and other elements reach surface waters from irrigation runoff, oil drilling operations, numerous industrial processes, urban storm runoff, and natural runoff.

Each year sodium and calcium chloride salts used during winter to deice U.S. roads cause an estimated $2.9 billion in damages from corroded cars and bridges, road damage, destruction of roadside vegetation, and pollution of drinking-water wells located near highways. Tests indicate that widespread use of a new deicing salt, calcium magnesium acetate (CMA), would eliminate most of these harmful effects. Discharges of salts produced by mining, industrial processes, and sewage treatment plants can contaminate water with toxic and sometimes cancer-causing compounds of heavy metals such as arsenic, cadmium, chromium (as chromates), lead, and mercury (Table 20-2 and Enrichment Study on pp. 510–12).

Inorganic Plant Nutrients Two key nutrients needed for plant growth in aquatic systems are phosphorus (as phosphate) and nitrogen (as nitrate and ammonia). Major sources of these water-soluble inorganic plant nutrients include point source discharges from sewage treatment plants and industries and nonpoint inputs from natural runoff and runoff from urban areas, cropland (commercial inorganic fertilizers), animal feedlots (manure), and phosphate mines (especially in Florida).

In excess amounts these plant nutrients cause rapid algal growth, called blooms, and dense growths of weeds that spoil the water's odor, taste, and beauty

Table 20-2 Health Effects of Common Chemical Contaminants in Drinking Water

Contaminant	Effects*
Inorganic Substances	
Arsenic	Cancer; liver, kidney, blood, and nervous system damage
Cadmium	Kidney damage, anemia, pulmonary problems, high blood pressure, possible fetal damage, and cancer
Chromium	Suspected cancer from some forms such as chromate
Lead	Headaches, anemia, nerve disorders, birth defects, and cancer; mental retardation, learning disability, and partial hearing loss in children
Mercury	Nervous system and kidney damage; biologically amplified in food webs
Nitrates	Respiratory distress and possible death in infants; possible formation of carcinogenic nitrosoamines
Synthetic Organic Substances	
Aldicarb (Temik)	High toxicity to nervous system
Benzene	Chromosomal damage, anemia, blood disorders, and leukemia
Carbon tetrachloride	Cancer; liver, kidney, lung, and central nervous system damage
Chloroform	Liver and kidney damage and suspected cancer
Dioxin	Skin disorders, cancer, and genetic mutations
Ethylene dibromide (EDB)	Cancer and male sterility
Polychlorinated biphenyls (PCBs)	Liver, kidney, and pulmonary damage
Trichloroethylene (TCE)	In high concentrations, liver and kidney damage, central nervous system depression, skin problems, and suspected cancer and mutations
Vinyl chloride	Liver, kidney, and lung damage; pulmonary, cardiovascular, and gastrointestinal problems; cancer and suspected mutations

*Based primarily on studies of laboratory animals.

and block sunlight. The algae then die and their decay by aerobic decomposers can deplete dissolved oxygen so that many forms of aquatic life cannot survive.

Phosphate in drinking water is not a health problem because it is a nutrient required by humans. However, excessive levels of nitrate in drinking water are a hazard to human health. In rural areas underground wells can become contaminated with nitrate seeping downward from septic tanks, animal feedlots, and heavily fertilized cropland. In the intestines of humans, nitrates (NO_3^-) are converted to nitrites (NO_2^-), which in large amounts can be fatal to infants under three months old. During the last 45 years over 2000 cases of infant nitrate poisoning, including 165 deaths, have been reported in North America and Europe. The incidence of this disease in the United States may be higher because it is not on the list of diseases that must be reported to public-health authorities. A 1984 survey the U.S. Geological Survey found that one-third of the 24,000 wells sampled had nitrate concentrations exceeding the EPA's drinking-water standard.

Organic Chemicals Thousands of different organic chemicals find their way into surface and underground water supplies. Some, such as crude oil seeping from fissures in the ocean floor and various substances produced by algae and bacteria, are of natural origin. But most are synthetic organic chemicals (SOCs) introduced into the hydrosphere as a result of human activities.

Crude and refined oil is discharged into rivers and oceans from blowouts of offshore oil wells, tanker accidents, pipeline breaks, and disposal of lubricating oil and grease from machines and automobile crankcases. Pesticides run off crop fields and home gardens into nearby surface water. Groundwater can be contaminated by leaks of gasoline, heating oil, and industrial solvents stored in underground tanks and by the leaching of numerous toxic synthetic organic chemicals from landfills and toxic dump sites. Synthetic organic plastics, detergents, and widely used degreasing solvents, such as cancer-causing trichloroethylene (TCE), are discharged into surface water by industries and can also seep into groundwater.

Figure 20-4 The oil-polluted Cuyahoga River, which runs through Cleveland, Ohio, caught fire in 1969.

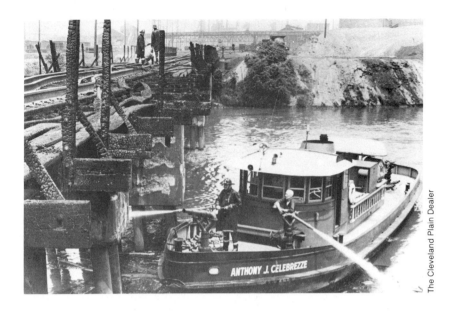

The Cleveland Plain Dealer

Studies indicate that a few of the organic chemicals found in surface water may be formed by chemical reactions between substances discharged into bodies of water or used to disinfect water. For example, potentially harmful trihalomethane (THM) compounds, such as chloroform ($CHCl_3$), may be formed when the chlorine used to kill bacteria in drinking water combines with natural organic matter in untreated water or with other SOCs discharged into some rivers.

Some of the more than 700 SOCs found in trace amounts in surface and underground drinking-water supplies in the United States can cause kidney disorders, birth defects, and various types of cancer in laboratory test animals (Table 20-2). It is not known what levels of these chemicals in drinking water can cause such acute effects in humans. We also do not know the long-term health effects of chronic ingestion of trace amounts of such compounds. Some SOCs such as chloroform and TCE can also be released into the air as vapors from hot water used for showers and washing clothes and dishes; humans can breathe and ingest these compounds at a rate about 100 times that of drinking the same water.

Some floating organic liquids can catch fire, causing economic damage and air pollution. In 1969 the Cuyahoga River in northeastern Ohio was so contaminated with oil and other floating flammable organic wastes that it caught fire in Cleveland (Figure 20-4). A 1986 report by the National Wildlife Federation revealed that it is still polluted significantly with numerous toxic chemicals because of lack of enforcement of water pollution control laws. The best approaches to reducing the hazards to human health and aquatic life from organic chemicals is to minimize their entry into surface water and groundwater, find short-

lived biodegradable substitutes for them, and use advanced but expensive methods to remove them at water treatment plants.

Sediments Water-insoluble particles of soil and rock and numerous inorganic and organic compounds wash into surface waters from natural runoff and from agricultural development, mining, lumbering, ranching, and construction activities. Sediments with large particles, such as sand and silt, settle to the bottom of bodies of water rapidly and are often deposited along the banks near their points of entry. Smaller particles, such as clays and fine organic particulates, can remain suspended in water for weeks and months before settling to the bottom or being deposited in deltas and estuaries near the mouths of rivers or on floodplains during floods.

Most sediment is easily filtered from water in treatment plants and thus rarely poses health hazards to humans. One exception is asbestos fibers reaching water supplies from deteriorating asbestos-reinforced pipes used to carry water from treatment plants to homes and businesses. Fine suspended solid particles not removed by water treatment can also adsorb and concentrate particles of toxic metals, pesticides, bacteria, and other harmful substances. Suspended particulate matter makes surface waters muddy or cloudy, kills or reduces growth of aquatic plants by reducing the penetration of light necessary for photosynthesis, kills aquatic animals by clogging gills of fish and filters of filter feeders such as clams, reduces ability of some organisms to find food, and damages pumps and turbines at hydroelectric plants.

Bottom sediment destroys feeding and spawning grounds of fish and clogs and fills lakes, reservoirs, river and stream channels, and harbors. This reduces sport and commercial fishing and recreational use of surface waters, and requires expensive dredging to keep shipping channels open. Sediment pollution can be reduced by making better use of soil conservation practices on croplands, logged forests, and construction sites (Section 10-5).

Radioactive Substances Radioisotopes such as radium-226, radium-228, strontium-90, and uranium-238 can get into surface water from geothermal wells (Section 17-1), accidental releases from various steps in the nuclear fuel cycle associated with nuclear power plants (Figure 17-8, p. 369) and the production of nuclear weapons, and from hospitals, industry, and research laboratories. Radon-222—found in underground deposits of uranium, granite, and phosphate rock—can contaminate groundwater supplies (see Enrichment Study at the end of Chapter 19). Ionizing radiation from such isotopes can cause DNA mutations leading to birth defects, cancer, and genetic damage (Section 3-2). The best ways to reduce the hazards to human health from these pollutants is to prevent their entry into water supplies and ban the use of contaminated supplies.

Heat Large amounts of water are withdrawn from nearby rivers, lakes, and ocean bays and circulated through parts of electric power and industrial plants to remove waste heat. When this heated water is returned to surface waters, it can have adverse effects on aquatic ecosystems.

20-2 POLLUTION OF RIVERS, LAKES, AND RESERVOIRS

Natural Processes Affecting Pollution Levels in Surface Water The concentrations and chemical forms of most pollutants change once they are added to bodies of surface water as a result of four natural processes: dilution, biodegradation, biological amplification, and sedimentation. The degree of dilution of all pollutants and biodegradation of oxygen-consuming wastes by decomposers taking place in a body of surface water depends on its volume and flow rate. In a large, rapidly flowing river, relatively small amounts of pollutants are quickly diluted to low concentrations and the supply of dissolved oxygen needed for aquatic life and for biodegradation of oxygen-consuming wastes is rapidly renewed. However, such rivers can be overloaded with pollutants. In addition, dilution and biodegradation are sharply reduced when flow is decreased during dry spells or when large amounts

of water are withdrawn for irrigation or cooling and returned in smaller amounts because of evaporation or returned at high temperatures, which decrease DO content.

In lakes, reservoirs, estuaries, and oceans, dilution is often less effective than in rivers because these bodies of water frequently contain stratified layers that undergo little vertical mixing (Figure 5-12, p. 104 and Figure 5-13, p. 105). Stratification also reduces the levels of dissolved oxygen, especially in bottom layers. In addition, lakes and reservoirs have little flow, further reducing dilution and replenishment of DO.

Another problem with relying on dilution to disperse pollution is that some substances, especially synthetic organic chemicals, can have harmful effects on aquatic life and humans at extremely small concentrations. Biodegradation is ineffective in removing nonbiodegradable and persistent pollutants. Also, concentrations of some of these pollutants (such as DDT, PCBs, some radioactive isotopes, and some mercury compounds) are biologically amplified to higher concentrations as they pass through food webs (Figure 4-20, p. 86).

Sedimentation can remove trace amounts of some organic and inorganic pollutants, which become attached to particles that settle and accumulate in the mud at the bottom of lakes, reservoirs, and slow-flowing rivers. However, toxic substances stored in bottom sediments can become resuspended if the bottom is dredged or if it is stirred up by high flow rates during flooding. Although the natural processes of dilution, biodegradation, and sedimentation can reduce many pollutants to harmless levels, we have learned that the solution to most forms of water pollution is to prevent or reduce their entry.

Rivers and Degradation of Oxygen-Consuming Wastes Because they flow, most rivers recover rapidly from some forms of pollution—especially excess heat and oxygen-demanding wastes—as long as they are not overloaded. How long this recovery process takes depends on the river's volume, flow rate, and the volume of incoming biodegradable wastes. Changes in the amount of DO at various points in a river lead to changes in the types and diversity of fish and other aquatic organisms (Figure 20-5).

Rivers are particularly susceptible to being overloaded with oxygen-demanding wastes during hot summer months, when stream flow and turbulence are low and the effects of dilution and oxygen transfer from the air are reduced. DO levels are also reduced because the warm water holds less oxygen and speeds up bacterial decay. In the United States many once-rapid major rivers, such as the Ohio, have been converted into chains of long, slow-flowing lakes by construction of flood control, navigational, and rec-

Figure 20-5 The oxygen sag curve (solid) versus oxygen demand (dashes). Depending on flow rates and the amount of pollutants, rivers recover from oxygen-demanding wastes and heat if given enough time and if they are not overloaded.

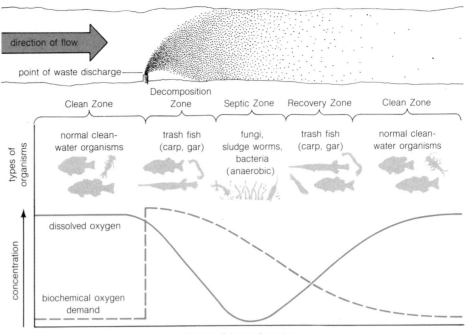

reational dams. As a result, they are less effective in biodegrading oxygen-demanding wastes and in dissipating inputs of heated water from power and industrial plants.

Along many rivers, water for drinking is removed upstream from a town, and industrial and sewage wastes are discharged downstream. This pattern is usually repeated hundreds of times. If a river or stream receives heavy loads of oxygen-demanding wastes along most or all of its path, the river can suffer from severe oxygen depletion, loss of most fish, and buildup of high levels of disease-carrying human and animal wastes. Requiring each town or city to withdraw its drinking water downstream rather than upsteam, would lead to a dramatic improvement in the quality of river water. Each town would be forced to clean up its own waste outputs rather than passing them on to downstream areas.

U.S. River Water Quality   Since 1972 about 13% of the 570,000 kilometers (354,000 miles) of U.S. rivers and streams on which the EPA has information have improved in quality in terms of increased DO, diversity of aquatic life, and decreased biological oxygen demand. National water quality surveys indicate that by 1985 about 73% of monitored stream miles fully supported their designated uses, mainly fishing, boating, and swimming. This improvement in water quality is primarily a result of water pollution control laws, which have greatly increased the number and quality of sewage treatment plants and required industries to reduce or eliminate discharges into surface waters.

Since 1972 about 3% of monitored U.S. stream miles have suffered a decrease in quality. Of these, about 6% are too polluted to support fishing and other designated uses and 14% only partially support such uses. One river still suffering from major pollution problems is the Ohio River, which runs through the industrial heartland from Pittsburgh, before joining the Mississippi River at Cairo, Illinois. It receives discharges and runoff from factories, cities, and farms in parts of 12 states making up the Ohio River Basin. About 20 million people live and work in this basin, where 75% of the nation's coal and one-third of its steel are produced. Although industrial discharges have been reduced considerably since 1972, no more than 50% of the industries along the Ohio meet current federal water discharge standards.

The quality of about 84% of monitored U.S. stream miles has remained about the same since 1972. Primarily by reducing discharges from point sources, the country is holding the line against pollution of most of its rivers and streams—an impressive accomplishment considering the rise in economic activity and population since 1972. Further improvements will require stricter monitoring and enforcement of existing standards for discharges from point sources and massive efforts to reduce inputs from nonpoint sources.

River Water Quality in Other Parts of the World   Pollution control laws have also led to improved water quality in many rivers and streams in Canada, Japan, and most western European countries since 1970. Many rivers in the Soviet Union, however, have become more

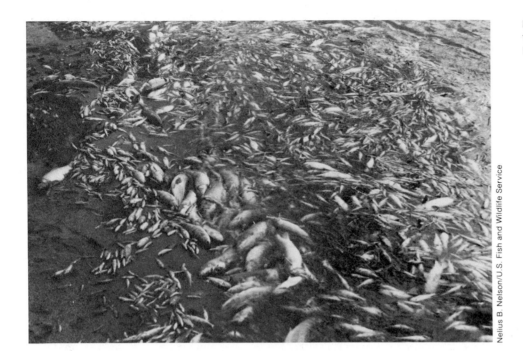

Nelius B. Nelson/U.S. Fish and Wildlife Service

polluted with industrial wastes, as industries have expanded without adequate pollution controls.

A spectacular river cleanup has occurred in Great Britain. In the 1950s the river Thames was little more than a flowing anaerobic sewer. But after more than 30 years of effort, $250 million of British taxpayers' money, and millions more spent by industry, the Thames has made a remarkable recovery. Dissolved oxygen levels have risen to the point where the river now supports increasing populations of at least 95 species of fish, including the pollution-sensitive salmon. Commercial fishing is thriving, and many species of waterfowl and wading birds have returned to their former feeding grounds.

Despite important progress, stretches of some rivers in MDCs are still polluted with excessive quantities of wastes from point and nonpoint sources. Large fish kills and contamination of drinking water still occur because of accidental or deliberate releases of toxic inorganic and organic chemicals by industries (see Spotlight on p. 464), malfunctioning sewage treatment plants, and runoff of pesticides from cropland.

Available data indicate that pollution of rivers in most LDCs is a serious and growing problem. Of India's 3,119 towns and cities, only 218 have any type of sewage treatment facilities. India's Ganges River, in which millions of Hindus regularly immerse themselves to wash away their sins, is highly contaminated. It receives untreated sewage and industrial wastes from millions of people in 114 cities, along with pesticide and fertilizer runoff. It has even caught fire twice. In 1985 the Indian government began a five-year, $252 million project that will treat the human sewage from the 27

largest cities on the river and convert it to methane gas, to be used as fuel to produce electricity, and a nutrient-rich sludge for use as fertilizer. Presently more than two-thirds of India's water resources are polluted.

Of the 78 rivers monitored in China, 54 are seriously polluted with untreated sewage and industrial wastes. In Latin America many rivers are severely polluted. The Bogotá River, for example, is contaminated by sewage from 5 million people and industrial wastes from Bogotá, Columbia. At the town of Tocaima, 120 kilometers (75 miles) downstream, the river has an average coliform bacteria count that is 36,500 times the maximum level allowed for swimming in the United States. Nearly all the children in a nearby village have sores on their skin from swimming in the river.

Pollution Problems of Lakes and Reservoirs The flushing and changing of water in lakes and large reservoirs can take from one to a hundred years, compared to several days to several weeks for rivers. As a result, these bodies of surface water are more susceptible than rivers to contamination with plant nutrients, oil, and toxic substances that can destroy bottom life and kill fish (Figure 20-6). Runoff of acids into lakes is a serious and increasing problem in areas subject to acid deposition (Figure 19-11, p. 432) and has killed most fish and other forms of aquatic life in thousands of lakes in western Europe, northwestern Canada, and the northeastern United States.

In 1985 the EPA reported that the water quality in 78% of the area of 3,755 U.S. lakes and reservoirs mon-

The Rhine River winds 1,320 kilometers (820 miles) through Switzerland, France, West Germany, and the Netherlands before emptying into the North Sea (Figure 20-7). Numerous cities and chemical, steel, and other plants border this heavily used and abused river.

In 1970 the Rhine was so heavily polluted that it was devoid of most fish and contained only about 25 forms of aquatic animal life. Between 1970 and 1986 cleanup efforts increased DO levels by almost 60%, decreased BOD by 50%, and raised the number of types of aquatic animal life to 100, including 15 species of fish reintroduced by scientists.

This progress was set back when a fire broke out on November 1, 1986, near Basel, Switzerland, at a chemical warehouse owned by Sandoz—a large, Swiss-based, international chemical and pharmaceutical company. The fire ruptured drums of chemicals, and water hosed onto the flames flushed at least 27 metric tons (30 tons) of toxic chemicals—mostly herbicides, mercury-containing fungicides, and dyes (which break down into cyanide)—into the Rhine. Then came the news that a neighboring chemical firm, Ciba-Geigy, had accidentally leaked at least 377 liters (100 gallons) of a highly toxic pesticide (Atrazin) into the Rhine four days later. At least eight other spills of toxic chemicals occurred between November 6 and December 2—causing environmentalists to charge that some were deliberately done.

Within a week after their discharge, most of the chemicals had flowed into the already polluted North Sea, where it is hoped most will be diluted to harmless levels or broken down into harmless substances. Villages and cities in the four countries depending on the river for drinking water had to temporarily find other supplies. Near Strasbourg, France, sheep that drank water from the river died. Most countries banned all fishing in the river and tributaries until further notice.

At least half a million fish and large numbers of eels, mussels, snails, aquatic insects, and waterfowl were killed. About 328 kilometers (205 miles) of the river, from Basel to Mainz, West Germany, suffered severe ecological damage. Of greatest concern are the estimated 200 kilograms (440 pounds) of highly toxic mercury compounds, most of which settled to the bottom of the river. Scientists fear that eventually much of this mercury will be biologically amplified in food webs, killing fish-eating birds, and poisoning humans eating contaminated fish.

Officials of countries downstream from Switzerland complained that Swiss authorities had failed to notify them of the accident for 24 hours and even then had not warned them about the severity of the spill. Although they broke no laws, Sandoz officials had decided five years earlier not to act on recommendations made by an insurance company to improve warehouse safety. A small investment would have saved the company the huge sums of money it is now expected to pay as compensation for the accident. More important, it would have prevented a major ecological disaster.

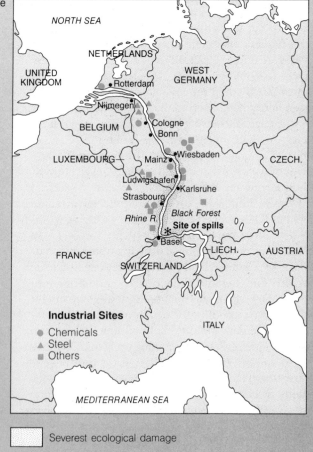

Figure 20-7 The Rhine River, site of a major industrial spill in 1986.

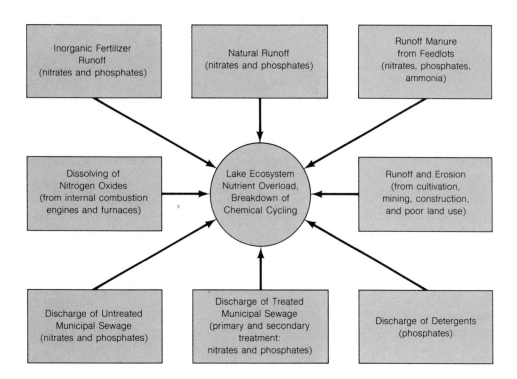

Figure 20-8 Major sources of nutrient overload from human activities, or cultural eutrophication.

Boxes surrounding central circle:

Inorganic Fertilizer Runoff (nitrates and phosphates)

Natural Runoff (nitrates and phosphates)

Runoff Manure from Feedlots (nitrates, phosphates, ammonia)

Dissolving of Nitrogen Oxides (from internal combustion engines and furnaces)

Lake Ecosystem Nutrient Overload, Breakdown of Chemical Cycling

Runoff and Erosion (from cultivation, mining, construction, and poor land use)

Discharge of Untreated Municipal Sewage (nitrates and phosphates)

Discharge of Treated Municipal Sewage (primary and secondary treatment: nitrates and phosphates)

Discharge of Detergents (phosphates)

itored fully support their designated uses such as boating, commercial and sport fishing, and swimming. Despite this encouraging news, significant water pollution problems remain, especially as a result of runoff of plant nutrients and toxic wastes from nonpoint sources.

The most widely reported problem impairing some uses of relatively shallow lakes and reservoirs, especially those near urban or agricultural centers, is accelerated eutrophication as a result of human activities (Figure 20-8). **Eutrophication** is a natural process by which a lake gradually becomes enriched in plant nutrients such as phosphate and nitrate as a result of natural erosion and runoff from the surrounding land basin (Figure 5-12, p. 104). The stepped-up addition of phosphates and nitrates as a result of human activities, sometimes called **cultural eutrophication,** can produce in a few decades the same degree of plant nutrient enrichment that takes thousands to millions of years by natural processes.

Overloading of shallow lakes and reservoirs with plant nutrients during the summer produces dense growths of rooted plants like water chestnuts and water hyacinths near the shore. It also causes population explosions, or blooms, of floating algae, especially the blue-green species, which give the water the appearance of green soup and which release substances that make the water taste and smell bad.

Dissolved oxygen in the surface layer of water near the shore and the bottom layer in areas covered with algae is depleted when large masses of these algae die, fall to the bottom, and are decomposed by aerobic bacteria (Figure 20-9). Then lake trout and other deep-water species of game fish die of oxygen starvation, leaving the lake populated by panfish species like carp, which need less oxygen. Cultural eutrophication may cause the actual number of fish to increase, but there will be fewer of the kinds of game fish that most people prefer. If excess nutrients continue to flow into a lake, the bottom water becomes foul and almost devoid of animals, as anaerobic bacteria take over and produce their smelly decomposition products.

In the United States about one-third of the 100,000 medium to large lakes and about 85% of the large lakes near major population centers suffer from some degree of cultural eutrophication. The Great Lakes, for example, receive massive inputs of plant nutrients and numerous toxic water pollutants from point and non-point sources (see Enrichment Study at the end of this chapter). Severe cultural eutrophication jeopardizes the use of lakes and reservoirs for drinking, sport and commercial fishing, recreation, irrigation, and cooling of electric power and industrial plants.

Control of Cultural Eutrophication The solution to cultural eutrophication is to use input methods to reduce the flow of nutrients into lakes and reservoirs and output methods to clean up lakes that suffer from excessive eutrophication.

Cultural Eutrophication: Input Control Methods

1. Use advanced waste treatment (Section 20-5) to remove 90% of phosphates from effluents of sewage treatment and industrial plants before they reach the lake.

2. Ban or set low limits on phosphates in household detergents and other cleaning agents to reduce the amount of phosphate reaching sewage treatment plants and nonpoint sources such as septic tanks (Figure 20-10).

3. Control land use, use sound soil conservation practices, and clean streets regularly to reduce runoff of fertilizers, manure, and soil from nonpoint sources.

4. Divert wastewater to fast-moving streams or to the ocean. This approach is not possible in most places; where it is possible, it may transfer the problem from a lake to a nearby estuary.

Cultural Eutrophication: Output Control Methods

1. Dredge bottom sediments to remove excess nutrient buildup. Impractical in large, deep lakes; not very effective in shallow lakes; often reduces water quality by resuspending toxic pollutants; dredged material must go somewhere—usually into the ocean.

2. Remove or harvest excess weeds and debris. Disruptive to some forms of aquatic life and difficult and expensive in large lakes.

3. Control nuisance plant growth with herbicides and algicides. Can pollute water and kill off desirable plants.

4. Aerate lakes and reservoirs to avoid oxygen depletion (Figure 20-11). Expensive.

As with other forms of pollution, input approaches are the most effective. Input control methods have to be tailored to each situation based on the **limiting factor principle:** When a number of nutrients are needed for the growth of various plant species, the one in smallest supply will limit or stop growth. For example, because phosphorus is the limiting factor in most freshwater lakes, its control should be emphasized.

But there is disagreement over whether this should be done by banning or limiting phosphates in laundry detergents, by removing phosphates from wastewater at sewage treatment plants, or both. Studies of over 400 bodies of water indicate that a reduction of 20% in the total phosphate load must be achieved to produce a discernible effect on water quality. By 1987 eight states—Indiana, Maryland, Michigan, Minnesota, New York, Vermont, Virginia, and Wisconsin—and many

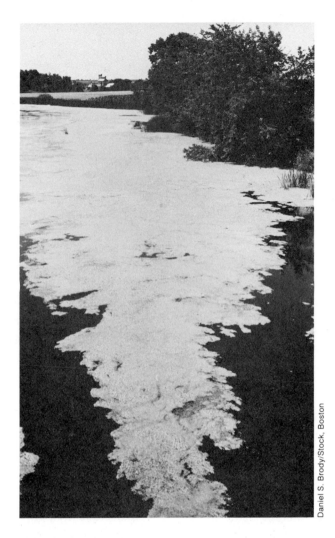

Daniel S. Brody/Stock, Boston

Figure 20-9 Mass of dead and dying algae from cultural eutrophication of a lake in Minnesota.

parts of Canada had banned the use of phosphate detergents. Such bans have made a major contribution to reducing cultural eutrophication in the Great Lakes and other areas (see Enrichment Study at the end of this chapter) and have saved consumers and taxpayers money.

In some lakes and in coastal waters and estuaries, emphasis should be on reducing inputs of nitrogen because it is the limiting factor. Fortunately, if excessive inputs of limiting plant nutrients stop, the lake will usually return to its previous state.

Thermal Pollution of Rivers and Lakes Almost half of all water withdrawn in the United States each year is for cooling electric power plants. The cheapest and easiest method is to withdraw cool water from a nearby ocean bay or inlet, major river, or large lake, pass it through heat exchangers in the plant, and return the heated water to the same body of water.

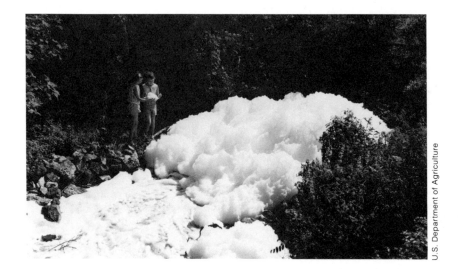

Figure 20-10 Foam on a creek caused by the use of nonbiodegradable components in synthetic detergents prior to 1966.

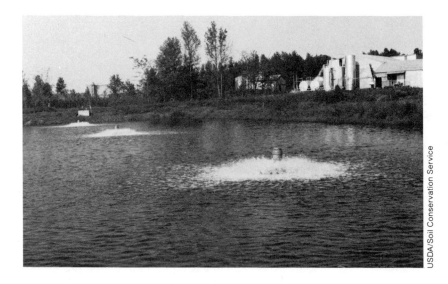

Figure 20-11 Lakes and reservoirs can be aerated to increase dissolved oxygen and reduce the harmful effects of cultural eutrophication.

Small amounts of heat have no serious effects on aquatic ecosystems. Large rivers with rapid flow rates can dissipate heat rapidly and suffer little ecological damage unless their flow rates are sharply reduced during summer months or prolonged drought. However, large inputs of heated water from a single plant or a number of plants using the same lake or slow-moving river can have an adverse ecological effect called **thermal pollution.**

Warmer temperatures lower DO content by decreasing the solubility of oxygen in water. Warmer water also causes aquatic organisms to increase their respiration rates and consume oxygen faster, and it increases their susceptibility to disease, parasites, and toxic chemicals. Although some fish species can survive in heated water, many game fish cannot because they have lower temperature tolerance limits and higher oxygen requirements. Discharge of heated water into shallow water near the shore also disrupts spawning and kills young fish.

Fish and other organisms adapted to a particular temperature range can also be killed from **thermal shock:** sharp changes in water temperature when new power plants open up or when plants shut down for repair. Many fish die on intake screens used to prevent fish and debris from clogging the heat exchanger pipes. Pumping large volumes of cold, nutrient-rich water from the bottom layer of moderate-size lakes also speeds up the eutrophication process.

While some scientists call the addition of excess heat to aquatic systems thermal pollution, others talk about using heated water for beneficial purposes, calling it **thermal enrichment.** They point out that heated water results in longer commercial fishing seasons and reduction of winter ice cover in cold areas and can be used for irrigation to extend the growing season in frost-prone areas.

Warm water from power plants can also be cycled through aquaculture pens to speed the growth of commercially valuable fish and shellfish. For example, waste

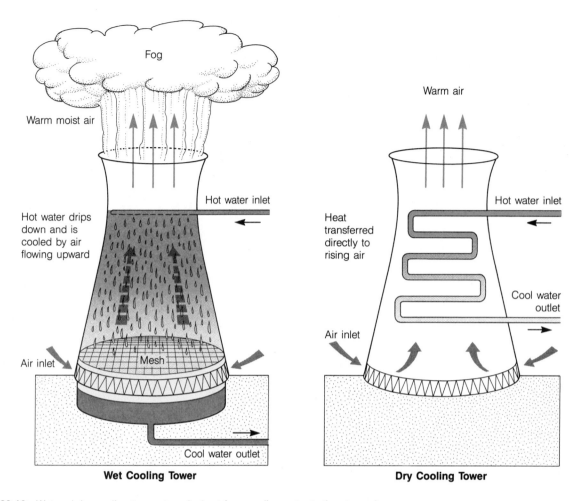

Figure 20-12 Wet and dry cooling towers transfer heat from cooling water to the atmosphere.

hot water is used to cultivate oysters in aquaculture lagoons in Japan and in New York's Long Island Sound and to cultivate catfish and redfish in Texas. Heated water could also be used to heat nearby buildings and greenhouses, melt snow, desalinate ocean water, and provide low-temperature heat for some industrial processes. However, because of dangers from air pollution and release of radioactivity, most coal-burning and electric power plants are usually not located near enough to aquaculture operations, buildings, and industries to make thermal enrichment economically feasible.

Reduction of Thermal Water Pollution There are a number of ways to minimize the harmful effects of excess heat on aquatic ecosystems. We can use and waste less electicity (Section 18-1) and limit the number of power and industrial plants discharging heated water into the same body of water. The heated water can also be returned at a point away from the ecologically vulnerable shore zone. In areas particularly susceptible to thermal pollution, heat in the water can be transferred to the atmosphere by means of wet or dry cooling towers (Figure 20-12). Water can also be discharged into shallow cooling canals, left to transfer its heat to the atmosphere, and then withdrawn for reuse as cooling water (Figure 20-13).

Most new power plants use wet cooling towers. This approach, however, has several disadvantages: larger withdrawals of surface water to replace water lost by evaporation, visual pollution from the gigantic cooling towers (Figure 20-14), high construction costs (about $100 million per tower for a 1,000-megawatt plant), high operating costs, and excessive fog and mist in nearby areas. Dry towers are seldom used because they cost two to four times more to build than wet towers. Cooling ponds and canals are useful where enough affordable land is available (about 1,000 acres for a 1,000-megawatt plant).

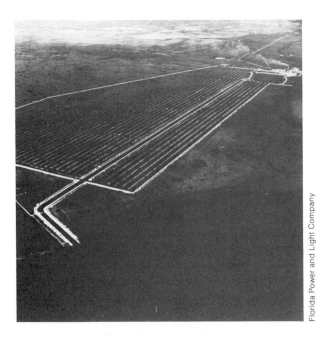

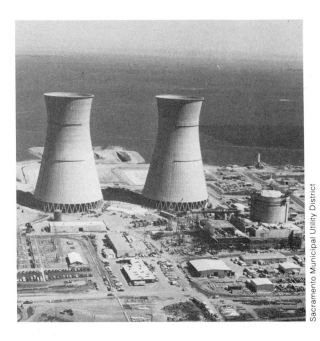

Florida Power and Light Company

Sacramento Municipal Utility District

Figure 20-13 A 2,400-hectare (6,000-acre) canal system is used to transfer heat from cooling water into the atmosphere at the Turkey Point power plant site near Miami, Florida, rather than discharging the heated water into Biscayne Bay. One of the four units—two nuclear and two fossil fuel—is located at the upper right.

Figure 20-14 Wet cooling towers for the Rancho Seco nuclear power plant near Sacramento, California. Compare the size of the towers with the power plant and automobiles. Each tower is more than 120 meters (400 feet) high and could hold a baseball field in its base.

20-3 OCEAN POLLUTION

Are the Oceans Dying? Oceans are the ultimate sink for natural and human wastes. They receive a variety of contaminants from multiple sources. These include runoff from urban areas and farms via streams and rivers, point source discharges by cities and industries into coastal zones, direct dumping of dredged materials and urban wastes by barges, dumping of sewage and garbage by merchant ships and pleasure boats, atmospheric fallout, natural oil seepage, and accidental oil spills from tankers and offshore oil drilling platforms. The major pollution problems of the oceans occur around their edges—the harbors, estuaries, wetlands, and inland seas, like the Baltic and Mediterranean, near large cities, industrial centers, and the mouths of polluted rivers.

Reports of the death of the oceans in the late 1960s and the 1970s were premature. Fortunately, the vastness of ocean waters and their constant mixing dilute and disperse many types of waste to harmless levels. Biodegradable wastes are broken down and recycled by natural chemical cycles in ocean ecosystems. Marine life has also proved to be more resilient than some scientists had expected.

Although the ocean can dilute, disperse, and break down large amounts of sewage and some types of industrial waste, especially in its deep-water areas, it does have limits. The sheer magnitude of discharges, especially near coasts, can overload natural purifying systems (see Spotlight on p. 470). In addition, these natural processes cannot readily degrade many of the plastics, pesticides, and other synthetic chemicals created by human ingenuity. For example, studies indicate that each year one to two million seabirds and more than 100,000 marine mammals, including whales, seals, dolphins, and manatees, die as a result of ingestion of plastic cups, bags, six-pack yokes, fishing gear, and other forms of plastic trash thrown or washed into the ocean.

Ocean Dumping Barges and ships dump large volumes of waste into the sea. About 80% of these wastes are **dredge spoils,** materials scraped from the bottoms

The Chesapeake Bay, the largest estuary in the United States, is an ecosystem in decline from pollution by toxic chemicals and excessive inputs of nitrogen and phosphorus plant nutrients. This generally shallow, 320-kilometer-long (200 miles) estuary receives wastes from point and nonpoint sources scattered throughout a massive drainage basin including nine large rivers and parts of six states (Figure 20-15). The bay becomes a massive pollution sink because only 1% of the waste entering it is flushed into the Atlantic Ocean. Between 1940 and 1986 the number of people living close to the bay grew from 3.7 million to 13.2 million and is projected to reach 14.5 million by 2000.

Nutrient levels have risen sharply in many parts of the bay, causing algal blooms and oxygen depletion. Levels of heavy metals and toxic organic chemicals have increased in the water and in the bottom sediment, and some of these toxic contaminants have been biologically amplified in food webs. As a result of these ecologi-cal changes, harvests of oysters, crabs, and commercially important fish such as striped bass (rockfish) and other species, which spawn in fresh water and feed on organisms that thrive in rapidly disappearing bay grasses, have fallen sharply since 1960. However, populations of bluefish, menhaden, and other species that spawn in salt water and feed around algae blooms have increased.

Studies have shown that point sources, primarily sewage treatment plants, are the major contributors of phosphorus, while nonpoint sources, primarily runoff from urban and suburban areas and agricultural activities, are the main sources of nitrogen. Between 1983 and 1985 over $550 million in federal and state funds were spent on a cleanup program that could ultimately cost several billion dollars. Emphasis has been placed on upgrading and building new sewage treatment plants and hiring more inspectors to track down industrial and municipal sewage treatment plants violating their discharge permits. Funds have also been used to entice farmers near the bay and its tributaries to switch to no-till farming to reduce soil erosion, plant grass buffers between cropland and river banks, contour fields, and install tanks and ponds to hold animal wastes.

Between 1980 and 1985 discharges of phosphorus from point sources dropped by about 20%, but there is a long way to go to reverse severe eutrophication in areas where phosphorus is the limiting factor. Bans on household detergents and other cleaning agents that contain phosphates will probably have to be enacted throughout the entire six-state drainage basin. Since nitrogen may be the limiting factor in many parts of the bay, reducing nitrogen inputs from millions of dispersed nonpoint urban and rural sources to levels sufficient to halt cultural eutrophication will be difficult and expensive. In addition to billions of dollars, halting the ecological deterioration of this vital estuary will require prolonged, cooperative efforts by officials in six states and thousands of cities, towns, and industries and by millions of individual homeowners and farmers.

---

of harbors and rivers to maintain shipping channels. Typically about one-third of these dredged materials are contaminated with effluents from industries and urban areas and runoff from farmlands. Most dredge spoils, too costly to transport to the land for disposal, pose relatively little risk to aquatic ecosystems.

Most of the remaining 20% of the wastes barged out and dumped into the ocean are industrial wastes and **sewage sludge,** a gooey mixture of bacteria- and virus-laden organic matter, toxic metals, synthetic organic chemicals, and settled solids removed from wastewater at sewage treatment plants. As a result of more stringent ocean-dumping laws, the volume of industrial wastes dumped at sea in U.S. coastal waters declined by about 75% between 1975 and 1985. However, the volume of sewage sludge dumped into coastal waters increased by almost 60% during the same period.

This increase occurred because of the greatly increased levels of sewage treatment required by water pollution control laws enacted in the 1970s and the lack of suitable and affordable land dumping sites. Great Britain also dumps large quantities of sewage sludge at sea.

Presently all dredge spoils, industrial wastes, and sewage sludge are dumped at designated sites near the Atlantic, Gulf, and Pacific coasts. The most intensely used ocean dumping site is the New York Bight, a shallow (80-feet-deep) area 19 kilometers (12 miles) off the New York-New Jersey coast near the mouth of the Hudson River (Figure 20-16).

After over 60 years of dumping, a 105-square-kilometer (40-square-mile) area of the ocean bottom in the New York Bight is covered with a black sludge containing high levels of bacteria, long-lived viruses, toxic metals, and organic compounds. During storms

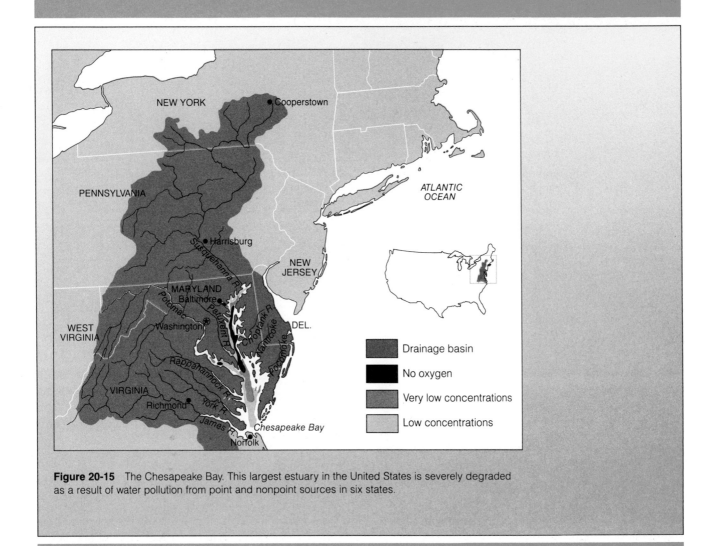

Figure 20-15 The Chesapeake Bay. This largest estuary in the United States is severely degraded as a result of water pollution from point and nonpoint sources in six states.

some of this sludge has washed ashore on Long Island and New Jersey beaches. It has also contaminated shellfish beds and caused disease outbreaks among people consuming raw clams and oysters illegally harvested from closed beds. Some experts have called the New York Bight one of the most severely polluted and degraded ocean areas in the world.

For 15 years federal officials and environmentalists have been trying to relocate the dumping of all sewage sludge to a deepwater site 170 kilometers (106 miles) east of New York City just beyond the continental shelf. Because of its 2,000-meter (610-foot) water depth and nearness to Gulf Stream currents, this site has a much greater capacity to dilute and disperse wastes than the New York Bight.

In 1985, after years of legal maneuvering by urban officials wishing to avoid the extra costs of hauling the sludge farther, the EPA and the municipalities agreed to phase out all dumping of sewage sludge in the New York Bight between March 1986 and December 1987. Even if this schedule is met, the bight will continue to receive substantial inputs of contaminants from coastal wastewater discharges, urban runoff, atmospheric fallout, and dumping of dredged material.

Although the deep ocean is better equipped than land to handle sewage and some forms of industrial waste, most scientists believe that the ocean should not be used for the dumping of slowly degradable or nondegradable pollutants like PCBs, some pesticides and radioactive isotopes, and toxic mercury compounds that can be biologically amplified in ocean food webs. Unfortunately, many of these materials are mixed with some types of sewage sludge and industrial waste being dumped into the oceans in large quantities.

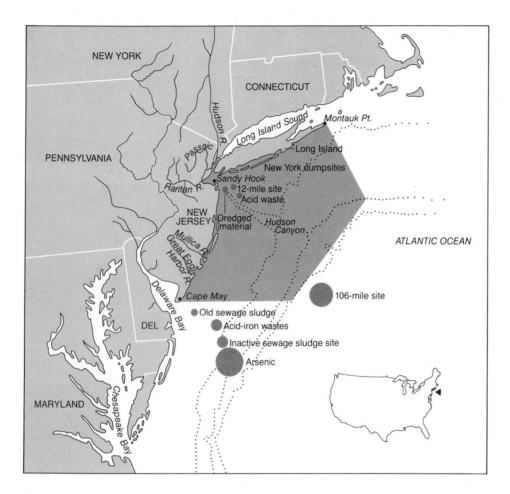

Figure 20-16 The New York Bight has served as an ocean dumping site for massive amounts of wastes for over 60 years.

Ocean Oil Pollution Crude petroleum (oil as it comes out of the ground) and refined petroleum (fuel oil, gasoline, and other products obtained by distillation and chemical processing of crude petroleum) are accidentally or deliberately released into the environment from a number of sources (Figure 20-17). The bad news is that in 1985 about 3.3 million metric tons (3.6 million tons) of crude and refined oil were added to the world's oceans from various sources (Figure 20-18). The good news is that the estimated input of oil into the ocean in 1985 was almost half the input in 1975.

The most publicized releases of oil into the oceans are tanker accidents and blowouts (oil escaping under high pressure from a borehole in the ocean floor) at offshore drilling rigs. However, releases of oil from offshore wells during normal operations and during transport of the oil to shore add a much larger volume of oil to the oceans than occasional blowouts. About 32% of the annual input of oil into the oceans comes from intentional discharges during routine cleaning, loading, and unloading operations of tankers.

Tanker accidents account for only 10% to 15% of the annual input of oil into the world's oceans. There has been a decrease in the average annual number of major tanker accidents from 38 between 1973 and 1981 to 12 between 1982 and 1985. This trend is due to improved safety measures including better navigational equipment, training, and control; tougher safety standards for tankers; and improved certification and inspection standards.

Effects of Oil Pollution There is considerable dispute and uncertainty over the short-term and long-term effects of oil on ocean ecosystems. The effects of oil spills are difficult to predict because they depend on a number of factors, including the type of oil spilled (crude or refined), amount, distance of the spill from shore, time of year, weather conditions, and ocean and tidal currents.

Crude oil and refined oil are collections of hundreds of substances with widely differing properties. After an oil spill, low-boiling, aromatic hydrocarbons are the primary cause of the immediate killing of a number of aquatic organisms, especially in their larval forms.

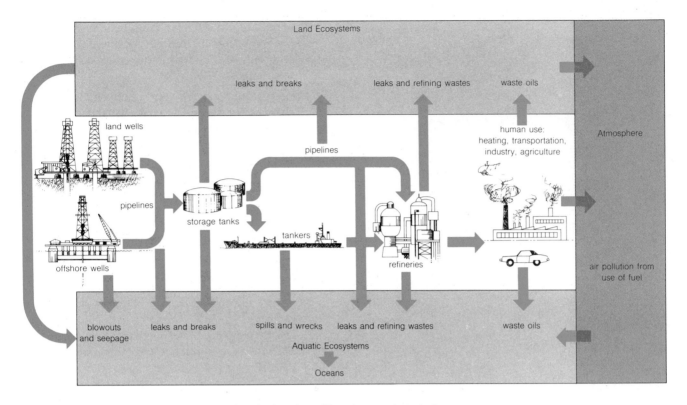

Figure 20-17 Major sources of oil pollution of the hydrosphere, lithosphere, and atmosphere.

Fortunately, most of these toxic chemicals evaporate into the atmosphere within a day or two. Some other chemicals remain on the surface and form floating, tarlike globs that range from the size of marbles to the size of tennis balls. These floating substances are gradually broken down by bacteria over several weeks or months, although they persist much longer in cold polar waters.

Floating oil can coat the feathers of marine birds, especially diving birds (Figure 20-19), and the fur of marine mammals such as seals and sea otters. This oily coating destroys the animals' natural insulation and buoyancy and most drown or die of exposure from loss of body heat. It is estimated that in the North Sea and North Atlantic regions between 150,000 and 450,000 marine birds are killed each year by chronic oil pollution, mostly from routine tanker releases. As a consequence, a number of species including the puffin, razorbill, and quillemont are threatened with extinction.

Heavy oil components that sink to the ocean floor or wash into estuaries are believed to have the greatest long-term impact on marine ecosystems. These components can kill bottom-dwelling organisms such as

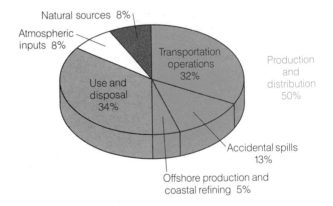

Figure 20-18 Sources of ocean oil pollution. (Data from the National Academy of Sciences)

crabs, oysters, mussels, and clams or make them unfit for human consumption because of their oily taste and smell. Some petroleum chemicals can cause major changes in the behavior patterns of aquatic organisms. For example, lobsters and some fish lose their abilities

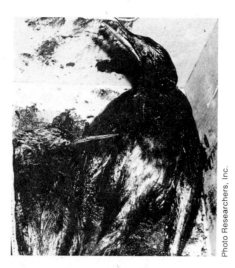

Figure 20-19 These birds were coated with crude oil from an underwater, offshore oil leak that occurred near Santa Barbara, California, in 1969. Such birds die unless the oil is removed with a detergent solution.

to locate food, avoid injury, escape enemies, find a habitat, communicate, migrate, and reproduce.

Oil slicks that wash onto beaches can have serious economic effects on coastal residents, who lose income from fishing and tourist activities. Oil-polluted beaches washed by strong waves or currents are cleaned up fairly rapidly, but beaches in sheltered areas remain contaminated for several years. Oil cleanup is very expensive for oil companies and coastal communities.

Studies of the effects of several crude oil spills in the open sea between 1969 and 1978 found that most forms of marine life recovered nearly completely within three years. In contrast, spills of oil, especially refined oil, near shore or in estuarine zones, where sea life is most abundant, have much more damaging and long-lasting effects. For example, damage to estuarine species from the 1969 spill of refined oil at West Falmouth, Massachusetts, was still being detected ten years later.

Controlling Ocean Oil Pollution The best way to deal with oil pollution is to use various input approaches to prevent it from happening in the first place. Output strategies can be used to deal with oil pollution once it has occurred, but these have not been very effective.

Ocean Oil Pollution: Input Control Methods

1. Use and waste less oil (Section 18-1).
2. Collect used oils and greases from service stations and other sources and reprocess them for reuse.

3. Strictly regulate the building, maintenance, loading and unloading procedures, training of crews, and routing of oil tankers to reduce accidental releases.
4. Require all tankers to have double hulls to reduce chances of a spill and to have separate tanks for the oil cargo and ballast water used to provide stability for empty ships. In older ships, the empty oil tanks were filled with salt water for ballast. When the ships arrived at port to be refilled with oil, the oil-contaminated water was dumped at sea.
5. Eliminate the rinsing of sludge from empty oil tanks and dumping it onto the sea by requiring crude oil to be cleaned before loading to prevent buildup of sludge in the ship's holding tanks.
6. Strictly regulate safety, training, and operation procedures for offshore wells.
7. Strictly regulate safety, operation, and disposal procedures for refineries and industrial plants.

Ocean Oil Pollution: Output Control Methods

1. Use mechanical barriers to prevent oil from reaching the shore and then vacuum it up or soak it up with pillows filled with chicken feathers. Ineffective in high seas and bad weather conditions and in ice-congested water.
2. Treat spilled oil with detergents so that it will disperse, dissolve, or sink. Experience has shown that the detergents kill more marine life than the oil does.
3. Use genetic engineering techniques to develop bacterial strains that can degrade compounds in oil faster and more efficiently than natural bacterial strains. Possible ecological side effects of the "superbugs" should be carefully investigated before widespread use.
4. Use helicopters equipped with lasers to ignite and burn as much as 90% of an oil spill in a few seconds. Cheaper and more effective than most other approaches and is the only effective method in ice-congested seas. Creates air pollution.

20-4 GROUNDWATER POLLUTION

Is It Safe to Drink the Water? Groundwater is a vital resource that provides drinking water for one out of two Americans and 95% of those in rural areas. About 75% of American cities depend on groundwater for all or most of their supply of drinking water.

The EPA estimates that roughly 1% to 2% of the country's usable groundwater is polluted moderately or severely. Although this may seem small, it is significant because most contaminated aquifers are near heavily populated areas. Thus, contaminated aquifers affect 5 million to 10 million people.

Furthermore, according to the Office of Technology Assessment, the EPA estimate is probably low; there has been no uniform or comprehensive testing of the country's groundwater resources. By 1986 only 38 of the 700 different chemicals found in groundwater were covered by federal water quality standards and routinely tested for in municipal drinking water supplies. No testing at all is required for the country's millions of private wells.

Groundwater contamination has occurred in every state, and incidents of contamination are being reported with increasing frequency as more supplies are tested. In a 1982 survey the EPA found that 45% of the large public water systems served by groundwater were contaminated with synthetic organic chemicals that posed potential health threats (Table 20-2). Another EPA survey found that two-thirds of the rural household wells tested violated at least one federal health standard for drinking water.

Vulnerability of Groundwater to Pollution   Some bacteria and most suspended solid pollutants are removed as contaminated surface water percolates through the soil into aquifers. But this process can be overloaded by large volumes of wastes, and its effectiveness varies with the type of soil. For example, these pollutants are not effectively filtered out in porous, sandy soils such as those in much of Florida. No soil is effective in filtering out viruses and most synthetic organic chemicals. Bacterial degradation of oxygen-demanding wastes reaching aquifers does not occur readily because of the lack of dissolved oxygen and sufficient microorganisms in groundwater.

Once contaminants reach groundwater, they are not effectively diluted and dispersed because the rate of movement of most groundwater is very slow. Thus, concentrations of groundwater contaminants are often much greater than those in surface waters.

Once an aquifer becomes contaminated, it remains that way for decades or centuries, depending on how rapidly it is replenished. Because groundwater flows so slowly, contamination being discovered in wells today may be the result of pollutants that seeped into an aquifer many years ago. And water from a well may test pure one day and then be contaminated the next day by water that has been flowing toward the well for years. Thus, we can see why most analysts believe that groundwater pollution is the most serious U.S. water quality problem today and why they expect it to get much worse.

Sources of Groundwater Contamination   Groundwater can be contaminated from a number of point and nonpoint sources (Figure 20-20). Two major sources of groundwater contamination are leaks of hazardous organic chemicals from underground storage tanks (see Spotlight on p. 477) and seepage of such chemicals and toxic heavy metal compounds from landfills, abandoned toxic waste dumps, and lagoons. There are at least 22,000 abandoned hazardous waste disposal sites, 1,500 active hazardous waste landfills, and 15,000 active municipal landfills that are unlined and located above or near aquifers in the United States (Section 21-4).

Another concern is leaks into groundwater from deep wells used to inject hazardous wastes deep underground. As a result of stricter regulation of surface water pollution and more recently of disposal of hazardous wastes in landfills, industries have found that injection of wastes into deep wells is a much cheaper and less carefully regulated solution. At least 30%, and according to some estimates 60%, of the hazardous wastes produced in the U.S. in 1986 were injected in about 1,000 deep wells. Such wells are bored through aquifers and separated from them by an impermeable layer of rock that theoretically seals the waste in an underground tomb. In practice, however, liquid wastes from some wells have migrated into aquifers and surface waters through other abandoned and unplugged gas and oil wells, blowouts, and cracks caused by earth tremors and by dynamite used to expand the disposal area. Wastes can also escape through faulty casings and joints.

Laws regulating deep-well injection are weak and poorly enforced. There are no limits on the types of wastes that can be injected, no required reporting of the types of wastes injected, and no national inventory of active and abandoned wells. Operators are not required to monitor nearby aquifers and are not liable for any damages from leaks once the well is abandoned and plugged. By 1986 Alabama, Florida, Louisiana, and California had either banned or were phasing out deep-well disposal. Environmentalists believe that there should be a national ban on all deep-well disposal of hazardous waste since there are other, less risky alternatives (Section 21-5).

Control of Groundwater Pollution   Groundwater pollution is much more difficult to detect and control than surface water pollution. Locating and monitoring groundwater pollution is expensive (up to $10,000 per monitoring well) and usually many monitoring wells must be sunk to determine the area of contamination. Pumping water out of a contaminated aquifer, cleaning it up, and then returning it is usually prohibitively expensive—$5 million to $10 million for a single aquifer. Cleaning up a small area can cost over $250,000.

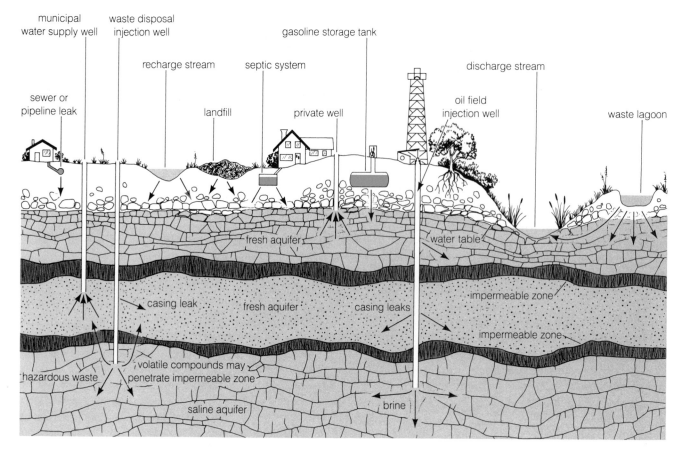

Figure 20-20 Major sources of groundwater contamination in the United States.

Some scientists propose that genetic engineering techniques be used to develop strains of anaerobic bacteria that could be injected into polluted aquifers to break down specific pollutants under low-oxygen conditions. Other scientists, however, are concerned about the possible side effects of such bacteria, including mutations into other strains.

Because of these difficulties, it is generally recognized that preventing contamination in the first place is the only effective long-range way to protect groundwater resources. Despite the seriousness of the threat to U.S. drinking water supplies, by 1986 there was no single federal law designed to protect groundwater. Some aspects of groundwater pollution, however, can be controlled by parts of existing water pollution control laws (Section 20-6).

In 1984 the EPA suggested that each state classify its groundwater resources into one of three categories. Class I, consisting of irreplaceable sources of drinking water and ecologically vital sources, should be given the highest protection. Class II includes all other groundwater currently in use or potentially available

for drinking water or for other beneficial uses. Class III groundwater is not a potential source of drinking water and is of limited beneficial use, usually because it is already too contaminated.

Protecting groundwater, however, will require enacting and strictly enforcing many unpopular laws at the federal and state levels. Any potentially polluting activities would have to be banned in Class I and II areas, but they could be encouraged in Class III areas. Essentially all disposal of hazardous wastes in landfills and deep wells would have to be banned except perhaps in Class III areas. Expensive monitoring would be required for aquifers near existing landfills, underground tanks, and other potential sources of groundwater contamination. Much stricter controls would have to be placed on the application of pesticides and fertilizers by millions of farmers and homeowners—regulations that would also be a key factor in protecting surface water from contamination by nonpoint sources. People using private wells for drinking water would probably have to have their water tested once a year. Unless nationwide federal laws are enacted, states that

Leaks of gasoline, home-heating oil, industrial-cleaning solvents, and other hazardous chemicals from 1.5 million underground storage tanks may be responsible for as much as 40% of the country's groundwater contamination. About 90% of these tanks contain motor fuel and 10% contain hazardous chemicals.

While most are located at gas stations, tanks are also found at airports, farms, industries, hospitals, dry-cleaning establishments, and bus, taxi, and rental car garages. EPA surveys indicate that up to 35% of these tanks may be leaking some of their contents into groundwater as a result of improper installation, corrosion (most are steel tanks designed to last only 15 to 20 years), cracking (fiberglass tanks), and overfilling. An additional 350,000 aging tanks are expected to become leakers between 1987 and 1990.

A gasoline leak of just one gallon a day can seriously contaminate the water supply for 50,000 persons. Such slow leaks usually remain undetected until someone discovers that a well is contaminated. Determining the extent of a leak can cost $25,000 to $250,000. Cleaning up the pollutant costs from $10,000 for a small spill to $250,000 and up if the chemical reaches an aquifer. Replacing a leaking tank adds an additional $10,000 to $60,000, and damages to injured parties and legal fees can run into the millions.

Most gasoline tanks are owned by independent operators or local petroleum suppliers and distributors, who tend not to report leaks for fear of bankruptcy. By 1986 only two states, Florida and Connecticut, required monitoring of underground tanks. In 1986 Congress passed legislation placing a tax on motor fuel to create a $500 million fund for cleaning up leaking underground tanks.

The EPA requires that all tanks installed after 1988 have double walls or concrete vaults built around them to help prevent leaks into groundwater. But this does not solve the problem of leaks from existing tanks. Environmentalists believe that monitoring of all underground tanks should be required by law. Operators should also be required to carry sufficient liability insurance to cover cleanup and damage costs and be liable for leaks from abandoned tanks. Environmentalists also urge that construction standards for tanks should be strict and well enforced and that all tank installers be certified by having to pass strict tests. In West Germany such a program has been quite successful in reducing underground tank leaks for 20 years. Most business owners oppose such regulations because they are too costly and increase government regulation. What do you think should be done?

take such measures to protect their water supplies and the health of their citizens might lose industries and jobs to states with less regulation.

20-5   WATER POLLUTION CONTROL

Control of Nonpoint Source Pollution   Although most U.S. surface waters have not declined in quality since 1970, they have also not improved. The primary reason is the absence of any national strategy for controlling water pollution from nonpoint sources. Such a strategy will require greatly increased efforts to control soil erosion through conservation and land-use control for farms, construction sites, and suburban and urban areas.

Fertilizer runoff and leaching can be reduced by avoiding excessive application, applying fertilizer only during the growing season, not using it on steeply sloped land, requiring buffer zones of vegetation between fields and surface water, using slow-release fertilizers, and using crop rotation with nitrogen-fixing plants to reduce the need for fertilizer.

Pesticide runoff and leaching can be reduced by applying no more pesticide than needed and by applying it only when needed; increased reliance on biological methods of pest control can significantly reduce the need for pesticides (Section 22-5). Methods to control runoff and infiltration of animal wastes from feedlots and barnyards include regulating animal density, not locating such operations on land sloping toward nearby surface water, and diverting runoff into lagoons or detention basins (Figure 20-21) from which the nutrient-rich water can be pumped and applied as fertilizer to cropland or forestland.

Control of Point Source Pollution: Wastewater Treatment   In many LDCs and parts of MDCs, sewage and waterborne industrial wastes from point sources are not treated and are discharged into the nearest waterway or into a storage basin such as a cesspool or lagoon. Widespread discharge of untreated

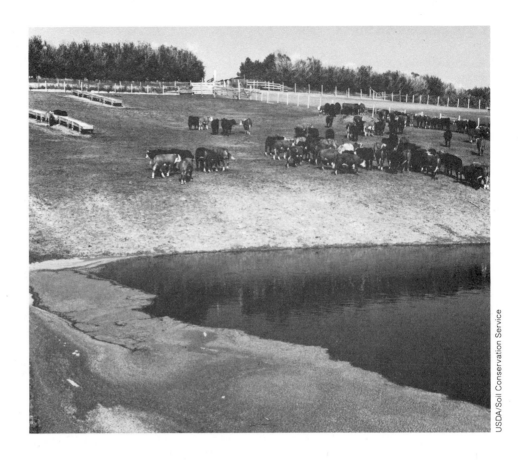

Figure 20-21 A detention basin such as this one in Cass County, Michigan, can be used to capture runoff from animal feedlots. Nutrient-rich water can be pumped out and used to fertilize cropland.

USDA/Soil Conservation Service

human and livestock wastes into surface water is a major cause of illness and death.

In most MDCs, however, most of the wastes from point sources are purified to varying degrees. In rural and suburban areas with suitable soils, sewage and wastewater from each individual house is usually discharged into a **septic tank,** which traps greases and large solids and discharges the remaining wastes over a large drainage field for filtration by the soil and biodegradation by soil bacteria (Figure 20-22). In the United States, septic tanks are regulated by all states to ensure that they are installed in soils with adequate drainage, not placed too close together or too near well sites, and installed properly. In most states, systems must be reinspected whenever a house is sold. To prevent backup and overflow, grease and solids must be periodically pumped out of the tank.

In urban areas most waterborne wastes from homes, businesses, factories, and storm runoff flow through a network of sewer pipes to sewage treatment plants. Some urban areas have separate lines for sewage and storm water runoff, but in other areas (such as parts of Boston) lines for these two sources are combined because it is cheaper (Figure 20-23). The problem with a combined sewer system is that during heavy rains the total volume of wastewater and storm runoff flowing through the system usually exceeds— by as much as 100 times—the amount that can be handled by the sewage treatment plant. As a result, the overflow, which contains untreated sewage, is discharged directly into surface waters.

When sewage reaches a treatment plant, it can undergo various levels of purification, depending on the sophistication of the plant and the degree of purity desired. **Primary sewage treatment** is a mechanical process that uses screens to filter out debris like sticks, stones, and rags; then suspended solids settle out as sludge in a sedimentation tank (Figure 20-24). These operations remove about 60% of suspended solids, 30% of oxygen-demanding wastes, 20% of nitrogen compounds, 10% of phosphorus compounds, and little or none of other chemical pollutants. Chemicals are sometimes added to speed up sedimentation.

Secondary sewage treatment is a biological process that uses aerobic bacteria to remove biodegradable organic wastes (Figure 20-25). It removes up to 90%

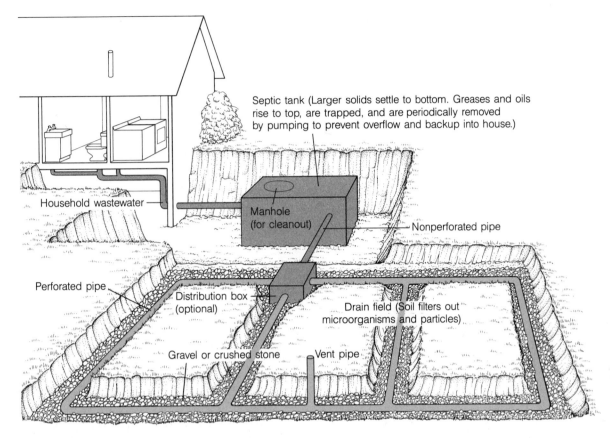

Figure 20-22 Septic tank system used for disposal of domestic sewage and wastewater in rural and suburban areas.

of the oxygen-demanding wastes by using either **trickling filters,** where aerobic bacteria degrade sewage as it seeps through a large vat bed filled with crushed stones covered with bacterial growths (Figure 20-26), or an **activated sludge process,** in which the sewage is pumped into a large tank and mixed for several hours with bacteria-rich sludge and air bubbles to increase bacterial degradation. The water then goes to a sedimentation tank, where most of the suspended solids settle out as sludge. The sludge is removed and then is broken down in an anaerobic digestor, disposed of by incineration, dumped in the ocean or a landfill, or applied to land as fertilizer.

The primary and secondary treatments combined still leave about 10% of the oxygen-demanding wastes, 10% of the suspended solids, 50% of the nitrogen (mostly as nitrates), 70% of the phosphorus (mostly as phosphates), 30% of most toxic metal compounds, 30% of most synthetic organic chemicals, and essentially all the long-lived radioactive isotopes and dissolved persistent organic substances such as some pesticides. In the United States, secondary treatment must be used in all communities served by sewage treatment plants. Preliminary experiments have shown that wastewater can also be purified by allowing it to flow slowly through long ponds filled with plants such as water hyacinths. These plants also remove toxic organic chemicals and metals, which are not removed by conventional primary and secondary treatment.

Tertiary sewage treatment is a series of specialized chemical and physical processes that reduce the quantity of specific pollutants still left after primary and secondary treatment (Figure 20-27). Types of tertiary treatment vary depending on the contaminants in specific communities and industries. The most common methods of tertiary treatment are precipitation (settling out as insoluble solids) to remove up to 90% of suspended solids and phosphates, filtration with activated carbon (finely powdered carbon) to remove dissolved organic compounds and any remaining suspended solids, and reverse osmosis by passage through a membrane to remove dissolved organic and inorganic substances. Tertiary treatment is rarely used, except in Sweden and Denmark, because the plants are roughly twice as expensive to build and four times as costly to operate as secondary plants.

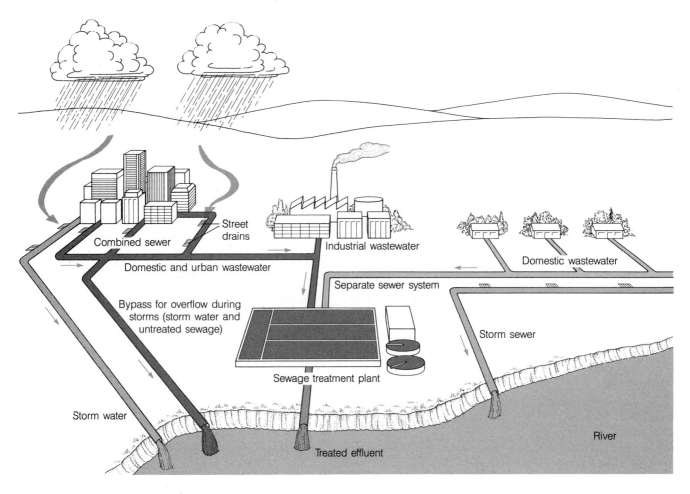

Figure 20-23 Separated and combined storm and sewer systems used in cities.

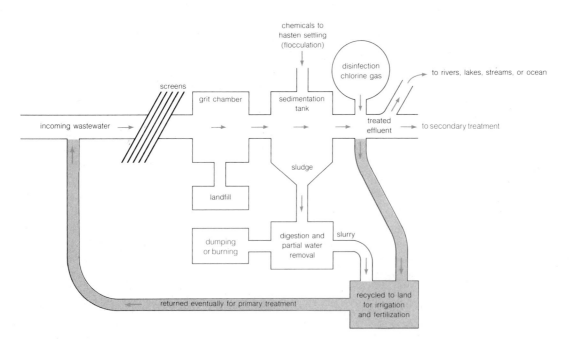

Figure 20-24 Primary sewage treatment. Shaded areas show recycling of plant nutrients in sludge and treated wastewater to land instead of discharge into surface waters.

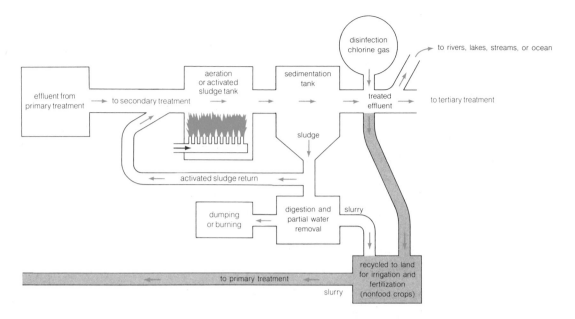

Figure 20-25 Secondary sewage treatment. Shaded areas show recycling of nutrients to land.

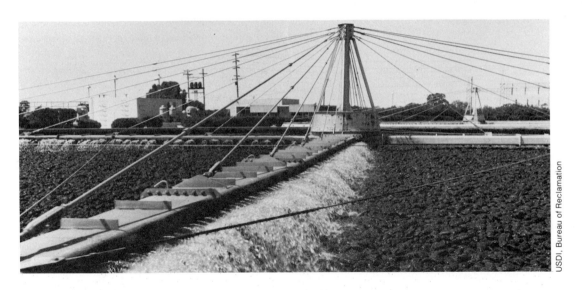

USDI, Bureau of Reclamation

Figure 20-26 Trickling filter used as part of secondary sewage treatment.

One of the last steps in any form of sewage treatment is to disinfect the water before it is discharged into nearby waterways or applied to land for further filtering and use as fertilizer. Disinfection removes water coloration and kills disease-carrying bacteria and some (but not all) viruses. The usual method is to add chlorine gas. A problem is that chlorine reacts with organic materials in the wastewater or in surface water to form small amounts of chlorinated hydrocarbons, some of which, such as chloroform, are known carcinogens. Consequently, several other disinfectants are being tested, and one of the leading contenders is ozone.

Ozone is more expensive than chlorine but is more effective against viruses.

Most large industrial plants have their own wastewater treatment facilities for primary and secondary, and if needed, tertiary treatment. The treated effluent is discharged into the nearest suitable surface water.

Alternatives to Large-Scale Treatment Plants Small-scale, **package sewage treatment plants** are sometimes used for secondary treatment of small quantities of wastes from shopping centers, apart-

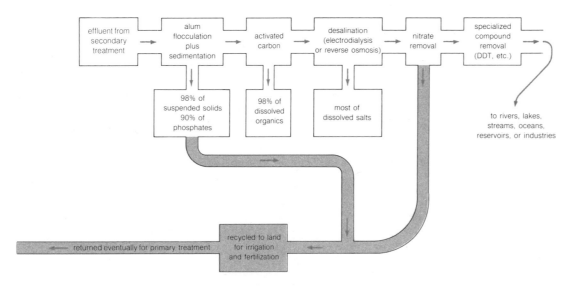

Figure 20-27 Tertiary sewage treatment. Shaded areas show recycling of nutrients to land.

ment complexes, villages, and small housing subdivisions. However, many of these do not work properly and require considerable attention and maintenance.

Some small rural villages and suburban developments where groundwater used for drinking is being polluted by large numbers of septic tanks have installed a small-diameter, gravity flow sewer system to link the septic tanks of all residences and carry wastewater to large soil-absorption drainage fields or beds of sand several feet thick. Such systems cost about one-third to one-half as much as conventional sewage treatment plants used in larger cities.

Purification of Drinking Water   Treatment of water for drinking by urban residents is much like wastewater treatment. The degree of treatment required varies with the purity of the water coming into the treatment plant. Areas depending on surface water usually store it in a reservoir for several days to improve clarity and taste by allowing the dissolved oxygen content to increase and suspended matter to settle out. The water is then pumped to a purification plant and given the degree of primary and secondary and, in some cases, tertiary treatment needed to meet federal drinking water standards. In areas with very pure sources of groundwater, little if any treatment is necessary.

Land Disposal of Sewage Effluent and Sludge
Building secondary sewage treatment plants throughout the United States is an important step in water pollution control, especially in reducing oxygen-

demanding wastes, suspended solids, and bacterial contamination. However, without more expensive tertiary treatment, sewage plant effluents can overload lakes and slow-moving rivers with phosphates and nitrates, triggering algae blooms and oxygen depletion. Sewage treatment also produces large volumes of sludge to be disposed of.

An alternative is to spray sewage plant effluent or untreated wastewater or to spread sludge as fertilizer to forestlands, parks, surface-mined lands, croplands, wetlands, and aquaculture ponds. By 1986 about 25% of all U.S. municipal sludge was returned to the land as fertilizer (Figure 20-28).

One problem with land disposal of wastewater and sludge is that bacteria, viruses, toxic metals, and hazardous synthetic, organic chemicals can contaminate food and groundwater. Several ways have been used to avoid or minimize the problem. Before it is applied, sludge can be heated to kill harmful bacteria, as is done in West Germany and Switzerland, or composted and allowed to decay. Sludge and wastewater can be treated to remove toxic metals and organic chemicals before application, or they can be applied only on land not used to grow crops or raise livestock, such as forests, surface-mined land, and highway medians in areas where groundwater is already contaminated or is not used as a source of drinking water. Land disposal is not a panacea, but with careful management and control it is a useful ecological approach to waste handling in some areas.

Individual Waste Management   As individuals we can reduce pollution of water by safely disposing of products containing harmful chemicals. They should

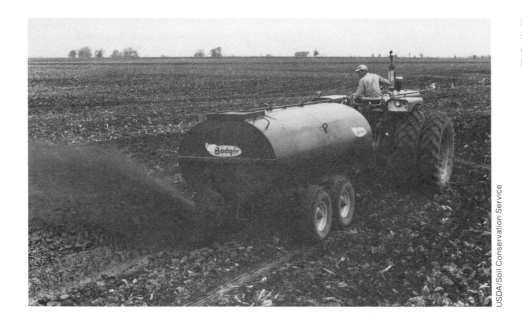

Figure 20-28 Use of treated sewage effluent as fertilizer on cropland near Monticello, Missouri.

never be poured down house or street drains or flushed down the toilet. Waste oil drained from automobiles should be put in a container and taken to a local service station, where it will be turned in for recycling. Antifreeze drained from motor vehicles should be collected and poured onto a porous surface, such as gravel, away from water supplies. Call your local health or water department for information about proper disposal of insecticides, herbicides, paints, lacquers, thinners, brush cleaners, wood preservatives, turpentine, and household cleaners containing organic solvents.

We can also reduce water pollution by using less water and by using low-phosphate or nonphosphate detergents and cleaners. Commercial inorganic fertilizers, pesticides, detergents, bleaches, and other chemicals should be used only if necessary and then in the smallest amounts possible (see Table 21-1, p. 509).

20-6 U.S. WATER POLLUTION CONTROL LAWS

Protecting Drinking Water Before 1974 the United States had no enforceable national standards for drinking water. Each state set its own standards, and these varied in range and rigor from state to state. This began changing with passage of the Safe Drinking Water Act of 1974, which required the EPA to establish national drinking water standards, called maximum contaminant levels (MCLs), for any pollutants that "may" have adverse effects on human health.

The law specifies that the levels set should prevent any known or anticipated adverse health effects with an adequate margin of safety. But it also specifies that these levels must be technically feasible taking cost into account. In conjunction with states and communities, the EPA is required to monitor water supplies to be sure standards are being met.

The first MCLs went into effect in 1977. By 1986 the EPA had set MCLs for 26 water pollutants, including 2 microbiological contaminants, 10 inorganic chemicals, 10 organic chemicals, and 4 radioisotopes. According to the EPA, 87% of the country's 59,000 municipal water systems were in compliance with these MCLs in 1985.

Environmentalists and health officials, however, have criticized the EPA for not setting MCLs for more of at least 700 potential pollutants found in municipal drinking water supplies. Amendments added to the Safe Drinking Water Act in 1986 require the EPA to set MCLs for 83 new contaminants by 1989 and for 25 more by 1991. The act also designates the use of granular activated carbon for removal of synthetic organic chemicals, requires disinfection for all public water supplies, bans the use of lead pipe and solder in any new public water system, and requires the EPA to establish regulations for monitoring deep waste-injection wells.

Wells for millions of individual homes in suburban and rural areas are not required to meet federal drinking water standards, primarily because of the cost (at least $1,000) of testing each well regularly and because of political problems associated with verifying individual compliance. A study conducted for the EPA by Cornell University scientists in 1982 indicated that 39 million rural residents—two out of three of all rural

Americans—were drinking water from private wells that did not meet one or more federal water quality standards.

Contaminated wells and concern about possible contamination of public drinking water supplies has led about 1 out of every 20 Americans to drink bottled water at an average cost of $1 a gallon. Bottled water is regulated by the Food and Drug Administration (FDA) based on standards that are required to be equivalent to EPA standards for drinking water. However, the FDA does little testing of bottled water and generally relies on tests by the bottled water industry. Furthermore, there is no assurance that such water won't contain synthetic organic chemicals and other chemicals not regulated by EPA standards.

Most activated-charcoal filter units (costing from $500 to $2,500) for attachment under home sinks remove most synthetic organic chemicals if filters are changed regularly. But they are not effective in removing bacteria, viruses, and toxic metals. Filter units that contain "bacteriocides" prevent bacteria from building up in the filter only—not in the water. Coupling of a reverse osmosis system (costing from $500 to $1,000) with an activated-charcoal filter removes just about all pollutants if both systems are properly maintained at a cost of about $100 a year.

U.S. Control Efforts   The Federal Water Pollution Act of 1972 and the Clean Water Act of 1977, along with amendments in 1981 and 1987 (passed after Congress overrode a veto by President Reagan), form the basis of U.S. water pollution control efforts, with the goals of making all U.S. surface waters safe for fishing and swimming. These acts require the EPA to establish national effluent standards limiting the amounts of conventional and toxic water pollutants that can be discharged into surface waters from factories, sewage treatment plants, and other point sources and to set up a nationwide system for monitoring water quality. All municipalities are required to use secondary sewage treatment by 1988—a deadline that will not be met in a number of areas.

Between 1972 and 1986 the federal government provided almost $45 billion to municipalities for the construction, operation, and maintenance of municipal wastewater treatment facilities. State and local governments provided an additional $15 billion in matching grants for these purposes. Amendments to the Clean Water Act in 1987 authorized expenditure of an additional $18 billion between 1987 and 1996.

By 1986 about 67% of the country's municipalities had completed the construction needed to ensure full compliance with national effluent limits, and only 12% of the municipalities where construction had been completed were still in significant noncompliance. The failure of almost one-third of the country's municipalities to complete construction by 1986 is attributed to fraud, overbuilding, bureaucratic and construction delays, and a 37% cut in federal funding for water pollution control between 1981 and 1986 by the Reagan administration.

By 1986 an impressive 94% of all industrial dischargers were officially in compliance with their discharge permits. However, a 1984 study by the General Accounting Office showed that most of the 33 industries studied violated their EPA waste discharge permits; the GAO accused the EPA of doing little to enforce compliance of water pollution control laws.

These water pollution control laws also require states to establish local and regional planning to reduce water pollution from nonpoint sources. But no goals and standards have been established, and relatively little funding has been provided to reduce water pollution from nonpoint sources. The country also has no comprehensive legislation, goals, or funding designed to protect its groundwater supplies from contamination.

Future Water Quality Goals   Since 1972 improved control of discharges of oxygen-demanding wastes from point sources has meant that about 75% of the country's monitored areas of rivers and lakes are fishable and swimmable. Environmentalists believe that future water pollution control efforts in the United States should be focused on three major goals. First, existing legislation controlling the discharge of conventional and toxic pollutants into surface waters from point sources should be strictly enforced and not weakened. Second, new legislation should be enacted and funded to establish national goals and regulations for sharply reducing runoff of conventional and toxic pollutants into surface waters from nonpoint sources. Finally, comprehensive and well-funded legislation should be enacted to protect the country's groundwater drinking supplies from pollution by point and nonpoint sources.

The reason we have water pollution is not basically the paper or pulp mills. It is, rather, the social side of humans—our unwillingness to support reform government, to place into office the best-qualified candidates, to keep in office the best talent, and to see to it that legislation both evolves from and inspires wise social planning with a human orientation.

Stewart L. Udall

Importance of the Great Lakes

The five interconnected Great Lakes are the largest surface body of fresh water on earth, stretching from Duluth, Minnesota, to the St. Lawrence River between the industrial heartlands of the United States and Canada (Figure 20-29). These lakes play a key role in both the American and Canadian economies by serving as an important conduit for iron ores from the mines of Duluth to the steel mills of Gary, Indiana, and grain from the nation's breadbasket to the Mississippi and St. Lawrence Rivers for distribution and export. The lakes also support profitable recreational and fishing industries.

The massive Great Lakes watershed contains thousands of industries and over 60 million people—one-third of Canada's population and one-eighth of the U.S. population. The lakes also serve as a source of drinking water for 24 million people.

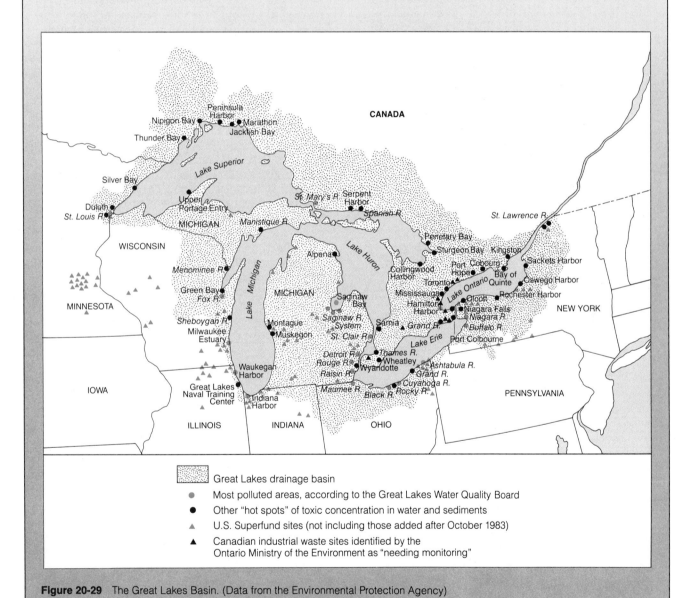

Figure 20-29   The Great Lakes Basin. (Data from the Environmental Protection Agency)

Sensitivity to Pollution

The Great Lakes are a massive sink for toxic industrial wastes and runoff of pesticides, plant nutrients, and sediment from urban and agricultural areas. Despite their massive size, the lakes are especially sensitive to pollution from point and nonpoint sources throughout their vast drainage basin because only 1% of the water entering them flows out at the St. Lawrence River in any single year.

During the 1950s and 1960s billions of gallons of untreated sewage along with toxic industrial and agricultural wastes were discharged into the Great Lakes. Scientists and officials had little concern for any harmful effects, believing that dilution is the solution to pollution. By the 1960s many areas of the lakes were suffering from severe cultural eutrophication, massive fish kills, and contamination with bacteria and other wastes, forcing the closing of many bathing beaches and severely reducing commercial and sport fishing.

Although all five lakes were affected, the impact on Lake Erie was particularly intense. It is the shallowest of the Great Lakes, has the smallest volume of water, and its drainage basin is heavily industrialized and contains the largest population of any of the lakes. At one time in the mid-1960s, massive algae blooms choked off oxygen to 65% of the lake's bottom, and populations of many of its most desirable species of commercial and game fish were sharply reduced. The press reported that Lake Erie was dying. Although many of its fish and other aerobic aquatic organisms died out, its main problem was that it was alive with too much plant life such as blue-green algae. Lake Ontario's small size and shallowness also make it susceptible to cultural eutrophication and other forms of water pollution.

Cleanup Efforts

Since 1972 a joint $15 billion pollution control program by Canada and the United States has led to significant decreases in levels of phosphates, coliform bacteria, and many toxic industrial chemicals along with decreases in algal blooms and increases in dissolved oxygen, aquatic life, and sport and commercial fishing. The rate of cultural eutrophication has been slowed in most areas, and even reversed in some areas; all the lakes, except Erie and Ontario, met joint U.S. and Canadian goals for reduction in phosphorus levels by 1986. Only 8 of 516 swimming beaches remained closed because of pollution by 1986. These accomplishments were mainly the result of decreases in discharges from point sources brought about by building and upgrading sewage treatment plants, improving treatment of industrial wastes, and banning or limiting the amount of phosphate in detergents, household cleaners, and water conditioners in many areas of the Great Lakes drainage basin.

Major Remaining Problems

Despite these improvements, runoff of phosphates from nonpoint sources is still a problem in some areas. The most serious problem, however, is contamination from toxic wastes that enter the lakes from atmospheric deposition, runoff from poorly constructed toxic waste dumps and landfills, accidental spills, industries and sewage treatment plants not in compliance with government water pollution standards, and dredging of contaminated harbor sediments. Most "toxic hot spots" are in harbors or near the mouths of tributaries emptying into the lakes, especially Lake Erie and Lake Ontario (Figure 20-29).

Many Great Lakes area residents are concerned both about the safety of eating Great Lakes fish and about supplies of drinking water obtained from the lake. Scientists are particularly concerned about the health effects of eating large fish that have become contaminated with large concentrations of persistent and fat-soluble chemicals such as PCBs (80% of which are deposited from the atmosphere), some pesticides, and mercury compounds as a result of biological amplification. It is estimated, for example, that a person would have to drink Great Lakes water for 1,000 years to receive as much PCB as from eating a pound of PCB-contaminated fish. The risk is particularly severe for unborn children and nursing infants who can receive dangerous levels of such chemicals from mothers who consume contaminated fish.

Scientists consider parts of Lake Ontario to be the most seriously polluted portions of the Great Lakes. Hazardous waste dumps lie at both ends. Four-fifths of its water comes from the heavily polluted Niagara River, which receives more than half of its toxic wastes from 160 dumps located within three miles of the river. About 90% of these wastes come from the American side of the river. Residents of Toronto, Canada, are drinking more bottled water after the discovery of over 50 potentially hazardous chemicals in the city's drinking water, drawn from Lake Ontario. Significant progress has been made in reducing pollution of the Great Lakes, but more remains to be done.

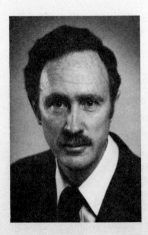

Philip R. Pryde

Philip R. Pryde is a specialist on land use planning, water resources, energy resources, and environmental impact analysis in the Department of Geography at San Diego State University. He is also the leading U.S. expert on environmental problems and resource conservation in the USSR. He serves on the San Diego County Planning Commission and the San Diego Growth Management Review Task Force, and he is director of the San Diego County Water Authority. In addition to numerous articles, he is author of Nonconventional Energy Resources *(Wiley, 1983) and* Conservation in the Soviet Union *(Cambridge University Press, 1972).*

Lake Baikal is perhaps the most remarkable lake in the world. It is located in the Soviet Union just north of the border with Mongolia and is the most voluminous body of fresh water in the world. At 1,620 meters (5,311 feet), it is also the deepest. It stretches for approximately 700 kilometers (435 miles) between steep mountain ranges, in a geological depression called a *graben*. The faults that produced the graben also subject the entire region to severe earthquakes.

However, the lake's uniqueness is not limited to just its size. In Lake Baikal's unusually clear waters can be found about 600 species of plants and about 1,200 species of animal life. About three-quarters of these species occur nowhere else on earth. Among them are the world's only freshwater seal and freshwater sponge. Because of its uniqueness and scientific value, controversy over the potential pollution of Lake Baikal has drawn considerable interest, not just within the Soviet Union, but throughout the world.

Timber cutting and small industrial facilities have existed in the Lake Baikal basin for decades. But in the 1960s, plans were prepared for two new wood-processing plants to be constructed on its shores. To keep them supplied with timber, large increases were planned in the logging activities on the surrounding mountain slopes, which would not only be an eyesore but could also result in considerable soil erosion.

Wood-processing plants of the type proposed inherently produce large amounts of potential water pollutants. A debate began almost immediately over whether the proposed wastewater treatment plants at the two factories would be adequate to preserve the quality of Lake Baikal's waters. This debate was noteworthy, as it was the first major environmental issue to be widely publicized in the Soviet press.

Despite the pleas of many leading Soviet scientists, artists, and writers, there was never any real likelihood that the plans for the factories would be abandoned. The most feasible goal of the protesters was to ensure that the highest possible degree of protection would be provided for the lake. And indeed, in addition to more advanced wastewater treatment plants, several other safeguards to protect the lake were adopted.

First, it was agreed that in the event of serious pollution from the plant at the south end of the lake, a pipeline would be built to divert the effluents away from it and into a nearby river which does not drain into the lake. A special decree was passed on the need to protect Lake Baikal, and a commission was appointed to monitor water quality in the lake. A later decision required that the wood pulp manufactured by the plants be transported to other industrial centers for processing to prevent further addition of pollutants to Lake Baikal. Finally, natural reserves and other types of protected areas have been established around the lake.

As a result of all this controversy, planning, and replanning, can we feel confident that Lake Baikal has been saved from pollution? Unfortunately, the differences of opinion go on. The industrial planners continue to defend their operations, claiming no serious harm has come to the lake, that the treatment facilities are adequate, and that the lake itself can act as a purifier of pollutants.

But the chief Soviet scientist in charge of protecting the lake stated in the early 1980s that he still had serious doubts that the steps taken were sufficient. The problem is that even a small amount of pollution, an amount that might be acceptable in an ordinary lake or river, could do irreversible harm in such a unique water body as Lake Baikal. Not all of the pollutants discharged into the lake are biodegradable and some are highly toxic. Further, it is known that wastewater purification facilities at the wood-processing plants have been closed down on more than one occasion for improvements.

Thus, after decades of controversy, Lake Baikal's amazing storehouse of biotic treasures, including many that are quite rare, must still be viewed as possibly in jeopardy. The Lake Baikal saga shows clearly that environmental pollution is a worldwide phenomenon inherent in any country experiencing large-scale industrial development. Its cure involves a combination of increased funding for improved pollution abatement facilities and the political determination to see that they are used effectively.

Guest Essay Discussion

1. Should it be forbidden to construct any additional industrial activities around Lake Baikal? Why or why not?
2. Can you think of any important bodies of water in the United States, perhaps in your state, that have problems similar to Lake Baikal? What is being done about these problems?

CHAPTER SUMMARY

Water pollution comes from *point sources* such as industries and sewage treatment plants at specific and usually easily identifiable locations and from scattered and more diffuse *nonpoint sources* such as crop fields and urban and surburban lands. The major types of water pollutants are disease-causing agents, oxygen-demanding wastes, water-soluble inorganic chemicals, inorganic plant nutrients (mostly nitrates and phosphates), insoluble and water-soluble organic chemicals, sediment, radioactive substances, and heat. Tests used to determine water quality include coliform bacteria counts to indicate the presence of disease-causing agents, measurements of dissolved oxygen (DO) content and biological oxygen demand (BOD) for oxygen-demanding wastes, and specific chemical tests for various inorganic and organic compounds.

Disease-causing agents (pathogens) and trace amounts of various toxic organic and inorganic compounds and radioactive substances are the major threats to human health. Fish and other forms of aquatic animals can be damaged or killed by an excess of oxygen-demanding wastes and plant nutrients (which can deplete dissolved oxygen), various organic and inorganic chemicals, sediment, and heat. Economic losses occur when water is too polluted to be used for fishing, boating, or swimming.

Concentrations of pollutants entering surface waters such as rivers, lakes, and oceans can be decreased by *dilution*, *biodegradation* (oxygen-demanding wastes), and *sedimentation* (settling out). These natural cleaning processes work much better in large, fast-flowing rivers than in slow-flowing rivers and lakes but can be overloaded in any body of water by excessive waste inputs. Concentrations of some persistent and fat-soluble substances such as DDT, PCBs, and some toxic mercury compounds can be increased through *biological amplification* in aquatic food webs.

Treatment of sewage and industrial wastes has reduced point source inputs of many pollutants—especially oxygen-demanding wastes—into many rivers and lakes in the U.S. and other MDCs. Most rivers and lakes near population centers in LDCs, however, receive massive loads of untreated sewage and industrial wastes. Contamination with toxic metals and synthetic organic chemicals is a major problem in many rivers and lakes in the U.S. and other MDCs. Many lakes and reservoirs located near urban and agricultural areas in the U.S. and other MDCs suffer from *cultural eutrophication*—explosive growths of algae and other aquatic plants that deplete dissolved oxygen when they die and decay—caused by massive inputs of nitrate and phosphate plant nutrients. Slow-moving rivers and lakes can also suffer from oxygen depletion and fish kills from *thermal pollution*—large inputs of heated water used to cool electric power and industrial plants.

Vast quantities of waste materials flow or are dumped into the oceans and are especially damaging to aquatic life around their edges in estuaries, wetlands, and small inland seas. Large quantities of sewage sludge containing toxic metals, organic compounds, and low-level radioactive wastes are dumped into the ocean with unknown long-term consequences. Fish, shellfish, and diving birds can be killed and beaches can be contaminated by oil reaching the ocean from urban and river runoff, routine discharges by tankers and refineries, and occasional tanker accidents and blowouts of offshore oil rigs.

A serious and growing water pollution problem is contamination of groundwater that serves as a source of drinking water for 50% of the U.S. population. Dilution, dispersion, and biodegradation of wastes are not very effective in groundwater because of its slow flow and lack of aerobic bacteria; thus, a contaminated aquifer remains that way for decades to centuries. Because cleanup of a contaminated aquifer is usually too costly, pollutants must be prevented from entering groundwater from point and nonpoint sources. At present, the U.S. has no comprehensive program for protecting its vital groundwater resources from pollution.

Waterborne wastes from households, industries, and businesses are collected by sewer systems and sent to sewage treatment plants for *primary and secondary treatment* and, in some cases, more advanced *tertiary treatment*. The solids or sludge removed from treated sewage can be disposed of by incineration or dumping in the ocean or a landfill. With proper precautions it can also be applied to land as a fertilizer. Household wastes in rural areas can be filtered and biodegraded in soil through the use of *septic tank systems*. Water drawn from surface water or groundwater sources can also be purified by similar treatment at water treatment plants. Such practices are widely used in MDCs but not in LDCs.

Since 1972 the U.S. and most MDCs have passed laws requiring municipalities and industries to install facilities for the secondary treatment of household and industrial wastewater and purification of drinking water in order to meet certain national standards. In the U.S. this control of discharges from point sources has prevented deterioration of most of the country's rivers and lakes in terms of dissolved oxygen and loss of aquatic life. However, little attention and funding have been devoted to reducing runoff of conventional and toxic pollutants into surface waters from nonpoint sources and to protecting groundwater drinking supplies from pollution by point and nonpoint sources.

DISCUSSION TOPICS

1. How would you control **(a)** nondegradable pollutants, **(b)** slowly degradable (persistent) pollutants, and **(c)** rapidly degradable (nonpersistent) pollutants?

2. Explain why dilution is not always the solution to water pollution. Cite examples and conditions for which this solution is, and is not, applicable.

3. Explain how a river can cleanse itself of oxygen-demanding wastes. Under what conditions will this natural cleansing system fail?

4. Give your reasons for agreeing or disagreeing with the idea that we should deliberately dump most of our wastes in the ocean because it is a vast sink for diluting, dispersing, and degrading wastes, and if it becomes polluted, we can get food from other sources.

5. Should all dumping of wastes in the ocean be banned? Explain. If so, where would you put these wastes? What exceptions, if any, would you permit? Under what circumstances? Explain why banning ocean dumping alone will not stop ocean pollution.

6. Contact local officials to find out the source of drinking water in your area. How is it treated? Has it been analyzed recently for the presence of synthetic organic chemicals, especially chlorinated hydrocarbons? If so, were any found and are they being removed?

7. Contact local officials to determine whether during the past ten years any swimming areas in your area have been closed because of high coliform bacteria counts. How often are swimming areas tested for coliform bacteria?

8. What are the major nonpoint sources of contamination of surface water and groundwater in your area?

9. Should the injection of hazardous wastes into deep underground wells be banned? Explain.

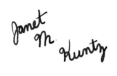

21

Solid Waste and Hazardous Waste

GENERAL OBJECTIVES

1. How much urban solid waste is produced in the United States?

2. What options do we have for dealing with this waste?

3. How can we recover some of the valuable resources in this waste?

4. What are the major types, sources, and effects of the hazardous waste we produce?

5. What can we do with hazardous waste?

6. What are some important examples of hazardous waste?

The shift from a throwaway society to a recycling one can help restore a broad-based gain in living standards.

Lester R. Brown and Edward C. Wolf

Since 1970 air and water quality in the United States have improved—or at least not worsened—in most areas. But these improvements have resulted in large quantities of solid waste, such as fly ash removed from smokestack exhaust and toxic sludge removed from wastewater at sewage treatment plants. To this increasing volume of waste are added massive quantities of other solid and hazardous wastes produced every day by individuals, businesses, and factories in our throwaway society. Complicating matters even further are the highly toxic wastes disposed of in thousands of land dump sites before environmental laws were passed—and now threatening the health and lives of entire communities. Thus, the control and management of solid and hazardous waste is one of our most urgent environmental problems.

21-1 SOLID WASTE PRODUCTION IN THE UNITED STATES

What Is Solid Waste and How Much Is Produced? Any useless, unwanted, or discarded material that is not a liquid or a gas is classified as **solid waste.** It is yesterday's newspaper and junk mail, today's dinner scraps, raked leaves and grass clippings, nonreturnable bottles and cans, worn-out appliances and furniture, abandoned cars, animal manure, crop residues, food-processing wastes, sewage sludge, fly ash, mining and industrial wastes, and an array of other cast-off materials.

The total amount of solid waste from all sources produced each year in the United States is staggering—estimated to be at least 4.6 billion metric tons (5.1 billion tons). This amounts to an average of 19 metric tons (21 tons) a year for each American, or 53 kilograms (115 pounds) a day. About 89% of this solid

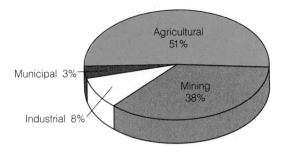

Figure 21-1 Sources of solid waste in the United States. (Data from the Environmental Protection Agency)

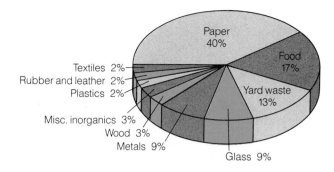

Figure 21-2 Composition of the approximately 1.8 kilograms (4 pounds) of urban solid waste thrown away in a typical day by each American. (Data from National Solid Wastes Management Association)

waste is produced as a result of agricultural and mining activities (Figure 21-1). Over half the country's solid waste consists of animal manure, crop residues, and other by-products of agriculture. Fortunately, over 90% of these wastes are recycled into the soil by being plowed under or used as fertilizer (manure). But much of what remains is an important nonpoint source of water pollution (Section 20-1).

The second largest category of solid waste consists of piles of rock, dirt, sand, and slag left behind from the mining and processing of energy resources and nonfuel mineral resources. With the implementation of the Surface Mining Act, some mining wastes are being recycled as strip-mined lands are returned to their original contour and replanted. However, piles of mining waste still pollute surface and groundwater through runoff and leaching, as well as contaminating the atmosphere when winds blow particulate matter into the air.

Industrial solid waste makes up about 8% of the total produced each year. Much of this is scrap metal, plastics, slag, paper, fly ash from electrical power plants, and sludge from sewage treatment plants. In 1985 an average of 3.2 metric tons (3.5 tons) of fly ash and 400 kilograms (880 pounds) of sewage sludge were produced per person in the United States. These two categories of industrial solid waste will increase even more rapidly as more coal-burning plants are built, as older plants are required to install air pollution control equipment, and as sewage plants that are now under construction or are still being planned are put into operation.

Urban solid waste produced by homes and businesses in or near urban areas makes up the remaining 3% of the solid waste produced in the United States. Each American produces an average of about 1.8 kilograms (4 pounds) per day, or 657 kilograms (1,460 pounds) per year. About 70% of what the typical American throws away as garbage and rubbish consists of paper, food, and yard waste (Figure 21-2). Because this solid waste is concentrated in highly populated areas, it must be removed quickly and efficiently to prevent health problems, infestation by rats and other disease-carrying organisms, and buildup of massive piles of unsightly trash.

Strategies for Dealing with Solid Waste There are three major ways to deal with solid waste: throwaway output approaches, resource recovery output approaches, and input approaches. Today we rely primarily on *throwaway output approaches* to dump these wastes in the ocean (Section 20-3) or on the land or to burn them in incinerators. Environmentalists, however, believe we should begin shifting from this throwaway approach (Figure 3-18, p. 65) to a sustainable-earth or low-waste approach (Figure 3-19, p. 66). With this approach most of the things we throw away would not be viewed as solid wastes but as wasted solids, which should be reused, recycled, or burned to provide energy. Even hazardous solid materials produced by one industry can often be sold as raw materials to another industry or detoxified and converted to useful materials.

This *resource recovery output approach* can be coupled with *input approaches* designed to produce less solid waste. Examples include reducing average per capita consumption by wasting fewer resources and buying things we really need rather than merely want, increasing the average lifetime of products, decreasing the amount of material used in some products (smaller cars, for example), and designing products for easier repair, reuse, and recycling (Section 15-5).

Because solid waste from agricultural, mining, and industrial activities is discussed elsewhere in this book, the next two sections of this chapter are devoted to evaluating the throwaway output and resource recovery strategies for dealing with urban solid waste.

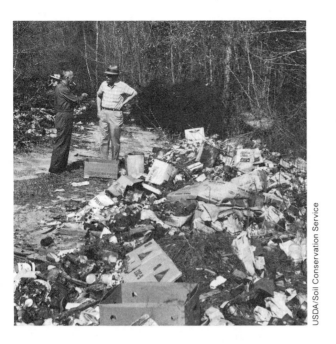

Figure 21-3 An unsightly and illegal roadside dump.

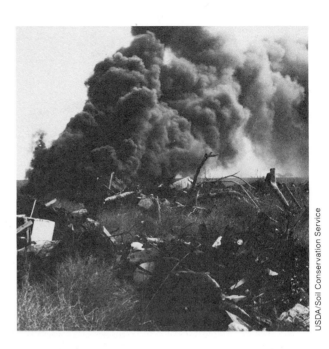

Figure 21-4 Burning of solid waste at an open dump near Ralls, Texas. This practice pollutes the air and is now banned, but it is still done illegally in some places.

21-2 DISPOSAL OF URBAN SOLID WASTE: DUMP, BURY, BURN, OR COMPOST?

Littering and Open Dumps Some people are litterbugs who get rid of their solid waste by throwing bottles, cans, fast-food containers, and other items on the street or out of car windows. In addition to creating visual pollution, this adds to the taxpayers' burden because collecting widely dispersed litter is very expensive. Although it is illegal, some people in rural areas, who must dispose of their own trash, dump it along roadsides rather than haul it to dumpster locations or county landfills (Figure 21-3).

In cities and suburban areas, solid waste from residences and commercial establishments is put in dumpsters, garbage bags, or cans for pickup. Most people don't care what happens to this trash as long as they don't have to smell it, see it, or pay too much to have it taken away—out of sight, out of mind. In 1986 Americans spent about $10 billion to have this urban waste collected and disposed of by local sanitation departments or privately owned services. Between 1975 and 1986, average urban waste collection and disposal costs doubled and are continuing to rise as many urban areas run out of convenient places to dispose of their refuse and have to haul it farther or find other alternatives.

Before passage of the 1976 Resource Conservation and Recovery Act (RCRA), most urban solid waste was merely dumped on the ground at selected sites—sometimes ecologically valuable wetlands and marshes.

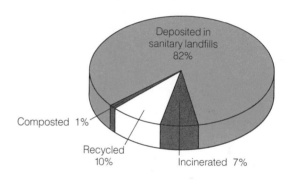

Figure 21-5 Fate of solid waste in the United States. (Data from the Environmental Protection Agency)

These unsightly **open dumps** supported large populations of disease-carrying rodents and insects and often contaminated groundwater and surface water through leaching and runoff. The dumps also created air pollution when they caught on fire from spontaneous combustion or when they were set on fire to reduce the volume of wastes (Figure 21-4). The RCRA, however, required that all existing open dumps in the United States be closed or upgraded to sanitary landfills by 1983 and banned the creation of new open dumps.

Sanitary Landfills Currently 82% of the urban solid waste collected in the United States is deposited in sanitary landfills. The remainder is burned in municipal incinerators, recycled, or composted (Figure 21-5). A **sanitary landfill** is a land waste disposal site

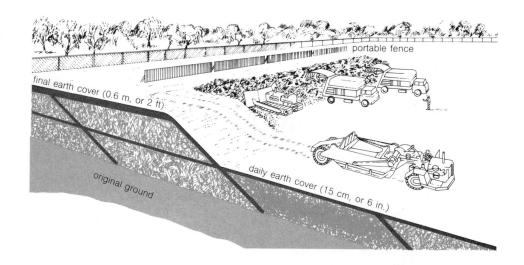

Figure 21-6 A sanitary landfill. Wastes are spread in a thin layer and then compacted with a bulldozer. A scraper (foreground) covers the wastes with a fresh layer of soil at the end of each day. Portable fences are used to catch and hold windblown debris.

portable fence

final earth cover (0.6 m, or 2 ft)

original ground

daily earth cover (15 cm, or 6 in.)

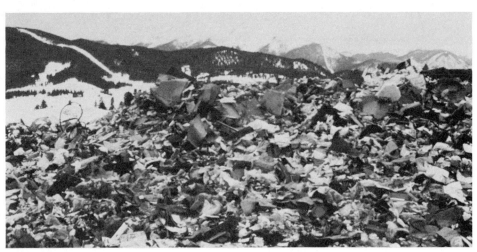

Figure 21-7 A mountain of solid waste is deposited in a sanitary landfill each day before it is covered with soil.

that eliminates most of the problems associated with open dumps by spreading waste in thin layers, compacting it, and covering it with a fresh layer of soil each day (Figure 21-6). No open burning is allowed, odor is seldom a problem, and rodents and insects cannot thrive. In addition, sanitary landfills are supposed to be situated so as to minimize water pollution from runoff and leaching.

A landfill can be put into operation fairly quickly, has low operating costs, and can handle a massive amount of solid waste (Figure 21-7). Some landfills are created by digging out an area and then refilling it with successive layers of trash and earth. Others involve filling in natural valleys, canyons, or abandoned mining pits and stone quarries. In areas where the water table is too close to the surface for excavation, successive layers of compacted waste and dirt can be built up to form a large hill, which is then contoured and vegetated to prevent erosion once it becomes too high for further use. In some large landfills a pipe system can be inserted underground to collect methane gas

produced by the anaerobic decomposition of organic waste; the gas can then be used as fuel. At a large landfill on Staten Island in New York City, enough methane gas is collected to heat 10,000 homes a year.

Once a landfill is filled, it is allowed to settle for a few years. Although a filled and settled landfill is not a suitable building site, it can be regraded and used as a site for a park, golf course, athletic field, wildlife area, or other recreational purposes (Figure 21-8). For example, filled landfills are used as sites for an amphitheater in Virginia Beach, Virginia (the site is known as Mt. Trashmore), and the Mile High Stadium in Denver; a landfill in Evanston, Illinois, is now a recreational area with sledding hills, tennis courts, and a baseball diamond.

Landfills do have some drawbacks. Wind can scatter litter and dust during the day before each day's load of trash is covered with soil. There is a danger that explosive methane gas and toxic hydrogen sulfide gas, produced by anaerobic decomposition, can seep into nearby buildings and cause explosions or asphyxi-

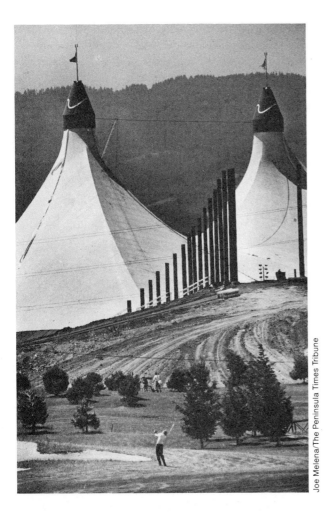

Figure 21-8 This entertainment center in Mountain View, California, was once a landfill.

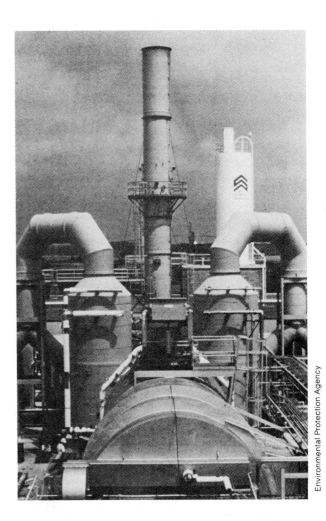

Figure 21-9 Main combustion chamber of a Chicago incinerator. There is a scrubber tower on each side to remove air pollutants.

ation. If located near buildings, the landfills must be equipped with vent pipes to collect these gases so they can be burned or allowed to escape into the air. In addition to saving energy, collecting and burning methane gas from all landfills worldwide would reduce annual atmospheric emissions of methane by 6% to 18%. This factor would significantly help to reduce depletion of the ozone layer and global warming from greenhouse gases (Section 19-5).

Contamination of groundwater is a potential problem without proper siting, construction, and monitoring. This is especially true for thousands of older landfills filled and abandoned before stricter landfill siting and operating regulations were established. To reduce this hazard, since 1983 the EPA has required that all sanitary landfills have a synthetic liner, a cap of clay or plastic, and a leachate system to collect water that seeps through waste. This contaminated water is then hauled or pumped to a sewage treatment system. The groundwater in the vicinity of the landfill is to be checked frequently to determine whether it

has been contaminated from leaks in the landfill liner. Studies have shown, however, that enforcement of these regulations by states and local communities is often lax.

Even if it is eventually converted to a useful purpose, most people do not want a landfill nearby because of the traffic, noise, and dust that are inevitable during the years the landfill is being filled. Because of citizen opposition, escalating land prices, and lack of environmentally acceptable sites, more than half of the cities in the United States will exhaust their present landfill capacity and run out of acceptable new sites by 1990.

Incineration Another way to deal with solid waste is to burn combustible materials and melt certain noncombustible materials in municipal incinerators (Figure 21-9). The ash or residue left after incineration can then be deposited in landfills or in the ocean. Incineration kills disease-carrying organisms and reduces the volume of solid waste by 80% to 90%. Salvaged metals and glass can generate income, and the waste energy can be used to produce electricity or heat for nearby buildings. Incinerators do not pollute groundwater and add very little air pollution if equipped with adequate air pollution control devices, which are required by present environmental laws.

However, construction, maintenance, and operating costs are much higher for incinerators than for landfills, except in areas where land prices are high or waste must be hauled long distances to the landfills. Appropriate incinerator sites are difficult to find because of citizen opposition. But as urban areas run out of acceptable landfills, incineration will become more economically attractive. By the end of this century incinerators are projected to be burning 30% of the country's trash, compared to 7% today. Existing and new incinerators, however, will have to be equipped with more effective air pollution control devices to reduce emissions of particles of toxic metals and their compounds and highly toxic dioxins formed during incineration (see Enrichment Study at the end of this chapter). Sweden, which burns half its solid waste, now requires such controls after high levels of dioxins turned up in crabmeat and mother's milk. Even with air pollution control devices, incinerators emit large quantities of fine particulate matter.

In addition, for every ten tons of municipal waste fed into an incinerator, one ton of ash is produced. This ash is usually contaminated with toxic metals and dioxins and may soon be classified as hazardous waste by the EPA. By 1986, Ohio, Maine, and California had passed laws restricting the disposal of incinerator ash in sanitary landfills. Disposal of these wastes at hazardous waste facilities costs about 15 times more than their disposal at sanitary landfills. Such restrictions, along with more effective air pollution controls, may make incineration—already the most costly method of solid waste management—too expensive for widespread use in the United States.

Composting   Biodegradable solid waste from slaughterhouses, food-processing industries, and kitchens can be mixed with soil and decomposed by aerobic bacteric to produce a material known as **compost,** which can be used as a soil conditioner and fertilizer. Kitchen waste, paper, leaves, and grass clippings can be decomposed in backyard compost heaps and used in gardens and flower beds. With food processing and other industries, the large supply of organic waste can be collected and degraded in large composting plants, as is done in many European countries such as the Netherlands, West Germany, and Italy. The compost is then bagged and sold.

Composting, however, has some drawbacks. It is not economically feasible with mixed urban waste because sorting out the glass, metals, and plastics is too expensive. Thus, composting requires that consumers and plants separate food and yard waste for collection. In some countries, such as the United States, the demand for compost is not great enough to justify its large-scale production.

21-3   RESOURCE RECOVERY FROM SOLID WASTE

The High-Technology Approach   By various methods of **resource recovery,** usable materials or energy can be salvaged from solid waste. Whether most resources should be recycled by a centralized high-technology approach or by a decentralized low-technology approach is the subject of debate. In the ideal high-technology approach, large, centralized **resource recovery plants** would shred and automatically separate mixed urban waste to recover glass, iron, aluminum, and other valuable materials, which would be sold to manufacturing industries for recycling (Figure 21-10). The remaining paper, plastics, and other combustible wastes would be incinerated to produce steam, hot water, or electricity, which could then be used in municipal facilities or sold to nearby buildings and manufacturing plants. The incinerator residue, including particulates removed to prevent air pollution, could be used as landfill to reclaim damaged land or processed into cinder blocks, bricks, or other building materials.

By 1986, the United States had 65 resource recovery plants and at least 100 others were under construction or in the planning stage. Although a few of these plants separate and recover some iron, aluminum, and glass for recycling, most are sophisticated incinerators used to produce energy by burning trash. Hundreds of such energy resource recovery plants are in operation in European and Japanese cities. Denmark uses incinerator plants to convert about 60% of its burnable waste to energy, Sweden 50%, Switzerland 40%, and the Netherlands 30%—compared to only 7% in the United States.

Unlike their European counterparts, most U.S. energy resource recovery plants have been a bitter disappointment. They have been expensive to build ($50 million to $500 million per plant) and have suffered from delays, breakdowns, high operating and maintenance costs, lack of enough daily waste for economical operation, and continuing financial losses. They also cause air pollution if not properly controlled and maintained.

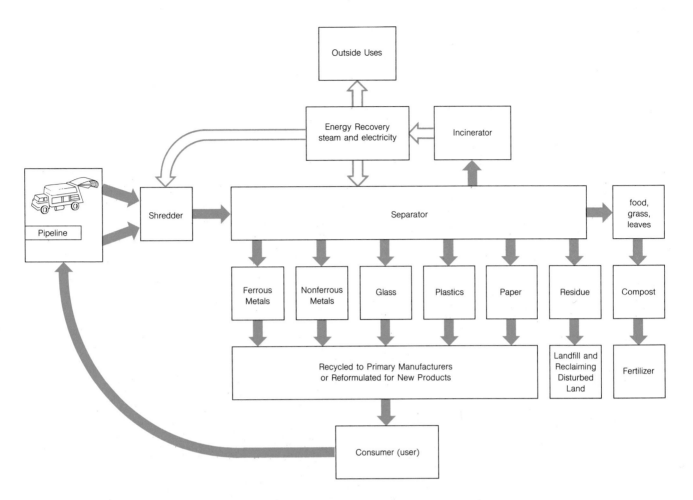

Figure 21-10 Generalized urban resource recovery system. At present, most resource recovery plants are designed primarily to burn paper and other combustible materials in an incinerator; the energy produced by the incinerator is used to produce electricity or for heating nearby buildings.

Even though 55% of the cost of these facilities was subsidized by federal funds, several have gone bankrupt and have been abandoned. One notable exception is a steam-producing plant in Saugus, Massachusetts, which has a steady, reliable supply of refuse and was built using tried-and-true European technology. Even so, it took the plant four years to make a profit—the only profitable U.S. resource recovery plant operating in 1984. Some cities have talked about a new wave of resource recovery plants based on the Saugus model. Such efforts, however, are hindered by the drastic cuts in federal funds since 1981, by citizens campaigning against locating landfills or resource recovery plants in their communities, and by the need to add more expensive air pollution control devices to reduce emissions of toxic metal particles and dioxins to acceptable levels.

Small-scale, high-tech resource recovery systems can be used for apartment buildings, hospitals, and housing developments. With this approach, which is widely used in Sweden, occupants of an apartment building, for example, dump their trash into chutes. It is then sucked through a vacuum-powered pipeline to a central incinerator (Figure 21-11). Glass and metals are mechanically sorted for recycling before or after incineration. The heat generated is used for melting snow and ice on sidewalks and roads, making electricity, and warming buildings and residences up to 3.2 kilometers (2 miles) away. By 1986, over 700 of these pneumatic waste collection systems were in operation in Sweden, England, West Germany, France, the Soviet Union, and other countries. The largest system in the world is at Disney World in Florida.

The Low-Technology Approach Most waste materials recovered in the United States are recycled in a *low-technology approach* involving source separation. In this simpler, small-scale approach, homes and businesses place waste materials—such as glass, paper, metals, and food scraps—into separate containers. Compartmentalized city collection trucks, private

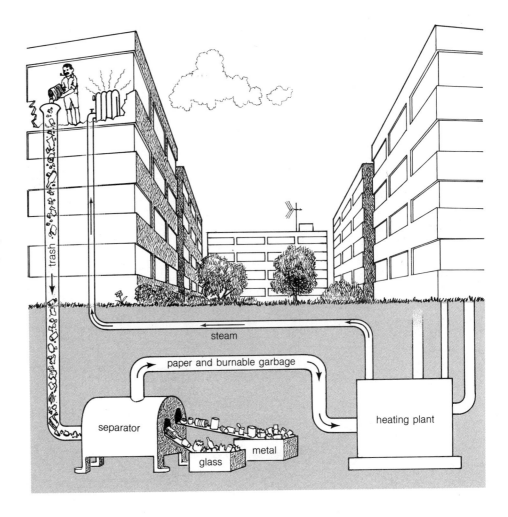

Figure 21-11 Pneumatic pipeline systems for the disposal and resource recovery of urban solid waste have been used in Sweden since 1960.

trash

steam

paper and burnable garbage

separator

glass

metal

heating plant

haulers, or volunteer recycling organizations pick up the segregated wastes, clean them up if necessary, and sell them to scrap dealers, compost plants, and manufacturers. Studies have shown that this source separation takes only 16 minutes a week for the average American family.

By 1986, more than 250 U.S. cities had curbside pickup of separated wastes. More than 3,000 municipal or community-based recycling centers together recycle 12 million tons of trash for an annual cash return exceeding $380 million. A number of U.S. cities are using this approach to recycle a significant percentage of their solid waste—Davis, California (25%), Berkeley, California (20%), San Francisco (23%), Seattle (20%), and Pennsauken, New Jersey (15%).

If all combustible urban solid waste was burned in high-technology energy recovery plants, this would provide only 1% of the country's annual energy use. By contrast, a comprehensive low-technology recycling program could save 5% of the annual U.S. energy use—more than the energy generated by all U.S. nuclear power plants—at perhaps one-hundredth of the capital and operating costs.

The low-technology approach produces little air and water pollution, has low start-up costs, moderate operating costs, and saves more energy and provides more jobs for unskilled workers than high-technology resource recovery plants. While it costs an average of $30 a ton to recycle solid waste, it costs $50 a ton to place such waste in a landfill, and $65 to $75 a ton to incinerate it. Mixing wastes and sending them off to landfills or resource recovery plants also hinders the recycling of paper and encourages the use of throwaway cans and bottles. Indeed, proponents of large-scale resource recovery plants have opposed federal and state laws to ban or discourage nonreturnable cans and bottles and to encourage the recycling of paper, because removal of these materials from mixed urban refuse could make such plants unprofitable.

However, the low-tech approach requires the public to separate waste into recyclable categories and requires large and stable markets for the recycled materials. Presently, with discriminatory tax policies and no guaranteed market, prices for recycled materials are subject to sharp and sudden changes, making recycling a highly risky business.

Some observers argue that the best approach may be to combine the centralized and decentralized approaches. Decentralized source separation would be used primarily for the recovery of metals and glass, and centralized plants would be used for energy recovery by burning paper and other combustible solid waste, as several European countries are doing. The Institute for Self-Reliance estimates that low-tech source separation and recycling could easily take care of 30% to 40% of U.S. solid waste. High-tech resource recovery plants can handle another 30% to 40% of the waste, and the remaining 20% to 40% would then be land-filled or incinerated. Regardless of what resource recovery methods are used, there is considerable room for improvement in the United States, where only about 8% of salvageable glass, metals, and paper in urban solid waste is presently recycled or burned as a source of energy (see Spotlight on p. 500).

21-4 TYPES, SOURCES, AND EFFECTS OF HAZARDOUS WASTE

What Is Hazardous Waste?   Any discarded material that may pose a substantial threat or potential hazard to human health or the environment when managed improperly is a **hazardous waste.** These wastes may be in solid, liquid, or gaseous form and include a variety of toxic, ignitable, corrosive, or dangerously reactive substances. Examples include acids, cyanides, and pesticides; solvents from dry cleaners; compounds of lead, mercury, arsenic, and cadmium; soil contaminated with toxic PCBs and dioxins; fly ash from power plants; infectious waste from hospitals and research laboratories; obsolete explosives, herbicides, and nerve gas that have been stockpiled by the Department of Defense; and radioactive materials (Section 17-2). Sewage sludge (which often contains toxic metals and toxic and carcinogenic organic compounds), hazardous household products, and recycled hazardous waste are exempt from the regulation requirements governing hazardous waste under present U.S. laws.

Until recently there was little concern over hazardous waste in the United States. This changed in 1977 when it was discovered that hazardous chemicals leaking from an abandoned waste dump had contaminated homes in a suburban development known as Love Canal, located in Niagara Falls, New York (see Spotlight on p. 502). This event triggered the realization that one of the country's primary environmental problems is dealing with the large amounts of hazardous waste we are producing today and dealing with what was stored in the past in up to 50,000 sites before any laws were established for disposal.

How Much Has Been Dumped on the Land in the Past?   Between 1950 and 1975 an estimated 5 trillion kilograms (6 billion tons) of hazardous waste has been deposited on or under land throughout the United States. The EPA estimates that there are at least 26,000 U.S. sites where hazardous materials were dumped before present laws regulating disposal of such materials were enacted in 1976. These sites include abandoned chemical dump sites like the one at Love Canal, abandoned chemical waste disposal plants, municipal landfills, farm fields, and junkyards. The full extent of the problem is unknown, because no one knows where they all are or what is in them. Every country in Europe (except Sweden and Norway) also contains a number of abandoned and active hazardous waste sites needing urgent attention. For example, small and densely populated Holland has 5,000 identified hazardous waste sites with at least 350 posing an immediate danger to public health.

By early 1987 the EPA had placed 951 sites on a priority cleanup list because of their threat to nearby populations from actual or potential pollution of the air, surface water, and groundwater. The largest number of these sites is in New Jersey (94), followed by Michigan (66), New York (64), and California (53). Many of these dump sites are located over major aquifers and pose a serious threat to groundwater (Figure 21-13). By early 1987 cleanup had begun at 819 of the priority sites but had been completed at only 13. As more sites are assessed, the EPA estimates that the list of priority sites could grow to 2,000. But the Office of Technology Assessment published a study in 1985 estimating that the final list may include 10,000 sites, with cleanup costs absorbing as much as $100 billion over the next 50 years.

How Much Is Produced Today?   Each year more than 265 million metric tons (292 million tons) of hazardous waste is produced in the United States—an average of 1 metric ton (1.1 tons) for each person in the country. Each day enough hazardous waste is produced in the United States to fill the New Orleans Superdome from floor to ceiling four times. About 96% of this waste is generated and treated on site by large companies—chemical producers, petroleum refiners, and manufacturers. The remaining 4% is handled by commercial facilities that take care of the hazardous waste generated by others.

However, the calculated amount of hazardous waste produced each year does not include radioactive waste, sewage sludge, and household toxic waste not regulated by the EPA. In addition, a 1984 study by the National Academy of Sciences revealed that only about 20% of the almost 710,000 different chemicals in com-

Although paper can be recycled at a fairly high rate, only about 25% of the world's wastepaper is now recycled (Figure 21-12). The Netherlands, Mexico, and Japan have high paper recycling rates primarily because they are sparsely forested. In Sweden the separation of wastepaper from all garbage in homes, shops, and offices has been required by law since 1980. A number of analysts believe that with sufficient economic incentives and laws, at least half the world's wastepaper could be recycled by the end of the century. During World War II the United States recycled about 45% of its wastepaper when paper drives and recycling were national priorities.

Directly or indirectly, each American uses an average of about 275 kilograms (600 pounds) of paper per year—about 8 times the world average and about 40 times the average in LDCs. Every Sunday edition of the *New York Times* consumes about 0.6 square kilometers (150 acres) of forest. Almost three-fourths of the U.S. paper production ends up in the trash, with wastepaper making up about 40% the volume of urban solid waste produced each year. Americans spend 9% of their grocery bills on paper packaging they throw out. Product overpackaging—packages inside of packages and oversized containers designed to trick consumers into thinking they are getting more for their money—is a major contributor to paper use and waste. Each year product packaging accounts for 65% of the paper, 15% of the wood, and 3% of all energy used in the United States.

In addition to saving trees and land, recycling paper saves about 30% to 55% of the energy needed to produce paper from virgin pulpwood and can reduce air pollution from pulp mills by about 95%. If

half the discarded paper were recycled, the country would save enough energy to provide 10 million people with electrical power each year.

Having individual homes and businesses sort out paper for recycling is an important key to increased recycling. Otherwise, the paper becomes so contaminated with other trash that wastepaper dealers will not buy it. Such source separation is feasible primarily for newspapers from homes, corrugated boxes from commercial and industrial establishments, and printing and writing paper from offices. Slick paper magazines, magazine sections, and advertising supplements, however, cause contamination problems and must not be included. By 1986, more than 150 U.S. cities required residences and businesses to sort out newspapers and cardboard for pickup and recycling, and at least 700 American companies and organizations were separating and selling computer cards and high-grade office wastepaper for recycling.

Factors hindering wastepaper recycling in the United States

include federal tax subsidies and other financial incentives that make it cheaper to produce new paper from trees than from recycling, widely fluctuating prices that make recycling paper a risky financial venture, and increased burning of paper in resource recovery plants to produce energy.

In the mid-1970s, the government attempted to create a fixed demand and make recycling paper more profitable by requiring that all federal agencies purchase the highest practical percentage of recycled products. But the Procurement of Papers and Secondary Materials Act has failed miserably because it contained so many exemptions—for copying paper, writing paper, and packaging paper—that almost nothing had to be recycled. In contrast, since 1977 Maryland has complied with a similar law and has increased the amount of recycled paper stock purchased by the state to 25%. Simple things like educating teachers to instruct their students to write on both sides of the paper would also go a long way toward reducing the amount of paper used and wasted. What do you think should be done?

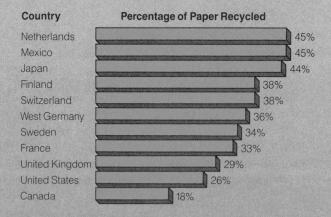

Figure 21-12 Percentage of paper recycled in various countries. (Data from Organization for Economic Cooperation and Development)

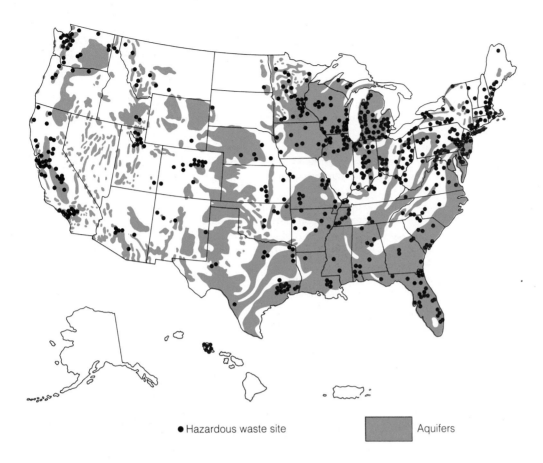

Figure 21-13 Hazardous waste sites on the EPA's priority list for cleanup. Many of these dump sites are located over the country's main aquifers and thus pose a threat to groundwater. (Data from the Environmental Protection Agency)

mercial use have been subjected to extensive toxicity testing, and one-third of these chemicals have never been tested at all for toxicity. If such tests were run, many of these chemicals would be classified as hazardous waste.

About 93% of the hazardous waste produced in the United States comes from the chemical, petroleum, and metal-related industries (Figure 21-14). Hazardous wastes are produced by approximately 850,000 different plants and businesses that generate more than 100 kilograms (220 pounds) a month—about half a 55-gallon drum—and thus fall under EPA regulations. Some are industrial plants that produce large quantities of hazardous waste, but most are small businesses like gas stations, dry cleaners, paint and leather manufacturers, and electroplating shops. Although all states produce hazardous waste, about 65% of the volume is produced, in decreasing order, by Texas, Ohio, Pennsylvania, Louisiana, Michigan, Indiana, Illinois, Tennessee, West Virginia, and California.

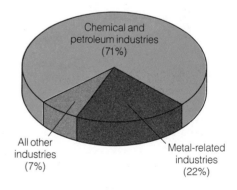

Figure 21-14 Major sources of hazardous waste in the United States in 1985. (Data from the Environmental Protection Agency)

At present, the regulation of the 3,500 industrial plants that make and handle the 15,000 most hazardous chemicals is a patchwork affair, divided among several federal agencies and overtaxed and under-

In 1977, the residents of a suburb of Niagara Falls discovered that "out of sight, out of mind" often does not apply. Hazardous industrial waste buried decades earlier bubbled to the surface, found its way into groundwater supplies, and ended up in backyards and basements. Between 1942 and 1953, Hooker Chemicals and Plastics Corporation, which produced pesticides and plasticizers, dumped more than 19,000 metric tons (21,000 tons) of highly toxic and carcinogenic chemical wastes (mostly contained in steel drums) into an old canal excavation, known as the Love Canal, and sealed the dump with a clay cap and topsoil.

In 1953 Hooker Chemicals sold the canal area to the Niagara Falls school board for one dollar on the condition that the company would have no future liability for any injury or property damage caused by the dump's contents. The company says that it warned the school board against carrying out any kind of construction at the disposal site. An elementary school and a housing project, eventually containing 949 homes, were built in the Love Canal area (Figure 21-15). Residents began complaining to city officials in 1976 about chemical smells and chemical burns received by children playing in the canal, but these complaints were ignored. In 1977 chemicals from badly corroded barrels filled with hazardous waste began leaking into storm sewers, gardens, and basements of homes adjacent to the canal. As the dirt in the dump continued to settle, barrels and chemical wastes were exposed.

Informal health surveys conducted by alarmed residents revealed an unusually high incidence of birth defects, miscarriages, assorted cancers, and nerve, respiratory, and kidney disorders among people who lived near the canal. Complaints to local elected and health officials had little effect. Pressure from residents and unfavorable publicity, however, led state officials to conduct a preliminary health survey and tests. They found that women age 30 to 34 in one area of the canal had a miscarriage rate four times higher than normal; they also found that the air, water, and soil of the canal area and basements of nearby houses were contaminated with a wide range of toxic and carcinogenic chemicals.

In 1978 the state closed the school and permanently relocated the 239 families whose homes were closest to the dump. This area was fenced off. In 1980, after protests from the outraged 710 families still living nearby, President Carter declared Love Canal a federal disaster area and had these families temporarily relocated. Federal and New York State funds were then provided to buy the homes of those who wanted to move permanently.

Since that time the homes and the school within a block and a half of the canal have been torn down, and the state has purchased 570 of the remaining homes. Most other homes, churches, and businesses have been boarded up. In 1987 about 50 families remained in the desolate neighborhood, unwilling or unable to sell their houses and move. The dump site has been covered with a clay cap and surrounded by a drain system that pumps leaking wastes to a new treatment plant. A chain-link fence surrounds the entire contaminated area. Local officials have pressed the federal government for a clean bill of health so that the state can resell the homes it bought from fleeing homeowners and begin rehabilitating the neighborhood. But cleanup has proved to be quite difficult. The EPA hopes to complete its evaluation of cleanup efforts by 1988.

As yet no definitive study has been made to determine the long-term effects of exposure to these hazardous chemicals on the former Love Canal residents. All studies made so far have been criticized on scientific grounds. Even if the effects of exposure to these chemicals prove to be less harmful than expected, the psychological damage to the evacuated families is enormous. For the rest of their lives, they will wonder whether a disorder will strike and will worry about the possible effects of the chemicals on their children and grandchildren.

budgeted state agencies, with no agency having overall responsibility.

Transporting hazardous waste, mostly by truck and train, is another area of increasing concern. According to the EPA, between 1980 and 1985 there were 7,000 accidents involving the release of 191,000 metric tons (210,000 tons) of toxic chemicals in the United States. These accidents killed 139 people, injured 1,478, led to the evacuation of 217,000 people, and caused at least $50 million in property damage.

21-5 CONTROL AND MANAGEMENT OF HAZARDOUS WASTE

Methods for Dealing with Hazardous Waste There are three basic ways of dealing with hazardous waste, as outlined by the National Academy of Sciences in 1983 (Figure 21-16). The first and most desirable approach aims at reducing the total amount of waste produced—by modifying industrial or other

In 1985 former Love Canal residents received payments from a 1983 out-of-court settlement from Occidental Petroleum (now parent company of Hooker Chemicals), the city of Niagara Falls, and the Niagara Falls school board. The payments ranged from $2,000 to $400,000 for claims of injuries ranging from persistent rashes and migraine headaches to cancers and severe mental retardation. The federal government and the state of New York have sued Occidental to recover the more than $250 million spent for cleanup and relocation. The incident is a vivid reminder that we can never throw anything away.

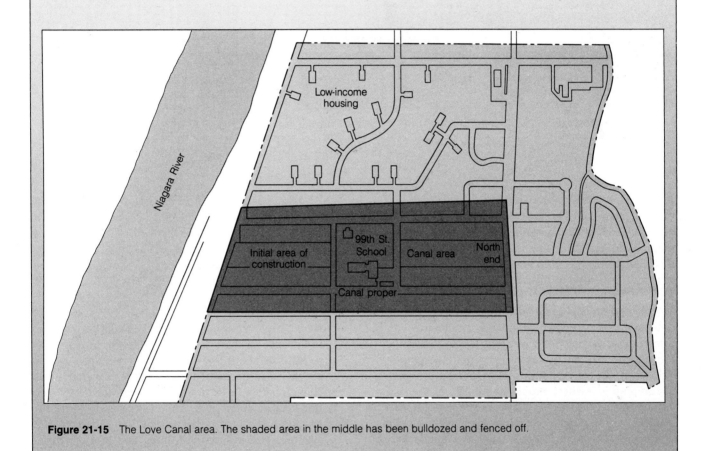

Figure 21-15 The Love Canal area. The shaded area in the middle has been bulldozed and fenced off.

processes to eliminate or reduce the waste output and by reusing or recycling the hazardous wastes that are produced.

Any wastes that are produced should then be converted to less hazardous or nonhazardous materials—by spreading them on the land where they can decompose biologically, by incinerating them on land or at sea using specially designed incinerators, by thermally decomposing them, by treating them chemically or physically, or, in some cases by diluting them to acceptable levels in the ocean or atmosphere. Any waste still remaining after such detoxification processes should then be placed in perpetual storage in a geologically and environmentally secure place that is carefully monitored for leaks.

Present Management of Hazardous Waste So far most hazardous waste produced in the United States is managed by the third and least desirable option.

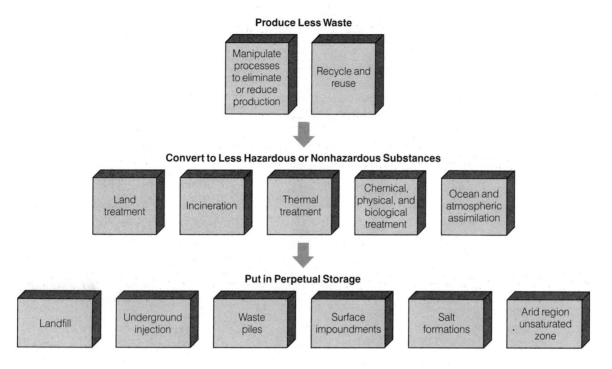

Produce Less Waste

Manipulate processes to eliminate or reduce production

Recycle and reuse

Convert to Less Hazardous or Nonhazardous Substances

Land treatment

Incineration

Thermal treatment

Chemical, physical, and biological treatment

Ocean and atmospheric assimilation

Put in Perpetual Storage

Landfill

Underground injection

Waste piles

Surface impoundments

Salt formations

Arid region unsaturated zone

Figure 21-16 Options for dealing with hazardous waste. (National Academy of Sciences)

About 80% of the hazardous waste produced each year in the United States is disposed of legally or illegally on the land using environmentally unacceptable methods (deep wells, unlined lagoons, and unlined landfills), discharged into sewage systems, rivers, and streams, or burned in unacceptable incinerators (Figure 21-17). Only 10% are stored in environmentally acceptable landfills and 7% are recycled, recovered, detoxified, or burned in acceptable incinerators. An unmeasured amount of hazardous waste is illegally dumped on the land or into water supplies (see Spotlight on p. 508). In most European countries, where vacant land is in short supply, about 50% of the hazardous waste is burned in incinerators equipped with sophisticated air pollution controls; much of the energy released by the incinerators is used to produce electricity or heat.

In 1984 Congress added amendments to the 1976 Resource Conservation and Recovery Act that made it national policy to minimize or eliminate land disposal of hazardous waste in landfills, surface impoundments, land treatment facilities, injection wells, concrete vaults or bunkers, and underground salt domes, mines, or caves. Congress established a 1990 deadline for stopping all land disposal of hazardous waste unless the EPA has determined that land disposal is an acceptable or the only feasible approach for a particular hazardous material. Even then, each chemical is to be treated to the fullest extent possible to reduce its toxicity before land disposal of any type is allowed.

Any specific chemical not found to be acceptable for land disposal by the EPA will automatically be banned from such disposal after 1990. Although it is unlikely that the deadline will be met, this national policy represents a much more ecologically sound approach to dealing with these wastes.

Recycling, Reuse, and Industrial Process Redesign
In Europe, waste exchanges or clearinghouses are used to transfer about one-third of a firm's waste so that another firm can use it as raw material. By 1986 at least 30 regional waste exchanges in the United States were transferring about 10% of the listed wastes, and this fraction could increase significantly in the future. For example, the Minnesota Mining and Manufacturing Company (3M) of St. Paul, Minnesota, sells ammonium sulfate, a corrosive by-product of videotape manufacture, to fertilizer makers. Between 1975 and 1985, 3M also reformulated products and redesigned manufacturing processes to eliminate—each year— more than 82,000 metric tons (90,000 tons) of air pollutants, 4 billion liters (1 billion gallons) of wastewater, and 136,000 metric tons (150,000 tons) of solid waste. In doing this, 3M has saved about $200 million. Since 1980, 25 companies in North Carolina have cut waste production between 25% and 100%.

Although the EPA estimates that at least 20% of the hazardous materials currently generated in the United States could be recycled or reused, presently only about 5% are managed in this manner. Despite

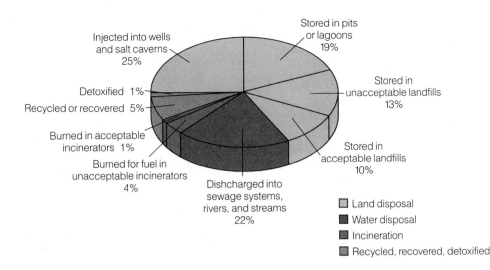

Figure 21-17 Fate of hazardous waste in the United States in 1985. (Data from the Congressional Budget Office)

Injected into wells and salt caverns 25%

Stored in pits or lagoons 19%

Detoxified 1%

Recycled or recovered 5%

Burned in acceptable incinerators 1%

Burned for fuel in unacceptable incinerators 4%

Stored in unacceptable landfills 13%

Stored in acceptable landfills 10%

Dishcharged into sewage systems, rivers, and streams 22%

☐ Land disposal
■ Water disposal
■ Incineration
■ Recycled, recovered, detoxified

enormous potential for recycling and waste trading, between 1979 and 1985 the EPA spent almost no money and assigned only one person to promote this approach. However, this picture should change as the phasing out of land disposal for most hazardous waste and the greatly increased cost of such disposal for even acceptable waste cause companies to find ways to cut costs—through reduced production, recycling, or reusing such wastes.

Conversion to Less Hazardous or Nonhazardous Materials Hazardous organic compounds that contain little or no toxic metal compounds, volatile materials, and persistent organic compounds can be detoxified biologically by landfarming. In **landfarming,** wastes are applied onto or beneath surface soil and mixed to expose the contamined material to oxygen; then microorganisms and nutrients are added as needed to ensure biological decomposition. This method is particularly useful for sewage, petroleum refinery wastes, and paper mill sludges, which can be applied to forest lands and for reclamation of surface-mined land.

Other biological treatment and decomposition processes include the use of composting, trickling filters, activated sludge, and aerated lagoons. There are also experiments using mutant bacteria produced by genetic manipulation to detoxify specific waste materials. But critics worry that these "superbugs" may get out of control and destroy other material before it has a chance to become waste.

Physical processes for detoxifying waste include neutralization of acidic or alkaline waste, oxidation or reduction by chemical reactions into different substances, removal of toxic metals and other compounds by precipitation or absorption (by a chemical such as

activated carbon), and selective ion removal in ion exchangers by passing wastewater over a packed bed of resin.

In the geographical center of Denmark, a plant detoxifies as much as 90% of the country's hazardous waste, while providing 30% of the heating needs for the 18,000 residents of a nearby town. In West Germany, 15 regional waste treatment centers, designed and built partially by several U.S. firms, detoxify almost 85% of the country's hazardous waste. The Netherlands incinerates about half its hazardous waste, and the EPA estimates that about 60% of all U.S. hazardous waste could be incinerated.

With proper air pollution controls, incineration has a number of advantages. It can detoxify complex organic compounds by breaking them down into harmless gases; it is potentially the safest method of disposal for most types of hazardous waste; and it is the most effective method of waste disposal and can destroy 99.99% to 99.9999% of organic waste material, such as pesticides, solvents, and PCBs. Incineration also greatly reduces the volume of waste to be disposed of in the form of ash, and does not require large land areas; and the energy produced can be converted to steam and used to generate electricity or heat.

But there are also some disadvantages. Incineration is the most expensive method, which explains why in 1986 only about 5% of the hazardous waste in the United States was burned and only 1% in environmentally acceptable incinerators. The ash that is left must be disposed of and often contains toxic metals. Not all hazardous wastes are combustible, and the gaseous and particulate combustion products emitted by incinerators can be a health hazard if not controlled.

In 1985 the EPA developed a prototype mobile incinerator, which can be hauled on seven tractor trailers, for detoxifying small amounts of dioxin-

Figure 21-18 Mobile incinerator used by the EPA to detoxify hazardous waste at some of the country's priority dump sites.

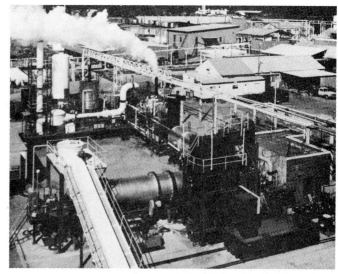

Environmental Systems Company

contaminated soil at various toxic waste dump sites (Figure 21-18). It was used to decompose 99.9999% of the dioxin in contaminated soil. However, this approach is too expensive (up to $1,250 a ton) to decontaminate toxic waste sites such as Times Beach, Missouri, where 364 million kilograms (400,000 tons) of soil are contaminated with dioxin (see Enrichment Study at the end of this chapter).

Between 1983 and 1985, 15 different proposals were made around the country for development of hazardous waste incineration facilities and small environmentally acceptable landfills for the disposal of incinerated and detoxified residues. None of these proposals succeeded due to community resistance.

Because most people object to living near incinerators, interest has been growing in incinerating liquid hazardous waste at sea in specially designed ships, as several European countries are doing. These ships would burn waste without the expensive smokestack scrubbers required for land-based incinerators. This approach is about one-third cheaper than on-land incineration and minimizes the accidental dangers to people. Since 1977, the United States has conducted several experimental hazardous waste burnings in incinerator ships in the Pacific Ocean and the Gulf of Mexico. Although these test burns were declared successful, several scientists contend that the measurements were inadequate or invalid.

Environmentalists have opposed burning of hazardous waste at sea, fearing that accidental chemical spills—resulting from human error, fog, storms, or reefs—or residue—from incomplete destruction of toxic waste—could threaten marine life. In addition, they suspect that some companies would take money-saving shortcuts or would cover up accidents at sea, far away from scrutiny. Although a land-based incinerator equipped with scrubbers injects only a tiny

amount of unburned toxic ash into the atmosphere, an incinerator ship burning the same volume of waste without such controls injects a large amount of unburned toxic particulate matter into the atmosphere, where winds carry it long distances and allow it to settle on land and inland surface waters. Environmentalists also point out that at-sea incineration works only for liquid waste and thus is not appropriate for most of the hazardous waste generated in the United States.

Because of the upcoming ban on land disposal of most hazardous waste, land or ocean incineration with proper controls is likely to become more popular. In 1986 the EPA was developing a comprehensive set of regulations governing the incineration of liquid hazardous waste at sea.

Land Disposal of Hazardous Waste Since 1976, the Resource Conservation and Recovery Act has required that any landfill used for the storage of hazardous waste be a secured landfill, that operators of such landfills show financial responsibility for up to $10 million in accidental damages, and that the facilities be monitored for at least 30 years to minimize the chance of hazardous waste escaping into the environment. A **secured landfill** is a site for the containerized burial and storage of hazardous solid waste (Figure 21-19); the site has restricted access and is continually monitored. Ideally, a secured landfill is situated in thick natural clay deposits, isolated from surface or subsurface water supplies, not subject to flooding, earthquakes, or other disruptions, and unlikely to transport leachate to an underground water source.

In addition, such a landfill must have two plastic liners about 30 times the thickness of a plastic trash bag to help prevent leakage; a bottom layer of gravel

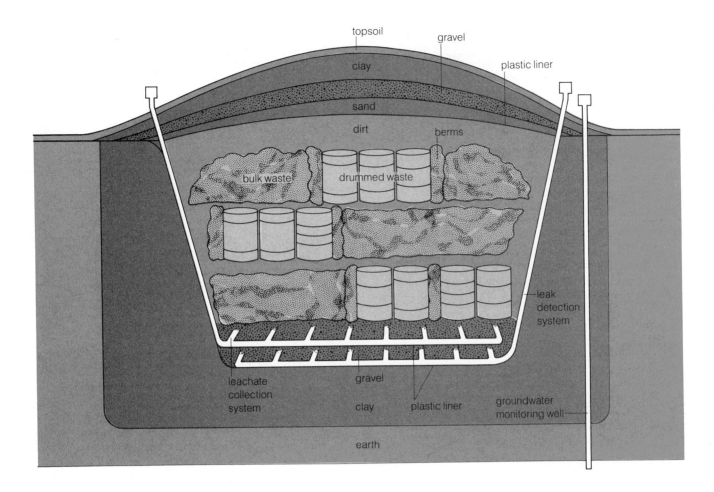

Figure 21-19 A secured landfill for the long-term storage of hazardous waste.

and perforated pipes to collect the leachate that inevitably seeps to the bottom of the pit and must be pumped to the surface for treatment; drainage ditches to prevent flooding from surface water; a cover consisting of another plastic liner plus layers of sand, gravel, and packed clay shaped to divert rainwater; and a monitoring well system to check for chemicals leaking into groundwater. Liquid hazardous waste cannot be stored in secured landfills unless the waste is solidified to reduce volume and encased in cement, asphalt, glass, or organic polymers to decrease the chance of escape into the air or water. By 1986 there were about 525 EPA-approved hazardous waste land disposal facilities operating in the United States, 49 of them commercial operations.

In evaluating hazardous waste control methods in 1983, the Office of Technology Assessment stated: "All land disposal methods will eventually fail." The only question is *when*. Sooner or later, any secured landfill will leak—from tears in the plastic liners caused by bulldozers or freezing temperatures, from leachate disintegration of the liner, from crushing of leachate collection pipes by the weight of the waste, from clogging of the perforations in the leachate collection pipes

by debris, or from disruption of the protective cover by erosion, new construction, or subsidence.

Federal Legislation and Control of Hazardous Waste The Resource Conservation and Recovery Act of 1976, as amended in 1984, requires the EPA to identify hazardous wastes, set standards for their management, and provide guidelines and some financial aid to establish state programs for managing such wastes. The RCRA also requires all firms that store, treat, or dispose of more than 100 kilograms (220 pounds) of hazardous waste per month to apply to the EPA for a permit.

To reduce illegal dumping, hazardous waste producers granted disposal permits by the EPA must use a "cradle-to-grave" manifest system; that is, they must keep track of the 4% of hazardous waste transferred from point of origin to offsite approved disposal facilities. EPA administrators, however, point out that this requirement is almost impossible to enforce because the EPA and state regulatory agencies do not have enough personnel to review the paper trails of more than 750,000 hazardous waste generators and 15,000

Spotlight   Illegal Disposal of Hazardous Waste

A large and probably growing amount of hazardous waste is dumped into municipal landfills, rivers, sewer drains, wells, empty lots and fields, old quarries, abandoned mines, and along the roadsides. Some truckers carrying liquid hazardous waste drive along freeways or rural roads, especially at night, with their spigots open. In Tennessee, illegal dumpers have sent freight cars loaded with hazardous waste to fictitious addresses, C.O.D. Some companies pick up hazardous waste from customers, charge them $50 to $150 a barrel for disposal, and then deposit the barrels in a rented warehouse. Once the warehouse is filled, the disposal company may declare bankruptcy and move out of state, leaving the building owner liable for disposing of the waste and for damages.

Hazardous wastes are also sprayed on ordinary trash, and garbage collectors are bribed to dispose of the trash in landfills not designed to handle such substances. Some are illegally mixed with heating oil and burned in the boilers of schools, hospitals, and office and apartment buildings, resulting in the release of toxic chemicals into the air.

Law enforcement officials warn that illegal dumping is becoming more frequent as waste generators and haulers try to cut costs. Some officials warn that the lure of large profits and generally lax law enforcement has led to increased involvement of organized crime in every aspect of the hazardous waste disposal industry. For example, mob-controlled garbage collection companies, principally in New York, New Jersey, Ohio, and Florida, are picking up toxic waste from client firms, mixing it with regular garbage, and then dumping the deadly mixture at municipal landfills and other sites not authorized to receive hazardous waste.

haulers each year—let alone verify them and prosecute offenders.

Environmentalists argue that the Resource Conservation and Recovery Act of 1976 and 1984 has several serious loopholes. The EPA has been too slow in inventorying and identifying which of the 710,000 different chemicals produced for commercial use should be classified as hazardous wastes. Sampling and testing procedures used by waste producers to determine whether their wastes are classified as hazardous under federal guidelines are inadequate. At least 4.5 million metric tons (5 million tons) of hazardous waste discharged down sewers is not regulated and is a major source of contamination of sewage sludge (which limits its use as a fertilizer) and surface waters. By early 1987 the EPA had listed only 450 of the estimated 35,000 potentially hazardous chemicals as being hazardous.

States are not required to regulate all hazardous wastes identified by the EPA, making states with weaker programs more attractive choices as dumping grounds for certain wastes. In addition, because federal money for inspections ended in 1982, few states regularly monitor city and county landfills to determine whether leachate is percolating into groundwater. Furthermore, in 1985 the EPA budget for drafting and enforcing hazardous waste control regulations was a fourth less than it was in 1981. Most violators draw only a warning, and with only 35 EPA criminal investigators, most illegal dumpers have little chance of being caught.

In 1980 Congress passed the Comprehensive Environmental Response, Compensation and Liability Act (CERCLA), known as the Superfund program, and added amendments in 1986. CERCLA was designed primarily to deal with the problems of financing the cleanup of abandoned or illegal hazardous waste sites. The original act established a $1.6 billion fund, financed jointly by federal and state governments and taxes on chemical and petrochemical industries; the EPA was authorized to use the funds to clean up abandoned or inactive hazardous waste dump sites. The EPA is authorized to collect fines and sue the owners later (if they can be found and held responsible) to recover up to three times the cleanup costs.

This legislation also requires states to provide 10% of the cleanup costs for sites located on private property and 50% of the costs for those on public land. The EPA cannot use any money from the Superfund for cleanup unless the states make their contributions. By 1985, only eight states had such cleanup funds in their budgets. The 1986 amendments also require states by 1990 to have 20 years of hazardous waste disposal capacity lined up. Until this is done, they cannot obtain federal funds to clean up hazardous sites.

Drastic EPA budget cuts since 1981 have made it difficult to implement the Superfund legislation. In 1983, critics charged the EPA with letting some non-complying firms off too easily and settling for superficial cleanups. Congressional investigations of Superfund mismanagement and alleged inside deals led to the firing of the director of the program and the resignation of the head of the EPA.

In 1986, amendments to the Superfund program authorized $9 billion more to be used for cleanup of sites between 1987 and 1994. The EPA was required

Table 21-1	Alternatives for Some Hazardous Household Chemicals
Chemical	Alternative
Oven cleaner	Using baking soda for scouring. For baked-on grease, apply ¼ cup of ammonia in oven overnight to loosen; scrub the next day with baking soda.
Drain cleaner	Pour ½ cup salt down drain, followed by boiling water; flush with hot tap water.
Glass polish	Use ammonia and soap.
Wall and floor cleaners containing organic solvents	Use detergents to clean large areas and then rinse with water.
Toilet bowl, tub, and tile cleaner	Mix borax and lemon juice in a paste. Rub on paste and let set two hours before scubbing.
Mildew stain remover and disinfectant cleaner	Chlorine bleach
Furniture polish	Melt 1 pound carnauba wax into 2 cups of mineral oil. For lemon oil polish, dissolve 1 teaspoon of lemon oil into 1 pint of mineral oil.
Shoe polish	Use polishes that do not contain methylene chloride, trichloro-ethylene, or nitrobenzene.
Spot removers	Launder fabrics when possible to remove stains. Also try cornstarch or vinegar.
Carpet and rug shampoos	Cornstarch
Detergents and detergent boosters	Washing soda and soap powder
Water softeners	Washing soda
Pesticides (indoor and outdoor)	Use natural biological controls (Section 22-5); boric acid for roaches
Mothballs	Soak dried lavender, equal parts of rosemary and mint, dried tobacco, whole peppercorns, and cedar chips in real cedar oil and place in a cotton bag.

to start work at 376 new sites between 1987 and 1992; in addition, the amendments required all cleanups to meet certain minimum health standards and provided $500 million to clean up leaking underground fuel tanks. The amendments also required manufacturers to provide citizens with detailed information about any hazardous chemicals produced or stored in their community and made it easier for citizens to sue polluters for damages.

The estimated cost for cleaning up all present priority hazardous waste dump sites, and those projected to be added to the priority list, ranges from $12 billion to $260 billion, with a 1985 study by the Office of Technology Assessment estimating a cost as high as $100 billion—an average of $1,000 per household. A 1983 study by the Office of Technology Assessment concluded that in the long run the Superfund program might be ineffective because many wastes are simply moved from one burial site to another, and leakage eventually will occur. A 1985 study by a congressional research team found that of the 1,246 hazardous waste dumps it surveyed, nearly half showed signs of polluting nearby groundwater. This team of investigators charged that the EPA's monitoring of these sites was "inaccurate, incomplete, and unreliable."

Individual Action Individuals can reduce their own exposure to hazardous waste by insisting that existing laws governing hazardous waste be enforced and strengthened and that the EPA and state agencies administering these laws be adequately funded and staffed. Used motor oil should be taken to a local auto service center for recycling. Less hazardous (and usually cheaper) household cleaning products should be used (Table 21-1), and hazardous chemicals such as pesticides should only be used when absolutely necessary and in the least amount possible.

Hazardous household chemicals should not be mixed because many react and produce deadly chemicals. For example, when ammonia and household bleach are combined, or even get near one another, they react to produce deadly poisonous chloramine gas. Hazardous chemicals should also not be flushed down the toilet, poured down the drain, buried in the yard, or dumped down storm drains. They should not be thrown away in the garbage because they will end up in a landfill, where they can contaminate drinking water supplies. Instead, contact your local health department or environmental agency for information on what to do with such chemicals. It has been pro-

---

Cadmium, Lead, and Mercury

A number of widely used metallic elements and some of their compounds are either known hazards (Table 21-2) or potential hazards to human health. In 1955 Japanese physicians reported that some people living along the Zintsu River in northern Japan had *itai-itai byo*, or "ouch-ouch disease," because of high levels of cadmium entering the water from industrial and mining wastes. The victims had excruciating pain in their joints, and their bones slowly weakened as they lost calcium; even standing or coughing could break their bones. Between 1955 and 1968, several hundred people became sick and at least 100 people died from eating rice and soybeans grown in fields using the contaminated water.

The greater threat to most of us comes from long-term exposure to low levels of cadmium, especially from food and cigarette smoke. Leafy vegetables tend to pick up cadmium from the soil from phosphate fertilizers, sludge application, and air deposition; they are a major dietary source of cadmium. Pack-a-day smokers carry about twice as much cadmium in their bodies as nonsmokers. People in the same room with smokers are also exposed to cadmium and other dangerous chemicals in cigarette smoke. Cadmium gradually accumulates in the liver and kidneys and at low levels can cause high blood pressure (hypertension) and atherosclerosis. Sweden banned most products containing cadmium in 1980. Adequate and balanced dietary intake of iron, zinc, calcium, copper, protein, and vitamins D and C reduces the absorption of cadmium from food and water.

Levels of lead in the environment have been increasing throughout the world since humans began mining and using lead, about 800 B.C. As a result, the typical body burden of lead today is 500 times higher than it was in people living before the industrial age (except early Romans, who suffered a high incidence of lead poisoning linked to lead pipes and beverage vessels).

We acquire small amounts of lead in the air we breathe, the food we eat, and the water we drink. A 1986 EPA study revealed that 77% of the U.S. population—including 88% of all children under 5—have

---

Table 21-2   Sources and Effects of Some Widely Used Toxic Metals

Metal	Major Sources	Major Health Effects
Arsenic (As)	Burning of coal and oil; smelting of nonferrous ores; additive to glass; pesticides; mine tailings	Cumulative poison at high levels; carcinogen
Beryllium (Be)	Burning of coal and oil; cement plants; alloys; ceramics; rocket propellants	Skin lesions; ulcers; respiratory disease (berylliosis); carcinogen
Cadmium (Cd)	Burning of coal and oil; zinc mining and processing; batteries; incineration; fertilizer processing and application	Carcinogen; teratogen; high blood pressure; heart disease; liver, kidney, and lung disease
Lead (Pb)	Automobile exhaust (leaded gasoline); lead batteries; lead-based paint; smelting of nonferrous metals	Brain damage; behavioral disorders; hearing damage to children; death
Mercury (Hg) and methyl mercury (CH_3Hg^+)	Burning of coal; many industrial uses; seed fungicides; antifouling paint	Nerve damage; kidney damage; birth defects; death

---

posed that a deposit tax, like those on bottles and cans, be placed on all containers of hazardous household chemicals. The deposit would be returned when the empty or partially filled container is returned to a store or authorized hazardous waste reclamation center.

Waste is a human concept. In nature nothing is wasted, for everything is part of a continuous cycle. Even the death of a creature provides nutrients that will eventually be reincorporated in the chain of life.

Denis Hayes

unsafe lead levels in their blood. Some of this comes from inhalation of tiny particles of lead compounds emitted into the atmosphere from the burning of leaded gasoline (which contains tetraethyl lead as an antiknock additive) and from lead smelters and steel factories. Vehicle emissions of lead have declined due to the gradual reduction of the lead allowed in gasoline in the United States—from about 2.5 grams per gallon in 1973 to 1.1 grams per gallon in 1982, to 0.1 gram per gallon in 1986. Studies show that the 68% drop in gasoline lead content between 1977 and 1982 caused lead concentrations in the atmosphere and in human blood to drop by almost two-thirds.

Environmentalists and many health officials have been pushing for a complete ban of lead in gasoline since 1972. But the gasoline industry and tetraethyl lead manufacturers have stretched the phaseout to over 13 years through delays and legal challenges. The EPA is considering a total ban on lead in gasoline beginning as early as 1988, but this is being vigorously opposed by the gasoline additives industry.

Brazil is phasing out gasoline entirely, in favor of ethanol. The European Common Market countries have agreed to set maximum standards of 0.15 to 0.40 gram per gallon. In Japan, where the lead standard is 0.13 gram per gallon, over 90% of all gasoline is unleaded. In the Soviet Union, leaded gasoline has been prohibited in all large cities since 1959. Canada is also phasing out the lead content of gas, but has not adopted the more stringent 1986 U.S. standard.

Another source of lead is ingesting food contaminated with airborne particles that have settled on agricultural and grazing areas, especially those near highways. Some of this lead is absorbed by plants, but most can be removed by careful washing. Solder used to seal the seams on food cans is another source of lead in food, especially in acidic foods such as tomatoes and citric juices.

As leaded gasoline is phased out, the remaining source of lead for many people is drinking water. According to the EPA, nearly one in five Americans drinks tap water containing excess levels of lead, caused when acidic "soft" water erodes lead conduits and the lead solder used to join copper pipe. Since 1987, the use of pipes and solder containing lead in

public water systems has been banned. However, a large percentage of existing houses and buildings contain pipes and solder joints containing lead.

For about 40 dollars homeowners can have private laboratories test tap water for lead and other contaminants (check with local health department officials). Running the water for two to three minutes before using will flush out most lead. Home water filtration systems using activated charcoal filters don't remove lead or other toxic metals. An alternative is to drink bottled water, most of which is spot-checked for lead content by the bottler. In building or remodeling, homeowners should use plastic pipes or ask plumbers to use lead-free solder, which costs only a few dollars more.

Before 1950 lead oxide and other lead compounds were added to interior and exterior paint to make it shinier, last longer, and to fix colors. Acceptable levels of lead in paint were lowered in the 1950s, but it was not until 1976 that the U.S. Consumer Products Safety Commission reduced the amount of lead in paint sold for home use to 0.06%. In the United States, it is estimated that 40 million older houses (built before 1950) and 20% of those built between 1960 and 1975 are potential sources of heavily leaded paint. These houses are a major source of lead poisoning for children betwen ages 1 and 3, who crawl around the floor and inhale harmful amounts of lead dust from cracking and peeling paint or ingest it by sucking their thumbs or putting toys in their mouths. Many infants also eat chips of leaded paint that have peeled off, apparently because they taste sweet.

Another common household source of lead is in burning certain types of paper. Homeowners who burn used paper in woodstoves should not burn comic strips, Christmas wrapping paper, and painted wood, which can be a source of lead contamination indoors and outdoors.

Once lead enters the blood, about 10% is excreted and the rest is stored in the bones. Children up to about age 9 are particularly vulnerable to lead poisoning because their bodies absorb lead very readily. Pregnant women can also transfer dangerous levels of lead to unborn children. Studies indicate that 15% to 20% of all preschool children in the United States may suffer some degree of lead poisoning. About 200 American children die each year from lead poisoning, especially from ingesting large quantities of leaded paint chips.

Another 12,000 to 16,000 children each year are treated for lead poisoning. About 30% of those who survive suffer from palsy, partial paralysis, blindness, and mental retardation. According to the EPA, each year lead poisoning lowers the intelligence—up to five IQ points—in 143,500 children. Studies have also indicated that even low levels of lead in the blood can lead to significant hearing loss in children and to high blood pressure in children and adults.

Mercury enters the air and water when we burn coal (which contains mercury as a contaminant) and through industrial discharges into sewers and surface waters. Yet these discharges are small compared to natural inputs of mercury vaporizing from the earth's crust and from the vast amounts stored as bottom sediments in the ocean. It is dangerous to eat large amounts of tuna, swordfish, and other large ocean species that contain high levels of mercury. But most, if not all, of this mercury comes from natural sources, and the danger has probably always been present. Although the human input of mercury into the ocean is insignificant compared to natural sources, dangerous levels of mercury compounds are sometimes discharged by industries into lakes, rivers, bays, and estuaries.

Figure 21-20 shows the major forms of mercury and the ways they are transformed. Metallic mercury is dangerous when inhaled, but it isn't as dangerous when swallowed. While preparing fillings, for example, dentists and dental workers can be exposed to high levels of mercury vapor because of leaky containers, spills, and poor ventilation. This condition can cause neurologic problems, such as anxiety or depression, and even death.

The major threat posed by mercury is in an extremely toxic organic mercury compound known as methyl mercury (CH_3Hg^+). It can remain in the body for months, can attack the central nervous system, kidneys, liver, and brain tissue, and can cause birth defects. Under acidic conditions, anaerobic bacteria dwelling in the bottom mud of lakes and other surface waters can convert elemental mercury and mercury salts into methyl mercury. Most surface waters apparently aren't acidic enough to cause this, but acidification of an increasing number of lakes from acid deposition may aggravate the problem (Section 19-2).

One tragic episode occurred in the late 1950s when 649 people died and 1,385 suffered mercury poisoning from methyl mercury discharged into Minamata Bay, Japan, from a nearby chemical plant. Most victims in this seaside area had eaten the mercury-contaminated fish and shellfish three times a day. In another incident in 1969, a New Mexico farm laborer fed seed grain treated with methyl mercury to his hogs. After he and his family ate the meat from these animals, three of the children became severely crippled. A fourth child, poisoned in his mother's womb, was born blind and mentally retarded. Another tragedy occurred in 1972 when Iraqi villagers, who had received a large shipment of seed grain fumigated

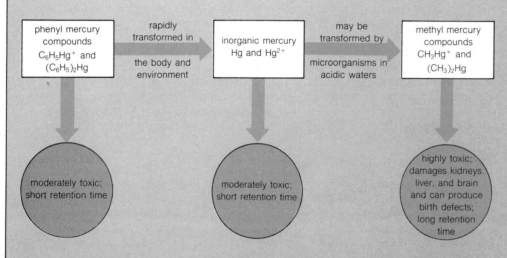

Figure 21-20 Some chemical forms of mercury and how they may be transformed in the environment.

with methyl mercury, fed it to their animals and baked bread with it instead of planting it. Reportedly, 459 people died and 6,530 were injured.

Dioxins

In 1971, dirt roads in several St. Louis, Missouri, suburbs were sprayed with waste automobile oil to control dust, a widely used procedure in many states. The day after the oil was sprayed, the owner of a horse ranch in the Moscow Hills suburb found dozens of dead sparrows on the floor of a barn near the road. Most dogs and cats on the ranch became thin and dehydrated, lost their fur, and died within a month of the spraying. Within a year, 43 horses that had regularly exercised in an arena near the road died, and most of the pregnancies of the horses bred in 1971 resulted in spontaneous abortions. All but one of the foals born alive that year died within a few months after birth. During 1971, one of the ranch owners suffered from headaches, diarrhea, and chest pains. One of his daughters suffered from bad sores and severe headaches, and another daughter had to be hospitalized as a result of severe internal bleeding.

Several years later, tests on the oil sprayed on the road revealed that it was contaminated with several highly toxic compounds, including a number of toxic chlorinated hydrocarbon compounds known as **dioxins.** Further investigation revealed that the contaminated oil had been sold to a chemical company that was supposed to clean it up for reuse but instead sprayed it on roads at several sites in Missouri. Soil in the Times Beach suburb was found to be so contaminated that in 1983 the EPA bought out the entire town at a cost of $36.7 million and had to relocate 2,200 people. Twenty-six other sites in Missouri are known to be contaminated with dioxins, and 75 more are suspected. Significant levels of dioxins have also been found in rivers in Michigan, in fish taken from the Great Lakes, and in flooded basements of homes near the Love Canal in Niagara Falls. In 1986, 128 residents of Times Beach and other Missouri areas who sued over dioxin contamination accepted a $19 million settlement from the company that failed to clean up the contaminated waste oil before it was to be used.

Dioxins are a family of 75 different chlorinated hydrocarbon compounds. One form in particular, usually referred to as TCCD, has been shown to be extremely toxic and to cause liver cancer, birth defects, and death in laboratory animals at extremely low levels. This chemical also persists in the environment, especially in soil and fatty tissue in the human body, and can apparently be biologically amplified to higher levels in food webs. Workers and others exposed to TCCD in industrial plant accidents have complained of headaches, weight and hair loss, liver disorders, irritability, insomnia, nerve damage in the arms and legs, loss of sex drive, and chloracne (a severe, painful, and often disfiguring form of acne). A study of 154 people in the Times Beach, Missouri, area exposed to soil contaminated with at least 2,200 ppb of TCCD showed some damage to their immune systems along with minor liver damage.

TCCD frequently appears as an unavoidable trace contaminant formed as a by-product in the chemical reactions used to make the herbicides Silvex and 2,4,5–T, and Agent Orange (a 50–50 mixture of 2,4–D and 2,4,5–T), widely sprayed to defoliate trees during the Vietnam War (Section 22–3). TCCD and several other dioxins also form in trace amounts during the high-temperature combustion of various organic compounds in incinerators and other combustion processes. In 1981 the EPA concluded that the quantity of TCCD and other dioxins released into the atmosphere during combustion processes is small enough and diffuse enough to be relatively harmless, though this finding is disputed by some scientists. The major potential threat comes from the large quantities of the chemical present in industrial dump sites, many of which are abandoned.

Measurements have shown that Americans and Canadians carry an average of 5 ppt to 10 ppt of TCCD in their fatty tissues. The effects, if any, of human long-term exposure to such trace levels is unknown. The U.S. Centers for Disease Control (CDC) considers a concentration of TCCD in soil as low as 1 ppb potentially hazardous to humans in residential areas. In 1986 the CDC found that through the fat in mother's milk, nursing infants may be exposed to TCCD levels 1,300 times the recommended daily maximum exposure level.

But there is some possible good news. The EPA had assumed that dioxins are highly mobile in soil, thus making disposal of dioxin-contaminated soil and waste on land quite hazardous. However, in 1986 a preliminary study indicated that dioxins apparently move very slowly in soil, perhaps as little as 1 centimeter in 400 years to 5,000 years. If this finding is substantiated, the EPA hopes to be able to dispose of soils containing low concentrations of dioxins in abandoned surface mines.

Polychlorinated Biphenyls (PCBs)

Since 1966, scientists have found widespread contamination from a widely used group of toxic, oily synthetic organic chemicals known as **polychlorinated biphenyls (PCBs).** PCBs are mixtures of about 70 different but closely related chlorinated hydrocarbon compounds that are made, like DDT and dioxins, of carbon, hydrogen, and chlorine. PCBs, which were manufactured in the United States from 1929 to 1979, are still widely used as insulating and cooling fluids in electrical transformers and capacitors. Until 1979, PCBs were also used in the production of plastics, paints, rubber, adhesives, sealants, printing inks, carbonless copy paper, waxes, pesticide extenders, and for dust control on roads.

There was little concern about PCBs until 1968, when some 1,300 Japanese came down with skin lesions (chloracne) and suffered liver and kidney damage after they had eaten rice oil accidentally contaminated with PCBs that had leaked from a heat exchanger. Statistical analysis suggests that victims of this accident may suffer from an abnormally high incidence of stomach and liver cancer. As a result of this incident, Japan banned all uses of PCBs.

Like DDT and dioxins, PCBs are insoluble in water, soluble in fats, and very resistant to biological and chemical degradation; thus they are biologically amplified in food webs. PCBs entering the body through food, skin contact, and inhalation accumulate in fatty tissues and body organs. Also like DDT, dioxins, and other chlorinated hydrocarbons, the long-term health effects on humans exposed to low levels of PCBs are unknown. But tests have shown that PCBs produce liver damage, kidney damage, gastric disorders, reproductive disorders, skin lesions, and tumors in laboratory animals.

In 1974 the U.S. chemical industry voluntarily stopped producing PCBs for all uses except in closed systems, such as electrical transformers, and in 1976 Congress banned the further manufacture and use of PCBs, except in existing electrical transformers. How-ever, prior to this ban, the EPA estimates that at least 68,000 metric tons (75,000 tons) of PCBs had entered the environment because of indiscriminate dumping at landfills, fields, sewers, and roadsides. Traces of PCBs have been found all over the world in soil, surface and groundwater, fish, human breast milk and fatty tissues—even in Arctic snow.

Since 1980 the EPA has required that all material containing PCBs be labeled and disposed of only at EPA-approved, secured landfills or high-temperature incinerators. Until 1981 the major risk of exposure to PCBs was thought to be from leaks and spills and improper disposal of PCBs and PCB equipment.

But since 1981, fires involving PCB-filled electrical transformers in several cities have exposed people in or near office buildings, apartment complexes, shopping malls, and train and subway stations, where some 80,000 transformers are located, to much more severe risks. During a transformer fire, PCBs, and even more toxic by-products produced by their combustion, spread throughout buildings and are also flushed into storm sewers and surface waters by the water used to extinguish the fire. A 1981 transformer fire in the basement of a state office building in Binghamton, New York, for example, spread PCBs and toxic by-products throughout the 18-story building through the ventilation system. In 1986 the building was still closed and decontamination and cleanup costs had amounted to $30 million—for a building that originally cost $20 million (Figure 21-21).

In 1985, the EPA ordered that by 1990 PCBs be removed from all electrical transformers in U.S. apartment and office buildings, hospitals, and shopping

CHAPTER SUMMARY

Massive amounts of solid waste are produced in the United States through agricultural, mining, and industrial processes, as well as urban solid waste from homes and commercial establishments. The three major ways to deal with solid wastes are (1) *throwaway output approaches,* in which they are dumped on the land, in the ocean, or burned in incinerators, (2) *resource recovery output approaches,* in which some of the waste is recycled, reused, or burned to provide energy, and (3) *input approaches,* in which products and manufacturing processes are designed to produce less solid waste.

Some urban solid waste is thrown out as roadside litter or dropped illegally in open dumps. Most solid waste in the United States is deposited in sanitary landfills and covered each day with a layer of soil. If selected in suitable sites and properly managed, landfills are a satisfactory method for solid waste disposal; once filled, they can be reclaimed and used for recreational and other purposes. However, many are located above aquifers and can contaminate groundwater; many urban areas are running out of economically and environmentally acceptable landfill sites. A small amount of urban solid waste in the United States is incinerated, and a tiny fraction is converted to soil fertilizer and conditioner by composting. With proper air pollution controls, incineration is a costly but environmentally acceptable method, provided there is a secured landfill or other option for disposal of the relatively small amounts of toxic ash left over after burning.

A number of urban areas in Europe and a few in the United States have built large-scale resource recovery plants

malls and banned the further installation of PCB-filled transformers in or near commercial buildings. This will still leave about 140,000 sealed electrical transformers and capacitors (owned mostly by utility companies) containing some 341 million kilograms (375,000 tons) of PCBs. Each year PCBs are released into the environment when these transformers and capacitors leak, catch fire, or explode.

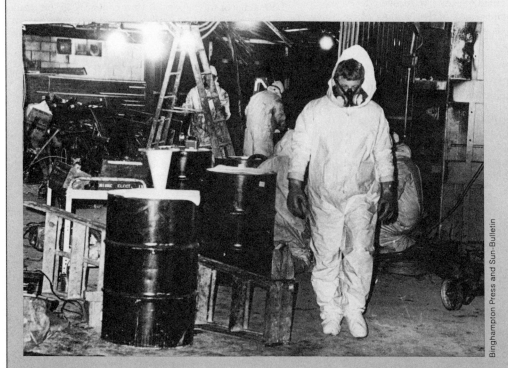

Binghampton Press and Sun-Bulletin

Figure 21-21 Cleanup begins after a 1981 fire in a basement transformer spread PCBs throughout a state office building in Binghamton, New York.

to separate urban solid waste into recycling materials (for example, glass and metals) and combustible materials (such as paper) to produce energy. U.S. plants, however, have been expensive to build and operate and have suffered from breakdowns and financial losses. Instead of using this high-technology approach, a number of cities use a low-technology approach in which homes and businesses separate waste materials—such as glass, metals, paper, and organic food and yard waste—into containers for pickup and recycling. This approach is much less costly, saves more energy, and provides more jobs for unskilled workers than the high-technology approach.

A serious and growing form of pollution results from the production and improper handling of solid, liquid, and gaseous *hazardous waste*. There are at least 26,000 sites throughout the country where hazardous waste was dumped before present laws regulating its disposal were enacted in 1976. The EPA has placed 951 of these sites on a priority cleanup list because they threaten nearby populations from actual or potential pollution of the air, surface water, or groundwater. By 1987 cleanup had started at 819 sites but had been completed at only 12. Eventually 10,000 sites might have to be cleaned up over the next 50 years at a cost of at least $100 billion. Examples of hazardous waste include toxic metals and metal compounds of cadmium, lead, and mercury, dioxins, and PCBs.

The major ways of dealing with hazardous waste are (1) input approaches in which the amount produced is decreased by redesigning industrial processes and products and by recycling and reuse, (2) detoxification to harmless or less hazardous substances by various physical, chemical, or biological processes, and (3) disposal on the land in specially designed secured landfills, lagoons, sewage systems, injection wells, and incinerators equipped with sophisticated air pollution control devices.

Most hazardous waste in western Europe is detoxified and incinerated. So far most hazardous waste in the United States is disposed of legally or illegally in unlined landfills, lagoons, and injection wells, or discharged into sewage systems or surface waters, and burned in environmentally unacceptable incinerators. In 1985 only about 17% of this waste was disposed of in environmentally acceptable landfills or incinerators or was detoxified, recycled, or recovered. This situation may change soon because of the banning of land disposal of most hazardous waste in the United States after 1990. Federal laws enacted between 1976 and 1986 require each hazardous waste producer to obtain a permit from the EPA and to keep track of all such wastes from point of origin to point of dispoal at EPA-approved secured landfills or incinerators. But this is difficult to enforce. Congress has appropriated $10.6 billion for cleanup between 1980 and 1994 of abandoned hazardous waste dump sites. Individuals can reduce their exposure to hazardous waste by using alternative substances that are less hazardous or nonhazardous, and by disposing of hazardous household products properly.

DISCUSSION TOPICS

1. List the advantages and disadvantages of each of the following methods for disposal of solid waste: (a) sanitary landfill, (b) incineration, and (c) composting.

2. How is solid waste collected and disposed of in your community? Is the groundwater near sanitary landfills periodically monitored for contamination? Does the community have any EPA-approved secured landfill sites for disposal of hazardous waste?

3. Keep a list for a week of the solid waste materials you dispose of. What percentage is composed of materials that could be recycled, reused, or burned as a source of energy? How much of this material is a result of unnecessary packaging?

4. List the advantages and disadvantages of the high-technology (resource recovery plant) and the low-technology (source separation) approaches to recycling materials from solid waste. Would you favor requiring all households and businesses to sort recyclable materials for curbside pickup in separate containers? Explain.

5. Determine whether (a) your college and your city have recycling programs, (b) your college and your local government require that a certain fraction of all paper purchases contain recycled fiber, (c) teachers in your college and in local schools expect everyone to write on both sides of the paper, (d) your college sells soft drinks in throwaway cans or bottles, and (e) your state has, or is contemplating, a law requiring deposits on all beverage containers.

6. What responsibility, if any, do you feel Hooker Chemicals has for damages and cleanup costs resulting from the leakage of hazardous waste at Love Canal? Explain.

7. Would you oppose locating a secured landfill in your community for the storage of hazardous waste? How about an incinerator to detoxify such wastes? Explain. If you oppose both of these alternatives, how would you propose that the hazardous waste generated in your community be managed?

8. Give your reasons for agreeing or disagreeing with each of the following proposals for dealing with hazardous waste in the United States:
   a. Burn all liquid hazardous waste in federally approved at-sea incinerator ships.
   b. Reduce the production of hazardous waste, and encourage recycling and reuse of such materials by levying a tax or fee on producers for each unit of waste generated.
   c. Ban all land disposal of hazardous waste as a means of encouraging recycling, reuse, and treatment, and technologies for dealing with hazardous wastes and as a means of protecting groundwater from contamination.
   d. Provide low-interest interest loans, tax breaks, and other financial incentives for industries that produce hazardous waste to encourage them to recycle, reuse, treat, destroy, and reduce generation of such waste.

22

Pesticides and Pest Control

GENERAL OBJECTIVES

1. Why has the need for pest control increased, and what major types of pesticides have been used since 1945?

2. What are the major advantages and disadvantages of using insecticides and herbicides?

3. How is pesticide usage regulated in the United States?

4. What alternatives are there to using pesticides?

A weed is a plant whose virtues have not yet been discovered.

Ralph Waldo Emerson

A **pest** is any unwanted organism that directly or indirectly interferes with human activity. Since 1945, vast fields planted with only one crop or only a few crops, as well as home gardens and lawns, have been blanketed with a variety of chemicals called **pesticides** (or *biocides*) to kill organisms that humans consider to be undesirable. The substances in this arsenal kill unwanted insects *(insecticides),* plants *(herbicides),* rodents such as rats and mice *(rodenticides),* fungi *(fungicides),* and other organisms.

Pesticides can improve crop yields and help control populations of disease organisms. However, there is considerable evidence that the widespread use of pesticides can have harmful effects on wildlife, ecosystem structure and function, and human health. Their overuse can even lead to an increase in crop losses and a resurgence of the diseases and pests they are supposed to control. In 1962 Rachel Carson's book *Silent Spring* dramatized the potential dangers of pesticides to wildlife and people and set off a controversy between environmentalists and pesticide industry officials that is still raging. A number of pesticides, such as DDT, have been banned for most uses in the United States and other MDCs but continue to be widely used in LDCs.

22-1 PESTICIDES: TYPES AND USES

Natural Control of Pests in Diverse Ecosystems We consider only about 10,000—or 1%—of the at least 1 million catalogued insect species to be pests. Only about 100 of these insects cause about 90% of the damage to food crops. Indeed, most insects, fungi, rodents, and soil microorganisms help to cycle essential life chemicals (Section 4-2) and pollinate plant species. In a diverse, relatively undisturbed natural ecosystem, populations of natural insect predators, disease organisms, and parasites usually keep populations of poten-

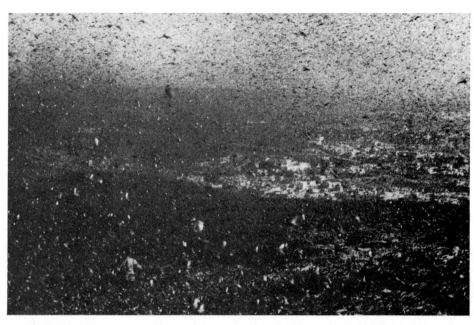

Figure 22-1 Throughout recorded history periodic outbreaks of locusts (such as these in Somalia, Africa) have devoured wild and cultivated plants used to feed the world's human population.

Jean Manuel, FAO

tially harmful species from reaching the levels that cause significant economic loss of food crops or livestock. Furthermore, through natural selection many plants and insects contain or give off chemicals that tend to protect them from certain predators, parasites, and diseases.

Why the Need for Pest Control Has Increased Locusts have always ravaged the wild and cultivated plants that people eat (Figure 22-1). Over the past 200 years, however, an increasing number of insects and other pests have become serious threats to crops that feed the world's mushrooming population. The major reason for this is that large areas of diverse ecosystems, containing small populations of many species, have been replaced with greatly simplified agricultural ecosystems and lawns, containing large populations of only one or two desired plant species. In such biologically simplified ecosystems, organisms can grow in number and achieve pest status, whereas their populations would have been controlled in more diverse ecosystems. As a result, people have had to spend an increasing amount of time, energy, and money to control pests in crop fields, lawns, and other simplified ecosystems. The most widely used approach has been to spray fields with certain synthetic chemicals.

The Ideal Pest Control Method The ideal pest-killing chemical would kill only the target pest; have no short- or long-term health effects on nontarget organisms, including human beings; be broken down into harmless chemicals in a relatively short time; not cause target organisms to acquire genetic resistance to its

effects; and be more economical than not using pest control. Unfortunately, no known pest control method meets all these criteria.

First Generation Pesticides Before 1940 there were only a few dozen pesticides on the market. Many of these *first generation pesticides* were nonpersistent organic compounds, made or extracted from insect poisons found naturally in plants. For example, pyrethrum, a powder obtained from the heads of chrysanthemums (Figure 22-2), was used by the Chinese 2,000 years ago and is still in use today. Caffeine is also an excellent insecticide that can be used to control tobacco hornworms, mealworms, milkweed bugs, and mosquito larvae. Other insecticides derived from natural plant sources include nicotine (as nicotine sulfate) from tobacco, rotenone from the tropical derris plant, and garlic oil and lemon oil, which can be used against fleas, mosquito larvae, houseflies, and other insects.

A second type of first generation commercial pesticide in use before 1940 consisted of persistent inorganic compounds, made from toxic metals such as arsenic, lead, and mercury. Most of these compounds are no longer used because they are highly toxic to people and to animals, they contaminate the soil for 100 years or more, and they tend to accumulate in soil to the point of inhibiting plant growth.

Second Generation Pesticides A major revolution in insect pest control occurred in 1939 when it was discovered that **DDT** (dichlorodiphenyltrichloroethane), a chemical known since 1874, was a potent insecticide. Since 1945, chemists have developed many

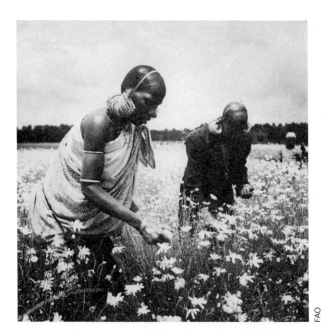

Figure 22-2 The heads of these pyrethrum flowers being harvested in Kenya, Africa, are ground into a powder and used directly as commercial insecticides or converted to other chemically related pyrethroid insecticides.

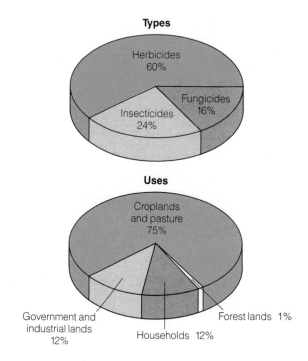

Figure 22-3 Major types of pesticides and their uses in the United States. (Data from the EPA and David Pimentel)

varieties of such synthetic organic chemicals for killing insects, weeds, rodents, and other pests. The chemicals in this array are known as *second generation pesticides*.

DDT and many related second generation pesticides have been widely used for two reasons: they are easy and cheap to produce, and they can kill many types of pest organisms over a long period of time because they are not broken down readily in the environment and are not dissolved and removed from crop fields by rain or irrigation water.

Worldwide, about 2.3 million metric tons (2.5 million tons) of second generation pesticides are used each year—amounting to an average of about 0.45 kilograms (1 pound) of pesticide for each person on earth. About 85% of all pesticides are used in MDCs, but use in LDCs is growing rapidly and is projected to increase at least fourfold between 1985 and 2000. Between 1972 and 1985, world pesticide sales grew from $8.1 billion to $14 billion.

In the United States about 600 active ingredients and 900 inert ingredients are mixed to make some 50,000 individual pesticide products. In 1985 about 500,000 metric tons (550,000 tons)—an average of 2 kilograms (4.6 pounds) for each American—were used in the United States (Figure 22-3).

Although we usually think of pesticide in terms of cropland, an EPA study showed that 92% of all U.S. households use one or more types of pesticide to control insects, weeds, fungi, or rodents. This study also showed that the average homeowner applies much more pesticide per unit of land area than do farmers; each year more than 250,000 Americans become sick because of pesticides used in the home. Thus, everyone—not just farmers—has an important role to play in reducing unnecessary pesticide use and in seeing that unused pesticides are not thrown in the trash to end up in landfills and pollute groundwater.

Major Types of Insecticides and Herbicides Most of the thousands of different insecticides used today fall into one of four classes of compounds: chlorinated hydrocarbons, organophosphates, carbamates, and pyrethroids (Table 22-1). Most of these chemicals are broad-spectrum poisons that kill most of the target and nontarget insects in the sprayed area by disrupting their nervous systems. They vary widely in their persistence, the length of time they remain active in killing insects (Table 22-1).

Organophosphates are generally much less persistent than DDT and most other chlorinated hydrocarbons now banned or restricted in the United States and many MDCs. However, they are more water soluble and can leach into groundwater; they also are much more toxic to birds, human beings, and other mammals than chlorinated hydrocarbons. Furthermore, to compensate for their fairly rapid breakdown, farmers usually apply nonpersistent insecticides at regular intervals to ensure more effective insect con-

Table 22-1 Major Types of Insecticides

Type	Examples	Persistence
Chlorinated hydrocarbons	DDT, DDE, DDD, aldrin, dieldrin, endrin, heptachlor, toxaphene, lindane, chlordane, kepone, mirex	High (2–15 years)
Organo-phosphates	Malathion, parathion, Azodrin, Phosdrin, methyl parathion, Diazinon, TEPP, DDVP	Low to moderate (normally 1–12 weeks, but some can last several years)
Carbamates	Carbaryl (Sevin), Zineb, maneb, Baygon, Zectran, Temik, Matacil	Usually low (days to weeks)
Pyrethroids	Pyrethrums extracted from flowers (Figure 22-2) and used directly or modified chemically	Usually low (days to weeks)

Table 22-2 Major Types of Herbicides

Type	Examples	Effects
Contact	Triazines such as atrazine	Kills foliage by interfering with photosynthesis
Systemic	Phenoxy compounds such as 2,4-D, 2,4,5-T, and Silvex; substituted ureas such as diuron, norea, and fenuron	Absorption creates excess growth hormones; plants die because they cannot obtain enough nutrients to sustain their greatly accelerated growth
Soil sterilants	Treflan, Dymid, Dowpon, Sutan	Kills soil microorganisms essential for plant growth; most also act as systemic herbicides

trol. As a result, these chemicals are often present in the environment almost continuously, like persistent pesticides. Use of pyrethroids is growing rapidly because they are generally nonpersistent, effective at low doses, and not highly toxic to mammals.

Herbicides can be placed in three classes based on their effect on plants: contact herbicides, systemic herbicides, and soil sterilants (Table 22-2). Most herbicides are active for only a short time.

22-2 THE CASE FOR PESTICIDES

Using Insecticides to Control Disease During World War II, DDT was sprayed directly on the bodies of soldiers and war refugees to control body lice, which spread typhus. The World Health Organization (WHO) also used DDT and related second generation pesticides to control the spread of insect-transmitted diseases such as malaria (carried by the *anopheles* mosquito), bubonic plague (rat fleas), typhus (body lice and fleas), sleeping sickness (tsetse fly), and Chagas' disease (kissing bugs).

Thanks largely to DDT, dieldrin, and several other chlorinated hydrocarbon insecticides, more than 1 billion people have been freed from the risk of malaria,

and the lives of at least 7 million people have been saved since 1947. Thus, *DDT and other insecticides have probably saved more human lives than any other synthetic chemicals since human beings have inhabited the earth.*

Although DDT and several other chlorinated hydrocarbon insecticides deserve their reputation as life-givers, they are no longer effective in many parts of the world. By early 1985, the World Health Organization reported that 51 of the 60 malaria-carrying species of mosquitoes had become genetically resistant to DDT and one or more of the other chlorinated hydrocarbons widely used to control the disease. At least ten of the species are also resistant to the widely used organophosphates malathion and fenitrothion. As a result, between 1970 and 1985 there was a thirty- to fortyfold increase in malaria in countries where it had been almost eradicated (Section 23-2). Despite the increasing ineffectiveness of DDT and other insecticides, the WHO points out that a ban on chlorinated hydrocarbon and organophosphate insecticides would lead to large increases in disease, human suffering, and death.

Using Insecticides and Herbicides to Increase Food Supplies Each year pests and disease consume or destroy about 45% of the world's food supply: 33% of

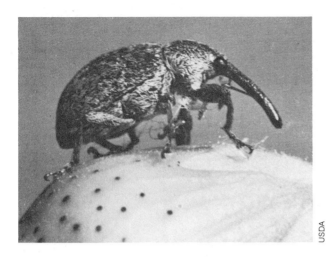

Figure 22-4 The cotton boll weevil accounts for about 35% of the pesticides used in the United States, but farmers are now increasing their use of natural predators to control this major pest.

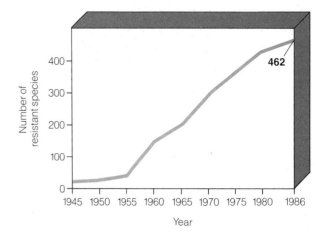

Figure 22-5 The number of insect pest species showing genetic resistance to one or more pesticides has increased dramatically since 1945 when pesticides were first applied in large doses. (Data from World Resources Institute)

this loss occurs before harvest and 12% after harvest. Even in the United States, which uses vast amounts of pesticides and has sophisticated food storage and transportation networks, the total loss due to pests and disease is estimated to be 42% of the potential yearly production—33% before harvest and 9% after. This leads to annual crop losses worth about $20 billion.

The yearly $3 billion that the United States invests in pest control yields about $12 billion in increased crop yields, an excellent investment return. This economic benefit has to be reduced by the $1 billion in annual losses as a result of social and environmental damages from using pesticides. However, pesticides are still a good investment in economic terms. The Department of Agriculture estimates that food prices in the United States are 30% to 50% lower than they would be without the country's widespread use of pesticides and extensive after-harvest storage facilities.

The use of pesticides to help increase crop yields in the United States has meant that more land is available for recreation, forests, and wildlife reserves. Thus, there is less pressure on farmers to expand crop production to lands subject to excessive erosion; another indirect effect of pesticide use is that reduced soil erosion has helped maintain water quality by limiting the flow of sediment into surface waters.

There are alternatives to relying on insecticides and herbicides to control insects and weeds (Section 22-5). But proponents argue that these chemicals have several advantages over other approaches. They can control most insect pests quickly and at a reasonable cost, they have a relatively long shelf life, they are easily shipped and applied, and they are safe when handled properly. When genetic resistance occurs in

pest insects and weeds, farmers can usually switch to other pesticides.

22-3 THE CASE AGAINST PESTICIDES

Development of Genetic Resistance The most serious drawback to using chemicals to control pests is that most pest species, especially insects, can develop genetic resistance to any chemical poison through natural selection (Section 6-2). When an area is sprayed with a pesticide, most of the pest organisms are killed. However, a few organisms in a given population of a particular species survive because they have genes that make them resistant or immune to a specific pesticide.

Because most pest species—especially insects and disease organisms—have short generation times, a few surviving organisms can reproduce a large number of similarly resistant offspring in a short time. For example, the boll weevil (Figure 22-4), a major cotton pest, can produce a new generation every 21 days. When populations of offspring of resistant parents are repeatedly sprayed with the same pesticide, each succeeding generation contains a higher percentage of resistant organisms. Thus the widespread use of any chemical to control a rapidly reproducing insect pest species typically becomes ineffective within about five years—even sooner in the tropics, where insects and disease organisms adapt quickly to new environmental conditions. Weeds and plant diseases also develop genetic resistance, but not as quickly as most insects.

Since 1950 there has been a dramatic increase in the number of insect species with genetic resistance to one or more insecticides (Figure 22-5). Worldwide,

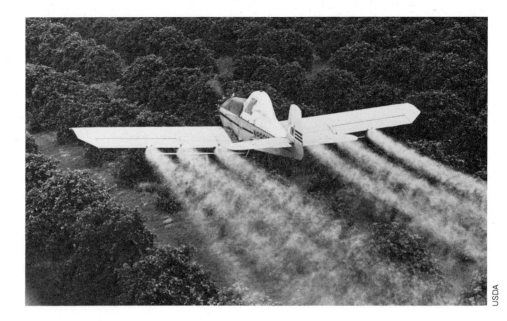

Figure 22-6 Crop duster spraying a Florida orange grove with fungicide. No more than 1% of the chemical being applied reaches the target organisms.

USDA

by 1986, at least 462 species of insects, 150 species of plant pathogens, 50 species of fungi, 50 species of weeds, and 10 species of small rodents (mostly rats) had strains resistant to one or more pesticides. About 20 species of particularly damaging pests have become resistant to virtually every pesticide thrown at them. According to insect expert Robert Metcalf, by 1995 the number of insect pest species resistant to one or more insecticides could exceed 1,500, and by the turn of the century, virtually all insect pest species will probably show some form of genetic resistance. Because half of all pesticides applied worldwide are herbicides, genetic resistance in weeds is also expected to increase significantly.

When genetic resistance develops, pesticide sales representatives usually recommend more frequent applications, stronger doses, or switching to a different chemical to keep the resistant species under control, rather than suggesting alternative methods. This can put farmers on a **pesticide treadmill,** in which the cost of using pesticides increases while their effectiveness decreases. Eventually insecticide costs can exceed the economic loss resulting from not using these chemicals. Thus, when farmers and homeowners apply pesticides to their fields and gardens, they are accelerating the natural selection and contributing to the population growth of the pest species they are trying to eliminate—another example of short-term economic gain leading to long-term economic loss. For example, even though insecticide use in the United States increased tenfold between 1940 and 1980, crop losses from insects during the same period almost doubled (from 7.1% to 13%).

Killing of Natural Pest Enemies Most pesticides are broad-spectrum poisons that kill not only the target pest species but also a number of natural predators and parasites that may have been holding the pest species at a reasonable level. Without sufficient natural enemies, and with lots of food available, a rapidly reproducing insect pest species can make a strong comeback a few days or weeks after being initially controlled. This revival of the pest population requires the use of more pesticides, again placing farmers on a pesticide treadmill.

For example, in California's San Joaquin Valley, farmers sprayed cotton crops with heavy dosages of the organophosphate insecticide Azodrin to control the cotton bollworm. After only three sprayings, so many natural predators had been killed that the cotton bollworm was able to destroy 20% of the cotton crop. Scientists at the University of California estimated that if no pesticide had been used, only about 5% of the cotton crop would have been destroyed by the bollworms.

Creation of New Pests The repeated use of broad-spectrum pesticides also creates new pests and converts minor pests to major pests—the reverse of what pesticides are supposed to do. This occurs when pesticides kill off not only the natural predators of the pest species but also the predators of minor pests, since predators like parasites and mites are not usually species-specific. Then minor pests become major pests. Additional pesticides are needed, and the pesticide treadmill occurs again.

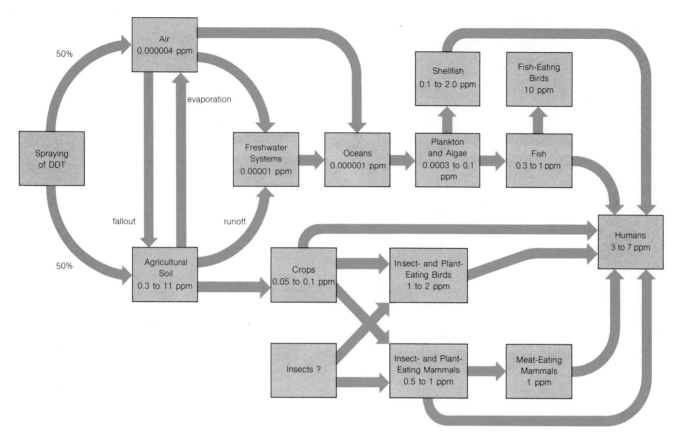

Figure 22-7 The movement and biological amplification of DDT in the biosphere.

Mobility and Biological Amplification of Persistent Pesticides Aircraft are used to apply about one-fourth of all pesticides used on U.S. cropland (Figure 22-6). Even under ideal application conditions, only about 50% of the spray reaches the target area. Most of this spray, as well as pesticides applied by ground sprayers, is washed or leached off the land or blown into the air. As a result, it is estimated that only 1% (ranging from 0.1% to 5%, depending on the chemical and its method of application) of pesticides applied to crops reaches the target pests. The remaining 99% ends up in the air, water, and other nontarget organisms, including people. In 1986 the EPA reported that traces of 17 different pesticides were found in groundwater supplies in 23 states. Water from almost 1,500 wells in California's Central Valley cannot be used for drinking, bathing, or cooking because of pesticide contamination.

DDT and other fat-soluble pesticides can be biologically amplified in food chains and webs to levels hundreds to millions of times higher than those in the soil or water (Figure 4-20, p. 86, and Figure 22-7). The high levels of pesticide stored in the fatty tissues of organisms feeding on pesticide-contaminated organisms that are lower in the food chain can kill many forms of wildlife outright or interfere with their reproduction. Because of biological amplification, all people born after 1950 have carried several parts per million (ppm) of DDT in their fatty tissues, with unknown long-term harmful effects.

Threats to Wildlife Marine organisms, especially shellfish, can be killed by minute concentrations of chlorinated hydrocarbon pesticides. The young offspring of some species are often particularly susceptible to pesticides. For example, adult mink remain healthy after consuming DDT-contaminated fish, but about 80% of their newborn infants die within a few days. Honeybees, which pollinate crops that provide one-third of the food consumed in the United States, are extremely susceptible to pesticide poisoning. Each year an estimated 20% of all honeybee colonies in the United States are killed by pesticides and another 15% of the colonies are damaged—causing annual losses of at least $135 million from reduced pollination of vital crops.

During the 1950s and 1960s there were drastic declines in populations of fish-eating birds, such as the osprey, cormorant, brown pelican, and bald eagle.

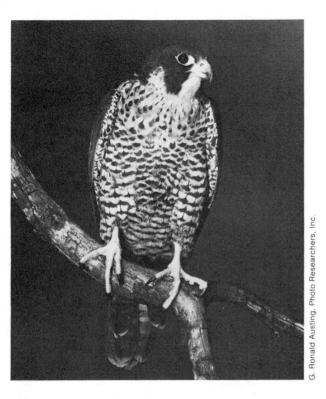

G. Ronald Austing, Photo Researchers, Inc.

Figure 22-8 The population of peregrine falcons in the United States was sharply reduced between 1950 and 1970 when high levels of DDT and its breakdown products caused the birds to produce eggs with shells so thin that many chicks died.

There were also sharp declines in populations of predatory birds, such as the prairie falcon, sparrow hawk, Bermuda petrel, and peregrine falcon (Figure 22-8); these birds help control populations of rabbits, ground squirrels, and other crop-damaging small mammals.

Research has shown that these population declines occurred because DDE, a chemical produced by the breakdown of high levels of DDT, accumulated in the bodies of the affected bird species and reduced the calcium deposition in the shells of their eggs. The resulting thin-shelled eggs are so fragile that many of them break, and the unborn chicks die before they can hatch normally.

Since the U.S. ban on DDT in 1972, populations of most of these bird species have made a comeback. By 1980, however, it was discovered that levels of DDT and other banned pesticides were beginning to rise again in some areas and in some species, such as the peregrine falcon—probably the result of illegal use of banned pesticides.

Short-Term Threats to Human Health Humans can be exposed to high levels of pesticides that are being manufactured, poured, or sprayed without proper safety precautions, or sprayed too close to homes. Farm workers and children can also be exposed to danger-ous levels of pesticides when they enter sprayed fields before the substances have broken down. By conservative estimates, about 400,000 farm workers, pesticide plant employees, and children become seriously ill, and about 10,000 die, each year around the world from exposure to toxic insecticides, especially organophosphates. Insecticide-related illnesses and deaths are particularly high among farm workers in LDCs, where educational levels are low, warnings are few, and pesticide regulation and control methods are often lax.

In the United States pesticides cause an estimated 45,000 illnesses and at least 25 deaths each year among the country's 7 million farm workers. Studies by the World Resources Institute (WRI) indicate that pesticide-related illness among farm workers in the United States and throughout the world is probably greatly underestimated because of poor records, lack of doctors and reporting in rural areas, and faulty diagnosis. In the United States many workers—particularly illegal immigrants—are reluctant to report illness for fear of being fired or deported. According to the WRI, the true number of pesticide-related illnesses each year probably runs in the millions, including 300,000 in the United States. Injuries and deaths can also occur from the manufacture of pesticides (see Spotlight on p. 525).

In the 1960s a controversy began over the possible health effects from the use of the herbicides 2,4,5-T and 2,4-D. Between 1962 and 1970, Agent Orange, a 50–50 mixture of 2,4-D and 2,4,5-T, was sprayed to defoliate swamps and forests in South Vietnam to prevent guerrilla ambushes, discourage the movement of troops and supplies through demilitarized zones, clear areas around military camps, and destroy crops that could feed Vietcong and North Vietnamese soldiers. This campaign of biological warfare destroyed vast areas of farmland, more than half the mangrove forests of South Vietnam, and about 5% of the country's hardwood forests—a supply of wood worth at least $500 million that could have lasted the country for 30 years.

In 1965 and 1966 a study commissioned by the National Cancer Institute found that low levels of 2,4,5-T caused high rates of birth defects in laboratory animals. This report was not released to the public until 1969. Because of the resulting pressure from environmentalists and health officials, however, the Vietnam defoliation program was halted in 1970. Investigations revealed that the birth defects in laboratory animals were probably caused by a highly toxic dioxin called TCCD, formed in minute quantities as an unavoidable contaminant during the manufacture of 2,4,5-T. Soil and industrial waste contaminated with TCCD have also been deposited in numerous sites in the United States (see Enrichment Study at the end of Chapter 21).

In the late 1970s as many as 40,000 previously healthy Vietnam veterans began experiencing a variety of medical disorders including dizziness, blurred

In 1975 state officials found that 70 of the 150 employees in a pesticide manufacturing plant in Hopewell, Virginia (near Richmond), had been poisoned by exposure to high levels of kepone (chlorodecone)—a persistent, chlorinated hydrocarbon pesticide used as an ant and roach poison. Inside the plant kepone dust filled the air, covered equipment, and was even found in the employees' lunch area. Some workers also brought kepone dust home on their clothes and contaminated family members.

The plant, associated with Allied Chemical Company, was shut down in 1975, and 29 workers were hospitalized with uncontrollable shaking, slurred speech, apparent brain and liver damage, inability to concentrate, joint pain, and, in some cases, sterility. Because kepone causes cancer in test animals, scientists have tried to reduce the risk of cancer by using a drug called cholestryamine to remove most of the kepone from the systems of exposed workers. Allied Chemical Company has paid out $13 million in damage suits to the victims and their families.

Further investigation revealed that a large area of the James River, the largest river in Virginia, and its fish and shellfish were contaminated with kepone. Between 1966 and 1975, the manufacturer illegally dumped kepone into the Hopewell municipal sewage system. The compound disrupted the bacterial decomposition processes in the sewage treatment plant and led to the discharge of untreated, kepone-laden sewage into the nearby James River. In 1975 more than 160 kilometers (100 miles) of the river and its tributaries were closed to commercial fishing, resulting in a loss of jobs and millions of dollars. By 1987, fish were still too contaminated with kepone for the ban to be lifted.

In 1984 the world's worst industrial accident occurred at a Union Carbide pesticide plant located in Bhopal, India. More than 2,300 people were killed when highly toxic methyl isocyanate gas, used in the manufacture of pesticides, leaked from a storage tank. Official Indian government figures indicate that 500,000 of Bhopal's population of about 1 million suffered some sort of injury. At least 14,000 were seriously injured and suffered blindness, sterility, kidney and liver infections, tuberculosis, brain damage, and other disorders that can lead to premature death. The victims sued Union Carbide for $3.1 billion in damages in a Bhopal district court.

This tragedy could probably have been prevented by the expenditure of perhaps no more than a million dollars to ensure more adequate plant safety. This incident has aroused concern about the safety of the almost 11,600 chemical plants located in the United States, especially after a toxic gas leak in 1985 from another Union Carbide plant in Institute, West Virginia, sent 135 nearby residents to the hospital.

vision, insomnia, fits of uncontrollable rage, nausea, chloracne on large areas of their skin, and depression. An abnormally high percentage of these veterans fathered infants who were aborted prematurely, stillborn, or had multiple birth defects. Other veterans had higher than expected incidences of leukemia, lymphoma, and rare testicular cancer.

By 1980, more than 1,200 Vietnam veterans had filed claims with the Veterans Administration for disabilities allegedly caused by exposure to Agent Orange. The VA and chemical manufacturers of Agent Orange, however, continue to deny any connection between the medical disorders and Agent Orange and attribute the problems to post-Vietnam stress syndrome. In 1984, the companies making Agent Orange agreed to an out-of-court settlement with the Vietnam veterans, without admitting any guilt or connection between the disorders and the use of the herbicide.

In 1986 a National Cancer Institute study indicated a strong statistical link between 2,4-D—a component of Agent Orange and the active ingredient in more than 1,500 herbicide products used by farmers and home gardeners—and a rare form of cancer known as non-Hodgkin's lymphoma. A study found that farmers who used 2,4-D were more than twice as likely as nonfarmers to develop this form of cancer. Earlier, Swedish researchers had shown an association between 2,4,5-T and 2,4-D and two other cancers—soft-tissue sarcoma and Hodgkin's disease.

Long-Term Threats to Human Health   Many scientists are concerned about the possible long-term effects on people of low-level exposure to DDT and other persistent pesticides. Such effects, if any, won't be known for several decades because the people who have carried these chemicals in their bodies the longest were only 43 years old by 1988. The results of this long-term worldwide experiment, with human beings involuntarily playing the role of guinea pigs, may never be known, because it is almost impossible to determine that a specific chemical such as DDT caused a particular cancer or other harmful effect.

However, some disturbing but inconclusive evidence has emerged. DDT, aldrin, dieldrin, heptachlor, mirex, endrin, and 19 other pesticides have all been found to cause cancer in test animals, especially liver cancer in mice. In addition, autopsies have shown that the bodies of people who died from cancer, cirrhosis of the liver, hypertension, cerebral hemorrhage, and softening of the brain contained fairly high levels of DDT or its breakdown products DDD and DDE.

22-4 PESTICIDE REGULATION IN THE UNITED STATES

Is the Public Adequately Protected? Because of the potentially harmful effects of pesticides on wildlife and people, Congress passed the Federal Insecticide, Fungicide, and Rodenticide Act (FIFRA) in 1972. This act, which was amended in 1975 and 1978, requires that all commercially available pesticides be registered with the Environmental Protection Agency. Using information provided by the pesticide manufacturer, the EPA may refuse to approve the use of the pesticide or may classify it for general or restricted use. The EPA can also cancel or suspend the use of a pesticide already on the market if new evidence of harmful side effects to wildlife or human beings is established.

Since its passage in 1972 environmentalists have considered the FIFRA the weakest environmental law on the books because of strong lobbying by the powerful agricultural chemicals industry and because the committee that draws up the legislation is controlled by pro-industry elected officials from farm states. Unlike other environmental laws, the FIFRA authorizes the EPA to allow a dangerous chemical to stay on the market if the supposed economic benefits (substantiated by the pesticide industry) outweigh the risk to human health or the environment.

Since 1972 the EPA has used the FIFRA to ban the use, except for emergency situations, of DDT and several other persistent chlorinated hydrocarbon pesticides such as aldrin, dieldrin, heptachlor, lindane, chlordane, and toxaphene. These pesticides were banned because their persistence and biological amplification in food chains and webs threaten some forms of wildlife and because laboratory tests show they cause birth defects, cancer, and neurologic dis-

orders in laboratory test animals. Between 1975 and 1985 the EPA banned all use of five pesticides, including the herbicides Silvex and 2,4,5-T, and restricted the use of 23 others because of their potential hazards to human health.

However, even when the health and environmental effects are shown to outweigh the economic benefits of continued use of a particular pesticide, the procedural labyrinth the EPA must follow to cancel or restrict the use of a pesticide can take ten years. During this time consumers continue to be exposed to health hazards from the product. For example, the National Cancer Institute established that low dosages of ethylene dibromide (EDB)—widely used for decades as a fumigant on grains and citrus fruits—caused stomach cancer and genetic mutations in all test animals in a relatively short time. But the EPA did not ban this chemical until 1984. Even this action came only after several states, fed up with inaction by the EPA, began removing EDB-contaminated products from grocery store shelves after finding alarming levels of EDB in groundwater supplies in fruit-growing areas and in some cake and muffin mixes and other grain products.

Most Americans might assume that the 600 active ingredients and 900 inert ingredients approved for use in 50,000 different pesticide products in the United States have been carefully examined by the EPA and have passed rigorous health and safety tests to determine their potential for producing cancer, genetic mutations, and birth defects. However, according to a 1984 study by the National Academy of Sciences, 84% of the pesticide ingredients in use had not been tested adequately by their manufacturers or any regulatory agency to determine whether they cause cancer. In addition, 93% had not been tested for their capacity to cause genetic mutations, and 70% had not been evaluated for their ability to cause birth defects. According to the National Academy of Sciences, only 10% of the ingredients used in pesticides in 1984 had sufficient health and safety data for an adequate assessment of their dangers to human health.

The FIFRA required the EPA to reevaluate the 600 active ingredients approved for use in pesticide products before 1972 to determine whether any of these substances caused cancer, birth defects, or other health risks. The EPA was supposed to complete this analysis by 1975. Yet, by 1986 the EPA had only completed its evaluation for six of these ingredients. In addition, during the late 1970s, the EPA discovered that data had been falsified by a now-defunct test laboratory on over 200 pesticides approved for use (including at least 90 used on food crops). Under the FIFRA, the EPA is not required to ban a pesticide even if it can be shown that its registration was based on faulty data. By 1986 repeated attempts by environmentalists to have Congress strengthen the FIFRA has failed.

Export of Banned Pesticides In response to a slow-down in the pesticide use rate in the United States since 1981, the U.S. chemical industry has increased exports of pesticides or their basic ingredients to countries (mostly LDCs) where they have not been banned. In most LDCs, up to 70% of these pesticides are applied to crops such as cotton, coffee, cocoa, and bananas destined for export to Europe, Japan, and the United States.

In 1984 tests by the Food and Drug Administration found that 30% to 50% of the imported coffee was tainted with residues of pesticides banned in the United States. Although high levels of residues on imported foods are illegal, enforcement is lax. Each year the FDA samples less than 1% of imported food products for pesticide contamination. Even then, in 1985 only 3% of the foods found to be contaminated were not allowed to be sold.

In 1978 Congress amended the FIFRA to require foreign purchasers of such pesticides to acknowledge their awareness that these chemicals are not approved for use in the United States. The EPA then notifies the government of the importing country that unregistered products are being shipped. However, many of these shipments arrive and are used long before this information reaches the appropriate official with the power to refuse to accept the cargo.

In 1983, the United Nations passed a resolution calling for stringent restrictions on the export of products whose use has been banned or severely restricted in the exporting nation; in addition, the UN asked for widespread publication of a list of such products. Under orders from President Reagan, the United States was the only country opposing this resolution. It was argued that countries receiving exports of banned or unregistered pesticides, drugs, and other chemicals from the United States should be free to use these chemicals if they so desire and that if U.S. companies do not sell these substances to them, someone else will.

Has DDT Really Been Banned? A 1983 study showed that 44% of the fruits and vegetables grown in California contained higher than expected residues of 19 different pesticides, including DDT and other banned substances. Investigators suspect that this is due to a combination of illegal smuggling from Mexico and a loophole in the FIFRA that allows the sale of insecticides that contain up to 15% DDT by weight. This DDT is allowed because it is classified by the EPA as an "unintentional impurity" that occurs when certain insecticides are manufactured. For example, dicofol (usually sold under the trade name Kelthane) contains as much as 15% DDT. Although dicofol is not manufactured in the United States, more than 910,000 kilograms (2 million pounds) are imported each year and used to control mites on cotton and citrus crops.

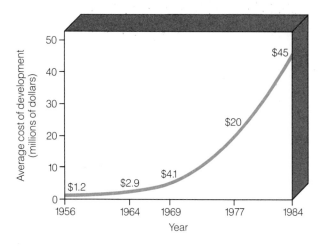

Figure 22-9 The average cost of developing a new pesticide in the United States has soared since 1956. (Data from Robert Metcalf)

22-5 ALTERNATIVE METHODS OF INSECT CONTROL

Modifying Cultivation Procedures There are a number of alternatives to relying on conventional pesticides to control pest populations. For centuries farmers have used cultivation methods that discourage or inhibit pests. Rotating the type of crop grown in a given field from year to year can be used to reduce populations in the soil or crop residues of nonmigrating pests that feed on a particular crop. Planting times can also be adjusted to ensure that most of the pest population starves to death before the crop is available or adjusted to favor natural predators over the pests. Rows of hedges around or through fields can serve as barriers to insect invasion and create refuges for enemies of pests. Crops can also be grown in areas where their major pests do not exist. Unfortunately, to increase profits and in some cases to avoid bankruptcy, many farmers in MDCs such as the United States have abandoned these cultivation methods.

Biological Control For decades, agricultural scientists have been using biological control to regulate the populations of insects, weeds, rodents, and other pests by reintroducing effective natural predators, parasites, and pathogens (disease-causing bacteria and viruses) or by importing new ones. Worldwide, there have been more than 300 successful biological control projects, especially in China and the Soviet Union.

Use of biological control is increasing rapidly not only because it often works but also because it is cheaper than pesticides. In the 1950s and 1960s, chemicals such as DDT cost 20 cents a pound. Today's pesticides cost from $20 to $400 a pound (Figure 22-9).

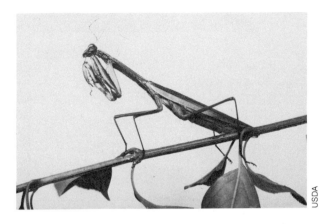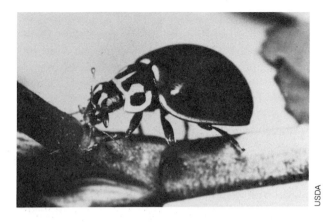

USDA

USDA

Figure 22-10 The praying mantis (left) and the ladybug (on the right eating an aphid) are used to control insect pests.

Examples of biological control include using ladybugs and praying mantises (Figure 22-10) to control aphids and using speck-sized parasitic wasps to control various crop-eating moths and flies such as the leaf miner. A bacterial agent *(Bacillus thuringiensis)*, sold commercially as a dry powder, is effective in controlling many strains of leaf-eating caterpillars, mosquitoes, and gypsy moths. Mycorrhizae, a category of molds, are being produced commercially and applied to the roots of seedling pines and other conifers to protect the trees against disease and to accelerate absorption of water and nutrients from the soil. The treated seedlings can grow twice as fast as untreated ones, making them especially useful in reclaiming sites that have been strip-mined or logged. As pesticide prices continue to climb, it will become economically feasible to mass produce many biological control agents.

Biological control has a number of important advantages. It normally effects only the target species and is nontoxic to other species, including human beings. Once a population of predators or parasites is established, control is often self-perpetuating and does not have to be reintroduced each year. Development of genetic resistance is minimized because both pest and predator species usually undergo natural selection to maintain a stable interaction (coevolution). In the United States biological control has saved farmers an average of $30 for every $1 invested, compared to $4 saved for every $1 invested in pesticides.

No method of pest control, however, is perfect. Typically, 10 to 20 years of research may be required to understand how a particular pest interacts with its various enemies and to determine the best control agent; also, mass production is often difficult. Farmers find that pesticides are faster acting and simpler to apply than biological agents. Biological agents must also be protected from pesticides sprayed in nearby fields, and there is a chance that some agents can also become pests. In addition, some pest organisms can

develop genetic resistance to viruses and bacterial agents used for biological control.

Genetic Control by Sterilization Males of an insect species can be raised in the laboratory, sterilized by radiation or chemicals, and then released in an infested area to mate unsuccessfully with fertile wild females. If sterile males outnumber fertile males by 10 to 1, a pest species in a given area can be eradicated in about four generations, provided reinfestation does not occur. This sterile male technique works best if the females mate only once, if the infested area is isolated so that it can't be periodically repopulated with nonsterilized males, and if the insect pest population has already been reduced to a fairly low level by weather, pesticides, or other factors.

The screwworm fly is a major livestock pest in South America, Central America, and the southeastern and southwestern United States. This metallic blue-green insect, about two to three times the size of the common housefly, deposits its eggs in open wounds of warm-blooded animals, such as cattle and deer. Within a few hours the eggs hatch into parasitic larvae that feed on the flesh of the host animal (Figure 22-11). A severe infestation of this pest can kill a mature steer within ten days. The Department of Agriculture used the sterile male approach to essentially eliminate the screwworm fly from the southeastern states between 1962 and 1971. In 1972, however, the pest made a dramatic comeback, infesting 100,000 cattle and causing serious losses until 1976, when a new strain of the males was developed, sterilized, and released to bring the situation under temporary control. To prevent resurgences of this pest, new strains of male flies will have to be developed, sterilized, and released every few years.

Major problems with this approach include ensuring that sterile males are not overwhelmed numeri-

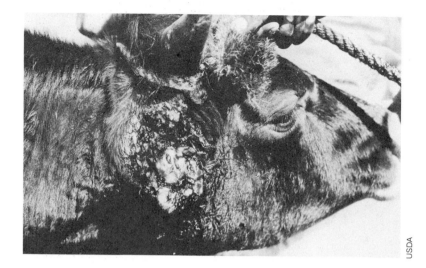

USDA

cally by nonsterile males, knowing the mating times and behavior of each target insect, risking that laboratory-produced strains of sterile males will not be as sexually active as normal wild males, preventing reinfestation with new nonsterilized males, and high costs.

Genetic Control by Breeding Resistant Crops and Animals For many decades agricultural scientists have used artificial selection, cross-breeding, and genetic engineering to develop new varieties of plants and animals resistant to certain insects, fungi, and diseases. For example, scientists developed a number of wheat strains resistant to the Hessian fly, a major wheat pest that was accidentally introduced into the United States in the straw bedding of German mercenaries during the Revolutionary War.

Breeding new resistant strains of crops and animals is expensive and can require from 10 to 20 years of painstaking work by highly trained scientists. The new strains must also produce high yields. Furthermore, insect pests and plant diseases can develop new strains that attack the once resistant varieties, forcing scientists to continually develop new resistant strains.

Chemical Control Using Natural Sex Attractants and Hormones Various pheromones and hormones can be used to control populations of insect pest species. Some observers believe that these two new types of chemical agents, sometimes called *third generation pesticides,* may eventually replace the present use of less desirable second generation pesticides.

In many insect species, when a virgin female is ready to mate she releases a minute amount (typically about one-millionth of a gram) of a species-specific chemical sex attractant called a pheromone. Males of the species up to a half-mile away can detect the chem-

ical with their antennal receptors and follow the scent upwind to its source. Pheromones extracted from an insect pest species or synthesized in the laboratory can be used to lure pests such as Japanese beetles into traps containing toxic chemicals. An infested area can also be sprayed with the appropriate pheromone or covered with millions of tiny cardboard squares impregnated with the substance so that the males become confused and are unable to find a mate because they detect the smell of virgin females everywhere. Recent research indicates that instead of using pheromones to trap bad bugs, it is more effective to use them to lure the pests' natural predators into fields and gardens. Pheromones are now commercially available for use against 30 major pests.

Pheromones have a number of advantages: They work on only one species, they are effective in extremely minute concentrations, they usually break down within a week, they have relatively little chance of causing genetic resistance, and they are not poisonous to animals, thus not affecting wildlife and not creating new pests. However, the difficulties with pheromones include identifying and isolating the specific sex attractant for each pest species, determining the mating behavior of the target insect, and coping with periodic reinfestation from surrounding areas. Pheromones have also failed for some pests because only adults are drawn to the traps; for most species, the juvenile forms—such as caterpillars—do most of the damage. The major problem with pheromones is their lack of availability for most pests or natural predators.

Hormones are chemicals produced in an organism's cells that travel through the bloodstream and control various aspects of the organism's growth and development. Each step in the life cycle of a typical insect is regulated by the timely release of juvenile hormones (JH) and molting hormones (MH) (Figure 22-12). If extracted or laboratory-synthesized juvenile hormones or molting hormones are applied at certain

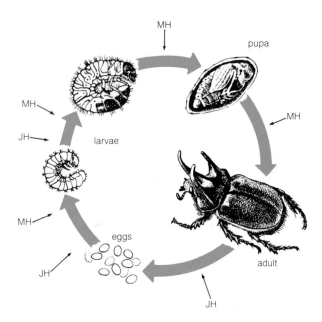

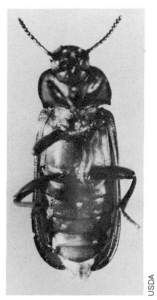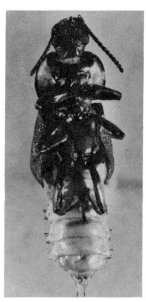

Figure 22-12 For normal growth, development, and reproduction certain juvenile hormones (JH) and molting hormones (MH) must be present at genetically determined stages in the typical life cycle of an insect. If applied at the right time, synthetic hormones can be used to disrupt the life cycle of insect pests.

Figure 22-13 Chemical hormones can prevent insects from maturing completely, thus making it impossible for them to reproduce. Compare a normal mealworm (left) with one that failed to develop an adult abdomen after being sprayed with a synthetic hormone.

stages in an insect's life cycle, they can produce abnormalities that cause the insect to die before it can reach maturity and reproduce (Figure 22-13).

Insect hormones have the same advantages as pheromones, except that they sometimes affect natural predators of the target insect species and other nonpest species. However, hormones require weeks rather than minutes to kill, are often ineffective with a large infestation, sometimes break down chemically in the environment before they can act, must be applied at the right time in the life cycle of a target insect, and are difficult and costly to isolate and produce.

Irradiation of Foods Exposing certain foods to various levels of radiation is being touted by the nuclear industry and the food industry as a means of killing or preventing insects from reproducing in certain foods after harvest, extending the shelf life of some perishable foods, and destroying parasites such as trichinae and bacteria such as salmonella that each year kill 2,000 Americans (Table 22-3). In 1986 the FDA approved use of up to 100 kilorads of ionizing radiation on fruits, vegetables, and fresh pork, and it may soon be approved for use on poultry and seafood. Irradiated foods are already sold in 33 countries including the Soviet Union, Japan, Canada, Brazil, Israel, and many west European countries.

Because tests show that consumers will not buy food if it is labeled as irradiated, foods exposed to

radiation sold in the United States bear a characteristic logo and a label stating that the product has been picowaved (Figure 22-14)—information that will be meaningless to many consumers, but better than no label. The label, however, is only required on foods that have been directly irradiated, not on those that contain irradiated components such as various spices used in processed cheese spreads and luncheon meats.

The irradiation treatment process is simple. Foods put on a conveyor belt pass near a concrete, lead-shielded chamber housing the radioactive source, typically gamma rays emitted by cobalt-60. The gamma rays passing through the food destroy insects and bacteria. Exposure to higher doses—generally above those presently allowed by the FDA—also could extend the shelf life of some perishable foods. A food does not become radioactive when it is irradiated, just as being X-rayed does not make the body radioactive.

The FDA and the World Health Organization say that over 1,000 studies show that foods exposed to low radiation doses are safe for human consumption. However, critics of irradiation argue that not enough animal studies have been done and tests of the effects of irradiated foods on people have been too few and brief to turn up any long-term effects, which typically require 30 to 40 years to be evaluated. The focus of this controversy is the fact that irradiation produces trace amounts of at least 65 chemicals in foods, some of which cause cancer in test animals.

Scientists in favor of irradiating foods respond that

Table 22-3	Effects of Radiation on Food
Dosage	**Effects**
Low (up to 100 kilorads)	Inhibits sprouting of potatoes, onions, and garlic; kills or prevents insects from reproducing in grains, fruits, and vegetables after harvest; inactivates trichinae in pork; delays ripening of certain fruits
Moderate (100–1,000 kilorads)	Delays spoilage of meat, poultry, and fish by reducing spoilage microorganisms; reduces salmonella and other food-borne pathogens in meat, fish, and poultry; extends shelf life by delaying mold growth on strawberries and other fruits
High (1,000–10,000 kilorads)	Sterilizes meat, poultry, fish, and other foods; kills microorganisms and insects in spices and seasonings

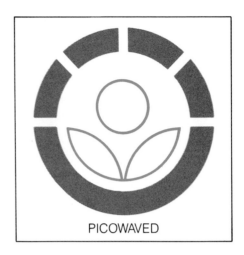

PICOWAVED

Figure 22-14 Logo used on irradiated foods in the United States.

23 of these chemicals are also formed by certain cooking methods—frying, for example—and 36 are found in some other nonirradiated foods. The FDA estimates that 10% of the chemicals produced in irradiated foods are probably unique—that is, they are chemicals not found in nonirradiated foods—and assumes that the concentrations of these chemicals will be too small to affect human health. Opponents of food irradiation say this assumption is unwarranted until these chemicals have been identified and thoroughly tested.

Opponents also fear that more people might die of deadly botulism because present levels of irradiation do not destroy the spore-enclosed bacteria that cause this disease, but they do destroy the microbes that give off the rotten odor warning of the presence of botulism bacteria. They also note that irradiation can be expensive, adding as much as five cents a pound to the price of some fresh vegetables. Proponents, however, respond that, on balance, irradiation of food is likely to reduce health hazards to people by decreasing the use of some potentially damaging pesticides and food additives.

Integrated Pest Management An increasing number of experts believe that in many cases our present, eventually self-defeating pesticide-based approach to pest control can be replaced with a carefully designed ecological approach—called **integrated pest management (IPM).** In IPM, each crop and its major pests are considered as an ecological system, and a control program is developed that uses a variety of biological, chemical, and cultivation methods in proper sequence and timing. The overall aim is not eradication but keeping pest populations just below the level of economic loss (Figure 22-15). Fields are carefully monitored to check whether pests have reached an economically damaging level. When such a level is reached, farmers first use biological and cultural controls. Pesticides are applied only when absolutely necessary, and in small amounts, with different chemicals cycled to retard development of genetic resistance.

Over the past 30 years, more than three dozen IPM programs have been used successfully. These experiments have shown that a properly designed IPM program can reduce preharvest pest-induced crop losses by 50%, reduce pesticide use and pesticide control costs by 50% to 75%, reduce fertilizer and irrigation needs, and at the same time increase crop yields and reduce costs. By 1979 IPM was being used on more than a third of all cotton acreage in 14 major cotton-producing states in the United States.

Integrated pest management has a number of advantages. It requires minimal use of pesticides and therefore reduces their harmful side effects, including genetic resistance. Also, it decreases soil erosion and use of fertilizer and irrigation water, and it is cheaper on a long-term basis than the increasingly expensive pesticide treadmill. However, there are some drawbacks to IPM. It requires expert knowledge about each

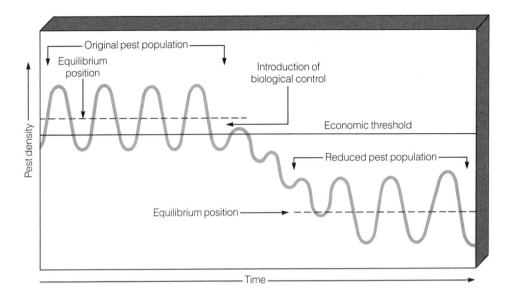

Figure 22-15 The goal of biological control and integrated pest management is not to eliminate pests but to keep the pest population beneath the level of economic damage.

In the figure: Original pest population; Equilibrium position; Introduction of biological control; Economic threshold; Reduced pest population; Equilibrium position; Pest density; Time

pest–crop situation and is slower acting and more labor intensive than the use of conventional pesticides. Methods developed for a given crop in one area may not be applicable to another area with slightly different growing conditions. Although long-term costs are typically lower than those using conventional pesticides, initial costs may be higher.

A massive switch to IPM in the United States is very difficult primarily because of the political clout of the agricultural chemical companies that see little profit in such methods. As a result, IPM will have to be developed through financial and technical support from federal and state agencies. Environmentalists also urge that its use be promoted by providing government subsidies and perhaps government-backed lost crop insurance to farmers who use IPM or other approved alternatives to the widespread use of pesticides. They also ask that the government greatly increase the funding for research on biological controls, natural insect pheromones and hormones, and effective IPM strategies for all major pests.

Changing the Attitudes of Consumers and Farmers Three attitudes tend to increase the use of pesticides and lock us into the pesticide treadmill. First, many people believe that the only good bug is a dead bug. Second, most consumers insist on buying only perfect, unblemished fruits and vegetables, even though a few holes or frayed leaves do not significantly affect the taste, nutrition, or shelf life of such produce. Third, most farmers and consumers want pests to be controlled instantly, but they have not seriously considered the long-term effects of such a demand. This last attitude, encouraged by the pesti-

cide industry, leads to the mistaken belief that there are no alternatives to the widespread use of pesticides and that without them diseases such as malaria would be rampant and crop losses would be great enough to cause mass starvation. Educating farmers and consumers to change these three attitudes would go a long way toward reducing the use of pesticides.

Individuals can also reduce the dangers of pesticides by using the smallest amount possible only when absolutely necessary and by disposing of unused pesticides in a safe manner (call your local health department). Elected representatives should also be pressured to significantly strengthen the Federal Insecticide, Fungicide, and Rodenticide Act in order to better protect human health and the environment.

Homeowners should seriously consider planting all or most of the land around a house site not used for gardening with a diverse mix of wildflowers, herbs (for cooking), low-growing ground cover, small bushes, and other forms of vegetation natural to the area. Create paths covered with wood chips or stones through the area so that little if any mowing is ever required. This approach, based on natural diversity rather than the traditional monoculture of grass, saves time, energy, money (no lawn mower, gasoline, or frequent lawn mower repairs), and strife over why the lawn hasn't been cut. This type of yard also reduces infestations by mosquitoes and other insects by providing a diversity of habitats for their natural predators. The largest homesite infestations by insect pests and weeds such as crabgrass usually occur in yards planted with grass that is kept cut below three inches in height. In other words, work with, not against, nature by establishing a diversity of vegetation and letting grass grow at least three inches.

We need to recognize that pest control is basically an ecological, not a chemical, problem.

Robert L. Rudd

CHAPTER SUMMARY

In a diverse natural ecosystem, the populations of insects and vegetation considered pests are usually kept in check by populations of natural predators, disease organisms, and parasites. Because such natural controls are sharply reduced in simplified croplands and gardens, people have increasingly used various chemicals called pesticides to control pest populations. A number of chlorinated hydrocarbon, organophosphate, carbamate, and pyrethroid compounds are used as insecticides to kill insects and a number of contact herbicides, systemic herbicides, and soil sterilants are used to kill unwanted vegetation.

Since 1945 pesticides such as DDT and related chlorinated hydrocarbon insecticides have been used to help control the number of cases and the spread of insect-transmitted diseases such as malaria; they have prevented the deaths of at least 7 million people. Pesticides have also been used to help reduce loss of crops to pests before and after harvest. These chemicals can control pests quickly at a reasonable cost, have a long shelf life, are shipped and applied easily, and when properly handled are safe.

There is considerable evidence, however, that widespread pesticide use causes undesirable and harmful effects in ecosystems and in nonpest organisms, including human beings. The major problems associated with the widespread use of insecticides are: (1) development of genetic resistance by target species, (2) killing of the target species's natural enemies, (3) creation of new pests, (4) global mobility and biological amplification of persistent insecticides, (5) threats to wildlife, and (6) threats to human health. Because of these problems, some analysts question the long-term value of pesticides in increasing food supplies and in controlling diseases spread by insects.

Pesticide use in the United States is regulated by the Federal Insecticide, Fungicide, and Rodenticide Act (FIFRA) of 1972, which requires all commercially available pesticides to be registered with the EPA. Although the EPA has used this act to ban or restrict the use of a number of pesticides, environmentalists consider the FIFRA to be a weak law that does not adequately protect human health and the environment from the harmful effects of pesticides. So far attempts to strengthen this law have failed.

There are a number of alternatives to relying almost exclusively on conventional pesticides to control insect pest populations. These include modifying cultivation procedures; biological control by natural predators; genetic control by sterilizing male insects; genetic control by breeding resistant crop and animal varieties; chemical control using natural sex attractants and hormones; irradiation of certain foods to kill insects and pathogens after harvest and to extend shelf life; and integrated pest management in which a variety of biological, chemical, and cultivation methods are used in proper sequence and timing to keep pest populations just below the economic loss level.

Farmers and consumers can also be educated to buy not only perfect fruits and vegetables and to realize that, because of genetic resistance, widespread use of any chemical is self-defeating: It eventually causes an outbreak of the pest species that is larger and stronger than before. Individuals should also use pesticides only when absolutely necessary in the smallest amounts possible, dispose of unused pesticides safely, and plant a diverse array of plants around house sites rather than planting only grass and keeping it cut low to the ground.

DISCUSSION TOPICS

1. Should the United States abandon or sharply decrease pesticide use and replace it with integrated pest management? Explain. What might be the consequences for LDCs? For the United States? For you?

2. Explain how the use of insecticides can actually increase the number of insect pest problems and threaten some carnivores and omnivores, including humans.

3. How does genetic resistance to a particular pesticide occur? What major advantages do insects have over humans in this respect?

4. Debate the following resolution: Because DDT and the other banned chlorinated hydrocarbon pesticides pose no demonstrable threat to human health and have probably saved more lives than any other chemicals in history, they should again be approved for use in the United States.

5. What ways, if any, do you believe the U.S. Federal Insecticide, Fungicide, and Rodenticide Act should be strengthened? Explain. What changes, if any, have been made in this act since this book was written in early 1987?

6. Should certain types of foods in the United States be irradiated? Explain.

7. List the major advantages and disadvantages of pest control by (a) biological control, (b) sterilization of male insects, (c) sex attractants, (d) juvenile hormones, (e) resistant crop varieties, (f) cultivation practices, (g) integrated pest management, and (h) conventional pesticides.

23

The Environment and Human Health: Disease, Food Additives, and Noise

GENERAL OBJECTIVES

1. What are the major types of disease?
2. What are some major infectious diseases found in LDCs?
3. What are the major environmental factors that can increase the incidence of cancer in MDCs?
4. What risks do food additives pose to human health?
5. What risks does excessive noise pose to human health?

Though their health needs differ drastically, the rich and the poor do have one thing in common: both die unnecessarily. The rich die of heart disease and cancer, the poor of diarrhea, pneumonia, and measles. Scientific medicine could vastly reduce the mortality caused by these illnesses. Yet, half the developing world lacks medical care of any kind.

William U. Chandler

When the complex, delicate balance that normally exists between our bodies and the environment is upset, we can become afflicted with a disease. The upset may result from factors in the physical environment (air, water, food, and sun), the biological environment (bacteria, viruses, plants, and animals, including people), the social environment (work, leisure, and cultural habits and patterns such as smoking, diet, drugs, or excessive drinking), or any combination of these three sources. Other potential threats to human health are the thousands of food additives in processed foods in the United States and other MDCs and exposure to excessive noise.

23-1 TYPES OF DISEASE

Infectious and Noninfectious Diseases Human diseases can be broadly classified as infectious and noninfectious. An **infectious disease** occurs when we are hosts to disease-causing living organisms called agents, such as bacteria, viruses, and parasitic worms. Infectious diseases can be classified according to the method of transmission (Table 23-1).

Vector-transmitted infectious diseases are carried from one person to another by a living organism (usually an insect), known as a vector. Examples include malaria, schistosomiasis, and elephantiasis (Figure 23-1). **Nonvector-transmitted infectious diseases** are transmitted from person to person without an

Table 23-1   Major Vector-Transmitted Infectious Diseases

Disease	Infectious Organism (Agent)	Vector	Estimated Number of People Infected (millions)
Malaria	*Plasmodium* (parasite)	*Anopheles* (mosquito)	500*
Schistosomiasis	*Schistosoma* (trematode worm)	Certain species of freshwater snails	100
Filariasis (elephantiasis and onchocerciasis, or river blindness)	Several species of parasitic worms	Certain species of mosquitoes and blood-sucking flies (elephantiasis); female black flies (onchocerciasis)	270
Trypanosomiasis (African sleeping sickness and Chagas' disease)	*Trypanosoma* (parasites)	Tsetse fly (African sleeping sickness); kissing bugs (Chagas' disease)	100

*250 million new cases each year.

intermediate carrier. Examples include the common cold, tuberculosis, cholera, measles, mononucleosis, syphilis, gonorrhea, and AIDS. Transmission of such diseases usually takes place by one or a combination of methods. Close physical contact with infected persons can transmit diseases such as mononucleosis and sexually transmitted diseases such as syphilis, gonorrhea, herpes, and AIDS. Contact with water, food, soil, or hands contaminated by fecal material or saliva from infected persons spreads diseases such as cholera, typhoid fever, and infectious hepatitis. Inhalation of air containing tiny droplets of contaminated fluid that is expelled when infected persons cough, sneeze, or talk transmits diseases such as the common cold, influenza, and tuberculosis.

Noninfectious diseases are not relayed by disease-causing organisms, and except for genetic diseases, are not transmitted from one person to another. Examples include cardiovascular (heart and blood vessel) disorders, cancer, diabetes, chronic respiratory diseases (bronchitis and emphysema, Section 19-3), allergies, nerve and other degenerative diseases (cerebral palsy and multiple sclerosis), and genetic diseases (hemophilia and sickle cell anemia). Many of these diseases have several often unknown causes and tend to develop slowly and progressively over time.

Acute and Chronic Diseases   Diseases can also be classified according to their effect and duration. An **acute disease** is an infectious disease such as measles or typhoid fever from which the victim either recovers or dies in a relatively short time. A **chronic disease** lasts for a long time (often for life) and may flare up

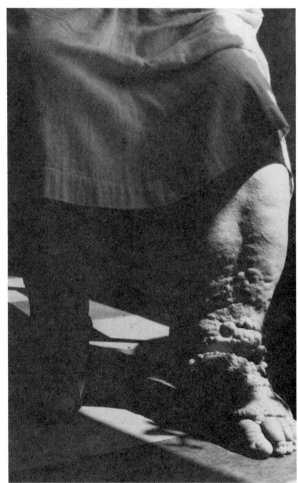

Photo Researchers, Inc.

Figure 23-1   A severe case of elephantiasis.

Table 23-2   Comparison of Acute Infectious, Chronic Infectious, and Chronic Noninfectious Diseases

Characteristic	Acute Infectious: Measles, Typhoid Fever, Whooping Cough, Smallpox	Chronic Infectious: Malaria, Schistosomiasis, Tuberculosis	Chronic Noninfectious: Cardiovascular Disorders, Cancer, Diabetes, Emphysema
Cause	Living organism	Living organism	Usually several, often unknown environmental and/or genetic factors
Transmission	Usually nonvector	Vector and nonvector	Not transmitted directly but some may be transmitted genetically
Time for development (latent period)	Short (hours or days)	Long (usually years)	Long (usually years)
Duration	Usually brief (days)	Long (often for life)	Long (often for life)
Effects	Usually temporary or reversible	Usually irreversible if untreated or not treated in early stages	Usually irreversible
Age group	Children and adults	Adults, middle to old age	Adults, middle to old age
Prevalence	High in LDCs, low in MDCs	High in LDCs, low in MDCs	High, especially in MDCs where longer life spans allow diseases to develop
Mortality	High in LDCs, low in MDCs	High in LDCs, low in MDCs	High in MDCs
Prevention	Sanitation, clean drinking water, vaccination	Sanitation, clean drinking water, vaccination, vector control	Control of environmental factors such as smoking, diet, and exposure to polluted air, water, and food

periodically (malaria), become progressively worse (cancer and cardiovascular disorders), or disappear with age (childhood asthma). Table 23-2 summarizes the major characteristics of acute infectious diseases, chronic infectious diseases, and chronic noninfectious diseases.

The Social Ecology of Disease   Although there is considerable room for improvement, impressive achievements have been made in human health in both MDCs and LDCs over the past 25 years. Since 1960 the average life expectancy at birth has increased from 41 years to 58 years in LDCs and from 70 years to 73 years in MDCs (Figure 7-4, p. 138).

People in LDCs tend to have shorter average life spans than those in MDCs, largely because of the complex interactions among poverty, malnutrition, and infectious diseases (Figure 12-11, p. 243). According to the World Health Organization, about 80% of all infectious disease in LDCs is caused by unsafe drinking water and inadequate sanitation.

The tropical or equatorial location of most LDCs also increases the chances of infection, because the hot, wet climates and the absence of winter enable disease vectors to thrive year round. In addition, poor people—especially infants—tend to be more susceptible to diseases because they are more likely to be weakened by malnutrition.

Fortunately, major improvements in human health in LDCs can be made with preventive and primary health care measures at a relatively low cost. One important goal should be to provide better nutrition and birth assistance for pregnant women in LDCs, where half of all births are delivered without any assistance from a trained midwife or doctor. Another would be to provide family planning and greatly improved child care (including the promotion of breast-feeding) to reduce the infant mortality rate. Finally, infant mortality rates can be significantly lowered and average life expectancy rates can be extended by providing clean drinking water and sanitation facilities to the third of the world's population that lacks them. Extending such primary health care to all the world's people would cost an additional $10 billion a year, one twenty-fifth as much as the world spends each year on cigarettes.

In most MDCs, safe water supplies, public sanitation, adequate nutrition, and immunization have nearly stamped out many infectious diseases. In 1900 pneumonia, influenza, tuberculosis, and diarrhea were the leading causes of death in MDCs. By contrast, the four leading causes of death in MDCs today are heart disease and strokes (48%), cancer (21%), respiratory infections (8%), and accidents, especially automobile accidents (7%).

These deaths are largely a result of environmental and lifestyle factors rather than infectious agents invading the body. Except for auto accidents, these

Excessive alcohol consumption and alcoholism are major forms of personal pollution that have damaging effects on individuals, friends and family members, and society as a whole. An estimated 21 million Americans are alcoholics (people so addicted to alcohol that they have lost control of their drinking) or problem drinkers (people in the early stages of alcoholism). This includes 4 million teenagers age 13 to 17.

Each year alcohol kills at least 100,000 Americans, more than twice the number of soldiers who were killed in the nine-year Vietnam War. In 1985, alcoholism cost Americans about $120 million in lost work time, medical bills, property damage, rehabilitation programs, and other expenses—costs borne by everyone, not just those who abuse alcohol.

Excessive alcohol consumption causes damage to the liver (cirrhosis or buildup of fatty tissue), esophagus, and digestive tract. The family members and loved ones of millions of alcoholics are psychologically injured each year. Pregnant women who have as little as two drinks or beers a day pass alcohol into the bloodstream of the fetus. Babies born to alcoholic mothers can be physically addicted to alcohol. Women who have three to nine alcoholic drinks per week face a 30% higher chance of developing breast cancer.

At least half of the 50,000 deaths and hundreds of thousands of serious injuries from automobile accidents in the United States each year are related to alcohol. Analysts argue that these alcohol-related deaths could be reduced sharply by requiring all passengers to use seat belts (as is done in essentially all MDCs except the United States), raising the drinking age to 21, significantly increasing the enforcement and penalties for driving under the influence of alcohol, and discouraging happy hours, chug-a-lug contests, and other practices that foster excessive alcohol consumption over a short period of time. It has also been suggested that bars and people hosting parties should have simple blood alcohol detection devices and should provide transportation for those who can't drive safely.

Although millions took to the streets to protest the Vietnam War, few protest the death and destruction caused by alcohol because it is a socially acceptable drug. Two-thirds of all Americans drink to some degree and one-third are moderate to heavy drinkers (Figure 23-2).

Because alcohol is so widely used in the United States and many other countries, reducing its destructive effects is difficult. One way to reduce alcohol abuse would be to provide better education on its effects and early symptoms. People should also be informed about how to help family members and friends who are alcoholics or who are becoming alcoholics. Government and private funding should also be increased for research on factors contributing to alcoholism and its treatment, for family members of alcoholics to cope with their own problems and help addicted family members, and for establishment of alcoholic treatment centers. Some of these funds could be provided through greatly increased taxes levied on the sale of alcoholic beverages. What do you think?

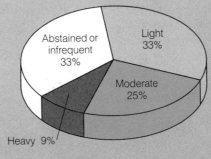

Figure 23-2   Drinking habits of American adults. (Data from National Institutes of Health)

deaths result from chronic diseases that take a long time to develop, have multiple causes, and are largely attributable to the area in which we live (urban or rural), our work environment, our diet, whether we smoke, and the amount of alcohol we consume (see Spotlight above).

Most of us are a bundle of contradictions when it comes to reducing risks from disease and premature death. We get angry about risks imposed on us but become fatalistic about the risks and forms of personal pollution we choose for ourselves. Even though most people know that ultraviolet rays from the sun cause

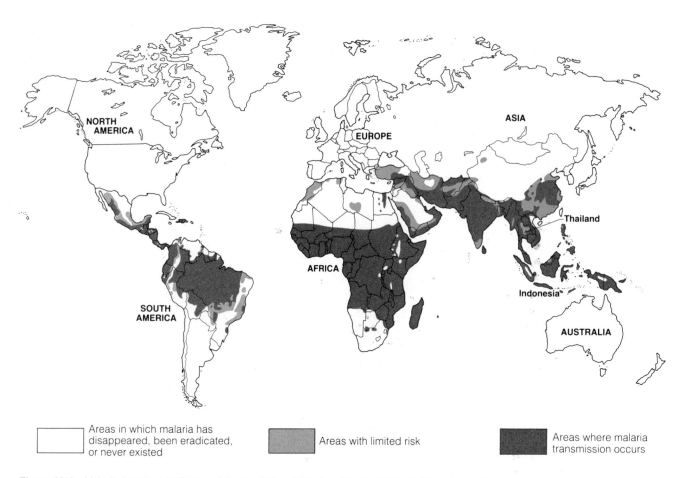

Areas in which malaria has disappeared, been eradicated, or never existed

Areas with limited risk

Areas where malaria transmission occurs

Figure 23-3 Malaria threatens half the world's population. (Data from the World Health Organization)

skin cancer and premature wrinkling, they bake in the sun or in even more dangerous tanning booths. Widely known statistics linking smoking with a greatly increased risk of lung cancer and heart disease don't stop many people from smoking. People forget the latest reports linking cholesterol to increased risk of heart disease when they see a bowl of chocolate chip ice cream.

23-2 INFECTIOUS DISEASES: MALARIA AND SCHISTOSOMIASIS

Malaria People in the United States and in most MDCs tend to view malaria as a disease of the past. But in the tropical and subtropical regions of the world, malaria is still the single most serious health problem—killing from 2 million to 4 million people a year and incapacitating tens of millions more. Today more than half the world's people live in malaria-prone regions in about 100 different countries (Figure 23-3). Even in the United States, each day an average of four people discover they have malaria.

Malaria's symptoms come and go; they include fever and chills, anemia, an enlarged spleen, severe abdominal pain and headaches, extreme weakness, and greater susceptibility to other diseases. Caused by one of four species of protozoa (one-celled organisms) of the genus *Plasmodium*, the disease is transmitted from person to person by a bite from the female of about 60 of the 400 different kinds of *anopheles* mosquito, which act as vectors (Figure 23-4).

Malaria can also be transmitted when a person receives the blood of an infected donor and when a drug user shares a needle with an infected user. For this reason heroin is usually "cut" or diluted with quinine, an antimalarial drug.

One way to control malaria is to administer antimalarial drugs like quinines, which protect people against infection from *Anopheles* mosquitoes. Although these drugs are helpful, they cannot be used effectively to rid an area of malaria—people in infested areas would have to take the drugs continuously throughout their lives. In addition, new strains of carrier mosquitoes eventually develop with genetic resistance to any widely used antimalarial drug.

Another approach is vector control—trying to get rid of the mosquito carriers by draining swamplands

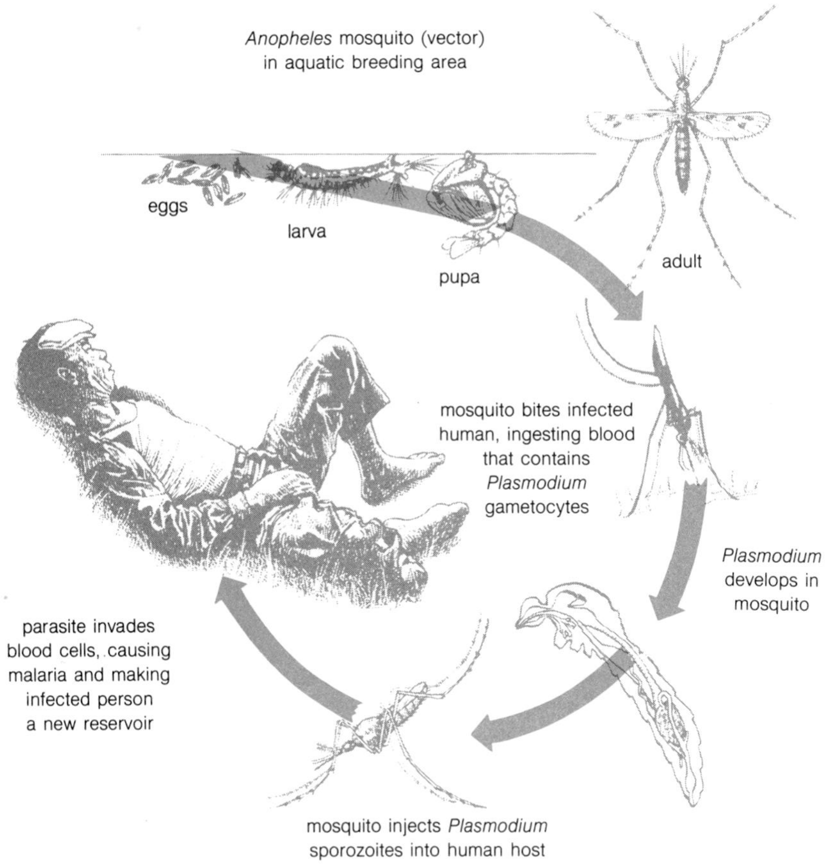

Anopheles mosquito (vector)
in aquatic breeding area

Figure 23-4 The life cycle of malaria.

eggs

larva

pupa

adult

mosquito bites infected
human, ingesting blood
that contains
Plasmodium
gametocytes

Plasmodium
develops in
mosquito

parasite invades
blood cells, causing
malaria and making
infected person
a new reservoir

mosquito injects *Plasmodium*
sporozoites into human host

and marshes and by spraying breeding areas with DDT and other pesticides. During the 1950s and 1960s, the WHO made great strides in reducing malaria in many areas, eliminating it in 37 countries by widespread spraying of DDT and the use of antimalarial drugs. In India malaria cases dropped from 100 million in 1952 to only 40,000 in 1966, and in Pakistan cases were reduced from 7 million in 1961 to 9,500 in 1967.

Since 1970, however, malaria has made a dramatic comeback in many parts of the world. By 1978 the number of cases had risen to 50 million in India and to 10 million in Pakistan. According to the WHO, there are now at least 250 million new cases of the disease each year. Epidemiologists at the U.S. Centers for Disease Control estimate that a more accurate figure may be 800 million new cases a year. Approximately 1 million people, mostly children under the age of 5, die of malaria each year. Major factors contributing to this tragic resurgence are the mosquito's increased genetic resistance to DDT and other insecticides and to antimalarial drugs (Section 22-3), rising costs of pesticides and antimalarial drugs, the spread of irrigation ditches that provide new mosquito breeding grounds, and reduced budgets for malaria control due to the misbelief that the disease has been eliminated.

Research is being carried out to develop biological controls for *Anopheles* mosquitoes and to develop antimalaria vaccines, but such approaches are in the early stages of development and lack adequate funding. The WHO estimates that only 3% of the money spent each year on biomedical research is spent on malaria and other tropical diseases, even though more people suffer and die from these diseases than from all others combined.

Schistosomiasis Schistosomiasis is caused by the trematode worm *Schistosoma*, which is transmitted between human and animal hosts by tiny snails found in freshwater streams, rivers, lakes, and irrigation canals (Figure 23-5). The adult worms lodge in the human host's veins and deposit eggs in surrounding organs and tissues, causing chronic inflammation, swelling, and pain. The urine and feces of newly infected humans can generate the entire cycle again.

Victims suffer from cough, fever, enlargement of the spleen and liver, a general wasting away of the body, filling of the abdomen with fluid (which produces the characteristic bloated belly), and constant pain; they are more susceptible to other diseases and

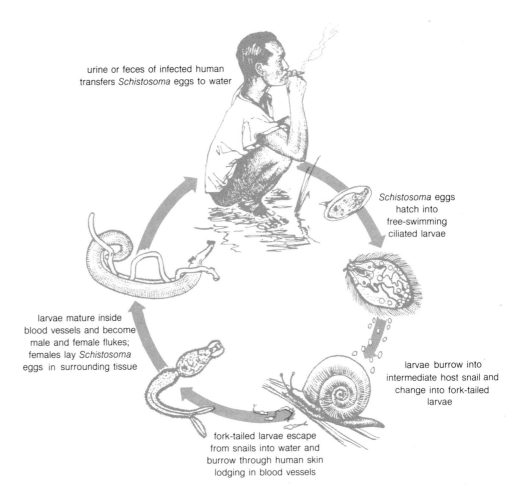

Figure 23-5 The life cycle of schistosomiasis.

urine or feces of infected human transfers *Schistosoma* eggs to water

Schistosoma eggs hatch into free-swimming ciliated larvae

larvae burrow into intermediate host snail and change into fork-tailed larvae

fork-tailed larvae escape from snails into water and burrow through human skin lodging in blood vessels

larvae mature inside blood vessels and become male and female flukes; females lay *Schistosoma* eggs in surrounding tissue

are often too weak to work. Although the disease itself is rarely fatal, people who are severely malnourished or severely infected may die.

In rural areas of Africa and Asia it is difficult for villagers to avoid contact with infested water because they collect it for drinking, cooking, and washing clothes; they also bathe and swim in it. Some are infected while washing cattle, fishing, planting rice, working in irrigation ditches (Figure 23-6), and engaging in *wadu*, the ritual washing that devout Muslims perform five times a day before praying. The building of dams for hydroelectric power and irrigation, such as the Aswan High Dam in Egypt, tends to intensify the spread of the disease because the slow-moving, often stagnant water in irrigation ditches makes them ideal breeding places for the snails that transmit the disease. As workers urinate and wade in the ditches, schistosomiasis spreads widely.

Although there are several ways to reduce the number of cases of schistosomiasis, in practice it is a difficult disease to control. Improved sanitation can prevent human excreta from reaching the snails. People can be prevented from swimming or washing in contaminated water, and those who farm or fish in contaminated waters can be encouraged to wear boots and protective clothing. These approaches, however,

require funding for improved sanitation and require rural people to change their cultural habits.

Several drugs have been developed that can kill most of the worms in the human body. But so far none works on all people or all species of the parasites. Such drugs usually have serious and occasionally lethal side effects, must be administered periodically to prevent reinfestation, and fail after a few years because of parasitic drug resistance or relaxed use when the incidence of the disease has fallen off. However, there is some hope. Preliminary results indicate that the dried, ground berries of the *endod*, used by villagers in Ethiopia as a detergent for washing clothes, may be effective in killing the snails without hurting other animals and plants.

Projects in Israel, Japan, China, and the Philippines have shown that a combination of engineering approaches can help prevent an increase in the incidence of schistosomiasis. These include draining marshlands where snails breed, increasing the water velocity in irrigation canals to prevent infestation by snails, draining irrigation projects to prevent stagnant pools and seepages, removing the aquatic vegetation from irrigation ditches that serve as snail habitats, and keeping irrigation ditches relatively far from houses. However, until more money is spent worldwide on

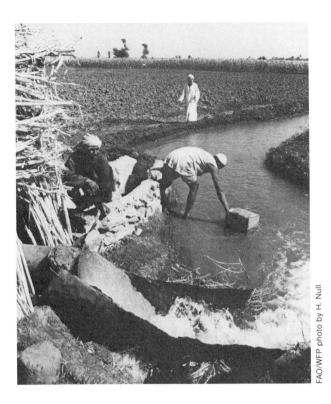

Figure 23-6 Irrigation ditches below the Aswan High Dam in Egypt are excellent habitats for the tiny snails that transmit schistosomiasis.

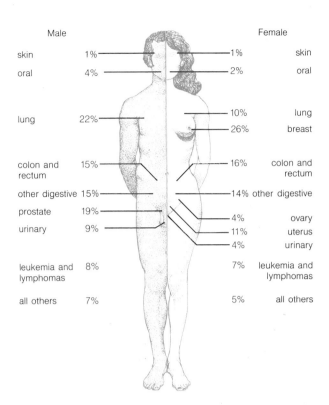

Figure 23-7 Where fatal cancer strikes; percentages of all U.S. cancer deaths in 1982. (Data from the National Cancer Institute)

schistosomiasis research, reducing the incidence of this disease in LDCs is going to be very difficult.

23-3 CHRONIC NONINFECTIOUS DISEASES: CANCER

Nature and Effects Tumors are growths of cells that enlarge and reproduce at higher than normal rates. A benign tumor is one that remains within the tissue where it develops. **Cancer** is the name for a group of more than 120 different diseases—one for essentially each major cell type in the human body—all characterized by a tumor in which cells multiply uncontrollably and invade the surrounding tissue. If not detected and treated in time, many cancerous tumors undergo **metastasis;** that is, they release malignant (cancerous) cells that travel in body fluids to various parts of the body, making treatment much more difficult.

Evidence suggests that human cancer is the result of a genetic error or mutation in one or more of the 100,000 normal genes found in each human cell. Because most types of cancer are not inherited, genes are usually mutated after birth spontaneously or from exposure to an environmental agent like radiation

(X rays, radioactivity, and the sun's ultraviolet rays) or one or more chemicals called **carcinogens,** such as several substances in tobacco smoke.

Cancer is usually a latent disease, requiring a time lag of 15 to 40 years between the initial cause and the appearance of symptoms. The long latency period and limited knowledge about the causes of different cancer types make it extremely difficult to identify what causes a particular cancer. This time lag also prevents many people from taking simple precautions that would greatly decrease their chances of getting the disease. For instance, it is difficult for healthy high school students and young adults to accept the fact that their smoking, drinking, and eating habits *today* will be major influences on whether they will die prematurely from cancer.

Incidence of Cancer in the United States Although cancer is mostly a disease of middle and old age because of its long latency period, it is second only to accidents as the leading cause of death in children between the age of 5 and 14 in the United States. American males and females have different incidences and death rates from different types of cancer (Figure 23-7). In 1986 about 472,000 Americans died from

Skin cancer is by far the most common form of cancer with about one in seven Americans getting it sooner or later. Each year about 500,000 Americans get some form of skin cancer. Cumulative sun exposure over a number of years is the major cause of basal-cell and squamous-cell skin cancers. These two types of skin cancer can be cured if detected early enough, although their removal may leave disfiguring scars.

However, evidence suggests that just one severe, blistering burn as a child or teenager is enough to double the risk of contracting deadly malignant melanoma later in life, regardless of skin type or the amount of cumulative exposure to the sun. This form of skin cancer spreads rapidly to other organs and killed about 7,500 Americans in 1986. Between 1950 and 1986 the incidence of malignant melanoma in Americans rose by 700%—from 1 in 600 to 1 in 150.

Although anyone can get skin cancer, those with very fair and freckled skin run the highest risk. White Americans who spend long hours in the sun or under sun lamps (which are even more hazardous than direct exposure to the sun) greatly increase their chances of developing skin cancer and also tend to have wrinkled, dry skin by age 40. Blacks with darker skin are almost immune to sunburn but do get skin cancer, although at a rate ten times lower than whites. Clouds are dangerously deceptive because they admit as much as 80% of the sun's harmful UV radiation and allow people to stay out in the sun longer because it isn't as hot. A dark sunburn also doesn't prevent skin cancer. Outdoor workers are particularly susceptible to cancer of the exposed skin on the face, hands, and arms.

Sunbathers and outdoor workers can reduce this risk greatly and still get a tan (although more slowly) by using lotions containing sunscreen agents to block out the most harmful ultraviolet rays given off by the sun and sun lamps. People should also stay away from tanning booths and sun lamps, wear wide-brimmed hats, and avoid prolonged exposure to the sun, especially between the hours of 10 A.M. and 3 P.M.

Physicians advise people to check themselves frequently for early signs of skin cancer, using a full-length mirror and a hand mirror for checking the back and hard-to-see places. The warning signs of skin cancer are a change in the size, shape, or color of a mole or wart (the major sign of malignant melanoma, which needs to be treated quickly), sudden appearance of dark spots on the skin, or a sore that keeps oozing, bleeding, and crusting over but does not heal. People should also be on the watch for precancerous growths that appear as reddish brown spots with a scaly crust. If any of these signs are observed, one should immediately consult a physician.

cancer—an average of 1,293 a day or 1 every 66 seconds. One of every three Americans now living will eventually have some type of cancer (see Spotlight above). But the good news is that almost half of the nearly 1 million people in the United States diagnosed as having cancer will survive for five years or more because of improved early diagnosis and treatment.

Diagnosis and Treatment   Many people automatically think of death when they hear the word *cancer,* but considerable progress has been made in early cancer diagnosis and treatment. Physicians who specialize in cancer consider that any patient who survives for five years after treatment and shows no trace of the disease is cured. On this basis, *about 49% of all Americans who get cancer can now be cured because of a combination of early detection and improved use of surgery, radiation, and drug treatments, compared to only a 25% cure rate 30 years ago.* Survival rates for many types of cancer now range from 66% to 88% (Table 23-3). On the other hand, there has been little improvement in the survival rates for people with cancer of the pancreas, esophagus, lung, stomach, and brain.

The major ways to treat cancer are surgery to remove cancerous growths, and radiation (Figure 23-8) and drugs (chemotherapy) to kill malignant cells. Radiation and today's anticancer drugs, however, are somewhat like shotgun blasts—they kill not only the cancerous cells but also hair follicles, gut cells, and other normal fast-growing cells. As a result, common side effects of radiation and chemotherapy are extreme fatigue, diarrhea, weight and hair loss, severe nausea and vomiting, reduced resistance to infection, and destruction of blood platelets.

Experts are exploring entirely new kinds of treatment that should lead to greatly increased survival rates and fewer harmful side effects. One approach is immunotherapy, using chemicals and laboratory-produced monoclonal antibodies to stimulate the body's

Type of Cancer	Diagnosed 1960–1963	Diagnosed 1977–1982	Type of Cancer	Diagnosed 1960–1963	Diagnosed 1977–1982
Among Adults			**Among Adults (Continued)**		
Testes	63	88	Brain	18	23
Lining of uterus	73	84	Stomach	11	16
Skin (melanoma)	60	80	Lung	8	13
Bladder	53	76	Esophagus	4	6
Breast	63	74	Pancreas	1	2
Hodgkin's disease	40	73	**Among Children**		
Prostate	50	71	Hodgkin's disease	52	86
Uterine cervix	58	66	Wilm's tumor	57	81
Colon	43	53	Acute lymphocytic leukemia	4	68
Rectum	38	50	Brain and central nervous system	35	52
Kidney	37	48	Neuroblastoma	25	51
Non-Hodgkin's lymphoma	36	48	Non-Hodgkin's lymphoma	18	50
Ovary	32	38	Bone	20	47
Leukemia	14	33	Acute granulocytic leukemia	3	25

*Data from the National Cancer Institute.

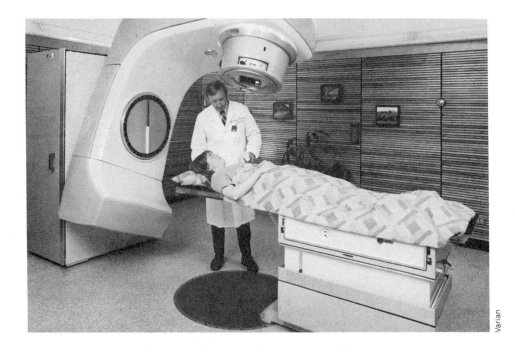

Figure 23-8 Deep-seated cancerous tumors can be treated with gamma rays emitted by cobalt-60.

Varian

own disease defenses to attack cancer cells. Scientists hope to develop a series of monoclonal antibodies for each type of cancer. Such antibodies would be used to carry drugs or radioactive isotopes directly to tumors without harm to healthy tissues. This rifle-shot approach to cancer treatment could eliminate most of the side effects associated with present treatment approaches. By the year 2000, the National Cancer Institute estimates that the average five-year cancer survival rate in the United States will be 75%.

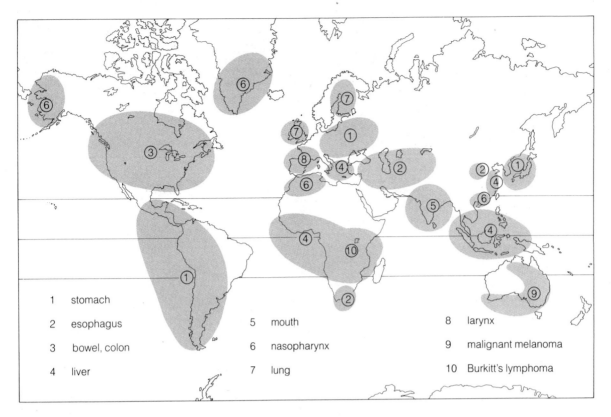

Figure 23-9 Areas around the world where incidence rates of certain types of cancer are much higher than normal. These differences are believed to be caused primarily by environmental factors such as diet, smoking, and pollution. (Data from the American Cancer Society)

1	stomach	5	mouth	8	larynx
2	esophagus	6	nasopharynx	9	malignant melanoma
3	bowel, colon	7	lung	10	Burkitt's lymphoma
4	liver				

Cancer Risk Factors Hereditary factors are involved in an estimated 10% to 30% of all cancers. Examples of genetically transferable cancer risks include leukemia in children with Down's syndrome, breast cancer, ovarian cancer, malignant melanoma, retinoblastoma (a rare form of eye cancer), and lung cancer (although heredity is not nearly as important as smoking).

Environmental factors—including such lifestyle elements as diet, smoking, and environmental pollution—are believed to contribute to or directly cause the remaining 70% to 90% of all cancers. For example, studies show that U.S. Mormons, who do not smoke or drink alcohol, have one-fourth the incidence of lung, esophagus, and larynx cancers, compared to the average U.S. white population. Higher than normal incidences of certain types of cancer in various parts of the world indicate the effects of diet, industrialization, and other environmental factors, such as soil and water contamination, on cancer rates (Figure 23-9). In the United States cancer death rates for males are much higher in large cities and in the heavily urbanized and industrialized Northeast, Great Lakes region, and Gulf Coast (Figure 23-10).

Thus, the risks of developing cancer can be greatly reduced by working in a less hazardous environment,

by not smoking, by drinking in moderation (maximum consumption of two beers or drinks a day) or not at all, by adhering to a healthful diet (see Spotlight on p. 547), and by shielding oneself from the sun. According to experts, 60% of all cancers could be prevented by such lifestyle changes.

Cancer and Smoking Tobacco is by far the cause of more death and suffering among adults than any other environmental factor. Over a billion people—one out of every five—throughout the world now smoke. They consume almost 5 trillion cigarettes a year—twice as many as in 1960. Greece leads the world in average per capita cigarette consumption, followed closely by Japan, the United States, Canada, Yugoslavia, and Poland. China, the world's largest producer of tobacco, uses a quarter of the world's tobacco.

Worldwide, between 2 million and 2.5 million smokers die prematurely each year from heart disease, lung cancer, bronchitis, and emphysema—all related to smoking. In the United States, tobacco is estimated to cause 375,000 deaths each year—one out of every five deaths—far more than all the deaths caused by

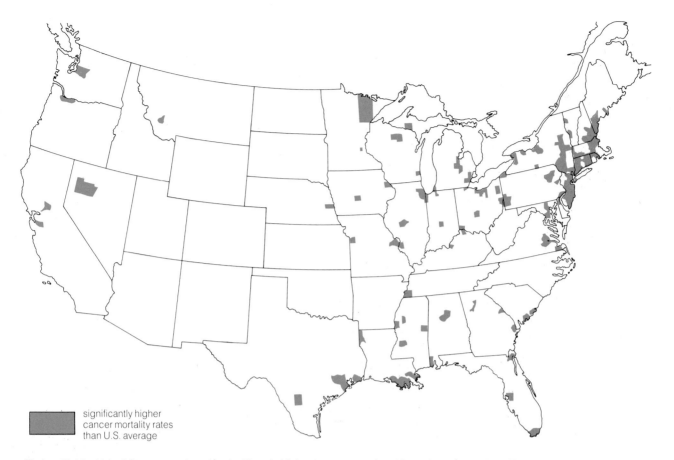

significantly higher
cancer mortality rates
than U.S. average

Figure 23-10 United States counties with significantly higher cancer rates for white males, 1960–1969. (Data from U.S. Department of Health, Education, and Welfare)

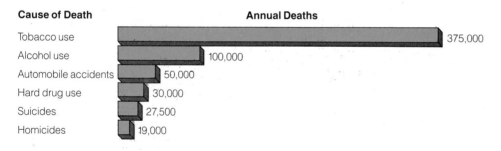

Cause of Death	Annual Deaths
Tobacco use	375,000
Alcohol use	100,000
Automobile accidents	50,000
Hard drug use	30,000
Suicides	27,500
Homicides	19,000

Figure 23-11 Annual deaths in the United States related to tobacco use and other causes in 1985. (Data from National Center for Health Statistics)

alcohol, automobile accidents, hard drugs, suicide, and homicide (Figure 23-11).

It is estimated that every cigarette smoked reduces one's average life span by five-and-a-half minutes. Overwhelming statistical evidence from more than 30,000 studies shows that smoking causes an estimated one-third of all cancer deaths in the United States, 30% of all heart disease deaths, and three-fourths of all lung cancer deaths in American men. People who smoke two packs of cigarettes a day increase their risk of getting lung cancer 15 to 25 times over nonsmokers. Tobacco use also contributes to cancer of the bladder, lip, mouth, pancreas, esophagus, and pharynx, although alcohol also plays a significant role in the last two types. Fires caused by cigarettes kill between 2,000 and 4,000 Americans each year.

In the United States, smoking costs from $38 billion to $95 billion per year in increased health care and insurance costs, lost work due to illness, and other economic losses. This amounts to an average cost to

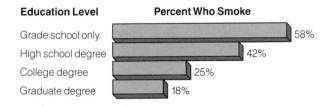

Education Level	Percent Who Smoke
Grade school only	58%
High school degree	42%
College degree	25%
Graduate degree	18%

Figure 23-12 Relationship between smoking and educational level among U.S. males in 1982. (Data from Worldwatch Institute)

society of $1.25 to $3.15 per pack of cigarettes sold, excluding the cost of the tobacco and packaging. By one estimate every nonsmoking American adult pays at least $100 a year in taxes and increased insurance premiums to help cover the health costs of smokers.

Smokers also cost their employers at least $650 a year more in health insurance, lost work time, and cleanup costs. One study showed that the average worker who smokes uses up about 50% more sick leave than one who does not smoke. To reduce these losses and protect nonsmokers, about 2% of American companies have prohibited smoking on the job. Some hire nonsmokers over smokers when skills and experience of applicants are roughly equal, and a few refuse to hire smokers. On a strictly economic basis, tobacco's economic costs to society exceed its benefits in terms of income and jobs of tobacco farmers and employees of tobacco companies by more than two to one.

Nicotine in tobacco is a highly addictive drug that, like heroin, can quickly hook its victims. A British government study showed that adolescents who smoke more than one cigarette have an 85% chance of becoming smokers. Other studies have shown that a child is about twice as likely to become a smoker if either parent smokes and that 75% of smokers who quit start smoking again within six months.

There is some good news, however. Studies show that 10 to 15 years after smokers quit, they have about the same risk of dying from lung cancer as those who never smoked. There is also evidence that very high doses of vitamin B-12 (half a milligram a day) and folic acid (10 milligrams a day) given to people for four months after they quit smoking reduced the number of premalignant cells in their lungs.

Between 1955 and 1985 the percentage of adult American men who smoked dropped from 52% to 35%, but the average male smoker now smokes more cigarettes than in 1955. During the same period the percentage of adult women who smoke increased from 24% to 30%; a higher percentage of teenage American females now smoke than teenage males, which should show up in greatly increased death rates for females

from heart disease, lung cancer, and emphysema over the next 20 years. The higher the educational level, the less likely is a person to smoke (Figure 23-12).

Smoke from cigarettes and other tobacco products harms more than just the smoker. About 86% of Americans who do not smoke involuntarily inhale smoke from other people's cigarettes, amounting to an average of about one cigarette a day. People working in smoky bars or living with a chainsmoker passively smoke the equivalent of 14 cigarettes a day. A 1985 study by the EPA indicated that passive smoke kills from 500 to 5,000 Americans a year.

Studies have shown that children whose parents smoke a pack or more of cigarettes a day get sick with respiratory illnesses such as colds, influenza, bronchitis, and pneumonia twice as often as children of nonsmokers. Pregnant women who smoke ten or more cigarettes a day give birth to underweight babies twice as often as nonsmokers and have children with reduced lung capacity, higher rates of respiratory illness, and slower intellectual development.

Many attempts have been made to prevent young people from smoking. In 1986 the American Medical Association passed a resolution calling for a total ban on cigarette advertising in the United States, the prohibition of the sale of cigarettes and other tobacco products to anyone under 21, and a ban on cigarette vending machines. Presently the U.S. tobacco industry spends almost $2 billion a year on advertising designed to create the impression that smokers are young, attractive, sophisticated, healthy, and sexy. By comparison, the federal government's Office on Smoking and Health has a yearly budget of about $3.5 million.

Seventeen states and several hundred cities have enacted laws banning smoking in enclosed public places and public transportation. Designating nonsmoking areas in buildings, buses, and planes is only a partial solution because air conditioning and heating systems recycle the smoke. By 1986 only nine states had no existing or pending laws restricting smoking in workplaces or restaurants, and early in 1987 smoking by employees as well as visitors was severely restricted in federal buildings throughout the country. A 1986 Gallup poll found that 87% of both smokers and nonsmokers in the United States favored a ban on smoking in the workplace or creation of nonsmoking areas, and 94% believed that smoking is a health hazard.

It has been suggested that all financial subsidies to U.S. tobacco farmers and tobacco companies be eliminated; instead, aid and subsidies would be provided to allow farmers to grow more healthful crops. Others have suggested that cigarettes be taxed at $1.25 to $3.15 a pack to discourage smoking and to make smokers—not nonsmokers—pay for the health and productivity losses now borne by society as a whole.

Cancer and Diet   A second major cause of cancer is improper diet, causing an estimated 35% of all cancer deaths. However, evidence linking specific dietary habits to specific types of cancer is difficult to obtain and controversial. The major factors—especially in cancers of the breast, bowel (colon and rectum), liver, kidney, stomach, and prostate—seem to be fats, nitrosamines, and nitrites. The incidence of cancers of the colon, rectum, and female breast is about five times higher in Americans than in Japanese, who have low-fat diets. Third generation offspring of Japanese immigrants, however, have about the same incidence of these types of cancer as other Americans. A high-fat, high-protein diet may also be a factor in cancers of the prostate, testis, ovary, pancreas, and kidney.

Others have proposed that high incidences of bowel cancer may result from the low fiber content in Western diets, a by-product of the use of highly refined foods. Studies have given conflicting results, however, and the low-fiber hypothesis is still controversial. Recent work indicates that the incidence of bowel cancer is lower in test animals and in individuals whose diets include daily intakes of vegetables such as cauliflower, carrots, broccoli, and cabbage. There is also some evidence that the incidence of stomach and bowel cancer may be reduced by adequate amounts of beta-carotene, vitamin C (and perhaps vitamin E), and trace minerals such as selenium and zinc.

High levels of nitrate and nitrite food preservative (Section 23-4), found in smoked and cured meats and in some beers, may increase the risk of stomach cancer because the body converts them to carcinogenic compounds known as nitrosamines. These compounds have been implicated in the very high incidence of stomach cancer in Japan, where large amounts of dried, salted, pickled, and smoked fish are consumed. Despite the uncertainty in linking specific cancers to excessive consumption of specific foods, there is enough evidence to suggest a diet that should reduce cancer risks (see Spotlight).

Cancer and the Workplace   The third major cause of cancer, occupational exposure to carcinogens and radiation, causes about 5% to 20% of cancer deaths according to health scientists. Roughly one-fourth of U.S. workers run the risk of some type of illness from routine exposure to one or more toxic compounds. The National Institute for Occupational Health and Safety estimates that as many as 100,000 deaths a year—

Spotlight   The Prudent Diet

The National Academy of Sciences and the American Heart Association advise that the risk of certain types of cancer—lung, stomach, colon, and esophagus cancer—and heart disease can be significantly reduced by a daily diet that cuts down on certain foods and includes others. Such a diet limits **(1)** total fat intake to 30% of total calories, with no more than 10% saturated fat (compared to the 40% fat diet of the average American); **(2)** protein (particularly meat protein) to 15% of total calories; **(3)** alcohol consumption to 15% of total caloric intake—no more than two drinks or beers a day; **(4)** cholesterol consumption to no more than 300 milligrams a day; and **(5)** sodium intake to no more than three grams a day. We should avoid salt-cured, nitrate-cured, and smoked ham, bacon, hot dogs, sausages, bologna, salami, corned beef, and fish.

The diet should include fruits (especially vitamin C rich oranges, grapefruit, and strawberries), minimally cooked orange, yellow, and green leafy vegetables such as spinach and carrots, which are rich in beta-carotene, and cabbage-family vegetables such as cauliflower, cabbage, kale, brussels sprouts, and broccoli. It should also incorporate 10 to 15 grams of whole-grain fiber a day from raw bran (the cheapest source), bran in cereals, and fibers in vegetables and fruits, and a daily intake of selenium not exceeding 200 micrograms. Recent preliminary evidence also suggests that eating coldwater fish such as bluefish, salmon, herring, and sardines, which are rich in certain types of fish oils, two or three times a week may help prevent heart disease and help prevent and arrest the growth of breast, colon, and prostate cancers.

at least half from cancer—are linked to workplace diseases in the United States (Table 23-4). An estimated 100,000 U.S. workers have died as a result of exposure to asbestos, and 350,000 additional asbestos-caused deaths are projected over the next 30 to 35 years. Most work-related deaths could be prevented by stricter laws and enforcement of existing laws governing exposure of workers to radiation and dangerous chemicals. If enforced, the Occupational Safety and Health Act of 1970 and the Toxic Substances Control Act of 1975 could establish such controls. However, political

Table 23-4 Cancer Risks in the Workplace in the United States*

Substance	Workers Exposed (millions)	Industries	Cancer Risks
Asbestos	2.5	Asbestos, textiles, insulation, mining	Lung, larynx, mesothelioma, bowel, stomach
Vinyl chloride	3.5	Vinyl chloride and vinyl plastic	Liver, brain, breast
Benzene	3.0	Tire, shoe, paint, cement, glue, varnish, chemicals	Leukemia
Arsenic	1.5	Pesticide, copper, leather tanning, mining, vineyards	Lung, skin, liver, testis, lymphatic system
Chromium	1.5	Bleaching, glass, pottery, battery, linoleum	Lung, nasal
Nickel	1.4	Nickel refiners	Lung, nasal, larynx
Cadmium	1.4	Electrical, paint, metal alloy	Prostate, renal, respiratory
Carbon tetrachloride	1.4	Dry cleaning, machinists	Liver
Formaldehyde	1.3	Wood finishing, plastics, synthetic resins	Nasal

*Data from Occupational Safety and Health Administration and the AFL-CIO.

pressure by industry officials has hindered effective enforcement of these laws (see Spotlight on p. 549).

Cancer and Pollution A fourth cause of cancer is air and water pollution, estimated to contribute from 1% to 5% of cancer deaths in the United States. This contribution may be more significant, however, for residents of airtight, energy-efficient housing without air-to-air heat exchangers because of abnormally high levels of indoor air pollution, for nonsmokers who work or live in an environment that exposes them to cigarette smoke, and for residents of cities whose drinking water is contaminated with one or more toxic metals or carcinogenic synthetic organic compounds.

23-4 FOOD ADDITIVES

Use and Types of Food Additives In LDCs many rural and urban dwellers consume harvested crops directly. In MDCs and in a growing number of cities in LDCs, harvested crops are used to produce processed foods for sale in grocery stores and restaurants. A large and increasing number of natural and synthetic chemicals, called **food additives,** are deliberately added to such processed foods to retard spoilage, to enhance flavor, color, and texture, and to provide missing amino

acids and vitamins. Although some food additives are useful in extending shelf life and preventing food poisoning, most are added to improve appearance and sales. For example, the following letter to the editor of the Albany *Times-Union* lists only a few of the 93 different chemicals that may be added to the "enriched" bread you buy in a grocery store:

Give us this day our daily calcium proprianate (spoilage retarder), sodium diacetate (mold inhibitor), monoglyceride (emulsifier), potassium bromate (maturing agent), calcium phosphate monobasic (dough conditioner), chloramine T (flour bleach), aluminum potassium sulfate acid (baking powder ingredient), sodium benzoate (preservative), butylated hydroxyanisole (antioxidant), mono-isopropyl citrate (sequestrant); plus synthetic vitamins A and D.
Forgive us, O Lord, for calling this stuff BREAD.

*J. H. Read, Averill Park**

All food, of course, is a mixture of chemicals, but today at least 2,800 different chemicals are deliberately added to processed foods in the United States. Each year the average American consumes about 55 kilograms (120 pounds) of sugar, 7 kilograms (15 pounds) of salt, and about 4.5 kilograms (10 pounds) of other food additives. Each day the average American eats one teaspoon of artificial colors, flavors, and preser-

---

*Used by permission of the *Times-Union*, Albany, New York.

Maximum allowed levels of air pollutants in U.S. mines and factories are set by the Occupational Safety and Health Administration (OSHA); for many major pollutants, the legal workplace levels range from 2 to 100 times higher than those set by the EPA for outdoor exposure. Occupational health experts point out that U.S. workers in general are denied knowledge of the types and concentrations of chemicals to which they are exposed, and are often not informed whether chemicals have been adequately tested and whether they are potentially toxic or carcinogenic under plant conditions.

Industry officials argue that enforcing stricter standards to protect workers would cause many mines and factories to close or to raise prices, hindering competition with the same items produced in other countries. So far, industry officials have been able to restrain Congress and OSHA from imposing stricter air pollution standards in the workplace and from strictly enforcing existing standards.

Environmentalists, however, argue that indoor workplace air pollution standards should be at least as stringent as outdoor standards, as is the case in the Soviet Union and many east European countries. Believing that it is morally wrong for companies to sacrifice the health of their workers in order to enhance short-term profits and economic growth, environmentalists argue that protecting worker health is a more cost-effective approach than having taxpayers pay for the health damage resulting from inadequate worker protection.

Environmentalists also contend that plant closings and the increasing competition with foreign industries are rarely the result of stricter controls on air pollutants. Instead, these industry problems result primarily from failure of most companies to use past profits to switch to newer production processes that reduce unnecessary and costly waste of matter and energy resources and that produce less pollution. Workers are caught in the middle—not wanting to sacrifice their health but also needing their jobs. What do you think?

vatives. Table 23-5 summarizes the major classes of food additives. The most widely used groups of additives—coloring agents, natural and synthetic flavoring agents, and sweeteners—are solely used to make food look and taste better.

The extremes of the controversy over food additives range from "Essentially all food additives are bad" and "We should eat only natural foods" to "There's nothing to worry about because there is no absolute proof that chemical X has ever harmed a human being." As usual, the truth probably lies somewhere in between.

Natural Versus Synthetic Foods   *The presence of synthetic chemical additives does not necessarily mean that a food is harmful, and the fact that a food is completely natural is no guarantee that it is safe.* A number of natural or totally unprocessed foods contain potentially harmful and toxic substances.

Polar bear or halibut liver can cause vitamin A poisoning. Lima beans, sweet potatoes, cassava, sugarcane, cherries, plums, and apricots contain chemicals (glucosides) that our intestines convert to small amounts of deadly hydrogen cyanide. Eating cabbage, cauliflower, turnips, rutabagas, mustard greens, collard greens, or brussels sprouts can cause goiter in susceptible individuals. Blood pressure can be raised by certain chemicals (amines) found in bananas, pineapples, various acid cheeses (such as Camembert), and some beers and wines. Safrole (a flavoring agent once used in root beer) and a component of tarragon oil cause liver tumors in rats. Three chemicals that cause cancer are formed when parsnips, celery, figs, and parsley are exposed to light. Chemicals (aflatoxins) produced by fungi sometimes found on corn and peanuts are extremely toxic to humans and are not legal in U.S. foods at levels above 20 ppb. Clams, oysters, cockles, and mussels can concentrate natural and artificial toxins in their flesh.

In addition, natural foods can be contaminated with food-poisoning bacteria, such as *Salmonella* and the deadly *Clostridium botulinum*, through improper processing, food storage, or personal hygiene. The botulism toxin from *Clostridium botulinum* is one of the most toxic chemicals known. As little as one ten-millionth of a gram (0.0000001 gram) can kill an adult, and it is estimated that 227 grams (half a pound) would be enough to kill every human being on earth. However, because of modern food-processing methods,

Table 23-5 Commonly Used Food Additives and Food Processes

Class	Function	Examples	Foods Typically Treated
Preservatives	To retard spoilage caused by bacterial action and molds (fungi)	Processes: drying, smoking, curing, canning (heating and sealing), freezing, pasteurization, refrigeration	Bread, cheese, cake, jelly, chocolate syrup, fruit, vegetables, meat
		Chemicals: salt, sugar, sodium nitrate, sodium nitrite, calcium and sodium propionate, sorbic acid, potassium sorbate, benzoic acid, sodium benzoate, citric acid, sulfur dioxide	
Antioxidants (oxygen interceptors, or freshness stabilizers)	To retard spoilage of fats (excludes oxygen or slows down the chemical breakdown of fats)	Processes: sealing cans, wrapping, refrigeration	Cooking oil, shortening, cereal, potato chips, crackers, salted nuts, soup, toaster tarts, artificial whipped topping, artificial orange juice, many other foods
		Chemicals: lecithin, butylated hydroxyanisole (BHA), butylated hydroxytoluene (BHT), propyl gallate	
Nutritional supplements	To increase nutritive value of natural food or to replace nutrients lost in food processing*	Vitamins, essential amino acids	Bread and flour (vitamins and amino acids), milk (vitamin D), rice (vitamin B_1), corn meal, cereal
Flavoring agents	To add or enhance flavor	Over 1,700 substances, including saccharin, aspartame (NutraSweet®), monosodium glutamate (MSG), essential oils (such as cinnamon, banana, vanilla)	Ice cream, artificial fruit juice, toppings, soft drinks, candy, pickles, salad dressing, spicy meats, low-calorie foods and drinks, most processed heat-and-serve foods
Coloring agents	To add aesthetic or sales appeal, to hide colors that are unappealing or that show lack of freshness	Natural color dyes, synthetic coal tar dyes	Soft drinks, butter, cheese, ice cream, cereal, candy, cake mix, sausage, pudding, many other foods
Acidulants	To provide a tart taste or to mask undesirable aftertastes	Phosphoric acid, citric acid, fumaric acid	Cola and fruit soft drinks, desserts, fruit juice, cheese, salad dressing, gravy, soup
Alkalis	To reduce natural acidity	Sodium carbonate, sodium bicarbonate	Canned peas, wine, olives, coconut cream pie, chocolate eclairs
Emulsifiers	To disperse droplets of one liquid (such as oil) in another liquid (such as water)	Lecithin, propylene glycol, mono- and diglycerides, polysorbates	Ice cream, candy, margarine, icing, nondairy creamer, dessert topping, mayonnaise, salad dressing, shortening
Stabilizers and thickeners	To provide smooth texture and consistency; to prevent separation of components; to provide body	Vegetable gum (gum arabic), sodium carboxymethyl cellulose, seaweed extracts (agar and algin), dextrin, gelatin	Cheese spread, ice cream, sherbet, pie filling, salad dressing, icing, dietetic canned fruit, cake and dessert mixes, syrup, pressurized whipped cream, instant breakfasts, beer, soft drinks, diet drinks
Sequestrants (chelating agents, or metal scavengers)	To tie up traces of metal ions that catalyze oxidation and other spoilage reactions in food; to prevent clouding in soft drinks; to add color, flavor, and texture	EDTA (ethylenediamine-tetraacetic acid), citric acid, sodium phosphate, chlorophyll	Soup, desserts, artificial fruit drinks, salad dressing, canned corn and shrimp, soft drinks, beer, cheese, frozen foods

*Adding small amounts of vitamins to breakfast cereals and other "fortified" and "enriched" foods in America is basically a gimmick used to raise the price. The manufacturer may put vitamins worth about 5¢ into 340 grams (12 ounces) of cereal and then add 45% to the retail price. Vitamin pills are normally a far less expensive source of vitamins than fortified foods. The best way to get vitamins, however, is through a balanced diet.

there are only about 10 to 20 cases of botulism annually in the United States.

Because there are potentially harmful chemicals in both natural and synthetic foods, the question is whether enough of a chemical is present to cause harmful effects, and whether the effects are cumulative. The answers are not simple because individuals vary widely in their susceptibility to chemicals. Some chemicals are harmful at any level, but others are harmful only above a certain level. In addition, a chemical that has been thoroughly tested and found to be harmless by itself may interact synergistically with another chemical to produce a hazard.

Consumer Protection: FDA and the GRAS List   In the United States the safety of foods and drugs has been monitored by the Food and Drug Administration since its establishment by the Pure Food and Drug Act of 1906, which was amended by the 1938 Food, Drug, and Cosmetic Act. Yet, it was not until 1958 that federal laws required that the safety of any new food additive be established by the manufacturer and approved by the FDA *before* the additive was put into common use. Today the manufacturer of a new additive must carry out extensive toxicity testing, costing up to a million dollars per item, and the results must be submitted to the FDA. The FDA itself does no testing but merely evaluates data submitted by manufacturers.

However, these federal laws did not apply to the hundreds of additives that were in use before 1958. Instead of making expensive, time-consuming tests on additives, the FDA drew up a list of the food additives in use in 1958 and asked several hundred experts for their professional opinions on the safety of these substances. A few substances were deleted, and in 1959 a list of the remaining 415 substances was published as the "generally recognized as safe" or *GRAS* (pronounced "grass") *list*.

Since 1959 further testing has led the FDA to ban several substances on the original GRAS list, including cyclamate sweeteners (1969), brominated vegetable oil (1970), and a number of food colorings, such as red dye no. 2 (1976). The ban on the most widely used artificial food color, red dye no. 2, came five years after Soviet scientists reported that it caused cancer in laboratory mice. Between 1969 and 1980 the FDA reviewed all 415 items on the GRAS list: 371 of the additives were considered to be safe as currently used; 19 (including caffeine, BHA, and BHT) needed further study; 7 (including salt and 4 modified starches) can be used only at restricted levels; and 18 were recommended for removal from the list. By 1982 the FDA had reviewed all other food additives approved for use since the publication of the original GRAS list.

As a regulatory agency, the FDA is caught in the crossfire between consumer groups and the food industry. It is criticized by consumer groups as being overly friendly to industry and for hiring many of its executives from the food industry—a practice the FDA contends is the only way it can recruit the most experienced food scientists. At the same time, the food industry complains that the FDA sometimes gives in too easily to demands from consumer groups. Both industry and consumer groups have criticized the agency for bureaucratic inefficiency.

Some Controversial Food Additives   Table 23-6 shows the major food additives that consumers are advised to avoid or use with caution, according to the Center for Science in the Public Interest. Many of these are food colorings made from coal tar. About half the food additives banned by the FDA have been coal tar food colorings; by early 1987, only six were still approved for use in food. Even with so small a number, public exposure to coal tar food dyes can be extensive. The FDA estimates that by age 12, about 10% of all U.S. children have eaten more than 454 grams (1 pound) of these dyes.

Critics charge that the remaining dyes should be banned because studies have linked them to cancer in laboratory test animals. For the past 20 years, however, the FDA has placed these dyes in an interim "provisional listing" category, meaning that they can be used pending a final decision. Since 1981, the FDA has proposed to ban red no. 3 at least 12 times, but each time the dye has been given a reprieve.

The Delaney Clause   One powerful weapon the FDA has is the Delaney Clause.* This 1958 amendment to food and drug laws prohibits the deliberate use of any food additive shown to cause cancer in test animals or people. The FDA must evaluate the evidence linking an additive to cancer; if the FDA finds a risk, however slight, it must ban the chemical. The amendment is absolute, allowing for no extenuating circumstances or consideration of benefits versus risks. Between 1958 and 1986, the FDA used this amendment to ban only nine chemicals.

Critics say the Delaney Clause is too rigid and not needed because the FDA already has the power to ban

---

*Named after Representative James J. Delaney of New York, who fought to have this amendment passed despite great political pressure and heavy lobbying by the food industry.

Table 23-6 Suggested Food Additives to Avoid*

Additive	Major Uses	Possible Problems
Coal tar dyes (reds no. 3, 8, 9, 19, and 37, and orange no. 17)	Cherries in fruit cocktail, candy, beverages	May cause cancer; poorly tested
Citrus red no. 2	Skin of some Florida oranges	May cause cancer
Yellow no. 5	Gelatin dessert, candy, baked goods	May cause cancer; allergic reaction in some people; widely used
BHA	Antioxidant in chewing gum, potato chips, oils	May cause cancer; stored in body fat; can cause allergic reaction; safer alternatives available
BHT	Same as BHA	Appears safer than BHA, but needs better testing; safer alternatives available
Propyl gallate	Antioxidant in oils, meat products, potato stock, chicken soup base, chewing gum	Not adequately tested; use is frequently unnecessary
Quinine	Flavoring in tonic water, quinine water, bitter lemon	Poorly tested; may cause birth defects
Saccharin	Noncaloric sweetener in diet foods	Causes cancer in animals
Sodium nitrite, sodium nitrate	Preservative and flavoring agent in bacon, ham, hot dogs, luncheon meats, corned beef, smoked fish	Prevents formation of botulism bacteria but can lead to formation of cancer-causing nitrosamines in stomach
Sodium bisulfite, sulfur dioxide	Preservative and bleach in wine, beer, grape juice, dehydrated potatoes, imported shrimp, dried fruit, cake and cookie mixes, canned and frozen vegetables, breads, salad dressings, fruit juices, soft drinks, some baked goods and snacks, some drugs	Causes severe allergic reaction in about 500,000 Americans; implicated in 12 deaths between 1982 and 1986

*Data from Center for Science in the Public Interest.

any chemical it deems unsafe. In general, the food industry would like to see the amendment removed, and some scientists and politicians would like it to be modified to allow a consideration of benefits versus risks. Others point out that it requires chemicals to be banned even when the dosage causing cancer in test animals is 10 to 10,000 times greater than the amount a person might be expected to consume. These critics also argue that cancer tests in animals don't necessarily apply to human beings.

Supporters of the Delaney Clause say that because people can't serve as guinea pigs, animal tests are the next best thing. Such tests don't prove that a chemical will cause cancer in humans, but they do strongly suggest that a risk is present. Moreover, all but two substances known to cause cancer in people also cause cancer in laboratory animals. Supporters also argue that the high doses of chemicals are necessary to compensate for the test animals' relatively short life spans and relatively fast metabolism and excretion rates. Tests using low doses not only would be inaccurate but also would require thousands of test animals to establish that an effect was not due to chance. Such tests would be prohibitively expensive.

Indeed, instead of revoking the Delaney Clause, some scientists feel it should be strengthened and expanded. Some even argue that the clause gives the FDA too much discretion, including the right to reject the validity of well-conducted animal experiments that show carcinogenicity. These critics cite the FDA's infrequent use of the clause as evidence that the law is too weak. They also argue that because the clause is absolute, it protects FDA officials from undue pressure from the food industry and politicians. If the FDA had to weigh benefits versus risks, political influence and lobbying by the food industry could delay the banning of a dangerous chemical while it underwent years of study.

What Can the Consumer Do? It is almost impossible for a consumer in an affluent country to avoid all food additives. Indeed, as mentioned, many additives perform important functions, and there is no guarantee that natural foods will always be better and safer. However, to minimize risk, individuals can follow a prudent diet and avoid additives and natural foods that have come under suspicion (Table 23-6).

23-5 NOISE POLLUTION

Sonic Assault According to the Environmental Protection Agency, nearly half of all Americans, mostly urban dwellers, are regularly exposed in their neighborhoods and jobs to levels of noise that interfere with communication or sleep. The American Speech and Hearing Associates report that every day, one of every ten Americans lives, works, or plays around noise of sufficient duration and intensity to cause some permanent loss of hearing and that this number is rising rapidly.

Industrial workers head the list, with 19 million hearing-damaged people out of an industrial work force of 75 million. Workers who run a high risk of temporary or permanent hearing loss include boilermakers, weavers, riveters, bulldozer and jackhammer operators, taxicab drivers, bus and truck drivers, mechanics, machine shop workers, bar and nightclub employees, and performers who use sound systems to amplify their music. Millions of people who listen to music at loud levels using home stereos, portable stereos ("jam boxes") held close to the ear, and earphones are also incurring hearing damage. Studies have shown that 60% of the incoming first-year students at the University of Tennessee have significant hearing loss in the high frequency range. In effect, these and many other young people are entering their twenties with the hearing capability of persons between the ages of 60 and 69.

Measuring and Ranking Noise To determine harmful levels of noise, sound pressure measurements in **decibels (db)** can be made with a decibel meter. A mathematical equation is used to convert sound pressure measurements to loudness levels.

Sound pressure and loudness, however, are only part of the problem. Sounds also have pitch (frequency), and high-pitched sounds seem louder and more annoying than low-pitched sounds at the same intensity. Normally, sound pressure is weighted for high-pitched sounds and reported in dbA units, as shown in Table 23-7. Sound pressure becomes damaging at about 75 dbA, painful at around 120 dbA, and deadly at 180 dbA. Because the db and dbA sound pressure scales are logarithmic, a tenfold increase in sound pressure occurs with each 10-decibel rise. Thus, a rise in sound pressure on the ear from 30 dbA (quiet rural area) to 60 dbA (normal restaurant conversation) represents a 1,000-fold increase in sound pressure.

Effects of Noise Excessive noise is a form of stress that can cause both physical and psychological damage. As noise control advocate Robert Alex Baron reminds us, "Air pollution kills us slowly but silently; noise makes each day a torment." Continued exposure to high sound levels permanently destroys the microscopic hairlike cells (cochlear cells) in the fluid-filled inner ear, which wave back and forth to convert sound energy to nerve impulses. Sound experts list the following signs of sound levels high enough to cause permanent hearing damage: You need to raise your voice to be heard above the racket, a noise causes your ears to ring, or nearby speech seems muffled.

In addition to hearing damage, sudden noise causes automatic stress reactions including constricted blood vessels, dilated pupils, tense muscles, increased heart rate and blood pressure, wincing, holding of breath, and stomach spasms. Constriction of the blood vessels can become permanent, increasing blood pressure and contributing to heart disease. Migraine headaches, gastric ulcers, and changes in brain chemistry can also occur.

What Can Be Done? Industrial employers can control noise by substituting quieter machines and operations. Workers can shield themselves from excessive noise by wearing hearing protectors such as wax or plastic plugs, bulky headsets, and custom-made plastic inserts with valves that close automatically in response to noise. Noisy factory operations can be totally or partially enclosed. Houses and buildings can be insulated to reduce sound transfer (and energy waste). Trucks, motorcycles, vacuum cleaners, and other noisy machines are available in quieter versions but are often not purchased because consumers falsely equate loudness of engines with their power or effectiveness.

The Soviet Union and many western European and Scandinavian nations are far ahead of the United States in reducing noise and in establishing and enforcing noise control regulations. Europeans have developed quieter jackhammers, pile drivers, and air compressors that do not cost much more than their noisy counterparts. Most European countries also require that small sheds and tents be used to muffle

Table 23-7 Effects of Common Sound Pressure Levels

Example	Sound Pressure (dbA)	Effect with Prolonged Exposure
Jet takeoff (25 meters away*)	150	Eardrum rupture
Aircraft carrier deck	140	
Armored personnel carrier, jet takeoff (100 meters away), earphones at loud level	130	
Thunderclap, textile loom, live rock music, jet takeoff (161 meters away), siren (close range), chain saw	120	Human pain threshold
Steel mill, riveting, automobile horn at 1 meter, jam box stereo held close to ear	110	
Jet takeoff (305 meters away), subway, outboard motor, power lawn mower, motorcycle at 8 meters, farm tractor, printing plant, jackhammer, garbage truck	100	Serious hearing damage (8 hours)
Busy urban street, diesel truck, food blender, cotton spinning machine	90	Hearing damage (8 hours), speech interference
Garbage disposal, clothes washer, average factory, freight train at 15 meters, dishwasher	80	Possible hearing damage
Freeway traffic at 15 meters, vacuum cleaner, noisy office or party	70	Annoying
Conversation in restaurant, average office, background music	60	Intrusive
Quiet suburb (daytime), conversation in living room	50	Quiet
Library, soft background music	40	
Quiet rural area (nighttime)	30	
Whisper, rusting leaves	20	Very quiet
Breathing	10	
	0	Threshold of hearing

*To convert meters to feet, multiply by 3.3.

construction noise, and some countries reduce the clanging associated with garbage collection by using rubberized collection trucks. Subway systems in Montreal and Mexico City have rubberized wheels to reduce noise. In France, cars are required to have separate highway and city horns.

The government standard for overexposure to noise in any U.S. workplace is 90 dbA for eight hours a day—still significantly above the standard of 85 dbA considered to be the minimum safe level. Industry officials oppose lowering the standard to 85 dbA because implementation would cost an estimated $20 billion. In 1972 Congress passed the Noise Control Act, which directed the EPA to set standards for major sources of noise and to support research on the effects of noise and its control.

By 1986, 14 years after the act was passed, the EPA had issued maximum noise standards only for air conditioners, buses, motorcycles, power mowers, some trucks and trains, and some construction equipment. Standards have not been set for aircraft noise, which affects millions. Enforcement of noise regulations has been almost nonexistent because the law merely fines violators. In addition, since 1981 the Reagan administration has virtually eliminated the EPA budget for curbing noise pollution.

The EPA has proposed a national plan for noise control. But noise control experts point out that unless Congress strengthens existing noise control laws and penalties and increases the amount of money appropriated for noise research and control, this plan will continue to collect dust in bureaucratic files.

Health and a good state of body are above all gold, and a strong body above infinite wealth.

Ecclesiastes 40:15

CHAPTER SUMMARY

Poor people in LDCs are more likely to suffer or die from *infectious diseases* such as malaria and schistosomiasis, which are transmitted by insects or by polluted water or food. People in MDCs are more likely to suffer or die from *noninfectious diseases* such as heart disease, stroke, cancer, and respiratory infections, caused by lifestyle factors such as smoking, alcohol or other drug abuse, diet, and pollution.

Half of the world's people live in malaria-prone regions. *Malaria*, transmitted from person to person by 60 kinds of *Anopheles* mosquito, is the world's single most serious health problem—killing from 2 million to 4 million people a year and incapacitating tens of millions. Control of malaria involves use of antimalarial drugs, draining of swamplands and marshes, and spraying mosquito breeding areas with DDT and other insecticides. However, most species of the *Anopheles* mosquito have developed genetic resistance to DDT and other insecticides, allowing malaria to make a dramatic comeback in many parts of the world.

Another major infectious disease in many LDCs is *schistosomiasis*, which is caused by a trematode worm usually transmitted to humans by tiny snails found in freshwater streams, rivers, lakes, and irrigation canals. Control of this disease involves improving sanitation, preventing people from swimming or working in contaminated water, using drugs that kill the worm in the body, using chemicals to kill the snails that transmit the worms, and trying to prevent infestation of freshwater bodies by the snails.

One of the major killers in MDCs is *cancer*, a name for a group of more than 120 diseases characterized by the uncontrolled growth and multiplication of certain cells. Most cancers take 15 to 40 years to develop. If not detected and treated in time, many cancerous tumors *metastasize*, or release cancerous cells that travel in body fluids to other parts of the body, making treatment much more difficult. Almost half of all Americans who get cancer now survive for five years or more (considered a cure) because of a combination of early detection and treatment by surgery, radiation, and drugs (chemotherapy). New treatment methods designed to stimulate the body's immune system to attack cancer cells look promising and may raise the cure rate to 75% by 2000.

About 10% to 30% of all cancers are caused by *hereditary factors*, and 70% to 90% are caused by *environmental factors* such as smoking, diet, occupation, and pollution. *Tobacco causes more death and suffering among adults than any other environmental factor*, causing between 2 million and 2.5 million smokers to die each year throughout the world, primarily from heart disease, lung cancer, bronchitis, and emphysema. Each year in the United States tobacco causes an estimated 375,000 premature deaths and economic losses ranging from $38 billion to $95 billion. Smoking also causes death and health problems for nonsmokers. Cancer risks from smoking can be reduced by not smoking, by banning smoking in all public places and work environments, and by taxing tobacco products so that those using them pay the full cost of the damage to health and the lost work productivity now borne by everyone.

Improper diet causes an estimated 35% of all cancer deaths in the United States, primarily as a result of excessive intake of fats, nitrosamines, and nitrites and insufficient intake of fish, vegetables, and fruits. About 5% to 20% of all cancer deaths are caused by *occupational exposure* to radiation and carcinogens. This exposure can be reduced by enacting stricter workplace standards that reduce or eliminate exposure to hazardous chemicals and radiation.

In MDCs large numbers of chemicals, known as *food additives*, are added to processed foods to retard spoilage, to enhance flavor, color, and texture, and to provide missing amino acids and vitamins. The presence of synthetic chemical additives does not necessarily mean that a food is harmful, and the fact that a particular food is completely natural is no guarantee that it is safe. Although most food additives are probably safe, some are harmful. So far there has been inadequate testing to determine which of the 2,800 different chemicals added to food in the United States do not increase the risks of cancer, birth defects, and other disorders.

Excessive noise affects the physical and mental health of most urban dwellers throughout the world and nearly half of all Americans. Harmful effects from noise pollution include permanent hearing loss, high blood pressure, migraine headaches, gastric ulcers, and psychological stress. Noise control can be accomplished by reducing noise at its source, by isolating it to reduce sound transfer, by using less noisy motorcycles, trucks, and other machines, and by wearing protective devices to reduce the amount of noise entering the ears. Control of noise pollution in the United States has lagged behind that in some other MDCs because of industry pressure against establishing stricter workplace noise standards and the virtual elimination of the EPA's budget for noise pollution control since 1981.

DISCUSSION TOPICS

1. Why are infectious diseases more common in LDCs? Why do so many infants and young children in LDCs die from measles, diarrhea, and other common childhood diseases?

2. Discuss malaria and schistosomiasis in terms of the life cycle, mode of transmission, effects, and possible controls.

3. Should DDT and other pesticides be banned from use in malaria control? Explain.

4. Analyze your lifestyle and diet to determine the relative risks of developing some form of cancer before you reach age 55. Which type of cancer are you most likely to get? How could you significantly reduce your chances of getting this cancer?

5. Give your reasons for agreeing or disagreeing with each of the following proposals:
   a. All advertising of cigarettes and other tobacco products should be banned.
   b. All smoking should be banned in public buildings and commercial airplanes, buses, subways, and trains.
   c. All government subsidies to tobacco farmers and the tobacco industry should be eliminated.

d. Cigarettes should be taxed at three dollars a pack so that smokers—not nonsmokers—pay for the health and productivity losses now borne by society as a whole.

6. Give your reasons for agreeing or disagreeing with the following suggestions made by some environmentalists and health scientists:

a. All new and presently used food additives should be reviewed and tested not only for toxicity and carcinogenicity but also for their ability to induce birth defects and long-term genetic effects.

b. All testing of food additives should be performed by a third party, independent of the food industry.

c. All food additives, including specific flavors, colors, and sodium content (for people on salt-free diets), should be listed on the label or container of all foods and drugs.

d. All food additives should be banned unless extensive testing establishes that they are safe and that they enhance the nutritive content of foods or prevent food spoilage or contamination by harmful bacteria and molds.

7. Compare brands of various foods found in the grocery store. See if there are some that contain no controversial additives.

8. Explain the fallacies in the following statements:

a. All synthetic food additives should be banned, and we should all return to safe, nutritious natural foods.

b. All foods are chemicals, so we shouldn't worry about artificial additives.

c. Because some natural foods contain harmful chemicals, we should not be so concerned about synthetic food additives.

d. Food additives are essential; without them we would suffer from malnutrition, food poisoning, and spoiled food.

9. Do you believe that the Delaney Clause should be revoked, left as is, altered to allow an evaluation of risks and benefits, or strengthened and broadened? Explain.

10. As a class or group project, try to borrow one or more sound pressure decibel meters from the physics or engineering department or from a local stereo or electronics repair shop. Make a survey of sound pressure levels at various times of day and at several locations; plot the results on a map. Include a room with a stereo, and take readings at an indoor concert or nightclub at various distances from the sound system speakers. Also measure sound pressure levels from earphones at several different loudness settings. Correlate your findings with those in Table 23-7.

11. Give your reasons for agreeing or disagreeing with the proposal that it should be illegal to play music above 85 dbA in any form of public transportation, in the streets, and in public buildings except nightclubs, auditoriums, and other places where live music is performed.

PART SIX

Environment and Society

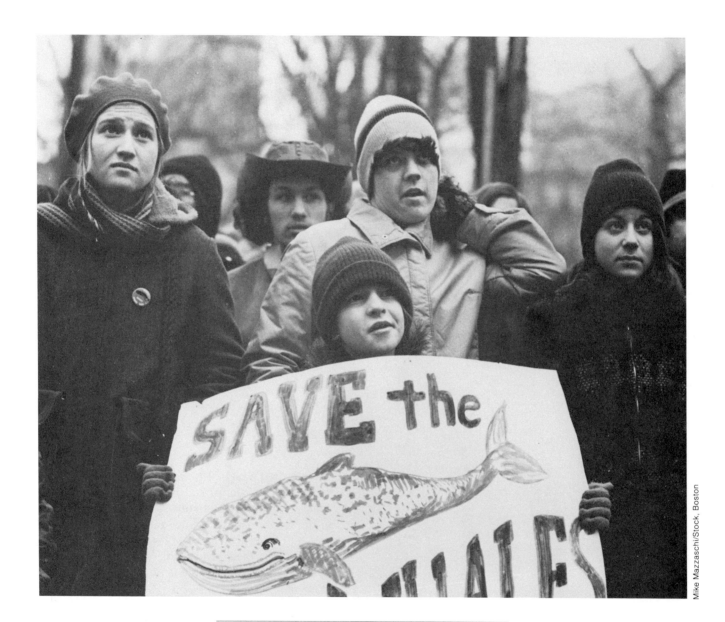

Mike Mazzaschi/Stock, Boston

We cannot hope for world peace when 20 percent of the people in the world have 80 percent of the goods.
Father Theodore Hesburgh

There is a need for a revolution in our thinking as basic as the one introduced by Copernicus, who first pointed out that the earth was not the center of the universe.

Lester Pearson

24

Economics and Environment

GENERAL OBJECTIVES

1. What are the three major types of economic systems found throughout the world?

2. Is economic growth good or bad?

3. What are some problems with present economic systems, and what are the characteristics of a sustainable-earth economic system?

4. How can economic systems be used to protect and improve environmental quality?

5. Are the economic costs of environmental protection and improvement too high?

As important as technology, politics, law, and ethics are to the pollution question, all such approaches are bound to have disappointing results, for they ignore the primary fact that pollution is primarily an economic problem, which must be understood in economic terms.

Larry E. Ruff

The words *economics* and *ecology* come from the same Greek root, *oikos*, meaning house or home. **Ecology** is the study of our earthly home—an analysis of interactions among species and between species and their environment. **Economics** literally means household management; today the term refers to the study of principles and customs that affect the production, consumption, growth, and distribution of material wealth for human needs. In spite of the common origin of these two terms, ecology and economics have scarcely interacted until recently, as discussed in this chapter.

24-1 ECONOMIC GROWTH, GNP, AND THE QUALITY OF LIFE

Economic Systems The world has three major types of economic systems: subsistence, commercial, and centrally planned. In a **subsistence economy,** found in the few remaining hunter-gatherer societies (Section 2-2), those who produce resources also consume them to meet their basic needs for food, shelter, and clothing. As a result, there is no surplus production of goods.

A **capitalist** or **commercial economy,** found in the United States and most MDCs, is based on producing a surplus of goods that are exchanged between producers and consumers in the marketplace. Three major characteristics of such an economy are profit, specialization, and interdependence. The economic driving force is a desire for profit. Individuals, or groups of individuals who pool their resources to form a company, usually produce a particular product or provide a particular service (specialization) and rely on other companies to provide raw materials and market the goods or services (interdependence). Such an economy is based on free market trade, profit maximization, and competition, with supply and demand governing the price and quantity of goods and services exchanged. When the supply exceeds demand, prices fall, and when demand exceeds supply, prices rise.

In practice, however, free market competition rarely exists. Some companies selling particular goods or services try to avoid free market competition and maximize profits by dominating or monopolizing the market through driving out competitors and obtaining special tax breaks or other subsidies from the government. Some companies also try to minimize production costs and maximize profits by passing on environmental and waste disposal costs to consumers in the form of increased taxes, rather than having them reflected in the cost of products and services. As a result of this distortion of free market competition, consumers have little idea of the true life-cycle costs of the items they purchase.

In a **centrally planned economy,** found in the Soviet Union and China, the central government controls and allocates resources and thus determines the type, supply, and price of goods and services. The government, not supply and demand market forces, determines the value or price placed on each good or service to be traded in the marketplace. In practice, many economies have a mixture of the capitalist and centrally planned approaches. For example, in China some free market competition is allowed and in the United States the federal government plays a major role in distorting free market competition.

The Economic Growth Debate   Economic growth is based on increasing consumption by a growing population and greater average per capita consumption. To most economists, city planners, and industrialists, economic growth is equated with progress. Only a vigorously growing economy coupled with maximum production and maximum consumption is considered healthy and sound. People are conditioned by advertising and the education system to expect to achieve self-satisfaction through individual consumption of more and more things, rather than distinguishing between what they really need and what they want. LDCs are encouraged to become economically developed like today's MDCs so they can then purchase more goods from MDCs.

Economic growth is assumed to increase well-being, provide more jobs, control inflation, help cure poverty, and provide enough funds to clean up the environment (Table 24-1). Since 1970 the growth mania goal of ever-increasing economic growth at any cost has come under attack by environmentalists and some

economists and industrialists who believe that the harmful consequences of such growth often outweigh the benefits.

The issue is more complicated than economic growth at any cost versus no economic growth. A number of economists and environmentalists generally agree on the following points:

1. Some forms of economic growth are neither desirable, necessary, nor inevitable. In the words of economist Herman E. Daly, "What we need is growth in things that really count, rather than in things that are merely countable."

2. We need to use economic rewards and penalties to redirect growth and eliminate waste. Some things need to grow and some need to decline, because the earth's resources and the ability of the environment to absorb pollution are finite.

3. We still know relatively little about which types of growth have good effects and which have bad effects, or about how to measure these effects.

4. We disagree over whether emphasis should be placed on short-term or long-term good and bad effects. Economists focus on the short-term economic effects of various forms of growth on a particular business and country, over a one- to five-year period. They assume that technology will always be able to overcome any long-term harmful effects. Ecologists focus on the long-term effects on the quality and quantity of basic ecological resources—air, water, soil, minerals, and genetic diversity—that provide the basis of human survival and all economic activity. They assume that technological advances can help but cannot prevent severe ecological and economic disruption once the limits of the environment to absorb, dilute, or degrade the society's wastes are exceeded.

Gross National Product: A Misleading Indicator   The **gross national product (GNP)** is the market value of all goods and services produced by the economy of a given area (usually a country) in a given year. **Average per capita GNP,** the GNP divided by the total population, is often used to show how economic growth is distributed among the population of a country. For example, a country that experiences a 3% growth in its GNP and a 3% growth in its population during a given year experiences no increase in average per capita GNP. In contrast, a country with 2% growth in GNP and 1% growth in population experiences a 1% increase in average per capita GNP.

To most economists a rising GNP or per capita GNP indicates improved well-being or a higher stan-

Table 24-1 Views on Economic Growth

Pro	Con
Economic growth promotes well-being.	Some types of economic growth promote the well-being of some, but worsen the well-being of others. In spite of decades of worldwide economic growth, the gap between the rich and the poor is growing (Figure 1-9, p. 11).
Economic growth promotes full employment and controls inflation.	Some labor-intensive types of economic growth such as pollution control and energy conservation do create jobs and help control inflation. However, many forms of economic growth such as defense spending and increasingly automated factories tend to decrease employment and raise taxes by increasing the number of people in legitimate need of welfare and related social programs.
Economic growth is the cure for poverty and makes it easier for rich countries to help poor countries. As long as the economic pie is growing, more wealth can "trickle down" to the world's poor.	Even if this hypothesis is valid, most economic growth in rich countries has not been used to help the poor. The gap between the rich and the poor is growing, and most rich countries are giving less and less aid to poor countries. In most cases, this argument is merely a smokescreen to direct attention from the important ethical and political issue of a more just distribution of the world's wealth.
The benefits of economic growth outweigh its harmful effects.	As we approach environmental thresholds, the harmful effects of air, water, heat, and noise pollution, land disruption, traffic jams, and other environmental and social disturbances that result from growing production and consumption begin to outweigh the benefits of economic growth.
Economic growth is necessary to fund environmental cleanup and to pay for higher-priced energy.	It is economically and ecologically unsound to use and waste more matter and energy at ever higher costs. Decreasing the rate of wasteful growth is a cheaper approach in the long run and is the only way to avoid the limits to growth imposed by finite resources and the second law of energy.
Economic growth promotes technological innovation, which can solve the problems of resource depletion and pollution.	Substitutes for some resources will not be found; other approaches, such as mining lower grade resources, are too expensive. Technology often creates as many problems as it solves. No technological development will overcome the unalterable limits imposed by the second law of energy.

dard of living for a country's citizens. Some economists have pointed out that the GNP was not meant to be a measure of well-being, but most economists still equate them that way.

To environmentalists, GNP and average per capita GNP are misleading indicators of quality of life. These figures do not reveal the average prices of goods and services, how well they are meeting human needs, or how they are distributed among the people. One problem is that the costs of goods and services vary widely from country to country. For example, the cost of housing, food, and fuel in a country where the average per capita GNP is high, say $15,000, may be

much higher than in a poorer country with an average per capita GNP of $2,000, where costs for these items may be much lower. Thus, people with an average per capita GNP of $2,000 may have more purchasing power than this figure indicates. Average per capita GNP also gives an inflated idea of average well-being in a poor country where most of the wealth is enjoyed by a small number of individuals.

Another major problem with GNP and average per capita GNP as indicators of well-being is that they include expenditures for both beneficial and harmful goods and services. Producing more cigarettes raises the GNP, but it also causes more cancer. This increases

Between 1950 and 1986 the U.S. federal debt, when adjusted for inflation, more than doubled from $1 trillion to $2.08 trillion. Most of this increase occurred since 1980 when President Reagan took office, primarily as a result of increased defense spending with no increase in taxes. During the six years between 1980 and 1986 the United States accumulated almost as much debt as during the preceding 200 years. The 1986 federal debt was equivalent to half the money in the world, and each American's share amounted to $8,595.

The interest on the federal debt in 1986 amounted to $138.1 billion, an average of $571 per American or $2,284 for a family of four. This interest accounted for 15% of all government expenditures and cost U.S. taxpayers $263,000 a minute. According to conservative estimates by the Congressional Research Service, just to finance the interest charges on today's federal deficit will cost the average citizen now entering the work force an extra $10,000 in taxes over his or her lifetime. All of these expenditures increase the GNP but decrease average well-being by draining off funds that could be used to improve health, educa-

tion, welfare, environmental quality, and research and development of new products to make the U.S. more economically competitive.

Such a large federal debt also crowds other borrowers out of the money market, keeps interest rates higher than necessary, and makes it difficult for the government to function without either raising taxes or further increasing the national debt. Economists point out that this debt must sooner or later be paid, or the country will in effect be bankrupt and experience an economic crash that will disrupt the entire world economy.

The already massive federal deficit does not include an additional $10.5 trillion in state and local government debt and off-the-books federal debt for future obligations such as Social Security and other federal pension plans. If we include all these debts, in 1986 each American owed an average of almost $52,000, excluding personal debts.

Between 1980 and 1986 the U.S. **trade deficit**—the difference between the larger amount the United States spent on goods from other countries and the smaller amount other countries spent on U.S. goods—increased

more than fivefold from $32.1 billion to $170 billion. Even in high-tech goods such as TVs, VCRs, computers, scientific instruments, and aircraft parts, the United States went from a $26.7 billion trade surplus in 1980 to a $2.6 billion trade deficit in 1986. This trade deficit, which represents a huge hemorrhage of capital from the U.S. economy, also increased the GNP. Sometime in the 1990s Japan is projected to supplant the United States as the world's leading trading power.

So far the president and members of Congress have been unable to come to grips with the federal deficit because it requires politically dangerous choices: decrease expenditures for defense and domestic programs or raise taxes. Some state constitutions forbid deficit spending and require a balanced budget each year. A growing number of people believe that an amendment should be added to the constitution requiring a balanced budget and setting up a schedule to pay off the existing national debt. Such a measure would cause a short-term drop in expenditures for many federally supported programs, but in the long run could prevent economic ruin. What do you think?

medical expenditures, which increases the GNP, but in a way that decreases life quality for the people who must pay for these additional costs. More automobiles cause more accidents, more congestion, and more pollution, causing the GNP to grow, but again by incurring costs of a harmful activity. Thus, a country that has greatly increased health, corrosion, and cleaning costs as a result of polluted air and water, and increased fertilizer costs, because of excessive soil erosion, experiences an increase in its GNP and average per capita GNP. Yet these expenditures result from a decrease in average life quality.

Waste in government is also included in the GNP. A 1983 government-sponsored study by a task force of business executives and experts gave detailed suggestions showing how $100 billion a year could be saved by eliminating government waste. By 1987 hardly any of the suggestions had been implemented. An increasing amount of the annual federal budget, also included in the GNP, goes to pay off or pay interest on the **federal deficit**—the amount of money the government has to borrow to make up the difference between what it spends and what it takes in from taxes (see Spotlight above).

1. The system is dynamic—not dull and static.

2. It is not a no-growth system, as opponents contend. Although it strives for a constant GNP, some things grow, some decline, and some remain fairly constant. These dynamic ups and downs help prevent the system from exceeding its limits. Some of the things that could grow are art, music, education, physical fitness, philosophy, aesthetics, religion, cultural diversity, scientific research, and positive human behavior and interactions. Areas of business and technology encouraged to grow would include birth control, pollution control, recycling, appropriate technology, production of long-lasting goods, medical research and health care, efficient energy use, resource recovery, and renewable energy resources. Industries that couldn't conserve resources and decrease harmful outputs would decline.

3. A sustainable-earth economy does not necessarily require a fixed level of pollution or resource use. Many possible combinations of population size and resource use allow a system to exist without exceeding environmental limits. Technological advances or other changes may make growth desirable. However, in such cases growth is viewed as a temporary situation needed to move from one steady state level to another, not as an economic norm.

4. The system is based on greatly increased use of renewable energy resources (sun, wind, water, and biomass) and decreased use and unnecessary waste of nonrenewable matter and energy resources.

5. A sustainable-earth economy is based on the often neglected fact that biological capital is as important as financial capital

for achieving long-term ecological and economic sustainability.

6. The system uses money to reward those who produce long-lasting goods and services and consume little matter and energy resources. In such a low-waste economic system, waste and scrap matter—what we now call secondary materials—would become the primary matter resources, and our natural, untapped resources would become our backup supplies—the reverse of our present situation.

7. A sustainable-earth economy emphasizes production and use of essential goods and services. People would be guided by two well-known principles: *The more things you own, the more you are owned by things*, and *The best things in life aren't things*.

8. The system would strive for a more equitable distribution of wealth.

Gross National Quality   Most economists agree that we need a better indicator than GNP for determining the quality of life. In theory, we could list and put a price tag on all the "negative" products and services included in the GNP. The total value of these negative factors could be subtracted from the GNP to obtain the **gross national quality,** or **GNQ.**

It is difficult to develop definitions and measures of the quality of life. For example, how do we put a value on clean air, clean water, a human life, and redwood trees? Should values be based on the present or the future? Even when we agree on values, it is often hard to put numbers on them. However, analysts argue that the inability to find perfect social indicators should not prevent us from improving the imperfect ones we now use. The Overseas Development Council has devised a Physical Quality of Life Indicator (PQLI) based on three social indicators—life expectancy, infant mortality, and literacy—to be used instead of per capita GNP.

24-2   TOWARD A SUSTAINABLE-EARTH ECONOMY

Problems with Conventional Economic Systems Existing capitalistic and centrally planned economic systems throughout the world are devoted to economic growth by continually increasing the rate of flow of matter and energy resources through each national economy (Figure 3-18, p. 65). The resulting problems with pollution and environmental degradation occur in all industrialized countries and can cause regional and global environmental problems. Each year more time, energy, and money must be devoted to preventing local, regional, and global environmental overload. At some point, the costs of preventing environmental destruction exceed the benefits of economic growth.

Economists are also finding that modern economic models cannot predict and control conven-

Table 24-2 Characteristics of Throwaway and Sustainable-Earth Economic Systems

Throwaway Economic System	Sustainable-Earth Economic System
Assumes essentially infinite matter and energy resources.	Assumes finite matter and energy resources (unless solar, wind, or some form of almost unlimited energy can be developed at an affordable economic and environmental cost).
One-way flow of both matter and energy (Figure 3-18, p. 65).	One-way flow of energy but recycling of matter (Figure 3-19, p. 66).
Increases flow rates of matter and energy through the system (maximizes throughput).	Reduces the flow rate of energy and the flow and cycling rate of matter by deliberately reducing waste of matter and energy resources and not exceeding the biosphere's capacity to handle waste heat and matter.
Emphasis on efficiency, quantity of goods, simplification, and cultural, biological, and physical homogeneity to maintain short-term stability.	Emphasis on quality of goods and preservation of cultural and biological diversity to attain long-term ecological sustainability at the expense of some efficiency.
Emphasis on output control of pollution.	Greater emphasis on input control to reduce costs and prevent pollution and environmental degradation from reaching crisis levels.
Continued growth provides capital for output pollution control and redistribution of wealth (trickle down theory).	If growth continues, capital must be increasingly devoted to maintenance and repair, thus decreasing life quality and inhibiting a more equitable distribution of wealth.
Emphasis on initial cost of goods—buy now and pay more for the external costs later through increased taxes.	Emphasis on the life-cycle cost of goods—buy now and pay less in the long run.
Assumes that a free competitive market system or a centralized controlled economy will respond to undesirable side effects.	Market responds only if quality of life indicators help determine the prices of goods and services; free market competition rarely exists.
Local or national outlook.	Global outlook.

tional economies as well as they had hoped, suggesting that the problem is economic theory itself. This was expressed by the editors of *Business Week:* "When all forecasts miss the mark, it suggests that the entire body of economic thinking accumulated during the past 200 years is inadequate to describe and analyze the problems of our times." Instead of tampering with dangerously out-of-date economic models, economists may have to develop a more comprehensive and realistic body of economic theory based on preserving the health of basic biological systems (fisheries, forests, grasslands, and croplands), which form the foundation of the entire global economy.

A Sustainable-Earth or Steady State Economy
Economists like Herman E. Daly (see Guest Essay at the end of this chapter) have proposed that the United States and other MDCs move from the present throwaway economy to a **sustainable-earth** or **steady state** economy: one in which the number of people and the quantity of goods (stock) are maintained at some constant level that is ecologically sustainable over time and that provides a good life for the population size that can be accommodated under these conditions (see Spotlight p. 562).

Table 24-2 summarizes some of the important differences between the throwaway economy found in most MDCs and a sustainable-earth economy. The transition to a sustainable-earth economy will not be painless and will require economists to question old economic models and develop new ones.

Barriers and Problems There are two major barriers hindering an orderly transition to a sustainable-earth economy: ignorance of how the world really works and human greed. Most decision makers in societies throughout the world do not believe there is an urgent need to adopt such an economy. The economists who advise these world leaders are too narrowly trained to be aware of how the biosphere works and how physical laws—such as the law of conservation of matter and the two laws of thermodynamics—place limits on what we can and cannot do (Section 3-7). Many economists believe that there are no physical limits to economic and population growth because human ingenuity can always develop technologies that raise the carrying capacity of the environment (Section 1-5). Others accept the existence of physical limits to growth but believe that we are too far removed from these limits to be concerned about them now.

Other analysts contend that a sustainable-earth economy cannot be achieved, even if desirable, because most countries would not agree to such a system and because most people are fundamentally selfish and greedy. They point to the fact that most people will not voluntarily do anything to diminish their power or wealth.

Critics of a sustainable-earth economy also argue that it could be instituted only by greatly reducing human freedom. They contend that attempts to control population and resource use would create a bureaucratic nightmare, promote inefficient management, and decrease incentives for discovering new and cheaper ways to find, extract, and use resources.

But proponents of a sustainable-earth economy respond that running our present high-waste economy at full speed until environmental disorder and resource depletion overwhelm us is a much worse alternative and would lead to an even greater loss of individual freedom. They also dispute that such an economy would necessarily become a bureaucratic nightmare or dampen creativity. Instead, the development of such a system calls for us to redirect human ingenuity to develop social and economic systems that are more compatible with the biosphere. Laws and regulations in free societies are attempts to prevent undue loss of individual freedom and accumulation of power. Shifting to a steady state would merely follow this tradition of using laws, education, and economic rewards to encourage resource conservation rather than waste, product durability rather than planned obsolescence, and zero population growth.

24-3 ECONOMICS AND POLLUTION CONTROL

Internal and External Costs   Pollution can be controlled by a number of methods in existing economic systems or in a sustainable-earth economy. To understand these methods, we must distinguish between what economists call internal costs and external costs.

In making or using anything there are **internal costs.** For example, the price one pays for a new car reflects the costs of construction and operation of the factory, raw materials and labor, marketing expenses, and shipping costs, as well as automobile company and dealer profits. There are also economic and health side effects not directly associated with the act of production. These **external costs** are passed on to someone else, usually the public. For example, the public pays the external costs of a new car resulting from land disruption and air and water pollution caused by mining and processing the manufacturing materials, noise and air pollution caused by driving the vehicle, and losses of productivity, health, and life due to automobile accidents. In addition, we all pay more in taxes for water purification because of the additional water pollution—again a cost not included in the car's price.

Unless it includes both internal and external costs, the initial cost of an item or service does not provide the consumer with accurate information about its **true cost:** its internal costs plus its external costs.

Approaches to Environmental Improvement   It is easy to suggest that we reduce environmental degradation by internalizing external costs, but how do we accomplish this? The major methods for environmental control are evaluated in Table 24-3.

No method of pollution control will be fair to everyone. Industries usually favor the subsidy or taxpayer-pays approach, by which they receive public monies for refraining from doing something—namely, polluting—that they shouldn't be doing in the first place. This approach, however, benefits the few at the expense of the many.

Most environmentalists favor reducing pollution levels by requiring that the price of any item or service include both its internal and external costs, through both direct regulation and pollution charges. For example, taxes on air pollutant emissions and on the use of nonrenewable resources would not only reduce air pollution and the depletion of nonrenewable resources but also generate about $80 billion in federal revenue. These funds could be used for further environmental improvement or to help reduce the federal budget deficit.

Opponents of adding pollution control costs to prices point out that an inequitable share of such costs would be borne by the poor. However, those favoring internalizing external costs argue that by paying a higher initial price to avoid the cost of pollution, we reduce later health and other pollution costs. In addi-

Table 24-3   Evaluation of Major Methods for Environmental Improvement

Method	Advantages	Disadvantages
Moral persuasion	1. Educates and sensitizes people. 2. Prepares people for action through other methods.	1. Often produces more guilt and discontent than action. 2. Rewards the socially irresponsible (those who refuse to buy pollution control equipment can make a bigger profit).
Suing for damages (torts)	1. Allows the individual or group to be compensated for damages.	1. Difficult to establish who damaged whom and to what degree. 2. Time consuming and expensive for both parties. 3. Output approach that does little to prevent damage.
Prohibition	1. Eliminates the damages. 2. May be required for some pollutants, such as toxic metals and radioactive materials. 3. Protects the individual from irresponsible acts by others.	1. Often not economically feasible; due to second energy law, removal of all pollution is prohibitively expensive. 2. May not be politically feasible (excessive control may lead to a political backlash that threatens even moderate control). 3. Zero or very low pollution levels are not always necessary (if not overloaded, natural chemical cycles can absorb, degrade, or recycle some types of waste).
Direct regulation	1. Can be used to keep pollution below a threshold level. 2. Protects the individual from irresponsible acts by others. 3. May be more just than prohibition.	1. Hard to enforce, especially when there are many pollution sources, such as cars, trucks, and buses. 2. Standards tend to be ones that are enforceable rather than optimal. 3. No incentive for polluters to reduce pollution below the standard. 4. Airsheds and watersheds cross political boundaries, so effective regulation by one government unit may be nullified by inaction of another. 5. Polluters can use courts and administrative procedures to delay compliance. 6. Often treats all polluters alike, regardless of amount of pollution contributed. This can discriminate against small polluters and can make the cost of effective pollution control higher than need be.
Payments and incentives	1. Makes it profitable not to pollute and encourages polluters to reduce pollution to lowest possible level. 2. A positive rather than negative approach. 3. Requires fewer enforcement procedures and expenses.	1. May encourage people or industries to pollute so they can qualify for payment.* 2. Pollution costs are still hidden and not internalized in the direct prices of items and services. 3. Drains public funds. 4. Taxpayers' money is used to pay individuals and corporations not to do something wrong.
Pollution rights and pollution charges	1. Makes it profitable not to pollute and encourages polluters to reduce pollution to lowest possible level. 2. Generates public revenue instead of draining public funds. 3. May reduce political maneuvering to influence or take over regulatory agencies. 4. Biggest polluters will have the greatest incentive to reduce pollution. 5. Administrative and enforcement machinery should be simpler and cheaper.	1. Hard to estimate what to charge for each pollutant. 2. The idea of being able to buy a license to pollute could encourage people to pollute up to a certain level. 3. Increases prices, putting a country's products at a disadvantage in international trade.

*The old joke that farm subsidies send people into the no-growing business could apply again if some enter the no-polluting business at taxpayers' expense.

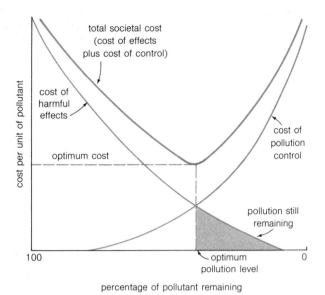

Figure 24-1 Cost-effectiveness analysis involves comparing the costs from the harmful effects of pollution with the costs of pollution control; the total costs of pollution control are minimized while still reducing the pollution to an acceptable level. The shaded area shows that some harmful effects remain, but removing these residual damages would make the costs of pollution control too high.

tion, because the poor now bear the brunt of environmental pollution, any scheme that reduces pollution will benefit them the most.

24-4 COST-BENEFIT AND COST-EFFECTIVENESS ANALYSIS

Cost-Benefit Analysis   When people buy groceries, cars, home heating systems, or other items, they usually purchase those products whose benefits appear to outweigh the costs by the largest margin. For example, does one benefit more by buying a small car that gets very good gas mileage or a larger, more powerful one that gets relatively poor gas mileage? Which type of car has the best repair record and thus will probably cost less in terms of life-cycle costs? Or which car will protect you best in an accident, and is thus potentially more beneficial in terms of health costs?

This same evaluation of costs and benefits is often used in decisions such as whether to build a large hydroelectric dam, to clean up a polluted river, or to enforce reduced pollution emissions to protect most of the public and still not drive industries out of business. The process of estimating and comparing the expected *costs* or losses associated with a particular project or degree of pollution control with the expected *benefits* or gains over a given period of time is known

as **cost-benefit analysis.** If the economic benefits exceed the costs, the project or activity is usually considered to be worthwhile.

For example, in 1987 the EPA proposed that the amount of lead permitted in drinking water be reduced from 50 parts per billion (ppb) to 20 ppb. An estimated 40 million Americans drink water that exceeds the 50 ppb standard. According to cost-benefit analysis, achieving the 20 ppb goal would cost from $115 million to $145 million a year but would yield from $800 million to $1 billion in health benefits. Thus the projected benefits exceed the projected costs by about 7 to 1. Another related approach, *risk-benefit analysis*, compares the projected health or environmental risks of a particular activity or product to its projected benefits (see Enrichment Study at the end of Chapter 6).

Cost-Effectiveness Analysis   Evaluation of alternative methods of achieving a desired goal while incurring the least cost is done by means of **cost-effectiveness analysis.** The goal of cost-effectiveness analysis is to minimize the total costs of pollution control and still reduce harmful environmental effects to a reasonable or acceptable level (Figure 24-1). Reducing pollution below this level might mean that the high costs would outweigh the economic benefits. Likewise, not reducing a given pollutant to the acceptable level means that the manufacturer is passing on hidden costs to taxpayers. The cost of pollution control climbs with each additional increment of control and rises very steeply for removing the last few percent. For example, reducing the pollutants emitted by a coal-burning power plant or an industrial plant by 90% might cost $20 million. However, to reduce emissions by 95% might cost $30 million and a 99% reduction might cost $75 million. Cost-effectiveness analysis can be used to decide what degree of control should be required.

Proponents of cost-benefit and cost-effectiveness analysis believe that they should be used in making all environmental decisions in order to use private capital and taxpayers' dollars in an economically efficient manner. These analyses encourage industry to develop new and more effective approaches to pollution control.

Problems with Cost-Benefit and Cost-Effectiveness Analysis   The controversy over the use of cost-benefit and cost-effectiveness analysis involves several key questions: Who decides what costs, risks, and benefits are considered in these calculations? Who should evaluate whether such analyses are valid and not distorted in favor of a particular position? Who gets the benefits and runs the risks? How do you put monetary values on such things as a human life, a wilderness area, and whooping cranes?

When asked to put a price tag on their life, most people would either call it infinite or contend that it is impossible or even immoral to do so. Yet the average American has been allowing industry and government officials to do so for decades, at least informally. Since 1980 the Reagan administration, under the urging of industry, has been proposing that such calculations become a mandatory part of all environmental and health decisions.

Values assigned to a human life in various cost-benefit and cost-effectiveness studies are plucked out of the air and vary from nothing to about $2 million; the most frequently assigned values range from $200,000 to $300,000. The callousness of this purely economic approach was revealed by an oil company representative who protested clean air standards affecting his firm's operations in Montana: "Some of the people who will die from air pollution are unemployed, and therefore have *no* economic value." An evaluation of a number of cost-benefit and cost-effectiveness studies also reveals that from a purely economic perspective, women are less valued than men, housewives less than women working outside the home, retired people less than workers, the sick less than the healthy, low-paid workers less than high-paid workers, and the unemployed less than the employed.

When the EPA did a cost-benefit analysis in 1984 on the proposed revision of the Clean Air Act, it concluded that the net benefits (after deducting the projected costs) ranged from a loss of $1.4 billion to a gain of as much as $110 billion—depending primarily on the monetary value assigned to things such as human life, human health, and a cleaner environment. From this calculation, we can see why cost-benefit and cost-effectiveness analyses are so vulnerable to partisan manipulation and value judgments. What value, if any, do you believe should be placed on your life? Do you think that cost-benefit, risk-benefit, and cost-effectiveness analysis should be made a part of all environmental and health decisions?

Environmentalists contend that cost-benefit and cost-effectiveness analyses often distort economic reality by exaggerating regulatory costs and underestimating benefits. They believe that such analyses are often used to weaken environmental regulation. Thus, it matters a great deal who carries out the analysis. Industries favoring a particular project or degree of pollution control have a strong financial incentive to exaggerate present costs of pollution control, to downgrade the economic value of a future benefit, and thus to confine their calculations only to the near future.

Similarly, environmentalists tend to place a much higher value on clean air and water and other benefits and to put more emphasis on long-term benefits and costs. Environmentalists also argue that all such evaluations should be open to review and challenge during administrative deliberations. Furthermore, regulatory agencies should be required to consider several different evaluations, including those from parties for and against a particular action as well as from an impartial party.

Another problem is that those who receive the benefits often don't run the risks, and those who run the risks often receive the fewest benefits. For example, in the chemical industry, workers and those living in the plant vicinity often bear the risks of not reducing air pollution emissions below a certain level, while those living far away reap the benefits of being able to purchase less expensive chemicals. Similarly, the poor, who are the most likely to live and work under hazardous and unhealthful conditions, bear the risks of unnecessarily low workplace and general environmental standards. For example, congressional investigators found that 75% of the South's worst hazardous waste dumps are located near low-income black communities.

The most serious objection to the automatic use of cost-benefit and cost-effectiveness analysis is that many things we value cannot be reduced to dollars and cents. For example, some of the costs of air pollution—such as extra laundry bills, house repainting, and ruined crops—are fairly easy to estimate. But how do we put a price tag on human life (see Spotlight above), clean air and water, beautiful scenery, and the ability of natural ecosystems to degrade and recycle our wastes? Such quantifications involve political, social, and ethical issues as well as economic ones. Furthermore, regarding a human life or an environmental value such as clean air solely in monetary terms reduces them to commodities that can be priced, bought, and sold.

Environmentalists contend that ethics and common sense—not economic analysis alone—should be the overriding factors in evaluating proposed projects. For example, the benefit of electricity from a nuclear power plant and a coal-burning power plant over their 30- to 40-year lifetime is fairly easy to calculate. But what are the long-term environmental and social costs of protecting our descendants from the radioactive wastes that the nuclear plant produces and the possibility of a catastrophic accident? And what are the long-term environmental and social costs associated with the air pollution produced by a coal-burning plant and the increased risk of altering global climate from carbon dioxide emissions?

What Obligation Do We Have to Future Generations? In making costs-benefit analyses, economists use a **discount factor,** a measure of how much something may be worth in the future compared with what it is worth now. A discount factor less than 1 indicates that something is considered to be worth more now than it will be worth in the future, and a discount factor greater than 1 means that something is expected to be worth more in the future than it is now.

In most conventional cost-benefit analyses the future is discounted or deemphasized by assuming discount factors less than 1. Reasons for this include uncertainty over the future rate of inflation, which if high enough can reduce future profits in constant dollars below present profits, and fear that innovation or changed consumer preferences may render a product or service obsolete. It is also assumed that economic

growth will automatically raise living standards in the future. Thus, why should the current generation sacrifice consumption or pay higher prices and taxes to benefit future generations who will be better off anyhow? In addition, many depletable resources located in LDCs are exploited by multinational firms. Such firms usually discount the future altogether and try to remove the resource as fast as possible because of their fear that the government may nationalize and take over their mines, factories, and other facilities.

Environmentalists argue that the external costs associated with a particular product or service should be internalized—not only to give consumers a better idea of the risks associated with its use but also because we have an ethical obligation to future generations to leave the environment in the best condition possible. Thus in economic calculations, the future value of the environment should be equal to or be greater than its present value; that is, we should use discount factors of 1 or higher rather than the less than 1 factor as is done in most present cost-benefit calculations.

Environmentalists also question the belief that continuing economic growth as measured by GNP and average per capita GNP will automatically lead to improved living standards. If much of the present environmental degradation and pollution is not prevented by input approaches, then an increasingly larger proportion of a country's GNP must be devoted to cleanup and restoration, leaving less capital, time, and talent available for improving life quality. This fundamental difference of opinion over our obligation to

Guest Essay The Steady State Economy in Outline

Herman E. Daly is professor of economics at Louisiana State University. His research centers on the economics of ecology, analysis of a steady state economy and society, and population issues. He has written a number of articles and three important books on the steady state economy (see Further Readings). He is one of a small number of economists seriously thinking about sustainable-earth economics.

The steady state economy is basically a physical concept but with important social and moral implications. It is defined as a constant stock of physical wealth and people, each maintained at some desirable, chosen level by a low rate of throughput of matter and energy resources so the longevity of people

and goods is high. Throughput is roughly equivalent to GNP, the annual flow of new production. It is the cost of maintaining the stocks of goods and services by continually importing low-entropy matter and energy resources from the environment and exporting high-entropy matter waste and low-quality heat energy back to the environment (Figure 3-18, p. 65).

Currently we attempt to maximize the growth of the gross GNP, whereas the reasoning just given suggests that we should relabel it gross national cost or GNC, and minimize it, subject to maintenance of a chosen level of stocks of essential items. For example, if we can maintain a desired, self-sufficient stock of items such as cars with a lower throughput of iron, coal, petroleum, and other resources, we are better off, not worse off.

future generations is a major source of disagreement between most environmentalists and conventional economists and corporate leaders.

24-5 HOW MUCH SHOULD BE SPENT ON ENVIRONMENTAL IMPROVEMENT?

Are the estimated costs of environmental protection and improvement in the United States and other countries so high that they outweigh the benefits? Have environmental protection standards in the United States caused massive unemployment?

Industrialists often argue that the costs of reducing pollution make their businesses unprofitable, causing them difficulty in raising capital and forcing them to close down plants and lay off employees. They argue that the economic benefits of jobs outweigh the need for stricter environmental control.

In 1985, U.S. government and industry were spending about $70 billion a year—an average of $289 for every American—on pollution control. This amounted to only about 1.6% of the GNP and 2.7% of capital expenditures by U.S. businesses. By contrast, it is estimated that environmental damage cost the United States and other Western industrialized countries about 4% of their GNP in 1985.

Of course, all costs of protecting the environment are ultimately paid for by consumers through increased taxes and prices. But numerous studies show that failure to control pollution will cost even more in the form of declining health, skyrocketing medical costs, absenteeism, and damage to food crops and other forms of vegetation, farm animals, and wildlife.

Moreover, the pollution control business is growing at about 18% per year—twice the annual growth rate for all U.S. manufacturing. Pollution control creates many more jobs than it eliminates and by 1985 provided employment for about 2.5 million people. For example, according to a report published by Management Information Services, the $70 billion spent on pollution control in 1985 created 167,000 jobs, $19.3 billion in pollution industry sales, and $2.6 billion in corporate profits.

Pollution control can also save industry money in the long run. For example, an $8 million pollution control system installed by Great Lakes Paper Company reduced the plant's operating cost by $4 million a year and paid for itself in only two years. The Ciba-Geigy chemical complex in Basel, Switzerland, has eliminated 50% of its pollution and saved about $400,000 a year. The Elf Oil Refinery in France has turned its hydrocarbon pollution into usable products with an annual profit of $1.3 million.

The first step is to stop the waste. Perhaps the next might be a greater willingness to share the wealth that has made the waste possible.

Barbara Ward

To maximize GNP throughput for its own sake is absurd. Physical and ecological limits to the volume of throughput imply the eventual necessity of a steady state economy. Less recognizable but probably more stringent social and moral limits imply the desirability of a steady state economy long before it becomes a necessity. For example, the effective limit to the use of nuclear fission breeder reactors (Section 17-3)—as long as development of this technology is heavily subsidized by the government—will more likely be the social problem of safeguarding plutonium from theft to make nuclear weapons than, say, thermal water pollution or low-level radiation. If breeder and conventional nuclear power were forced to operate in an open market without government subsidies, neither would probably be developed because of too low an economic return on the investment.

Once we have attained a steady state economy at some level of stocks, we are not forever frozen at that level. Moral and technological evolution may make it both possible and desirable to grow (or decline) to a different level. But growth will then be seen as a temporary process necessary to move from one steady state level to another, not as an economic norm. Moreover, technical and moral evolution will no longer be pushed by growth along the dangerous path of least short-run resistance. This requires a substantial shift in economic thought. Ecological conservatism of resources breeds economic radicalism that questions and replaces current economic ideas and models.

The major challenges facing us today are **(1)** for physical and biological scientists to define more clearly the limits and interactions within ecosystems and the biosphere (which determine the feasible levels of the steady state) and to develop technologies more in conformity with such limits; **(2)** for social scientists to design the institutions that will bring about the transition to a steady state and permit its continuance; and **(3)** for philosophers and theologians to stress the neglected traditions of stewardship and distributive justice that exist in our cultural and religious heritage. The latter is of paramount importance because the problem of sharing a fixed amount of resources and goods is much greater than that of sharing a growing amount. Indeed, this has been the major reason for giving top priority to growth. If the pie is always growing, there will be crumbs for the poor so that the moral question of a more equitable distribution of the world's resources and wealth is avoided.

The kinds of economic institutions required to make this transition follow directly from the definition of a steady state economy. We need an institution for maintaining a constant population size within the limits of available resources. For example, economic incentives can be used to encourage each woman or

CHAPTER SUMMARY

The three major types of economic systems found throughout the world are *subsistence, capitalist* or *commercial,* and *centrally planned,* with the latter two predominating. All capitalist and centrally planned economies are based on increasing economic growth by a combination of a larger population and greater average per capita consumption. Such growth, as measured by *gross national product (GNP)* and *average per capita GNP,* is assumed to increase average well-being, provide jobs, control inflation, help cure poverty, and provide funds for environmental protection and improvement.

Environmentalists, however, question the idea of economic growth at any cost. They point out that some types of growth increase average well-being and environmental quality, whereas other types do the opposite. They also point out that GNP and average per capita GNP are misleading indicators of life quality because they include expenditures for both beneficial and harmful goods and services. They suggest that economists devise a *gross national quality (GNQ)* index obtained by subtracting the negative or harmful factors from the GNP.

Environmentalists contend that all existing capitalist and centrally planned economic systems are based on increasing economic growth continually by increasing the rate of flow of matter and energy resources through each national economy, eventually leading to environmental overload and depletion of nonrenewable resources or bankruptcy. To prevent such environmental and ecological collapse, they believe that the United States and other MDCs should begin making a transition from their present throwaway economy to a sustainable-earth economy—one in which the number of people and the quantity of goods would be maintained at some constant level that is ecologically sustainable over the long run and that provides a good life for whatever population size can be accommodated under such conditions. In such a system goods and services that improve health and well-being and the condition of the environment would be encouraged to grow economically and those that don't serve these goals would be discouraged. Emphasis would be on preserving the biological capital of soil, grasslands, forests, fisheries, and biological diversity upon which all life and economic activities depend, producing goods and services that are essential not frivolous, decentralizing the manufacture of many goods, increased use of renewable energy resources, decreased waste of matter and energy resources, and more equitable distribution of wealth.

Critics of a sustainable-earth economy believe that it is unnecessary because there are no limits to physical growth that cannot be overcome by technological advances. In addition, they contend we are too far from such limits to be concerned about them now. Others contend that even if a sustainable-earth economy is desirable, most people are too selfish and greedy to make the necessary changes and sacrifices such an economy demands and that such a change would involve a significant loss of individual freedom by requiring excessive bureaucratic control. Proponents respond that the alternative of running our present high-waste economies at full speed until environmental overload and resource depletion overwhelm us would lead to an even greater loss of individual freedom.

In making or using anything, there are *internal costs,* passed on to consumers in the price of goods and services, and *external costs,* passed on to all taxpayers, regardless of whether they use the goods or services themselves. Thus, the health, cleaning, and other external costs associated with various products and services are either paid for by consumers who use the items or services (the *consumer-pays approach*) or by society as a whole (the *taxpayer-pays approach*). Environmentalists favor passing laws that require the prices of all items and services to include their internal and external costs. This allows consumers to see the true costs of using various items and services so they can make more informed choices. The taxpayer-pays approach would then be used primarily for cleaning up the air, water, and land that was contaminated or degraded as a result of past practices.

Reducing pollution and environmental degradation can be accomplished by several methods: **(1)** moral persuasion, **(2)** suing for damages, **(3)** prohibition, **(4)** direct regulation, **(5)** payments and other incentives, **(6)** selling transferable rights to pollute up to a certain level, and levying taxes or charges on each unit of pollution produced. Industries usu-

couple to have no more than a certain number of children, or each woman or couple could be given a marketable license to have a certain number of children. We also need an institution for maintaining a constant stock of physical wealth and limiting resource throughput. For example, the government could set and auction off transferable annual depletion quotas for key resources. Finally, there must be an institution to limit inequalities in the distribution of the constant physical wealth among the constant population in a steady state economy. For example, there might be minimum and maximum limits on personal income and maximum limits on personal wealth.

Many such institutions could be imagined. The problem is to achieve the necessary global and societal (macro) control with the least sacrifice of freedom at the individual (micro) level.

Guest Essay Discussion

1. Does a steady state economy imply the end of technologial growth? Explain.
2. Why does the concept of the steady state economy force us to face up to the moral issue of the distribution of wealth?
3. Should minimum and maximum limits on personal income and wealth be established? Explain.

ally favor the subsidy or taxpayer-pays approach, whereas environmentalists favor the consumer-pays approach through a combination of direct regulation and pollution taxes to internalize all external costs.

Cost-benefit analysis is used to estimate and compare the costs associated with a particular project, product, or form of pollution control with the expected benefits. If cost-benefit analysis is favorable, *cost-effectiveness analysis* is then used to evaluate alternative methods of achieving a desired goal at the lowest estimated cost. Proponents of these evaluation methods contend that they are the best ways to keep consumer costs down and to use private capital and taxpayers' dollars efficiently. Environmentalists contend that these analyses are often distorted to make a project or product more economically attractive than it really is and to get around environmental regulation. They also argue that it is impossible and in some cases immoral to place an economic value on things such as human life and clean air and water that are not commodities to be priced, bought, and sold in the marketplace.

Economists and environmentalists also disagree on how much emphasis should be placed on the present and future economic value of something, such as a virgin forest, crude oil, aluminum ore, or other resource. Economists tend to emphasize present worth by using a *discount factor* less than 1. Environmentalists believe that discount factors should be equal to or greater than 1 so that we meet our ethical obligation to future generations to leave the environment in at least as good a condition as we found it.

Industrialists often argue that the economic costs of reducing pollution under present and proposed environmental regulations often outweigh the benefits—forcing them to close down plants and put people out of work. However, in 1985 total private and government expenditures for environmental control and improvement amounted to only about 1.6% of the GNP compared to environmental damages amounting to about 4% of the GNP. Some factories have closed down because of inability or unwillingness to reduce the amount of pollution they produce. Overall, however, pollution control is a major growth business that creates many more jobs than it eliminates.

DISCUSSION TOPICS

1. What are the major advantages and disadvantages of the present capitalist economy in the United States?
2. What are the major advantages and disadvantages of a sustainable-earth economy? Do you favor making a gradual shift to such a system? Explain.
3. Discuss the desirability of a sustainable-earth economy in terms of the first and second laws of thermodynamics (Chapter 3).
4. Do you agree with the proposition that maximizing economic growth is the only way or the best way of providing enough money to eliminate poverty and to protect the environment? Explain and cite specific evidence for your position.
5. If you wanted to develop an index of gross national quality (GNQ), what specific items would you include?
6. What are the social and environmental costs associated with **(a)** smoking cigarettes, **(b)** driving a car, and **(c)** living or working in an air-conditioned building? Do you believe that the benefits outweigh the costs in each case?
7. What good and bad effects would internalizing the external costs of pollution have on the U.S. economy? Do you favor doing this? How might it affect your lifestyle? The lifestyle of the poor? If possible, have an economist discuss these problems with your class.
8. What obligations concerning the environment do we have to future generations? Try to list the major beneficial and harmful aspects of the environment that were passed on to you during the past 50 years by the last two generations.
9. Who should pay for pollution control—industry, and thus consumers, taxpayers, or all three? Explain.
10. Who should pay for cleaning up past environmental damage—industry, and thus consumers, taxpayers, or all three? Explain.

25

Politics and Environment

1. What are the major ways of bringing about social change?
2. What are some of the major achievements of environmental law in the United States?
3. What progress has been achieved in the United States through enactment of environmental legislation?
4. What are the key characteristics and tactics of a sustainable-earth political system?
5. How can the United States achieve a sustainable-earth political system?
6. How can we influence elected officials?

Mourn not the dead . . .
But rather mourn the apathetic throng—
The cowed and meek
Who see the world's great anguish and its wrong,
And dare not speak.
Ralph Chaplin

Politics is concerned with the distribution of resources in an orderly fashion—who gets what, where, when, how, and why. Because resources such as food, water, air, land, minerals, and energy are provided by the biosphere, politics—like economics—rests on an ecological foundation. As resources become scarce, this fundamental dependence of politics on ecology becomes more apparent.

25-1 POLITICS AND SOCIAL CHANGE

Is Politics the Art of the Possible? Because there is always competition for resources, politicians must deal with conflicting groups, each asking for resources or for money that will enable them to purchase or control certain resources. Because of these conflicts, politics has been called the art of the possible.

For most politicians in democratic countries the art of the possible is focused on ensuring their own reelection, primarily by not taking stands on controversial or long-range issues and by avoiding change. A favorite strategy of traditional politicians is to say "I agree with you, but what you are suggesting is not feasible."

Throughout history, however, the significant political acts have been those of making the seemingly impossible—or the highly improbable—possible. True political leadership, then, is the art of creating new possibilities for progress. As George Bernard Shaw put it, "Some see things as they are and say why? I dream of things that never were and say why not?"

Ecology and Politics Ecology has been called the subversive science because its findings challenge most of the economic, political, and ethical foundations of modern society. Modern learning is based on specialization—putting everything in neat, separate compartments and treating each problem that arises in isolation from other problems and influences. Ecology, however, is based on a holistic or generalist view that seeks to understand how the individual parts of the biosphere and culturesphere interact.

A major reason that many conventional scientists, economists, and politicians resent and even fear ecology is that it violates the idea that a science should be politically and ethically neutral. Ecology is a combination of holistic scientific principles, which when formulated and understood imply both a moral obligation and a political imperative to effect changes that bring the culturesphere of thought and action into harmony with the workings of the biosphere. Instead of hiding behind ethical and political neutrality, ecologists and environmentalists confront politicians with scientific limits and imperatives that sooner or later cannot be violated without severe disruption of society. Accordingly, politics must become anticipatory rather than merely reactionary, and politics cannot be divorced from ecology.

Politicians complain, however, that if everything is connected to everything as ecology reveals, then how can they understand any single ecological problem without understanding how the entire biosphere—even the universe—works. There is, of course, an element of truth in this complaint. Our knowledge of how the biosphere works is still in its infancy and will never be complete. But we have learned a lot, and the fact that our knowledge is incomplete should not be used as an excuse for not applying what we do know.

25-2 ENVIRONMENTAL LAW

Some Principles of Environmental Law There are two types of laws: statutory and common. A **statutory law** is one passed by a state legislature or by Congress. Environmental statutes, many of which are listed in Appendix 3, govern how the environment and human health should be protected and how resources are to be managed. Many of these laws have been discussed throughout this book. **Common laws,** a large body of unwritten principles and rules based on thousands of past legal decisions, are used by judges to resolve disputes in the absence of applicable statutory law.

In any court case the **plaintiff** is the individual, group of individuals, or corporation bringing the charges, and the **defendant** is the individual, group of individuals, or corporation being charged. Citizens can bring two types of lawsuits. In the first type the plaintiff can request the court to issue a permanent

injunction forbidding the defendant to commit or to continue to commit a specific wrongful act. The plaintiff might also ask for issuance of a temporary injunction to prevent the alleged act from occurring until the case is finally decided by the court. This type of lawsuit can be used to force a polluter to clean up a polluted site or to comply with existing statutory environmental laws.

The other type of lawsuit, known as a **civil suit,** seeks to collect damages for injuries or for economic loss, have the court issue a permanent injunction against any further wrongful action, or both. In this case the plaintiff makes a civil complaint alleging that he or she has been harmed by the defendant. If the court decides that harm has occurred, it orders the defendant to pay the plaintiff to offset the damage and may also issue an injunction forbidding any further harm. Such suits may be brought by an individual plaintiff or a group of clearly identified plaintiffs.

Another type of civil suit is the **class action suit,** in which a group, often a public interest or environmental group such as the Environmental Defense Fund or the Sierra Club, files a suit on behalf of a larger number of citizens who allege similar damages but who need not be listed and represented individually. The class, for example, might consist of all people who worked in a certain chemical plant between certain dates when pollution was known to have caused a number of illnesses. A public notice of the intention to file the class action suit is published in a local newspaper. Unless people who believe they are in the class request that they be excluded from the suit, they are automatically included in the class and the lawsuit. In 1973, however, the U.S. Supreme Court restricted federal class action suits by requiring that each person in the class claim to have suffered at least $10,000 in damage.

Problems with Environmental Lawsuits To use the courts for a civil action, the plaintiff must (1) allege that an act forbidden by a specific statutory law has been committed or that the plaintiff has suffered injuries to health or economic loss as a result of actions by the defendant; (2) file the complaint in the court that has jurisdiction over the alleged action; and (3) demonstrate that he or she has standing—the right to bring the case to court. Then, of course, the plaintiff must prove that the actions of the accused caused the alleged damage. As in a criminal case, the accused is presumed innocent until proven guilty.

Unfortunately, there are problems with this procedure:

- A plaintiff may not have standing to file a suit against a defendant. Standing for damage suits is granted only if it is clear that the harm to an individual plaintiff is unique and different enough to be distinguished from that to the general public. For example, you could not sue the Department of the Interior for actions leading to the commercialization of a wilderness area on the grounds that you do not want your taxes used to bring about environmental harm. The harm to you could not be distinguished from that to the general public. However, if the government damaged property you own, you would have standing to sue.

■ Bringing any suit is expensive. Often the defendant in an environmental action is a large corporation or government agency with ample funds for legal and scientific advice. In contrast, the plaintiffs in such cases usually use volunteer legal and scientific talent and rely on donations.

■ The court, or series of courts if the case is appealed, may take years to reach a decision. During this time, the defendant may continue the alleged damage unless the court issues a temporary injunction forbidding the allegedly harmful actions until the case is decided. Furthermore, each new violation requires a new case because a particular decision is not generally binding on future offenses.

■ It is often difficult for the plaintiff to prove that the accused is liable. For example, suppose that one company is charged with bringing harm to individuals by polluting a river. If hundreds of other industries and cities dump waste into that river, establishing that the defendant company is the culprit will be extremely difficult, requiring extensive, costly scientific testing and research.

Despite these handicaps, proponents of environmental law have accomplished a great deal since the 1960s. Now there are more than 100 public interest law firms specializing partially or totally in environmental and consumer law, and hundreds of other lawyers and scientific experts participate in environmental and consumer law cases as needed. Major public interest law groups concerned with environmental issues include the Environmental Defense Fund, the Sierra Club's Legal Defense Fund, the National Resources Defense Council, the Center for Science in the Public Interest, and others listed in Appendix 1.

Most successful environmental lawsuits have involved preventing damage—by seeking to enjoin the construction of a jetport, a nuclear power plant, or a superhighway through an urban park, a conservation area, or a poor neighborhood, for example. Environmental and public interest lawyers and groups, however, are limited by lack of money. In 1976 environmental lawyers received a serious setback when the Supreme Court ruled that public interest law firms

cannot recover attorneys' fees unless Congress has specifically authorized such recovery in the law they have sued to enforce. If you believe in the efforts of public interest groups to protect the country's resources from abuse, you might consider becoming a supporting member of one or more of the environmental public interest law groups listed in Appendix 1.

25-3 U.S. ENVIRONMENTAL LEGISLATION

Environmental Legislation Environmentalists, with backing from many other citizens, have pressured Congress to enact a number of important environmental and resource protection laws, as discussed throughout this text and listed in Appendix 3. Similar laws, and in some cases even stronger laws, have been passed by most states.

These laws attempt to provide environmental protection using five major approaches:

1. Setting pollution level standards or limiting emissions or effluents for various classes of pollutants (such as the Federal Water Pollution Control Act of 1972 and the Clean Air Acts of 1965, 1970, and 1977)

2. Screening new substances before they are widely used in order to determine their safety (for example, the Toxic Substances Control Act of 1976)

3. Requiring a comprehensive evaluation of the environmental impact of an activity before it is undertaken (for example, the National Environmental Policy Act of 1969)

4. Setting aside or protecting various ecosystems, resources, or species from harm (such as the Wilderness Act of 1964 and the Endangered Species Act of 1973)

5. Encouraging resource conservation (for example, the Resource Conservation and Recovery Act of 1976 and to some extent the National Energy Act of 1978)

The Environmental Protection Agency, created by administrative reorganization in 1970, has the responsibility for enforcing most federal environmental laws, for administering the Superfund to clean up abandoned toxic waste sites, and for awarding grants for local sewage treatment plants. These laws give the EPA broad powers, including the imposition of jail terms for criminal pollution violations and fines of up to $25,000 a day for polluters, and the power to sue almost any U.S. citizen or company for violation of antipollution laws.

However, responsibility for managing the nation's environmental and resource policy is widely frag-

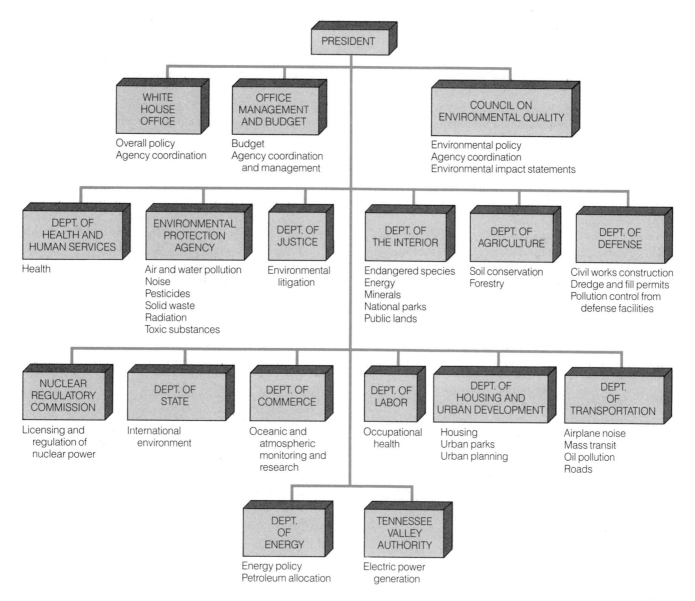

Figure 25-1 Major agencies of the executive branch of the federal government with responsibilities for environmental protection and resource management. (Data from U.S. General Accounting Office)

mented among many different agencies within the executive branch of the federal government (Figure 25-1) and among state agencies. This often leads to contradictory policies, duplicated efforts, and wasted funds, while preventing an effective holistic approach to interrelated problems. For example, while the EPA has tried to limit or ban the use of certain pesticides, the Department of Agriculture has defended the use of some of these chemicals. The EPA has attempted to reduce the burning of coal and has proposed that Congress enact more stringent emission standards for coal-burning plants, while the Department of Energy has encouraged the burning of coal to reduce U.S. dependence on oil imports.

Another problem is that an environmental law is no better than its enforcement. Budget cuts by the Reagan administration have reduced the ability of the EPA and other federal environmental and resource agencies to carry out their responsibilities. Thus, in the 1980s, environmentalists are increasingly turning their attention to seeing that existing laws and regulations are enforced and not weakened by amendments favored by special interest groups.

NEPA and Environmental Impact Statements One important environmental law is the National Environmental Policy Act of 1969 (NEPA). This landmark legislation declared that the federal government has a responsibility to restore and maintain environmental quality; it established in the executive office of the president a three-member Council on Environmental

Quality. The CEQ determines the condition of the national environment, prepares an annual environmental quality report, develops and recommends to the president new environmental policies and programs, appraises and coordinates federal environmental programs and activities, advises the president on environmental problems and solutions, and establishes guidelines for the preparation of environmental impact statements. The importance and influence of the CEQ, however, has been sharply reduced since 1981 when President Reagan, who had planned to abolish the council, cut its budget by 70% and slashed its staff from 60 to 10.

NEPA requires that all federal agencies (except the EPA) file an environmental impact statement (EIS) for any proposed legislation or project having a significant effect on environmental quality. A draft EIS must be made public for review by the EPA, other appropriate federal, state, and local agencies, and the general public at least 90 days before a proposed action. A final statement, incorporating all comments and objections to the draft statement, must be made public at least 30 days before the proposed action is undertaken. Each EIS must include:

1. The purpose and need for the proposed action

2. The probable environmental impact (positive, negative, direct, and indirect) of the proposed action and of possible alternatives

3. Any adverse environmental effects that could not be avoided should the project be implemented

4. Relationships between the probable short-term and long-term impacts of the proposal on environmental quality

5. Irreversible and irretrievable commitments of resources that would be involved should the project be implemented

6. Objections raised by reviewers of the preliminary draft of the statement

7. The names and qualifications of the people primarily responsible for preparing the EIS

8. References to back up all statements and conclusions

The EIS process has forced government agencies to think more seriously about the side effects of proposed projects and in many cases to analyze alternatives more carefully. As a result, scores of planned dams, highways, and airports have been modified or canceled. In addition, by 1985, 34 states had laws or executive orders requiring EISs for state projects. The EIS process has also spread to Australia, Canada, France, Ireland, New Zealand, and Sweden.

Despite its successes, the EIS process in the United States has been criticized. EISs are often prepared to justify a decision that has already been made. An agency can sometimes avoid preparing an EIS by denying that a given project will have a significant environmental impact. An unfavorable EIS does not necessarily mean that the project will be canceled, that a less harmful option will be selected, or that the federal agency has to follow the terms of the EIS. The process has diverted the efforts and funds of environmentalists away from questioning and defining agency powers and responsibilities by forcing them to analyze large numbers of often irrelevant EIS documents. Most EISs do not receive careful scrutiny because only a few, highly controversial projects are important enough to be evaluated.

Environmentalists have suggested that the NEPA should be amended to correct some of these major weaknesses by requiring a federal agency to pick and follow the terms of the least harmful option and by allowing public interest groups to recover attorneys' fees when they sue to enforce NEPA or any other environmental laws—thus putting public interest law groups on a more equitable footing with federal agencies and large corporations.

25-4 SUSTAINABLE-EARTH POLITICS

Characteristics of a Sustainable-Earth Political System An effective sustainable-earth political system is adaptable to change and can anticipate and prevent short- and long-term problems from reaching crisis proportions rather than merely reacting to crises in an uncoordinated, fragmented manner. Such a system is based on corrective negative feedback of information to anticipate and respond to problems (Figure 6-1, p. 116). The major characteristics of such a system are:

1. *Multiple negative feedback loops:* Checks and balances with different time lags ensure long-term sustainability, prevent takeover by a single part of the system, and continue self-renewal and adaptation to change.

2. *Minimum number of feedback loops necessary for long-term sustainability:* Too many feedback loops block, distort, or overload information flow—causing chaos, overcorrection, undercorrection, and even breakdown rather than gentle and steady oscillation.

3. *Sophisticated methods for short-range, intermediate-range, and long-range forecasting and planning:* Deal-

ing only with the present or the near future often leads to disastrous long-term results. Short-range goals should always be developed and related by feedback and time lags to intermediate and long-term goals.

4. *An array of niches (roles) with a balance between specialists and generalists:* Excessive specialization (bureaucracy) leads to waste, inefficiency, obsolete government agencies, and inability to develop or act on long-range goals. A government with too many generalists does not have the necessary detailed information and facts.

5. *Accurate information flow (feedback) among all levels of government and between the government and the people:* Proper anticipatory and corrective political action is possible only with accurate and high-quality information and biological, physical, economic, and social indicators that clearly signal whether conditions are improving or deteriorating. Capital and labor must be expended to obtain such information. Three major problems are **(a)** blocked and distorted information flow to decision makers, **(b)** information overload when more information is received than can be evaluated (an increasingly serious problem in a computer age), and **(c)** blocked and distorted information flow from government to the people because of excessive government secrecy and media manipulation.

6. *Responsive and responsible decision makers and controllers:* The persons and organizations responsible for making decisions must be willing to bring about rather than avoid significant change when it is needed. This willingness will depend on their ability as generalists to evaluate conflicting information sources, to get accurate information, and to relate decisions to short-term, intermediate, and long-term goals.

7. *Flexibility:* It should be possible to change parts of the system as conditions change. The people need an orderly mechanism for removing and changing leaders and parts of the political system.

Sustainable-Earth Political Tactics Traditional attempts to change the social system tend to be frontal and single purpose—marches, demonstrations, sit-ins, education, persuasion, legislation, and the like. Although these tactics attract media attention, inform others about the need for change, build and maintain morale, and counter undesirable trends, they often stop too soon. When facing the massive inertia of the status quo, many political activists decide that it is

useless to buck the system and give up. Thus, it is usually more effective to couple traditional political tactics with those of sustainable-earth politics to bring about change.

An important tactic of sustainable-earth politics is to use *positive synergy* so that the final effect is greater than the sum of individual efforts. Positive synergy can be used to amplify a desirable trend or to counteract an undesirable trend. In this way a small group of people can bring about major changes. For example, in 1970 a small organization called Environmental Action initiated the "Dirty Dozen Campaign"—a program that in every election year attempts to defeat 12 congressional representatives who have consistently opposed sound environmental legislation. Of the 54 persons named to the list between 1970 and 1982 (some were named more than once), 41, or 76%, are no longer in Congress either because they were defeated at the polls or because they decided not to seek reelection. A handful of workers, using the scarce funding provided by private contributions, instigated this important change—a remarkable example of sustainable-earth politics in action. Additional tactics for bringing about political change are discussed in the Enrichment Study at the end of this chapter.

Sustainable-earth tactics also make use of *lag times* and *threshold effects*. Exerting pressure on a slow-moving, complex political or social system may seem to have no effect, but if pressure is maintained long enough, a threshold level may eventually be reached, thus prompting a major change.

In traditional linear politics, if someone wins, someone else loses (a win-lose game). By contrast, a major goal of sustainable-earth politics is to seek ways in which everyone wins (*win-win games*). A sustainable-earth value system emphasizes cooperation rather than competition (see Guest Essay at the end of the chapter).

One important method for setting up win-win games is the *tunnel effect*. Think of bringing about change as getting over a mountain. Statutory laws can be passed that force everyone to go over the mountain (traditional politics), or positive synergy can be used to vault everyone over the mountain. But usually the best way is to tunnel through the mountain—to find a social, technological, or scientific innovation that avoids old attitudes and resistance (Figure 25-2); then no one has to struggle over the mountain (a win-win solution).

The tunnel effect can be described as a social catalyst that lowers the resistance barrier. It is a social chain reaction that is so obvious and effective that resistance disappears. The social catalyst may be a charismatic leader, like M. K. Gandhi, or persuasive rhetoric, as exemplified by Henry Thoreau's essay on

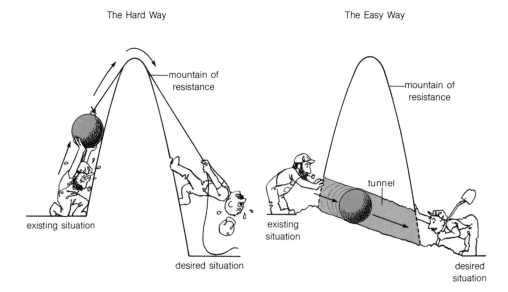

Figure 25-2 The tunnel effect. When an easier path becomes available through some technological or social innovation, rapid political and social change occur automatically.

The Hard Way

The Easy Way

mountain of resistance

existing situation

desired situation

mountain of resistance

existing situation

tunnel

desired situation

civil disobedience. Gandhi skillfully used Thoreau's ideas to develop a nonviolent strategy to win India's independence from Great Britain. Thoreau's catalytic ideas were also used later by Martin Luther King, Jr., in the civil rights movement in the United States.

A social catalyst may also be a scientific or technological innovation like oral contraceptives, which have revolutionized birth control and made effective population control possible. Another example is the silicon microchip, which has greatly expanded communication and the processing of information.

25-5 TOWARD A SUSTAINABLE-EARTH GOVERNMENT IN THE UNITED STATES

The U.S. Government as a Corrective Feedback System The founders of the United States had to decide what form of government would maximize individual freedom without intruding on the rights of others. They also had to guard against authoritarian takeovers and yet encourage the development of the land and its resources. In other words, the founders wanted to preserve national stability but still allow a range of choices.

The framers of the Constitution, which was drafted and agreed upon by less than 40 people in only four months, attempted to develop a sustainable political system by creating a diversity of structures all connected by negative feedback loops. The Constitution calls for three major loops and control subsystems—the legislative, executive, and judicial branches—all connected by multiple checks and balances, or negative feedback (Figure 25-3).

For the entire system to work, all three branches must cooperate and interact, but checks and balances (corrective negative feedback mechanisms) are built in to prevent one branch from gaining too much power. The government established by the Constitution was not designed for efficiency. Instead it was designed for consensus and accommodation as a key to survival. Thus, by staying as close to the middle of the road as possible, the government attempts to muddle through crises. Ralph Waldo Emerson once said, "Democracy is a raft which will never sink, but then your feet are always in the water."

The grand design of the Constitution is like a finely balanced watch with gears and springs moving and responding at different lag times. For immediate response, there is the executive branch. But to avoid hasty changes and to ensure responsiveness to the diversity of national interests, the Congress was created. It, in turn, contains two feedback loops: The House of Representatives has the faster response time, because its members are elected every two years; the Senate, whose members are elected every six years, can take a longer view and guard against abuse of power by the executive branch. The counterbalance to the entire system is the Supreme Court, whose members are appointed for life. The functions of the Court are to protect the Constitution, to interpret it, and to settle disputes of power between the executive and legislative branches and the states. The Supreme Court tends to move slowly; but in times of crisis, Court action may come faster than either congressional or executive action.

The founders of the U.S. system of government were concerned primarily with growth and expanding the frontier. Thus, the system they devised contains several defects that can hinder the orderly transition to a sustainable-earth society.

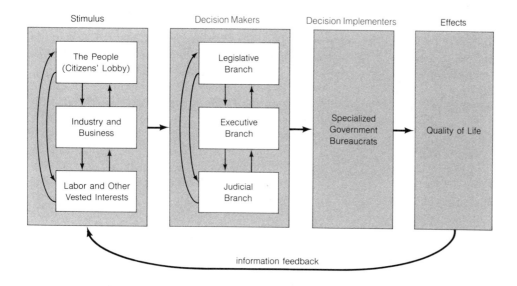

Stimulus   Decision Makers   Decision Implementers   Effects

The People (Citizens' Lobby)

Industry and Business

Labor and Other Vested Interests

Legislative Branch

Executive Branch

Judicial Branch

Specialized Government Bureaucrats

Quality of Life

information feedback

Figure 25-3 A crude model of the U.S. political system.

Lack of Long-Range Planning   Everyone is in favor of long-range planning, but nobody in the federal government seems to be able to do it. As futurist Harlan Cleveland put it: "We are still tackling 20-year problems with 5-year plans staffed by 2-year personnel working with 1-year appropriations. It's simply not good enough."

Lack of long-range planning has several causes. There are no mechanisms built into the Constitution to require long-range planning or to ensure that the results of such planning be taken into account. Indeed, the short terms of office specified in the Constitution mean that any politician who wishes to get reelected cannot afford to support policies that require the electorate to make short-term sacrifices (such as sharply increased taxes on gasoline to encourage conservation) in the interests of long-term gains (such as lower future energy bills, cleaner air, and fewer health problems).

The system is also designed to expose policymakers to constant competing pressures from mostly single-issue groups seeking relief from short-term problems. As a result, elected leaders are forced to focus on one problem at a time, to seek compromises that attempt to give a little to each side, and to pass legislation that promises quick results with little regard for long-term consequences. Most political leaders also have not been exposed to ecological principles and holistic thinking and thus do not understand that comprehensive long-range planning and action are essential for biosphere and culturesphere sustainability.

Several suggestions have been made to require or encourage long-range planning and action without destroying the important concept of checks and balances. Some have suggested that effective methods for long-range planning should be a major federal budget priority. It has also been suggested that a national long-range planning board might be created at the executive level or as a separate bureaucratic agency, the Department of Long-Range Planning and Coordination. The Congress and citizens would need similar boards as checks and balances.

Others have indicated that a better approach might be amending the Constitution to add a fourth branch of government, the planning branch, with members appointed for staggered terms of 15 to 25 years. Ideally, highly respected generalists and sustainable-earth thinkers would be appointed to the planning branch of government. This planning branch could form and direct task forces or councils of urgent studies. Such councils would examine and make projections of major national and global problems and direct efforts to find social and technologial innovations and tunnel effects for solving short-, intermediate-, and long-range problems. The members of the planning branch would evaluate and integrate what ordinary people think needs to be done with what specialists think the people need. The amendment creating this fourth branch of government would also set up a mechanism requiring the other branches of government to take into account recommendations from the planning branch in decisions, laws, and budget allocations.

It has also been suggested that the terms of office of elected officials be expanded by changing the Constitution so that members of the House of Representatives serve for four rather than two years, members of the Senate for eight rather than six years, and presidents for six rather than four years.

Election Reform and Electing Sustainable-Earth Leaders   A major problem in the executive branch and the legislative branch is undue influence on elections by wealthy people and special interest groups.

This problem plagues all democratic governments and will never be completely eliminated. But a number of analysts believe that a powerful and active citizens' lobby can help to counterbalance the disproportionate influence of business, industry, labor, and other powerful and well-financed vested interests by providing additional checks and balances.

It has also been suggested that federal election campaigns be financed by an assessment of all taxpayers, with *no other contributions of any type allowed* and with maximum spending limits rigidly enforced. This would require the banning of all political action committees (PACs), whose contributions to congressional candidates increased from $12.5 million to $130 million between 1974 and 1986.

To hold down election costs, some have urged that campaigns (including primaries) for presidential and congressional races be shortened to no more than six months. In addition, each candidate meeting certain specific qualifications would be given a fixed number of hours of free television and radio time and a certain amount of free advertising space in the print media (as part of the media's public service requirements). There would also be a limit on the air time and printed advertising space candidates could purchase, and strict ethical guidelines would ban negative advertising.

Because incumbents running for reelection can more easily command and manipulate media attention, new candidates might be given more media time and space. In addition, all major candidates for the presidency would be expected—if not required—to participate in a series of in-depth, televised debates, each focused on one topic. A single moderator would force the candidates to stick to the topic and to address the questions raised. States might require similar debates for congressional and gubernatorial candidates.

In criticizing and evaluating political leaders, we should keep in mind the Spanish verse "Advice pours down from the stadium full, But only the matador faces the bull." Instead of merely criticizing, some observers urge that we elect a new breed of leaders—sustainable-earth leaders, whose primary loyalty is to the biosphere and to the future of humanity. Table 25-1 compares the characteristics of traditional, nationalistic leaders to those of sustainable-earth leaders.

Congressional Reform   In addition to lengthening terms of office and bringing about reforms in election funding, many analysts, including present and former members of Congress, have called for a sharp reduction in the number and nature of the committees and subcommittees used to write and evaluate legislation. The 132 committees and subcommittees in the Senate and the 180 in the House of Representatives have overlapping and often conflicting responsibilities. These committees and subcommittees have more to do with the desire for personal power than with present and future needs of society. They can also tie up bills and bring the whole legislative process to a grinding halt. For example, some energy bills may be dealt with by up to 83 different committees and subcommittees. Reform, however, is unlikely because most members of Congress want to be in charge of at least one subcommittee, and the more subcommittees there are, the better their chances.

Bureaucratic Reform   A government bureau is created as a response to a specific problem. In its early stages a vigorous, small agency with dynamic leadership can make progress. But as it grows, its effectiveness and sense of mission decline. Eventually the agency can become so large, complex, and rigid that it chokes on all the highly specialized rules and regulations it has created. More energy and money are then used to keep the agency operating, while it accomplishes less and sometimes creates more problems than it solves.

Many government regulations are necessary to protect the environment and consumers from abuse by private industry. However, most observers agree that the number and complexity of government regulations can and should be reduced. On the other hand, many regulations must be complex and detailed. Government officials know that most regulated industries have teams of lawyers who will find even the tiniest loophole that will allow these industries to circumvent the intention of the law.

Much of the blame for overregulation lies with Congress—not federal regulatory agencies. In a number of cases, Congress writes vague laws in order to avoid controversy and to satisfy competing interests; it leaves it up to federal agencies and the courts to fill in the details. On the other hand, Congress has learned that vague legislation also allows a regulatory agency to avoid implementing the general intent of the law. For example, Congress became so frustrated by the EPA's failure to implement much of the intent of the 1980 Superfund law for identifying and cleaning up hazardous waste dumps that it added detailed amendments in 1986 telling the EPA exactly what it must do (Section 21-5).

Because of bureaucratic overspecialization, government has become an enormous organism composed of separate cells of experts, often remote from

Table 25-1 Comparison of Nationalistic Leaders and Sustainable-Earth Leaders

Nationalistic Leader	Sustainable-Earth Leader
International view. Thinks and acts internationally but in terms of national prestige, honor, and power.	Biosphere view. Thinks in terms of preserving the biosphere and the world's resources for everyone now and in the future.
Thinks national loyalty is the primary driving force.	Thinks biosphere loyalty is the only viable approach in the long run.
Thinks and acts in terms of win-lose games and uses sports and battle analogies. ("We won," "Honor is in winning," "This play will win," "Right is right," "Frontiers to conquer," "God is on our side.")	Sees the goal as having everyone in the world win now as well as in the future (win-win games).
Politics of the possible. Avoids really difficult problems or declares them solved. Calls people who talk of the impossible "naive idealists."	Politics of the seemingly impossible or improbable made possible by use of vision, sustainable-earth politics, and outstanding leadership. Willing to propose solutions for complex and controversial problems.
Simplistic view. Problems are due to a single variable or culprit and can be solved by enacting a short-term simple cure.	Holistic view. Everything interacts with everything. Problems are complex and ever changing and require multivariable approaches over long periods of time.
Primarily concerned with his or her role in history.	Primarily concerned with ensuring survival and human dignity for all.
Emphasizes short-term planning. Defends or talks mostly of past accomplishments rather than future goals.	Emphasizes long-term planning, with all short-term planning done in relation to intermediate and long-term goals. Talks of where we must go instead of where he or she has taken us.
Thinks a nation should do whatever can be done technologically to maintain or win national prestige, honor, and supremacy.	Thinks a nation should assess all technological solutions to determine possible long-range side effects on the biosphere and to determine whether the solutions improve human dignity and life quality.
Chooses advisers who say only what he or she wants to hear (information blockage and distortion).	Insists that the best minds project and evaluate major alternatives.
Tries to control the press, which is portrayed as a threat to national security and to individual freedom.	Realizes that a free but accountable press is essential to uncover and prevent information blockage and distortion. Recognizes that politicians have seized or controlled the press in many countries, but the press has not seized power from any government.
Uses secrecy to block information flow to the people.	Operates openly to ensure maximum and accurate information flow to the people.
Believes economic growth is the only way a nation can win or dominate. Sees a dynamic sustainable-earth economy as stagnant.	Evaluates growth on the basis of long-term biosphere goals. A dynamic sustainable-earth economy is the only viable long-term goal.
Thinks the problem of social justice will be solved only by economic growth—the trickle-down approach.	Believes that in a finite world nearing its limit of resource availability, the problem of social justice must be solved by a more equitable distribution of wealth.
Believes the greatest threat to peace and individual freedom is some outside -ism that a nation must overcome.	Thinks the greatest threats to peace and individual freedom are the arms race, overpopulation, overexploitation of finite resources by rich nations, and a world economic system that tends to make the rich richer and the poor poorer.
Talks about peace, poverty, population, and pollution but spends most of the money on armaments so that a nation can act from a position of strength.	Acts to promote peace, eliminate poverty, stabilize population, control pollution, and drastically reduce military expenditures and arms buildup throughout the world.
Thinks the solution to most problems is to buy or build things (more missiles, guns, computers, and highways).	Thinks the solution to most problems is to deliberately slow the flow rate of matter and energy in the industrialized nations and to encourage appropriate technologies in LDCs to meet the people's needs and to foster self-reliance.

the people, unable to see the overall picture, competing rather than cooperating with one another, and incapable of dealing with the multiplicity of interlocking problems that characterizes society today.

Another problem is that each overspecialized bureau becomes more concerned with its own survival than with its mission; some bureaus are even taken over by the groups they are supposed to regulate. For example, a 1981 study by Common Cause showed that 14 of the top 16 officials appointed to the Department of the Interior by the Reagan administration came from the five major industries regulated by the Department of the Interior—oil and gas, mining, utilities, timber, and grazing. President Harry S Truman recognized this problem when he said "You don't set foxes to watching the chickens just because they have a lot of experience in the hen house."

Often by the time a new agency is fully functioning, public attention has shifted to other problems. Agencies often want a share of such new issues so that they can justify their existence to the public. As a result, responsibility for a given problem may be spread among many agencies (Figure 25-1).

New reforms that have been suggested to reduce the size of the bureaucracy and to increase its efficiency include:

1. Streamlining dismissal procedures

2. Overhauling the evaluation and merit raise system

3. Empowering the president to appoint more high-level departmental officials

4. Providing better protection and rewards for whistle blowers who expose fraud and waste in government

5. Giving state and local officials more authority over the spending of federal grants

6. Turning more of the federal tax revenues directly back to the states

7. Having the states assume full responsibility for some areas, such as education

8. Enacting and strictly enforcing sunset laws (under which government agencies and programs are evaluated periodically and eliminated unless they can be shown to be necessary, effective, and efficient)

All Is Not Lost Despite shortcomings in the U.S. political system, environmental laws and agencies have improved the quality of the environment. Many streams, rivers, and lakes are less polluted and air pollutant levels in some metropolitan areas are lower than they were in the 1960s and 1970s. Strip-mined areas must now be restored, and we are slowly beginning to clean up thousands of abandoned hazardous waste dumps.

The U.S. national park, wilderness, wildlife refuge, and forest systems and endangered species programs are among the best in the world. On a per capita basis, few others countries spend as much as the United States does to protect the environment. Thus, the system is muddling through. But new environmental problems keep arising, often as by-products of solutions to old problems treated in isolation rather than as an interacting system.

Since 1970 numerous polls have revealed that Americans remain strongly committed to environmental protection. Almost two-thirds of American adults polled in 1984 believe that priority should be given to protecting the environment even if this means restricting economic growth. Sixty percent of those polled in 1984 believed that the U.S. government was spending too little on environmental protection; 63% believed that present environmental laws are not being enforced strictly enough by the agencies involved; 45% felt that existing U.S. environmental laws don't go far enough. It is because of the strong public support for environmental protection that repeated attempts by the Reagan administration to weaken or overthrow environmental laws were largely unsuccessful.

25-6 ACHIEVING GLOBAL SECURITY AND COOPERATION

The Arms Race Many consider the sharp rise in world military expenditures to be the most dangerous J-shaped curve in the world (Figure 25-4). In 1986 world military expenditures amounted to $900 billion—an average of about $2.5 billion a day or $17.4 million a minute. This sum exceeds the total income of the poorest one-half of the world's population. The United States and the Soviet Union account for almost two-thirds of the world's military expenditures and 97% of the world's nuclear bombs and warheads. The $286.1 billion U.S. military budget for 1986 amounted to an average expenditure of over half a million dollars a minute. Military spending is also increasing rapidly in LDCs, which buy 74% of their arms from the United States and the Soviet Union.

This situation drains financial, natural, and human resources that could be used for peaceful, constructive purposes. About one-half the world's physical scientists and engineers (or one-fourth the world's scientific community) devote their talents and skills to military research and development. By comparison, only 8% of scientists and engineers are working on energy research and development (with most of these working on nuclear power), 7% on health, 5% on trans-

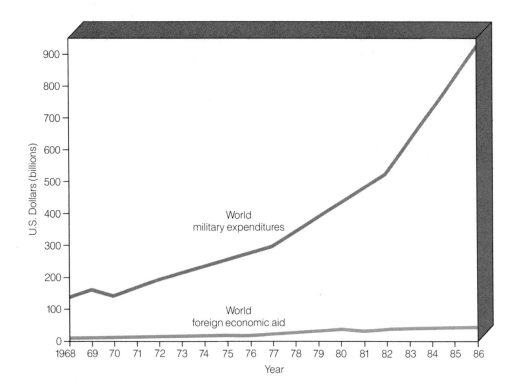

Figure 25-4 Comparison of world military expenditures and world foreign economic aid.

portation, and 3% on agriculture. Furthermore, in the 1980s over 70% of all federally funded research and development expenditures in the United States were devoted to military purposes, up from 50% in the 1970s. About 29% of all federal taxes in the United States and at least an equivalent amount in the Soviet Union are presently being used for national defense. As President Dwight D. Eisenhower warned in the 1960s:

Every gun that is made, every warship launched, every rocket fired, signifies in the final sense, a theft from those who are hungry and are not fed, those who are cold and not clothed. This world in arms is not spending money alone. It is spending the sweat of its laborers, the genius of its scientists, the hopes of its children.

Redefining National Security Many people believe that more guns, tanks, planes, and bombs equal more national security. But some are beginning to see that real national security doesn't come from having an enormous military establishment, but from having a highly productive, efficient, and modern economy. They see that the arms race is draining the treasuries of the United States and the Soviet Union, weakening their economies, and lowering their global economic position.

Many analysts warn that the United States is rapidly losing its ability to compete in the world marketplace and thus threatening its own economic and national security. This is occurring primarily because a large fraction of its capital and scientific and engineering talent is being used for military buildup. Without this drain of capital and technological talent, the United States could experience an unprecedented industrial and economic renaissance.

Although most Americans support a strong defense, they are beginning to ask some important questions: Why is it necessary to spend billions to build strategic nuclear weapons when the United States could destroy the Soviet Union several times over and vice versa? Why isn't it possible to have a strong defense without budget increases by eliminating vast areas of wastefulness in military expenditures?

Indeed, several studies have estimated that reducing unnecessary waste by requiring cost-effective military spending and restructuring military forces could produce a stronger national defense system with a 40% reduction in military expenditures. To do this, citizens must demand that their elected representatives prohibit the Pentagon and its industrial suppliers from building every weapons system they can dream up in order to further political patronage or satisfy military fantasies. Such an approach will lead to a leaner and tougher military and will free resources needed to revitalize the U.S. economy and protect the environment.

The Soviet Union is also paying a heavy price for its role in the arms race. Despite its wealth of natural resources, its average per capita GNP is half that of most other MDCs. And despite this fact, 14% of its GNP is used for military purposes, compared to about 7% in the United States. During the 1970s the Soviet economy grew at roughly 5% a year. In the 1980s Soviet industrial growth, like the United States's, slowed to a crawl.

The Japanese have realized that in a nuclear age economic strength is power; they have concentrated their financial resources and human creativity on becoming the world's leading economic power by the 1990s. A few other governments are also redefining national security in terms of economic strength rather than military strength. Between 1972 and 1985 China cut its military spending in half, from 14% to 7.5% of its GNP, and expects to make further cuts. After years of military spending hikes, Argentina and Peru have also joined the ranks of countries beginning to make cuts in military expenditures.

Paths to Global Peace and Cooperation   Many people are beginning to try to find ways out of the arms race, rather than leaving the fate of the world up to politicians. One approach to arms reduction is to bring about an attitude change in which people see themselves as members of a global community, bearing loyalty to the planet, not merely to a particular country. They are also urging that mediation, conciliation, and binding arbitration be used to bring about nonviolent resolution of conflict among nations. Another approach is to develop a global network of mutual understanding and trust among individual citizens in different countries, instead of relying on high-level talks among political leaders.

The roots of this global pacification, cooperation, and security network are being established at the local level, where individuals have the most influence. Then it can be expanded to regional, national, and global levels. Individuals have come up with a number of creative ideas for defusing the threat of nuclear war and allowing people in the United States and the Soviet Union to gain an understanding of one another (see Spotlight above).

The basic idea in this international grass-roots drive for global peace and cooperation is for individual citizens to *think globally and act locally* to bring about change. Individuals involved in this global movement recognize that their chances for defusing the arms race are not great. However, they believe that the grass-roots approach has a better chance of avoiding economic bankruptcy and global nuclear war—the ultimate lose-lose game—than continuing the present buildup of arms. They agree with historian Arnold Toynbee's observation: "If you make the world ever so little better, you will have done splendidly, and your life will have been worthwhile."

Some call for a world government to end the arms race and to solve other global problems. Others argue that the world is too diverse for a single government—even if it could be instituted without war. Further-

more, they point out that preserving cultural diversity is crucial for long-term survival and adaptability of the human race and of other species (Figure 25-5). A political monoculture, like a vast agricultural monoculture, could easily topple with changing conditions. Preserving biological and cultural diversity is probably best achieved by a loose federation of politically autonomous states—like the European Community. A federation of nations would cooperate to prevent nuclear and ecological destruction and to improve the quality of life for everyone.

In effect, we must simultaneously live and act on three cultural levels: a *microculture* of families and local communities based on personal relationships; a *macroculture* of national interests based on common economic and political arrangements, laws, and customs; and a *global culture* based on economic, political, and ethical arrangements in which global loyalty and cooperation are viewed as the only forms of patriotism that can lead to long-term sustainability of the biosphere and culturesphere.

Indifference is the essence of inhumanity.
George Bernard Shaw

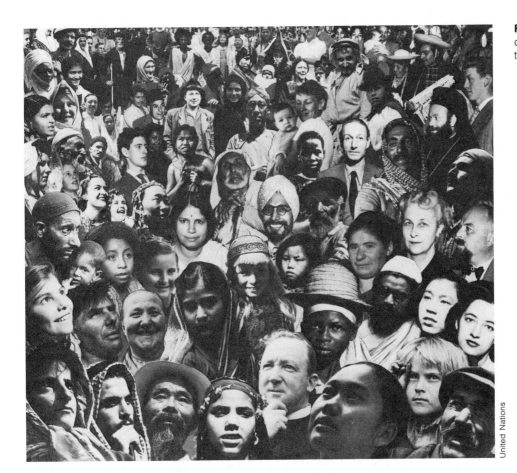

United Nations

Enrichment Study   How to Influence Elected Officials

How to Write Elected Officials

Do you write your congressional representatives and senators opposing or supporting environmental legislation or complimenting them for a particular stand? You may be thinking, "What can my one letter or one vote do?" But letters supporting or opposing a particular position can slowly accumulate until elected officials are forced to recognize that if they don't vote in a certain way for the people they represent, they are not likely to be reelected. The following are guidelines for communicating with elected officials effectively:*

---

*A list of the elected federal officials for your state and district is usually available at the local post office. Each year the League of Women Voters publishes a pamphlet "When You Write to Washington," which lists all elected officials and includes a list of all committee members and chairpersons. This pamphlet can be obtained from the League of Women Voters, 1730 M St., N.W., Washington, D.C. 20036.

1. Address the letter properly:
   a. *The president:*
   The President
   The White House
   1600 Pennsylvania Avenue, N.W.
   Washington, DC 20500

   Dear Mr. President:

   b. *Your senators:*
   The Honorable _____
   Senate Office Building
   Washington, DC 20510

   Dear Senator _____ :

   c. *Your representatives:*
   The Honorable _____
   House Office Building
   Washington, DC 20515

   Dear Representative _____ :

2. Always concentrate on your own representatives, but also write the chair or members of the com-

mittee that is holding hearings on legislation that interests you. Try to write the original committee chair and members, the conference committee members, and the chair and members of the correct appropriations committee.

3. Be brief (a page or less), cover only one subject, and come to the point quickly. Write the letter in your own words and express your own views—don't send a form or mimeographed letter. Make the letter personal, and don't say that you are writing for an organization (the representative should know the official positions of organizations).

4. If possible, identify the bill by number (for example, "H.R. 123" or "S. 313") or name, and ask the representative or senator to do something specific (cosponsor, support, or oppose it). You can get a free copy of any bill or committee report by writing to the House Document Room, U.S. House of Representatives, Washington, DC 20515, or the Senate Document Room, U.S. Senate, Washington, DC 20510.

5. Give specific reasons for your position. Try to explain the impact of the legislation on yourself or—better yet—on your district or state.

6. If you have expert knowledge, share it. You may give your representative much-needed information.

7. Be courteous and reasonable. Don't be rude, threaten, or berate. Don't pretend that you have vast political influence. Don't begin on a righteous note ("as a citizen and taxpayer . . .").

8. Don't become a constant pen pal. Quality at the right time, rather than quantity, is what counts.

9. Include your name and return address.

10. If you don't have time to write a letter, send a telegram or make a phone call. Telegrams are particularly useful in the last few days before a vote. You can send a Western Union mailgram of 50 words or less with overnight delivery or a Public Opinion Message of 20 words or less to the president or any member of Congress at a relatively low cost. All you have to do is telephone Western Union, which will bill your home phone. A member of Congress (or his or her staff) can also be reached by telephone through the Capitol switchboard: (202) 224–3121. As in letters, be polite, concise, and specific. Introduce yourself as a constituent, and ask to speak to the staff member who works on the issue you are concerned about.

11. Use positive reinforcement. After the vote write your representative a short note of thanks. A general rule here (as well as for life in general) is to give at least two compliments for every criticism.

12. If you are going to Washington, D.C., consider visiting your representative to lobby for your position. But go prepared or you risk destroying your credibility and effectiveness. It helps to call or write ahead to ask for an appointment, but you can probably get an appointment (at least with a staff member) by calling after you arrive in Washington. You can also try to make an appointment to talk with your congressional representative when he or she is in your district.

13. Become a contributing member of Common Cause, the Sierra Club, the League of Women Voters, the Environmental Defense Fund, or other groups (see the list of organizations in Appendix 1), which have full-time professional lobbyists working for you. These organizations exist only by individual support.

14. Remember that getting a bill passed is only the first step. You need to follow up by writing the president to be sure that the bill isn't vetoed or, once the bill has been signed, that the money appropriated by Congress is spent as required. Finally, write the federal agency (see addresses in Appendix 1) charged with carrying out the program, asking it to establish effective regulations or to be more active in enforcing the law. It is even more important to monitor and influence action at the state and local levels, where all federal and state laws are either ignored or enforced. As Thomas Jefferson once said, "The execution of laws is more important than the making of them."

Rules for Effective Political Action

Writing letters is essential. But to use positive synergy, citizens need to support national lobbying organizations to counteract the massive lobbying activities of industry and other vested interests. Join or form local organizations or temporary task forces on particular issues. The late John W. Gardner, former cabinet official and founder of Common Cause (see *In Common Cause*, 1972), has summarized the basic rules for effective political action:

1. Have a full-time continuing organization.

2. Limit the number of targets and hit them hard. Most groups dilute their efforts by taking on too many issues.

3. Get professional advisers to provide you with accurate, effective information and arguments.

4. Increase positive synergy by forming alliances with other organizations on a particular issue.

5. Have effective communication that will state your position in an accurate, concise, and moving way.

6. Persuade and use positive reinforcement—don't attack. Confine your remarks to the issue; do not make personal attacks on individuals. Try to find allies within the institution, and compliment individuals and organizations when they do something you like. Do your homework and then privately approach public officials whose support you need, without lecturing them or using high pressure tactics. In most cases it is best not to bring up something at a public meeting unless you have the votes lined up ahead of time. Most political influence is exerted behind the scenes through one-on-one conversations.

7. Organize for action—not just for study, discussion, or education. Minimize regular meetings, titles, and minutes. Have a group coordinator, a series of task forces with a project leader, a press and communications contact, legal and professional advisers, and a small group of dedicated workers. A small cadre can accomplish more than a large, unwieldy group. Work in groups but always keep in mind the Abilene paradox: People in groups will tend to act collectively in ways they individually know to be stupid.

8. Don't work exclusively at the national level. Concentrate much of your efforts at the state and particularly at the local level (see Further Readings for guidelines).

9. Be honest, accessible, and on good terms with your local press.

William Ophuls is a writer and lecturer working on the politics of ecological transformation to a sustainable-earth society. His background is unusually broad and varied: an officer in the merchant marine and the U.S. Coast Guard; a U.S. foreign service officer stationed in Washington, D.C., West Africa, and Japan; and a political scientist teaching at several universities, including Yale and Northwestern. In addition to numerous articles, he is author of Ecology and the Politics of Scarcity: Prologue to a Political Theory of the Steady State *(W. H. Freeman, 1977), which received awards from the American Political Science Association and the International Studies Association.*

The social and political implications of ecology are radical. We stand on the threshold of an ecological transformation of human culture that will bring epochal changes in every sphere of life. Life in the age of ecology now dawning will be as different from our own as our life today has been from the life of our medieval ancestors. However, in a curious fashion, our ecological future may closely resemble our past in many important aspects—because both eras, unlike our own, have scarcity as their organizing principle.

The age of affluence in today's MDCs has shaped essentially all the institutions and beliefs of the modern world. Once humankind left behind the original affluent society of the hunter-gatherer for an agricultural existence, the resulting population growth and scarcity of matter and energy resources created societies that, however admirable, were closed, hierarchical, and predominantly concerned with spiritual matters. When a combination of unique factors—such as the "discovery" and greedy exploitation of the wealth found in the New World—suddenly lifted the burden of resource scarcity from Europe, the political, social, and economic structures of these countries were transformed and "modernized." They became much more open and accepting of the view that all human beings are created equal, and became primarily concerned with material things.

The problem is that the whole process of economic development as we know it strongly resembles a chain letter: The first people to get in on the scheme get rich, but the latecomers (either classes within a country or entire countries) do not do nearly so well, and the game can only go on for so long before exhausting its finite resources. We are now entering this stage. What one historian has called "the 400-year boom" is about to collapse, returning us to the usual historical state of scarcity. The inevitable consequence is that all our values, practices, and institutions, which were created and nurtured in affluence, must now adapt to a wholly new situation.

We have certainly learned a thing or two during the abnormal age of affluence. This knowledge will stand us in good stead in coping with the reemergence of scarcity. We need not simply revert to pre-modern existence—although a combination of ecological heedlessness and nuclear warfare could well bring about such an undesirable outcome. In fact, we possess enough material wealth and technical understanding to create a semiutopian civilization. But to do so we shall have to change our present values, practices, and institutions to take into account current ecological realities.

The new political ideals that we must adopt and live by can be summed up in two words—frugality and fraternity. Frugality means making a little go a long way. Fraternity means making this a cooperative instead of a competitive venture. Nothing less than these actions will do: We must scale down our demands on the environment, yet we must at the same time ensure that the shrinking of the resource pie does not simply cause increased conflict or oppression, as the few try to force the many to maintain them in the style to which they have become accustomed.

Implicit in the rediscovery and implementation of these values are two ideas. First, selfish individualism has to go, for it is totally antithethical to both frugality and fraternity. But the individual need not be and must not be abandoned. Whatever the excesses of individualism, we surely have no wish to return to a state in which all but a tiny handful of people at the top of the social and economic pyramid are consid-

ered worthless. Our task is therefore to find social structures for our future that continue to permit individuals to seek fulfillment but in ways that do not harm the community and the biosphere directly or indirectly.

Second, and closely related to the above, we shall have to rediscover the ancient truth that the real purpose, meaning, and joy of life are not found in the material things of this world, but rather in the limitless realm of the spirit. It is so simple: Because the artistic and intellectual frontiers are endless, all we need to create a civilization more advanced and sustainable than our own is a small amount of material well-being, not endless growth in the material realm. Furthermore, because spiritual and cultural ideas and goods can be fully shared—indeed, only have real meaning when shared—we can participate in their creation and enjoyment fraternally in ways that simultaneously enhance our own self-development and the welfare of the community and biosphere.

Utopia, of course, cannot be realized here on earth. But even if we must abandon certain destructive forms of material growth, that does not mean that progress itself must end. To the contrary, we can turn the ecological crisis we face into a grand opportunity to build a better world than any that humankind has known thus far. Whether this happens is up to us.

Guest Essay Discussion

1. Do you agree that we are entering an age of scarcity? Explain.
2. What things have we learned that might help us cope with the reemergence of scarcity?
3. How should progress be defined in a sustainable-earth society?

CHAPTER SUMMARY

Politics is concerned with the distribution of resources in an orderly fashion. Although politics has been called the art of the possible, throughout history important political changes have involved making the seemingly impossible—or the highly improbable—a reality. Social change can be brought about by education and persuasion, legal action, enacting laws, and revolution.

Ecology has been called the subversive science because its findings challenge most of the economic, political, and ethical foundations of modern society. Unlike compart-

mentalized sciences whose findings are politically and ethically neutral, ecology is a holistic science whose findings imply a moral obligation and a political imperative to preserve the long-term sustainability of the culturesphere and the biosphere. It tells politicians that there are limits, that they must treat problems as part of an interacting system, rather than in isolation, that they must anticipate and prevent problems rather than merely react to crises, and that politics cannot be divorced from ecology.

Since the 1960s environmental law has played an important role in protecting the environment. Citizens, scientists, and public interest groups have successfully lobbied to see that a number of important *statutory laws* have been passed and enforced. The system of *common laws* based on past legal precedents have also been used to prevent environmentally harmful projects from being executed and to improve or modify others.

A number of analysts believe that the United States and other governments should gradually transform their present political systems to *sustainable-earth political systems*. Such systems would be designed to be more adaptable to change and to anticipate and prevent short- and long-term problems from reaching crisis proportions. Several political tactics can be used to bring about such a transformation. *Positive synergy* can be used to amplify desirable trends or to block or slow down undesirable ones. People can use *lag times* and *threshold effects* built into political systems to see that enough pressure is exerted at critical points long enough to achieve results. Major efforts are devoted to seek solutions in which everyone wins (*win-win games*) rather than the *win-lose games* associated with traditional politics. Efforts are also devoted to development of social and technological innovations that wipe out resistance to change by offering an irresistible alternative (the *tunnel effect*).

The U.S. political system consists of a number of checks and balances designed to promote sustainability through gradual rather than revolutionary change. Although it has many of the elements needed for a sustainable-earth political system, there are some flaws. There is no mechanism for long-range planning, primarily because terms of office for elected officials allow politicians to focus only on short-term problems if they wish to be reelected. There is also undue influence on elections by wealthy or influential special interest groups. Passage of effective legislation is hindered by a bloated number of congressional committees and subcommittees with overlapping and competing responsibilities that have more to do with personal power than with the present and future needs of society. Even when effective legislation is passed, its implementation is sometimes hindered by a specialized, entrenched, and outmoded system of bureaucratic agencies that are more concerned with obtaining an increasing share of the budget pie than with carrying out their original missions. Correcting these flaws is essential to developing a sustainable-earth political system.

Many consider the sharp rise in world military expenditures, especially by the United States and the Soviet Union, to be the greatest threat to global and national security. Increased military expenditures drain capital and talent needed to maintain a strong, healthy economy that is the base of any country's national security. Primarily because of this drain of capital and talent, the United States has a massive national debt and trade deficit and is rapidly losing its position as a global economic leader. The Soviet Union is experiencing similar difficulties because so much of its funds are devoted to arms buildup. Analysts believe that the present economic decline will continue until the superpowers begin to redefine their national security in economic rather than military terms and cut out massive waste and cost-ineffectiveness in military spending.

Many people are beginning to work together to try to find ways out of the arms race, rather than leaving the fate of the world up to politicians. They are educating people to see themselves as members of a global community with ultimate loyalty to the planet or biosphere, not merely to a particular country. The basic idea in this international grassroots drive for global peace and cooperation is that individual citizens *think globally and act locally to bring about change*. Chances of success may be slim, but the increasingly probable alternatives of global nuclear war, widespread environmental destruction, and economic decline make such efforts an ethical imperative. Individuals can join these and other drives for social change by learning how to influence elected officials through writing effective letters and organizing or joining groups designed to bring about change.

DISCUSSION TOPICS

1. Do you agree that real politics is the art of making the seemingly impossible possible? Why or why not? On this basis, what have been the major political events of this century, and who was mainly responsible for each of them?

2. What major trends do you see in society today? Which ones are desirable and which are undesirable? Use various combinations of these trends to construct three scenarios of what the world might be like in 2020. Identify the scenario you favor and outline a program for achieving this alternative future.

3. Do you think it is desirable to have a sustainable-earth political system in the United States? Explain.

4. As a class, analyze the Constitution and the Bill of Rights in terms of the principles of sustainable-earth systems. Use these principles to revise or write a new constitution that would enhance the chances of making the transition to a sustainable-earth society.

5. As a class, design a sustainable-earth constitution for your student government. Design a strategy for passage based on the tactics of sustainable-earth politics.

6. Should the U.S. Constitution be amended to create a long-range planning board as a fourth branch of government? Explain.

7. Evaluate the past five U.S. presidents in terms of nationalistic and sustainable-earth characteristics (see Table 25-1). Can you identify any existing sustainable-earth politicians or citizens who should be elected to local, state, or federal office because of such potential?

8. Do you believe that all presidential and congressional elections should be funded entirely by taxpayers, with fixed spending limits for each candidate and no donations from other sources allowed? Explain.

9. Debate the following resolution: The U.S. military budget could be cut by at least one-third through elimination of unnecessary waste.

10. Debate the following resolution: National patriotism is both irrelevant and dangerous. The only viable patriotism is primary loyalty to sustaining the biosphere.

11. Do you agree or disagree with the "guestage" proposal for helping prevent nuclear war between the United States and the Soviet Union? Explain. How could such a proposal be implemented?

26

Environmental Ethics

Through our scientific and technological genius we have made this world a neighborhood. Now through our moral and spiritual genius we must make it a brotherhood.

Martin Luther King, Jr.

Although we will not get rid of pollution and environmental degradation, the world can be made a better place to live for present and future generations. Ecological understanding and less destructive economic and political systems can bring about a gradual and orderly transition from a throwaway society to a sustainable-earth society. However, such a transformation will not take place unless enough people change their worldview and their ethical and moral system of beliefs—their perception of how the world works and what is right and wrong behavior. Regardless of what we say we believe is right or wrong, how we act in the world reveals our true beliefs.

26-1 ETHICS AND MORALS

What Is Ethical and What Is Moral? **Ethics** is a branch of philosophy that seeks to define what is right and what is wrong on a universal basis. For example, stealing, lying, cheating, killing, and indifference to the well-being of others are considered to be unethical. Preserving human life, concern for others, honesty, and truthfulness are considered to be ethical. Some also believe it is unethical for people to encourage the extinction of any species.

Morals reflect the dominant beliefs of a particular culture about what is right or wrong. Although killing someone is considered unethical, most people believe that killing an enemy in wartime or executing a murderer are not immoral acts. Indeed, they are considered moral acts that are necessary to protect other lives and freedom. No country has ever declared what it considered to be an immoral war; throughout history hundreds of millions have been killed in the name of religious wars.

Most societies also do not consider it immoral for leaders or for individuals to tell lies to protect national security or to avoid unnecessarily hurting someone's feelings by being brutally honest. It is considered unethical to allow others to starve given the fact that there is more than enough food to feed everyone. Yet, the fact that most people and governments (including those whose people are starving) are largely indifferent to this problem reveals that it is not considered immoral to allow people to starve.

It is difficult to define what is right or wrong because of such differences in what is considered unethical and immoral in and between various cultures. For example, some individuals consider it unethical and immoral to unnecessarily waste resources; as a result, they have reduced their use and waste of resources. Others do not believe there are any serious environmental or resource problems and thus do not consider resource waste unethical or immoral. Indeed, they would argue that maximizing their consumption is a moral act because it promotes the economic growth that is a source of jobs and funds for helping the poor and protecting the environment (Table 24-1, p. 560). Others are indifferent to all or most problems except their own and will consume as many resources as their financial situation allows.

Some Important Questions Differences over what is considered ethical and moral behavior raise a lot of other complex and important issues:

- Is it ethical and moral for people to have more than two children in a world that many consider to be overpopulated?

- Do people have an ethical or moral right to have as many children as they want?

- Is it ethical and moral for a company to attempt to avoid installing pollution controls and to provide funds to lobby for weakening environmental laws because pollution control might reduce the profits of their stockholders?

- Is it unethical and immoral for a company not to do everything it can within the bounds of existing laws to maximize the profits of its stockholders, even if this leads to increased pollution and environmental degradation?

- Do we have an ethical and moral responsibility to leave the environment for the next generation in a condition at least as good as we found it?

- Is it unethical and immoral to ask members of this generation to make financial or other sacrifices in order to protect the environment for future generations?

26-2 THROWAWAY SOCIETY ETHICS

Some Basic Beliefs Most people in industrialized countries hold an attitude toward nature that can be expressed in eight basic beliefs:

1. Humans are the source of all value (anthropocentrism). We are apart from and above nature.

2. Nature exists only for our use. Our role is to conquer and subdue wild nature so it can be used to further human goals.

3. Our primary purpose is to produce and consume material goods. Material wealth is the best measure of success.

4. Matter and energy resources are unlimited because of human ingenuity in making them available.

5. Production and consumption of goods must rise endlessly because we have a right to an ever-increasing material standard of living.

6. We need not adapt ourselves to the natural environment because we can remake it to suit our own needs by means of science and technology.

7. A major function of the state is to help individuals and corporations exploit the environment to increase wealth and power. The most important nation-state is the one that can command and use the largest fraction of the world's resources.

8. The ideal person is the self-made individualist who does his or her own thing and hurts no one.

Although we may not accept these statements, most of us act individually, corporately, and politically as if we did.

Roots of the Throwaway Mentality How did we get such attitudes toward nature? Part of the reason that we exploit and degrade the environment is a biological imperative built into all species to ensure survival. Every organism seeks to maximize the use of resources available in its ecological niche and to perpetuate itself through offspring to maintain a position of dominance. The human species is no different, except that people have used their brains to develop technologies that have allowed them to expand their niche to a global scale. The problem is that there are so many people trying to maximize their use of matter and energy resources that this biological imperative now threatens not only the human species but also many other species sharing the planet with us.

Self-preservation does not mean self-centeredness, where individuals concentrate primarily on satisfying their present *wants* (a now-oriented society) instead of their own present and future *needs* and the needs of future generations, as well as those of other life forms on earth. Some analysts argue that people are born wanting to have everything and wanting to be in charge of the world. This egotism causes people to connect their sense of worth with the power they have over others and the environment and with their ability to accumulate material things to achieve status.

Others, however, point out that maturity involves learning that we cannot have everything and that true joy, happiness, and meaning come from cooperation, sharing, caring, and love. The question is whether enough people will learn to balance their innate drive to exploit the environment with their learned drive to cooperate with one another and with nature before we exceed various environmental limits.

Anthropocentric or human-centered beliefs mean that people believe they are in charge of—not merely a part of—nature. Historian Lynn White, Jr., among others, argues that the attitudes of Western civilization toward nature are linked to the Judeo-Christian teachings that direct us to "be fruitful and multiply, fill the earth and subdue it, and have dominion over the fish of the sea and over the birds of the air and over every living thing" (Genesis 1:28). This ethical foundation tells us that nature is here to serve us and that it is God's will for human beings to exploit nature for their own purposes.

Theologians and other scholars, however, have pointed out that this hypothesis treats the Judeo-Christian tradition as a monolithic structure instead of as a rich diversity of beliefs operating differently throughout history. They also point out that the Bible calls for stewardship of nature and commands us to "hurt not the earth."*

Some have suggested that the answer lies in Eastern religions, which emphasize human beings *in* nature rather than human beings *against* nature. For example, Taoism and Zen Buddhism stress the harmony and unity of people with nature, and Buddhism fosters reverence for all living creatures and an appreciation of the beauty of nature. But people guided by these and other Eastern religions have also ruined land through overgrazing, soil erosion, and excessive deforestation. Thus, some scholars argue that it is not one's professed religion or philosophy that is to blame, but the failure of people to put their religious or philosophical beliefs into practice. Others argue that all the world's religions and philosophies contain anthropocentric (human-centered) views that can and usually do lead to environmental degradation.

There are also four traps or excuses many people use to avoid involvement in caring for the earth and following their professed religious or ethical beliefs. One is *gloom-and-doom pessimism*—the belief that the world is doomed by nuclear war or environmental catastrophe so why not enjoy life while we can. The second trap is *blind technological optimism*—the belief that human ingenuity will always be able to come up with technological advances that will solve our problems.

A third excuse for inaction is *fatalism*—the belief that whatever will be will be, and that we have no control over our actions. Most people believe in free will or our ability to control many of our actions but lapse into the fatalism excuse when confronted with something they can only do with great effort. A fourth excuse is *extrapolation to infinity*—the idea that "If I can't change the entire world quickly, I won't try to change any of it." This rationalization is reinforced by modern society's emphasis on instant gratification and quick results with as little effort as possible.

26-3 SUSTAINABLE-EARTH SOCIETY ETHICS

Sustainable-Earth Ethics Many analysts argue that ecological concern will be short-lived and ecological action crippled unless we deal with the attitudes and values that have led to environmental degradation. As E. F. Schumacher said, "Environmental deterioration does not stem from science or technology, or from a lack of information, trained people, or money for research. It stems from the lifestyle of the modern world, which in turn arises from its basic beliefs or its religion."

A number of environmentalists urge that we adopt a sustainable-earth or conservation worldview based on replacing the eight attitudes toward nature listed earlier with the following ethical guidelines:

1. Human beings are not the source of all value. We are part of nature, not apart from and above nature, as expressed in the philosophy of the international Greenpeace environmental organization: "Ecology has taught us that the whole earth is part of our body and that we must learn to respect it as we respect ourselves. As we feel for ourselves, we must feel for all forms of life— the whales, the seals, the forests, the seas."

2. Nature does not exist primarily for human use but for all living species. In the words of Aldo Leopold, each of us is "to be a plain member and citizen of nature."

---

*Examples are found in Genesis 2:15; Leviticus 25:2–5; Deuteronomy 8:17, 20:19–20, 22:6; Job 38; Psalms 24:1–6, 65:11–13, 84:3, 148; Isaiah 24:4–6; Malachi 3:11–12; Matthew 6:12, 26–29; Luke 12:16–21, 16:1–2.

Table 26-1   Comparison of Shallow and Deep Ecology

Shallow Ecology (Spaceship Earth)	Deep Ecology (Sustainable Earth)
Views human beings as separate from nature.	Views human beings as part of nature.
Emphasizes the right of human beings to live (anthropocentrism).	Emphasizes the idea that every species has in principle a right to live (biocentrism); recognizes that we have no right to destroy other living species without sufficient reason based on ecological understanding.
Concerned with human feelings (anthropocentrism).	Concerned with the feelings of all living things; deep ecologists feel sad when another human being or a cat or dog feels sad and grieve when trees and landscapes are destroyed.
Concerned with the wise management of resources for human use (traditional resource conservation).	Concerned about resources for all living species.
Concerned with stabilizing the population—especially in LDCs.	Concerned not only with stabilizing the human population worldwide, but also with reducing the size of the human population to a sustainable size without revolution or dictatorship.
Either accepts by default or positively endorses the ideology of continued economic growth.	Replaces this ideology with that of ecological sustainability and preservation of biological and cultural diversity.
Bases decisions on cost-benefit analysis.	Bases decisions on ethical intuitions about how the natural world really works.
Bases decisions on short-term planning and goals.	Bases decisions on long-range planning and goals and on ecological intuition when all facts not available.
Tries to work within existing political, social, economic, and ethical systems.	Questions these systems and looks for better systems based on the way the natural world works.

3. Our primary purposes should be to share the earth's finite resources, care for human beings and all other species, and interfere with nonhuman species only to satisfy vital—not frivolous—needs. Success is based on the degree to which we achieve these goals.

4. Matter and energy resources are finite and must not be wasted. As Arthur Purcell puts it: "A conservation ethic means simply a desire to get the most out of what people use, and a recognition that the wasteful use of precious resources is harmful and detrimental to the quality of everyone's life."

5. Production and consumption of material goods need not increase endlessly—no individual, corporation, or nation has a right to an ever-increasing share of the earth's finite resources. "There is enough for everybody's need but not for anybody's greed" (M. K. Gandhi).

6. As part of nature, humans should work with—not against—nature. In the words of Aldo Leopold, "A thing is right when it tends to preserve the integrity, stability, and beauty of the biotic community. It is wrong when it tends otherwise."

7. The major functions of the state are to prevent individuals and corporations from exploiting or damaging the environment, and to preserve human freedom and dignity.

8. We can never completely "do our own thing" without exerting some effect now or in the future on other human beings and on other living species. All past, present, and future actions have effects, most of which are unpredictable.

It won't be easy to achieve a sustainable-earth world-view because it requires changing many of the things most people believe. In general, it involves working our way through four levels of environmental awareness (see Spotlight on p. 594).

Shallow and Deep Ecology   In 1973 the Norwegian ecophilosopher Arne Naess pointed out two approaches to environmental problems, which he called "shallow ecology" and "deep ecology." Shallow ecology corresponds roughly to the Spaceship Earth world-view and deep ecology corresponds roughly to the sustainable-earth worldview. Some of the major differences between these two approaches are summarized in Table 26-1 and are also discussed in the guest essay at the end of this chapter.

First Awareness Level: Pollution and Environmental Degradation

We must discover the symptoms. At this level, we must point out and try to stop irresponsible acts of pollution and environmental degradation by individuals and organizations and resist being duped by slick corporate advertising. But we must at the same time change our own lifestyles. We have all been working toward our own destruction by "drilling holes in the bottom of the boat." Arguing over who is drilling the biggest hole only diverts us from working together to keep the boat from sinking. The problem of remaining at the first awareness level is that individuals and industries see their own impact as too tiny to matter, not realizing that millions of individual impacts together threaten our life-support systems. Remaining at this first level of awareness also leads people to see the crisis as a problem comparable to a moon shot, and to look for a quick technological solution: "Have technology fix us up, send me the bill at the end of the month, but don't ask me to change my way of living."

Second Awareness Level: Consumption Overpopulation

We must recognize that the cause of pollution is not just people but their level of consumption and the environmental impact of various types of production (Figure 1–10,

p. 14). At this second level, the answers seem obvious. We must control the world's population, but we must also reduce wasteful consumption of matter and energy resources—especially in MDCs, which, with less than 26% of the world's population, account for about 80% of the world's resource consumption and environmental pollution.

Third Awareness Level: Spaceship Earth (Shallow Ecology)

We must become aware that population and resource use will not be controlled until enough world leaders and citizens stress that protecting and preserving the environment must be our primary purpose. The goal at this level is to use technology, economics, and conventional politics to control population growth, pollution, and resource depletion to prevent ecological overload. Some argue that the Spaceship Earth metaphor is a sophisticated expression of our arrogance toward nature—the idea that through technology we can control nature and create artificial environments to avoid environmental overload. They point out that this approach eventually poses a dire threat to individual freedom because to protect the life-support systems that are necessary in space, a centralized authority (ground control) must rigidly control astronauts' lives. Instead of novelty, spontaneity, joy, and free-

dom, the spaceship model is based on cultural homogenization, social regimentation, artificiality, monotony, and gadgetry. In addition, it is argued that this approach can cause environmental overload in the long run because it is based on the false idea that we have essentially complete understanding of how nature works. Furthermore, this awareness level does not seriously question the economic, political, social, and ethical foundations of modern industrial society, which some see as the major causes of the environmental problems.

Fourth Awareness Level: Sustainable Earth (Deep Ecology)

We must recognize that (1) all living species are interconnected; (2) the role of human beings is not to rule and control nature but to work with nature to meet human needs on the basis of ecological understanding; (3) because the earth's organisms and their interactions are so diverse, attempts at excessive control will sooner or later backfire; (4) our major goal should be to preserve the ecological integrity, sustainability, and diversity of the life-support systems for all species; (5) the forces of biological evolution, not technological control, should determine which species live or die; and (6) human beings have no right to interfere destructively with nonhuman life except to satisfy vital needs.

Naess believes that if people seriously question what is going on in the world, they will eventually emerge with a worldview that can "provide a single motivating force for all the activities and movements aimed at saving the planet from human exploitation and domination." He argues that such a search for meaning would reveal that we need practically nothing of what we have been culturally conditioned to believe we need for a rich and fulfilling life. Deep ecology gives people the confidence to take stands on complex issues based on intuition about how the natural world works instead of deferring a stand until all the facts are in.

Deep ecology does not reject technology. But it does insist that technology be used in just and humane ways to protect—not to degrade and destroy—all forms of life on earth. It also rejects the idea that a technology should be developed and encouraged just because it is possible.

Deep ecology calls for us to distinguish between our wants and our true needs by making our lifestyles more harmonious with natural cycles and by adopting a philosophy of *voluntary simplicity* based on doing more with less. Deep ecologists have found that simplifying their material lives—learning to be happy with the simple things that come from a life of self-reliance—gives them more time to focus on their inner lives and on the enjoyment that goes with recognizing that one is a part of nature (see Spotlight on p. 596). However, voluntary simplicity by those who have more than they really need should not be confused with the forced simplicity of the poor, who do not have enough to meet their most basic needs for food, clothing, shelter, and health.

Deep ecologists recognize that to truly commit ourselves to the protection of the biosphere in general, we need to experience nature directly. We need to become emotionally, not just intellectually, involved in appreciating the worth of the biosphere.

This is accomplished by finding a *sense of place*—a river, mountain, or piece of the earth that we feel truly at one with. When we become part of a place and it is a part of us, we are driven to defend it against damage and to heal its ecological wounds.

26-4 WHAT CAN YOU DO?

The key to transforming the culturesphere so that it is more in harmony with the biosphere is to combine sustainable-earth ethical beliefs with realistic optimism based on a balanced view of how much has been accomplished since 1965 (Section 2-5) and how much more needs to be done. As the Chinese philosopher Confucius reminded us centuries ago: "The journey of a thousand miles begins with one step."

Although we can read and talk about environmental and resource problems, it finally comes down to what you and I are willing to do individually and collectively. Begin with yourself.

1. **You can evaluate the way you think the world works and sensitize yourself to the environment.** Stand up, look around, compare what is with what could and should be. Examine your room, your home, your school, your place of work, your street, and your city, state, country, and world. What things around you really improve the quality of your life? What are your own environmental bad habits? What is your own worldview? Do the assumptions on which it is based represent a valid view of the real world?

2. **You can become ecologically informed.** Give up your throwaway thinking and immerse yourself in sustainable-earth thinking. Specialize in one particular area of environmental knowledge and awareness, relate this to holistic, sustainable-earth thinking, and share your knowledge and understanding with others (networking). Everyone doesn't need to be an ecologist, but you do need to "ecologize" your lifestyle. Keep in mind Norman Cousins's statement: "The first aim of education should not be to prepare young people for careers but to enable them to develop respect for life."

3. **You can become emotionally involved in caring for the earth by experiencing nature directly and by trying to find a place that you love and thus must defend as a part of you.** Intellectual ecological knowledge of how the world works is vitally important but will not be enough until it is combined with a sense of place—a feeling of oneness with and thankfulness for some piece of the earth that you truly love and respect. Poet-philosopher Gary Snyder urges us to "find [our] place on the planet, dig in, and take responsibility from there . . ."

4. **You can choose a simpler lifestyle to reduce resource consumption and waste and pollution production.** Do this by distinguishing between your true needs and your wants and by using trade-offs. For every high-energy, high-waste, or highly polluting thing you do (buying a car, living or working in an air-conditioned building), give up a number of other things. Such a lifestyle will be less expensive and may bring you joy as you learn how to break through the technological barrier that artificially separates many people from nature, one another, and their true selves.

5. **You can become more self-reliant by trying to unhook yourself from dependence on large, centralized systems for your water, energy, food, and livelihood.** You don't need to move to the country to become more self-reliant and to lower your impact on the environment (see Farralones Institute, 1979; Leckie et al., 1975; Todd and Todd, 1984; Van der Ryn and Calthorpe, 1986, in Further Readings). Learn to use organic, intensive gardening techniques to grow some of your own food in a small plot, roof garden, or windowbox planter. Accumulate basic hand tools and learn skills such as plumbing, wiring, and carpentry so that you can save money and survive on your own if necessary.

I am writing this book deep in the midst of some beautiful woods in a structure that Peggy, my wife and earthmate, and I designed to work with nature. First, we purchased a 1954 school bus from a nearby school district and then resold the tires for the same price that we paid for the bus. We constructed an insulated foundation, rented a crane for two hours to lift and set the gutted bus on the foundation, placed heavy insulation around the bus, and added a wooden outside frame.

A solar room—a passive solar collector with double-paned conventional sliding glass windows (for ventilation)—was then attached to the entire south side of the recycled bus structure (Figure 26-1). The solar room serves as a year-round sitting and work area and contains a small kitchen area with a stove and refrigerator that run on LP natural gas. The room collects enough solar energy to provide at least 60% of our heating needs during the cold months. A solar-assisted water stove (Figure 18-17, p. 410) in a small building outside provides backup heat as needed by burning wood (from dead limbs and trees and selective pruning) and paper and other burnable materials that are not recycled (there is no nearby recycling center).

Hot water is provided by active solar collectors connected to the water stove, which serve as preheaters for a tankless, instant heater fueled by LP natural gas. Most of the light bulbs we use last an average of six years and use about 60% less electricity than conventional bulbs. Electricity is now provided by the power company, but we plan to obtain our electricity from roof-mounted panels of solar photovoltaic cells (Figure 18-12, p. 401) when their prices become lower, probably sometime in the 1990s. We hope to be able to sell any excess power we produce back to the power company. Our present monthly electricity bills run around $30.

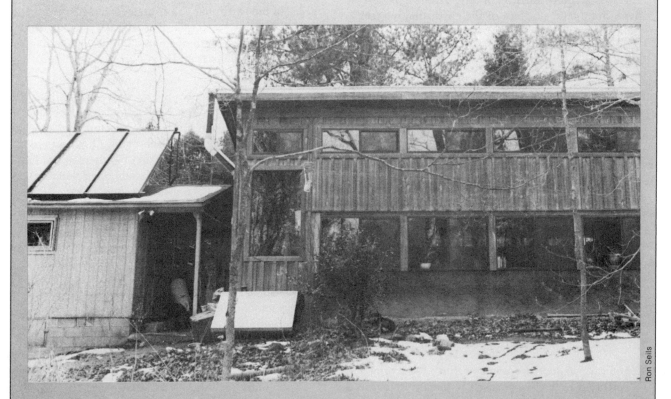

Figure 26-1 Eco-Lair. A south-facing solar room collects solar energy passively and distributes it to a recycled school bus. Backup heat is provided by a solar-assisted water stove housed in the separate structure on the left (see Figure 18-17, p. 410).

We cool the structure in moderate weather by opening windows to capture breezes from any direction. During hot and humid North Carolina summers, we get additional cooling by using earth tubes or cool tubes (Figure 18-7, p. 395). Four plastic pipes were buried about 18 feet underground, extending down a gently sloping hillside until their ends emerge some 100 feet away. The other ends of these tubes come up into the foundation of the bus and connect to a duct system containing a small fan whose speed can be varied by a rheostat. When the fan is turned on, outside air at a temperature of 95°F is drawn slowly through the buried tubes (which are surrounded by earth at about 55°F) and enters the structure at about 72°F. This form of natural air conditioning costs about one dollar per summer for running the fan.

Additional passive cooling is provided by several large oak trees and other deciduous trees in front of the south-facing solar room. These trees provide shade during the summer and drop their leaves to let the sun in during the winter. Because of allergies, we have had to install a recycled conventional air conditioning unit for occasional short-term use (typically no more than 15 to 30 minutes) a day when excessive pollen counts or heat and humidity overwhelm the immune system and the earth tubes. Life always involves some trade-offs.

The entire structure, which we call Eco-Lair, is surrounded by natural vegetation including flowers and low-level ground cover; thus, there is no grass to cut and no lawnmower to repair, feed with gasoline, and listen to. To the natural diversity of the landscape we have added plants that repel various insects, so we have few insect pest problems. We have reduced the use of water by installing water-saving faucets and low-flush toilets and have also experimented with a waterless composting toilet that gradually converts wastes to a dry, odorless powder that can be used as a soil conditioner. Kitchen wastes also are composted and recycled to the soil.

Much of our furniture (which we keep to a minimum) and clothes are obtained from garbage dumpsters we pass on the way into the nearest town (seven miles away) and from a thrift shop that donates most of the money it makes to the local school system. We are constantly amazed at the things (often new) that people throw away. Two additional school buses are used for storage of extra furniture, clothes, and other items we find and recycle to family, friends, and people in need.

Eco-Lair lies near the end of a narrow, one-mile-long dirt road that at times can only be traversed by a four-wheel-drive vehicle. As a result, we have had to compromise and use a vehicle that consumes much more gasoline than we would like. If the technology becomes available and economically feasible in the future, we hope to have a vehicle that runs on hydrogen gas produced by using solar photovoltaic cells to decompose water into hydrogen and oxygen gas. When burned, hydrogen fuel would emit small amounts of nitrogen oxides and harmless water vapor into the atmosphere—in sharp contrast to the variety of pollutants spewing out the exhaust pipes of today's vehicles. Because of laziness and allergies, we get most of our food from the grocery store rather than growing it ourselves.

We feel a part of the piece of land we live on and love. To us, ownership of this land means that we are ethically driven to vigorously defend and protect it from environmental degradation. We feel that the trees, flowers, deer, squirrels, hummingbirds, songbirds, and other forms of wildlife we often see are a part of us and we are a part of them. As temporary caretakers of this small portion of the biosphere, we are also obligated to pass it on to future generations in a way that preserves its ecological integrity and sustainability.

Most of our political activities involve thinking globally but acting locally. They include attempts to prevent an economically unnecessary nuclear power plant from opening about 15 miles away (it opened anyway), to prevent an ecologically unsound development along a nearby river that is already badly polluted (successful so far), to prevent the building of a large, conventional housing development that would double the size of the closest town (still undecided), and to financially support numerous environmental organizations working at the national and global levels (see Appendix 1). We are not opposed to all forms of development—only those that are ecologically unsound and destructive.

We have found that working with nature gives us an immense sense of joy and purpose, and also saves us money. We are taking our stand in a rural area. But it is only one example of many thousands of possible low-environmental-impact, high-quality lifestyles that one can implement in or out of cities, as an increasing number of people are discovering (see Further Readings).

Get as much of your energy as possible from renewable sources such as the sun, wind, water, or biomass. An organic garden of any size, a solar house, or solar window collectors in an apartment not only save energy and money on a lifetime cost basis, they also put you in direct contact with other parts of nature by bringing sun, soil, and plants into your life.

6. **You can remember that environment begins at home.** Before you start trying to convert others, begin by changing your own living patterns. If you become an environmental activist, be prepared to have everyone looking for and pointing out your own environmental sins. People are most influenced by what we do, not by what we say.

7. **You can avoid the four do-nothing traps of blind technological optimism, gloom-and-doom pessimism, fatalism, and extrapolation to infinity.** Most people talk about the difficulties of changing the system, but others get involved in bringing about ecologically sound changes.

8. **You can become politically involved on local and national levels.** Start or join a local environmental group, and also join national organizations (see the list in Appendix 1). Become the biosphere citizen of your block, school, apartment building, or dormitory. Learn how to cooperate with others to amplify or synergize your efforts. The environment would improve noticeably if each of us made an annual donation of money, time, or both to one or more politically active environmental organizations working for causes we believe in. Work to elect sustainable-earth leaders and to influence officials once they are elected to public office (see Enrichment Study at the end of Chapter 25).

9. **You can do the little things based on thinking globally and acting locally.** Individual acts of consumption and litter have contributed to the mess. When you are tempted to say "This little bit won't hurt," remember that hundreds of millions of others are saying the same thing. Picking up a single beer can, joining a carpool, bicycling to work, writing on both sides of a piece of paper, not discarding clothing and other items just to be fashionable, and not buying overpackaged products are all very significant acts. Turning off a light when leaving a room or not using more light than is necessary ultimately reduces the need for nuclear and coal-burning electric power plants. Each small act reminds us of ecologically sound practices. Start now with a small, concrete, personal act, and then add more such acts.

10. **You can work on the big polluters and big problems, primarily through political action.** Individual actions help reduce pollution, give us a sense of involvement, and help us develop a badly needed ecological consciousness. Our awareness must then expand to recognize that large-scale pollution and environmental disruption are caused by industries, governments, and big agriculture. The ethic of the international Greenpeace movement, for example, is "not only to personally bear witness to atrocities against life; it is to take direct nonviolent action to prevent them."

11. **You can start a movement of awareness and action.** You can change the world by changing the two people next to you. For everything, big or little, that you decide to do, make it your primary goal to convince two others to do the same thing and persuade them in turn to convince two others. Carrying out this doubling process only 28 times would convince everyone in the United States. But it is not necessary to convince everybody. Most major changes occur when a critical mass of people—probably only 5% to 10% of the population of a country or of the world—begins to work actively for a common goal. The national and global environmental movement is nearing this critical mass and needs your help.

12. **Don't make people feel guilty.** If you know people who are overconsuming or carrying out environmentally harmful acts, don't make them feel bad. Instead, find the things that each individual is willing to do to help the environment. There is plenty to do, and no one can do everything. Use positive rather than negative reinforcement (win-win rather than win-lose games). We need to nurture, reassure, and understand rather than to threaten one another.

Begin at the individual level and work outward by joining with others to amplify your knowledge and actions. This is the way the world is changed. Envision the world as made up of all kinds of cycles and flows in a beautiful and diverse web of interrelationships; it is a kaleidoscope of patterns and rhythms whose very complexity and multitudinous potentiality remind us that cooperation, honesty, humility, and love must be the guidelines for our behavior toward one another and the earth.

The main ingredients of an environmental ethic are caring about the planet and all of its inhabitants, allowing unselfishness to control the immediate self-interest that harms others, and living each day so as to leave the lightest possible footprints on the planet.

Robert Cahn

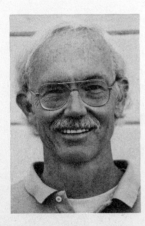

Bill Devall

Bill Devall is a professor of sociology at Humboldt State University, Arcata, California. He is coauthor, with George Sessions, of Deep Ecology: Living as If Nature Mattered *(1985). He has written a number of articles on the deep ecology movement and has taught environmental politics and ethics at universities in Canada and Australia.*

Nearly fifty years ago the great ecologist Aldo Leopold wrote: "To be trained as an ecologist is to live alone in a world of wounds." Leopold was talking about wounds to the earth—massive strip mining, urban blight, and human-caused desertification and species extinction. He wrote these words before the development of nuclear weapons and before the arms race between the United States and the USSR began to threaten the integrity of the whole earth. And he was not thinking, it seems, about other wounds—the wounds of our psyche. We all have been wounded just from living in the late twentieth century. We have been wounded by dominating attitudes toward nature, by the cult of egoism, by violence, and by competitiveness and consumerism.

But we no longer live alone, not even scientific ecologists. The deep, long-range ecology movement is a collective affirmation of a different way of being-in-the-world and of working cooperatively to prevent and heal ecological wounds. Supporters of deep ecology see the earth not just as a launching pad into outer space (as interesting as space travel may be) or a bus stop between heaven and hell (although salvation is vital to many people). The earth is our homeland, and our species, although a special and perhaps unique species, has no special claim on being superior to and in charge of all other species. We are one of many species—all moving toward self-realization.

Although many people intellectually accept the earth as their homeland, many still feel and act as if they were homeless. And at a deep level we are homeless. The more we rely on technocratic modes of understanding our homeland, the more we attempt to conquer earth's great spaces with macro engineering projects—freeways, dams, huge mining operations—the more homeless and alienated we become from our real Self. Driven by our desire for more power over nature, we lack the wisdom to empower ourselves as mature beings-in-the-world.

Our task, it seems to me, is to cultivate ecophilosophy or ecosophy—earth wisdom. Arne Naess, who first used the phrase "deep ecology," contends that ecosophy springs not from intellectual arguments alone but from the great underground river that gives life to the way we experience the world. We can articulate sophisticated intellectual statements and write and read learned papers about ecophilosophy and self-realization, but such intellectual exercises alone have only limited usefulness in cultivating ecosophy.

If we are experiencing the world as part of our Self, not apart from our Self, then we identify with the earth—our homeland. From such identification springs solidarity with and desire to defend our homeland against deterioration. On the other hand, if we see nature as the Other, as a collection of natural resources useful to some humans, then—most likely—we won't have much solidarity with our homeland and won't defend it.

This search for ecosophy may involve what Aldo Leopold calls "thinking like a mountain." That is, only when we make a fundamental shift in our mode of thinking can we understand what it means to be-in-the-world and to cultivate our authentic place in the world. But how can we "think like a mountain"? Being open and vulnerable to our personal experiences in wild nature is one way.

We can respect the Other—some species such as grizzly bears, for example—without cultivating our ecosophy, and we can have aesthetic appreciation for a river or a mountain. We can also seek to conserve natural resources or natural biotic diversity for the narrow commodity values these resources have for us. We can understand what ecologist Paul Ehrlich calls "nature's machinery," and this appreciation can "provide the basis for the necessary changes in attitudes and the guidelines for the safe development of new technologies."

But when we limit our study of nature to modern scientific methods of study, we tend to objectify and dissect nature into isolated parts and thus separate our minds from the Other—nature. If we merely change our words, our concepts, theories, and ideas, we never really live, never "touch the earth," and never enter into the waters of the underground river that gives life to ecosophy.

I am talking here of the need for environmental education, but not the usual sort of environmental education. Information about environmental problems and ecological concepts, biology, natural history, and even environmental ethics are important, but they are not nearly enough. Indeed what passes for environmental education in many schools perpetuates the separation we have from the rest of nature; it teaches that nature is only "dead matter" to be understood by disciplinary dissection rather than by interdisciplinary holism or that nature is a collection of natural resources put on earth primarily for human use.

Indeed, the very word *environment* contains and reinforces the separation between ourselves and nature—the Other. But when we understand our Self as a pond, extending outward and inward, then the artificially erected barriers between us and nature begin to dissolve. According to historian Neil Everdon, the great subversive insight of ecology is not that everything is connected with everything else but that everything is intermingled. There are no boundaries.

If we live richly, fully, deeply, and simply, we might be more open to experiences that contribute to ecosophy. Thus, any exercises that help us to become alert, centered, open, calm, and caring can help us discipline our unruly minds, integrate our body and mind, and truly connect with our surroundings.

Any activity that brings us physically closer to mountains, rivers, deserts—or any wild place in our neighborhood—enhances our possibility to become emotionally closer to those places and to identify with them. What we are searching for, whether we recognize it or not, is to have a true sense of place and belonging. Developing a sense of place—whether it be in an urban, suburban, or rural area, or a large geographical region—means that we have located a piece of the earth that we feel at peace with, a part of, and intermingled with. It means that we become sensitive to the spiritual as well as biological needs of a place that we reinhabit, or attempt to restore to ecological health.

When this happens we are driven to defend the place or places we love against degradation and heal ecological wounds because we identify them as part of ourselves. This also leads to political activism to help others preserve the places they identify with. Surrounding ourselves with material possessions and using objects to bring the world to us indirectly and imprecisely through TV images, photos, and sound recordings merely enhance our sense of alienation from ourselves and nature.

John Muir, the godfather of the American preservationist movement, consistently urged his readers to go to the mountains to get their "good tidings." But this does not automatically empower us nor lead us to actions in defense of the environment unless we have developed a true mental and physical sense of place. In his book *The Journey Home*, Edward Abbey confesses, "Like so many others in this century I found myself a displaced person shortly after birth and have been looking half my life for a place to take my stand. Now that I think I've found it, I must defend it. My

CHAPTER SUMMARY

Ethics seeks to define what is right and wrong on a universal basis, whereas *morals* reflects the dominant beliefs of a particular culture about what is right and wrong. It is difficult to define what is right or wrong because of differences in and between various cultures

The *throwaway ethical beliefs* upon which most industrial societies are built assume that human beings are apart from and above nature and that their role is to conquer and subdue nature to further human goals. Matter and energy resources are assumed to be unlimited because of human ingenuity, and endlessly rising production and consumption of material goods is considered to be the primary goal of the culturesphere.

This worldview is based on a biological imperative in which every organism seeks to maximize the use of resources available in its ecological niche and to perpetuate itself through offspring to maintain a position of dominance. Another contributing cause of this attitude is ignorance of the fact that all parts of nature are interconnected, as well as religious and cultural teachings that direct human beings to be fruitful and multiply and to have dominion over the earth. These same religious teachings, however, also direct people to not hurt the earth and to assume a role of stewardship.

Some argue that the causes of environmental degradation are not in cultural, religious, and ethical beliefs but in the failure of people to follow such beliefs. They also argue that the innate biological imperative includes a need for cooperation within and between species to enhance their long-term survival. Many people use *gloom-and-doom pessi-*

home is the American West. All of it." Abbey eloquently describes the feelings, tones, and sounds of the American West and his relationship with it. His broad and deep identification inspires him to "resist much, obey little" in defense of the American West.

Many people choose recreational activities that bring them closer to wild places—skiing, kayaking, bicycling, canoeing, hiking, surfing, climbing—to name only a few. But we must engage in these activities in the correct way, with the correct attitude—without competitiveness, without dominating attitudes. If we approach a mountain with the intent to climb the mountain, we pause for a moment and honor the mountain and bow to it before beginning to climb. Many people feel uncomfortable, even awkward at first, bowing to the mountain, and those feelings indicate our separation from the mountain. If we are respectful and receptive, however, we can open a way to the heart of the mountain and be open to what the mountain might teach us. On a simpler scale, walking outside and thanking plants for the beauty, oxygen, joy, and companionship they provide us with recognizes them as part of us. Aware of our own mortality, alert to new possibilities, accepting our vulnerability and dependence on other species, we empower our Self.

Some people, such as Dave Foreman of Earth First!, suggest that acts of civil disobedience or ecodefense can be a "patch with a heart" in the defense of a forest, river, or other threatened place. In his writings, Edward Abbey talks about Mark Dubois, a young man with the true right stuff, who chained himself to a rock in a river, in a hidden place known only to a single friend. He did this to save a river—the Stanislaus in northern California—he had learned to know and love from being tamed by the New Melones Dam. His action halted work on the project.

In sum, involving our Self in the world rather than pursuing only things in the world, is a process that grounds us to our homeland, our place of being-with-our-fellow-creatures. Or as Chief Seattle of the Duwamish Native American tribe of Washington State said in 1855, "Whatever befalls the earth befalls the sons of the earth. Continue to contaminate your bed and you will one day suffocate in your own waste. Man did not weave the web of life; he merely is a strand in it. Whatever he does to the web, he does to himself."

Guest Essay Discussion

1. Do you feel that you are homeless, alienated from the earth, and without a sense of place? If not, describe the place you love and feel a part of to other members of your class. If you do not have a sense of place, try to explain why and identify changes in your lifestyle that might enable you to obtain a sense of place.

2. Do you agree with the basic ideas of deep ecology, or do you believe that it is a naive, romantic, unrealistic—perhaps dangerous and subversive—system of beliefs? Explain.

3. Is your understanding of nature intellectual, emotional, or both? Give concrete examples and feelings to support your answer based on your own life.

mism, blind technological optimism, fatalism, and *extrapolation to infinity* as excuses to avoid change and to avoid becoming involved in caring for the earth.

Sustainable-earth ethics are based on the beliefs that humans are part of nature and that our primary purpose is to share the earth's finite resources, care for all people and all nonhuman species, interfere with nonhuman species only to satisfy vital human needs, and work with—not against—nature. Matter and energy resources are finite and must not be wasted, and production and consumption of material goods need not increase endlessly.

Achieving a sustainable-earth worldview involves working through four levels of awareness: *pollution and environmental degradation* (the symptoms), *consumption overpopulation* (some of the causes), *Spaceship Earth or shallow ecology* (the solution is to use technology and conventional economics and politics to prevent environmental overload), and *sustainable-earth or deep ecology* (the solution is to work with nature and selectively modify small parts of the biosphere to meet human needs on the basis of ecological understanding, humility, love, and caring for the earth and its species).

Deep ecology calls for us to distinguish between our wants and our true needs by making our lifestyles more harmonious with natural cycles and by adopting a philosophy of *voluntary simplicity* based on doing more with less. True commitment to working with nature requires not only intellectual understanding of the general ways nature works but also direct emotional involvement with nature. This is accomplished by finding a *sense of place*—a piece of the earth that we love and become a part of and it a part of us so that we are driven to defend it against damage and to heal its ecological wounds.

The key to transforming the culturesphere so that it is more in harmony with the biosphere is to combine sustainable-earth ethical beliefs with *realistic optimism* based on a balanced view of how much has been done since 1965 and how much more needs to be done. To accomplish this each of us can become sensitized to the way the world works, become ecologically informed, and become emotionally involved in caring for the earth by experiencing nature directly. We can also choose a simpler lifestyle to reduce resource consumption and waste and pollution production, become more self-reliant, avoid do-nothing rationalizations, become politically involved on local and national levels, do the little things based on thinking globally and acting locally, work on big problems and big polluters through political action, bring about change by changing the two people next to us, and not make people feel guilty. Cooperation, honesty, humility, and love must be the guidelines for our behavior toward one another and the earth.

DISCUSSION TOPICS

1. As a class, list the rationalizations that we typically use to avoid thought, action, and responsibility.

2. Do you agree with the cartoon character Pogo that "we have met the enemy and he [or she] is us"? Why or why not? Criticize this statement from the viewpoint of the poor. From the viewpoint that large corporations and government are the really big polluters.

3. Distinguish carefully between the Spaceship Earth worldview and the sustainable-earth worldview.

4. Do you agree with the hypothesis that the throwaway mentality in Western societies comes primarily from the Judeo-Christian teachings that humans are to have dominion over the earth? Explain.

5. Do you agree with the sustainable-earth ethical guidelines listed in Section 26-3? Explain. Can you add others? Which ones do you try to follow?

6. Do you agree that the sustainable-earth worldview is an unrealistic, hypocritical, probably dangerous idea that does not recognize the true nature of human beings and thus gives people false hope? Explain. If you do agree, what alternatives do you propose?

7. Why is it so important to do the little things? As a class, make a list of all the little things you can do to help protect the environment.

8. Make a list of the products sold in a typical suburban shopping center that are really essential for survival and for a meaningful life.

Epilogue

Where there is no dream, the people perish.
Proverbs 29:18

This book is based on nine deceptively simple theses:

1. The biosphere is not only more complex than we think but more complex than we can ever think.

2. In Garrett Hardin's terms, the basic principle of ecology is "that everything and everyone are all interconnected." Truly accepting this will require a basic change in our patterns of living. But because we can never completely know how everything is connected, we must function in the biosphere and culturesphere with a sense of humility and creative cooperation rather than blind domination.

3. On earth there are no consumers, only users of materials. We can never really throw anything away, and natural resources are so interdependent that the use or misuse of one will affect others, often in unpredictable ways. This is a threat to a throwaway society, but an opportunity for reuse, recycling, and conservation of matter resources in a sustainable-earth society.

4. Because of the first law of thermodynamics, we can't get anything for nothing, and because of the second law of thermodynamics, almost every action we take has some undesirable present or future impact on the environment.

As a result, there can be no completely technological solution to pollution and environmental degradation, although appropriate forms of technology can help.

5. The earth's resources and matter recycling systems can support only a limited number of people living at a particular average level of affluence.

6. Because we have rounded the bend on the J-shaped curves of increasing population, natural resource use, pollution, and environmental degradation, we now have the power to disrupt the earth's life-support systems.

7. Our primary task must be to move from a simplistic, nonsustainable, throwaway society to a diverse, adaptable, sustainable-earth society that is more harmonious with the ecological cycles and fundamental rhythms of life that sustain us and other species.

8. Informed individual and collective action based on a combination of realistic hope, ecological understanding, and becoming a part of, rather than apart from, nature offers humanity the opportunity to make the transition to a sustainable-earth society.

9. It is not too late. There is time to deal with the complex, interacting problems we face and to make an orderly rather than catastrophic transition to a sustainable-earth society if enough of us really care. It's not up to "them," it's up to "us." Don't wait.

Periodicals, Environmental and Resource Organizations, and Federal and International Agencies

PERIODICALS

The following publications can help you keep well informed and up to date on environmental and resource problems. Those marked with an asterisk (*) are recommended as basic reading. Subscription prices, which tend to change, are not given.

Acid Precipitation Digest, Center for Environmental Information, 33 S. Washington St., Rochester, NY 14608. Summarizes current news and research related to acid deposition.

Alternate Sources of Energy, Alternate Sources of Energy, Inc., 107 S. Central Ave., Milaca, MN 56353. Useful source of information on renewable energy alternatives.

American Demographics, American Demographics, Inc., P.O. Box 68, Ithaca, NY 14851. Basic information.

*American Forests, American Forestry Association, 1319 18th St., N.W., Washington, DC 20036. Popular treatment, "seeks to promote an enlightened public appreciation of natural resources."

*Annual Energy Review, National Energy Information Center, Energy Information Administration, Forrestal Building, Room 1F-048, 1000 Independence Ave., S.W., Washington, DC 20585. Useful summary of data.

*Audubon, National Audubon Society, 950 Third Ave., New York, NY 10022. Conservationist viewpoint; covers more than bird watching. Good popularizer of environmental concerns; well-produced, sophisticated graphics.

*Audubon Wildlife Report, National Audubon Society, 950 Third Ave., New York, NY 10022. Superb annual summary of wildlife conservation.

BioScience, American Institute of Biological Sciences, 1401 Wilson Blvd., Arlington, VA 22209. Official monthly publication of AIBS; gives major coverage to biological aspects of the environment, including population. Style ranges from semipopular to technical. Features and news sections attentive to legislative and governmental issues.

*Bulletin of the Atomic Scientists, 935 E. 60th St., Chicago, IL 60637. Includes coverage of environmental issues, particularly in relation to nuclear power and nuclear testing and fallout.

Catalyst for Environmental/Energy, 274 Madison Ave., New York, NY 10016. High-level, popular treatment; substantial articles on all aspects of environment, including population control. Reviews books and films suited to environmental education.

Ceres, Food and Agriculture Organization of the United Nations (FAO), UNIPUB, Inc., 650 First Avenue, P.O. Box 433, New York, NY 10016. Contains articles on the population-food problem.

*The CoEvolution Quarterly, P.O. Box 428, Sausalito, CA 94965. Covers a wide range of environmental and self-sufficiency topics.

*Conservation Biology, Blackwell Scientific Publications, Inc., 52 Beacon St., Boston, MA 02108. Excellent coverage of wildlife conservation.

*Conservation Foundation Letter, Conservation Foundation, 1717 Massachusetts Ave., N.W., Washington, DC 20036. Usually 12 pages long. Good summaries of key issues.

*Conservation News, National Wildlife Foundation, 1412 16th St., N.W., Washington, DC 20036. Good coverage of wildlife issues.

Demographic Yearbook, Department of International Economic and Social Affairs, Statistical Office, United Nations Publishing Service, United Nations, NY 10017. Excellent source of population data.

Design and Environment, 355 Lexington Ave., New York, NY 10017. Useful for architects, engineers, and city planners.

*Earth Island Journal, Earth Island Institute, 300 Broadway, Suite 28, San Francisco, CA 94133. Excellent summaries of national and global environmental issues.

*The Ecologist, Ecosystems Ltd., 73 Molesworth St., Wadebridge, Cornway PL27 7DS, United Kingdom. Wide range of articles on environmental issues from an international viewpoint.

Ecology, Ecological Society of America, Dr. Ralph E. Good, Business Manager, Department of Biology, Rutgers University, Camden, NJ 08102. Good source of information on more technical ecology research.

Ecology Law Quarterly, University of California, Boalt Hall School of Law, Berkeley, CA 94720. Good treatment of latest developments in environmental law.

Ekistics, Athens Center of Ekistics, 24 Strat Syndesmou, Athens 136, Greece. Reviews the problems and science of human settlements. Reflects ideas of such planners as Constantine Doxiadis, R. Buckminster Fuller, and John McHale.

The Energy Consumer, U.S. Department of Energy, Office of Consumer Affairs, Forrestal Building, 1000 Independence Ave., S.W., Washington, DC 20585. Free monthly summaries of energy information.

*Environment, Heldref Publications, 4000 Albemarle St., N.W., Washington, DC 20016. Seeks to put environmental information before the public. Excellent in-depth articles on key issues.

Environmental Abstracts, Environment Information Center, Inc., 48 W. 38th St., New York, NY 10018. Compilation of environmental abstracts; basic bibliographic tool. Too expensive for individual subscription but should be available in your library.

*Environmental Action, 1525 New Hampshire Ave., N.W., Washington, DC 20036. Political orientation. Excellent coverage of environmental issues from legal, political, and social action viewpoints.

Environmental Ethics, Department of Philosophy, University of Georgia, Athens, GA 30602. Major journal in the field.

*The Environmental Professional, Editorial Office, Department of Geography, University of Iowa, Iowa City, IA 52242. Excellent discussion of environmental issues.

*Environmental Quality, Council on Environmental Quality, 722 Jackson Place, N.W., Washington, DC 20006. Annual report on environmental problems and progress in environmental protection and improvement.

Environmental Science & Technology, American Chemical Society, 1155 16th St., N.W., Washington, DC 20036. Emphasis on water, air, and solid waste chemistry. Basic reference on current technological developments.

*EPA Journal, Environmental Protection Agency. Order from Government Printing Office, Washington, DC 20402. Broad coverage of environmental issues and updates on EPA activities.

Family Planning Perspectives, Planned Parenthood-World Population, Editorial Offices, 666 Fifth Ave., New York, NY 10019. Excellent coverage of population issues and latest information on birth control methods.

FDA Consumer, U.S. Department of Health and Human Services, Public Health Service, 5600 Fishers Lane, Rockville, MD 20857. Useful source of information on health issues and food additives.

*The Futurist, World Future Society, P.O. Box 19285, Twentieth Street Station, Washington, DC 20036. Covers wide range of societal problems, including environmental, population, and food issues. A fascinating and readable journal.

Impact of Science on Society, UNESCO, 317 East 34th St., New York, NY 10016. Essays on the social consequences of science and technology.

Journal of the Air Pollution Control Association, 4400 Fifth Ave., Pittsburgh, PA 15213. Technical research articles.

Journal of the American Public Health Association, 1015 18th St., N.W., Washington, DC 20036. Some coverage of environmental health issues.

Journal of Environmental Education, Heldref Publications, 4000 Albemarle St., N.W., Suite 504, Washington, DC 20016. Good for teachers.

Journal of Environmental Health, National Environmental Health Association, 1600 Pennsylvania Ave., Denver, CO 80203. Good coverage of technical research.

Journal of the Water Pollution Control Federation, 2626 Pennsylvania Ave., N.W., Washington, DC 20037. Technical research articles.

Journal of Wildlife Management, Wildlife Society, Suite 611, 7101 Wisconsin Ave., N.W., Washington, DC 20014. Good coverage of basic issues and information.

*Living Wilderness, Wilderness Society, 1901 Pennsylvania Ave., N.W., Washington, DC 20006. Strong statement of "wild areas" viewpoint.

Monthly Energy Review, National Energy Information Center, Energy Information Administration, Forrestal Building, Room 1F-048, 1000 Independence Ave., S.W., Washington, DC 20585. Useful monthly summaries of U.S. energy production and consumption.

*Mother Earth News, P.O. Box 70, Hendersonville, NC 28739. Superb articles on organic farming, alternative energy systems, and alternative lifestyles.

*National Parks and Conservation Magazine, National Parks and Conservation Association, 1701 18th St., N.W., Washington, DC 20009. Good coverage of parks and wildlife issues.

*National Wildlife, National Wildlife Federation, 8925 Leesburg Pike, Vienna, VA 22180. Good summaries of issues with wildlife emphasis. Action oriented, with a "Washington report."

Natural History, American Museum of Natural History, Central Park West at 79th St., New York, NY 10024. Popular; wide school and library circulation. Regularly concerned with environment.

Nature, 711 National Press Building, Washington, DC 20045. British equivalent to Science; enjoys outstanding reputation.

New Scientist, 128 Long Acre, London, WC 2, England. Excellent general science journal with extensive coverage of environmental issues.

*Not Man Apart, Friends of the Earth, 1245 Spear St., San Francisco, CA 94105. Excellent capsule summaries and a few in-depth articles on national and international environmental issues.

Organic Gardening & Farming Magazine, Rodale Press, Inc., 33 E. Minor St., Emmaus, PA 18049. The best guide to organic gardening.

Pollution Abstracts, Data Courier, Inc., 620 S. 5th St., Louisville, KY 40202. Basic bibliographic tool. Too expensive for individual subscription but should be available in your library.

Population and Vital Statistics Report, UN Publications Sales Section, New York, NY 10017. Latest world figures.

*Population Bulletin, Population Reference Bureau, 2213 M St., N.W., Washington, DC 20037. Nontechnical articles on population issues. Highly recommended.

Population Bulletin, UN Publications Sales Section, New York, NY 10017. Statistical summaries. English and French editions.

Population Reports, Population Information Program, Johns Hopkins University, Hampton House, 624 N. Broadway, Baltimore, MD 21205. Useful information on population issues and birth control.

*Practical Homeowner, Rodale Press, Inc., 33 E. Minor St., Emmaus, PA 18049. Excellent nontechnical articles for homeowners on energy conservation and alternative energy systems.

PV News, PV Energy Systems, 2401 Childs Lane, Alexandria, VA 22308. Monthly newsletter summarizing developments in solar photovoltaic cell technology.

Renewable Energy News, Solar Vision, Inc., 7 Church Hill, Harrisville, NH 03450. Useful summary of latest technological and political developments.

Resource Recycling, Resource Recycling, P.O. Box 10540, Portland, OR 97210. Useful summaries of ways consumers can profit from recycling, reuse, and waste reduction.

Resources, Resources for the Future, Inc., 1755 Massachusetts Ave., N.W., Washington, DC 20036. Free on request; summarizes information and research on natural resources.

Science, American Association for the Advancement of Science, 1515 Massachusetts Ave., N.W., Washington, DC 20036. Useful source of information. Formerly an excellent source of key environmental articles, but under new editorship a technical research journal with greatly decreased coverage of environmental and interdisciplinary issues.

Science News, Science Service, Inc., 1719 N St., N.W., Washington, DC 20036. Good popular summaries of scientific developments, including environmental topics.

Scientific American, 415 Madison Ave., New York, NY 10017. Outstanding journal for the intelligent citizen who wants to keep up with science. Many general articles on environment and ecology.

Sierra, 530 Bush St., San Francisco, CA 94108. Excellent coverage of a wide range of environmental problems and of citizen action. Beautiful photographs.

Solar Age, Solar Vision, Inc., 7 Church Hill, Harrisville, NH 03450. Summary of advances in solar technology.

State of the World, Worldwatch Institute, 1776 Massachusetts Ave., N.W., Washington, DC 20036. Superb annual summary of environment and resource issues.

Statistical Yearbook, Department of International Economic and Social Affairs, Statistical Office, United Nations Publishing Service, United Nations, NY 10017. Useful annual summary of data on population, food production, resource production and consumption, energy, housing, and forestry.

Sun Times, Solar Lobby, Suite 510, 1001 Connecticut Ave., N.W., Washington, DC 20036. Quarterly newsletter summarizing political developments related to alternative energy options.

Technology Review, Room E219-430, Massachusetts Institute of Technology, Cambridge, MA 02139. Not specialized or always technical, but addressed to a sophisticated audience. Devotes more than half its pages to environment-related material; strong on issues of science policy.

Transition, Laurence G. Wolf, ed., Department of Geography, University of Cincinnati, Cincinnati, OH 45221. Quarterly journal of the Socially and Ecologically Responsible Geographers.

UNESCO Courier, UNESCO Publications Center, 317 E. 34th St., New York, NY 10016. A magazine for the general reader; frequently attentive to environmental issues.

World Development Report, World Bank, Publications Department, 1818 H St., N.W., Washington, DC 20433. Useful annual summary.

World Resources, World Resources Institute, 1735 New York Ave., N.W., Washington, DC 20006. Superb annual summary of environment and resource problems published jointly by the World Resources Institute and the International Institute for Environment and Development.

Worldwatch Papers, Worldwatch Institute, 1776 Massachusetts Ave., N.W., Washington, DC 20036. A series of reports designed to serve as an early warning system on major environmental problems. Worldwatch also publishes an annual *State of the World* in book form. Highly recommended.

Yearbook of World Energy Statistics, Department of International Economic and Social Affairs, Statistical Office, United Nations Publishing Service, United Nations, NY 10017. Useful annual summary of data on worldwide energy production.

ENVIRONMENTAL AND RESOURCE ORGANIZATIONS

For a more detailed list of national, state, and local organizations, see *Conservation Directory*, published annually by the National Wildlife Federation, 1412 16th St., N.W., Washington, DC 20036.

Air Pollution Control Association, P.O. Box 2861, Pittsburgh, PA 15230. Education on air pollution and its control. Publishes *Journal of the Air Pollution Control Association*.

Alliance for Environmental Education, Inc., 1619 Massachusetts Ave., N.W., Washington, DC 20036. Works to further environmental education activities at all levels.

American Association for World Health, 515 22nd St., N.W., Washington, DC 20037. Provides general information on national health problems and publishes a quarterly newsletter.

American Fisheries Society, 5410 Grosvenor Lane, Bethesda, MD 20014. Professional society to promote conservation of fisheries.

American Forestry Association, 1319 18th St., N.W., Washington, DC 20036. Focuses on forest and soil conservation, although active in air and water pollution concerns. Doesn't lobby directly, but pushes indirectly for preserving and creating parklands. Publishes *American Forests*.

American Geographical Society, Suite 1501, 25 W. 39th St., New York, NY 10018. Sponsors research and publishes scientific and popular books and periodicals.

American Institute of Biological Sciences, Inc., 1401 Wilson Blvd., Arlington, VA 22209. Professional organization. Publishes *BioScience*.

American Society for Environmental Education, P.O. Box 800, Hanover, NH 03755. Education of teachers and the public concerning environmental issues. Publishes *Environmental Education Report*.

American Water Resources Association, 5410 Grosvenor Lane, Suite 220, Bethesda, MD 20014. Publishes *Water Resources Bulletin*.

Animal Protection Institute of America, P.O. Box 22505, Sacramento, CA 95822. Provides education and information on the humane treatment of animals.

Association of American Geographers, 1710 16th St., N.W., Washington, DC 20009. Professional association.

Center for Action on Endangered Species, 175 West Main St., Ayer, MA 01432. Develops educational materials, including teaching units, on endangered wildlife.

Center for Environmental Education, Inc., 625 Ninth St., N.W., Washington, DC 20001. Dedicated to encouraging informed citizen involvement. Also sponsors the Whale Protection Fund.

Center for Science in the Public Interest, 1755 S St., N.W., Washington, DC 20009. Group of public interest scientists concerned especially with energy, environmental, food, and nutrition issues. Publishes many informative reports.

Center for the Study of Responsive Law, P.O. Box 19367, Washington, DC 20036. A research organization working in the public interest; areas investigated include problems of the environment. Publishes research reports from the Ralph Nader study groups.

Citizens' Clearinghouse for Hazardous Waste, P.O. Box 7097, Arlington, VA 22207. Research, information, and organizing on this issue.

Citizens Energy Project, 1110 Sixth St., N.W., Suite 300, Washington, DC 20001. Emphasis on research and education, alternative energy, nuclear power, and appropriate technology.

Clean Water Action Project, 1341 G St., N.W., Suite 204, Washington, DC 20005. National citizen action organization lobbying for strict water pollution control and safe drinking water.

Common Cause, 2030 M St., N.W., Washington, DC 20036. Citizens' lobby with over 100,000 members, who work hard on a broad range of political issues including nuclear freeze, arms control, and campaign financing reform.

Congress Watch, 215 Pennsylvania Ave., S.E., Washington, DC 20003. Lobbying group concerned with corporate responsibility, nuclear energy, and campaign financing.

Conservation Foundation, 1717 Massachusetts Ave., N.W., Washington, DC 20036. Active in conservation, analysis of the ecological impact of foreign aid, and conservation education in the schools. Publishes *Conservation Foundation Letter.*

Cousteau Society, 777 Third Avenue, New York, NY 10017. Research and education with emphasis on preservation of the world's oceans.

Critical Mass Energy Project, P.O. Box 1538, Washington, DC 20003. Sponsors national conferences on issues such as nuclear energy, alternative energy sources, and legislative and citizen activities; publishes monthly newspaper promoting safe and efficient energy.

Defenders of Wildlife, 1244 19th St., N.W., Washington, DC 20036. Works for preservation of all forms of wildlife. Research, education, lobbying.

Ducks Unlimited, P.O. Box 66300, Chicago, IL 60666. Has acquired or protected over 2 million acres of vital breeding habitats for migrating waterfowl.

Ecological Society of America, Dr. Paul G. Risser, Secretary, Department of Botany and Microbiology, University of Oklahoma, Norman, OK 73069. Professional society.

Energy Conservation Coalition, 1725 Eye St., N.W., Suite 610, Washington, DC 20036. Education and lobbying.

Environmental Action Foundation, Inc., 724 DuPont Circle Building, Washington, DC 20036. Research and education on a broad range of environmental issues.

Environmental Action, Inc., 1525 New Hampshire Ave., N.W., Washington, DC 20036. Nonprofit organization that evolved from Earth Day 1970. Lobbies for effective legislation for environmental reform. Publishes *Environmental Action.*

Environmental Defense Fund, Inc., 444 Park Ave. South, New York, NY 10016. A public benefit organization composed of scientists, lawyers, and laypersons; works to link law and science in defense of the environment before courts and regulatory agencies. Other offices at 1525 18th St., N.W., Washington, DC 20036; 2606 Dwight Way, Berkeley, CA 97404.

Environmental Fund, Inc., 1302 18th St., N.W., Washington, DC 20036. Works to educate the public about the need for population control.

Environmental Law Institute, 1346 Connecticut Ave., N.W., Suite 600, Washington, DC 20036. Conducts a wide program of research and education in environmental law.

Environmental Policy Center, 317 Pennsylvania Ave., S.E., Washington, DC 20003. Research, education, and lobbying on a range of environmental issues.

Food and Agriculture Organization of the United Nations, Via delle Terme di Caracalla, Rome 00100 Italy. Conducts surveys and research and provides information on world food problems and nutrition.

Friends of the Earth, Inc., 1045 Sansome St., San Francisco, CA 94111. Education, lobbying, and litigation on a variety of environmental issues. Its political arm, the League of Conservation Voters, raises funds for congressional candidates with sound environmental records.

Fund for Animals, Inc., 1765 P St., N.W., Washington, DC 20036, and 140 W. 57th St., New York, NY 10019. Education, lobbying, and litigation on animal rights, endangered species, and wildlife conservation.

Fund for Renewable Energy and the Environment (FREE), 1001 Connecticut Ave., N.W., Suite 638, Washington, DC 20036. Offers technical assistance to grass-roots organizers, conducts policy research, and provides educational materials on solar energy and key environmental problems.

Greenpeace, USA, Inc., 2007 R St., N.W., Washington, DC 20009. Lobbying, organizing, and direct action with emphasis on whales, seals, nuclear energy, and toxic wastes.

Institute for Local Self-Reliance, 1717 18th St., N.W., Washington, DC 20009. Research and education; promotion of appropriate technology for communities.

International Association of Fish and Wildlife Agencies, 1412 16th St., N.W., Washington, DC 20003. Promotes conservation, protection, and management of wildlife and related natural resources.

International Planned Parenthood Federation, 105 Madison Ave., 7th Floor, New York, NY 10016. Provides information, education, and services; attempts to persuade governments to establish family planning programs.

International Union for the Conservation of Nature and Natural Resources (IUCN), Av. du Mont Blanc, CH-1196 Gland, Switzerland (022.64 71 81). Promotes scientifically based action for the conservation of wildlife.

Izaak Walton League of America, 1800 North Kent St., Suite 806, Arlington, VA 22209. Research and education on wildlife conservation, renewable natural resources, and water quality.

John Muir Institute for Environmental Studies, 743 Wilson St., Napa, CA 94558. Research and education on a wide range of environmental issues.

Keep America Beautiful, 99 Park Ave., New York, NY 10016. Education to combat litter as a necessary first step toward solving broader environmental problems and a program to increase knowledge of solid waste disposal techniques. Provides assistance, materials, and advice for grass-roots efforts by some 7,000 comunity groups and 32 statewide affiliates.

League of Conservation Voters, 317 Pennsylvania Ave., S.E., Washington, DC 20003. Political action and national campaign committee working to promote the election of legislators pledging to seek a healthy environment. Publicizes roll call votes on environmental issues. Political arm of Friends of the Earth.

League of Women Voters of the United States, 1730 M St., N.W., Washington, DC 20036. Lobbies for a wide range of environmental issues; local and state leagues work for political responsibility through an informed and active citizenry. Played a central role in bringing water pollution to the public's attention. Research and education by the League of Women Voters Education Fund (same address).

National Audubon Society, 645 Pennsylvania Ave., S.E., Washington, DC 20003; 950 Third Ave., New York, NY 10022. Research and lobbying on a wide range of environmental issues. Operates 40 wildlife sanctuaries across the country and provides a wide variety of ecology education services. Publishes *Audubon* and *Audubon Wildlife Report.*

National Parks and Conservation Association, 1701 18th Street, N.W., Washington, DC 20009. Research and education. Urges acquisition and protection of public parklands. Now active in general environmental issues, such as resource management, pesticides, and pollution. Publishes *National Parks and Conservation Magazine.*

National Recreation and Park Association, 3101 Park Center Drive, 12th Floor, Alexandria, VA 22302. Promotes recreation and park conservation and development.

National Science Teachers' Association, 1742 Connecticut Ave., N.W., Washington, DC 20009. Educational affiliate of the American Association for the Advancement of Science. Dedicated to improving the teaching of science (including environmental issues) from preschool through college.

National Solid Waste Management Association, 1730 Rhode Island Ave., N.W., Suite 100, Washington, DC 20036. Compiles statistics and provides information on waste management and resource recovery.

National Wildlife Federation, 1412 16th St., N.W., Washington, DC 20036. Research and education. Encourages citizen and governmental action for conservation. Publishes *National Wildlife* and a comprehensive annual conservation directory.

Natural Resources Defense Council, 122 East 42nd St., New York, NY 10017; 1725 Eye St., N.W., Suite 600, Washington, DC 20006. Research, organizing, and litigation on a wide range of environmental issues.

The Nature Conservancy, 1800 N. Kent St., Suite 800, Arlington, VA 22209. Research and preservation of natural areas. Often acquires endangered property and holds it for later resale to public agencies.

New Alchemy Institute, 237 Hatchville Road, East Falmouth, MA 02536. Research and education with emphasis on self-sufficient agriculture, aquaculture, passive solar energy, wind power, and energy conservation.

The Oceanic Society, Executive Offices, Stamford Marine Center, Magee Ave., Stamford, CT 06902. Promotes protection and sensible management of ocean and coastal resources.

Physicians for Social Responsibility, 639 Massachusetts Ave., Cambridge, MA 02139. Research and education on the health effects of nuclear weapons and nuclear war.

Planet/Drum Foundation, P.O. Box 31251, San Francisco, CA 94131. Research and education with emphasis on wise use of land and watersheds.

Planned Parenthood Federation of America, 810 Seventh Ave., New York, NY 10019. Education and research on fertility control and family planning.

Population Reference Bureau, 2213 M Street, N.W., Washington, DC 20037. Clearinghouse for data concerning the effects of worldwide population growth. Publishes *Population Bulletin.*

The Public Citizen, 1346 Connecticut Ave., N.W., Washington, DC 20036. Ralph Nader's political action and lobbying organization.

Public Interest Research Group, P.O. Box 19312, Washington, DC 20036. Organizes research and education in environmental issues.

RAIN, 2270 N.W. Irving, Portland, OR 97210. Research and education on appropriate technology and community and regional self-reliance.

Resources for the Future, 1775 Massachusetts Ave., N.W., Washington, DC 20036. Research and education in the development, conservation, and use of natural resources and in the quality of the environment. Publishes *Resources.*

Scientists' Institute for Public Information, 355 Lexington Ave., New York, NY 10017; 1256 National Press Building, Washington, DC 20045. Utilizes scientists of all disciplines in public information programs dealing with many social issues; serves as national coordinating body for local scientific information committees.

Sierra Club, 530 Bush St., San Francisco, CA 94108; 330 Pennsylvania Avenue, S.E., Washington, DC 20003. Lobbying and education on a wide range of environmental issues. Provides films, manuals, exhibits, and speakers; publishes books and a monthly bulletin.

Smithsonian Institution, 1000 Jefferson Drive, S.W., Washington, DC 20560. Promotes environmental education through a wide variety of programs.

Soil Conservation Society of America, 7515 N.E. Ankeny Road, Ankeny, IA 50021. Professional society dedicated to soil and water conservation.

Student Conservation Association, Inc., P.O. Box 550, Charlestown, NH 03603. Promotes and coordinates work and learning opportunities during summer vacations for students at the high school, college, and graduate levels.

Union of Concerned Scientists, 1346 Connecticut Ave., N.W., Suite 1101, Washington, DC 20036; 1384 Massachusetts Ave., N.W., Cambridge, MA 02238. Lobbying, research, education, and litigation with emphasis on nuclear power safety and arms control.

Water Pollution Control Federation, 2626 Pennsylvania Ave., N.W., Washington, DC 20037. Professional society devoted to research and dissemination of technical information.

The Wilderness Society, 1901 Pennsylvania Ave., N.W., Washington, DC 20006. Research, education, and lobbying with emphasis on wilderness, parks, and public lands. Publishes *Living Wilderness.*

Wildlife Management Institute, 1000 Vermont Ave., N.W., 709 Wire Building, Washington, DC 20005. Promotes better use of wildlife and related natural resources.

Wildlife Society, Suite 611, 7101 Wisconsin Ave., N.W., Washington, DC 20014. Major concern is wildlife preservation, but its base is broadening.

World Environment Center, Inc., 605 Third Ave., New York, NY 10158. Information and education with emphasis on international environment and development issues.

World Resources Institute, 1735 New York Ave., N.W., Washington, DC 20006. Research center providing analysis and information on environment and resource policy options. Publishes numerous reports including *World Resources,* an annual summary of resource and environment problems.

Worldwatch Institute, 1776 Massachusetts Ave., N.W., Suite 701, Washington, DC 20036. Research, early warning, and education on major environmental problems. Publishes several very informative and well-researched *Worldwatch Papers* and *State of the World* each year on selected environmental issues.

World Wildlife Fund, 1601 Connecticut Ave., N.W., Washington, DC 20009. Research and education on endangered species and acquisition of wildlife habitats.

Zero Population Growth, 1346 Connecticut Ave., N.W., Washington, DC 20036. Education and lobbying on population and immigration issues.

ADDRESSES OF FEDERAL AND INTERNATIONAL AGENCIES

Bureau of the Census, U.S. Department of Commerce, Washington, DC 22161

Bureau of Land Management, Interior Building, Room 5660, Washington, DC 20240

Bureau of Mines, 2401 E St., N.W., Washington, DC 20241

Bureau of Reclamation, Interior Building, Room 7654, Washington, DC 20240

Congressional Research Service, 101 Independence Ave., S.W., Washington, DC 20540

Council on Environmental Quality, 722 Jackson Place, N.W., Washington, DC 20006

Department of Agriculture, 14th St. and Jefferson Dr., S.W., Washington, DC 20250

Department of Commerce, 14th St. between Constitution Ave. and E St., N.W., Washington, DC 20230

Department of Energy, Forrestal Building, 1000 Independence Ave., S.W., Washington, DC 20585

Department of Health and Human Services, 200 Independence Ave., S.W., Washington, DC 20201

Department of Housing and Urban Development, 451 Seventh St., S.W., Washington, DC 20410

Department of the Interior, 18th and C Sts., N.W., Washington, DC 20240

Department of Transportation, 400 Seventh St., S.W., Washington, DC 20590

Environmental Protection Agency, 401 M St., S.W., Washington, DC 20460

Federal Energy Regulatory Commission, 825 N. Capitol St., N.E., Washington, DC 20426

Fish and Wildlife Service, Department of the Interior, 18th and C Sts., N.W., Washington, DC 20240

Food and Drug Administration, Department of Health and Human Services, 5600 Fishers Lane, Rockville, MD 20852

Forest Service, P.O. Box 2417, Washington, DC 20013

Geological Survey, 12201 Sunrise Valley Drive, Reston, VA 22092

Government Printing Office, Washington, DC 20402

National Academy of Sciences, 2101 Constitution Ave., N.W., Washington, DC 20418

National Center for Appropriate Technology, 3040 Continental Dr., Butte, MT 59701

National Oceanic and Atmospheric Administration, Rockville, MD 20852

National Park Service, Department of the Interior, 18th and C Sts., N.W., Washington, DC 20240

National Science Foundation, 1800 G St., N.W., Washington, DC 20550

National Solar Heating and Cooling Information Center, P.O. Box 1607, Rockville, MD 20850

National Technical Information Service, Department of Commerce, 5285 Port Royal Rd., Springfield, VA 22161

Nuclear Regulatory Commission, 1717 H St., N.W., Washington, DC 20555

Occupational Safety and Health Administration, Department of Labor, 200 Constitution Ave., N.W., Washington, DC 20210

Office of Coastal Zone Management, 3300 Whitehaven St., N.W., Washington, DC 20235

Office of Technology Assessment, U.S. Congress, 600 Pennsylvania Ave., S.E., Washington, DC 20510

Soil Conservation Service, P.O. Box 2890, Washington, DC 20013

Solar Energy Research Institute, 6536 Cole Blvd., Golden, CO 80401

Surface Mining Reclamation and Enforcement, U.S. Department of Interior, 1951 Constitution Ave., N.W., Washington, DC 20240

United Nations Environment Program, New York Liaison Office, Room DC2-0816, United Nations, New York, NY 10017

U.S. International Development Cooperation Agency, 320 21st St., N.W., Washington, DC 20523

2

Units of Measurement

Length
  Metric
    1 kilometer (km) = 1,000 meters (m)
    1 meter (m) = 100 centimeters (cm)
    1 meter (m) = 1,000 millimeters (mm)
    1 centimeter (cm) = 0.01 meter (m)
    1 millimeter (mm) = 0.001 meter (m)
  English
    1 foot (ft) = 12 inches (in)
    1 yard (yd) = 3 feet (ft)
    1 mile (mi) = 5,280 feet (ft)
  Metric-English
    1 kilometer (km) = 0.621 mile (mi)
    1 meter (m) = 39.4 inches (in)
    1 inch (in) = 2.54 centimeters (cm)
    1 foot (ft) = 0.305 meter (m)
    1 yard (yd) = 0.914 meter (m)
    1 nautical mile = 1.85 kilometers (km)

Area
  Metric
    1 square kilometer (km^2) = 1,000,000 square meters (m^2)
    1 square meter (m^2) = 1,000,000 square millimeters (mm^2)
    1 hectare (ha) = 10,000 square meters (m^2)
    1 hectare (ha) = 0.01 square kilometer (km^2)
  English
    1 square foot (ft^2) = 144 square inches (in^2)
    1 square yard (yd^2) = 9 square feet (ft^2)
    1 square mile (mi^2) = 27,880,000 square feet (ft^2)
    1 acre (ac) = 43,560 square feet (ft^2)
  Metric-English
    1 hectare (ha) = 2.471 acres (ac)
    1 square kilometer (km^2) = 0.386 square mile (mi^2)
    1 square meter (m^2) = 1.196 square yards (yd^2)
    1 square meter (m^2) = 10.76 square feet (ft^2)
    1 square centimeter (cm^2) = 0.155 square inch (in^2)

Volume
  Metric
    1 cubic kilometer (km^3) = 1,000,000 cubic meters (m^3)
    1 cubic meter (m^3) = 1,000,000 cubic centimeters (cm^3)
    1 liter (L) = 1,000 milliliters (mL) = 1,000 cubic centimeters (cm^3)
    1 milliliter (mL) = 0.001 liter (L)
    1 milliliter (mL) = 1 cubic centimeter (cm^3)
  English
    1 gallon (gal) = 4 quarts (qt)
    1 quart (qt) = 2 pints (pt)
  Metric-English
    1 liter (L) = 0.265 gallon (gal)
    1 liter (L) = 1.06 quarts (qt)
    1 liter (L) = 0.0353 cubic foot (ft^3)
    1 cubic meter (m^3) = 35.3 cubic feet (ft^3)
    1 cubic meter (m^3) = 1.307 cubic yard (yd^3)
    1 cubic kilometer (km^3) = 0.24 cubic mile (mi^3)

    1 barrel (bbl) = 159 liters (L)
    1 barrel (bbl) = 42 U.S. gallons (gal)

Mass
  Metric
    1 kilogram (kg) = 1,000 grams (g)
    1 gram (g) = 1,000 milligrams (mg)
    1 gram (g) = 1,000,000 micrograms (µg)
    1 milligram (mg) = 0.001 gram (g)
    1 microgram (µg) = 0.000001 gram (g)
    1 metric ton (mt) = 1,000 kilograms (kg)
  English
    1 ton (t) = 2,000 pounds (lb)
    1 pound (lb) = 16 ounces (oz)
  Metric-English
    1 metric ton = 2,200 pounds (lb) = 1.1 tons
    1 kilogram (kg) = 2.20 pounds (lb)
    1 pound (lb) = 454 grams (g)
    1 gram (g) = 0.035 ounce (oz)

Energy and Power
  Metric
    1 kilojoule (kJ) = 1,000 joules (J)
    1 kilocalorie (kcal) = 1,000 calories (cal)
    1 calorie (cal) = 4.184 joules (J)
  Metric-English
    1 kilojoule (kJ) = 0.949 British thermal unit (Btu)
    1 kilojoule (kJ) = 0.000278 kilowatt-hour (kW-h)
    1 kilocalorie (kcal) = 3.97 British thermal units (Btu)
    1 kilocalorie (kcal) = 0.00116 kilowatt-hour (kW-h)
    1 kilowatt-hour (kW-h) = 860 kilocalories (kcal)
    1 kilowatt-hour (kW-h) = 3,400 British thermal units (Btu)
    1 quad (Q) = 1,050,000,000,000,000 kilojoules (kJ)
    1 quad (Q) = 2,930,000,000,000 kilowatt-hours (kW-h)
  Approximate crude oil equivalent
    1 barrel (bbl) crude oil = 6,000,000 kilojoules (kJ)
    1 barrel (bbl) crude oil = 2,000,000 kilocalories (kcal)
    1 barrel (bbl) crude oil = 6,000,000 British thermal units (Btu)
    1 barrel (bbl) crude oil = 2,000 kilowatt-hours (kW-h)
  Approximate natural gas equivalent
    1 cubic foot (ft^3) natural gas = 1,000 kilojoules (kJ)
    1 cubic foot (ft^3) natural gas = 260 kilocalories (kcal)
    1 cubic foot (ft^3) natural gas = 1,000 British thermal units (Btu)
    1 cubic foot (ft^3) natural gas = 0.3 kilowatt-hour (kW-h)
  Approximate hard coal equivalent
    1 ton (t) coal = 20,000,000 kilojoules (kJ)
    1 ton (t) coal = 6,000,000 kilocalories (kcal)
    1 ton (t) coal = 20,000,000 British thermal units (Btu)
    1 ton (t) coal = 6,000 kilowatt-hours (kW-h)

Temperature Conversions

Fahrenheit (°F) to Celsius (°C): $°C = \dfrac{(°F - 32.0)}{1.80}$

Celsius (°C) to Fahrenheit (°F): $°F = (°C \times 1.80) + 32.0$

3

Major U.S. Environmental Legislation

General

National Environmental Policy Act of 1969 (NEPA)

Energy

National Energy Acts of 1978 and 1980

Water Quality

Federal Water Pollution Control Act of 1972

Ocean Dumping Act of 1972

Safe Drinking Water Act of 1974, 1984

Toxic Substances Control Act of 1976

Clean Water Act of 1977, 1987

Air Quality

Clean Air Act of 1965, 1970, 1977

Noise Control

Noise Control Act of 1972

Quiet Communities Act of 1978

Resources and Solid Waste Management

Solid Waste Disposal Act of 1965

Resources Recovery Act of 1970

Toxic Substances

Toxic Substances Control Act of 1976

Resource Conservation and Recovery Act of 1976

Comprehensive Environmental Response, Compensation, and Liability (Superfund) Act of 1980, 1986

Wildlife

Species Conservation Act of 1966

Federal Insecticide, Fungicide, and Rodenticide Control Act of 1972

Marine Protection, Research, and Sanctuaries Act of 1972

Endangered Species Act of 1973

Land Use

Multiple Use Sustained Yield Act of 1960

Wilderness Act of 1964

Wild and Scenic River Act of 1968

National Coastal Zone Management Acts of 1972 and 1980

Federal Land Policy Management Act of 1976

Forest Reserves Management Act of 1974, 1976

National Forest Management Act of 1976

Surface Mining Control and Reclamation Act of 1977

Endangered American Wilderness Act of 1978

Alaskan National Interest Lands Conservation Act of 1980

4

Average U.S. Water Use

Use or Product	Average Amount Withdrawn		Use or Product	Average Amount Withdrawn	
	Liters	Gallons		Liters	Gallons
Total Use	7,402	1,953			
Home Use					
Total per person (per day)	341	90	454 grams (1 pound) of corn	645	170
Drinking water (per day)	2	0.5	454 grams (1 pound) of sugar from sugarbeets	872	230
Shaving, water running (per minute)	8	2	454 grams (1 pound) of rice	2,122	560
Shower (per minute)	19	5	454 grams (1 pound) of grain-fed beef	3,032	800
Toilet (per flush)	23	6	454 grams (1 pound) of cotton	7,732	2,040
Cooking (per day)	30	8	**Industrial and Commercial**		
Washing dishes, water running (per meal)	38	10	Total per person (per day)	4,518	1,192
Watering lawn or garden (per minute)	38	10	Cooling water for electric power plants per person (per day)	3,707	978
Automatic dishwasher (per load)	60	16	Industrial mining and manufacturing per person (per day)	695	183
Bath	135	36	Refine 3.8 liters (1 gallon) of gasoline from crude oil	38	10
Washing machine (per load)	230	60	454 grams (1 pound) of steel	133	35
Leaky toilet (per day)	90–455	24–120	Refine 3.8 liters (1 gallon) of synthetic fuel from coal	1,000	265
Leaky faucet (per day)	180–910	48–240	One Sunday newspaper	1,060	280
Agricultural Use (irrigation)			454 grams (1 pound) of synthetic rubber	1,140	300
Total per person (per day)	2,543	671	454 grams (1 pound) of aluminum	3,790	1,000
One egg	150	40	One automobile	379,000	100,000
454 grams (1 pound) flour	284	75			
Orange	380	100			
Glass of milk	380	100			
Loaf of bread	570	150			

Source: U.S. Geological Survey, *Estimated Use of Water in the United States in 1980,* 1984.

5

National Ambient Air Quality Standards
for the United States

Pollutant	Averaging Time	Primary Standard Levels [micrograms (μg) or milligrams (mg) per cubic meter (m³) and parts per million (ppm)]	Secondary Standard Levels [micrograms (μg) or milligrams (mg) per cubic meter (m³) and parts per million (ppm)]
SPM	Annual (geometric mean)	75 μg/m³	60 μg/m³
	24 hours*	260 μg/m³	150 μg/m³
Sulfur dioxide	Annual (arithmetic mean)	80 μg/m³ (0.03 ppm)	—
	24 hours*	365 μg/m³ (0.14 ppm)	—
	3 hours*		1300 μg/m³ (0.5 ppm)
Carbon monoxide	8 hours*	10,000 μg/m³ (9 ppm)	same as primary
	1 hour	40 mg/m³ (35 ppm)*	same as primary
Nitrogen dioxide	Annual (arithmetic mean)	100 μg/m³ (0.05 ppm)	same as primary
Ozone	1 hour	235 μg/m³ (0.12 ppm)	same as primary
Volatile organic compounds[†]	3 hours (6 to 9 A.M.)	160 μg/m³ (0.24 ppm)	160 μg/m³ (0.24 ppm)
Lead	3 months	1.5 μg/m³	same as primary

Source: Environmental Protection Agency.
*Not to be exceeded more than once a year.
[†]A non-health-related standard used as a guide for ozone control. Does not include methane.

Further Readings

Chapter 1 Population, Resources, Environmental Degradation, and Pollution

Brown, Lester R., et al. Annual. *State of the World*. New York: W. W. Norton. Superb overview published annually since 1984 by the Worldwatch Institute, Washington, D.C.

Cahn, Robert, ed. 1985. *An Environmental Agenda for the Future*. Covelo, Calif.: Island Press. Outline of action recommended by the chief executive officers of the ten principal environmental organizations in the United States.

Callahan, Daniel, ed. 1971. *The American Population Debate*. Garden City, N.Y.: Doubleday. Superb collection of articles on whether the United States is overpopulated.

Commoner, Barry. 1971. *The Closing Circle: Nature, Man and Technology*. New York: Alfred A. Knopf. Well-written presentation of Commoner's view that the misuse of technology is the cause of most pollution. See the critique of this view by Holdren and Ehrlich (1974).

Conservation Foundation. 1984. *State of the Environment: An Assessment at Mid-Decade*. Washington, D.C.: Conservation Foundation. Excellent summary. Describes progress in environmental improvement in the United States and documents attempts of the Reagan administration to undo much of that progress.

Council on Environmental Quality. *Annual Report*. Washington, D.C.: Government Printing Office. Annual summaries since 1970 of environmental problems and progress. Useful source of information.

Council on Environmental Quality. 1981. *Environmental Trends*. Washington, D.C.: Government Printing Office. Excellent presentation of graphs and tables documenting trends in environmental problems in the United States and the world.

Council on Environmental Quality and U.S. Department of State. 1980. *The Global 2000 Report to the President*. 3 vols. Washington, D.C.: Government Printing Office.

Outstanding summary of global population, resource, environmental degradation, and pollution problems with projections to the year 2000.

Council on Environmental Quality and U.S. Department of State. 1981. *Global Future: Time to Act*. Washington, D.C.: Government Printing Office. Recommendations for action based on *The Global 2000 Report to the President*.

Dahlberg, Kenneth A., et al. 1985. *Environment and the Global Arena*. Durham, N.C.: Duke University Press. Superb overview of problems, policies, and possible environmental futures.

Durrell, Lee. 1986. *State of the Ark: Conservation in Action*. Garden City, N.Y.: Doubleday. Superb overview.

Eckholm, Erik P. 1982. *Down to Earth: Environment and Human Needs*. New York: W. W. Norton. Summary of global environmental problems and progress by an outstanding multidisciplinary thinker.

Editorial Research Reports. 1986. *Earth's Threatened Resources*. Washington, D.C.: Congressional Quarterly. Useful summaries of key environmental problems.

Fund for Renewable Energy and the Environment. 1987. *The State of the States*. Washington, D.C.: Fund for Renewable Energy and the Environment. Informative evaluation and ranking of environmental and energy programs in each state.

Goldfarb, Theodore D. 1983. *Taking Sides: Clashing Views on Environmental Issues*. Guilford, Conn.: Dushkin Publishing Group. Useful source of information.

Hardin, Garrett. 1968. "The Tragedy of the Commons." *Science*, vol. 162, 1243–1248. Classic environmental article describing how land and other resources are abused when they are shared by everyone.

Hardin, Garrett. 1985. *Filters Against Folly*. East Rutherford, N.J.: Viking. Thought-provoking series of essays by a prominent neo-Malthusian.

Holdren, John P., and Paul R. Ehrlich. 1974. "Human Population and the Global Envi-

ronment." *American Scientist*, vol. 62, 282–292. Excellent analysis of the relationships between population size, resource use, and harmful technology; an answer to Commoner's (1971) view that technology is the key factor in producing pollution. An environmental classic.

Kahn, Herman. 1982. *The Coming Boom: Economic, Political, and Social*. New York: Simon & Schuster. Predictions of a rosy future by a prominent cornucopian. Kahn, who died in 1983, considered population, resource, and pollution problems as solved or on the way to being solved through economic growth and technological advances.

Maurice, Charles, and Charles W. Smithson. 1984. *The Doomsday Myth*. Stanford, Calif.: Hoover Institution Press. Two cornucopian economists argue that there will be no resource shortages in the future as long as the free market is allowed to function.

Meadows, Donella H., et al. 1972. *The Limits to Growth*. New York: Universe Books. Controversial nontechnical summary of a computer model of the relationships among population, food, resource use, economic growth, and pollution (see Enrichment Study at the end of Chapter 8 for more details). An environmental classic.

Meadows, Donella, et al. 1982. *Groping in the Dark: The First Decade of Global Modeling*. New York: Wiley. Superb summary and evaluation of the successes and failures of various global models of the interactions among population, resource use, and pollution.

Myers, Norman, ed. 1984. *Gaia: An Atlas of Planet Management*. Garden City, N.Y.: Anchor Press/Doubleday. Outstanding overview of the planet's resources, environmental problems, and possible solutions. Excellent illustrations.

Organization for Economic Cooperation and Development (OECD). 1985. *The State of the Environment 1985*. Washington, D.C.: OECD. Excellent summary of data and case studies.

Pryde, Philip R. 1983. "The Decade of the Environment in the U.S.S.R." *Science*, vol.

220, 274–279. Excellent discussion of environmental degradation in the Soviet Union.

Ramade, François. 1984. *Ecology of Natural Resources*. New York: John Wiley. Good overview at a somewhat higher level than this textbook.

Repetto, Robert, ed. 1986. *The Global Possible: Resources, Development, and the New Century*. New Haven, Conn.: Yale University Press. Useful collection of articles outlining major environmental problems and possible solutions.

Schumacher, E. F. 1973. *Small Is Beautiful: Economics As If People Mattered*. New York: Harper & Row. Eloquent presentation of the need for appropriate technology. An environmental classic.

Simon, Julian L. 1981. *The Ultimate Resource*. Princeton, N.J.: Princeton University Press. Very good presentation of the cornucopian position. However, the author bases some of his conclusions on the false idea that energy can be recycled.

Simon, Julian L., and Herman Kahn, eds. 1984. *The Resourceful Earth: A Response to "Global 2000."* Useful collection of articles by a group of mostly cornucopian thinkers who argue that increased economic growth and technology can solve the world's population, resource, and pollution problems and that these problems were exaggerated in *The Global 2000 Report to the President* (1980).

Smith, Vaclav. 1984. *The Bad Earth*. Armonk, N.Y.: Sharpe. Useful description of environmental degradation and ecological mismanagement in China.

Southwick, Charles H., ed. 1985. *Global Ecology*. Sunderland, Mass.: Sinauer Associates. Useful collection of key articles.

Watt, Kenneth E. F. 1982. *Understanding the Environment*. Newton, Mass.: Allyn & Bacon. Outstanding high-level treatment of how population, resource use, pollution, technology, economics, politics, and ethics interact to cause or intensify environmental problems, usually in unpredictable ways.

Wattenberg, Ben J. 1984. *The Good News Is the Bad News Is Wrong*. New York: Simon & Schuster. Useful attack on gloom-and-doom pessimism by a cornucopian showing how, by most indicators, the average quality of life in the United States has improved since the 1950s.

World Resources Institute and International Institute for Environment and Development. Annual. *World Resources*. New York: Basic Books. Excellent annual report since 1986 that updates *The Global 2000 Report to the President* (1980).

Chapter 2 Human Impact on the Earth

Bennett, Charles F. 1975. *Man and Earth's Ecosystems*. New York: Wiley. Excellent survey of human impact on the earth with a geographic emphasis.

Bronowski, Jacob, Jr. 1974. *The Ascent of Man*. Boston: Little, Brown. Outstanding overview of human cultural change.

Brooks, Paul. 1980. *Speaking for Nature: How Literary Naturalists from Henry Thoreau to Rachel Carson Have Shaped America*. Boston: Houghton Mifflin. Excellent overview.

Carson, Rachel. 1962. *Silent Spring*. Boston: Houghton Mifflin. An environmental classic.

Carter, V. G., and T. Dale. 1974. *Topsoil and Civilization*. Norman: University of Oklahoma Press. Superb account of the impact of early societies on the soil.

Clawson, Marion. 1983. *The Federal Lands Revisited*. Washington, D.C.: Resources for the Future. Excellent survey of federal land use with suggestions for future policies.

Clepper, H. 1966. *Origins of American Conservation*. New York: Ronald Press. Excellent history of conservation.

Congressional Quarterly. 1983. *The Battle for Natural Resources*. Washington, D.C.: Congressional Quarterly, Inc. Excellent overview of the history of federal land use.

Conservation Foundation. 1982. *State of the Environment 1982*. Washington, D.C.: Conservation Foundation. Excellent summary of environmental problems with detailed analysis of the environmental policies of the Reagan administration.

Culhane, Paul J. 1981. *Public Land Politics: Interest Group Influences on the Forest Service and the Bureau of Land Management*. Washington, D.C.: Resources for the Future. Excellent in-depth study.

Ferguson, Denzel, and Nancy Ferguson. 1983. *Sacred Cows at the Public Trough*. Bend, Ore.: Maverick Publications. Excellent investigative reporting of environmental degradation of western public rangelands by the cattle industry.

Fox, Stephen. 1981. *John Muir and His Legacy: The American Conservation Movement*. Boston: Little, Brown. Superb overview.

Friends of the Earth et al. 1982. *Reagan and Environment*. San Francisco: Friends of the Earth. Excellent summary of administration environmental policies; compiled by ten environmental groups.

Graham, Frank. 1971. *Man's Dominion: The Story of Conservation in America*. New York: M. Evans. Outstanding history of conservation.

Hyams, Edward. 1976. *Soils and Civilization*. New York: Harper & Row. Excellent discussion of the impact of our species on the earth.

Lash, Jonathan, et al. 1984. *A Season of Spoils*. New York: Pantheon. Well-researched analysis of Ronald Reagan's environmental policies during most of his first term.

Lee, R. B., and I. DeVore, eds. 1968. *Man the Hunter*. Chicago: Aldine. Classic study of hunter-gatherer societies.

Leopold, Aldo. 1949. *A Sand County Almanac*. New York: Oxford University Press. An environmental classic describing Leopold's ecological land use ethic.

Livingston, John A. 1973. *One Cosmic Instant*. Boston: Houghton Mifflin. Highly readable account of human cultural evolution.

Marsh, George Perkins. 1864. *Man and Nature*. New York: Scribners. An environmental classic considered to be one of the greatest American works on the environment.

Moore, John A. 1985. "Science as a Way of Knowing—Human Ecology." *American Zoology*, vol. 25, 483–637. Superb article detailing environmental abuse in earlier societies.

Mumford, Lewis. 1962. *The Transformations of Man*. New York: Collier. Superb analysis of human cultural change.

Nash, Roderick. 1968. *The American Environment: Readings in the History of Conservation*. Reading, Mass.: Addison-Wesley. Excellent collection of articles.

Nash, Roderick. 1982. *Wilderness and the American Mind*. 3d ed. New Haven, Conn.: Yale University Press. Outstanding book on American attitudes toward wilderness and conservation.

Odell, Rice. 1980. *Environmental Awakening: The New Revolution to Protect the Earth*. Cambridge, Mass.: Ballinger. Important book describing environmental progress since 1965.

Osborn, Fairfield. 1948. *Our Plundered Planet*. Boston: Little, Brown. An environmental classic that attempted to alert readers to the environmental problems we face today.

Repetto, Robert, ed. 1986. *The Global Possible: Resources, Development, and the New Century*. New Haven, Conn.: Yale University Press. Excellent series of articles.

Robinson, Glen O. 1975. *The Forest Service: A Study in Public Land Management*. Baltimore: Johns Hopkins Press. Excellent historical overview.

Roszak, Theodore. 1986. *The Cult of Information: The Folklore of Computers and the True Art of Thinking.* New York: Pantheon. Excellent analysis of problems with the high-tech information society.

Sabaloff, Jeremy A., and C. C. Lamberg-Karlovsky. 1975. *The Rise and Fall of Civilizations.* Menlo Park, Calif.: Benjamin-Cummings. Excellent analysis.

Sears, Paul B. 1980. *Deserts on the March.* Norman: University of Oklahoma Press. Probably the best account of how human activities have contributed to the spread of deserts. Originally published in 1935.

Shanks, Bernard. 1984. *This Land Is Your Land.* San Francisco: Sierra Club Books. Outstanding history of the use and abuse of public lands in the United States.

Spencer, J. E., and W. L. Thomas. 1977. *Introducing Cultural Geography.* 2d ed. Excellent account of how human activities have affected the earth's surface and resources.

Stroup, Richard L., and John A. Baden. *Natural Resources: Bureaucratic Myths and Environmental Management.* 1986. San Francisco: Pacific Institute for Public Policy Research. Useful in-depth study.

Tucker, William. 1982. *Progress and Privilege: America in the Age of Environmentalism.* Garden City, N.Y.: Anchor Press/Doubleday. Accuses U.S. environmentalists of being upper-middle-class liberals whose primary concern is to protect their own wealth and power. Makes some useful points but greatly oversimplifies the diversity of citizens in the environmental movement.

Udall, Stewart L. 1963. *The Quiet Crisis.* New York: Holt, Rinehart & Winston. An environmental classic.

U.S. Department of Agriculture, Forest Service. 1976. *Highlights in the History of Forest Conservation.* Washington, D.C.: Government Printing Office. Useful overview.

Vig, Norman J., and Michael J. Craft. 1984. *Environmental Policy in the 1980s.* Washington, D.C.: Congressional Quarterly Press. Useful summary of President Reagan's environmental policy during his first term.

Zaslowsky, Dyan, and Wilderness Society. 1986. *These American Lands.* New York: Henry Holt. Superb history of use of federal lands.

Chapter 3 Matter and Energy Resources: Types and Concepts

American Physical Society. 1975. *Efficient Use of Energy.* New York: American Institute of Physics. Summary of energy waste and opportunities for energy conservation based on second-law energy efficiencies in the United States.

Bent, Henry A. 1971. "Haste Makes Waste: Pollution and Entropy." *Chemistry,* vol. 44, 6–15. Excellent and very readable account of the relationship between the second law of thermodynamics and environmental problems.

Bent, Henry A. 1977. "Entropy and the Energy Crisis." *Journal of Science Teaching,* vol. 44, no. 4, 25–29. Readable introduction to implications of the second law of thermodynamics.

Bertell, Rosalie. 1986. *No Immediate Danger.* New York: Women's Press. Excellent analysis of dangers of low-level radiation.

Boulding, Kenneth E. 1964. *The Meaning of the 20th Century.* New York: Harper & Row. Penetrating discussion of our planetary situation by one of our foremost thinkers. See especially Chapters 4, 6, and 7 on the war, population, and entropy traps. A classic.

Christensen, John W. 1981. *Energy, Resources, and Environment.* Dubuque, Iowa: Kendall/Hunt. Excellent overview.

Clark, Wilson, and Jake Page. 1981. *Energy, Vulnerability, and War: Alternatives for America.* New York: W. W. Norton. Excellent analysis of vulnerability of centralized U.S. energy system to nuclear attack and to cutoffs of imported oil. Based on a study carried out by energy expert Clark for the Department of Defense.

Colorado Energy Research Institute. 1976. *Net Energy Analysis: An Energy Balance Study of Fossil Fuel Resources.* Golden, Colo.: Colorado Energy Research Institute. Excellent source of data.

Cook, Earl. 1976. *Man, Energy, Society.* San Francisco: W. H. Freeman. Excellent introduction to energy concepts, problems, and alternatives.

Fowler, John M. 1984. *Energy and the Environment.* 2d ed. New York: McGraw-Hill. Excellent overview.

Gofman, John W. 1981. *Radiation and Human Health.* San Francisco: Sierra Club Books. An expert's detailed and controversial evaluation of the health effects of exposure to low-level radiation.

Hurley, Patrick M. 1982. *Living with Nuclear Radiation.* Ann Arbor: University of Michigan Press. Useful evaluation of the risks of exposure to low-level radiation.

Lovins, Amory B. 1977. *Soft Energy Paths.* Cambridge, Mass.: Ballinger. Superb analysis of energy alternatives. See also Nash (1979).

Miller, G. Tyler, Jr. 1971. *Energetics, Kinetics and Life: An Ecological Approach.* Bel-mont, Calif.: Wadsworth. An attempt to show the beauty of thermodynamics and its wide application to life. Amplifies and explains the material in Chapter 3 of *Living in the Environment* at a slightly higher level.

Nash, Hugh, ed. 1979. *The Energy Controversy: Soft Path Questions and Answers.* San Francisco: Friends of the Earth. Pros and cons of the soft energy path.

National Academy of Sciences. 1980. *The Effects on Populations of Exposure to Low Levels of Ionizing Radiation.* Washington, D.C.: National Academy Press. Controversial report by a team of experts who disagreed widely on the subject.

Odum, Howard T., and Elisabeth C. Odum. 1980. *Energy Basis for Man and Nature.* New York: McGraw-Hill. Outstanding discussion of energy principles and energy options, with emphasis on net energy analysis.

Pochin, Edward. 1985. *Nuclear Radiation: Risks and Benefits.* New York: Oxford University Press. Excellent overview.

Rifkin, Jeremy. 1980. *Entropy: A New World View.* New York: Viking. Superb nontechnical description of the need to develop a sustainable-earth society based on the second law of thermodynamics.

Simon, Julian L., and Herman Kahn, eds. 1984. *The Resourceful Earth: A Response to "Global 2000."* Useful cornucopian analysis.

Steinhart, Carol E., and John S. Steinhart. 1974. *Energy: Source, Use, and Role in Human Affairs.* North Scituate, Mass.: Duxbury Press. Excellent treatment of energy principles and options.

Sternglass, Ernest J. 1981. *Secret Fallout: Low-Level Radiation from Hiroshima to Three Mile Island.* New York: McGraw-Hill. An expert's controversial evaluation of effects of exposure to low-level radiation.

United Nations Scientific Committee on Effects of Atomic Radiation (UNSCEAR). 1977. *Sources and Effects of Ionizing Radiation.* New York: United Nations. Evaluation by an international team of experts similar to that by the National Academy of Sciences (1980).

Upton, Arthur C. 1982. "The Biological Effects of Low-Level Ionizing Radiation." *Scientific American,* vol. 246, no. 2, 41–49. Excellent overview.

Chapter 4 Ecosystems: What Are They and How Do They Work?

Bolin, B., and R. B. Cook. 1983. *The Major Biogeochemical Cycles and Their Interactions.* New York: Wiley. Comprehensive analysis.

Colinvaux, Paul A. 1978. *Why Big Fierce Animals Are Rare*. Princeton, N.J.: Princeton University Press. Fascinating and very readable description of major ecological principles.

Colinvaux, Paul A. 1986. *Ecology*. New York: Wiley. Excellent basic text.

Ehrlich, Paul R. 1985. "Human Ecology for Introductory Biology Courses." *American Zoologist*, vol. 25, 379–394. Excellent overview.

Ehrlich, Paul R. 1986. *The Machinery of Life: The Living World Around Us and How It Works*. New York: Simon & Schuster. Superb nontechnical description.

Ehrlich, Paul R., Anne H. Ehrlich, and John P. Holdren. 1977. *Ecoscience: Population, Resources and Environment*. San Francisco: W. H. Freeman. Excellent, more detailed text at a higher level than *Living in the Environment*.

Emmel, Thomas C. 1973. *An Introduction to Ecology and Population Biology*. New York: W. W. Norton. Superb introduction.

Gates, David M. 1985. *Energy and Ecology*. Sunderland, Mass.: Sinauer. Excellent analysis at a higher level than *Living in the Environment*.

Kormondy, Edward J. 1984. *Concepts of Ecology*. 3d ed. Englewood Cliffs, N.J.: Prentice-Hall. First-rate introduction at a slightly higher level than *Living in the Environment*.

Krebs, Charles J. 1978. *Ecology*. 3d ed. New York: Harper & Row. Splendid basic text using the evolutionary approach to ecology.

Lovelock, James E. 1979. *Gaia: A New Look at Life*. Oxford, England: Oxford University Press. Superb analysis of interactions in the biosphere.

McIntosh, R. P. 1985. *The Background of Ecology: Concept and Theory*. New York: Cambridge University Press. Useful summary of ecological ideas from the mid–nineteenth century to the present.

Moore, John A. 1985. "Science as a Way of Knowing: Human Ecology." *American Zoologist*, vol. 25, 483–637. Excellent overview of ecological principles.

Odum, Eugene P. 1983. *Basic Ecology*. Philadelphia: Saunders. Outstanding textbook on ecology by a prominent ecologist.

Ramade, Francois. 1984. *Ecology of Natural Resources*. New York: Wiley. Excellent introduction.

Richardson, Jonathan L. 1977. *Dimensions of Ecology*. Baltimore: Williams & Wilkins. Excellent brief introductory text.

Rickleffs, Robert E. 1976. *The Economy of Nature*. Portland, Ore.: Chiron Press. Beautifully written introduction to ecology.

Smith, Robert L. 1980. *Ecology and Field Biology*. 3d ed. New York: Harper & Row. Outstanding basic text in ecology using the ecosystem approach.

Smith, Robert L. 1980. *The Ecology of Man: An Ecosystem Approach*. 3d ed. New York: Harper & Row. Excellent collection of ecological articles with extremely useful introductory commentaries.

Smith, Robert L. 1985. *Elements of Ecology*. 2d ed. New York: Harper & Row. Outstanding basic text.

Watt, Kenneth E. F. 1973. *Principles of Environmental Science*. New York: McGraw-Hill. Excellent high-level discussion of ecological principles.

Watt, Kenneth E. F. 1982. *Understanding the Environment*. Newton, Mass.: Allyn & Bacon. Excellent introduction.

Chapter 5 Ecosystems: What Are the Major Types?

See also the readings for Chapter 4.

Andrewartha, H. G., and L. C. Birch. 1984. *The Ecological Web*. Chicago: University of Chicago Press. Useful high-level description of ecosystems.

Attenborough, David. 1984. *The Living Planet*. Boston: Little, Brown. Superb survey of life in the biosphere.

Brown, J. H., and A. C. Gibson. 1983. *Biogeography*. St. Louis: C. V. Mosby. Excellent analysis of factors affecting distribution of plants and animals in various parts of the earth.

Clapham, W. B., Jr. 1984. *Natural Ecosystems*. 2d ed. New York: Macmillan. Useful introduction.

Clark, J. R. 1977. *Coastal Ecosystem Management*. New York: Wiley. Useful detailed analysis.

Council on Environmental Quality. 1978. *Our Nation's Wetlands*. Washington, D.C.: Government Printing Office. Interagency task force description of wetlands, the problems they face, and federal policies designed to protect them.

Culliney, John L. 1979. *The Forest of the Sea: Life and Death on the Continental Shelf*. Garden City, N.Y.: Anchor/Doubleday. Detailed description.

Daiber, Franklin C. 1986. *Conservation of Tidal Marshes*. New York: Van Nostrand Reinhold. Detailed analysis.

Gedzelman, Stanley L. 1980. *The Science and Wonders of the Atmosphere*. New York: Wiley. Superb introduction to climate and weather.

Goldman, C., and A. Horne. 1983. *Limnology*. New York: McGraw-Hill. Good basic introduction to freshwater biology.

Griggs, Gary, and Lauret Savoy, eds. 1985. *Living with the California Coast*. Durham, N.C.: Duke University Press. Comprehensive analysis of the processes and problems that anyone living on the coastline needs to understand.

Hynes, H. B. N. 1970. *The Biology of Running Waters*. Toronto: University of Toronto Press. Excellent description of stream biology.

Jordan, Carl F. 1985. *Nutrient Cycling in Tropical Forest Ecosystems*. New York: Wiley. Useful detailed analyses.

Kaufman, Wallace, and Orin Pilkey. 1979. *The Beaches Are Moving*. Garden City, N.Y.: Anchor Press/Doubleday. Superb analysis of hazards of development on barrier islands.

Lehr, Paul E., et al. 1975. *Weather*. New York: Golden Press. Excellent introduction to weather and climate.

McArthur, R. H. 1972. *Geographical Ecology*. New York: Harper & Row. Basic text on biogeography.

Maltby, Edward. 1986. *Waterlogged Wealth*. Washington, D.C.: Earthscan. Excellent overview of destruction of wetlands in the United States.

Marx, Wesley. 1981. *The Oceans: Our Last Resource*. San Francisco: Sierra Club Books. Excellent discussion of how to preserve the ocean's resources.

Office of Technology Assessment. 1984. *Wetlands: Their Use and Regulation*. Washington, D.C.: Government Printing Office. Excellent overview.

Parker, Henry S. 1985. *Exploring the Ocean: An Introduction for the Traveler and Amateur Naturalist*. Excellent overview of ocean ecosystems.

Pilkey, Orin H., Sr., et al. 1984. *Coastal Design, A Guide for Builders, Planners, & Homeowners*. New York: Van Nostrand Reinhold. Excellent analysis.

Ringold, Paul L., and John Clark. 1980. *The Coastal Almanac for 1980—The Year of the Coast*. San Francisco: W. H. Freeman. Useful source of information.

Simon, Anne W. 1978. *The Thin Edge: Coast and Man in Crisis*. New York: Harper & Row. Superb discussion of stresses on estuarine zones and possible solutions.

Sutton, A., and M. Sutton. 1979. *Wildlife of the Forests*. New York: Harry N. Abrams, Inc. Useful source of information.

Teal, J., and M. Teal. 1969. *Life and Death of a Salt Marsh*. New York: Ballantine. A classic work on estuaries.

Wagner, F. H. 1980. *Wildlife of the Deserts.* New York: Harry N. Abrams, Inc. Useful source of information.

Wetzel, R. G. 1983. *Limnology.* Philadelphia: Saunders. Excellent advanced treatment of lake ecology.

Whittaker, R. H. 1975. *Communities and Ecosystems.* 2d ed. New York: Macmillan. One of the best discussions of biomes.

Chapter 6 Ecosystems: What Can Happen to Them?

See also the readings for Chapters 4 and 5.

Adams, Ruth, and Susan Culen, eds. 1982. *The Final Epidemic: Physicians and Scientists on Nuclear War.* Chicago: University of Chicago Press. Excellent summary of the effects of nuclear war.

Barrett, G. W., and R. Rosenberg, eds. 1981. *Stress Effects on Natural Ecosystems.* New York: Wiley. Useful high-level analysis.

Bradshaw, A. D., and T. McNeilly. 1981. *Evolution and Pollution.* Baltimore, Md.: Edward Arnold Publishers. Useful detailed analysis.

Caldicott, Helen. 1979. *Nuclear Madness: What Can You Do?* New York: Bantam Books. Excellent summary by a physician and early leader of the nuclear freeze movement.

Conservation Foundation. 1985. *Risk Assessment and Risk Control.* Washington, D.C.: Conservation Foundation. Superb overview.

Crutzen, Paul J. 1985. "The Global Environment After Nuclear War." *Environment,* vol. 27, no. 8, 6–11, 34–37. Excellent overview of research on the nuclear winter effect.

Dotto, Lydia. 1986. *Planet Earth in Jeopardy: Environmental Consequences of Nuclear War.* New York: Wiley. Excellent overview.

Douglas, Mary, and Aaron Wildavsky. 1982. *Risk and Culture.* Berkeley: University of California Press. Excellent overview.

Ehrlich, Paul R. 1980. "Variety Is the Key to Life." *Technology Review.* March/April. Excellent summary of the need to preserve biological diversity.

Ehrlich, Paul R., et al. 1984. *The Cold and the Dark: The World After Nuclear War.* New York: W. W. Norton. Superb overview of ecological and health effects of nuclear war.

Ehrlich, Robert. 1985. *Waging Nuclear Peace.* Edison, N.Y.: State University of New York Press. Excellent summary of effects of nuclear war and control of nuclear weapons.

Farvar, M. Taghi, and John P. Milton, eds. 1972. *The Careless Technology: Ecology and International Development.* Garden City, N.Y.: Natural History Press. Documents numerous cases of unexpected environmental consequences of transferring technology from rich to poor countries.

Fischoff, Baruch, et al. 1984. *Acceptable Risk: Science and Determination of Safety.* New York: Cambridge University Press. Excellent analysis.

Futuyma, D. J. 1979. *Evolutionary Biology.* Sunderland, Mass.: Sinauer Associates. Excellent textbook presenting the modern view of natural selection and evolution.

Grover, Herbert D. 1984. "The Climatic and Biological Consequences of Nuclear War." *Environment,* vol. 26, no. 4, 4–13, 34–38. Outstanding summary.

Hattis, Dale, and David Kennedy. 1986. "Assessing Risks from Health Hazards: An Imperfect Science." *Technology Review.* May/June, pp. 60–71. Excellent discussion of some limitations of risk-benefit analysis.

Hiroshima and Nagasaki. 1981. New York: Basic Books. The most complete description available of the effects of the atomic attack on these two cities; written by 34 Japanese physicians, physicists, and social scientists.

Holling, C. S. 1985. "Resilience of Ecosystems: Local Surprise and Natural Change." In *Global Change,* edited by T. F. Malone and J. G. Roederer. New York: Cambridge University Press, pp. 228–269. Excellent detailed analysis.

Imperato, P. J., and Greg Mitchell. 1985. *Acceptable Risks.* New York: Viking. Excellent nontechnical overview.

Katz, Arthur M. 1982. *Life After Nuclear War.* Cambridge, Mass.: Ballinger. Superb description of the effects of nuclear war.

Lowrance, W. W. 1976. *Of Acceptable Risk.* Los Altos, Calif.: William Kaufmann. Excellent overview.

Morone, Edward J., and Edward J. Woodhouse. 1986. *Averting Catastrophe: Strategies for Regulating Risky Technologies.* Berkeley: University of California Press. Excellent analysis.

National Academy of Sciences. 1985. *The Effects on the Atmosphere of a Major Nuclear War.* Washington, D.C.: National Academy Press. Authoritative summary of nuclear winter/autumn effect.

Odum, Eugene P. 1969. "The Strategy of Ecosystem Development." *Science,* vol. 164, 262–270. Excellent summary of succession.

Office of Technology Assessment. 1981. *The Effects of Nuclear War.* Washington, D.C.: Government Printing Office. Very informative and detailed analysis of the effects of nuclear war on the United States and the Soviet Union.

Oldfield, Margery. 1984. *The Value of Conserving Genetic Resources.* Washington, D.C.: U.S. Department of Interior, National Park Service. Excellent overview.

Olsen, Steve. 1986. *Biotechnology.* Washington, D.C.: National Academy Press. Useful summary of a conference of experts on the nature and possible regulation of genetic engineering.

Perrow, Charles. 1985. *Normal Accidents: Living with High-Risk Technologies.* New York: Basic Books. Excellent analysis.

Rescher, Nicholas. 1983. *A Philosophical Introduction to the Theory of Risk Evaluation and Management.* Washington, D.C.: University Press of America. Excellent introduction.

Rifkin, Jeremy. 1985. *Declaration of a Heretic.* Boston: Routledge & Kegan Paul. Excellent summary of potential problems with genetic engineering by its most active and effective critic.

Rowe, William D. 1977. *An Anatomy of Risk.* New York: Wiley. Excellent introduction.

Schell, Jonathan. 1982. *The Fate of the Earth.* New York: Alfred A. Knopf. Outstanding attempt to make us think about the unthinkable effects of nuclear war.

Thompson, Starley L., and Stephen H. Schneider. 1986. "Nuclear Winter Reappraised." *Foreign Affairs,* summer. Research indicating that effects of nuclear war might be a less severe nuclear autumn.

Thompson, Starley L., and Stephen H. Schneider. 1986. "The Nuclear Winter Debate: Comment and Correspondence." *Foreign Affairs,* vol. 65, no. 1, 171–178. Useful analysis.

Turco, R. P., et al. 1983. "Nuclear Winter: Global Consequences of Multiple Nuclear Explosions." *Science,* vol. 22, 1283–1291. Outstanding analysis by a team of experts.

Whittaker, Robert H., and George M. Woodwell. 1972. "Evolution of Natural Communities." In *Ecosystem Structure and Function,* edited by John A. Wiens. Corvallis: Oregon State University Press. Good summary of diversity and succession.

Wilson, E. O. 1975. *Sociobiology.* Cambridge, Mass.: Harvard University Press. Superb analysis of behavioral aspects of ecology.

Winner, Langdon. 1986. *The Whale and the Reactor.* Chicago: University of Chicago Press. Excellent summary of risk-benefit analysis.

Woodwell, G. M. 1970. "Effects of Pollution on the Structure and Physiology of Ecosystems." *Science,* vol. 168, 429–433. Excellent analysis.

Chapter 7 Population Dynamics

Bouvier, Leon F. 1980. "America's Baby Boom Generation: The Fateful Bulge." *Population Bulletin*, April, pp. 1–35. Superb discussion of the implications of the baby boom for American society.

Bouvier, Leon F. 1984. "Planet Earth 1984–2034: A Demographic Vision." *Population Bulletin*, vol. 39, no. 1, 1–39. Outstanding overview of future population trends and problems.

Bouvier, Leon F., and Robert W. Gardner. 1986. "Immigration to the U.S.: The Unfinished Story." *Population Bulletin*, vol. 41, no. 4, 1–50. Superb overview of the impact of immigration on U.S. population growth.

Brown, Lester R., et al. 1984. *State of the World 1984*. New York: W. W. Norton. Superb overview of population trends in Chapter 2.

Brown, Lester R., and Edward C. Wolf. 1985. *Reversing Africa's Decline*. Washington, D.C.: Worldwatch Institute. Excellent summary of population, food, and environmental problems in Africa with suggested solutions.

Chandler, William U. 1985. *Investing in Children*. Washington, D.C.: Worldwatch Institute. Excellent analysis of how to reduce infant mortality.

Council on Environmental Quality. 1980. *The Global 2000 Report to the President*, vol. 2. Washington, D.C.: Government Printing Office. Useful model with projections of world food, population, land, water, energy, minerals, and pollution to the year 2000.

Davis, Cary, et al. 1983. "U.S. Hispanics: Changing the Face of America." *Population Bulletin*, vol. 38, no. 3, 1–43. Superb overview.

Dickenson, J. P., et al. 1983. *A Geography of the Third World*. New York: Methuen. Excellent overview.

Faux, Marian. 1984. *Childless by Choice: Choosing Childlessness in the Eighties*. New York: Anchor Press/Doubleday. Excellent analysis of increasing reluctance of American women to become mothers.

Haupt, Arthur, and Thomas T. Kane. 1978. *The Population Handbook*. Washington, D.C.: Population Reference Bureau. Superb introduction to demographic terms and concepts.

Loup, Jacques. 1983. *Can the Third World Survive?* Baltimore: Johns Hopkins University Press. Excellent overview of past and future problems of LDCs with a proposed strategy for the future.

Merrick, Thomas W. 1986. "World Population in Transition." *Population Bulletin*, vol. 41, no. 2, 1–51. Superb overview.

Newland, Kathleen. 1981. *Infant Mortality and the Health of Societies*. Washington, D.C.: Worldwatch Institute. Useful overview.

Population Reference Bureau. Annual. *World Population Data Sheet*. Washington, D.C.: Population Reference Bureau. This concise annual summary is the source for most of the population data used in this book.

Population Reference Bureau. 1982. "U.S. Population: Where We Are; Where We're Going." *Population Bulletin*, vol. 37, no. 2. Excellent summary.

Rosa, Jean-Jacques, ed. 1982. *The World Crisis in Social Security*. San Francisco: Institute for Contemporary Studies. Excellent overview of this serious problem and proposed solutions.

Senderowitz, Judith, and John M. Paxman. 1985. "Adolescent Fertility: Worldwide Concerns." *Population Bulletin*, vol. 40, no. 2, 1–51. Excellent overview.

Teitelbaum, Michael, and Jay M. Winter. 1985. *The Fear of Population Decline*. Orlando, Fla.: Academic Press. Excellent overview of this problem feared by some MDCs.

UNICEF. 1985. *The State of the World's Children*. New York: United Nations. Excellent overview.

United Nations Fund for Population Activities. 1985. *State of World Population: 1985*. New York: United Nations Fund for Population Activities. Excellent source of data.

Weller, Robert, and Leon Bouvier. 1981. *Population: Demography and Policy*. New York: St. Martin's Press. Excellent college text.

Chapter 8 Population Control

Birdsall, Nancy. 1980. "Population Growth and Poverty in the Developing World." *Population Bulletin*, vol. 35, no. 5, 1–48. Excellent discussion of the relationships between poverty and population growth.

Borjas, George J., and Marta Tienda. 1987. "The Economic Consequences of Immigration." *Science*, vol. 235, 645–651. Useful analysis.

Boughey, Arthur S. 1976. *Strategy for Survival: An Exploration of the Limits to Further Population and Industrial Growth*. Menlo Park, Calif.: W. A. Benjamin. Excellent introductory text explaining and evaluating computer models.

Boyd, Robert. 1972. "World Dynamics: A Note." *Science*, vol. 177, 516–519. Shows effects of adding an exponentially growing technology function to the Forrester-Meadows model so that disaster is averted.

Brown, Lester R. 1978. *The Twenty-Ninth Day: Accommodating Human Needs and Numbers to the Earth's Resources*. New York: W. W. Norton. Superb discussion of the need to control world population growth.

Brown, Lester R. 1981. *Building a Sustainable Society*. New York: W. W. Norton. An outstanding discussion of the need for population control and the conservation of renewable and nonrenewable resources.

Brown, Lester R., and Jodi L. Jacobson. 1986. *Our Demographically Divided World*. Washington, D.C.: Worldwatch Institute. Superb analysis of demographic transition.

Callahan, Daniel. 1972. "Ethics and Population Limitation." *Science*, vol. 175, 487–494. Superb analysis of the ethical implications of various population policies.

Clark, J., and S. Cole. 1975. *Global Simulation Models: A Comparative Survey*. New York: Wiley. Useful comparison and evaluation of global models.

Commission on Population Growth and the American Future. 1972. *Population and the American Future*. Washington, D.C.: Government Printing Office. Also available in paperback (Signet, New American Library). Important historical document showing the need for controlling U.S. population growth.

Connery, John. 1977. *Abortion: The Development of the Roman Catholic Perspective*. Chicago: Loyola University Press. Excellent overview.

Crewdson, John. 1983. *The Tarnished Door*. New York: New York Times Books. Excellent overview of U.S. immigration policies and problems.

Croll, Elisabeth, et al. 1985. *China's One-Child Family Policy*. New York: St. Martin's Press. Excellent overview.

Davis, Kingsley. 1973. "Zero Population Growth: The Goal and Means." *Daedalus*, vol. 102, no. 2, 15–30. Superb analysis of ZPG.

Day, Lincoln H. 1978. "What Will a ZPG Society Be Like?" *Population Bulletin*, vol. 33, no. 3, 1–42. Useful description of life in a ZPG society.

Djerassi, Carl. 1980. *The Politics of Contraception*. New York: W. W. Norton. Inside view by an expert of how drug companies and the government control the development of new contraceptive drugs and devices.

Forrester, Jay W. 1971. "Counterintuitive Behavior of Social Systems." *Technology Review*, vol. 73, no. 3. Readable summary of results of the first world model.

Forrester, Jay W. 1971. *World Dynamics.* Cambridge, Mass.: Wright-Allen Press. Detailed description of the first world model.

Goliber, Thomas J. 1985. "Sub-Saharan Africa: Population Pressures on Development." *Population Bulletin*, vol. 40, no. 1, 1–45. Excellent summary of problems and possible solutions.

Gray, Elizabeth Dodson. 1979. *Why the Green Nigger: Remything Genesis.* Wellesley, Mass.: Roundtable Press. Excellent discussion of women's rights and environmental problems.

Greenhalgh, Susan, and John Bongaarts. 1987. "Fertility Policy in China: Future Options." *Science*, vol. 235, 1167–1172. Useful analysis.

Grupte, Pranay. 1984. *The Crowded Earth: People and the Politics of Population.* New York: W. W. Norton. Superb summary of population problems and what is being done about them in selected countries.

Hardin, Garrett. 1974. *Mandatory Motherhood: The True Meaning of "Right to Life."* Boston: Beacon Press. Superb discussion of the abortion issue.

Hardin, Garrett. 1982. *Naked Emperors, Essays of a Taboo Stalker.* Los Altos, Calif.: William Kaufmann. Thought-provoking essays on a variety of subjects including overpopulation and abortion.

Hatcher, Robert A., et al. 1982. *It's Your Choice.* New York: Irvington Press. Excellent overview of contraceptive methods.

Henshaw, Stanley, and Christopher Tietze. 1986. *Induced Abortion: A World Review.* New York: Alan Guttmacher Institute. Excellent source of data.

Hernandez, Donald J. 1985. *Success or Failure? Family Planning Programs in the Third World.* Westport, Conn.: Greenwood. Useful evaluation.

Jacobsen, Judith. 1983. *Promoting Population Stabilization: Incentives for Small Families.* Washington, D.C.: Worldwatch Institute. Excellent discussion of the use of economic incentives and disincentives to help control population growth.

Jaffe, Frederick S., et al. 1980. *Abortion Politics.* New York: Alan Guttmacher Institute. Excellent balanced approach.

Kahn, Herman, et al. 1976. *The Next 200 Years: A Scenario for America and the World.* New York: William Morrow. A dazzling example of linear extrapolation by a leading cornucopian. Unfortunately, the assumptions and the reasoning used to arrive at the conclusions generated by this intuitive mental model are not clearly specified.

Keely, Charles B. 1982. "Illegal Migration." *Scientific American,* March, pp. 41–47. Excellent analysis.

Keyfitz, Nathan. 1984. "The Population of China." *Scientific American*, vol. 250, no. 2, 38–47. Excellent overview.

Lamm, Richard D., and Gary Imhoff. 1985. *The Immigration Time Bomb.* New York: Dutton. Excellent analysis arguing for greater control of legal and illegal immigration in the United States.

Meadows, Dennis L., et al. 1974. *The Dynamics of Growth in a Finite World.* Cambridge, Mass.: M.I.T. Press. Detailed technical documentation of the second world model, presented in popularized form as *The Limits to Growth.*

Meadows, Donella H., et al. 1972. *The Limits to Growth.* New York: Universal Books. Popular description of the second world model.

Meadows, Donella, et al. 1982. *Groping in the Dark: The First Decade of Global Modeling.* New York: Wiley. Superb summary and evaluation of the successes and failures of global models developed by various teams since *The Limits to Growth* was published.

Menken, Jane, ed. 1986. *World Population and U.S. Policy: The Choices Ahead.* New York: W. W. Norton. Eight experts provide an insightful analysis of population policy.

Mesarovic, Mihajlo, and Eduard Pestel. 1974. *Mankind at the Turning Point.* New York: E. P. Dutton. Popular presentation of a regional model of the world. Compare it with *The Limits to Growth.*

Morgan, Robin. 1984. *Sisterhood Is Global.* Garden City, N.Y.: Doubleday. Excellent analysis of improving conditions for women throughout the world.

Murphy, Elaine M., and Patricia Cancellier. 1982. *Immigration: Questions and Answers.* Washington, D.C.: Population Reference Bureau. Superb and concise summary of this important issue.

Murphy, Francis X. 1981. "Catholic Perspectives on Population Issues II." *Population Bulletin*, vol. 35, no. 6, 1–43. Superb overview.

NARAL Foundation. 1984. *Legal Abortion: Arguments Pro & Con.* Washington, D.C.: National Abortion Rights Action League. Excellent summary.

National Academy of Sciences. 1985. *Immigration Statistics: A Story of Neglect.* Washington, D.C.: National Academy Press. Useful source of data.

Newland, Kathleen. 1980. *Women, Men, and the Division of Labor.* Washington, D.C.: Worldwatch Institute. Excellent summary.

Office of Technology Assessment. 1982. *World Population and Fertility Planning Technologies: The Next 20 Years.* Washington, D.C.: Government Printing Office. Excellent survey of prospects for development of new contraceptives between 1980 and 2000.

O'Hare, William P. 1985. "Poverty in America: Trends and New Patterns." *Population Bulletin*, vol. 40, no. 3, 1–44. Useful summary of data.

Oltmans, Willem L. 1974. *On Growth.* New York: G. P. Putnam. Useful collection of interviews of 70 of the world's great thinkers in many disciplines on the debate over the Forrester-Meadows model.

Pearce, Fred. 1984. "In Defense of Population Growth." *The New Scientist*, Aug. 9, pp. 21–26. Excellent presentation of the cornucopian position.

Population Reference Bureau. 1986. *Women in the World: The Women's Decade and Beyond.* Washington, D.C.: Population Reference Bureau. Excellent summary of condition of women throughout the world.

Religious Coalition for Abortion Rights. 1985. *Point, Counterpoint.* Washington, D.C.: Religious Coalition for Abortion Rights. Excellent summary of arguments for and against abortion by a group of 31 national religious organizations.

Seager, Joni, and Ann Olson. 1986. *Women in the World: An International Atlas.* Superb summary of the status of women throughout the world.

Simon, Julian L. 1981. *The Ultimate Resource.* Princeton, N.J.: Princeton University Press. Argues against population control because people will use their creativity and ingenuity to solve the world's population, resource, and pollution problems.

Sivard, Ruth L. 1985. *Women: A World Survey.* Washington, D.C.: World Priorities. Excellent overview.

Starr, Chauncey, and Richard Rudman. 1973. "Parameters of Technological Growth." *Science*, vol. 182, 358–364. Presentation of the view that technology can grow exponentially and thus avert the problems projected by the Forrester-Meadows and Mesarovic-Pestel models.

Steiner, Gilbert Y., ed. 1983. *The Abortion Dispute and the American System.* Washington, D.C.: Brookings Institution. Useful analysis.

Stokes, Bruce. 1980. *Men and Family Planning.* Washington, D.C.: Worldwatch Institute. Superb discussion of the male's role and responsibilities in preventing unwanted births.

Teitelbaum, Michael S. 1975. "Relevance of Demographic Transition Theory for

Developing Countries." *Science*, vol. 188, 420–425. Excellent summary of why the demographic transition may or may not work for today's LDCs.

van de Kaa, Dirk J. 1987. "Europe's Second Demographic Transition." *Population Bulletin*, vol. 42, no. 1, 1–57. Excellent analysis of population decline in much of Europe.

Wattenberg, Ben, and Karl Zinsmeister, eds. 1985. *Are World Population Trends a Problem?* Washington, D.C.: American Enterprise Institute for Public Policy Research. Useful arguments by cornucopians that continued population growth may be desirable.

Wilbur, Amy E. 1986. "The Contraceptive Crisis." *Science Digest*, September, pp. 54–61, 84–85. Excellent summary of problems with development of new contraceptives in the United States.

Zero Population Growth. 1977. *The Benefits of Zero Population Growth*. Washington, D.C.: Zero Population Growth. Superb summary.

Chapter 9 Population Distribution: Urbanization

Brenneman, Russell L., and Sarah M. Bates, eds. 1984. *Land-Saving Action*. Covelo, Calif.: Island Press. Useful collection of articles telling how individuals and groups can save land from development.

Brown, David L., and John M. Wardwell, eds. 1980. *New Directions in Urban-Rural Migration: The Population Turnaround in Rural America*. New York: Academic Press. Excellent overview of the metropolitan-to-nonmetropolitan shift.

Brown, Lester R., et al. 1980. *Running on Empty: The Future of the Automobile in an Oil-Short World*. New York: W. W. Norton. Excellent analysis.

Brown, Lester R., and Jodi Jacobson. 1987. "Assessing the Future of Urbanization." In *State of the World 1987*, by Lester R. Brown et al. New York: W. W. Norton, pp. 38–56. Excellent overview.

Burby, Raymond J., et al. 1976. *New Communities U.S.A.* Lexington, Mass.: Lexington Books. Excellent overview of new towns in the United States.

Butler, Stuart M. 1980. *Enterprise Zones: Pioneering in the City*. Washington, D.C.: Heritage Foundation. Excellent presentation of the case for encouraging private industry to develop businesses and create jobs in declining urban areas.

Cassidy, Robert. 1980. *Livable Cities: A Grass-Roots Guide to Rebuilding Urban America*. New York: Holt, Rinehart & Winston.

Excellent guide to efforts by people to rebuild their own neighborhoods.

Choate, Pat, and Susan Walter. 1981. *America in Ruins: Beyond the Public Works Pork Barrel*. Washington, D.C.: Council on State Planning Agencies. Superb discussion of the deterioration of America's physical plant and suggestions for correcting the problem.

Dantzig, George B., and Thomas L. Saaty. 1973. *Compact City: A Plan for a Liveable Environment*. San Francisco: W. H. Freeman. Outstanding analysis of urban design for a more ecologically sound and self-reliant city.

Department of International Economic and Social Affairs, United Nations. 1986. *Population Growth and Policies in Mega-Cities*. New York: Population Division, United Nations. Excellent overview.

Dorney, R. S., and P. Wagner McLellan. 1984. "The Urban Ecosystem: Its Spatial Structure, Its Scale Relationships, and Its Subsystem Attributes." *Environments*, vol. 16, no. 1, 9–20. Excellent overview of urban areas as ecosystems.

Exline, Christopher H., et al. 1982. *The City: Patterns and Processes in the Urban Ecosystem*. Boulder, Colo.: Westview Press. Excellent overview.

Fabos, Julius G. 1985. *Land-Use Planning*. New York: Chapman and Hall. Excellent examples.

Farallones Institute. 1979. *The Integral Urban House: Self-Reliant Living in the City*. San Francisco: Sierra Club Books. Superb guide to those wishing to live a more ecologically sound lifestyle in cities.

Goodman, Percival. 1977. *The Double E*. Garden City, N.Y.: Doubleday. Exciting ideas for the design of small, self-sufficient, and ecologically sound cities.

Hartshorn, Truman A. 1980. *Interpreting the City: An Urban Geography*. New York: Wiley. Fine basic text.

Healy, Robert G., and John S. Rosenberg. 1981. *Land Use and the States*. 2d ed. Baltimore: Johns Hopkins University Press. Excellent overview of land-use policies and in-depth studies of land-use planning and control by several states.

Heller, Alfred, ed. 1972. *The California Tomorrow Plan*. Los Altos, Calif.: William Kaufmann. Superb example of an integrated, ecological land-use plan for a state.

Jacobs, Jane. 1984. *Cities and the Wealth of Nations*. New York: Random House. Excellent overview of the vitality and decline of the world's great cities.

League of Women Voters Education Fund. 1977. *Growth and Land Use: Shaping Future*

Patterns. Washington, D.C.: League of Women Voters. Excellent summary of methods for land-use control.

Leckie, Jim, et al. 1975. *Other Homes and Garbage: Designs for Self-Sufficient Living*. San Francisco: Sierra Club Books. Excellent guide for those wishing to live a more ecologically sound lifestyle.

McHarg, Ian L. 1969. *Design with Nature*. Garden City, N.Y.: Natural History Press. A beautifully written and illustrated description of an ecological approach to land-use planning. Also available in paperback from Doubleday.

Meyer, John R., and Jose A. Gomez-Ibanez. 1981. *Autos, Transit, and Cities*. Cambridge, Mass.: Harvard University Press. Excellent analysis of problems and possible solutions.

Morris, David. 1982. *Energy and the Transformation of Urban America*. San Francisco: Sierra Club Books. Excellent discussion of how urban areas, particularly small cities, can take steps toward increased energy efficiency and resource self-reliance.

Mumford, Lewis. 1968. *The Urban Prospect*. New York: Harcourt Brace Jovanovich. An important classic on urban life.

Naisbitt, John. 1982. *Megatrends: Ten New Directions Transforming Our Lives*. New York: Warner Communications. Superb discussion of major national and global trends. See especially Chapter 9 on the North to South and West population shift.

National Academy of Sciences. 1983. *Future Directions of Urban Public Transportation*. Washington, D.C.: National Academy Press. Excellent analysis.

Odum, Eugene P. 1969. "The Strategy of Ecosystem Development." *Science*, vol. 164, 262–270. Classic article on ecological principles and land use.

Popper, Frank J. 1981. *The Politics of Land-Use Reform*. Very useful analysis of the political problems associated with attempts at regional, state, and federal land-use planning and control.

Rudofsky, B. 1969. *Streets for People: A Primer for Americans*. Garden City, N.Y.: Doubleday. A classic describing how we should design and use city streets.

Ryn, Sin van der, and Peter Calthorpe. 1982. *Sustainable Communities: A New Design Synthesis for Cities, Suburbs, and Towns*. San Francisco: Sierra Club Books. Outstanding analysis and suggestions.

Steiner, Frederick. 1980. *Ecological Planning for Farmlands Preservation*. Pullman, Wash.: Student Book Corp., Washington State University. Story of how Whitman County, Washington, is preserving its farmland using Ian McHarg's ecological planning method.

Stokes, Bruce. 1981. *Global Housing Prospects: The Resource Constraints.* Washington, D.C.: Worldwatch Institute. Excellent analysis of the difficulties and possibilities of providing housing for the world's growing population.

Todd, Nancy Jack, and John Todd. 1984. *Bioshelters, Ocean Arks, City Farming: Ecology As the Basis of Design.* San Francisco: Sierra Club Books. Excellent suggestions for urban design and how to live a more ecologically sound lifestyle in cities.

Ward, Barbara. 1976. *The Home of Man.* New York: W. W. Norton. Superb discussion of urban problems in LDCs.

Whyte, William H. 1968. *The Last Landscape.* Garden City, N.Y.: Doubleday. Classic analysis of land use and discussion of open space.

Whyte, William H. 1980. *The Social Life of Small Urban Spaces.* Washington, D.C.: Conservation Foundation. Superb analysis of how small urban open spaces should be designed for maximum use by people. These research findings are also discussed in the Nova television program "City Spaces, Human Places," originally broadcast on PBS November 29, 1981, and available for classroom use.

Chapter 10 Soil Resources

Batie, Sandra S. 1983. *Soil Erosion: Crisis in America's Croplands?* Washington, D.C.: Conservation Foundation. Useful and objective analysis.

Beasley, R. P. 1972. *Erosion and Sediment Pollution Control.* Ames: Iowa State University Press. Excellent discussion of soil conservation.

Brady, Nyle C. 1974. *The Nature and Properties of Soils.* New York: Macmillan. Excellent introductory text.

Brown, Lester R., et al. 1984. *State of the World 1984.* New York: W. W. Norton. See Chapter 4 for a superb summary of world and U.S. soil erosion.

Dale, Tom, and V. G. Carter. 1955. *Topsoil and Civilization.* Norman, Okla.: University of Oklahoma Press. Classic work describing soil abuse throughout history.

Donahue, Roy L., et al. 1971. *Soils: An Introduction to Soils and Plant Growth.* Englewood Cliffs, N.J.: Prentice-Hall. Excellent introductory text.

Hausenbuiller, R. L. 1972. *Soil Science: Principles and Practices.* Dubuque, Iowa: Wm. C. Brown. Another excellent introductory text.

National Academy of Sciences. 1986. *Soil Conservation.* 2 vols. Washington, D.C.: National Academy Press. Superb overview of soil conservation needs and opportunities in the United States.

Paddock, Joe, et al. 1987. *Soil and Survival: Land Stewardship and the Future of American Agriculture.* San Francisco: Sierra Club Books. Superb overview.

Pritchett, W. L. 1979. *Properties and Management of Forest Soils.* New York: Wiley. A must for those interested in soil ecosystems.

Ramade, François. 1984. *Ecology of Natural Resources.* New York: Wiley. See Chapter 5 for an excellent discussion of soil erosion.

Sanchez, P. A., and S. W. Buol. 1975. "Soils of the Tropics and the World Food Crisis." *Science,* vol. 188, 598–603. Useful description of the potential and limitations for growing more food in the tropics.

Sophen, C. D., and J. V. Baird. 1982. *Soils and Soil Management.* Reston, Va.: Reston Publishing. Excellent introductory text that is easy to read and scientifically sound.

Steila, Donald. 1976. *The Geography of Soils.* Englewood Cliffs, N.J.: Prentice-Hall. Easy-to-read and accurate treatment of basic properties, formative processes, and spatial distributions of soils.

Swanson, Earl R., and Earl O. Heady. 1984. "Soil Erosion in the United States." In *The Resourceful Earth,* edited by Julian L. Simon and Herman Kahn. New York: Basil Blackwell, pp. 202–222. Useful overview.

Chapter 11 Water Resources

Academy of Natural Sciences. 1982. *Groundwater.* Philadelphia: Academy of Natural Sciences. Superb nontechnical guide.

Anderson, Terry L., ed. 1986. *Water Rights: Scarce Resource Allocation, Bureaucracy, and the Environment.* San Francisco: Pacific Institute for Public Policy. Excellent analysis.

Ashworth, William. 1982. *Nor Any Drop to Drink.* New York: Summit Books. Outstanding overview of the water crisis in the United States.

Berk, Richard A., et al. 1981. *Water Shortage: Lessons in Conservation from the Great California Drought, 1976–77.* Cambridge, Mass.: Abt Books. Useful overview of water conservation.

Brown, Lester R., et al. 1985. *State of the World 1985.* New York: W. W. Norton. See Chapter 3 for excellent discussion of water resources.

Conservation Foundation. 1984. *America's Water: Current Trends and Emerging Issues.* Washington, D.C.: Conservation Foundation. Excellent overview.

Cousteau, Jacques-Yves, et al. 1981. *The Cousteau Almanac: An Inventory of Life on Our Water Planet.* Garden City, N.Y.: Doubleday. Superb source of information.

Dennis, Harry. 1981. *Water and Power.* San Francisco: Friends of the Earth. Useful discussion of the politics of water resources in California.

Dregnue, H. E. 1983. *Desertification of Arid Lands.* New York: Academic Press. Excellent overview by an expert.

El-Ashry, Mohamed T., and Diana C. Gibbons. 1986. *Troubled Waters: New Policies for Managing Water in the American West.* Washington, D.C.: World Resources Institute. Excellent analysis.

Engelbert, Ernest, and Ann Scheuring. 1982. *California Water.* Berkeley: University of California Press. Useful, fairly technical overview of California's water problems.

Fradkin, Phillip L. 1981. *A River No More: The Colorado and the West.* New York: Alfred A. Knopf. Overview of politics and water resources in the West.

Franco, David A., and Robert G. Wetzel. 1983. *To Quench Our Thirst: The Present and Future Status of Freshwater Resources of the United States.* Ann Arbor: University of Michigan Press. Excellent source of information.

Goldsmith, Edward, and Nicholas Hidyard, eds. 1986. *The Social and Environmental Effects of Large Dams.* 3 vols. Detailed analysis. Useful source of data.

Grainger, Alan. *Desertification.* 1983. Washington, D.C.: Earthscan. Excellent overview.

Kahrl, William L. 1982. *Water and Power.* Berkeley: University of California Press. Excellent discussion of fight over water supplies for Southern California.

Leopold, L. B. 1974. *Water: A Primer.* San Francisco: W. H. Freeman. Outstanding, easy-to-read introduction to the fundamentals of water resources.

Marx, Wesley. 1977. *Acts of God, Acts of Man.* New York: McCann & Geoghegan. Excellent discussion of adverse impacts of building dams for flood control.

Micklin, Philip P. 1985. "Diversion of Soviet Rivers." *Environment,* vol. 27, no. 2, 12–20, 41–45. Excellent analysis of a proposed project.

Okun, Daniel L. 1975. "Water Management in England: A Regional Model." *Environmental Science and Technology,* vol. 9, no. 10, 918–923. Excellent description of the integrated regional water resource and waste treatment system used in England with great success since 1974.

Pimentel, David, et al. 1982. "Water Resources in Food and Energy Production." *BioScience*, vol. 32, no. 11, 861–867. Excellent analysis and source of data.

Postel, Sandra. 1984. *Water: Rethinking Management in an Age of Scarcity*. Washington, D.C.: Worldwatch Institute. Excellent overview.

Postel, Sandra. 1985. *Conserving Water: The Untapped Alternative*. Washington, D.C.: Worldwatch Institute. Excellent overview.

Pringle, Laurence. 1982. *Water—The Next Great Resource Battle*. New York: Macmillan. Superb overview of the water crisis in the United States.

Ramade, François. 1984. *Ecology of Natural Resources*. New York: Wiley. See Chapter 4 for an informative overview of world water resources.

Resner, Marc, and Ronald H. McDonald. 1986. "The High Costs of Dams." In *Bordering on Trouble: Resources and Politics in Latin America*, edited by Andrew Maguire and Janet Welsh Brown. Bethesda, Md.: Alder & Alder. Excellent overview of ecological side effects of large dam construction in Latin America.

Rogers, Peter P. 1986. "Fresh Water." In *The Global Possible: Resources, Development, and the New Century*, edited by Robert Repetto. New Haven, Conn.: Yale University Press, pp. 255–297. Excellent overview of use of water resources throughout the world.

Sheaffer, John, and Leonard Stevens. 1983. *Future Water*. New York: William Morrow. Excellent overview of U.S. water resource problems with suggested solutions.

Stokes, Bruce. 1983. "Water Shortages: The Next Energy Crisis." *The Futurist*, April, pp. 38–47. Excellent overview.

U.S. Geological Survey. 1984. *Estimated Use of Water in the United States in 1980*. Washington, D.C.: Government Printing Office. Useful source of data.

U.S. Water Resources Council. 1979. *The Nation's Water Resources, 1975–2000*. 4 vols. Washington, D.C.: Government Printing Office. Excellent source of data.

Ward, Roy. 1978. *Flood: A Geographical Perspective*. New York: Macmillan. Useful overview.

Welsh, Frank. 1985. *How to Create a Water Crisis*. New York: Johnson. Former employee of U.S. Army Corps of Engineers presents suggestions for solving the problem of water distribution in the West.

Wijkman, Anders, and Lloyd Timberlake. 1984. *Natural Disasters: Acts of God or Acts of Man?* Washington, D.C.: Earthscan. Excellent overview of effects of human activities on damages from floods and drought.

World Resources Institute and International Institute for Environment and Development. Annual. *World Resources*. New York: Basic Books. Excellent annual summary of water resources published since 1986.

Worster, Donald. 1985. *Rivers of Empire: Water, Aridity, and the Growth of the American West*. New York: Pantheon. Excellent overview of history of water development and politics in the West.

Chapter 12 Food Resources and World Hunger

Aliteri, Miguel A. 1983. *Agroecology: The Scientific Basis of Alternative Agriculture*. Berkeley: Division of Biological Control, University of California, Berkeley. Excellent overview of sustainable-earth agriculture.

Batie, Sandra S., and Robert G. Healy. 1983. "The Future of American Agriculture." *Scientific American*, vol. 248, no. 2, 44–53. Superb overview.

Bourlag, Norman E. 1983. "Contributions of Conventional Plant Breeding to Food Production." *Science*, vol. 219, 689–693. Excellent analysis of the second green revolution by the father of the movement.

Brewer, Michael. 1981. "The Changing U.S. Farmland Scene." *Population Bulletin*, vol. 36, no. 5, 1–39. Excellent analysis of the pros and cons of conversion of U.S. cropland to nonagricultural uses.

Brown, Larry. 1987. "Hunger in America." *Scientific American*, vol. 256, no. 2, 37–41. Useful source of data.

Brown, Lester R. 1981. *Building a Sustainable Society*. New York: W. W. Norton. Outstanding analysis of the limitations and side effects of modern industrialized agriculture with proposals for alternatives.

Brown, Lester R., and Edward C. Wolf. 1985. *Reversing Africa's Decline*. Washington, D.C.: Worldwatch Institute. Superb overview of Africa's problems.

Brown, Lester R., et al. Annual. *State of the World*. New York: W. W. Norton. Excellent annual summary published since 1984.

Calder, Nigel. 1986. *The Green Machines*. New York: Putnam. Excellent summary of the potential of genetic engineering and other forms of biotechnology.

Crosson, Pierre R. 1984. "Agricultural Land: Will There Be Enough?" *Environment*, vol. 26, no. 7, 17–20, 40–45. Excellent analysis.

Dando, William A. 1980. *The Geography of Famine*. New York: Wiley. Very useful data on the persistent problem of famine in many parts of the world.

Douglas, Gordon K., ed. 1984. *Agricultural Sustainability in a Changing World Order*. Boulder, Colo.: Westview Press. Useful collection of articles.

Doyle, Jack. 1985. *Altered Harvest: Agriculture, Genetics, and the Fate of the World's Food Supply*. New York: Viking. Excellent overview of the potential of genetic engineering techniques to produce future green revolutions.

Dudal, R. 1982. "Land Degradation in a World Perspective." *Journal of Soil and Water Conservation*, vol. 37, no. 5, 245–249. Excellent overview of the limitations and requirements for increasing the amount of land under cultivation.

Eckholm, Erik P. 1976. *Losing Ground: Environmental Stresses and World Food Prospects*. New York: W. W. Norton. Outstanding survey of environmental problems associated with agriculture throughout the world.

Eckholm, Erik P. 1979. *The Dispossessed of the Earth: Land Reform and Sustainable Development*. Washington, D.C.: Worldwatch Institute. Discussion of how land ownership by the wealthy in LDCs contributes to world poverty and hunger.

Eckholm, Erik P., and Frank Record. 1976. *The Two Faces of Malnutrition*. Washington, D.C.: Worldwatch Institute. Superb summary of the undernutrition of the poor and the overnutrition of the rich.

Editorial Research Reports. 1984. *Where Farm Policy Comes From*. Washington, D.C.: Congressional Quarterly. Useful and concise reports on past and present U.S. farm policies and problems.

Fletcher, W. Wendell, and Charles E. Little. 1982. *The American Cropland Crisis*. Bethesda, Md.: American Land Forum. Useful analysis of ways to save U.S. cropland.

Forbes, Malcolm H., and Lois J. Merrill, eds. 1986. *Global Hunger: A Look at the Problem and Potential Solutions*. Evansville, Ind.: University of Evansville Press. Useful overview.

General Accounting Office. 1976. *Disincentives to Agricultural Production in Developing Countries*. Washington, D.C.: Government Printing Office. Informative examples of how governments have discouraged food production in LDCs by setting prices too high or too low.

Goliber, Thomas J. 1985. "Sub-Saharan Africa: Population Pressures on Development." *Population Bulletin*, vol. 40, no. 1,

1–47. Excellent overview of Africa's problems.

Hart, John Fraser. 1984. "Cropland Change in the United States." In *The Resourceful Earth*, edited by Julian L. Simon and Herman Kahn. New York: Basil Blackwell, pp. 224–248. Useful source of data.

Hrabovszky, Janos P. 1986. "Agriculture: The Land Base." In *The Global Possible: Resources, Development, and the New Century*, edited by Robert Repetto. New Haven, Conn.: Yale University Press. Excellent overview.

Huessy, Peter. 1978. *The Food First Debate*. San Francisco: Institute for Food and Development Policy. Pros and cons of the proposals made by Lappé and Collins (1977).

Hunger Project. 1985. *Ending Hunger: An Idea Whose Time Has Come*. New York: Praeger. Superb discussion of world food problems and possible solutions.

Jackson, Wes. 1980. *New Roots for Agriculture*. San Francisco: Friends of the Earth. Thought-provoking analysis of problems with modern industrialized agriculture; proposals for alternatives.

Jackson, Wes, Wendell Berry, and Bruce Coleman, eds. 1985. *Meeting the Expectations of the Land: Essays in Sustainable Agriculture and Stewardship*. Berkeley, Calif.: North Point Press. Excellent overview.

Johnson, D. Gale. 1984. "World Food and Agriculture." In *The Resourceful Earth*, edited by Julian L. Simon and Herman Kahn. New York: Basil Blackwell, pp. 67–112. Useful overview.

Lappé, Francis M., and Joseph Collins. 1977. *Food First*. Boston: Houghton Mifflin. Provocative discussion of world food problems.

Linburg, Peter R. 1981. *Farming the Waters*. New York: Beaufort Books (Scribner). Excellent overview of aquaculture.

Lockeretz, W. G., et al. 1981. "Organic Farming in the Corn Belt." *Science*, vol. 211, 540–547. Useful comparison of organic and conventional industrialized farming.

Lowrance, Richard, et al., eds. 1984. *Agricultural Ecosystems: Unifying Concepts*. New York: Wiley. Useful series of articles.

Mollison, Bill. 1979. *Permaculture Two*. Tasmania, Australia: Tagari Books. Excellent overview of sustainable-earth agriculture.

Mollison, Bill, and David Holmgren. 1978. *Permaculture One*. Tasmania, Australia: Tagari Books. Excellent description of an approach to sustainable-earth agriculture.

Montclair, Susan G. 1977. *How the Other Half Dies: The Real Reasons for World Hunger*.

Montclair, N.J.: Allanheld, Osmun, & Co. Excellent analysis of the political and economic causes of world hunger, with emphasis on the role played by MDCs.

Morgan, Dan. 1980. *Merchants of Grain*. New York: Penguin Books. Useful political analysis of the major companies controlling the global grain trade.

Murphy, Elaine M. 1984. *Food and Population: A Global Concern*. Washington, D.C.: Population Reference Bureau. Excellent overview.

Myers, Norman, ed. 1984. *Gaia: An Atlas of Planet Management*. Garden City, N.Y.: Anchor/Doubleday. Superb overview of world food problems and possible solutions. Outstanding graphics.

Nicholaides, J. J., et al. 1985. "Agricultural Alternatives for the Amazon Basin." *BioScience*, vol. 35, no. 5, 279–284. Summary of technological options for growing food on acidic and infertile soils in the tropics.

Oldfield, Margery L. 1984. *The Value of Conserving Genetic Resources*. Washington, D.C.: Government Printing Office. Useful analysis.

Parr, J. F., et al. 1983. "Organic Farming in the United States: Principles and Perspectives." *Agro-Ecosystems*, vol. 8, 183–201. Excellent overview.

Paulino, Leonardo A. 1986. *Food in the Third World: Past Trends and Projections*. Research Report 52. Washington, D.C.: International Food Policy Research Institute. Useful source of data.

Pimentel, David. 1987. "Down on the Farm: Genetic Engineering Meets Ecology." *Technology Review*, January, pp. 24–30. Excellent analysis of usefulness and potential harmful effects of genetic engineering.

Pimentel, David, and Marcia Pimentel. 1979. *Food, Energy, and Society*. New York: Wiley. Outstanding discussion of food problems and possible solutions, with emphasis on energy use and food production.

Plucknett, Donald L., and Nigel J. H. Smith. 1982. "Agricultural Research and Third World Food Production." *Science*, vol. 217, 215–219. Excellent summary of positive effects of the green revolution and directions of future research.

Prescott-Allen, Robert, and Christine Prescott-Allen. 1983. *Genes from the Wild: Using Wild Genetic Resources for Food and Raw Materials*. Washington, D.C.: Earthscan. Excellent overview.

Ramade, François. 1984. *The Ecology of Natural Resources*. New York: Wiley. See Chapters 4 and 5 for useful discussion of food resources from the sea and land.

Reichert, Walt. 1982. "Agriculture's Diminishing Diversity." *Environment*, vol. 24, no. 9, 6–11, 39–43. Excellent summary.

Sampson, R. N. 1981. *Farmland or Wasteland: A Time to Choose*. Emmaus, Pa.: Rodale Press. Superb overview of agricultural systems used throughout the world.

Sanchez, Pedro A., et al. 1982. "Amazon Basin Soils: Management for Continuous Crop Production." *Science*, vol. 216, 821–827. Excellent overview of problems and potential of tropical soils.

Short, R. V. 1984. "Breast Feeding." *Scientific American*, vol. 250, no. 4, 35–41. Excellent overview.

Smil, Vaclav. 1985. "China's Food." *Scientific American*, December, 116–125. Excellent overview of progress and potential problems.

Steiner, Frederick. 1981. *Ecological Planning for Farmlands Preservation*. Chicago: A.P.A. Planners Press. Excellent overview.

Timberlake, Lloyd. 1985. *Africa in Crisis*. Washington, D.C.: Earthscan. Excellent overview.

Todd, Nancy J., ed. 1977. *The Book of the New Alchemists*. New York: E. P. Dutton. Description of important experiments in developing a decentralized, self-sufficient agricultural system.

Todd, Nancy J., and John Todd. 1984. *Bioshelters: Ocean Arks, City Farming: Ecology as a Basis for Design*. San Francisco: Sierra Club Books. Outstanding description of how individuals can practice sustainable-earth agriculture.

United States Department of Agriculture. 1980. *Report and Recommendations on Organic Farming*. Washington, D.C.: U.S. Department of Agriculture. Excellent summary of research.

Vietmeyer, Noel D. 1986. "Lesser-Known Plants of Potential Use in Agriculture." *Science*, vol. 232, 1379–1384. Excellent summary.

Wijkman, Anders, and Lloyd Timberlake. 1984. *Natural Disasters: Acts of God or Acts of Man?* Washington, D.C.: Earthscan. Excellent overview of the causes of famine and the pros and cons of famine relief.

Witt, Steven. 1985. *Briefbook: Biotechnology and Genetic Diversity*. San Francisco: California Agricultural Lands Project. Excellent discussion of pros and cons of biotechnology for increasing food production.

Wolf, Edward C. 1986. *Beyond the Green Revolution: New Approaches for Third World Agriculture*. Washington, D.C.: Worldwatch Institute. Excellent analysis.

World Resources Institute and International Institute for Environment and

Development. Annual. *World Resources*. New York: Basic Books. Excellent annual summary since 1986.

Chapter 13 Land Resources: Wilderness, Parks, Forests, and Rangelands

See also the readings for Chapter 2.

Allin, Craig W. 1982. *The Politics of Wilderness Preservation*. Westport, Conn.: Greenwood Press. Excellent political history of efforts to preserve wilderness.

Anderson, Dennis, and Robert Fishwich. 1985. *Fuelwood Consumption and Deforestation in African Countries*. Washington, D.C.: The World Bank. Excellent overview.

Arrandale, Thomas. 1983. *The Battle for Natural Resources*. Washington, D.C.: Congressional Quarterly Books. Excellent overview of conflicts over use of public lands.

Beattie, Mollie, et al. 1983. *Working with Your Woodland*. Hanover, N.H.: University Press of New England. Outstanding guide to management of small private forests.

Blonston, G. 1982. "Coyote." *Science 82*, vol. 3, no. 8, 62–71. Excellent discussion of coyote predation and control.

Brown, Lester R., et al. 1984. *State of the World 1984*. New York: W. W. Norton. See Chapter 5 for an excellent overview of the status of the world's forests and ways to protect them.

Brown, Lester R., et al. 1986. *State of the World 1986*. New York: W. W. Norton. See Chapter 4 for an excellent overview of use and management of rangelands.

Camp, Orville. 1984. *The Forest Farmer's Handbook*. Ashland, Ore.: Sky River Press. Excellent manual for sustainable management of small to medium-sized forest areas.

Caufield, Catherine. 1985. *In the Rainforest*. New York: Alfred A. Knopf. Excellent summary of tropical forest problems.

Chase, Alston. 1986. *Playing God in Yellowstone: Destruction of America's First National Park*. New York: Atlantic Monthly Press. Excellent analysis of problems stemming from elimination of wolves and other natural predators from Yellowstone.

Clawson, Marion. 1975. *Forests for Whom and for What?* Baltimore: Johns Hopkins University Press. Excellent discussion of forest uses and policy.

Clawson, Marion. 1983. *The Federal Lands Revisited*. Washington, D.C.: Resources for the Future. Excellent survey of federal land use with suggestions for future policies.

Connally, Eugenia, ed. 1982. *National Parks in Crisis*. Washington, D.C.: National Parks and Conservation Association. Useful collection of articles on problems facing national parks with recommendations for future policies and actions.

Conservation Foundation. 1985. *National Parks and the New Generation*. Washington, D.C.: Conservation Foundation. Excellent analysis of problems, with proposed solutions.

Dana, Samuel T., and Sally K. Fairfax. 1980. *Forest and Range Policy: Its Development in the United States*. 2d ed. New York: McGraw-Hill. Very useful analysis of federal policies.

Daniel, T. W., et al. 1979. *Principles of Silviculture*. New York: McGraw-Hill. Excellent standard text.

Deacon, Robert T., and M. Bruce Johnson, eds. 1986. *Forestlands: Public and Private*. San Francisco: Pacific Institute for Public Policy Research. Useful analysis of forest management policies in the United States.

Defenders of Wildlife. 1982. *1080: The Case Against Poisoning Our Wildlife*. Washington, D.C.: Government Printing Office. Excellent discussion of why the poison 1080 should not be used.

Eckholm, Erik. 1979. *Planning for the Future: Forestry for Human Needs*. Washington, D.C.: Worldwatch Institute. Excellent suggestions for preserving and renewing more of the world's forests.

Eckholm, Erik. 1982. *Down to Earth: Environment and Human Needs*. New York: Norton. See Chapter 9 for an excellent summary of world deforestation and the global firewood crisis.

Ferguson, Denzel, and Nancy Ferguson. 1983. *Sacred Cows at the Public Trough*. Bend, Ore.: Maverick Publications. Excellent investigative reporting of environmental degradation of western public rangelands by the cattle industry.

Francis, John G., and Richard Ganzel, eds. 1984. *Western Public Lands: The Management of Natural Resources in a Time of Declining Federalism*. Totowa, N.J.: Rowman & Allanheld. Useful collection of articles.

Frome, Michael. 1974. *The Battle for the Wilderness*. New York: Praeger. Excellent overview of politics of wilderness preservation.

Frome, Michael. 1983. *The Forest Service*. Boulder, Colo.: Westview Press. Excellent overview.

Hales, L. 1983. "Who Is the Best Steward of America's Public Lands?" *National Wildlife*, vol. 21, no. 3, 5–11. Excellent analysis.

Heady, H. F. 1975. *Rangeland Management*. New York: McGraw-Hill. Excellent in-depth coverage.

Hendee, John, et al., eds. 1977. *Principles of Wilderness Management*. Washington, D.C.: Government Printing Office. Useful collection of articles.

Hewett, Charles E., and Thomas E. Hamilton, eds. 1982. *Forests in Demand: Conflicts and Solutions*. Boston: Auburn Publishing. Useful discussion of controversies over forest use with recommendations for future policies.

Horowitz, E. C. J. 1974. *Clearcutting*. Washington, D.C.: Acropolis Books. Excellent presentation of the case for clearcutting of some species.

Jordan, Carl F. 1982. "Amazon Rain Forests." *American Scientist*, vol. 70, July–August, pp. 394–400. Excellent overview of the unique problems of forest management in these ecosystems; suggestions for new techniques of management.

Leopold, Aldo. 1949. *A Sand County Almanac*. New York: Oxford University Press. An environmental classic describing Leopold's ecological land use ethic.

Libecap, Gary D. 1986. *Locking Up the Range: Federal Land Control and Grazing*. San Francisco: Pacific Institute for Public Policy Research. Excellent analysis.

McNeely, Jeffery A., and Kenton R. Miller, eds. 1984. *National Parks, Conservation, and Development*. Washington, D.C.: Smithsonian Institution Press. Excellent analysis.

Minckler, Leon S. 1980. *Woodland Ecology*. 2d ed. Syracuse, N.Y.: Syracuse University Press. Superb introduction to ecological management of forests.

Myers, Norman. 1979. *The Sinking Ark*. New York: Pergamon Press. Excellent discussion of the disappearance of the world's tropical moist forests.

Myers, Norman. 1984. *The Primary Source: Tropical Forests and Our Future*. New York: W. W. Norton. Superb analysis by an expert.

Nash, Roderick. 1982. *Wilderness and the American Mind*. 3d ed. New Haven, Conn.: Yale University Press. Outstanding book on American attitudes toward wilderness and conservation.

National Academy of Sciences. 1980. *Conversion of Tropical Moist Forests*. Washington, D.C.: National Academy of Sciences. Authoritative study of the loss of the world's tropical moist forests and what can be done about it.

National Audubon Society. 1986. *Audubon Wildlife Report 1986*. New York: National Audubon Society. Excellent summary of management of national forests by the Forest Service.

National Park Service. 1980. *The State of the Parks—1980*. Washington, D.C.: U.S.

Department of the Interior. Excellent overview.

Office of Technology Assessment. 1984. *Technologies to Sustain Tropical Forest Resources*. Washington, D.C.: Government Printing Office. Excellent analysis.

Olson, Sigurd F. 1969. *The Hidden Forest*. New York: Viking. A beautifully illustrated classic that will heighten your powers of observation and appreciation of the beauty and diversity of forest life.

Ramade, François. 1984. *Ecology of Natural Resources*. New York: Wiley. See Chapters 6, 7, and 8 for overviews of forest, rangeland, national park, and wilderness resources.

Repetto, Robert, ed. 1985. *The Global Possible: Resources, Development, and the New Century*. New Haven, Conn.: Yale University Press. Excellent overview of land and other resources.

Runte, Alfred. 1979. *National Parks: The American Experience*. Lincoln: University of Nebraska Press. Excellent history of the National Park System.

Sax, Joseph. 1980. *Mountains Without Handrails: Reflections on the National Parks*. Ann Arbor: University of Michigan Press. Excellent discussion of the types of recreation the parks should provide.

Shanks, Bernard. 1984. *This Land Is Your Land*. San Francisco: Sierra Club Books. Excellent description of misuse of public lands and suggestions for better management.

Sheridan, D. 1981. "Western Rangeland: Overgrazed and Undermanaged." *Environment*, vol. 23, no. 4, 37–39. Excellent overview.

Sierra Club. 1982. *Our Public Lands: An Introduction to the Agencies and Issues*. San Francisco: Sierra Club Books. Excellent overview.

Smith, D. M. 1982. *The Practice of Silviculture*. New York: Wiley. Excellent standard text.

Spurr, Stephen H., and Buron V. Barnes. 1980. *Forest Ecology*. 3d ed. New York: Ronald Press. Very good forestry text.

Steen, H. K. 1976. *The U.S. Forest Service: A History*. Seattle: University of Washington Press. Superb history of forest management.

Timberlake, Lloyd. 1985. *Africa in Crisis*. Washington, D.C.: Earthscan. Excellent description of destruction of tropical forests and rangelands in Africa.

U.S. Department of Agriculture. 1980. *An Assessment of the Forest and Range Situation in the United States*. Washington, D.C.: U.S.

Department of Agriculture. Useful source of data.

U.S. Department of Interior. 1984. *50 Years of Public Land Management: 1934–1984*. Washington, D.C.: Bureau of Land Management. Useful overview of range management.

Waring, R. H., and W. R. Schlesinger. 1985. *Forest Ecosystems: Concepts and Management*. Orlando, Fla.: Academic Press. Useful source of information.

World Resources Institute and International Institute for Environment and Development. Annual. *World Resources*. New York: Basic Books. Excellent annual summary since 1986 of land resources.

World Resources Institute, World Bank, and United Nations Development Program. 1985. *Tropical Forests: A Call for Action*. Washington, D.C.: World Resources Institute. A plan for saving some of the world's tropical forests.

Wright, H. A., and A. W. Bailey. 1982. *Fire Ecology: United States and Southern Canada*. New York: Wiley. Good in-depth treatment.

Chapter 14 Wild Plant and Animal Resources

Allen, Robert L. 1980. *How to Save the World*. London: Kogan Page. Superb presentation of a strategy to preserve more of the world's vanishing wildlife and land ecosystems.

Anderson, S. H. 1985. *Managing Our Wildlife Resources*. Columbus, Ohio: Charles Merrill. Excellent textbook.

Ayensu, Edward, et al. 1984. *Our Green and Living World: The Wisdom to Save It*. Excellent analysis of need to save plants from extinction.

Bailey, J. A. 1984. *Principles of Wildlife Management*. New York: Wiley. Excellent basic textbook.

Baker, Ron. 1985. *The American Hunting Myth*. New York: Vantage Press. Useful analysis of arguments for and against sport hunting.

Credlund, Arthur G. 1983. *Whales and Whaling*. New York: Seven Hills Books. Excellent overview.

Daiber, Franklin C. 1986. *Conservation of Tidal Marshes*. New York: Van Nostrand Reinhold. Useful source of information.

Dasmann, Raymond F. 1981. *Wildlife Biology*. 2d ed. New York: Wiley. Excellent high-level text.

Davis, Steven D., et al. 1986. *Plants in Danger: What Do We Know?* Cambridge, UK:

Conservation Monitoring Center, International Union for Conservation of Nature and Natural Resources. Excellent source of information.

Durrell, Lee. 1986. *State of the Ark: An Atlas of Conservation in Action*. Garden City, N.Y.: Doubleday. Superb overview.

Eckholm, Erik. 1978. *Disappearing Species: The Social Challenge*. Washington, D.C.: Worldwatch Institute. One of the best overviews of the need for wildlife conservation.

Ehrenfeld, David W. 1970. *Biological Conservation*. New York: Holt, Rinehart & Winston. Superb introduction.

Ehrlich, Paul, and Anne Ehrlich. 1981. *Extinction*. New York: Random House. One of the best treatments of the value of wildlife and the causes of extinction, with suggestions for preventing extinction.

Elton, Charles S. 1958. *The Ecology of Invasions by Plants and Animals*. London: Methuen. An environmental classic on species invasions and introductions.

Gaskin, D. E. 1982. *The Ecology of Whales and Dolphins*. London: Heinemann. Excellent overview.

Hunter, Robert. 1979. *Warriors of the Rainbow: A Chronicle of the Greenpeace Movement*. New York: Holt, Rinehart & Winston. Excellent account of this environmentalist group, which has used commandolike tactics to prevent whaling.

Huxley, Anthony. 1984. *Green Inheritance*. Garden City, N.Y.: Anchor/Doubleday. Superb discussion of importance of plants and how to save them from extinction.

IUCN. 1980. *World Conservation Strategy*. New York: Unipub. Important document.

IUCN. 1984. *National Conservation Strategies*. Gland, Switzerland: IUCN. Excellent summary of what some countries are doing.

Kennedy, David M. 1987. "What's Now at the Zoo?" *Technology Review*, April, 67–73. Excellent overview of the role of zoos in breeding endangered species.

Klausner, A. 1985. "Food From the Sea." *Biotechnology*, vol. 3, no. 1, 27–32. Excellent overview.

Koopowitz, Harold, and Hilary Kaye. 1983. *Plant Extinctions: A Global Crisis*. Washington, D.C.: Stone Wall Press. Useful summary with suggestions for preventing plant extinctions.

Laycock, G. 1966. *The Alien Animals*. Garden City, N.Y.: Natural History Press. Classic reference on effects of introducing alien species.

Leepson, Marc. 1985. "Whaling: End of an Era." *Editorial Research Reports*, Sept. 27, pp. 143–160. Excellent overview.

Leopold, Aldo. 1933. *Game Management*. New York: Scribner's. A classic.

Livingston, John. 1981. *The Fallacy of Wildlife Conservation*. London: McClelland & Stewart. Excellent critique of the idea that wildlife resources should be managed to benefit humans.

Miller, Harlan B., and William H. Williams, eds. 1983. *Ethics and Animals*. Clifton, N.J.: Humana Press. Excellent collection of articles on animal rights.

Myers, Norman. 1983. *A Wealth of Wild Species: Storehouse for Human Welfare*. Boulder, Colo.: Westview Press. Superb presentation of the value of wild species to humans.

National Audubon Society. Annual. *Audubon Wildlife Report*. New York: National Audubon Society. Excellent detailed annual summary published since 1985.

Norton, Bryan G., ed. 1986. *The Preservation of Species*. Princeton, N.J.: Princeton University Press. Excellent collection of articles on why and how to preserve biological diversity.

Oldfield, Margery. 1984. *The Value of Conserving Genetic Resources*. Washington, D.C.: National Park Service. Excellent overview.

Passmore, John. 1974. *Man's Responsibility for Nature*. New York: Scribner's. Useful discussion of the inherent right of species to exist.

Prescott-Allen, Robert, and Christine Prescott-Allen. 1982. *What's Wildlife Worth?* Washington, D.C.: Earthscan. Excellent analysis.

Reagan, Tom. 1983. *The Case for Animal Rights*. Berkeley: University of California Press. Excellent analysis.

Reagan, Tom, and P. Singer. 1976. *Animal Rights and Human Obligation*. Englewood Cliffs, N.J.: Prentice-Hall. Excellent discussion of this controversial issue.

Reed, Nathaniel, and Dennis Drabelle. 1984. *The United States Fish and Wildlife Service*. Boulder, Colo.: Westview Press. Excellent overview.

Roe, Frank G. 1970. *The North American Buffalo*. Toronto: University of Toronto Press. Documented discussion of the rise and fall of the American bison.

Roots, Clive. 1976. *Animal Invaders*. New York: Universe Books. Excellent discussion of good and bad results from introducing species to new areas.

Shaw, James H. 1985. *Introduction to Wildlife Management*. New York: McGraw-Hill. Excellent text at a high level.

Smith, Robert Leo. 1976. "Ecological Genesis of Endangered Species: The Philosophy of Preservation." *Annual Reviews of Ecology and Systematics*, vol. 7, 33–56. Excellent discussion of how some species are vulnerable to extinction.

Soulé, Michael, ed. 1986. *Conservation Biology*. Sunderland, Mass.: Sinauer. Excellent collection of articles providing more advanced information on wildlife resource management.

Steiner, Stan. 1976. *The Vanishing White Man*. New York: Harper & Row. Excellent discussion of the American Indian philosophy of the sacredness of the earth and all its inhabitants.

Stone, Christopher D. 1975. *Should Trees Have Standing? Toward Legal Rights for Natural Objects*. Los Altos, Calif.: William Kaufmann. Useful discussion of the dispute over development at Mineral King, which went to the U.S. Supreme Court.

Trefethen, J. B. 1975. *An American Crusade for Wildlife*. New York: Winchester Press. Excellent history of wildlife conservation in the United States.

U.S. Fish and Wildlife Service. 1984. *Endangered and Threatened Wildlife and Plants*. Washington, D.C.: U.S. Fish and Wildlife Service. Useful source of data.

Vecsey, C., and R. Venables. 1980. *American Indian Environments*. Syracuse, N.Y.: Syracuse University Press. Good discussion of the ecological wisdom of some American Indian tribes.

Wilson, Edward O. 1984. *Biophilia*. Cambridge, Mass.: Harvard University Press. Excellent discussion of the need to preserve wildlife.

World Resources Institute and International Institute for Environment and Development. Annual. *World Resources*. Excellent annual summary of state of wildlife resources published since 1986.

Yalden, D. W., and P. A. Morris. 1975. *The Lives of Bats*. New York: Quadrangle/New York Times. Excellent discussion of ecological importance of bats.

Chapter 15 Nonrenewable Mineral Resources: Raw Materials from the Earth's Crust

Barnet, Richard J. 1980. *The Lean Years: Politics in an Age of Scarcity*. New York: Simon & Schuster. Superb discussion of the politics and economics of resource use and increasing scarcity.

Barnett, Harold J. 1967. "The Myth of Our Vanishing Resources." *Transactions—Social Sciences & Modern Society*, June, pp. 7–10. Statement of the cornucopian view of our resource situation. Compare with the article by Cloud (1975).

Berry, Stephen. 1972. "Recycling, Thermodynamics and Environmental Thrift." *Bulletin of the Atomic Scientists*, May, pp. 8–15. Good discussion of the limits of recycling.

Borgese, Elisabeth Mann. 1985. *The Mines of Neptune: Minerals and Metals from the Sea*. New York: Abrams. Excellent overview.

Broadus, James M. 1987. "Seabed Minerals." *Science*, vol. 235, 853–860. Excellent overview.

Brown, Lester R., et al. 1984. *State of the World 1984*. New York: W. W. Norton. See Chapter 6 for excellent overview of recycling.

Chandler, William U. 1983. *Materials Recycling: The Virtue of Necessity*. Washington, D.C.: Worldwatch Institute. Superb overview.

Clark, Joel P., and Frank R. Field, III. 1985. "How Critical Are Critical Materials?" *Technology Review*, August/September, pp. 38–46. Argues that the United States will not run short of critical materials because of conservation and substitution.

Cloud, Preston E., Jr. 1975. "Mineral Resources Today and Tomorrow." In *Environment: Resources, Pollution and Society*, 2d ed., edited by William W. Murdoch. Sunderland, Mass.: Sinauer. Superb summary of the neo-Malthusian view. Compare with Barnett (1967), Kahn et al. (1976), Simon (1981), and Smith (1979).

Council on Economics and National Security. 1981. *Strategic Minerals: A Resource Crisis*. Washington, D.C.: Council on Economics and National Security. Useful analysis.

Dorr, Ann. 1984. *Minerals—Foundations of Society*. Montgomery County, Md.: League of Women Voters of Montgomery County. Outstanding introduction to mineral resources.

Fischman, Leonard F. 1980. *World Mineral Trends and U.S. Supply Problems*. Washington, D.C.: Resources for the Future. Excellent summary of future availability of U.S. mineral supplies.

Franchot, Peter. 1978. *Bottles and Cans: The Story of the Vermont Deposit Law*. Washington, D.C.: National Wildlife Federation. Excellent summary.

Garbor, D., et al. 1978. *Beyond the Age of Waste*. New York: Pergamon Press. Useful discussion of resource conservation.

Hamrin, Robert D. 1983. *A Renewable Resource Economy*. New York: Praeger Scientific. Excellent overview of resource principles, supplies, and conservation.

Hayes, Denis. 1978. *Repairs, Reuse, Recycling—First Steps Toward a Sustainable Society*. Washington, D.C.: Worldwatch Institute. Splendid overview of resource recovery and conservation.

Huls, Jon, and Neil Seldman. 1985. *Waste to Wealth*. Washington, D.C.: Institute for Local Self-Reliance. Superb discussion of recycling and reuse.

Kahn, Herman, et al. 1976. *The Next 200 Years: A Scenario for America and the World*. New York: William Morrow. A cornucopian view on mineral supplies.

Lean, Geoffrey. 1978. *Rich World Poor World*. London: Allen & Urwin. Excellent discussion of the need for a new international economic order.

Leontief, Wassily, et al. 1983. *The Future of Nonfuel Minerals in the U.S. and World Economy: 1980–2030*. Lexington, Mass.: Lexington (Heath). Excellent analysis.

Maurice, Charles, and Charles W. Smithson. 1984. *The Doomsday Myth*. Stanford, Calif.: Hoover Institution Press. Cornucopian view of mineral resource supplies by two economists.

Office of Technology Assessment. 1985. *Strategic Materials: Technologies to Reduce U.S. Import Vulnerability*. Washington, D.C.: Government Printing Office. Excellent analysis.

Park, Charles F., Jr. 1975. *Earthbound: Minerals, Energy, and Man's Future*. San Francisco: W. H. Freeman. Superb overview emphasizing the neo-Malthusian view.

Purcell, Arthur H. 1980. *The Waste Watchers: A Citizen's Handbook for Conserving Energy*. Garden City, N.Y.: Anchor Press/Doubleday. Superb guide for achieving a low-waste society.

Ridker, Ronald G., and William D. Watson. 1980. *To Choose a Future: Resources and Environmental Consequences of Alternative Growth Paths*. Baltimore: Johns Hopkins University Press. Excellent and fairly optimistic overview.

Seaborg, Glenn T. 1974. "The Recycle Society of Tomorrow." *The Futurist*, June, pp. 108–115. Stirring vision of what a low-waste society would be like.

Simon, Julian L. 1981. *The Ultimate Resource*. Princeton, N.J.: Princeton University Press. Effective presentation of the cornucopian position.

Skinner, Brian J. 1976. *Earth Resources*. 2d ed. Englewood Cliffs, N.J.: Prentice-Hall. Excellent survey of the world's resources.

Smith, V. Kerry. 1979. *Scarcity and Growth Reconsidered*. Baltimore: Johns Hopkins University Press. Excellent analysis of the cornucopian view of world resource supplies.

Trainer, F. E. 1982. "Potentially Recoverable Resources: How Recoverable?" *Resource Policy*, vol. 8, no. 1, 41–50. Superb analysis.

U.S. Bureau of Mines. 1983. *The Domestic Supply of Critical Minerals*. Washington, D.C.: Government Printing Office. Useful source of data.

U.S. Geological Survey. 1986. *Subsea Mineral Resources* (Bulletin 1698-A). Denver, Colo.: USGS Federal Center. Useful source of data.

Ward, Barbara. 1979. *Progress for a Small Planet*. New York: W. W. Norton. Superb discussion of the need for a new international world economic order.

Westing, Arthur H. 1986. *Global Resources and International Conflict*. New York: Oxford University Press. Excellent analysis.

Chapter 16 Nonrenewable Energy Resources: Fossil Fuels

See also the readings for Chapter 3.

Ackerman, Bruce A., and William T. Hassler. 1981. *Clean Coal/Dirty Air*. New Haven, Conn.: Yale University Press. Excellent discussion of air pollution from coal plants with suggestions for improvement.

Allar, Bruce. 1984. "No More Coal-Smoked Skies?" *Environment*, vol. 26, no. 2, pp. 25–30. Excellent summary of fluidized-bed combustion of coal.

Brown, Lester R., et al. Annual. *State of the World*. New York: W. W. Norton. Excellent annual overviews of oil use and trends published since 1984.

Brown, William M. 1984. "The Outlook for Future Petroleum Supplies." In *The Resourceful Earth*, edited by Julian L. Simon and Herman Kahn. New York: Basil Blackwell. Cornucopian view of future oil supplies.

Congressional Quarterly Editors. 1985. *Energy and Environment: The Unfinished Business*. Washington, D.C.: Congressional Quarterly. Excellent overview.

Edmonds, Jae, and John M. Reilly. 1985. *Global Energy: Assessing the Future*. New York: Oxford University Press. Excellent overview of energy supplies, alternatives, and policy over the next 50 to 75 years.

Environmental Protection Agency. 1980. *Environmental Perspective on the Emerging Oil Shale Industry*. Washington, D.C.: Government Printing Office. Excellent overview of environmental impacts of oil shale development.

Flavin, Christopher. 1980. *The Future of Synthetic Materials: The Petroleum Connection*. Washington, D.C.: Worldwatch Institute. Explains the importance of using oil to produce petrochemicals and evaluates alternatives.

Flavin, Christopher. 1985. *World Oil: Coping with the Dangers of Success*. Washington, D.C.: Worldwatch Institute. Explains problems of the temporary oil glut of the 1980s and suggests ways to avoid serious energy problems in the future.

Gates, David M. 1985. *Energy and Ecology*. Sunderland, Mass.: Sinauer. Excellent detailed analysis of all major energy alternatives.

Hayes, Earl T. 1979. "Energy Resources Available to the United States, 1985 to 2000." *Science*, vol. 203, 233–239. Superb overview.

Hirsch, Robert L. 1987. "Impending United States Energy Crisis." *Science*, vol. 235, 1467–1473. Excellent analysis of what we may face in the 1990s.

Holdren, John. 1982. "Energy Hazards: What to Measure, What to Compare." *Technology Review*, April, pp. 32–38. Excellent guide to comparing risks and benefits of various energy technologies.

Hughes, Barry B., et al. 1985. *Energy in the Global Arena: Actors, Values, Policies, and Futures*. Durham, N.C.: Duke University Press. Outstanding overview and analysis of energy alternatives and policy.

Humphrey, Craig R., and Frederick R. Buttel. 1982. *Environment, Energy, and Society*. Belmont, Calif.: Wadsworth. Excellent overview of energy problems and possible alternatives.

Leon, George de Lucenay. 1982. *Energy Forever: Power for Today and Tomorrow*. New York: Arco Publishing. Excellent nontechnical overview of nonrenewable and renewable energy alternatives.

Masters, Charles D. 1985. *World Petroleum Resources: A Perspective*. Open-File Report 85-248. Reston, Va.: U.S. Department of Interior Geological Survey. Useful source of data on latest estimates.

Perry, Harry. 1983. "Coal in the United States: A Status Report." *Science*, vol. 222, no. 4622, 377–394. Excellent overview.

Shahinpoor, Mohsen. 1982. "Making Oil from Sand." *Technology Review*, February–March, pp. 49–54. Excellent summary of oil sands.

Woodwell, G. M. 1974. "Success, Succession and Adam Smith." *BioScience*, vol. 24, no. 2, 81–87. Outstanding overview of the world's energy problems and their ecological implications.

Chapter 17 Nonrenewable and Perpetual Energy Resources: Geothermal and Nuclear Energy

See also readings for Chapter 3.

American Nuclear Society. 1985. *Report of the Special Committee on Source Terms*. La Grange, Ill.: American Nuclear Society. Analysis suggesting that U.S. nuclear power plants are much safer than earlier studies indicated.

American Physical Society. 1985. *Radionuclide Release from Severe Accidents at Nuclear Power Plants*. New York: American Physical Society. Analysis of whether U.S. nuclear power plants are safer than earlier studies indicated.

Atomic Industrial Forum. 1985. *Nuclear Power Plant Response to Severe Accidents*. Bethesda, Md.: Atomic Industrial Forum. Analysis by the nuclear industry suggesting that U.S. nuclear power plants are much safer than earlier studies indicated.

Beckmann, Peter. 1976. *The Health Hazards of Not Going Nuclear*. Boulder, Colo.: Golem Press. Readable, hard-hitting defense of nuclear power.

Brown, Lester R., et al. Annual. *State of the World*. New York: W. W. Norton. Excellent annual overviews of economics of nuclear power (1984), decommissioning nuclear power plants (1986), and nuclear power safety (1987).

Browne, Corinne, and Robert Munroe. 1981. *Time Bomb: Understanding the Threat of Nuclear Power*. New York: WIlliam Morrow. Excellent overview.

Caldicott, Helen. 1981. *Nuclear Madness*. New York: Bantam Books. Attack on nuclear power by a physician and leading antinuclear activist.

Cohen, Bernard L. 1983. *Before It's Too Late: A Scientist's Case for Nuclear Power*. New York: Plenum Press. Probably the best available case for nuclear power by an expert.

Cummings, Ronald G., et al. 1979. "Mining Earth's Heat: Hot Dry Rock Geothermal Energy." *Technology Review*, February, pp. 58–78. Very good summary.

Department of Energy. 1980. *Geothermal Energy and Our Environment*. Washington, D.C.: Department of Energy. Superb summary.

Faculty Members at M.I.T. 1984. *Nuclear Almanac: Confronting the Atom in War and Peace*. Reading, Mass.: Addison-Wesley. Excellent source of information.

Flavin, Christopher. 1987. *Reassessing Nuclear Power: The Fallout from Chernobyl*. Washington, D.C.: Worldwatch Institute. Excellent analysis.

Ford, Daniel F. 1983. *Three Mile Island: Thirty Minutes to Meltdown*. New York: Penguin Books. Excellent overview by a nuclear power expert.

Ford, Daniel F. 1986. *Meltdown*. New York: Simon & Schuster. Excellent analysis of nuclear power plant safety by an expert.

Gray, Mike, and Ira Rosen. 1982. *The Warning: Accident at Three Mile Island*. New York: W. W. Norton. Useful description.

Harding, Jim. 1984. "Lights Dim for Nuclear Power." *Not Man Apart*, April, pp. 21–22. Excellent summary of economics of nuclear power in the United States and elsewhere.

Hilgartner, Stephen, et al. 1982. *Nukespeak*. San Francisco: Sierra Club Books. Excellent discussion of the history and dangers of nuclear power.

Hippenheimer, T. A. 1984. *The Man-Made Sun: The Quest for Fusion Power*. Boston: Little, Brown. Excellent overview.

Hunt, Charles B. 1984. "Disposal of Radioactive Wastes." *Bulletin of the Atomic Scientists*, April, pp. 44–46. Summary by a prominent geologist of problems associated with geologic disposal of radioactive wastes.

Kaku, Michio, and Jennifer Trainer. 1982. *Nuclear Power: Both Sides*. New York: W. W. Norton. Useful collection of pro and con essays.

Kemeny, John G. 1980. "Saving American Democracy: The Lessons of Three Mile Island." *Technology Review*, June–July, pp. 65–75. Excellent analysis by the head of the presidential panel that investigated the nuclear accident.

Komanoff, Charles. 1981. *Power Plant Cost Escalation*. New York: Van Nostrand Reinhold. An expert's detailed analysis of the unfavorable economics of nuclear power.

Kulcinski, G. L., et al. 1979. "Energy for the Long Run: Fission or Fusion." *American Scientist*, vol. 67, 78–89. Superb evaluation of nuclear fusion.

League of Women Voters Education Fund. 1982. *A Nuclear Power Primer: Issues for Citizens*. Washington, D.C.: League of Women Voters. Outstanding, readable, balanced summary.

League of Women Voters Education Fund. 1985. *The Nuclear Waste Primer*. Washington, D.C.: League of Women Voters. Excellent, readable, balanced summary.

Lidsky, Lawrence M. 1983. "The Trouble with Fusion." *Technology Review*, October, pp. 32–44. Superb evaluation by one of the world's most prominent nuclear fusion scientists.

Lidsky, Lawrence M. 1984. "The Reactor of the Future," *Technology Review*, February–March, pp. 52–56. Excellent summary of new and safer designs for nuclear fission reactors.

Lindholm, Ulf, and Paul Gnirk. 1982. *Nuclear Waste Disposal: Can We Rely on Bedrock?* New York: Pergamon Press. Useful analysis.

Lipschultz, Ronnie. 1980. *Radioactive Waste: Politics, Technology, and Risk*. Cambridge, Mass.: Ballinger. Useful analysis of this problem.

Loeb, Paul. 1986. *Nuclear Culture: Living and Working in the World's Largest Atomic Complex*. Philadelphia: New Society. Fascinating discussion of Hanford Nuclear Reservation.

Lovins, Amory B., and L. Hunter Lovins. 1980. *Energy/War: Breaking the Nuclear Link*. San Francisco: Friends of the Earth. Superb discussion by two experts of the relationship of the development of commercial nuclear power to the proliferation of nuclear weapons.

Lovins, Amory B., and L. Hunter Lovins. 1982. *Brittle Power: Energy Strategy for National Security*. Andover, Mass.: Brick House. Outstanding discussion of how centralized power plants threaten national security.

McCracken, Samuel. 1982. *The War Against the Atom*. New York: Basic Books. Excellent defense of nuclear power.

Murray, Raymond L. 1982. *Understanding Radioactive Waste*. Columbus, Ohio: Battelle Press. Useful overview by an expert.

National Academy of Sciences. 1980. *Energy in Transition 1985–2010: Final Report of the Committee on Nuclear and Alternative Energy Systems*. Washington, D.C.: National Academy Press. Useful analysis.

O'Banion, Kerry. 1981. "Long-Term Nuclear Options." *Environmental Science & Technology*, vol. 15, no. 10, 1130–1136. Excellent comparison of the environmental effects of nuclear fission breeder reactors and nuclear fusion reactors.

Office of Technology Assessment. 1984. *Managing the Nation's Commercial High-Level Radioactive Waste*. Washington, D.C.: Government Printing Office. Excellent sourcebook.

O'Hefferman, Patrick, Amory Lovins, and L. Hunter Lovins. 1984. *The First Nuclear World War*. New York: Morrow Books. Excellent overview of how terrorists could steal plutonium and start a nuclear war and suggestions for preventing such a scenario.

Organization for Economic Cooperation and Development (OECD). 1986. *Decommissioning of Nuclear Facilities: Feasibility, Needs, and Costs.* Washington, D.C.: OECD. Useful analysis.

Patterson, Walter C. 1984. *The Plutonium Business and the Spread of the Bomb.* San Francisco: Sierra Club Books. Superb overview.

Pollack, Cynthia. 1986. *Decommissioning: Nuclear Power's Missing Link.* Washington, D.C.: Worldwatch Institute. Superb analysis of this unsolved problem.

President's Commission on the Accident at Three Mile Island. 1979. *Report of the President's Commission on the Accident at Three Mile Island.* Washington, D.C.: Government Printing Office. Useful analysis of nuclear reactor safety.

Ramberg, Bennett. 1985. *Nuclear Power Plants as Weapons for the Enemy.* Berkeley: University of California Press. Thought-provoking analysis.

Resnikoff, Marvin. 1983. *The Next Nuclear Gamble: Transportation and Storage of Nuclear Waste.* Washington, D.C.: Council on Economic Priorities. Excellent analysis.

Shapiro, Fred C. 1981. *Radwaste: A Reporter's Investigation of a Growing Nuclear Menace.* New York: Random House. Excellent overview.

Spector, Leonard S. 1985. *The New Nuclear Nations.* New York: Vintage Press. Excellent analysis of proliferation of nuclear weapons.

Union of Concerned Scientists. 1985. *Safety Second: A Critical Evaluation of the NRC's First Decade.* Washington, D.C.: Union of Concerned Scientists. Excellent analysis.

U.S. Office of Technology Assessment. 1984. *Nuclear Power in an Age of Uncertainty.* Washington, D.C.: Government Printing Office. Excellent analysis of the future of commercial nuclear power in the United States.

Weinberg, Alvin M. 1985. *Continuing the Nuclear Dialogue.* La Grange Park, Ill.: American Nuclear Society. Thoughtful defense of nuclear power.

Weinberg, Alvin M., et al. 1985. *The Second Nuclear Era: A New Start for Nuclear Power.* New York: Praeger. Detailed analysis of how nuclear power might grow out of its present economically imposed moratorium in the United States.

Chapter 18 Perpetual and Renewable Energy Resources: Conservation, Sun, Wind, Water, and Biomass

See also the readings for Chapter 3.

Bockris, J. O. 1980. *Energy Options: Real Economics and the Solar-Hydrogen System.* London: Taylor & Francis. Excellent analysis by an expert on this energy alternative.

Brown, Lester R., and Pamela Shaw. 1982. *Six Steps to a Sustainable Society.* Washington, D.C.: Worldwatch Society. Excellent overview.

Brown, Lester R., et al. Annual. *State of the World.* New York: W. W. Norton. Various chapters in these annual reports published since 1984 give excellent summaries of progress in renewable energy resources and energy conservation.

Butti, Ken, and John Perlin. *A Golden Thread: 2500 Years of Solar Architecture and Technology.* New York: Cheshire Books. Superb overview.

Calvin, Melvin. 1979. "Petroleum Plantations for Fuels and Materials." *BioScience,* vol. 29, no. 9, 533–538. Nobel Prize-winning chemist discusses his proposal to grow plants that yield petroleum.

Center for Science in the Public Interest. 1977. *99 Ways to a Simple Lifestyle.* Garden City, N.Y.: Doubleday. Superb summary of how you can conserve matter and energy.

Chandler, William U. 1985. *Energy Productivity: Key to Environmental Protection and Economic Progress.* Washington, D.C.: Worldwatch Institute. Excellent discussion of ways to save energy.

Chapman, Duane. 1983. *Energy Resources and Energy Corporations.* Ithaca, N.Y.: Cornell University Press. Useful analysis of the economic and political roles of energy companies.

Charlier, Roger Henri. 1982. *Tidal Energy.* New York: Van Nostrand Reinhold. Excellent description and analysis of this option.

Clarke, Robin. 1977. *Building for Self-Sufficiency.* New York: Universe Books. How to prepare for the energy and economic crunch that may come in the 1990s.

Commoner, Barry. 1983. "A Reporter at Large: Ethanol." *New Yorker,* October 10, pp. 125–140. Excellent overview of ethanol as a biofuel.

Darmstadter, Joel, et al. 1983. *Energy Today and Tomorrow—Living with Uncertainty.* Englewood Cliffs, N.J.: Prentice-Hall. Useful analysis of energy problems and possible solutions.

Demand and Conservation Panel of the Committee on Nuclear and Alternative Energy Systems, National Academy of Sciences. 1978. "U.S. Energy Demand: Some Low Energy Futures." *Science,* vol. 200, 142–152. Useful analysis showing how the United States could get along with much less energy without affecting lifestyles.

Deudney, Daniel, and Christopher Flavin. 1983. *Renewable Energy: The Power to Choose.* 1983. New York: W. W. Norton. Probably the best overview of renewable energy resources.

Editorial Research Reports. 1982. *Energy Issues: New Directions and Issues.* Washington, D.C.: Congressional Quarterly. Useful overview.

Energy Conservation Research. 1979. *Energy for Today and Tomorrow.* Malvern, Pa.: Energy Conservation Research. One of the best lists of ways to avoid energy waste.

Energy Policy Project. 1974. *A Time to Choose: The Final Report of the Energy Policy Project of the Ford Foundation.* Cambridge, Mass.: Ballinger. Excellent overview by a high-level task force.

Farallones Institute. 1979. *The Integral Urban House: Self-Reliant Living in the City.* San Francisco: Sierra Club Books. Excellent discussion of how to survive in the city.

Finneran, Kevin. 1983. "Solar Technology: A Whether Report." *Technology Review,* April, pp. 48–59. Excellent overview.

Flavin, Christopher. 1980. *Energy and Architecture: The Solar and Conservation Potential.* Washington, D.C.: Worldwatch Institute. Excellent summary.

Flavin, Christopher. 1982. *Electricity from Sunlight: The Future of Photovoltaics.* Washington, D.C.: Worldwatch Institute. Superb overview.

Flavin, Christopher. 1984. *Electricity's Future: The Shift to Efficiency and Small-Scale Power.* Washington, D.C.: Worldwatch Institute. Superb overview of energy conservation efforts and possibilities.

Flavin, Christopher. 1986. *Electricity for a Developing World: New Directions.* Washington, D.C.: Worldwatch Institute. Superb overview.

Fowler, John W. 1984. *Energy and the Environment.* 2d ed. New York: McGraw-Hill. Excellent summary of energy problems and alternatives at a slightly higher level than this text.

Gever, John, et al. 1986. *Beyond Oil.* Washington, D.C.: Carrying Capacity. Excellent computer-projected assessment of U.S. energy supplies well into the next century.

Gibbons, John H., and William U. Chandler. 1981. *The Conservation Revolution*. New York: Plenum Press. Excellent and informative overview.

Glasner, David. 1986. *Politics, Prices, and Petroleum: The Political Economy of Energy*. San Francisco: Pacific Institute for Public Policy Analysis. Useful analysis.

Hayes, Denis. 1977. *Rays of Hope: The Transition to a Post-Petroleum World*. New York: W. W. Norton. Outstanding analysis of energy problems and alternatives.

Heede, H. Richard L., et al. 1985. *The Hidden Costs of Energy*. Washington, D.C.: Center for Renewable Resources. Superb summary of federal subsidies provided for development of various energy alternatives.

Hill, Ray. 1980. "Alcohol Fuels—Can They Replace Gasoline?" *Popular Science*, March, pp. 25–34. Very good summary.

Holdren, John P. 1982. "Energy Hazards: What to Measure, What to Compare." *Technology Review*, April, pp. 34–75. Excellent discussion of how to evaluate risks of various energy options.

Holdren, John P., et al. 1980. "Environmental Aspects of Renewable Energy Sources." In *Annual Review of Energy*, vol. 5, edited by Jack M. Hollander et al. Palo Alto, Calif.: Annual Reviews. Excellent analysis of the environmental impacts of renewable energy alternatives by an expert. Compare with Inhaber's less favorable estimate (1982) of the impact of these alternatives.

Hollander, Jack M., et al., eds. Annual. *Annual Review of Energy*. Palo Alto, Calif.: Annual Reviews. Excellent series of articles.

Inhaber, Herbert. 1982. *Energy Risk Assessment*. New York: Gordon & Breach. Updating of a controversial 1978 analysis indicating that solar, wind, biomass, and other renewable energy options have a more severe impact than most energy options, with nuclear power having the lowest impact. Compare with Holdren et al. (1980).

Kash, Don E., and Robert W. Rycroft. 1984. *U.S. Energy Policy: Crisis and Complacency*. Norman, Okla.: University of Oklahoma Press. Useful analysis.

Kendall, Henry, and Steven Nadis. 1980. *Energy Strategies: Toward a Solar Future*. Cambridge, Mass.: Ballinger. Splendid analysis of energy alternatives.

Knowles, R. S. 1980. *American's Energy Famine: Its Causes and Cures*. Norman, Okla.: University of Oklahoma Press. Useful analysis.

Mazria, Edward. 1979. *The Passive Solar Energy Book: A Complete Guide to Passive Solar Home, Greenhouse, and Building Design*.

Emmaus, Pa.: Rodale Press. Excellent description.

Medsker, Larry. 1982. *Side Effects of Renewable Energy Resources*. New York: National Audubon Society. Excellent summary of environmental effects.

Miller, Alan S., et al. 1986. *Growing Power: Bioenergy for Development and Industry*. Washington, D.C.: World Resources Institute. Excellent overview.

National Academy of Sciences. 1983. *Alcohol Fuels: Options for Developing Countries*. Washington, D.C.: National Academy Press. Useful analysis.

Penny, Terry R., and Desikan Bharathan. 1987. "Power from the Sea." *Scientific American*, vol. 286, no. 1, 86–92. Excellent overview.

Pimentel, David, et al. 1984. "Environmental and Social Costs of Biomass Energy." *BioScience*, February, pp. 89–93. Excellent overview.

Pryde, Philip R. 1983. *Nonconventional Energy Resources*. New York: Wiley-Interscience. Excellent overview with emphasis on nonrenewable energy resources.

Purcell, Arthur. 1980. *The Waste Watchers: A Citizen's Handbook for Conserving Energy and Resources*. Garden City, N.Y.: Anchor Press/Doubleday. Superb guide.

Rosenbaum, Walter A. 1987. *Energy, Politics, and Public Policy*, 2d ed. Washington, D.C.: Congressional Quarterly. Superb analysis.

Ross, Marc H., and Robert H. Williams. 1981. *Our Energy: Regaining Control*. New York: McGraw-Hill. Excellent overview of opportunities for energy conservation.

Sant, Roger W., and Dennis W. Bakke. 1983. *Creating Energy Abundance*. New York: McGraw-Hill. Excellent summary of why saving energy saves money.

Sawyer, Stephen W. 1986. *Renewable Energy: Progress, Prospects*. Washington, D.C.: Association of American Geographers. Outstanding evaluation.

Simon, Julian L. 1981. *The Ultimate Resource*. Princeton, N.J.: Princeton University Press. Optimistic view by a cornucopian economist who argues that we will always have affordable supplies of energy. His view is based in part on the idea that energy can be recycled—ignoring the second law of energy.

Skelton, Luther W. 1984. *The Solar-Hydrogen Economy: Beyond the Age of Fire*. New York: Van Nostrand Reinhold. Excellent overview.

Smith, Nigel. 1981. *Wood: An Ancient Fuel with a New Future*. Washington, D.C.: Worldwatch Institute. Outstanding overview.

Solar Energy Research Institute. 1981. *A New Prosperity: Building a Sustainable Energy Future*. Andover, Mass.: Brick House. Outstanding study showing that more efficient use of energy and greatly expanded use of renewable energy could lead to a 25 percent reduction in U.S. energy consumption and virtually eliminate oil imports.

Stephenson, Richard M. 1982. *Living with Tomorrow: A Factual Look at America's Resources*. New York: Wiley-Interscience. Balanced analysis of the energy and related environmental problems facing the United States.

Stobaugh, Robert, and Daniel Yergin, eds. 1979. *Energy Future: Report of the Energy Project at the Harvard Business School*. New York: Random House. Superb analysis of U.S. energy alternatives.

Swan, Christopher C. 1986. *Suncell: Energy, Economy, Photovoltaics*. New York: Random House. Outstanding overview of the potential of this emerging energy alternative.

Underground Space Center, University of Minnesota. 1979. *Earth-Sheltered Housing Design*. Princeton, N.J.: Van Nostrand Reinhold. One of the best sources.

Chapter 19 Air Pollution

Barth, Michael C., and James G. Titus. 1984. *Greenhouse Effect and Sea Level Rise*. New York: Van Nostrand Reinhold. Excellent summary of possible effects on coastal areas.

Borman, F. H. 1982. "The Effects of Air Pollution on the New England Landscape." *Ambio*, vol. 11, no. 5, pp. 338–346. Excellent source of information.

Boyle, Robert H., and R. Alexander Boyle. 1983. *Acid Rain*. New York: Schocken Books. Excellent overview.

Brodeur, Paul. 1985. *Outrageous Conduct: The Asbestos Industry*. New York: Pantheon. Excellent investigative reporting.

Bryson, Reid A., and Thomas J. Murray. 1977. *Climates of Hunger: Mankind and the World's Changing Weather*. Madison: University of Wisconsin Press. Excellent summary of the position that the world may be cooling.

Council on Environmental Quality. 1981. *Global Energy Futures and the Carbon Dioxide Problem*. Washington, D.C.: Council on Environmental Quality. Superb overview.

Cowling, Ellis B. 1982. "Acid Precipitation in Historical Perspective." *Environmental*

Science and Technology, vol. 16, no. 2, 110A–122A. Useful survey of the literature and knowledge of this problem since 1661.

Davies, J. Clarence, III, and Barbara S. Davies. 1975. *The Politics of Pollution*. 2d ed. Indianapolis, Ind.: Pegasus. Superb discussion of the politics of air pollution control.

Ember, Lois R., et al. 1986. "Tending the Global Commons." *Chemistry and Engineering News*, Nov. 24, pp. 14–64. Superb analysis of effects of human activities on global climate.

Environmental Protection Agency. 1983. *Can We Delay a Greenhouse Warming?* Washington, D.C.: EPA. Useful evaluation of effects of policies to delay the effects of increasing CO_2 levels.

Fennelly, Paul F. 1976. "The Origin and Influence of Airborne Particulates." *American Scientist*, vol. 64, 46–56. Superb overview.

Gould, Roy. 1985. *Going Sour: Science and Politics of Acid Rain*. Cambridge, Mass.: Birkhauser. Useful analysis.

Government Institutes. 1983. *Acid Deposition: Causes and Effects*. Rockville, Md.: Government Institutes. Excellent overview.

Gribbin, John. 1982. *Future Weather and the Greenhouse Effect*. New York: Delacorte Press. Useful overview of factors affecting global climate and the greenhouse effect.

Heywood, John, and John Wilkes. 1980. "Is There a Better Automobile Engine?" *Technology Review*, November–December, pp. 19–29. Superb overview of advantages and disadvantages of possible new engines.

Holdren, John P. 1971. "Global Thermal Pollution." In *Global Ecology*, edited by J. P. Holdren and P. R. Ehrlich. New York: Harcourt Brace Jovanovich. Clear summary of the principles and calculations of predicting the effects of human heat inputs on climate.

Kellogg, William W., and R. Schware. 1981. *Climate Change and Society: Consequences of Increasing Atmospheric Carbon Dioxide*. Boulder, Colo.: Westview Press. Outstanding overview.

Landsberg, Helmut E. 1981. *The Urban Climate*. New York: Academic Press. Useful overview of research.

Lave, Lester B., and Eugene B. Seskin. 1977. *Air Pollution and Human Health*. Baltimore: Johns Hopkins University Press. Useful source of data.

League of Women Voters Education Fund. 1981. *Blueprint for Clean Air*. Washington, D.C.: League of Women Voters. Excellent

description of the Clean Air acts of 1970 and 1977 and suggested changes for the future.

Lovins, Amory B., et al. 1981. *Least-Cost Energy: Solving the CO_2 Problem*. Andover, Mass.: Brick House. Excellent summary of how the CO_2 problem could be minimized by a combination of energy conservation and a switch to solar, wind, hydro, biomass, and other forms of renewable energy.

Lundquist, Lennart J. 1980. *The Hare and the Tortoise: Clean Air Policy in the United States*. Ann Arbor: University of Michigan Press. Superb analysis of the politics of air pollution.

Luoma, Jon R. 1984. *Troubled Skies, Troubled Waters: The Story of Acid Rain*. New York: Viking. Excellent overview.

McKormick, John. 1985. *Acid Earth: The Global Threat of Acid Pollution*. Washington, D.C.: Earthscan. Excellent analysis.

National Academy of Sciences. 1981. *Indoor Pollutants*. Washington, D.C.: National Academy Press. Excellent summary.

National Academy of Sciences. 1983. *Acid Deposition: Atmospheric Processes in the United States*. Washington, D.C.: National Academy Press. Excellent overview and source of data.

National Academy of Sciences. 1983. *Changing Climate*. Washington, D.C.: National Academy Press. Excellent overview of the CO_2 problem.

National Academy of Sciences. 1986. *Acid Deposition: Long-Term Trends*. Washington, D.C.: National Academy Press. Excellent summary.

National Clean Air Coalition. 1983. *The Clean Air Act*. Washington, D.C.: National Clean Air Coalition. Useful analysis.

Office of Technology Assessment. 1985. *Acid Rain and Transported Air Pollutants: Implications for Public Policy*. New York: Unipub. Excellent analysis.

Pawlick, Thomas. 1986. *A Killing Rain: The Global Threat of Acid Precipitation*. San Francisco: Sierra Club Books. Readable overview by a journalist.

Postel, Sandra. 1984. *Air Pollution, Acid Rain, and the Future of Forests*. Washington, D.C.: Worldwatch Institute. Superb overview.

Postel, Sandra. 1986. *Altering the Earth's Chemistry: Assessing the Earth's Risks*. Washington, D.C.: Worldwatch Institute. Superb overview of effects of air pollution on ecosystems and human health.

Roberts, Walter Orr, and Henry Lansford. 1979. *The Climate Mandate*. San Francisco: W. H. Freeman. Superb discussion of cli-

mate and possible climatic effects of human activities.

Rose, David J., et al. 1984. "Reducing the Problem of Global Warming." *Technology Review*, May–June, pp. 49–58. Excellent overview.

Schneider, Stephen H. 1976. *The Genesis Strategy: Climate and Global Survival*. New York: Plenum Press. Outstanding overview of possible effects of human activities on climate, with a detailed plan for action.

Schneider, Stephen H. 1987. "Climate Modeling." *Scientific American*, vol. 256, no. 5, 72–80. Excellent overview.

Schneider, Stephen H., and Robert S. Chen. 1980. "Carbon Dioxide Warming and Coastline Flooding: Physical Factors and Climatic Impact." In *Annual Review of Energy*, vol. 5, edited by Jack M. Hollander et al., pp. 107–140. Palo Alto, Calif.: Annual Reviews. Excellent summary of the CO_2 problem and its possible effects.

Schneider, S. H., and R. S. Londer. 1984. *The Coevolution of Climate and Life*. San Francisco: Sierra Club Books. Excellent overview of possible effects of human activities on global climate.

Strauss, W., and S. S. Mainwaring. 1983. *Air Pollution*. Baltimore, Md.: Edward Arnold. Excellent advanced treatment.

Turiel, Isaac. 1985. *Indoor Air Quality and Human Health*. Stanford, Calif.: Stanford University Press. Superb nontechnical overview.

Waldbott, George L. 1978. *Health Effects of Environmental Pollutants*. 2d ed. St. Louis: C. V. Mosby. Excellent overview at a slightly higher level. Detailed bibliography.

Ward, Morris A. 1981. "The Clean Air Controversy: Congress Confronts the Issues." *Environment*, vol. 23, no. 6, pp. 8–20, 42–45. Superb summary of proposed changes in the Clean Air acts of 1970 and 1977.

Wark, Kenneth, and Cecil F. Warner. 1981. *Air Pollution: Its Origin and Control*, 2d ed. New York: Harper & Row. Excellent high-level treatment.

Wilson, Richard, et al. 1981. *Health Effects of Fossil Fuel Burning: Assessment and Mitigation*. Cambridge, Mass.: Ballinger. Useful overview and source of data.

Woodwell, George M., et al. 1983. "Global Deforestation: Contribution to Atmospheric Carbon Dioxide." *Science*, vol. 222, 1081–1086. Excellent overview of effect of land-clearing activities on CO_2 levels.

World Resources Institute. 1985. *The American West's Acid Rain Test*. Holmes, Pa.: World Resources Institute Publications. Useful source of data.

Aberley, Richard C., and Susan Berg. 1986. "Finding Uses for Sludge." *American City and County,* vol. 101, 38–46. Excellent overview.

Agarwahl, Anil, et al. 1981. *Water, Sanitation, Health—for All? Prospects for the International Drinking Water Supply and Sanitation Decade, 1981–1990.* Washington, D.C.: Earthscan. Excellent overview.

Ashworth, William. 1986. *The Late, Great Lakes: An Environmental History.* New York: Alfred A. Knopf. Excellent overview.

Bascom, Willard. 1974. "The Disposal of Waste in the Ocean." *Scientific American,* vol. 231, no. 2, 16–25. Argues that with careful control we can safely dispose of many types of waste in the ocean.

Bastow, Thomas F. 1986. *This Vast Pollution: United States of America v. Reserve Mining Company.* Washington, D.C.: Green Fields Books. Excellent behind-the-scenes look at an environmental confrontation and the difficulty in enforcing existing water pollution legislation.

Borgese, Elisabeth Mann. 1986. *The Future of the Oceans.* New York: Harvest House. Excellent overview of ocean pollution and ocean resources.

Burmaster, David E. 1982. "The New Pollution: Groundwater Contamination." *Environment,* vol. 24, no. 2, 4–12, 33–36. Excellent overview.

Conservation Foundation. 1984. *America's Water: Current Trends and Emerging Issues.* Washington, D.C.: Conservation Foundation. Useful overview of water pollution.

Conservation Foundation. 1987. *Groundwater Pollution.* Washington, D.C.: Conservation Foundation. Excellent overview.

Council on Environmental Quality. 1981. *Contamination of Groundwater by Toxic Chemicals.* Washington, D.C.: Government Printing Office. Excellent source of data.

Crites, R. W. 1984. "Land Use of Wastewater and Sludge." *Environmental Science and Technology,* vol. 18, no. 5, 140A–147A. Useful review of the application of sewage effluent to land.

Davies, J. Clarence, III, and Barbara S. Davies. 1975. *The Politics of Pollution.* 2d ed. Indianapolis, Ind.: Pegasus. Excellent account of the political realities of pollution control.

D'Elia, Christopher R. 1987. "Nutrient Enrichment of the Chesapeake Bay." *Environment,* vol. 29, no. 2, 6–11, 30–35. Excellent source of data.

Edmondson, W. T. 1973. "Lake Washington." In *Environmental Quality and Water Development,* edited by Charles R. Goldman et al. San Francisco: W. H. Freeman. Excellent summary of this success story by one of its planners.

Environmental Protection Agency. 1984. *A Ground-Water Protection Strategy.* Washington, D.C.: Government Printing Office. Description of EPA strategy.

Goldstein, Jerome. 1977. *Sensible Sludge.* Emmaus, Pa.: Rodale Press. Useful overview of how to recycle sludge from waste treatment plants.

Gordon, Wendy. 1984. *A Citizen's Handbook on Groundwater Protection.* New York: Natural Resources Defense Council. Excellent source of information and ideas.

Grundlach, Erich R., et al. 1983. "The Fate of *Amoco Cadiz* Oil." *Science,* vol. 221, 122–129. Useful scientific study of the recovery of marine life after an oil spill.

Hodges, Laurent. 1977. *Environmental Pollution.* 2d ed. New York: Holt, Rinehart & Winston. See Chapters 8, 9, 10, 11, and 14 for a discussion of water pollution and water pollution control at a slightly higher level than that in this book.

Hutchinson, G. Evelyn. 1973. "Eutrophication." *American Scientist,* July, pp. 269–279. Outstanding summary.

Keogh, Carol. 1980. *Water Fit to Drink.* Emmaus, Pa.: Rodale Press. Excellent overview of threats to drinking water quality and how individuals can combat such problems.

Ketchum, Bostwick H., et al. 1981. *Ocean Dumping of Industrial Wastes.* New York: Plenum Press. Useful source of technical details on the chemical and biological aspects of ocean dumping.

King, Jonathan. 1985. *Troubled Water.* Emmaus, Pa.: Rodale Press. Excellent overview of pollution of the country's drinking water supplies.

Lahey, William, and Michael Connor. 1983. "The Case for Ocean Waste Disposal." *Technology Review,* August–September, pp. 61–68. Excellent overview.

Lee, G. Fred, et al. 1978. "Eutrophication of Water Bodies: Insights for an Age-Old Problem." *Environmental Science and Technology,* vol. 12, no. 8, 900–908. Superb overview.

Leich, Harold H. 1975. "The Sewerless Society." *Bulletin of the Atomic Scientists,* November, pp. 38–44. How waterless toilets can save money, water, and energy and reduce our need for sewage treatment plants.

Lieber, Harvey. 1975. *Federalism and Clean Waters.* Lexington, Mass.: D. C. Heath. Useful case study of the Federal Water Pollution Control Act of 1972.

Loer, Raymond C. 1984. *Pollution Control for Agriculture.* 2d ed. New York: Academic Press. Excellent analysis.

Merkel, James A. 1981. *Managing Livestock Wastes.* Westport, Conn.: AVI Publishing. Authoritative source.

National Academy of Sciences. 1983. *Drinking Water and Health.* Vol. 5. Washington, D.C.: National Academy Press. Up-to-date information on the effects on human health of 21 drinking water contaminants.

National Academy of Sciences. 1984. *Disposal of Industrial and Domestic Wastes: Land and Sea Alternatives.* Washington, D.C.: National Academy Press. Excellent overview.

National Academy of Sciences. 1984. *Groundwater Contamination.* Washington, D.C.: National Academy Press. Excellent overview.

National Academy of Sciences. 1984. *Ocean Disposal Systems for Sewage Sludge and Effluent.* Washington, D.C.: National Academy Press. Excellent overview.

National Academy of Sciences. 1985. *Oil in the Sea: Inputs, Fates, and Effects.* Washington, D.C.: National Academy Press. Excellent overview and source of data.

National Groundwater Policy Forum. 1985. *Groundwater: Saving the Unseen Resource.* Washington, D.C.: The Conservation Foundation. Excellent analysis.

Office of Technology Assessment. 1984. *Protecting the Nation's Groundwater from Contamination.* Washington, D.C.: Government Printing Office. Excellent analysis.

Organization for Economic Cooperation and Development. 1982. *Eutrophication of Waters: Monitoring, Assessment, and Control.* Washington, D.C.: OECD. Excellent overview.

Organization for Economic Cooperation and Development. 1986. *Water Pollution by Fertilizers and Pesticides.* Washington, D.C.: OECD. Excellent overview.

Pye, Veronica I., et al. 1983. *Groundwater Contamination in the United States.* Philadelphia: University of Pennsylvania Press. Excellent overview.

Simon, Anne W. 1985. *Neptune's Revenge: The Ocean of Tomorrow.* New York: Franklin Watts. Superb overview of stresses on the oceans and ways to protect them from excessive abuse.

Warren, C. E. 1971. *Biology and Water Pollution Control.* Philadelphia: W. B. Saunders. Excellent introduction.

Westman, Walter E. 1972. "Some Basic Issues in Water Pollution Control Legislation." *American Scientist,* November–December, pp. 767–773. Excellent summary of the ecological versus the technological-economic approach to water pollution control.

Woodwell, George M. 1977. "Recycling Sewage Through Plant Communities." *American Scientist*, vol. 65, 556–562. Excellent overview of this natural alternative to expensive waste treatment plants.

World Health Organization. 1981. *Drinking Water and Sanitation 1981–1990: A Way to Health*. Albany, N.Y.: WHO Publications Center. Useful overview of world problems and proposed solutions.

Chapter 21 Solid Waste and Hazardous Waste

Barnes, Donald. 1983. "An Overview on Dioxin." *EPA Journal*, November, pp. 16–19. Excellent summary by an EPA science advisor.

Berry, Stephen R. 1972. "Recycling, Thermodynamics and Environmental Thrift." *Bulletin of the Atomic Scientists*, May, pp. 8–15. Recycling is not always the answer and must be coupled with other approaches.

Block, Alan A., and Frank R. Scarpatti. 1984. *Poisoning for Profit: The Mafia and Toxic Waste in America*. New York: William Morrow. An alarming and useful study.

Bloom, Gordon F. 1986. "The Hidden Liability of Hazardous Waste Cleanup." *Technology Review*, February/March, pp. 59–67. Useful analysis of effects of cleanup on business.

Bond, Desmond H. 1984. "At-Sea Incineration of Hazardous Wastes." *Environmental Science and Technology*, vol. 18, no. 5, 148A–152A. Raises concerns about the risks of this option.

Brown, Lester R., et al. 1984. *State of the World 1984*. New York: W. W. Norton. Chapter 6 is an excellent summary of recycling.

Brown, Lester R., et al. 1987. *State of the World 1987*. New York: W. W. Norton. Chapter 6 is an excellent summary of the potential for recycling.

Brown, Michael. 1979. *Laying Waste: The Poisoning of America by Toxic Wastes*. New York: Pantheon. Critical attack with detailed discussion of the Love Canal disaster.

Chemistry and Engineering News. 1983. "Dioxin Report." June 6, pp. 20–64. Excellent series of articles.

Citizens' Advisory Committee on Environmental Quality. 1976. *A New Look at Recycling Waste Paper*. Washington, D.C.: Citizens' Advisory Committee on Envi-ronmental Quality. Excellent discussion of paper recycling problems and possibilities.

D'Itri, Patricia R., and Frank M. D'Itri. 1977. *Mercury Contamination*. New York: Wiley. Superb summary.

Dowling, Michael. 1985. "Defining and Classifying Hazardous Wastes." *Environment*, vol. 27, 18–20, 36–41. Useful analysis.

Efron, Edith. 1984. *The Apocalyptics: Cancer and the Big Lie*. New York: Simon & Schuster. Contends that concern over hazardous wastes, pollutants, and other toxic and hazardous materials has been overblown and has little or no scientific foundation.

Environmental Defense Fund. 1985. *To Burn or Not to Burn*. New York: Environmental Defense Fund. Excellent analysis of incineration of garbage.

Environmental Planning Lobby. 1985. *The Financial and Environmental Impact of Garbage Incineration*. Albany, N.Y.: Environmental Planning Lobby. Excellent analysis.

Environmental Protection Agency. 1976. *Decision-Maker's Guide in Solid Waste Management*. Washington, D.C.: Government Printing Office. Superb analysis of advantages and disadvantages of the major methods of solid waste collection, disposal, and high-technology resource recovery.

Environmental Protection Agency. 1977. *Fourth Report to Congress: Resource Recovery and Waste Reduction*. Washington, D.C.: Environmental Protection Agency. Superb analysis of solid waste disposal, high- and low-technology resource recovery, and resource conservation in the United States.

Environmental Protection Agency. 1979. *Operating a Recycling Program: Citizens Guide*. Washington, D.C.: Environmental Protection Agency. Excellent source of information.

Environmental Protection Agency. 1980. *Damages and Threats Caused by Hazardous Material*. Washington, D.C.: Environmental Protection Agency. Authoritative overview.

Environmental Protection Agency. 1980. *Hazardous Waste Generation and Commercial Hazardous Waste Management Capacity: An Assessment*. Washington, D.C.: Environmental Protection Agency. Useful source of data.

Epstein, Samuel S., et al. 1982. *Hazardous Waste in America*. San Francisco: Sierra Club Books. Superb analysis of the problems, along with suggested solutions.

Fortuna, Richard C., and David J. Lennett. 1987. *Hazardous Waste Regulation: The New Era*. New York: McGraw-Hill. Excellent overview.

General Accounting Office. 1981. *Hazardous Waste Sites Pose Investigation, Evaluation, Scientific, and Legal Problems*. Washington, D.C.: Government Printing Office.

Gibbs, Lois. 1982. *The Love Canal: My Story*. Albany: State University of New York Press. Useful description by a former Love Canal area resident who led the fight by homeowners to have the area condemned as unsafe.

Gordon, Wendy, and Jane Bloom. 1985. *Deeper Problems: Limits to Underground Injection as a Hazardous Waste Disposal Method*. New York: Natural Resources Defense Council. Excellent analysis.

Gough, Michael. 1986. *Dioxin, Agent Orange: The Facts*. New York: Plenum Press. Excellent case study.

Harrison, R. M., and D. P. H. Laxon. 1981. *Lead Pollution: Causes and Control*. London: Chapman and Hall/Meuthen. Excellent overview.

Hay, Alstair. 1982. *The Chemical Scythe: Lessons of 2,4,5-T and Dioxin*. New York: Plenum Press. Excellent overview.

Hayes, Dennis. 1978. *Repairs, Reuse, Recycling—First Steps Toward a Sustainable Society*. Superb overview of resource recovery and conservation.

Hiatt, V., and J. E. Huff. 1975. "The Environmental Impact of Cadmium." *International Journal of Environmental Studies*, vol. 7, no. 4, 277–285. Good overview.

Institute for Local Self-Reliance. 1986. *Environmental Review of Waste Incineration*. Washington, D.C.: Institute for Local Self-Reliance. Excellent analysis.

Kriebel, David. 1981. "The Dioxins: Toxic and Still Troublesome." *Environment*, January–February, pp. 6–13. Excellent overview.

LaDouc, Joseph. 1984. "The Not-So-Clean Business of Making Chips." *Technology Review*, May–June, pp. 24–36. Excellent survey of hazardous waste problem in the microelectronics industry.

League of Women Voters Education Fund. 1981. *A Hazardous Waste Primer*. Washington, D.C.: League of Women Voters. Excellent overview.

Levine, Adeline G. 1982. *Love Canal: Science, Politics, and People*. Lexington, Mass.: Lexington (Heath). A useful study by a former area resident.

Montague, Katherine, and Peter Montague. 1976. *No World Without End: The New Threats to Our Biosphere*. New York: G. P. Putnam. Excellent overview of threats from lead, mercury, cadmium, and other toxic metals.

Moore, Dennis. 1982. "Recycling: Where Are We Now?" *New Shelter*, February, pp. 56–69. Excellent overview.

Morrell, David, and Christopher Magorian. 1982. *Siting Hazardous Waste Facilities: Local Opposition and the Myth of Preemption.* Cambridge, Mass.: Ballinger. Excellent analysis of the politics of siting.

Nader, Ralph, et al. 1981. *Who's Poisoning America?* San Francisco: Sierra Club Books. Useful description of several case studies.

National Academy of Sciences. 1980. *Lead in the Human Environment.* Washington, D.C.: National Academy Press. Authoritative review.

National Academy of Sciences. 1983. *Transportation of Hazardous Materials: Toward a National Strategy.* Washington, D.C.: National Academy Press. Excellent overview and source of data.

National Academy of Sciences. 1984. *Toxicity Testing: Strategies to Determine Needs and Priorities.* Washington, D.C.: National Academy Press. Study showing that most chemicals in use in the United States have not been tested adequately for toxicity.

National Science Foundation. 1977. *Lead in the Environment.* Washington, D.C.: National Science Foundation. Authoritative review.

Needleman, Herbert L. 1980. "Lead Exposure and Human Health: Recent Data on an Ancient Problem." *Technology Review,* March–April, pp. 39–45. Excellent overview.

Office of Technology Assessment. 1983. *Technologies and Management Strategies for Hazardous Waste Controls.* Washington, D.C.: Government Printing Office. Excellent evaluation.

Office of Technology Assessment. 1986. *Serious Reduction of Hazardous Waste.* Washington, D.C.: Government Printing Office. Excellent evaluation.

Piaeski, Bruce, ed. 1984. *Beyond Dumping: New Strategies for Controlling Toxic Contamination.* Westport, Conn.: Quorum Books, Greenwood Press. Excellent collection of essays.

Pollack, Cynthia. 1987. *Mining Urban Wastes: The Potential for Recycling.* Washington, D.C.: Worldwatch Institute. Superb overview.

Purcell, Arthur H. 1980. *The Waste Watchers: A Citizen's Handbook for Conserving Energy and Resources.* Garden City, N.Y.: Anchor Press/Doubleday. Superb guide for achieving a low-waste society.

Randers, Jorgen, and Dennis L. Meadows. 1972. "The Dynamics of Solid Waste." *Technology Review,* March–April, pp. 20–32. Computer simulation of various proposed solutions to the solid waste problem.

Ratcliffe, J. M. 1981. *Lead in Man and the Environment.* New York: Halsted Press. Excellent technical summary.

Regenstein, Lewis. 1982. *America the Poisoned.* Washington, D.C.: Acropolis Books. Useful description of the hazardous waste problem.

Robinson, William D., ed. 1986. *The Solid Waste Handbook.* New York: Wiley. Excellent source of information.

Rose, David J., et al. 1972. "Physics Looks at Waste Management." *Physics Today,* February, pp. 32–41. Outstanding evaluation of alternative solutions.

Schroeder, Henry A. 1974. *The Poisons Around Us: Toxic Metals in Food, Air, and Water.* Bloomington: Indiana University Press. Superb summary by an expert toxicologist.

Segel, Edward, et al. 1985. *The Toxic Substances Dilemma: A Plan for Citizen Action.* Washington, D.C.: National Wildlife Federation. Excellent source of information.

Senkan, Selim M., and Nancy W. Stauffer. 1981. "What To Do with Hazardous Waste?" *Technology Review,* November–December, pp. 34–47. Excellent summary.

Small, W. E. 1971. *Third Pollution: The National Problem of Solid Waste Disposal.* New York: Praeger. Somewhat dated but still a useful analysis of solid waste problems and possible solutions.

Smith, W. Eugene, and Aileen M. Smith. 1975. *Minamata.* New York: Holt, Rinehart & Winston. Well-researched description of methyl mercury poisonings in Japan.

Tschirley, Fred H. 1986. "Dioxin." *Scientific American,* vol. 254, no. 2, 29–35. Useful overview.

Whelan, Elizabeth M. 1985. *Toxic Terror.* Ottawa, Ill.: Jameson Books. Argues that threats from hazardous wastes have been overblown and that hazardous wastes have been overregulated.

Chapter 22 Pesticides and Pest Control

Barrons, Keith C. 1981. *Are Pesticides Really Necessary?* Chicago: Regnery Gateway. Excellent presentation of both sides of the pesticide controversy, with emphasis on the benefits of pesticides.

Brown, Joseph E. 1983. *The Return of the Brown Pelican.* Baton Rouge: Louisiana State University Press. Excellent case history of the comeback of this species since the 1972 ban of DDT in the United States.

Bull, David. 1982. *A Growing Problem: Pesticides and the Third World Poor.* London: Oxfam. Very useful description of the problems from increased pesticide use in LDCs.

Carson, Rachel. 1962. *Silent Spring.* Boston: Houghton Mifflin. An environmental classic that provided the first major warning about the dangerous side effects of pesticides.

Dover, Michael J. 1985. *A Better Mousetrap: Improving Pest Management for Agriculture.* Washington, D.C.: World Resources Institute. Excellent analysis.

Dover, Michael J., and Brian A. Croft. 1986. "Pesticide Resistance and Public Policy." *BioScience,* vol. 36, no. 2, 78–91. Excellent overview of use and problems.

Dunlap, Thomas R. 1981. *DDT: Scientists, Citizens, and Public Policy.* Princeton, N.J.: Princeton University Press. Excellent discussion of the history of the use of DDT and the problems that led to its banning in the United States.

Entomological Society of America. 1975. *Integrated Pest Management.* Washington, D.C.: Entomological Society of America. Excellent overview.

Galston, Arthur W. 1979. "Herbicides: A Mixed Blessing." *BioScience,* vol. 29, no. 2, 85–90. Useful evaluation.

Goldstein, Jerome. 1978. *The Least Is Best Pesticide Strategy.* Emmaus, Pa.: J.G. Press. Excellent discussion of integrated pest management.

Gough, Michael. 1986. *Dioxin, Agent Orange: The Facts.* New York: Plenum Press. Excellent source of information.

Graham, Frank, Jr. 1984. *The Dragon Hunters.* New York: E. P. Dutton. Excellent summary of biological control.

Hussey, N. W., and N. Scopes. 1986. *Biological Pest Control.* Ithaca, N.Y.: Cornell University Press. Excellent overview.

Metcalf, R. L., and A. Kelman. 1981. "Integrated Pest Management in China." *Environment,* vol. 23, no. 4, 6–13. Excellent overview.

Metcalf, R. L., and William H. Luckmann, eds. 1982. *Introduction to Insect Pest Management.* New York: Wiley. Useful source of information.

Morehouse, Ward, and M. Arun Subramaniam. 1986. *The Bhopal Tragedy: What Really Happened and What It Means for American Workers and Communities at Risk.* New York: Council on International and Public Affairs. Excellent overview of this accident.

National Academy of Sciences. 1986. *Pesticide Resistance: Strategies and Tactics for Management.* Washington, D.C.: National Academy Press. Excellent analysis.

National Academy of Sciences. 1986. *Pesticides and Groundwater Quality: Issues and Problems in Four States.* Washington, D.C.: National Academy Press. Useful case studies.

Pimentel, David, et al. 1980. "Environmental and Social Costs of Pesticides: A Preliminary Assessment." *Oikos,* vol. 34, no. 2, 126–140. Superb overview.

Regenstein, L. 1982. *America the Poisoned.* Washington, D.C.: Acropolis. Revealing account of the use and effects of pesticides.

Shrivastava, Paul. 1987. *Bhopal: Anatomy of a Crisis.* New York: Harper & Row. Excellent source of information.

van den Bosch, Robert. 1978. *The Pesticide Conspiracy.* Garden City, N.Y.: Doubleday. Pest management expert exposes political influence of pesticide companies in preventing widespread use of biological controls and integrated pest management.

van den Bosch, Robert, and Mary L. Flint. 1981. *Introduction to Integrated Pest Management.* New York: Plenum Press. Superb presentation.

Wasserstrom, Robert F., and Richard Wiles. 1985. *Field Duty: U.S. Farmworkers and Pesticide Safety.* Washington, D.C.: World Resources Institute. Excellent analysis.

Wilcox, F. A. 1983. *Waiting for an Army to Die: The Tragedy of Agent Orange.* New York: Vintage Books. Description of possible effects of Agent Orange on Vietnam veterans.

Yepsen, Roger B., Jr. 1984. *The Encyclopedia of Natural Insect and Disease Control.* Emmaus, Pa.: Rodale Press. Excellent source of information.

Chapter 23 The Environment and Human Health: Disease, Food Additives, and Noise

American Medical Association. 1986. *Journal of the American Medical Association,* vol. 228. Entire February 28 issue devoted to effects of smoking.

Armstrong, David. 1984. *The Insider's Guide to Health Foods.* New York: Bantam Books. Excellent source of information.

Beattie, Edward J. 1980. *Toward the Conquest of Cancer.* New York: Crown Publishers. Superb analysis showing how 40% to 50% of cancers can be prevented and about 50% can be cured.

Benarde, Melvin A. 1971. *The Chemicals We Eat.* New York: American Heritage Press. Readable introduction to additives by a prominent health scientist. A moderate view, weighted somewhat toward the food industry.

Benenson, A. S., ed. 1979. *Control of Communicable Diseases in Man.* 13th ed. Washington, D.C.: American Public Health Association. Basic reference.

Bergin, Edward J., and Ronald Grandon. 1984. *The American Survival Guide: How to Survive Your Toxic Environment.* New York: Avon. Many useful suggestions.

Campbell, T. C. 1980. "Chemical Carcinogens and Human Risk Assessment." *Federation Proceedings,* vol. 39, no. 8, 2467–2484. Excellent overview.

Carmen, Richard. 1977. *Our Endangered Hearing.* Emmaus, Pa.: Rodale Press. Excellent overview of noise problems, effects, and possible solutions.

Chandler, William U. 1986. *Banishing Tobacco.* Washington, D.C.: Worldwatch Institute. Superb analysis.

Chemistry and Engineering News. 1977. "Should the Delaney Clause Be Changed? A Debate on Food Additive Safety, Animal Tests, and Cancer." June 27, pp. 24–46. Informative debate by four experts on the Delaney clause.

Davis, Devra L. 1981. "Cancer in the Workplace: The Case for Prevention." *Environment,* vol. 23, no. 6, 25–37. Excellent overview.

Derr, Patrick, et al. 1981. "Worker/Public Protection: The Double Standard." *Environment,* vol. 23, no. 7, 6–15, 31–36. Useful overview showing how standards for protecting the general public from carcinogens and other hazardous chemicals in the environment are much stricter than those protecting workers.

Doll, Richard, and Richard Petro. 1981. "The Causes of Cancer: Quantitative Estimates of Avoidable Risks of Cancer in America Today." *Journal of the National Cancer Institute.* June. Useful summary of cancer risk factors showing that diet and smoking together account for about 65% of all cancer deaths. Authors' estimate that about 4% of cancer deaths are related to occupational exposure is considered too low by experts such as Epstein (1979) and by the authors of a 1978 study conducted jointly by the National Cancer Institute, the National Institute of Environmental Health Sciences, and the National Institute for Occupational Safety and Health.

Eckholm, Erik P. 1977. *The Picture of Health: Environmental Sources of Disease.* New York: W. W. Norton. Superb overview of environmental health problems throughout the world.

Eckholm, Erik P. 1978. *Cutting Tobacco's Toll.* Washington, D.C.: Worldwatch Institute. Superb overview of smoking problems and possible solutions in the United States and throughout the world.

Efron, Edith. 1984. *The Apocalyptics: Cancer and the Big Lie.* New York: Simon & Schuster. A freelance writer accuses environmentalists of overstating the effects of human-produced chemicals as a cause of cancer.

Environmental Protection Agency. 1977. *Toward a National Strategy for Noise Control.* Washington, D.C.: U.S. Government Printing Office. Excellent plan; implementing it is the problem.

Environmental Protection Agency. 1978. *Noise: A Health Problem.* Washington, D.C.: Environmental Protection Agency. Good overview of the problems and effects of excessive noise.

Epstein, Samuel S. 1979. *The Politics of Cancer.* Garden City, N.Y.: Anchor/Doubleday. Excellent overview of cancer by an expert, with emphasis on occupational exposure to carcinogens.

Faber, M. M., and A. M. Reinhardt. 1982. *Promoting Health Through Risk Reduction.* New York: Macmillan. Excellent analysis.

Freydberg, N., and W. Gortner. 1982. *The Food Additives Book.* New York: Bantam. Useful source of information.

Goldsmith, Edward. 1980. "The Ecology of Health." *The Ecologist,* vol. 10, nos. 6/7, 225–245. Eloquent summary of an ecological—as opposed to a modern medical—approach to health.

Gorman, James. 1979. *Hazards to Your Health: The Problem of Environmental Disease.* New York: New York Academy of Sciences. Superb overview.

Halpern, Steven, and Louis Savary. 1985. *Sound Health.* New York: Harper & Row. Excellent overview of the effects of noise pollution and ways to minimize exposure to excessive noise.

Highland, Joseph, et al. 1980. *Malignant Neglect.* New York: Random House. Excellent discussion of cancer and the environment.

Holleb, Arthur I., ed. 1986. *The American Cancer Society Cancer Book.* New York: Doubleday. Excellent overview.

Jacobson, Michael F. 1972. *Eater's Digest: The Consumer's Factbook of Food Additives.* Garden City, N.Y.: Doubleday. Outstanding moderate overview. Consult this paperback book to determine which additives you might want to avoid.

Kasperson, R. E. 1983. "Worker Participation in Protection: The Swedish Alternative." *Environment,* vol. 25, no. 4, 13–20, 40–43. Excellent discussion of worker protection in Sweden.

Kessler, David A. 1984. "Food Safety: Revising the Statute." *Science,* vol. 223,

1034–1040. Excellent analysis of whether food safety laws should be changed.

Kryter, Karl D. 1985. *The Effects of Noise.* 2d ed. Orlando, Fla.: Academic Press. Authoritative source of data.

Leepson, Marc. 1980. "Noise Control." *Editorial Research Reports,* Feb. 22, pp. 83–96. Excellent overview.

Lipscomb, David M. 1974. *Noise: The Unwanted Sound.* New York: Nelson-Hall Publishers. Authoritative review of the health hazards of excessive noise and methods for noise control.

Mellinkoff, Sherman H. 1973. "Chemical Intervention." *Scientific American,* vol. 229, no. 3, 103–112. Excellent overview of overuse of drugs and food additives.

Milne, Anthony. 1979. *Noise Pollution: Impact and Countermeasures.* New York: David Charles. Superb basic reference.

National Academy of Sciences. 1981. *Effects on Human Health from Long-Term Exposure to Noise.* Washington, D.C.: National Academy Press. Excellent overview of research studies on the effects of noise.

National Academy of Sciences. 1982. *Diet, Nutrition, and Cancer.* Washington, D.C.: National Academy Press. Authoritative review of relationships between diet and cancer.

National Academy of Sciences. 1982. *The Health Effects of Nitrate, Nitrite, and N-Nitroso Compounds.* Washington, D.C.: National Academy Press. Expert evaluation of this potential problem, with recommendations.

Nelkin, M. M., and M. S. Brown. 1984. *Workers at Risk: Voices from the Workplace.* Chicago: University of Chicago Press. Excellent overview of worker safety in the United States.

Office of Technology Assessment. 1985. *Status of Biomedical Research and Related Technology for Tropical Diseases.* Washington, D.C.: Government Printing Office. Excellent overview.

Organization for Economic Cooperation and Development (OECD). 1986. *Fighting Noise.* Washington, D.C.: OECD. Excellent analysis.

Reif, Arnold E. 1981. "The Causes of Cancer." *American Scientist,* vol. 69, 437–447. Excellent overview.

Schell, Orville. 1984. *Modern Meat: Antibiotics, Hormones, and the Pharmaceutical Farm.* New York: Random House. If you like meat, don't read this revealing book.

Smedley, Howard, et al. 1985. *Cancer: What It Is and How It's Being Treated.* London: Basil Blackwell. Excellent overview.

Stein, Jane. 1977. "Water for the Wealthy." *Environment,* vol. 19, no. 4, 6–14. Good overview of infectious waterborne diseases.

Sylvester, Edward J. 1986. *Target: Cancer.* New York: Scribner's. Excellent summary of recent breakthroughs in cancer detection and treatment.

Thumann, Albert, and Richard K. Miller. 1976. *Secrets of Noise Control.* Atlanta, Ga.: Firmont Press. Useful overview with good tips.

U.S. Department of Health and Human Services. 1983. *Alcohol and Health.* Washington, D.C.: Government Printing Office. Useful survey of research.

U.S. Surgeon General. 1981. *The Health Consequences of Smoking.* Washington, D.C.: Government Printing Office. Useful survey of research.

Verrett, Jacqueline, and Jean Carper. 1974. *Eating May Be Hazardous to Your Health.* New York: Simon & Schuster. Excellent over view of the potential dangers of food additives and the problems of consumer protection.

Whelan, Elizabeth M., and Frederick J. Stare. 1983. *The 100% Natural, Purely Organic, Cholesterol-Free, Megavitamin, Low-Carbohydrate Nutrition Hoax.* New York: Atheneum Press. Presentation heavily weighted toward the food industry that debunks concern over the dangers of food additives and pesticides and derides people who grow and eat health foods and use vitamin supplements.

Winter, Ruth A. 1978. *A Consumer's Dictionary of Food Additives.* New York: Crown Publishers. Extremely useful guide, suggesting which additives to avoid.

Chapter 24 Economics and Environment

Abernathy, William, et al. 1983. *Industrial Renaissance.* New York: Basic Books. Useful description of the decline of American industry.

Andrews, Richard N. L. 1981. "Will Benefit-Cost Analysis Reform Regulations?" *Environmental Science and Technology,* vol. 15, no. 9, 1016–1021. Excellent summary of cost-benefit and cost-effective analysis.

Baram, Michael S. 1980. "Cost-Benefit Analysis: An Inadequate Basis for Health, Safety, and Environmental Regulatory Decisionmaking." *Ecology Law Quarterly,* vol. 8, 473–479. Excellent analysis.

Beckerman, Wilfred. 1974. *Two Cheers for the Affluent Society.* New York: St. Martin's Press. A vigorous defense of the need for an economy based on continued growth. Compare with Daly (1977) and Georgescu-Roegen (1977).

Bluestone, Barry, and Bennett Harrison. 1983. *The Deindustrialization of America.* New York: Basic Books. Useful presentation of the case for reindustrializing America.

Boulding, Kenneth E. 1974. "What Went Wrong, If Anything, Since Copernicus?" *Bulletin of the Atomic Scientists,* January, pp. 17–23. Penetrating analysis of the possible types of sustainable society.

Bowles, Samuel, et al. 1983. *Beyond the Wasteland.* New York: Anchor Press. Excellent analysis showing how eliminating waste in the American economy would allow continued economic growth.

Brown, Lester R. 1981. *Building a Sustainable Society.* New York: W. W. Norton. Excellent overview of how interlocking pollution, energy, and resource problems are helping create global economic problems.

Brown, Lester R. 1986. *State of the World 1986.* New York: W. W. Norton. See Chapter 1 for an excellent discussion of connections between economic and ecological deficits.

Burness, Stuart, et al. 1980. "Thermodynamic and Economic Concepts as Related to Resource-Use Policies." *Land Economics,* vol. 56, February, pp. 1–9. Useful analysis.

Butlin, J. A., ed. 1981. *The Economics of Environmental and Natural Resource Policy.* Boulder, Colo.: Westview Press. Useful analysis at a higher level.

Canterberry, E. Ray. 1976. *The Making of Economics.* Belmont, Calif.: Wadsworth. A readable critique of contemporary economic theory. Explains why economics so long ignored ecology and points the way to a reconstruction of economics on a humanistic base.

Chandler, William U. 1986. *The Changing Role of the Market in National Economies.* Washington, D.C.: Worldwatch Institute. Excellent and revealing analysis.

Cottrell, Alan. 1978. *Environmental Economics.* New York: Halsted. Good introduction.

Daly, Herman E. 1973. *Toward a Steady-State Economy.* San Francisco: W. H. Freeman. Outstanding analysis.

Daly, Herman E. 1977. *Steady-State Economics.* San Francisco: W. H. Freeman. Superb discussion of a sustainable-earth economy and how we can make the transition to such a system.

Daly, Herman E., ed. 1980. *Economics, Ecology, and Ethics.* San Francisco: W. H. Freeman. Superb collection of essays.

Fisher, Anthony C. 1981. *Resource and Environmental Economics.* Cambridge,

England: Cambridge University Press. Excellent high-level analysis.

Freeman, A. Myrick, III. 1982. *Air and Water Pollution Control: A Benefit-Cost Assessment.* New York: Wiley. Detailed look at a complex benefit-cost analysis study.

Georgescu-Roegen, Nicholas. 1971. *The Entropy Law and the Economic Process.* Cambridge, Mass.: Harvard University Press. Important advanced work on the relationships between the second law of energy and economics.

Georgescu-Roegen, Nicholas. 1977. "The Steady State and Ecological Salvation: A Thermodynamic Analysis." *BioScience*, vol. 27, no. 4, 266–270. Superb analysis of steady-state and sustainable-earth economic systems by one of the world's outstanding economic thinkers. See also his article in Daly (1980).

Goldsmith, Edward. 1978. *The Stable Society.* Cornwall, England: Wadebridge Press. Useful description of a sustainable-earth economy and society.

Hamer, John. 1976. "Pollution Control: Costs and Benefits." *Editorial Research Reports*, vol. 1, no. 8, 147–164. Excellent overview of approaches to pollution control.

Hamrin, Robert D. 1983. *A Renewable Resource Economy.* New York: Praeger. Useful analysis of some aspects of a sustainable-earth economy.

Hardin, Garrett. 1968. "The Tragedy of the Commons." *Science*, vol. 162, 1243–1248. Classic article describing how common property is ruined by individual actions.

Hartwick, John M., and Nancy D. Olewiler. 1986. *The Economics of Natural Resource Use.* New York: Harper & Row. Excellent advanced analysis.

Hawken, Paul. 1983. *The Next Economy.* New York: Holt, Rinehart & Winston. Useful and readable analysis showing how ordinary citizens can buy smartly by substituting knowledge for energy.

Hueting, R. 1980. *New Scarcity and Economic Growth.* New York: Oxford University Press. Superb analysis of the interaction of ecology and economics.

Huisingh, Donald, and Vicky Bailey, eds. 1982. *Making Pollution Prevention Pay.* Elmsford, N.Y.: Pergamon Press. Excellent analysis.

Institute for Policy Studies. 1985. *Alternatives to the International Debt Crisis.* Washington, D.C.: Institute for Policy Studies. Excellent overview.

Johnson, Warren. 1978. *Muddling Toward Frugality.* San Francisco: Sierra Club Books. Outstanding economic and political

analysis of how we might make it to the end of this century.

Kahn, Herman. 1982. *The Coming Boom: Economic, Political, and Social.* New York: Simon & Schuster. Useful projections by a pro-growth, technological optimist.

Kasis, Richard, and Richard L. Grossman. 1982. *Fear at Work: Job Blackmail, Labor, and the Environment.* New York: Pilgrim Press. Useful study showing how environmental legislation has created far more jobs than it has eliminated.

League of Women Voters. 1977. "Growth: An Invitation to the Debate." *Current Focus*, no. 146, 1–5. Superb summary of the debate over economic growth.

Mishan, E. J. 1977. *The Economic Growth Debate: An Assessment.* London: Allen & Unwin. Superb analysis.

Naisbitt, John. 1982. *Megatrends: Ten New Directions Transforming Our Lives.* New York: Warner Books. Superb discussion of major trends, economic and other.

O'Hare, William P. 1985. "Poverty in America: Trends and New Patterns." *Population Bulletin*, vol. 40, no. 3, 1–42. Excellent overview.

Riddel, Robert. 1981. *Ecodevelopment: An Alternative to Growth Imperative Models.* Hampshire, England: Gower Publishing. Useful summary of how LDCs can develop by using ecological principles to become more self-reliant and self-sufficient.

Rifkin, Jeremy. 1980. *Entropy: A New World View.* New York: Viking. Important book with a discussion of sustainable-earth economics based on the second law of energy.

Royston, Michael G. 1980. "Making Pollution Pay." *Harvard Business Review*, November–December. Excellent summary of how businesses have saved money and made profits through pollution control.

Ruff, Larry E. 1970. "The Economic Common Sense of Pollution." *Public Interest*, spring, pp. 69–85. Readable introduction to the various economic approaches to pollution control.

Schumacher, E. F. 1973. *Small Is Beautiful: Economics as if People Mattered.* New York: Harper & Row. Important environmental classic describing the need for and the nature of appropriate technology.

Science Council of Canada. 1980. *Entropy and the Economic Process.* Ottawa: Science Council of Canada. Useful analysis of relationships between the second law of thermodynamics and economics.

Siebert, Horst. 1981. *Economics of the Environment.* Lexington, Mass.: Lexington Books. Useful analysis.

Spencer, Milton H. 1981. *Contemporary Economics.* 4th ed. New York: Worth. Understandable basic text with a discussion of ecology and economics.

Swartzman, Daniel, et al., eds. 1982. *Cost-Benefit Analysis and Environmental Regulations: Politics, Ethics, and Methods.* Washington, D.C.: Conservation Foundation. Useful analysis.

Theobald, Robert. 1970. *The Economics of Abundance.* New York: Pitman. Detailed plan for the transition to a sustainable-earth economy and a more just distribution of wealth.

Tietenberg, Tom. 1984. *Environmental and Natural Resource Economics.* Glenview, Ill.: Scott, Foresman. Useful overview at a higher level.

Walter, Edward. 1981. *The Immorality of Limiting Growth.* Albany: State University of New York Press. Effective presentation of arguments for continuing economic growth.

Woodward, Herbert N. 1977. *Capitalism Can Survive in a No-Growth Economy.* New York: Brookdale. Useful analysis.

Chapter 25 Politics and Environment

Abbey, Edward. 1985. *The Monkey Wrench Gang.* Salt Lake City, Utah: Dream Garden Press. Thought-provoking guide to environmental guerrilla warfare to prevent unsound development.

Alderson, George, and Everett Sentman. 1979. *How You Can Influence Congress: The Complete Handbook for the Citizen Lobbyist.* New York: E. P. Dutton. Superb guide.

Arbuckle, J. G., et al. 1985. *Environmental Law Handbook.* Rockville, Md.: Government Institutes. Useful overview of environmental law.

Axelrod, Robert. 1984. *The Evolution of Cooperation.* New York: Basic Books. Superb analysis of the strategy of getting people to cooperate.

Barnett, Richard J. 1980. *The Lean Years: Politics in an Age of Scarcity.* New York: Simon & Schuster. One of the best discussions of politics and the environment.

Berger, John. 1986. *Restoring the Earth: How Americans Are Working to Renew Our Damaged Environment.* New York: Alfred A. Knopf. Inspiring descriptions of what people have done to improve the environment.

Brown, Lester R. 1986. "Redefining National Security." In *State of the World 1986*, edited by Lester R. Brown et al. Washington, D.C.: Worldwatch Institute, pp.

196–211. Superb analysis of national security in ecological rather than military terms.

Caldwell, Lynton K., et al. 1976. *Citizens and the Environment: Case Studies in Popular Action.* Bloomington: Indiana University Press. Outstanding collection of case studies showing what informed and concerned citizens can do.

Capra, Fritjof, and Charlene Spretnok. 1984. *Green Politics.* New York: E. P. Dutton. Informative description of the history of the ecologically oriented West German Green political party.

Congressional Quarterly. 1983. *How Congress Works.* Washington, D.C.: Congressional Quarterly. Useful guide.

Cotgrove, Stephen. 1982. *Catastrophe or Cornucopia: The Environment, Politics, and the Future.* New York: Wiley. Useful overview.

Davies, J. Clarence, III, and Barbara S. Davies. 1975. *The Politics of Pollution.* 2d ed. Indianapolis, Ind.: Pegasus. Superb introduction to pollution control by government regulation.

Dumas, Lloyd J. 1986. "The Military Burden on the Economy." *Bulletin of the Atomic Scientists,* October, 22–26. Excellent analysis.

Ehrlich, Robert. 1985. *Waging Nuclear Peace.* Albany: State University of New York Press. Superb analysis of nuclear war and how to avoid it.

Elgin, Duane S., and Robert A. Bushnell. 1977. "The Limits to Complexity: Are Bureaucracies Becoming Unmanageable?" *The Futurist,* December, pp. 337–349. Excellent analysis.

Falk, Richard A. 1975. *A Study of Future Worlds.* New York: Free Press. Superb detailed plan for achieving world order.

Findley, R. W., and D. A. Farber. 1981. *Environmental Law: Cases and Materials.* St. Paul, Minn.: West Publishing. Detailed information on key environmental law cases.

Firestone, David B., and Frank C. Reed. 1983. *Environmental Law for Non-Lawyers.* Woburn, Mass.: Butterworth. Excellent introduction.

Foreman, Dave, ed. 1985. *Ecodefense: A Field Guide to Monkeywrenching.* Tucson, Ariz.: Earth First! Excellent guide to environmental guerrilla warfare.

Friends of the Earth, et al. 1982. *Ronald Reagan and the American Environment.* Andover, Mass.: Brick House. Detailed analysis by a coalition of major environmental groups of President Reagan's attempts to weaken environmental protection.

Gardner, John W. 1970. *The Recovery of Confidence.* New York: W. W. Norton. A classic describing how to accomplish change.

Gardner, John W. 1972. *In Common Cause.* New York: W. W. Norton. Explains how to bring about political change.

Johnson, Warren. 1978. *Muddling Toward Frugality.* San Francisco: Sierra Club Books. Superb analysis of economics, politics, and environment.

Kennard, Byron. 1982. *Nothing Can Be Done, Everything Is Possible.* Andover, Mass.: Brick House. Superb discussion of bringing about change through networking.

League of Women Voters. Annual. *When You Write to Washington.* League of Women Voters, 1730 M St., N.W., Washington, D.C. 20005. The best guide on how to write elected officials.

Milbrath, Lester R. 1984. *Environmentalists: Vanguard for a New Society.* Albany: State University of New York Press. Summary of views of environmentalists and argument for a major change in our worldview.

Morris, David, and Karl Hess. 1975. *Neighborhood Power: The New Localism.* Boston: Beacon Press. Excellent guide for local action.

Ophuls, William. 1977. *Ecology and the Politics of Scarcity.* San Francisco: W. H. Freeman. Outstanding book on environment and politics.

Papageorgiou, J. C. 1980. *Management Science and Environmental Problems.* Springfield, Ill.: Charles C. Thomas. Useful overview.

Peters, Charles. 1980. *How Washington Really Works.* Reading, Mass.: Addison-Wesley. Superb and revealing guide.

Petulla, Joseph M. 1980. *American Environmentalism: Values, Tactics, and Priorities.* College Station: Texas A&M University. Useful historical analysis.

Pezzuti, Thomas. 1974. *You Can Fight City Hall and Win.* Los Angeles: Sherbourne Press. Fact-filled guide.

Pirages, Dennis. 1978. *Global Ecopolitics.* North Scituate, Mass.: Duxbury Press. Excellent overview.

Robertson, James, and John Lewallen, eds. 1975. *The Grass Roots Primer: The Spare Time, Low Cost, At Home Guide to Environmental Action.* New York: Scribner's. Superb guide.

Rodgers, William H. 1977. *Environmental Law.* St. Paul, Minn.: West Publishing. Useful, advanced treatment.

Rosenbaum, Walter A. 1985. *Environment Politics and Policy.* Washington, D.C.: Congressional Quarterly. Excellent overview.

Ross, Donald K. 1973. *A Public Citizen's Action Manual.* New York: Grossman. Superb guide.

Schaiberg, Allan, et al., eds. 1984. *Distributional Conflicts in Environmental Resource Policy.* New York: St. Martin's. Excellent evaluation of environmental regulation.

Shuck, Peter H. 1986. *Agent Orange on Trial: Mass Toxic Disasters in the Courts.* Cambridge, Mass.: Harvard University Press. Engaging account of Vietnam veterans' suit for compensation for damages to health inflicted by exposure to herbicides.

Sivard, Ruth L. 1986. *World Military and Social Expenditures.* Washington, D.C.: World Priorities. Excellent source of data.

Smith, Dorothy. 1979. *In Our Own Interest (A Handbook for the Citizen Lobbyist in State Legislatures).* Seattle, Wash.: Madrona. Outstanding handbook.

Sommer, Mark. 1985. *Beyond the Bomb.* New York: Expro Press. Excellent analysis of how to abolish nuclear weapons.

Stokes, Bruce. 1981. *Helping Ourselves: Local Solutions to Global Problems.* New York: W. W. Norton. Superb examples.

Stone, Christopher D. 1974. *Should Trees Have Standing? Toward Legal Rights for Natural Objects.* Los Altos, Calif.: William Kaufmann. Useful discussion.

Tarlock, Anthony Dan. 1979. "Environmental Law: What It Is, What It Should Be." *Environmental Science and Technology,* vol. 13, no. 11, 1344–1348. Good summary.

Time. 1981. "American Renewal." February 23, pp. 34–49. Superb in-depth report on governmental reform, which includes some of the suggestions given in this chapter.

Tucker, William. 1982. *Progress and Privilege: America in the Age of Environmentalism.* Garden City, N.Y.: Anchor Press/Doubleday. Attacks U.S. environmentalists as elitist liberals whose primary concern is to protect their own wealth and power. This book has been used as intellectual support for the environmental policies of the Reagan administration. The author makes some good points but greatly oversimplifies environmental problems.

Vig, Norman J., and Michael E. Kraft. 1984. *Environmental Policy in the 1980s: Reagan's New Agenda.* Washington, D.C.: Congressional Quarterly. Useful analysis and source of information.

Wenner, Lettie M. 1982. *The Environmental Decade in Court.* Bloomington: Indiana University Press. Useful summary of environmental litigation during the 1970s.

Westman, Walter E. 1985. *Ecology, Impact Assessment, and Environmental Planning.*

New York: Wiley. Excellent overview of environmental impact assessment.

Wolfe, Joan. 1983. *Making Things Happen: The Guide for Members of Volunteer Organizations.* Andover, Mass.: Brick House. Excellent guide.

Chapter 26 Environmental Ethics

Barbour, Ian G., ed. 1973. *Western Man and Environmental Ethics.* Reading, Mass.: Addison-Wesley. Outstanding collection of essays.

Berger, John J. 1986. *Restoring the Earth.* New York: Alfred A. Knopf. Excellent series of case studies showing how small groups of Americans have restored ravaged and polluted habitats.

Bodian, Stephan. 1982. "Simple in Means, Rich in Ends: A Conversation with Arne Naess." *The Ten Directions (Zen Center Los Angeles),* summer–fall, pp. 7–9. Superb description of the deep ecology movement by the prominent Norwegian philosopher and environmental activist.

Bookchin, Murray. 1982. *The Ecology of Freedom.* Palo Alto, Calif.: Cheshire Books. Excellent discussion of environmental ethics.

Boyer, William H. 1984. *America's Future: Transition to the 21st Century.* New York: Praeger. Excellent overview.

Brown, Lester R. 1981. *Building a Sustainable Society.* New York: W. W. Norton. Superb overview of our environmental problems and plans for attaining a sustainable-earth society.

Cahn, Robert. 1978. *Footprints on the Planet: A Search for an Environmental Ethic.* New York: Universe Books. Outstanding book on environmental ethics and progress by a former member of the Council on Environmental Quality.

Cahn, Robert, ed. 1985. *An Environmental Agenda for the Future.* Covelo, Calif.: Island Press. Useful insights from the leaders of the country's major environmental organizations.

Cailiet, G., et al. 1971. *Everyman's Guide to Ecological Living.* New York: Macmillan. Superb summary of what you can do.

Caldwell, Lynton K., et al. 1976. *Citizens and the Environment: Case Studies of Popular Action.* Bloomington: Indiana University Press. Excellent summary describing what citizens have done to improve the environment.

Callahan, Daniel. 1973. *The Tyranny of Survival.* New York: Macmillan. Magnificent analysis contrasting sustainable-earth ethics and Spaceship Earth ethics.

Callenbach, Ernest. 1975. *Ecotopia.* Berkeley, Calif.: Banyan Tree Books. Stirring vision of what the world would be like if we became a sustainable-earth society.

Callenbach, Ernest. 1981. *Ecotopia Emerging.* Des Plaines, Ill.: Bantam Books. Superb discussion of how a utopian ecological revolution is taking place in northern California.

Capra, Fritjof. 1983. *The Turning Point.* New York: Bantam. Excellent discussion of how we are moving into a new phase of human cultural evolution built around the concepts of deep ecology.

Devall, Bill. 1981. "The Deep Ecology Movement." In *Ecological Consciousness,* edited by J. Donald Hughes and Robert Schults. Washington, D.C.: University Press of America. Excellent summary.

Devall, Bill, and George Sessions. 1984. "The Development of Natural Resources and the Integrity of Nature." *Environmental Ethics,* winter, 293–322. Superb analysis of resource use based on principles of deep ecology.

Devall, Bill, and George Sessions. 1985. *Deep Ecology: Living as if Nature Mattered.* Salt Lake City, Utah: Gibbs M. Smith. Superb description of deep ecology and its profound implications.

Eckholm, Erik P. 1982. *Down to Earth: Environment and Human Needs.* New York: W. W. Norton. Superb overview of problems and possible solutions.

Ehrenfeld, David. 1978. *The Arrogance of Humanism.* New York: Oxford University Press. Superb discussion of environmental ethics and the dangers of the Spaceship Earth worldview.

Elder, Frederick. 1970. *Crisis in Eden: A Religious Study of Man and Environment.* Nashville, Tenn.: Abingdon Press. Reply to White's charge (1967) that Christianity is the culprit. Calls for a theology of nature based on reverence for all life.

Elgin, Duane, and Arnold Mitchell. 1977. "Voluntary Simplicity (3)." *CoEvolution Quarterly,* summer, pp. 4–27. Superb description of the trend toward sustainable-earth lifestyles in the United States.

Environmental Ethics Journal. Department of Philosophy, University of Georgia, Athens, GA 30602. Excellent source of research articles.

Fackre, Gabriel. 1971. "Ecology and Theology." *Religion in Life,* vol. 40, 210–224. Superb overview.

Falk, Richard A. 1975. *A Study of Future Worlds.* New York: Free Press. Superb discussion of how to achieve a sustainable-earth society.

Fanning, Odum. 1986. *Opportunities in Environmental Careers.* West Bethesda, Md.: Bradley Hills Books. Useful survey of career possibilities and how to plan an educational curriculum for an environmental career.

Farallones Institute. 1979. *The Integral Urban House: Self-Reliant Living in the City.* San Francisco: Sierra Club Books. Superb guide to those wishing to live a more ecologically sound urban lifestyle.

Foster, Thomas W. 1981. "Amish Society." *Futurist,* December, pp. 33–40. Description of a sustainable-earth community that has long existed in America.

Fritsch, Albert J. 1980. *Environmental Ethics: Choices for Concerned Citizens.* New York: Anchor Books. Outstanding book. Highly recommended.

Fritsch, Albert J., et al. 1977. *99 Ways to a Simple Lifestyle.* Bloomington: Indiana University Press. Read and pass on to others.

Fromm, Eric. 1968. *The Revolution of Hope: Toward a Humanized Technology.* New York: Harper & Row. A classic analysis of hope, going beyond the typical superficial approach.

Granberg-Michaelson, Wesley. 1984. *A Worldly Spirituality.* New York: Harper & Row. Excellent discussion of religion and environmental ethics.

Hardin, Garrett, 1977. *The Limits of Altruism: An Ecologist's View of Survival.* Bloomington: Indiana University Press. Superb and controversial discussion of environmental ethics.

Hardin, Garrett. 1978. *Exploring New Ethics for Survival.* 2d ed. New York: Viking. Superb exploration of ethics of population control policies.

Hardin, Garrett. 1985. "Human Ecology: The Subversive, Conservative Science." *American Zoologist,* vol. 25, 469–476. Excellent overview.

Hargrove, Eugene C., ed. 1985. *Religion and Environmental Crisis.* Athens, Ga.: University of Georgia Press. Informative series of essays.

Henderson, Hazel. 1978. *Creating Alternative Futures.* New York: Berkley. Excellent description of exciting experiments and trends that could lead to a sustainable-earth society.

Hughes, J. Donald, and Robert Schults, eds. 1981. *Ecological Consciousness.* Washington, D.C.: University Press of America. Excellent collection of essays.

Johnson, Warren. 1978. *Muddling Toward Frugality.* San Francisco: Sierra Club Books. Important and hopeful book showing how we might make it to a sustainable-earth society.

Leckie, Jim, et al. 1975. *Other Homes and Garbage: Designs for Self-Sufficient Living*. San Francisco: Sierra Club Books. Excellent guide for those wishing to live a more ecologically sound lifestyle.

Leopold, Aldo. 1949. *A Sand County Almanac*. New York: Oxford University Press. An environmental classic describing Leopold's deep ecology land-use ethic.

Marchant, Carolyn. 1981. "Earthcare: Women and the Environmental Movement." *Environment*, vol. 23, no. 5, 6–13, 38–42. Excellent overview.

Partridge, Ernest, ed. 1981. *Responsibilities for Future Generations: Environmental Ethics*. New York: Prometheus Books. Useful collection of articles.

Regan, Tom. 1984. *Earthbound: New Introductory Essays in Environmental Ethics*. New York: Random House. Excellent collection of essays.

Repetto, Robert. 1986. *World Enough and Time: Successful Strategies for Resource Management*. New Haven, Conn.: Yale University Press. Useful blueprint for the future.

Rifkin, Jeremy. 1980. *Entropy: A New World View*. New York: Viking. Important book giving a nontechnical overview of the transition to a sustainable-earth society based on the second law of energy.

Rolston, Holmes, III. 1986. *Philosophy Gone Wild*. Buffalo, N.Y.: Prometheus. Excellent collection of articles on environmental ethics.

Roszak, Theodore. 1978. *Person/Planet*. Garden City, N.Y.: Doubleday. Stimulating discussion of a low-technology, spiritual, ecological utopian vision.

Ryn, Sin van der, and Peter Calthorpe. 1982. *Sustainable Communities: A New Design Synthesis for Cities, Suburbs, and Towns*. San Francisco: Sierra Club Books. Outstanding analysis and suggestions.

Sessions, George S. 1974. "Anthropocentrism and the Environmental Crisis." *Humbolt Journal of Social Relations*, vol. 2, fall–winter, 1–12. Superb discussion of our view of the world as a major cause of the environmental crisis.

Sessions, George. 1980. "Shallow and Deep Ecology: A Review of the Philosophical Literature." In *Ecological Consciousness*, edited by J. Donald Hughes and Robert Schults. Washington, D.C.: University Press of America. Outstanding summary of deep ecology.

Shrader-Frechette, Kristin. 1986. "Environmental Ethics and Global Imperatives." In *The Global Possible: Resources, Development, and the New Century*, edited by Robert Repetto. New Haven, Conn.: Yale University Press, pp. 97–127. Excellent overview.

Soloman, Lawrence. 1978. *The Conserver Society*. Garden City, N.Y.: Doubleday. Excellent discussion of a sustainable-earth society.

Squires, Edwin R., ed. 1982. *The Environmental Crisis: The Ethical Dilemma*. Mancelona, Minn.: AuSable Trails Institute. Excellent collection of essays.

Stivers, Robert L. 1976. *The Sustainable Society*. Philadelphia: Westminster. Excellent discussion of environmental ethics and a sustainable-earth society.

Tiger, Lionel. 1979. *Optimism: The Biology of Hope*. New York: Simon & Schuster. Useful antidote for despair.

Todd, Nancy Jack, and John Todd. 1984. *Bioshelters, Ocean Arks, City Farming: Ecology as the Basis of Design*. San Francisco: Sierra Club Books. Excellent suggestions for urban design and a more ecologically sound urban lifestyle.

Valaskakis, Kimon, et al. 1979. *The Conserver Society: A Workable Alternative for the Future*. New York: Harper & Row. Useful description of a sustainable-earth society.

White, Lynn, Jr. 1967. "The Historical Roots of Our Ecologic Crisis." *Science*, vol. 155, 1203–1207. Classic and controversial thesis that the root of the ecological crisis lies in the Judeo-Christian tradition.

Wilkinson, Loren, ed. 1980. *Earthkeeping: Christian Stewardship of Natural Resources*. Grand Rapids, Mich.: Erdmans. Excellent collection of articles by conservative Christians.

Worster, Donald. 1977. *Nature's Economy: The Roots of Ecology*. San Francisco: Sierra Club Books. Outstanding discussion of why we must work with—not against— nature.

Glossary

Abiotic Nonliving.

Abyssal zone Bottom zone of the ocean consisting of dark, deep water. Compare *Bathyal zone, Benthic zone, Euphotic zone.*

Accelerated eutrophication See *Cultural eutrophication.*

Acid deposition Combination of wet deposition from the atmosphere of droplets of sulfuric acid and nitric acid dissolved in rain, sleet, and snow (acid precipitation) and dry deposition from the atmosphere of particles of sulfate and nitrate salts. These acids and salts are formed when water vapor in the air reacts with the air pollutants sulfur dioxide (SO_2) and nitrogen dioxide (NO_2).

Acidic See *Acid solution.*

Acid mine drainage Dissolving and transporting of sulfuric acid and toxic metal compounds from abandoned underground coal mines to nearby streams and rivers when surface water flows through the mines.

Acid rain See *Acid deposition.*

Acid solution Any aqueous solution that contains more hydrogen ions (H^+) than hydroxide ions (OH^-); any aqueous solution with a pH less than 7. Compare *Basic solution, Neutral solution.*

Activated sludge process Form of secondary sewage treatment in which wastewater is pumped into a large tank and mixed for several hours with bacteria-rich sludge and air bubbles to increase biodegradation of organic wastes by aerobic bacteria.

Active solar heating System that uses solar collectors to capture energy from the sun as heat and then uses mechanical devices such as pumps and fans to move the captured heat to a storage system (usually an insulated tank of water or bed of rocks) or throughout a dwelling. Compare *Passive solar heating.*

Acute disease An infectious disease such as measles or typhoid fever that normally lasts for a relatively short time before the victim either recovers or dies. Compare *Chronic disease.*

Acute effect Serious effect such as a burn, illness, or death which occurs shortly after exposure to a pollutant or other stress.

Advanced industrial society Highly industrialized society based on extensive use of fossil fuels and efficient machines and techniques for mass production of goods.

Aerobic organism Organism that requires oxygen to live. Compare *Anaerobic organism.*

Aerosols Tiny droplets of liquid and solid particles suspended in air.

Age structure Number or percentage of persons of each sex at each age level or age group (cohort) in a population.

Agriculture-based urban society A society consisting of villages, towns, and cities that produce specialized goods and services which are traded for food and fibers produced by farmers in nearby agricultural land.

Air pollutant Chemical whose concentration in the atmosphere builds up to the point of causing harm to humans, other animals, vegetation, or materials such as metals and stone.

Alga (algae) Simple one-celled or many-celled plant(s), usually aquatic, capable of carrying on photosynthesis.

Algal bloom Population explosion of algae in surface waters due to an increase in plant nutrients such as nitrates and phosphates.

Alkaline solution See *Basic solution.*

Alpha particle Positively charged chunks of ionizing radiation consisting of two protons and two neutrons which are spontaneously emitted by the nuclei of some radioisotopes.

Alveoli Tiny sacs at the end of the bronchiole tubes in the lungs, where oxygen is inhaled, air is transferred to hemoglobin in the blood, and carbon dioxide in the blood is transferred to inhaled air and exhaled.

Ambient air Surrounding outdoor air.

Ambient air quality standard (AAQS) Maximum permissible concentration of a specific pollutant allowed by the federal government in the air. Compare *Emission standard.*

Amino acids Basic building block molecules of proteins. A long chain of certain amino acid molecules linked together chemically forms a specific protein molecule.

Anadromous species Species of fish, such as salmon, which migrate from fresh water to salt water and back again.

Anaerobic organism Organism that does not require oxygen to survive. Compare *Aerobic organism.*

Animal A form of life that is unable to make its own food the way plants do, that can usually move about voluntarily, and that has specialized sensory organs that enable it to react more quickly to stimuli than plants. Compare *Plant.*

Animal feedlot Confined area where hundreds or thousands of livestock animals are fattened for sale to slaughterhouses and meat processors.

Animal manure Dung (fecal matter) and urine of animals.

Annual population change rate See *Natural change rate.*

Annuals Terrestrial plants which die off each year during periods of temperature and moisture stress but leave behind seeds to germinate during the next favorable climatic season. Compare *Perennials.*

Antagonistic effect Result of the interaction of two or more factors so that the net effect is less than that resulting from adding their independent effects. Compare *Synergistic effect*.

Anthracite Hard coal with a low to moderate sulfur content, a very low moisture content (2%), and a high heat content. Compare *Bituminous coal, Lignite, Peat, Subbituminous coal*.

Anthropocentric Human-centered. Compare *Biocentric*.

Appropriate technology Technology that is usually characterized by simple, easy-to-repair, small- to medium-sized machines that are used on a decentralized basis, are inexpensive to build and maintain, and that utilizes locally available materials and labor. Compare *High technology*.

Aquaculture Growing and harvesting of fish and shellfish for human use in freshwater ponds, irrigation ditches, and lakes or fenced-in portions of coastal lagoons and estuaries.

Aquatic Pertaining to water. Compare *Terrestrial*.

Aquatic ecosystem Any major ecosystem such as a river, pond, lake, and ocean found in the hydrosphere. Compare *Biome*.

Aquifer Water-bearing layer of the earth's crust; water in an aquifer is known as groundwater. See *Confined aquifer, Unconfined aquifer*.

Aquifer depletion Withdrawal of groundwater from an aquifer faster than it is recharged by precipitation.

Aquifer overdraft See *Aquifer depletion*.

Arable land Land that is capable of being cultivated and supporting agricultural production.

Area strip mining Type of surface mining in which minerals such as coal and phosphate are removed by cutting deep trenches in flat or rolling terrain. Compare *Contour strip mining, Open-pit surface mining*.

Arid Dry, parched with heat.

Artesian aquifer See *Confined aquifer*.

Artesian well A water well drilled into a pressurized confined aquifer where the hydraulic pressure is so great that the water flows freely up the bore hole to the level of the water in the earth without any need for pumping.

Asbestosis Scarring of lung tissue and decrease in breathing capacity brought about by prolonged inhalation of tiny fibers of asbestos (silicate fibers).

Asthma Lung disorder characterized by a narrowing of the bronchial passages (bronchioles) and excessive mucus production that result in periodic shortness of breath, difficulty in breathing, and coughing. Usually caused by allergies and is often aggravated by air pollution.

Atmosphere Layer of air surrounding the earth's surface.

Atoms Extremely small particles that are the basic building blocks of all elements and thus all matter.

Average per capita GNP The gross national product (GNP) of a country divided by its total population.

Background ionizing radiation Ionizing radiation in the environment from naturally radioactive materials and from cosmic rays entering the atmosphere.

Bacteria Smallest living organisms; with fungi, they comprise the decomposer level of the food chain.

Balanced chemical equation Shorthand representation of a chemical change that contains the same number of atoms of each element on each side of the equation.

Baleen whales Species of whales, such as the blue, gray, humpback, and finback, which feed on zooplankton, krill, and other small marine animal organisms by using horny plates in their jaws to filter the organisms from seawater. Compare *Toothed whales*.

Barrier beach Gently sloping land along a coastline that normally contains two rows of sand dunes that help protect the land behind them from ravages of the sea. Compare *Rocky shore*.

Barrier islands Thin, sandy islands off the coast, separated from the mainland by bays or lagoons.

Basic See *Basic solution*.

Basic solution Any water solution containing more hydroxide ions (OH^-) than hydrogen ions (H^+); any water solution with a pH greater than 7. Compare *Acidic solution, Neutral solution*.

Bathyal zone Cold, fairly dark zone in an ocean below the euphotic zone in which there is some penetration by sunlight but not enough for photosynthesis. Compare *Abyssal zone, Euphotic zone*.

Benthic zone Bottom of a body of water. Compare *Abyssal zone, Bathyal zone, Euphotic zone, Limnetic zone, Littoral zone*.

Beta particle Swiftly moving electron emitted by the nucleus of a radioisotope.

Biocentric Ecosystem-centered. Compare *Anthropocentric*.

Biodegradable Material that can be broken down into simpler substances (elements and compounds) by bacteria or other decomposers.

Biofuels Gas or liquid fuels (such as ethyl alcohol) made from biomass (plants and trees).

Biogas Mixture of methane (CH_4) and carbon dioxide (CO_2) gases produced when anaerobic bacteria break down plants and organic waste (such as manure).

Biogeochemical cycle Mechanism by which chemicals such as carbon, oxygen, phosphorus, nitrogen, and water are continuously moved through the biosphere to be renewed over and over again for use by living organisms.

Biological amplification Increase in concentration of certain fat-soluble chemicals such as DDT in successively higher trophic levels of a food chain or web.

Biological control Use of natural predators, parasites, or disease-causing bacteria and viruses (pathogens) to regulate the population of a pest species.

Biological diversity See *Genetic diversity*.

Biological evolution See *Evolution*.

Biological magnification See *Biological amplification*.

Biological oxygen demand (BOD) Amount of dissolved oxygen gas required for bacterial decomposition of organic wastes in water; usually expressed in terms of the parts per million (ppm) of dissolved oxygen consumed over 5 days at 20°C (68°F) and normal atmospheric pressure. See also *Chemical oxygen demand*.

Biomass Total dry weight of all living organisms in a given area. See also *Biomass fuel*.

Biomass fuel Plant and animal matter such as wood that can be burned directly as a source of heat or converted to a more convenient gaseous or liquid biofuel.

Biome Large land ecosystem such as a forest, grassland, or desert. Compare *Aquatic ecosystem*.

Biosphere Total of all the ecosystems on the planet, along with their interactions; parts of the lithosphere, atmosphere, and hydrosphere in which living organisms can be found.

Biota The living plant and animal life of a region.

Biotic Living or of life.

Biotic potential The maximum rate at which members of a species can reproduce, given unlimited resources and ideal environmental conditions. Compare *Environmental resistance*.

Birth rate Number of live births per 1,000 persons in the population at the midpoint of a given year. Compare *Death rate*.

Bitumen Black, high-sulfur, tarlike heavy oil extracted from tar sands and then upgraded to synthetic fuel oil. See *Tar sands*.

Bituminous coal Soft form of coal with a moderate to high heat content and usually a high sulfur content (2% to 4%). Compare *Anthracite, Lignite, Peat, Subbituminous coal*.

Black lung disease Respiratory disorder that impairs breathing capacity as a result of the accumulation of fine particles of coal dust and other particulate matter in the lungs of coal miners over a prolonged period.

Breeder nuclear fission reactor Nuclear fission reactor that produces more nuclear fuel than it consumes, usually by converting nonfissionable uranium-238 into fissionable plutonium-239.

Broad-spectrum pesticide Chemical that kills organisms besides the target species.

Bronchitis See *Chronic bronchitis*.

Bronchiole tubes Tiny ducts entering the lungs which are subdivisions of the bronchus tubes and eventually lead to the alveoli.

Bronchus Either of the two main branches of the trachea, or windpipe, which enter the lungs.

Calorie Amount of energy required to raise the temperature of 1 gram of water 1°C. See also *Kilocalorie*.

Cancer A group of more than 120 different diseases—one for essentially each major cell type in the human body—all characterized by a tumor in which cells multiply uncontrollably and invade surrounding tissue.

Capitalist economy Economic system based on producing a surplus of goods that are exchanged between producers and consumers in the marketplace for profit. The United States and most MDCs have such an economy. Compare *Centrally planned economy, Subsistence economy*.

Carbon cycle Cyclic flow of carbon in various chemical forms through various components of the biosphere.

Carcinogen A chemical or physical agent (such as ionizing radiation) capable of causing cancer.

Carcinogenic Cancer causing.

Carnivore Animals that obtain their food by feeding only on other animals.

Carrying capacity Maximum population size of a species that a given ecosystem or area can support indefinitely under a given set of environmental conditions.

Cartel Group of companies or producers of a resource or product who agree to control production so as to keep the price of the resource or product high in order to enhance profits. OPEC is an example of a cartel.

Cell Basic structural unit of all organisms.

Cellular respiration Complex process that occurs in the cells of plants and animals in which food molecules such as glucose ($C_6H_{12}O_2$) combine with oxygen (O_2) and break down into carbon dioxide (CO_2) and water (H_2O), releasing usable energy. Compare *Photosynthesis*.

Census A count of the population.

Centrally planned economy One in which some or all of the decisions about allocation of resources, production, investment, and distribution of resources and wealth are made by the government. The Soviet Union and China have centrally planned economies. Compare *Capitalist economy, Subsistence economy*.

Chain reaction Series of multiple nuclear fissions taking place within the critical mass of a fissionable isotope and resulting in the emission of an enormous amount of energy.

Chemical Any one of the millions of different elements and compounds found in the universe.

Chemical change Process in which one or more elements or compounds interact in a way that changes them into one or more different elements or compounds. For example, the element carbon (C) can combine with oxygen (O_2) to form the compound carbon dioxide (CO_2). Compare *Physical change*.

Chemical cycles See *Biogeochemical cycles*.

Chemical energy Potential energy stored in the chemical bonds that hold together the atoms or ions in chemical compounds.

Chemical equation Shorthand representation of a chemical change in which symbols are used to represent each element involved. See *Balanced chemical equation*.

Chemical oxygen demand (COD) Measure of the total depletion of dissolved oxygen in polluted water. See also *Biological oxygen demand*.

Chemical reaction See *Chemical change*.

Chemosynthesis Process in which certain organisms such as specialized bacteria can convert chemicals obtained from the environment into chemical energy stored in nutrient molecules without the presence of sunlight. Compare *Photosynthesis*.

Chlorinated hydrocarbon insecticides Class of synthetic, organic compounds containing chlorine, hydrogen, and carbon that are persistent, fat soluble, and can be biologically amplified in food chains and webs. Examples include DDT, aldrin, and dieldrin.

Chlorination Addition of chlorine to drinking water or treated sewage plant effluent to kill germs (disinfection).

Chlorofluorocarbons (CFCs) Organic molecules containing varying numbers of chlorine, fluorine, carbon, and hydrogen atoms.

Chronic bronchitis Lung disorder characterized by persistent inflammation of the bronchi, excessive mucus buildup, recurrent coughing, and throat irritation. It appears to be caused and aggravated by smoking and air pollution.

Chronic disease Disease that lasts for a long time (often for life) and may flare up periodically (malaria), become progressively worse (cancer and cardiovascular disorders), or disappear with age (childhood asthma). Compare *Acute disease*.

Chronic effect A condition such as emphysema that lasts a long time and usually takes a long time to appear, often due to long-term exposure to low concentrations of one or more pollutants or other stresses. Compare *Acute effect*.

Chronic exposure Continuous or recurring prolonged exposure to potentially harmful chemicals or ionizing radiation.

Class action suit Filing of a lawsuit by a group on behalf of a larger number of citizens who allege similar damages but who need not be listed and represented individually.

Clay soil Low-porosity soil with a high clay content and little, if any, silt and sand.

Clearcutting Method of timber harvesting in which all trees in a forested area are removed.

Climate Average of day-to-day weather conditions at a given place on earth over a fairly long period, usually 30 years or more. Also includes extremes in weather behavior during the same period.

Climax ecosystem (climax community) A relatively stable, self-sustaining stage of ecological succession; a mature ecosystem with a diverse array of species and ecological niches, capable of using energy and cycling critical chemicals more efficiently than simpler, immature ecosystems. Compare *Immature ecosystem*.

Closed forest Land surface with an almost complete cover of trees. Compare *Open forest*.

Coal A solid, combustible material usually containing from 40% to 98% carbon mixed with varying amounts of water (2%

to 50%) and small amounts of nitrogen (0.2% to 1.2%) and sulfur (0.6% to 4%) compounds. See *Anthracite, Bituminous coal, Lignite, Peat, Subbituminous coal*.

Coal gasification Process in which solid coal is converted to either low-heat-content industrial gas or high-heat-content synthetic natural gas (SNG).

Coal liquefaction Process in which solid coal is converted to liquid hydrocarbon fuel such as methanol or synthetic gasoline.

Coastal wetland Land along a coastline that remains flooded with saltwater all or part of the year. Compare *Inland wetland*.

Coastal zone See *Neritic zone*.

Cogeneration The production of two useful forms of energy from the same process. In a factory, for example, excess steam produced for industrial processes or space heating is run through turbines to generate electricity, which can be used by the industry or sold to power companies.

Coliform bacteria A normally harmless type of bacteria that resides in the intestinal tract of humans and other animals and whose presence in water is an indicator that the water may be contaminated with other disease-causing organisms found in untreated human and animal waste.

Coliform bacteria count Number of colonies of fecal coliform bacteria present in a 100-milliliter sample of water.

Combined sewer Sewer system that transports both storm runoff and sewage through one large pipe to a sewage treatment plant.

Combustion Burning. Any very rapid chemical reaction in which heat and light are produced.

Commercial economy See *Capitalist economy*.

Commercial extinction Depletion of the population of a species to a point where it is no longer economical to harvest the species.

Commercial hunting Killing of wild animals for profit from sale of their furs or other parts. Compare *Sport hunting, Subsistence hunting*.

Commercial inorganic fertilizer Commercially prepared mixtures of plant nutrients such as nitrates, phosphates, and potassium applied to the soil to restore fertility and increase crop yields. Compare *Organic fertilizer*.

Common law Large body of unwritten principles and rules based on many thousands of past legal decisions that are used by judges to resolve disputes in the absence

of applicable statutory laws. Compare *Statutory law*.

Common property resource A resource, such as the air, oceans, sunshine, or public land to which a population has free and unmanaged access and thus can be abused. See *Tragedy of the commons*.

Commons See *Common property resource*.

Community (natural) All the populations of plant and animal species living and interacting in a given habitat or area at a given time.

Competition Two or more individual organisms of a single species (intraspecific competition) or two or more individuals of different species (interspecific competition) in the same ecosystem attempting to use the same scarce resources.

Competitive exclusion principle No two species in the same ecosystem can occupy exactly the same ecological niche indefinitely.

Compost See *Composting*.

Composting Accelerated breakdown of grass clippings, leaves, paper, and other organic solid waste in the presence of oxygen by aerobic (oxygen-needing) bacteria to produce a humus-like product that can be used as a fertilizer or soil conditioner.

Compound Substance composed of two or more atoms (molecular compounds) or oppositely charged ions (ionic compounds) of two or more different elements held together in fixed proportions by chemical bonds. Compare *Element*.

Concentration Amount of a chemical in a given volume of air, water, or other medium.

Confined aquifer Deposit of groundwater sandwiched between two layers of relatively impermeable rock, such as clay or shale. Compare *Unconfined aquifer*.

Conifer See *Coniferous trees*.

Coniferous trees Cone-bearing trees, mostly evergreens that have needle-shaped or scale-like leaves.

Conservation Wise use and careful management of resources, so as to obtain the maximum possible social benefits from them for present and future generations. Methods include preservation, balanced multiple use, reducing unnecessary waste, recycling, reuse, and decreased resource use.

Conservationists People who express their concern for the present and future survival of human beings and other species by not wasting and not irreversibly depleting or degrading the biological, physical, and chemical wealth of the world

upon which all life depends. Compare *Shallow conservatives*.

Conservation tillage farming Method of cultivation in which the soil is disturbed very little (minimum-tillage farming) or not at all (no-till farming) in order to reduce soil erosion, lower labor costs, and save energy.

Consumer Organism that relies on other organisms for its food. Generally divided into primary consumers (herbivores), secondary consumers (carnivores), and microconsumers (decomposers).

Consumption overpopulation Situation in the world or a given country or region in which a relatively small number of people use resources at such a high rate and without sufficient pollution control that the resulting pollution, environmental degradation, and resource depletion can threaten the health and survival of human beings and other species and disrupt the natural processes that cleanse and replenish the air, water, and soil. Compare *People overpopulation*.

Consumptive use Water use that results in water being lost by evaporation or transpiration or degraded by pollution so that it is no longer available for reuse in a particular area. Compare *Withdrawal use*.

Continental shelf Submerged sea floor that slopes gradually from the exposed edge or shore of a continent for a variable distance to a point where a much steeper descent to the ocean bottom begins.

Contour farming Plowing and planting along rather than up and down the sloped contours of land to reduce soil erosion and conserve water.

Contour strip mining Form of surface mining carried out in hilly or mountainous terrain by cutting out a series of shelves or terraces on the side of a hill or mountain and dumping the overburden from each new terrace onto the one below. Used primarily for coal. Compare *Area strip mining, Open-pit surface mining*.

Contraceptive Any physical, chemical, or biological method used to prevent fertilization of the human ovum by a male sperm.

Control rod Neutron-absorbing rods that are raised or lowered in the core of a nuclear reactor to control the rate of nuclear fission.

Cooling pond A lake or pond used to cool heated water from an electric power plant or factory.

Cooling tower A large towerlike structure used to cool hot water used to cool an electric power plant or factory by transferring the heat to water which is evaporated into the atmosphere (wet, or evap-

orative, cooling tower) or to air forced upward through the tower (dry cooling tower).

Coral reef Shallow area near the coast of a warm tropical or subtropical ocean consisting of calcium-containing material secreted by photosynthesizing red and green algae and small coral animals.

Core (of the earth) Central or innermost portion of the earth. Compare *Crust, Mantle.*

Cornucopians People, mostly economists, who believe that if present trends continue, economic growth and technological advances based on human ingenuity will produce a less crowded, less polluted, world in which most people will be healthier, live longer, and will have greater material wealth. Compare *Neo-Malthusians.*

Cosmic rays Streams of highly penetrating charged particles composed of protons, alpha particles, and a few heavier nuclei that bombard the earth from outer space.

Cost-benefit analysis Technique used to estimate and compare the expected costs or losses associated wtih a particular project or degree of pollution control with the expected benefits or gains over a given period of time.

Cost-effectiveness analysis Technique to determine how a particular goal, such as pollution control, can be achieved for the least cost.

Cover Place where an organism can go to escape predators or to find shelter from harsh environmental conditions.

Critical mass The quantity of fissionable material needed to initiate and maintain a nuclear fission chain reaction.

Critical mineral As defined by the U.S. government, a mineral necessary for national security.

Crop rotation Farming practice that involves planting the same field with a different series of crops from year to year in order to prevent plant nutrient depletion.

Crown fire Intensely hot fire that can destroy all or most of the forest vegetation, kill wildlife, and accelerate erosion. Compare *Ground fire.*

Crude birth rate See *Birth rate.*

Crude death rate See *Death rate.*

Crude oil A gooey liquid mixture of hydrocarbon compounds (90% to 95% of its weight) and small quantities of compounds containing oxygen, sulfur, and nitrogen that can be extracted from underground deposits and then sent to refiner-

ies to convert it to useful materials such as heating oil, diesel fuel, gasoline, and tar.

Crust (of the earth) Solid, outer layer of the earth. Compare *Core, Mantle.*

Cultural eutrophication Overnourishment of aquatic ecosystems with plant nutrients due to human activities such as agriculture, urbanization, and industrial discharge. See *Eutrophication.*

Culturesphere Use of human ingenuity and knowledge to extract, produce, and manage the use of matter, energy, and biological resources to enhance human survival and life quality.

DDT *Dichlorodiphenyltrichloroethane*, a chlorinated hydrocarbon that has been widely used as a pesticide.

Death rate Number of deaths per 1,000 persons in the population at the midpoint of a given year. Compare *Birth rate.*

Decibel (db) Unit used to measure sound power or sound pressure.

Deciduous plants Plants such as oak and maple that lose all their leaves during part of the year.

Decomposers Organisms such as bacteria, mushrooms, and fungi, which obtain nutrients by breaking down complex matter in the wastes and dead bodies of other organisms into simpler chemicals, most of which are returned to the soil and water for reuse by producers.

Deep well injection Method of disposing of liquid wastes by pumping them under pressure into deep subsurface cavities.

Defendant Individual, group of individuals, or a corporation charged in a court action. Compare *Plaintiff.*

Deforestation Removal of trees from an area without adequate replanting.

Degradable See *Biodegradable.* Compare *Nondegradable*

Degree of urbanization Percentage of a country's population living in areas with a population of 2,500 or more.

Delta Built-in deposit of river-borne sediments found near the mouth of a river near the ocean.

Demographic transition Gradual change, supposedly brought about by economic development, from a condition of high birth and death rates to substantially lower birth and death rates for a given country or region.

Demography Study of the characteris-

tics and changes of the human population in a particular area.

Dependency load Ratio of the number of old and young dependents in a population to the work force.

Depletion time Period required to use up a certain fraction—usually 80%—of the known reserves or estimated resources of a mineral, at an assumed rate of use.

Desalinization Purification of salt or brackish water by removing the dissolved salts.

Desert Biome characterized by very low average annual precipitation (less than 25 centimeters or 10 inches per year) and sparse, mostly low vegetation.

Desertification Conversion of productive grassland, cropland, or forest into desert, usually through a combination of overgrazing, prolonged drought, and global climate change.

Desirability quotient Number used to determine the desirability of using a particular technology; it is obtained by dividing the estimated short- and long-term benefits of using the technology by its estimated short- and long-term risks. See *Risk-benefit analysis.*

Detritus Dead plant material, bodies of animals, and fecal matter.

Deuterium (D: hydrogen-2) Isotope of the element hydrogen with a nucleus containing one proton and one neutron, thus having a mass number of 2. Compare *Tritium;* see also *Heavy water.*

Developed country See *More developed country.*

Diminishing returns Situation in which increased inputs of money, fertilizer, water, energy, or other factors does not lead to increased outputs such as crop productivity.

Dioxins Family of at least 75 different highly toxic chlorinated hydrocarbon compounds.

Discount factor Measure of how much something may be worth in the future compared to what it is worth now.

Dissolved oxygen (DO) content Amount of oxygen gas (O_2) dissolved in a given quantity of water at a given temperature and atmospheric pressure. It is usually expressed in parts per million (ppm).

Diversity Physical or biological complexity of a system. Usually a measure of the number of different species in an ecosystem (species diversity).

DNA (deoxyribonucleic acid) Large molecules found in the cells which carry genetic information.

Doubling time Length of time (usually years) it takes for a population to double in size if present annual population growth continues unchanged.

Drainage basin See *Watershed.*

Dredge spoils Materials scraped from the bottoms of harbors and rivers to maintain shipping channels.

Dredging Surface mining of seabeds and streambeds, primarily for sand and gravel.

Drip irrigation Method of irrigation in which small pipes deliver water to plant roots.

Drought Prolonged period of dry weather.

Dry cooling tower Large structure used in electric power plants to cool water by transferring heat to the air. Compare *Wet cooling tower.*

Dry farming Cultivation of agricultural crops without the use of irrigation.

Dust dome A dome-shaped accumulation of particulate matter that often forms over urban-industrial areas.

Early industrial society Society in which there is increasing use of inventions such as the coal-burning steam engine, the steam locomotive, the internal combustion engine, and other machines to replace dependence on draft animals and human muscle power for carrying out most tasks. Compare *Advanced industrial society.*

Early-successional species Wild animal species found in pioneer communities of plants found at the early stage of ecological succession. Compare *Late-successional species, Mid-successional species, Wilderness species.*

Ecological conservatives See *Conservationists.*

Ecological efficiency (food chain efficiency) The percent transfer of useful energy from one trophic level to the next higher trophic level in a food chain.

Ecological equivalents Species that occupy the same or similar ecological niches in similar ecosystems located in different parts of the world. For example, cattle in North America and kangaroos in Australia are both grassland grazers, hence are ecological equivalents.

Ecological niche Description of all the physical, chemical, and bilogical factors that a species needs to survive, stay healthy, and reproduce in an ecosystem.

Ecological succession Process in which communities of plant and animal species are replaced in a particular area over time

by a series of different and usually more complex communities. See *Primary succession, Secondary succession.*

Ecology Study of the interactions of living organisms with each other and with their environment; study of the structure and function of nature.

Economic resources See *Reserves.*

Economics Study of the principles and customs that affect the production, consumption, growth, and distribution of material wealth for human needs.

Ecosphere See *Biosphere.*

Ecosystem Self-regulating natural community of plants and animals interacting with one another and with their nonliving environment.

Efficiency See *Ecological efficiency, Energy efficiency.*

Effluent Any substance, particularly a liquid, that enters the environment from a point source. Generally refers to wastewater from a sewage treatment or industrial plant.

Electromagnetic radiation Radiant energy that can move through a vacuum or through space as waves of oscillating electric and magnetic fields.

Electromagnetic spectrum Span of electromagnetic energy ranging from short-wavelength gamma waves to long-wavelength radio waves.

Electron Fundamental particle found moving around outside the nucleus of an atom. Each electron has one unit of negative charge (-1) and has extremely little mass.

Electrostatic precipitator Device for removing particulate matter from smoke-stack emissions by causing the particles to become electrostatically charged and then attracting them to an oppositely charged plate, where they are removed from the air.

Element Chemical such as iron (Fe), sodium (Na), carbon (C), nitrogen (N), and oxygen (O) whose distinctly different atoms serve as the basic building blocks of all matter. Compare *Compound.*

Emergency core cooling system System designed to prevent meltdown if the core of a nuclear reactor overheats by instantaneous flooding of the core with large amounts of water.

Emigration Movement of people out of one country to take up permanent residence in another. Compare *Immigration.*

Emigration rate Number of people migrating out of a country each year per 1,000 people in its population. Compare *Immigration rate, Net migration rate.*

Emission Discharge of one or more gases or liquids into the environment.

Emission standard Maximum amount of a pollutant that is permitted by the federal government to be discharged into the air or a body of water from a point source.

Emphysema Lung disease in which the alveoli enlarge, fuse together, and lose their elasticity, thus impairing the transfer of oxygen to the blood.

Endangered species A wild species having so few individual survivors that the species could soon become extinct in all or most of its natural range. Compare *Threatened species.*

Energy Ability to do work or produce a change by pushing or pulling some form of matter or to cause a heat transfer between two objects at different temperatures.

Energy conservation Reduction or elimination of unnecessary energy use and waste.

Energy crisis A shortage or catastrophic price rise for one or more forms of useful energy, or a situation in which energy use is so great that the resulting pollution and environmental degradation threaten human health and welfare.

Energy efficiency The percentage of the total energy input that does useful work and is not converted into low-quality, essentially useless, low-temperature heat in an energy conversion system or process.

Energy pyramid Diagram representing the loss or degradation of useful energy at each step in a food chain. About 80% to 90% of the energy in each transfer is lost as waste heat, and the resulting shape of the energy levels is pyramidal.

Energy quality Ability of a form of energy to do useful work. See *High-quality energy, Low-quality energy.*

Enhanced oil recovery Removal of some of the heavy oil remaining in an oil well after primary and secondary recovery by methods such as pumping in steam or igniting the oil to increase its flow rate so that it can be pumped to the surface. Compare *Primary oil recovery, Secondary oil recovery.*

Entropy A measure of randomness or disorder. The higher the randomness or disorder of a system of matter, the higher its entropy. See *Second law of thermodynamics.*

Environment All of the external conditions that affect an organism or other specified system during its lifetime.

Environmental degradation Depletion or destruction of some renewable resource by using it at a faster rate than it is naturally replenished. See also *Sustained yield.*

Environmental resistance All the limiting factors that act together to regulate the maximum allowable size, or carrying capacity, of a population.

Epilimnion Upper layer of warm water with high levels of dissolved oxygen in a stratified lake. Compare *Hypolimnion, Thermocline.*

Erosion Removal of soil by flowing water or wind.

Essential amino acid One of the eight chemical building blocks for proteins that cannot be made in the human body and must be included in the diet for good health.

Estuarine zone Area near the coastline that consists of estuaries and coastal saltwater wetlands, and that extends out to the edge of the continental shelf.

Estuary Thin zone along a coastline where freshwater from rivers mixes with salty ocean water.

Ethics Branch of philosophy that seeks to define what is right and wrong on a universal basis. Compare *Morals.*

Euphotic zone Surface layer of an ocean, lake, or other body of water through which there is sufficient sunlight for photosynthesis. Compare *Abyssal zone, Bathyal zone.*

Eutrophication (natural) Natural process in which lakes receive inputs of plant nutrients (mostly nitrates and phosphates) as a result of natural erosion and runoff from the surrounding land basin. See also *Cultural eutrophication.*

Eutrophic lake Lake with a large or excessive supply of plant nutrients (mostly nitrates and phosphates). Compare *Mesotrophic lake, Oligotrophic lake.*

Evaporation Change of a liquid into vapor.

Evapotranspiration Combination of evaporation and transpiration of liquid water in plant tissue and in the soil to water vapor in the atmosphere.

Even-aged Where all the plants in a community such as a forest are about the same age.

Evergreen plants Plants such as pines, spruces, and firs that retain some of their leaves or needles throughout the year. Compare *Deciduous plants.*

Evolution The process by which a population of a species changes its characteristics (genetic makeup) over time in response to changes in environmental conditions. See *Natural selection.*

Exponential growth Growth in which some quantity, such as population size, increases by a constant percentage of the whole during each year or other time period; yields a J-shaped curve.

External cost Portion of the cost of production and marketing of a product that is borne by society, not by the producer, and thus is not included in the price of the product. Compare *Internal cost.*

Extinction Complete disappearance of an entire species.

Fallout See *Radioactive fallout.*

Family planning Provision of information and contraceptives to help couples choose the number of children and spacing of any children they choose to have.

Famine Situation in which people in a particular area suffer from widespread lack of access to enough food for good health as a result of catastrophic events such as drought, flood, earthquake, or war.

Fauna Animal population of a particular area. Compare *Flora.*

Federal deficit The amount of money the government has to borrow to make up the difference between what it spends and what it takes in from taxes.

Feedback Signal sent back into a self-regulating system to induce some system response.

Fertility The average number of live babies born to women in the population during their normal childbearing years (ages 15–44).

Fertilizer Substance that makes the land or soil capable of producing more vegetation or crops. See *Commercial inorganic fertilizer, Organic fertilizer.*

First law of ecology When humans interfere or modify an ecosystem there are always numerous short- and long-term effects, many of which are unpredictable.

First law of energy See *First law of thermodynamics.*

First law of thermodynamics (energy) In any chemical or physical change, movement of matter from one place to another, or change in temperature, energy is neither created nor destroyed, but merely converted from one form to another. In terms of energy quantity you can't get something for nothing; you can only break even; or, there is no free lunch.

Fissionable isotopes Isotopes that are capable of undergoing nuclear fission.

Floodplain Land along a river that is subject to periodic flooding when the river overflows its banks.

Flora Plant population of a region. Compare *Fauna.*

Fluidized-bed combustion Process for burning coal more efficiently, cleanly, and cheaply by using a flowing stream of hot air to suspend a mixture of powdered coal and limestone during combustion. About 90% to 98% of the sulfur dioxide produced during combustion is removed by reaction with limestone to produce solid calcium sulfate.

Fly ash Small, solid particles of ash and soot generated when coal, oil, or waste materials are burned.

Food additive Chemical deliberately added to a food, usually to enhance its color, flavor, shelf life, or nutritional characteristics.

Food chain Sequence of transfers of energy in the form of food from organisms in one trophic level to organisms in another trophic level when one organism eats or decomposes another.

Food web Complex network of many interconnected food chains and feeding interactions.

Forest Region with sufficient average annual precipitation of 75 centimeters (30 inches) or more to support various species of trees and smaller forms of vegetation. See also *Closed forest, Open forest.*

Forest fire presuppression Techniques used to prevent a forest fire from spreading once it has started. Compare *Forest fire prevention, Forest fire suppression.*

Forest fire prevention Educational and regulatory measures designed to prevent forest fires. Compare *Forest fire presuppression, Forest fire suppression.*

Forest fire suppression Methods used to put out a forest fire once it has started. Compare *Forest fire presuppression, Forest fire prevention.*

Fossil fuel Buried deposits of decayed plants and animals that have been converted to crude oil, coal, natural gas, or heavy oils by exposure to heat and pressure in the earth's crust over hundreds of millions of years.

Fossil fuel era Period of time in which nonrenewable deposits of crude oil, natural gas, coal, and other fossil fuels formed over millions of years are being used up in several hundred years.

Freons Chlorofluorocarbon compounds composed of atoms of carbon, chlorine, and fluorine.

Freshwater fish management Methods used to encourage the growth of populations of desirable commercial and sport freshwater fish species and to reduce or eliminate populations of less desirable species.

Frontier society See *Throwaway society.*

Frontier worldview See *Throwaway worldview.*

Fungicide Substance or mixture of substances used to prevent or kill fungi.

Fungus Simple or complex organism without chlorophyll. The simpler forms are unicellular; the higher forms have branched filaments and complicated life cycles. Examples are molds, yeasts, and mushrooms.

Game See *Game species.*

Game species Wildlife animal resources that provide sport for humans in the form of hunting and fishing.

Gamma rays High-energy electromagnetic waves emitted by the nuclei of some radioisotopes.

Gasohol Vehicle fuel consisting of a mixture of gasoline and ethyl or methyl alcohol that typically contains 10% to 23% by volume alcohol.

Gene pool Total genetic information possessed by a given reproducing population.

Genetic adaptation Changes in the genetic makeup of organisms of a species that allows the species to reproduce and gain a competitive advantage under changed environmental conditions.

Genetic damage Damage by radiation or chemicals to reproductive cells, resulting in mutations that can be passed on to future generations in the form of fetal and infant deaths and physical and mental disabilities.

Geometric growth See *Exponential growth.*

Geothermal energy Heat transferred from the earth's intensely hot molten core to underground deposits of dry steam (steam with no water droplets), wet steam (a mixture of steam and water droplets), hot water, or rocks lying relatively close to the earth's surface.

Global net population change Difference between the total number of live births and the total number of deaths throughout the world during a given period (usually a year).

GNP See *Gross national product.*

GRAS list List of food additives used in the United States that are generally recognized as being safe.

Grassland Biome found in regions where moderate average precipitation, ranging from 25 to 75 centimeters (10 to 30 inches) a year, is enough to allow grass to prosper but not enough to support large stands of trees.

Greenhouse effect Trapping of heat in the atmosphere. Incoming short-wavelength solar radiation penetrates the atmosphere, but the longer wavelength outgoing radiation is absorbed by water vapor, carbon dioxide, ozone, and several other gases in the atmosphere and is reradiated to earth, causing a rise in atmospheric temperature.

Greenhouse gases Gases present in the earth's atmosphere that cause the greenhouse effect.

Green manure Fresh or still-growing green vegetation plowed into the soil to increase the organic matter and humus available to support crop growth. Compare *Animal manure.*

Green revolution Popular term for the introduction of scientifically bred or selected varieties of a grain (rice, wheat, maize) that with high enough inputs of fertilizer and water can give greatly increased yields per area of land planted.

Gross national product (GNP) Total market value of all goods and services produced per year in a country.

Gross national quality (GNQ) Measure of life quality obtained by subtracting all the "negative" products and services that decrease the quality of life from a country's GNP.

Ground fire Low-level fire that typically burns only undergrowth. Compare *Crown fire.*

Groundwater Water that sinks into the soil, where it may be stored for long times in slowly flowing and slowly renewed underground reservoirs known as aquifers. See *Confined aquifer, Unconfined aquifer.*

Groundwater contamination Dissolving of substances at harmful levels in groundwater primarily as a result of human activities.

Growth rate (population) Percentage of increase or decrease of a population. It is the number of births minus the number of deaths per 1,000 population, plus net migration, expressed as a percentage.

Gully reclamation Using small dams of manure and straw, earth, stone, or concrete to collect silt and gradually fill in channels of eroded soil.

Habitat Place or type of place where an organism or community of organisms naturally or normally thrives.

Half-life Length of time taken for half the atoms in a given amount of a radioactive substance to emit one or more forms of ionizing radiation and, in the process, change into another nonradioactive or radioactive isotope.

Hazard Something that can cause injury, disease, death, economic loss, or environmental deterioration.

Hazardous waste Discarded solid, liquid, or gaseous material that may pose a substantial threat or potential hazard to human health or the environment when managed improperly.

Heat Form of kinetic energy that flows from one body to another as a result of a temperature difference between the two bodies.

Heavy oil Black, high-sulfur, thick oil found in deposits of crude oil, tar sands, and oil shale. See *Enhanced oil recovery.*

Heavy water Water (D_2O) in which all the hydrogen atoms have been replaced by deuterium (D).

Herbicide Chemical that injures or kills plant life by interfering with normal growth.

Herbivore Organism that feeds on plants. Compare *Carnivore, Omnivore.*

High-grade ore An ore that contains a relatively large concentration of a desired metallic element. Compare *Low-grade ore.*

High-quality energy Energy that is concentrated and has great ability to perform useful work. Examples include high-temperature heat and the energy in electricity, coal, oil, gasoline, sunlight, and nuclei of uranium-235. Compare *Low-quality energy.*

Humus Complex mixture of partially decomposed, water-insoluble material found in the topsoil layer; it helps retain water and water-soluble nutrients so they can be taken up by plant rocks.

Hunters and gatherers People who obtain their food by gathering edible wild plants and other materials and by hunting wild game and fish from the nearby environment.

Hydrocarbons Class of organic compounds containing carbon (C) and hydrogen (H).

Hydroelectric plant Electric power plant in which the energy of falling water is used to spin a turbine generator to produce electricity.

Hydrologic cycle Biogeochemical cycle that moves and recycles water in various forms through the biosphere.

Hydropower Electrical energy produced by falling water.

Hydrosphere Region that includes all the earth's moisture as liquid water (oceans, smaller bodies of fresh water, and underground aquifers), frozen water (polar ice caps, floating ice, and frozen upper layer of soil known as permafrost), and small amounts of water vapor in the earth's atmosphere.

Hypolimnion Bottom layer of cold, denser water in a lake. Compare *Epilimnion, Thermocline.*

Identified resources Specific bodies of a particular mineral-bearing material whose location, quantity, and quality are known or have been inferred from geological evidence and measurements. Compare *Reserves, Resources,* and *Undiscovered resources.*

Immigration Process of entering one country from another to take up permanent residence. Compare *Emigration.*

Immigration rate Number of people migrating into a country each year per 1,000 people in its population. Compare *Emigration rate, Net migration rate.*

Incineration Controlled process by which combustible wastes are burned and changed into gases.

Incomplete protein Protein lacking one or more of the eight essential amino acids. Compare *Complete protein.*

Industrialized agriculture Supplementation of solar energy with large amounts of energy derived from fossil fuels (especially oil and natural gas) to produce large quantities of crops and livestock for sale within the country where it is grown and to other countries. Compare *Subsistence agriculture.*

Industrial smog Air pollution, primarily from sulfur dioxide and suspended particulate matter, produced by the burning of coal and oil in industries and power plants. Compare *Photochemical smog.*

Inertia stability Ability of a living system to resist being disturbed or altered. See also *Resilience stability.*

Infant mortality rate Number of deaths of infants under one year of age in a given year per 1,000 live births in the same year.

Infectious disease Disease resulting from presence of disease-causing living organisms called agents, such as bacteria, viruses, and parasitic worms. See also *Nonvector-transmitted infectious disease, Vector-transmitted infectious disease.*

Information feedback Process by which information is fed back into a system and causes it to change in order to maintain a particular state or set of desired conditions. See *Negative feedback, Positive feedback.*

Inland wetland Land such as a swamp, marsh, or bog found inland that remains flooded all or part of the year with fresh water. Compare *Coastal wetland.*

Inorganic compounds Substances that consist of chemical combinations of two or more elements other than those used to form organic compounds. Compare *Organic compounds.*

Inorganic fertilizer See *Commercial inorganic fertilizer.*

Input pollution control Any method that prevents potential pollutants from entering the environment or sharply reduces the amount entering the environment. Compare *Output pollution control.*

Insecticide Substance or mixture of substances intended to prevent, destroy, or repel insects.

Integrated pest management (IPM) Use of a combination of biological, chemical, and cultivation methods in proper sequence and timing in order to keep pest population sizes just below the level of economic loss.

Intensive forest management Clearing an area of all vegetation, planting it with a single tree species, and then fertilizing and spraying the resulting even-aged stand of trees with pesticides. Compare *Moderate forest management.*

Internal costs Costs of production that are directly paid by the user or producer of a product. Compare *External costs.*

Interspecific competition Two or more species in the same ecosystem attempting to use the same scarce resources.

Intraspecific competition Two or more individual organisms of a single species in an ecosystem attempting to use the same scarce resources.

Intrauterine device (IUD) Small plastic or metal device inserted into the uterus to prevent contraception.

Inversion See *Thermal inversion.*

Ionizing radiation Fast-moving alpha or beta particles or high-energy electromagnetic radiation emitted by radioisotopes which have enough energy to dislodge one or more electrons from atoms it hits to form charged ions, which can react with and damage living tissue.

Ions Atoms or groups of atoms with one or more net positive ($+$) or negative ($-$) electrical charges.

Isotopes Two or more forms of a chemical element that have the same number of protons but different mass numbers or numbers of neutrons in their nuclei.

IUD See *Intrauterine device.*

J-shaped curve Curve with the shape of the letter J that depicts exponential or geometric growth (1, 2, 4, 8, 16, 32, . . .).

Kerogen Solid, waxy mixture of hydrocarbons that is intimately mixed with a fine-grained sedimentary rock. When the rock is heated to high temperatures, the kerogen is vaporized and much of the vapor can be condensed to yield shale oil, which can be refined to give petroleumlike products. See also *Oil shale, Shale oil.*

Kilocalorie (kcal) Unit of energy equal to 1,000 calories. See *Calorie.*

Kilowatt (kW) Unit of electrical power equal to 1,000 watts. See *Watt.*

Kinetic energy Energy that matter has because of its motion and mass. Compare *Potential energy.*

Kwashiorkor Nutritional deficiency (malnutrition) disease that occurs in infants and very young children when they are weaned from mother's milk to a starchy diet that is relatively high in calories but low in protein. See also *Marasmus.*

Lake Large natural body of standing fresh water formed when water from precipitation, land runoff, or groundwater flow fills depressions in the earth created by glaciation, earthquakes, volcanic activity, or crashes of giant meteorites.

Landfarming Spreading and mixing of hazardous or other solid or liquid wastes with surface soil to allow biodegradation to less hazardous or nonhazardous materials.

Landfill Land waste disposal site that is located without regard to possible pollution of groundwater and surface water due to runoff and leaching. Waste is covered intermittently with a layer of earth to reduce scavenger, aesthetic, disease, and air pollution problems. Compare *Open dump, Sanitary landfill, Secured landfill.*

Land-use planning Process for deciding the best use of each parcel of land in an area.

Laterite Soil found in some tropical areas in which an insoluble concentration of such metals as iron and aluminum is present; soil fertility is generally poor.

Late-successional species Wild animal species found in moderate-sized mature forest habitats. Compare *Early-successional species, Mid-successional species, Wilderness species.*

Law of conservation of energy See *First law of thermodynamics.*

Law of conservation of matter In any ordinary physical or chemical change, matter is neither created nor destroyed but merely changed from one form to another.

Law of conservation of matter and energy In any nuclear change the total amount of matter and energy involved remains the same.

Law of tolerance The existence, abundance, and distribution of a species is determined by whether the levels of one or more physical or chemical factors fall above or below the levels tolerated by the species.

LDC See *Less developed country.*

Leaching Process in which various soil components found in upper layers are dissolved and carried to lower layers and in some cases to groundwater.

Less developed country (LDC) Country that typically has low to moderate industrialization, a very low to moderate average GNP per person, a high rate of population growth, a large fraction of its labor force employed in agriculture, and a high level of adult illiteracy. Compare *More developed country.*

Life-cycle cost Initial cost plus lifetime operating costs.

Life expectancy Average number of years a newborn can be expected to live.

Lifetime cost See *Life-cycle cost.*

Light-water reactor (LWR) A nuclear reactor in which ordinary water, called light water, is used as a moderator inside its core to slow down the neutrons emitted by the fission process and thus sustain the chain reaction.

Lignite Form of coal with a low heat content and usually a low sulfur content. Compare *Anthracite, Bituminous coal, Peat, Subbituminous coal.*

Limiting factor Factor such as temperature, light, water, or a chemical that limits the existence, growth, abundance, or distribution of an organism.

Limiting factor principle The single physical or chemical factor that is most deficient in an ecosystem determines the presence or absence and population size of a particular species.

Limnetic zone Open-water surface layer of a lake through which there is sufficient sunlight for photosynthesis. Compare *Benthic zone, Littoral zone, Profundal zone.*

Liquified natural gas (LNG) Natural gas which is converted to liquid form by cooling to a very low temperature and then transported by sea in specially designed, refrigerated tanker ships.

Liquified petroleum gas (LPG) Mixture of liquified propane and butane gas removed from a deposit of natural gas.

Lithosphere Region of soil and rock consisting of the earth's upper surface or crust, a mantle of partially molten rock beneath this crust, and the earth's inner core of molten rock.

Littoral zone Shallow waters near the shore of a body of water. Compare *Benthic zone, Limnetic zone, Profundal zone.*

Livestock ranching Raising livestock for personal use and sale as meat by having them graze on rangeland grass.

Loams Medium porosity soils consisting of almost equal amounts of sand and silt and somewhat less clay; considered to be the best soil for growing crops.

Longwall method Method of subsurface mining for a mineral such as coal in which a narrow tunnel is cut and then supported by movable metal pillars. After the coal or ore is removed the roof supports are moved forward, allowing the earth behind them to collapse. Compare *Room-and-pillar method.*

Low-grade ore An ore that contains a relatively low concentration of a desired metallic element. Compare *High-grade ore.*

Low-quality energy Form of energy such as low-temperature heat that is dispersed or dilute and has little ability to do useful work. Compare *High-quality energy.*

LP-gas See *Liquified petroleum gas.*

Lung cancer Abnormal, runaway growth of cells in the mucous membranes of the bronchial passages.

Macronutrient Chemical needed in a relatively large quantity to sustain life in an organism. Carbon, hydrogen, nitrogen, and oxygen are examples. Compare *Micronutrient.*

Magma Molten rock material within the earth's core.

Malnutrition Condition in which quality of diet is inadequate and an individual's minimum daily requirements (for proteins, fats, vitamins, minerals, and other specific nutrients necessary for good health) are not met. Compare *Overnutrition, Undernutrition.*

Malthusian overpopulation Result of the tendency for the size of the human population in the world or a given portion of the world to outrun the ability of people to produce or buy sufficient food, so that poor health due to disease, malnutrition, and starvation begins to restore the balance between births and deaths. Compare *Neo-Malthusian overpopulation.*

Malthusian theory of population The theory of economist Thomas Malthus that population tends to increase as a geometric progression while food tends to increase as an arithmetic progression. The conclu-sion is that human beings are destined to misery and poverty unless population growth is controlled.

Manure See *Animal manure, Green manure.*

Marasmus Nutritional deficiency disease that results from a diet that is low in both calories and protein. See also *Kwashiorkor.*

Mass number Sum of the number of neutrons and the number of protons in the nucleus of an atom. It is a measure of the approximate mass of that atom.

Mass transit Transportation systems (such as buses, trains, and trolleys) that use vehicles that carry large numbers of people.

Matter Anything that has mass and occupies space.

Matter-recycling society Society based on significant recycling of nonrenewable, nonfuel matter resources. Compare *Sustainable-earth society, Throwaway society.*

MDC See *More developed country.*

Megawatt (MW) Unit of electrical power equal to 1,000 kilowatts, or 1 million watts. See *Watt.*

Meltdown Complete melting of the fuel rods and core of a nuclear reactor.

Mesotrophic lake Lake with a moderate supply of plant nutrients. Compare *Eutrophic lake, Oligotrophic lake.*

Metabolic reserve Lower half of rangeland grass plants that can grow back as long as it is not consumed by herbivores.

Metallic mineral Inorganic substance found in the earth's crust that contains a useful metallic element such as aluminum, iron, or uranium.

Metastasis Release of malignant (cancerous) cells from a tumor into other parts of the body.

Microconsumer See *Decomposer.*

Microorganism Generally, any living thing of microscopic size; examples include bacteria, yeasts, simple fungi, some algae, slime molds, and protozoans.

Mid-successional species Wild species which are found around abandoned croplands and partially open areas characterized by vegetation at the middle stages of ecological succession. Compare *Early-successional species, Late-successional species, Wilderness species.*

Migration rate Difference between the numbers of people leaving and entering a given country or area per 1,000 persons in its population at midyear.

Mineral An inorganic substance (element or compound) occurring naturally in the earth's crust. See *Metallic mineral, Nonmetallic mineral.*

Mineral deposit Any naturally occurring concentration in the lithosphere of a free element or compound in solid form.

Mineral resource Nonrenewable chemical element or compound in solid form that is used by humans. Mineral resources are classified as metallic (such as iron and tin) or nonmetallic (such as fossil fuels, sand, and salt).

Minimum tillage farming Planting crops by disturbing the soil as little as possible and keeping crop residues and litter on the ground instead of turning them under by plowing.

Moderate forest management Partial harvesting of timber from existing commercially exploitable forests, usually consisting of uneven-aged stands of several tree species. Compare *Intensive forest management.*

Molecule Chemical combination of two or more atoms of the same chemical element (such as O_2) or different chemical elements (such as H_2O). Compare *Atom.*

Monoculture Cultivation of a single crop (such as maize or cotton) to the exclusion of other crops on a piece of land.

Morals The dominant beliefs of a particular culture about what is right and wrong. Compare *Ethics.*

More developed country (MDC) Country with significant industrialization, a high average GNP per person, a low rate of population growth, a small fraction of its labor force employed in agriculture, a low level of adult illiteracy, and a strong economy. Compare *Less developed country.*

Mortality The death rate.

Multiple use Principle for managing a forest so that it is used for a variety of purposes, including timbering, mining, recreation, grazing, wildlife preservation, and soil and water conservation.

Municipal waste Combined residential and commercial waste materials generated in a given municipal area.

Mutagen Any substance capable of increasing the rate of genetic mutation of living organisms.

Mutation Inheritable changes in the DNA molecules found in genes as a result of exposure to various environmental factors such as radiation and certain chemicals or during cell division (asexual reproduction) or when a sperm and egg cell fuse (sexual reproduction).

National ambient air quality standard (NAAQS) Federal standard that speci-

fies the maximum allowable level, averaged over a specific time period, for a certain pollutant in outdoor (ambient) air.

Natural change rate How fast a population is growing or decreasing per year; usually expressed in percent and obtained by subtracting the crude death rate from the crude birth rate and dividing the result by 10.

Natural community See *Community.*

Natural eutrophication See *Eutrophication.*

Natural gas Underground deposits of gases consisting of 50% to 90% methane (CH_4) and small amounts of heavier gaseous hydrocarbon compounds such as propane (C_3H_8) and butane (C_4H_{10}).

Natural increase (or decrease) Difference between the birth rate and the death rate in a given population during a given period.

Natural ionizing radiation See *Background ionizing radiation.*

Natural radioactivity A nuclear change in which unstable nuclei of atoms spontaneously shoot out "chunks" of mass, energy, or both, at a fixed rate.

Natural resource Anything obtained from the physical environment to meet human needs.

Natural selection Mechanism for evolutionary change in which individual organisms in a single population die off over time because they cannot tolerate a new stress and are replaced by individuals whose genetic traits allow them to cope with the stress and reproduce successfully to pass these adaptive traits on to their offspring. See also *Evolution.*

Negative feedback Process by which information is fed back into a system and causes it to change in order to maintain a particular desired state. Compare *Positive feedback.*

Neo-Malthusians People who believe that if present trends continue, the world will become more crowded and more polluted, leading to greater political and economic instability and increasing the threat of nuclear war as the rich get richer and the poor get poorer. Compare *Cornucopians.*

Neritic zone Relatively warm, nutrient-rich, shallow portion of the ocean that extends from the high-tide mark on land to the edge of the continental shelf. Compare *Open Sea.*

Net energy See *Net useful energy.*

Net migration rate For a given place on earth, the difference between the numbers of persons immigrating and emigrating during a given period (usually a year) per 1,000 persons in the population at the midpoint of the year.

Net population change Difference between the total number of live births and the total number of deaths throughout the world or a given part of the world during a specified period (usually a year).

Net primary productivity Rate at which all the plants in an ecosystem produce net useful chemical energy. It is equal to the difference between the rate at which the plants in an ecosystem produce useful chemical energy and the rate at which they use some of this energy through cellular respiration.

Net useful energy Total useful energy available from an energy resource or energy system minus the useful energy used, lost, and wasted in finding, processing, concentrating, and transporting it to a user.

Neutral solution Water solution containing an equal number of hydrogen ions (H^+) and hydroxide ions (OH^-); has a pH of 7. Compare *Acid solution, Basic solution.*

Neutron (n) Elementary particle present in the nuclei of all atoms (except hydrogen-1). It has a relative mass of 1 and no electric charge.

Niche See *Ecological niche.*

Nitrogen cycle Biogeochemical cycle in which nitrogen is converted into various forms and transported through the biosphere.

Nitrogen fixation Process in which bacteria and other soil microorganisms convert atmospheric nitrogen into nitrates, which become available to growing plants.

Nonbiodegradable pollutant Material such as toxic mercury and lead compounds that is not broken down to an acceptable level or form in the environment by natural processes. Compare *Rapidly biodegradable pollutant, Slowly biodegradable pollutant.*

Noninfectious disease Illness not relayed by disease-causing organisms and except for genetic diseases, are not transmitted from one person to another. Examples include heart disease, bronchitis, cancer, diabetes, asthma, multiple sclerosis, and hemophilia. Compare *Infectious disease.*

Nonmetallic mineral Inorganic substance found in the earth's crust that contains useful nonmetallic compounds such as those in sand, stone, and nitrate and phosphate salts used as commercial fertilizers. Compare *Metallic mineral.*

Nonpoint source Source of pollution in which wastes are not released at one specific, identifiable point but from a number of points that are spread out and difficult to identify and control. Compare *Point source.*

Nonrenewable resource Resource that is available in a fixed amount (stock) in various places in the earth's crust and either is not replenished by natural processes or is replenished more slowly than it is used so that it can ultimately be totally depleted or depleted to the point where it is too expensive to extract and process for human use. Compare *Perpetual resource, Renewable resource.*

Nonthreshold pollutant Substance or condition harmful to a particular organism at any level or concentration. Compare *Threshold pollutant.*

Nonvector-transmitted infectious disease Disease that is transmitted from person to person without an intermediate nonhuman live carrier. Compare *Vector-transmitted infectious disease.*

No-till cultivation See *Conservation tillage farming.*

Nuclear autumn effect Moderate drop in atmospheric temperature and degree of light penetration to the earth's surface as a result of large amounts of smoke, soot, dust, and other debris lifted into the atmosphere as a result of a limited nuclear war. Compare *Nuclear winter effect.*

Nuclear change Process in which the isotope of an element changes into one or more different isotopes by altering the number of protons, neutrons, or both in its nucleus. Compare *Chemical change.*

Nuclear energy Energy released when atomic nuclei undergo fission or fusion.

Nuclear fission Nuclear change in which the nuclei of certain heavy isotopes with large mass numbers such as uranium-235 are split apart into two lighter nuclei when struck by slow- or fast-moving neutrons; this process also releases more neutrons and a substantial amount of energy. Compare *Nuclear fusion.*

Nuclear fusion Nuclear change in which two nuclei of light elements such as hydrogen are forced together at high temperatures of 100 million to 1 billion °C until they fuse to form a heavier nucleus with the release of a substantial amount of energy. Compare *Nuclear fission.*

Nuclear winter effect Significant drop in atmospheric temperature and degree of light penetration to the earth's surface as a result of massive amounts of smoke, soot, dust, and other debris lifted into the atmosphere as a result of a limited nuclear war. Compare *Nuclear autumn effect.*

Nucleus The extremely tiny center of an atom, which contains one or more positively charged protons and in most cases one or more neutrons with no electrical charge. The nucleus contains most of an atom's mass.

Nutrient Element or compound needed for the survival, growth, and reproduction of a plant or animal.

Ocean thermal energy conversion (OTEC) Use of a floating power plant located in a suitable tropical ocean area to produce electricity by taking advantage of the temperature difference between warm surface waters and cold bottom waters in an ocean.

Oil See *Petroleum.*

Oil shale Underground formation of a fine-grained rock which contains varying amounts of a solid, waxy mixture of hydrocarbon compounds known as kerogen. When the rock is heated to high temperatures the kerogen is converted to a vapor which can be condensed to form a slow-flowing heavy oil called shale oil. See *Kerogen, Shale oil.*

Oligotrophic lake A lake with a low supply of plant nutrients. Compare *Eutrophic lake, Mesotrophic lake.*

Omnivore Organism such as a pig, rat, cockroach, or human being that can use both plants and other animals as food sources. Compare *Carnivore, Herbivore.*

Open dump Land disposal site where wastes are deposited and left uncovered with little or no regard for control of scavenger, aesthetic, disease, air pollution, or water pollution problems. Compare *Sanitary landfill, Secured landfill.*

Open forest Land area covered only partially with trees. Compare *Closed forest.*

Open-pit surface mining Surface mining of materials (primarily stone, sand, gravel, iron, and copper) that creates a large pit.

Open sea The part of an ocean that is beyond the continental shelf.

Ore Mineral deposit containing a high enough concentration of at least one metallic element to permit the metal to be extracted and sold at a profit. See *High-grade ore, Low-grade ore.*

Ore deposit See *Ore.*

Organic compounds Molecules that typically contain atoms of the elements carbon and hydrogen; carbon, hydrogen, and oxygen; or carbon, hydrogen, oxygen, and nitrogen. Compare *Inorganic compounds.*

Organic farming Method of producing crops and livestock naturally by using organic fertilizer (mature, legumes, composting, crop residues), crop rotation, and natural pest control (good bugs that eat bad bugs, plants that repel bugs, and environmental controls such as crop rota-

tion) instead of using commercial fertilizer and synthetic pesticides and herbicides.

Organic fertilizer Organic material such as animal manure, green manure, and compost applied to cropland as a source of plant nutrients. Compare *Commercial inorganic fertilizer.*

Organism Any form of life.

Organophosphates Diverse group of nonpersistent synthetic chemical insecticides that act chiefly by breaking down nerve and muscle responses; examples are parathion and malathion.

Output pollution control Method for reducing the level of pollution once a pollutant has entered the environment. Compare *Input pollution control.*

Overburden Layer of soil and rock overlying a mineral deposit that is removed during surface mining.

Overdeveloped country (ODC) Hypothesis that affluent and technologically advanced countries are hastening the depletion and degradation of many of the world's vital resources through a throwaway lifestyle based on unnecessary resource waste—thus helping make it difficult or impossible for many of today's LDCs to undergo significant economic and industrial development. Compare *Less developed country, More developed country.*

Overfishing Harvesting so many fish, especially immature individuals, of a species that there is not enough breeding stock left for adequate annual renewal.

Overgrazing Excessive grazing of rangeland by livestock to the point where it cannot be renewed or is slowly renewed because of damage to the root system.

Overnutrition Diet so high in calories, saturated (animal) fats, salt, sugar, and processed foods, and so low in vegetables and fruits that the consumer runs high risks of diabetes, hypertension, heart disease, and other health hazards. Compare *Malnutrition, Undernutrition.*

Overpopulation Impairment of the life-support systems in a country, a region, or the world when its people use nonrenewable and renewable resources to such an extent that the resource base is degraded or depleted and air, water, and soil are severely polluted. See *Consumption overpopulation, People overpopulation.*

Oxygen cycle Biogeochemical cycle in which oxygen is converted into various forms and transported through the biosphere.

Oxygen-demanding wastes Organic water pollutants that are usually degraded by aerobic (oxygen-consuming) bacteria if there is sufficient dissolved oxygen (DO) in the water. See also *Biological oxygen demand*.

Ozone layer Layer of gaseous ozone (O_3) in the upper atmosphere that protects life on earth by filtering out harmful ultraviolet radiation from the sun.

Package sewage treatment plant Small plant sometimes used for treatment of small quantities of wastewater from shopping centers, apartment complexes, villages, and small housing subdivisions.

PANs Group of chemicals (photochemical oxidants) known as *peroxyacyl nitrates*, found in photochemical smog.

Paratransit Transit system such as carpools, vanpools, jitneys, and dial-a-ride systems that carry a relatively small number of passengers per vehicular unit.

Particulate matter Solid particles or liquid droplets suspended or carried in the air.

Parts per billion (ppb) Number of parts of a chemical found in one billion parts of a particular gas, liquid, or solid mixture.

Parts per million (ppm) Number of parts of a chemical found in one million parts of a particular gas, liquid, or solid mixture.

Parts per trillion (ppt) Number of parts of a chemical found in one trillion parts of a particular gas, liquid, or solid mixture.

Passive solar heating System which captures sunlight directly, usually through large windows or an attached greenhouse, and distributes and stores some of it without the use of fans, pumps, or other mechanical devices. Compare *Active solar heating*.

Pastoralists Livestock farmers who herd livestock over vast areas of natural rangeland.

Pathogen Organism that produces disease.

PCBs (*polychlorinated biphenyls*) Mixture of at least 50 widely used compounds containing chlorine that can be biologically magnified in the food chain with unknown effects.

Peat A fuel with a low heat content and a high moisture content (70% to 95%) that is the first step in the formation of various types of coal. Compare *Anthracite, Bituminous coal, Lignite, Subbituminous coal*.

People overpopulation Condition in which there are more people in a particular country, region, or the world than the available supplies of food, water, and other vital resources can support, or where the rate of population growth so exceeds the rate of economic growth and the equitable distribution of wealth that a number of people are too poor to grow or buy sufficient food. Compare *Consumption overpopulation*.

Perennials Terrestrial plants which flower and produce and set seeds year after year despite seasonal climatic fluctuations. Compare *Annuals*.

Permafrost Water permanently frozen year-round in thick underground layers of soil found in tundra.

Perpetual resource One such as solar energy that comes from an essentially inexhaustible source and thus will always be available on a human time scale regardless of whether or how we use it. Compare *Nonrenewable resource, Renewable resource*.

Persistence See *Inertia stability*.

Pest Unwanted organism that directly or indirectly interferes with human activities.

Pesticide Any chemical designed to kill weeds, insects, fungi, rodents, and other organisms that humans consider to be undesirable.

Pesticide treadmill Situation in which the costs of using pesticides increase while their effectiveness decreases primarily as a result of genetic resistance to the chemicals by target organisms.

Petrochemicals Chemicals obtained by refining (distilling) crude oil which are used as raw materials in the manufacture of most industrial chemicals, fertilizers, pesticides, plastics, synthetic fibers, paints, medicines and numerous other products.

Petroleum See *Crude oil*.

pH Numeric value that indicates the relative acidity or alkalinity of a substance on a scale of 0 to 14, with the neutral point at 7.0. Acid solutions have pH values lower than 7.0 and basic solutions have pH values greater than 7.0.

Phosphorus cycle Biogeochemical cycle in which phosphorus is converted into various chemical forms and transported through the biosphere.

Photochemical reaction Chemical reaction activated by light.

Photochemical smog Complex mixture of air pollutants produced in the atmosphere by the reaction of hydrocarbons and nitrogen oxides under the influence of sunlight. Especially harmful components include ozone, peroxyacyl nitrates (PANs), and various aldehydes. Compare *Industrial smog*.

Photosynthesis Complex process that occurs in the cells of green plants whereby radiant energy from the sun is used to combine carbon dioxide (CO_2) and water (H_2O) to produce oxygen (O_2) and simple sugar or food molecules, such as glucose ($C_6H_{12}O_6$). Compare *Cellular respiration, Chemosynthesis*.

Photovoltaic cell (solar cell) Device in which radiant (solar) energy is converted directly into electrical energy.

Physical change Process that alters one or more physical properties of an element or compound without altering its chemical composition. Examples include changing the size and shape of a sample of matter (crushing ice and cutting aluminum foil) and changing a sample of matter from one physical state to another (boiling and freezing water). Compare *Chemical change*.

Phytoplankton Free-floating, mostly microscopic aquatic plants.

Pioneer community First successfully integrated set of plants, animals, and decomposers that is found in an area undergoing primary ecological succession.

Plaintiff Individual, group of individuals, or corporation bringing charges in a court case. Compare *Defendant*.

Plankton Microscopic floating plant and animal organisms of lakes, rivers, and oceans.

Plantation agriculture Growth of specialized crops such as bananas, coffee, and cacao in some tropical LDCs, primarily for sale to MDCs.

Plasma "Gas" of charged particles (ions) of elements that exists only at such high temperatures (40 million to several billion degrees Celsius) that all electrons are stripped from the atomic nuclei.

Point source Source of pollution that involves discharge of pollutants from an identifiable point, such as a smokestack or sewage treatment plant. Compare *Nonpoint source*.

Pollution A change in the physical, chemical, or biological characteristics of the air, water, or soil that can affect the health, survival, or activities of humans or other living organisms in a harmful way.

Polychlorinated biphenyls See *PCBs*.

Pond Small, shallow, usually human-created impoundment of fresh water.

Population Group of individual organisms of the same species that occupy particular areas at given times.

Population crash Extensive deaths over a relatively short time resulting when a population exceeds the ability of the environment to support it.

Population density Number of organisms in a particular population per square kilometer or other unit of area.

Population distribution Variation of population density over a given country, region, or other area.

Porosity See *Soil porosity*.

Positive feedback Flow of information into a system that causes the system to change continuously in the same direction; as a result, the system can go out of control. Compare *Negative feedback*.

Potential energy Energy stored in an object as a result of its position or the position of its parts. Compare *Kinetic energy*.

Power tower See *Solar furnace*.

ppb See *Parts per billion*

ppm See *Parts per million*.

ppt See *Parts per trillion*.

Precipitation Water in the form of rain, sleet, hail, and snow that falls from the atmosphere onto the land and bodies of water.

Predation Situation in which an organism of one species (the predator) captures and feeds on an organism of another species (the prey).

Predator Organism that captures and feeds on parts or all of an organism of another species (the prey).

Preservationists People who believe that large areas of public land resources should be protected and preserved from mining, lumbering, and other forms of development by establishing parks, wilderness areas, and wildlife refuges which can be enjoyed by present generations and passed on unspoiled to future generations. Compare *Scientific conservationists*.

Prey Organism that is captured and serves as a source of food for an organism of another species (the predator).

Primary air pollutant Chemical that has been added directly to the air and occurs in a harmful concentration. Compare *Secondary air pollutant*.

Primary consumer See *Herbivore*.

Primary oil recovery Pumping out all of the crude oil that will flow by gravity into the bottom of an oil well. Compare *Enhanced oil recovery, Secondary oil recovery*.

Primary succession Sequential development of communities in a bare or soilless area that has never been occupied by a community of organisms. Compare *Secondary succession*.

Primary treatment (of sewage) Mechanical treatment in which large solids, like old shoes and sticks of wood, are screened out, and suspended solids settle out as sludge. Compare *Secondary treatment, Tertiary treatment*.

Prime reproductive age Years between ages 20 and 29 during which most women have most of their chidren. Compare *Reproductive age*.

Producer Organism that uses solar energy (green plant) or chemical energy (some bacteria) to manufacture its own organic substances (food) from inorganic nutrients. Compare *Consumer, Decomposer*.

Profundal zone Deep-water region of a lake, which is not penetrated by sunlight. Compare *Benthic zone, Limnetic zone, Littoral zone*.

Proton Positively charged particle found in the nuclei of all atoms. Each proton has a relative mass of 1 and a single positive charge.

Pyramid of biomass Diagram representing the biomass, or total dry weight of all living organisms, that can be supported at each trophic level in a food chain.

Pyramid of numbers Diagram representing the number of organisms of a particular type that can be supported at each trophic level from a given input of solar energy at the producer trophic level in a food chain.

Pyrolysis High-temperature decomposition of material in the absence of oxygen.

Radiation Propagation of energy through matter and space in the form of fast-moving particles (particulate radiation) or waves (electromagnetic radiation).

Radioactive fallout Radioactive dirt and debris that fall back to the earth after being released into the atmosphere as a result of the detonation of a nuclear weapon or an accident at a nuclear power plant or other facility handling radioactive materials.

Radioactive isotope See *Radioisotope*.

Radioactive waste End products of nuclear power plants, research, medicine, weapons production, or other processes involving nuclear reactions.

Radioactivity See *Natural radioactivity*.

Radioisotope Isotope of an atom whose unstable nuclei spontaneously emit fast-moving particles (such as alpha or beta particles), high-energy electromagnetic radiation in the form of gamma rays, or both, to form nonradioactive or radioactive isotopes of a different kind.

Rangeland Land on which the vegetation is predominantly grasses, grasslike plants, or shrubs such as sagebush and that is capable of providing forage for grazing or browsing animals.

Range of tolerance Range or span of

chemical and physical conditions that must be maintained for populations of a particular species to stay alive and grow, develop, and function normally.

Rapidly biodegradable pollutant Substance such as human sewage that can be rapidly broken down in the environment into an acceptable level or form by natural processes. Compare *Nondegradable pollutant, Slowly biodegradable pollutant*.

Rate of natural change Measure of population change obtained by finding the difference between the birth rate and the death rate.

Rate of population change Difference between the birth rate and the death rate plus net migration rate for a particular country or area.

Recharge area Area in which an aquifer is replenished with water by the downward percolation of precipitation through soil and rock.

Recharging Replenishment of water in an aquifer.

Recycling Collecting and remelting or reprocessing a resource so it can be used again, as when used glass bottles are collected, melted down, and made into new glass bottles. Compare *Reuse*.

Renewable resource Resource that can be depleted in the short run if used or contaminated too rapidly but normally will be replaced through natural processes in the long run. Compare *Nonrenewable resource, Perpetual resource*.

Replacement level of fertility Number of children a couple must have to replace themselves; the average for a country or the world is usually slightly higher than 2 (2.1 in the United States) because some children die before reaching their reproductive years.

Reproductive age Ages 15 to 44, when most women have all their children. Compare *Prime reproductive age*.

Reproductive potential See *Biotic potential*.

Reserves Identified deposits of a particular resource in known locations that can be extracted profitably at present prices and with current mining technology. Compare *Identified resources, Resources, Undiscovered resources*.

Reservoir Large and deep, human-created body of standing fresh water often built behind a dam. Compare *Lake*.

Resilience stability Ability of a disturbed living system to restore itself to its condition before the disturbance. See also *Inertia stability*.

Resource (natural) See *Natural resource*.

Resource conservation Developing and protecting natural resources for the greatest good of the greatest number of people for the longest length of time by reducing unnecessary resource use and waste.

Resource recovery Extraction of useful materials or energy from waste materials. This may involve recycling or conversion into different and sometimes unrelated products or uses. Compare *Recycle, Reuse.*

Resource recovery plant Centralized facility in which mixed urban solid waste is shredded and automatically separated to recover glass, iron, aluminum, and other valuable materials. The remaining paper, plastics, and other materials are incinerated to produce steam, hot water, or electricity.

Resources Identified and unidentified deposits of a particular mineral that cannot be recovered profitably with present prices and mining technology but may be converted to reserves when prices rise or mining technology improves. Compare *Identified resources, Reserves, Undiscovered resources.*

Respiration See *Cellular respiration.*

Reuse To use a product over and over again in the same form, as when returnable glass bottles are washed and refilled. Compare *Recycle.*

Risk Probability that something undesirable will happen from deliberate or accidental exposure to a hazard.

Risk assessment Process of determining the short- and long-term adverse consequences to individuals or groups from the use of a particular technology in a particular area.

Risk-benefit analysis Estimating the short- and long-term societal benefits and risks involved in using a particular technology; the benefits can be divided by the risks to find a desirability quotient which can be used to help determine whether the technology should be used. See also *Cost-benefit analysis.*

Risk management The administrative, political, and economic actions taken to decide how, and if, a particular societal risk is to be reduced to a certain level and at what cost.

River Fairly wide and deep flowing body of water that usually empties into an ocean.

Rocky shore Steep, rock-laden coastline. Compare *Barrier beach.*

Room-and-pillar method Type of subsurface mining in which a mineral deposit such as coal is removed in a manner that created a series of rooms supported by pillars of unremoved mineral. Compare *Longwall mining.*

Ruminant animals Animals such as cattle, sheep, goats, and buffalo with four-chambered stomachs that digest cellulose.

Runoff Surface water entering rivers, freshwater lakes, or reservoirs from land surfaces.

Rural area Area in the United States with a population of fewer than 2,500 people.

S-shaped curve Leveling off of an exponential or J-shaped curve.

Salinity Amount of dissolved salts (especially sodium chloride) in a given volume of water.

Salinization Accumulation of salts in soils that can eventually make the soil incapable of supporting plant growth.

Saltwater intrusion Movement of saltwater into freshwater aquifers in coastal areas as groundwater is withdrawn faster than it is recharged by precipitation.

Sandy soil Highly porous soil containing a large amount of sand and little, if any, silt and clay. Compare *Clay soil, Loams.*

Sanitary landfill Land waste disposal site that is located to minimize water pollution from runoff and leaching; waste is spread in thin layers, compacted, and covered with a fresh layer of soil each day. Compare *Open dump, Secured landfill.*

Scientific conservationists People guided by the belief that public land resources should be used to enhance economic growth and national strength and protected from depletion and degradation by being managed using the principles of sustained yield and multiple use. Compare *Preservationists.*

Scrubber Common antipollution device that uses a liquid spray to remove pollutants from a stream of air.

Secondary air pollutant Harmful chemical formed in the atmosphere through a chemical reaction among air components. Compare *Primary air pollutant.*

Secondary consumer See *Carnivore.*

Secondary oil recovery Injection of water to force some of the remaining crude oil from a well after primary recovery. Usually primary and secondary recovery remove about one-third of the crude oil in a well. Compare *Enhanced oil recovery, Primary oil recovery.*

Secondary sewage treatment Second step in most waste treatment systems, in which aerobic bacteria break down biodegradable organic wastes in wastewater; usually accomplished by bringing the sewage and bacteria together in trickling filters or in the activated sludge process. Compare *Primary sewage treatment, Tertiary sewage treatment.*

Secondary succession Sequential development of communities in an area in which natural vegetation has been removed or destroyed, but the soil or bottom sediment is not destroyed. Compare *Primary succession.*

Second law of energy See *Second law of thermodynamics.*

Second law of thermodynamics (1) In any conversion of heat energy to useful work, some of the initial energy input is always degraded to a lower-quality, more-dispersed, less useful form of energy, usually low-temperature heat that flows into the environment; *or,* you can't break even in terms of energy quality. (2) Any system and its surroundings (environment) as a whole spontaneously tends toward increasing randomness, disorder, or entropy; *or,* if you think things are mixed up now, just wait.

Secured landfill A land site for the storage of hazardous solid and liquid wastes, which are normally placed in containers and buried in a restricted-access area that is continually monitored. Such landfills are located above geologic strata that are supposed to prevent the leaching of wastes into groundwater. Compare *Open dump, Sanitary landfill.*

Sediment Soil particles, sand, and minerals washed from the land into aquatic systems as a result of natural and human activities.

Seed tree cutting Removal of nearly all trees on a site in one cut, with a few of the better, commercially valuable trees left uniformly distributed as a source of seed to regenerate the forest. Compare *Clearcutting, Selective cutting, Shelterwood cutting, Whole-tree harvesting.*

Selective cutting Cutting of intermediate-aged or mature or diseased trees in an uneven-aged forest stand either singly or in small groups to encourage younger trees to grow and to produce an uneven-aged stand with trees of different species, ages, and size. Compare *Clearcutting, Seed tree cutting, Shelterwood cutting, Whole-tree harvesting.*

Septic tank Underground receptacle for wastewater from a home in rural and suburban areas. The bacteria in the sewage decompose the organic wastes, and the sludge settles to the bottom of the tank. The effluent flows out of the tank into the ground through a field of drain pipes.

Sewage sludge See *Sludge.*

Shale oil A slow-flowing, dark brown heavy oil obtained when kerogen in shale oil rock is vaporized at high temperatures and then condensed. Shale oil can be refined to yield petroleum products. See *Kerogen, Oil shale*.

Shallow conservatives Persons who are primarily concerned with preserving the societal arrangements that have led to their own increased power, material wealth, and sense of stability and security. Compare *Ecological conservatives*.

Shelterbelt See *Windbreak*.

Shelterwood cutting Removal of all mature trees in an area in a series of cuts over one or more decades. Compare *Clearcutting, Seed tree cutting, Selective cutting, Whole-tree harvesting*.

Shifting cultivation Clearing and planting a plot of ground in a forest for 2 to 5 years, until no further cultivation is worthwhile because of a reduction of soil fertility or invasion by a dense growth of vegetation, and then clearing a new plot to grow crops by slash-and-burn cultivation. See *Slash-and-burn cultivation*.

Silviculture Cultivation and management of forests to produce a renewable supply of timber.

Slash-and-burn cultivation In many tropical areas, the practice of clearing a patch of forest, leaving the cut vegetation on the ground to dry, burning the dried residue to add nutrients to the soil, and planting crops. Ideally, the patch is abandoned after 2 to 5 years of cultivation to prevent depletion of soil fertility. See *Shifting cultivation*.

Slowly biodegradable pollutant A pollutant such as DDT that is broken down in the environment by natural processes to an acceptable level or form at a relatively slow rate. Compare *Nonbiodegradable pollutant, Rapidly biodegradable pollutant*.

Sludge Gooey solid mixture of bacteria- and virus-laden organic matter, toxic metals, synthetic organic chemicals, and solid chemicals removed from wastewater at a sewage treatment plant.

Smog Originally a combination of *smoke* or *fog*; now applied also to the photochemical haze produced by the action of sun and atmosphere on automobile and industrial exhausts. Compare *Industrial smog, Photochemical smog*.

Soil Complex mixture of inorganic minerals (mostly clay, silt, and sand), decaying organic matter, water, air, and living organisms.

Soil conservation Methods used to reduce soil erosion and to prevent depletion of soil nutrients.

Soil erosion Movement of soil components, especially topsoil, from one place to another usually by exposure to wind and flowing water.

Soil horizons Horizontal layers that make up a particular type of soil.

Soil porosity Number of pores and the average distances between pores in a given sample of soil.

Soil profile Cross-sectional view of the horizons in a soil.

Solar cell Device that converts radiant energy from the sun directly into electrical energy.

Solar collector Device for collecting radiant energy from the sun and converting it into heat.

Solar energy Direct radiant energy from the sun plus indirect forms of energy—such as wind, falling or flowing water (hydropower), ocean thermal gradients, and biomass—that are produced when solar energy interacts with the earth.

Solar furnace System for concentrating direct solar energy to produce electricity or high-temperature heat for direct use. Also called a power tower.

Solar pond Relatively small body of fresh water or saltwater in which stored solar energy can be extracted as a result of the temperature difference between the hot surface layer exposed to the sun during daylight and its cooler bottom layer.

Solid waste Any unwanted or discarded material that is not a liquid or a gas.

Speciation Splitting of a single species over thousands to millions of years into two or more different species in response to new environmental conditions.

Species All organisms of the same kind; a group of plants or animals that is potentially capable of breeding with other members of its group but normally not with organisms outside its group.

Species diversity Number of different species and their relative abundances in a given area.

Sport hunting Killing of animals for recreation. Compare *Commercial hunting, Subsistence hunting*.

Stability Ability of a living system to withstand or recover from externally imposed changes or stresses. See *Inertia stability, Resilience stability*.

Statutory law Law passed by state or federal legislature. Compare *Common law*.

Steady-state economy See *Sustainable-earth economy*.

Strategic materials Fuel and nonfuel minerals vital to the industry and defense of a country. Ideally, supplies are stock-piled to cushion against supply interruptions and sharp price rises.

Stream Relatively small, flowing body of fresh water that empties into a river.

Strip cropping Planting regular crops and close-growing plants such as hay or nitrogen-fixing legumes in alternating rows or bands.

Strip mining See *Surface mining*.

Subatomic particles Extremely small particles such as electrons, protons, and neutrons that make up the internal structure of atoms.

Subbituminous coal Form of coal with a low heat content and usually a low sulfur content. Compare *Anthracite, Bituminous coal, Lignite, Peat*.

Subsidence Sinking down of part of the earth's crust due to underground excavation, such as a coal mine, or removal of groundwater.

Subsistence agriculture Supplementation of solar energy with energy from human labor and draft animals to produce enough food to feed one's self and family members; occasionally some may be left over to sell or put aside for hard times. Compare *Industrialized agriculture*.

Subsistence economy Economic system in which individuals produce only enough resources to meet their basic needs for food, shelter, and clothing with no surplus left over for trade. Found in a few remaining hunter-gatherer societies. Compare *Capitalist economy, Centrally planned economy*.

Subsistence farming See *Subsistence agriculture*.

Subsistence hunting Killing of animals to provide enough food and other materials for survival. Compare *Commercial hunting, Sport hunting*.

Subsurface mining Underground extraction of a metal ore or fuel resource such as coal. Compare *Surface mining*.

Succession See *Ecological succession*.

Succulent plants Plants such as cacti that store water and produce the food they need in the thick, fleshy tissue of their green stems and branches.

Sulfur cycle Biogeochemical cycle in which sulfur is converted to various chemical forms and transported through the biosphere.

Superinsulated house House that contains massive amounts of insulation, is extremely airtight, typically uses active or passive solar collectors to heat water, and has an air-to-air heat exchanger to prevent buildup of excessive moisture and indoor air pollutants.

Surface mining The process of removing the overburden of topsoil, subsoil, and other strata to permit the extraction of underlying mineral deposits. See *Area strip mining, Contour strip mining, Open-pit surface mining*; Compare *Subsurface mining*.

Surface water Precipitation that does not infiltrate into the ground or return to the atmosphere and becomes runoff that flows into nearby streams, rivers, lakes, wetlands, and reservoirs. Compare *Groundwater*.

Surroundings (environment) Everything outside a specified system or collection of matter.

Sustainable-earth agriculture Method of growing crops and raising livestock that places heavy reliance on organic fertilizers, soil conservation, water conservation, biological control of pests, and minimal use of nonrenewable fossil fuel energy.

Sustainable-earth economy Economic system in which the number of people and the quantity of goods are maintained at some constant that is ecologically sustainable over time and that provides a good life for the population size that can be accommodated under these conditions.

Sustainable-earth society Society based on working with nature by recycling and reusing discarded matter, conserving matter and energy resources by reducing unnecessary waste and use, and by building things that are easy to recycle, reuse, and repair. Compare *Matter-recycling society, Throwaway society*.

Sustainable-earth worldview Belief that the earth is a place with finite room and resources so that continuing population growth, production, and consumption inevitably put severe stress on natural processes that renew and maintain the resource base of air, water, and soil that supports all life. To prevent environmental overload and resource depletion, people should work with—not against—nature by controlling population growth and reducing unnecessary use and waste of matter and energy resources. Compare *Throwaway worldview*.

Sustained yield The highest rate at which a renewable resource can be used without impairing or damaging its ability to be fully renewed. See also *Environmental degradation*.

Synergism Interaction in which the total effect is greater than the sum of two effects taken independently.

Synergistic effect Result of the interaction of two or more substances or factors that cause a net effect greater than that expected from adding together their independent effects. Compare *Antagonistic effect*.

Synfuels Synthetic gaseous and liquid fuels produced from coal or sources other than natural gas or crude oil.

Synthetic natural gas (SNG) Gaseous fuel containing mostly methane that is produced from solid coal.

System Any collection of matter under study. Compare *Surroundings*.

Tailings Rock and other waste materials removed as impurities when minerals are mined and mineral deposits are processed. These materials are usually dumped on the ground in piles or dumped into ponds.

Tar sands Swamplike deposits of a mixture of fine clay, sand, water, and variable amounts of a tarlike heavy oil known as bitumen. The bitumen or heavy oil can be extracted from the tar sand by heating and purified and upgraded to synthetic crude oil. See *Bitumen*.

Temperatuare inversion See *Thermal inversion*.

Teratogen Substance that, if ingested by a pregnant female, causes malformation of the developing fetus.

Terracing Planting crops on a long, steep slope that has been converted into a series of broad, nearly level terraces with short vertical drops from one to another following the slope of the land in order to retain water and reduce soil erosion.

Terrestrial ecosystem See *Biome*.

Tertiary sewage treatment Series of specialized chemical and physical processes that reduce the quantity of specific pollutants still left in wastewater after primary and secondary sewage treatment. See also *Primary sewage treatment, Secondary sewage treatment*.

Thermal enrichment Beneficial effects in an aquatic ecosystem as a result of a rise in water temperature. Compare *Thermal pollution*.

Thermal gradient Temperature difference between two areas.

Thermal inversion Layer of cool air trapped under a layer of less dense warm air, thus reversing the normal situation. In a prolonged inversion, air pollution may rise to harmful levels.

Thermal pollution Increase in water temperature that has harmful ecological effects on an aquatic ecosystem. Compare *Thermal enrichment*.

Thermal shock Harmful ecological effects in an aquatic ecosystem as a result of a sharp rise or drop in water temperature.

Thermocline Fairly thin transition zone in a lake that separates an upper warmer zone (*epilimnion*) from a lower colder zone (*hypolimnion*).

Threatened species A wild species that is still abundant in its natural range but is considered likely to become endangered within the foreseeable future because of a decline in numbers. Compare *Endangered species*.

Threshold effect A harmful or fatal effect that does not occur until the level of a particular physical or chemical factor exceeds the limit of tolerance of an organism. See *Threshold pollutant*.

Threshold pollutant Substance that is harmful to a particular organism only above a certain concentration, or threshold level. Compare *Nonthreshold pollutant*.

Throwaway society Society such as that found in most advanced industrialized countries in which ever-increasing economic growth is sustained by maximizing the rate at which matter and energy resources are used with little emphasis on resource conservation. Compare *Matter-recycling society, Sustainable-earth society*.

Throwaway worldview Belief held by cornucopians that the earth is a place of unlimited resources. Any type of resource conservation that hampers short-term economic growth is unnecessary because if we pollute or deplete the resource in one area, we will find substitutes, control the pollution through technology, and if necessary obtain additional resources from the moon and asteroids in the "new frontier" of space. Compare *Sustainable-earth worldview*.

Time delay Lag between the receipt of an information signal or stimulus by a system and the time when the system makes a corrective action by negative feedback.

Tolerance limit Point at and beyond which a chemical or physical condition (such as heat) becomes harmful to a living organism.

Toothed whales Species of whales such as the porpoise, sperm whale, and killer whale which have teeth that enable them to feed mostly on squid, octopus, and other marine animals. Compare *Baleen whale*.

Total fertility rate (TFR) Estimate of the number of children the average woman will bear during her reproductive years, assuming she lives to age 44.

Total resources Total amount of a particular mineral that exists on earth.

Trade deficit Difference between the larger amount a country such as the United States spent on goods from other countries and the smaller amount other countries spent on U.S. goods.

Tragedy of the commons Depletion or degradation of a resource such as clean air or clean water to which a population has free and unmanaged access.

Transpiration Transfer of water from exposed parts of plants through leaf pores to the atmosphere.

Trickling filters Form of secondary sewage treatment in which aerobic bacteria degrade organic wastes in wastewater as it seeps through a large vat filled with crushed stones covered with bacterial growths.

Tritium (T: hydrogen-3) Isotope of hydrogen with a nucleus containing one proton and two neutrons, thus having a mass number of 3. Compare *Deuterium*.

Trophic level All organisms that consume the same general types of food in a food chain or food web. For example, all producers belong to the first trophic level and all primary consumers belong to the second trophic level in a food chain or a food web.

Tropical moist forests Tropical rain and evergreen forests found on each side of the equator.

Troposphere Innermost layer of the atmosphere, which contains about 95% of the earth's air, and extends about 8 to 12 kilometers (5 to 7 miles) above the earth's surface.

True cost All internal and external costs associated with the production and use of a product.

Turnover Mixing of the thermally stratified layers of a lake during one or more of the year's seasons which brings plant nutrients from the bottom to the surface and allows the bottom to replenish its supply of dissolved oxygen by being exposed to the atmosphere.

Unconfined aquifer Water-bearing layer of the earth's crust when groundwater collects above a layer of relatively impermeable rock or compacted clay. Compare *Confined aquifer*.

Undernutrition Condition characterized by an insufficient quantity or caloric intake of food to meet an individual's minimum daily energy requirement. Compare *Malnutrition, Overnutrition*.

Undiscovered resources Potential supplies of a particular mineral resource believed to exist on the basis of broad geological knowledge and theory, although location, quality, and amounts are unknown. Compare *Identified resources, Reserves, Resources*.

Upwelling Area along a steep coastal area where winds blow surface water away from the shore and allow cold, nutrient-rich bottom water to rise to the surface.

Urban area Place with a population of 2,500 or more.

Urban growth Rate of growth of urban population.

Urban heat island Buildup of heat in the atmosphere above an urban area as a result of the dense concentration of cars, buildings, factories, and other heat-producing activities.

Urbanization The percentage of the total population of the world or a country concentrated in urban areas.

Urban open space Any large, medium-size, or small area of land or water in or near an urban area that can be used for recreational, aesthetic, or ecological purposes.

Vector Living organism (usually an insect) that carries an infectious disease from one host (person or animal) to another.

Vector-transmitted infectious disease Disease carried from one host to another by a living organism (usually an insect), called a vector. Examples include malaria, schistosomiasis, and African sleeping sickness. Compare *Nonvector-transmitted infectious disease*.

Voluntary simplicity A lifestyle in which people voluntarily decide to reduce unnecessary consumption and waste of matter and energy resources by distinguishing between their wants and true needs.

Water cycle See *Hydrologic cycle*.

Waterlogging Saturation of soil with irrigation water so that the water table rises close to the surface.

Water pollution Any physical or chemical change in surface water or groundwater that can adversely affect living organisms.

Watershed Land area that delivers runoff water, sediment, and dissolved substances to a major river and its tributaries.

Water table Top of the water-saturated portion of an unconfined aquifer.

Water table aquifer See *Unconfined aquifer*.

Watt Unit of power, or rate at which electrical work is done.

Wavelength Distance between the crest (or trough) of one wave of electromagnetic radiation and that of the next.

Weather Moment-to-moment and day-to-day variation in atmospheric conditions.

Weathering Process in which bedrock is gradually broken down into small bits and pieces that make up most of a soil's inorganic material as a result of exposure to physical and chemical processes.

Wetland Land that remains flooded all or part of the year with fresh or saltwater. See *Coastal wetland, Inland wetland*.

Whole-tree harvesting Use of machines to pull entire trees from the ground and reduce them to small chips.

Wilderness Area where the earth and its community of life have not been seriously disturbed by humans and where humans are only temporary visitors.

Wilderness species Wild animal species which flourish only in relatively undisturbed climax vegetational communities such as large areas of mature forest, tundra, grassland, and desert. Compare *Early-successional species, Late-successional species, Mid-successional species*.

Wildlife All free, undomesticated species of plants and animals on earth.

Wildlife conservation The worldwide social movement to bring about the protection, preservation, management, and study of wildlife and wildlife resources.

Wildlife management Manipulation of populations of wild species and their habitats for human benefit, the welfare of other species, and the preservation of threatened and endangered wildlife species.

Wildlife resources Species of wildlife that are actually or potentially useful to humans. See also *Game species*.

Windbreaks Rows of trees or hedges planted in a north-to-south direction to partially block wind flow and reduce soil erosion on cultivated land that is exposed to high winds.

Wind farm Clusters of 50 to 100 small to medium-sized wind turbines located in windy areas to capture wind energy and convert it to electrical energy.

Withdrawal use Use of water when it is taken from a surface or ground source and conveyed to its place of use. Compare *Consumptive use*.

Work What happens when a force is used to push or pull a sample of matter over some distance. Energy is defined as the capacity to do such work.

Zero population growth (ZPG) State in which the birth rate (plus immigration) equals the death rate (plus emigration) so that population is no longer increasing.

Index

Note: Page numbers appearing in **boldface** indicate where definitions of key terms can be found in the text; these terms also appear in the glossary. Page numbers in *italics* indicate illustrations, tables, and figures.

Abbey, Edward, 600–601
Abortion, *158,* 160–61
 should it be banned in the U.S., 162
Abyssal zone, **108**
Accelerated eutrophication, **103**
Acid deposition, 12–13, 76, **276,** 354, 430, **432,** *433,* 458
 effect on aquatic life, 437
 effect on plants, *436*
 in North America, *433,* 437
 ozone depletion and increase in, 439–40
Acidic. *See* Acid solution
Acidity, soil, 192–93
Acid mine drainage, **352**–53
Acid rain. *See* Acid deposition
Acid solution, **192,** *193*
Activated carbon, 483, 484, 511
Activated sludge process, **479**
Active solar heating, **395**–98
 hot water heating system, *396*
Acute disease, **535**
 compared to chronic infectious/noninfectious disease, *536*
Acute effect on human health, **13**
Advanced industrial society, **30**
Africa
 food production in, 240, *241, 242*
 region infested by tsetse fly, *251*
 water resources and food production, *215*
Agency for International Development (AID), 156
Agent Orange herbicide, 524–25
Age structure, and population, **146**–49
Agricultural societies, 27–29
Agriculture. *See also* Crop yields; Irrigation
 breeding pest resistant crops and livestock, 529
 burning waste from, for energy, 412
 components of industrialized, *236*
 effect on ecosystems, 126–27
 effect of nuclear war on, 129
 energy use and, 238, *239*
 industrialized (*see* Industrialized agriculture)
 inputs into, *238*
 major types of, *237,* 238
 sustainable-earth, 258–60
 world systems of, 234–39
Agriculture-based urban societies, **28,** *29,* 30
Air, atmospheric. *See* Atmosphere
Air conditioning and lighting, conservation in, *397*
Air pollutant, **423**
 classes of, 423, *424*
 emissions in the U.S., *424*
Air pollution, 422–54
 acid deposition (*see* Acid deposition)
 from burning coal, 354–55
 controlling, 443–51
 effects of, on human health, 432–35

effects of, on ozone layer and global climate, 438–43
effects of, on plants, animals, and materials, 435–38
from mineral mining/processing, 324
in mines and factories, 549
in the past, 426
protecting forests from, 276
radioactive radon gas in homes, 451–53
smog, 427–30
types and sources of, 422–27
urban heat islands, 430
from wood burning, 409
Air quality and emissions trends in the U.S., 444–45
Air quality control regions (AQCRs), 443
Alcoholism, 537
Alfisols, 193, *196*
Alfvén, Hannes, 364
 on the threat of nuclear war, 40–41
Algae bloom, 465, *466*
Alkaline solution, **192,** *193*
Alligator, ecological importance of, *294*
Alpha particle, **48,** *49*
Amazon River, 217
Ammonia (NH_3), 47
Animal(s). *See also* Wild plant and animal resources
 adaptations of, 92
 effect of air pollution on, 436–37, *438*
 as food sources, 234, *235*
Animal feedlot, *236,* 477, *478*
Animal manure, **203**
Annual population change rate, **139,** *140*
 doubling time and, *141*
Annuals, **92**
Antagonistic effect, **117**
Anthracite, **351**
Appropriate technology, **15**
Aquaculture, **254**–55
Aquariums, 305–6
Aquatic ecosystems, **71**
 coastal zones, 110–13
 freshwater, 102–6
 marine, 106–9
Aquifer, **211**
 depletion (overdraft), **224,** *225, 226*
Arabian oryx, 306, *307*
Area strip mining, **321**
Argentina, 246
Aridisols, *196, 197*
Arms race, 582, *583. See also* Nuclear war
Arsenic, *510*
Artesian aquifer, **212**
Asbestos, 435, 460
Asbestosis, 435
Ashworth, William, 230
Aswan Dam, benefits/costs of, 223
Atmosphere, 69, *70,* 71, **422**
 elements in, 48, 422
 global circulation of, 94, *95*
 zones, *423*
Atoms, **46**
Audubon Society, 35, 297

Australia, 300–301, 327
Automobile. *See* Motor vehicles
Average per capita GNP, 5, *6–7,* **559**
 LDCs vs. MDCs, *11*

Background ionizing radiation, **52.** *See also* Ionizing radiation
Bacon, Francis, 115
Bacteria, as water pollutant, 456, *457*
Baghouse filter, *447*
Balanced chemical equation, **47**
Baleen whales, **310**
Baron, Robert Alex, 553
Barrier beach, **107,** *109*
Barrier islands, **107,** 111–12
Basic solution, **192,** *193*
Bathyal zone, **108**
Bats, *304*
Bay Area Rapid Transit (BART) system, *178*
Beaches
 barrier, **107,** *109*
 erosion, 110, *111*
Beef imports, and tropical deforestation, 280
Bennett, Hugh, 199
Benthic zone, **103**
Beryllium, *510*
Beta particle, **48,** *49*
Beverage container deposit laws, 331, *332*
Bhopal, India, pesticide disaster, *525*
Bicycles, 179
Biofuels, **408**
 converting biomass to, 412–13
Biogas, 412
Biogeochemical cycle, 69, 73–74
Biological amplification, **86**–87
 of pesticides, *523*
Biological control, of insect pests, **527,** *528*
Biological diversity. *See* Genetic diversity
Biological evolution. *See* Evolution
Biological magnification. *See* Biological amplification
Biological oxygen demand (BOD) and water quality, **458**
Biomass, 337, **408**–13
 burning agricultural and urban waste, 412
 converting to biofuels, 412–13
 energy plantations, 412
 major types of, *408*
 renewable, as a versatile fuel, 408–9
 solar-assisted water stove, *410–11*
 wood, 409–11
Biomass fuel, 337, **408**
Biome, **70.** *See also* Ecosystems
Biosphere, **69**
 and ecosystems, 68–72
 energy flow in, *81*
Biotic potential, **118**
Birth control, 158–62
Birth rate, **137**
 controlling, 154, 158–62

Bison, 297–98, *299*
Bitumen, **347**
Bituminous coal, **351**
Black-footed ferret, 288, *289*
Black lung disease, **352,** 435
Blue whales, 311
Boll weevil, *521*
Borgstrom, Georg, 168
Botanical gardens, 305–6
Bouvier, Leon F., on demographic behavior, 149–50
Bray, Phil, 364
Brazil, 156, 246
 hydroelectric power in, 402
 pollution in, *425*
Breastfeeding, 159–60
Breeder fission reactor, 381–82, 385
Bridges, maintenance of, 180
Bronchitis. *See* Chronic bronchitis
Brower, David, 33
Brown, Lester, 204, 246, 252, 491
Brown-air cities, 429
Brown lung disease, 435
Buildings
 improving energy efficiency of, 391–92
 solar electricity production for, 400, *401, 402*
Bureau of Land Management (BLM), 34, 35, 267, 283, 284, 286
Burford, Anne Gorsuch, 36, 37
Burford, Robert, 36
Bus mass transit, 179

Cadmium, *510*
Caffeine, 518
Cahn, Robert, 598
Calcutta, India, urbanization in, 171
California Water Plan, 222, *224*
Calorific Recovery by Anaerobic Processes (CRAP), 412
Canada, 327
 acid deposition in, 432, *433,* 437
 oil resources in, 347–48
 water use in, *213*
Cancer, **541**–48
 diagnosis and treatment, 542–43
 diet and, 547
 incidence in the U.S., 541–42, *545*
 lung, **434**–35
 nature and effects, 541
 and pollution, 548
 risk factors, *544,*
 skin, 439, 542
 smoking and, 544–47
 survival rate, 542, *543*
 and the workplace, 547, *548*
Capitalist (commercial) economy, **558**
Carbon cycle, 69, 74–75
Carbon dioxide (CO_2), 47
 produced by fossil fuels, *354*
 rising atmospheric levels of, *441*
Carbon monoxide (CO), 47

Carcinogen, **541**
Carcinogenic, **541**
Carnivore, **72**
Carrying capacity, **118**
Carson, Rachel, 35, 517
Cartel, **327**
Carter, Jimmy, 35, 66
Catlin, George, 32
Cell fusion, 250
Cellular respiration, **74**
Central America, beef exports and tropical deforestation, 280
Central Arizona Project, 222, 224
Centrally planned economy, **559**
Chain reaction, nuclear, **49**, *50*
Chandler, William U., 534
Chaplin, Ralph, 572
Chateaubriand, François-Réné de, 287
Chemical(s),
   alternatives to household, *509*
   and water quality
      common pollutants, *459*
      inorganic plant nutrients, 458–59
      organic, 459–60
      water-soluble inorganic, 458
Chemical change of matter, **47**
Chemical oxygen demand (COD), and water quality, **458**
Chemical reaction, **47**
Chemosynthesis, **109**
Chernobyl nuclear power plant accident, 51, 130, 132, 372, 373
Chesapeake Bay, pollution in, 470, *471*
China, 258
   biomass energy conversion, 412
   economy in, 559
   food production, 240, 242
   hydroelectric power in, 402
   population control in, 162, 163–65
   soil erosion in, 197
   water use in, *213*
Chlorofluorocarbons (CFCs), 438–39
Chronic bronchitis, **434**
Chronic disease, **535**
   compared to acute infectious, *536*
Chronic effects on human health, 13
Cities. *See also* Urbanization
   building new, 181–82
   early agriculture-based, 28, *29*
   fostering self-suffiency in, 182
   repairing existing, 180
   world's largest, *169*
Citizens of the earth concept, 37. *See also* Sustained-earth worldview
Civilian Conservation Corps, 34
Civil suit, **573**
Clarke, Arthur C., 334
Class action suit, **573**
Clay soil, 192
Clean Air Acts, 39, 443–44, 451, 567, 574
Clean Water Act, 484
Clearcutting forests, **274**, *275*
Cleveland, Grover, 34
Climate, **94**
   global air/water circulation and, 94, *95*
   global changes in, due to greenhouse effect, *440*, *441*, 442–43
   and major ecosystem types, *96*
   topography, smog and, 429–30
Climax ecosystem (climax community), **124**
Cloning, 250
Closed forest, **271**
Cloud seeding, 228
Cluster development, 184, *185*
Coal, 350–57
   advantages/disadvantages of, 356–57
   air pollution from burning, 354–55

burning more cleanly/efficiently, 355–56
   conventional types of, 350, *351*
   distribution of, 351, *352*
   historical use of, 336–37, *338*
   mining health/environmental hazards of, 352–54
   synfuels from, 356
   uses of, 354
Coal-burning power plants
   risk-benefit analysis, 131–32
   scrubber on, to reduce air pollution, 446–50
Coal gasification, 356
Coal liquification, 356
Coastal wetland, 106, *107*
   service provided by, *110*
Coastal zone, **107**–8. *See also* Neritic zone
   importance of, 110–12
   use and protection of, 112–13
Cogeneration, 63, **389**, 392
Cohen, Bernard L., 364
Cold (high-latitude) northern coniferous forests, *102*
Coliform bacteria, 457
Coliform bacteria count, **457**
Combined sewer, *480*
Commercial economy. *See* Capitalist (commercial) economy
Commercial extinction, 310
Commercial hunting, 296
Commercial inorganic fertilizer, **203**, 236
Commoner, Barry, 35
Common law, **573**
Common property resource, **11**
Commons, **11**
Community, natural, **70**
Competition, between species, 87–89
Competitive exclusion principle, **88**
Compost/composting, **203**, 496
Compounds, 46–47
Comprehensive Environmental Response, Compensation and Liability Act (CERCLA), 508
Computer modeling, of population growth and resource use, 164–66
Condoms, 159
Condor, 297
Cone of depression, *212*
Confined aquifer, *212*
Congressional reform, 580
Coniferous trees, *102*
Conservation. *See* Resource conservation
Conservationists
   on forest management, 282
   vs. Reagan, on the national park system, 270, *271*
   scientific, 33–34
Conservation tillage farming, **200**–201
Consumers
   attitudes of, and pesticide use, 532
   avoiding food additives, *552*, *553*
   in ecosystems, **72**
Consumption of water, *213*, *214*
Consumption overpopulation, 15, *16*
Consumptive use, 213
Continental shelf, *107*
Contour farming, **201**
Contour strip mining, 321, *322*
Contraceptives, 158–60
Convention on International Trade in Endangered Species, 301–2
Cooking, conserving energy in, *397*
Coral reef, *107*
Cornucopians, **17**
   on energy, 61
   guest essay (J. Simon), 22–23
   vs. neo-Malthusians, 18–19
   on nuclear energy, 384–85
   on oil reserves, 343–44
   on population control, 153, 155
Cost-benefit analysis, 566
   problems with, 566–69

Cost-effectiveness analysis, **566**
   problems with, 566–59
Council of Agricultural Science and Technology, 199
Council on Environmental Quality, 575–76
Cousins, Norman, 1
Coyote, 287
Critical mass, **49**
Crop rotation, **204**
Crop yields, 247–50
Crown fire, *275*, *276*
Crude birth rate, **137**
Crude death rate, **137**
Crude oil, *342*
Crust of the earth, *70*
Cultural beliefs, and use of natural resources, 9
Cultural changes, future, and the environment, 37, *38*, 39
Cultural eutrophication, **103**, **465**
   control of, 465–66
Culturesphere, **69**
Cuyahoga River, *460*
Cyclone separator, *447*

Daly, Herman E., on the steady-state economy, 568–70
Dams, 220–22. *See also* Reservoir
   Aswan Dam in Egypt, 223
Darling, Jay N. "Ding," 314
Darwin, Charles, 120
DDT (dichlorodiphenyltrichloroethane), **518**–19
   biological amplification of, 86–87, *523*
   continued use of, 527
   control of malaria by, 520
   genetic adaptation to, 88
Death rate, **137**
   caused by motor vehicles, 176–77
   controlling, 154
Decibel (db), **553**
Deciduous plants, **92**
Decomposers in an ecosystem, **72**
Deep ecology, **593**–95
   becoming a deep ecologist (B. Devall), 599–601
Deep well injection of waste, 475, *476*
Defendant, **573**
Deforestation, 11, 251
   tropical, 277–78, *279*
Degree of urbanization, **168**
Delaney Clause, on food additives and cancer, 551–52
Delta, **106**
Demographic transition, **154**, *155*
Denmark, 505
Depletion time of minerals, **326**
Desalinization, **227**–28
Desert, **96**, *97*
Desertification, 11, 28, **231**, *232*
Desirability quotient, **130**–31
Deudney, Daniel, 417
Deuterium (D: hydrogen-2), 49, *50*, 382
Devall, Bill, on becoming a deep ecologist, 599–601
Developed country. *See* More developed country (MDC)
Dieldrin, 124
Diet and cancer, 547
Diminishing returns, 248
Dingell-Johnson Act, 315
Dioxins, 513, 524–25
Discount factor, **568**
Disease, 126
   acute and chronic, 535–36
   alcoholism, 537
   cancer, 541–48
   caused by water pollution, 456–58
   controlled by insecticides, 520
   infectious/noninfectious, 534–35
   malaria, 538–39
   and malnutrition, *243*
   protecting forests from, 276
   schistosomiasis, 539–41
   sexually transmitted, 159
   social ecology of, 536–38

Dismantlement of nuclear reactors, 378
Dissolved oxygen (DO) content, and water quality, **458**
Diversity. *See* Species diversity
Doubling time, of population growth, 140, *141*
Drainage basin, **105**, *107*, **209**
Dredge spoils, 469–70
Drinking water
   diseases carried by polluted, 456–58
   insufficient, 217, *218*
   laws protecting, 483–84
   lead contamination of, 511
   purification of, 482
Drought, 214–15
Drugs, medicinal
   for cancer treatment, 542
   risk-benefit analysis of, 131
   from tropical forests, 288–89
   from wildlife resources, 292–93, 299
Dry steam deposits, geothermal, 362
Dubois, Mark, 601
Dubos, Réné, 37, 421
Dust Bowl, 199
Dust dome, *430*, *431*

Early industrial society, 30
Early-successional species, **309**
Earth-sheltered housing, *395*, 399
Ecological conservatives. *See* Conservationists
Ecological niche, **87**–89
Ecological succession, 123, *124*, *125*
   mature and immature, 125–26, *127*
Ecology, **68**, **558**
   ecological future (W. Ophuls), 587–88
   first law of, 127
   importance of wildlife to, 293–94
   major features of living systems, 129
   and politics, 572–73
   realm of, 69–71
   shallow vs. deep, 593–95
Economic development, and population control, 154–55
Economic growth, debate on, 559
Economic resources. *See* Reserves, mineral
Economics, and the environment, 9, **558**–71
   cost-benefit and cost-effectiveness analysis, 566–69
   cost of environmental improvement, 569
   economic growth, GNP and quality of life, 558–62
   and pollution control, 564–66
   the steady-state economy (H. Daly), 568–70
   sustainable-earth economy, 562–64
Ecosphere. *See* Biosphere
Ecosystems
   approach of, to wildlife protection, 306–7
   the biosphere and, 68–72
   climate and major terrestrial ecosystems, 94–96, *98–99*
   components of, 71, 72, *73*
   defined, **68**, *70*
   deserts, grasslands, and forests, 97–102
   ecological niches of species in, 87–89
   energy flows in, 81–82
   freshwater aquatic, 102–6
   human impact on, 126–29
   importance of coastal zones, 110–13
   limits in (E. Kormondy), 88–89
   marine aquatic, 106–9
   matter cycling in, 73–80
   mature vs. immature, 125–26, *127*

natural vs. human simplified, 127, *128*
net primary productivity of plants in different, *85*
population responses to stress, 117–22
responses of, to stress, 122–26
risk analysis and management in, 130–33
species' adaptations and limits of adaptation, 91–94
stability in living systems, 115–17
structure/function, 74
unexpected results of interference in, 124
and urban systems, 173–76
Edberg, Rolf, 109
Eddington, Arthur S., 67
Efficiency. *See* Energy efficiency
Egypt
benefits/costs of Aswan Dam, 223, *541*
water use in, *213*
Ehrlich, Paul, 35, 599
Eisenhower, Dwight D., 583
Eisley, Loren, 208
Elderly population, U.S., 148, *149*
Election reform, and electing sustainable-earth leaders, 579–80
Electricity
cost of heating with, 388, *389*
costs of generating by various methods, *379*
production of, with solar energy, 399, 400–402
production of, with water resources, 402–6
production of, with wind, 406–8
Electron (e), 46
Electrostatic precipitator, 447, *449*
Elements, 45–46
percentage by weight in the earth's crust, *318*
Elephantiasis, *535*
Eliot, Charles W., 32
Emerson, Ralph Waldo, 32, 517, 578
Emigration, 141
Emigration rate, 141
Emphysema, **434**
Endangered species, **296**
Endangered Species Act, 302–4, 574
Energy, 53
energy resources and laws of, 59–64
first law of, **55**
flow of, in the biosphere and ecosystems, 80–87
high quality, available in food chains, *84*
input into a U.S. city, *174*
matter, energy laws and environmental problems, 65–67
needed for food production, 240
needed for production of fish as food, *253*
net useful, 63–64
second law of, 55–58
summary of matter and energy laws, *58*
types and changes, 53–55
Energy, U.S. Department of, 35, 376
Energy conservation, 39, **387**–93
in different countries, *393*
improving building efficiency, 391–92
improving industrial efficiency, 389
improving transportation efficiency, 389–91
personal plan for, 392–93
reducing waste, 387–88
Energy efficiency, **59**
automobile engines, 62, *63*
in housing, 391–92
increasing, 59–62
industrial, 389
of some energy conversion devices, *59*

space heating, *60, 61, 62*
transportation, 389–91
water heating, 62, *63*
Energy fraud, spotting, 57
Energy plantation, 412
Energy resources, 53–55
cornucopians vs. neo-malthusians on, 61
energy resources and laws of, 59–64
energy services and technology (A. Lovins), 357–59
evaluating resources of, 341–42
industrialized agriculture and use of, 238, *239*
and laws of energy, 59–64
major resources, 54
nonrenewable (*see* Fossil fuels)
nonrenewable and perpetual (*see* Geothermal energy; Nuclear energy)
perpetual and renewable (*see* Biomass; Energy conservation; Solar energy; Wind energy)
strategy (*see* Energy strategy)
use, history of, 336–41
used by humans, 53–55
Energy strategy, 413–17
alternatives evaluation, for the U.S, 413, *414–15*
economics and a national, 414–15
free market competition as, 415–16
high pricing as, 416
low pricing as, 416
personal plan for, 417–18
why the U.S. has no long-term, 416–17
Enhanced oil recovery, 342
Entombment of nuclear reactors, 378
Entropy, **57**
Environment
cost-benefit/cost-effectiveness of improving the, 566–69
economics and (*see* Economics and the environment)
evaluating costs of improving the, 569
evaluating methods of improving the, 565
effect of increased food production on, 246, *247*
effect of mining and processing minerals on, 322–25
future cultural changes and, 37–39
impact of early agricultural societies on, 28–29, *30*
impact of energy alternatives, 342
impact of industrial societies, 31
legislation (*see* Legislation and laws, environmental)
politics and (*see* Politics and the environment)
Environmental and resource organizations, A-3–6
Environmental Defense Fund (EDF), 35
Environmental degradation, **10**. *See also* Pollution
caused by coal mining/burning, 352–57
caused by mineral mining/processing, 322–25
early agricultural societies and, *30*
guest essays on, 20–23
matter, energy laws and, 65–67
multiple-factor model of, *16, 17*
relationship to population growth, 13, *14*, 15
relationship to technologies, 15–16
from shale oil production, 347
spotlight on, *11*
Environmental ethics, 590–602
author's personal progress report, 596–97
becoming a deep ecologist (B. Devall), 599–601

environmental awareness levels, *594*
ethics and morals, 590–92
individual actions toward, 595, 598
sustainable-earth ethics, 592–95
throwaway society ethics, 591–92
Environmental impact statements (EIS), 575–76
Environmental movement, 34–35
Environmental principles, 43
Environmental protection, history of, in the U.S., 31–37. *See also* Legislation and laws, environmental
Environmental Protection Agency, U.S., 35
and air pollution, 443–44, *445*, 450–51
on asbestos, 435
creation of, 574
pesticide control under, 526–27
on solid/hazardous wastes, 501, 508–9
on water pollution, 477, 483, 484
Environmental resistance, **118**
Environmental stress
ecosystem responses to, 122–26
population responses to, 117–22
some effects of, *117*
Epilimnion, **104**
Erosion
beach, 110, *111*
soil (*see* Soil erosion)
Estuaries, **107**
pollution in Chesapeake Bay, 470–71
services provided by, 110
Ethanol, 412–13
Ethics, **590**
importance of wildlife to, 294–95
morals and, 590–91
Ethiopia, food relief aid in, 259
Ethylene dibromide (EDB), 526
Euphotic zone, **108**
Eutrophication, 103, **465**
Eutrophic lake, 103, *104*
Evapotranspiration, **79**
Everdon, Neil, 600
Evergreen plants, 92
Evolution, **120**
in response to environmental stress, 119–22
Exponential growth of human population, 2
annual rates of, *4*
spotlight on, *3*
External cost, **564**
Extinction of species, **295**
average annual rate of, *295*
characteristics of species prone to, 301, *303*
how it happens, 295–301
protecting from, 301–7

Fallout. *See* Radioactive fallout
Family planning, and population control, 154, **155**–57
should U.S. federal funds be used for, 157
Famine, **242**–43
insufficient water resources causing, *215*
Farmers, attitudes of, and pesticide use, 532
Fast breeder reactors, 381
Federal Aid in Wildlife Restoration Act, 314
Federal deficit, **561**
Federal government, U.S. *See also* Legislation and laws, environmental
agencies' addresses, A-6
agricultural policies of, 256
bureaucratic reform, 580, 582
as a corrective feedback system, 578, *579*

history of role in resource conservation, 32–37
land ownership/use by, 264, *265, 267, 268*
responsibility for environmental protection in, *575*
soil conservation programs, 204
Federal Insecticide, Fungicide and Rodenticide Act (FIFRA), 526, 532
Federal Land Policy and Management Act of 1976, 35
Federal Water Pollution Control Act, 484, 574
Feedback, system information, 116
Fernow, Bernard E., 32
Fertility
human, 142–46
soil, 203–4
Fertilizers, soil, 203–4, 236
as pollutants, 476, 477
sewage as, 482, *483*
First-generation pesticides, 518
First law of ecology, **127**
First law of energy. *See* First law of thermodynamics (energy)
First law of thermodynamics (energy), **55**
Fish
effect of air pollution on, 436–37
effect of dams on, 221, *222*
increasing use of, as food, 252–55
Fish and Wildlife Conservation Act, 315
Fish and Wildlife Service, 267, 314
Fish catch, trends in, 253, *254*
Fisheries, commercial marine, 252, 253
laws regulating, 255
management of, 310–11, 315
Fish farming, 254, *255*
Flavin, Christopher, 417
Floodplain, **216**
Floods, 215–16
risks/benefits of living in flood-prone areas, 216, *217*
Flue gas desulfurization (FGD), 447. *See also* Scrubbers
Fluidized-bed combustion, of coal, 355–56, 448
Fluorosis, 436, *438*
Flyways, *309, 310*
Food(s)
irradiation of, 530, *531*
natural vs. synthetic, 549–51
reducing waste of, 259–60
relief aid, 258, *259*
unconventional, 249
using pesticides to increase supplies of, 520–21
vitamin/protein supplements and fabricated, 250
Food additives, **548**–53
consumer protection and the GRAS list, 551
controversial, 551, *552*
Delaney Clause and cancer causing, 551–52
natural vs. synthetic, 549–51
use and types of, 548–49, *550*
Food and Drug Administration, U.S., 161, 484
on food additives, 551
Food chain, 81–82
biological amplification in, *86–87*
energy losses in, *235*
and the second law of energy, 82–83
Food niche, 87
Food resources, 234–61
agricultural systems/food production, 234–39
catching fish/fish farming, 252–55
cultivating more land, 251–52
global warming, and production of, 442, *443*
increasing crop yields/using new foods, 247–51
major problems of, 239–47

Food resources (continued)
  profits in food production/
    food aid/land distribution,
    256–58
  sustainable earth agriculture,
    258–60
Food web, 81–82
  biological amplification in,
    86–87
  of organisms in soil, 189, 190
  and the second law of energy,
    82, 83
Ford Foundation, 156
Foreign aid, 258, 259
Foreman, Dave, 601
Forest(s), 96, 101–2
  diversity and stability in, 123
  federal reserve, 32, 33
  importance and resource man-
    agement of, 271–76
  status of world and U.S.,
    277–82
Forest fire protection, 275–76
  presuppression, 275–76
  prevention, 275
  suppression, 276
Forest Reserve Act of 1891, 33
Forest Service, U.S., 32, 281,
  282, 283, 284, 286
Forrester-Meadows computer
  model, of resource use and
  population growth, 164–66
Fossil fuel era, 10
Fossil fuels, 9, 75, 336–59
  carbon dioxide emissions
    from, 354
  coal, 350–54
  energy use history, 336–41
  energy services and technol-
    ogy (A. Lovins), 357–59
  evaluating energy resources,
    341–42
  global warming and 440–45
  natural gas, 348–50
  oil, 337–48
France
  energy end uses and sources
    in (A. Lovins), 359
  nuclear energy in, 365, 381
Free enterprise zones, 181
Free-standing new towns, 181
Freshwater aquatic ecosystems,
  102–6
Freshwater fish management, 310
Friends of the Earth, 33, 35
Frontier worldview. See Throwaway worldview
Fuelwood shortage in LDCs,
  277, 278, 337
Fund for Population Activities,
  U.N., 153, 156
Fungicide, 517, 522
Future generations, present obli-
  gation to, 568–69

Game species, 292
Gamma rays, 48, 49
Gandhi, M. K., 577–78
Gasohol, 413
Gene banks, plant, 305–6
Gene pool, 120
Generalist niche, 87
Genes, 120
Genetic adaptation, 88
  to pesticides, 521–22
Genetic diversity, 10
  loss of, in green revolutions,
    248–49
Genetic engineering
  agricultural, 250
  risk-benefit analysis of,
    132–33
  risks/benefits of, 121
Genotypes, 120
Gentrification, 180
Geometric growth. See Exponen-
  tial growth of human
  population
Geopressurized zones, geother-
  mal, 364
Geothermal energy, 361–64
  direct-flash and binary-cycle
    methods, 363
  U.S. resources, 362
Global net population change,
  136–37

Global security and cooperation,
  achieving, 582–84
Global 2000 Report to the Presi-
  dent, The, Gus Speth on,
  20–21
Glucose, 47, 71
GNP. See Gross national product
  (GNP)
Grand Council Fire of American
  Indians, 89
Grant, Ulysses S., 32
GRAS (generally recognized as
  safe) list, 551
Grassland, 96, 100
  diversity and stability in, 123
Gray-air cities, 427
Great Britain, 338
Great Lakes, pollution in, and
  cleanup efforts, 485, 486
Greeley, Horace, 32
Greenhouse effect, 440–43
Greenhouse gases, 440
Green manure, 203
Greenpeace, 311
Green revolution, 247
  benefits of, to the poor, 249
  crop increases with, 247, 248
  future of, 250
  limitations of, 247–48
  loss of genetic diversity in,
    248–49
Groins, beach, 111, 113
Gross national product (GNP),
  4, 559
  average (see Average per capita
    GNP)
  misleading as an indicator,
    559–61
Gross national quality (GNQ),
  562
Ground fire, 275, 276
Groundwater, 210–13
  contamination of, 225, 495
  effects of withdrawing, 212
  pollution of, 474–77
  systems of, 211
  tapping, 224–27
Guano, 77
Gully reclamation, 201

Habitat, 70
  loss of, and species extinction,
    296, 306–7
  niche, 87
  wildlife management through,
    308–9
Haeckel, Ernst, 68
Half-life, 48
Hardin, Garrett, 35, 127, 149
Harrison, Benjamin, 32
Hayes, Denis, 511
Hazard, 130
Hazardous waste, 499
  affecting groundwater, 475,
    476, 477
  alternatives for household
    chemicals, 509
  control and management of,
    502–11
  EPA identified sites, 501
  fate of, in the U.S., 505
  illegal disposal of, 508
  Love Canal tragedy, 502–3
  major sources of, 501
  toxic metals, PCBs, and diox-
    ins, 510–15
  types, sources and effects of,
    499–502
Health. See Human health, and
  the environment
Health mat, 125
Heat, as a water pollutant, 461,
  466–69
Heating
  conservation, 397
  energy efficiency in, 388, 389,
    391–92
  passive solar vs. nuclear, 60,
    61, 62
  with solar energy, 393–402
  using waste, 63
  water, 396
Heavy oil, 342
  from oil shale and tar sands,
    346–48
Heavy-rail mass transit, 178

Hemingway, Ernest, 25
Herbicide, 126, 200, 236, 517
  Agent Orange, 524–25
  major types of, 519, 520
  using to increase food sup-
    plies, 520–21
Herbivore, 72
Hesburgh, Theodore, 557
Heyerdahl, Thor, 317
High-grade ore, 318
High grading of forests, 273
High-quality energy, 55
Hiroshima, 51, 127, 128
Homes, water conservation in,
  229–30, 231
Homestead Act of 1862, 32
Hopewell, Virginia, pesticide
  disaster, 525
Hormones, using to control
  insect pests, 529, 530
Horticulture, 27
Hot dry-rock zones, geothermal,
  364
Hot water deposits, geothermal,
  363
Hough, Franklin B., 32
Housing
  earth-sheltered, 395, 399
  energy conservation in, 388,
    389, 391–92
  inadequate, 3, 4
  passive solar design, 394–95
  solar electricity production for,
    401
Human body
  defenses of, against air pollu-
    tion, 433, 434
  effect of ionizing radiation on,
    51
  overloading defense mecha-
    nisms of, 434–35
Human health, and the environment, 534–56
  acute and chronic effects on,
    13
  air pollution in mines and fac-
    tories, 549
  cancer, 541–48
  disease types, 534–38. See also
    Disease
  food additives and, 548–53
  hazards to
    of air pollution, 432–35
    of asbestos, 435
    of chemicals in drinking
      water, 459
    of coal mining, 352–54
    of ionizing radiation, 51
  long-term threat of pesticides
    to, 525–26
  malaria and schistosomiasis,
    538–41
  noise pollution and, 553–54
  short-term threat of pesticides
    to, 524–25
  of toxic metals, PCBs and
    dioxins, 510–15
Human impact on the earth,
  25–42
  on ecosystems, 126–29
Human ingenuity, and use of
  natural resources, 8
Human life, price value of, 567
Human nutrition, 244, 245, 246
Human population. See Population, human
Humus, 189
Hunger. See Famine; Food
  resources
Hunger Project, 260
Hunters and gatherers, 25–27
  advanced societies, 26–27
  spotlight on rights to live
    undisturbed, 26
Hunting
  and species extinction, 296–98
  and wildlife management, 308
Hurricanes, 110–11
Hydroelectric power, 402–4
Hydrogen
  energy cycle, 417
  isotopes of, 46
  as a replacement for oil, 417,
    418
Hydrologic cycle, 69, 79–80
Hydrosphere, 69, 70, 71, 208
Hypolimnion, 104

Icebergs, as a water source, 228
Iceland, 311
Identified resources, mineral,
  325, 326
Immigration, 141
  rate, 141, 142
  restricting into the U.S.,
    157–58
In situ processing of oil shale,
  347, 348
Incineration of solid waste,
  495–96, 505, 506
India
  Bhopal pesticide disaster, 525
  floods in, 215
  food production in, 247, 248,
    249
  hunger in, 246
  population control in, 162,
    163
  urbanization in, 171
  water pollution in, 463
  water use in, 213
Indians. See Native Americans
Individual transit, 176–77
Indoor air pollution, 426, 427
Industrial smog, 427–28
Industrial societies, 30–31
Industrialized agriculture, 237
  effects of, 239
  energy use in U.S., 238, 239
  spotlight on, 236
Industry
  energy conservation in, 389,
    390
  process design, to decrease
    hazardous waste, 504–5
  solid waste from, 492
  water conservation in, 229
Inertia stability, 115, 123
Infant mortality rate, 138, 139
Infanticide, 26
Infectious disease, 534–35
  malaria and schistosomiasis,
    538–41
Information feedback, 116
Inland wetland 106
Inorganic fertilizer. See Commercial inorganic fertilizer
Input pollution control, 13,
  445–46
  on cultural eutrophication, 466
  on motor vehicle emissions,
    450
  on nitrogen oxides, 448–49
  on ocean oil pollution, 474
  on sulfur dioxide emissions,
    446–47
  on suspended particulate mat-
    ter, 449
Insecticide, 126, 517. See also
  Pesticides
  major types of, 519, 520
  using to control disease, 520
  using to increase food sup-
    plies, 520–21
Insect pests. See Pest(s), insect
Integrated pest management
  (IPM), 531, 532
Intensive forest management,
  272
Internal costs, 564
International Conference on
  Population, 153
International Council for Bird
  Preservation, 301
International environmental
  agencies, A-6
International Planned Parent-
  hood Federation, 153, 156
International Union for the Con-
  servation of Nature and Nat-
  ural Resources, 301
International Whaling Commis-
  sion, 310, 311
Interspecific competition, 87
In-town new towns, 181–82
Intraspecific competition, 564
Intrauterine device (IUD), 159
Inversion. See Thermal inversion
Ionic compounds, 46
Ionizing radiation, 48
  average annual dose, 52
  as cancer treatment, 542, 543
  effect on the human body, 51,
    128
  food exposure to, 530, 531

human exposure to, 52–53
three major types of, *49*
Ions, **46**
Ireland, 19th century population crash in, 119
Ironstone, 196
Irrigation, 218–19, 224
reducing losses in, 229
Isotopes, **46**
of hydrogen and uranium, *46*
radioactive, 48
Israel
energy in, 395, 398, 405
water conservation in, 229
Italy, 362
IUD. *See* Intrauterine device (IUD)

J-shaped curve,
of human population growth, **2**, *3*
of population size, and environmental stress, 118, *119*
Jackson, Jesse, 39
Japan, 311, 561, 584
energy in, 362, 363, 365, 389, 398
nuclear accidents in, 372
PCB contamination in, 514
pollution control in, 39
population in, 153, 155
Jetties, 111, *113*
Jitneys, 180
Johnson, Lyndon B., 35
Johnson, Warren, 387

Kennedy, John F., 35, 187
Kenya, 204
Kepone contamination, 525
Kerogen, **346**
Kinetic energy, **53**
King, Martin Luther, Jr., 578, 590
Komanoff, Charles, 365
Kormondy, Edward J., on limits of ecosystems, 88–89
Krill, 255
Kudzu vine, *301*
Kwashiorkor, **244**

Lacey Act of 1901, 297
Lake(s), **103**–4
eutrophic/oligotrophic, *104*
thermal pollution of, 466–69
water pollution in, 463, 465
zones of life in, *103*
Lake Baikal, 487–88
Landfarming, **505**
Landfill. *See* Sanitary landfill
Land ownership
types of, *263*
by U.S. government, *264*, *265*, *267*, 268
in the U.S., *263*, *265*
Land resources, 262–90
classification of, *251*
disappearing tropical forests (N. Myers), 288–89
forest resources management, 271–76
land use in the world and U.S., 262–65
limitations on cultivating, for food, 251–52
parks, 269–71
rangelands, 282–87
status of world and U.S. forests, 277–82
wilderness, 265–69
Land use
appropriate, for soil conservation, *202*, *203*
control, 183
for motor vehicles, *176*, *177*
planning, **182**, *183*
in the world and the U.S., 262–65
Laser inertial confinement, nuclear fusion, *383*
Laterite, 196, 251
Late-successional species, **309**
Law, environmental. *See* Legislation and laws, environmental

Law of conservation of energy. *See* First law of thermodynamics (energy); Second law of thermodynamics (energy)
Law of conservation of matter, **47**–53
Law of conservation of matter and energy, **52**
Law of the Sea, 255
Law of tolerance, **93**
LDC. *See* Less developed countries (LDCs)
Leaching, **190**
Lead, 510–12
Legislation and laws, environmental, 35–39, 573–74, A-8
air pollution, 443–44
beverage container deposit, 331, 332
on controlling hazardous waste, 507–9
energy conservation, 392
pesticide regulation, 526–27
to protect endangered species, 301–4, 310
to protect fisheries, 255, 311
in the U.S., 574–76
water pollution, 483–84
for wildlife management, 314–15
Lehrer, Tom, 455
Leopold, Aldo, 33, 262, 294, 295, 599
Less developed countries (LDCs), **4**
annual population change rate, 139, *140*
average GNP per person, *5*, *6–7*, 11
average population size, *8*
birth/death rates, 137, *138*
decline in food production in, *241*
degree of industrial development, *6–7*
energy use and problems in, 337, *339*
fuelwood crisis in, 277, *278*
life conditions in, *5*, 8
mineral resources of, 329
population characteristics in, *4*, *5*
social ecology of disease in, 536
sustainable earth agriculture in, 258–59, *260*
urbanization in, 169, *170*, *171*
water supply in, 457
withdrawal of water resources, *212*
Life-cycle cost, **59**
Life expectancy, human, 26, 137, *138*
Lifetime cost. *See* Life-cycle cost
Light-rail mass transit, 179
Light-water reactor (LWR), **366**, *366*
Lignite, **351**
Limestone injection multiple burning (LIMB), 446, *447*, 448–49
Limiting factor principle, **94**, 466
Limnetic zone, **103**
Liquid ethanol, 412
Liquid methanol, 412
Liquified natural gas (LNG), **348**
Liquified petroleum gas (LPG), **348**
Lithosphere, **69**, *70*, *71*
Littering of solid waste, 493
Littoral zone, **103**
Livestock ranching, **237**. *See also* Rangeland
Loams, **192**
Long-range planning and environmental protection, 579
Longwall method of mining, **321**
Love Canal disaster, 499, 502, *503*
Lovins, Amory, 60–61
on energy services and technology, 357–59
Low-grade ore, **318**
Low-quality energy, **55**
LP-gas. *See* Liquified petroleum gas (LPG)
Lung cancer, **434**–35

McHale, John, 1
McNamara, Robert S., 152, 336
Magma, **364**
Magnetic containment, nuclear fusion, **383**
Malaria, 124, 520, 538, *539*
Malnutrition, **8**, 234, **242**
and disease, *243*
Malthus, Thomas Robert, 17
Malthusian theory. *See* Neo-malthusians
Manganese, 329, *330*
Mantle of the earth, *70*
Manure. *See* Animal manure; Green manure
Marasmus, **243**, *244*
Mariculture. *See* Aquaculture
Marine aquatic ecosystems, 106–9
Markandaya, Kamala, 234
Marriage age, and fertility, 143
Marsh, George P., *32*, 35
Marshall, Robert, 33
Mass number, **46**
Mass transit, 177–80
Materials, effect of air pollution on, *438*, *439*
Matter, **44**
cycling of, in the ecosystems, **69**, 73–80
environmental problems, energy laws and, 65–67
forms and structure of, 44–47
input into a U.S. city, *174*
law of conservation and changes in, 47–53
organizational levels of, *45*
summary of laws of, *58*
Matter-recycling society, **65**
Maximum contaminant levels (MCLs), water, 483
Maximum sustained yield. *See* Sustained yield
MDC. *See* More developed countries (MDCs)
Measurements, units of, A-7
Medical research, 290–300
Medicare, 148
Meltdown, **369**
Mencken, H. L., 17
Mercury, 510, 512–13
Mesotrophic lake, **104**
Metabolic reserve, plant, **284**
Metallic mineral, **9**, **317**
Metastasis, **541**
Metcalf, Robert, 522
Methane (CH$_4$), 47, 412
Methanol, 412
Methyl isocyanate gas, 525
Methyl mercury, *510*, 512–13
Mexico, 363
oil production in, 339, 344
population in, *146*, 155, *156*, 171
urbanization in Mexico City, 171
water pollution in, 455
Microconsumer. *See* Decomposer in an ecosystem
Mid-successional species, **309**
Migration rate, human, 141, *142*
controlling, 154
Migration route, waterfowl, *309*
Migratory Bird Hunting Stamp Act, 310
Mineral deposit, **317**
Mineral resources, nonrenewable, **9**, 317–35
environmental impact of mining and processing, 322–25
extending supplies of, through conservation, 331–34
geographic distribution of, *319*
increasing supplies of, 328–30
locating/extracting, 317–21
sufficiency of, 325–28
Minimum tillage farming, 200
Mining, 320–21
air pollution and, 549
environmental impact of, 322–24
improving technology of, 330
of the ocean, 329–30
uranium, 367–68, *369*
Moderate forest management, **272**
Moderately-restricted-use lands, 267

Molecular compounds, 46
Molecule, **46**
Mollisols, 193, *196*
Molten rock (magma), geothermal energy, 364
Money, as limiting factor in food production, 252
Morals, **590**–91
More developed countries (MDCs), **4**. *See also* Overdeveloped countries (ODCs)
annual population change rate, 139, *140*
average GNP per person, *5*, *6–7*, 11
average population size, *8*
birth/death rates, 137, *138*
degree of industrial development, *6–7*
energy use, 337–38, *339*
population characteristics in, *4*, *5*
social ecology of disease in, 536
sustainable earth agriculture in, 259
teen pregnancy rate, 143, 144
urbanization in, 169, *170*
use of natural resources, 10, 15, 329
withdrawal of water resources, *212*
Mothballing nuclear power plants, 378
Motor vehicles
controlling emissions from, 450
energy efficiencies of, 62, *63*, 390
fuel economy, *388*
as urban transportation, 176–77
Muir, John, *32*, 33, 91, 266, 600
Multiple use
of federally owned lands, 267
of forests, 33
Municipal waste. *See* Urban solid waste
Muskie, Edmund, 35
Mutation, **120**
Myers, Norman, on disappearing tropical forests, 288–89

Naess, Arne, 593–94, 599
Nagasaki, 51, 127
Nash, Roderick, 266
National ambient air quality standard (NAAQS), **443**, A-10
National Cancer Institute, 289
National Coastal Zone Management Acts, 113
National Energy Act, 574
National Environmental Policy Act, 574
and environmental impact statements, 575–76
National Forest Management Act, 281
National forests, 267
conflicting demands on, 281–82
importance/use of, 280–81
timber harvesting from, *282*
National Park Service, U.S., 33
National Park System, U.S., 32, 33, 267, 269–71
external threats to, 270
internal stresses on, 269–70
Reagan administration vs. conservationists on, 270, 271
recreational visits to, *269*
wolves in Yellowstone Park, 270
National resource lands, 267
National security, redefining for a sustainable-earth, 583–84
National Wild and Scenic Rivers Act, 265–66, 403
National Wilderness Preservation System, 265, 267, 268
National Wildlife Federation, 35
National Wildlife Refuge System, 33, 267, 304–5

Native Americans
  beliefs about life of, 294
  land loss by, *31*
Natural change rate. *See* Annual
  population change rate
Natural community. *See* Community, natural
Natural eutrophication. *See* Eutrophication
Natural gas, **348**–50
  advantages/disadvantages of, 350
  historical use of, 337, *338*
Natural ionizing radiation, 52.
  See also Ionizing radiation
Natural products, replaced by
  synthetic products, 15
Natural radioactivity, 48, *52*. *See
  also* Ionizing radiation
Natural resource(s), **8**. *See also*
  Energy resources; Food
  resources; Fossil fuels; Land
  resources; Mineral
  resources, nonrenewable;
  Soil resources; Water
  resources; Wild plant and
  animal resources
  computer modeling of uses of,
  164–66
  conservation (*see* Resource
  conservation)
  decrease in, 10–12
  definition of, 8–9
  major types of, *9*
  MDCs and ODCs overuse of,
  10, 15
  nonrenewable, 9–10
  renewable and perpetual, 10
Natural Resources Defense
  Council (NRDC), 35
Natural selection, **120**
  in response to environmental
  stress, 119–22
Nature Conservancy, 35
Negative feedback, **116**
Nelson, Gaylord, 35
Neo-Malthusians, **17**
  vs. cornucopian view, 18–19
  on energy, 61
  guest essay (G. Speth), 20–21
  on nuclear energy, 385
  on oil reserves, 344
  on population control, 153,
  155
Neritic zone, **107**–8. *See also*
  Coastal zone
Net energy, **63**
Netherlands, 505
Net migration rate, **141**
Net population change, **136**–37
Net primary productivity, **83**
  of plants, 83–86
Net useful energy, **63**–64
  ratios for various energy systems, *64*
Neutral solution, *192*, *193*
Neutron (n), **46**
New source performance standards (NSPS), air quality,
  444
New York Bight, 470–71, *472*
New Zealand, 363
Niche. *See* Ecological niche
Nicotine, 518
Nitric oxide, 46, 48
Nitrogen cycle, 69, *75*, *76*
Nitrogen dioxide, 47
Nitrogen fixation, 75
Nitrogen oxides, controlling
  emissions of, 448–49
Nixon, Richard, 35
Noise Control Act, 554
Noise pollution, **553**–54
  effects of, 553, *554*
  measuring and ranking, 553
  solutions for, 553–54
  sonic assault, 553
Nonbiodegradable pollutant, **12**
Noninfectious disease, **535**–36
Nonmetallic mineral, **9**, **317**
Nonpoint source of water pollution, 455, **456**
  control of, 477, *478*
Nonrenewable resource, **9**–10
Non-urban lands, importance
  of, *262*, *263*

Nonvector-transmitted infectious disease, **534**–35
Norway, 311, 338
No-till cultivation, *200*
Nuclear autumn effect, **129**
Nuclear changes, in matter,
  48–52
Nuclear energy, 40, 53
  efficiency of, vs. solar energy,
  60, *61*, *62*
  fission (*see* Nuclear fission
  energy)
  fusion, **49**, 50, 382–85
Nuclear fission energy, 48, *49*,
  364–81
  accepting risks of (A. Weinberg), 384–85
  accidents and incidents with,
  371–73
  advantages/disadvantages of,
  380–81
  breeder nuclear fission reactor,
  381–82, 385
  controversy on, 364–65
  costs of, 379–80
  decommissioning plants,
  376–78
  France's commitment to, 381
  how it works, 365–67
  nuclear fuel cycle, 367–68, *369*
  nuclear weapons, 378–79
  radioactive waste disposal/
  storage, 375–76, *377*
  reactor safety, 369–75
  reducing oil imports with, 380
Nuclear fission reactors. *See also*
  Chernobyl nuclear power
  plant accident; Three Mile
  Island nuclear plant accident
  accidents, 371–73
  decommissioning, 376–78
  graphite, 366
  light-water, 366, *367*
  risk-benefit analysis, 131–32
  safety, 369–75
  in the U.S., *366*
  use in various countries, *365*
  workings of, 365–67
Nuclear fuel cycle, 367–68, *369*
Nuclear Regulatory Commission
  (NRC), 370
Nuclear war. *See also* Arms race
  risk-benefit analysis, 131
  threat of (H. Alfvén), 40–41
  as the ultimate ecological
  catastrophe, 127–29
Nuclear Waste Policy Act, 376
Nuclear weapons, 378–79
Nuclear winter effect, **129**
Nucleus of atoms, **46**
Nutrient, **45**

Occupational Safety Health Act
  of 1970, 547
Ocean(s)
  currents, 95
  importance of, 106–7
  major life zones in, *108*
  mining minerals from, 329,
  330
Ocean pollution, 469–74
  dumping in, 469–71
  oil pollution in, 472–74
Ocean thermal energy conversion (OTEC), **404**, *405*
Ogallala Aquifer, depletion of,
  225, *226*
Oil, 327, 342–48
  advantages/disadvantages of,
  345
  average price of, *340*
  conserving, 389–90
  conventional crude oil,
  342–43
  crisis of 1970s, 337–40
  evaluation of low prices for,
  340
  glut of 1980s, 340
  heating with, vs. wood, *409*
  hydrogen as a replacement for,
  417–18
  next crisis in, 340–41
  oil shale and tar sands,
  346–48

reducing dependence on, with
  nuclear power, 380
  refining process, 344
  supplies of, 343–45
  U.S. deposits of, 346
  U.S. use of, 39, *340*
  world locations of, *345*
Oil pollution, ocean, 472
  controlling, 474
  effects of, 472–74
  sources of, 473
Oil shale, 346, *347*
  in situ processing, *347*, *348*
Oligotrophic lake, **104**
Olmstead, Frederick Law, 32
Omnivore, **72**
OPEC. *See* Organization of
  Petroleum Exporting Countries (OPEC)
Open dump, **493**
Open forest, 271
Open pit surface mining, *320*
Open sea, **108**
Open space, urban, 184–85
Ophuls, William, on politics of
  the ecological future, 587–88
Oral contraceptives, 158–59
Ore, **318**
Organic fertilizer, **203**
Organism, **69**
Organization of Petroleum
  Exporting Countries
  (OPEC), 327, 337–40
Osborn, Fairfield, 35
Outdoor air pollutants, 422–23
  sources of, 423–25
Output pollution control, **13**,
  445–46
  on cultural eutrophication, 466
  on motor vehicle emissions,
  450
  on nitrogen oxides emissions,
  449
  on ocean oil pollution, 474
  on sulfur dioxide emissions,
  447–48
  on suspended particulate matter, 449–50
Overburden, **320**
Overdeveloped countries
  (ODCs), **15**. *See also* More
  developed countries (MDCs)
Overfishing, **254**
Overgrazing, 11, **284**
Overnutrition, 234, **245**
Overpopulation, 14–15
Oxisols, 196, *197*
Oxygen cycle, 69, 74–75
Oxygen-demanding wastes, as
  water pollution, **458**
  in rivers, *461*, *462*
Ozone layer depletion, 438–40

Package sewage treatment
  plants, **481**–82
Pakistan, 163
Pampas, 100
Paper, recycling, 500
Parasites, as water pollutants,
  456, *457*
Paratransit, 179–80
Passenger pigeon, 291, *292*
Passive solar heating, **393**–95
  housing design, 394–95
  water heating system, *396*
Pastoralists, 27
PCBs (polychlorinated biphenyls), **513**–14, *515*
Pearson, Lester, 557
Peat, 351
Pelican, 304, *306*
Peregrine falcons, 524
Perennials, 92
Periodicals, environmental,
  A-1–3
Permafrost, 100
Perpetual resource, **10**
Persistence. *See* Inertia stability
Peruvian anchovy, 254
Pest(s), insect, 126, 251, **517**
  alternative methods of controlling, 527–33
  control of (*see* Pesticides)
  control of, and extinction, 298

creating new, 522
  genetic adaptation to pesticides, 521–22
  ideal control of, 518
  locusts, 518
  natural control of, 517–18, 522
  protecting forests from, 276
Pesticides, 236, 300, **517**–53
  case against, 521–26
  case for, 520–21
  cost of developing new, 527
  export of banned, 527
  Hopewell and Bhopal tragedies involving, 525
  regulation of, in the U.S.,
  526–27
  types and uses of, 517–20
  as a water pollutant, 459, *463*,
  464, 476, 477
Pesticide treadmill, **522**
Petrochemicals, 343
Petroleum. *See* Oil
Pets, 298–300
pH, **192**, *193*
Pheromone, using to control
  insect pests, 529–30
Phosphorus cycle, 69, 76–77
Photochemical smog, **428**–29,
  439
Photosynthesis, **74**
Photovoltaic cell, 65–66, 392,
  400, *401*, *402*
Physical and chemical niche, 87
Physical change of matter, **47**
Physical Quality of Life Indicators (PQLI), 562
Phytoplankton, 108
Pimentel, David, on land degradation, 205–6
Pinchot, Gifford, 32, 33, 34
Pioneer community, **124**
Pittman-Robertson Act, 314–15
Plaintiff, **573**
Planned Parenthood Federation
  of America, 156
Planned unit development
  (PUD), 184
Plant(s). *See also* Wild plant and
  animal resources
  adaptations of, 92
  effects of air pollution on, 435,
  436–38
  as food sources, 234, *235*
  net primary productivity of,
  83–86
  nutrients, as water pollutant,
  458–59
  photosynthesis, 74–75
  rangeland, 284
Plantation agriculture, **237**
Plasma, nuclear fusion, 382–84
Plutonium-239, 365, 378, 381
Pneumatic waste collection system, 497, *498*
Point source of water pollution,
  455, **456**
  control of, 477–81
Poland, spotlight on pollution
  in, 13
Polar grasslands, 100
Political leaders
  election reform and electing,
  579–80
  influencing, 585–87
  nationalistic vs. sustainable-earth, *581*
Politics and the environment,
  572–89
  achieving global security and
  cooperation, 582–84
  the ecological future
  (W. Ophuls), 587–88
  environmental law, 573–74
  influencing elected officials,
  585–87
  social change and, 572–73
  sustainable-earth, 576–78
  toward a sustainable-earth
  government, 578–82
  U.S. environmental legislation, 574–76
Pollution, **12**. *See also* Air pollution; Water pollution
  and cancer, 548
  control of, 13
  defined, 12

economics and control of, 564–66
generated by natural and human activities, 12, 560
in Poland, 13
relationship to population growth, 13, 14
threat to wildlife, 300
types, sources, effects of, 12–13
Pollution standards index (PSI), 444, 445
Polychlorinated biphenyls (PCBs), 513–14, 515
Pond, 105
Population, human, 70
computer modeling on growth of, 164–66
control (see Population control)
decline of growth in, 39
distribution (see Urbanization)
dynamics (see Population dynamics)
growth in, 2–8
growth in, and food quantity, 239–42
overpopulation, 14–15
relationship to environmental degradation and pollution, 13, 14
Population control, 152–67
birth control methods for, 158–62
in China, 162, 163–65
computer modeling of, 164–66
in India, 162, 163
means of, 154–58
should growth be controlled, 152–53
socioeconomic methods for, 162–63
Population crash, 119
Population Crisis Committee, 156
Population dynamics, 136–51
age structure, 146–49
birth/death rates and net population change, 136–40
demographic behavior (L. Bouvier), 149–50
fertility, 142–46
migration, 141–42
Population(s) of organisms, 70
responses to environmental stress, 117–22
Porosity, soil, 191, 192
Positive feedback, 116
Potential energy, 53
Poverty and the poor
effect of green revolutions on, 149
and hunger, 246
land reform and, 258
malnutrition, disease and, 243
Powell, John Wesley, 34
Prairies, 100
Precipitation, 79
effect on climate and ecosystems, 96, 97
fate of, 211
major routes of local, 209, 210
Predation, 82
Predator, 82
control of, 287, 298
Pregnancy rate, teenage, 143, 144
Preservationists, 33
Prevailing ground winds, 94, 95
Prevention of significant deterioration (PSD) of air quality, 443–44
Prey, 82
Primary air pollutant, 425
Primary consumer. See Herbivore
Primary oil recovery, 342
Primary sewage treatment, 478, 480
Primary succession, 124, 125
Prime reproductive age, 143
Procurement of Papers and Secondary Materials Act, 500
Producers, in ecosystems, 72
Products in chemical changes, 47
Profundal zone, 103

Protein, 250
energy required to produce, 240
Protons (p), 46
Protozoa, as water pollutant, 456, 457
Pryde, Philip R., on environmentalism in the Soviet Union and Lake Baikal, 487–88
Public housing projects, revitalizing, 180, 181
Pyrethrum, 518, 519

Quality of life. See Gross national quality (GNQ)

Rabbits, introduction into Australia, 300–301
Radiant energy, 80
Radiation, ionizing. See Ionizing radiation
Radioactive fallout, 128
Radioactive isotope, 48
Radioactive waste
disposal and storage of, 375–76, 377
storages sites, 374
as a water pollutant, 461
Radioactivity. See Natural radioactivity
Radioisotope, 48
Radon gas, contamination of homes by, 451–53
Rain shadow effect, 95, 96
Rangeland, 282–87
carrying capacity and overgrazing, 284–85
grazing fees on public, 286
management of, 285–87
poison use on predators in, 287
quality of, 285
in the U.S., 283–84
vegetation characteristics, 284
in the world, 283–84
Range of tolerance, 92, 93
for temperatures, 94
Rapidly biodegradable pollutant, 12
Reactants in chemical changes, 47
Reagan, Ronald, 36, 37
economy and deficit under, 561
environmental policies, 36, 66, 287, 444, 450, 484
national forest policies, 282
national park policies, 270, 271
population policies, 153, 161
price value of human life under administration of, 567
transportation policies, 177
Recharge area, 211
Recharging aquifers, 211
Recombinant DNA, 250
Recycling, 10, 65–66, 496–99
to extend mineral resources, 331–32
hazardous materials, 504–5
obstacles to, 332–33
paper, 500
reusable containers, 333
Refrigeration, conservation in, 397
Renewable resource, 10
Replacement level fertility, 142
Reproductive age, 147
Reproductive niche, 87
Reproductive potential. See Biotic potential
Reserves, mineral, 325, 326
Reservoir, 104–5, 106
to increase water supply, 220–22
water pollution in, 463, 465
Resilience stability, 115
Resource, natural. See Natural resource(s)
Resource conservation, 12
energy (see Energy conservation)
history of, in the U.S., 31–37

soil, 198–204
water, 228–30
Resource Conservation and Recovery Act (RCRA), 493, 504, 507, 508, 574
Resource exploitation in the U.S., 31–37
Resource recovery from solid waste, 492, 496–99
high-technology approach, 496–97
low-technology approach, 497–99
Resource recovery plant, 496, 497
Resources, mineral, 325, 326
Respiration. See Cellular respiration
Restricted-use lands, federal, 267
Retrofitting for energy conservation, 392
Reusable containers, 333
Reuse of natural resources, 10
Rhine River pollution disaster, 464
Rhinoceros, 297, 298
Rickover, Hyman, 365
Risk, 130
Risk assessment, 130
Risk-benefit analysis, 130–33
Risk management, 133
River(s), 105–6
degradation of oxygen-consuming wastes in, 461, 462
quality of, in the U.S., 462
quality of, in the world, 462–63
Rhine River disaster, 464
thermal pollution of, 466–69
wild and scenic, 265–66
Rocky shore, 107
Rodenticides, 517
Room-and-pillar method of mining, 321
Roosevelt, Franklin, 34
Roosevelt, Theodore, 32, 33, 34, 304
Rotenone, 518
Rowland, Sherwood, 451
Rudd, Robert L., 533
Ruminant animals, 283
Runoff, water, 209

S-shaped curve, of population size, and environment stress, 118, 119
Saccharin, risk-benefit analysis of, 132
Safe Drinking Water Act, 483
Sagebrush rebellion, 35–37
Salinity, in water bodies, 102
Salinization of soil, 11, 218, 219, 220
desalinization, 227–28
Salk, Jonas, 136
Salk, Jonathan, 136
Saltwater intrusion, 224, 225, 226
Sandy soil, 192
Sanitary landfill, 493, 494, 495
secured, for hazardous waste, 506, 507
Satellite towns, 181, 182
Saudi Arabia, 338, 344
Savannas, 100
Schistosomiasis, 223, 539, 540, 541
Schumacher, E. F., 592
Scientific conservationists, 33–34
Scrubbers, on fossil fuel burning plants, 443, 447, 448
Sears, Paul B., 35
Seasons, 94, 95
Seawalls, 111, 112
Seawater, mining minerals from, 329–30, 382
Secondary air pollutant, 425
Secondary consumer. See Carnivore
Secondary oil recovery, 342
Secondary sewage treatment, 478–79, 481
Secondary succession, 125, 126

Second generation pesticides, 518–19
Second law of energy. See Second law of thermodynamics (energy)
Second law of thermodynamics (energy), 56–57, 67
and energy quality, 55–56
food chains, food webs and, 82–83
and increasing disorder, 57–58
Secured landfill, 506, 507
Sediment, as water pollutants, 460–61
Seed tree cutting, 274
Selective cutting of forests, 273
Self, Peter, 183
Septic tank, 478, 479
Sewage sludge and effluent, 470, 482, 499
Sewage treatment, 477–81
alternatives to, 481–82
Sewer systems, separated and combined, 480
Sexually transmitted disease, 159
Shale oil, 346, 347
Shallow ecology, 593–95
Shelterbelt, 201
Shelterwood cutting of forests, 273
Shifting cultivation, 27
Sierra Club, 33, 35
Silent Spring (Carson), 517
Silicosis, 435
Silviculture, 272–73
Simon, Julian, 57
on myth of environmental crisis, 22–23
Skin cancer, 439, 542
Slash-and-burn cultivation, 27
Slowly biodegradable pollutant, 12
Sludge, 470
methane production from, 412
Small, J. Kenneth, 584
Smith, Robert Leon, on wildlife restoration, 314–15
Smog
climate, topography and, 429–30
industrial, 427–28
origin of the term, 426, 439
photochemical, 428–29
Smoking and cancer, 544–47
Snail darter controversy, 305
Snowy egret, 297, 298
Social Security system, U.S., 148, 149
Socioeconomic methods of population control, 162–63
Soddy, Frederick, 44
Soil conservation, 198–204
achieving more effective, 204
appropriate land use, 202–3
conservation tillage, 200–201
contour farming, terracing, strip cropping, 201
gully reclamation and shelterbelts, 201–2
maintaining fertility, 203–4
management methods, 198, 200
Soil Conservation Service (SCS), 34, 199
Soil erosion, 196–98
caused by water, 196, 198
caused by wind, 196–97, 198
natural and human-accelerated, 196–97
D. Pimentel on, 205–6
possibility of another Dust Bowl, 199
in the U.S., 198
in the world, 197–98
Soil horizons, 188, 189
Soil profile, 188, 189, 196–97
Soil resources, 188–207. See also Salinization of soil; Waterlogging soil
conservation (see Soil conservation)
erosion (see Soil erosion)
formation, porosity, and acidity, 190–93
land degradation (D. Pimentel), 205–6

Soil resources (continued)
major types of, 193–96
uses, components, and profiles, 188–90
water in, 189, 191
world distribution of, 194–95
Solar-assisted water stove, 410–11
Solar cell. See Photovoltaic cell
Solar energy, 54, 65–66
availability of, in the U.S., 398
in the biosphere, 80–81
converting to electricity, 400–402 (see also Photovoltaic cell)
to create high-temperature heating and electricity, 399
to create low-temperature heating, 393–99
efficiency of, vs. nuclear energy, 60, 61, 62
photosynthesis and, 74
wavelength range, 80
Solar furnace, 399, 400
Solar pond, 404–6
Solar power towers, 399, 400
Solid waste, 491–99. See also Hazardous waste
disposal of urban, 493–96
fate of, in the U.S., 493
production of, in the U.S., 491–93
resource recovery from, 496–99
South Africa, mineral resources of, 327, 328, 356
South Korea, 311
Soviet Union, 311
arms race in, and global security, 582–84
economics vs. ecology at Lake Baikal, 487–88
economy of, 559
energy resources, 363
mineral resources, 327
noise reduction in, 553
nuclear accidents in, 371, 372, 373
nuclear energy, 365
oil resources, 345
soil erosion, 197
water diversion, 224
water use, 213
Spaceship Earth concept, 17. See also Shallow ecology
Specialist niche, 87
Speciation, 122, 123
Species, 70
adaptations/limits of, 91–94
characteristics of extinction prone, 301, 303
competition between, 87–89
early-, mid-, late-successional, 309
ecological niche of, 87
estimated number of, 292
extinction rate, 295
how they become extinct, 295–301
introduction of alien, 300–301, 302
protecting wild, from extinction, 301–7
reasons for preserving wild, 292–95
wilderness, 309
Species diversity, 122, 123
Speed limits, energy conservation with, 390
Speth, Gus, on the Global 2000 and World Resources reports, 20–21
Spodosols, 193, 196, 197
Spoil banks, 321, 322
Sponge effect of forests, 289
Sport hunting, 296, 308
Sprinkler systems, water-saving, 220, 229
Spun vegetable protein (SVP), 250
Stability, 115–16
information feedback and, 116
time delays, synergistic/antagonistic effects and, 116–17
Statutory law, 573

Steady-state economy. See Sustainable-earth economy
Stegner, Wallace, 266
Steppes, 100
Sterilization,
human, 158
of insect pests, 528–29
Stevenson, Adlai E., 2
Stone ripraps, 111, 112
Storm and sewer systems, 480
Storms, damage to coastline caused by, 110–11
Strategic materials, 327
Stream, 105–6
Stress. See Environmental stress
Strip cropping, 200, 201
Strip mining, 320. See also Surface mining
area, 321
contour, 321, 322
Subatomic particles, 46
Subbituminous coal, 351
Subsidence
coal mining, 353
groundwater depletion, 224, 225, 226, 227
Subsistence agriculture, 28, 237
Subsistence economy, 558
Subsistence hunting, 296
Subsurface mining, 321
Succession. See Ecological succession
Succulent plants, 92
Sulfur cycle, 78–79
Sulfur dioxide (SO₂), 12, 47, 78–79
controlling, 446–48
Sun, as energy source, 80–81. See also Solar energy
Superfund program, 508–9, 574
Superinsulated house, 391
Supreme Court, U.S., abortion decision, 160–61
Surface mining, 320–21, 353
environmental impact, 322, 323, 324
restoration after, 323, 325
Surface Mining Control and Reclamation Act of 1977, 353
Surface water, 209–10
natural processes affecting pollution in, 461
Surface-litter layer of soil, 188, 189
Suspended particulate matter (SPM), 423, 424
input-output controls on, 449–50
Sustainable-earth agriculture, 258, 259, 260
Sustainable-earth economy, 563
barriers and problems, 563–64
H. Daly on, 568–70
key characteristics of, 562
problems with conventional economic systems, 562–63
as a steady-state economy, 563
vs. throwaway economic systems, 563
Sustainable-earth politics, 576–78
and the ecological future, 587–88
global security and cooperation with, 582–84
influencing elected officials with, 585–87
nationalistic vs. sustainable-earth leaders, 581
political system, 576–77
political tactics, 577–78
toward a U.S. government based on, 578–82
Sustainable-earth society, 37, 38, 66–67
beyond recycling/reuse, 333, 334
Sustainable-earth worldview, 17
ethics of, 592–95
Sustained yield
of forests, 33
of natural resources, 10
Sweden, 204
acid deposition, 437
energy use/conservation in, vs. U.S., 393

nuclear energy in, 365
population in, 146, 155, 156
radon gas in, 453
teen fertility rate, 144
waste management in, 496, 497, 498
Swift, Ernest, 33
Synergistic effect on human health, 13, 117
Synfuels, 356–57
Synthetic natural gas (SNG), 356
Synthetic organic chemicals (SOCs), 459–60
Synthetic products, substituted for natural products, 15

Tailings, mining, 324, 368
Taiwan, land reform in, 258
Tapiola, Finland, 182
Tar sands, 347
processing, 347–48, 349
Taylor Grazing Act of 1934, 285
Technology
relationship to environmental degradation, 15–16
risk assessment, 130
Teenage pregnancy, 143, 144
Temperate deserts, 97
Temperate grasslands, 100
Temperate (mid-latitude) deciduous forests, 102
Temperature
control system based on information feedback, 116
effect on climate and ecosystems, 96, 97
lake zones of, 105
range of tolerance, 94
Temperature inversion. See Thermal inversion
Tennessee Valley Authority, 34, 305
Terracing, 201
Terrestrial ecosystem, 70
Tertiary sewage treatment, 479, 482
Thalidomide, risk-benefit analysis, 131
Thermal enrichment, 467
Thermal inversion, 429, 440
Thermal pollution of water, 461, 466, 467, 468–69
reduction of, 468
Thermal shock, 467
Thermocline, 104
Third-generation pesticides, 529
Thoreau, Henry David, 17, 32, 577–78
Threatened species, 296
Three Mile Island nuclear plant accident, 130, 132, 371–72, 374
Threshold effect, 94
Throwaway society, 65–66
ethics of, 591–92
vs. sustainable-earth economy, 563
Throwaway worldview, 17, 333
and solid waste, 492
Tidal power, 403
Time delay, in self-regulating systems, 116–17
Times Beach, Missouri, dioxin contamination, 513
Tolerance limits, 92–94
Toothed whales, 310
Topography, local climate and smog, 429–30
Top soil layer, 189
Total fertility rate (TFR), 142, 143
to project population stabilization, 143, 144, 145
in the U.S., 145
Total resources of a mineral, 325, 326
Toxic metals, 510–13
Toxic Substances Control Act of 1975, 547, 574
Trade deficit, 561
Tragedy of the commons, 11
Trans-Alaska pipeline, 343, 350
Transpiration, 79

Transportation, urban, 176–80
conservation, 397
improving efficiency in, 389–91
Tree(s)
effects of air pollution on, 436, 437–38
harvesting and regeneration methods, 273–75
Trickling filters, 479, 481
Tritium, 50, 382
Trophic level, 82
Tropical climates, 96
deserts, 97
grasslands, 100
Tropical rain (moist) forests, 101, 102, 277
deforestation of, 277–78, 279, 280, 288–89
as potential crop land, 251
Troposphere, 422
True cost, 564
Tsetse fly, 251
Tundra, 100
Tunnel effect and social change, 577, 578
Turner, Frederick Jackson, 32
Turnover, lake water, 104, 105
2,4-D herbicide, 524–25
2,4,5-T herbicide, 524–25

Udall, Stewart L., 33, 35, 129, 484
Unconfined aquifer, 211
Underground storage tanks, as sources of water pollution, 477
Undernutrition, 8, 234, 242
and disease, 243
Undiscovered resources, mineral, 325, 326
United States. See also Federal government, U.S.
acid deposition in, 432, 433, 437
air pollution control legislation in, 443–44
air quality and emissions in, 444–45
arms race in, and global security, 582–84
availability of solar energy in, 398
beef importation into, and tropical deforestation, 280
birth control and abortion in, 159, 160, 161, 162
cancer incidence in, 541–42, 545
coal in, 351, 352
energy conservation in, 388, 389, 390, 393
energy strategy for, 413–17
ethnic composition of, 142
evaluation of population growth in, 153
family planning in, 157
farm crisis in, 256, 257, 258
flood-prone areas, 216, 217
food waste in, 259–60
forests in, 279–80, 281 (see also National forests)
geothermal resources in, 362
groundwater depletion/contamination, 224, 225, 226
hazardous waste sites, 501
history of resource exploitation/conservation and environmental protection in, 31–37
hydroelectric power in, 402–3
immigration to, 141, 142, 157–58
industrialized agriculture in, 236, 238–39
land ownership in, 262, 263, 264, 265
life expectancy/infant mortality in, 138, 139
mineral import dependence, 327
mineral resources, 327–28
nuclear energy in, 365, 366, 370

oil and natural gas deposits in, *346*
pesticide regulation in, 526–27
pollution disaster in, 426
population projections and age structure, 147, *148*
population shifts in, 172
population stabilization, 145–46
radioactive wastes storage sites, *374*, *375*–76
radon gas in, *452*
rangelands, 283–84, 286
reducing dependence on oil, with nuclear power, 380
river quality in, *462*
soil erosion in, 198
solid waste production in, 491, *492*
surface-mined land in the, *320*
teenage pregnancy in, 144
toward a sustainable-earth government in, 578–82
transportation in, 176–80
urbanization in, 171, *172*
water deficit regions, *221*
water diversion in, *222*, *224*
water pollution control laws, 483–84
water resource problems in, 219–20
water use, *213*, *214*, A-9
Upwelling, **107**, *109*
Uranium, 378. *See also* Radon gas
fission, *49*, *50*, 365–67, *368*
isotopes of, *46*
Urban areas. *See also* Urbanization
burning waste from, for energy, 412
solid waste from (*see* Urban solid waste)
world's largest, *169*
Urban growth, **168**, *169*
Urban heat island, **430**, *431*
Urban homesteading programs, 180
Urbanization, 168–86
preserving open space, 184–85
in the U.S., 171–73
U.S. population shifts, 173
urban land-use planning and control, 182–83
urban problems, 180–82
urban systems and natural ecosystems, 173–76
urban transportation, 176–80
in the world, 168–71
Urban open space, **184**–85
Urban problems, 180–82
Urban solid waste, **492**
disposal of, 493–96
resource recovery from, 496–99

Urban spatial structure, 174, *175*, 176
Urban systems, and natural ecosystems, 173–76

Van Hise, Charles, 34
Vector, **534**
Vector-transmitted infectious disease, **534**
major, *535*
Veld, 100
Viruses, as water pollutants, 456, *457*
Vitamins
needed in human nutrition, 244, *245*, 246
supplements in food, 250

Wald, George, 135
Ward, Barbara, 569
Warm rock deposits, geothermal, 364
Waste. *See also* Hazardous waste; Solid waste; Wastewater treatment
burning agricultural and urban, for energy, 412
burning wood, for energy, 409–11
ocean dumping of, 469–71
Wastewater treatment, 477–81
alternatives to, 481–82
individual management of, 482–83
Water, 46. *See also* Water resources
average U.S. use of, A-9
drinking (*see* Drinking water)
global circulation of, 94, *95*
physical properties of, 208–9
in soil, 189, *191*
solar heating system, *396*
waste (*see* Wastewater treatment)
Water conservation, 228–30
in heating, 62, 63, 397
importance of, 228–29
reducing irrigation losses, 229
wasting less in homes, 229, *230*, *231*
wasting less in industry, 229
Water cycle. *See* Hydrologic cycle
Water diversion projects, 222–24
Waterfowl, management of migratory, *309*, 310
Waterlogging soil, 11, *218*, **219**
Water pollutants, 456
disease-causing, 456, *457*, *458*
heat as, 461
organic chemicals, *459*, 460
inorganic plant nutrients, 458–59
oxygen-demanding wastes, 458

radioactive substances, 461
sediments, 460–61
Water pollution, **455**–88
caused by surface mining, 323, *324*
control of, 477–83
in the Great Lakes, 485–86
groundwater, 474–77
in Lake Baikal, 487–88
in the ocean, 469–74
related to agricultural fertilizers, 204
Rhine River disaster, 464
of rivers, lakes, and reservoirs, 461–68
sources, types and effects of, 455–61
U.S. laws controlling, 483–84
Water resources, 208–33
average and per capita withdrawal of, *212*
conservation (*see* Water conservation)
desertification, 231–32
energy from flowing and falling, 402–6
energy from heat stored in, 404–6
increasing usable supply of, 220–28
management methods, 220, *222*
physical properties of, 208–9
portion usable by humans, *210*
problems of, 214–20, 252
supply, renewal and use of, 209–14
Water stove, solar-assisted, *410*
Water table, *210*, **211**, 212
Water table aquifer. *See* Unconfined aquifer
Watershed, **105**, *107*, **209**
Watt, James G., 36, 37
Wave power, 404
Wavelengths, solar, **80**
Weather, **94**
Weathering, soil, **190**, 191
Weeds, 126
Weinberg, Alvin M., 361, 364
on accepting risks of nuclear fission energy, 384–85
Wells, contaminated water, 483–84
West Germany, 154, 365, 505
Wet steam deposits, geothermal, 362–63
Wetlands, **106**
Whales, 310–11, *312–13*
Whaling industry, 310–11
White, Lynn, Jr., 592
Whitehead, Alfred North, 17
Whole-tree harvesting, **274**, *275*
Whooping crane, *297*
Wild plant and animal resources, 291–315
fishing management, 310–11

how species become endangered and extinct, 295–301
management of, 307–10
protecting from extinction, 301–7
reasons for preserving, 292–95
threat of pesticides to, 523–24
wildlife restoration in the U.S. (R. L. Smith), 314–15
Wilderness, **35**, 265–69
amount needed, 268–69
Congressional definition of, **267**
reasons for preserving, 266–68
U.S. expansion of, 265–66
use/abuse of, 266
Wilderness Act of 1964, 35, 574
Wilderness Society, 33, 35
Wilderness species, **309**
Wildlife conservation, **292**
Wildlife management, **307**–10
Wildlife refuge system, 33, 267, 304–5
Wildlife resources, **292**–95
Wilson, Alexander, 291
Wilson, Edward O. 295
Wind energy, 406–8
Wind farms, **406**, *407*
Wind turbines, 406
Windbreaks, **201**–2
Withdrawal of water, **213**, *214*, A-9
Wolf, Edward C., 491
Women, changing roles of, and population control, 162–63
Wood
as energy source, 336, *338*, 409–11
fuelwood crisis in LDCs, 277, *278*, 337
heating with, vs. oil, *409*
Work, **53**
Workplace
air pollution in, 549
cancer risks in, 547, *548*
World Bank, 156
World Resources 1986 report, Gus Speth on, 20–21
World Wildlife Fund, 301

X rays, risk-benefit analysis, 131

Youth, numbers of, in various countries, *147*

Zaire, 328
Zaire River, 216–17
Zero population growth (ZPG), **8**
and total fertility rate, 143, 145
Zooplankton, 72, 108
Zoos, 298–300, 305–6

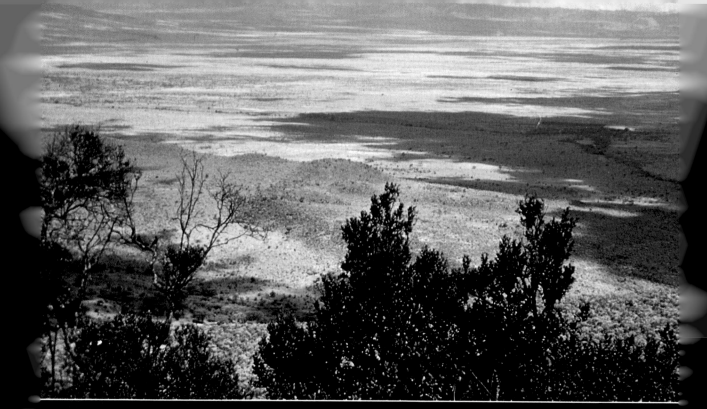

Tropical savana biome

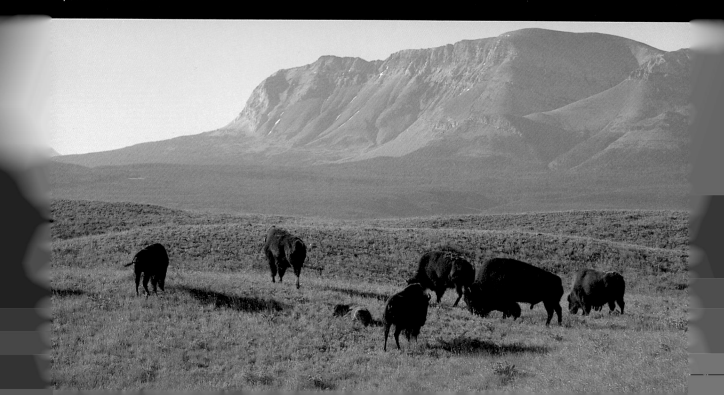

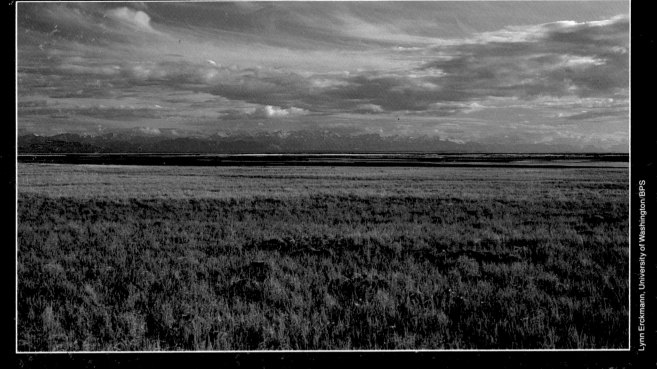

Arctic tundra biome

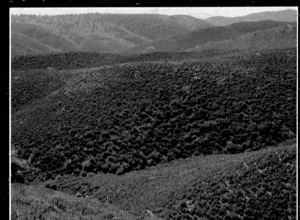

Chaparral biome

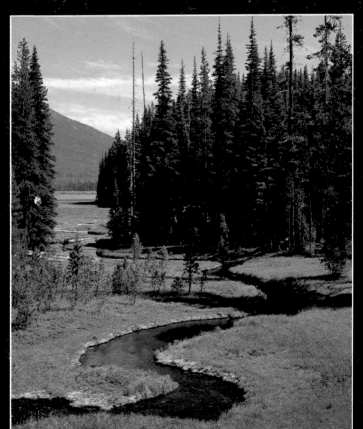